Ordeal by Fire

The Civil War and Reconstruction

James M. McPherson, *Princeton University*

Third Edition

Mc
Graw
Hill

Boston   Burr Ridge, IL   Dubuque, IA   Madison, WI
New York   San Francisco   St. Louis
Bangkok   Bogotá   Caracas   Lisbon   London   Madrid   Mexico City
Milan   New Delhi   Seoul   Singapore   Sydney   Taipei . Toronto

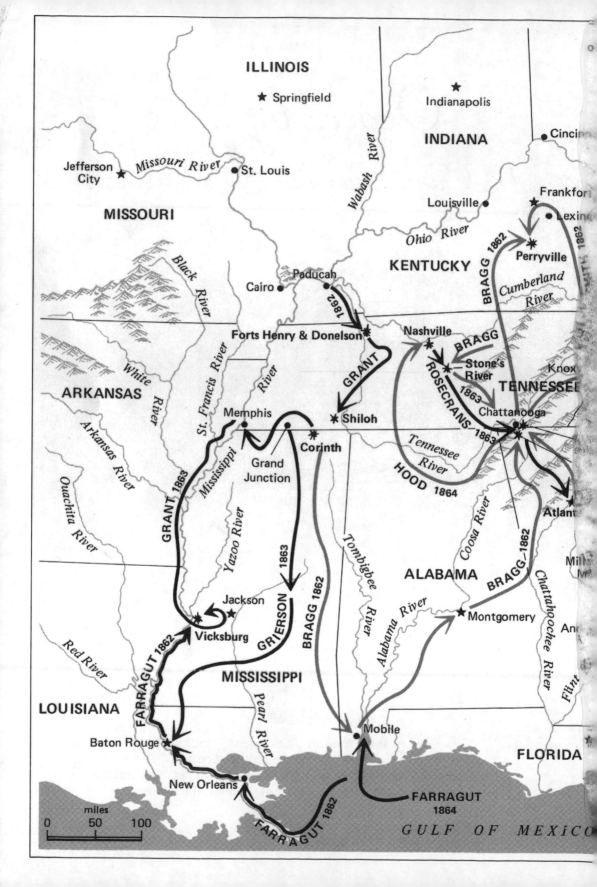

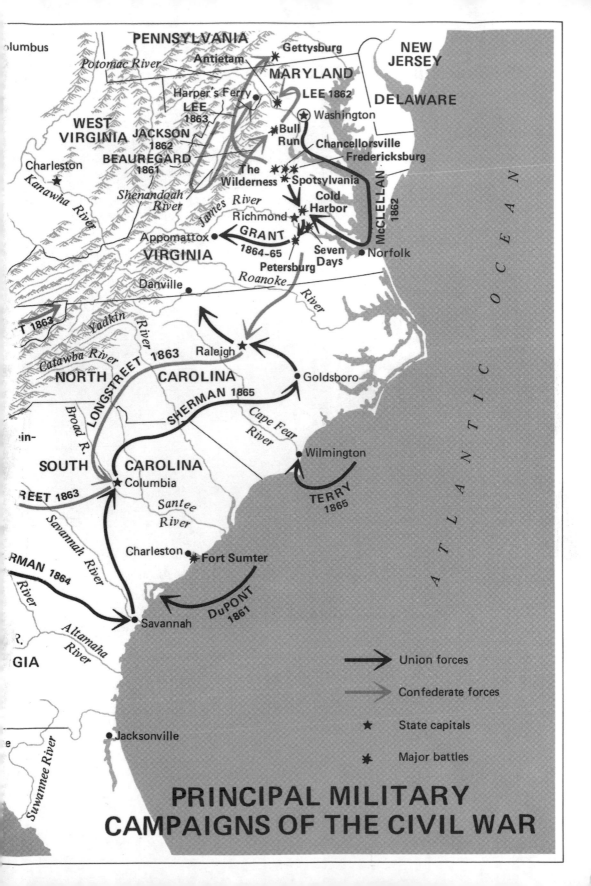

PRINCIPAL MILITARY
CAMPAIGNS OF THE CIVIL WAR

McGraw-Hill Higher Education

A Division of The **McGraw-Hill** *Companies*

ORDEAL BY FIRE: THE CIVIL WAR AND RECONSTRUCTION
THIRD EDITION

Published by McGraw-Hill, an imprint of The McGraw-Hill Companies, Inc., 1221 Avenue of the Americas, New York, NY 10020. Copyright © 2001, 1992, 1982 by The McGraw-Hill Companies, Inc. All rights reserved. No part of this publication may be reproduced or distributed in any form or by any means, or stored in a database or retrieval system, without the prior written consent of The McGraw-Hill Companies, Inc., including, but not limited to, in any network or other electronic storage or transmission, or broadcast for distance learning.

Some ancillaries, including electronic and print components, may not be available to customers outside the United States.

This book is printed on acid-free paper.

9 0   B K M / B K M   0 9 8 7 6

ISBN-13: 978-0-07-231736-7
ISBN-10: 0-07-231736-1

Vice president and editor-in-chief: *Thalia Dorwick*
Editorial director: *Jane E. Vaicunas*
Senior sponsoring editor: *Lyn Uhl*
Developmental editor: *Kristen Mellitt*
Marketing manager: *Janise A. Fry*
Project manager: *Vicki Krug*
Senior media producer: *Sean Crowley*
Production supervisor: *Kara Kudronowicz*
Design director: *Keith J. McPherson*
Senior photo research coordinator: *Carrie K. Burger*
Photo research: *PhotoSearch, Inc.*
Compositor: *Carlisle Communications, Ltd.*
Typeface: *10/12 ITC Garamond Light*

Cover image: *The Century Association, New York, Guerilla Warfare by Albert Bierstadt.*

Library of Congress Cataloging-in-Publication Data

McPherson, James M.
    Ordeal by fire : the Civil War and Reconstruction / James M. McPherson.—3rd ed.
        p.   cm.
    Includes bibliographical references (p.   ) and index.
    ISBN 0–07–231736–1
    1. United States—History—Civil War, 1861–1865.   2. United States—History—Civil War,
    1861–1865—Causes.   3. Reconstruction.   4. United States—History—1865–1898.   I. Title.

E468 .M23   2001
973.7—dc21   00–025043
                                                          CIP

www.mhhe.com

About the Author

JAMES M. McPHERSON is George Henry Davis '86 Professor of American History at Princeton University, where he has taught since 1962. He was born in Valley City, North Dakota, in 1936. He received his B.A. from Gustavus Adolphus College in 1958 and his Ph.D. from The Johns Hopkins University in 1963. He has been a Guggenheim Fellow, a National Endowment for the Humanities Fellow, a Fellow at the Center for Advanced Studies in Behavioral Sciences at Stanford, and a Seaver Institute Fellow at the Henry E. Huntington Library in San Marino, California. In 1982, he was Commonwealth Fund Lecturer at University College, London.

A specialist in Civil War and Reconstruction history and in the history of race relations, McPherson is the author of *The Struggle for Equality: Abolitionists and the Negro in the Civil War and Reconstruction* (1964); *The Negro's Civil War* (1965); *Marching Toward Freedom: The Negro in the Civil War* (1968); *The Abolitionist Legacy: From Reconstruction to the NAACP* (1975); *Battle Cry of Freedom: The Civil War Era* (1988); *Abraham Lincoln and the Second American Revolution* (1991); *What They Fought For, 1861–1865* (1994); *Drawn With the Sword: Reflections on the American Civil War* (1996); and *For Cause and Comrades: Why Men Fought in the Civil War* (1997).

v

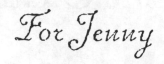

For Jenny

Contents in Brief

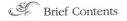

Contents

Chapter Twenty-One
Behind the Lines

Chapter Twenty-Two
Wartime Reconstruction and the Freedpeople

Chapter Twenty-Three
Military Stalemate, 1864

Chapter Twenty-Four
The Third Turning Point: The Election of 1864

Maps

Tables

Figures

Preface

The Civil War is the central event in the American historical consciousness. While the Revolution of 1776–1783 created the United States, the Civil War of 1861–1865 preserved this creation from destruction, and determined in large measure what sort of nation it would be. The war settled two fundamental issues for the United States: whether it was to be a nation with a sovereign national government or a dissoluble confederation of sovereign states; and whether this nation, born of a declaration that all men are created with an equal right to liberty, was to continue to exist as the largest slaveholding country in the world. The Constitution of 1789 had left these issues unresolved. By 1861, there was no way around them; one way or another, a solution had to be found.

The Civil War shaped the institutions of modern America. It did so at the cost of 620,000 soldiers' lives—almost equal to the number of American deaths in all the rest of the nation's wars combined. The Civil War was the largest and most destructive conflict in the Western world between 1815 and 1914. It was a total war. It mobilized the total resources of the two societies that fought it, and utterly devastated the resources of the loser. The principal issues of the war, sovereignty and freedom, proved to be uncompromisable. All efforts for a negotiated peace failed, and the war ended—could only have ended—in unconditional surrender. The war destroyed not only slavery and the Confederacy but also the socioeconomic foundations on which these institutions had been built.

This book is intended to fill the need for a comprehensive one-volume study of the United States during the era of the Civil War and Reconstruction. It seeks both to tell an important story and to explain the meaning of that story. It blends the most up-to-date scholarship with the author's own interpretations based on decades of teaching, research, and writing about this era. The first three chapters describe the social, economic, and ideological context of the sectional conflict during the first half of the nineteenth century. The remaining six chapters in Part One trace the political processes from 1844 to 1861 by which that conflict exploded into secession and war. Part Two chronicles the four crucial, dramatic years of war. All aspects of the war are treated: military leadership, strategy, technology, campaigns, and battles; political leadership and behavior in the Union and Confederacy; the foreign policy of both sides; economic mobilization in North and South; life behind the lines; emancipation and the wartime role of freed slaves. Part Three deals with the postwar problems of reuniting the nation and defining the rights of the freed slaves in the new South. The final chapter departs from the traditional practice of ending Reconstruction in 1877 and shows how the issues growing out of the war remained vital until the 1890s, when Southern states formally disfranchised their black citizens without significant opposition from the North or the national government. Then, and only then, came an end to the preoccupation with sectional and racial issues that had dominated American politics for more than half a century.

New Material

The extraordinary level of interest in the American Civil War has, if anything, increased even more during the 1990s. The updated and expanded bibliography at the end of this third edition provides evidence of the continued outpouring of books on all aspects of the war, its causes, and its consequences. To the extent possible, I have incorporated new findings and perspectives on the social and economic history of the era, especially with respect to women (including those who passed as men to enlist in the armies), the home front during the war, and the black experience during Reconstruction. This edition also contains a new section on the motivations of common soldiers and their understanding of what they were fighting for. I have added new material on the war in the trans-Mississippi West, on intelligence and espionage operations, on the assassination of Lincoln, on the psychological impact of the war in the South and the origins of the Lost Cause mentality, and on Ulysses S. Grant's presidency.

Learning Aids for Students

As always, a new edition has provided the opportunity to correct a few minor errors that had somehow survived in or crept into the previous edition. More exciting has been the chance to expand or clarify several battlefield maps, to add three new black and white maps in the text, and especially to create the new foldout full-color map poster, which provides five additional maps not found in the text. The book also contains photographs accompanied by brief essays explaining their settings and significance. Many of the terms or concepts that might be unfamiliar to some readers, especially military terms, are defined in the glossary at the back of the book. New in this third edition, brief outlines begin each chapter, providing students with an overview of what the chapter will cover, and a timeline of key events concludes each Part.

Website

Also new for this edition is a website that provides helpful resources for instructors, including electronic versions of maps and images from the textbook. Learning tools for students, including quizzes and Web-based research exercises, are also available on the site.

Acknowledgments

I am grateful to reviewers of the second edition who offered suggestions both for new content and for revising the map program: Dale Baum, Texas A&M University; Stephen Kantrowitz, University of Wisconsin—Madison; Peter Maslowski, University of Nebraska—Lincoln; Kenneth T. Osborne, Roger Williams University; Roger Ransom, University of California—Riverside; Alice E. Reagan, North Virginia Community College; Louis T. Scirrotto, Northhampton Community College; Paul D. Travis, Texas Woman's University; Vernon L. Volpe, University of Nebraska—Kearney; and Kenneth J. Winkle, University of Nebraska—Lincoln. My thanks go also to students and colleagues whose feedback and advice have helped me make these improvements in the third edition. I am most appreciative of the skilled editorial blue pencil of a Princeton University graduate student, Jenny Weber, which has sharpened my prose. The copy editor, Jane Stembridge, has eliminated inconsistencies and crudities in punctuation and usage. The editorial and production staff of McGraw-Hill College Division, especially Kristen N. Mellitt and Vicki Krug, have been unfailingly supportive and efficient.

James M. McPherson

The Setting of Conflict

During the first half of the nineteenth century, the United States grew at a rate unparalleled in modern history. This growth occurred in three dimensions: territory, population, and economy. The Louisiana Purchase in 1803 doubled the nation's territory. The acquisitions of Florida (1810 and 1819), Texas (1845), and Oregon (1846) and the cessions from Mexico (1848 and 1854) nearly doubled it again. Population growth exceeded this fourfold increase of territory: the six million Americans of 1803 became twenty-six million by 1853. The economy grew even faster: during these fifty years, the gross national product increased sevenfold. No other country could match any single one of these components of growth; the combined impact of all three made the United States a phenomenon of the Western world.

This growth, however, was achieved at high cost to certain groups in North America. White men ruthlessly and illegally seized Indian lands and killed the native Americans or drove them west of the Mississippi. The land hunger of Americans provoked armed conflicts with Spaniards and Mexicans whose territory they seized by violence and war. American economic expansion was based in part on slave-grown tobacco and cotton. Born of a revolution that proclaimed all men free and equal, the United States became the largest slaveholding country in the world.

The social and political strains produced by rapid growth provoked repeated crises that threatened to destroy the republic. From the beginning, these strains were associated mainly with slavery. The geographical division of the country into free and slave states ensured that the crises would take the form of sectional conflict. Each section evolved institutions and values based on its labor system. These values in turn generated ideologies that justified each section's institutions and condemned those of the other.

For three-quarters of a century, the two sections coexisted under one flag because the centripetal forces of nationalism—the shared memories of a common struggle for nationhood—proved stronger than the centrifugal forces of sectionalism. But as early as 1787, conflict over slavery at the constitutional convention almost broke up the Union before it was fairly launched. To forestall Southern threats to reject the Constitution, Northern states finally accepted three compromises to protect slavery: a provision adding three-fifths of the slaves to the free population as a basis of representation in the lower house and in the electoral college (Article I, Section 2); a clause forbidding for twenty years the passage of a federal law to prohibit the importation of slaves (Article I, Section 9); and a clause requiring the return of slaves who escaped into free states (Article IV, Section 2).

In subsequent decades a powerful impetus for territorial expansion came from the South, which hoped to gain new slave states to counterbalance the more rapid population growth of the free states. The Louisiana Purchase, the annexation of Texas, and the conquest of the Southwest from Mexico were accomplished by Southern presidents and Southern-dominated congressional majorities over significant Northern opposition. Southern-born settlers tried unsuccessfully to legalize slavery in Indiana and Illinois, in defiance of the provision in the Northwest Ordinance banning the institution in the territories from which these states were formed.

Northern antislavery leaders produced their own counterthrusts to Southern maneuvers. In 1819, Northern congressmen tried to exclude slavery from the proposed new state of Missouri, part of the Louisiana Purchase. The ensuing sectional conflict in Congress provoked angry rhetoric and fears of disunion. The lawmakers resolved the impasse in 1820 by a compromise that admitted Missouri as a slave state but prohibited slavery in the remaining portion of the Louisiana Purchase that lay north of 36°30′.

The Missouri Compromise settled the question of slavery in the territories for a generation, until the Mexican War caused it to flare up anew. Before 1850, Congress admitted free and slave states alternately to the Union, enabling the South to maintain parity in the Senate (at fifteen slave states and fifteen free states by 1848) even though the region's slower population growth reduced the South to a permanent minority in the House and in the electoral college. The selection of Supreme Court justices by geographical circuits gave the slave states, with their larger territory, a majority on the Supreme Court. And the South's domination of the Democratic party allowed the section to wield political power out of proportion to its population. For two-thirds of the years from 1789 to 1861, the Presidents of the United States, the Speakers of the House and presidents pro tem of the Senate, and the chairmen of key congressional committees were Southerners.

But this Southern domination of national politics could not last forever. By 1860, the free states had a population of nineteen million, and the slave states just over twelve million. Four million of the latter were slaves. The election of a President by a Northern antislavery party in 1860 was the handwriting on the wall. To escape the perceived threat to their way of life, most of the slave states seceded and brought on a civil war.

Part One The Coming of War

Chapter One

American Modern- ization, 1800—1860

Everything new is quickly introduced here, and all the latest inventions. There is no clinging to old ways, the moment an American hears the word "invention" he pricks up his ears.

-Friedrick List,
a Prussian visitor to the United States, 1829

5

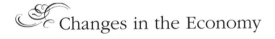

Changes in the Economy

A middle-aged American in the 1850s could look back on remarkable economic changes during his or her lifetime. The first half of the nineteenth century brought the industrial revolution to the United States, where it greatly transformed the material conditions of life.

In 1800, when steam power, machines, and factories had already turned Britain into the world's leading industrial power, the United States was still an agricultural society whose few manufactured goods were made by hand in homes and in small artisan shops or were imported from Britain. Only 6 percent of the population lived in towns or cities larger than 2,500 people, a percentage that had remained roughly constant for more than a century. Sailing vessels carried most of the trade between cities. Overland travel had improved little since the days of the Roman Empire; indeed, the Roman highway was probably superior to the American—with few exceptions, the American road was little more than a dirt path almost impassable in wet weather. Inland water transport was mainly confined to downriver flatboats that were broken up and sold for firewood when they reached their destinations. Farming techniques had undergone little alteration since the arrival of the first colonists. Output per farm worker was no higher—and in some areas lower—than a century earlier. Farms more than a few miles from population centers or navigable rivers existed largely on a subsistence basis, for the absence of adequate transportation made it difficult to get crops to market.

All of this began to change after the War of 1812. Before then, the American colonies and states had experienced what economists call "extensive" economic growth: a growth rate little if any greater than the increase in population. After 1815, the economy sustained "intensive" growth: a rate of increase in wealth and output exceeding population growth. This intensive, or *per capita,* economic growth averaged about 1.5 percent annually from 1815 to 1860—enough to double per capita output during those forty-five years.

The economic changes during the first half of the nineteenth century were qualitative as well as quantitative. One can conceive of intensive economic growth without any important changes in economic structures or techniques. An agricultural economy, for example, may increase its per capita output by moving onto more fertile land or by utilizing traditional methods more efficiently. This happened in the Southern states between 1800 and 1860. The Northern economy, however, underwent a process of *development*—that is, qualitative as well as quantitative growth—during this period. The following analysis of economic development, therefore, will apply mainly to the North.[1]

Changes in Transportation

The first and probably most important qualitative changes came in transportation. The decades from 1800 to 1830 constituted the turnpike era in early American history. Construction crews built thousands of miles of new or improved all-weather, macadamized roads (compacted stones and crushed rock), mostly in the Northern states. The turnpike era overlapped the canal era, which began with the astounding success of the Erie Canal, completed from Albany to Buffalo in 1825. By 1850, the United States had 3,700 miles of canals, also mostly in the free states. The canal era in turn overlapped the beginning of the railroad age. The opening of the first railroad westward from Baltimore in 1830 was followed by a boom in railroad construction, especially during the 1850s. As early as 1840, the United States had 3,328 miles of rail—more than Britain, the pioneer in this mode of transport. By 1860, the United States had nearly 31,000 miles of rail—as much as the rest of the world combined.

These decades also witnessed the great age of the river steamboat. Robert Fulton introduced the first successful steamboat on the Hudson River in 1807. After the War of 1812, this novel form of transport developed rapidly and became the principal

---

[1]In this book, geographical terms will be defined as follows: "South" refers to the slave states and "North" to the free states, except during the Civil War when the four "border states" that did not secede—Delaware, Maryland, Kentucky, and Missouri—are included in the "North." These "border states" plus Virginia, North Carolina, and Tennessee will sometimes be referred to as the "upper South"; all other slave states are designated the "lower South" and sometimes the "cotton South." "Section" and "sectional" refer, according to context, to the slave states or the free states and to comparisons or relations between them. "Region" will designate smaller groupings of states within each section: "New England" and the "Mid-Atlantic states" (New York, Pennsylvania, and New Jersey) will sometimes be grouped together as the "Northeast"; the "Old Northwest," or after the acquisition of the Oregon Territory in 1846, the "Midwest," will be the label for states west of the Appalachian Mountains and north of the Ohio River; the "Southeast" will refer to slave states east of the Appalachians; the "Old Southwest" will be used for the slave states west of the Appalachians and should not be confused with the new "Southwest"—the territory acquired from Mexico in 1848.

Principal Canals in 1860

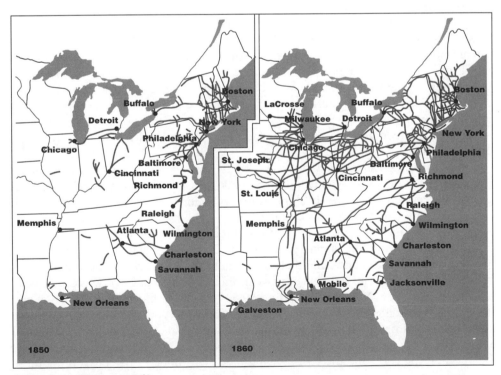

Railroads in 1850 and 1860

7

means of transport in the area served by the Ohio and Mississippi rivers. The dozen or so steamboats on American rivers in 1815 multiplied to about 3,000 by 1860. Canals were widened and deepened in the 1840s to accommodate steamboats. These paddlewheeled vessels also plied the Great Lakes. The ocean steamer had appeared before the Civil War, but the United States continued to rely mainly on sailing ships for its salt-water merchant marine.

The expansion of canals and railroads plus the development of Great Lakes shipping had an impact on regional alignments. Before 1840, most interregional trade flowed in a north-south direction. Coastal shipping along the Atlantic seaboard and river transport along the Ohio-Mississippi network dominated trading patterns. But the major canals and railroads ran generally in an east-west direction to link the Northeast with the Old Northwest. By the 1840s, the tonnage transported over the Great Lakes-Erie Canal route exceeded tonnage on the Mississippi; by the 1850s, tonnage on the east-west water and rail routes was more than twice the north-south river volume. This reorientation of trade patterns strengthened interregional ties among the free states—a development that would help weld them together against the South in the secession crisis of 1861.

Nineteenth-century Americans called their transport facilities "internal improvements." Modern economists term them "infrastructure" or "social overhead capital." This is a form of capital investment that, because construction takes a long time, does not yield quick returns. Indeed, even the ultimate direct profits to investors may be low or nonexistent, though the benefits to society in the form of improved transportation are high. Private capital is often unwilling or unable to undertake such projects. Thus the state governments built most of the canals, and the state and federal governments built most of the improved roads outside of New England. Turnpikes constructed by private capital rarely returned a profit, and the states eventually took over many of them. The federal as well as state governments dredged harbors and river channels, built levees, and in other ways helped to improve and maintain inland waterways. Although private capital built most of the railroads, many cities, states, and the federal government provided vital assistance with loans, land grants, and guarantees of bond issues.

These investments provided the basis for intensive economic growth. By reducing the time and costs of transportation, they made possible the creation of an interregional market economy. Freight shipped from Cincinnati to New York in 1817 took more than fifty days to reach its destination; by 1852, it required only six days. The same trip for passengers was reduced from three weeks to two days. The accompanying graph of inland freight rates illustrates the dramatic reduction in transport costs. Western farmers could now ship their products to the East, where consumers could afford to buy them. The difference between the wholesale price of western pork in Cincinnati and New York declined from $9.53 to $1.18 a barrel between 1818 and 1858. The price difference between Cincinnati and New York for a barrel of western flour declined from $2.48 to $0.28 during the same years. The cumulative effect of many such cost reductions lowered the wholesale price index for the United States by about 40 percent, and the cost-of-living index by about 15 percent, during these four decades.

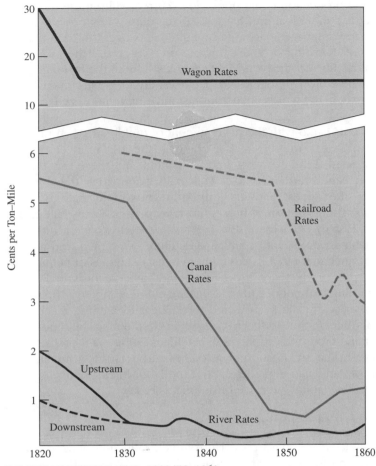

INLAND FREIGHT RATES, 1820 TO 1860
(Adapted from Douglass C. North, *Growth and Welfare in the American Past,* 2d ed., Englewood Cliffs, N.J. 1974, p. 108.)

Increased Food Production

By creating a national market, improved transportation enabled farmers and manufacturers to achieve specialization and economies of scale (lower unit costs because of larger volume). During the four antebellum decades, the total output of food crops increased fourfold and the percentage of that production sold in the market instead of consumed on the farm nearly doubled. This made it possible for farmers to feed the rapidly growing cities even though the proportion of the labor force in agriculture declined from 76 to 57 percent between 1820 and 1860. The urban population grew three times as fast as the rural population during these four decades, raising the urban proportion of the total from 7 percent in 1820 to 20 percent in 1860. This was the fastest rate of urbanization in American history.

The increase in food production could not have occurred without the numerous technological innovations in agriculture that took place during this period. Before 1800, there had been few improvements in farm implements over the centuries. "In culture, harvesting, and threshing of grains," wrote one historian, "the [American] colonists were not much advanced beyond Biblical times." But in the first half of the nineteenth century, a host of inventors developed a variety of horse-drawn implements and machines that, in the words of another historian, "revolutionized the technology of agriculture."[2]

The first improvements came with the development of moldboard iron plows in the 1810s and steel plows in the 1830s. Beginning in the 1820s, inventors also patented a variety of seed drills, harrows, and cultivators. But these implements, which increased the acreage a farmer could sow, actually made worse the chief bottleneck of agriculture—the harvest. Farmers could now grow more grain than they could reap and thresh. The invention of horse-drawn reapers by Cyrus McCormick of Virginia and Obed Hussey of Maine in the 1830s was therefore one of the most important developments in nineteenth-century agriculture. Two men and a horse could now harvest as much grain in a day as eight men using cradles or twenty men using sickles. This leap in productivity, however, would have meant little if similar improvements in threshing had not occurred at the same time. John and Hiram Pitts of Maine patented a successful horse-powered threshing and fanning machine in 1834. By the 1850s, farmers in the Northern states were overcoming their traditional conservatism and buying thousands of the new machines being mass-produced by factories in the Midwest. This substitution of machines and horses for human labor began the transition of American agriculture from the labor-intensive livelihood it had been until then to the capital-intensive business it is today.

The American System of Manufactures

Similar changes took place in manufacturing. Household production of hand-crafted goods for subsistence and for local markets reached a peak about 1815 and then gave way to shop- and factory-produced goods for regional and national markets. In the United States, as in Britain, textiles were the leading sector of the industrial revolution. The factory system (defined as wage-earning employees with different skills working together in a large building to manufacture a product with the aid of power-driven machinery) came first to this industry in the 1810s with the introduction of the power loom at Waltham, Massachusetts. New England textile mills increased their annual output of cloth from 4 million yards in 1817 to 308 million yards in 1837.

The factory system spread from textiles to other industries after 1830, as inventors and entrepreneurs developed new machines and new methods of organizing production. Britain, of course, pioneered many of these developments. Other western

---

[2]Ulysses Prentiss Hedrick, *A History of Agriculture in the State of New York* (Albany, 1933), p. 67; Clarence H. Danhof, *Change in Agriculture: The Northern United States, 1820–1870* (Cambridge, Mass., 1969), p. 181.

European countries also led the United States in basic science and in early industrial technology. But American businessmen and engineers had a knack for adapting foreign technology to their own needs and improving it. Thus, while the basic inventions of textile machinery were British, most of the improvements during the 1820s and 1830s were American. Perhaps the most important American contribution to the clothing industry was the sewing machine, invented by Elias Howe of Massachusetts in the 1840s.

American technology was more change oriented than its European counterpart. Americans built cheap and light textile machinery, often of wood. This horrified British engineers, who built their machines of metal to last for decades. But there was method in the apparent American madness. Technology was advancing so rapidly that when an American machine wore out after a few years, it could be cheaply replaced by a better one, while the heavier and more expensive British machines could not be so readily scrapped. "Everything new is quickly introduced here," wrote a foreign visitor to the United States in 1829. "There is no clinging to old ways, the moment an American hears the word 'invention' he pricks up his ears."[3]

By the 1840s, the United States had partly reversed the earlier flow of technology from Europe to America. British industrialists discovered that they could learn much from their upstart rivals across the Atlantic. Perhaps the most important Yankee contribution to the industrial revolution was what the British called "the American system of manufactures"—the mass production of machine-made, interchangeable parts. Introduced first in the manufacture of firearms in the early nineteenth century, the concept of interchangeable parts was a revolutionary one. Previously, skilled craftsmen had fashioned each part of a musket, and each musket had been a unique creation whose parts were not exactly the same as the similar parts of other muskets. The manufacture of muskets (or any other item) was therefore a slow process requiring many skilled workers. The final product was expensive, and if any of its parts broke or wore out they could be replaced only by a craftsman, who would make a new and expensive replacement. If each part, on the other hand, was machine-produced in large quantities, all the parts in one musket would be interchangeable with the similar parts of another one. Both the manufacturing and the replacement costs would be reduced. The first crude machine tools did not always produce parts that were perfectly interchangeable, but as the century advanced and machine-tool technology improved, the American system of mass production expanded to include scores of products: clocks and watches, nails, screws, nuts and bolts, locks, furniture, plows, sewing machines, boots and shoes—even large items such as the parts for steam engines, locomotives, and McCormick reapers.

Impressed by American methods of firearms manufacture, the British imported Yankee engineers and machinists to help build their new Enfield Armoury for the production of army rifles. Britain also sent industrial commissions to visit American factories in the 1850s and invited Samuel Colt, the Connecticut inventor of the six-shooting revolver, to testify before Parliament in 1854. In his testimony, Colt summed

---

[3]Stuart Bruchey, *The Roots of American Economic Growth, 1607–1861* (New York, 1965), p. 166.

up the American system of manufactures in a single sentence: "There is nothing that cannot be produced by machinery."[4] This attitude enabled the United States to become the world leader in machine-tool technology by the third quarter of the nineteenth century.

✑ Causes of American Modernization

From its beginnings, therefore, American industry—like much of American agriculture—was capital intensive rather than labor intensive. There were four basic reasons for this: a shortage of labor, especially skilled labor; a generous endowment of resources; a high level of mass education and literacy; and an openness to change, a willingness to innovate and experiment.

The low population density of the United States, the lure of cheap land on the frontier, and the rapid growth of the economy kept the supply of labor below the demand. American wage levels were consequently higher than European. The shortage and high cost of labor impelled technological innovation, to substitute machines for human workers.

If labor was scarce and expensive in comparison with Europe, the opposite was true of key resources, especially water and wood. Water powered the textile mills of New England, and wood fueled the steam engines that powered steamboats, locomotives, and some factories. American forests also supplied a plentiful and cheap source of building material for machinery, ships, railroad ties and cars, and a host of other items whose cost was greater in wood-deficient Europe. Just as the abundance of resources, in the form of cheap land, stimulated capital-intensive agriculture, so the abundance of raw materials and power stimulated capital-intensive industry.

Education and values also played crucial roles in American economic development. Not counting the slave population, the United States in 1850 had the highest literacy rate (89 percent) and the highest percentage of children in school of any country in the world save Sweden and Denmark. The free states, when considered alone, surpassed the Scandinavian countries, while New England stood in a class by itself. Foreign observers pointed out the importance of education in producing the "adaptative versatility" of Yankee workers. A visiting British industrial commission reported in 1854 that having been "educated up to a far higher standard than those of a much superior social grade in the Old World, the American working boy develops rapidly into the skilled artisan, and having once mastered one part of his business, he is never content until he has mastered all." With examples "constantly before him of ingenious men who have solved economic and mechanical problems to their own profit and elevation . . . there is not a working boy of average ability in the New England States, at least, who has not an idea of some mechanical invention

---

[4]Eugene S. Ferguson, "Technology as Knowledge," in Edwin T. Layton (ed.), *Technology and Change in America* (New York, 1973), p. 23.

or improvement in manufactures."[5] Many American technological innovations were indeed contributed by the workers themselves: Elias Howe, for example, was a journeyman machinist in Boston when he invented the sewing machine.

Americans were less bound than Europeans by tradition and by inherited institutions that inhibited change. The heritage of revolution and republicanism gave them a sense of being a new and unique people. They oriented themselves toward the future rather than the past; they valued change more than tradition; they proclaimed their belief in "progress," "advancement," "improvement"; they exhibited a "go-ahead spirit," a belief that "the sky is the limit." "We are THE PEOPLE OF THE FUTURE," exulted American nationalists in the 1840s. "Custom hath lost its sway, and Time and Change are the Champions against the field."[6] This optimism, this willingness to experiment, underlay the Yankee genius for innovation.

Many Americans considered machinery an agent of moral improvement and democratic equality. The railroads, said one enthusiast, were God's instrument "to quicken the activity of men; to send energy and vitality where before were silence and barrenness; to multiply cities and villages, studded with churches, dotted with schools." A writer in *Scientific American* asserted in 1851 that "every new and useful machine, invented and improved, confers a general benefit upon all classes,— the poor as well as the rich." The Whig political leader William H. Seward believed that "popular government follows in the track of the steam-engine and the telegraph." The increased output and rising standard of living produced by technological progress, declared an early economist, were "marked by a tendency to equality of physical and intellectual condition."[7]

The antebellum United States was undergoing a process that some social scientists term "modernization": heavy investment in social overhead capital, which transforms a localized subsistence economy into a nationally integrated market economy; rapid increases in output per capita, resulting from technological innovation and the shift from labor-intensive toward capital-intensive production; the accelerated growth of the industrial sector compared with other sectors of the economy; rapid urbanization, made possible by an increase in agricultural productivity that enables farmers to feed the growing cities; an expansion of education, literacy, and mass communications; a value system that emphasizes change over tradition; an evolution from the traditional, rural, village-oriented system of personal and kinship ties, in which status is "ascriptive" (inherited), toward a fluid, cosmopolitan, impersonal, and pluralistic society, in which status is achieved by merit. In most of these respects, the United States—with the partial and significant exception of the South—was the most rapidly modernizing country in the world in the mid-nineteenth century.

---

[5]Nathan Rosenberg (ed.), *The American System of Manufactures* (Edinburgh, 1969), pp. 203–204.

[6]Arthur A. Ekirch, *The Idea of Progress in America, 1815–1860* (New York, 1944), p. 52.

[7]Ibid., pp. 102, 119; Eric Foner, *Free Soil, Free Labor, Free Men: The Ideology of the Republican Party Before the Civil War* (New York, 1970), p. 39.

The Modernizing Ethos

American modernization had its roots in a value system associated with the Protestant work ethic. Nearly a century ago, the German sociologist Max Weber called attention to the connection between *The Protestant Ethic and the Spirit of Capitalism*—to cite the title of his most famous book. Weber wondered why the most advanced capitalist societies were Protestant—and in particular, Calvinist. He pointed to Calvinist theology as an explanation: the doctrine of salvation by election; the belief that worldly success was a sign of God's favor; the concept of the "calling," according to which all people are called by God to vocations that, no matter how great or humble, are equal in his sight and whose diligent performance is a sacred duty; and the injunction against waste, according to which wealth must be used for the glory of God through stewardship to humankind rather than squandered in conspicuous consumption and easy living. This combination of beliefs created a value system that Weber described as "worldly asceticism": hard work, thrift, sobriety, reliability, self-discipline, self-reliance, and the deferral of immediate gratification for long-range goals. These were precisely the values best suited to modernizing capitalism.[8]

In a more secular age, these values have become known as the work ethic. But during the nineteenth century, they were still very much anchored in religion. And because in Britain and America they were exhibited most forcefully by the Puritans (as well as by those seventeenth- and eighteenth-century offshoots of Puritanism, the Quakers and Unitarians), they are sometimes known as the Puritan ethic. Puritan theology, sermons, and maxims contained many biblical quotations and aphorisms emphasizing work as the glorification of God and idleness as the instrument of Satan: "If any would not work, neither shall he eat" (2 Thess. 3:10); "The hand of the diligent shall bear rule: but the slothful shall be under tribute" (Prov. 13:24), "Satan finds mischief for idle hands to do" (Isaac Watts).

These maxims were also disseminated by schoolbooks and by the extraordinary outpouring of "how to succeed" books. The main message of the latter was that success is attainable through hard work, good works, sobriety, and thrift. Many of the authors were clergymen, who told their readers that, in the words of a New England minister, "religion will teach you that industry is a SOLEMN DUTY you owe to God, whose command is, 'BE DILIGENT IN BUSINESS!' " American schoolbooks, especially the widely used Speller by Noah Webster and the Readers by Presbyterian clergyman William Holmes McGuffey, inculcated the same message: "Persevering industry will enable one to accomplish almost anything."[9]

---

[8]Although influential, the Weber thesis is not universally accepted. Critics maintain that religious factors alone cannot explain economic developments and point out that several non-Protestant societies—for example, Japan—have also experienced remarkable economic growth and modernization.

[9]Irvin G. Wyllie, *The Self-Made Man in America: The Myth of Rags to Riches* (New Brunswick, N.J., 1954), pp. 63, 42–43.

Table 1.1   Origins of Nineteenth-Century American Business Executives and Inventors

| Region | AMERICAN BUSINESS EXECUTIVES (MEDIAN BIRTH DATE 1825) | | Birthplace and/or Residence of Inventors of Main Technological Innovations, 1790–1860 | Residence of All Americans in 1825 |
	Birthplace (N = 247)	Father's Birthplace (N = 175)		
New England	51%	65%	42%	16%
Rest of North	34	22	51	38
South	3	2	7	46
Abroad or unspecified	12	11		

Table 1.2   Religious Affiliations of Nineteenth-Century Business Executives

Denomination	Business Executives (N = 144)	American Population c. 1840 (Estimated)
Congregational	22% ⎫	5% ⎫
Presbyterian	14 ⎬ 54%	10 ⎬ 17%
Unitarian	10 ⎪	1 ⎪
Quaker	8 ⎭	1 ⎭
Episcopal	25	2
Other Protestant	21	51

The Puritan work ethic was strongest among New Englanders in general and among Congregationalists, Unitarians, Presbyterians, and Quakers in particular. It was no coincidence that New England was at the cutting edge of American modernization or that a disproportionate number of entrepreneurs and inventors were New England Yankees of Calvinist background. Tables 1.1 and 1.2 illustrate this predominance.[10]

Other studies have confirmed the data in these tables. An analysis of property ownership based on the 1860 census revealed that, no matter where they lived, men of New England birth enjoyed greater average wealth than men born in any other part of the country. Surveys of prominent businessmen and of millionaires during

---

[10]The data on business executives are from Frances W. Gregory and Irene Neu, "The American Industrial Elite in the 1870's: Their Social Origins," in William Miller (ed.), *Men in Business* (Cambridge, 1952), pp. 193–204. Data on inventors were calculated from the list in Roger Burlingame, *March of the Iron Men: A Social History of Union Through Invention* (New York, 1938), pp. 468–476. Data on religious affiliation of the American population were calculated from Edwin S. Gaustad, *Historical Atlas of Religion in America* (New York, 1962), pp. 52, 140.

the nineteenth century found that New Englanders were represented in both groups at twice their proportion of the population. Two studies of scientists found Yankees overrepresented by two and a half times their population percentage.[11]

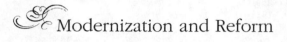

Modernization and Reform

The modernizing ethos of Yankee Protestantism also gave rise to some of the principal reform movements in antebellum America: temperance, education, women's rights, and antislavery.[12] These movements grew out of the Second Great Awakening, a prolonged series of Protestant revivals in the first third of the nineteenth century. Inspired by a zealous sense of mission, many evangelicals—especially those of Yankee heritage—strove not only for the conversion of individual sinners but also for the purification of society from such sins as drunkenness, prostitution, ignorance, and above all slavery. The evangelicals hoped to reform society by first reforming individuals—by inculcating in them the Protestant ethic values of industry, piety, sobriety, thrift, and self-improvement through self-discipline.

The Temperance Movement

The temperance movement displayed all of these reform traits. In the early nineteenth century, Americans consumed an extraordinary amount of alcohol—more than three times as much per person as today. No social occasion was complete without heavy drinking. Liquor was cheap, untaxed in most areas, and constituted a considerable portion of people's caloric intake. Many persons greeted each day with a gill (four ounces) of whiskey or rum; John Adams regularly drank a pint of hard cider (about 20 proof) before breakfast. European visitors voiced astonishment at the "universal practice of sipping a little at a time [every] half an hour to a couple of hours, during the whole day."[13]

The temperance movement arose as a reaction against such heavy drinking. Beginning as a local religious and moral reform, it expanded into a national crusade by the 1830s. At the height of its influence in 1836, the American Temperance Union (ATU), a federation of local and regional societies, claimed a membership of a million and a half. But the ATU fragmented thereafter as its members divided over the question of temperance versus prohibition. At first, the movement had favored moderation in drinking; but by the 1830s its radical wing was pushing the organization toward the goal of prohibiting all alcoholic beverages. The requirement that members pledge total abstinence caused a dramatic drop in ATU membership by 1840.

Up to this point, temperance had been a middle-class Protestant movement. It had tried by moral suasion to infuse values of sobriety and self-restraint into the whole society. In this respect, the temperance movement fostered the process of modern-

---

[11]Lee Soltow, *Men and Wealth in the United States 1850–1870* (New Haven, 1975), pp. 148–149, 152; C. Wright Mills, "The American Business Elite: A Collective Portrait," in Economic History Association, *Tasks of Economic History* (New York, 1945), pp. 20–44; Pitirim Sorokin, "American Millionaires and Multi-Millionaires," *Journal of Social Forces,* 3 (1925), 634 (this article includes data on scientists also); *American Men of Science* (New York, 1910).

[12]The antislavery movement is discussed in Chapter 3.

[13]J. C. Furnas, *The Americans: A Social History* (New York, 1969), p. 505.

ization. Work patterns in pre-industrial societies were task oriented rather than time oriented. Artisans worked in bursts of effort to complete a particular job, then took several days off, perhaps to spend their time and money in tippling. This irregularity did not fit the clockwork pace of factories, in which the operation of machines required punctuality, reliability, and sobriety. Work became time oriented instead of task oriented, a transition aided by the mass production of clocks and watches, itself an achievement of the American system of manufactures. It was not merely an accident of history that the temperance movement in both Britain and America coincided with the industrial revolution. As part of the effort to inculcate discipline and steadiness among workers, many employers supported the temperance movement, and some forbade their employees to drink on *or* off the job.

Many workers, especially Irish and German immigrants, resented and resisted such efforts to impose temperance. But by 1840 some skilled Protestant workingmen had internalized temperance values and had begun to form "Washington Temperance Societies."[14] Proudly declaring themselves reformed drunkards, they expanded the membership of these societies to a purported 600,000 by 1847. The Washingtonian movement rejuvenated the temperance crusade, which turned from moral suasion to legal coercion in the 1840s. Fifteen states legislated against the sale of liquor during the decade after Maine passed the first such law in 1846.

These laws, however, were poorly enforced, and most were eventually repealed or struck down by the courts. The phenomenal success of the temperance movement was due chiefly to moral suasion and self-denial. Between 1830 and 1850, the per capita consumption of alcohol declined fourfold. During the same years, the per capita consumption of coffee and tea nearly doubled. The impact of these changes on the values associated with the work ethic—such as sobriety, punctuality, and reliability—scarcely needs to be spelled out.

Education

Another major focus of antebellum reform was public education. Economists consider education a means of "human capital formation" crucial to economic growth and modernization. Investment in education temporarily removes young people from the labor force but in the long run increases their aptitudes, skills, and productivity. "Intelligent laborers," wrote a businessman in 1853, "can add much more to the capital employed in a business than those who are ignorant."[15] As noted earlier, British industrialists explained the adaptative versatility of American workers and the technological proficiency of American industry by reference to the high level of education and literacy in the United States.

Like other aspects of modernization, education owed much of its impetus to Protestantism. The Puritan emphasis on the ability to read the Bible and to understand theology made New England the most literate society in the world during the seventeenth century. The same religious motivation underlay education in Presbyterian Scotland and Lutheran Sweden, which caught up with New England during

---

[14]Named for George Washington, in order to symbolize their professed patriotic and republican virtues.
[15]Ekirch, *Idea of Progress*, p. 197.

the eighteenth century. In nineteenth-century America, higher education was sustained primarily by Protestant denominations, and Protestant influences imbued even the public schools.

As early as 1830, New England and New York had public school systems that reached at least three-quarters of the population. Although in other areas a combination of local free schools, church schools, private schools, apprenticeship programs, and home tutoring provided education for most of the white population, little in the way of a public school *system* existed outside New England and New York. And even there the system was haphazard; formal teacher training scarcely existed; educational standards varied widely; classes were ungraded and rarely went beyond the grammar-school level.

Under the tutelage of New England progressives, especially Horace Mann, educational reforms spread through much of the North beginning in the 1830s. As secretary of the Massachusetts State Board of Education, Mann led a drive to rationalize the patchwork pattern of public schools, to professionalize the teachers, and to carry the message of reform into other states. Mann founded the first "normal" school for teacher training in 1839. During the next two decades, several Northern states established such institutions. Massachusetts also pioneered in other innovations: a standardized graded curriculum, the first compulsory attendance law (1852), and extension of public education to the secondary level. By 1860, most Northern states sustained public school systems at least through the eighth grade, and about three-quarters of the Northern children between five and sixteen years of age were enrolled in school. Although some Southern states began modest educational reforms in the 1850s, the South lacked an effective public school system before the Civil War.

An essential task of education, wrote the Massachusetts superintendent of schools in 1857, was "by moral and religious instruction daily given" to "inculcate habits of regularity, punctuality, constancy, and industry." Although religious overtones remained strong, many educational reformers began to view the function of schooling in more secular terms. Horace Mann in particular had a modern vision of the schools as agents of economic growth and social mobility. Education "[is] the grand agent for the development or augmentation of national resources," he wrote in 1848, "more powerful in the production and gainful employment of the total wealth of a country than all the other things mentioned in the books of the political economists." Schooling would also uplift the poor by equipping them with the values and skills necessary to function in a modern capitalist economy. Education "does better than to disarm the poor of their hostility toward the rich; it prevents their being poor."[16] If this belief proved to be too optimistic, it nevertheless bespoke the faith that most Americans have placed in education as a lever of upward mobility.

Not all education took place in schools. In addition to such institutions as the family and the church, many channels existed for the dissemination of information and ideas. One of the most important was the public lecture. Reformers dis-

---

[16]Michael B. Katz, *The Irony of Early School Reform: Educational Innovation in Mid-Nineteenth Century Massachusetts* (Cambridge, Mass., 1968), p. 43; Horace Mann, "Annual Report of 1848," in *The Life and Works of Horace Mann,* 5 vols. (Boston, 1891), IV, 245–251.

covered lecturing to be the most effective way to spread their message. In 1826, Josiah Holbrook, a Massachusetts educator, founded the American Lyceum of Science and the Arts. The lyceum was the first national agency for adult education. It brought lecturers on almost every conceivable subject to cities and hamlets throughout the country.

Overshadowing all other means of communication in the nineteenth century was the press. The United States was the world's preeminent newspaper-reading country. Technological advances in printing caused explosive growth in newspaper circulation after 1830. The installation of the first steam press in 1835 increased the capacity of a single press from 200 to 5,500 copies per hour. New machines for making and cutting paper also lowered prices and thereby boosted circulation. In the 1820s, a single issue of a newspaper cost five or six cents; less than two decades later, several New York dailies sold for a penny. The growth of the railroads enabled urban dailies to print weekly editions for rural areas. By 1860, the weekly edition of Horace Greeley's *New York Tribune* reached the unprecedented circulation of 200,000 copies. The commercial development of the telegraph after 1844 made possible the instantaneous transmission of news over long distances and led to the formation of the Associated Press in 1848. The number of newspapers doubled between 1825 and 1840 and doubled again by 1860, reaching a total of 3,300. Circulation grew twice as fast as population. By 1860, the United States had twice as many newspapers as Britain—indeed, it had nearly one-third of the newspapers in the entire world.

Women

Economic modernization had an ambivalent impact on women. When most Americans lived on farms or in farm villages, before 1815, the family had been the principal unit of production as well as of consumption. Mothers and daughters had tended gardens and farm animals, spun and woven cloth, sewed garments, dipped candles, and helped to make many other items for family use. But as the economy diversified and industrialized after 1815, production of cloth, shoes, candles, and even food moved increasingly outside the home. Some girls and unmarried young women went to work in the new textile mills; others stayed at home and helped their mothers bind shoes or sew shirts for low piecework wages in the "putting out" system organized by the shoemaking and ready-made clothing industry during the 1820s. But very few married women worked for wages outside the home, and only the poorest did so within the household. As production shifted from household to shop, factory, office, and commercial agriculture, husbands went *out* of the home to work while wives stayed at home to raise children and manage the household. Thus there arose "separate spheres" for men and women. Man's sphere was the bustling world of work, commerce, politics; woman's sphere was the domestic circle of household and children.

In some respects this marked a decline in woman's status. But in other ways it laid the groundwork for modern feminism. The young women who earned wages in New England textile mills experienced a degree of independence that often carried into their marriages, which were more of an equal partnership with husbands than their mothers' marriages had been. "I regard it as one of the privileges of my

THE CHANGING STATUS OF WOMEN.

By the second quarter of the nineteenth century, a growing number of young, unmarried women were joining the wage labor force, especially in New England textile mills such as the one above. At the same time, middle-class women like Elizabeth Cady Stanton, photographed here in the 1840s with two of her children, obtained an excellent education at women's secondary schools (called "seminaries") but were denied political rights and excluded from many occupations. Having broken through some traditional barriers, women led by Stanton launched the modern women's rights movement at a convention in Seneca Falls, New York, in 1848, calling for removal of remaining obstacles to their equal rights and opportunities.

youth," wrote one such woman later in life, "that I was permitted to grow up among those active, interesting girls, whose lives were not mere echoes of other lives, but had principle and purpose distinctly their own."[17]

Even within the confined sphere of the home, many women practiced what has been called "domestic feminism." The old patriarchal domination of wife and children eroded as the father went out of the house each day to his sphere, leaving mother in charge of nurturing, socializing, and educating the children. As the family became less of a productive unit, it became a locus of love and nurture of children. Childhood emerged as a separate stage of life. As middle-class parents lavished more affection on children, they began having fewer of them by practicing a rudimentary form of birth control (mainly sexual abstinence). The birth rate declined by 23 percent between 1810 and 1860. This meant that a woman in the 1850s was less continuously burdened by pregnancy, childbirth, and nursing of children than her mother and grandmother had been. This freed women, especially those of the middle and upper classes, for more activities outside the home.

Thus in a seeming paradox, the notion that woman's sphere was in the home became a sort of springboard for extension of that sphere outside the home. Many of the activists in the temperance movement, antislavery societies, church-related and missionary organizations, and other reform movements of this era were women. But perhaps the most important change during these decades was the rising prominence of women in the enlarged public education system. As families began having fewer children, they sent them to school longer and more frequently. As the function of schools expanded beyond the Three R's to include socializing of children in the values of the society, women began to play a larger role in the process. In a sense, this represented an expansion of woman's "sphere" of nurturing and training children. By the 1850s, nearly three-fourths of the public school teachers in New England were women, and the institution of the "schoolma'am" was spreading through the rest of the North and into the South.

And, of course, if women were to be teachers, they must themselves become better educated. In every society before the middle of the nineteenth century, men were more literate than women. The United States in 1860 was the first country in which as many girls as boys went to school and in which literacy rates for the two sexes were about equal. Higher education was still mostly a male domain, but a few women's "seminaries" got started during this period, and Oberlin College in the 1830s became the first coeducational college. Women also forged to the front in two important media of communication during this era: magazines and popular literature. More than one hundred "ladies' magazines" flourished in the antebellum generation, to which women were principal contributors. The best-selling novelists and short-story writers, whose work was serialized in newspapers and magazines, were mainly women—including Harriet Beecher Stowe, author of one of the most popular and powerful novels of all time, *Uncle Tom's Cabin*.

In many ways, American women by midcentury had emerged into more prominent social and public roles than women had previously played in any Western society. All the more galling, then, were laws that turned their property over to husbands when

---

[17]Catherine Clinton, *The Other Civil War: American Women in the Nineteenth Century* (New York, 1999), p. 25.

they married, made divorce from cruel, exploitative, or philandering husbands almost impossible, and denied women the right to vote or hold public office. It was to attack these injustices that Elizabeth Cady Stanton, Lucretia Mott, and other feminists held a convention at a church in the upstate New York village of Seneca Falls in 1848 to launch the modern women's rights movement. Although the movement's crowning achievement—enfranchisement of women on an equal basis with men—was not secured until the twentieth century, the movement did win more liberal divorce laws, married women's property acts in most states, broader educational and professional opportunities for women, and other gains during the quarter century after 1848.

Modernization and Social Tensions

Not all groups in American society participated equally in the modernizing process or accepted the values that promoted it. The most important dissenters were found in the South (see Chapter 2). In the North, three groups resisted aspects of modernization and the Yankee Protestant hegemony that accompanied it: Catholics, especially the Irish; residents of the southern Midwest, most of them descendants of settlers from the slave states; and some wage laborers.

Catholic versus Protestant Values

The Catholic Irish in both Ireland and America during the nineteenth century possessed cultural values that were in many ways antithetical to modernization. The experience of poverty and oppression had bred in the Irish a profound pessimism that amounted almost to fatalism. Since others possessed all the wealth and power, the practice of self-discipline, self-denial, and investment in the future seemed pointless. Many Irish did not share the conviction that reform or "progress" could lead to improvement for either individuals or society.

Roman Catholic doctrine reinforced this conservatism. A prominent Catholic layman wrote in 1859: "The age attaches . . . too much importance to what is called the progress of society or the progress of civilization, which, to the man whose eye is fixed on God and eternity, can appear of not great value." The church opposed the ferment of reform that flourished in the yeast of Yankee Protestantism. Such reform movements, said Catholic leaders, are "against all the principles and maxims of the past, and all the moral, religious, social, and political institutions of the present." The "spirit of radical Protestantism" had "infected our whole society and turned a large portion of our citizens into madmen." Under the influence of this fanaticism, said a New York Catholic newspaper in 1856, "the country has for a number of years been steadily tending toward revolution."[18] The pope from 1846 to 1878 was Pius IX, whose opposition to modernism and liberalism set the tone for the entire church. In

---

[18]Ekirch, *Idea of Progress,* p. 173; Benjamin J. Blied, *Catholics and the Civil War* (Milwaukee, 1945), p. 30; Oscar Handlin, *Boston's Immigrants: A Study in Acculturation,* rev. ed. (Cambridge, Mass., 1959), pp. 132, 139; *Freeman's Journal,* June 7, 1856.

his *Syllabus of Errors* (1864) Pius declared: "It is an error to believe that the Roman Pontiff can and ought to reconcile himself to, and agree with, progress, liberalism, and contemporary civilization."

These ethnic and religious values contributed to the gulf between the conservative, antireformist Catholic population and the modernizing, reform-minded Yankee Protestants. Class distinctions widened the gulf, for native-born Protestants predominated in the upper and middle classes while Irish Catholics clustered in the lower. Each group viewed the other with suspicion, which increased after the onset of heavy Irish and German immigration in the 1840s (see Chapter 5). Yankee reform movements such as those promoting temperance and public education tried to impose middle-class Protestant values and behavior patterns on the Catholic population. But drinking remained popular among the Irish and Germans even as it declined among Protestants of native or English birth. The proportion of immigrant children attending school in 1850 was only one-third that of native-born children of native-born parents. Catholic parents resented the reading of the King James Bible and the recital of Protestant prayers in the public schools. During the 1840s, a movement began to establish Catholic parochial schools.

The Midwest: Butternuts versus Yankees

The "Butternuts" of the southern Midwest constituted another antimodernization subculture. American westward migration tended to follow the lines of latitude. Thus the southern part of the Midwest was settled mostly by emigrants from the upper South and Pennsylvania, and the northern part mostly by emigrants from New England and upstate New York (which in turn had been settled by New Englanders). The two streams of migration met in central Ohio, Illinois, and Indiana, where they mixed about as readily as oil and water. The Butternuts (so-called because many of them wore homespun clothing dyed with an extract from butternuts or walnuts) were mostly Methodists and Baptists of Southern origin who developed a largely rural economy based on corn, hogs, and whiskey. Their economic as well as cultural orientation was Southern, for the region's transportation network was tied into the southward-flowing tributaries of the Ohio and Mississippi rivers.

The somewhat later-arriving Yankees in the northern half of the Midwest developed a diversified commercial-agricultural economy. This region grew faster and became more prosperous than the Midwest's southern tier during the last two antebellum decades. Its trade orientation along the newly built canal and railroad networks linked it to the industrializing Northeast. The "Yankee" Midwesterners gained control of the major economic institutions in their states: banks, railroads, commercial enterprises, industries, and so on. They also organized temperance, antislavery, and other reform movements. In nearly every index of modernization—per capita wealth and economic growth, schools and literacy, railroads and commerce, rate of urbanization, technological innovation, and support for measures favoring social and economic change—the Yankee areas were ahead of Butternut areas by 1850. Butternuts disliked what they viewed as Yankee economic dominance and "Puritan" cultural imperialism. The politics of these states were marked by bitter conflicts over banking laws, corporation charters, temperance legislation, antislavery agitation, and anti-Negro measures, with the Butternuts consistently hostile to banks, corporations, temperance, and blacks.

Workers

Some urban wage earners as well as farmers looked sourly on what historians have labeled the "market revolution" in the American economy between 1815 and 1860.[19] This was not because the economic transition impoverished the working class. On the contrary, real wages (a combined index of changes in actual wages and in the cost of living) increased at least 50 percent during those years. Nevertheless, workers did not share equally with other segments of society in the economic benefits of the market revolution, or modernization, for the average per capita income of all Americans increased nearly 100 percent during the same period. The poor were getting richer, but not as fast as the rich and middle class were, leading to a widening gap between rich and poor and a growing sense of class consciousness among wage earners. And the emergence of child labor in the textile industry, sweatshop conditions for women in the garment industry of big cities, and other low-wage occupations for recent immigrants, women, and children created a substantial group of workers who earned less than a living wage and could make ends meet only if several members of the family worked.

Even when earnings were adequate, the whole concept of "wages" seemed alien to the American notion of independence and equality among white men. In the Jeffersonian world of landowning farmers and independent artisans, the great majority of white males owned the means of production—and/or the tools of their trade. But in the post-1815 era of capitalist modernization, more and more men owned nothing but their labor power, which they sold to employers in return for wages. Those who worked for wages were dependent for a living on the owner of the business who paid them; they were not equal in status or independence to the "boss" or "capitalist" (words that entered the American language during the first half of the nineteenth century). Skilled craftsmen like shoemakers, tailors, cabinetmakers, gunsmiths, handloom weavers, and others resented the downgrading or displacement of their skills by the new techniques of production or new machines. Spokesmen for these workers, and others, protested the granting by state legislatures of bank and corporation charters, or subsidies to transportation companies, as a form of "special privilege" that enriched the few at the expense of the many. Labor unions and workingmen's political parties proliferated during the 1830s. Their protests against privilege and in favor of preserving the old status of independence for skilled workers fueled political activism during the presidencies of Andrew Jackson and Martin Van Buren (1829–1841). But the economic depression from 1837 to 1843 killed off many labor unions. Thereafter most workers seemed to accept, with varying degrees of reluctance or enthusiasm, the economic changes that transformed and expanded the working class, because rising wages brought a higher standard of living and technological innovation created new high-status occupations like telegrapher, railroad

---

[19]Charles Sellers, *The Market Revolution: Jacksonian America, 1815–1846* (New York, 1991); Melvyn Stokes and Stephen Conway, eds., *The Market Revolution in America . . . 1800–1880* (Charlottesville, Va., 1996).

engineer, steamboat pilot, machinist, and the like that enabled many workers to achieve upward occupational mobility. Nevertheless, an undercurrent of hostility to modernization persisted among elements of the working class.

Political Parties and Modernization

By the 1830s, a two-party system had emerged as an apparently permanent feature of American politics. Issues associated with modernizing developments in the first half of the nineteenth century helped to define the ideological position of the two parties and the constituencies to which they appealed. Democrats inherited the Jeffersonian commitment to states' rights, limited government, traditional economic arrangements, and religious pluralism; Whigs inherited the Federalist belief in nationalism, a strong government, economic innovation, and cultural homogeneity under the auspices of established Protestant denominations. Catholics and Butternuts provided the most solid support for the Democratic party in the North, while Protestants of New England and British birth formed the strongest Whig constituency. In areas with few Catholics or Butternuts, different but analogous patterns emerged. In states as dissimilar as Alabama and New Hampshire, the Whigs were most prevalent in urban areas and in prosperous farming regions linked by good transportation to the market economy. Merchants and skilled workers in New Hampshire and merchants and large planters in Alabama tended to be Whigs; farmers on poorer soils—those less involved with the market economy—leaned toward the Democrats. Similar patterns existed in other states—though often with significant exceptions.

These patterns suggest a generalization that can be stated, at the risk of oversimplification, as follows: Whigs were the party of modernization, Democrats the party of tradition. Whigs wanted to use the federal and state governments to promote economic growth through aid to internal improvements and the chartering of banks; Democrats tended to oppose such institutions of economic growth as banks and corporations, especially after 1840, because they feared that state-legislated economic privilege would threaten equal rights. Most advocates of temperance and public schools and black rights and prison reform were Whigs; most opponents were Democrats. Most Whigs subscribed to an entrepreneurial ethic that favored industrialization and urban growth; many Democrats retained the Jeffersonian agrarian heritage of hostility or at least unease toward these things. Most Whigs welcomed the future; many Democrats feared it. In the words of historian Marvin Meyers, "the Whig party spoke to the explicit hopes of Americans" while the Democrats "addressed their diffuse fears and resentments."[20] Table 1.3, showing the roll-call votes in seven state legislatures (New Hampshire, New Jersey, Pennsylvania, Ohio, Virginia, Alabama, and Missouri) from 1832 to 1849, illustrates these party differences.[21]

---

[20]Marvin Meyers, *The Jacksonian Persuasion* (Stanford, 1957), p. 13. See also Michael F. Holt, *The Rise and Fall of the American Whig Party* (New York, 1999).

[21]This table is derived from the tables in Herbert Ershkowitz and William G. Shade, "Consensus or Conflict? Political Behavior in State Legislatures During the Jacksonian Era," *Journal of American History,* 58 (December 1971), 591–621, and in J. Mills Thornton, *Politics and Power in a Slave Society: Alabama, 1800–1860* (Baton Rouge, 1978), pp. 463–471.

Table 1.3   Roll-Call Votes in Seven State Legislatures, 1832–1849

Legislation Favoring	Whigs	Democrats
Banks ($N = 92$)	83%	31%
Incorporation of business enterprises ($N = 49$)	77	39
Internal improvements ($N = 49$)	63	45
Incorporation of nonprofit voluntary associations ($N = 10$)	71	37
Social reforms (temperance, prison and asylum reform, abolition of capital punishment) ($N = 22$)	66	41
Public schools ($N = 15$)	68	47
Antislavery and pro black measures (N.H., Pa., and Ohio) ($N = 19$)	82	10
Total (unweighted average) ($N = 256$)	74%	38%

In national politics, the most dramatic Whig-Democratic conflicts occurred over the issues of rechartering the Second Bank of the United States in the 1830s and the Mexican War in the 1840s. The Whigs favored the bank and opposed the war, but lost both contests. The latter issue points up another difference between the parties. Both believed in American expansion. But the Whigs favored expansion *over time* by means of economic growth and modernization. Democrats supported expansion *over space* by the acquisition of new territory in which to replicate the traditional institutions of older states. Democrats believed in the removal of Indians from their lands east of the Mississippi; Whigs provided what little defense existed for Indian rights in antebellum America—feeble and ineffective though it was. To the Whigs, "progress" meant internal development; to the Democrats it meant external growth. In a pamphlet entitled *Why I Am a Whig,* Horace Greeley explained: "Opposed to the instinct of boundless acquisition stands that of Internal Improvement. A nation cannot simultaneously devote its energies to the absorption of others' territories and the improvement of its own."[22]

The Democratic ideology of Jeffersonian agrarianism, small government, states' rights, and territorial expansion best suited the interests of the South and slavery. Chattel slavery in the United States became known as "the peculiar institution," not least because it seemed like an anomaly in a modernizing society. In the end, the party contests over banks, tariffs, internal improvements, and the like faded into the background of the greater conflict over slavery.

---

[22](New York, 1851), p. 6.

Chapter Two

The Ante- bellum South

We are an agricultural people. . . . We have no cities—we don't want them. . . . We want no manufactures; we desire no trading, no mechanical or manufacturing classes. As long as we have our rice, our sugar, our tobacco, and our cotton, we can command wealth to purchase all we want.

-Louis T. Wigfall,
Confederate senator from Texas, 1861

 The Southern Economy

The South was the great exception to many of the foregoing generalizations about American modernization. The slave states remained overwhelmingly rural and agricultural. Their economy grew, but it did not develop a substantial commercial and industrial sector. Southern agriculture was as labor intensive in 1860 as it had been in 1800. Upward social mobility was impossible for the half of the Southern labor force who lived in slavery. In contrast to the vigorous educational system and near-universal literacy of the North, the South's commitment to education was weak, and nearly half of its population was illiterate. The proliferation of voluntary associations, reform movements, and self-improvement societies that flourished in the free states largely bypassed the South. The slave states valued tradition and stability more than change and progress. As the North hurtled toward a future of competitive, meritocratic, free-labor capitalism, many Southerners responded with distaste and alarm. Southern separatism was rooted in resistance to this Northern vision of what America should become.

Some North-South Comparisons

Tables 2.1 through 2.5 illustrate some key statistical differences between North and South. In the tables, the category "slave states" includes the four border states that remained in the Union in 1861; had it included only the eleven states that eventually seceded, the North-South contrasts would have been even greater.

Table 2.1   Percentage of Urbanized Population (Living in Towns of 2,500 or More)

	Free States	Slave States
1820	10%	5%
1840	14	6
1860	26	10

Table 2.2   Percentage of Labor Force in Agriculture

	Free States	Slave States
1800	68%	82%
1860	40	81

Table 2.3   Value of Farmland and Implements, 1860

	Value of Farmland per Acre	Value of Farm Machinery and Implements per Acre	Value of Farm Machinery and Implements per Worker
Free states	$25.67	$0.89	$66
Slave states	10.40	0.42	38

Table 2.4   Capital Invested in Manufacturing

	FREE STATES		SLAVE STATES	
	Percentage of U.S. Total	Per Capita	Percentage of U.S. Total	Per Capita
1840	80%	$21.92	20%	$ 7.25
1860	84	43.73	16	13.25

Table 2.5   Literacy and Education, 1860

	PERCENTAGE OF POPULATION LITERATE			Percentage of Free Population Aged 5–19 Enrolled in School	Average Number of School Days per Year
	Total Population	Free Population	Slaves		
Free states	94%	94%	—	72%	135
Slave states	58	83	10% (est.)	35	80

Other kinds of data confirm the picture presented by these tables. In 1860, Massachusetts produced more manufactured goods than all the future Confederate states combined, while New York and Pennsylvania *each* produced more than twice the goods manufactured by all the future Confederate states combined. The states that grew all the cotton possessed only 6 percent of the nation's cotton manufacturing capacity. New York state had nearly as much banking capital in 1860 as all fifteen slave states combined. The per capita circulation of newspapers and magazines among Southern whites was less than half that among the Northern population. With one-third of the country's white population, Southerners contributed only 7 percent of the important inventions from 1790 to 1860. The inventor of the cotton gin, which revolutionized the Southern economy, was the Massachusetts native Eli Whitney, who had gone to Georgia in 1792 as a tutor. A large proportion of antebellum Southern college presidents and professors, academy principals, tutors, and newspaper editors came from the North.

The South as a "Colonial" Economy

From the first Virginia experiments with tobacco culture in the 1610s, the growing of staple crops for the world market dominated Southern economic life. Four-fifths of all colonial exports to England before 1776 came from the Southern colonies—tobacco from Virginia and Maryland, rice and indigo and naval stores from the Carolinas and Georgia. Indigo virtually disappeared and tobacco underwent a relative decline after the Revolution. But Whitney's invention of the cotton gin made the commercial growing of short-staple cotton feasible,[1] while the rise of the textile industry in England and in New England created a vast new demand for cotton. Southern plantations and farms doubled their cotton output each decade from 1800 to 1860. Cotton exports provided more than half of all American exports from 1815 to 1860. Defenders of slavery and of the South argued with much truth that King Cotton ruled the American economy.

Much of the capital and entrepreneurship to finance and market Southern crops came from outside the South. The key figure in this process was the "factor," or commission merchant. The origins of factoring went back to the colonial period, when tobacco-importing firms in London sent their agents to Virginia to buy and ship the crop. The factor advanced credit to the planter, with future crops as collateral, and functioned as the planter's purchasing agent to obtain consumer goods from London or elsewhere. This system adapted itself easily to the marketing of cotton in the nineteenth century, except that factors became increasingly the representatives of Northern rather than British firms. Although they lived in the South, most of the factors—two-thirds by a contemporary estimate—were Yankees or Britons.

The factor took charge of the planter's crop when it reached Memphis or New Orleans or Mobile or Charleston or Savannah—or any of several other cities. He provided storage facilities and contracted for transportation and sale to the ultimate purchaser. He arranged for insurance and credit and supplies for the planter. For each of these services he charged a commission. The total amount of the commissions—including interest if the planter went into debt, as many of them did—might be as

---

[1]Before 1793, little "short-staple" cotton was grown, as the amount of hand labor required to remove the seeds from the short and tenacious cotton fibers made this crop commercially unprofitable. The cotton gin was a simple device in which a spiked cylinder rotating through a grid of bars separated the fiber from the seeds. The higher-quality (but more expensive) long-staple cotton, in which the seed could be easily separated from the fibers, had been grown commercially before 1793, but its growing area was limited to the coastal and sea-island areas of Georgia and South Carolina. The adaptability of short-staple cotton to widespread areas of the South set off a veritable cotton boom after Whitney's invention in 1793.

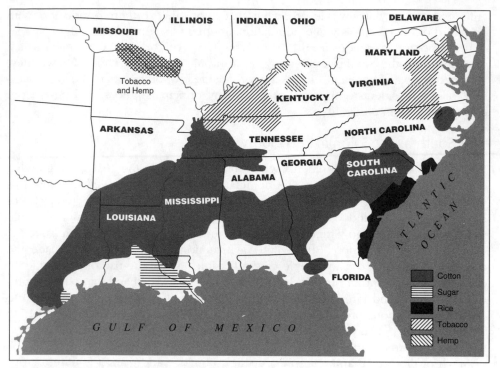

Principal Staple Crop Regions of the South, 1860

much as 20 percent of the value of the crop. Factoring represented a drain of wealth from the South estimated at between $100 million and $150 million annually in the late antebellum period.

Thus while plantation agriculture was a profitable enterprise, many of the profits on marketing the crop—not to speak of the profits on its manufacture into finished goods—went to outsiders. Indeed, as an exporter of raw materials and an importer of manufactured goods, the South sustained something of a colonial economic relationship to the North and with Britain. Complained a resident of Mobile in 1847, "our whole commerce except a small fraction is in the hands of Northern men. 7/8 of our Bank Stock is owned by Northern men. . . . Our wholesale and retail business— everything in short worth mentioning is in the hands of [Yankees]. . . . Financially we are more enslaved than our negroes."[2] "At present, the North fattens and grows rich upon the South," declared an Alabama newspaper in 1851.

We purchase all our luxuries and necessities from the North. . . . Northerners abuse and denounce slavery and slaveholders, yet our slaves are clothed with Northern manufactured goods, have Northern hats and shoes, work with Northern hoes, ploughs, and other implements. . . . The slaveholder dresses in Northern goods, rides in a Northern saddle . . . sports his Northern carriage . . . reads Northern books. . . . In Northern vessels his products are carried to market, his cotton is ginned with Northern gins, his sugar is crushed and preserved by

[2]J. Mills Thornton, *Politics and Power in a Slave Society: Alabama, 1800–1860* (Baton Rouge, 1978), p. 255.

Northern machinery; his rivers are navigated by Northern steamboats. . . . His son is educated at a Northern college, his daughter receives the finishing polish at a Northern seminary; his doctor graduates at a Northern medical college, his schools are furnished with Northern teachers, and he is furnished with Northern inventions.[3]

In 1852, Southerners who wanted to do something about this state of affairs revived the Southern Commercial Convention (originally founded in 1837), which met annually through the rest of the 1850s. Its purpose was to promote the construction with Southern capital of railroads, steamship lines, port facilities, banks, factories, and other enterprises to achieve economic independence from the North. The leaders of this movement exhorted fellow Southerners to buy only Southern-made goods, to boycott Northern textbooks and teachers, to patronize only Southern authors and vacation resorts. South Carolina's William Gregg urged the creation of a Southern textile industry, and led the way by building a model textile mill at Graniteville in the 1840s. The fierce Southern partisan Edmund Ruffin wore only clothes of Southern manufacture. Senator James Mason of Virginia proudly appeared in the U.S. Senate wearing a homespun suit.

But all of this availed little. The achievements of the Southern Commercial Convention turned out to be more political than economic. The Convention became increasingly a forum for secessionists. While Southern per capita investment in manufacturing nearly doubled between 1840 and 1860, as illustrated by Table 2.4 on page 28, this increase lagged behind the Northern growth rate, and the South's share of the nation's manufacturing capacity actually declined. James B. D. DeBow of New Orleans, publisher of the commercial magazine *DeBow's Review* and a leading advocate of Southern economic independence, found it necessary to have his *Review* printed in New York because of inadequate facilities in New Orleans. Three-quarters of DeBow's advertising income came from Northern businesses, and an important collection of *Review* articles on the industrial potential of the South sold six times as many copies in the North as in the South. Even William Gregg was obliged to hire a Northern superintendent and Yankee foremen for his Graniteville textile mill.

A crucial aspect of the Southern economy helps to explain its failure to modernize: slaves were both capital and labor. On a typical plantation, the investment in slaves was greater than the investment in land and implements combined. Slave agriculture could not follow the path blazed by Northern agriculture and become more capital intensive because, paradoxically, an increase of capital became an increase of labor. Instead of investing substantial sums in machinery, planters invested in more slaves. As a contemporary observer put it: "To sell cotton in order to buy negroes—to make more cotton to buy more negroes, 'ad infinitum,' is the aim and direct tendency of all the operations of the thorough going cotton planter." A planter explained why: "Having abundance of prime cotton land, I can make three or four times as much annual income by vesting capital in Negroes, as I can by any Stock annuities."[4]

---

[3]Quoted in Robert R. Russel, *Economic Aspects of Southern Sectionalism, 1840–1861* (Urbana, Ill., 1924), p. 48.

[4]Harold D. Woodman, *King Cotton and His Retainers: Financing and Marketing the Cotton Crop of the South, 1800–1925* (Lexington, Ky., 1968), p. 135; Stuart Bruchey, *Enterprise: The Dynamic Economy of a Free People* (Cambridge, Mass., 1990), p. 241.

Antebellum Southern agriculture underwent little technological change after the invention of the cotton gin in 1793. As indicated by Table 2.3 (page 28), the absorption of capital by labor meant that the per-unit value of land and machinery in the South was less than half the Northern average. The per capita output of Southern agriculture did increase between 1800 and 1860, but the cause was not primarily technological change. Rather, it was the improved organization of the plantation labor force and the westward movement of the plantation frontier to virgin soil, as indicated by the maps on pages 30 and 33.

Thus the Southern economy *grew,* but it did not *develop.* As indicated by Table 2.2, the proportion of the Southern labor force in agriculture was virtually the same in 1860 as it had been in 1800. The South failed to develop a substantial urban middle class and skilled-labor population or to generate a diversified economy producing a wide variety of goods and services. Because slaves along with other kinds of personal and real property were counted as wealth, the per capita wealth of Southern whites in 1860 ($3,978) was nearly double the Northern average ($2,040). With only 30 percent of the nation's free population, the South furnished 60 percent of the nation's wealthiest men. Southern per capita income for the free population was 6 percent greater than the Northern average. But when the slaves are included, Southern per capita income was 27 percent *less* than Northern.[5]

Economic historians have demonstrated that slavery was profitable. But profitable for whom? Certainly for cotton and sugar planters (probably less so for tobacco, rice, and hemp planters), whose average return on investment probably equaled that of Northern industrialists and exceeded that of Northern farmers. It was also profitable for the many slave owners in the upper South who sold their surplus slaves to the thriving cotton plantations of the Southwest. But it was not "profitable" for the slaves. Two economic historians have calculated that slaves on cotton plantations received in the form of food, clothing, and shelter only 22 percent of the earnings produced by these plantations. With emancipation, the proportion of output retained by labor rose to 56 percent.[6] It was also not profitable for the small-holding Southern farmers, who were crowded off the best land by large planters and could scarcely afford to buy slaves in the rising market.

Another way to look at the economics of slavery is to ask whether the institution promoted or inhibited Southern development. Many contemporaries believed that in this respect slavery's impact was negative. Observers of Southern life—ranging from the French visitor Alexis de Tocqueville to the British economist John Elliott Cairnes to the Yankee traveler Frederick Law Olmsted—maintained that slavery caused Southern backwardness. As de Tocqueville steamed down the Ohio River in 1831, with Kentucky on his left and Ohio on his right, he mused on the contrast between slave and free society.

---

[5]Lee Soltow, *Men and Wealth in the United States 1850–1870* (New Haven, 1975), pp. 65, 101; Roger L. Ransom, *Conflict and Compromise: The Political Economy of Slavery, Emancipation, and the American Civil War* (Cambridge, 1989), p. 76.

[6]Roger L. Ransom and Richard Sutch, *One Kind of Freedom: The Economic Consequences of Emancipation* (Cambridge, 1977), pp. 3–4.

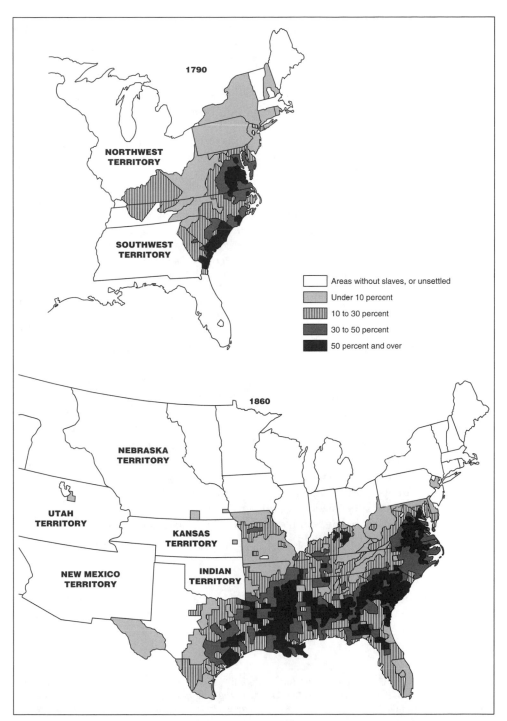

1790

NORTHWEST
TERRITORY

SOUTHWEST
TERRITORY

Areas without slaves, or unsettled
Under 10 percent
10 to 30 percent
30 to 50 percent
50 percent and over

1860

NEBRASKA
TERRITORY

UTAH
TERRITORY

KANSAS
TERRITORY

NEW MEXICO
TERRITORY

INDIAN
TERRITORY

Percentage of Slaves in Total Population, 1790 and 1860

On the left bank of the river the population is sparse; from time to time one sees a troop of slaves loitering through half-deserted fields. . . . One might say that society had gone to sleep. But on the right bank a confused hum proclaims from afar that men are busily at work; fine crops cover the fields . . . there is evidence of comfort; man appears rich and contented; he works.

Equally harsh were Olmsted's conclusions after three extended trips through the South in the 1850s, each of which resulted in a book. The slave states, wrote Olmsted, lacked "the characteristic features of a free-labor community, including an abundance and variety of skilled labor, a home market for a variety of crops, dense settlements [and] a large body of small proprietors." If a man returned to a Northern state after twenty years' absence, he would be struck by:

. . . what we call the "improvements" which have been made: better buildings, churches, schoolhouses, mills, railroads . . . roads, canals, bridges . . . the better dress and evidently higher education of the people. But where will the returning traveler see the accumulated cotton profits of twenty years in Mississippi? Ask the cotton–planter for them, and he will point in reply, not to dwellings, libraries, churches, schoolhouses, mills, railroads, or anything of the kind; he will point to his negroes—to almost nothing else.[7]

A fundamental reason for the South's failure to modernize and become economically independent was a lack of diversity in its economy—that is, too great a dependence on a single staple crop, cotton. The soaring demand for cotton in the 1850s intensified this problem. As the nation's economy recovered from the 1837–1843 depression, cotton prices rose from their 1844 low of five cents a pound to an average of eleven cents a pound throughout the 1850s. Planters scrambled to put every available acre into cotton, and they set new production records almost every year. This also bid up the price of slaves, which nearly doubled during the 1850s and thereby absorbed most of the available capital in the South. A discouraged promoter of textile mills in Georgia asked rhetorically: "Why should all our cotton make so long a journey to the North, to be manufactured there, and come back to us at so high a price? It is because all spare cash is sunk here in purchasing negroes."[8] Although the cotton South enjoyed unprecedented prosperity in the 1850s, its economy became even more narrowly specialized in staple-crop agriculture.

Yet another reason for the South's failure to develop economically was rooted in the values of Southern society.

Southern Values versus Economic Change

In the South the voices of those calling for industrial development were sometimes drowned out by the voices of those who branded the entrepreneurial ethic a form of vulgar Yankee materialism. The South's ideal image of itself portrayed country

---

[7]Alexis de Tocqueville, *Democracy in America*, ed. J. P. Mayer, trans. George L. Lawrence (Garden City, N.Y., 1969), pp. 345–346; Frederick Law Olmsted, *The Cotton Kingdom: A Selection*, ed. David Freeman Hawke (Indianapolis, 1971), pp. 184–185; Frederick Law Olmsted, *The Slave States Before the Civil War*, ed. Harvey Wish (New York, 1959), p. 253.

[8]Ulrich B. Phillips, *American Negro Slavery* (New York, 1918), p. 396.

gentlemen as practicing the arts of gracious living, hospitality, leisure, the ride and the hunt, chivalry toward women, honor toward equals, and kindness toward inferiors. The Yankees, on the other hand, appeared as a nation of shopkeepers—always chasing the almighty dollar, shrewd but without honor, hardworking but lacking the graces of a leisured class. "The Northerner loves to make money," said a Mississippian, "the Southerner to spend it." The author George Cary Eggleston recalled after the Civil War how he had come from Indiana to Virginia to inherit the family plantation. "I quitted the rapidly developing, cosmopolitan, kaleidoscopic West [for] the restful leisureliness of life in Virginia [with] its repose, the absence of stress or strain or anxious anticipation, the appreciation of tomorrow as the equal of today in the doing of things."[9]

Many leading Southerners in the 1850s echoed Thomas Jefferson's praise of farmers as the "peculiar deposit for substantial and genuine virtue" and his warning against the industrial classes in the cities as sores on the body politic. "We have no cities," said a Texas politician at the outset of the Civil War. "We don't want them. . . . We want no manufactures; we desire no trading, no mechanical or manufacturing classes. As long as we have our rice, our sugar, our tobacco, and our cotton, we can command wealth to purchase all we want." In 1857, Governor Henry Wise of Virginia gloried in the gentleman slaveholder class, "civilized in the solitude, gracious in the amenities of life, and refined and conservative in social habits . . . who have leisure for the cultivation of morals, manners, philosophy, and politics." A South Carolina planter rejected the concept of progress as defined in Northern terms of commerce, industry, internal improvements, cities, and reform. The goals of these "noisy, brawling, roistering *progressistas*," he warned, could be achieved in the South "only by the destruction of the planter class."[10] The popularity of such views posed a powerful obstacle to economic change in the South.

Slavery in the American South

Slavery formed the foundation of the South's distinctive social order. Although some historians have argued that plantation agriculture rather than slavery per se was the basic institution of the Southern economy, the distinction scarcely seems important. Slavery and the plantation were inextricably linked from the seventeenth century onward. In the 1850s, only 10 percent of the slave labor force worked in mining, transportation, construction, lumbering, and industry; another 15 percent were domestic servants or performed other nonagricultural labor. The overwhelming majority of slaves, about 75 percent, worked in agriculture—55 percent raising cotton,

---

[9]Eugene D. Genovese, *The Political Economy of Slavery* (New York, 1965), p. 30; George Cary Eggleston, *Recollections of a Varied Life* (New York, 1910), pp. 46–49.

[10]William Howard Russell, *My Diary North and South* (Boston, 1861), p. 179; David Bertelson, *The Lazy South* (New York, 1967), p. 190, "The Prospects and Policy of the South, as They Appear to the Eyes of a Planter," *Southern Quarterly Review*, 26 (October 1854), 432, 448.

10 percent tobacco, and the remaining 10 percent sugar, rice, or hemp. Slave labor raised more than half of the tobacco, three-quarters of the cotton, and nearly all of the rice, sugar, and hemp, as well as a major portion of the South's food crops.

Although only one-third of the South's white families owned slaves, this was a remarkably widespread distribution of ownership for such expensive property. By contrast, only 2 percent of American families in 1950 owned corporation stocks comparable in value to one slave a century earlier. Nearly half of all owners in the 1850s held fewer than five slaves, but more than half of all slaves belonged to the 12 percent of owners who possessed twenty or more—the number that unofficially distinguished a plantation from a farm.

Herrenvolk Democracy

What stake did nonslaveholding whites have in the slave system? A number of different views have existed concerning this group. To some observers they have appeared as an undifferentiated mass of ragged, dirty, illiterate "poor whites" eking out a miserable living on the margins of the plantation economy. At the opposite pole, some Southern historians have portrayed these "plain folk" as a proud, intelligent, prosperous, and politically important rural middle class who raised food crops and small amounts of tobacco or cotton or hogs for the market. Many contemporaries, Northern and Southern alike, viewed the nonslaveholding whites as a potential antislavery force who, because they had no stake in the plantation system, might feel that slavery degraded all labor to the level of bond labor.

None of these viewpoints is entirely correct, though all possess elements of truth. To disentangle truth from stereotype, one must distinguish among three distinct groups of rural nonslaveholding whites. One group consisted of the residents of the "hill country"—the Appalachian highlands and valleys stretching from western Maryland and eastern Kentucky to northern Alabama, and the Ozark Plateau of southern Missouri and northern Arkansas. These regions contained few slaves. Their inhabitants were mainly small-holding farmers who raised food crops and livestock. In politics, the hill-country residents often opposed the piedmont and lowland areas of their states over matters of legislative apportionment, state aid to internal improvements, and taxation of land and slaves. No friends of the plantation regime, the hill-country folk came closest to fitting the image of an antislavery fifth column within the South. During the Civil War, many of them remained loyal to the Union.

A second group of nonslaveholders lived in the "piney woods" or "wiregrass" regions—areas of sandy or marshy soil in eastern North Carolina, southern Georgia and Alabama, eastern Mississippi, and numerous pockets elsewhere. These people came closest to fitting the traditional image of poor whites. Many of them were tenants or squatters rather than landowners. They raised a few acres of corn and grazed scraggy herds of livestock in the woods. Although they sold some of their hogs to richer areas of the South, these whites, like those in the upcountry, participated minimally in the staple-crop economy.

The largest group of nonslaveholding whites, however, played an important role in that economy. They lived in the piedmont districts or in the less fertile areas of the tidewater, where they raised each year a bale or two of cotton or a hogshead of tobacco, as well as food crops. They were linked to the plantation regime by numerous ties of self-interest and sentiment. They ginned their cotton and perhaps sold some of their pork at the nearest plantation. Many of them aspired to become slaveholders, and the more successful or lucky achieved this goal. Moreover, given the traditional patterns of kinship in the South, a nonslaveholder was quite likely to be a cousin or a nephew of the planter down the road. The big planter was in the habit of treating his poorer neighbors once or twice a year to a barbecue—especially if he happened to be running for the legislature.

While subtle ties of kinship and mutual interest blunted potential class conflict between slaveholders and some nonslaveholders, the most important tie was the bond of race. Not all Southern whites owned slaves, but they all owned white skins. Slavery was not only a system of labor exploitation, it was also a method of racial control. However much some nonslaveholders may have disliked slavery, few could see any alternative means of preserving white supremacy. An Alabama farmer told Frederick Law Olmsted that he believed slavery to be wrong—but he did not believe emancipation to be right. "Now suppose they was free, you see they'd all think themselves just as good as we. . . . How would you like to hev a nigger feelin' just as good as a white man? How'd you like to hev a nigger steppin' up to your darter?" Another dirt farmer said to Olmsted that he wished "there warn't no niggers here. They are a great cuss to this country. . . . But it wouldn't never do to free 'em and leave 'em here. I don't know anybody, hardly, in favor of that. Make 'em free and leave 'em here and they'd steal everything we made. Nobody couldn't live here then."[11]

Olmsted perceptively concluded that "from childhood, the one thing in their condition which has made life valuable to the mass of whites has been that the niggers are yet their inferiors." The South's leading proslavery political spokesman, John C. Calhoun of South Carolina, also grasped this truth. "With us," said Calhoun in 1848, "the two great divisions of society are not the rich and the poor, but white and black; and all the former, the poor as well as the rich, belong to the upper class, and are respected and treated as equals . . . and hence have a position and pride of character of which neither poverty nor misfortune can deprive them."[12]

The sociologist Pierre L. van den Berghe has described this rationalization for slavery and white supremacy as "Herrenvolk democracy"—the equal superiority of all who belong to the Herrenvolk (master race) over all who do not.[13] The Herrenvolk concept had a powerful appeal in both the South and the North. "Your fathers and my fathers built this government on two ideas," said the Alabama champion of Southern rights William L. Yancey. "The first is that the white race is the citizen, and the master race, and the white man is the equal of every other white man. The second idea is that the Negro is the inferior race." The Jacksonian Democrats aggressively championed white supremacy; their Herrenvolk ideology helped attract Irish, Butternuts, and unskilled

---

[11]Olmsted, *Cotton Kingdom,* pp. 106, 192.

[12]Olmsted, *Slave States Before the Civil War,* p. 251; *The Works of John C. Calhoun,* ed. Richard K. Crallé, 6 vols. (New York, 1854–57), IV, 505–506.

[13]Pierre van den Berghe, *Race and Racism: A Comparative Perspective* (New York, 1967). George M. Fredrickson, *The Black Image in the White Mind* (New York, 1971), chap. 2, applies this concept to antebellum race relations in a penetrating analysis.

laborers in the North to the Democratic party, for it proclaimed that no matter how poor they might be, these people were still better than blacks. Like the Southern nonslaveholders, they feared emancipation because it would render their whiteness meaningless. "Slavery is the poor man's best government," wrote Governor Joseph E. Brown of Georgia, because "the poor white laborer is respected as an equal. . . . He belongs to the only true aristocracy, the race of white men."[14] Here was the central paradox of American history: slavery was for many whites the foundation of liberty and equality.

The Conditions of Slavery

For the slaves there was no paradox: slavery was slavery, and freedom was its opposite. Chattel bondage gave the master great power over his slaves to buy or sell, to punish without sanction of the courts, to separate families, to exploit sexually, even to kill with little fear of being held legally responsible. As a form of property, the slaves had few human rights in the eyes of the law. They could not legally marry, nor own property, nor be taught to read or write in most states. Owners might let them have a family, earn money, or (in rare cases) even buy their freedom; but until they were free, money, spouse, and children could be taken away at any moment. Several states permitted manumission only on condition that the manumitted slave leave the state. Of the 250,000 free blacks in the slave states in 1860, only 35,000 lived in the eight lower-South cotton states, where they suffered galling restrictions that made life for many of them little better than slavery.

In practice, the master's power over his slaves was often tempered by economic self-interest and sometimes by paternalism. Masters and overseers could not rule by the whip alone. Dead, maimed, brutalized, or runaway slaves could grow little if any cotton. Persuasion, inducement, rewards for good work, and concessions were necessary in this as in other relationships between employer and employees. The slaves spoke the same language and worshipped the same Christian God as their owners. Relations of trust and affection as well as alienation and hatred could exist between slave and master.

Slavery was, in short, a human institution as well as a legal and economic one. This helped to neutralize its dehumanizing tendencies and to give the slaves latitude to create cultural institutions that sustained them through generations of bondage. Natural leaders in the slave quarters often became eloquent preachers in the "invisible institution" of the black church, whose congregations worshipped apart from whites (sometimes secretly) in spite of laws to the contrary. The slaves created the most original and moving music in antebellum America—the spirituals—which expressed their longing for freedom as well as their resignation to sorrow, and evolved after the Civil War into the blues and eventually into jazz. While slavery made stable family life difficult, a majority of slaves nevertheless formed strong ties of kinship and family. Thus, although slavery's impact on black people could be repressive, the countervailing force of a positive black culture provided an impressive example of survival in the face of adversity.

---

[14]Yancey quoted in Fredrickson, *Black Image*, p. 61; Brown quoted in Michael A. Morrison, *Slavery and the American West: The Eclipse of Manifest Destiny and the Coming of the Civil War* (Chapel Hill, 1997), p. 175.

SLAVES IN THE AMERICAN SOUTH.
The photograph above portrays a typical slave cabin—this one in Georgia—with dirt floors and no glass in the windows. The photograph below shows slaves gathered before "the Great House" and outbuildings on a large plantation near Baton Rouge, Louisiana.

Slavery in the United States operated with less physical harshness than in most other parts of the Western Hemisphere. For most slaves on West Indian sugar plantations or Brazilian coffee plantations, life was indeed nasty, brutish, and short. Climatic conditions and disease took a higher toll of black lives there than in North America. Food, clothing, medical care, and the material necessities of life were less abundant, and the pace of work on tropical sugar plantations was more brutally demanding than work in the cotton or tobacco fields further north.

Slavery in the Caribbean and in South America flourished while the African slave trade was still open. In the United States, by contrast, the slave system reached its height only after the African slave trade had ended in 1808. This had important implications for the physical treatment of slaves. In Latin America, many planters had considered it cheaper to import slaves from Africa and almost literally work them to death than to create an environment in which the slaves could raise families and maintain their population through natural reproduction. In the United States, the cutoff of imports made planters dependent on natural reproduction for the maintenance and increase of their slave "stock." It was in the slave owner's interest to encourage good health and a high birth rate among his slaves. One former slave said that his master "fed us reg'lar on good, 'stantial food, just like you'd tend to you hoss, if you had a real good one." Another former slave recalled a Louisiana planter who liked to point out healthy slave children to visitors. " 'Dat one be worth a t'ousand dollars,' or 'Dat one be a whopper.' You see, 'twas just like raisin' young mules."[15]

The U.S. slave population increased by an average of 27 percent per decade after 1810, almost the same natural growth rate as for the white population. This rate of increase was unique in the history of bondage. No other slave population in the Western Hemisphere even maintained, much less increased, its population through natural reproduction. At the time of emancipation, the black population of the United States was ten times the number of Africans who had been imported, but the black population of the West Indies was only half the number of Africans who had been imported. Of the estimated eleven million Africans brought across the Atlantic by the slave trade, the United States received only 5 percent; yet at the time of emancipation it had more than 30 percent of the hemisphere's black population.

Important social implications underlie these bare demographic facts. For example, Spanish and Portuguese laws in Latin America allowed slaves to marry and provided some protection to their families, whereas slave marriages had no legal basis in the United States. But because West Indian and Latin American countries relied on the slave trade to maintain their supply of slaves, and because twice as many male as female Africans were imported, marriage and a family were impossible for large numbers of male slaves in these countries. By contrast, the sex ratio among slaves in the United States was virtually equal from 1820 onward. This enabled most slaves to form families, and helps to explain why the natural reproduction rate was so much higher in North America than elsewhere. It also helps to explain why large-scale slave revolts were rarer in the United States than in the Caribbean or in Latin America: men with family responsibilities were less likely to start an insurrection.

---

[15]Paul D. Escott, *Slavery Remembered: A Record of the Twentieth-Century Slave Narratives* (Chapel Hill, N.C., 1979), p. 25.

Lacking legal protection, however, slave families in the United States were fragile. One of the most tragic aspects of slavery was the breakup of families. Even a
master who refused to sell family members apart from each other could not always
prevent such sales to settle debts after his death. Several studies of slavery have
found that from one-fifth to one-third of slave marriages were broken by owners—
generally by selling one or both of the partners separately.[16] The percentage of children sold apart from their parents or siblings cannot even be estimated.

Slavery and the Work Ethic

In a modernizing society, status depends on achievement as well as on ascription.
But most slaves could achieve upward mobility only within the narrowest of ranges:
from field hand to driver or house servant, for example. Even those few slaves who
earned their freedom found their mobility blocked by racism and by the legal restrictions on free blacks.

Slavery also undermined the work ethic among Southern whites. When most
kinds of manual labor are associated with bondage, work becomes servile rather
than honorable. The Virginia statesman George Mason acknowledged that "slavery
discourages arts and manufactures. The poor despise labor when performed by
slaves." The South Carolina industrialist William Gregg lamented that his state was
"destitute of every feature which characterizes an industrious people."[17] Primarily because of the paucity of employment opportunities and the lack of esteem for white
labor, only one-eighth of the immigrants to the United States settled in the South.
Twice as many native-born whites migrated from slave to free states as vice versa.

Perhaps the most outspoken critic of the work habits of both whites and blacks
in the South was Frederick Law Olmsted, whose writings on the South portrayed
slipshod farming practices, wretched roads and public services, trains and steamboats that ran late or not at all, and a general air of shiftlessness. The root of the
problem, as Olmsted and others saw it, was the inefficiency of slave workers. Forced
labor was reluctant labor. Slaves "seem to go through the motions of labor without
putting strength into them," wrote Olmsted, who believed that the average free
worker in the North accomplished twice as much as the average slave. Most slaves,
he argued, had little motivation to improve their output through harder work or
greater efficiency. They lacked the time discipline of modern work habits. "Their
time isn't any value to themselves," said one Southern white in a remark that Olmsted considered profound.[18]

Planters' records as well as black folklore also provide evidence that slaves engaged in slowdowns and careless practices as a form of resistance to compulsory
labor. They feigned illness, ceased to work when the overseer looked the other

---

[16]John W. Blassingame, *The Slave Community* (New York, 1972), pp. 89–92; Herbert Gutman and
Richard Sutch, "The Slave Family: Protected Agent of Capitalist Masters or Victim of the Slave Trade?" in
Paul A. David et al., *Reckoning with Slavery* (New York, 1976), pp. 127–129; Herbert Gutman, *The
Black Family in Slavery and Freedom* (New York, 1976), pp. 146–147; Escott, *Slavery Remembered*,
pp. 46–48; Peter Kolchin, *American Slavery 1619–1877* (New York, 1993), pp. 125–127.

[17]Mason and Gregg quoted in Bertelson, *Lazy South*, pp. 159, 195.

[18]Olmsted, *Cotton Kingdom*, pp. 28, 153–154.

way, pretended to misunderstand orders, broke tools, abused work animals, ran away to the woods or swamps. Slavery helped cause the technological lag in Southern agriculture. Southern hoes were heavy and clumsy because slaves were said to break the lighter ones customarily used on Northern farms. Slaves continued to use hoes for tillage and cultivation long after Northern farmers had begun to use horse-drawn plows and cultivators. The plows that *were* used in Southern agriculture tended to be the old shallow-furrow mule-drawn shovel plows, rather than the new deep-furrow horse-drawn moldboard plows common in the North by the 1830s. Mules were the common Southern draft animals because, while less strong than horses, they could better withstand the reputed carelessness and abuse of slaves. In 1860, the slave states contained 90 percent of the mules but only 40 percent of the horses in the United States.[19]

The denial of education to slaves produced the most jarring disjunction between slavery and modernization. At least 90 percent of the slave population was illiterate. Although the slaves developed a vigorous oral tradition, their inability to read and write barred them from the principal means of communicating knowledge, ideas, and culture in a modernizing society. The low level of literacy was one of the chief features distinguishing the slave from the free population and the South from the North (see Table 2.5, page 28). In the eyes of abolitionists, it was one of the main reasons for the "backwardness" of the South and the immorality of slavery.

---

[19]Two economic historians, Robert Fogel and Stanley Engerman, have challenged the thesis of slave inefficiency. Indeed, they maintain that because of careful management, high morale among slave workers, and economies of scale on large plantations, Southern agriculture was more efficient than Northern. Few other historians, however, have accepted this argument. See Robert W. Fogel and Stanley L. Engerman, *Time on the Cross: The Economics of American Negro Slavery* (Boston, 1974), and two volumes criticizing these arguments: Paul A. David et al., *Reckoning with Slavery* (New York, 1976), and Herbert G. Gutman, *Slavery and the Numbers Game* (Urbana, Ill., 1975). In a subsequent study, Robert Fogel reiterated the thesis about the superior efficiency of slave-labor agriculture, but now attributed it mainly to "the enormous, almost unconstrained degree of force available to masters." Fogel, *Without Consent or Contract: The Rise and Fall of American Slavery* (New York, 1989), p. 34.

Chapter Three

The Ideological Conflict over Slavery

Many in the South once believed that slavery was a moral and political evil. That folly and delusion are gone. We see it now in its true light, and regard it as the most safe and stable basis for free institutions in the world.

-John C. Calhoun,
1838

The Antislavery Movement

Few white men questioned the morality of black slavery before the eighteenth century. Bondage was the most ancient and universal form of labor in the history of civilization. Philosophy and religion in the premodern era justified slavery as one of many forms of subordination to authority necessary for social order. But by the second half of the eighteenth century, four currents of Anglo-American and French thought converged to form the basis for an emerging international antislavery movement.

The first was the growth of post-Reformation radical Protestant denominations, especially the Quakers. Traditional Christianity had justified slavery as God's will, a necessary part of the divine order. But the explosive forces loosed by the Reformation generated numerous sectarian challenges to the status quo. The Quakers became one of the most successful sects in England and America. By 1760, they had begun to purge themselves of slaveholding. In 1775, they founded the first American antislavery organization, the Pennsylvania Society for Promoting the Abolition of Slavery. Meanwhile the Great Awakening of the 1740s (the first of several major revival movements in the history of American Protantism) had produced an evangelical faith in conversion and spiritual regeneration. This in turn caused many Congregationalists and Methodists as well as Quakers to transform the traditional Christian view of sin as a form of slavery into a conviction that slaveholding was a sin.

The second current of thought that helped to undermine the intellectual rationalizations for bondage was the Enlightenment, which questioned slavery's place in a social order designed to produce the greatest good for the greatest number. The third was the maturation of a laissez-faire economic theory that rejected feudal and mercantilistic restrictions on free enterprise and free labor. Adam Smith's *Wealth of Nations* (1776) was the most influential statement of this theory. The labor of slaves, wrote Smith, "though it appears to cost only their maintenance, is in the end the dearest of any. A person who can acquire no property, can have no other interest but to eat as much, and to labour as little as possible."[1]

The fourth development that worked against slavery was the series of revolutions that rocked the transatlantic world in the half-century after 1775. The Age of Revolution produced the abolition of slavery in all of the new states of the Union north of Maryland, in the French West Indies,[2] and in most of the Central and South American countries that won their independence from Spain. In 1808, Britain and the United States prohibited their citizens from engaging in the international slave trade; in subsequent years, Britain used diplomacy and naval power to enforce this prohibition on a growing list of additional nations. In 1833, Britain abolished slavery in its own West Indian colonies, and in 1848, during a second wave of European revolutions, France and Denmark followed suit.

These were impressive achievements. Nearly two million slaves attained freedom. The slave trade was curtailed if not fully halted. On the other hand, slavery survived in the southern United States, Brazil, and Cuba, where the increasing production respectively of cotton, coffee, and sugar after 1800 entrenched the institution more firmly than ever. The expansion of slavery in these countries produced a slave population in the Western Hemisphere larger in 1850 than it had been a half-century earlier. Americans and the nationals of other countries participated in a flourishing illicit slave trade to Brazil and Cuba. The illegal slavers even continued to bring Africans to the United States after 1808.[3]

Abolition versus Colonization

After the achievements of the Revolutionary generation, the antislavery movement in the United States lost some of its impetus. The libertarian sentiments of Southern Jeffersonians were neutralized by the class benefits they derived, as planters, from slavery. Whites also feared the racial consequences of "letting loose" a large number of black people whose assumed inferiority and "savage instincts" would constitute a threat to society. As Thomas Jefferson put it in 1820, the South had "the wolf by the ears" and could not let it go.[4]

---

[1] Quoted in David Brion Davis, *The Problem of Slavery in the Age of Revolution 1770–1823* (Ithaca, 1975), p. 352.

[2] Napoleon reinstated slavery in French possessions in 1803.

[3] Probably fewer than one thousand annually.

[4] Jefferson to John Holmes, April 22, 1820, in H. A. Washington (ed.), *The Writings of Thomas Jefferson,* 9 vols. (New York, 1853–1854), VII, 159.

One popular solution to this dilemma was the idea of gradual emancipation coupled with "colonization"—the settlement of freed blacks in their African "homeland." In 1817, a number of prominent Americans, including Henry Clay and Bushrod Washington (nephew of George Washington), formed the American Colonization Society. The society acquired land in West Africa and founded the country of Liberia as a haven for free black Americans whose transportation and settlement there the society financed. Begun with high hopes, the American Colonization Society did nothing to solve the problems of slavery and race. Although Liberia became an independent republic in 1847, the society and its state auxiliaries managed to send fewer than ten thousand blacks there by 1860—about 0.3 percent of the increase in the American black population during that period.

Opposition to the American Colonization Society came from three principal sources: proslavery advocates in the lower South, who resented any effort, however moderate, to interfere with bondage; most free blacks, especially in the North, who considered themselves Americans, not Africans; and the post-1830 abolitionist movement, which denounced the colonization society as racist for assuming the race problem could be solved only by sending black people out of the country.

Militant Abolitionism

The most important underlying cause for the emergence of militant abolitionism after 1830 was the religious phenomenon known as the Second Great Awakening. The revisionist Calvinists who led this movement in the North emphasized the free will of anyone to choose the path to salvation. God's grace was available not just to the predestined elect, but to all who experienced conversion, abjured sin, and placed themselves in a state of belief and behavior to receive His grace. This was an activist faith. It spawned a host of reform crusades against "sin"—the sin of infidelity, of Sabbath breaking, of prostitution, of intemperance, and of enslaving human beings. These crusades inherited the Puritan doctrine of collective accountability and collective judgment. Every man *was* his brother's keeper. All Americans were therefore accountable for the sin of slavery so long as one American held slaves.

The principal evangelical preacher of the Second Great Awakening was Charles Grandison Finney. Among his followers were the eloquent lecturer Theodore Weld and the wealthy merchant brothers Arthur and Lewis Tappan. Along with William Lloyd Garrison, these men became, in 1833, the principal founders of the American Anti-Slavery Society. The next few years saw a remarkable growth of this organization and its state and local auxiliaries. By 1838, there were 1,350 such auxiliaries with a total claimed membership of 250,000. These societies published pamphlets and newspapers, sponsored lectures, and gathered signatures of petitions to Congress calling for action against slavery.

The scope and fervor of this crusade were unprecedented. The abolitionists of the 1830s spurned the moderation and gradualism of their predecessors. They rejected colonization as a proslavery trick to strengthen the institution by merely appearing to ameliorate it. There must be no compromise with slavery, they insisted; one does not compromise with sin, one vanquishes it. William Lloyd Garrison published the manifesto of the new militancy in the first issue of his famous newspaper, the *Liberator,* on January 1, 1831:

> I *will* be as harsh as truth, and as uncompromising as justice. On this subject, I do not wish to think, or speak, or write, with moderation. No! No! Tell a man whose house is on fire to give a moderate alarm; tell him to moderately rescue his wife from the hands of the ravisher; tell the mother to gradually extricate her babe from the fire into which it has fallen;—but urge me not to use moderation in a cause like the present. I am in earnest—I will not equivocate—I will not excuse—I will not retreat a single inch—AND I WILL BE HEARD.

In the 1830s, abolitionists had two primary goals: to convert Americans, including Southerners and slaveholders, to a belief that slaveholding was a sin; and to win equal rights for free blacks. These goals, and the methods to achieve them, were modeled on the religious crusades, or "revivals," of the Second Great Awakening. Having themselves experienced "conversion" to abolitionism, the reformers hoped to convert others. Once convinced that slavery and racial discrimination were sins against God and humanity, Americans would cease sinning, surmount racism, abolish slavery, and grant equal rights to the freed people.

But these hopes were doomed to failure. The South closed its mind to the abolitionists. Some Southern states and cities put a price on the head of Garrison and other leading reformers. Intrepid abolitionists who ventured into the South were mobbed and driven out or imprisoned. Mobs broke into Southern post offices and seized and burned abolitionist pamphlets. President Andrew Jackson approved of this type of action and ordered his postmaster general to ban abolitionist literature from the mails, on the ground that it might incite a slave rebellion. Those few Southern whites who did become abolitionists—such as the Kentuckian James G. Birney and the South Carolina sisters Angelina and Sarah Grimké—had to move to the North to proclaim their beliefs.

Nor did most Northerners accept the abolitionist message of total emancipation and equal rights. Such objectives threatened too many economic and racial interests. Northern mobs attacked abolitionist lecturers, destroyed printing presses, and burned abolitionist property in the 1830s. Some of these mobs also attacked free blacks. The mobs consisted mainly of lower-class whites, who feared that emancipation would loose a horde of blacks to come north and compete with them for jobs and social equality. But some mobs included "gentlemen of property and standing"—merchants or lawyers who had business connections with the South, or conservative men who believed that abolitionist radicalism threatened the Union and the very basis of the social order.

The Politics of Abolitionism

The failure of moral suasion to convert the nation to abolition prompted some abolitionists to go into politics. In 1839, they founded the Liberty party, which nominated James G. Birney for president in 1840. But Birney received a mere seven thousand votes—0.3 percent of the total.

WILLIAM LLOYD GARRISON.
The scholarly countenance that gazes out from this photograph gives little evidence Garrison's fiery rhetoric that seared slaveholders and their allies. Something of a universal reformer, Garrison also embraced women's rights, pacifism, temperance, Indian rights, diet reform, and opposition to capital punishment.

The formation of the Liberty party was one of several factors that caused a split in the antislavery movement. William Lloyd Garrison led a faction of abolitionists who opposed political action, arguing that it would lead to compromises of principle. The Garrisonians refused to vote under the U.S. Constitution, which they branded as a proslavery document. Several Garrisonians even called for the withdrawal of free states from a Union that sanctioned slavery. In their disappointment with the refusal of major church denominations to endorse militant abolitionism, some followers of Garrison attacked organized religion as a "den of thieves." This angered evangelical abolitionists. The Garrisonians also endorsed equal rights for women, which offended some male abolitionists who, though they believed in equality for black men, could not bring themselves to support equality for women. The women's rights movement grew out of women's participation in abolitionist organizations. As female abolitionists wrote and spoke about the sin of racial subordination, some of them also began to speak out against their own subordination to men. This growing feminist consciousness helped spark the movement that resulted in the first national women's rights convention at Seneca Falls in 1848. Eight years earlier, the Garrisonians' success in electing a woman to the executive board of the American Anti-Slavery Society had provoked a schism in the society. Those who withdrew—including Finney and the Tappan brothers—supported the Liberty party and founded other antislavery societies in the 1840s.

The most important of these was the American Missionary Association. This organization grew out of a successful effort by the Tappan brothers to win the freedom of Africans who had captured the slave ship *Amistad,* which was carrying them to slavery in Cuba. They steered it to Long Island instead, where abolitionists took up their cause and carried the case to the Supreme Court. The Court declared the Africans to be free, and the abolitionists repatriated them to their homeland. The American Missionary Association, founded in 1846 to bring Christianity to these and other Africans, became, two decades later, the principal agency for bringing education to freed slaves in the American South.

Although split, the abolitionist movement remained active and important after 1840. Indeed it broadened its impulse: as events unfolded, the widening gulf between free and slave states won more converts to antislavery politics than abolitionists ever did. But as Garrisonians had predicted, this broadening of the movement diluted its religious and humanitarian thrust. Although some political abolitionists continued to support the ultimate goals of total emancipation and equal rights, they and their less radical colleagues focused primarily on restricting the further spread of slavery and pledged to not interfere with it in the states where it already existed. This represented *antislavery* sentiment, but not abolition. It considered slavery wrong but proposed to take no direct action against the institution in the states. Instead, antislavery hoped that restrictions against expansion of slavery into the territories would produce a slow decline of the institution, leading to its gradual extinction at some future date. In the meantime, the territories and new states would fill up with free labor and replicate the social and economic institutions of the free states. This antislavery impulse became politically institutionalized in the Free Soil party of 1848 and in the more powerful Republican party in 1854. Most Free Soilers, in contrast to most abolitionists, cared more about the rights of white men than about the rights of black people. "There are Republicans who are Abolitionists:; there are others who anxiously desire and labor for the good of the slave," explained the *New York Tribune* in 1856, "but there are many more whose main impulse is to secure the new Territories for Free White Labor, with little or no regard for the interests of negroes, free or slave."[5]

Antislavery and Modernization

Both abolition and antislavery took deepest root in New England and in areas of the North settled by New Englanders. All of the principal founders and leaders of the movement—Finney, Weld, the Tappan brothers, Garrison, and Wendell Phillips— were natives of Massachusetts or Connecticut. Salmon P. Chase, the Ohioan who took over leadership of the Liberty party in the 1840s and helped to broaden it into the Free Soil party in 1848, was born and raised in New Hampshire. Of 567 abolitionist leaders, 63 percent were born in New England—at a time when that region contained

---

[5]October 15, 1856.

Table 3.1 Origins of Abolitionists and Entrepreneurs

	Abolitionist Leaders	Ratio to Population*	Entrepreneurs	Ratio to Population*
New England-born	63%	3:1	51%	3:1
Congregational	34 ⎫	7:1 ⎫	22 ⎫	5:1 ⎫
Unitarian	13 ⎬ 67%	13:1 ⎬ 10:1	10 ⎬ 40%	10:1 ⎬ 6:1
Quaker	20 ⎭	20:1 ⎭	8 ⎭	8:1 ⎭

*This ratio expresses the relationship between the percentage of abolitionist leaders or entrepreneurs and the percentage of the whole American population in these categories. That is, the proportion of all Americans living in New England at the median birth date of the abolitionist leaders (1805) was 21 percent, hence the proportion of abolitionists born in New England was three times that of the whole population. The proportion of Americans living in New England at the median birth date of entrepreneurs (1825) was about 18 percent. The church affiliation ratios are calculated for the 1840s. The size of the samples was:

Abolitionist birthplace: $N = 567$ Entrepreneur birthplace: $N = 247$

Abolitionist religious affiliation: $N = 504$ Entrepreneur religious affiliation: $N = 144$

but 21 percent of the country's population. Studies of counties in upstate New York and Ohio where abolitionism was strongest have found a significant correlation between Yankee settlement, evangelical revivals, and antislavery organizations.[6]

A similarity existed in the social origins of entrepreneurial and abolitionist leaders—both in Britain and in the United States. Quakers, especially in England, were prominent among both groups. English Quaker families, such as the Darbys, the Lloyds, the Barclays, and the Wedgwoods, formed the vanguard of the industrial revolution and furnished many eighteenth-century British antislavery leaders. Likewise, Quakers were prominent in eighteenth-century American commercial enterprises and dominated the early antislavery societies. After 1830, abolitionist leadership in the United States passed to the evangelical Protestants and Unitarians in New England—at precisely the time these groups and this region were forging the most modernized sector of the economy. Table 3.1 illustrates the similarities between abolitionist and industrial leadership in the mid-nineteenth-century United States.[7] In an occupational survey of abolitionist leaders ($N = 622$), the proportion of businessmen (21 percent) was exceeded only by clergymen (34 percent).

---

[6]Data on the birthplace of abolitionist leaders are from the author's research. For studies of New York and Ohio counties, see Whitney R. Cross, *The Burned-over District: The Social and Intellectual History of Enthusiastic Religion in Western New York, 1800–1850* (Ithaca, 1950); Alan M. Kraut, "The Forgotten Reformers: A Profile of Third Party Abolitionists in Antebellum New York," in Lewis Perry and Michael Fellman (eds.), *Antislavery Reconsidered: New Perspectives on the Abolitionists* (Baton Rouge, 1979), pp. 119–145; Gerald Sorin, *The New York Abolitionists: A Case Study of Political Radicalism* (Westport, Conn., 1971); and John L. Hammond, "Revival Religion and Antislavery Politics," *American Sociological Review,* 39 (April 1974), 175–186.

[7]The data for abolitionists in Table 3.1 are based on the author's research. For other studies of abolitionist leaders and rank and file that come up with roughly similar data, see Lawrence J. Friedman, *Gregarious Saints: Self and Community in American Abolitionism, 1830–1870* (Cambridge, 1982); Edward Magdol, *The Antislavery Rank and File: A Social Profile of the Abolitionists' Constituency* (Westport, Conn., 1986); and Paul Goodman, *Of One Blood: Abolitionism and the Origins of Racial Equality* (Berkeley, 1998). Data for entrepreneurs and the data for the estimated ratio to the religious affiliations of the whole population are based on the sources cited in chap. 1, note 10.

The Free-Labor Ideology

The abolitionist-entrepreneur correlation was no coincidence. The capitalist ideology was a free-labor ideology. It held that the internalized self-discipline of the Protestant ethic created more efficient workers than the coercive external discipline of slavery. The positive incentives of wages or advancement and the negative incentive of poverty provided stronger motivation than the lash. "The whip," said an abolitionist, "only stimulates the flesh on which it is laid. It does not reach the parts of the man where lie the springs of action." "Enslave a man," wrote the antislavery Whig editor Horace Greeley, "and you destroy his ambition, his enterprise, his capacity. In the constitution of human nature, the desire of bettering one's condition is the mainspring of effort."[8]

The ideal of upward social mobility was central to the free-labor ideology. "Our paupers to-day, thanks to free labor, are our yeomen and merchants of to-morrow," said the *New York Times,* in a typical glorification of the Northern free-labor system. "I am not ashamed to confess," said Abraham Lincoln in 1860—then a successful lawyer—"that twenty-five years ago I was a hired laborer, mauling rails, at work on a flat-boat." But "free society" enables the poor man "to better his condition; he knows that there is no fixed condition of labor, for his whole life." This principle, "that *all* should have an equal chance, " wrote Lincoln, was "the principle that clears the *path* for all, gives hope to all, and, by consequence, *enterprize,* and *industry,* to all."[9]

Because slaves were, in Lincoln's words, "fatally fixed in that condition for life," the free-labor ideology portrayed the South as a region in which the masses were mired in backwardness and poverty while their labor piled up wealth for the privileged few. Although Southerners could point to numerous examples of white men who had risen from poverty to prominence, Free Soilers nevertheless insisted that "slavery withers and blights all it touches. . . . It is a curse upon the poor, free, laboring white [men]. . . . They are depressed, poor, impoverished, degraded in caste, because labor is disgraceful." Wherever slavery goes, said a New York congressman in 1849, "there is in substance no middle class. Great wealth or hopeless poverty is the settled condition."[10]

In short, slavery and modernizing capitalism were irreconcilable. After a trip through Virginia in 1835, the future Whig and Republican leader William H. Seward wrote of "an exhausted soil, old and decaying towns, wretchedly-neglected roads . . . an absence of enterprise and improvement. . . . Such has been the effect of slavery." The institution undermined "intelligence, vigor, and energy," said Seward, and was therefore "incompatible with all . . . the elements of the security, welfare, and greatness of nations."[11]

---

[8]Lewis C. Gray, *History of Agriculture in the Southern United States to 1860,* 2 vols. (Washington, D.C., 1933), I, 463; Eric Foner, *Free Soil, Free Labor, Free Men* (New York, 1970), p. 46.

[9]Foner, *Free Soil,* p. 16; Roy P. Basler (ed.), *The Collected Works of Abraham Lincoln,* 9 vols. (New Brunswick, N.J., 1953–1955), IV, 24, II, 364, IV, 169.

[10]Basler, *Works of Lincoln,* III, 478; Foner, *Free Soil,* pp. 42, 47.

[11]John Ashworth, *Slavery, Capitalism, and Politics in the Antebellum Republic,* Vol. I: *Commerce and Compromise, 1820–1850* (Cambridge, 1995), p. 80; Foner, *Free Soil,* p. 51.

This view of Northern virtues and Southern vices was of course distorted. Nevertheless, as the conflict over the expansion of slavery into new territories heated up after 1845, an increasing number of Northerners adopted this viewpoint. Those in the antislavery camp regarded the conflict as no less than a contest over the future of America. "We are opposed to the extension of slavery because . . . it diminishes the productive power of its population," declared a Free Soil newspaper. "It is an obstacle to compact settlements, and to every general system of public instruction. [If slavery goes into the territories,] the free labor of all the states will not. . . . If the free labor of the states goes there, the slave labor of the southern states will not, and in a few years the country will teem with an active and energetic population."[12]

The Proslavery Counterattack

From Necessary Evil to Positive Good

The antislavery movement struck a raw nerve in the South. As heirs of the Revolutionary tradition, Southern leaders at first recognized the incompatibility of slavery with the ideals of liberty for which Americans of 1776 had fought. For nearly half a century after the Revolution, most Southerners apologized for slavery as a "necessary evil." As an evil, it would eventually die out under the beneficent influences of time and progress. But as a *necessary* evil, it could not be abolished precipitously or the South might be plunged into chaos. Hence the popularity in the upper South of colonization, which looked toward the elimination of the evil by gradual, ameliorative means.

By the 1830s, two developments undermined the necessary evil viewpoint. One was the phenomenal growth of the cotton kingdom, which seemed to make slavery more necessary than ever to the Southern economy. The second was the abolitionist movement, which placed the South on the defensive and provoked a sweeping ideological counterattack that took the form of an assertion that slavery, far from being a necessary evil, was in fact a "positive good." All great societies in history, went the argument, rested on slavery or serfdom—ancient Egypt, biblical Israel, Greece, Rome, the France of Charlemagne, the England of the Magna Charta. "There is not a respectable system of civilization known to history," said Senator R. M. T. Hunter of Virginia, "whose foundations were not laid in the institution of domestic slavery."[13] Even the Bible sanctioned bondage: the apostle Paul urged slaves to obey their masters and advised an escaped slave to return to his master. In 1850, a Southern clergyman wrote a pamphlet, typical of many similar publications, whose title summed up the positive good thesis: *A Defense of the South Against the Reproaches and Encroachments of the North: In Which Slavery Is Shown to Be an Institution of God Intended to Form the Basis of the Best Social State and the Only Safeguard to the Permanence of a Republican Government.*

---

[12]*New York Evening Post,* November 8, 1847; April 14, 1857.
[13]Quoted in David Donald, *Charles Sumner and the Coming of the Civil War* (New York, 1960), p. 349.

The proponents of the positive good thesis were confident that they had won the argument, at least in their own section. "Many in the South once believed that slavery was a moral and political evil," said John C. Calhoun in 1838. "That folly and delusion are gone. We see it now in its true light, and regard it as the most safe and stable basis for free institutions in the world." Two decades later, Senator James H. Hammond, also from South Carolina, recalled the days when misguided Southerners:

. . . believed slavery to be an evil—weakness—disgrace—nay a sin . . . and in fear and trembling [they] awaited a doom that seemed inevitable. But a few bold spirits took the question up—they compelled the South to investigate it anew and thoroughly, and what is the result? Why, it would be difficult to find a Southern man who feels the system to be the slightest burthen on his conscience.[14]

To achieve this result, the South spurned outside criticism and suppressed internal dissent. The section developed a siege mentality; unity in the face of external attack and vigilance against the internal threat of slave insurrections became mandatory. After the Nat Turner revolt in 1831,[15] Southern states imposed new restrictions on both blacks and whites, in the name of preserving order. Nearly every state passed laws limiting freedom of speech. Louisiana, for example, legislated penalties—ranging from twenty-one years at hard labor to death—for speeches or writings "having a tendency to promote discontent among free colored people, or insubordination among slaves." Several states empowered justices of the peace or other officials to confiscate objectionable material sent through the mails. Some communities established a "vigilance committee" or a "committee of public safety" to employ "all energetic means in ferreting out, and detecting any person or persons that may attempt to circulate among the community, any pamphlet, tract, or other seditious publication of any kind whatever." James Hammond insisted that abolitionists "can be silenced in but one way—*Terror*—*death*." Numerous Northern visitors to the South fell victim to mob violence, including lynching.[16]

Proslavery spokesmen expressed pride in the South's conservative social order, which resisted the "isms" that convulsed Northern society—not only abolitionism, but feminism, socialism, utopianism, transcendentalism, and millennialism, among a host of others. The slave states, declared a South Carolinian, were "the breakwater" which was "to stay that furious tide of social and political heresies." Only two of more than a hundred utopian communities in the antebellum United States were located in the South. The women's rights movement made no headway south of the Potomac, where white women remained safely on the pedestal that elevated them

---

[14]Calhoun in *Congressional Globe,* 25th Cong., 2nd sess. (1838), Appendix, 61–62; Hammond quoted in William W. Freehling, *Prelude to Civil War: The Nullification Controversy in South Carolina, 1816–1836* (New York, 1966), p. 299.

[15]Inspired by apocalyptic religious visions, Nat Turner led a group of his fellow Virginia slaves in an uprising in August 1831 that killed at least fifty-five whites and produced a wave of terror and reprisals throughout the South.

[16]Russel B. Nye, *Fettered Freedom: Civil Liberties and the Slavery Controversy, 1830–1860* (East Lansing, Mich., 1949), pp. 175, 178, 182–193; Hammond quoted in William W. Freehling, *The Road to Disunion: Secessionists at Bay 1776–1854* (New York, 1990), p. 294.

above the man's world of politics and public affairs. A Southern editor pointed with horror to the "ism-smitten people of Massachusetts," who "crowd to hear a Bloomer-clad unsexed lecturer, who has left her husband at home to take care of the children." Such things could never happen in a slave society, where "the bondsmen, as a lower class, as the substratum of society, constitute an always reliable, never wavering foundation whereon the social fabric rests securely, rooted and grounded in stability, and entirely beyond the reach of agitation."[17]

The South must insulate itself from heresy by shunning Northern magazines and books, said a Richmond newspaper in 1855. It must keep its young men at home instead of sending them to college in the North, where "every village has its press and its lecture room, and each lecturer and editor, unchecked by a healthy public opinion, opens up for discussion all the received dogmas of faith," where unwary youth are "exposed to the danger of imbibing doctrines subversive of all old institutions, and of all the established tenets respecting religion, law, morality, property, and government." Young men should be educated in the South, where "their training would be moral, religious, and conservative, and they would never learn, or read a word in school or out of school, inconsistent with orthodox Christianity, pure morality, the right of property, the sacredness of marriage."[18]

The Wage-Slavery Theme

In their war of words against outside critics, proslavery protagonists soon learned that the best defense was a good offense. "In the Northern states," said a New Orleans newspaper in 1856, "free society has proved a failure. It is rotten to the core." Southerners wrote numerous pamphlets to prove that black slaves on the plantations enjoyed a higher living standard than "wage slaves" in the factories. Southern slaves never suffered from unemployment or wage cuts; they received free medical care; they were taken care of in old age, rather than cast out to starve or depend on charity. Nowhere in the South did one see such "scenes of beggary, squalid poverty, and wretchedness" as one could find in any Northern city. The South Carolinian William Grayson published a long poem in 1855, *The Hireling and the Slave*, which pungently expressed the wage-slavery theme:

The Hireling

Free but in name—the slaves of endless toil . . .
In squalid hut—a kennel for the poor,
Or noisome cellar, stretched upon the floor,
His clothing rags, of filthy straw his bed,
With offal from the gutter daily fed. . . .
These are the miseries, such the wants, the cares,
The bliss that freedom for the serf prepares. . . .

---

[17]Clement Eaton, *The Freedom-of Thought Struggle in the Old South* (New York, 1964), p. 350; Avery Craven, *The Coming of the Civil War*, 2d ed. (Chicago, 1957), p. 300.

[18]Craven, *Coming of the Civil War*, pp. 301–302.

The Slave

> Taught by the master's efforts, by his care
> Fed, clothed, protected many a patient year,
> From trivial numbers now to millions grown,
> With all the white man's useful arts their own,
> Industrious, docile, skilled in wood and field,
> To guide the plow, the sturdy axe to wield. . . .
> Guarded from want, from beggary secure,
> He never feels what hireling crowds endure,
> Nor knows, like them, in hopeless want to crave,
> For wife and child, the comforts of the slave,
> Or the sad thought that, when about to die,
> He leaves them to the cold world's charity.[19]

The titles of some of the novels written in response to Harriet Beecher Stowe's *Uncle Tom's Cabin* illustrate the same theme; for example, *Uncle Robin in His Cabin in Virginia and Tom Without One in Boston.* So did the title of the most extreme proslavery indictment of free society, George Fitzhugh's *Cannibals All! Or Slaves Without Masters.* By 1852, the wage-slavery theme so pervaded Southern literature that one partisan could write: "It is needless to repeat the evidence that the average condition of the slave at the South is infinitely superior, morally and materially, in all respects, to that of the labouring class under any other circumstances in any other part of the world."[20]

 The Cavalier Image

Many planters conceived of their class as an aristocracy. "Slavery does indeed create an aristocracy," said James Hammond, "an aristocracy of talents, of virtue, of generosity and courage."[21] The habit of command was instilled into the youth of slaveholding families almost from birth. Planters subscribed to the code of chivalry with its requirements of honor, courtesy, gallantry toward women, and *noblesse oblige.* This helps to explain the popularity of Sir Walter Scott's novels in the South: the planter class could identify with the knights of *Ivanhoe* and the Scottish aristocrats of the *Waverly* novels. As Southern nationalism waxed in the 1850s, some residents of Dixie began to call themselves "Southrons," a term borrowed from Scott. The Southern upper class delighted in jousting tournaments, at which young men designated as the Knight of Malvern, the Knight of the Old Dominion, and the like, competed for the favor of fair maidens before crowds of thousands.

---

[19]Allan Nevins, *Ordeal of the Union*, 2 vols. (New York, 1947), I, 515; Eric McKitrick (ed.), *Slavery Defended: The View of the Old South* (Englewood Cliffs, N.J., 1963), pp. 58–59, 66–67. For a provocative interpretation of the wage-slavery theme, see David R. Roediger, *The Wages of Whiteness: Race and the Making of the American Working Class* (London, 1991).

[20]McKitrick, *Slavery Defended,* pp. 109–110.

[21]William S. Jenkins, *Pro-Slavery Thought in the Old South* (Chapel Hill, NC, 1935), p. 289.

From this self-image arose the notion that Southern planters were descended from the seventeenth-century English Cavaliers, while Yankees were descended from the Roundheads, or Puritans. The Cavaliers, in this theory, were in turn descended from the Norman knights who had conquered Saxon England in the eleventh century, while the Puritans were descended from those conquered Saxons. "The Norman Cavalier of the South cannot brook the vulgar familiarity of the Saxon Yankee," remarked a Kentucky editor in a typical comment. In 1860, the *Southern Literary Messenger* published an article entitled "The Difference of Race Between the Northern People and the Southern People." This difference was none other than that between Cavalier and Puritan, Norman and Saxon. The Southern colonies, the article claimed, had been settled by:

> . . . persons belonging to the blood and race of the reigning family . . . recognized as Cavaliers . . . directly descended from the Norman-Barons of William the Conqueror, a race distinguished in its earliest history for its warlike and fearless character, a race in all times since renowned for its gallantry, chivalry, honor, gentleness, and intellect. . . . The Southern people come of that race.[22]

The reference to "warlike and fearless character" in this quotation pointed to an aspect of Southern life more real than the mythical descent from Cavaliers and Normans. Contemporary observers—Southern, Northern, and foreign alike—agreed that familiarity with weapons and the habit of using them were more common in the South than in the North. The homicide rate was higher below the Mason-Dixon line than above it. Dueling became rare in the North after Aaron Burr killed Alexander Hamilton in 1804, but it persisted in the South until the Civil War.

Dueling was linked to the South's aristocratic code of honor and to the Southerner's reliance on personal action, rather than law, to avenge insult. Many prominent Southern statesmen fought duels. Andrew Jackson killed one of his antagonists, and a South Carolina governor reputedly fought fourteen duels and wounded his man every time. As sectional tensions escalated after 1830, Southern congressmen occasionally challenged their Northern counterparts to duels. The latter usually refused (though in 1838 a Maine congressman was killed by a Kentucky representative in a duel), which tended to confirm the Southern stereotype of Yankees as poltroons.[23]

The martial spirit appeared to be stronger in the South than in the North. More Southern than Northern volunteers fought in the Mexican War, where the principal generals were also Southerners. From 1841 to 1861, the general in chief of the U.S. army was a Southerner. During the 1850s, two of the three brigadier generals and all but one commander of the army's geographical divisions were natives of the South. All four secretaries of war from 1849 to 1860 were Southerners. The proportion of Southerners admitted to West Point, and of regular army officers from the South, was

---

[22]Rollin G. Osterweis, *Romanticism and Nationalism in the Old South* (New Haven, 1949), p. 101; *Southern Literary Messenger*, 30 (June 1860), 401–409.

[23]For perceptive discussions of this theme, see John Hope Franklin, *The Militant South 1800–1861* (Cambridge, Mass., 1956); Dickson D. Bruce, Jr., *Violence and Culture in the Antebellum South* (Austin, Tex., 1979); Bertram Wyatt-Brown, *Southern Honor: Ethics and Behavior in the Old South* (New York, 1982); and Kenneth S. Greenberg, *Honor and Slavery* (Princeton, 1996).

THE RICHMOND GRAYS IN 1859.
Note the healthy appearance and self-confident mien of these men and boys. By 1865, several would be maimed for life and one-third would be dead.

COOK COLLECTION, VALENTINE MUSEUM

30 percent greater than the section's proportion of the nation's white population. The camaraderie among Southerners at the Point became important in 1861: eleven of the cadets who had been there together in 1828 and 1829 became top generals or leaders in the Confederacy, including Robert E. Lee, Albert Sidney Johnston, Joseph E. Johnston, and Jefferson Davis.

Perhaps even more significant than the Southern presence at West Point was the large number of military schools in the South. The best known were Virginia Military Institute and the Citadel; but by the 1850s, nearly every Southern state had its military institute. The census of 1860 listed five times as many military colleges in the South as in the North (the North had more than twice as many colleges and professional schools of other types). This too became important when the fighting began in 1861.

Volunteer military companies were popular in both North and South. Some of them were social organizations whose training in military drill was indifferent at best. But others were genuine armed units that took their duties seriously. Although the evidence is inconclusive, the latter seem to have been more numerous in the South than in the North, in proportion to population, especially by the late 1850s.[24] In 1859, a Savannah lawyer wrote an account of a trip that his artillery company had taken to Nashville and back:

At Macon we were received with a salute from the artillery company newly formed, were escorted by the Macon Volunteers, the Floyd Rifles, and the Bibb County Cavalry. . . . Midway between Macon and Atlanta we were met by a delegation from the Gate City Guards. . . . As we passed through Marietta the cadets from the military institute gave us a salute with a small battery of six-pounders. . . . [In Nashville] we were received by the German *Yagers,* the Shelby Guards, and the cadets from the military institute. . . . [Upon our return to Savannah] the Guards, the Blues, the Oglethorpe Light Infantry, and the Irish Jasper Greens were all out in full ranks to meet us.[25]

An important purpose of the South's armed readiness was the control of slaves. A central feature of Southern life was the slave patrol, a mounted detachment of three or four white men under a captain that patrolled its "beat" each night to apprehend slaves without passes and to prevent secret gatherings of bondsmen. Since each patrol rode about once every two weeks, some fifty or more white men in each beat performed this duty. The patrols included nonslaveholders and formed another link that bound them to the system.

Although large-scale slave insurrections occurred rarely in the United States, Southern whites lived in constant fear of an uprising. It took only a few such examples—Nat Turner's revolt in 1831, or the aborted conspiracies of Gabriel Prosser and Denmark Vesey, the first near Richmond in 1800, the second in Charleston in 1822—to keep alive that dread. One function of the volunteer military companies was preparedness "to quell sudden insurrection." As the Savannah lawyer quoted above put it in 1856: "I think it a duty which every citizen owes in our citizen-soldier state of society . . . to connect himself if possible with one of these military companies. It is certainly a police service very necessary in its character."[26]

Slavery and National Politics

Slavery was the main issue in national politics from 1844 to the outbreak of the Civil War. And many times before 1844 this vexed question had set section against section, as in the Missouri debates of 1819–1820. Even the nullification crisis of 1832,

---

[24]Marcus Cunliffe, in *Soldiers and Civilians: The Martial Spirit in America, 1775–1865* (Boston, 1968), maintains that the military ethos was equally vigorous in North and South. In particular, he argues that the volunteer companies were if anything more common in the North than in the South. But much of his own evidence demonstrates the contrary. Cunliffe sometimes fails to interpret the evidence on a per capita basis: that is, with less than half the North's white population, the South could have fewer West Point alumni or fewer volunteer companies than the North but still have a larger number in proportion to population.

[25]Robert Manson Myers (ed.), *The Children of Pride* (New York, 1972), pp. 489–494.

[26]Ibid., pp. 211–212.

ostensibly over the tariff, had slavery as its underlying cause. The South Carolina nullifiers feared that the centralization of government power, as manifested by the tariff, might eventually threaten slavery itself. Nullification was the most extreme assertion of states' rights—a constitutional theory whose fundamental purpose was to protect slavery against potential federal interference. In the eyes of some Southerners, *any* exercise of federal power constituted a potential threat to slavery. "If Congress can make banks, roads, and canals under the Constitution," said Senator Nathaniel Macon of North Carolina, "they can free any slave in the United States."[27]

The Democratic party served as the main political bulwark of slavery. The South formed the backbone of the Jacksonian Democratic coalition. In 1828, Andrew Jackson won 71 percent of the popular vote in the slave states, compared with only 50 percent in the free states. Three-fifths of his electoral votes came from the South. Four years later, Jackson carried 70 percent of the popular vote in the slave states and 51 percent in the North. The Jacksonians rewarded their Southern support. Three of Jackson's four appointees to the Supreme Court were Southerners. President Martin Van Buren, Jackson's hand-picked successor, appointed two more Southern justices but no Northerners to the Court. Jackson's veto of bills to recharter the Second Bank of the United States and to appropriate funds for road construction pleased Southern proponents of states' rights. So did the administration's willingness to ban antislavery materials from the Southern mails. And congressional Democrats supplied most of the votes for the "gag rule"—a resolution that barred the reception of antislavery petitions in the House from 1836 to 1844.

Despite Van Buren's reputation as a "doughface" (a Northern man with Southern principles), many Southerners did not trust the New Yorker. Although Van Buren won the presidency in 1836, the newly organized Whig party (whose principal leader was Henry Clay of Kentucky) carried a slight majority of the Southern popular vote that year. For the next fifteen years, the Democratic and Whig parties remained evenly balanced in both the North and the South. Party leaders strove to keep the divisive slavery issue out of national politics. But this effort succeeded for only a few years. The annexation of Texas and the subsequent war with Mexico pushed the question of slavery's expansion to the forefront of national politics and divided both parties along sectional lines.

---

[27]Norman K. Risjord, *The Old Republicans: Southern Conservatism in the Age of Jefferson* (New York, 1965), p. 242.

Chapter Four

Texas, Mexico, and the Compromise of 1850

We must "satisfy the northern people . . .
that we are not to extend the institution of
slavery as a result of this war."

-Gideon Welles,
Connecticut Democrat, 1846

The Annexation of Texas

Americans began migrating to Texas in the 1820s at the invitation of a Mexican government that had just won its independence from Spain. By 1830, however, Mexico was alarmed at the influx of a population alien in language and culture, suspect in political allegiance, and committed to slavery in defiance of Mexico's recent abolition of the institution. The growing number of American settlers produced controversies over land claims and political rights. In 1836, tensions between Texans and the central government in Mexico City reached the breaking point. The Texans proclaimed their independence and, after suffering the massacre of the defenders of the Alamo, won the decisive battle of San Jacinto on April 21, 1836. They also captured the Mexican leader Antonio Lopez de Santa Anna. In return for his release, Santa Anna signed a treaty granting Texas independence. Although the Mexican Congress repudiated the treaty, joyful Texans established the Lone Star Republic and petitioned for annexation to the United States.

But this request ran into a snag in Washington, where antislavery Whigs charged collusion between Southern Democrats and Texans to foment revolution and annexation in the hope of expanding slave territory. Several Northern Democrats also opposed annexation. To preserve peace with Mexico and harmony in the Democratic party, Presidents Andrew Jackson and Martin Van Buren kept Texas at arm's length. The disappointed Texans turned their energies to strengthening their republic, and the Texas issue subsided in American politics.

It did not subside for long. The death, from pneumonia, of the first Whig President, William Henry Harrison, one month after his inauguration in 1841 brought John Tyler into the White House. A Virginia Whig who opposed much of his party's legislative program for higher tariffs, a new national bank, and federal aid for roads and waterways, Tyler broke with congressional Whigs on these issues and soon found himself a president without a party. He turned to Southern Democrats for support, appointed several Southerners to his cabinet—including fellow Virginian Abel Upshur as secretary of state—and cast about for an issue on which he might win the 1844 election. He settled on the annexation of Texas as "the only matter, that will take sufficient hold of the feelings of the South to rally it on a southern candidate."[1]

Upshur opened secret negotiations with Texas for a treaty of annexation. At the same time, pro-administration newspapers began to point with alarm at alleged maneuvering by the British government in Texas. Britain had negotiated a treaty of recognition and commerce with the republic. English abolitionists expressed hope that their country's expected influence in Texas would promote emancipation there. Southerners magnified this into the first stage of a British plot to set up satellite free states in the Western Hemisphere as barriers to further American expansion and as beachheads for an assault, in alliance with Northern abolitionists, on slavery in the United States itself.

This made good propaganda. Anglophobia was still a potent force in American politics. Southerners feared that the confinement of slavery to its present boundaries would mean ultimate asphyxiation. Unless they could increase the number of slave states, the South would become a helpless minority in the national government. Southerners must "*demand* . . . the admission of Texas . . . as indispensable to their security," wrote Secretary of State Upshur to John C. Calhoun, the South's foremost partisan. "Both parties [in the South] may unite on that, for it is a *Southern* question, and not one of whiggism and democracy."[2]

When an accident killed Upshur in February 1844, his successor was none other than Calhoun, who completed the annexation treaty and submitted it to the Senate in April. At the same time, Calhoun publicly informed the British minister that annexation was necessary to forestall abolitionist plots against slavery, an institution "essential to the peace, safety, and prosperity" of the United States.[3] This open avowal of a proslavery purpose did not sit well with Northern senators. Nor did southern Whigs wish to support the renegade Tyler and risk war with Mexico by ap-

[1]Charles Sellers, "Election of 1844," in Arthur M. Schlesinger, Jr. (ed.), *History of American Presidential Elections,* 4 vols. (New York, 1971), I, 760.
[2]Frederick Merk, *Slavery and the Annexation of Texas* (New York, 1972), p. 20.
[3]Sellers, "Election of 1844," p. 821.

proving annexation. They joined Northern Whigs and several Northern Democrats to defeat the treaty in June. But even before this happened, Texas had become the chief issue in the presidential campaign.

The two leading presidential contenders, Henry Clay and Martin Van Buren, were wounded by the Texas whiplash. Both of them had come out against annexation in letters published simultaneously on April 27. Clay's position was standard Whig doctrine, even in the South, and the party nominated him unanimously four days later. But Van Buren's letter sent shock waves among Southern Democrats. It accelerated the drive by Calhoun Democrats to defeat the New Yorker's nomination. This drive succeeded because of the Democratic rule requiring a two-thirds majority to name a candidate at national conventions. Southern delegations used the rule through eight ballots to block Van Buren's nomination, even though he had received a simple majority on the first ballot. On the ninth ballot, the exhausted Democrats finally nominated dark horse James K. Polk of Tennessee, an ardent annexationist. "We have triumphed," exulted one of Calhoun's allies. "Polk is nearer to *us* than any public man who was named. He is a large Slave holder and [is for] Texas—States rights *out & out.*"[4]

Polk's success undercut Tyler's forlorn hope to be a third-party candidate, and the President withdrew from the race. "Texas fever" swept the South as the campaign warmed up. "The people seem literally to have taken fire on this subject of Texas," wrote a Virginian, "& nothing short of *immediate annexation* will serve them." Clay was alarmed by the slippage of his strength among Southern Whigs vulnerable to the annexation pressure. In July he wrote two public letters explaining that while he still opposed annexation if it would mean war with Mexico, "I should be glad to see it, without dishonor, without war, with the common consent of the Union."[5] This provoked anger among antislavery Whigs, some of whom vowed to vote for Liberty party candidate James G. Birney. In the end Clay's equivocation on Texas won back few votes in the South while losing perhaps decisive votes to the Liberty party in New York. That state went for Polk by a margin of only five thousand votes and thereby gave him the presidency.

Polk carried all but two of the future Confederate states. At the same time, the Liberty party vote in the North increased ninefold from 1840. Although the Liberty ballots added up to no more than 3 percent of the Northern total, the 1844 election drove in the thin edge of the wedge that would eventually split the intersectional two-party system into predominantly sectional parties.

Manifest Destiny and the Mexican War

Although Polk's margin of victory was narrow (49.6 percent of the popular vote to Clay's 48.1 percent), annexationists chose to consider the outcome a mandate. Hoping to acquire Texas as the crowning achievement of his administration, Tyler in December 1844

---

[4]William J. Cooper, *The South and the Politics of Slavery, 1828–1856* (Baton Rouge, 1978), p. 206.

[5]Sellers, "Election of 1844," pp. 762, 855–856.

outflanked the required two-thirds Senate majority for approval of treaties by submitting to Congress a joint resolution of annexation, which required a simple majority of both houses. Despite the doubtful constitutionality of this procedure, both houses passed the joint resolution on the eve of Tyler's retirement from office in March 1845. Although several Northern Democrats broke ranks to vote initially against the joint resolution, these dissenters wheeled into line on the final vote to adopt annexation. Texas came in as a state at the end of 1845.

Northern Democrats were willing to swallow Texas because in return they expected Southern support for the acquisition of an equally large slice of territory in the Pacific Northwest. The 1844 Democratic platform had pledged the party to acquire "the whole of the territory of Oregon" as well as Texas. Both the United States and Britain claimed Oregon, which then stretched all the way from the northern borders of present-day California and Nevada to the southern border of Russian Alaska. Since 1818, the two countries had by agreement jointly occupied this huge area. But in the 1840s American settlers began pouring into the fertile valley of the Willamette River. Like the Texans, they wanted to become part of the United States. In 1845, President Polk recommended termination of the joint Anglo-American occupation agreement and reasserted the American claim to the whole territory—stretching north to the latitude of 54°40′. Inspired by the bombastic eloquence of Democratic orators, who announced America's "manifest destiny" to acquire the whole continent, Democrats proclaimed the slogan "Fifty-four forty or fight!" To Northern Democrats, Oregon became a test of whether their Southern colleagues would support the expansion of free territory as vigorously as they supported the expansion of slave territory. The Tennessean Polk failed the test. While he was willing to provoke war with Mexico to obtain the Southwest, he was unwilling to risk war with Britain to acquire all of Oregon. But this did not become clear until the Mexican War was already under way.

Relations with Mexico deteriorated from the outset of Polk's administration. Three issues divided the two countries. The first was American annexation of Texas. This was probably negotiable, because Texas had maintained its independence for a decade and Mexico had no realistic hope of regaining it. The second was the Texas border. As a Mexican province, Texas's southern border had been the Nueces River. The Texans, backed by the Polk administration, claimed an area more than twice as large, with the Rio Grande as the border. The third issue was the future of sparsely populated California and New Mexico, which Polk was determined to acquire.

The President employed a carrot-and-stick approach in 1845. He sent the Louisianian John Slidell to Mexico City as a "minister plenipotentiary" empowered to offer up to $30 million for California and New Mexico, as well as the U.S. assumption of Mexican debts to American citizens in return for Mexican acceptance of the Rio Grande boundary. At the same time, Polk ordered American troops under General Zachary Taylor into the disputed territory south of the Nueces and dispatched a naval squadron to patrol the Mexican coast. He authorized the American consul in Monterey, California, to act as a secret agent to stir up pro-American sentiment among the local population, which included several hundred American settlers. The administration also sent contingency orders to the Pacific fleet to seize California ports if war broke out between Mexico and the United States.

The Mexican government refused to receive Slidell. Soon thereafter a revolution in Mexico City brought a militant anti-American regime into power, which vowed to recover the "stolen province" of Texas. In response, Polk in January 1846 ordered Taylor's troops to the Rio Grande while American ships blockaded the river. A Mexican army camped across the river from Taylor. Hoping for an incident that would justify a declaration of war, the impatient Polk was ready by May 9 to send a war message to Congress even without an incident when word arrived that Mexicans had killed several American soldiers north of the Rio Grande in a skirmish on April 25. Polk dispatched his war message on May 11. "Notwithstanding all our efforts to avoid it," said the President disingenuously, war "exists by the act of Mexico herself, [for she has] invaded our territory and shed American blood upon American soil."[6]

Since Mexico's claim to the disputed territory was at least as strong as the American claim, it would have been equally true to say that the United States had started the war by shedding Mexican blood on Mexican soil. This was the view of abolitionists, antislavery Whigs, and even many Southern Whigs. A Whig senator from Ohio created a sensation when he declared: "If I were a Mexican, I would tell you, 'Have you not room in your own country to bury your dead men? If you come into mine we will greet you with bloody hands, and welcome you to hospitable graves.' " The abolitionists won new converts to their belief that Texas and the Mexican War were steps in a nefarious "slave power conspiracy" to expand slave territory. James Russell Lowell's antiwar dialect poems, supposedly written by the Yankee rustic Hosea Biglow, achieved a wide popularity in New England:

> They jest want this Californy
> So's to lug new slave-states in
> To abuse ye, an' to scorn ye,
> And to plunder ye like sin.

The Massachusetts legislature agreed with Lowell: in 1847, it resolved that this "unconstitutional" war was being waged for "the triple object of extending slavery, of strengthening the slave power, and of obtaining control of the free states."[7]

The demand for "all Oregon" became one of the war's first casualties. Not wanting to fight two wars at the same time, Polk retreated from "fifty-four forty" and negotiated a compromise with Britain on the 49th parallel. Twelve Northern Democratic senators rebelled and voted against this treaty. Only the unanimous support of the Whigs, who were cool toward Manifest Destiny and wanted peace with Britain, permitted ratification of the treaty. Bitter Northern Democrats accused their Southern colleagues of bad faith: "Texas and Oregon were born in the same instant, nursed and cradled in the same cradle," but having used Northern votes to

---

[6]James D. Richardson (comp.), *Messages and Papers of the Presidents, 1789–1897,* 20 vols. (Washington, D.C., 1897–1913), V, 2292.

[7]Louis Filler, *The Crusade against Slavery 1830–1860* (New York, 1960), p. 186; *The Works of James Russell Lowell,* Standard Library ed., 11 vols. (Boston, 1890), VIII, 46–47; H. V. Ames (ed.), *State Documents on Federal Relations* (Philadelphia, 1906), pp. 241–242.

get Texas, "the peculiar friends of Texas turned and were doing all they could to strangle Oregon."[8] Still, most Northern Democrats continued to support the administration's war policy.

Despite Whig dislike of "Mr. Polk's War," few congressmen were willing to risk political suicide by voting against a war that was popular in most parts of the country. Some Whigs remembered that opposition to the War of 1812 had killed the Federalist party. Only fourteen Whigs in the House and two in the Senate voted against the declaration of war. Most Whigs voted appropriations for troops and supplies. But in preliminary roll calls on this legislation and in congressional votes on auxiliary legislation connected with the war, a clear antiwar faction emerged, consisting of nearly all Northern Whigs, plus several Southern Whigs and a few Northern Democrats. Antiwar sentiment was partly responsible for a Whig gain of thirty-eight House seats in 1846 and 1847, most of them in the Northeastern states.

Had the American forces not enjoyed such remarkable success in Mexico, the antiwar opposition might have evolved into a powerful coalition. But mixed armies of regulars and volunteers led by Generals Zachary Taylor and Winfield Scott won a string of stunning victories over numerically larger Mexican forces that resulted in the capture of Mexico City itself in September 1847. A small American army also captured Santa Fe, New Mexico, and then marched overland to help the Pacific naval squadron and volunteer units of American settlers subdue Mexican resistance in California.

American armies in Mexico owed their success to excellent artillery, the élan of the infantry, the low morale of Mexican soldiers, and especially to the superiority of American officers—from Scott and Taylor down to the lieutenants. The roster of junior officers included men who would play the leading roles in a far bloodier conflict fifteen years later: Robert E. Lee, Ulysses S. Grant, Thomas J. Jackson, Albert S. and Joseph E. Johnston, George B. McClellan, Pierre G. T. Beauregard, James Longstreet, Braxton Bragg, Joseph Hooker, George Gordon Meade, George H. Thomas, and Jefferson Davis.

American conquests whetted the appetite of expansionists for an additional slice of Mexico south of the Rio Grande. This desire prompted Polk in October 1847 to recall his peace negotiator Nicholas Trist, who seemed too willing to compromise with the Mexicans. Trist ignored the recall, negotiated the Treaty of Guadalupe Hidalgo, and sent it to Washington in February 1848. By this treaty Mexico gave up all claim to Texas north of the Rio Grande and, in return for a payment of $15 million and assumption of Mexican debts to Americans, ceded New Mexico and California to the United States. (This territory included present-day California, Nevada, Utah; most of Arizona and New Mexico; and part of Oklahoma, Colorado, and Wyoming.) In the Senate, seven Whigs who wanted no Mexican territory and five Democrats who wanted more voted against the treaty, but the remaining votes were sufficient to approve it on March 10.

In the preceding three years, the United States had acquired a million and a quarter square miles of new territory. Nearly half of it lay south of the old Missouri Compromise line of 36°30'. It had been won largely by the exertions of two

---

[8]Chaplain W. Morrison, *Democratic Politics and Sectionalism: The Wilmot Proviso Controversy* (Chapel Hill, N.C., 1967), pp. 11–12.

Southern presidents and of armies commanded by Southern generals (Scott was a Virginian and Taylor a Louisianian) in which two-thirds of the volunteer soldiers were from slave states. One can thus readily imagine the anger of Southerners when Northern congressmen tried to exclude slavery from the territory won in the Mexican War.

The Wilmot Proviso

On August 8, 1846, when the war was barely three months old, an obscure first-term Democratic congressman from Pennsylvania named David Wilmot offered an amendment to an appropriations bill: "that, as an express and fundamental condition to the acquisition of any territory from the Republic of Mexico . . . neither slavery nor involuntary servitude shall ever exist in any part of said territory."[9] The principle embodied in this amendment—the Wilmot Proviso, as it came to be known—remained the lodestone of sectional conflict for the next fifteen years.

Wilmot acted in behalf of a group of Northern Democrats whose grievances had reached the boiling point. Some of these grievances concerned economic legislation. The Polk administration came into power pledged to dismantle the last vestiges of Whig programs for federal aid to economic development. Most Northern Democrats approved of this, but significant blocs were alienated by two actions: the Walker Tariff of 1846, which reduced duties for many commodities below the level of a supposed administration commitment to Democratic congressmen from tariff-conscious Pennsylvania; and Polk's veto of a rivers and harbors improvements bill supported by Midwestern Democrats—the same Democrats who were angered by the administration's compromise with Britain on the Oregon question. Other grievances were political. Van Buren's supporters had not forgotten the denial of the 1844 presidential nomination to their leader. Polk added insult to injury by refusing to appoint any Van Buren Democrats to his cabinet and by turning the rich federal patronage in New York over to Van Buren's factional enemies.

Underlying all these grievances was a burgeoning resentment at Southern domination of the party. Southern Democrats had sabotaged Van Buren in 1844; they had formulated the Walker Tariff and sustained the rivers and harbors veto; a Southern president had conceded away half of Oregon while insisting on all of Texas, and had provoked Mexico into a war that a growing number of Northerners regarded as wicked aggression to expand slavery. Northern Democrats feared punishment at the polls if they appeared to support the war for proslavery purposes. "There have been enough northern democrats who have sacrificed themselves to southern interests and I do not wish to see any more," said a New York party leader. "The South has never yielded anything to conciliate the North, [and] we have yielded too much to conciliate the South," wrote Connecticut Democrat Gideon Welles in July 1846. We must "satisfy the northern people . . . that we are not to extend the institution of slav-

---

[9]*Congressional Globe*, 29th Cong., 1st sess. (1846), 1217.

ery as a result of this war."[10] Antislavery Whigs shared these sentiments. The South, wrote one, "[has] trampled on the rights and just claims of the North sufficiently long and have fairly shit upon all our Northern statesmen and are now trying to rub it in and I think now is the time and just the time for the North to take a stand."[11]

Northern Whigs voted unanimously for Wilmot's proviso; so did all but four Northern Democrats, while every Southern Democrat and all but two Southern Whigs voted against it. Having passed the House, the proviso failed to come to a vote in the Senate at this session. At the next session, in February 1847, the House repassed the proviso; but the Senate, with five Northern Democrats joining the Southerners, passed the appropriations bill without the antislavery amendment. Under heavy administration pressure, twenty-three Northern House Democrats then receded from the proviso and cast the necessary votes to pass the bill unamended.

Parties Split along Sectional Lines

Despite this victory for the South, the political system had experienced an ominous wrenching of the normal party division of congressional votes into an almost completely sectional division. This was an ill omen for the future of the parties and of the Union itself. Before the Wilmot Proviso, the political system had been able to accommodate sectional differences because slavery was a state institution beyond the power of Congress. But with the imminent acquisition of territory whose status was a matter for congressional legislation, the question of slavery exploded beyond party lines and became an arena for sectional conflict.

Every Northern state legislature but one endorsed the Wilmot Proviso. Southern legislatures responded with pledges of "determined resistance [at] all hazards and to the last extremity." The proviso affronted the South with regard to its most cherished value—honor. To prevent slave owners from taking their property into the territories was to stigmatize them. It was an imputation of "degrading inequality . . . which says to the Southern man, Avaunt! you are not my equal, and hence are to be excluded as carrying a moral taint." The South could not accept such "degradation," said dozens of spokesmen. "Death is preferable to acknowledged inferiority."[12]

Most of all, Southerners feared encirclement by free territory that, like a boa constrictor, would slowly squeeze slavery to death. Some antislavery men avowed precisely this purpose. "If you drive on this bloody war of conquest to annexation," warned an Ohio Whig congressman, "we will establish a cordon of free States that will surround you; and then we will light up the fires of liberty on every side, until they melt your present chains, and render all your people free." Such statements reinforced Southern fears. James H. Hammond of South Carolina warned that adoption of the Wilmot Proviso would insure ten new free states west of the Mississippi. "Long before the North gets this vast accession of strength she will ride over us rough shod, proclaim freedom or something equivalent to it to our Slaves and reduce us to

---

[10]Eric Foner, "The Wilmot Proviso Revisited," *Journal of American History,* 61 (September 1969), 270, 277, and 277n.

[11]Michael F. Holt, *The Political Crisis of the 1850s* (New York, 1978), p. 51.

[12]Cooper, *The South and the Politics of Slavery,* pp. 235, 239; Holt, *Political Crisis of the 1850s,* p. 54.

the condition of Hayti. . . . If we do not act now, we deliberately consign our children, not our posterity, but *our children* to the flames."[13] One after another, Southern congressmen invoked the threat of disunion as the inevitable consequence of the Wilmot Proviso.

As he had often done before, John C. Calhoun made the formal presentation of the Southern position. And as before, Calhoun based his presentation on a rigorous exegesis of constitutional rights. The territories, he said in a series of resolutions introduced in the Senate on February 19, 1847, were the "common property" of the several states; as the "joint agent" of the states, Congress had no power to deny the citizens of any state the right to take their property into a territory; therefore slavery was legal in all of the territories. If the institution was "entirely excluded from the territories," said Calhoun in a speech supporting his resolutions, the balance of fifteen slave and fifteen free states would be destroyed and the former would be "at the entire mercy of the non-slaveholding States." "If this scheme should be carried out—if we are to be reduced to a mere handful . . . wo, wo, I say to this Union." In a private letter written the same day, Calhoun told a friend: "You will see that I have made up the issue between North and South. If we flinch we are gone, but if we stand fast on it, we shall triumph either by compelling the North to yield to our terms, or declaring our independence of them."[14]

Between the polar opposites of the Wilmot and Calhoun positions ranged a spectrum of opinions that seemed to offer room for compromise. One compromise proposal, supported by Polk and his cabinet and backed by a coalition of moderate Whigs and Democrats, was to extend the Missouri Compromise line of 36°30' to the Pacific. Thus Oregon territory (present-day Oregon, Washington, and Idaho) plus the area now comprising Utah, Nevada, western Colorado, and the northern half of California would have been organized without slavery; the area now comprising Oklahoma, New Mexico, Arizona, and southern California would have been organized with no restrictions against slavery. This compromise attracted some antislavery Northerners, who believed that climate and geography would prevent slavery from taking root in the new Southwest. But most antislavery people were concerned not only about these territories but also about additional territory the United States might acquire in the future. The hard-line supporters of both the Wilmot Proviso and the Calhoun resolutions refused to recede from their positions.

Failure of the 36°30' solution opened the way for another possible compromise, which became known as "popular sovereignty." The early champion of this approach was Michigan Democrat Lewis Cass, an aspirant for his party's presidential nomination in 1848 (Polk was not a candidate for reelection). At the end of 1847, Cass proposed "leaving to the people of the territory to be acquired the business of settling the matter for themselves." This was consistent with democracy and self-government. It also had the political virtue of ambiguity. Nowhere did Cass specify at what stage the people of a territory would have the right to regulate slavery. Could a territorial

---

[13] *Congressional Globe*, 29th Cong., 2nd sess. (1847), Appendix, 281; William L. Barney, *The Road to Secession: A New Perspective on the Old South* (New York, 1972), pp. 105–106.

[14] *Congressional Globe*, 29th Cong., 2nd sess. (1847), 454–455; Morrison, *Democratic Politics and Sectionalism*, p. 35.

legislature prohibit slavery if it wished? Northern Democrats understood popular sovereignty to mean that it could. Or did the Cass formula mean that the people of a territory could decide on slavery only when they applied for statehood? Southern Democrats, who believed that nothing less sovereign than a state could legislate against property in slaves, interpreted popular sovereignty in this way. Thus slavery might gain a legal foothold in territories where it was economically feasible, and one or more of the new states might come into the Union with slavery. Although aware of these opposing sectional interpretations, most Northern and Southern Democrats endorsed popular sovereignty and tacitly agreed to preserve the ambiguity for the sake of harmony in the forthcoming presidential campaign.

 The Election of 1848

But the Democratic national convention could not prevent the slavery-extension issue from splitting the party. The issue first confronted the convention in the form of rival delegations from New York. The Van Burenites (or "Barnburners" in the political lexicon of the time) were pledged to the Wilmot Proviso, while the "Hunkers" were willing to conciliate the South.[15] The Barnburners rejected a compromise proposal to seat both delegations and stomped out of the convention to nominate Van Buren on a splinter ticket. A combination of Southern and Western Democrats nominated Cass, on a platform whose vague references to slavery failed to satisfy Southern Calhounites. William Lowndes Yancey of Alabama offered a resolution affirming the Calhoun position on slavery in the territories. When a six-to-one majority voted it down, Yancey walked out of the convention. Although only one other delegate followed him, this symbolic gesture portended trouble in the future.

The Whigs attempted to minimize sectional damage to their party by adopting no platform at all and by nominating a nonpolitician for President. The party passed over its two venerable leaders, Henry Clay and Daniel Webster, to nominate war hero Zachary Taylor, who had never voted in his life and was not even sure until 1848 that he was a Whig. The nomination of a Mexican War general by the antiwar party provided one more illustration of the strange convolutions of American politics.

Taylor owned many slaves. Although this did not prevent most Northern Whigs from supporting him, a vigorous antislavery minority refused to do so. The nomination brought to a boil the long-simmering dispute between "Conscience" and "Cotton" Whigs in Massachusetts. The former consisted of younger men influenced by the antislavery movement. They resented the domination of the state's Whig party by textile manufacturers who were economically dependent on Southern cotton. Although these Cotton Whigs had opposed the annexation of Texas and had supported the Wilmot Proviso, they sought a détente with Southern Whigs in 1848. In response,

---

[15]The Barnburners were the progressive wing of the New York Democrats. They resented Southern domination of the national Democratic party and patronage-machine control of the state party. Like the proverbial Dutchman who burned his barn to rid it of rats, they were said to be willing to bolt the party (and therefore to cripple it) in order to punish the opposing faction. The Hunkers were said to be men without principle who only hankered or "hunkered" for office.

the Conscience faction under the leadership of Charles Francis Adams and Charles Sumner denounced Taylor's nomination as the product of an unholy alliance between "the Lords of the Lash" and "the Lords of the Loom." They bolted the party and prepared to join a third-party coalition.

The time appeared to be ripe for such a coalition. "The whole country seems to be arousing at last!" wrote Charles Sumner to Salmon P. Chase of Ohio in July 1848. "The spirit of Freedom is spreading in Massachusetts now as in the days of the earlier Revolution."[16] Chase headed a group within the Liberty party working for a fusion with antislavery defectors from the major parties. Since 1844, the Liberty party had suffered its own defection—of a minority who interpreted the Constitution as authorizing the federal government to abolish slavery in the states. Since few abolitionists took this extreme position, these Liberty purists found themselves as isolated on one wing of the antislavery movement as were the Garrisonians—who believed that the Constitution should be repudiated as a proslavery document—on the other. The mainstream Liberty men followed Chase's lead in late 1847 by nominating Senator John P. Hale of New Hampshire for President, on a platform calling for the prohibition of slavery wherever the national government had the constitutional power to ban it—in the territories, in the District of Columbia, and in all federal installations. This platform paved the way for a coalition with like-minded Whigs and Democrats.

Hale was willing to step aside for a candidate who might be able to mobilize broader support, especially in the key state of New York. Such a candidate was Martin Van Buren, who had already received the Barnburner nomination. During the summer, complicated negotiations between Liberty men, Conscience Whigs, and Barnburner Democrats laid the groundwork for a Free Soil convention at Buffalo in August. The sticking point was Van Buren. It came hard for antislavery Whigs and abolitionists to accept this former doughface Democrat. But in return for Barnburner support of a strong antislavery platform, the Liberty men and Conscience Whigs swallowed Van Buren. They also managed to nominate Charles Francis Adams as his running mate. Choosing as its slogan "Free Soil, Free Speech, Free Labor, and Free Men," the Free Soil party was born.

Its birth upset the Whig and Democratic strategy of trying to keep the slavery issue out of the campaign. "Nothing is talked of—but Slavery—free territory—& the Wilmot Proviso,"complained an Illinois Whig. In the North, both major parties were forced to adopt an antislavery stance: Democrats insisted that popular sovereignty would keep the territories free, while Whigs cited their support for the Wilmot Proviso. In the South, however, each party presented a different face: Democrats pointed with pride to their record of territorial expansion as evidence of friendship to Southern interests, while Whigs emphasized that Louisiana slaveholder Taylor would better protect Southern rights than Midwesterner Cass. "We prefer Old Zack with his sugar and cotton plantations and four hundred negroes to all their compromises," proclaimed a Richmond newspaper.[17]

---

[16]Kinley J. Brauer, *Cotton versus Conscience: Massachusetts Whig Politics and Southwestern Expansion, 1843–1848* (Lexington, Ky., 1967), p. 240.

[17]Michael A. Morrison, *Slavery and the American West* (Chapel Hill, 1997), p. 87; Cooper, *The South and the Politics of Slavery*, p. 265.

Such appeals apparently won votes. The Whig tally in the South increased by 10 percent over 1844 while the Democratic vote declined by 4 percent. Taylor carried eight of the fifteen slave states. He also carried seven of the fifteen free states, including crucial New York, and thereby won a majority in the electoral college. Van Buren carried no states but won 14 percent of the Northern popular vote. His candidacy did not affect the outcome, however; for while he took enough Democratic votes from Cass in New York to put that state in the Whig column, he neutralized this electoral impact by attracting enough Whig voters in Ohio to give that state to the Democrats.

The Compromise of 1850

During the lame-duck session of Congress before Taylor's inauguration on March 4, 1849, the smoldering embers of sectionalism flamed up anew. The Northern-controlled House reaffirmed the Wilmot Proviso, passed a resolution condemning the slave trade in the District of Columbia, and came close to passing a bill to abolish slavery itself there. In retaliation, a caucus of Southern congressmen asked Calhoun to draft an address setting forth Southern grievances. Calhoun eagerly seized this opportunity to write a platform for what he hoped would become a new Southern rights party. But fewer than two-thirds of the Southern Democrats signed the address, and Southern Whigs wanted no part of it at all. Having just won the presidential election, Whigs looked forward to a rejuvenation of their fortunes with Taylor in the White House. Alexander Stephens of Georgia expressed this viewpoint: We "feel *secure* under General Taylor."[18]

Once in office, however, Taylor shocked his Southern allies. He considered himself President of the whole country, not merely the South. Forty years in the army had given him a national perspective and an unsuspected distaste for proslavery extremists whom he branded in 1850 as "intolerant and revolutionary."[19] William H. Seward, New York's antislavery senator, became one of Taylor's principal advisers. The President faced an imminent decision on the question of slavery in the territories. The discovery of gold at Sutter's Mill in 1848 brought an avalanche of settlers into California, making it necessary to provide political organization for the region. Taylor's solution was to bypass the aggravating territorial problem by admitting California and New Mexico immediately *as states*. This provoked howls of protest from the South, for under Mexican law slavery had not existed in these areas and they would therefore come in as free states. To many Southerners, Taylor's policy was the Wilmot Proviso in disguise.

The President sent emissaries to San Francisco and Santa Fe to encourage the citizens to adopt state constitutions and to apply for admission. Californians needed no urging. In the fall of 1849, they held a convention and wrote a state constitution—

---

[18]Cooper, *The South and the Politics of Slavery,* p. 271.

[19]Thelma Jennings, *The Nashville Convention: Southern Movement for Unity, 1848–1851* (Memphis, 1980), p. 49.

which prohibited slavery. With a population already larger than that of two existing states (Delaware and Florida), California petitioned for admission to statehood. Affairs in New Mexico were too confused for the same thing to happen there. For one thing, a boundary dispute with Texas (which claimed the eastern half of the present state of New Mexico) threatened to break out into a shooting war. For another, the recently established Mormon settlement near the Great Salt Lake had adopted a constitution for a proposed new state named Deseret. Although slavery did not exist in Deseret, polygamy did, and it was equally unacceptable to many congressmen. Statehood would have to wait until these problems could be sorted out.

The question of California became a touchstone of Southern rights and power. Its admission as a free state would set a fatal precedent. Whether or not slavery could be expected to flourish in the Southwest, said Robert Barnwell Rhett of South Carolina, "the right is important because it applies to future acquisitions of territory, and by refusing to acknowledge [the South's rights] you force open the whole question of power." Alexander Stephens insisted: "Principles, sir, are not only outposts, but the bulwarks of all constitutional liberty; and if these be yielded, or taken by superior force, the citadel will soon follow." "Our only safety," said Hammond of South Carolina, "is in *equality* of POWER."[20]

The California controversy pumped new life into Calhoun's Southern rights movement. A groundswell of sentiment led in the fall of 1849 to a call for a convention to meet in Nashville the following June. Southern radicals, soon to be called fire-eaters, began to speak openly of secession. They hoped to use the Nashville convention to promote this cause. The backlash against Taylor in the South weakened the Whigs there. Several state elections in 1849 produced sharp declines in the Whig vote. In self-defense, Whigs began to vie with Democrats in protestations of loyalty to Southern rights. Secession rhetoric became commonplace. Calhoun observed that Southern senators and representatives were "more determined and bold than I ever saw them. Many avow themselves disunionists, and a still greater number admit, that there is little hope of any remedy short of it." If the North did not allow the South permanent equality in the Senate, said James Hammond to Calhoun, "we should kick them out of the Capitol & set it on fire."[21] Such violent rhetoric was matched by physical violence, as several fistfights broke out in Congress. On April 17, 1850, Senator Henry S. Foote of Mississippi pulled a revolver against a colleague on the Senate floor.

In 1850, the republic faced a crisis of the first order. To the center of the stage in this high drama strode three of the country's foremost statesmen, for their last appearance before the footlights of history: Senators Henry Clay, Daniel Webster, and John C. Calhoun. All three had been born during the Revolution and had been in public life for nearly half a century. All three had tried without success for the country's highest office. Their crucial roles in the great debate of 1850 marked the passing of leadership to the next generation. Calhoun would die in the midst of the debate; Clay and Webster would follow him to the grave two years later. Four junior

---

[20]Barney, *The Road to Secession,* pp. 106–107, 110.

[21]J. Franklin Jameson (ed.), *Correspondence of John C. Calhoun,* in American Historical Association, *Annual Report, 1899* (Washington, D.C., 1900), II, 780; Holman Hamilton, *Prologue to Conflict: The Crisis and Compromise of 1850* (New York, 1964), p. 74.

LIBRARY OF CONGRESS

LIBRARY OF CONGRESS

BRADY COLLECTION, NATIONAL ARCHIVES

HENRY CLAY, DANIEL WEBSTER, AND JOHN C. CALHOUN

senators who played a prominent role in the debate—Stephen A. Douglas, William H. Seward, Jefferson Davis, and Salmon P. Chase—would emerge as four of the most influential politicians of the next decade.

In 1820 and 1833, Henry Clay had earned a reputation as "the Great Pacificator" by constructing compromises to prevent disunion. In 1850 he stepped forward once more to propose compromise. On January 29, 1850, Clay presented eight resolutions to the Senate. The first six were paired in groups of two, each pair offering something to each section. California would be admitted with its free-state constitution, but the remainder of the Mexican cession would be organized as territories "without the adoption of any restriction or condition on the subject of slavery"; the Texas boundary dispute would be settled in favor of New Mexico, but Texas would be compensated by federal assumption of its public debt; the slave trade in the District of Columbia would be abolished, but slavery there would itself be guaranteed against federal interference. These six resolutions perhaps conceded more to the North than to the South. All of California would be free, and New Mexico probably would be. The area of slavery would be scaled down by the reduction of Texas' size, thereby putting a crimp in Southern hopes for the division of Texas into two or more slave states. But the reaffirmation of slavery in the District would be a Southern gain, and the rejection of the Wilmot Proviso would be an antislavery defeat. The last two resolutions offered concessions to the South. One declared that Congress had no authority to interfere with the interstate slave trade, the other called for a stronger federal law to help slave owners recover fugitive slaves who had escaped to the North.

Clay's eloquent plea for his resolutions was followed by some of the great set speeches in the history of the Senate. On March 4, Calhoun, ill and soon to die, sat wrapped in flannels while a Virginia senator read aloud his speech. Opposing the compromise, Calhoun warned that the Union was in danger. National institutions had already been split or gravely weakened by the sectional conflict: the Methodist and Baptist churches had divided into Northern and Southern branches over such questions as whether a slaveholder could be a bishop or a missionary; voluntary associations were splitting over the issue of slavery; political parties were going the same way. In each of these schisms, said Calhoun, the North had been the aggressive party. The only hope for preserving the Union was to adopt a constitutional amendment restoring to the South "the power she possessed of protecting herself before the equilibrium between the sections was destroyed." Calhoun probably had in mind his proposal for a "concurrent majority," by which the country would have two presidents, one from each section, each having veto power over national legislation.[22]

Three days later, Daniel Webster rose to deliver what many would later refer to as his "Seventh of March" address. "I wish to speak to-day," he began, "not as a Massachusetts man, nor as a Northern man, but as an American. . . . I speak to-day for the preservation of the Union. 'Hear me for my cause.' " Despite his antislavery constituency and his previous support for the Wilmot Proviso, Webster now spoke for compromise. Nature would exclude slavery from the Mexican cession; why insult Southern honor by legislating exclusion? "I would not take pains uselessly to reaffirm an act of nature, nor to reenact the will of God."[23] But such an assertion was unacceptable to Free Soilers, who were by no means certain that God would exclude slavery from New Mexico. Webster compounded his sin in their eyes by endorsing the proposed fugitive slave law. Although Webster's speech won praise from conservatives in both North and South, it earned him obloquy among antislavery people, whose anguish was best captured by John Greenleaf Whittier's poem "Ichabod":

All else is gone; from those great eyes
The soul has fled:
When faith is lost, when honor dies,
The man is dead!

Much more to abolitionist taste was Seward's "Higher Law" address on March 11. "Under the steady action of moral, social, and political causes . . . emancipation is inevitable," said Seward. "Whether it shall be peaceful or violent depends on the question whether it be hastened or hindered. . . . All measures which fortify slavery, or extend it, tend to the consummation of violence; all that check its extension and abate its strength tend to its peaceful extirpation." Clay's compromise was therefore "radically wrong and essentially vicious." Not only did the Constitution justify the prohibition of slavery in the territories, "but there is a higher law than the Constitution," the law of God; under it, all men are free and equal in his sight. The South pronounced Seward's speech "monstrous and diabolical"; Clay condemned the higher law doctrine as "wild, reckless, and abominable."[24]

---

[22]*Congressional Globe,* 31st Cong., 1st sess. (1850), Appendix, 451–455. Calhoun outlined his proposal for a concurrent majority in his posthumously published *Disquisition on Government.*

[23]*Congressional Globe,* 31st Cong., 1st sess. (1850), Appendix, 269–276.

[24]Ibid., pp. 260–269; Allan Nevins, *Ordeal of the Union,* 2 vols. (New York, 1947), I, 301.

After the oratory was over, the Senate in April created a "committee of thirteen," with Clay as chairman, to fashion his resolutions into legislation. By this time a discernible bloc of compromise supporters had emerged, consisting mainly of Midwestern Democrats and upper-South Whigs. This bloc constituted less than a quarter of all senators and representatives, however, for Northern Whigs (and some Northern Democrats) opposed those parts of the compromise they considered proslavery, while Southern Democrats and lower-South Whigs opposed those they considered antislavery. Clay introduced the various components of the compromise as a package, in the hope that this would induce a majority from both sections to vote for the whole bill in order to get the parts of it they favored.[25] But this strategy backfired. Instead, the opponents of each part voted against the whole in order to defeat the part they opposed. After nearly three months of complex maneuvering, in which party and sectional coalitions formed and dissolved in kaleidoscopic fashion, the Senate killed the measure on July 31. An exhausted and disheartened Clay left steaming Washington for the sea breezes of Newport.

Stephen A. Douglas of Illinois replaced Clay as the leader of the procompromise forces. A pragmatic Democrat and a skilled parliamentarian, who said later that he cared not whether slavery in the territories was voted up or down, Douglas had never believed in the package approach. He was confident that he could put together separate coalitions in favor of each part of the compromise. During the next two months, aided by his lieutenants in the House, he did exactly that.

Two events during the summer assisted Douglas's efforts. In June the Nashville convention, billed in advance as a conclave of fire-eaters, had failed to ignite. So long as compromise proposals remained before Congress, most Southerners favored deferral of extreme actions. The delegates from nine Southern states adopted restrained resolutions and adjourned to await events. One month later, sudden death from gastroenteritis removed President Taylor from the scene. To the end, Taylor had insisted on his plan for the admission of California and New Mexico as states, with no quid pro quo for the South. The new President, Millard Fillmore of New York, favored the compromise. Fillmore used his influence to persuade several Whig congressmen to abstain from roll calls on compromise measures distasteful to them, which reduced the number of opposition votes.

From mid-August to mid-September of 1850, Congress passed five separate bills: the admission of California; the adjustment of the Texas border; the organization of the New Mexico and Utah territories with the provision that when admitted as states they "shall be received into the Union, with or without slavery, as their constitution may prescribe at the time of their admission"; the enactment of a stringent fugitive slave law; and the abolition of the slave trade in the District of Columbia.

---

[25]The bill admitted California as a state, organized New Mexico and Utah as territories without reference to slavery, adjusted the Texas boundary in New Mexico's favor, and compensated Texas with $10 million to finance its public debt. A fugitive slave law and a bill to abolish the slave trade in the District of Columbia were separately reported.

This, then, was the "compromise" of 1850. But if a compromise is "an agreement among adversaries, by which each consents to certain terms desired by the other," one may question whether this was a genuine compromise. In no case did a majority of the "adversaries" on either side consent to the terms desired by the other side; on the contrary, a majority of Northerners voted against those measures they considered proslavery, and a majority of Southerners voted against those they considered anti-slavery. The bills passed only because the procompromise bloc of Northern Democrats and upper-South Whigs supported each one, and a large number of Northern congressmen abstained on the bills pertaining to Utah, New Mexico, and fugitive slaves. Because of this, and because of events that followed ten years later, historian David Potter's appellation, "the Armistice of 1850," seems more appropriate.[26]

In any event, the consequences of some parts of the 1850 settlement turned out to be different from those anticipated. Although California came in as a free state, its voters sent mostly proslavery representatives and senators to Washington. California could scarcely have given the South more aid and comfort in national politics if it had been a slave state. On the other hand, the territorial provisions for New Mexico and Utah proved to be a hollow victory for the South. Although Utah adopted a slave code in 1852, the territory contained only twenty-nine slaves by 1860. Southerners took a few slaves to New Mexico and pushed through a slave code in 1859, but the 1860 census found no slaves in the territory. While the District of Columbia bill ended the transportation of slaves into the District for purposes of sale and transfer, it did not end the buying and selling of slaves within the District itself. And the Fugitive Slave Law, which had been one of the least-debated parts of the Compromise of 1850, turned out to be its most explosive feature.[27]

Whatever the ambiguities and ironies of the Compromise, it did avert a grave crisis in 1850—or at least postponed it. Most Americans—even those who disliked the Compromise—breathed a sigh of relief. Moderates in both parties and in both sections took their cue from President Fillmore, who announced that the Compromise was "a final and irrevocable settlement" of sectional differences. Acceptance of the Compromise was more hearty in the South than in the North. Most Southerners, especially Whigs, regarded it as a Southern victory. "We of the South had a new lease for slave property," wrote a North Carolina Whig. "It was more secure than it had been for the last quarter of a century."[28]

These sentiments blunted the fire-eaters' drive to keep disunionism alive. In four lower-South states—South Carolina, Georgia, Alabama, and Mississippi—Unionist coalitions of Whigs and moderate Democrats defeated efforts by Southern Rights Democrats to win control of the state governments and to call secession conventions. The Georgia Unionists in December 1850 adopted resolutions that furnished a platform for the South during the next decade. It was a platform of conditional Unionism. Although Georgia did "not wholly approve" of the Compromise, she would "abide by it as a permanent adjustment of this sectional controversy." But if

---

[26]David Potter, *The Impending Crisis 1848–1861* (New York, 1976), pp. 90, 113.

[27]For an account of the law and its consequences, see pages 79 to 84.

[28]Cooper, *The South and the Politics of Slavery*, p. 301.

Congress or the North took any of certain actions, Georgia would be obliged to resist even to the point of secession. Those actions were abolition of slavery in the District of Columbia, repeal or nonenforcement of the Fugitive Slave Law, prohibition of slavery in the territories of Utah or New Mexico, refusal to admit a new slave state, or suppression of the interstate slave trade. Since these were precisely the policies advocated by Free Soilers and a growing number of Northern Whigs, antislavery men viewed the Georgia platform as a species of political blackmail.

As moderates and Unionists, Southern Whigs stood to gain by their section's acceptance of the 1850 Compromise. But the Democrats ultimately reaped most of the benefits. Indeed, by 1852, the Whig party was in serious trouble in the South, for three reasons: (1) The memory of the late President Taylor's "betrayal" of the South remained fresh; (2) the Democrats had proven themselves to be stronger Southern rights advocates than the Whigs, and thus the first hint of renewed Northern aggression was sure to cause Whig defections to the Democrats; and (3) a groundswell of Northern hostility to the Fugitive Slave Law produced resistance to its enforcement and strengthened the antislavery wing of the Whig party in the North. Several antislavery radicals had recently been elected to Congress: John P. Hale of New Hampshire, Salmon Chase and Benjamin Wade of Ohio, Seward of New York, and Sumner of Massachusetts to the Senate; Thaddeus Stevens of Pennsylvania and George W. Julian of Indiana to the House, where they joined the doughty veteran Joshua Giddings of Ohio, who had battled the "slave power" in Congress for many years. Nearly all of these men were of New England birth or parentage. Most of them were Whigs. Southern Whigs therefore suffered at home from their party affiliation with these Yankee "fanatics."

C The Election of 1852

The 1848 Barnburners had been an aberration caused more by intraparty Democratic factionalism than by genuine antislavery convictions. By 1851, most Barnburners had tamely returned to the party, leaving their Wilmot Proviso principles behind them. In 1852, the Democrats nominated dark horse Franklin Pierce of New Hampshire for President on a states' rights platform that denounced abolitionists and reaffirmed the Compromise of 1850. Despite his Yankee heritage, Pierce had a safe proslavery record. The Democrats became again a united, intersectional party.

Northern Whigs remained divided between a pro-Compromise Fillmore faction and an antislavery Seward faction, while Southern Whigs determined to bolt the party if the latter prevailed. The Whig national convention of 1852 illustrated the sectional tensions and paradoxes that were crippling the party. Northern antislavery Whigs supported the nomination of Winfield Scott, the Southern general who had conquered Mexico. Southern Whigs backed Fillmore, a New Yorker. The convention managed to adopt a platform that "acquiesced in" the Compromise of 1850. But half of Scott's delegates voted against this plank, and many of the remainder supported it only as part of an implicit bargain to secure conservative support for Scott. Through fifty-two ballots, the convention deadlocked between the two candidates, with 96 percent of Scott's votes coming from free states and 85 percent of Fillmore's from slave states. A handful of Webster delegates held the balance of power. On the fifty-third ballot, Scott picked up enough Fillmore support to win the nomination, but he received only one-tenth of his votes from the South.

The Free Soilers nominated John P. Hale on a platform that denounced the Compromise of 1850, demanded the repeal of the Fugitive Slave Law, opposed any future admission of slave states, and branded slavery "a sin against God and a crime against man", adding that "Christianity, humanity, and patriotism, alike demand its abolition."[29]

Southern Whigs knew that more than a few of their Northern brethren harbored similar sentiments. They suspected that Scott, like Taylor before him, would become prey to Seward's wiles. Believing that the South "must not *offer Bounties for Anti-Slavery Agitation and Aggression* by supporting a candidate forced upon her by abolition influences," several prominent Southern Whigs repudiated the ticket and went over to the Democrats.[30] In six states of the lower South, Scott won only 35 percent of the popular vote, compared with 50 percent for Taylor in 1848. Scott carried only two of the fifteen slave states. He also carried just two free states, but the Whig popular vote in the North declined only slightly from 1848. The Free Soil vote dropped to 6 percent of the Northern total, as the Barnburners' return to the Democratic fold swelled Pierce's victory margin.

In the South Alexander Stephens, the former Whig party leader, said bluntly, "the Whig party is dead."[31] By 1853, the Democrats controlled every one of the future Confederate states. The Whigs elected only fourteen of the sixty-five congressmen from these states. For all practical purposes, the Whigs had become a Northern party, with Northern Whigs badly divided among themselves. The intersectional two-party system tottered on the edge of the grave.

---

[29]Roy and Jeannette Nichols, "Election of 1852," in Arthur M. Schlesinger, Jr. (ed.), *History of American Presidential Elections,* 4 vols. (New York, 1960), II, 954.
[30]Cooper, *The South and the Politics of Slavery,* p. 330; Michael F. Holt, *The Rise and Fall of the American Whig Party* (New York, 1999), pp. 732–733.
[31]Cooper, *The South and the Politics of Slavery,* p. 343.

Chapter Five

Filibusterers, Fugitives, and Nativists

*I want Cuba. . . . I want Tamaulipas,
Potosi, and one or two other Mexican States
. . . and a foothold in Central America. . . .
Yes, I want these Countries for the spread of
slavery.*

—Albert Gallatin Brown,
senator from Mississippi, 1850s

Manifest Destiny and Slavery in the 1850s

An exasperated Southern congressman complained in 1850 that the conflict over slavery in the territories was quarrel about "an imaginary negro in an impossible place." Many contemporaries echoed Daniel Webster's contention that Nature would ban slavery from the Mexican cession. "The right to carry slaves to New Mexico or California is no very great matter, whether granted or denied," wrote the Kentuckian John J. Crittenden in 1848, "the more especially when it seems to be agreed that no sensible man would carry his slaves there if he could."[1] If this was true, then the Civil War was indeed caused by fanatics on each side who tore the country apart over a "pernicious abstraction."

But it was by no means certain that Nature would keep slavery out of the Southwest. Given the existing level of agricultural technology, the cultivation of cotton and tobacco had almost reached their western limits by the 1850s, but this did not necessarily mean that slavery was unfeasible in the new territories. Slave labor had proved successful in mining and other industries in the South and in

---

[1] Harold M. Hyman and William M. Wiecek, *Equal Justice under Law: Constitutional Development 1835–1875* (New York, 1982), p. 134; Michael F. Holt, *The Political Crisis of the 1850s* (New York, 1978), p. 77.

Latin America. In a Senate speech opposing the Compromise of 1850, Jefferson Davis insisted that slavery could flourish in the California gold mines. The *Southern Quarterly* maintained that "California is by nature peculiarly a slaveholding State." If the government had not interfered, "thousands of young, intelligent, active men would have been in that region, having each carried with them from one to five slaves." Several hundred slaves did work in the California mines before the state constitution prohibited slavery. Some of them even continued to work as slaves after 1850, under legislation allowing the temporary residence of slaveholders in the state. Noting the mineral resources of New Mexico, the *Charleston Mercury* declared: "The right to have property protected in the territory is not a mere abstraction. . . . There is no vocation in the world in which slavery can be more useful and profitable than in mining."[2]

The real crux of the issue, however, was not the territories already owned but those likely to be acquired in the future. In 1850, an American aged sixty-five had seen the country quadruple in size during his adult life. There was little reason for him to expect this process to stop. President Pierce's inaugural address pledged further annexations. Since a strong power (Britain) controlled the land to the north, the obvious direction for expansion was to the south. Antislavery congressmen, therefore, felt apprehension not only about slavery in existing territories but even more about slavery in future territories.

There was good reason for their apprehension. Proslavery expansionists were casting covetous eyes on Cuba, Central America, and Mexico. Jefferson Davis pressed for the acquisition of Cuba and of additional Mexican territory to "increase the number of slave-holding constituencies." His Mississippi Senate colleague, Albert Gallatin Brown, declared: "I want Cuba. . . . I want Tamaulipas, Potosi, and one or two other Mexican States . . . and a foothold in Central America. . . . Yes, I want these Countries for the spread of slavery." Many Southern voices echoed these sentiments: "I look to the acquisition of Cuba as of great importance to the South"; "Our destiny is intertwined with that of Cuba. . . . The safety of the South is to be found only in the extension of its peculiar institutions"; "The desire that Cuba should be acquired as a Southern conquest, is almost unanimous among Southern men." The South's leading monthly, *DeBow's Review,* hammered away in almost every issue on the need to expand southward: "We have a destiny to perform, a manifest destiny over all Mexico, over South America, over the West Indies."[3]

The fulfillment of this destiny was the goal of a shadowy, fantastic organization known as the Knights of the Golden Circle, founded at Louisville in 1854 by a Virginian named George Bickley. A fraternal organization with elaborate rituals and regalia, the Knights proposed to establish a "golden circle" of slave states starting in the South and extending in a wide arc through Mexico, Central America, northern

---

[2]Davis and the *Mercury* quoted in Robert S. Starobin, *Industrial Slavery in the Old South* (New York, 1970), pp. 219–220; *Southern Quarterly* quoted in William R. Brock, *Parties and Political Conscience: American Dilemmas 1840–1850* (Millwood, N.Y., 1979), p. 319.

[3]Davis and Brown quoted in Robert E. May, *The Southern Dream of a Caribbean Empire, 1854–1861* (Baton Rouge, 1973), pp. 11, 9; many Southern voices quoted in John McCardell, *The Idea of a Southern Nation: Southern Nationalists and Southern Nationalism, 1830–1860* (New York, 1979), pp. 248, 258–259; *DeBow's Review* quoted in John Hope Franklin, *The Militant South* (Cambridge, Mass., 1956), p. 99.

South America, and the West Indies. This would add twenty-five new slave states to the Union, said Bickley. If Congress refused to admit them, the South could secede and become the center of a vast new slave empire that would produce most of the world's cotton, tobacco, sugar, and coffee. Although Bickley was something of a charlatan and his organization accomplished little, the Knights did manage to provoke controversy. During the Civil War, Bickley tried to organize antiwar groups in the North.

Realistic American expansion efforts after the Mexican War focused mainly on Cuba. In 1848, the Polk administration offered Spain $100 million for the island. When the Spanish government indignantly refused, Southerners tried other means. They hoped to foment a Texas-style revolution among dissident Cuban sugar planters who wanted American annexation. For this purpose they supported Narciso Lopez, a Venezuelan-born Cuban adventurer who had fled the island in 1848 after an abortive uprising. Lopez recruited American volunteers to invade Cuba. This was the first of many American filibustering[4] expeditions after the Mexican War.

The unsympathetic Taylor administration ordered the navy to seize the ships of the Lopez expedition before they could sail. The undaunted Lopez reorganized a force of several hundred men and slipped out of New Orleans in 1850. He captured Cardenas and burned the governor's mansion, but the Cubans failed to rise and a Spanish counterattack forced the filibusterers to scurry for Key West. The U.S. government prosecuted the leaders for violation of neutrality laws, but New Orleans juries failed to convict. Instead, the city treated Lopez as a hero. Prominent Southerners helped him raise men and money for a third attempt. With five hundred men Lopez again invaded Cuba, in August 1851. But once more the expected uprising failed to materialize. Many of Lopez's troops were cut off and killed; more than fifty were captured and executed as pirates, including Lopez and young William Crittenden of Kentucky, nephew of the U.S. attorney general. This put a temporary damper on filibustering.

But it did not discourage American efforts to acquire Cuba. The Pierce administration made acquisition of Cuba a primary foreign policy goal. The President appointed the flamboyant Pierre Soulé of Louisiana as minister to Spain. Within months of his arrival in Madrid, Soulé offended the Spaniards with his denunciations of monarchy, wounded the French ambassador in a duel, and tried to present an ultimatum to the Spanish government over an incident concerning an American merchant ship in the Havana harbor. In the spring of 1854, Secretary of State William Marcy instructed Soulé to offer Spain $130 million for Cuba and, if this failed, to "direct your efforts to the next desirable object, which is to detach that island from Spanish dominion." When the Spanish government refused to sell, Soulé began intriguing with revolutionary groups bent on overthrowing the government. Meanwhile, Marcy authorized Soulé and the U.S. ministers to Paris and London—John Mason and James Buchanan—to meet at Ostend, Belgium, to exchange views concerning the acquisition of Cuba. The three ministers sent to Washington a remarkable memorandum. "Cuba is as necessary to the North American republic as any of its present

---

[4]From the Spanish *filibustero,* meaning freebooter or pirate.

. . . family of states," they declared. If Spain refused to sell and if the United States considered Cuba essential to its security, then "by every law, human and Divine, we shall be justified in wresting it from Spain."[5]

When this "Ostend Manifesto" leaked to the press, it produced an uproar in both Europe and America. Antislavery groups denounced it as a "manifesto of the Brigands," which proposed "to grasp, to rob, to murder, to grow rich on the spoils of provinces and toils of slaves."[6] The House subpoenaed the diplomatic correspondence and published it. Already in political trouble over the Kansas-Nebraska act,[7] the Pierce administration recalled Soulé and gave up the Cuba project.[8]

In 1854, a major filibustering enterprise overlapped the official efforts to buy Cuba. The leader of this venture was former Governor John A. Quitman of Mississippi. With the support of Cuban exiles in New York, Quitman raised money and recruited volunteers for an invasion of the island. Numerous public men in the South openly aided the undertaking. Through his friendship with Secretary of War Jefferson Davis, Quitman thought he had obtained the administration's tacit support for the venture. Senator John Slidell of Louisiana even introduced a motion on May 1, 1854, to suspend the neutrality laws. But Quitman failed to strike while the iron was hot. By the fall of 1854, the backlash against the Kansas-Nebraska Act and the Ostend Manifesto caused Pierce to announce that he would enforce the neutrality laws. Quitman finally called off the invasion in April 1855.

These failures caused expansionist attention to shift toward Mexico and Central America. The minister to Mexico, James Gadsden, tried in 1853 to buy an additional 250,000 square miles of the country. The ostensible purpose was to obtain land for a railroad to the Pacific. But Northern senators suspected, with good reason, that a hidden purpose was to gain potential slave territory. Mexico refused to sell this much territory and reduced the purchase to 54,000 square miles; Northern senators cut out another 9,000 miles before approving in 1854 the Gadsden Purchase—which resulted in the acquisition of what is now southern Arizona and New Mexico.

During the 1850s, American filibusterers, mostly from Texas and California, launched dozens of raids into Mexico. Some of them had simple plunder as their goal; others were part of a sporadic border warfare that continued for years after the Mexican War. But some were animated by a desire to create "a chain of slave states from the Atlantic to the Pacific" across northern Mexico.[9] None of these raids succeeded; some turned out disastrously for the invaders—particularly the Crabb expedition of 1857. Henry Crabb, a Tennessee-born Californian, led an army of ninety men into the province of Sonora, where they were surrounded and all executed in cold blood after surrendering to Mexican authorities.

---

[5]William R. Manning (ed.), *Diplomatic Correspondence of the United States: Inter-American Affairs, 1831–1860,* 12 vols. (Washington, D.C., 1932–1939), XI, 175–178, 193–194.

[6]Allan Nevins, *Ordeal of the Union,* 2 vols. (New York, 1947), II, 362.

[7]See pages 90 to 95.

[8]This did not end official efforts to obtain Cuba, however. After his election as President in 1856, Buchanan tried to buy the island; and as late as 1860, the Democratic platform pledged the party to further efforts in that direction.

[9]John R. Wells to John Quitman, April 26, 1856, in May, *Southern Dream of a Caribbean Empire,* p. 137.

Crabb's boyhood friend William Walker eventually met the same fate, but not until he had won a reputation as the greatest of all filibusterers, "the grey-eyed man of destiny." A restless native of Tennessee who had moved to California, Walker recruited other footloose men for an invasion of Baja California in 1853. After some initial success, they were driven back across the border to stand trial in San Francisco for violation of the neutrality laws. A sympathetic jury acquitted Walker after deliberating for eight minutes. Two years later, Walker went after bigger game. With a small army he invaded Nicaragua; in alliance with local rebels, he overthrew the government and in June 1856 proclaimed himself president. Walker pronounced his conquest to be the first step toward "regeneration" of the Central American republics by Anglo-Saxon settlers. Many of Walker's predominantly Southern backers also saw it as the first step toward reintroducing slavery in Central America and creating several new slave states.

But the other Central American republics had different ideas. They formed an alliance to invade Nicaragua and expel Walker. To rally support and recruits from the South to meet this threat, Walker in September 1856 issued a decree reinstituting slavery in Nicaragua. This elicited enthusiasm and some recruits from the South, but they were too late to save Walker's regime. The remnants of the defeated and cholera-decimated filibusterers were rescued by a U.S. naval vessel in May 1857.

Walker returned to a hero's welcome in the South, which furnished men and supplies for a second invasion of Nicaragua. But the American navy stepped in to prevent it. Southerners in Congress denounced the naval commander who detained Walker. A hung jury in New Orleans voted 10 to 2 to acquit Walker of violating the neutrality laws. Walker made a triumphal tour of the South. He wrote a book about his experiences in which he urged Southern backing for another invasion. "If the South wishes to get her institutions into tropical America she must do so before treaties are made to embarrass her action," wrote Walker. "The hearts of Southern youth answer the call of honor. . . . The true field for the exertion of slavery is in tropical America."[10] He received enough encouragement to launch a new filibustering expedition. But this time his luck ran out. The Honduras militia stopped his small force, and on September 12, 1860, Walker's remarkable career came to an end before a Honduran firing squad.

Southern support for these efforts to acquire new slave territory did much to undermine the fragile sectional armistice that followed the Compromise of 1850. So did Northern reaction to the Fugitive Slave Law.

The Fugitive Slave Law

The issue of fugitive slaves went back to the framing of the Constitution. Article IV, Section 2, specified that persons "held to Service or Labour in one State" who escaped to another "shall be delivered up on Claim of the Party to whom such Service or Labour may be due." In plain English, this meant that slaves who fled to a free state were still slaves and liable to be returned to bondage. In 1793, Congress enacted a

---

[10]William Walker, *The War in Nicaragua* (New York, 1860), pp. 278–280.

fugitive slave law that authorized slave owners to recapture their escaped slaves beyond state lines and bring them before any state or federal court to establish proof of ownership. This procedure worked well enough for a time. But when militant abolitionism emerged in the 1830s, the fugitive slave question became a major controversy.

For Northerners, the escaped bondsman transformed slavery from an abstraction into a flesh-and-blood reality. The antislavery press publicized stories about the heroic flights of fugitives who outwitted the bloodhounds and followed the North Star to freedom. Abolitionists found that escaped slaves made the most effective antislavery lecturers. The autobiographies of fugitives (sometimes ghost-written) became the most effective antislavery literature. The organization of an "underground railroad" to help fugitives on their way gave antislavery Yankees an opportunity to do something practical against slavery. Although the underground railroad was never as extensive in fact as in legend, the exaggerated rumors about it inflamed Southern anger and exacerbated sectional tensions. And although the number of slaves who escaped to the North was a tiny fraction of the total (probably fewer than a thousand per year), their symbolic importance magnified the issue out of proportion to their numbers.

What made it worse, in Southern eyes, was the enactment by several Northern states of "personal liberty laws." The main purpose of these statutes was to prevent the kidnapping of free blacks for sale into slavery. The personal liberty laws of some states also prohibited state officials from participating in the recapture of slaves and assured fugitives the rights of habeas corpus and trial by jury.

The constitutionality of these laws came before the U.S. Supreme Court in *Prigg v. Pennsylvania* (1842), a case that concerned a Maryland slave owner convicted in Pennsylvania of kidnapping after he had forcibly carried his runaway slave back to Maryland. In a divided decision, the Court overturned the conviction and ruled the Pennsylvania antikidnapping statute unconstitutional. But the Court also ruled that enforcement of the fugitive slave clause of the Constitution was entirely a federal responsibility. Pennsylvania's law prohibiting state officers from enforcing the 1793 federal statute was therefore valid. This complex decision produced a new wave of personal liberty laws in the 1840s, by which seven states prohibited their officials from helping to recapture fugitives or forbade the use of state and local jails to hold fugitives pending a decision on their return. These laws provoked Southern demands for a new federal statute to put teeth into the fugitive slave clause.

The 1850 Fugitive Slave Act did just that. In fact, it was one of the strongest national laws yet enacted by Congress. The act included the following provisions: (1) it created a category of U.S. commissioners who were empowered to issue warrants for the arrest and return of fugitives to slavery; (2) it allowed an affidavit by the claimant to be sufficient evidence of ownership, and denied the fugitive the right to testify in his or her own behalf; (3) the commissioner would earn a fee of $10 if he found for the claimant but only $5 if he released the fugitive; and (4) the commissioner could deputize any citizen to serve as a member of a posse to aid in enforcement of the law, and stiff fines or jail sentences could be meted out to those who refused such orders or who resisted the law. Attempts by Northern congressmen to mandate a jury trial for fugitives were defeated.

HARRIET TUBMAN: © CORBIS/BETTMANN

HARRIET TUBMAN.   Known as "the Moses of her people," Tubman was the most famous "conductor" on the underground railroad. She appears here on the far left with a group of ex-slaves she had led northward to freedom. After escaping from Maryland herself in 1849, Tubman risked recapture by returning numerous times to help at least sixty slaves escape along a network of "stations" maintained by Quakers and free blacks in Delaware and Pennsylvania.

This law proved to be the most consequential product of the Compromise of 1850. Southerners insisted that its enforcement was the *sine qua non* of union. Antislavery Northerners denounced it. In Ralph Waldo Emerson's words, it was "a filthy law" that no one could obey "without loss of self-respect." Although supporters of the statute claimed that the extra paperwork involved if a commissioner remanded a fugitive to slavery justified the doubled fee, opponents regarded this fee as a shameless bribe. As one Free Soiler put it, the law fixed the price of a slave at a thousand dollars and the price of a Yankee soul at five. Many Northerners considered the prohibitions against fugitive testimony and jury trials to be denials of due process. Worst of all was the provision authorizing federal commissioners to deputize citizens, which might compel anyone to become a slave catcher. Many Yankees vowed civil disobedience. Congressman Joshua Giddings predicted that even the army could not enforce the statute: "Let the President . . . drench our land of freedom in blood; but he will never make us obey that law."[11]

---

[11]Emerson quoted in James Ford Rhodes, *History of the United States from the Compromise of 1850 . . .* , 7 vols. (New York, 1893–1906), I, 207–208; Giddings quoted in Frederick J. Blue, *The Free Soilers: Third Party Politics 1848–54* (Urbana, Ill., 1973), p. 204.

Northern anger was intensified by a sharp increase in attempts to recapture fugitives during the first year of the law's operation. A class of professional slave catchers came into existence. Ostensibly the agents of Southern owners, some of them were no better than kidnappers bearing forged affidavits who saw a chance to make a tidy sum by selling captured free blacks to the South. In February 1851, a black man in Madison, Indiana, was seized in front of his wife and children and returned to an owner who claimed that he had run away nineteen years earlier. Slave catchers grabbed a hard-working black Methodist in New York and spirited him away to Baltimore before his wife and children knew what had happened. A black tailor who had lived in Poughkeepsie for many years was arrested and carried to South Carolina, where he was held for a price of $1,750. A black woman who said she had lived in Philadelphia all her life was claimed by a Maryland man who insisted that she had run away twenty-two years earlier. The Marylander also claimed ownership of her six children, all born in Philadelphia. In this case, the commissioner ruled against the claimant. In the cases of the New York Methodist and Poughkeepsie tailor, local blacks and whites raised funds to buy their freedom. But no such ransoms redeemed most of the other eighty-one fugitives returned from the North to slavery in 1850–1851.

Nor was there a happy ending to the most tragic fugitive slave case of the decade—the Margaret Garner affair. Margaret Garner and her four children escaped with three other slaves across the Ohio River to Cincinnati in January 1856. The owner traced them and obtained a warrant for their arrest. As the fugitives were about to be captured by a U.S. marshal's posse, Margaret Garner tried to kill her children to prevent their return to slavery. She managed to cut her daughter's throat but was stopped before she could do the same to her sons. Ohio courts tried to retain custody in order to try her for murder, but the federal commissioner overrode the state and ordered Garner and her children returned to their Kentucky owner, who promptly sold them down the river. A steamboat accident killed Garner's infant child before she and her two surviving sons were finally sold in the New Orleans slave market.

The Fugitive Slave Law had a devastating impact on Northern black communities. Many "free" blacks were in fact escaped slaves; even if they were not, their inability to testify in their own behalf left them helpless in the face of an affidavit certified by a Southern court. Thousands of Northern blacks fled to Canada. The law pumped new life into black nationalism in the North by seeming to provide evidence that blacks could never live safely in the United States. Projects for emigration to Haiti, Central America, and Africa gained momentum during the 1850s.

But flight was not the only response to the Fugitive Slave Law. Blacks and whites in several Northern cities formed vigilance committees to hide or protect fugitives from slave catchers, and to give them legal assistance if arrested. People holding a variety of antislavery opinions came together on these committees, along with others who had not previously professed any such opinions. The vigilance committees urged nonviolent resistance. But many members did not shrink from violence. The black leader and one-time fugitive slave Frederick Douglass said that the best way to make the Fugitive Slave Law a dead letter was "to make a dozen or more dead kidnappers."[12]

---

[12]Philip Foner (ed.), *The Life and Writings of Frederick Douglass,* 4 vols. (New York, 1950–1955), II, 207.

Vigilance committees played a role in some of the spectacular fugitive rescues of the decade. In October 1850, the Boston committee spirited away two famous fugitives, William and Ellen Craft, from under the nose of a Georgia jailer who had come to claim them. Four months later a black waiter named Fred Wilkins, who was known to his friends as Shadrach, was arrested in Boston as a fugitive. While he was being held in the federal courthouse, a crowd of black men burst through the door and snatched him away before the astonished deputy marshal realized what was happening. In April 1851, the government managed to foil another attempt in Boston to rescue a fugitive, Thomas Sims, only by guarding him with three hundred soldiers who took him away at four o'clock in the morning for shipment South. In September 1851, a group of black men in the Quaker community of Christiana, Pennsylvania, shot it out with a Maryland slave owner and his allies who had come to arrest two fugitives. The slave owner was killed and his son severely wounded in the affray. The following month a group of black and white abolitionists broke into a Syracuse police station, carried off the arrested fugitive William McHenry (alias Jerry), and sent him across Lake Ontario to Canada.

The Millard Fillmore administration, committed to making the Compromise of 1850 work, was determined to punish these violations of the Fugitive Slave Law. The government indicted several dozen men involved in the Shadrach, Christiana, and McHenry rescues. But with the exception of one man convicted in the William McHenry case, all the defendants were acquitted or released after mistrials by hung juries. Northern juries would no more convict violators of the Fugitive Slave Law than Southern juries would convict violators of the neutrality laws.

Perhaps because most available fugitives had gone into hiding or fled to Canada, the number of arrests and returns—as well as of rescues—decreased after 1851. Excitement over the fugitive slave issue cooled down in 1852. Moderates in the North and in the South seemed to gain control of affairs with their affirmations of support for all parts of the Compromise of 1850, including the Fugitive Slave Law.

But beneath this surface calm, the volcano of Northern discontent continued to rumble. The astounding popularity of Harriet Beecher Stowe's novel, *Uncle Tom's Cabin,* both reflected and reinforced the North's feelings of guilt and revulsion toward the hunting down of slaves on its own soil. Mrs. Stowe was moved to write it by her own anguish at the Fugitive Slave Law. The story ran serially in an antislavery newspaper for nearly a year, beginning in the spring of 1851, and was published as a book in the spring of 1852. Within months it became one of the bestsellers of all time. It provoked tears in the North and angry rebuttals in the South. A decade later, when Mrs. Stowe was introduced to Abraham Lincoln, the President reportedly said: "So you're the little woman who wrote the book that made this great war."

Two events in the spring of 1854 rekindled Northern defiance of the Fugitive Slave Law. The first was the passage of the Kansas-Nebraska Act, which repealed the Missouri Compromise's ban on slavery in the Louisiana Purchase territory north of 36°30′ (see pages 95 to 99). The Kansas-Nebraska Act outraged many Northern moderates who had previously urged obedience to the Fugitive Slave Law. Since the South had repudiated one key sectional compromise, they felt no obligation to respect the other. A second jarring event in 1854 was the Anthony Burns affair.

The Burns Affair, *Ableman* v. *Booth*

Anthony Burns was a Virginia slave who had escaped to Boston and gone to work in a clothing store, where he was suddenly seized on May 24. News of the arrest spread quickly. The vigilance committee organized mass rallies; antislavery protesters poured into Boston from surrounding areas; black and white abolitionists mounted an ill-coordinated assault on the federal courthouse that killed one of the deputies guarding Burns but failed to rescue the fugitive. Determined to make an example of this case and to prove that the law could be enforced "even in Boston," the Pierce administration refused an offer from the city's leaders to purchase Burns's freedom at three times his market value. Instead, the government sent in federal troops. They marched Burns to the harbor, where a ship waited to carry him back to Virginia, while tens of thousands of bitter Yankees looked on and bells tolled the death of liberty in the cradle of the American Revolution.

It is impossible to exaggerate the impact of this event. "When it was all over," wrote a conservative Boston attorney who had previously counseled obedience to the law, "and I was left alone in my office, I put my face in my hands and wept. I could do nothing less." Another conservative, Edward Everett, commented that "a change has taken place in this community within three weeks such as the 30 preceding years had not produced." And Amos A. Lawrence, formerly a leader of the Cotton Whigs, said that "we went to bed one night old fashioned, conservative, Compromise Union Whigs & waked up stark mad Abolitionists."[13]

Anthony Burns (whose freedom a Boston committee later managed to buy) was the last fugitive returned from Boston—or from anywhere in New England. Nine Northern states passed new personal liberty laws in the wake of the Burns affair. These laws included one or more of the following provisions: the appointment of state attorneys to defend fugitives, state payment for all defense costs, the denial of the use of any public building for the detention of fugitives, new and stringent antikidnapping statutes, and jury trials in state courts for accused fugitives. The purpose of these laws was to harass slave catchers and to make their enterprise so costly, time consuming, and precarious that they would give it up. In this the laws were successful, for the number of fugitives returned from states that had passed new personal liberty laws declined after 1854.[14]

The personal liberty laws of some states virtually nullified federal law. Inevitably, therefore, the issue came before the U.S. Supreme Court, in *Ableman v. Booth* (1859). This case arose when a Wisconsin abolitionist named Sherman Booth was convicted by a federal court and imprisoned for leading a raid in 1854 that had freed a fugitive held in custody. The Wisconsin Supreme Court ruled the Fugitive Slave Law unconstitutional and ordered Booth's release. The federal attorney appealed to the U.S. Supreme Court, where Chief Justice Roger Taney spoke for the majority in ruling the

---

[13]Attorney quoted in Nevins, *Ordeal of the Union*, II, 151–152; Everett and Lawrence quoted in Jane H. and William H. Pease (eds.), *The Fugitive Slave Law and Anthony Burns* (Philadelphia, 1975), pp. 51, 43.

[14]In these states during the 1850s, sixty-two slaves were returned before passage of new laws, and twenty-seven afterwards.

Fugitive Slave Law constitutional and declaring any state interference with its enforcement unconstitutional. Booth went back to prison. Thus the supremacy of federal law, supported by the South, was upheld, and state sovereignty, supported by the North, was struck down—indeed an ironic commentary on the South's traditional commitment to states' rights.

Free Soilers and Free Blacks

Although the personal liberty laws might seem to have indicated a liberalization of Northern racial attitudes, that interpretation would be an oversimplification. Indeed, in some parts of the North the opposite was true. While several Northern states were passing personal liberty laws, others were adopting new "black laws" that imposed degrading restrictions on free blacks. Most of the legislation to protect fugitives came out of the upper North (New England, upstate New York, Michigan, Wisconsin, and Minnesota), while several lower-North states and the new Western states of California and Oregon retained or passed black laws.

The Indiana constitutional convention of 1851 adopted a provision forbidding black migration into the state. This supplemented the state's laws barring blacks already there from voting, serving on juries or in the militia, testifying against whites in court, marrying whites, or going to school with whites. Iowa and Illinois had similar laws on the books and banned black immigration by statute in 1851 and 1853, respectively. These measures reflected the racist sentiments of most whites in those states. The exclusion laws also served as a conciliatory assurance to the South that no fugitives would be welcomed in these states. There was little likelihood of black migration to Oregon, but upon admission to the Union in 1859, that state also adopted the full range of black laws—among them an exclusion statute. A decade earlier, California had refrained from excluding blacks by law only because it feared this might harm the state's chances for admission. But the Golden State adopted all the other discriminatory legislation that prevailed in the lower North. Even the territory of Kansas, a Free Soil stronghold by the end of the decade, voted at one point for a constitutional clause excluding blacks, though this provision was dropped before Kansas came in as a state in 1861. Most Western settlers clearly wanted no black people in their midst—slave *or* free.

This antiblack animus infected even a portion of the Free Soil movement. David Wilmot himself insisted that his proviso did not arise from any "squeamish sensitiveness upon the subject of slavery, nor morbid sympathy for the slave. . . . The negro race already occupy enough of this fair continent." Wilmot was perfectly willing to call his resolution "the white man's proviso."[15]

Wilmot spoke mainly for the Democratic or "Barnburner" constituency of the Free Soil party. Liberty men and Conscience Whigs expressed more liberal attitudes. The 1844 Liberty party platform contained several planks affirming equal rights and pledging to work for the removal of racial discrimination in Northern states. In Massachusetts,

---

[15] *Congressional Globe,* 29th Cong., 2nd sess. (1847), Appendix, 317.

where blacks enjoyed almost full civil and political equality, a coalition of Liberty men, Garrisonian abolitionists, and Conscience Whigs worked to remove the last vestiges of legal discrimination. They managed to repeal the anti-intermarriage law in 1843 but failed in their attempts to remove the ban on blacks in the militia. In 1855, they finally won passage of a law prohibiting school segregation. In 1846, an effort by Liberty men and antislavery Whigs in New York to abolish the discriminatory $250 property qualification for black voters was defeated by Democrats, including many Barnburners who voted Free Soil two years later. The Free Soilers achieved one of their greatest successes in Ohio, whose black laws until 1849 were the most restrictive in the North. The election of 1848 gave the Free Soilers the balance of power in Ohio politics. They used this leverage to strike a bargain with the Democrats whereby the latter grudgingly voted to elect Salmon P. Chase to the Senate and to repeal laws prohibiting black migration into the state, testimony against whites in court, and attendance at public schools. These concessions were made in return for Free Soil votes that would enable the Democrats to control the legislature.

Before the Civil War, only the New England states (except Connecticut) allowed blacks to vote on equal terms with whites. During the 1850s, the Free Soilers and Republicans tried to enact black suffrage in a few other Northern states, but failed. Democrats made much political capital by calling their opponents the "nigger party" or "amalgamation party." So pervasive was racism in many parts of the North that no party could win if it endorsed full racial equality. Thus the Free Soil platforms of 1848 and 1852 failed to include the earlier Liberty party planks demanding equal rights. Free Soil and Republican campaigns for state black suffrage laws in the 1850s sometimes seemed halfhearted.

Apart from the question of political expediency, many Free Soilers also harbored prejudices and stereotypes that inhibited a commitment to racial equality. They could hate slavery and sympathize with fugitive slaves but at the same time favor the colonization abroad of black people to preserve America as a white man's country. The ambivalence of the Free Soil party—and later of the Republican party—toward racial equality was one reason why some abolitionists remained aloof from these parties.

Nativism and the Rise of the Know-Nothings

For a few years in the 1850s, ethnic conflict among whites rivaled sectional conflict as a major political issue. The immediate origins of this phenomenon lay in the sharp increase of immigration after 1845. In the 1820s, the number of immigrants had averaged fewer than 13,000 per year. The average quadrupled in the 1830s. But even this paled in comparison with the immigration of the late 1840s. Land shortages and labor surpluses in Europe, plus the potato blight in Ireland and the revolutions of 1848 on the Continent, caused millions to emigrate. High wages, cheap land, and the booming American economy attracted most of them to the United States. During the decade 1846–1855, more than three million immigrants entered the United States—equivalent to 15 percent of the 1845 population. This was the largest proportional increase in the foreign-born population for any ten-year period in American history. Because 87 percent of the immigrants settled in free states, their impact was felt mainly in the North, where several cities by 1855 had a foreign-born population approaching or exceeding half of the total population.

Equal in significance to the increase in the foreign-born population were changes in its composition. Before 1840, three-quarters of the immigrants were Protestants, mostly from the British Isles. Only one-fifth of them became unskilled laborers or servants, while the remainder were farmers, skilled workers, and white-collar or professional men. In the 1840s and 1850s, however, more than half of the immigrants were Catholics, two-thirds of whom came from Ireland and most of the rest from German-speaking countries. Moreover, the proportion of unskilled laborers among this much larger wave of immigration was double that among the earlier immigrants. Irish Catholics, who settled primarily in the large cities of the Northeast, became the poorest, most concentrated, and most visible of the immigrants.

Anti-immigrant sentiment, or "nativism," manifested itself less against the foreign-born in general than against Roman Catholics in particular. Indeed, some of the fiercest nativists were Scots-Irish Presbyterians and Welsh or English Methodists, who brought their anti-Catholic feelings with them from the old country. Anti-Catholicism had deep roots in Britain and in America. Bloody Mary, Guy Fawkes Day, the Glorious Revolution, and similar memories formed part of the cultural baggage of Anglo-American Protestantism. British Catholics had suffered deprivation of certain civil and political rights even after the Catholic Emancipation Act of 1829. In the United States, the Protestant evangelicalism of the Second Great Awakening produced a heightened anti-Catholicism. Protestant perceptions of Irish and German drinking habits, the Irish and German tendency to vote for the Democratic party and to oppose equal rights for blacks, and the resistance of Catholics to the Protestant-dominated public schools further intensified the prejudices of evangelical Protestants and reformers.

Even before the post-1845 increase in immigration, ethnic and religious tensions had sometimes burst into violence: a Protestant mob destroyed a convent in Charlestown, Massachusetts, in 1834; riots between Protestants (including Scots-Irish) and Catholics in Philadelphia in 1844 left at least sixteen dead, hundreds injured, and two Catholic churches as well as thirty other buildings destroyed. Increased immigration exacerbated these tensions. Seventeen people were killed and fifty wounded in an 1854 election-day clash between Protestant gangs and Catholic Democrats in Baltimore; an election riot the same year killed ten in St. Louis; similar violence between natives and Irish immigrants in Louisville in 1855 left twenty-two dead.

Election-day riots were one outcome of nativism's having entered the realm of politics. In 1843 and 1844, so-called American parties had contested local elections in New York and Philadelphia. Several secret fraternal organizations of a nativist hue had been founded in the 1840s. One of these was the Order of the Star Spangled Banner, organized in New York in 1849. When questioned about this order, members replied, "I know nothing." By 1854, the "Know-Nothings" had achieved national prominence and had an estimated membership of a million. Their main goal was to restrain the growing political power of immigrants. Several states allowed foreign-born men to vote even before they were naturalized; in other states, the short five-year wait for naturalization meant that by the early 1850s the heavy immigration of the late 1840s

Immigration to the United States
1820 to 1860

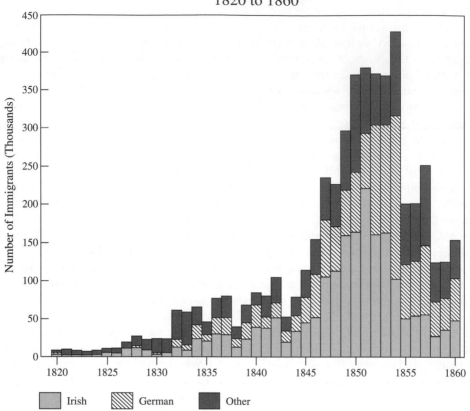

was showing up on the voting rolls. Angry nativists accused Democratic machines in several cities of illegally enrolling alien voters prior to naturalization—and there was much truth in the charge. In Boston, the number of foreign-born voters increased by 200 percent from 1850 to 1855 while the number of native-born voters increased by only 14 percent. To counter this development, the Know-Nothings went into politics themselves, organizing under the American party name. They proposed to lengthen the naturalization period from five to twenty-one years; to permit only citizens to vote; and to restrict officeholding to native-born citizens.

The temperance and education issues became linked to nativism (see pages 16 to 19). Maine's passage of a law banning the manufacture and sale of liquor set off a "Maine law" crusade that produced similar statutes in several other states during the 1850s. Many Irish and German Americans considered these laws an attack on their cultural autonomy. At the same time, a drive by Catholic leaders in some states to end the reading of the King James Bible in public schools and to secure tax support for parochial schools aroused fears of a Roman threat to American institutions. "Are American Protestants to be taxed for the purpose of nourishing Romish vipers?"

asked one nativist. Since Romanism was "diametrically opposed to the genius of American republicanism," the election of "true Americans" was necessary to "guarantee the three vital principles of Republican Government—*Spiritual Freedom, Free Bible, and Free Schools.*"[16]

The Know-Nothings capitalized on this nativist ferment in the 1854 state and local elections. Old-line party leaders were dumbfounded by what they described as a "hurricane," a "tornado," "a freak of political insanity." A baffled Pennsylvania Democrat declared that "nearly everybody appears to have gone altogether deranged on Nativism here." A despairing Whig leader in New York confessed that "the new questions have destroyed everything like party discipline, and many staunch old Whigs are floating off they don't know where."[17] The Know-Nothing hurricane swept away the old parties in Massachusetts, winning 63 percent of the vote and electing all the state officers, all the congressmen, and all but two members of the legislature. The new party polled more than 40 percent of the vote in Pennsylvania and 25 percent in New York. The next year it won control of three more New England states, made further gains in the Mid-Atlantic states, and moved southward to carry Maryland, Kentucky, and Texas, and to become the main rival of the Democrats in several other Southern states.

In the border states and in the South, Know-Nothings recruited former Whigs looking for a new political home. In the Northeast, they drew voters from both major parties but cut more into Whig than Democratic strength. While some native-born Democrats bolted their party because of resentment at its increasingly immigrant cast, the Whigs, having traditionally attracted the majority of middle-class and skilled working-class Protestants, were most susceptible to nativist appeals. Already crippled by the sectional conflict over slavery, the Whigs suffered a mortal blow in the nativist defections of 1854–1855.

Nativists and Free Soilers maintained an ambivalent relationship. On the one hand, the antislavery movement grew out of the same milieu of evangelical Protestantism as did nativism. The ideology of free-labor capitalism viewed both Catholicism and slavery as symbolic of backward, autocratic, and repressive social systems. "The Catholic press upholds the slave power," noted a Free Soil paper. "These two malign powers have a natural affinity for each other." A Know-Nothing convention in Massachusetts resolved that since "Roman Catholicism and slavery" were both "founded and supported on the basis of ignorance and tyranny . . . there can exist no real hostility to Roman Catholicism which does not [also] embrace slavery."[18] Many Free Soilers voted for Know-Nothings in 1854. And in some states, the "anti-Nebraska" parties that sprang up in reaction to the Kansas-Nebraska Act entered into coalitions with nativist parties. Most of the congressmen elected on antislavery tickets in the 1854 elections also received some degree of nativist support, and vice versa.

---

[16]Tyler Anbinder, *Nativism and Slavery: The Northern Know Nothings and the Politics of the 1850s* (New York, 1992), p. 25; Holt, *Political Crisis of the 1850s*, p. 162.

[17]Holt, *Political Crisis of the 1850s*, pp. 157–158.

[18]Eric Foner, *Free Soil, Free Labor, Free Men* (New York, 1970), p. 231; Ray Allen Billington, *The Protestant Crusade 1800–1860: A Study of the Origins of American Nativism* (New York, 1938), p. 425.

On the other hand, most abolitionists, Free Soil leaders, and antislavery Whigs denounced nativism both as a form of bigotry and as a red herring that distracted attention from the main goal of restricting slavery. "Neither the Pope nor the foreigners ever can govern the country or endanger its liberties," said one Republican, "but the slave-breeders and slavetraders do govern it." The editor of the Free Soil *National Era* (the newspaper in which *Uncle Tom's Cabin* was first serialized) described the Know-Nothings as a "detestable organization . . . as repugnant to the doctrine of equal rights, as Slavery. . . . You have no more right to disfranchise your brother man, seeking a home in this country, than you have to disfranchise your colored neighbor."[19] In New York, William H. Seward had been fighting nativists for a decade or more. And from the Illinois prairie came some pertinent words from an antislavery Whig who was soon to join the Republican party. "I am not a Know-Nothing," said Abraham Lincoln.

How can any one who abhors the oppression of negroes, be in favor of degrading classes of white people? Our progress in degeneracy appears to me to be pretty rapid. As a nation, we began by declaring that *"all men are created equal."* We now practically read it "all men are created equal, *except negroes."* When the Know-Nothings get control, it will read "all men are created equal, except negroes, *and foreigners, and catholics."* When it comes to this I should prefer emigrating to some country where they make no pretense of loving liberty—to Russia, for instance, where despotism can be taken pure, and without the base alloy of hypocrisy.[20]

For reasons detailed in the next chapter, the political power of the Know-Nothings in the North collapsed in 1856. By then the American party was mainly a Southern party, a way station for Southern Whigs who did not yet know where else to go. But while it lasted, the Know-Nothing phenomenon had wrenched the normal patterns of politics in the Northeast completely out of shape. It delivered the *coup de grâce* to the Whig party. In the long run, however, the Kansas-Nebraska Act proved to be more important than nativism in producing a fundamental political realignment, for it gave birth to an antislavery party that soon became the dominant political force in the North.

---

[19]Foner, *Free Soil,* p. 234; Richard H. Sewell, *Ballots for Freedom: Antislavery Politics in the United States 1837–1860* (New York, 1976), p. 268.

[20]Lincoln to Joshua Speed, August 24, 1855, in Roy P. Basler (ed.), *The Collected Works of Abraham Lincoln,* 9 vols. (New Brunswick, N.J., 1953–1955), II, 323.

Chapter Six

Kansas and the Rise of the Republican Party

We are playing for a mighty stake; if we win we carry slavery to the Pacific Ocean, if we fail we lose Missouri, Arkansas, and Texas and all the territories; the game must be played boldly.

—David R. Atchison,
senator from Missouri, 1854

The Kansas-Nebraska Act

On January 4, 1854, Senator Stephen A. Douglas, chairman of the Committee on Territories, reported a bill to organize the area west and northwest of Missouri as Nebraska territory. This action set off a new and fateful controversy over slavery in the territories.

The origins of the Nebraska bill stretched back nearly a decade. Land-hungry pioneers pressed for territorial organization to extinguish Indian titles and to open the fertile acres for settlement. Interests supporting a railroad from the Midwest to California likewise clamored for establishment of a territory, to facilitate surveys and the acquisition of a right of way. In February 1853, the House passed a territorial bill. Since Nebraska was north of 36°30′, the Missouri Compromise banned slavery there.

The Southern faction in the Senate therefore killed the bill. Missourians were particularly sensitive on this matter, for "if Nebraska be made a free Territory," explained a St. Louis newspaper, "then will Missouri be surrounded on three sides by free territory, where there will always be men and means to assist in the escape of our slaves. . . . This species of property would become insecure, if not valueless in Missouri." A meeting of Missouri slaveholders resolved: "If the Territory shall be opened to settlement, we pledge ourselves to each other to extend the institutions of Missouri over the Territory at whatever sacrifice of blood or treasure." Missouri's Senator David Atchison vowed that he would see Nebraska "sink in hell" before it became a free territory.[1]

Atchison had the power to make his threat good. As president pro tem of the Senate, he was next in line for the presidency, the vice president having died in 1853. Atchison boarded at a house on F Street in Washington with a trio of other powerful Southern senators: James M. Mason and Robert M. T. Hunter of Virginia and Andrew P. Butler of South Carolina, chairmen respectively of the Foreign Relations, Finance, and Judiciary committees. This "F Street Mess," as they called themselves, exerted potent pressure for repeal of the Missouri Compromise as a prerequisite for the organization of Nebraska.

Recognizing the potential for a Northern backlash if the ban on slavery north of 36°30′ was repealed, Stephen Douglas initially tried to circumvent this pressure by equivocation. Contemporaries and historians have ascribed various motives to Douglas in this matter: sympathy for the expansion of slavery, or at least indifference toward its expansion; an eagerness to win Southern support for his Democratic presidential nomination in 1856; a desire to promote the building of a transcontinental railroad with its eastern terminus in his own state of Illinois. Whatever the weight of these factors, Douglas's chief motive probably grew out of his belief in Manifest Destiny. He wanted to organize Nebraska territory in order to speed American westward expansion. To prevent further delay, he hoped to bypass the troublesome slavery question. His original version of the Nebraska bill in 1854 merely copied the language of the 1850 Utah and New Mexico bills. Douglas's draft specified that when admitted as a state, Nebraska would come in "with or without slavery as its constitution may prescribe." This was not good enough for the Southerners, however, because by banning slavery during the territorial stage, the Missouri Compromise would guarantee a free state. So Douglas tried another tactic. Discovering that a "clerical error" had omitted a key section of the bill, he added it: "All questions pertaining to slavery in the Territories, and in the new States to be formed therefrom, are to be left to the people residing therein, through their appropriate representatives." This was popular sovereignty, which Douglas had championed since 1848. Although it was an implied repeal of the Missouri Compromise, it still did not go far enough for Southern senators.

At this point a Whig senator from Kentucky, eager to rehabilitate his party's Southern rights image, introduced an amendment to repeal the part of the Missouri Compromise that prohibited slavery north of 36°30′. Douglas at first resisted this

---

[1]Allan Nevins, *Ordeal of the Union,* 2 vols. (New York, 1947), II, 92–93.

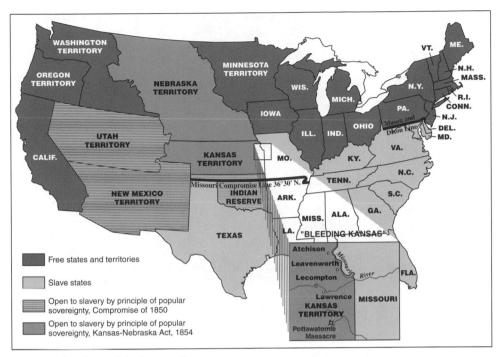

WASHINGTON TERRITORY

OREGON TERRITORY

NEBRASKA TERRITORY

MINNESOTA TERRITORY

WIS.

MICH.

IOWA

UTAH TERRITORY

CALIF.

KANSAS TERRITORY

MO.

NEW MEXICO TERRITORY

Missouri Compromise Line 36°30' N.

INDIAN RESERVE

ARK.

TEXAS

MISS.   ALA.   GA.

LA.   "BLEEDING KANSAS"

VT.   ME.

N.H.
MASS.

N.Y.   R.I.
CONN.

PA.   N.J.

OHIO   Mason and Dixon Line   DEL.
MD.

ILL.   IND.   VA.

KY.

TENN.   N.C.

S.C.

FLA.

Atchison

Leavenworth

Lecompton   Missouri River

Lawrence   MISSOURI

KANSAS TERRITORY

Pottawatomie Massacre

- ■ Free states and territories
- □ Slave states
- ▨ Open to slavery by principle of popular sovereignty, Compromise of 1850
- ▩ Open to slavery by principle of popular sovereignty, Kansas-Nebraska Act, 1854

Kansas-Nebraska and the Slavery Issue

amendment, which he knew would provoke outrage in the North. But after a meeting with the Kentucky senator, Douglas reportedly capitulated with the words: "By God, Sir, you are right. I will incorporate it in my bill, though I know it will raise a hell of a storm."[2]

Douglas and a delegation of Southern senators persuaded a reluctant but weak-willed President Pierce to endorse repeal, thereby making it a Democratic party measure with the lever of patronage to prod reluctant Northern Democrats into line. When Douglas introduced his revised bill on January 23, it contained an additional feature dividing the territory in two: Kansas immediately to the west of Missouri, and Nebraska to the north of Kansas. Observers interpreted this as marking out Kansas for slavery and Nebraska for freedom. The question of *when* the inhabitants of these territories would be able to decide on slavery—at the time of the first territorial legislature, as Northern Democrats believed, or not until statehood, as Southerners insisted—was deliberately left unresolved, to preserve the precarious intersectional Democratic support for the measure.

Douglas's action certainly did raise a hell of a storm. The first thunderclap was an *Appeal of the Independent Democrats*[3] written by Salmon P. Chase and Joshua Giddings, signed by the leading Free Soilers in Congress, and published in the *National Era* on January 24. The *Appeal* arraigned the Kansas-Nebraska bill as "a gross violation of a

---

[2]David M. Potter, *The Impending Crisis 1848–1861* (New York, 1976), p. 160.

[3]Something of a misnomer, since nearly all the signers were former Whigs.

STEPHEN A. DOUGLAS. One of the most talented men in public life, the 5-foot, 4-inch Douglas was called "the Little Giant." Combative in his public style, he was skilled at behind-the-scenes political compromise. He attained national leadership of the Democratic party by the mid-1850's, but his ambition for the presidency was thwarted by Southern opposition and by his fellow Illinoisian Abraham Lincoln. Douglas was a hard drinker as well as a hard worker; in 1861, the combination killed him. He was forty-eight.

LIBRARY OF CONGRESS

sacred pledge" (the Missouri Compromise); as a "criminal betrayal of precious rights; as part and parcel of an atrocious plot to exclude from the vast unoccupied region immigrants from the Old World and free laborers from our own States, and convert it into a dreary region of despotism, inhabited by masters and slaves."[4] This became the Free Soil theme in the bitter congressional debates that followed and in hundreds of protest rallies held throughout the North.

With energy and skill, Douglas piloted the Kansas-Nebraska bill through the Senate. He maintained that the Compromise of 1850, by introducing popular sovereignty in territory north of 36°30', had implicitly repealed the Missouri Compromise. Although this was a specious argument—the 1850 legislation applied only to territory acquired from Mexico, not to the Louisiana Purchase—it was to become Southern and Democratic orthodoxy. Douglas also insisted—as he had in 1850—that Nature would prevent slavery from gaining a foothold in the new territory. This was questionable, for the eastern third of present-day Kansas possesses about the same

---

[4]Nevins, *Ordeal,* II, 112.

climate and soil conditions as the Missouri River basin in Missouri, where most of that state's slaves resided and raised hemp and tobacco, which could also be grown in Kansas.

The quintessence of the Senate debate was captured in an exchange between George Badger of North Carolina and Benjamin Wade of Ohio. Badger: "If some Southern gentlemen wishes to take the. . . old woman who nursed him in childhood, and whom he called 'Mammy'. . . into one of these new Territories for the betterment of the fortunes of his whole family—why, in the name of God, should anybody prevent it?" Wade: "We have not the least objection. . . to the senator's migrating to Kansas and taking his old 'Mammy' along with him. We only insist that he shall not be empowered to sell her after taking her there."[5]

Douglas drove the bill to Senate passage on March 3 by a vote of 37 to 14. Northern Democratic senators voted 14 to 5 for the bill. The struggle in the House was harsher and more prolonged, for Northern Democrats there had to face the voters in November. At one point in the House debate, some congressmen drew weapons, and bloodshed was narrowly avoided. The House finally passed the bill on May 22 by a vote of 113 to 100. Northern Democrats divided 44 to 44 on the measure, a sure sign of trouble for the party in the North. In the combined vote of both houses, Southerners provided 61 percent of the aye votes and Northerners 91 percent of the nay votes. It was clearly a Southern victory, a "triumph of Slavery [and] Aristocracy over Liberty and Republicanism," in the bitter words of a Northern newspaper.[6]

But it was an expensive triumph. As Horace Greeley later remarked, the bill created more abolitionists in two months than William Lloyd Garrison and Wendell Phillips had created in twenty years.

The Rise of the Republican Party

Throughout the North during the spring and summer of 1854, angry meetings protested the "Nebraska outrage" and organized new political coalitions. In some states Free Soilers took the lead; in others, antislavery Whigs. Anti-Nebraska Democrats in the Northwest and nativists in the Northeast contributed significant strength to these coalitions. The new organizations took various names: Anti-Nebraska; Fusion; People's; Independent. But the name that caught on was Republican, which linked the struggle of 1854 with the country's first battle for freedom in 1776. Many towns later claimed credit for having held the first "Republican" meeting. The honor seems to belong to Ripon, Wisconsin, where an anti-Nebraska rally in the Congregational church on February 28, 1854, adopted the name Republican. A meeting of about thirty antislavery congressmen in Washington on May 9 suggested that the anti-Nebraska coalition appropriate this name. A state convention in Michigan on July 6 officially chose the name Republican for the state party.

---

[5]James Ford Rhodes, *History of the United States from the Compromise of 1850 . . .* , 7 vols. (New York, 1893–1906), I, 452–453.

[6]James A. Rawley, *Race and Politics: "Bleeding Kansas" and the Coming of the Civil War* (Philadelphia, 1969), p. 36.

In 1854, several other state organizations also adopted the name. In some states, however, Whig leaders refused to give up their old allegiance and still hoped to turn their party into the vehicle of the Northern political revolution. William Seward's Whigs fought the 1854 campaign under their own name in New York. In Illinois, Abraham Lincoln stayed with the Whig party. But the Whigs faced two handicaps in their efforts to control the anti-Nebraska movement: in some states the conservative, "cotton" wing of the party wanted no part of a coalition with Free Soilers and bolting Democrats; in others, the latter groups refused to subsume themselves under the name of Whig. Although former Whigs would eventually become the dominant element in the Republican party, they would lose their identity as Whigs in the process. By the end of 1855, the Whig party had quietly expired.

Under whatever name, the anti-Nebraska parties reaped rewards from the political realignment of 1854. The elections that fall were a disaster for the Democrats. Perhaps as many as a quarter of the Northern Democratic voters deserted their party. A startling sixty-six of the ninety-one free-state Democratic incumbents went down to defeat in the congressional elections. Only seven of the forty-four representatives who had voted for the Kansas-Nebraska bill won reelection. Having carried all but two Northern states in 1852, the Democrats lost all but two in 1854. As a result, the party became even more a Southern party. In the next Congress, Southern Democrats would outnumber their Northern colleagues by two to one. With the exception of the abnormal years of the Civil War and Reconstruction, Northern Democrats did not again reach parity with their Southern colleagues in Congress until 1931.

The new Republican party was the chief beneficiary of the Democratic disaster. But this was not immediately apparent. Not all anti-Nebraska men were yet Republicans. In several states the Know-Nothings won more votes than the Republicans. But in 1855–1856, the latter scored a major coup by outmaneuvering the Know-Nothings to gain most of their antislavery adherents. Some antislavery men who had supported the Know-Nothings in 1854, especially in Massachusetts, had done so with the intention of taking over the movement and converting it into a new antislavery party. A meeting of the National Council of the American party in June 1855 gave them a chance to take the first step in that direction. Delegates from twelve free states walked out after the meeting adopted resolutions endorsing the Kansas-Nebraska Act. In February 1856, a second Northern bolt took place when another American party convention voted down a resolution calling for repeal of the Kansas-Nebraska Act.[7]

Meanwhile in the winter of 1855–1856, a protracted struggle over the election of a Speaker of the House further strengthened the Republicans at the expense of the Know-Nothings. About two-thirds of the one hundred or so anti-Nebraska congressmen elected in 1854 now classified themselves as Republicans, though some of

---

[7]The best account of this complex story is Tyler Anbinder, *Nativism and Slavery: The Northern Know Nothings and the Politics of the 1850s* (New York, 1992), esp. chaps. 8–9. For somewhat different interpretations, which emphasize the persistence of nativism in the Republican party, see William E. Gienapp, *The Origins of the Republican Party 1852–1856.* (New York, 1987), and Michael F. Holt, *The Rise and Fall of the American Whig Party* (New York, 1999), chaps. 23–26.

these had been elected with Know-Nothing support. The Republican caucus nominated Nathaniel P. Banks of Massachusetts for Speaker. Banks, formerly a Know-Nothing, was now a Republican. Since neither the Republicans nor the Democrats had a majority in the House, the Know-Nothings held the balance of power and prevented either party from winning a majority. Day after day, week after week, the balloting dragged on. Finally the House changed its rules to allow election of a Speaker by a plurality. Banks thereupon won on the 133rd ballot with 103 votes. About 30 of these votes came from Northern Know-Nothings, who thereby declared themselves Republicans. This marriage was consummated in June 1856 when the "North Americans" endorsed the Republican presidential nominee, John C. Frémont. For them, slavery had proved to be a more potent negative image than immigration. The Republicans thereby absorbed most Northern nativists into their ranks.

In the process, Republicanism took on some of the cultural baggage of nativism. The Republicans became the party of reformist, antislavery Protestantism. They also became the party of dynamic, innovative capitalism, whose ideology of modernization attracted mainly the native-born Yankees of the upper North. A map showing Republican strength in the 1856 presidential election (see page 106) is remarkably congruent with a map of New England settlement patterns, of antislavery and temperance societies, of a high density of public schools and literacy, and of areas that opposed black laws and favored black suffrage but contained few if any black residents. Although the Republicans officially spurned nativism, many party members inherited a hostile view of slavery and Catholicism as dual manifestations of repression, ignorance, and backwardness.

Southerners and Catholics returned the hostility. Their epithets of "Black Republicans," "Yankees," and the "Puritan party" summed up in turn a host of negative symbols associated with the Republicans: abolitionism and racial equality, material acquisitiveness and sharp practice, hypocrisy, bigotry, and an offensive eagerness to reform other people's morals or to interfere with their property. The Butternuts of the southern Midwest (see pages 23 to 25) shared these anti-Republican attitudes. Most of the Democrats who left their party after Kansas-Nebraska and eventually became Republicans lived in the upper North; the Butternuts remained loyal Democrats and, along with Catholics and Southerners, continued to form the backbone of the party.

Bleeding Kansas

The Republicans took over the Free Soil commitment to the principle of the Wilmot Proviso as their central tenet: no slavery in the territories, no more slave states. When the antislavery forces lost the congressional battle for a free Kansas, they vowed to carry the struggle to the territory itself. "Since there is no escaping your challenge," Senator Seward told his Southern colleagues, "I accept it in behalf of the cause of freedom. We will engage in competition for the virgin soil of Kansas, and God give the victory to the side which is stronger in numbers as it is in right." On the other side, Senator Atchison of Missouri wrote: "We are playing for a mighty stake; if we win we carry slavery to the Pacific Ocean, if we fail we lose Missouri, Arkansas, and Texas and all the territories; the game must be played boldly."[8]

And boldly did he play. Although the Free Soil forces organized first, forming the New England Emigrant Aid Company in the summer of 1854 to finance settlements in Kansas, it was Atchison's people who did the first settling. Most of the early migrants to Kansas came from Missouri. Some brought their slaves with them. Most of the Free Soil settlers came from Midwestern states. Only a sprinkling of New Englanders migrated to Kansas, but the publicity surrounding the New England Emigrant Aid Company provoked proslavery partisans to portray a Yankee conspiracy to abolitionize the West. Much of the subsequent conflict between Free Soil and proslavery settlers was of the sort typical in frontier communities: clashes over land claims or town sites or water rights, and the inevitable violence of settlements without established institutions of law and order. But because Kansas was the national cockpit of the slavery question, all conflicts became polarized around this issue.

In the fall of 1854, Andrew Reeder, a Pennsylvania Democrat, arrived in Kansas to begin his duties as territorial governor. His first task was to supervise an election for the territory's delegate to Congress. The proslavery men were determined to make this initial test of popular sovereignty come out in their favor. On election day, 1,700 armed Missourians crossed the border to vote in Kansas. These "border ruffians," as the antislavery press dubbed them, swelled the overwhelming majority that sent a proslavery delegate to Washington.

The border ruffians repeated their tactics in the election of a territorial legislature in March 1855. This time, four or five thousand of them swarmed across the border. Atchison returned home from the Senate to lead the invasion. "There are eleven hundred coming over from Platte County to vote," he told his followers, "and if that ain't enough we can send five thousand—enough to kill every God-damned abolitionist in the Territory."[9] Although by this time bona fide settlers from free states were in the majority, the proslavery voters cast 5,247 ballots, the Free Soilers 791. A congressional investigation later concluded that 4,968 of the proslavery votes were fraudulent. But Governor Reeder, intimidated by the Missourians, refused to order a new election. Although urged to take corrective action, President Pierce did nothing. The Southern press applauded. "Missourians have nobly defended *our* rights," declared an Alabama newspaper.[10] The legislature (or "bogus legislature," as antislavery men called it) passed a draconian slave code. It restricted officeholding to avowed proslavery men. Anyone who questioned the legality of slavery in Kansas could be imprisoned, and anyone who advocated a slave rebellion or aided the escape of fugitive slaves could be put to death.

---

[8]Seward quoted in *Congressional Globe,* 33rd Cong., 1st sess. (1854), Appendix, 769; Atchison quoted in Rawley, *Race and Politics,* p. 81.

[9]Gienapp, *Origins of Republican Party,* p. 170.

[10]Rawley, *Race and Politics,* p. 89.

SOUTHERN CHIVALRY — ARGUMENT versus CLUB'S.

VIOLENCE IN CONGRESS. This Northern cartoon depicts Preston Brooks's assault on Senator Charles Sumner on May 22, 1856. The pen in Sumner's hand symbolizes the words of "truth," to which the only Southern response was the brutality of the cane wielded as a club. Note other Southern senators in the background smiling on the scene or preventing Northern senators from coming to Sumner's aid. Reaction to this incident intensified sectional polarization.

Outraged free-state settlers began to organize in self-defense. They turned the town of Lawrence into an antislavery stronghold and began arming themselves with "Beecher's Bibles" (so called because antislavery clergyman Henry Ward Beecher had said that Sharps rifles would do more than Bibles just then to enforce morality in Kansas). They organized a free-state party, held an election for a constitutional convention (boycotted by the proslavery voters), met in Topeka to draw up a constitution prohibiting slavery, and established their own legislature in the winter of 1855–1856. To prove that they were not the "abolitionist fanatics" portrayed by the proslavery press, the free-staters adopted an ordinance banning the entry of free blacks as well as of slaves.[11]

Kansas now had two territorial governments—one legal but fraudulent, the other illegal but representing a majority of settlers. In Washington, the President and the Democratic-controlled Senate recognized the former, while the Republican-organized House favored the latter. When Governor Reeder declared his sympathy with the free-staters, Pierce replaced him with a solid proslavery man, Wilson Shannon. The Republican party benefited from Northern anger at the border ruffians, whose buccaneering practices the antislavery press played up for all they were worth.

---

[11]Of the thirty-seven delegates who signed the Topeka constitution, thirteen had been born in the South and twenty-one were former Democrats. These were the elements that supported black exclusion. In the referendum on this provision, the New England settlers voted against it but were overwhelmed by the more numerous Midwesterners.

Meanwhile in Kansas the sporadic violence took more organized form. In November 1855, each side mobilized several hundred armed men along the Wakarusa River. The Missourians prepared to attack Lawrence, but at the last minute Governor Shannon persuaded them to desist. This "Wakarusa War" amounted to nothing more than a few skirmishes. The harsh winter that followed kept everyone indoors for several months. But with the coming of spring, violence burst forth once again. On May 21, an army of seven hundred proslavery men rode into Lawrence, destroyed the offices of two newspapers and threw their presses into the river, burned down the hotel and the house of the free-state "governor," and pillaged the stores.

Even before news of this affair reached the East, violence in Washington had inflamed sectional passions. On May 19 and 20, Charles Sumner of Massachusetts delivered in the Senate a long philippic entitled "The Crime Against Kansas." Given to florid rhetoric and provocative assertions of superior Northern morality, Sumner lashed the South with sexual metaphors about the "rape" of Kansas. Included in his speech were abusive references to Senator Andrew Butler of South Carolina. Two days later Butler's cousin, Representative Preston Brooks, entered the Senate chamber after adjournment, walked over to Sumner's desk, and began beating him over the head with a cane. His legs trapped under the desk, Sumner was unable to defend himself. Trying to stand up, he finally wrenched the bolted desk from the floor, stumbled forward and collapsed, while the enraged Brooks continued to hit him until pulled away by other congressmen who had rushed to the scene. Suffering from shock as well as from his injuries, Sumner did not return to the Senate for three years. But the Massachusetts legislature reelected him in 1857 and kept his seat vacant as a silent but eloquent symbol of martyrdom to the "barbarism" of slavery.

Brooks's act provoked wrath in the North. "Bleeding Sumner" along with "Bleeding Kansas" became potent Republican rallying cries. Southern moderates deplored Brooks's caning of Sumner. But their voices were decidedly in the minority. "Every Southern man is delighted," Brooks wrote the day after the event. "The fragments of the stick are begged for as sacred relics."[12] The *Richmond Whig* expressed the opinion of many Southern newspapers when it endorsed "this elegant and effectual caning. . . . The only regret we feel is that Mr. Brooks did not employ a horsewhip or cowhide upon his slanderous back instead of a cane." A solid Southern vote against the expulsion of Brooks by the House prevented the necessary two-thirds majority. Brooks resigned anyway, won unanimous reelection in his district, and returned triumphantly to Washington. While Brooks was in South Carolina, the mayor of Columbia gave him a hickory cane with a gold head. From all over the South Brooks received canes; one presented by the city of Charleston bore the inscription "Hit Him Again"; his own constituents gave him one inscribed "Use Knock-Down Arguments."[13]

---

[12]Robert L. Meriwether (ed.), "Preston S. Brooks on the Caning of Charles Sumner," *The South Carolina Historical and Genealogical Magazine,* 52 (January 1951), 3.

[13]Nevins, *Ordeal,* II, 446–447; John Hope Franklin, *The Militant South 1800–1861* (Cambridge, Mass., 1956), pp. 54–55.

Thus far, Southerners had committed most of the violence in the Kansas controversy. But out in Kansas was a man who believed in an eye for an eye. John Brown looked and acted like an Old Testament prophet. A Connecticut-born abolitionist who had failed in most of his business and farming enterprises, Brown had drifted west and in 1855 settled in Kansas with several of his sons. He commanded a free-state military company that participated in the Wakarusa War. In May 1856, this company was on its way to defend Lawrence when word reached it that the town had already been sacked. When he heard this news, Brown was seized with "frenzy." It was time to "fight fire with fire," he said, to "strike terror in the hearts of the proslavery people." When the company learned the next day about the caning of Sumner, Brown "went crazy—*crazy,*" according to witnesses. "It seemed to be the finishing, decisive touch."[14] Brown led a party containing four of his sons and two other men on a nighttime raid along Pottawatomie Creek. They seized five proslavery settlers from their cabins and murdered them by splitting their skulls with broadswords.

This butchery launched full-scale guerrilla war in Kansas. Although shocked antislavery people in the East denied—or chose not to believe—the truth about these killings,[15] most Kansans knew who had done them. For the next four months, hit-and-run attacks by both sides raged in Kansas and were exaggerated by the national press into full-scale battles. Several newspapers had a standing headline for news from Kansas: "Progress of the Civil War." John Brown participated in these skirmishes, and one of his sons was killed. About two hundred other men died in the Kansas fighting during 1856. In September, President Pierce finally replaced the ineffective Governor Shannon with John Geary, a tough but fair-minded Pennsylvanian who had won his spurs as a captain in the Mexican War and as San Francisco's first mayor. Combining persuasion with a skillful deployment of federal troops, Geary imposed a truce on the two sides and brought an uneasy peace to Kansas in the fall of 1856. By this time the larger question of which Kansas was a part—slavery in the territories—was the focus of the presidential election.

The Election of 1856

The Republicans were the first entirely sectional major party in American history. A few delegates from four upper-South states attended the national convention, but the party had no hope of carrying a single county in the slave states. The Republican platform called for a free Kansas, denounced Democratic efforts to acquire Cuba, and affirmed the duty of Congress "to prohibit in the Territories those twin relics of barbarism—Polygamy, and Slavery." Although four-fifths of the platform dealt with slavery, the party also endorsed government aid for the construction of a transcontinental railroad and for river and harbor improvements—measures that had been blocked by Southern congressmen or vetoed by President Pierce.

---

[14]Stephen B. Oates, *To Purge This Land With Blood: A Biography of John Brown* (New York, 1970), pp. 128–129, 133.

[15]Proof of Brown's responsibility did not come out until years later.

By nominating John C. Frémont—whose father was a Catholic and who had himself been married by a Catholic priest—the Republicans dismayed some of their nativist supporters. But Frémont's nomination was a calculated gamble to attract ex-Democrats. The established Republican leaders, Seward and Chase, were radicals whose notoriety might offend timid voters. The dashing young Frémont, by contrast, had little political experience but had won popularity by his explorations in the West and his role in the California Bear Flag Revolt against Mexican rule.[16]

"Availability" also dictated the Democratic nomination of James Buchanan. The incumbent, Pierce, and the party's most prominent leader, Douglas, were too closely identified with the Kansas-Nebraska Act. Buchanan had the good fortune to have been out of the country as minister to Britain during the previous three years. After sixteen deadlocked ballots at the Democratic convention, Douglas withdrew in favor of Buchanan. The platform reiterated all the Jeffersonian-Jacksonian states' rights planks, coming out against any government role in the economy or in social reform. It also reaffirmed the Fugitive Slave Law, denounced the Republicans as abolitionists in disguise, and endorsed popular sovereignty in the territories.

What was left of the American party nominated Millard Fillmore, who also received the endorsement of the remnant of Whigs who vainly hoped to revive their moribund party. The 1856 contest was really two elections: between Buchanan and Fillmore in the South, and between Buchanan and Frémont in the North. Although Fillmore ran well in the upper South and in former Whig strongholds of the lower South, he carried only Maryland. Frémont won the upper North—Wisconsin, Michigan, all of New England, and New York (where heavy upstate majorities outweighed a dismal showing in New York City). Large pluralities in the "Yankee" areas of Ohio and Iowa gave the Republicans these states also. But the crucial struggle took place in the lower North—New Jersey, Pennsylvania, Indiana, and Illinois. Whoever could carry Pennsylvania plus any one of the others would be elected. Both sides concentrated most of their efforts in these states.

On the Republican side, the campaign evoked a moral fervor unprecedented in American politics. "The process now going on in the politics of the United States," wrote a Republican journalist, "is a *Revolution*." Young Republicans organized Wide Awake clubs and marched in huge torchlight parades. They chanted the slogan "Free Soil, Free Labor, Free Men, Frémont." Republican rhetoric presented the election as a struggle between democracy and aristocracy, progress and reaction. "We require for our country a government of the people, instead of a government by an oligarchy; a government maintaining before the world the rights of men rather than the privilege

---

[16]When war broke out between Mexico and the United States in 1846, a group of American settlers in California's Sacramento Valley, aided by Captain Frémont of the U.S. Topographical Corps who happened to be there mapping the country, captured the headquarters of the Mexican commandant at Sonoma. They raised a flag bearing a grizzly bear facing a red star and proclaimed the independent Bear Flag Republic. Three weeks later, American troops entered California and the joyful settlers lowered their bear flag in favor of the stars and stripes.

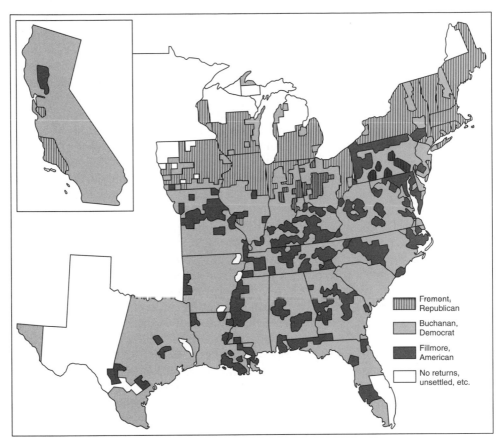

Counties Carried by Candidates in the 1856 Presidential Election

of masters," declared a Republican meeting in Buffalo. "The contest ought not to be considered a *sectional* one but the war of a *class*—the slaveholders—against the laboring people of *all classes*."[17]

Southern rhetoric seemed to confirm this Republican argument. "The great evil of Northern *free* society is that it is burdened with a *servile class of mechanics and laborers,* unfit for self-government," declared a South Carolina newspaper. A Virginia editor explained that "we have got to hating everything with the prefix *free,* from free negroes up and down the whole catalogue—*free farms, free labor, free society, free will, free thinking, free children, and free schools*—all belonging to the same brood of damnable *isms*."[18]

---

[17]Roy F. Nichols and Philip S. Klein, "Election of 1856," in Arthur M. Schlesinger, Jr., *History of American Presidential Elections,* 4 vols. (New York, 1971), II, 1031; Michael F. Holt, *The Political Crisis of the 1850s* (New York, 1978), pp. 196–197.

[18]Nevins, *Ordeal,* II, 498.

Democrats exploited two powerful issues in the lower North—racism and the fear of disunion. "The Black Republicans," a Democratic newspaper informed voters, intended to "turn loose. . . millions of negroes, to elbow you in the workshops, and compete with you in the fields of honest labor." The election would show whether the Northern people preferred "niggers . . . [and] a false, wretched, miserable and resultless philanthropy, to their own race and color and the Union and all its countless blessings." With Southern fire-eaters and even some moderates uttering threats of secession if Frémont won, Buchanan benefited from apprehensions about the future of the Union. After the Republicans carried Maine with 65 percent of the vote in that state's September balloting, Governor Henry A. Wise of Virginia put his militia on alert and wrote that "if Frémont is elected there will be a revolution."[19] Such statements caused many Northern conservatives of Whig background to rally behind Buchanan as the only alternative to disaster. The pacification of Kansas in October also helped the Democrats by robbing the Republicans of their best issue.

Buchanan carried all four of the crucial lower-North states (plus California) and was therefore elected. He won 45 percent of the popular vote nationwide—41 percent in the free states and 56 percent in the slave states. Fillmore won 44 percent of the popular vote in the South but only 13 percent in the North—though this was enough to deny Frémont the lower North. Buchanan carried fourteen of the fifteen slave states but only five of the sixteen free states. He was the first President since 1828 who failed to win a majority in both sections. His election was a Southern victory. But like earlier Southern victories—the annexation of Texas, the Mexican War, and the Kansas-Nebraska Act—it ultimately strengthened the antislavery cause in the North. This paradoxical process was carried a step further by an event that occurred two days after Buchanan's inauguration—the announcement of the Supreme Court's decision in the Dred Scott case.

---

[19]Stephen E. Maizlish, *The Triumph of Sectionalism: The Transformation of Ohio Politics, 1844–1856* (Kent, 1983), p. 232; Rawley, *Race and Politics,* p. 162; Roy F. Nichols, *The Disruption of American Democracy* (New York, 1948), p. 44.

Chapter Seven

The Deepening Crisis, 1857– 1859

Let us discard all this quibbling about this man and the other man, this race and . . . the other race being inferior . . . and unite as one people throughout this land, until we once more stand up declaring that all men are created equal.

—Abraham Lincoln,

1858

The Dred Scott Decision

The men who fashioned the Compromise of 1850 hoped their handiwork would lay to rest the issue of slavery in the territories. So did proponents of the Kansas-Nebraska Act. But both measures left unresolved the question of whether a territorial legislature could prohibit slavery before the territory achieved statehood. And both had backfired by stirring up rather than calming Northern passions. In 1857, the Dred Scott decision followed the same pattern. The Supreme Court intended to settle the legal status of slavery in the territories. Instead, it inflamed the embers of sectionalism.

The case followed a long and complex route to the Supreme Court. Dred Scott was a Missouri slave whose owner, an army surgeon, had taken him to Illinois and to Wisconsin territory when stationed at army posts there in the 1830s. In 1846, after the owner's death, Scott sued the heirs for his freedom, on the grounds that residence in a free state and in a territory made free by the Missouri Compromise had made him a free man. Scott first lost and then won his suit in a Missouri circuit court, only to see the state's supreme court overturn the lower court and deny him freedom in 1852. The legal owner having meanwhile moved to New York, Scott took his case to the federal circuit court, under the constitutional clause that allows a citizen of one state to sue a citizen of another in the federal courts. Scott again lost his bid for freedom when the federal court upheld the Missouri Supreme Court in 1854, whereupon Scott's lawyers appealed to the U.S. Supreme Court. The appeal was argued in the spring of 1856 and held over for reargument in the 1856–1857 term.

By then the case had acquired a significance far beyond the issue of Scott's freedom.[1] Three important questions came before the Court. (1) Did prolonged residence in a free state or territory make Scott free? (2) As a slave and a black, was Scott a citizen with the right to sue in federal courts? (3) Was the Missouri Compromise, which had prohibited slavery in the portion of Wisconsin territory where Scott resided, a constitutional law? The first of these questions was the least controversial. Precedents existed for upholding the ruling of the Missouri Supreme Court that Scott had been only a "sojourner" in a free state and territory and therefore remained a slave. The U.S. Supreme Court could have evaded the second and third questions by simply affirming the circuit court's decision. Indeed, on February 14, 1857, a majority of the justices decided to do just that, and Justice Samuel Nelson began to write the opinion.

But a few days later the Court reconsidered and decided to issue a comprehensive ruling covering all aspects of the case. What caused this change of mind? A definitive answer is shrouded in the secrecy of the Court's proceedings. But certain things are clear. For eleven years—ever since the Wilmot Proviso—the legal status of slavery in the territories had been the chief issue before the country. This issue had crippled one political party, given birth to another, and threatened to divide a third—the Democrats—over the question of whether slavery could be excluded by a territory's residents prior to statehood. For years, people had hoped for a judicial resolution of this question. The New Mexico and Utah territorial bills of 1850 and the Kansas-Nebraska Act of 1854 included provisions to expedite an appeal to the Supreme Court on the matter. But no case had arisen from these territories. Now came one from another part of the Louisiana Purchase.

During the winter of 1856–1857, Washington was alive with rumors that the Court would seize this opportunity to resolve the issue of whether slavery could legally be excluded from a territory. Confident that the Court would rule in their favor, Southerners were eager for a comprehensive decision. They had good reason for confidence. Five of the justices, including Chief Justice Roger Taney, were Southern Democrats. Two of the four Northern justices were also Democrats, and one of them, Robert Grier of Pennsylvania, was a proslavery partisan with Southern relatives. The temptation to settle the vexed territorial question by "judicial statesmanship" proved too strong. On a motion of Justice James M. Wayne of Georgia, the Court agreed that Taney, speaking for the majority, should write a decision that denied black citizenship and declared unconstitutional the Missouri Compromise's exclusion of slavery from northern territories.

The five Southern justices wanted to win the support of at least one free-state colleague, to avoid the appearance of a sectional decision. Justice John Catron of Tennessee urged President-elect Buchanan to bring pressure on his fellow Pennsylvan-

---

[1]Scott would obtain his freedom in any event. Three months after the Supreme Court handed down its negative ruling, his owner manumitted him. Scott died a year later.

ian Grier to concur with the majority. Buchanan needed little urging. Sympathetic to the proslavery position and owing his election mainly to Southern voters, Buchanan also hoped for a judicial resolution of the territorial question to prevent it from damaging his administration as it had his predecessor's. The President used his influence with Grier, who decided to go along with the Southern justices. Apprised of the forthcoming ruling, Buchanan made a disingenuous reference to it in his inaugural address: "To their decision, in common with all good citizens, I shall cheerfully submit, whatever this may be."[2]

Two days later, on March 6, the Court spoke. It spoke with many voices, for every justice wrote an opinion. This has made it difficult to know precisely what the Court ruled. Taney wrote the 7-to-2 majority decision; but some of the concurring opinions followed different lines of reasoning to arrive at approximately the same points. Taney ruled: (1) Dred Scott was still a slave. (2) As a slave *and* as a black,[3] he was not a citizen because at the time the Constitution was written, blacks "had for more than a century before been regarded as beings of an inferior order . . . so far inferior, that they had no rights which the white man was bound to respect."[4] By a tendentious process of reasoning, Taney concluded that neither these inferior beings nor their descendants in 1857 were citizens and therefore Scott's suit in federal court should have been denied in the first place. (3) Scott's sojourn in Illinois did not free him, for under interstate comity, Missouri law prevailed. (4) His sojourn in Wisconsin territory did not free him, because Congress had no power to exclude slavery from a territory and the exclusion clause of the Missouri Compromise was therefore unconstitutional.

Taney and the concurring justices based their territorial ruling on several principles: the Calhoun idea that the territories were the joint property of the states, not the creation of Congress; the principle that slave property had the same standing as any other property and that a master's slave could no more be excluded from a territory than could a farmer's horse (thus Taney denied the power of a territorial legislature as well as of Congress to exclude slaves); and the due process clause of the Fifth Amendment, which prohibited the federal government from depriving any person of life, liberty, or property without due process of law. Antislavery people, of course, emphasized the word "liberty" in the Fifth Amendment as the basis for banning slavery in all jurisdictions of the federal government. But for Taney, property superseded liberty, and the clause as a whole outweighed Article IV, Section 3, of the Constitution, which gave Congress the "Power to dispose of and make all needful Rules and Regulations respecting the Territory" of the United States. To Republicans, this section empowered Congress to exclude slavery; to a majority of justices, it did not.

Taney's ruling evoked almost universal praise below the Mason-Dixon line. "Southern opinion upon the subject of southern slavery . . . is now the supreme law of the land," exulted the *Augusta* (Georgia) *Constitutionalist*. "Opposition to

---

[2]Don E. Fehrenbacher, *The Dred Scott Case: Its Significance in American Law and Politics* (New York, 1978), p. 313.

[3]Three of the concurring opinions stated only that slaves were not citizens, without going into the question of whether free blacks, as the descendants of slaves, were also deprived of citizenship.

[4]Fehrenbacher, *Dred Scott Case*, p. 347.

NATIONAL ARCHIVES

ROGER TANEY

LIBRARY OF CONGRESS

DRED SCOTT

southern opinion upon this subject is now opposition to the Constitution, and morally treason against the Government." Many Northern Democrats were equally jubilant. A party newspaper in Pennsylvania called the decision "the funeral sermon of Black Republicanism. It . . . crushes into nothingness the whole theory upon which their party is founded."[5]

But the decision was not unanimous, and its obvious partisanship robbed it of respect among Republicans. Justice Nelson of New York submitted a separate opinion that merely affirmed the circuit court ruling and refused to comment on the other issues. Justices John McLean of Ohio (a former Whig turned Republican) and Benjamin Curtis of Massachusetts (who still called himself a Whig) submitted dissenting opinions that upheld the Missouri Compromise, affirmed black citizenship, and declared that Scott should be freed. Curtis's opinion was a powerful indictment of Taney's reasoning on every crucial point. He demonstrated that blacks were legal citizens of several states in 1787 and later, and that by Article IV, Section 2, of the Constitution ("The Citizens of each State shall be entitled to all Privileges and Immunities of Citizens in the several States"), they were entitled to the rights of U.S. citizens. Curtis riddled Taney's circumlocutions concerning the power of Congress in the territories, and stated that the exclusion of slavery was neither deprivation of property nor denial of due process.

Most modern scholars have judged Curtis's dissent to be better law than Taney's majority opinion. The most thorough study of the case demonstrates that Taney was an "intensely partisan" advocate of Southern rights, a "bitter sectionalist" who disliked the North and held Republicans in contempt. His Dred Scott decision was a calculated attempt to destroy the central principle of the Republican party. It was a ruling of "unmitigated partisanship, polemical in spirit though judicial in language, and more like an ultimatum than a formula for sectional accommodation."[6]

---

[5]Ibid., pp. 418–419.

[6]Ibid., pp. 3, 234, 311. See also Don E. Fehrenbacher, "Roger B. Taney and the Sectional Crisis," *Journal of Southern History,* 43 (November 1977), 555–566.

This modern appraisal almost echoes contemporary Republican opinions of the decision. "A wicked and false judgment," "an atrocious doctrine," a "willful perversion," a "collation of false statements and shallow sophistries," "the greatest crime in the judicial annals of the Republic," were some of the Republican epithets. Abolitionists condemned in particular the ruling against black citizenship, while Republicans concentrated most of their fire on the abrogation of congressional power over slavery in the territories. Republicans also pointed with alarm to the legal implications of the decision for the free states themselves. If Dred Scott's "sojourn" of two years in Illinois did not free him, what was to prevent slaveholders from bringing their slaves into the free states for two years or even longer? If slaves were no different from other property, what right did a state have to legislate against ownership of such property? Abraham Lincoln warned that Taney's Court would probably soon hand down a decision "declaring that the Constitution of the United States does not permit a *state* to exclude slavery from its limits."[7]

Antislavery people insisted that the Dred Scott ruling was not valid law. "The Decision of the Supreme Court is the Moral Assassination of a Race and Cannot be Obeyed," declared the *New York Independent*. The *Chicago Tribune* maintained that no "Free People can respect or will obey a decision so fraught with disastrous consequences to the People and their Liberties."[8] But such assertions brought Republicans into uncomfortable proximity with the civil disobedience theories of Garrisonian abolitionists. Democrats lost no opportunity to nail the Republicans on this point. The Court's decision, they said, was the law of the land. Defiance of the law was treason to the Constitution. To counter this accusation, Republicans seized upon Justice Curtis's contention that Taney's ruling on slavery in the territories was an *obiter dictum*—a comment in passing that had no direct bearing on the case and was therefore not binding. Since Taney had declared that Scott was not a citizen, his case—and thus the question of slavery in the territories—was not properly before the Court, and any opinion concerning it was a mere *dictum* "entitled to as much moral weight," said the *New York Tribune,* as "the judgment of a majority of those congregated in any Washington bar-room."[9]

The *dictum* thesis was a political godsend to the Republicans. It let them repudiate the decision without acquiring the stigma of lawlessness.[10] The legislature of Maine passed a resolution declaring the Dred Scott decision "not binding in law or conscience." Several other legislatures followed suit. Republicans capitalized on Northern hostility to the decision with a pledge to "reconstitute" the Court and obtain a new ruling. "The remedy is . . . the ballot box," said the *Chicago Tribune*. "Let the next President be Republican, and 1860 will mark an era kindred with that of 1776."[11]

---

[7]Charles Warren, *The Supreme Court in United States History,* rev. ed., 2 vols. (Boston, 1926), II, 302–309; Roy P. Basler (ed.), *The Collected Works of Abraham Lincoln,* 9 vols. (New Brunswick, N.J., 1953–1955), II, 467.

[8]*New York Independent* quoted in Fehrenbacher, *Dred Scott Case,* p. 429; *Chicago Tribune,* March 12, 1857.

[9]*New York Tribune,* March 7, 1857.

[10]For half a century the *dictum* thesis prevailed—even among legal scholars. But historians and jurists now recognize that whatever the legal soundness or political wisdom of Taney's decision, it was not mere *dictum*. All of the questions on which he ruled, except the power of territorial legislatures over slavery, were legal aspects of the case and therefore properly before the Court.

[11]Fehrenbacher, *Dred Scott Case,*p. 432; *Chicago Tribune,* March 19, 1857.

The Dred Scott decision confounded the hopes of its authors. It did not settle the slavery question. Instead of calming sectional rancor, it served to intensify it. It did not weaken the Republican party; rather, by lending credence to Republican charges of a conspiracy to nationalize slavery, it strengthened the party. Nor did it really establish the right of slavery in the territories, for the decision was not self-enforcing. Southerners therefore began to call for a federal slave code to protect slavery in the territories. Finally, the decision did not resolve the Democrats' intraparty division concerning *when* popular sovereignty became operational. Taney's ruling that a territorial legislature, as the creation of Congress, had no more right to exclude slavery than had Congress itself, conflicted with Stephen Douglas's conception of popular sovereignty. Douglas's efforts to reconcile popular sovereignty with the Dred Scott decision occurred during a new flareup over Kansas that forced Douglas into opposing the Buchanan administration and the Southern wing of his party.

✍ The Lecompton Constitution

While the Supreme Court was pondering the fate of Dred Scott, affairs in Kansas were building toward a new crisis. Although Governor Geary had pacified the territory, the struggle for power continued. The proslavery forces were clearly losing the population battle. Every observer conceded that the free-staters had at least a two-to-one majority of settlers, and the annual spring migration was expected to enlarge it even more. With a boldness born of desperation, the proslavery territorial legislature in February 1857 called a convention to write a constitution and apply for statehood without submitting the constitution to the voters. The legislature enacted a bill that put the preparation of voting lists and the counting of votes for convention delegates in the hands of proslavery officials. Governor Geary vetoed the bill, but the legislature passed it over his veto. Worn out by overwork and the strain of threats on his life, Geary resigned on March 4. He had survived the Mexican War and San Francisco's hell-roaring gold rush days, but Kansas proved too much for him.

President Buchanan appointed a diminutive but tough Mississippian, Robert J. Walker, to replace Geary. Although Walker was determined to be impartial, the whipsaw of Kansas politics soon cut him to pieces also. Territorial officials gerrymandered election districts to give the proslavery counties a majority of convention delegates. Denouncing the whole proceeding as a farce, free-state voters boycotted the election in June. This gave the slave-state faction control of the convention by default. Walker insisted, however, that any constitution it drew up must be submitted to the voters. For this he was denounced and threatened by his former friends in the South. The Buchanan administration at first backed Walker on this question. But events in the fall of 1857 caused Buchanan to cave in to the Southerners who dominated his administration.

The Kansas constitutional convention that met at Lecompton in September drafted a constitution intended to make Kansas a slave state. As it was doing so, a new election for a territorial legislature took place in October. Assured by Walker that this would be a fair election, the free-state voters took part. The results at first appeared to give the proslavery candidates a slight edge. But frauds soon came to light. In one district with 30 legitimate voters, a total of 1,601 names had been copied onto the voting rolls from the Cincinnati city directory. Walker threw out 2,800 fraudulent votes, which gave the Free Soilers a substantial majority in the next territorial legislature.

Although Southerners abused Walker for "going behind the returns," their censure constituted an admission that the Free Soilers had a majority in an honest election—one that would ensure the defeat of the Lecompton constitution in a referendum. Since Congress would almost certainly refuse to sanction statehood without a referendum, the leaders of the Lecompton convention worked out an ingenious method to save the constitution and have a referendum too. They prepared a new article that would guarantee slaveholders' rights to retain ownership of the two hundred slaves (and their progeny) then living in the territory but would prohibit future importations of slaves into Kansas. The voters could then ratify the constitution either including this article ("the constitution *without* slavery") or including the original provision, which allowed the future importation of slaves ("the constitution *with* slavery"). These were the only two choices in the referendum.

Republicans denounced this "Lecompton swindle" as a travesty of popular sovereignty. So did Senator Stephen Douglas and many other Northern Democrats. They saw it as a swindle because: (1) it gave voters no opportunity to reject the constitution outright, even though the document contained several controversial features besides the slavery provisions; (2) the constitution "without slavery" was a subterfuge that, by protecting slave property already in the territory, opened the door for future smuggling of additional slaves into the state despite the ban on importation.

Because they considered both the constitution and the convention that framed it illegitimate, Kansas Free Soilers boycotted the referendum on December 21. The constitution "with slavery" therefore won easy ratification by a vote of 6,226 (of which 2,720 were later declared fraudulent) to 569. Meanwhile, the new Free Soil territorial legislature mandated a second referendum on January 4, 1858, in which voters could accept or reject the constitution outright. The slave-state voters boycotted this election, which resulted in a vote of 138 for the constitution with slavery, 24 for the constitution "without slavery," and 10,226 against the constitution.

The Lecompton constitution became the central issue of an acrimonious congressional session in 1857–1858. Douglas declared political war on the administration over the issue, and led the fight in the Senate against admitting Kansas to statehood under the Lecompton constitution. At one point in February 1858, a wild sectional fistfight broke out among thirty congressmen during an all-night debate on Lecompton. Northern state legislatures denounced the constitution, but several Southern legislatures threatened secession unless Congress admitted Kansas under this "duly ratified" document: "Rather than have Kansas refused admission under the Lecompton constitution," said a South Carolinian, "let [the Union] perish in blood and fire."[12] Frightened by these threats and browbeaten by his Southern advisers, Buchanan reneged on his commitment to a referendum on the whole constitution. He now declared that the December 21 election was a legitimate referendum while the January 4 election—which was in fact more representative of Kansas

---

[12]Don E. Fehrenbacher, *The South and Three Sectional Crises* (Baton Rouge, 1980), p. 54.

opinion—was not. In his message transmitting the Lecompton constitution to Congress, the President declared that Kansas "is at this moment as much a slave State as Georgia or South Carolina."

Buchanan made Lecompton a test of party loyalty. During a political career of forty years that included service as a congressman, senator, minister to Russia and to Britain, and secretary of state, the sixty-seven-year-old bachelor President had come to love the Democratic party above all else on earth and to regard faithfulness to its policies as the highest virtue. Buchanan decided to use all of the administration's resources of patronage and power to bring wavering Democratic senators and representatives into line on Lecompton. Despite Douglas's bitter opposition, the Lecompton constitution was accepted by the Senate, where the greater Southern strength plus the proslavery inclinations of several Northern Democrats secured passage of a Kansas statehood bill on March 23. But the House was a different matter. Northern representatives had to face the voters in 1858. Nearly half of the Northern Democrats along with all of the Republicans opposed Lecompton and defeated it in a showdown vote on April 1.

In Kansas, the aftermath of this affair proved almost anticlimactic. The administration saved face by sponsoring a bill for renewed submission of the Lecompton constitution to the voters under the guise of adjusting the customary federal land grant to new states. Kansans rejected the constitution by a margin of six to one on August 2, 1858. When Kansas finally achieved statehood in 1861, it came in as the most Republican state in the Union.

For the Democratic party, the legacy of Lecompton was bitter. Douglas had broken with a president from his own party and had alienated most of his former supporters in the South, where he was now regarded as no better than a Black Republican. This ensured a divisive Democratic national convention in 1860, when Douglas was certain to command the support of most Northern delegates for the presidential nomination.

The Lecompton struggle also exposed the defects of popular sovereignty after the Dred Scott decision. Even though slavery still existed legally in Kansas territory after 1858, it ceased to exist there in fact because the predominance of Free Soilers created an environment in which it could not survive. In a speech at Springfield, Illinois, back in June 1857, Douglas had tried to reconcile the Dred Scott doctrine with popular sovereignty. Although the right of slave owners to hold their property in the territories was guaranteed by the Constitution, said Douglas on that occasion, "it necessarily remains a barren and worthless right, unless sustained, protected and enforced by appropriate police regulations and local legislation" which "must necessarily depend entirely upon the will and wishes of the people of the Territory."[13] This truism had provoked little controversy at the time. But in the aftermath of Lecompton it became an issue on which Southerners could flail Douglas. Popular sovereignty was ground between the upper millstone of Republican demands for the congressional exclusion of slavery from the territories and the nether millstone of Southern demands for a federal slave code to guarantee its protection there.

---

[13]Fehrenbacher, *Dred Scott Case,* p. 456.

The Lincoln-Douglas Debates

On June 16, 1858, a convention of Illinois Republicans nominated Abraham Lincoln for the U.S. Senate. This action was almost unprecedented, for senators were then elected by state legislatures and rarely nominated by a party convention before the legislative selection. But the unusual circumstances of 1858 called for unusual action. Douglas's break with the Buchanan administration had caused several Eastern Republicans to suggest an endorsement of his reelection to the Senate as the first step toward a broadened antislavery coalition. But Illinois Republicans would have none of this. They had fought Douglas for years. They knew he was no crypto-Republican. To endorse him would be to commit suicide as a party. Their nomination of Lincoln nailed Republican colors to the mast. It made the senatorship the sole issue in the election of the Illinois legislature. By forcing Douglas to fight for his political life, it cast a long shadow toward 1860. It also produced the most famous debates in American history.

Lincoln set the tone for the campaign with his acceptance speech, which has come down through history as the "House Divided" address. His purpose was to put the greatest possible distance between Douglas and the Republicans. Although Douglas had opposed the Lecompton constitution, he did so only on the grounds that Kansans had been denied a fair vote on the measure. Douglas had said repeatedly that he cared not whether slavery was voted up or down. The "care not" policy, said Lincoln, was anathema to Republicans who considered slavery a moral, social, and political evil. This had been the position of the republic's founders, who excluded slavery from the Northwest Territory and the northern part of the Louisiana Purchase, and hoped for its eventual demise everywhere. But in 1854 Douglas had pushed through the repeal of the Missouri Compromise. In 1857, he had supported the Dred Scott decision. Quoting the Bible, Lincoln said that " 'A house divided against itself cannot stand.' I believe this government cannot endure, permanently half *slave* and half *free*. . . . It will become *all* one thing, or *all* the other." Under Democratic leadership, it might become all slave. But the Republicans—true heirs of the founders—intended to "arrest the further spread of it, and place it where the public mind shall rest in the belief that it is in the course of ultimate extinction."[14]

This linkage of Douglas with the most extreme proslavery advocates was a challenge Douglas could not ignore. His campaign speeches lashed out at Lincoln's alleged misrepresentations. Lincoln replied, and for weeks the two candidates followed each other around the state engaging in long-range debates by speaking on the same platform only days apart. Douglas finally agreed to meet Lincoln in seven face-to-face debates. These debates have become part of the folklore of American history. Thousands of farmers crowded into the seven towns to listen to three hours of outdoor oratory in weather ranging from stifling heat to cold rain. The campaign took on the character of high drama. It was David versus Goliath—only this time David, at 6 feet 4 inches, was nearly a foot taller than Goliath.

---

[14]Basler, *Works of Lincoln,* II, 461.

Douglas tried to put Lincoln on the defensive by identifying him with the abolitionists. The country *could* survive half slave and half free, said Douglas. It had done so from the beginning and there was no reason why it could not do so indefinitely. Popular sovereignty gave the residents of territories the choice to have slavery or not. In all remaining territories they were sure to exclude slavery, said Douglas, if given a fair choice. This would achieve what most Northerners wanted without the risk of disunion, which the Black Republicans would provoke with their abolitionist doctrine of "ultimate extinction."

Moreover, said Douglas, the Republicans favored black equality. He hammered away at this theme ad nauseam, especially in the Butternut counties of southern Illinois. "I do not believe that the Almighty ever intended the negro to be the equal of the white man," thundered Douglas as his partisans roared approval. "He belongs to an inferior race, and must always occupy an inferior position." America was a white man's country, "made by white men, for the benefit of white men and their posterity for ever, and I am in favor of confining citizenship to white men." "Do you desire to strike out of our State Constitution that clause which keeps slaves and free negroes out of the State?" shouted Douglas, while his supporters shouted back, "No, no."

Do you desire to turn this beautiful State into a free negro colony, ("no, no,") in order that when Missouri abolishes slavery she can send one hundred thousand emancipated slaves into Illinois, to become citizens and voters, on an equality with yourselves? ("Never," "no.") If you desire negro citizenship, if you desire to allow them to come into the State and settle with the white man, if you desire them to vote on an equality with yourselves . . . then support Mr. Lincoln and the Black Republican party, who are in favor of the citizenship of the negro.[15]

These tactics put Lincoln on the defensive. His speeches in the southern and central counties denied Douglas's accusations. Differences existed between the races, he said, that would "forever forbid [them] living together on terms of social and political equality." Lincoln assured his listeners "[that] I am not, nor ever have been, in favor of bringing about in any way the social and political equality of the white and black races [applause]—that I am not nor ever have been in favor of making voters or jurors of negroes, nor of qualifying them to hold office, nor to intermarry with white people."[16] Nor did he favor repeal of the Fugitive Slave Law, abolition of the interstate slave trade, or emancipation in the District of Columbia against the wishes of slave owners there, as Douglas had charged.

Lincoln took a more conservative position on these issues than did most Republicans in the upper North. But he could scarcely speak otherwise and hope to win in Illinois, one of the most race conscious of the free states. And at other times in the debates, he soared to a higher level of eloquence. "Let us discard all this quibbling about this man and the other man, this race and. . . the other race being inferior . . . and unite as one people throughout this land, until we shall once more stand up declaring that all men are created equal." Whether or not the black man was equal to the white man in mental endowment, said Lincoln, "in the right to eat the bread, without leave of anybody else, which his own hand earns, he is *my equal and the*

---

[15]Ibid., III, 9–10.
[16]Ibid., III, 145–146.

equal of Judge Douglas, and the equal of every living man. [Great applause]." While the Republicans did not intend to interfere with slavery in the states where it existed, they did intend to prevent its expansion. Unlike the Democrats, they "hold that this government was instituted to secure the blessings of freedom, and that slavery is an unqualified evil to the negro, to the white man, to the soil, and to the State." The real question was the morality of bondage. If it was right, it should exist everywhere; if wrong, everything possible should be done to restrict and ultimately to end it. "It is the eternal struggle between these two principles—right and wrong—throughout the world." Douglas "*looks to no end of the institution of slavery.*" The Republicans, on the other hand, "will, if possible, place it where the public mind shall rest in the belief that it is in the course of ultimate extinction, in God's good time."[17]

Although these debates illustrated the deep differences between Republican and Democratic attitudes toward slavery, they also reflected Republican ambivalence toward racial equality and the contradictions inherent in Lincoln's commitment to both "ultimate" emancipation and the indefinite continuation of slavery where it already existed. Douglas's insistence that the Republicans could not have it both ways hit uncomfortably close to the mark. But in 1858 this was the only way for Republicans to mediate the tension between the competing values of antislavery and union.

In any case, the voters of Illinois divided almost evenly in the election. Pro-Douglas candidates for the legislature polled heavy majorities in the southern half of the state, while Lincoln supporters did similarly well in the north. Republican candidates tallied 125,000 votes, the Douglas Democrats 121,000, and a handful of anti-Douglas Democrats 5,000. But Douglas carried a larger number of counties, which preserved the Democratic majority on the joint ballot in the legislature and enabled the party to reelect him. Elsewhere in the free states, the Democrats suffered another calamity. Their fifty-three Northern congressmen were reduced to a paltry thirty-one. Republicans won pluralities in Pennsylvania and Indiana as well as in Illinois—states that would give them the presidency in 1860 if they could retain their hold.

Portents of Armageddon, 1858–1859

Wedges of Sectional Division

Historians once thought that Lincoln had cleverly ruined Douglas's chances for the presidency by the question he put to him in their debate at Freeport. Could the people of a territory, Lincoln asked, lawfully exclude slavery before achieving statehood? In other words, could popular sovereignty be reconciled with the Dred Scott decision? If Douglas answered no, he would alienate many Northern Democratic voters and probably lose the current Senate contest. But if he answered yes, he would alienate the South and lose his party's presidential nomination in 1860.

The trouble with this theory is that Douglas had already alienated the South by his opposition to Lecompton, and he had already answered this question many times, beginning with his speech in June 1857 endorsing the Dred Scott decision (see

---

[17]Ibid., II, 501, III, 16, 92–93, 315.

page 116). At Freeport he again answered yes: the people of a territory could in effect exclude slavery despite its legal right to be there, by refusing to pass the kind of police regulations necessary to protect it. Lincoln knew that Douglas would give this answer, and he placed less importance on the question than it assumed in retrospect—indeed, the question ran somewhat counter to Lincoln's purpose, which was to identify Douglas with proslavery elements, not to alienate him from them.

Many Southern newspapers did denounce Douglas's "Freeport Doctrine," it is true, but they had already been berating Douglas for nearly a year on the Lecompton issue. Nevertheless, the Freeport Doctrine became the focus of a bitter and growing dispute that in 1860 formally split the Democratic party into Northern and Southern halves. This dispute concerned the question of a federal code of laws to protect slavery in the territories. If a territorial legislature refused to pass police regulations for this purpose, said Southerners, then Congress must do so. In February 1859, Senator Albert G. Brown of Mississippi told the Senate that unless such a federal slave code was passed, he would urge his state to secede. This set off a rancorous sectional debate in which Brown's colleague Jefferson Davis, among others, clashed ferociously with Douglas.

The Buchanan administration's renewed attempt to acquire Cuba also exacerbated sectional tensions. The President's purpose was twofold. He was an ardent expansionist and hoped to make the annexation of Cuba the centerpiece of his foreign policy. At the same time, the Cuban question might heal Democratic sectional wounds. Most Northern Democrats believed in Manifest Destiny. Whatever their attitudes toward slavery in Kansas, most were willing to welcome Cuba as a slave state. Here was an issue to bring Northern and Southern Democrats together again. Douglas endorsed annexation. The American minister in Madrid made clumsy efforts to bribe various factions in Spain to secure their support for the sale of Cuba. In Washington, Southern senators sponsored a bill for $30 million as a down payment. Republicans denounced the bid for Cuba as an outrageous maneuver to expand slavery. They managed to block the appropriation by postponements until the expiration of Congress on March 4, 1859.

In the meantime, Southern senators killed a bill for the granting of 160-acre homesteads to settlers. This measure had passed the House in February 1859 with the support of nearly all Republicans and two-thirds of the Northern Democrats. But Southerners opposed it. They saw it as a device to fill up the West with Yankee farmers. Minnesota and Oregon had just come in as states; Kansas would soon be admitted as a free state; the South was acutely conscious of the growing Northern majority in Congress and in the electoral college. Therefore, Southern senators and a handful of their Northern colleagues blocked the homestead bill in the short 1858–1859 session. The simultaneous defeat of the Cuban bill by Northern votes and the homestead bill by Southern votes gave each section another issue for 1860.

The Slave-Trade Controversy

A drive to reopen the African slave trade also joined the growing list of divisive sectional issues. This movement began in the early 1850s and grew to significant proportions by 1859. Most Southerners opposed the revival of the trade. But a substantial number of prominent men endorsed repeal of the 1807 law banning the importation of slaves. Jefferson Davis condemned that law as unconstitutional and as insulting to the South. The governor of South Carolina demanded the reopening of the trade. Two-thirds of the Southern congressmen voted against a House resolution condemning the agitation to reopen the trade. In 1859, the Southern Commercial Convention passed a resolution favoring repeal of the anti-importation laws. J. B. D. DeBow, editor of the South's leading commercial periodical, became president of the African Labor Supply Association, organized in 1859 to work for repeal.

Three reasons underlay this movement. The first was the rapid escalation of slave prices in the 1850s. Between 1849 and 1859, the average price of a prime male field hand rose from $1,000 to $1,700. This not only stretched the resources of wealthy planters but also priced ordinary farmers out of the market. At a time of growing concern about the loyalty of nonslaveholders to the plantation regime, the idea of lowering prices by importation in order to widen ownership was attractive. "Our true purpose," wrote the governor of South Carolina, "is to diffuse the slave population as much as possible, and thus secure in the whole community the motives of self-interest for its support."[18]

A second reason was psychological. Many Southerners considered the African slave trade immoral. Proslavery extremists feared that such a feeling might be only the first step toward a conviction that the internal slave trade and even slavery itself were wrong. "If it is right to buy slaves in Virginia and carry them to New Orleans," asked William L. Yancey, "why is it not right to buy them in Africa and carry them there?" A Texas editor bluntly told his readers: "If you agree to slavery, you must agree to the trade, for they are one. Those who are not for us must be against us. Those who deny slavery and the slave-trade are enemies of the South."[19]

Thirdly, the drive to reopen the trade became a weapon of Southern nationalism. Instead of always standing on the defensive, said one fire-eater, the South should carry on "active aggression." The slave-trade agitation was the best means for this, because it would give "a sort of spite to the North and defiance of their opinions." Two of the foremost fire-eaters and slave-trade advocates, Yancey and Edmund Ruffin of Virginia, founded the League of United Southerners in 1858 to "fire the Southern heart, instruct the Southern mind . . . and at the proper moment, by one organized, concerted action, we can precipitate the Cotton States into a revolution."[20]

Whatever its success in firing the Southern heart, the campaign to revive the African trade did not achieve its concrete goals. The lower house of the Louisiana legislature did authorize in 1858 the importation of African "apprentices" (a legal subterfuge for slavery), but the state senate did not concur. No other legislative body took action on this question.

But there appears to have been an increase in the illegal smuggling of slaves into the United States during the late 1850s. The most notorious case was that of the schooner *Wanderer,* owned by a prominent Southerner, Charles A. L. Lamar. In 1858,

---

[18]David M. Potter, *The Impending Crisis 1848–1861* (New York, 1976), p. 399.

[19]Ibid., p. 398; Ronald T. Takaki, *A Pro-Slavery Crusade: The Agitation to Reopen the African Slave Trade* (New York, 1971), p. 79.

[20]Potter, *Impending Crisis,* p. 399; Eric H. Walther, *The Fire-Eaters* (Baton Rouge, 1992), p. 71.

the *Wanderer* took on five hundred slaves in Africa, evaded British patrols, and eventually landed the four hundred surviving Africans in Georgia. Arrested by federal officials, the crew was acquitted by a Savannah jury despite firm evidence of their guilt. Lamar was even allowed to repurchase his ship at government auction for $4,000! At about the same time, a Charleston jury also acquitted the crew of another illegal trader. In the North these actions provoked outrage, which in turn called forth denunciations of Yankee hypocrisy. "What is the difference," asked a Mississippi newspaper, "between a Yankee violating the fugitive slave law in the North, and a Southern man violating . . . the law against the African slave trade in the South?"[21]

Whatever the difference, the slave-trade controversy seemed to confirm William H. Seward's description, in an 1858 speech, of an "irrepressible conflict" between slavery and freedom. Two books published within weeks of each other in 1857 punctuated this conflict: George Fitzhugh's *Cannibals All, or Slaves Without Masters;* and Hinton Rowan Helper's *The Impending Crisis of the South*.

The Rhetoric of Sectional Conflict

A member of Virginia's tidewater gentry, Fitzhugh had written numerous articles about "the failure of free society." In 1854, he collected several of these essays in a book entitled *Sociology for the South,* and he followed it with *Cannibals All* in 1857. Capitalism was a form of social cannibalism, said Fitzhugh. Slavery, on the other hand, was an ancient institution that guaranteed the employer's paternal interest in his workers. "What a glorious thing to man is slavery, when want, misfortune, old age, debility and sickness overtake him." All the problems of the North stemmed from its belief in the false doctrine that all men are created equal. "Men are not born entitled to equal rights," insisted Fitzhugh. "It would be far nearer the truth to say that some were born with saddles on their backs, and others booted and spurred to ride them; and the riding does them good. . . . Slavery is the natural and normal condition of the laboring man, whether white or black. . . . We slaveholders say you must recur to domestic slavery, the oldest, the best, and most common form of Socialism."[22]

Other proslavery partisans echoed Fitzhugh's arguments. George McDuffie, former governor of South Carolina, asserted that "the laboring population of no nation on earth are entitled to liberty, or capable of enjoying it." A Georgia newspaper exclaimed: "Free Society! we sicken at the name. What is it but a conglomeration of greasy mechanics, filthy operatives, small-fisted farmers, and moon-struck theorists . . . hardly fit for association with a southern gentleman's body servant."[23] A few years later, some of the farmers and mechanics in General Sherman's army would remember these words as they marched through Georgia and South Carolina.

The minimal impact of the Panic of 1857 in the South underscored Southern boasts about the superiority of their system. While many Northern businesses failed, banks closed, and factories shut down during the depression, causing unemployment and suffering among Northern workers during the winter of 1857–1858, cotton

---

[21]Takaki, *A Pro-Slavery Crusade*, p. 220.

[22]Harvey Wish (ed.), *Ante-Bellum: Writings of George Fitzhugh and Hinton Rowan Helper on Slavery* (New York, 1960), pp. 58, 82, 9, 85; Nevins, *Emergence of Lincoln*, I, 200n.

[23]Vernon L. Parrington, *The Romantic Revolution in America, 1800–1861,* Harvest Books ed. (New York, 1954), p. 77; Arthur C. Cole, *The Irrepressible Conflict 1850–1865* (New York, 1934), p. viii.

prices held firm and cotton crops set new records. This led Senator James Hammond to deliver his famous "King Cotton" speech in the Senate on March 4, 1858. Southerners were "unquestionably the most prosperous people on earth." Only the continued exports of cotton during the Panic, Hammond told the North, "saved you from destruction." This was conclusive proof of slavery's virtues. For that matter, Hammond went on:

> . . . your whole hireling class of manual laborers and "operatives," as you call them, are essentially slaves. . . . In all social systems there must be a class to do the menial duties, to perform the drudgery of life. . . . It constitutes the very mudsill of society. . . . Fortunately for the South, she found a race adapted to that purpose. . . . We use them for our purpose, and call them slaves. . . . Yours are white.[24]

Republicans naturally made political capital of such speeches. Several prominent Republicans came from humble origins: Nathaniel Banks had started as a bobbin boy in a textile mill; Massachusetts Senator Henry Wilson's father was a manual laborer and Wilson himself had been a shoemaker; the fathers of Thaddeus Stevens and Horace Greeley scratched a poor living from the soil; Abraham Lincoln's parents were semi-literate pioneers. These men served as living examples of upward mobility in a free-labor society. If the South thought that such men constituted the mudsill of society, this only confirmed Republican opinions of the South.[25] During the Lincoln-Douglas debates, Republicans in the audience held up banners with such slogans as "SMALL-FISTED FARMERS," "MUD SILLS OF SOCIETY," "GREASY MECHANICS," "FOR A. LINCOLN."

Hinton Rowan Helper was at the opposite pole from George Fitzhugh. Helper grew up in western North Carolina, an area of small farmers. His 1857 book, *The Impending Crisis of the South,* dealt with slavery's impact on the Southern economy. Using selected statistics from the 1850 census, Helper portrayed a South stagnating in backwardness while the North strode forward in seven-league boots. His account contrasted the near-universal literacy and comfortable living standards of Northern farmers and workers with the ignorance and poverty of Southern poor whites. What was the cause for this? "Slavery lies at the root of all the shame, poverty, ignorance, tyranny and imbecility of the South." Slavery monopolized the best land, degraded all labor to the level of bond labor, denied schools to workers, and impoverished all but "the lords of the lash" who "are not only absolute masters of the blacks [but] of all non-slaveholding whites, whose freedom is merely nominal, and whose unparalleled illiteracy and degradation is purposely and fiendishly perpetuated."[26] Although he demanded the abolition of slavery, Helper wasted no sympathy on the slaves, whom he wanted shipped back to Africa. He aimed his book at the non-slaveholding whites. He urged them to rise up, organize state Republican parties, and use their votes to overthrow the planters' rule and disenthrall the South.

Few nonslaveholders read his message, however. No Southern printer would publish *The Impending Crisis.* Helper had to move north and get it published in New York. When the book appeared in the summer of 1857, it made an immediate hit

---

[24] *Selections from the Letters and Speeches of the Hon. James H. Hammond, of South Carolina* (New York, 1866), pp. 317–319.

[25] Ironically, several prominent Southern leaders had also worked their way up from modest beginnings—including Senator Hammond.

[26] Wish, *Ante-Bellum,* pp. 201, 179.

with Republicans. Horace Greeley's *New York Tribune* gave it an unprecedented eight-column review. Leading Republicans raised money to print and circulate an abridged edition as a campaign document. This infuriated Southerners, especially as the Republicans added such inflammatory captions in the abridged edition as: "Revolution—Peacefully if we can, Violently if we must."[27] Slaveowners denounced the book as "incendiary, insurrectionary, and hostile to the peace and tranquility of the country."[28] Several states made circulation or possession of it a crime.

Helper's book played a role in provoking one of the most serious deadlocks in the history of Congress. The Republicans had a plurality but not a majority in the House that convened in December 1859. They nominated John Sherman of Ohio for Speaker. A moderate on slavery, Sherman had nevertheless endorsed Helper's book (without having read it), along with sixty-seven other Republican congressmen. To win the speakership, Sherman needed the support of a few border-state congressmen of the American party. A resolution introduced by a Missouri representative stating that no one who had endorsed *The Impending Crisis* was "fit to be Speaker of the House" inhibited the border-state men from voting for Sherman. The House took ballot after ballot without being able to choose a Speaker. For eight weeks the contest dragged on while tempers grew short, Northern and Southern congressmen hurled insults at one another, and members came armed to the sessions. One observer claimed that "the only persons who do not have a revolver and knife are those who have two revolvers."[29] A shootout on the floor of the House seemed a real possibility. The deadlock was finally resolved on the forty-fourth ballot, when Sherman withdrew and enough border-state Americans voted with the Republicans to elect the colorless William Pennington of New Jersey as Speaker.

The tension in Washington was heightened by John Brown's raid at Harpers Ferry, which had occurred less than two months before Congress met. This violent event climaxed more than a decade of rising sectional tensions. It also launched a year of portentous political events leading up to the presidential election of 1860.

---

[27]Potter, *Impending Crisis,* p. 387.

[28]Avery O. Craven, *The Growth of Southern Nationalism 1848–1861* (Baton Rouge, 1953), p. 251.

[29]Potter, *Impending Crisis,* p. 389.

The Critical Year, 1859– 1860

I John Brown am now quite certain that the crimes of this guilty land: will never be purged away; but with Blood.

—John Brown,
1859

John Brown and the Harpers Ferry Raid

Since his exploits during 1856 as a free-state guerrilla chieftain in Kansas, John Brown had been evolving an audacious plan for a strike against slavery in the South itself. Brown was a Calvinist who believed in a God of wrath and justice. His favorite biblical passage was: "Without shedding of blood there is no remission of sins." He was certain that the sin of slavery must be atoned in blood. With the single-mindedness of religious fanaticism, he was also certain that he was God's instrument to carry out the task. He planned to lead a raiding party into the Virginia mountains. There he would attract slaves from lowland plantations to his banner. He would arm them, establish a provisional freedmen's republic that could defend the mountain passes against counterattack, and move southward along the Appalachians, inspiring slave insurrections until the whole accursed system of bondage collapsed.

It was a wild scheme, but Brown managed to persuade several leading abolitionists of its practicality. From 1856 to 1859, he shuttled back and forth between Kansas, the Northeast, and settlements of former slaves in Canada, recruiting volunteers, raising money, and writing the constitution for his proposed black republic. Gerrit Smith, Thomas Wentworth Higginson, Theodore Parker, and three other Massachusetts abolitionists constituted a "Secret Six" who helped Brown raise money in New England. Ostensibly intended for Kansas, these funds were used instead to buy arms and supplies for Brown's invasion of the South.

JOHN BROWN.
Unlike most abolitionists, Brown believed that slavery could be ended only by the sword. The fierce determination of the Old Testament patriarchs and warriors on whom Brown modeled himself is expressed by the piercing eyes in this photograph taken in 1859, the year of his raid on Harpers Ferry.

LIBRARY OF CONGRESS

The abolitionists who supported Brown had become convinced that moral and political actions against slavery had failed. With the Kansas-Nebraska Act, the election of Buchanan, and the Dred Scott decision, slavery had gone on from one victory to another. A violent counterstroke was the only answer. The Secret Six regarded Brown as "a Cromwellian Ironside introduced in the nineteenth century for a special purpose . . . to take up the work of the English Puritans where it had ended with the death of Cromwell—the work of social regeneration."

Brown planned to capture the federal arsenal at Harpers Ferry, Virginia, and with the weapons seized there, to arm the thousands of slaves he expected to join him. In the summer of 1859, he rented a farm in Maryland across the river from Harpers Ferry and began gathering his seventeen white and five black recruits. Brown tried to persuade the black leader Frederick Douglass to join him. "I want you for a special purpose," he told Douglass. "When I strike, the bees will begin to swarm, and I shall want you to help hive them." But Douglass refused to participate. He tried to dissuade Brown from the mad enterprise. He could see the hopeless folly of invading Virginia and attacking federal property with an "army" of two dozen men.[1]

Situated at the confluence of the Potomac and Shenandoah rivers and surrounded by commanding heights, Harpers Ferry was a military trap. Brown's tactical plans were amateurish. He failed to inform any of the relatively few slaves in the area of

---

[1]Stephen B. Oates, *To Purge This Land With Blood: A Biography of John Brown* (New York, 1970), pp. 237, 283.

his intentions. He neglected to reconnoiter the terrain around Harpers Ferry to work out an escape route. And he did nothing about laying in supplies or establishing a defensive line against an inevitable counterattack. When he took eighteen men to seize the arsenal on the night of October 16, 1859, they carried no rations.

The little band captured the undefended arsenal, armory, and rifle works. But having gained his initial objectives, Brown seemed not to know what to do next. He sat down to await slave reinforcements; but the only blacks who joined him were a handful of bewildered slaves gathered up—along with white hostages—by patrols sent out by Brown for the purpose.

Meanwhile, news of the affair spread quickly. Local citizens and nearby militia companies mobilized on October 17. They captured the bridges across the Potomac and Shenandoah, cutting off Brown's escape, and drove the raiders out of the armory, the arsenal, and the rifle works. Three local men (including a free black) and several of Brown's men, including two of his sons, were killed or mortally wounded in the fighting. Seven raiders escaped (two were later captured) and the rest were driven into the stout fire-engine house, where Brown and the remaining four unwounded invaders made their last stand. During the night of October 17-18, a detachment of U.S. marines commanded by Colonel Robert E. Lee and Lieutenant J. E. B. Stuart surrounded the engine house. Next morning, Brown having refused to surrender, the marines stormed and carried the building with the loss of one man. They killed two more raiders and wounded Brown.

Thirty-six hours after it began, John Brown's war to liberate the slaves was over. Seventeen men had been killed, including ten raiders. Brown and his six captured confederates would eventually be hanged. Not a single slave had voluntarily joined the insurrection. Brown had left behind in the Maryland farmhouse a suitcase full of correspondence with the Secret Six and other Northern sympathizers. When this was captured and publicized, the Secret Six (except Higginson, who defiantly stood his ground) went into hiding or fled to Canada. Some of them later testified before a congressional committee, but none was indicted as an accessory.

In one sense the Harpers Ferry raid was a tragic, wretched failure. But in a larger sense, perhaps, if Brown's goal was to provoke a violent confrontation and liberate the slaves, he succeeded beyond his dreams. There is some evidence that Brown realized this—that he anticipated a martyrdom that would translate him from madman to saint in the eyes of many Northerners while it provoked fear and rage in the South that would hasten the final showdown. During his swift trial by the state of Virginia for murder, treason, and insurrection, Brown discouraged all schemes to cheat the hangman's rope by forcible rescue or pleas of insanity. "I am worth inconceivably more to *hang* than for any other purpose," he told family and friends.[2]

During the month between Brown's sentencing November 2 and his execution December 2, his demeanor won the admiration of millions in the North. He faced death with dignity. Nothing in his life became him like the leaving of it. The peroration of his speech to the court upon his sentencing became an instant classic:

This Court acknowledges, too, as I suppose, the validity of the law of God. I see a book kissed, which I suppose to be the Bible, or at least the New Testament, which teaches me that all things whatsoever I would that men should do to me, I should do even so to them. It teaches

---

[2]Ibid., p. 335.

me, further, to remember them that are in bonds as bound with them. I endeavored to act up to that instruction. I say I am yet too young to understand that God is any respecter of persons. I believe that to have interfered as I have done, as I have always freely admitted I have done, in behalf of His despised poor, is no wrong, but right. Now, if it is deemed necessary that I should forfeit my life for the furtherance of the ends of justice, and mingle my blood further with the blood of my children and with the blood of millions in this slave country whose rights are disregarded by wicked, cruel, and unjust enactments, I say, let it be done.

As he walked calmly to the gallows on December 2, Brown handed one of his jailers a note: "I John Brown am now quite *certain* that the crimes of this *guilty land: will never be purged away;* but with Blood."[3]

Brown's post-trial behavior elevated him to a sort of sainthood in Northern anti-slavery circles. Ralph Waldo Emerson said that Brown would "make the gallows as glorious as the cross." Henry Wadsworth Longfellow marked the day of Brown's execution as "the date of a new Revolution,—quite as much needed as the old one." Louisa May Alcott put these sentiments into verse:

No breath of shame can touch his shield
Nor ages dim its shine.
Living, he made life beautiful
Dying, made death divine.

Although prominent Republicans scrambled to dissociate themselves from Brown, some of them endorsed the nobility of his aims even while condemning his means. John Brown's act may have been foolish, said John Andrew, a rising star in the Massachusetts Republican party, but "John Brown himself is right." The *Springfield Republican,* a moderate paper, declared that no event "could so deepen the moral hostility to slavery as this execution. This is not because the acts of Brown are generally approved, for they are not. It is because the nature and spirit of the man are seen to be great and noble." On the day Brown was hanged, church bells tolled in many Northern towns. Cannons fired salutes. Prayer meetings adopted memorial resolutions. This outpouring of grief was an amazing phenomenon, a symbol of how deeply the antislavery purpose had penetrated the Northern consciousness.[4]

These manifestations of Northern sympathy for Brown sent a shock wave through the South more powerful than the raid itself had done. No matter that Northern Republicans disavowed Brown's act. No matter that Northern conservatives and Democrats got up their own meetings to denounce Brown and all who sympathized with him. Southerners could see only the expressions of grief for Brown's martyrdom. They identified Brown with the abolitionists, the abolitionists with Republicans, and Republicans with the whole North. Panic seized many parts of the South. Slave patrols doubled their surveillance. Volunteer military companies cleaned their weapons and stood by for action. Despite their claims that slaves were happy in bondage, many white Southerners knew better. They were aware that they lived atop a volcano that

---

[3]Oswald Garrison Villard, *John Brown, 1800–1859: A Biography Fifty Years After* (Boston, 1910), pp. 498–499, 554.

[4]For Northern reaction to Brown's raid and its aftermath, see Oates, *To Purge This Land With Blood,* pp. 308–356, Allan Nevins, *The Emergence of Lincoln,* 2 vols. (New York, 1950), II, 98–101; and Maury Klein, *Days of Defiance: Sumter, Secession, and the Coming of the Civil War* (New York, 1997), pp. 58–59.

might erupt at any time. Brown's raid evoked the deepest, darkest fears of Southern whites. Northern abolitionists, charged Edmund Ruffin of Virginia, "designed to slaughter sleeping Southern men and their awakened wives and children."

Secession sentiment mushroomed after Brown's raid. "The day of compromise is passed," exulted the fire-eating *Charleston Mercury*. Harpers Ferry had convinced even "the most bigoted Unionist that there is no peace for the South in the Union." And a former Whig confirmed sadly that the affair had "wrought almost a complete revolution in the sentiments, the thoughts, the hopes, of the oldest and steadiest conservatives in all the Southern states."[5]

Northern Democrats hoped to capitalize on the raid by portraying it, in Stephen Douglas's words, as the "natural, logical, inevitable result of the doctrines and teachings of the Republican party." Because William H. Seward was the leading contender for the Republican presidential nomination, Democrats focused most of their fire on him. His "bloody and brutal" Irrepressible Conflict speech (see page 122), they charged, was the inspiration for Brown's bloody and brutal act. The Democrats succeeded in putting the Republicans on the defensive. "Brown's invasion," admitted Massachusetts Senator Henry Wilson, "has thrown us, who were in a splendid position, into a defensive position. . . . If we are defeated next year we shall owe it to that foolish and insane movement of Brown's."[6]

The Democratic Party Breaks in Two

But political events soon put the Democrats, not the Republicans, on the defensive in the North. Southern Democrats resolved to repudiate Douglas's Freeport Doctrine and to block his nomination for president by insisting that the platform include a plank calling for a federal legal code to guarantee protection of slavery in all territories. Douglas, pledged to popular sovereignty, could not run on such a platform. At the prompting of William Lowndes Yancey, the Alabama Democratic party in January 1860 instructed its delegates to walk out of the national convention if the slave code plank was defeated. Twelve years earlier only one delegate had followed Yancey out of the national convention when a similar plank was rejected (see page 68). But this time Yancey could expect plenty of company.

When the national Democratic convention met in Charleston, South Carolina, on April 23, Douglas appeared to command a majority of the delegates but to fall short of the two-thirds that since 1836 had been necessary for the Democratic nomination. Emotions were at a fever pitch in Charleston. Yankee delegates felt like aliens in a hostile land. The tension mounted as the platform committee presented majority and minority reports to the convention. Southern partisans cheered as Yancey strode to the podium to speak for the slave code plank. The South must have security for its property, he said. "We are in a position to ask you to yield. What right of yours, gentlemen

---

[5]For Southern reaction, see Nevins, *Emergence of Lincoln*, II, 102–112; Oates, *To Purge This Land With Blood*, pp. 320–324; David M. Potter, *The Impending Crisis 1848–1861* (New York, 1976), pp. 380–384; and Klein, *Days of Defiance*, pp. 59–60.

[6]Oates, *To Purge This Land With Blood*, p. 310; C. Vann Woodward, "John Brown's Private War," in Woodward, *The Burden of Southern History* (Baton Rouge, 1960), p. 46.

of the North, have we of the South ever invaded? . . . Ours are the institutions which are at stake; ours is the peace that is to be destroyed; ours is the property that is to be destroyed; ours is the honor at stake." Douglas's delegates supported a motion to reaffirm the 1856 popular sovereignty plank with an added provision promising to obey a definitive Supreme Court ruling on the powers of a territorial legislature over slavery.[7] Beyond this the Northern Democrats could not go. The slave code plank would rub their faces in the dirt. The South was asking them to pronounce the extension of slavery a positive good. "Gentlemen of the South," declaimed an Ohio delegate, "you mistake us—you mistake us! We will not do it!"[8]

When the platform finally came to a vote after several days of debate, the popular sovereignty plank prevailed by a vote of 165 to 138 (free states, 154 to 30; slave states, 11 to 108). In a prearranged move, forty-nine delegates from eight Southern states followed Yancey out of the convention. They met in another hall, adopted the Southern rights platform, and waited to see what the main convention would do. Even after the Southern walkout, Douglas could not win two-thirds of the remaining delegates, to say nothing of two-thirds of the *whole* number, which the chairman ruled necessary for nomination. After fifty-seven ballots, the weary delegates gave up and adjourned, to meet again six weeks later in Baltimore.

Democratic leaders hoped that the postponement would allow tempers to cool and wiser counsels to prevail. But the jubilant Southern bolters were in no mood for reconciliation, save on their own terms. Some of them considered secession from the Democratic party the first step toward secession from the Union. On the night after the Southern exodus from the convention, an excited crowd gathered in front of the courthouse at Charleston to hear Yancey speak. He did not disappoint them. He concluded his ringing oration: "Perhaps even now, the pen of the historian is nibbed to write the story of a new revolution." The huge throng gave "three cheers for the Independent Southern Republic."[9]

The Southern bolters expected to attend the second convention in Baltimore on June 18. In alliance with Northern administration Democrats, they hoped to defeat Douglas again. But Douglas Democrats organized their own delegations from several Southern states. After a bitter fight over readmission of the Southern bolters, the Baltimore convention admitted some but rejected most of those from states where competing Douglas slates had been elected. This prompted a second walkout of Southerners. This time 110 delegates, more than a third of the total, departed to hold a Southern rights convention of their own. While the bolters nominated John C. Breckinridge of Kentucky (Buchanan's Vice President) on a slave code platform, the loyalists nominated Douglas. The divided and dispirited Democrats headed into the campaign against a united and dynamic Republican party.

---

[7]Because the question of a territorial legislature's power over slavery was not before the Court in the Dred Scott case, Taney's pronouncement on that matter had been an *obiter dictum*.

[8]*Speech of William L. Yancey of Alabama, Delivered in the National Democratic Convention*, p. 4; William B. Hesseltine (ed.), *Three Against Lincoln: Murat Halstead Reports the Caucuses of 1860* (Baton Rouge, 1960), p. 54.

[9]Robert W. Johannsen, "Douglas at Charleston," in Norman A. Graebner (ed.), *Politics and the Crisis of 1860* (Urbana, 1961), p. 90.

The Republicans Nominate Lincoln

The Republican national convention met at Chicago May 16 in a confident mood. Much would depend on their candidate. The party was sure to carry all but five or six Northern states and not a single Southern state, no matter whom they chose. But to win a majority of the electoral votes, they would need to carry Pennsylvania plus either Illinois or Indiana—all three of which had gone Democratic in 1856. This ruled out Salmon P. Chase, who was too radical for these states. It seemed to strengthen the candidacy of Edward Bates of Missouri, a colorless ex-Whig whom the quixotic Horace Greeley supported on the grounds that only Bates could carry the lower North. But Bates had backed the American party in 1856, which would hurt his candidacy among German Americans. Bates's lukewarm commitment to free soil was also out of tune with the party's antislavery ideology. Simon Cameron of Pennsylvania commanded the loyalty of his own state but that was all. A man of somewhat dubious integrity, Cameron had at various times been a Democrat, a Whig, and a Know-Nothing.

The leading candidate was Seward, who was supported by most of the delegates from the upper North. But Seward suffered from two handicaps. The first was his long career in public life. As governor and senator, he had made many enemies, including Greeley, who worked against Seward within his own New York bailiwick. Second, Seward's opposition to the Compromise of 1850, his "Higher Law" speech at that time (see page 73) and his "Irrepressible Conflict" speech in 1858 had given him a reputation for radicalism. Republican leaders from the lower North feared that Seward could not carry their states.

All of these factors strengthened the candidacy of Abraham Lincoln. Before the convention met, Lincoln had the support of little more than the Illinois delegation. But his lieutenants worked skillfully to pick up additional votes here and there—and, more important, to get second-choice commitments from several key states. Lincoln had all the right credentials. He was a former Whig in a party containing a majority of ex-Whigs. He had condemned slavery as a moral evil but deprecated radical action against it. He was an experienced politician who had won favorable notice in his campaign against Douglas but had not been in public life long enough to make a host of enemies. He had opposed nativism but not, like Seward, so conspicuously as to alienate nativist voters. His humble origins and homespun "honest Abe" image as a railsplitter were political assets.

The 1860 Republican platform appeared to be less radical than that of 1856. The 1860 resolutions dropped the references to polygamy and slavery as "twin relics of barbarism," condemned John Brown's raid as "the gravest of crimes," softened the language on exclusion of slavery from the territories without changing its meaning, and affirmed "the right of each state to order and control its own domestic institutions." To shed the party's nativist image, the platform opposed "any change in our naturalization laws" by which the rights of immigrants would be "abridged or impaired." The 1860 platform paid more attention than its predecessor to the economic interests of regional groups: it contained a protective tariff plank for Pennsylvania; it endorsed a homestead act to attract votes in the Midwest; it sanctioned rivers and harbors appropriations and government aid to build a transcontinental railroad. The platform was a composite of Whig and Free Soil ideas, a moderate but firm expression of the free-labor ideology of modernizing capitalism. As party platforms go, it was one of the most concise and concrete in American history—and one of the most successful in appealing to a broad spectrum of Northern voters.

The candidate matched the platform. All through the hectic night of May 17–18, frantic meetings of delegates from the lower North tried to unite on a candidate to stop Seward. Lincoln's lieutenants circulated tirelessly with the message that only their man could carry the whole North. They probably promised cabinet posts to Caleb Smith of Indiana and Simon Cameron of Pennsylvania. Lincoln had instructed his campaign managers to "make no contracts that will bind me," but in the words of his chief manager, "Lincoln ain't here, and don't know what we have to meet, so we will go ahead as if we hadn't heard from him, and he must ratify it."[10]

On the first ballot, Lincoln tallied 102 votes to Seward's 173 ½ (233 necessary to nominate). In the upper North, Seward had 132 to Lincoln's 19; in the crucial tier of six states from New Jersey to Iowa, Lincoln had 62 to Seward's 3 ½. Pennsylvania and several New England delegates switched to Lincoln on the second ballot, bringing him to 181 while Seward climbed to only 184 ½. Still more votes trickled to Lincoln on the third ballot. At the end of the roll call he had 231 ½ votes, only 1 ½ short of the nomination. A dramatic hush fell over the hall as an Ohio delegate leaped to his feet and announced the switch of four votes to Lincoln. Pandemonium reigned in Chicago as the state's favorite son became the nominee. The ticket was balanced by giving the vice-presidential nomination to Hannibal Hamlin, a former Democrat from Maine.

A fourth party also entered the lists in 1860. A coalition of former Southern Whigs who could not bring themselves to vote Democratic and Northern Whigs who considered the Republican party too radical formed the Constitutional Union party. This was essentially a revival of the 1856 American party shorn of its nativism. The strength of the Constitutional Unionists was concentrated in the upper South. The party adopted a platitudinous platform endorsing "the Constitution of the Country, the Union of the States, and the enforcement of the laws." It nominated John Bell of Tennessee for president and Edward Everett of Massachusetts for vice president. These men had no chance to win; the best they could hope for was to prevent a Republican victory by carrying enough electoral votes to throw the election into the House. The country braced itself for a four-party election that everyone recognized as the most crucial in its history.

The Campaign

The contest soon resolved itself into a two-party campaign in each section: Lincoln versus Douglas in the North and Breckinridge versus Bell in the South. The Republicans did not even put up a ticket in ten Southern states. And Douglas had no hope of carrying any of the same ten states. In the North, most of the old Whig/American constituency had gone over to the Republicans. And while Breckinridge gained the

---

[10]Potter, *Impending Crisis,* p. 428.

support of prominent Northern Democrats identified with the Buchanan administration, the Southern rights party could expect no Northern electoral votes. It became clear that the only way to beat Lincoln was by a fusion of the three opposing parties that might enable them to carry a solid South plus three or four crucial Northern states.

But formidable barriers stood in the way of such a fusion. The bitter divisions among Democrats could scarcely be forgiven or forgotten. A good many fire-eaters had worked to break up the party precisely in order to ensure the election of a Black Republican president and thereby to fire the Southern heart for secession. Even among Southern Democrats who deplored the schism, the gulf was now too wide to be bridged. The only fusion achieved in the South was a joint Bell-Douglas ticket in Texas, which won a paltry 24 percent of the vote against Breckinridge. Herculean efforts by party leaders in New York, Pennsylvania, Rhode Island, and New Jersey patched together fusion tickets in those states. But this proved futile, for Lincoln won a majority against the combined opposition in the first three states and an electoral plurality in New Jersey.

The likelihood that Lincoln would carry nearly all of the free states created a mood of despondency and fatalism among conservatives. At the same time a wave of mass hysteria swept through the South. John Brown's ghost stalked the Southern imagination. The prospect of a Republican president provoked fears that an abolitionized North would let loose dozens of John Browns on the South. Every stranger became an abolitionist agent; every black man with an inscrutable face became a potential Nat Turner. Southern newspapers reported hundreds of cases of arson, poisoning, and murder attributed to slaves. Several suspected insurrectionists, black and white, were lynched; scores were whipped or tarred and feathered; hundreds of Northern whites were ordered to leave on pain of death. A severe drought in the South that summer intensified the climate of hysteria.

Southern newspapers supporting Bell or Douglas insisted that the Breckinridge press was stirring up the insurrection panic to win votes for their candidate. Most of the scare stories, said one newspaper, "turned out, on examination, to be totally false, and *all of them* grossly exaggerated."[11] Modern historians agree. But false or not, the stories contributed to the tension that made the South ripe for revolution. At one time or another in 1860, nearly every spokesman in the lower South threatened or warned of secession if a Republican president was elected. Even the Bell and Douglas press issued such warnings. "This Government and Black Republicanism cannot live together," said Benjamin H. Hill, a leader of the Constitutional Union party in Georgia. A Douglas newspaper in Atlanta proclaimed: "Let the consequences be what they may, whether the Potomac is crimsoned in human gore, and Pennsylvania Avenue is paved ten fathoms deep with mangled bodies . . . the South will never submit to such humiliation and degradation as the inauguration of Abraham Lincoln."[12]

Republicans refused to take these threats seriously. They suspected, with good reason, that the warnings were aimed at Northern voters to frighten them from voting Republican. Southerners had threatened disunion in 1850, during the 1856 presidential

---

[11]William L. Barney, *The Road to Secession: A New Perspective on the Old South* (New York, 1972), p. 149.

[12]Emerson D. Fite, *The Presidential Campaign of 1860* (New York, 1911), p. 165; Dwight L. Dumond, *The Secession Movement, 1860–1861* (New York, 1931), p. 106.

election, during the House speakership battle in 1859, and at various other times. The latest warnings, said the Republican mayor of Chicago, were part of "the old game of scaring and bullying the North into submission to Southern demands and Southern tyranny."[13] The German-American leader Carl Schurz recalled that when Pennington was elected Speaker of the House, Southern congressmen had walked out, taken a drink, and then come back. After Lincoln's election, said Schurz, they would take two drinks and come back again.

Lincoln also refused to believe that "there will be any formidable effort to break up the Union." During the campaign, he observed the customary public silence of presidential candidates. As the election approached, he rejected pleas from conservative friends that he publish a statement to calm the South. "What is it I could say which would quiet alarm?" Lincoln asked. "Is it that no interference by the government, with slaves or slavery within the states, is intended? I have said this so often, already, that a repetition of it is but mockery, bearing an appearance of weakness, and cowardice . . . [and] encouraging bold bad men to believe they are dealing with one who can be scared into anything."[14]

Subsequent events, of course, proved that Southern threats of secession were not bluffs. Yet it is hard to see what Republicans could have done about it before the election, short of repudiating everything they stood for. "We regard every man . . . an enemy to the institutions of the South who does not boldly declare that he . . . believes African slavery to be a social, moral, and political blessing," announced a Douglas newspaper in Atlanta.[15] Under such circumstances, the Republicans could not have obtained a Southern hearing no matter how conciliatory they had tried to be, unless they came out foursquare for slavery.

While the main issue for the South was the Republican threat to slavery, Northern Democrats exploited racism in a fashion that had become standard. Democratic cartoons and banners proclaimed that a Black Republican victory would turn the North into a bedlam of "nigger equality," racial amalgamation, and all manner of similar evils. Cartoons showed black men kissing white women while Lincoln and Horace Greeley looked on benevolently. Such propaganda flourished especially in New York, where the Republican legislature had placed on the ballot a constitutional amendment to eliminate the discriminatory $250 property qualification for black voters. Recognizing their vulnerability on this issue, most Republican speakers and newspapers ignored the amendment or endorsed it lukewarmly. While Lincoln carried New York with 54 percent of the vote, the amendment received just 37 percent. Only two-thirds of the state's Republicans voted for it, though most upstate antislavery counties gave the amendment solid majorities.

While in the upper North the Republicans concentrated on the slavery issue, in the lower North they stressed economic issues: the homestead plank in the Midwest, the tariff plank in Pennsylvania, and the rivers and harbors and Pacific railroad planks in areas that would benefit from these measures. Only two of twenty-seven

---

[13]*New York Herald,* August 1, 1860.

[14]Roy P. Basler (ed.), *The Collected Works of Abraham Lincoln,* 9 vols. (New Brunswick, N.J., 1953–1955), IV, 132–133.

[15]Barney, *Road to Secession,* p. 156.

ILLINOISE STATE HISTORICAL SOCIETY

ABRAHAM LINCOLN AT HOME DURING THE ELECTION OF 1860.   Observing the custom that presidential candidates did not campaign for themselves, Lincoln remained at home in Springfield, greeting delegations of supporters who came to visit him. His 6-foot, 4-inch frame towers above the crowd just to the right of the front door.

banners in a Republican rally at Lincoln's hometown of Springfield referred to slavery. "The Republicans, in their speeches, say nothing of the nigger question," complained a Pennsylvania Democrat, "but all is made to turn on the Tariff."[16] In truth, the Democrats had handed the Republicans these issues on a silver platter. During the 1859–1860 session of Congress, Democratic votes had defeated a Pacific railroad bill, a rivers and harbors bill, and an increase in the low 1857 tariff. And President Buchanan had vetoed a homestead act. Here was graphic proof to Northern voters, if any more was needed, that the South and its "doughface lackeys" were blocking measures vital to the growth and prosperity of the country.

The relationship between Republicans and abolitionists in 1860 was ambivalent. Many abolitionists denounced the Republican party as being, in Garrison's words, a "timeserving, a temporizing, a cowardly party" because it was pledged to restriction rather than destruction of slavery. Republicans' descriptions of themselves as the true "White Man's Party" because they wanted to reserve the territories for free white labor also drew abolitionist fire. So did Lincoln's statements opposing interference with

[16]Reinhard H. Luthin, *The First Lincoln Campaign* (Cambridge, Mass., 1944), pp. 183, 208.

slavery in the states, curtailment of the interstate slave trade, and repeal of the Fugitive Slave Law. In most areas, the Republicans held abolitionists at arm's length because association with these "fanatics" would lose votes.

But in parts of the upper North, especially New England, relations between Republicans and abolitionists were cordial. Republican gubernatorial candidates John Andrew of Massachusetts and Austin Blair of Michigan were abolitionists in all but name. So were numerous Republican senators and congressmen and virtually the whole Republican party of Vermont. Several out-and-out abolitionists campaigned for Lincoln. Most Garrisonians said privately that despite Republican shortcomings, "Lincoln's election will indicate growth in the right direction." The Radical Abolitionist party, a tiny remnant of Liberty party veterans, held a convention in 1860 and nominated Gerrit Smith for president. But this "fifth-party" nomination was little more than a gesture, and Smith received a negligible number of votes. Most political abolitionists had joined the Republican party, where they constituted a radical cell that gave the party a crusading, militant tone in the upper North.[17]

Emotion pervaded the campaign in the North as well as in the South. But whereas fear prevailed in the South, the Republicans mobilized zeal in the North. The free-labor symbolism of Lincoln the railsplitter was irresistible. Republican Wide Awakes marched in huge parades, singing political songs and bearing torches mounted on fence rails. (A year later many of these same men would be marching with muskets and singing "John Brown's Body.")

Douglas broke with tradition and campaigned personally in all parts of the country. From the outset he knew that he had little chance of victory. But he took seriously the Southern threats of disunion and strove courageously to meet them head-on. His speeches contained eloquent appeals for all Americans to rally behind the Union. Although ill and exhausted, Douglas maintained a killing pace (less than a year later, at the age of forty-eight, he died.) In many ways this was his finest hour—though reflective observers noted that part of the whirlwind the country was now reaping had been sown in Kansas six years earlier by Douglas himself.

While campaigning in Iowa, Douglas learned that the Republicans had carried the October state elections in Pennsylvania, Ohio, and Indiana. "Mr. Lincoln is the next President," said Douglas. "We must try to save the Union. I will go South." At considerable personal risk, he campaigned through the lower South, denouncing disunion at every stop. He rested in Mobile on the day of the election. When Douglas observed the reaction of Alabamians to Lincoln's victory, he returned to his hotel, said his secretary, "more hopeless than I had ever before seen him."[18]

The Outcome

From the Democratic viewpoint the result was indeed discouraging. Lincoln won all the electoral votes in the free states except New Jersey (where he won four and Douglas three); he carried 54 percent of the popular vote in the North; and he won an ab-

---

[17] James M. McPherson, *The Struggle for Equality: Abolitionists and the Negro in the Civil War and Reconstruction* (Princeton, 1964), chap. 1.

[18] Robert W. Johannsen, *Stephen A. Douglas* (New York, 1973), pp. 797–798, 803.

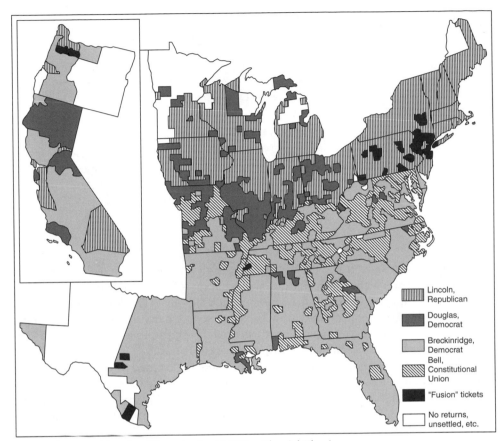

Counties Carried by Candidates in the 1860 Presidential Election

solute majority over his combined opponents in all but three Northern states (California, Oregon, New Jersey). Thus he would have garnered a majority of the electoral votes in the whole country even if his opposition had combined against him, as is shown in Table 8.1. Lincoln won no electoral votes in the slave states and scarcely any popular votes outside of a few urban counties in the border states. Douglas ran second in the North but won the electoral votes only of Missouri plus the three in New Jersey. Bell carried Virginia, Kentucky, and his native Tennessee, while Breckinridge carried the rest of the South.

In the upper North—New England and upstate New York, Michigan, Wisconsin, and Minnesota plus the Yankee counties of Ohio, Indiana, Illinois, and Iowa—Lincoln carried more than 60 percent of the vote. In the remaining portions of the free states, he barely won 50 percent. Thus it was the strongly antislavery portion of the North that had carried the election and would emerge as the dominating force among congressional Republicans. This fact did not go unnoticed in the South.

Until 1856, no major party had expressed a clear opposition to slavery. Only four years later, the Northern states elected a president who hoped for the ultimate extinction of the institution. According to a New Orleans newspaper, this was "full of

Table 8.1   Voting in the 1860 Election

	ALL STATES		FREE STATES (18)		SLAVE STATES (15)	
	Popular Votes	*Electoral Votes*	*Popular Votes*	*Electoral Votes*	*Popular Votes*	*Electoral Votes*
Lincoln	1,864,735	180	1,838,347	180	26,388	0
Opposition to Lincoln	2,821,157	123	1,572,637	3	1,248,520	120
Fusion	595,846	—	580,426	—	15,420	—
Douglas	979,425	12	815,857	3	163,568	9
Breckinridge	669,472	72	99,381	0	570,091	72
Bell	576,414	39	76,973	0	499,441	39

portentous significance. It shows, beyond all question or peradventure, the unmixed sectional animosity with which an enormous majority of the Northern people regard us of the South." The *Richmond Examiner* stated bluntly: "The idle canvass prattle about Northern conservatism may now be dismissed. A party founded on the single sentiment . . . of hatred to African slavery, is now the controlling power. . . . No clap trap about the Union . . . can alter [this] or weaken its force."[19]

The reaction of antislavery men to Lincoln's election seemed to confirm Southern fears. The abolitionists Wendell Phillips and Frederick Douglass had vigorously criticized Republican defects. But the day after the election, Phillips told a celebrating crowd in Boston: "For the first time in our history the *slave* has chosen a President of the United States (Cheers). We have passed the Rubicon." No longer would the slave power rule the country, said Douglass. "Lincoln's election has vitiated their authority and broken their power. . . . It has demonstrated the possibility of electing, if not an Abolitionist, at least an *anti-slavery reputation* to the Presidency." And Charles Francis Adams, the son and grandson of presidents, a founder of the Free Soil and Republican parties in Massachusetts, declared that with Lincoln's election "the great revolution has actually taken place. . . . The country has once and for all thrown off the domination of the Slaveholders."[20]

In response to this Northern revolution, the South launched its own counter-revolution of secession.

---

[19] *New Orleans Daily Crescent,* November 13, 1860, and *Richmond Semi-Weekly Examiner,* November 9, 1860, in Dwight L. Dumond (ed.), *Southern Editorials on Secession* (New York, 1931), pp. 237, 223.

[20] McPherson, *Struggle for Equality,* p. 27; Charles Francis Adams, Diary, November 7, 1860, quoted in Eric Foner, *Free Soil, Free Labor, Free Men* (New York, 1970), P. 223.

Chapter Nine

Secession and the Coming of War

*Our new government is founded upon . . .
the great truth that the negro is not equal to
the white man; that slavery—subordination
to the superior race—is his natural and
normal condition.*

—Alexander H. Stephens,
Confederate Vice President, March 21, 1861

Secession of the Lower South

As the telegraph flashed news of Lincoln's election, the South Carolina legislature called a convention to take the state out of the Union. Within six weeks the six other states of the lower South had also called conventions. Their voters elected delegates after short but intensive campaigns. Each convention voted by a substantial (in most cases an overwhelming) margin to secede.[1] By February 9, 1861, three months after Lincoln's election, commissioners from these states meeting in Montgomery, Alabama, had adopted a provisional constitution for the Confederate States of America and elected Jefferson Davis provisional president. By way of comparison, the second Continental Congress

---

[1]The dates and votes on secession ordinances were as follows:

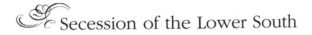

South Carolina, 20 Dec., 169-0	Georgia, 19 Jan., 208-89
Mississippi, 9 Jan., 85-15	Louisiana, 26 Jan., 113-17
Florida, 10 Jan., 62-7	Texas, 1 Feb., 166-8
Alabama, 11 Jan., 61-39	

The average vote in these seven conventions was 83 percent in favor of secession, 17 percent opposed. Five of the conventions took preliminary votes on whether to delay separate state secession in favor of some vaguely defined cooperative action by the South as a whole. These motions lost, but by a closer margin—an average of 40 percent in favor of delay, to 60 percent opposed. It is clear that a large majority of delegates in these seven states favored secession in some form.

took fourteen months to adopt the Declaration of Independence, and a full year elapsed between the first call for a convention in 1786 and the drafting of the U.S. Constitution; the National Assembly of France met for two years before promulgating the new constitution of 1791.

Although secession proceeded with extraordinary speed in the lower South, the appearance of solidarity masked some internal divisions. Three basic positions had emerged by December 1860. The first and most radical was "immediate secession." Proponents of this viewpoint believed that each state should secede on its own without waiting for collective action by the South as a whole. The immediate secessionists were strongest in the high-slaveholding counties that had gone for Breckinridge in 1860. But many nonslaveholding Democrats and slaveholding Whigs were also swept into the immediatist camp by the perceived Republican threat to white supremacy and slavery. The second position was known as "cooperation." Its supporters urged delay until the South could formulate a collective response to Lincoln's election. The cooperationists drew their greatest strength from upland counties with fewer slaves and from areas that had supported Bell or Douglas for president. The third position was one of outright opposition to secession. These "unconditional Unionists" lived mostly in the border states; they could scarcely be found in the lower South.

Except in South Carolina, where secessionist sentiment was overwhelming, cooperationist voters may have constituted 40 percent of the total in the lower South. This caused many Northerners to overestimate the strength of Southern Unionism. They failed to appreciate that cooperationism and Unionism were quite different things. The cooperationists divided into three overlapping and shifting groups, which can be labeled cooperative secessionists, ultimatumists, and conditional Unionists. All three groups believed in the right of secession, but they disagreed on method and timing. This led to much confusion. "Here in New Orleans nobody knows exactly what cooperation means," complained the *New Orleans Crescent* on January 5, 1861. "With some it means delay, with some conference with other states, with some it means submission." In essence, cooperative secessionists wanted the South to act as a unit, for they believed that individual state secessions would produce division and weakness. Ultimatumists wanted the Southern states to agree on an ultimatum to the Republicans demanding certain concessions. If the Republicans refused, the South would go out. Conditional Unionists urged the South to delay action to give the incoming Lincoln administration an opportunity to prove its peaceful intentions. Not until the North committed some "overt act" against Southern rights, they said, should the South take such an extreme step as secession.

Of the cooperationists, only the conditional Unionists offered much hope of preventing disunion. And they were strong only in Georgia and Louisiana. Cooperationists in other states insisted that their zeal for Southern rights was no less fervent than that of the immediate secessionists. "We do not associate with submissionists!" insisted Alabama cooperationists. "We scorn the Black Republican rule. . . . We intend to resist . . . but our resistance is based upon consultation, and in unity of action, with the other slave states."[2] The kinds of concessions that ultimatumists asked for would have required the Republican party to repudiate what it stood for. Ultimatumists demanded a federal slave code for all territories, a pledge not to interfere

---

[2]Dwight L. Dumond, *The Secession Movement, 1860–1861* (New York, 1931), pp. 201–202, 122.

with the interstate slave trade, repeal of personal liberty laws by Northern states, compensation to slaveholders for property lost through Northern failure to enforce the Fugitive Slave Law, and other concessions of similar purport.

Republican spokesmen soon made clear the party's opposition to such concessions. This put the cooperationists on the defensive. By January 1861, the momentum of individual state secession became irresistible in the lower South. As each state seceded, it appointed commissioners to the other conventions about to meet. These commissioners gave fiery speeches urging each of the remaining states to join those that had already gone out. The barrage of mass meetings and newspaper publicity added to the pressures that caused cooperationists to cave in. Even conditional Unionists jumped aboard the secession bandwagon, for to stay off would have looked like treason to the South. The most prominent conditional Unionist, Alexander H. Stephens of Georgia, became vice president of the Confederacy.

Secession: Revolution or Counterrevolution?

Many Southerners proclaimed secession to be a revolution in the image of 1776. "The tea has been thrown overboard," declared the *Charleston Mercury* when Lincoln's election was announced. "The revolution of 1860 has been initiated." Pierre Soulé, former leader of the Douglas Democrats in Louisiana, said after the election that faced with a choice between "ignominy and revolution, I choose revolution." Senator Judah P. Benjamin of Louisiana described the "wild torrent of passion" that was "carrying everything before it" as "a revolution; a revolution of the most intense character" that could "no more be checked by human effort than a prairie fire by a gardener's watering pot."[3]

Benjamin was right about the intense torrent of passion sweeping the South. Mass meetings roared their approval of speakers who called for Southern independence. Secession functioned as a catharsis for the tension that had been building to a level of near hysteria since the John Brown raid a year earlier. "The minds of the people are aroused to a pitch of excitement probably unparalleled in the history of our country," wrote one Southerner. And a Virginia conservative lamented that "the desire of some for change, the greed of many for excitement . . . seems to have unthroned the reason of men, and left them at the mercy of passion."[4]

Many secessionists expected their revolution to be a peaceful one. Robert Barnwell Rhett, editor of the *Charleston Mercury,* was quoted as saying that he would eat the bodies of all men slain as a consequence of disunion, while Senator James Chesnut of South Carolina was said to have offered to drink all the blood shed in the cause. A Georgia newspaper announced: "So far as civil war is concerned, we have no fears of that in Atlanta."[5]

---

[3] *Charleston Mercury,* November 8, 1860; Soulé quoted in Willie M. Caskey, *Secession and Restoration of Louisiana* (University La., 1938), pp. 21–22; Judah Benjamin to Samuel L. M. Barlow, December 9, 1860, S. L. M. Barlow Papers, Henry E. Huntington Library.

[4] Charles G. Sellers, "The Travail of Slavery," in Charles G. Sellers (ed.), *The Southerner as American* (Chapel Hill, 1960), pp. 69–70.

[5] E. Merton Coulter, *The Confederate States of America* (Baton Rouge, 1950), pp. 14–15; *Atlanta Daily Intelligencer,* January 28, 1861, quoted in Donald E. Reynolds, *Editors Make War: Southern Newspapers in the Secession Crisis* (Nashville, 1970), p. 174.

While hoping for peace, however, secessionists knew that most revolutions succeed only by violence. All the seceding states strengthened their militia and encouraged the formation of new volunteer military companies, which often called themselves Minute Men. As they declared themselves out of the Union, the states seized federal arsenals and forts to arm and equip these military organizations. One of the first acts of the provisional Confederate government was to authorize an army of 100,000 men.

Although many Confederates looked to 1776 as their model, secession was not a revolution in the usual sense of the word. Armed revolt against an established government is by definition illegal, but most secessionists insisted that their action was legal and constitutional. Senator Louis T. Wigfall of Texas would not have favored secession "if I believed that the act of secession was one of revolution, that it was one in direct conflict with the Constitution of the United States that I am sworn to obey."[6] But he did favor it, for like most Southerners he believed in the "compact" theory of the Constitution. This theory had a long history going back to the Virginia and Kentucky Resolutions of 1798. It held that the U.S. Constitution was a compact among states that had authorized the federal government to act as their agents in the exercise of certain functions of sovereignty. But the states had never transferred the sovereignty itself. Having delegated these functions by the ratifying act of a convention, a state could withdraw from the compact and reassert its full sovereignty by the act of another convention. This was precisely what the seceding states did in 1861.

Of course, a good many Confederates believed in both the legal and the revolutionary rights of secession. "There is no incompatibility between the right of secession by a State and the right of revolution by the people," said a Southern theorist. "The one is a civil right founded upon the Constitution; the other is a natural right resting upon the law of God."[7] But as time passed, the emphasis on the right of revolution diminished while that on the legal right of secession increased, as Confederate leaders pondered the possible consequences of their action. By insisting that secession was legal rather than revolutionary, they intended to place the Confederacy on firm and safe ground in the eyes of the world. Moreover, some feared that an outpouring of revolutionary rhetoric might happen to fall upon the wrong ears—after all, "liberty" and "rights" could mean something quite different to slaves than to masters. Although seceding states quoted the part of the Declaration of Independence that justified the dissolution of old governments and the formation of new ones, they did *not* quote the part that affirmed that all men are created equal and endowed with the inalienable right of liberty.

Abolitionists and Republicans were not slow to point out the incongruity—indeed the logical contradiction—of a revolution for the defense of slavery. Secession was "the oddest Revolution that History has yet seen," wrote an abolitionist editor, "a Revolution for the greater security of Injustice, and the firmer establishment of Tyranny!" The *New York Tribune* best summarized the Republican attitude: "Mr. Jefferson's Declaration of Independence was made in the interest of natural rights against Established Institutions. Mr. Jeff. Davis's caricature thereof is made in the interest of an

---

[6]*Congressional Globe*, 36th Cong., 2nd sess. (1860), 12.
[7]Jesse T. Carpenter, *The South as a Conscious Minority, 1789–1861* (New York, 1930), p. 196.

unjust, outgrown, decaying Institution against the apprehended encroachments of Natural Human Rights." It was therefore not a revolution but a counterrevolution, a "rebellion in the interest of darkness, of despotism and oppression."[8]

Thus challenged, Confederate leaders responded that indeed they were defending established institutions. "Ours is not a revolution," said Jefferson Davis. "We are not engaged in a Quixotic fight for the rights of man; our struggle is for inherited rights." We left the Union "to save ourselves from a revolution" that threatened to make "property in slaves so insecure as to be comparatively worthless." The South's foremost journalist, J. B. D. DeBow, maintained that "we are not revolutionists; we are resisting revolution. We are upholding the true doctrines of the Federal Constitution. We are conservative." On March 21, 1861, Confederate Vice President Stephens proclaimed that the "present revolution" was one to preserve "the proper status of the negro in our form of civilization." The affirmation of equality in the Declaration of Independence was wrong. "Our new government," said Stephens, "is founded upon exactly the opposite idea; its foundations are laid, its cornerstone rests, upon the great truth that the negro is not equal to the white man; that slavery—subordination to the superior race—is his natural and normal condition. This, our new government, is the first in the history of the world based upon this great physical, philosophical, and moral truth."[9]

During the secession crisis, Southerners quoted from hundreds of Republican speeches and editorials to prove that it was the Republicans who were the revolutionists, not they. Their favorites for this purpose were Seward and Lincoln. These men were the leaders of their party, said Southerners. If anyone truly represented Republican intentions, they did. In his "Irrepressible Conflict" speech, Seward had predicted the ultimate victory of the free-labor ideology. "I know, and you know, that a revolution has begun," he had said in 1858. "I know, and all the world knows, that revolutions never go backward." And in his "House Divided" address, Lincoln had announced that the Republicans intended to place slavery "where the public mind shall rest in the belief that it is in the course of ultimate extinction."[10]

Whether ultimate or imminent, the extinction of slavery was precisely what the South feared. No matter how moderate the Republicans professed to be, no matter how many assurances they gave that slavery in the states would be safe under their rule, nothing could gainsay their ultimate purpose to destroy the institution. No one should "be deluded . . . into the belief that the Black Republican party is a moderate and conservative, rather than a radical and progressive party," warned the *New Orleans Delta*. "It is, in fact, essentially a revolutionary party."[11]

Secessionists conjured up a frightening scenario of future Republican actions: exclusion of slavery from the territories would bring in so many new free states that the South would be overwhelmed in Congress and encircled by free territory; Lincoln

---

[8]*National Anti-Slavery Standard*, December 1, 1860; *New York Tribune*, May 21, 1862.

[9] Dunbar Rowland (ed.), *Jefferson Davis, Constitutionalist: His Letters, Papers and Speeches*, 10 vols. (Jackson, Miss., 1923), VI, 357, V, 50, 72; *DeBow's Review*, 33 (1862), 44; *Augusta Daily Constitutionalist*, March 30, 1861.

[10]George E. Baker (ed.), *The Works of William H. Seward*, 5 vols. (Boston, 1853–1884), IV, 302; Roy P. Basler (ed.), *The Collected Works of Abraham Lincoln*, 9 vols. (New Brunswick, N.J., 1953–1955), II, 461.

[11]*New Orleans Delta*, November 3, 1860.

would appoint Republican justices to the Supreme Court and thus turn this bastion of Southern protection into an engine of destruction; Congress would repeal the Fugitive Slave Law and slaves would flee northward by the thousands; Congress would abolish slavery in the District of Columbia and on all federal property such as forts and arsenals, navy yards and customs houses; the government would stand by and do nothing while new John Browns led armies of insurrection into the South. "Now that the black radical Republicans have the power I suppose they will [John] Brown us all," exclaimed a South Carolinian when he learned of Lincoln's election. "We shall be in a State of Revolution forthwith," echoed another.[12]

The greatest concern of some secessionists was the possibility that the Republican party might have some attraction for nonslaveholders, especially in the border South and the upcountry. What if Hinton Rowan Helper was right about the yeomen farmers' alienation from the planter elite? "The great lever by which the abolitionists hope to extirpate slavery in the States is the aid of non-slaveholding citizens in the South," worried one editor. If the Republicans used the patronage cleverly by appointing nonslaveholders to federal offices in the South, they might build up "a party with supporters for the incoming administration here in our midst." This might prove to be the entering wedge to "Helperize" the South.[13]

To prevent such a calamity, secessionists invoked Herrenvolk democracy to remind yeomen of their racial stake in defending slavery. Lincoln's election, declared an Alabama newspaper, "shows that the North [intends] to free the negroes and force amalgamation between them and the children of the poor men of the South." Thus nonslaveholders "will never consent to submit to abolition rule," said Georgia's secessionist governor Joseph E. Brown, for they "know that in the event of the abolition of slavery, they would be greater sufferers than the rich, who would be able to protect themselves. . . . When it becomes necessary to defend our rights against so foul a domination, I would call upon the mountain boys as well as the people of the lowlands, and they would come down like an avalanche and swarm around the flag of Georgia."[14] Most nonslaveholding whites in 1861—at least in the seven states that seceded by February—seemed to respond favorably to this argument that "democratic liberty exists solely because we have black slaves" whose presence "promotes equality among the free." They therefore supported the "political revolution" of secession whose purpose was to avert the "social revolution" that would come with Republican rule.[15]

Southern political skills and Southern domination of the Democratic party had given the slave states disproportionate power in the national government. From 1789 to 1861, twenty-three of the thirty-six Speakers of the House and twenty-four of the

---

[12] Mary Boykin Chesnut, *A Diary from Dixie,* ed. Isabel D. Martin and Myrta Lockett Avary (New York, 1905), p. 1; James L. Roark, *Masters Without Slaves: Southern Planters in the Civil War and Reconstruction* (New York, 1977), p. 6.

[13] Dumond, *The Secession Movement,* p. 117n.; Daniel W. Crofts, *Reluctant Confederates: Upper South Unionists in the Secession Crisis* (Chapel Hill, 1989), p. 154.

[14] Reynolds, *Editors Make War,* pp. 125–126; Michael P. Johnson, *Toward a Patriarchal Republic: The Secession of Georgia* (Baton Rouge, 1977), p. 48; Steven Hahn, *The Roots of Southern Populism: Yeoman Farmers and the Transformation of the Georgia Upcountry, 1850–1890* (New York, 1983), pp. 86–87.

[15] J. Mills Thornton III, *Politics and Power in a Slave Society: Alabama, 1800–1860* (Baton Rouge, 1978), pp. 320, 206–207; Johnson, *Toward a Patriarchal Republic,* p. 47.

thirty-six presidents pro tem of the Senate had been Southerners. Twenty of the thirty-five Supreme Court justices had come from slave states, and at all times since 1789 the South had had a majority on the Court. During forty-nine of these seventy-two years the president of the United States had been a Southerner—and a slave-holder. During twelve additional years, including most of the crucial 1850s, the presidents were Northern Democratic "doughfaces." Lincoln's election foreshadowed an end to all this. It was a signal that the country had turned a decisive political corner toward a future dominated by the ideology and institutions of the North. For the Old South this seemed to spell disaster, so its leaders launched a counterrevolution of independence to escape the dreaded consequences. "These are desperate means," admitted a secessionist, "but then we must recollect that we live in desperate times. Not only our property but our honor, our lives and our all are involved." We must decide, said fire-eater Edmund Ruffin of Virginia, "whether the institution of negro slavery on which the social and political existence of the south rests, is to be secured by our resistance, or . . . abolished . . . as the certain result of our present submission to northern domination."[16]

The Northern Response to Secession

While the lower South acted rapidly and decisively, the North floundered in uncertainty and confusion. The "lame-duck" syndrome crippled the government's will to act: President Buchanan and the current Congress held power but lacked a recent mandate; the President and Congress elected in November would not take office until March 4, by which time the Confederacy would be a fait accompli. But even if the Republicans had controlled the government during the winter, they would have been helpless to stem the tide of secession, for they had no clear conception of what to do about it.

For several weeks after the election, most Republicans urged a "Fabian policy" of "masterly inactivity." They would sit tight and do nothing to encourage secessionists or to undercut Southern Unionists. Lincoln and Seward were the chief exponents of this approach. They expected the secession fever to run its course without taking more than one or two states out of the Union. Then the good sense and basic loyalty of the South would reassert itself, and the "erring sisters" would return. This of course was a misreading of the situation in the lower South, as events soon revealed.

President Buchanan and the Crisis

Meanwhile, Buchanan took more seriously the gravity of the situation. He was in a difficult position. He believed that the crisis, having been precipitated by Lincoln's election, was Lincoln's responsibility. But Buchanan's term had nearly four months to go, and during that time the constitutional responsibility was his. He hoped that somehow he could keep the government afloat and preserve peace until relieved of

---

[16]Reynolds, *Editors Make War*, p. 150.; Maury Klein, *Days of Defiance: Sumter, Secession, and the Coming of the Civil War*, (New York, 1997),p. 23.

his duties on March 4. Yet he was buffeted by conflicting pressures from the Southern and Northern wings of his party. Most of his advisers were Southerners. Secretary of the Treasury Howell Cobb of Georgia and Secretary of the Interior Jacob Thompson of Mississippi were secessionists marking time in Washington until their states went out. Secretary of War John Floyd of Virginia, under fire for malfeasance in office and under suspicion of treason for having transferred arms to Southern arsenals, would soon declare openly his support for secession.

Despite the Southern orientation of his administration, Buchanan could not accept disunion. His annual message on December 3 declared secession illegal. The Union was more than a "mere voluntary association of states," said the President. It was a sovereign nation "not to be annulled at the pleasure of any one of the contracting parties." The founders of the republic were not "guilty of the absurdity of providing for its own dissolution." Thus "secession is neither more nor less than revolution." All peoples have a right of revolution against intolerable oppression, but the election of a president by constitutional procedures could not "justify a revolution to destroy this very Constitution." The Union "has been consecrated by the blood of our fathers, by the glories of the past, and by the hopes of the future." If it could be broken by the mere will of a state, the great experiment in republican self-government launched in 1776 became a failure. "Our example for more than eighty years would not only be lost, but it would be quoted as conclusive proof that man is unfit for self-government."[17]

Most Republicans and Northern Democrats applauded this part of the President's message. It expressed the themes of nationalism for which the North was to fight during the ensuing four years. But Buchanan's next point seemed to contradict his ringing Unionist phrases. While the government must continue to "enforce the laws" in all states, said the President, it could not "coerce" a seceding state back into the Union. Republicans ridiculed this distinction between enforcement and coercion. The President had proved, jeered Seward, that "no state has the right to secede unless it wishes to" and "that it is the President's duty to enforce the laws, unless somebody opposes him."[18]

The question of what constituted "coercion" was a matter of interpretation. A few Republicans urged invasion and war if necessary to crush treason. This would unquestionably be coercion. Most Republicans in December 1860 were not ready to go this far. But they did believe that the government should defend its forts and other property in the South, collect customs duties, and carry on other functions as usual. If Southern states resisted, they would be responsible for the consequences. To secessionists, of course, such a policy was coercion. "If the President of the United States were to send a fleet to Liverpool," said Senator Wigfall of Texas, "and attempt there to enforce the laws of the United States, and to collect revenues, and that flag were fired at, would anybody say that the British Government was responsible for the blood that might follow?"[19]

---

[17]James D. Richardson (comp.). *Compilation of the Messages and Papers of the Presidents, 1789–1897,* 20 vols. (Washington, D.C., 1897–1913), V, 628, 630, 632–634, 637.

[18]*Ibid.,* pp. 635–636; Klein, *Days of Defiance,* p. 125.

[19]Kenneth M. Stampp, *And the War Came: The North and the Secession Crisis, 1860–61* (Baton Rouge, 1950), p. 56.

Buchanan's message blamed Republicans and abolitionists for bringing on the crisis. "The incessant and violent agitation of the slavery question" had stirred "vague notions of freedom" among the slaves and created a climate of fear in the South. Unless Northerners stopped criticizing slavery and undertook in good faith to obey the Fugitive Slave Law, "disunion will become inevitable" and the South will "be justified in revolutionary resistance to the Government." To meet the South's just grievances, Buchanan recommended a constitutional amendment to protect slavery in the territories and to annul personal liberty laws in Northern states. For good measure, the President reaffirmed his recommendation to buy Cuba, which would help alleviate Southern discontent by adding a new slave state to the Union.[20]

Proposals for Compromise

Buchanan's recommendations were similar to dozens of compromise measures introduced in Congress during December. To sort all of these out, the House created a special Committee of Thirty-three (one member from each state) and the Senate a Committee of Thirteen. The proposed compromises had two things in common: the North would make all the concessions; and Republicans would be required to give up their intention to prohibit slavery in the territories—the issue on which the party had been founded. To most Republicans this was intolerable. The party "cannot be made to surrender the fruits of its recent victory," said a Republican newspaper in a typical editorial. "If the will of the majority is no longer the governing power in this country, free government is at an end."[21]

A good many abolitionists preferred disunion rather than a shameful bribe in the form of a "compromise" to purchase the South's loyalty. The Garrisonian abolitionists, of course, had long denounced the Constitution as a "covenant with death" and the Union as an "agreement with hell." They had urged the free states to break loose from the sinful slaveholding Union. Now that slave states had done the breaking loose, Garrisonians were happy to see them go. They believed that secession would isolate the South and bring its peculiar institution under the ban of world opinion, end the North's obligation to return fugitive slaves, relieve the U.S. army from the duty to suppress slave insurrections, and hasten the final collapse of bondage. Some non-Garrisonians also preferred disunion to compromise. "If the Union can only be maintained by new concessions to the slaveholders," said Frederick Douglass, "if it can only be stuck together and held together by a new drain on the negro's blood, then . . . let the Union perish."[22] During the winter of 1860–1861, abolitionists who preached such doctrines encountered mob violence in many parts of the North, for Democrats and conservative Republicans blamed them for having provoked the South into secession.

But some Republicans agreed with the abolitionists in wishing to let the South go if surrender to Southern demands was the price of union. Horace Greeley's powerful *New York Tribune* expressed a willingness to "let the erring sisters depart in

---

[20]Richardson, *Messages and Papers of the Presidents,* V, 626–627, 630, 638, 642.

[21]*Boston Daily Advertiser,* December 7, 1860, and *Des Moines Iowa State Register,* December 12, 1860, in Howard C. Perkins (ed.), *Northern Editorials on Secession* (New York, 1942), pp. 147, 157.

[22]*Douglass' Monthly,* January 1861.

peace." But Greeley and other radical Republicans hedged their apparent acquiescence in disunion with so many qualifications as to render it practically meaningless.
By January 1861, after congressional Republicans had stood firm against compromise
on the issue of slavery in the territories, Greeley and most other "go in peace" Republicans began to denounce secessionists as traitors.

Before January, however, some conservative Republicans had hinted at a willingness to compromise on the territorial question. They endorsed the idea of extending
the old Missouri Compromise line westward to the California border. This proposal
became the centerpiece of a complex compromise plan introduced in the Senate
Committee of Thirteen by John J. Crittenden of Kentucky. It consisted of a series of
constitutional amendments: to recognize and protect slavery in all territories south
of latitude 36°30′ "now held, *or hereafter acquired*"(italics added) while prohibiting
it north of that latitude; to prevent Congress from abolishing slavery in the District
of Columbia or in any national jurisdiction within a slave state (e.g., forts, naval
bases, arsenals); to forbid federal interference with the interstate slave trade; and to
indemnify owners who were prevented by local opposition from recovering escaped
slaves. These amendments were to be perpetually binding, unrepealable and una-
mendable for all time. Additional congressional resolutions that became part of the
Crittenden Compromise undertook to modify the Fugitive Slave Law and to request
states to repeal laws that conflicted with it.

Crittenden believed that his plan could win majority support in both North and
South. He proposed that it be submitted to a national referendum. But Republicans
in Congress opposed it. Not only did this "compromise" repudiate their platform, it
also promised to set off a new wave of imperialism in the Caribbean and Central
America to expand slavery into territories "hereafter acquired." Passage of Crittenden's proposal, said Republicans, "would amount to a perpetual covenant of war
against every people, tribe, and State owning a foot of land between here and Tierra
del Fuego." It would convert the United States into "a great slave-breeding and
slave-extending empire."[23] Republican votes killed the Crittenden Compromise in
the Senate Committee of Thirteen on December 28. When Crittenden brought the
measure to the Senate floor on January 16, Republican votes again provided the
margin of defeat.[24]

Lincoln's Position

Although Lincoln made no public statements during this period, he played a crucial
role in preventing concessions on the territorial issue. He quietly passed the word
for Republicans to "entertain no proposition for a compromise in regard to the *extension* of slavery. The instant you do, they have us under again; all our labor is lost,
and sooner or later must be done over. . . . Filibustering for all South of us, and making slave states of it, would follow. . . . The tug has to come & better now than later."

---

[23]Stampp, *And the War Came*, p. 169.

[24]The vote in the Senate committee was 7 to 6, with all five Republican members in the majority.
The vote on the Senate floor was 25 to 23. All 25 of the majority votes were cast by Republicans. Six
Southern Democratic senators, from states soon to secede, abstained from the floor vote.

Two years earlier, in his "House Divided" speech, Lincoln had said that "a crisis must be reached and passed" on the slavery question. The nation must face a decision whether it was to be ultimately a free or slave society. Now the "tug" had come, and Lincoln did not intend to back down. "If we surrender," he said in January, "it is the end of us, and of the government. They will repeat the experiment on us *ad libitum*. A year will not pass, till we shall have to take Cuba as a condition upon which they will stay in the Union."[25]

Lincoln privately assured Southern friends that his administration would not interfere with slavery in the states or in the District of Columbia, would do nothing against the interstate slave trade, would enforce the Fugitive Slave Law, and would urge Northern states to repeal or modify their personal liberty laws. Two Northern states did take such action during the secession winter. And with Lincoln's support, about two-fifths of the Republicans in Congress joined in the passage of a constitutional amendment to guarantee slavery in the states against future interference by the federal government.[26] But beyond this most Republicans would not go. As Lincoln put it in a December 22 letter to his old friend, Alexander Stephens: "You think slavery is *right* and ought to be extended; while we think it is *wrong* and ought to be restricted. That I suppose is the rub."[27]

It was indeed the rub. The lower South was seceding because a party that believed slavery wrong had come to power. No compromise could undo this fact. Although many contemporary observers, as well as some historians, believed the Crittenden Compromise commanded widespread support in the North and upper South, it is likely that no conceivable compromise could have stopped secession in the lower South.[28] Secessionists frankly said as much from the beginning of the crisis. On December 13, before any state seceded or any compromise was voted on, thirty congressmen and senators from the lower South issued an address to their constituents: "The argument is exhausted. All hope of relief in the Union, through the agency of committees, Congressional legislation, or constitutional amendments, is extinguished, and we trust the South will not be deceived by appearances or the pretense of new guarantees. . . . The honor, safety, and independence of the Southern people are to be found only in a Southern Confederacy." Jefferson Davis said on December 2 that "no human power can save the Union, all the cotton states will go." A week later Judah Benjamin declared that "a settlement [is] totally out of our power to accomplish."[29]

---

[25]Basler, *Works of Lincoln*, IV, 150, 154, 172.

[26]This Thirteenth Amendment was ratified by two states, Ohio and Maryland, before the Civil War broke out; eventually a quite different Thirteenth Amendment became part of the Constitution—one that abolished slavery in all the states.

[27]Basler, *Works of Lincoln*, p. 160.

[28]For discussions of popular support for the Crittenden Compromise, see Stampp, *And the War Came*, chaps. 8–9, David M. Potter, *Lincoln and His Party in the Secession Crisis* (New Haven, 1942), chap. 8, and Crofts, *Reluctant Confederates*, pp. 197–199.

[29]Edward McPherson, *The Political History of the United States of America During the Great Rebellion*, 2d ed. (Washington, 1865), p. 37; Davis quoted in Samuel C. Buttersworth to Samuel L. M. Barlow, December 3, 1860, Benjamin to Barlow, December 9, 1860, Barlow Papers.

Launching the Confederacy

Thus the delegates to the Confederate constitutional convention that met February 4 in Montgomery paid no attention to what was going on in Washington. They hammered out a provisional constitution in four days. They could do this so quickly because their constitution was in most respects a copy of the U.S. Constitution. The same was true of the permanent Confederate constitution adopted a month later. But the latter did contain some significant new provisions. The preamble omitted the general welfare clause of the U.S. Constitution and added that by ratifying the new charter, each state acted "in its sovereign and independent character." The Confederate constitution explicitly guaranteed slavery in territories as well as in states. It forbade protective (as distinguished from revenue) tariffs and outlawed congressional appropriations for internal improvements. All of these features were designed to strengthen slavery and states' rights.[30]

The Confederate constitution also departed from the U.S. model by limiting the president to one six-year term, by giving him the power to veto separate items in appropriation bills, and by authorizing Congress to grant cabinet officers the right to speak on the floor of Congress (this was never implemented). On February 9, the convention elected Davis and Stephens provisional president and vice president. Later legislation provided for the election of permanent officers in November and for their inauguration on February 22, 1862. Until then, the delegates to the constitutional convention (plus those elected by any additional seceding states) would function as a provisional Congress.

The fire-eaters who had done so much to spur the South to secession took a back seat at Montgomery. Yancey was not even a delegate. Although Davis had been a secessionist since Lincoln's election, he was considered a moderate. Stephens had been a conditional Unionist. Part of the convention's purpose in choosing these men was to present a moderate image to the upper South, which had not seceded—yet. The same reasoning lay behind the constitutional prohibition of the foreign slave trade. Some of the militant secessionists wanted to reopen the trade, but this would have alienated the upper South and crippled the Confederacy's hopes for European recognition. So instead of legalizing the trade, the convention proscribed it.

The Upper South

The question of what the eight slave states of the upper South would do was crucial. Without them, the Confederacy would have scarcely 5 percent of the industrial capacity of the Union states and less than one-fifth of the population (only one-tenth of the white population). The Confederate government sent commissioners to all

---

[30]The fullest study of the Confederate constitutional convention is William C. Davis, *"A Government of Our Own": The Making of the Confederacy* (New York, 1994).

eight states to woo them with appeals to interest and sentiment. But the momentum of secession seemed to have spent itself by February. Voters in Virginia, Missouri, and Arkansas elected large majorities of conditional Unionists to their state conventions. The Arkansas and Missouri conventions voted in March to reject secession. The Virginia convention did the same on April 4, though it thereafter remained in session to await further developments. The legislatures of Kentucky and Delaware refused to call conventions. In North Carolina and Tennessee, the voters rejected the calling of a convention. The Unionist governor of Maryland resisted pressure to call the legislature into session to consider the issue.

These events seemed to confirm Republican faith in Southern Unionism. But upper-South Unionists made clear that their loyalty was contingent on two factors: the incoming Republican administration must offer guarantees for the safety of slavery, and it must refrain from "coercion" of Confederate states. Many Republicans were willing to go at least halfway to meet these conditions. Seward put himself at the head of this element. Lincoln had already asked the New Yorker to serve as secretary of state. Most observers expected that Seward, a man of greater prominence and experience than Lincoln, would be the "premier" of the administration. Seward expected this himself. He became the foremost Republican proponent of a policy known as "voluntary reconstruction." This approach assumed that if the Republicans refrained from provocative acts against the seceded states and made a few timely concessions, the upper South would remain in the Union, and the lower South would eventually return. "Every thought that we think ought to be conciliatory, forbearing and patient," Seward advised Lincoln on January 27, "and so open the way for the rising of a Union Party in the seceding States which will bring them back."[31]

Accordingly, Seward backed a proposal to admit New Mexico (which included what is now Arizona) as a state. This was an apparent violation of the Republican platform, for slavery was legal in the territory. Lincoln grudgingly approved the proposal, since it was clear that the institution would not take root there. Several Southern congressmen, however, considered the New Mexico scheme a trick to divide the upper and lower South by the appearance of concession, and voted against it. So did three-quarters of the Republicans. The House killed the measure in March.

More significant was an invitation from the Virginia legislature for all states to send delegates to a "peace convention" in Washington on February 4. This was the upper South's major attempt to find some basis for voluntary reconstruction. But the enterprise was doomed from the start. Seward and his allies did manage to persuade most Republican states to send delegates as a gesture of goodwill. But the Confederate states did not participate, and the anticompromise Republicans were suspicious. Although many distinguished men attended the convention (ex-President John Tyler was chairman), they failed to develop any fresh proposals to resolve the crisis. After three weeks of labor, the convention could come up with nothing more than a modified version of the Crittenden Compromise. Congress rejected this as it had previously rejected similar proposals. Nevertheless, the peace convention did help to channel the energies of the upper South into Unionist rather than secession activities during the month before Lincoln's inauguration.

---

[31]Allan Nevins, *The Emergence of Lincoln*, 2 vols. (New York, 1950), II, 431.

Lincoln Takes the Helm

Seward's activities alarmed anticompromise Republicans. They feared that Lincoln would defer too much to the New Yorker. Like Seward, Lincoln hoped for voluntary reconstruction through the reassertion of Southern Unionism. But he was afraid that too much forbearance would legitimize secession. Lincoln wanted to maintain the symbols of national authority in the South as a beacon to Unionists while at the same time to reassure Southerners that the government threatened none of their vital interests. During his trip from Springfield to Washington in February, Lincoln made many brief speeches along the way to crowds eager to see the relatively unknown prairie lawyer. Because he wished to say nothing that could be distorted, most of the speeches contained platitudes that seemed to make light of the crisis. To many observers, these speeches revealed Lincoln as a lightweight unequal to the grave occasion.

　　Nothing could have been further from the truth. Lincoln intended to take a reassuring but firm line in his inaugural address. The initial draft stated that "all the power at my disposal will be used to reclaim the public property and places which have fallen; to hold, occupy and possess these, and all other property belonging to the government." Seward and other advisers persuaded Lincoln to delete the reference to reclaiming federal property already seized. Seward also suggested a number of other modifications to soften the general tone of the address. The final version of Lincoln's inaugural address—the most important such speech in American history— was a careful balancing of the sword and the olive branch. It began by assuring the South—for the hundredth time—that the administration had no intention of interfering with slavery where it existed. Where hostility to the federal government was so great "in any interior locality" as to prevent the normal functioning of federal activities, the government would suspend these activities "for the time." This was the olive branch. But the Union was "perpetual," said Lincoln; secession was the "essence of anarchy," for its success would mean that a disaffected minority could break up the government at will. Lincoln intended to "take care, as the Constitution itself expressly enjoins upon me, that the laws of the Union be faithfully executed in all the States." The government would "hold, occupy, and possess" its property and "collect the [customs] duties and imposts." There would be no "invasion—no using of force . . . beyond what may be necessary for these objects." The new President closed with an eloquent peroration, part of which had been suggested by Seward:

In *your* hands, my dissatisfied fellow countrymen, and not in *mine,* is the momentous issue of civil war. The government will not assail *you.* You can have no conflict, without being yourselves the aggressors. *You* have no oath registered in Heaven to destroy the government, while *I* shall have the most solemn one to "preserve, protect and defend" it.

　　. . . We must not be enemies. Though passion may have strained, it must not break our bonds of affection. The mystic chords of memory, stretching from every battle-field, and patriot grave, to every living heart and hearthstone, all over this broad land, will yet swell the chorus of the Union, when again touched, as surely they will be, by the better angels of our nature.[32]

---

[32]Basler, *Works of Lincoln,* IV, 249–271, reproduces the first and final drafts of the address, with annotations of all revisions and corrections.

Ever since March 4, 1861, contemporaries and historians have debated the meaning of this address. Did the promise to enforce the laws, to collect customs duties, and to "hold, occupy and possess" federal property mean coercion? Did it mean that arsenals and forts already seized by the Confederate states would be repossessed, or only that the four forts still in federal possession—Sumter in Charleston Bay, Pickens in Pensacola Bay, and two remote posts in the Florida keys—would be held? How would the duties be collected—by ships stationed offshore? How could the laws be executed at "interior localities" if the government left vacant the offices— federal courts, land offices, post offices, and the like—necessary to execute them? Lincoln intentionally left these matters ambiguous, to avoid alienating the upper South and to give himself maximum flexibility.

Reactions to the message varied by section and party. Secessionists denounced it as a "Declaration of War." Most Republicans praised its firmness. Many Northern Democrats criticized it as either too obscure or too warlike, but Stephen A. Douglas considered it a "peace offering." The address had been aimed above all at the conditional Unionists of the upper South, and reactions of many of them, while hardly ebullient, were gratifying. "What more does any reasonable Southern man expect or desire?" asked a North Carolinian. "Are not . . . these . . . cheering assurances enough to induce the whole South to wait for the sober second thought of the North?"[33]

꧁ Fort Sumter and the End of Peace

The main purpose of Lincoln's inaugural message was to buy time—time for the disunion fever to subside, time for the presumed legions of Southern Unionists to regain the upper hand, time for the process of voluntary reconstruction to get under way. But on the day after his inauguration, Lincoln received some bad news that seemed likely to deny him the necessary time. From Major Robert Anderson came word that the garrison at Fort Sumter would be forced to evacuate unless resupplied within a few weeks. For more than two months Sumter had been a symbol of the Union presence in the South, a symbol out of all proportion to its intrinsic military importance. Now the Union government would be forced to act—decisively and soon—or to abandon its last effective symbol of authority in the lower South.

Sumter was a nearly completed fort on an island at the entrance to Charleston Bay. When South Carolina seceded on December 20, the fort was still unoccupied. Most of the eighty-odd U.S. soldiers in the area were stationed at Fort Moultrie, an obsolete fortification on a spit of land a mile across the bay from Sumter. The commander of the garrison, Robert Anderson, had been sent to Charleston because as a Kentuckian he would be viewed as being less provocative than his Massachusetts-born predecessor. In response to Anderson's report that Moultrie was indefensible against an attack by land, the War Department on December 11 had given him discretionary orders to move his command to Sumter if he thought an attack imminent. Anderson had every reason to expect an attack. South Carolina was going out of the

---

[33]Crofts, *Reluctant Confederates,* pp. 261–262; James G. Randall, *Lincoln the President,* 4 vols. (New York, 1945–1955), I, 308–309.

Union; its officials were demanding surrender of the Charleston forts; militia companies were arming and drilling. After dusk on December 26, Anderson secretly
spiked Moultrie's guns and transferred the garrison to Sumter.

Anderson believed that this move would preserve peace, for Moultrie's weakness
invited attack while Sumter's strength would deter it. But the transfer outraged
South Carolinians and set off reverberations that reached the White House. Commissioners from the independent republic of South Carolina had just arrived in
Washington to negotiate a surrender of the forts and of other U.S. property—which
they now claimed as South Carolina's property. They regarded the occupation of
Sumter as a violation of an earlier pledge by Buchanan not to change the status quo
in Charleston.

But the administration felt that the South had pushed it around long enough. The
Northern press was hailing Anderson as a hero. "Never have I known the *entire people* more unanimous on any question," wrote an influential Buchanan Democrat. "We
are ruined if Anderson is recalled or if Sumter is given up. . . . There will be hardly
a man found who will not on this question be ready to attack the South."[34]
Buchanan's cabinet was undergoing a shakeup owing to the departure of secessionists and their replacement by Northerners of staunch Unionist fiber. Secretary of
State Jeremiah Black of Pennsylvania, Attorney General Edwin M. Stanton of Ohio,
and Secretary of War Joseph Holt, a Kentucky Unionist, emerged as the strong men
of the reconstructed cabinet. They stiffened the administration's backbone against
Southerners who demanded that Buchanan withdraw the troops from Sumter.
Buchanan astonished the South Carolinians by saying no.

The President went further and ordered reinforcements sent to Anderson. The
army decided to use an unarmed merchant vessel rather than a warship for this purpose, to minimize the publicity and provocation. The ship *Star of the West* left New
York with two hundred troops and supplies on January 5. Despite secrecy, word
leaked out, and the South Carolina militia was ready for her with shotted guns. They
were more ready than Fort Sumter was, for the official notification to Anderson of
the expedition had gone astray. When the *Star of the West* entered the bay on January 9, the shore batteries opened on her, scoring one direct hit before the captain
turned her around and headed back North. Lacking instructions and loath to start a
war, Anderson had withheld Sumter's fire during the incident.

The North erupted in anger at this affair, while South Carolina bristled with accusations of federal aggression and with new demands for Sumter's surrender. But despite war cries on both sides, war did not come. The Buchanan administration
worked out an informal truce with South Carolina that preserved the status quo for
the time being. Secessionists in other states persuaded the South Carolinians to lie
low until the Confederacy could complete its organization and begin to build an
army. On March 1, Jefferson Davis ordered Confederate General Pierre Gustave T.
Beauregard to take command at Charleston. This removed the Sumter question from
the hands of the hotheaded Carolinians. Meanwhile, the Confederacy also respected
a truce worked out earlier between the U.S. navy and the Florida militia whereby

---

[34]Samuel L. M. Barlow to Judah P. Benjamin, December 29, 1861, Barlow Papers.

Southern troops agreed not to attack Fort Pickens at Pensacola if the navy did not try to land reinforcements. The Confederacy sent commissioners to Washington to negotiate the surrender of both forts.

Lincoln and Fort Sumter

This was the situation confronting Lincoln when he learned on March 5, his second day as President, that Anderson's supplies would soon be exhausted. The status quo could not last much longer. The crucial question was what to do about it. The hawkish wing of the Republican party insisted that Sumter be reinforced even at the cost of war. From all over the North came letters and telegrams with the same message. "Give up Sumpter [sic], Sir, & you are as dead politically as John Brown is physically," a correspondent told Lincoln. "You have got to fight." The editor of an influential Connecticut newspaper told the secretary of the navy: "I will gladly be one of the volunteers to sail into that harbor past all the guns of hell rather than see the flag dishonored and the government demoralized."[35] But the doves, led by Seward, urged that the fort be evacuated to avoid war and keep the door open for voluntary reconstruction. Seward did more than merely recommend this policy. Without authorization from Lincoln, he virtually assured Confederate commissioners in Washington that Sumter would be surrendered. He leaked similar reports to the press.

Lincoln had made no such decision, although he did lean this way for a time. General in Chief Winfield Scott advised him that it would be impossible to reinforce the fort. A poll of the cabinet on March 15 disclosed that only Postmaster General Montgomery Blair unequivocally favored reinforcement. Faced with advice from his advisers to pull out, the President wavered in his determination to "hold, occupy, and possess" the fort. But during the last two weeks of March, the hawks gained the upper hand with Northern opinion. Republicans began to insist that the government *do* something to assert its sovereignty. Republican newspapers printed editorials with such titles as: "HAVE WE A GOVERNMENT?" "WANTED—A POLICY." "COME TO THE POINT." The restlessness and tension of the Northern people were approaching the breaking point. "Better almost anything than additional suspense," said one newspaper. The German-American leader Carl Schurz felt the pulse of public opinion for Lincoln and reported widespread dissatisfaction with the administration. But "as soon as one vigorous blow is struck," said Schurz, "as soon as, for instance, Fort Sumter is reinforced, public opinion in the free States will at once rally to your support."[36]

This stiffened Lincoln's initial resolve to hold the fort. So did the advice of Gustavus V. Fox, a former naval officer from Massachusetts, who suggested a plan whereby supplies and reinforcements could be run into Fort Sumter at night while cannoneers in the fort and on warships stood by to suppress the Confederate guns if they tried to interfere. Lincoln accepted the plan and on March 29 ordered Fox to prepare the expedition. At the same time, he also authorized—for the second time—

---

[35]Richard N. Current, *Lincoln and the First Shot* (Philadelphia, 1963), p. 119; Bruce Catton, *The Coming Fury* (Garden City, N.Y., 1961), p. 278.

[36]Stampp, *And the War Came,* pp. 267–268; Klein, *Days of Defiance,* p. 369.

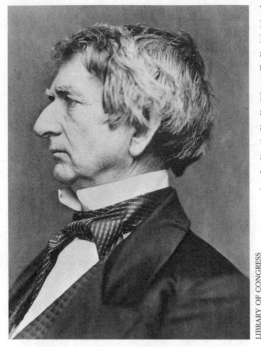

WILLIAM H. SEWARD.
Having served four years as governor of New York and twelve years as a U.S. senator, he was the odds-on favorite to win the Republican presidential nomination in 1860. When Lincoln won instead, Seward hoped to dominate the new administration as secretary of state and "premier," but soon discovered that Lincoln intended to run his own administration. Seward became an effective ally; in 1867, he crowned his career by negotiating the purchase of Alaska from Russia.

LIBRARY OF CONGRESS

an expedition to reinforce Fort Pickens.[37] In a switch from two weeks earlier, the entire cabinet except Seward and Secretary of the Interior Caleb Smith now approved the decision to hold Sumter.

This decision put Seward in a tight spot. His peace policy would collapse. His assurances to Confederate commissioners would be exposed as deceit. His aspirations to be premier would crumble. In an ill-advised attempt to repair the damage, he penned a memorandum to Lincoln on April 1. Seward again proposed to abandon Sumter (though to reinforce Pickens). But the most important feature of this document was its foreign policy recommendations. Spain had sent troops to intervene in the troubled politics of Santo Domingo. France was casting covetous eyes toward Mexico. Seward would "demand explanations" from Spain and France and, if the explanations were not "satisfactory," would declare war. He would also "seek explanations" from Britain and Russia concerning violations of the Monroe Doctrine. Seward believed that a foreign war would reunite the country. To execute this policy

---

[37]On March 12, Lincoln had ordered that Fort Pickens in Florida be reinforced. This was more feasible than reinforcement of Sumter, for Pickens was outside the harbor entrance and thus less vulnerable than Sumter, which was ringed by scores of Confederate cannon. It was also less provocative, for Pickens was not the powerful symbol to both sides that Sumter had become. But weeks passed and Lincoln received no word whether his order to reinforce Pickens had been carried out. On April 6, he finally learned that it had not. The naval commander there had cited the previous agreement not to reinforce so long as the Confederates refrained from attacking the fort and had refused to recognize new orders unless issued directly by his superiors in the Naval Department. Such orders were sent April 6; Pickens was reinforced and held by the Union through the Civil War.

there must be firm leadership, and Seward modestly offered to assume the responsibility. Lincoln gently but firmly rejected these extraordinary suggestions. He also reminded his secretary of state that whatever decisions were made or orders issued, "*I* must do it." The chastened Seward wrote no more such memoranda. There was no longer any doubt in his mind about who was premier of this administration.[38]

The President did agree to meet with a spokesman for Virginia Unionists before giving the final go-ahead for the Sumter expedition. Lincoln talked with the Virginia representative on April 4, but the meeting was unproductive. No record was kept of the conversation, and no reliable evidence of its nature exists. Whatever happened, it seems to have soured Lincoln's faith in Southern Unionism, at least temporarily. He made up his mind that very day (April 4) to proceed with the Sumter expedition. He sent a letter to Major Anderson advising him that relief was on the way.

The nature of this expedition had changed in a crucial way since Fox first suggested it. A full-scale attempt to reinforce Sumter was certain to provoke shooting, in which the North might appear to be the aggressor. This would drive the upper South into the Confederacy. Thus Lincoln conceived the idea of separating the question of reinforcement from that of provisions. He would send in supplies, but the troops and warships would stand by to go into action only if the Confederates stopped the supplies. And he would notify Southern officials of his intentions. If they opened fire on the unarmed tugs carrying provisions, they would stand convicted of attacking "a mission of humanity" bringing "food for hungry men."

Lincoln had some reason to believe that the Confederates would resist the landing of supplies. An emissary he had sent to Charleston reported the bellicose determination he found there. But if the Confederates stayed their hand, the status quo in Charleston Bay could be maintained, peace would be preserved for at least a while, and the policy of voluntary reconstruction would have a new lease on life. If Confederate guns did fire on the supply ships, the responsibility for starting a war would rest on Jefferson Davis's shoulders. On April 6, Lincoln sent a special messenger to Charleston with a dispatch notifying the governor of South Carolina "to expect an attempt will be made to supply Fort-Sumpter [sic] with provisions only; and that, if such attempt be not resisted, no effort to throw in men, arms, ammunition, will be made, without further notice, [except] in case of an attack on the Fort."[39]

The Confederates Fire the First Shot

The Confederacy accepted Lincoln's challenge. Given the assumptions that governed its policy, the Davis administration could scarcely do otherwise. Sumter had become to the South as potent a symbol of sovereignty as it was to the North. The Confederacy could not be considered a viable nation so long as a foreign power held a fort in one of its principal harbors. The Confederate provisional Congress had resolved on February 15 that Sumter and other forts must be acquired "as early as practicable . . . either by negotiation, or force." Negotiation had failed; the only option left was force. The prolonged suspense had stretched Southern as well as Northern nerves to the breaking point. Any action was better than continued uncertainty. Confederate leaders also

---

[38]Basler, *Works of Lincoln,* IV, 316–318.
[39]Ibid., p. 323.

believed that a shooting war would bring the upper South to their side. Virginia secessionists had descended on Charleston with the message that Virginia would join her sister states instantly if South Carolina would "strike a blow!"[40]

On April 9, the Confederate cabinet made the fateful decision to strike a blow at Sumter. Davis ordered Beauregard to demand the fort's surrender before the relief expedition arrived. If surrender was refused, he was to batter it into submission with the heavy guns that now bore on Sumter from four sides. Only Secretary of State Robert Toombs opposed this decision. It "will lose us every friend at the North," Toombs reportedly told Davis. "You will wantonly strike a hornet's nest. . . . Legions now quiet will swarm out and sting us to death. It is unnecessary. It puts us in the wrong. It is fatal."[41]

Anderson rejected the demand for surrender. But he remarked that if left alone, his lack of supplies would force him soon to vacate the fort. When Beauregard asked him to fix a time for such a withdrawal, Anderson named April 15—unless he received supplies before then. This was unsatisfactory, for the Confederates knew that the supply ships were approaching the harbor. At 4:30 A.M. on April 12, the Confederate guns opened fire. The Union relief expedition was helpless to intervene because a mix-up in orders had diverted its strongest warship to Fort Pickens, and high seas prevented the other ships from coming to Sumter's aid. Outmanned and outgunned (the Confederate batteries fired four thousand rounds to Sumter's one thousand), the Union garrison surrendered after thirty-three hours of bombardment that destroyed large portions of the fort—though not a man on either side was killed in this first engagement of what became America's bloodiest war.

On April 14, the Confederate stars and bars replaced the stars and stripes at Fort Sumter. War had begun. And it had begun in such a way as to fulfill Toombs's prediction. Seldom in history has a counterrevolution so effectively ensured the success of the very revolution it sought to avert.

---

[40]Current, *Lincoln and the First Shot,* pp. 138–139.

[41]These words were quoted by Toombs's first biographer, Pleasant A. Stovall, *Robert Toombs* (New York, 1892), p. 226. Although one may be permitted to doubt that Toombs uttered such prescient sentiments in precisely these words, subsequent biographers and most historians have accepted the quotation as authentic, including the most recent student of the firing on Fort Sumter, Klein, *Days of Defiance,* p. 399.

1793	Invention of cotton gin
1807	First successful steamboat
1808	Abolition of African slave trade
1817	Founding of American Colonization Society
1820	Missouri Compromise
1825	Completion of Erie Canal
1830	First railroad operates
1831	William Lloyd Garrison founds _Liberator_
	Nat Turner slave revolt in Virginia
1832	Nullification crisis over South Carolina's attempt to nullify federal law
1833	Founding of American Anti-Slavery Society
1836	Texas wins independence from Mexico
1839	Founding of Liberty party
1845	Annexation of Texas
1846	Settlement of Oregon boundary dispute
	Mexican War begins
	House passes Wilmot Proviso
1848	Treaty of Guadalupe Hidalgo ends Mexican War, acquires California, New Mexico, and Utah for U.S.
	First women's rights convention at Seneca Falls, New York
	Founding of Free Soil party
1850	Compromise of 1850
1852	_Uncle Tom's Cabin_ published
1854	Ostend Manifesto
	Anthony Burns returned to slavery

	Passage of Kansas-Nebraska Act
	Founding of Republican party
	Know-Nothings emerge as political force
1856	William Walker proclaims himself president of Nicaragua, reinstitutes slavery
	Brooks beats Sumner in Senate and John Brown goes on rampage in Kansas
	Republicans nominate John C. Frémont for president; Democrat James Buchanan wins election
1857	Dred Scott decision
	Lecompton Constitution legalizes slavery in Kansas
1858	Congress rejects admission of Kansas as slave state
	Lincoln-Douglas debates
1859	John Brown's raid at Harpers Ferry
1860	William Walker shot by firing squad in Honduras
	Democratic party splits
	Lincoln elected president
	South Carolina secedes
1861	
	January–February Six more states secede, Confederate States of America formed in Montgomery, Jefferson Davis elected president of CSA
	March Lincoln inaugurated
	April Firing on Fort Sumter Lincoln calls out militia to suppress insurrection

Part Two The Civil War

Chapter Ten

A Brothers' War: The Upper South

Chapter Outline

*Rather than concede to the State of Missouri
for one single instant the right to dictate to
my Government, I would see you . . . and
every man, woman, and child in the State
dead and buried. This means war.*

—Union General Nathaniel Lyon,
June 11, 1861

163

The Conflict Takes Shape

The day after the surrender of Fort Sumter, Lincoln called 75,000 state militia into federal service for ninety days to put down an insurrection "too powerful to be suppressed by the ordinary course of judicial proceedings."[1] With these words the President accepted the South's challenge to civil war, a war that would last not ninety days but four years and would destroy the Old South, transform the Union it preserved, and cost at least 620,000 lives.

During the weeks after the fall of Sumter, war fever swept both North and South. A New York woman wrote that "it seems as if we never were alive till now; never had a country till now." A Philadelphia diarist described "a wild state of excitement" on April 20. From Oberlin College a student wrote on the same day that "WAR! and volunteers are the only topics of conversation or thought. . . . I cannot study. I cannot sleep, I cannot work." In Goldsboro, North Carolina, a correspondent of the *Times* of London watched "an excited mob" with "flushed faces, wild eyes, screaming mouths, hurrahing for 'Jeff Davis' and 'the Southern Confederacy.' " In Charlottesville an eighteen-year-old

---

[1]Roy P. Basler (ed.), *The Collected Works of Abraham Lincoln,* 9 vols. (New Brunswick, N.J., 1953–1955), IV, 331–332.

student at the University of Virginia wrote on April 17: "No studying today. . . . 'War!' 'War!' 'War!' was on placards all about. My company was called at 4:45. All was excitement and 'go.' "[2]

The bombardment of Sumter united a divided North. Stephen Douglas went to the White House to assure Lincoln of Democratic support for a war to preserve the Union. "There can be no neutrals in this war," said Douglas; "*only patriots—or traitors.*" At the other end of the political spectrum, abolitionists who had opposed all attempts to coax the departing states back by compromise now acclaimed the effort to bring them back by force. Even though the states to be brought back had slavery, abolitionists believed that the institution would not survive the conflict. Amid the feverish war preparations, one abolitionist wrote: "I hear Old John Brown knocking on the lid of his coffin & shouting 'Let me out,' 'let me out!' The doom of slavery is at hand. It is to be wiped out in blood. Amen!"[3] In the difference between the Democrats' support for a war to restore the old Union and the abolitionists' vision of a war to create a new one lay the seeds of a bitter harvest. But in April 1861, the North was united as never before.

From Northern governors came a zealous response to Lincoln's call for troops. Nearly every state offered to send more men than were requested. But owing to the rundown condition of the militia in several states, many of these men were lacking in organization, training, arms, and equipment. One state ready immediately to send more than patriotic telegrams was Massachusetts. Governor John Andrew, who had foreseen war sooner than most of his contemporaries, had put the Massachusetts militia in shape for mobilization months before the firing on Sumter. When Lincoln's call came, he responded: "Dispatch received. By what route shall we send?" Two days later, April 17, he wired the War Department: "Two of our regiments will start this afternoon—one for Washington, the other for Fort Monroe; a third will be dispatched tomorrow, and the fourth before the end of the week."[4]

Lincoln's call for militia requisitioned a quota of troops from each loyal state. The governors of six of the eight slave states still in the Union sent defiant refusals. "Tennessee will furnish not a single man for the purpose of coercion," declared its governor, "but fifty thousand if necessary for the defense of our rights and those of our Southern brothers." Virginia's governor telegraphed the President that since he had "chosen to inaugurate civil war," Virginia would join her sister states of the South. From North Carolina and Arkansas came similar replies, while the secession-minded governors of Kentucky and Missouri also refused to comply with Lincoln's call.[5]

The governors of Tennessee, Virginia, North Carolina, and Arkansas were, for the most part, expressing the popular will of their states. A majority of people in these states were bound by ties of culture and ideology to the lower South. They were

---

[2]Henry Steele Commager (ed.), *The Blue and the Gray,* rev. ed. (Indianapolis, 1973), I, 47; James M. McPherson, *For Cause and Comrades: Why Men Fought in the Civil War* (New York, 1997), pp. 16–17.

[3]*Chicago Tribune,* May 2, 1861; Henry B. Stanton to Elizabeth Cady Stanton, April ?, 1861, E. C. Stanton Papers, Library of Congress.

[4]*War of the Rebellion: A Compilation of the Official Records of the Union and Confederate Armies* (Washington, D.C., 1880–1901), Ser. 3, Vol. 1, pp. 71, 79. Hereinafter cited as *O.R. (Official Records).*

[5]Ibid., pp. 70, 72, 76, 81, 83.

conditional Unionists only so long as Lincoln did nothing to "coerce" the Confederacy; when forced to a choice, they chose southernism over nationalism. On April 15, a cheering crowd in Richmond ran up a Confederate flag, dragged cannon from the state arsenal to the Capitol, and fired a one-hundred-gun salute to the flag. Similar scenes took place in Raleigh, Nashville, and Little Rock. On April 17, the Virginia state convention, still in session after two months of futile compromise efforts, passed a secession ordinance by a vote of 88 to 55. Arkansas followed on May 6 by a vote of 69 to 1; North Carolina voted unanimously on May 20 to secede. In Tennessee, where voters had earlier rejected the calling of a state convention, the legislature resolved to enter the Confederacy, an action ratified in a popular referendum on June 8 by a majority of more than two to one.

The allegiance of these four states was of great importance to the Confederacy. Virginia, Tennessee, and North Carolina ranked first, second, and third in white population among the eleven Confederate states. Along with Arkansas, these upper-South states possessed more than half of the manufacturing capacity of the Confederacy, produced half of its food crops, contained nearly half of its horses and mules, and furnished more than two-fifths of the men in the Confederate armies. Without the upper South, the Confederacy could scarcely have been a viable military power.

But large pockets of Union sentiment remained in the upland and mountain counties of these late-seceding states. Traditionally hostile to the slaveholding lowlands, eastern Tennessee and western Virginia voted strongly against secession even after the firing on Sumter. In Knoxville, the blunt-spoken editor William G. "Parson" Brownlow vowed to "fight the Secession leaders till Hell freezes over, and then fight them on the ice."[6] Senator Andrew Johnson of Tennessee refused to go with his state and remained in the U.S. Senate, the only senator from a Confederate state to do so. After Confederate Tennessee had held special congressional elections in August 1861, the victorious Unionist candidates from three east Tennessee districts went to Washington instead of Richmond and took their seats in the Union Congress. Three congressmen from Virginia west of the Shenandoah Valley also remained loyal. Unionists in these areas plus those in the rest of the Appalachian uplands—extending all the way to northern Alabama—were a thorn in the flesh of the Confederacy.

The First Clashes

Even before Virginia and North Carolina had officially seceded, state troops moved to seize federal property within their borders. When a thousand Virginia militia appeared on the heights above Harpers Ferry on April 18, the U.S. army garrison of forty-seven men fled after setting fire to the arsenal and armory. The Virginians moved in quickly and saved much of the rifle-making machinery from destruction. Meanwhile, several thousand Virginia militia entrained for Norfolk to seize the Gosport Navy Yard, largest shipbuilding and repair facility in the South. The elderly commander of this post, confused by vague orders from Washington, decided to

---

[6]Shelby Foote, *The Civil War: A Narrative, Fort Sumter to Perryville* (New York, 1958), p. 51.

abandon the yard and destroy its facilities before the militia could overwhelm his handful of sailors and marines. On the night of April 20, the Federals tried to burn the half-dozen warships in the yard, blow up the dry dock, and spike the 1,000 cannon. But in their haste they made a poor job of it, and the Virginians captured most of the machinery and artillery in good condition. Many of the cannon were soon on their way to forts throughout the South, while the Confederate navy began the task of raising and refitting a powerful steam frigate that had been burned to the waterline, the *U.S.S. Merrimack*.

The ease with which these key points had been seized showed the vulnerability of Union installations in the upper South. Surrounded by slave states and full of Confederate sympathizers, Washington also feared a secessionist *coup d'état* during the tense days of April 1861. Secession sentiment was strong in Maryland. On April 19, a mob in Baltimore attacked several companies of the 6th Massachusetts Regiment, Governor Andrew's first militia unit en route to Washington. The soldiers returned the fire. When the melee was over, four soldiers and twelve Baltimoreans lay dead and many wounded. The battered regiment arrived in Washington that evening, while behind them enraged Marylanders burned railroad bridges and tore down telegraph wires, cutting the capital off from the North.

Exultant at this turn of events, the *Richmond Examiner* urged Virginians to march into Washington and clean out "that filthy cage of unclean birds." The Confederate secretary of war predicted that his country's flag would fly over the U.S. Capitol by May 1.[7] More Northern troops were reported on the way to Washington, but having no communication with the outside world, the government did not know where they were. Finally, on April 25, a troop train puffed into the capital carrying the crack 7th New York Regiment, followed by other trains full of militia from Rhode Island and Massachusetts. Resourceful Benjamin Butler, a Massachusetts Democrat whom Andrew had reluctantly appointed commander of the state's four militia regiments, had detrained the 8th Massachusetts at the head of Chesapeake Bay, commandeered a steamer, brought his troops to Annapolis, and put mechanics and railwaymen from the regiment to work repairing the damaged rolling stock and branch line from Annapolis to Washington. By the end of April, 10,000 troops were in the capital, most of them having arrived over Butler's route.

The Eastern Border States: Maryland and Delaware

Washington was safe for the moment, but the problem of Maryland remained. Pro-Confederate units in the state were arming and drilling. Public pressure forced Unionist Governor Thomas Hicks to call the legislature into session. Lincoln decided that drastic measures were necessary to forestall disaster, for no government could function if its capital was surrounded by enemy territory. He suspended the writ of habeas corpus (virtually equivalent to declaring martial law) in part of Maryland.

---

[7]Ibid., p. 53; Allan Nevins, *The War for the Union: The Improvised War, 1861–1862* (New York, 1959), p. 78.

Federal troops occupied Baltimore and other important points. Intimidated by this show of force and by the rising tide of Union sentiment in the western counties, the legislature rejected secession.

Nevertheless, Maryland remained a divided state. While some 35,000 white men (and 9,000 blacks) from the state fought in the Union army and navy, an estimated 20,000 went South to fight for the Confederacy. The Union government arrested many Maryland citizens for pro-Confederate activities. One of these, John Merryman, appealed for release under a writ of habeas corpus in May 1861. Sitting as a circuit judge in this case, Chief Justice Roger Taney issued the writ in a ruling, *ex parte Merryman,* which denied the President's power to suspend habeas corpus. In refusing to obey Taney's injunction, Lincoln pointed to Article I, Section 9, of the Constitution, which authorized suspension of the writ "when in Cases of Rebellion or Invasion the public Safety may require it." Taney insisted that only Congress possessed this power, but Lincoln commanded the army and his interpretation prevailed.

Although Delaware contained numerous Southern sympathizers, the state's adherence to the Union was never in serious doubt. Slavery had virtually ceased to exist there (fewer than 1,800 of Delaware's 20,000 blacks were slaves). The economy of the most populous part of the state, Wilmington and environs, was oriented toward Pennsylvania. The governor was a Unionist, and the legislature on January 3, 1861, decisively rejected secession. Delaware furnished about 10,000 white men and 1,000 black men to the Union army and navy; probably not more than 1,000 men from the state fought for the Confederacy.

The Western Border States: Kentucky and Missouri

War brought bitter divisions and cruel violence to Kentucky and Missouri. Just as control of Maryland was vital to the security of Washington, control of these western border states was crucial for the war in the West. Missouri had a larger white population than any other slave state, while Kentucky had a larger white population than any Confederate state save Virginia. They possessed resources on a comparable scale. The Mississippi-Missouri river network added to the military importance of Missouri, while the confluence of the Ohio, Mississippi, Tennessee, and Cumberland rivers on the borders of Kentucky made the state a vital military nexus for the movement of troops and supplies. Lincoln reportedly said that while he hoped to have God on his side, he must have Kentucky.

Kentucky

Nowhere was the phrase "a brothers' war" more apt than in Kentucky. It was the native state of both Abraham Lincoln and Jefferson Davis. Heir to Henry Clay's nationalism, it was also drawn toward the South by ties of slavery and kinship. Kentucky regiments fought each other on battlefields from Shiloh to Atlanta. Three of Henry Clay's grandsons fought for the Union and four enlisted in the Confederate army. One son of Senator John J. Crittenden became a general in the Union army and the other a general in the Confederate army. The other senator from Kentucky in 1861,

John C. Breckinridge, resigned his seat to join the Confederate army, where he rose to major general. Three of his sons also fought for the Confederacy, while two Kentucky cousins joined the Union army. Four of Mrs. Lincoln's brothers and three brothers-in-law, one of them a general, served in the Confederate army.

Pulled both ways, Kentucky at first tried to remain neutral. Governor Beriah Magoffin responded to Lincoln's call for troops with a statement that Kentucky would send no men "for the wicked purpose of subduing her sister Southern States." Mindful of Union sentiment in large parts of the state, however, Magoffin also refused a request from Jefferson Davis for troops. Called into special session, the legislature issued a neutrality proclamation warning both the Union and the Confederacy against sending troops into or through the state.

For the time being, both Lincoln and Davis decided to respect Kentucky's neutrality, for it was clear that whichever side violated this neutrality would drive the state into the arms of the other. But the state soon became a rich source of horses, mules, leather, grain, and meat for Confederate forces mobilizing south of its border. The Louisville and Nashville Railroad served as a conduit for a brisk trade in military supplies to the South. Governor Magoffin secretly allowed Southern agents to begin recruiting in the state. Many Kentuckians slipped over the Tennessee border to join the Confederate army.

Lincoln's hands-off policy may have benefited the Confederacy militarily, but it paid handsome political dividends for the Union. Kentucky held three special elections in 1861: for a border-state convention in May, for a special session of Congress in June, and for the state legislature in August. Unionists won solid majorities in every election. Meanwhile, the partisans of each side were arming to prevent a coup by the other. Magoffin organized Confederate sympathizers into "state guard" regiments. Unionists countered by organizing "home guards." Lincoln authorized five thousand muskets for the home guards, and the Unionists secretly ferried these weapons across the Ohio River at night. The President also sent Robert Anderson, the defender of Fort Sumter and a native of Kentucky, to Cincinnati to receive Kentucky volunteers into the Union army.

As both sides built up their forces on the borders and as state guards confronted home guards inside the state, the days of Kentucky's neutrality appeared to be numbered. Several Union regiments under the command of General Ulysses S. Grant were poised just across the Ohio River at Cairo, Illinois. Fearing that these regiments were about to seize the strategic heights commanding the Mississippi River at Columbus, Kentucky, Confederate General Leonidas Polk decided to steal a march on them by occupying Columbus himself. His troops did so on September 3. Polk's fears were well founded, and his move was militarily sound. But by moving first he committed a political blunder. Kentucky's Unionist legislature denounced the Confederate "invaders" and invited the U.S. government to drive them out. On September 6, Grant obligingly occupied Paducah and Southland, at the mouths of the Tennessee and Cumberland rivers. A taciturn man whose iron will and quiet efficiency compelled obedience and got things done, Grant belied his reputation as a drunk and a drifter. His occupation of these key river points boded ill for the Confederacy.

The war that Kentucky had vainly hoped to avoid by neutrality was now at its doorstep. The state officially remained in the Union, even though in November 1861 its secessionist minority called a convention, passed an ordinance of secession, and "joined" the Confederacy. During the war nearly 50,000 Kentucky whites (and 24,000 blacks) fought in the Union army, while an estimated 35,000 served in the Confederate ranks.

Missouri

A quite different series of events kept Missouri in the Union. It would scarcely stretch the truth to say that the Civil War began along the Missouri-Kansas border in 1854 and lasted there eleven years instead of four. Many of the border ruffians continued their battle for slavery as members of the Confederate army, while the free-state Kansas "jayhawkers" donned Federal uniforms in 1861.[8] A former leader of the border ruffians, Claiborne Jackson had been elected governor of Missouri in 1860. When Lincoln called for militia from the state, Jackson sent a defiant reply: "Your requisition is illegal, unconstitutional, revolutionary, inhuman, diabolical, and cannot be complied with."[9] The governor moved quickly to place Missouri in the Confederacy before Unionist elements could organize. He took control of the St. Louis police and began to mobilize the militia under pro-Confederate officers. On April 21, some of these troops seized the U.S. arsenal at Liberty, near Kansas City. But Jackson had a bigger prize in mind—the arsenal in St. Louis, which held 60,000 muskets and other military equipment. He secretly asked Jefferson Davis for a battery of artillery to use against the arsenal. Davis complied, and on May 8 boxes marked "marble" but containing four cannons and ammunition arrived at St. Louis from downriver.

But Jackson had reckoned without two antagonists even more determined than he. The acting commander of the St. Louis arsenal was Captain Nathaniel Lyon of the 2nd U.S. Infantry. Lyon was a wiry, hard-bitten Connecticut Yankee who had acquired strong anti-Southern convictions when stationed in Kansas before the war. His aggressive Unionism was backed by Francis P. Blair, Jr., a congressman from Missouri and brother of Lincoln's postmaster general. Lyon and Blair arranged for the removal of most of the muskets across the river to Illinois and kept the rest to arm volunteer regiments organized mainly by the German-American population of St. Louis, the backbone of Unionism in Missouri. Lyon mustered four of these regiments into Federal service. On May 10, he led them with two companies of regulars to surround the pro-Confederate militia camp. Outnumbered, the militia surrendered. As the prisoners were marched through St. Louis, a crowd gathered. Growing increasingly raucous, members of the crowd cheered for Jefferson Davis, threw stones at the "Hessians," and threatened them with revolvers. Finally, a drunken man shot an officer, whereupon the soldiers opened fire. When it was over, thirty-three people including two soldiers lay dead or dying. That night mobs roamed the streets, and next day another affray broke out in which twelve civilians and soldiers were killed.

This affair blew the lid off Missouri. Many conditional Unionists went over to secession, including former Governor Sterling Price, who assumed command of the pro-Southern troops. The legislature adopted Governor Jackson's proposals to put

---

[8]For the border ruffians, see pages 101 to 102. The jayhawkers (from the name of an imaginary bird) were the free-soil counterparts of the border ruffians. They practiced the same guerrilla tactics of hit-and-run attacks, ambush, and terrorism as their enemies, which helped make the war in Missouri a particularly vicious affair.

[9]O.R., Ser. 3, Vol. 1, p. 83.

the state on a war footing. On the other side, Lyon was promoted to brigadier general and given command of the 10,000 Union troops now in Missouri. In a stormy meeting with Price on June 11, Lyon ended the armed truce that had prevailed while moderates tried to work out a Kentucky-style "neutrality" for Missouri. "Rather than concede to the State of Missouri for one single instant the right to dictate to my Government," Lyon told the aristocratic, Virginia-born Price, "I would see you . . . and every man, woman, and child in the State dead and buried. This means war."[10]

Lyon moved his troops up the Missouri River to the capital, Jefferson City. Price retreated farther upriver to Boonville. Lyon pursued him with 1,700 men, and in a skirmish on June 17 he routed Price's militia and drove them in disarray to the southwest corner of the state. There they hoped to regroup, arm new recruits, and combine with Confederate troops from Arkansas to win Missouri for the South. Meanwhile, the state convention, which had adjourned in March after rejecting a secession ordinance, reassembled and assumed the functions of a legislature. It declared the governorship vacant and appointed a new governor. Claiborne Jackson retaliated by forming a pro-Confederate shadow government, which was officially recognized by the Confederacy in November.

On July 25, John C. Frémont arrived in St. Louis as commander of the Union's Western Department. As a former explorer of the Rockies, hero of California's Bear Flag Revolt, and first Republican presidential candidate, Frémont had both military experience and political connections. But the chaotic situation in Missouri proved too much for him. Guerrilla warfare raged in all parts of the state. Two Confederate armies were gathering on the southern border for an invasion. Four days after Frémont arrived, a Rebel force of 6,000 crossed the Mississippi from Tennessee and occupied New Madrid, threatening the Union garrison at the river junction of Cairo, Illinois.

Frémont decided to reinforce Cairo, but to do so he had to withhold reinforcements from Nathaniel Lyon's army of 6,000 men at Springfield in southwest Missouri. Short of supplies, distant from his base, the enlistment time of the ninety-day regiments that comprised half his force about to expire, Lyon confronted a motley Southern army composed of Sterling Price's Missourians plus Confederates under General Ben McCulloch, a former Texas Ranger. Since this force numbered more than twice as many men as his own, Lyon's only choice seemed to be retreat. But he was loath to give up southern Missouri without a fight. Aggressive and impetuous, Lyon decided to make a surprise attack on the Confederate camp at Wilson's Creek, ten miles from Springfield. Boldly splitting his small army, he sent 1,200 men under General Franz Sigel to attack the Confederate rear while he himself with 4,200 men hit them in front. The two groups attacked at dawn August 10. The advantage of surprise gave the Federals an edge at first. The poorly armed Rebels fell back between the Union pincers. But at a critical point Sigel, seeing a regiment with the same color uniforms as the 1st Iowa emerge from the smoke in his front and assuming that Lyon had broken through the Confederate line, ordered his men to hold their fire. The approaching soldiers were not Iowans, however, but a Louisiana regiment that, like

[10]Thomas L. Snead, *The Fight for Missouri from the Election of Lincoln to the Death of Lyon* (New York, 1886), pp. 199–200; Christopher Phillips, *Damned Yankee: The Life of General Nathaniel Lyon* (Columbia, Mo., 1990), pp. 212–214.

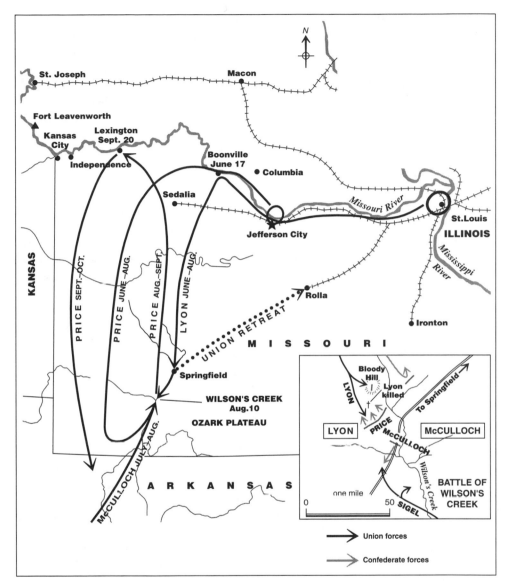

Missouri, 1861

many others on both sides in the early months of the war, had clothed itself in uniforms of a color and style of its own choosing. The Louisianians, unopposed, cut down Sigel's force with a withering fire and routed it from the field. Lyon's own command, now outnumbered three to one, held on desperately in the face of repeated counterattacks. But they lost many men and began to run short of ammunition. After Lyon had been killed, the top-ranking Federal officer left unwounded on the field (a major) ordered a retreat. The Unionists trudged back to Springfield and then one hundred miles northward to the railhead supply base at Rolla.

Confederate victory in this small but vicious battle of Wilson's Creek (each side suffered more than 1,200 casualties) exposed southern and western Missouri to Confederate invasion. Marching northward with 10,000 men and gathering recruits as he moved, Price went all the way to the Missouri River, where with 18,000 troops he laid siege to the 3,500-man Union garrison at Lexington. Frémont could spare few men from the task of fighting guerrillas, but he managed to scrape together two small brigades to reinforce Lexington. They were too little and too late. The garrison surrendered on September 20.

In two months Frémont had lost nearly half of Missouri. And military reverses were not his only problem. As commander of a department, he faced complex administrative problems with little help from Washington a thousand miles away. War contracts must be let; supplies, arms, horses, and wagons must be obtained in a hurry; gunboats for the river navy must be built; new recruits must be organized and trained; transport bottlenecks must be overcome; Rebel sympathizers must be watched; and quarreling factions of Unionists must be kept in line. Frémont was not equal to the task. Honest himself, he was overwhelmed by contractors eager to make profits from the army's needs. Reports of graft became commonplace. Congressman Blair, the most powerful political figure in Union Missouri and now a colonel as well, turned against Frémont and began scheming to have him removed.

Distracted by these problems and bedeviled by the increasing boldness of guerrillas, Frémont took a desperate step. On August 30, he issued an order that put the whole state under martial law, proclaimed the death penalty for guerrillas captured behind Union lines, and confiscated the property and freed the slaves of all Confederate sympathizers in Missouri. This order stirred up a hornet's nest. Abolitionists and many Republicans lionized Frémont as one general who knew how to destroy the taproot of rebellion. But a guerrilla commander in southeast Missouri announced that for every one of his men executed by the Yankees he would "HANG, DRAW AND QUARTER a minion of said Abraham Lincoln."[11] Slaveholding Unionists from Missouri to Maryland threatened to defect if Frémont's emancipation edict was carried out. Vitally concerned with keeping the allegiance of the border states, Lincoln believed he could not afford to let Frémont's action stand. He told the general he must execute no guerrillas without prior approval from Washington and suggested privately that he modify his confiscation and emancipation edict to make it conform with the confiscation act enacted by Congress on August 6 (see page 290), which authorized the seizure only of property and slaves used directly in the Confederate war effort. When Frémont refused, Lincoln publicly ordered him to modify the proclamation.

The President also decided to make a change of command in Missouri, where the war contract scandals had become notorious. Knowing that he could save himself only by military success, Frémont gathered 38,000 troops and took personal command of them. The Federals drove Price's army almost to the Arkansas line once again. But as Frémont was preparing for a showdown battle, on November 2 an order relieving him of command reached his headquarters. His successor, believing the army overextended, ordered a retreat to its bases in central Missouri. On November 19, General Henry W. Halleck took control of the newly created Department of Mis-

---

[11]Jay Monaghan, *Civil War on the Western Border 1854–1865* (New York, 1955), p. 185.

souri (which also included western Kentucky, bringing Grant under Halleck's command). A military scholar who had written and translated several works on strategy (which earned him the sobriquet "Old Brains."), Halleck was a cautious general who waged war by the book. He possessed the administrative capacity that Frémont lacked and soon brought order out of the organizational chaos in Missouri.

In the course of the war, about 80,000 white Missourians (and 8,000 blacks) served in the Union armies, while some 30,000 joined the Confederates and another 3,000 or more fought as Southern guerrillas. Among the latter was the notorious William Quantrill, whose band at one time or another included Cole Younger and Frank and Jesse James. These guerrilla bands wreaked havoc out of all proportion to their numbers. Counterguerrilla forces sprang up among the Kansas jayhawkers, whose raids across the border continued the vicious warfare of Bleeding Kansas days. Although peripheral to the principal military campaigns of the war, Missouri suffered more than any other state from raids, skirmishes, and guerrilla actions, leaving a postwar legacy of violence and outlawry in which "the terrible grudges of neighbor against neighbor created in the guerrilla conflict" persisted for decades.[12]

Each through a different process, then, the four border slave states remained in the Union, though a substantial minority of their people supported the Confederacy. The war itself created a fifth Union border state: West Virginia.

West Virginia

The western portion of Virginia was strategically important because the Baltimore and Ohio Railroad (the B&O) and the Ohio River ran through it or along its border for two hundred miles. The Confederates struck first in this vital area by cutting the B&O west of Harpers Ferry in May 1861. The task of driving them out fell to General George B. McClellan, who organized 20,000 troops in Ohio and sent a vanguard across the river in late May. This force occupied Grafton on the B&O and then moved fifteen miles south to rout a small Confederate outpost at Philippi on June 3. The Confederates sent reinforcements to western Virginia under General Robert Garnett, who fortified two passes through the mountains, twenty miles south of Philippi. Meanwhile, the Confederate garrison at Harpers Ferry, menaced by the Federal advance in its rear and by the buildup of another Union force across the Potomac in its front, retreated to a more defensible position near Winchester.

Union forces now controlled the B&O, but McClellan's plans had evolved beyond merely regaining the railroad. With 12,000 men he advanced in two columns against Garnett's 5,000. While one Union column demonstrated against the most strongly defended pass at Laurel Mountain, the other assaulted the Confederate position at Rich Mountain on July 11. Accepting the battle plan suggested by General William S. Rosecrans, McClellan sent Rosecrans's brigade to circle around and assail the Rebels from the rear while the main force attacked in front. Rosecrans did his job well, smashing through the Confederate defenses and driving the survivors into the town of Beverly,

---

[12]Michael Fellman, *Inside War: The Guerrilla Conflict in Missouri During the American Civil War* (New York, 1989), p. 232.

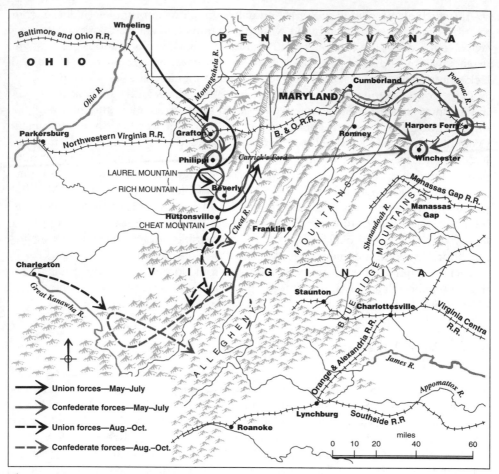

The War in Western Virginia, 1861

where more than 550 surrendered. The weakness of McClellan's frontal attack allowed the rest to escape northward, where they joined the other Confederate force retreating from Laurel Mountain. On July 13, the pursuing Federals fell on the Confederate rear guard at Carrick's Ford, where Garnett was killed trying to rally his broken regiments.

At a cost of fewer than a hundred casualties, the Federals had inflicted ten times that number of losses on the Confederates, including seven hundred prisoners. The defeated Southern army fled eastward, leaving most of Virginia west of the Alleghenies under Union control. Although much of the credit for these victories belonged to McClellan's subordinates, especially Rosecrans, McClellan proved adept at writing dispatches reflecting glory on himself. The Northern press lauded the thirty-four-year-old general as a "Young Napoleon" who would roll up the Confederate flank in the mountains and drive all the way to Richmond. McClellan's army was too small for this, however, even if the formidable problems of transport and supply across the rugged Alleghenies could have been solved. Most of McClellan's troops were needed to protect the railroad and other key points against guerrilla and cavalry raids and to prepare for an expected Confederate counterstroke.

The Richmond government sent Robert E. Lee to regain western Virginia. One of the most promising officers in the old army, Lee on April 18 had declined Lincoln's offer of command of the principal Union field army and had resigned his commission two days later. Lee was lukewarm toward slavery and opposed secession, but he was unwilling to "raise my hand against my birthplace." He chose state over nation. After an interval as a desk general in Richmond, he went west to the mountains on July 28 to assume overall command of the 15,000 reorganizing Confederate troops facing about 11,000 Federals now occupying trans-Allegheny Virginia. Lee decided to attack a Union brigade dug in at the Cheat Mountain pass through which ran the turnpike connecting Staunton in the Shenandoah Valley with Parkersburg on the Ohio River. Hampered by heavy rains and by epidemics of measles and typhoid that sidelined a third of his men, Lee's complicated enveloping maneuver fizzled on September 12 and he fell back without a battle.

Lee then moved south to the Kanawha Valley to take charge of the brigades under Generals John Floyd and Henry Wise, Virginia politicians who spent more energy feuding with each other than fighting the enemy. Jefferson Davis straightened out their conflict by recalling Wise to Richmond. But Lee's plan to trap a Union force under Rosecrans failed when Rosecrans pulled back to a defensive position too strong for Lee to attack. Disease, mud, feuding generals, and supply problems over terrible mountain roads had defeated Lee. Although he kept Rosecrans out of the Shenandoah Valley, his three months' expedition was counted a failure. Southern newspapers called him "Granny Lee" and criticized him for having failed even to bring the Yankees to battle, much less to disturb their control of western Virginia. Lee's first campaign almost ruined his reputation before it had a chance to become established.

The Union's military success in western Virginia had important political consequences. Few residents of this region owned slaves. For decades they had complained of overtaxation and underrepresentation in the state government. They had little in common with the "tidewater aristocrats." Their economy and culture were oriented toward Ohio and Pennsylvania. When Virginia seceded from the Union, many of the trans-Allegheny convention delegates returned home determined to secede from Virginia. They arrived to find mass meetings demanding the same thing. Many northwestern Virginians welcomed the Union troops as liberators. At the second of two conventions in Wheeling representing thirty-four trans-Allegheny counties, delegates voted June 19 to constitute themselves the legitimate government of Virginia. This convention later called a constitutional convention to meet in Wheeling in November 1861 to form a new state to be named Kanawha (later changed to West Virginia). This action was ratified by a popular referendum in which only those who took a Unionist oath could vote. In May 1862, a Unionist "legislature," which theoretically represented all of Virginia but in reality represented primarily the western counties, approved the creation of the new state. This technically fulfilled the stipulation of the U.S. Constitution (Article IV, Section 3) that no new state can be formed within the boundaries of an existing state without the consent of the latter's legislature.

Despite these irregular proceedings, the Union Congress finally admitted West Virginia as a state in 1863 (after requiring the abolition of slavery therein). This new state contained fifty counties, nearly half of which, however, probably had a pro-Southern majority that would have preferred to remain part of Confederate Virginia. West Virginia contributed about 25,000 men to the Union army, though many of these remained tied down by Rebel guerrilla bands that roamed the mountains throughout the war. Perhaps 15,000 West Virginians fought for the Confederacy. Like Missouri, West Virginia carried on its own civil war within the larger conflict.

East Tennessee

The Lincoln administration hoped to provoke a Unionist uprising in east Tennessee to restore that region to the Union on the West Virginia model. Soon after Union military forces had occupied northern Kentucky in September 1861, Federal agents established contact with east Tennessee Unionists to coordinate a local uprising with an invasion by Northern troops through the Cumberland Gap from Kentucky. The commander of the small invading army was General George H. Thomas, a Virginian who had remained loyal to the Union.

Right on schedule at the end of October, the Tennessee Unionists began burning bridges, attacking Confederate supply lines, and softening up the opposition for their Northern liberators. But the Yankees did not come. Nervous about an expected Confederate thrust in central Kentucky, the commander of the Union's Department of the Ohio, General Don Carlos Buell, canceled Thomas's invasion. The roads were terrible, said Buell, the mountains rugged, winter was coming on, and a Union occupying force could not be sustained in this difficult country even if it could get there. The true line of operations, he insisted, was along the rivers against central and west Tennessee. Without support from the outside, the east Tennessee resistance collapsed in November. Confederate soldiers rounded up scores of Unionists, executed five, and imprisoned the rest.[13]

Buell's pessimism about a winter offensive was justified. But continuing pressure from the administration caused him reluctantly to order Thomas southward in January 1862. Winter rains mired Thomas's wagons and artillery axle-deep in mud, on roads little better than Indian paths. A fifth of his 5,000 men fell out sick or as stragglers in the hundred-mile march to Mill Springs, the Confederate base sixty miles northwest of the Cumberland Gap. A Confederate force of 4,000 under Generals George Crittenden and Felix Zollicoffer marched out to strike Thomas in a surprise dawn attack on January 19 at Logan's Cross-Roads (see map, page 245). Although pushed back at first, the Federals rallied in a spirited counterattack that killed Zollicoffer and routed the Rebels. It was a decisive tactical victory for Thomas but its strategic consequences were negligible. The wild mountains south of the Cumber-

---

[13]Noel C. Fisher, *War at Every Door: Partisan Politics and Guerrilla Violence in East Tennessee, 1860–1869* (Chapel Hill, 1997), chap. 3.

land River made a farther advance impossible during the winter. By spring the important campaigns in west Tennessee diverted Federal attention to that theater. To Lincoln's sorrow, east Tennessee was fated to remain under Confederate control for another year and a half.

On balance, the outcome of the crucial struggle for the upper South in 1861 probably favored the Union. Although four of these states (Virginia, North Carolina, Tennessee, and Arkansas) went over to the Confederacy, they were offset by the five border states (including West Virginia) of equal population that declared for the Union. The production of food, draft animals, iron, lead, salt, and other items of military importance was greater in the five Union than in the four Confederate states. Union control of northern Kentucky and Missouri provided strategic access to the major river systems in the western war theater. This enabled the North to launch its victorious river-borne invasions deep into Confederate territory during 1862. And while close to 100,000 men from the Union border states fought for the Confederacy, this was equaled by 55,000 whites and 45,000 blacks from the upper-South Confederate states who eventually served in the Union armies.[14]

In the spring of 1861, however, most of these developments lay in the future. The main concern of both sides in these early months of the war was to mobilize, train, and equip their armies and navies, and to develop a strategy for using them.

---

[14]Richard Nelson Current, *Lincoln's Loyalists: Union Soldiers from the Confederacy* (Boston, 1992).

Mobi-lizing for War

Col. Roberts has showed himself to be ignorant of the most simple company movements. There is a total lack of system about our regiment. . . . We can only be justly called a mob & one not fit to face the enemy.

—Pennsylvania soldier,
July 1861

Organizing the Armed Forces

Unreadiness for War

Seldom has a country been less prepared for a major war than the United States was in 1861. The tiny regular army—fewer than 16,000 men—was scattered in small units all over the country, mostly west of the Mississippi. Nearly a third of the army's officers were resigning to join the Confederacy. The War Department in Washington drowsed in peacetime routine. All but one of the officers commanding the eight army bureaus had been in service since the War of 1812. General-in-Chief Winfield Scott was seventy-four years old and suffered from dropsy and vertigo. There was nothing resembling a general staff. There were no accurate military maps. When General Henry W. Halleck began to direct operations in the western theater in 1862, he used maps obtained from a bookstore. West Point's strong points were engineering, mathematics, and fortifications, but its students learned little of strategy, staff work, or the tactical command of troops in the field. Many of the Point's graduates, including George B. McClellan, Ulysses S. Grant, William T. Sherman, Thomas J. Jackson, Jefferson Davis, and Braxton Bragg, had the left the army to pursue civilian careers.

The navy was scarcely in better shape. Only forty-two of its ninety ships were in commission. Most of these were on station in distant waters; fewer than a dozen were available for immediate service along the American coast. Trained for deep-water operations, the navy had little experience with the coastal and inshore work that would be required of it during the Civil War. Indeed, its officers knew the coastal defenses and forts of foreign nations better than those of the South, for they had never contemplated operations against their own ports!

In theory, the state militias formed a ready reserve of all men of military age. But practice fell ludicrously short of theory. The militia had always been somewhat unreliable in war; by the 1830s, it had become a peacetime joke. Militia musters were the occasion for a drinking holiday. Rare was the company that took seriously the idea of drilling. Several militia regiments were called up during the Mexican War, but they saw little action because the principal reliance in that conflict was on regular and volunteer regiments. By the 1850s, the volunteer principle had largely replaced the concept of universal obligation for militia service. Socially elite volunteer companies sprang up in both North and South. Recognizing the inevitable, several states incorporated these units into the militia structure, making the militia for all practical purposes voluntary and selective rather than compulsory and universal. Being primarily social rather than military societies, few of these volunteer companies acquired any real training or discipline. Nevertheless, it was they who first answered the call to arms in 1861.

Both sides believed that the war would be a short one. The active phase of the Mexican War, which served as a reference point for Americans, had lasted only sixteen months and had resulted in the conquest of a country larger than the Confederacy. A more recent example, the Franco-Austrian War of 1859, had lasted less than three months. After Sumter fell, the *New York Times* predicted that this "local commotion" in the South would be put down "in thirty days." The *Chicago Tribune* thought it might take two or three months. General Winfield Scott, less optimistic than most, was confident of success by the spring of 1862. Confederate estimates were even more unrealistic. Many Southerners felt contempt for Yankees as "vulgar, fanatical, cheating counter-jumpers." Northerners were cowards: "Just throw three or four shells among those blue-bellied Yankees," said a North Carolinian, "and they'll scatter like sheep." Many Southerners believed that one Rebel could lick ten Yankees because "the Yankee army is filled up with the scum of creation and ours with the best blood of the grand old Southland."[1]

Of course, not everyone in the South or North lived in this dreamland. Jefferson Davis and his vice president, Alexander Stephens, tried to warn their followers that it would be a long, hard war. Just after the fall of Sumter, William T. Sherman wrote: "I think it is to be a long war—very long—much longer than any politician thinks." On Lincoln's call for 75,000 three-months militiamen, Sherman commented: "You might as well attempt to put out the flames of a burning house with a squirt-gun."[2]

But such were minority opinions amid the ebullient enthusiasm that existed in the spring of 1861. Men on both sides rushed to enlist before the war was over. They had only the vaguest and most romantic notions of what war was like. Their vision was of bands, banners, massed formations marching in brilliant sunshine to glorious vic-

---

[1] Allan Nevins, *The War for the Union: The Improvised War, 1861–1862* (New York, 1959), pp. 75, 95–96, 151; Bell I. Wiley, *The Life of Johnny Reb: The Common Soldier of the Confederacy* (Indianapolis, 1943), p. 310.

[2] Sherman to Thomas Ewing, Jr., June 3, 1861, Brooks D. Simpson and Jean V. Berlin (eds.) *Sherman's Civil War: Selected Correspondence of William T. Sherman, 1860–1865* (Chapel Hill, 1999), p. 98; Basil H. Liddell Hart, *Sherman: Soldier, Realist, American* (New York, 1929), p. 72.

tories in which death, if it came, would be painless and honorable. Few could envisage the mud or choking dust, the bone-deep fatigue, the searing thirst and gnawing hunger, the bitter cold or enervating heat of the march or bivouac; the boredom of camp life; the gut-tearing pain of dysentery or the delirious ravings of typhoid in a primitive army hospital; the smoke, noise, confusion, and terror of battle; the blood and screams and amputated limbs of the surgeon's tent. Even those who foresaw a long war could scarcely conceive of the massive mobilization of men and resources this war would require or the savage destruction of men and resources it would cause.

Recruitment and Supply

Lincoln realized that three-months militiamen would be inadequate for even a short war. On May 3, the President called for 42,000 three-year volunteers, expanded the regular army by authorizing an additional 23,000 men, and directed the recruitment of 18,000 sailors for the navy. Lincoln's only legal authorization for these measures was his emergency war powers as Commander in Chief, but he expected Congress to ratify his actions at its special session beginning July 4. Congress did so. In his message to the special session, Lincoln also asked for authority to raise at least 400,000 additional volunteers; Congress approved a million; and in the end more than 700,000 men enlisted, most of them for three years, under these presidential and congressional actions of 1861. Some of the three-months regiments reenlisted for three years; many individuals in other militia units reenlisted in the new three-year regiments after expiration of their initial service.

The process of raising a three-year regiment went something like this: Prominent citizens opened a recruiting office and organized recruiting rallies. When approximately one hundred men had signed up, they were formed into a company; ten companies were then enrolled as a regiment. In accordance with long-standing militia and volunteer tradition, the men in most companies elected the company officers (captain and lieutenants); these in turn elected the regimental officers (colonel, lieutenant colonel, and major). The state governor officially commissioned the regimental officers but usually appointed those elected by the junior officers. In practice, the selection of officers at all levels was often predetermined by their role in organizing a company or by their political influence. The election of officers was often a *pro forma* ratification of their leadership. The principal basis for recruitment and organization was geography. Companies and sometimes entire regiments came from the same township, county, or city. Ethnicity was also an affinity basis for numerous regiments in the Union army. Many regiments and sometimes whole brigades were composed primarily of German-Americans or Irish-Americans.

In the early months of the war, states or localities provided uniforms and other equipment. This led to a motley variety of colors and types of uniforms, ranging from the standard dark blue jacket and light blue trousers of the regular army to the gaudy "Zouave" colors based on the uniforms of the renowned French colonial regiments of Algeria. Some Union regiments at first wore gray uniforms (and some Confederates initially wore blue), leading to tragic mix-ups in the early battles. Not until 1862 were Union soldiers consistently uniformed in blue.

TYPICAL CONFEDERATE AND UNION INFANTRY COMPANIES EARLY IN THE WAR.
These pictures show typical Confederate and Union volunteer infantry companies in the early months of the war. The above photograph is of Co. K of the 4th Georgia Infantry in April 1861. Note the seven stars in the Confederate flag, indicating that the photograph was taken before the secession of the upper-South states. This "Stars and Bars" flag remained the official flag of the Confederacy. But its arrangement of stars and bars caused it to become confused with the Stars and Stripes of the U.S. flag in the first battle of Bull Run. Confederate General Beauregard therefore devised a battle flag based on the St. Andrew's cross, and it was this battle flag that has come down through history as the familiar banner of the Confederacy. The photograph on the next page shows Co. K of the 6th Vermont Infantry at the regiment's training camp near Washington in the fall of 1861. Note that healthy, spit-and-polish appearance of both companies before they saw combat. Still, by the time these pictures were taken, their numbers had been reduced, the Georgia company to 80 percent, and the Vermont company to 60 percent of its initial complement of one hundred men. The 6th Vermont was part of the Vermont Brigade, which would suffer greater losses than any other Union brigade. More than one-fourth of the men in the 6th Vermont would die in the war.

The process of Northern recruitment was marked by great energy at the local level and decreasing efficiency at each step up the ladder to the War Department. Secretary of War Simon Cameron was overwhelmed by his task. As the regiments poured in to state rendezvous points or training camps, shortages and confusion abounded. In a November 1861 report from his base at Cairo, Illinois, General Ulysses S. Grant complained of "a great deficiency in transportation. I have no ambulances. The cloth-

ing received has been almost universally of an inferior quality and deficient in quantity. . . . The quartermaster's department has been carried on with so little funds that government credit has become exhausted." Grant's superior in St. Louis, General Henry W. Halleck, put it succinctly: "Affairs here are in complete chaos."[3]

The need to sign war contracts hurriedly in 1861 led to scandals and charges of profiteering. A few clothing contractors supplied uniforms made from pressed scraps of shredded wool, called "shoddy," which fell apart after a few weeks' wear. Not until Congress set up a watchdog committee and Edwin M. Stanton replaced the blundering Cameron as war secretary in January 1862 did order and efficiency govern the business of contracts and supply for the Union army. By 1862, the Northern forces would become the best-equipped armies in the world's history, but a society unprepared for war required a full year to gear up for the conflict.

In some respects, the South mobilized more quickly than the North. Although the Confederacy began with no regular army or navy and few resources to create the latter, the South's numerous volunteer companies put themselves on a war footing as soon as their states seceded. On March 6, 1861, more than five weeks before the firing on Sumter, the Confederate Congress authorized 100,000 volunteers. Two more laws in May provided for an additional 400,000 men. Although the South's manpower pool was less than one-third as large as the North's, the Confederacy had nearly two-thirds as many men under arms as the Union by July 1861.

The recruiting process followed essentially the same pattern in the South as in the North. Localities and states took the initiative, swamping the government with more volunteers than it could equip. Some 150,000 muskets were stored in the U.S. arsenals seized by the seceding states, but most of these were obsolete and many were unserviceable. Confederate volunteers often brought their own weapons. Many companies initially carried shotguns, hunting rifles, and ancient flintlock muskets. Each regiment also uniformed itself in 1861, and the range of styles and colors was as great as in the Union army. The Confederate government adopted cadet

---

[3]Bruce Catton, *Grant Moves South* (Boston, 1960), p. 93.

gray as the official uniform color but was never able to clothe its armies uniformly. Many soldiers wore no distinguishable uniform at all; the most common hue was "butternut," a dust-brown color produced by a dye made from butternut bark or walnut hulls.

Why They Fought

Most soldiers on both sides in the Civil War were volunteers who considered them-selves citizens in uniform rather than professional soldiers. What caused hundreds of thousands to flock to recruiting offices in 1861? For many, simple patriotism was motive enough. Whether his family approved or not, wrote a young clerk in Massa-chusetts, "I *am going*. I am not laboring under any 'sea fit' . . . but a duty which everyone ought to perform—love of country." A married man in a small Michigan town defied the wishes of both his wife and parents to enlist in August 1861, trying to explain to them that "the state of the country" required "all true patriots to sustain her government." Of his family he said, "They admitted that our country needed men but their plea was that thare was anuff without me but I had made up my mind to enlist so thare was no stoping me." Just as Northern soldiers fought for the *United States* as their country, many Confederates swore allegiance to their new separate country, the Confederate States of America. "Sink or swim, survive or perish," wrote one, "I will fight in defence of my country."[4]

More than any other generation of Americans, Civil War soldiers had come of age in an era of political and ideological ferment. They carried into the army the con-victions they formed during the stirring events of 1854–1860. Union soldiers pro-fessed to fight for the preservation of constitutional government, majority rule, and the heritage of republican liberty. Lincoln had labeled secession "the essence of an-archy"; many Union soldiers echoed his words. "This contest is not the North against the South, " wrote a Philadelphia printer as he prepared to enlist. "It is government against anarchy, law against disorder." An immigrant working in a textile mill wrote to his father back in England explaining why he had joined the 3rd New Jersey Vol-unteer Infantry. "If the Unionists let the South secede, " he declared, "the West might want to follow and this country would be as bad as the German states. . . . There would have to be another form of a constitution wrote and after it was written who would obey it?" To an Ohio blacksmith, the cause for which he fought as a private in the 70th Ohio was "the cause of the constitution and law." He explained, "Admit the right of the seceding states to break up the Union at pleasure . . . and how long will it be before the new confederacies created by the first disruption shall be re-solved into still smaller fragments and the continent become a vast theater of civil war, military license, anarchy, and despotism? Better settle it at whatever cost and settle it forever."[5]

Confederate volunteers invoked the rights of property and self-government and the defense of home and hearth against "tyranny" and "subjugation." Three months before he was killed at Chancellorsville, a soldier in the 44th Virginia described the

---

[4]James M. McPherson, *For Cause and Comrades: Why Men Fought in the Civil War* (New York, 1997), pp. 17–18; James M. McPherson, *What They Fought For, 1861–1865* (Baton Rouge, 1994), p. 11.
[5]McPherson, *For Cause and Comrades,* pp. 18, 112.

war as "a struggle between Liberty on one side, and Tyranny on the other." A Missourian who cast his lot with the Confederacy wrote in 1862, two years before he was killed in action, that he fought for the "undying principles of Constitutional liberty and self government."[6]

Union and Confederate soldiers alike believed themselves custodians of the legacy of 1776. The crisis of 1861 was the great test of whether they were worthy of the heritage of liberty bequeathed to them by the founding fathers. On *their* shoulders rode the fate of the great experiment in republican government launched in 1776. The tragic irony of the Civil War is that Confederate and Union soldiers interpreted the heritage of 1776 in opposite ways. Like their forefathers (they believed), Confederates fought for liberty and independence from what they regarded as a tyrannical government. Unionists fought to save from dismemberment and destruction the nation created by the founders.

A young Virginia officer filled letters to his mother with comparisons of the North's "war of subjugation against the South" to "England's war upon the colonies." He was confident the Confederacy would win this "second War for American Independence" because "Tyranny cannot prosper" against "a people fighting for their liberties." Across the lines, a recruit in the 10th Wisconsin wrote in January 1862 that civil war "is a calamity to any country, " but "this second war I consider equally as holy as the first . . . by which we gained those liberties and privileges" now threatened by "this monstrous rebellion." Later the same year, a Minnesota sergeant recovering from a wound refused to seek a medical discharge as his wife had urged him to do. "My grandfather fought and risked his life to bequeath to his posterity . . . the glorious Institutions" under attack by "this infernal rebellion. . . . It is not for you and I, or us & our dear little ones, alone, that I was and am willing to risk the fortunes of the battle-field, but also for the sake of the country's millions who are to come after us."[7]

Several Union soldiers also invoked an idea frequently expressed by Lincoln, that the United States represented the last best hope for the survival of republican government in a world bestrode by kings, emperors, and despots of many stripes. If secession fragmented America into the dis-United States, European aristocrats and reactionaries would smile in smug satisfaction at the confirmation of their belief that this foolish experiment in government of, by, and for the people would indeed perish from the earth. In 1863, on the second anniversary of his enlistment, a private in the 2nd Ohio Cavalry wrote that he had not expected the war to last so long, but no matter how much longer it took, it must be prosecuted "for the great principles of liberty and self government at stake, for should we fail, the onward march of Liberty in the Old World will be retarded at least a century, and Monarchs, Kings and Aristocrats will be more powerful against their subjects than ever." An Irish-born soldier in the 28th Massachusetts drew a parallel between his fight for the Union and the struggle for liberty in the old country. "This is my country as much as the man who was born on the soil," he wrote in 1863. "I have as much interest in the maintenance of . . . the integrity of the nation as any other man." The war "is the first test of a modern free government in the act of sustaining itself against internal enemys . . . if

---

[6]McPherson, *What They Fought For,* p. 11.

[7]McPherson, *What They Fought For,* p. 9; McPherson, *For Cause and Comrades,* pp. 19, 111.

it fail all tyrants will succeed." The "old cry will be sent forth from the aristocrats of Europe that such is the common lot of all republics. . . . America is Irlands refugs Irlands last hope destroy this republic and her hopes are blasted."[8]

Soldiers on both sides used the word "liberty" more than any other to express what they fought for. But no Confederates and few Union soldiers at first meant liberty for the slaves. Indeed, many Confederates insisted that they were defending their society's "right" and "liberty" to own slaves. "I choose to fight for southern rights and southern liberty," wrote a Kentuckian, "against tyrants of the North . . . who are determined to destroy slavery." While, from the beginning, some Union soldiers professed to fight against the "slave power" that wanted "to secure the extension of that blighting curse—slavery—o'er our fair land," in 1861–1862 most believed that they had enlisted to preserve the Union, not to free the slaves. Not until 1864 would a majority of Northern soldiers agree with the sentiments of a sergeant in the 5th Iowa who thanked God that "we are fighting for *Liberty* and Union and not Union and Slavery."[9]

Americans of the Civil War generation were products of Victorian culture. For them the words "duty" and "honor" were not platitudes; they were vital principles that guided behavior. "No man now has a right to stay at home," wrote a forty-two-year-old Tennessee planter whose wife had opposed his enlistment in the Confederate army. "Duty, patriotism, and, aye, honour calls him to the field." Northern soldiers also filled their letters with references to the need to sacrifice "personal feelings and inclinations to . . . my duty in the hour of danger." Victorians understood duty to be a binding moral obligation involving reciprocity; one had a duty to defend the flag under whose protection one had lived. A Kentucky physician explained to his sister why he joined the Union army: "I know no reason why I should not be a subject to duty as any man, as I have had the protection of government all my life. . . . My absence from home is, of course, a source of grief to Lida and the children . . . but an all-absorbing, all-engrossing sense of duty, alike to country and family, impelled me."[10]

Honor reinforced duty. Honor involved one's public reputation. To shirk duty is a violation of conscience; to suffer dishonor is to be disgraced by public shame. To stay home when others were enlisting courted dishonor. Even though he was thirty-nine years old and father of several daughters (but no son), a South Carolina planter felt compelled to enlist because "I would be disgraced if I staid at home, and unworthy of my revolutionary ancestors. I stand alone in my family. There is no one bearing my name left to fight for our freedom. The honor of our family is involved. . . . A man who will not offer up his life . . . does dishonor to his wife and children." A Virginian enlisted for "the salvation of my reputation and honor (without which a man is not a man)."[11]

Contrary to popular stereotype, the sense of honor seemed as well developed among Northern as Southern men. "My honor is bound up with the Army," wrote an Ohio officer whose wife had pleaded with him to resign his commission. "The filing

---

[8]McPherson, *For Cause and Comrades,* p. 113.
[9]Ibid., pp. 19, 122.
[10]Ibid., pp. 22–24.
[11]Ibid., pp. 24, 136.

of a resignation would cover me with disgrace, no officer can resign in the face of the enemy." A soldier in the 136th New York wrote in his diary that "if I should come home alive, and live to be old, I want to be able to say that I fought willingly for my country and not have my name branded as coward."[12]

The codes of duty and honor were not exclusively masculine. Many young women who watched brothers march away were heard to exclaim, "I wish I were a man!" Some of them acted on this wish. Several hundred women, from Maine to Texas, disguised themselves as men and passed superficial medical examinations to enlist in volunteer regiments. Their motives ranged from patriotism and love of adventure to a desire to stay with husbands or lovers who had joined the army.

Some women soldiers were soon discovered and discharged. The usual reason for discovery was hospitalization for illness or wounds, as in the case of an Ohio private, "Charles Freeman," who was hospitalized for fever, found to be Mary Scaberry, and discharged for "sexual incompatibility." Six female soldiers were found out when they had babies. As a male soldier in a Massachusetts regiment described one of these cases in a letter home: "There was an orderly in one of our regiments & he & the Corporal always slept together. Well, the other night the Corporal had a baby, for the Cpl. turned out to be a woman! She has been in 3 or 4 fights."

A few women soldiers served through the war without discovery. The most famous was Albert Cashier of the 95th Illinois, whose name is inscribed on the Illinois monument at Vicksburg along with those of all other soldiers from the state who fought there. Cashier went to bachelor farming after the war, and not until an accident in 1911 required "his" hospitalization was Albert Cashier discovered to be Jennie Hodgers.[13]

War fever, patriotism, ideological conviction, duty, honor, and peer pressure—these were the sentiments that underlay the virtual self-mobilization of a million Union and Confederate soldiers in the first year of war and sustained both armies through four years of the bloodiest conflict in American history.

Army Organization

The Union and Confederate armies were similar in organization. The basic unit was the regiment; the three combat arms were infantry, artillery, and cavalry. The infantry was the backbone of both armies. The Union raised during the war the equivalent of 2,047 regiments: 1,696 infantry; 272 cavalry; and 78 artillery. The number of regiments or equivalents in the Confederacy is unknown because of the loss or destruction of records, but estimates range from 764 to 1,000.

Each of the ten companies in an infantry regiment had an official strength of eighty-two privates, thirteen sergeants and corporals, two lieutenants (some Confederate regiments had three), and a captain. The regiment itself was commanded by a colonel, with a lieutenant colonel and major as second and third in command plus a small regimental staff. Thus the official strength of an infantry regiment was

---

[12]Ibid., pp. 24, 137.

[13]Elizabeth D. Leonard, *All the Daring of the Soldier: Women of the Civil War Armies* (New York, 1999); quotation from Lauren Cook Burgess (ed.), *An Uncommon Soldier: The Civil War Letters of Sarah Rosetta Wakeman, alias Pvt. Lyons Wakeman . . . 1862–1864* (Pasadena, Md., 1994), p. xii.

about 1,000 men. When first enrolled, most regiments came close to this total. But sickness, casualties, and desertions soon reduced this number. By the second year of the war, the average combat strength of veteran regiments on both sides was less than 500; by the third and fourth years, 350 or fewer. Many regiments by 1863 went into battle with fewer than 200 men.

Instead of channeling new recruits into old regiments to keep them up to strength, localities often preferred to organize new companies and states to organize new regiments. Each new company and regiment provided opportunities for ambitious men to become officers and governors to exercise patronage through the appointment of field officers. Most localities eventually recruited some new men for "their" old regiments, but never enough to maintain anything near full strength. Of the 421,000 new three-year recruits for the Union army in the summer and fall of 1862, only 50,000 went into existing regiments. Commanding generals repeatedly denounced this inefficient and costly system. But it was the price that a democratic society paid to maintain a volunteer army. With the coming of conscription, draftees and substitutes could be assigned to old regiments. Because the Confederacy resorted to conscription earlier than the Union, it kept its regiments a little closer to full strength—but the difference was marginal.

Cavalry regiments were organized in the same fashion as the infantry, except that Union regiments had twelve instead of ten companies (called "troops" in the cavalry). The artillery was of two basic kinds: heavy artillery posted in permanent fortifications, and light or field artillery attached to mobile armies. Since the Confederates rarely attacked Union forts after the fall of Sumter, several Union "heavy" regiments converted to infantry in the latter part of the war. The basic tactical unit of field artillery was the battery, composed of four to six guns with their caissons and four or six horses to pull each gun and caisson. The battery was commanded by a captain and was comparable in size to an infantry company. But unlike the latter, it was generally kept near full strength because of the need for enough men to fire the guns and manage the equipment.

Infantry and sometimes cavalry regiments were grouped into brigades commanded by a brigadier general. Initially composed of four regiments, brigades expanded to five or six later in the war, as the size of regiments decreased. Three or four brigades were grouped into divisions. The division commander was usually a major general. In the first year or so of the war, armies consisted of two or more divisions. But in 1862, both sides adopted the corps organization for larger armies. Composed of two or more divisions (usually three), an army corps was normally commanded by a lieutenant general in the Confederacy but by a major general in the Union (except for Grant in 1864–1865, the North had no higher rank than major general). Artillery batteries were grouped with brigades, divisions, or corps as the situation required.

There was one interesting difference between the Union and Confederate armies. The Union government supplied the horses for its cavalry and artillery. The South expected men in these branches to provide their own horses. This tended to create class distinctions in the Confederate army, especially between the cavalry and infantry, since not every man could afford a cavalry mount. To a degree, the Confederacy preserved the medieval tradition of the cavalry ("chevaliers" or knights) as the

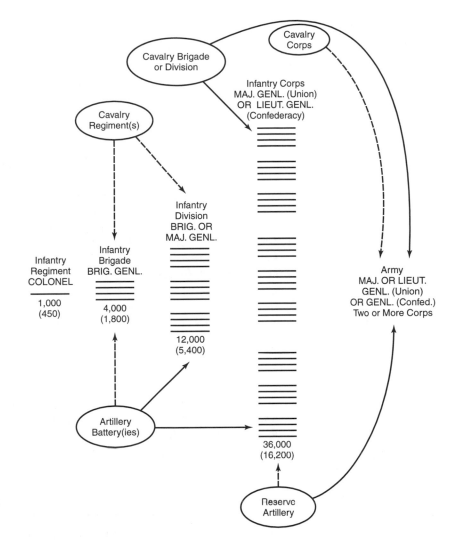

Normal commanding officer of each unit appears in capital letters. Numbers below each unit indicate full quota of men; numbers in parentheses indicate typical size of combat units by second year of war. (By the last two years of the war, brigades often contained five or size regiments; divisions sometimes contained four brigades; and corps sometimes contained four divisions.) Arrows indicate attachment of artillery and cavalry to infantry units; broken arrows indicate occasional attachments to these units. Cavalry often operated independently of infantry units

ORGANIZATION OF UNION AND CONFEDERATE ARMIES

preserve of the aristocracy. The actual practice was more egalitarian, however, especially in the western Confederate armies, where if a man did not own a horse he had a good chance of stealing one or capturing it from the enemy. Nathan Bedford Forrest's troopers scarcely fit one's idea of an aristocracy. Horse-stealing expeditions were an important cavalry function, which Forrest's men elevated to a fine art.

Leadership and Training

In most respects the Confederate army was fully as democratic as its enemy, perhaps more so. Johnny Reb also elected his company officers and sometimes his regimental officers too. Professional army men in both North and South deplored this practice. But in a volunteer army whose privates were accustomed to electing their governors, congressmen, and presidents, the logic of electing their army leaders seemed unassailable. As Jefferson Davis put it, "The troops were drawn from civil life. . . . Who so capable to judge the fitness to command a company, a battalion or a regiment as the men composing it?" It was part of the American creed that any intelligent citizen could learn the skills of statesman or soldier. Most civilians believed that the average lawyer or businessman could "give an average army officer all the advantage of his special training, at the start, and yet beat him at his own trade in a year."[14]

One can imagine the impact of this system on discipline. Privates tended at first to obey only those orders they considered reasonable. Men who regarded themselves as equals of their neighbors at home were slow to change their minds just because the neighbor now wore shoulder straps. Officers were reluctant to enforce discipline if it meant that they might be voted out of their commission or lose the election for county attorney after the war. All too often, officers deserved the contempt of their men. Many officers knew little or nothing about training or commanding soldiers. "Col. Roberts has showed himself to be ignorant of the most simple company movements," wrote a Pennsylvania soldier in 1861. "There is a total lack of system about our regiment. . . . We can only be justly called a mob & one not fit to face the enemy." But the enemy was in no better shape, if one is to believe Confederate professionals. General Joseph E. Johnston, commanding the Southern garrison at Harpers Ferry, complained in June 1861 that his officers and men were so lacking in "discipline and instruction" that it would be "difficult to use them in the field." Of one regiment Johnston said: "I would not give one company of regulars for the whole regiment."[15]

Recognizing the need for minimum standards of officer competence, the Union army in August 1861 instituted an examination for officers. Those who failed were to be replaced by others who had passed. Although this examination did not end the election of officers in new regiments, it did something toward ensuring that those elected met certain standards. Promotion within the ranks of old regiments was generally earned by merit, not election, though the continuing role of state governors in the appointment of officers meant that politics would never be absent from the process. By 1863, the Union army had virtually ended the practice of electing officers. The Confederates were slower to give it up. Although the South established officer examinations in October 1862, not until the war was almost over did the Confederate Congress abolish the practice of allowing companies to elect their officers.

---

[14]Dunbar Rowland (ed.), *Jefferson Davis, Constitutionalist: His Letters, Papers and Speeches*, 10 vols. (Jackson, Miss., 1923), IX, 543; Thomas Wentworth Higginson, "Regular and Volunteer Officers," *Atlantic Monthly*, 14 (September 1864), 349.

[15]Bell I. Wiley, *The Life of Billy Yank: The Common Soldier of the Union* (Indianapolis, 1952), p. 26; Douglas Southall Freeman, *Lee's Lieutenants: A Study in Command*, 3 vols. (New York, 1942–1944), I, 13.

Nevertheless, Confederate officers were probably of higher caliber than their Union counterparts during the first year or two of the war. The South's military tradition and its large number of graduates from such academies as Virginia Military Institute provided a reservoir of trained leaders. The North could not match this; most company and regimental officers for the Union had to learn their work on the job.

The 313 officers who resigned from the regular U.S. army in 1861 to fight for the South also gave Confederate armies a core of professional leadership. Of course, the other 767 regular army officers stayed with the Union. But because of a policy decision by General Winfield Scott, most of them remained in the regular army instead of being dispersed among the volunteer regiments to provide a cadre of professional instructors and officers. Scott wanted to preserve the tactical existence of the only force he considered wholly reliable—the regulars—as a model for the volunteer army rather than as leaders of it. Eventually, several hundred regular army officers were allowed to join the volunteer forces, but many others went through the war as captains or lieutenants in the tiny regular army while volunteer regiments blundered along under colonels from civilian life. The South got a big jump on the North in utilizing trained officers to leaven its volunteer armies.

The majority of generals on both sides came from civilian life. Of the 583 men who attained the rank of general in the Union army, only 194 (33 percent) were in the regular army when the war began. Another 70 (14 percent) had attended West Point or other military schools. In the Confederacy, 125 (29 percent) of the 425 generals came from the regular army, and another 69 (16 percent) had attended military academies, including West Point.

The nonprofessionals in both armies can be divided into two groups: the "political generals," who were appointed because of their influence and connections; and a larger group of "civilian generals," who started at lower ranks and achieved promotion largely through merit. The political generals acquired a reputation—partly deserved—for military incompetence. Although the South had its share of such men—one thinks of John Floyd, Gideon Pillow, Henry Wise, and Robert Toombs—the phrase "political general" usually referred to Northerners such as Benjamin Butler, Nathaniel Banks, John McClernand, and Francis Blair, Jr. Powerful political figures, several of them prewar Democrats, they were appointed in order to attract various Northern constituencies to support of the war. Some of them received their commissions as rewards for raising large numbers of volunteers. Others obtained appointment because of sponsorship by important governors or congressmen. Some were leaders of ethnic groups: Franz Sigel and Carl Schurz, for example, received commissions because of their prominence in the German-American community, while Thomas Meagher, commander of the "Irish Brigade," helped to rally his countrymen for the cause.

Political generals formed the counterpart at the command level of elected officers at the company level—both were necessary in the citizen armies of a democratic society. Professional soldiers did not like this situation but reluctantly accepted the necessity. "It seems but little better than murder to give important commands to such men as Banks, Butler, McClernand, Sigel and Lew Wallace," sighed General Halleck after he became chief of staff, "yet it seems impossible to prevent it."[16] And the system of

---

[16]Halleck to W. T. Sherman, April 29, 1864, in *O.R.*, Ser. 1, Vol. 34, pt. 3, pp. 332–333.

political patronage produced good as well as evil. Grant's initial appointment as brigadier general came through the influence of Elihu Washburne, a congressman from Illinois. Sherman's appointment to the same rank was aided by political connections that included his brother John, senator from Ohio. Some of the most political of generals developed into first-class soldiers, while many West Pointers proved to be spectacular failures. And in any case, professionals held most of the top commands: in fifty-five of the sixty largest battles, West Pointers exercised overall strategic command of both armies; in the other five, a professional commanded one of the two armies. In both North and South, some politicians and army nonprofessionals complained that the "West Point clique" formed a closed corporation that denied promotions to able outsiders.

During the first year of war, most officers and men alike were raw recruits. By the standards of European armies, the American levies were little more than armed mobs. Officers had to teach themselves before they could train their men. Civil War literature abounds with stories of colonels and captains burning the midnight oil studying manuals on drill and tactics to stay one step ahead of their men. This practice went right to the top in the North, for Abraham Lincoln read numerous books on strategy in an effort to learn his job as Commander in Chief. Eventually, these American volunteer armies became tough, battle-wise veterans—perhaps equal to any European army in military skills and superior in motivation, for as citizens and voters (most of them), with higher levels of literacy than any previous armies in history, they had a better idea of what they were fighting for.

The egalitarian ethos of these citizen armies also meant that officers must be leaders rather than merely commanders. Although the Civil War had its share of rear-echelon commanders, the successful officers led their men from the front, not the rear. Battle casualties were proportionately higher among officers than among enlisted men in both armies: 18 percent of all Confederate generals were killed in action, compared with 12 percent for the Confederate army as a whole; and 8 percent of the Union generals suffered battle deaths, compared with 5 1/2 percent for the entire army.

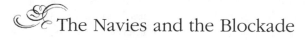 The Navies and the Blockade

The Confederate Navy

If the Confederate army was better prepared than its enemy at the outset, the reverse was true of the navies. Indeed, the Confederacy scarcely had a navy. Of the U.S. navy's 1,554 officers and 7,600 seamen in 1861, some 373 officers but only a handful of men defected to the Confederacy. Southerners were a martial but not a maritime people. The main shipbuilding facilities were in the North; the merchant marine was Northern-owned; most of the merchant seamen were Yankees. Under the circumstances, Confederate Secretary of the Navy Stephen Mallory did a remarkable job in creating a navy from scratch. The South built or acquired more than 130 vessels during the conflict, most of them small craft mounting only one or a few guns.

CONFEDERATE IRONCLAD RAM *ATLANTA*.   The *Atlanta* was typical of armored
Confederate ships, with an iron prow below the waterline to rip holes in Union wooden
warships. This picture was taken after the *Atlanta's* capture on the Savannah River; the men
posing on deck are Union sailors.

But by the end of the war, 37 armored warships had been built or were under construction. Several of these were "rams," with heavy iron prows designed to ram and
sink enemy ships. Such was the South's lack of industrial facilities, however, that not
a single machine shop in the Confederacy was capable of building an engine large
enough to power these ships adequately, and most of the rams never saw action.

But the Confederacy did contribute several technological innovations to naval
warfare. The rebuilding of the captured *Merrimack* as the first ironclad warship to
see combat action is well known. The South also developed various naval mines
(which were called "torpedoes"), which sank or damaged forty-three Union warships. The Confederates built several "torpedo boats," small half-submersed cigar-
shaped vessels carrying a contact mine on a spar extending in front of the bow. The
South also built the world's first combat submarine, the *H. L. Hunley,* which sank
with loss of its crew three times in trials before torpedoing a Union blockade ship
off Charleston on February 17, 1864, sinking the blockader and damaging the *Hunley,* which also sank before she could return to shore.

The most spectacular activity of the Confederate navy was commerce raiding. At
first this ancient form of official piracy was carried out by privateers (privately owned
ships commissioned by a belligerent government to capture enemy merchant ships).

On April 17, 1861, Jefferson Davis offered letters of marque to any ships that wished to prey upon Yankee commerce. Numerous privateers were soon darting out of coves along the Southern coast to snatch unarmed merchantmen.

Refusing to recognize the Confederacy as a legitimate government, Lincoln retaliated with a proclamation stating that captured privateer crews would be hanged as pirates. Davis came right back with a declaration that for every man so executed, a Union prisoner of war would be similarly treated. By the fall of 1861, several captured privateer crews languished in Northern jails awaiting trial. Although judges and juries showed a reluctance to convict, some of the crew of the *Jefferson Davis,* most notorious of the privateers, were convicted and sentenced to death in Philadelphia. True to his word, Davis had lots drawn among Union POWs, and the losers—including a grandson of Paul Revere—were readied for hanging if the Philadelphia sentence was carried out. Lincoln hesitated and finally backed down. He announced on February 3, 1862, that privateer crews would be treated as prisoners of war.

But by this time, the Union blockade and the refusal of neutral ports to admit prizes taken by privateers had put an end to privateering. Commerce raiding was taken over by Confederate naval cruisers, which unlike privateers usually destroyed their prizes instead of selling them. Sleek, fast, and heavily armed, twenty such Rebel cruisers roamed the seas searching out Yankee merchantmen. Several of these cruisers were built in Britain. The most famous was the *Alabama,* built at Liverpool and manned mostly by British sailors. Its captain was Raphael Semmes, an Alabamian who resigned from the U.S. navy to become the Confederacy's premier maritime hero. From September 1862 until sunk by the *U.S.S. Kearsarge* off Cherbourg, France, on June 19, 1864, the *Alabama* destroyed at least sixty-two merchant vessels and one ship of the U.S. navy. Other famous raiders were the *Sumter,* the *Florida,* and the *Shenandoah*. Their exploits crippled the U.S. merchant marine, which never recovered. The raiders destroyed 257 merchant ships and whalers, caused the transfer of at least 700 others to foreign flags, and forced most of the rest to remain in port. These were impressive achievements for a handful of ships, but they had a negligible impact on the outcome of the war.

The Union Navy

The Confederate navy was unable to challenge the enemy where it mattered most— on the coasts and rivers of the South. Union naval power was a decisive factor in the war. Although few ships were available for immediate service at the outset, Secretary of the Navy Gideon Welles and his dynamic Assistant Secretary, Gustavus V. Fox, both New Englanders, quickly chartered or purchased civilian vessels for conversion to warships and began contracting for the construction of new vessels. By the last year of the war, the 42 warships of 1861 had grown into the world's largest navy— a powerful fleet of 671 ships of all types, from shallow-draft river gunboats to ironclad monitors. These ships maintained a blockade of 3,500 miles of coastline, forced the surrender of Confederate ports from Norfolk to New Orleans, penetrated the South's river system into the heart of the Confederacy, and protected the huge fleet of Union coastal and river supply vessels. The joint army-navy operations on Southern rivers (to be described in later chapters) that played such a decisive role in the western theater contributed a major tactical innovation to warfare. Indeed, the navy's contribution to Northern victory was far out of proportion to its numbers. About 100,000 men served in the Union navy, only 5 percent of the number in the army.

The Union navy was more professional than the army. Few civilians sought commissions afloat as political plums. Even those Americans who believed that anyone could learn the art of war on land admitted that the sea demanded more specialized skills. The navy immediately established an officers' examination board and during 1861 appointed hundreds of new officers, drawn mostly from the merchant marine. Seamen were recruited from the same source. Unlike volunteer soldiers, they already knew their trade, except for gunnery. In June 1861, Welles appointed a naval strategy board, something the army never did.

The Blockade

The navy's chief task was the blockade. On April 19, Lincoln proclaimed a blockade of Confederate ports. Since international law recognized a blockade as a weapon of war between sovereign powers, this in effect granted the Confederacy the belligerent status that Lincoln simultaneously tried to deny it in his stated intention to treat privateers as pirates. The Union blockade was never wholly effective, though it became increasingly so with each month of the war. The task of patrolling all of the 189 harbors and coves in the South where cargo could be landed was impossible. But on May 1, eleven days after the declaration of blockade, the navy captured its first blockade runner. Within another three weeks, all major Southern ports were under surveillance. By the end of 1864, there were 471 ships on blockade duty.

The Confederacy's need for European arms and material, Europe's need for Southern cotton, and the profits to be made by carrying these items through the blockade created a bonanza business for blockade runners. Some of these were old, slow sailing ships that succeeded only because of the blockade's looseness in the first year of war. As the blockade tightened, the risks increased—but so did the profits. Fast, sleek steamers were built in Britain especially for blockade running. Painted gray for low visibility and burning almost smokeless anthracite—and designed with low freeboards, shallow drafts, and raked smokestacks that could be telescoped almost to deck level—these ships repeatedly evaded Yankee blockaders to slip in and out of Southern harbors on moonless or stormy nights. Nassau, Bermuda, and Havana became the chief ports from which the blockade runners operated. Wilmington became their main port of entry. The numerous inlets and shoals at the mouth of the Cape Fear River below Wilmington made it the hardest Confederate port for the Union navy to patrol.

Private individuals owned most of the blockade runners; but as the war went on, the state governments and Confederate government itself acquired an increasing number. The secretary of war tried to require privately owned runners to reserve at least one-third of their cargo space at reasonable rates for military freight. But the highest profits could be made on such items as silks, liquor, and other consumer goods, and many runners carried these in preference to arms or shoes or bacon for

the army. Finally, in February and March 1864, the Confederate government prohibited the importation of luxury goods and required all runners to allot at least half
their space to the government at fixed rates.

In July 1861, the Union navy's strategy board made a decision of far-reaching consequences. The naval bases for blockade squadrons at Hampton Roads and Key West
were 600 miles or more from such enemy ports as Charleston, Savannah, and New
Orleans. This meant that blockade ships spent as much time returning to their bases
for coal, supplies, and repairs as they did on blockade duty. Moreover, the navy
could not patrol every inlet from which blockade runners and privateers operated.
Thus the strategy board planned to seize several inlets and harbors along the Southern coast to close them to blockade runners and to establish additional bases for the
blockade fleet.

The first joint army-navy expedition for this purpose arrived off storm-swept Cape
Hatteras August 27 with seven ships and 900 soldiers under Benjamin Butler. The
fleet shelled into submission the two forts guarding Hatteras Inlet. Butler's troops occupied the forts, and the Yankees henceforth controlled the channel through which
at least 100 blockade runners had passed in the previous six weeks. Two weeks later
the navy seized without opposition Ship Island off Biloxi, Mississippi, and established there a base for blockade patrol of the Gulf ports.

The finest natural harbor on the Southern coast was Port Royal, South Carolina,
midway between Charleston and Savannah. Port Royal was the Union navy's first
choice as a base for the South Atlantic blockade fleet. Preparations for an army-navy
expedition to capture it went forward in secrecy during the fall of 1861. Flag Officer
(later Rear Admiral) Samuel Du Pont commanded the fleet of fourteen warships,
twenty-six collier and supply vessels, and twenty-five transports to carry 12,000 soldiers and marines. Although a gale off Hatteras wrecked or crippled several transports, the remainder of the fleet arrived intact off Port Royal Sound in early November. Two forts mounting forty-three heavy guns guarded the sound, but Du Pont's
warships carried more than 120 guns. Steaming between the forts in a long oval pattern on November 7, the fleet pounded them at a rate of two dozen shells per
minute. Confederate General Thomas Drayton (brother of Commander Percival
Drayton of the *U.S.S. Pocahantas,* one of the attacking warships) decided to abandon the ruined forts. The army and marines took possession of Port Royal and the
entire string of coastal islands from Savannah almost to Charleston. The Southern
white population fled to the mainland, leaving behind 10,000 slaves and hundreds
of rich long-staple cotton plantations.

The Port Royal attack was a success far beyond Union expectations. Unprepared
to follow it up with an invasion inland, the army consolidated its control of the islands while the navy built up a huge base. During the next few months, amphibious
expeditions seized coastal points as far south as St. Augustine. Army artillery operating from an island off the coast bombarded and captured Savannah's Fort Pulaski
in April, virtually closing the harbor to blockade runners.

Nor did North Carolina escape further incursions of the blue tide. General Ambrose E. Burnside, a Rhode Islander with mutton-chop whiskers, organized a division of New Englanders accustomed to working around water and boats. In January
1862, Burnside's 12,000 men accompanied by a naval flotilla of shallow-draft gun-

boats, tugs, transports, and barges crossed the shoals at Hatteras Inlet and steamed up Pamlico Sound to Roanoke Island. This island controlled the channels between the Pamlico and Albermarle sounds and therefore the river outlets of every North Carolina port except Wilmington. The Confederates had fortified the island, but their 3,000 troops were hopelessly outmatched. In an amphibious attack on February 7–8, steamers towed long strings of surfboats crammed with soldiers to the shallows while gunboats stood by to cover their landing. Burnside's men poured onto the beach, fanned out, and smashed through the Rebel trenches. They took the forts in the rear while the gunboats punched through the channel obstructions in their front. It was a well-executed operation that netted 2,675 Confederate prisoners at a cost of 278 Union casualties. During the next several weeks, the bluecoats occupied mainland North Carolina ports for 150 miles up and down North Carolina's sounds.

The *Monitor* and the *Merrimack*

For Confederates, the news from the coast was nothing but bad all through the fall and winter of 1861–1862. But they were counting on a powerful new weapon to turn the tide. Since their seizure of the Norfolk navy yard in April 1861, the Confederates had been rebuilding the captured *Merrimack* as an ironclad ram. Work went forward slowly because of shortages, but by winter the heavily armored ship was nearing completion. She was not the world's first ironclad. The French had used iron-sheathed "floating batteries" in the Crimean War, and in 1861 the French navy had one armored ship and the British two. The Union navy in October 1861 contracted with the Swedish-born inventor John Ericsson for an entirely new type of ironclad, the *Monitor*. With a hull low on the waterline and a revolving turret mounting two guns, she looked like "a tin can on a shingle." The *Monitor* was completed in Brooklyn about the time the *Merrimack* (rechristened *Virginia*) was getting ready to sally forth from Norfolk against the Federal blockade ships at Hampton Roads.

On March 8, 1862, the *Virginia* attacked. Before dark she had destroyed two ships and run three others aground, to be finished off on the morrow. Shots from Union ships had bounced harmlessly off her armor. Panic seized Washington. But that evening the *Monitor* arrived at Hampton Roads and next morning engaged the *Virginia* in history's first combat between ironclad ships. After more than three hours of close-in fighting, in which each vessel sustained more than two dozen direct hits without suffering crippling damage, the exhausted crews broke off the duel. The *Virginia's* threat to the Union blockade was neutralized. Though the engagement was a draw, the *Monitor* proved to be the superior ship. She was faster and more maneuverable because of a shallower draft (eleven feet as against the *Virginia's* twenty-two); her low hull presented two-thirds less target area; and her two-gun revolving turret generated as much firepower in a given direction as the *Virginia's* ten lighter guns. The *Virginia* had to be scuttled when Norfolk fell to the Federals in May 1862 because she was too unseaworthy to escape to open water and too deep-drafted to go up the James River. But the *Monitor* became the prototype for fifty-eight ironclad warships built or begun by the Union during the war. The Confederacy's major saltwater challenge to the Union navy failed.

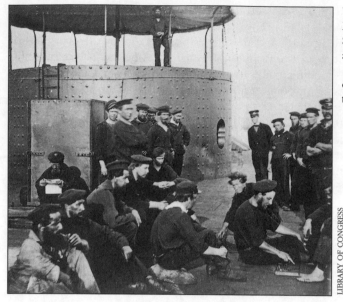

UNION SAILORS ON THE MONITOR.
Sailors relaxing on board after their fight with the *C.S.S. Virginia*. Note the dents in the turret below the gunport, caused by the *Virginia*'s cannonballs.

LIBRARY OF CONGRESS

Results of the Blockade

The effectiveness of the Union blockade was hotly argued during the Civil War—and has been debated ever since. The Confederate secretary of state insisted that it was a "paper blockade" undeserving of recognition under international law. In support, several historians have cited figures or estimates showing that the South exported at least a half-million bales of cotton and imported 600,000 rifles, a million pairs of shoes, and so on. In 1861, at least nine out of ten blockade runners were getting through. By 1865, the Union navy had cut this to one out of two. But for the war as a whole, there were an estimated 8,000 successful trips through the blockade, while the Union navy captured or destroyed only 1,500 blockade runners. Thus, it is argued, the blockade was ineffective.[17]

But these figures can sustain an opposite interpretation. The important fact is not how many blockade runners got through, but how much cargo would have gotten through had there been no blockade. The half-million bales of cotton exported during the last three years of the war (after the voluntary Confederate cotton embargo of 1861 discussed on page 238) contrasted with more than ten million exported in the three years prior to the war. Twenty thousand ships entered and cleared South-

---

[17]See especially Frank L. Owsley, *King Cotton Diplomacy* (Chicago, 1931); and Richard E. Beringer, Herman Hattaway, Archer Jones, and William N. Still, Jr., *Why the South Lost the Civil War* (Athens, Ga., 1986), pp. 53–63. Stephen R. Wise, in *Lifeline of the Confederacy: Blockade Running During the Civil War* (Columbia, S.C., 1988), maintains that of the 1,300 attempted trips in and out of Confederate ports by steam cargo ships (the rest were sailing ships), about 1,000 were successful.

ern harbors in the four antebellum years, most of them with greater cargo capacity than the 8,000 successful blockade runners of the war years. Many blockade runners had to jettison part of their cargoes to increase speed when pursued. The blockade cut the South's seaborne trade to less than a third of normal. And wartime was not normal because, lacking an industrial base, the South needed to import large quantities of material for its war effort. Although of minor military importance at first, the blockade in the end played a large part in the outcome of the war.

Chapter Twelve

The Balance Sheet of War

We shall have the enormous advantage of fighting on our own territory and for our very existence. All the world over are not one million of men defending themselves at home against invasion, stronger in a mere military point of view, than five millions [invading] a foreign country?

—Confederate diplomat John Slidell,
July 20, 1861

201

The American Civil War is often described as the first "modern" war. Many firsts are associated with the Civil War: the first extensive use of the railroad and telegraph for military purposes, the first combat between iron-plated warships, a much greater use of rifled field artillery and of rifled small arms than ever before, the first use of repeating rifles, the development of crude machine guns, the first combat use of a submarine, trench warfare on a scale that anticipated World War I, the first general conscription in American history, and the first extensive application of the "American system" of mass production to the manufacture of military goods.

But in many respects, the Civil War was more traditional than modern—that is, it more closely resembled the Napoleonic Wars of fifty years earlier than World War I a half-century later. Despite railroads and steamboats, the armies still depended on animal-powered transport for field supply. Campaigning slowed or halted during the winter and during heavy rains because of what Napoleon had once called the "fifth element" in war—mud. Despite advances in repeating arms and in rifling, most infantrymen carried muzzleloaders, and during the war's first year most of these were smoothbores. The cavalry was still an important military arm. Artillery had only a fraction of the range, accuracy, and power of World War I artillery. The modern concept of substituting firepower for men was yet in its infancy. Weapons and machines counted for much in this war—but men and horses still counted for more.

Manpower and Resources

In 1861, the Union states had nearly three and a half times as many white men of military age as had the Confederacy. Of course, the slaves were a military asset to the South, for they could do the home-front tasks done by free men in the North and thus release an equivalent number of whites for army service. On the other hand, the North also drew on former slaves for military labor and eventually enlisted more than 150,000 of them in its armed forces. Altogether an estimated 2,100,000 men fought for the Union and 850,000 for the Confederacy (the exact number is not known because the Union records enumerate the number of enlistments, which must be adjusted to avoid the double counting of men who reenlisted, and many Confederate records were destroyed). About half the men of military age in the North served in the army or navy; close to three-fourths of the white men in the South did so, a *levée en masse* made possible only by the existence of slavery.

Confederate Conscription

Ironically, the South, which went to war to protect individual and states' rights against centralized government, was compelled to enact a draft a year earlier than the North. By the fall of 1861, the romantic enthusiasm that had stimulated volunteering in the early months was wearing off. "I have seen quite enough of A Soldier's life," wrote one Johnny Reb to his family, "to satisfy me that it is not what it is cracked up to be." A Confederate general wrote from the Virginia front on October 20: "The first flush of patriotism led many a man to join who now regrets it. The prospect of winter here is making the men very restless and they are beginning to resort to all sorts of means to get home."[1] More than half the Confederate soldiers on the rolls were one-year volunteers who had enlisted in the spring of 1861 (the rest were three-year men). Faced with the prospect of part of their armies melting away just as the Yankees launched their spring offensives in 1862, the Confederate Congress in December passed an act offering to all one-year men who would reenlist a $50 bounty, one month's furlough, and the opportunity to join new regiments with new elected officers if the reenlistees did not like their old ones. But this failed to produce enough reenlistments. In March 1862, Robert E. Lee, then serving as Jefferson Davis's military adviser, urged passage of a national conscription law as the only way to avert disaster.

The Confederate Congress complied in April with legislation making able-bodied white males (including those whose enlistments were expiring) aged eighteen to thirty-five liable to conscription for three years' service. The law exempted persons in several war-production occupations plus militia officers, civil servants, clergymen, apothecaries, and teachers. These last two exemptions proved full of mischief, for many new drugstores and schools sprang up in excess of any apparent demand for them. A supplemental conscription law passed in October 1862 exempted one white

---

[1]Bell I. Wiley, *The Life of Johnny Reb: The Common Soldier of the Confederacy* (Indianapolis, 1943), pp. 128–129.

man on any plantation with twenty or more slaves. The Confederacy also allowed drafted men to hire substitutes to serve in their stead. A practice with roots in both the European and American past (state militia drafts during the Revolution had permitted substitutes), substitution was intended to ameliorate the coerciveness of conscription. But it favored those rich enough to afford substitutes. By 1863, the going price for substitutes had risen to $6,000 in Confederate currency (about $300 in gold). Along with the "20-Negro law," substitution produced the bitter saying that it was "a rich man's war and a poor man's fight."

As Confederate manpower needs became more desperate, the conscription law was strengthened. Congress raised the upper age limit to forty-five in September 1862 and fifty (with the lower limit reduced from eighteen to seventeen) in February 1864. The substitute clause was repealed in December 1863, and men who had previously furnished substitutes became eligible for the draft. The exempt categories were trimmed (though the controversial 20-Negro provision was retained in modified form). The new conscription act of February 1864 required all men then in the army to stay in, thus making sure that the three-year men of 1861 would not go home when their enlistments expired.

So unpopular was conscription that it was impossible to enforce in some parts of the South, especially in the upcountry and mountain regions. In nonslaveholding areas, the "rich man's war" theme was particularly strong. "All they want, " said an Alabama hill farmer, "is to get you pupt up and go to fight for their infurnal negroes and after you do there fighting you may kiss there hine parts for o they care."[2] Draft evaders and deserters in some upcountry regions formed armed bands, killed several draft officials, and resisted all Confederate authority.

Several of the South's leading politicians also denounced the draft as being contrary to the goals the Confederacy was fighting for. "No act of the Government of the United States prior to the secession of Georgia," said that state's pugnacious Governor Joseph E. Brown, "struck a blow at constitutional liberty so fell as has been stricken by this conscription act." Brown did everything he could to frustrate the draft. He appointed large numbers of Georgians to the exempt positions of civil servant and militia officer. The state militia became so top-heavy with officers that a disgusted Confederate general described a typical militia company as containing "3 field officers, 4 staff officers, 10 captains, 30 lieutenants, and 1 private with a misery in his bowels."[3] Other governors, particularly Zebulon Vance of North Carolina, criticized the way the draft was enforced. Their opposition became part of a larger conflict between states' rights and centralization, a conflict that afflicted the Confederate government.

But despite opposition, inefficiency and fraud in its enforcement, conscription produced men for the Confederate armies. Without the draft the South could scarcely have carried the war past 1862, for in addition to bringing new men into the army, it kept the veterans from leaving. A total of perhaps 120,000 draftees served in the Confederate army, while an estimated 70,000 men provided substitutes. How many

---

[2]Hugh C. Bailey, "Disloyalty in Early Confederate Alabama," *Journal of Southern History*, 23 (November 1957), 525.

[3]Albert B. Moore, *Conscription and Conflict in the Confederacy* (New York, 1924), pp. 256, 271.

of the latter actually served in the ranks is a moot question, since many substitute papers were fraudulent. In any event, perhaps 20 percent of the Confederate soldiers were draftees and substitutes, compared with 8 percent of the Union army.[4] The compulsory reenlistment of volunteers in the South meant that every Confederate soldier served for the duration unless killed or discharged because of wounds or disease. In the Union, by contrast, men whose terms expired could not be drafted or compelled to reenlist. Thus while the total number of men who fought for the Union was two and a half times greater than those who fought for the Confederacy, the difference in the number of veterans in the ranks at any given time was much smaller. Since one veteran was believed to be worth at least two recruits, the Confederacy's inferiority in manpower was less than it appeared to be.

In resources necessary to wage war, however, the South was at a greater disadvantage than in manpower. The North possessed close to 90 percent of the nation's industrial capacity. In certain industries vital to military production, Union superiority was even more decisive. According to the 1860 census, the North had eleven times as many ships and boats as the South and produced fifteen times as much iron, seventeen times as many textile goods, twenty-four times as many locomotives, and thirty-two times as many firearms (though an important market for the last had always been the South). In food production, the Northern superiority was little better than two to one (or about the same per capita as the South). But the Union had more than twice the density of railroad mileage per square mile and several times the amount of rolling stock. The South's inferiority in railroads, intensified by a lack of replacement capacity, produced transportation bottlenecks that created frequent shortages of food and supplies at the front. The North's advantage in horses and mules was less than two to one, but many of the Confederacy's animals were in portions of the upper South soon overrun by Union armies.

Confederate Advantages

With all these disadvantages, how could Southerners expect to win? "Something more than numbers makes armies," wrote a Confederate journalist. "Against the vast superiority of the North in material resources, " he insisted, the South had "a set-off in certain advantages."[5]

War Aims and Morale

The most important advantage stemmed from the contrasting war aims of two sides. To "win," the Confederates did not need to invade the North or to destroy its armies; they needed only to stand on the defensive and to prevent the North from destroying Southern armies. Southerners looked for inspiration to the American Revolution, when Britain's relative material superiority was even greater than the North's in 1861.

---

[4]For a discussion of the Union draft, see Chapter 20.

[5]Quoted in Richard N. Current, "God and the Strongest Battalions," in David Donald (ed.), *Why the North Won the Civil War* (Baton Rouge, 1960), p. 5.

They also looked to other successful revolutions by small countries. All the power of Spain under Philip II could not stamp out rebellion in the Netherlands. The legions of Austria marched in vain against tiny Switzerland. Like those liberty-loving rebels, said Jefferson Davis in his first war message to the Confederate Congress April 26, 1861, "we seek no conquest, no aggrandizement, no concession of any kind from the States with which we were late confederated; all we ask is to be let alone."[6]

To win the war, the North had to invade, conquer, and destroy the South's capacity and will to resist. Invasion and conquest are logistically far more difficult than defense of one's territory. Recalling their own army's experience in 1776, British military experts in 1861 agreed that a country as large as the Confederacy could not be conquered. "It is one thing to drive the rebels from the south bank of the Potomac, or even to occupy Richmond," observed the London *Times* early in the war, "but another to reduce and hold in permanent subjection a tract of country nearly as large as Russia in Europe. . . . Just as England during the revolution had to give up conquering the colonies so the North will have to give up conquering the South."[7]

The intangible but vital factor of morale favored an army fighting in defense of its homeland. When the Confederates became the invaders, this morale advantage went over to the Yankees. On the first day of the battle of Gettysburg, a Union officer wrote: "Our men are three times as Enthusiastic as they have been in Virginia. The idea that Pennsylvania is invaded and that we are fighting on our own soil proper, influences them strongly." On the Confederate retreat to Virginia after Gettysburg, one of Lee's staff officers said that "our men, it must be confessed, are far better satisfied when operating on this [south] side of the Potomac. . . . They are not accustomed to operating in a country where the people are inimical to them, and certainly every one of them is today worth twice as much as he was three days ago."[8]

Geography and Logistics

One of the South's important military advantages was geography. The Confederacy covered a large territory—750,000 square miles—twice as much as the thirteen colonies in 1776. The topography in the eastern part of the Confederacy favored the defense against invasion. The Appalachian chain was a formidable barrier that resisted penetration until Sherman's invasion of Georgia in 1864. The Shenandoah Valley of Virginia formed a natural route of invasion, but this favored the Confederacy rather than the Union because it ran southwest, away from Richmond and the main battle theater in Virginia. Indeed, the Confederacy used the valley three times for invasions

---

[6]Dunbar Rowland (ed.), *Jefferson Davis, Constitutionalist: His Letters, Papers and Speeches,* 10 vols. (Jackson, Miss., 1923), V, 84.

[7]London *Times,* July 18, 1861, August 29, 1862. For analyses of the reasons why the North eventually won, which emphasize not Northern manpower and industrial superiority but the way in which each side managed its resources and waged the war, see Herman Hattaway and Archer Jones, *How the North Won: A Military History of the Civil War* (Urbana, Ill., 1983); Richard E. Beringer, Herman Hattaway, Archer Jones, and William N. Still, Jr., *Why the South Lost the Civil War* (Athens, Ga., 1986); and Gabor S. Boritt (ed.) *Why the Confederacy Lost* (New York, 1992).

[8]Bell I. Wiley, *The Life of Billy Yank: The Common Soldier of the Union* (Indianapolis, 1952), p. 283; Douglas Southall Freeman, *Lee's Lieutenants: A Study in Command,* 3 vols. (New York, 1942–1944), III, 146n.

or threats against the North (Jackson in 1862, Lee in his Gettysburg campaign in 1863, and Jubal Early in 1864), for in that direction the valley pointed toward important Northern cities, including Washington itself. Much of the South was heavily wooded, providing cover for armies operating on the defensive. Between Washington and Richmond, six rivers and numerous streams ran from west to east, each of them a line of defense. In the western portion of the Confederacy, by contrast, the river system favored an invading force. The Cumberland and Tennessee rivers were highways of invasion into Tennessee, northern Mississippi, and northern Alabama, while the Mississippi River was an arrow thrust into the heart of the lower South.

But away from the rivers, an invading force was dependent on railroads or roads, and railroads were especially vulnerable to guerrillas and cavalry, who developed into a fine art the destruction of trackage, bridges, and rolling stock. The Union engineer corps became equally adept at repairing the damage (a Yankee construction battalion once built an 800-foot bridge containing 400,000 board feet of lumber in four and a half days from trees to trestle), but Northern military movements were repeatedly delayed or stopped by the destruction of supply lines in their rear. In this way, a few hundred guerrillas or cavalry could neutralize an entire army and force it to detach thousands of men to guard its communications.

Once an army moved away from its railhead or river-landing supply base, its marching men, artillery, and supply wagons had to move by road. Union armies campaigning in the South averaged one wagon for every forty men and one horse or mule for every two or three men. An army of 100,000 men would thus be encumbered with 2,500 wagons and at least 35,000 animals and would consume 600 tons or more of supplies a day. The South's wretched roads became an important Confederate military asset. Most of them were dirt tracks without ditches or anything else to prevent them from becoming impassable in wet weather. Wagons and artillery often sank to the axles, especially in Virginia, where the red clay soil formed a mud with the character almost of quicksand. Civil War literature is full of mud stories. A Union officer in the Virginia peninsula campaign of 1862 insisted that he saw an army mule sink out of sight except for its ears—though he admitted that "it was a small mule."

Of course, the roads were as bad for the Rebels as for the Yankees. But an army operating in its own territory is closer to its base and needs fewer wagons because it can gather much of its food and forage from the friendly countryside. Then, too, Johnny Reb traveled lighter than Billy Yank. Carrying his few necessities in a blanket roll rather than a knapsack, getting along without a shelter tent, subsisting on less food, the Confederate infantryman usually marched with thirty to forty pounds of equipment including rifle and ammunition. The fully equipped Union soldier carried about fifty pounds. The very abundance of Northern war production encouraged some generals to requisition so lavishly that their troops became bogged down in their own supplies. "This expanding, and piling up of *impedimenta*," an exasperated Lincoln told one general, "has been, so far, almost our ruin." Not until 1864 did some Northern commanders learn the dictum expressed by Confederate General Richard Ewell: "The road to glory cannot be followed with much baggage."[9]

---

[9]Roy P. Basler (ed.), *The Collected Works of Abraham Lincoln,* 9 vols. (New Brunswick, N.J., 1953–1955), V, 505; *O.R.,* Ser. 1, Vol. 12, pt. 3, p. 890.

LIBRARY OF CONGRESS

DESTRUCTION AND REBUILDING OF MILITARY RAILROADS.
The photo above shows the result of a Rebel raid on a Union rail supply line in Virginia.
Yankee repair crews have already relaid the ripped-up tracks but have not yet cleared away
the overturned locomotive and cars. The photo below shows a Union-rebuilt railroad bridge
over Potomac Creek in Virginia. President Lincoln admired the proficiency of the army
engineer corps in constructing trestles out of what appeared to be "nothing but bean-poles
and corn-stalks."

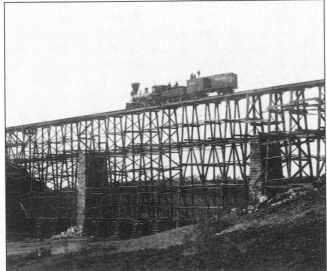

LIBRARY OF CONGRESS

The deeper the Union army penetrated into enemy territory, the longer became its supply lines and the greater became the necessity to detach troops to guard these lines. By the time Sherman reached Atlanta in 1864, only half of his total forces were at the front; the rest were strung out along his 470-mile rail lifeline back through Chattanooga and Nashville to Louisville. As an invading power, the Union army also had to assign large numbers of troops to occupation duties.

For these reasons, scarcely half of the 611,000 men present for duty in the Union armies at the beginning of 1864 were available for front-line combat service, while probably three-fourths of the Confederate total of 278,000 were so available. Thus the usual Southern explanation for defeat ("They never whipped us, Sir, unless they were four to one. If we had anything like a fair chance, or less disparity of numbers, we should have won our cause and established our independence"[10]) requires some modification. Indeed, one writer has maintained that in the war's fifty main battles, the number of Union combat soldiers averaged only 2 percent more than the enemy.[11] This probably understates Union numerical superiority. A calculation based on the sixty battles listed in the best statistical study of the subject shows that the Union armies averaged 37 percent more men than the Confederates.[12] But even this was a far cry from the "overwhelming numbers" portrayed in much Civil War historiography.

Other advantages accruing to the Confederacy from fighting on the defensive were interior lines of communication, better knowledge of topography and roads, and better means of gathering intelligence. The term "interior lines" means simply that armies fighting within a defensive arc can shift troops from one point to another over shorter distances than invading armies operating outside the perimeter of the arc. Several instances of this occurred in the Virginia theater. Most notable was Lee's transfer of his army from the peninsula to the Rappahannock in July-August 1862, a distance of about seventy-five miles, while the Union Army of the Potomac had to travel three times as far, partly by water. Some of these Union troops arrived too late to participate in the second battle of Bull Run.

The South was laced with obscure country roads not marked on any map. Only local knowledge could guide troops along these roads, many of which ran through thick woods that could shield the movement from the enemy but where a wrong turn could get a division hopelessly lost. Here the Confederates had a significant advantage. Rebel units used such roads to launch surprise attacks on the enemy. The outstanding example was Jackson's flank attack at Chancellorsville after a day-long march on a narrow track used to haul wood for a charcoal iron furnace, guided by the son of the furnace owner. Numerous examples could also be cited of Union troops getting lost on similar roads because of inaccurate or nonexistent maps.

"If I were mindful only of my own glory," wrote Frederick the Great of Prussia, "I would choose always to make war in my own country, for there every man is a spy, and the enemy can make no movement of which I am not informed."[13] Robert E.

---

[10]Quoted in Donald, *Why the North Won the Civil War,* p. ix.

[11]Franklin Marshall Pierce, *The Battle of Gettysburg* (New York, 1914), pp. 37–38.

[12]Thomas L. Livermore, *Numbers and Losses in the Civil War in America* (Boston, 1901).

[13]Quoted in J. F. C. Fuller, *Grant and Lee: A Study in Personality and Generalship* (London, 1933), p. 41.

Lee could have said the same. Operating amid a hostile population, the Union army was at a disadvantage in the matter of military intelligence. Even the women and children, reported a Northern officer, "vied with each other in schemes and ruses by which to discover and convey to the enemy facts which we strove to conceal."[14] Confederate officers often treated information obtained in this way with a grain of salt and relied mainly on their excellent cavalry for intelligence. But the cavalry, of course, functioned more effectively among a friendly than a hostile population. Southern women (who could travel more freely in the vicinity of armies than male civilians) brought important intelligence to Confederate commanders on several occasions; perhaps the best-known example is Belle Boyd's work during Jackson's Shenandoah Valley campaign of 1862. The Confederates maintained an intelligence network among Southern sympathizers in Washington, especially the romantic Rose O'Neal Greenhow, during the early part of the war. By the later years of the conflict, though, the Union had the most effective intelligence operation of the war operating in Richmond, headed by a Union sympathizer from a prominent Southern family, Elizabeth Van Lew, who used her reputation for eccentricity (she was known as "Crazy Bet") as cover for her espionage activities.[15] By 1864, Union cavalry scouts operating behind Confederate lines had also become more effective than their Confederate counterparts.

Confederate Guerrillas

There is disagreement among historians about the impact of Southern guerrillas on the war. Bruce Catton wrote that the numerous guerrilla attacks "befuddled the Federal high command, kept the invaders from getting accurate information about the strength and position of their opponents, disrupted supply and communication lines, and . . . went a long way to nullify the heavy advantage in numbers which the Federals possessed." The biographer of partisan leader John Singleton Mosby claims that the operations of guerrillas behind Union lines in Virginia in 1864 were "responsible largely for the war's extension into 1865."[16] But other historians maintain that partisan bands did the Confederate cause more harm than good. They drained potential manpower from the organized armies, it is claimed, and by their savage attacks on civilians and rear-area military personnel, they discredited the Southern cause and provoked ruthless reprisals. The credit for successful raids on Union supply lines, according to this interpretation, belongs less to guerrillas than to cavalry units under such commanders as Nathan Bedford Forrest and John Hunt Morgan.[17]

The truth probably lies somewhere between the two assertions. Although the claim that guerrillas prolonged the war by a year is an exaggeration, Mosby's band did give Union commanders no end of trouble and did hamper Federal operations in the

---

[14]Bruce Catton, *Glory Road* (Garden City, N.Y., 1952), p. 170.

[15]For a fascinating and well-researched account of women spies, see Elizabeth D. Leonard, *All the Daring of the Soldier: Women of the Civil War Armies* (New York, 1999), chaps. 1–2.

[16]Catton's introduction to Virgil Carrington Jones, *Gray Ghosts and Rebel Raiders* (New York, 1956), pp. vii–viii; and Jones's own assertion in ibid., 12.

[17]Albert Castel, *The Guerrilla War, 1861–1865* (Gettysburg, 1974).

JOHN SINGLETON MOSBY AND MEMBERS OF HIS PARTISAN BAND.   Mosby is the beardless, hatless man standing near the center.

Shenandoah Valley (see Chapters 23 and 24). Partisan bands in other theaters also wreaked havoc behind Union lines. The assertion that it was Confederate cavalry, not guerrillas, that accomplished these things fails to recognize that there was sometimes little if any difference between the two categories. Nearly all guerrillas were mounted, and most had some sort of relationship with the Confederate army as "rangers." Many of the troopers who rode with Morgan and Forrest were local men who melted back into the civilian population in classic guerrilla fashion after a raid.

Guerrilla warfare had a glamorous reputation in the South, stemming from the exploits of the "Swamp Fox," Francis Marion, during the Revolution. With the blessing of the Confederate War Department, several ranger companies sprang up in 1861—especially in western Virginia, where they harassed Union occupation troops and repeatedly cut the B&O. Confederate generals in Missouri and Arkansas encouraged the early operations of William Quantrill and other guerrilla leaders. Union generals organized counter-insurgency units to track down and destroy Rebel guerrilla bands, but these efforts met with more frustration than success.

In April 1862, the Southern Congress authorized the official formation of partisan ranger companies, which were to be enrolled as units of the Confederate army. Mosby's rangers were the most famous of these companies. Mosby's exploits (which included the capture of a Union general in his bed only ten miles from Washington) became legendary, earning him the praise of J. E. B. Stuart and Robert E. Lee. Unlike some other guerrilla outfits, Mosby's men usually wore Confederate uniforms, though they frequently concealed them under captured Union overcoats that enabled them to get through Yankee lines at will.

Despite the apparent success of ranger companies, several Confederate leaders by 1863 began to question their value. Many potential army recruits preferred to join these companies with their easy discipline, adventurous life, and prospects for loot. A good many guerrilla units were no better than "bushwhackers" (the Federals' term for them) who, in the words of a Union officer, "kill for the sake of killing and plunder for the love of gain."[18] Most notorious of the bushwhackers was Quantrill, who held a commission as captain in the Confederate army. In August 1863, he led his men on a raid into Lawrence, Kansas, the old Free Soil stronghold. He burned the defenseless town and murdered more than 150 male civilians in cold blood. This and other infamous raids by Missouri partisans gave all guerrillas a bushwhacker image. In January 1864, the Confederate Congress repealed the law authorizing partisan units and ordered their merger with regular commands. Even so, most ranger units continued to function.

The question of how to treat captured guerrillas vexed the Union government. Early in the war, several generals threatened to execute them, but this only produced retaliatory threats of an eye-for-an-eye execution of captured Yankees. In 1862, the Union War Department decided to treat partisans as ordinary prisoners of war so long as they were officially authorized by the Confederacy. But as the guerrillas escalated their violence and as more of them operated without uniforms or official sanction, Union commanders sometimes had them shot when captured. In July 1864, the Northern Congress approved this practice. When Philip Sheridan took command of Union forces in the Shenandoah Valley in August 1864, Grant told him: "Where any of Mosby's men are caught hang them without trial."[19] One of Sheridan's cavalry commanders, George A. Custer, executed six guerrillas, whereupon Mosby had six captured troops from Custer's brigade draw lots and go before a firing squad. In Missouri the war of ambush and massacre escalated beyond imagination, killing innocent civilians as well as bushwhackers and jayhawkers.

Probably no more than 10,000 men (not including official cavalry units) functioned as guerrillas in the Confederacy. It can be plausibly argued that they did more damage to the Union war effort than an equal number of front-line soldiers. In the fashion of guerrillas in other wars, they tied down several times their number of regular soldiers in guard duty or search-and-destroy missions. But whatever their military value, guerrilla raids and Union reprisals certainly increased the hatred and violence that made the Civil War a war of peoples as well as of armies.

---

[18]Bruce Catton, *The Coming Fury* (Garden City, N.Y., 1961), p. 413; Thomas Goodrich, *Black Flag: Guerrilla Warfare on the Western Border,* 1861–1865 (Bloomington, Ind., 1995); Goodrich, *Bloody Dawn: The Story of the Lawrence Massacre* (Kent, Ohio, 1991).

[19]Jones, *Gray Ghosts and Rebel Raiders,* p. 279.

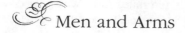

Men and Arms

With all the advantages of fighting a defensive war on its own territory, in which stalemate would be victory, perhaps the South was right in its belief that one Southerner could whip ten Yankees—or at least three. And in the war's early stages, the average Confederate cavalryman or infantryman probably *was* a better soldier than his enemy. Most Southern boys learned to ride and hunt as an essential part of growing up. Most Rebel soldiers did not have to be taught to shoot; many Yankees did. Martial values were more central to Southern than to Northern culture. The South's less modernized society proved a military advantage during the first half of a war in which the traditional martial qualities of man and horse gave way slowly to the modernized superiority of industry and the iron horse.

Cavalry

The Confederacy enjoyed its greatest early superiority in the cavalry. The mounted arm illustrated Karl von Clausewitz's[20] dictum that a nation will fight a war in a manner that resembles its social system. Lack of good roads in the South had compelled Southerners to ride from childhood, while most Northerners traveled on wheels *drawn* by horses. It took longer to train a cavalryman than an infantry or artillery soldier. A majority of the cavalry officers in the regular army had been Southerners. In leadership, horsemanship, and the equally important matter of taking care of horses, the Confederate trooper had a head start. The cavalry attracted the devil-may-care element of the South. General Sherman best described this element:

The young Bloods of the South, sons of Planters, Lawyers about Town, good billiard–players and sportsmen. . . . They hate Yankees *per se,* and don't bother their brains about the Past, present, or Future. As long as they have good horses, plenty of Forage, and an open country, they are happy. . . . They are splendid riders, shots, and utterly reckless. . . . They are the best Cavalry in the world.[21]

During the first two years of the war, Confederate troopers rode circles around Yankee horsemen, who, in the exaggerated words of a British observer, could "scarcely sit their horses even when trotting."[22] This was no small matter, for though cavalry were soon to become obsolete, they still performed vital functions during the Civil War. They were the eyes of the army. Their primary tasks were to obtain information about the size and movements of enemy forces while screening their own army from similar efforts by enemy cavalry. This reconnaissance function became particularly important in the wooded terrain of the South. It was in this task espe-

---

[20]A Prussian military officer (who rose to the rank of general) of the early nineteenth century. A brilliant strategist, von Clausewitz achieved renown as the author of *Vom Kriege* (3 vols., 1833) and several other texts of military science.

[21]Sherman to Henry W. Halleck, Sept. 17, 1863, Brooks D. Simpson and Jean V. Berlin (eds.) *Sherman's Civil War: Selected Correspondence of William T. Sherman, 1860–1865* (Chapel Hill, 1999), 545–546.

[22]H. C. B. Rogers, *The Confederates and Federals at War* (London, 1973), p. 51.

cially that the Rebel cavalry outshone the Yankees during the war's first two years. Another function of cavalry was to patrol the front or flanks of a marching or fighting army to prevent surprise attacks and detect enemy flanking movements. In this job, too, the Confederate cavalry performed better than the Yankees during the early part of the war. The logistical importance of the railroad also enhanced the cavalry's role as a raiding force deep in the enemy's rear.

The saber was becoming little more than a ceremonial arm, and some troopers did not bother to carry one. The principal cavalry weapon was the breechloading carbine. Since carbines were in short supply in the South, many Rebel cavalrymen carried shotguns. Most troopers also carried revolvers. Cavalry units did much of their actual fighting on foot, using their horses mainly as a means of rapid transportation to the scene of action. The Civil War produced new developments in dismounted cavalry tactics. Forrest was one of the principal innovators in this sphere. Sheridan carried the concept further when he took command of the Army of the Potomac's cavalry in 1864. Although the cavalry did less heavy fighting than the infantry, the foot soldier's half-sneering, half-envious question, "Whoever saw a dead cavalryman?" did not reflect reality. By late 1863, several Union cavalry brigades were armed with seven-shot repeating carbines, which greatly increased their firepower and made them more than a match, fighting dismounted, for an equal number of infantry. This increased firepower plus improved horsemanship, leadership, and experience brought Union cavalry to a par with Confederate horsemen by 1863 and gave them the edge, man for man, in the last year of the war.

LIBRARY OF CONGRESS

A UNION BATTERY POSING IN ACTION STATIONS FOR THE PHOTOGRAPHER IN VIRGINIA 1863.

Artillery

Just as the Confederacy's initial cavalry supremacy reflected the premodern aspects of Southern society, so the Union's superior artillery throughout the war reflected the technological ascendancy of the North. The industrial capacity for manufacturing cannon, shells, powder, and fuses was greater in the North than in the South. Artillery officers in the old army were mostly Northern-born. The mathematical training necessary to calculate range and elevation existed more widely in the North.

During the first two years of the war, the Confederacy captured more artillery than it manufactured or imported. By 1863, however, the South was producing most of its own artillery, chiefly at the Tredegar Iron Works in Richmond. The Confederacy manufactured nearly 3,000 cannon (compared with more than 7,000 in the Union) and built from scratch at Augusta, Georgia, one of the world's largest gunpowder mills. But many of the Southern-built cannon were defective and prone to crack. Shell fuses were also unreliable (so were Union fuses, but less so), causing most shells to explode too soon, too late, or not at all.

Civil War cannon were of two basic types: smoothbore and rifled. Rifled artillery was new and the Civil War produced its first widespread use. Rifled barrels gave projectiles greater distance, velocity, and accuracy. Nearly half of the Union cannon and about one-third of the Confederate cannon were rifled. Artillery projectiles were of three basic kinds: shells and solid shot for long-range work and case shot (canister or grape) for close-in defense against attacking infantry. Case shot was contained in shells that exploded to spray hundreds of small bullets (canister) or nine golf-ball-sized shot (grape). The effect of a cannon firing case shot into troops at close range was like that of a huge sawed-off shotgun. Despite the greater power and accuracy of rifled cannon, the twelve-pound smoothbore Napoleon remained the artillerists' favorite gun; the unreliability of shell fuses limited the value of longer-range rifled guns, and the versatile Napoleons, which could fire any kind of projectile, were the best for case shot.

The first crude predecessors of the machine gun were developed during the Civil War. For the Confederacy, Captain R. S. Williams invented a gun operated by a revolving camshaft that fed bullets from a hopper into the breech at the rate of twenty per minute. This gun was evidently used in combat as early as 1862. At least two dozen were built, but they were prone to malfunction and saw little action. The same was true of two types of rapid-fire guns developed in the North, the "coffee-mill gun" (so labeled by Lincoln because its feeder mechanism resembled a coffee grinder) and the Gatling gun, invented by Richard Gatling of Indiana. The multiple-barreled Gatling gun could fire 250 shots a minute—when it worked—and became the model for the postwar evolution of the modern machine gun. But its unreliability prevented significant combat use during the war itself.

Infantry

Despite the cavalry's glamour and the artillery's power, the infantry was by far the most important branch of Civil War armies. Combat troops in the Union army consisted of 80 percent infantry, less than 15 percent cavalry, and about 6 percent artillery. In the Confederate army, the proportion of artillery was the same, cavalry was

higher at nearly 20 percent, and infantry was lower at 75 percent. The infantry in-flicted and suffered 80 to 90 percent of the battle casualties. The infantry's relative importance was greater in the Civil War than in any other war. This was so because the rifle had replaced the smoothbore musket as the infantry weapon.

The Rifle

For centuries men had known that by cutting spiraled grooves inside a musket bar-rel to impart spin to the bullet, they could increase its range and accuracy.[23] Hunt-ing weapons were usually rifled, and some eighteenth-century armies contained spe-cial rifle regiments. But the smoothbore remained the principal infantry weapon until the 1850s. Why? Because a bullet large enough to "take" the rifling was hard to ram down the barrel of a muzzleloading weapon. After a rifle had been fired a few times, the residue from the black powder built up in the grooves and made the gun im-possible to load without cleaning. Since rapid loading and the reliability of repeated and prolonged firing were essential in a military weapon, the rifle could be used only for specialized purposes.

Gun designers had long been experimenting with methods to overcome these dif-ficulties. The man given credit for solving the problem was French army Captain Claude E. Minié, who in the 1840s invented an elongated bullet with an iron or wooden plug in the base that expanded when fired, to take the rifling. The bullet was of slightly smaller caliber than the barrel and thus could be easily loaded. The Minié ball was expensive and prone to malfunction because of its wooden or iron plug; the famous "minie ball" of Civil War rifles was developed by an American, James H. Bur-ton, at the Harpers Ferry armory. Instead of a plug, it had a cavity in the base which was expanded by gas from the powder explosion that fired the bullet.

This simple invention revolutionized military tactics. The maximum range of a smoothbore musket was about 250 yards, but a soldier could scarcely count on hit-ting anything at over 80 yards. In 1861, experienced marksmen in an Illinois regi-ment fired 160 shots from a smoothbore at a flour barrel 180 yards away and regis-tered only four hits. By contrast, the new Springfield and Enfield rifles had a maximum range of more than 1,000 yards and an effective range of about 400 yards. After a New Hampshire regiment received Springfields in October 1861, a private wrote home to his parents: "We went out the other day to try them. We fired 600 yds and we put 360 balls into a mark the size of old Jeff."[24] This fivefold increase in range greatly strengthened the infantry vis-à-vis the cavalry and artillery. It became suici-dal for cavalry to charge infantry, for most of the horses and many of their riders would be shot down before they reached the infantry. The Napoleonic tactics of ad-vancing field artillery along with or ahead of charging infantry would no longer work, for the cannoneers and horses would be picked off before the artillery got close enough to do much damage.

---

[23]To illustrate the principle: without spin, a bullet might behave as erratically as a knuckleball in baseball.
[24]Wiley, *Billy Yank,* p. 63.

CIVIL WAR TRENCHES.   This photo shows part of the Confederate entrenchments protecting Atlanta in 1864. The soldiers posing here are members of Sherman's army after they had captured Atlanta.

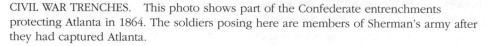

The rifle gave the tactical defense a big advantage over the offense. Traditional tactics had favored compact assaults by infantry against defensive positions. The defenders would have time for only one or two volleys with their smoothbore muskets before the attackers were upon them with bayonets. But with rifles, the defenders could hit attackers five times farther away than previously. Rarely did a charging line get close enough to use the bayonet (fewer than 1 percent of Civil War wounds were caused by bayonets). But commanders whose West Point textbooks had taught Napoleonic tactics and whose previous experience had been in the Mexican War, where compact assaults often succeeded, were slow to appreciate the new power of the rifle. Generals on both sides, as late as 1864, ordered frontal attacks that were beaten back with fearful slaughter.[25]

The defense also benefited from the evolution of trench warfare in the last two years of the conflict. Field trenches were not new, of course, but the advent of the rifle drove troops to seek cover more than ever before. By 1863, the men of both armies were constructing trenches and breastworks at virtually every place of deployment. The campaigns of 1864–1865 left the countryside of Virginia and Georgia scarred as if a race of giant moles had burrowed through it. Good troops in good

---

[25]For an opposing viewpoint, which argues that most Civil War firefights took place at short range, where the rifle had little advantage over the smoothbore, and that Civil War tactics were properly similar to those of the Napoleonic Wars, see Paddy Griffith, *Rally Once Again: Battle Tactics of the American Civil War* (Ramsbury, Eng., 1987). Griffith's evidence is shaky, however, and his arguments have struck most historians as unconvincing.

trenches could hold them against three or four times as many attacking troops. The rifle and the trench ruled the later Civil War battlefields as thoroughly as the machine gun and trench ruled those of World War I.

In 1861, however, most regiments on both sides carried smoothbores, for when the war began there were barely enough rifles to equip the tiny regular army. The Union and Confederate governments, several state governments, and some private firms sent agents to Europe, where they engaged in a bidding contest for the surplus arms of Britain and the Continent. Altogether the Union government and Northern states bought more than a million muskets and rifles in Europe, some worthless but most serviceable. By 1863, the domestic arms industry was turning out enough rifles for the Union army, so foreign purchases came to an end. The U.S. armory at Springfield, Massachusetts, produced nearly 800,000 rifles; private manufacturers made an additional 900,000 of the Springfield model. Northern factories and government armories turned out more than two and a half million small arms of all types during the Civil War, an unprecedented achievement that testified to the modernized efficiency of the arms industry.

The Confederacy could not come close to matching this output. Total Confederate domestic production of rifles is unknown, but it probably did not exceed 250,000. In addition the South imported 600,000 rifles, a large portion of them Enfields. In the war's first year, the Confederacy was starved for weapons; during 1862, victorious Rebel armies captured 100,000 Union rifles and blockade runners brought in nearly 200,000 more, ending the South's small-arms famine. By 1863, most infantrymen on both sides were armed with modern rifles.

"Modern" they may have been, but they were still single-shot muzzleloaders. To load this weapon was a complicated procedure: the soldier took a paper-wrapped cartridge containing bullet and powder from his cartridge pouch; tore open the paper with his teeth; poured the powder down the barrel; put the bullet in the barrel; rammed bullet and powder down with the ramrod; half-cocked the hammer; put a percussion cap on the nipple; cocked the hammer; aimed; and fired. An experienced soldier could get off two or three shots a minute. But in the noise and excitement of battle, many soldiers failed to do one or more of these steps properly, and the gun misfired. The exhausted or distracted soldier might fail to realize this, might ram down another load and misfire a second, third, or even several times. After the battle of Gettysburg, 24,000 loaded rifles were found on the field. Half of them had two bullets in the barrel, 6,000 had three or more loads, and one famous specimen had twenty-three loads jammed down the barrel. Even if a soldier did everything correctly, he normally had to stand or kneel to load his rifle (though some agile men learned how to load while lying on their backs), thereby exposing himself to enemy fire.

The obvious solution to these problems was a rifle that could be loaded at the breech. Military breechloaders had existed for many years. But they were plagued by problems, chiefly the escape of powder gas through the breech, which caused the gun to malfunction as the barrel heated with rapid use. In the 1850s, several inventors (including Ambrose E. Burnside, who became a Union general) developed copper cartridges or other devices that largely solved the problem of escaping gas. The Union cavalry received breechloading carbines as fast as they could be produced, and some Rebel horsemen also carried them when they could get them by capture or from the limited production of the Richmond armory. Ingenious Connecticut Yankees also invented breechloading repeaters. The most successful was the Spencer seven-shot carbine, fed by a springloaded clip in the stock, which became the favorite weapon of Yankee troopers in 1864–1865.

The breechloading and repeating techniques could be applied to rifles as well as carbines (the main differences between the two were the rifle's longer barrel and heavier powder charge). But the U.S. Ordnance Bureau was slow to accept the idea of breechloaders for the infantry. Angry progressives referred to Ordnance Bureau Chief James Ripley as "Ripley Van Winkle" because of his opposition to breechloading rifles. Several historians have maintained that if Ripley had contracted for large numbers of breechloaders and repeaters in 1861–1862, the war might have been shortened by a year or more. As it was, few breechloading infantry rifles were produced before Lincoln forced Ripley to retire in September 1863.[26]

But there is another side to this question. The initial skepticism of Ripley and other officers toward breechloaders and repeaters was not wholly unfounded. They argued that (1) the new weapons had not yet proven themselves in 1861–1862, and it would be foolish to divert resources from the production of muzzleloaders like the Springfield until all troops had been armed with these reliable weapons; (2) because of European purchases and domestic production of several types of muzzleloaders, the Ordnance Bureau had trouble enough supplying different regiments with the right kinds of ammunition without having to supply ammunition also for the dozen or so different breechloaders then in existence; (3) soldiers firing breechloaders might waste ammunition, thereby exacerbating the already serious logistics problem. Although it turned out in the end that men armed with breechloaders and repeaters became more efficient and accurate in their fire than before, there was enough wild and wasteful shooting early in the war to lend credence to this argument. And despite the disadvantages of muzzleloaders, the Springfield and Enfield were deadly weapons, as the carnage of Civil War battlefields cruelly attested.

Nevertheless, part of the indictment against Ripley is valid: despite malfunction problems, the breechloaders were better weapons, and more of them could have been produced earlier had it not been for Ripley's opposition. Altogether about 100,000 Sharps single-shot breechloaders (90,000 carbines and 10,000 rifles), 55,000 Burnside single-shot carbines, 85,000 Spencer seven-shot carbines and rifles, and at least 100,000 breechloaders and repeaters of other types were manufactured for the Union army. They gave Yankee soldiers who carried them a powerful advantage in the war's later stages.

Southern and Northern War Production and Supply

Although often less well armed than their enemies, Confederate soldiers did not suffer from ordnance shortages after 1862. The Confederate Ordnance Bureau was the one success story of Confederate logistics. The architect of this success, Chief of Ordnance Josiah Gorgas, was a native of Pennsylvania and a West Point graduate who had married a Southern woman. Starting with almost nothing except the Tredegar Iron Works in Richmond, Gorgas created dozens of factories that turned out large quantities of pow-

---

[26]See especially Robert V. Bruce, *Lincoln and the Tools of War* (Indianapolis, 1956), and Allan Nevins, *The War for the Union: The Improvised War 1861–1862* (New York, 1959), pp. 361–369.

der and ammunition. He was a genius at improvisation. Appeals went out to Southern churches and plantations to turn in their bells to be melted down and recast into cannon. Southern women saved the contents of chamber pots to be leached for niter to produce gunpowder. The Ordnance Bureau located limestone caves in the southern Appalachians that contained niter deposits. Army officers gleaned battlefields to retrieve and recycle lead for bullets. Ordnance officials scoured the countryside for stills, which they melted down to obtain copper for rifle percussion caps. Gorgas's achievement is best described in his own words: "From being the worst supplied of the Bureaus of the War Department, " he wrote in his diary on April 8, 1864, the Ordnance Bureau:

. . . is now the best. Large arsenals have been organized at Richmond, Fayetteville, Augusta, Charleston, Columbus, Macon, Atlanta and Selma. . . . A superb powder mill has been built at Augusta. . . . Lead-smelting works were established by me at Petersburgh. . . . A cannon foundry established at Macon for heavy guns, and bronze foundries at Macon, Columbus, Ga., and Augusta; a foundry for shot and shell at Salisbury, N.C. . . . a manufactory of carbines has been built up here [Richmond]; a rifle factory at Asheville (transferred to Columbia, S.C.). . . . Where three years ago we were not making a gun, a pistol nor a sabre, no shot nor shell (except at the Tredegar Works)—a pound of powder—we now make all these in quantities to meet the demands of our large armies.[27]

But when we turn from ordnance to the commissary and quartermaster bureaus of the Confederacy, a far different picture emerges. If an army marches on its stomach, as Napoleon said, the mobility of Rebel soldiers was all the more marvelous, for they seldom had enough to eat. The deterioration of Southern railroads, the disorganization of the economy by runaway inflation, and the inefficiency of Commissary General Lucius Northrop (who was said to retain his post only because of favoritism by President Davis) all combined to make food supply one of the Confederacy's worst problems. During the winter of 1862–1863, the daily ration in Lee's army was reduced to four ounces of bacon, eighteen ounces of cornmeal, and an occasional handful of rice or black-eyed peas. Thousands of men suffered from scurvy, which disappeared only when the arrival of spring enabled the soldiers to dig sassafras roots and wild onions. In January 1864, Lee wrote: "Unless there is a change, I fear the army cannot be kept effective and cannot be kept together."[28]

Men can fight in rags, and many Rebels did. But it is hard to march twenty miles a day or stand picket duty in winter without shoes. Yet Confederate soldiers did that also. When Lee's army invaded Maryland in 1862, several thousand stragglers stayed behind, mainly because they could not march on the macadamized Maryland roads in bare feet. These men might have made a difference had they been present at the battle of Antietam.

Union soldiers also sometimes suffered from lack of proper food. During the winter of 1862–1863, corruption and inefficiency in the Commissary Department caused food shortages and scurvy in the Army of the Potomac. But most of the time, Billy Yank was abundantly supplied. Quartermaster General Montgomery Meigs was a superb administrator. Northern industry and agriculture poured out uniforms, overcoats, shoes, pork and "hardtack" (a three-inch square of hard bread that formed the

---

[27]Frank E. Vandiver (ed.), *The Civil War Diary of General Josiah Gorgas* (University, Ala., 1947), pp. 90–91.

[28]Douglas Southall Freeman, *R. E. Lee: A Biography*, 4 vols. (New York, 1934–1935), III, 247.

staple of Union rations), and other items in such abundance that Yankee soldiers became prodigal of their provisions. "A French army of half the size of ours could be supplied with what we waste," confessed one Union general.[29]

In the end, the greater resources and productivity of the Northern economy enabled Union forces to overcome the Confederacy's advantages of fighting a defensive war in its own territory. Man for man, the Yankee soldier was no better than the Rebel; at first he may not have been as good. But there were more Yankees than Rebels and they were better armed and supplied.

Financing the War: The Confederacy

The most serious deficiency of the Confederate economy was its financial structure. With its capital invested primarily in land and slaves, the South had not developed a fiscal system capable of meeting the demands of a wartime economy. Forced to print paper money to prime its monetary pump, the Confederacy set in motion a dizzying spiral of inflation that could not be stopped.

This was one of the war's cruel ironies, for Confederate Secretary of the Treasury Christopher Memminger was a hard-money advocate who considered the printing press "the most dangerous of all methods of raising money."[30] Of the three methods to finance the war—taxation, loans, and treasury notes (paper money)—Memminger preferred the first. But the Confederate Congress was wary of imposing new taxes. For thirty-five years, Americans had paid no internal taxes to the federal government, whose modest prewar budgets had been funded by tariffs and the proceeds of land sales. Believing that the war would be short and that heavy taxes would diminish patriotic ardor, Southern lawmakers passed no general tax measure until August 1861. The small direct property tax then levied was weakened by offering the states a 10 percent reduction of their quotas if they paid the Confederate Treasury by April 1, 1862. All but three states did so not by collecting the tax but by floating state loans!

More palatable than taxes were bond issues, to be repaid by future generations who would presumably enjoy the benefits of independence won by the sacrifices of the war generation. The Confederacy's first bonds ($15 million) were fully subscribed in the patriotic fervor of 1861. But this loan soaked up most of the available specie in the South without coming close to meeting mounting costs. The shortage of capital spawned the ingenious idea of a "produce loan," which would enable farmers to pledge the proceeds from part of their crop in return for bonds equal to the market price of their pledge. First authorized in a $50 million bond issue of May 1861, the produce loan was expanded to $100 million in August. But the response was disappointing. Pledges were slow to come in, and the government had trouble collecting them. The mushrooming price of cotton encouraged planters to hold their crop for higher prices and even to smuggle it through enemy

---

[29]Russell F. Weigley, *Quartermaster-General of the Union Army: A Biography of Montgomery C. Meigs* (New York, 1959), p. 205.

[30]Eugene M. Lerner, "The Monetary and Fiscal Problems of the Confederate Government," *Journal of Political Economy,* 62 (December 1954), 520.

lines for Yankee gold. From the produce loan, the Confederacy realized only $34 million—most of it late in the war, when the currency had so far depreciated as to be almost worthless.

To fill the monetary gap, Congress authorized $119 million of treasury notes in 1861 and $400 million in 1862. These notes were to be redeemable in specie within two years of the end of the war. Once begun on this scale, the printing of money became like liquor to an alcoholic—the more printed, the more needed to achieve the same result. When coupled with the shortages caused by the blockade, by Union invasions, and by the deterioration of Southern railroads, these issues of paper money drove the price index up to 762 by the beginning of 1863 (January 1861 = 100). State and city governments added to the flood of paper money by printing their own notes. Counterfeiting of the crudely printed Confederate notes became widespread; indeed, the counterfeit notes could sometimes be detected because of their superior quality. The South moved toward a barter economy as creditors required payment in goods rather than in depreciated currency. Farmers complained that their crops were impressed by army commissary officers at far below the market value. Wages lagged behind prices: real wages in the South declined by at least 65 percent during the war. City dwellers could not afford skyrocketing food prices and rents, and food riots broke out in several cities during 1863.

By 1863, everyone realized that the printing press was a major cause of inflation. Newspapers that had opposed high taxes in 1861 reversed themselves and presented the strange spectacle of a people begging to be taxed. Congress responded with the passage on April 24, 1863, of a remarkably comprehensive tax bill. It included an 8 percent tax on certain consumer goods, a 10 percent profits tax on wholesalers, excise taxes, a license tax on businesses and professions (a later amendment added a 5 percent levy on land and slaves), and a graduated income tax ranging from 1 percent on incomes between $1,000 and $1,500 up to 15 percent on income over $10,000. A unique additional feature was the "tax in kind" on agricultural products. After reserving specified amounts of food crops for their own families, farmers were required to pay one-tenth of their remaining crops to the government.

These taxes were a failure. Evasion was widespread and enforcement erratic, under the pressures of Union invasion and the breakdown of Confederate authority. In two years the money taxes yielded only $119 million in badly depreciated currency. The tax in kind yielded products valued at only $62 million. This latter tax was particularly unpopular. Farmers living near the war theaters or near railroads found their full quotas seized by tax agents, while those remote from armies or transportation paid little or nothing. And when some tax-in-kind food crops rotted in warehouses for want of transportation, the bitterness of farmers knew no bounds.

After the Confederate military defeats at Gettysburg and Vicksburg in July 1863, inflation became even worse. The only remedy seemed to be to run the printing presses faster. By the spring of 1864, it took $46 to buy what $1 had bought three years earlier. The Confederate Congress tried to reverse the trend by requiring treasury notes to be converted to low-interest bonds (in effect, a forced loan) or exchanged for new notes at the rate of three old notes for two new ones. This partial repudiation did stabilize the currency for several months, but only at the cost of destroying whatever faith was left in Confederate finances. By the spring of 1865, prices had risen to ninety-two times their prewar level.

Unsound financial policies were one cause of Confederate defeat. Reliance on taxes for less than 10 percent of government revenues and on loans for 30 percent, leaving the remaining 60 percent to be created as fiat money, was a sure-fire recipe for disaster. It sapped civilian morale and embittered large segments of the population. Runaway inflation was in effect a form of confiscatory taxation that fell most heavily on the poor. But the Confederate Congress and Treasury do not deserve all the blame. Factors beyond their control—the Union blockade, Northern military victories, the refusal of European governments to recognize the Confederacy—were also responsible. The chief culprit, however, was the South's unbalanced agricultural economy, which was just not equal to the demands of modern war.

Financing the War: The Union

At first, the Union government seemed little better prepared than the Confederacy to finance a major war. The depression following the Panic of 1857 had reduced tax revenues. Just as the economy was recovering, the secession crisis plunged it into another recession. For the first time since the War of 1812, the federal budget had run a deficit for four consecutive years. When Lincoln became President, the national debt was higher than ever before, government bonds were selling below par, and the Treasury was nearly empty. The new Secretary of the Treasury, Salmon P. Chase, had been appointed not because of his financial knowledge (which was minimal) but because of his political influence.

Even if Chase had been a financial genius, the monetary system of the United States in 1861 would have been hard to mobilize for war. Although the North had one of the world's most advanced economies, Jacksonian Democrats had saddled the federal government with an antiquated financial structure. The Independent Treasury Act of 1846 had prohibited the government from depositing its funds in banks and had required all payments to or by the government to be made in specie. This had climaxed the campaign, begun fifteen years earlier, to destroy the Second Bank of the United States and to divorce the federal government from the country's banking and monetary system. Chartered by the separate states, banks and the banknotes that they circulated as currency varied widely in soundness. In 1861, seven thousand different kinds of banknotes were circulating, many of them counterfeit and others virtually worthless because the issuing bank had gone bankrupt. Out of this monetary chaos had emerged a degree of order and strength in the private sector, for the sound banks functioned mainly on a demand deposit basis (similar to the modern checking account), and the banknotes of even the less sound banks provided a medium of exchange that circulated at various rates of discount. But the federal government continued to operate in a monetary horse-and-buggy age: "tons of gold had to be hauled to and fro in dray-loads, with horses and heavers doing by the hour what bookkeepers could do in a moment."[31]

---

[31]Bray Hammond, *Sovereignty and an Empty Purse: Banks and Politics in the Civil War* (Princeton, 1970), p. 23.

Such a system was perhaps acceptable in peacetime, when the federal government played a small role in the economy. The government's annual budgets in the 1850s averaged less than 2 percent of the gross national product (compared with 20 percent today). But the Civil War changed all that. Government expenditures jumped to an average of 15 percent of the gross national product during the war. The conflict forcibly modernized the government's monetary structure. The underlying strength of the Northern economy enabled the Union to emerge in 1865 with a sounder financial system than before.

During the first year of fighting, however, the Union Treasury was in bad shape. In August 1861, Congress did take the unprecedented step of levying an income tax of 3 percent on incomes over $800. But most of this tax would not be collected until the second half of 1862. Meanwhile, the Treasury had to rely mainly on the borrowing authority granted by Congress. The government had traditionally gone to eastern banks for the short-term loans needed to carry on ordinary business. Chase wanted to change this and to offer bonds directly to the public. A people's war should be sustained by the people's loans. Here was the germ of the great bond drives of the two world wars in the twentieth century. But in the Civil War, this novel idea got off to a slow start. The banks underwrote the first $150 million loan in the fall of 1861. Jay Cooke's small banking house in Philadelphia successfully promoted the public subscription of these bonds. But elsewhere public sales were poor. The average citizen had never seen a government bond, much less thought of buying one. Moreover, the bonds had to be paid for in specie, and few people possessed any spare gold.

The specie problem also plagued the banks. Their reserves threatened to fall below the requirements necessary to support their notes and demand deposits. Then in November 1861, a potentially disastrous diplomatic crisis erupted between the North and Britain over the seizure of Confederate envoys traveling on the British ship *Trent* (see page 241). Stocks and bonds fell, gold and silver went into hoarding or left the country, and the North seemed to be heading toward another financial panic. Peaceful settlement of the *Trent* affair did little to ease the crisis. On December 30, all banks and the Treasury suspended specie payments. For a while soldiers and government contractors were not paid, and banks did not redeem their notes in gold. To pessimists it looked like the North was about to lose the war by default.

Creation of the Greenbacks

But Congress resolved the crisis in a way that was to have profound consequences for the nation's future monetary history. Three main proposals emerged during the congressional debate. Chase proposed to create a national banking system that would enable banks to issue notes backed by government bonds, which in turn would be backed by Treasury reserves. This was a far-reaching suggestion that eventually bore fruit, but it could not go into effect soon enough to meet the emergency of early 1862. Several bankers put forward a second alternative: a new issue of bonds to be sold "at the market"—that is, at whatever price they would bring, even if it meant selling them below par. This would bring specie out of hoarding, begin the flow of money, and supply the government with necessary funds. It would also make large profits for bankers and investors, who would buy at a discount and eventually receive par value plus interest. Thus Congress rejected the idea. The third proposal was to do what the Confederacy was already doing—to print fiat money. This was the alternative chosen by Congress, which on February 25, 1862, passed the Legal Tender Act authorizing the issue of $150 million in treasury notes—the famous greenbacks.

Congress enacted this law only after a great deal of soul searching. Was it constitutional? Was it a violation of contract to make greenbacks legal tender to pay debts previously contracted? Was it wise? Would the greenbacks depreciate? Were the greenbacks not immoral? "By common consent of the nations," said a banker, "gold and silver are the only true measure of value. These metals were prepared by the Almighty for this very purpose." Democrats in Congress voted against the Legal Tender Act by a three-to-one margin because, as one of them said, it launched the country "upon an ocean of experiment upon which the wise men who administered the government before we came into power . . . would not permit it even to enter."[32] More open to experimentation, Republicans voted three to one in favor of the act. But many of them did so with misgivings. "It shocks all my notions of political, moral, and national honor," said William Pitt Fessenden, chairman of the Senate Finance Committee. "The thing is wrong in itself, but to leave the government without resources at such a crisis is not to be thought of." Chase, a hard-money man at heart, came to reluctant support of the bill only because *immediate action is of great importance. The Treasury is nearly empty.*[33]

The Legal Tender Act fulfilled the hopes without confirming the fears of those who passed it. It gave the government money to pay its obligations, ended the banking crisis, and injected a circulating medium into the specie-starved economy. Although the greenbacks gradually depreciated in relation to gold, the Union did not experience the runaway inflation that ruined Confederate finance. Why not? First, the Union greenbacks, unlike Confederate notes, were made *legal tender,* receivable for all debts public or private except import duties and interest on the national debt. Banks, contractors, merchants, and the government itself had to accept greenbacks as lawful money at their face value, with the exceptions noted. Some Republican congressmen who opposed these exceptions asked why bondholders should receive interest in gold while soldiers who risked their lives were paid with paper money. But supporters of interest payments in gold argued that such a policy was necessary to attract foreign and domestic investors to buy at par the $500 million of 6 percent bonds authorized in February 1862. This argument was undoubtedly correct, for without the promise of interest in gold as a hedge against inflation these bonds could not have been sold at par.[34] The requirement that import duties be paid in specie guaranteed the government the means to maintain interest payments in gold.

---

[32]Hugh McCulloch, *Men and Measures of Half a Century* (New York, 1888), p. 201; *Congressional Globe,* 37th Cong., 2nd sess. (1862), 549.

[33]Francis Fessenden, *Life and Public Services of William Pitt Fessenden,* 2 vols. (Boston, 1907), I, 194; Chase quoted in Robert P. Sharkey, *Money, Class, and Party: An Economic Study of Civil War and Reconstruction* (Baltimore, 1959), p. 41. The best study of the Republicans' monetary and tax legislation to finance the war is Heather Cox Richardson, *The Greatest Nation of the Earth: Republican Economic Policies during the Civil War* (Cambridge, Mass., 1997), chaps. 1–4.

[34]The question of whether the principal of the bonds should also be paid in gold caused considerable controversy after the war. The Republicans insisted that it should, and they carried their point.

The fortuitous timing of the greenback issues was a second reason for their success. Union military and naval victories in the winter and spring of 1862 (see pages 244 to 256) lifted Northern morale and helped to float the greenbacks on a newly buoyant mood. A third reason why Union greenbacks depreciated less than any previous fiat money was Congress's belated recognition that new and heavy war taxes must be levied. The revenue measure signed by Lincoln on July 1, 1862, taxed practically everything: it imposed an income tax of 3 percent on incomes from $600 to $10,000 and 5 percent on those above $10,000 (revised upward in 1864 to 5 percent on incomes over $600 rising to 10 percent on those over $10,000); it laid excise taxes on everything from tobacco and liquor to yachts and billiard tables; and it levied license taxes, stamp taxes, inheritance taxes, and value-added taxes on hundreds of products. It also increased the tariff, to protect manufacturers from the added costs imposed by internal taxes. These levies raised more than $600 million in the last three years of the war. Along with $1.5 billion of bonds sold during the same period, the taxes soaked up part of the inflationary pressures of the war economy—even though three subsequent greenback issues raised the total amount of this currency to $447 million.

War Bonds

The U.S. Treasury marketed a bewildering variety of war bonds. The most common were the famous "five-twenty" bonds (redeemable in not less than five and not more than twenty years) at 6 percent, of which more than $600 million were sold. But during the summer of 1862, these bonds were not selling well. Confederate military victories in Virginia offset earlier Union gains in the West. European recognition of the Confederacy appeared imminent. And the 6 percent interest on the bond was not attractive to investors so long as the future seemed cloudy. By late summer, the Treasury faced a crisis almost as grave as in January. At this juncture, Chase appointed Jay Cooke as a special agent to market the lagging five-twenties. Cooke attacked the problem with energy and skill. He flooded the newspapers with advertisements that appealed both to patriotism and to profit. He organized 2,500 subagents who sold bonds in every corner of the North. Cooke democratized the purchase of government securities. Nearly a million Northerners—one out of every four families—bought war bonds. This helped to bind the average person not only to the war effort but also to the modernizing capitalist system by which it was financed. It also helped Cooke's banking house become one of the country's leading financial institutions.

National Banks

From the experience of Civil War finance developed the national banking system, which remained the backbone of the American monetary structure until superseded by the Federal Reserve system in 1913. The creation of national banks sprang from several motives: the need to create a market for war bonds, the desire of Whiggish Republicans to resurrect the centralized banking structure destroyed by the Jacksonians, and the desire of many leaders of the financial community, especially in the Northeast, to create a more stable banknote currency. In February 1863, Congress passed the National Bank Act (supplemented by a second act in June 1864), which established criteria by which a bank could obtain a federal charter and issue national banknotes in an amount up to 90 percent of the value of the U.S. bonds that it held. Designed to replace the plethora of state banks and banknotes with a uniform national system, this legislation was supported by 78 percent of the congressional Republicans, who narrowly overcame the 91 percent of the Democrats voting against it.

The chartering of national banks proceeded slowly at first, for many state banks saw no advantage in joining the federal system. By the end of 1864, fewer than five hundred national banks had been chartered while more than a thousand state banks were still doing business. Under the impulse of a triumphant nationalism, Congress in March 1865 enacted a tax of 10 percent on state banknotes. This soon accomplished its purpose of driving these notes out of circulation and forcing most state banks to apply for federal charters. By 1873, state banknotes had virtually disappeared.[35]

Whereas the Confederacy raised 60 percent of its funds by printing paper money and less than 10 percent by taxes, Union war finances included 13 percent paper money and 21 percent taxes. While the Confederacy suffered an inflation rate exceeding 9,000 percent, the cost of living rose about 80 percent in the North and fell gradually but steadily after the war was over.[36] This compares with 80 percent inflation in World War I and 72 percent in World War II. Because wages rose at a slower rate than prices during the Civil War, real wages declined by about 25 percent in the North, but they returned to the prewar level by 1866 and continued to rise thereafter. Without rationing or price controls, the Union government successfully financed the war after overcoming the inexperience and crises of the first year. Northern people suffered no serious shortages of food or other necessities except cotton cloth. To a remarkable degree, the Northern economy was able to produce both guns and butter.

---

[35]But not state banks. Indeed, by 1873 their number had grown to 1,330 and their assets totaled nearly half as much as the assets held by the 1,968 national banks. The requirement that national banks must purchase U.S. bonds in an amount equivalent to at least one-third of their capital discouraged many smaller banks, especially in the West and South, from applying for a national charter. Most of the national banks were therefore concentrated in the Northeast, and this fact, combined with the limitation of national banknotes to $300 million (later increased slightly), created a severe regional maldistribution of banknote currency that hurt the economy of the West and South and produced postwar demands in these regions for monetary reform and inflation.

[36]The inflation rate was distinct from the gold premium, another index of currency depreciation. The former measured changes in what a dollar would buy; the latter measured fluctuations in the value of a dollar in relation to the value of gold. Although this fluctuation had some impact on domestic prices, it mainly reflected the international status of the dollar. With the suspension of specie payments and the creation of the greenbacks in 1862, the United States in effect went off the gold standard, though it still used gold for international trade. The gold value of the dollar fluctuated wildly in response to changes in the military situation. The price of gold soared to 284 (i.e., it took $2.84 in currency to purchase a dollar of gold) in July 1864, when Grant and Sherman seemed stymied before Petersburg and Atlanta, and Confederate General Jubal Early led a raid to the very outskirts of Washington. By the end of the war, gold had dropped to 127.

The War at Home and Abroad

By some strange operation of magic I have become the power of the land. . . . God has placed a great work in my hands. . . . The people call on me to save the country. I must save it, and cannot respect anything that is in the way. . . . The President is an idiot and the old General is in his dotage.

—Union General George B. McClellan, 1861

The First Battle of Bull Run

One of the war's most consequential strategic developments was a political decision. On May 21, the Confederate Congress accepted Virginia's invitation to move the capital from overcrowded, wilting Montgomery to the bustling industrial and commercial center of Richmond. By locating their capital a hundred miles from Washington, the Confederates made northern Virginia the war's main battle theater. Although Richmond would have been a focal point of conflict in any case because of its industrial importance, its political significance concentrated most Confederate strategic thinking on the Virginia theater at the expense of the West, where in the end the South lost the war.

If a defensive strategy accorded with Southern war aims, the North's determination to restore the Union required some sort of offensive plan. On May 3, General in Chief Winfield Scott proposed such a plan. He would cordon the Confederacy on all sides with a blockade by sea and by the dispatch of an invasion flotilla down the Mississippi to the Gulf. This would "envelop the insurgent states and bring them to terms with less bloodshed than by any other plan."[1]

---

[1] *O.R.*, Ser. 1, Vol. 51, pt. 1, pp. 369–370.

Although the blockade already existed and Scott's proposed move down the Mississippi anticipated the later course of the war in the West, two things were wrong with his plan in 1861. First, having sealed off the South, Scott planned to wait for the Confederacy to die of suffocation and for Southern Unionists to regain power. A Virginian himself, Scott still cherished the illusion that his Southern brethren would come to their senses if the North acted firmly but with restraint. Second, Scott's plan would take time—five months to build the gunboats and train the soldiers; several more months for them to fight their way downriver and for the blockade to become effective. But Northern faith in Southern Unionism had worn thin, and public opinion clamored for an immediate invasion to "crush" the rebellion. When details of Scott's proposal leaked out, newspapers derisively labeled it "The Anaconda Plan." Editors called for action. On June 26, the powerful *New York Tribune* put the slogan "Forward to Richmond" on its masthead and kept it there day after day, thundering that the Rebel Congress must not be allowed to meet July 20.

The main Union army of 35,000 men under General Irvin McDowell was encamped across the Potomac from Washington. Twenty-five miles away, a Confederate force of 20,000 under General Beauregard deployed on the south bank of Bull Run covering the key rail junction at Manassas. Fifty miles to the northwest, in the Shenandoah Valley, 12,000 Rebels under General Joseph E. Johnston, former Quartermaster General of the U.S. army and now the ranking officer of the Confederacy, confronted a Union force half again as large under General Robert Patterson, a sixty-nine-year-old veteran of the War in 1812. Lincoln ordered McDowell to draw up a plan to attack Beauregard's army at Manassas. A former major in the regular army, McDowell had never commanded so much as a squad in battle. But he had experience in staff work; he had taught tactics at West Point; and the plan he submitted was a good one—for veteran troops. While Patterson advanced against Johnston's forces in the valley to prevent them from reinforcing Beauregard, McDowell would march from Washington, feint against the strongly held fords and bridges on Bull Run, and send a large column around the Confederate defenses to cross the river and attack their flank. Lincoln liked the plan, but McDowell protested that he needed more time—several weeks at least—to train and discipline his raw troops. Lincoln could not wait. "You are green, it is true," he said, "but they are green also; you are all green alike." The President told McDowell to get moving.[2]

McDowell issued orders for the advance to begin on July 16, but things went wrong from the start—as he had feared. Confused by ambiguous orders from Washington, Patterson demonstrated half-heartedly against Johnston in the valley and then pulled back. Meanwhile, the Confederates had learned of McDowell's plans from Rose O'Neal Greenhow, head of a Confederate spy ring in Washington. Jefferson Davis ordered Johnston to entrain most of his troops on the Manassas Gap Railroad and bring them to reinforce Beauregard. Johnston left a cavalry screen under Colonel James E. B. (Jeb) Stuart to deceive Patterson and marched most of his army to the railhead. So befuddled was Patterson by Stuart's aggressive maneuvers that he did not even discover Johnston's departure until July 20. By then all but one of the Con-

---

[2]T. Harry Williams, *Lincoln and His Generals* (New York, 1952), p. 21.

federate valley brigades had arrived at Manassas. Patterson's failure to hold Johnston in the valley proved to be of crucial importance in the upcoming battle. It also illustrated three of the Confederate advantages early in the war discussed in the previous chapter: superior intelligence sources, better cavalry, and the ability to move troops on interior lines.

Despite all this, the Federals might have kept the advantage if McDowell had been able to move as fast as planned. But his march from Alexandria to Bull Run turned into a nightmare of confusion and delays, which illustrated the military axiom that march discipline is harder to achieve with half-trained troops than is battle discipline. Soldiers had to halt in the July heat for hours while problems ahead bogged down the whole line. Troops fell out of line to pick blackberries or to take a nap in the shade. Inexperienced officers did not know how to keep thousands of men under control. It took two and a half days for the army to move twenty-two miles, a distance veterans later in the war could march in a day. The need to reissue rations and ammunition consumed or lost by careless troops and the necessity for reconnaissance in this little-known, ill-mapped terrain caused further delays. McDowell was finally ready for action on Sunday, July 21. On that day carriages from Washington filled with congressmen and other spectators drove out to "see the Rebels get whipped."

McDowell's flanking column of 12,000 men roused themselves at 2 A.M., stumbled through the underbrush in the dark, and deployed after crossing the Sudley Springs ford three hours behind schedule. In the meantime, other Union brigades feinted against the stone bridge over Bull Run and the fords downstream to hold the Confederates there while the flanking force rolled them up. At first it worked, despite all the delays. Union regiments came scrambling across the fields north of the Warrenton turnpike, attacking disjointedly but driving before them the outnumbered Confederates, who had changed front to meet this threat to their left flank. Other Union troops commanded by Colonel William T. Sherman forded the river to join the assault. To their crumbling left, the Confederates rushed reinforcements, including a brigade under Virginian Thomas J. Jackson, who took a defensive position on Henry House Hill. By noon the Rebels had been forced back to this hill. Attempting to reform his shattered brigade of South Carolinians, General Barnard Bee pointed toward Jackson's troops. "Look!" he shouted. "There is Jackson standing like a stone wall! Rally behind the Virginians!" Rally they did, even though Bee himself was killed. Thus was the legend of "Stonewall" Jackson born.

As Beauregard and Johnston arrived at Henry House Hill to direct their regrouping forces in person, the Union troops, jubilant but disorganized by their success, paused to reform for a renewed assault. Then for two hours, from 2 to 4 P.M., heavy fighting surged back and forth across the hill. At one point the confusion caused by a multiplicity of uniforms crippled a Union attack. A blue-clad regiment moved out of the woods toward two Union artillery batteries. Thinking they were supporting infantry, the Federals held their fire until the regiment, which turned out to be the 33rd Virginia, suddenly leveled their muskets and fired a volley at point-blank range, killing many of the gunners and knocking out the batteries. The fighting raged on, but the steam went out of the Union advance in that sector. McDowell was in the thick of the fighting, personally giving orders to brigades, even regiments, but he neglected the duties of overall command and failed to order up two reserve brigades from the rear.

Beauregard and Johnston, by contrast, now had firm control of their army, including the last brigade from the valley, just off the train at Manassas and marching into line at 4 P.M. Bolstered by these and other reinforcements, Beauregard ordered a counterattack with his fresh troops. The Southerners charged forward with the rebel yell on their lips. A high-pitched, wailing scream, this famous yell served the same function as the deeper-toned shout uttered by the Yankee soldiers in battle—it relieved tension and created a sense of solidarity among comrades. Of unknown origin (some said it came from the fox hunter's cry, others likened it to a hog-calling halloo), the rebel yell was by all accounts a fearsome thing. "There is nothing like it this side of the infernal region," wrote a Union veteran. "The peculiar corkscrew sensation that it sends down your backbone under these circumstances can never be told. You have to feel it, and if you say you did not feel it, and heard the yell, you have *never* been there."[3]

In the face of this screaming counterattack, the exhausted Yankees, many of whom had been marching and fighting with little food or water for more than thirteen hours on a hot July day, gave way—slowly at first, but with increasing disorder as they were forced back across Bull Run. As the sun dipped toward the horizon, panic infected many bluecoats, and the retreat became a rout. This illustrated another military maxim: an orderly retreat is the most difficult maneuver for raw troops to execute. Some of the army vehicles became entangled with the carriages of frantic civilians caught in the melee. One Northern congressman was captured; several other politicians tried to rally the fugitives but were pushed aside by wild-eyed soldiers who wanted only to get away. All night long the men streamed back toward Washington, making far better time in their retreat than they had in their advance.

The battle of Bull Run (or Manassas, as Southerners called it) was a decisive tactical victory for the Confederacy.[4] Of the 18,000 men on each side actually engaged (several brigades on both sides did not see action), 387 Confederates and 481 Yankees were killed, 1,582 and 1,011 respectively were wounded, and about 1,200 Northerners were missing, mostly captured. In Civil War battles, about one-seventh of the wounded later died of their injuries; so the total of killed and mortally wounded came to about 600 on each side. Although this was a small battle by later Civil War standards, it was by far the largest and most costly in American history up to that time.

When Jefferson Davis arrived on the Bull Run battlefield at the climax of victory, he asked Johnston and Beauregard if they could push on to Washington. But Johnston believed his army was "more disorganized by victory than that of the United States by defeat."[5] A controversy later developed in the South over responsibility for the failure to follow up the victory. Beauregard blamed Davis for vetoing an advance,

---

[3]Bruce Catton, *Glory Road* (Garden City, N.Y., 1952), p. 57.

[4]In several cases, North and South called battles by different names: Bull Run/Manassas and Antietam/Sharpsburg are the most familiar examples. In most cases of different names, Confederates named the battle after the town or supply depot that served as their base (Manassas, Sharpsburg, Murfreesboro, etc.) while the Union named it after a landmark, usually a river, nearest to their own lines or to the fighting: Bull Run, Antietam Creek, Stones River, etc.

[5]Joseph E. Johnston, "Responsibilities of the First Bull Run," *Battles and Leaders of the Civil War,* 4 vols. (New York, 1887), I, 252.

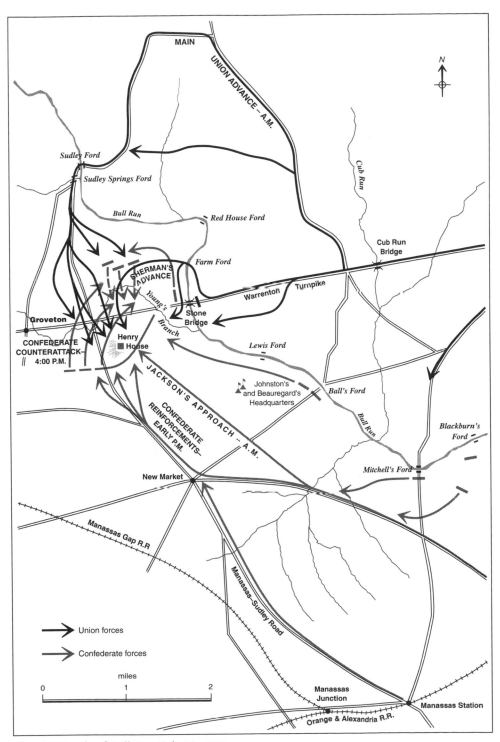

The First Battle of Bull Run, July 21, 1861

but in fact the opposite appears to have been the case. In any event, the Confederates could hardly have taken Washington. McDowell formed a strong rear guard of fresh troops at Centreville, which probably could have checked an enemy advance. Other Union soldiers rallied in the fortifications along the Potomac, a formidable barrier. A drenching rain the day after the battle turned roads into bottomless mud. Moreover, the Confederates did not have the logistical capacity for an advance; supplies at Manassas were almost exhausted, and some men went without food for more than twenty-four hours after the battle.

Bull Run made a profound impact on the country. To the Confederates, it seemed to confirm that one Southerner could whip ten Yankees—even though the numbers were equal and the Rebels had come within an ace of being whipped themselves. They had stood on the defensive for most of the battle, always an advantage but especially so with inexperienced troops. Nevertheless, this first decisive Confederate victory instilled Southern troops in Virginia with a confidence that gave them a psychological edge in future battles. More important, perhaps, it created a gnawing sense of inferiority among some Union officers and soldiers in this theater. Perhaps the Rebels were better fighters than the Yankees after all, just as Southerners had always claimed. This potential inferiority complex would prove to have significant military consequences in the eastern theater during the next two years.

McClellan and the Army of the Potomac

The tonic of triumph stimulated overconfidence on the Southern home front, causing many to believe the war was over. At the same time, the shock of defeat jolted the North into reality. A mood of grim determination replaced the incandescent optimism of the spring. If Southerners thought the Yankees would quit after one licking, they soon learned differently. Three-year volunteers flooded Northern recruiting offices. The administration reshuffled the top command in the East. George B. McClellan, fresh from his successes in western Virginia, came to Washington as commander of the newly named Army of the Potomac. McDowell suffered demotion to a division commander, and Patterson, who had failed to keep Johnston in the valley, was replaced by the Massachusetts political general Nathaniel P. Banks.

Only thirty-four years old, McClellan had served with distinction in the Mexican War, had studied military methods in Europe, and from 1857 to 1861 had been successively a chief engineer, vice president, and president of midwestern railroads. McClellan later wrote that when he arrived in Washington on July 26, he "found no army to command—only a mere collection of regiments cowering on the banks of the Potomac, some perfectly raw, others dispirited by the recent defeat."[6] Though this was an exaggeration, the situation was bad enough. McClellan took hold with a firm hand to reorganize and train these troops. Unfit officers found themselves discharged; enlisted men found themselves under a rigorous discipline that turned them from recruits into soldiers. They regained some of the pride lost at Bull Run. An excellent organizer, McClellan was just what the army needed in 1861.

---

[6]Kenneth P. Williams, *Lincoln Finds a General: A Military Study of the Civil War,* 5 vols. (New York, 1949–1959), I, 113.

GEORGE B. MCCLELLAN AND HIS WIFE, ELLEN MARCY MCCLELLAN. McClellan expressed his frank and unflattering judgments of Lincoln, Stanton, and Republicans in letters to his wife. Her father was a general on McClellan's staff.

LIBRARY OF CONGRESS

The press hailed McClellan as the man to save the country. Some enthusiasts talked of him as the next president (he was a Democrat). The adulation went to McClellan's head. He came to regard himself not as the subordinate of the President and of the general in chief but as their master. In letters to his wife and friends, McClellan unconsciously revealed his messiah complex. "I receive letter after letter, have conversation after conversation, calling on me to save the nation, alluding to the presidency, dictatorship, etc.," he wrote. "By some strange operation of magic I have become the power of the land. . . . God has placed a great work in my hands. . . . I was called to it; my previous life seems to have been unwittingly directed to this great end." His soldiers reinforced McClellan's ego. "You have no idea how the men brighten up now when I go among them," he wrote to his wife. "You never heard such yelling. . . . I can see every eye glisten." As for Lincoln and General in Chief Scott, McClellan wrote:

I am leaving nothing undone to increase our force; but the old general always comes in the way. . . . The people call on me to save the country. I must save it, and cannot respect anything that is in the way. . . . The President is an idiot and the old General is in his dotage. . . .

If [Scott] *cannot* be taken out of my path, I will not retain my position but will resign and let the administration take care of itself.[7]

On November 1, Scott finally resigned and McClellan took his place. When Lincoln warned McClellan that the dual jobs of general in chief and commander of the Army of the Potomac would be taxing, the general replied: "I can do it all."[8]

The three months after Bull Run saw no important action in the Virginia theater. While McClellan trained his growing army (120,000 men by October), Johnston was doing the same with fewer than 50,000 Confederates at Centreville. The Rebels pushed their outposts to within sight of Washington, where pickets of both armies watched each other and occasionally traded shots. It was during this period that a Northern woman wrote the poem "All Quiet Along the Potomac," which a Southern composer set to music. Its hauting strains and sentimental lyrics made it one of the most popular war songs on both sides of the Potomac.

These were McClellan's honeymoon months with Northern public opinion. But as the fine, clear days of October passed and McClellan made no move with his "magnificent army," the administration and the public began to grow impatient. McClellan had begun to exhibit the weaknesses that would ultimately bring his downfall. His first defect was perfectionism. He was superb at preparation, but the preparation was never complete enough to satisfy him. The army was perpetually *almost* ready to move. Linked to this was McClellan's chronic exaggeration of the forces opposing him. At a time when Johnston had only 41,000 men ready for duty, McClellan estimated enemy numbers at 150,000 and used this as a reason for delay until he could build up his own force to 200,000. McClellan's intelligence service, headed by Allan Pinkerton of the famous Pinkerton detective agency, fed the general's fears by constantly overestimating the size of Confederate forces. But McClellan believed what he wanted to believe. He too had absorbed notions of the South's martial superiority, which caused him always to magnify the strength of the enemy.

McClellan lacked that mental and moral courage required of great generals, the will to *act,* the willingness to confront the terrible moment of truth. To cover his weaknesses, he had an unhappy tendency to seek scapegoats. "I am here in a terrible place," he wrote his wife. "The enemy have three or four times my force; the President, the old general, cannot or will not see the true state of affairs. . . . I am thwarted and deceived . . . at every turn."[9]

McClellan's low opinion of Lincoln caused him to commit serious errors of judgment. For one thing, he failed to keep the administration informed of his plans. When pressed about his reasons for inaction, he replied petulantly or not at all. Privately, he described the cabinet as "geese" and the President as "the original gorilla." Once when Lincoln wished to learn something of McClellan's plans, the general made himself scarce "to dodge all enemies in the shape of 'browsing' Presidents,

---

[7]G. B. McClellan to Ellen Marcy McClellan, July 27, 20, August 8, 9, October 31, 1861, George B. McClellan Papers, Library of Congress.

[8]Michael Burlingame and John R. T. Ettlinger (eds.) *Inside Lincoln's White House: The Complete Civil War Diary of John Hay* (Carbondale, Ill., 1997), p. 30.

[9]McClellan to Ellen Marcy McClellan, August 16, November 2, 1861, McClellan Papers. For a detailed study of McClellan and Pinkerton's intelligence operations, see Edwin C. Fishel, *The Secret War for the Union: The Untold Story of Military Intelligence in the Civil War* (Boston, 1996), chaps. 5–6.

PRINCETON UNIVERSITY LIBRARY

SECRET SERVICE AGENTS, ARMY OF THE POTOMAC.   The man in the checkered shirt is Allan Pinkerton, known during the war by the alias E. J. Allen. His exaggerated reports of Confederate strength reinforced McClellan's defensive caution.

etc." A few evenings later, in November 1861, Lincoln and Secretary of State Seward called on McClellan and were informed that the general was out but would be home soon. When McClellan returned and learned of his visitors, he ignored them and went upstairs. Lincoln and Seward waited another half-hour until a servant finally deigned to inform them that the general had gone to bed.[10]

McClellan made no secret of his contempt for abolitionists and radical Republicans. A year earlier, his closest political friends had been Breckinridge Democrats. His proslavery learnings and his refusal to strike the Rebels a blow aroused dark thoughts among some Republicans. Montgomery Blair said on October 1 that "Lincoln himself begins to think he smells a rat." Suspicions of McClellan's loyalty to the Northern cause were unfounded. But he did appoint fellow Democrats to several important staff positions. Like himself, they wanted to restore the Union on the basis of something like the Crittenden Compromise. They were "soft" on slavery, and in a

---

[10]McClellan to Ellen Marcy McClellan, October 10, 31, November 17, 1861, McClellan Papers; Burlingame and Ettlinger, *Inside Lincoln's White House,* p. 32.

sense they were soft on the South too. Having attended West Point and served in the old army with Southern officers (several Confederate generals "were once my most intimate friends," wrote McClellan in November 1861), they could not share the Republicans' free-labor ideology. They did not want to fight the kind of war the abolitionists and radicals were beginning to demand—a war to destroy slavery and to reshape the South in the Free Soil image. "Help me to dodge the nigger," McClellan wrote to an influential Democratic friend. "I am fighting to preserve the integrity of the Union. . . . To gain that end we cannot afford to mix up the negro question."[11]

Thus did McClellan's personality and politics become mixed up with questions of military strategy and war aims. A dangerous polarization developed between top echelons of the army and of the Republican party. The Army of the Potomac became politicized, with serious consequences for its future effectiveness.

These developments came to a head in the battle of Ball's Bluff and its aftermath. This battle occurred when McClellan ordered General Charles P. Stone to send part of his division on a reconnaissance in force across the Potomac toward Leesburg, Virginia, to determine the strength and movements of a Confederate brigade there. Stone did so on October 21. The Rebels ambushed the blue regiments and forced them down the steep bluff into the river, where several men were shot or drowned as they tried to swim to safety. More than 200 Federals were killed and wounded, and 700 captured. One of the killed was Colonel Edward Baker, commander of the reconnaissance and also a Republican senator from Oregon and a close friend of President Lincoln. It was a humiliating defeat, although of little military consequence. Its political consequences, however, were large. In December 1861, Congress created a joint committee to investigate "the conduct of the present war," especially Ball's Bluff and Bull Run. Dominated by radical Republicans, the Committee on the Conduct of the War produced both good and evil. It investigated army medical services, illegal trade with the enemy, and war contracts, and helped to bring about greater efficiency and honesty in such matters. But it also harassed Democratic generals and intensified the political tensions infecting the Army of the Potomac.

General Stone was the committee's first target. A West Pointer and a Democrat from Massachusetts, Stone had ordered the return to their masters of fugitive slaves who came into his lines. For this he was reprimanded by Governor Andrew and denounced on the Senate floor by Charles Sumner. Stone was also reported to have been in contact with Confederate officers at Leesburg. Was he disloyal? Had he deliberately sent Baker and the Union troops into a trap a Ball's Bluff? The committee investigated all sorts of rumors against Stone. Although the general's convictions were undoubtedly proslavery and he may have maintained ill-advised contacts with Confederate friends, none of the stories of his disloyalty was ever proven. The committee bullied Stone, refused to let him cross-examine witnesses, and did not even inform him of the specific charges against him. Without receiving a trial or a military inquiry, he was imprisoned in February 1862 for six months. Though he was later restored to minor commands, his career was ruined.

---

[11]Montgomery Blair to Francis P. Blair, Sr., October 1, 1861, Blair-Lee Papers, Princeton University Library; McClellan to Samuel L. M. Barlow, November 8, 1861, S. L. M. Barlow Papers, Henry E. Huntington Library.

Europe and the War

The American Civil War proved an exception to the rule that large-scale internal wars become international wars. Although the South sought foreign intervention and European powers were tempted to fish in troubled American waters, the Confederacy failed to achieve even diplomatic recognition by a single foreign government. Many factors were responsible for this failure: the skill of Northern diplomacy, the diversion of European interests to international crises in Poland and Denmark, the antislavery sentiments of most Europeans, British and French fears of the consequences of a war with the North, and others. But the most important single factor was the inability of Confederate arms to win enough consecutive victories to convince European governments that the South could sustain its independence. Diplomatic success was contingent upon military success. The rhythm of foreign policy was dictated by the outcome of battles. Confederate military prowess came close to winning foreign intervention in the fall of 1862, but the Union victory at Antietam in September kept the fruits of diplomatic recognition just beyond the Southern grasp.

European attitudes toward the American war are often summarized by a series of generalizations. The upper classes, especially in Britain, are said to have been pro-Confederate because of an affinity between Southern planters and the European aristocracy. The British textile industry depended on Southern cotton. English manufacturers and shipping merchants welcomed the discomfiture of their Yankee competitors. European governments were not sorry to see the weakening of the North American republic whose remarkable growth threatened their own Western Hemisphere interests. The European ruling classes looked with pleasure on the downfall of the American democratic experiment, whose success inspired emulation by the restless masses in their own lands. The working classes and the liberal middle class, on the other hand, are said to have sympathized with the North as the great symbol of republicanism and progressivism in the world. Victory for the Union would be a triumph of free labor and democracy whose impact would advance the cause of liberalism in Europe; but the success of the Confederacy would represent the triumph of slavery and reaction.

Although they contain much truth, these generalizations are oversimplified. There were crosscurrents and ambivalences in European attitudes. While it was true that British workers in general sympathized with the North, unemployment in the textile industry of Lancashire caused some laborers there to favor intervention in behalf of the South to obtain cotton. On the other hand, many British manufacturers and merchants found the wartime North to be a profitable customer rather than a rival. Some European liberals saw no moral advantage in the Union cause so long as the North fought only for Union and not for emancipation. At the same time, as rebels against an established government, the Southern gentry inspired apprehension as well as admiration among European ruling classes. Although some British statesmen secretly hoped for the downfall of the Yankee republic, others feared that the resulting power vacuum would spawn intrigue and instability in the Western Hemisphere. The French ruler Napoleon III did take advantage of the American conflict to create a puppet monarchy in Mexico. But in the tradition of balance-of-power politics, France was no more eager than Russia to see a decline in American maritime strength, which had functioned as a counterweight to British naval supremacy.

Considerations of power and national self-interest, more than of ideology or public opinion, ultimately determined European policy toward the Civil War. And in the evolution of this policy, Britain was the country that really mattered. As the world's leading industrial and naval power, Britain's interests were the most affected by the American war, and Britain was also the nation best equipped to intervene. Napoleon toyed with the idea of unilateral intervention, but in the end he refused to take any action (except in Mexico) without British cooperation.

The King Cotton Illusion

In 1861, the South based its foreign policy on the theory that cotton was king. According to this theory, the British and French economies depended heavily on cotton. Four-fifths of Britain's cotton supply came from the South. Any interruption of this supply would disrupt the British economy, reduce the workers to starvation, and bring down the government. Britain would have to break the blockade and thereby provoke a war with the North that would ensure Confederate independence.

"What would happen if no cotton was furnished for three years?" Senator James Hammond of South Carolina had asked rhetorically in his famous "King Cotton" speech of 1858. "England would topple headlong and carry the whole civilized world with her, save the South. No, you dare not make war on cotton. No power on earth dares to make war upon it. Cotton is king!" Few Confederates in 1861 doubted the logic of this argument. Mississippi's governor told a British war correspondent that "the sovereign State of Mississippi can do a great deal better without England than England can do without her." "Why sir," said another Southerner, "we have only to shut off your supply of cotton for a few weeks and we can create a revolution in Great Britain." A Charleston merchant was confident that if the Union blockade reduced British imports of cotton, "you'll just send their ships to the bottom and recognize us. That will be before Autumn, I think."[12]

Confederates did not intend to rely on the Union blockade alone to invoke the sovereignty of King Cotton. Southern committees of public safety imposed an embargo on the export of cotton. Although never officially endorsed by the Confederate Congress, the cotton embargo enjoyed wide support in the South and was enforced with thoroughness. Most of the 1860 crop had already been shipped, but most of the 1861 crop stayed in the South. In 1862, Southern planters sowed only one-third of the usual cotton crop and gave over their remaining acres to food production. The 1863 and 1864 crops were even smaller, less than one-eighth the prewar average. British imports from the Confederacy in 1862 were about 1 percent of the 1860 level.

But unfortunately for the King Cotton theory, the bumper crops of the late 1850s had created an oversupply of raw cotton and cotton products. By a cruel irony, the cotton embargo of 1861 actually benefited British textile firms suffering from a glut-

---

[12]Frank L. Owsley, *King Cotton Diplomacy: Foreign Relations of the Confederate States of America* (Chicago, 1931), pp. 16–23.

ted market. Not until 1862 did the much-touted cotton famine seriously affect Britain and France. Even without the fortuitous circumstance of a cotton surplus in 1861, the embargo probably would not have produced British intervention. The world's most powerful nation was not likely to submit to economic blackmail. King Cotton's sovereignty was an illusion. The British developed alternative sources of cotton in India and Egypt. Although the quality of this cotton was poorer than that of Southern cotton and its quantity far less at first, by 1864 British cotton imports had risen to nearly three-quarters of the antebellum average. Most of this came from India and Egypt, but some came from Southern ports now in Union hands and some from the Confederacy itself. By 1863, the South had reversed its embargo policy and was trying desperately to ship cotton through the tightening blockade to pay for military imports.

The economic motives for British intervention were highest in late 1862, when the cotton famine was at its worst and thousands of Lancashire workers were suffering. But if this sector of the British economy was temporarily depressed by the American war, other sectors were booming. Even before the war, textiles had been losing their central importance in Britain. Union and Confederate war purchases stimulated the rapidly growing iron and shipbuilding and munitions industries. Linen and woollen production took up part of the slack in cotton textiles. The wartime boom in these sectors absorbed many unemployed cotton workers. An increase of poor relief tided over the rest until cotton textiles recovered in 1863. It turned out after all that Mississippi needed England more than England needed Mississippi.

The Blockade and Foreign Relations

The Union blockade emerged as the central diplomatic issue of the war's first year—not because of its economic effects but because of its legal and political implications. Lincoln's proclamation of a blockade undermined his insistence that the war was a mere domestic insurrection, since a blockade was a weapon of war between sovereign states. On May 13, 1861, the British government issued a proclamation of neutrality, thus granting belligerent status to the Confederacy. Other European nations followed suit. The recognition of belligerency gave the South the right to contract loans and purchase supplies in neutral nations and to exercise belligerent rights on the high seas. This produced anger in the North and jubilation in the South, for both sides considered it a prelude to diplomatic recognition of the Confederacy. But in truth the British had little choice but to recognize Confederate belligerency. As British Foreign Secretary Lord John Russell put it, "the question of belligerent rights is one, not of principle, but of fact."[13]

Contrary to Northern fears and Southern hopes, the recognition of belligerency was not a first step toward diplomatic recognition. In fact, the European proclamations of neutrality favored the Union in the long run, for they constituted official acceptance of the blockade. Under international law a blockade must be physically effective to be legally binding on neutral powers. But "physically effective" was a

---

[13]Robert H. Jones, *Disrupted Decades: The Civil War and Reconstruction Years* (New York, 1973), p. 363.

matter of definition. As a neutral power in previous wars, the United States had insisted that it meant every port had to be sealed off by a cordon of warships. But as the world's leading naval power, Britain had always maintained that a blockade was legal if patrolling warships made an effort to prevent vessels from entering or leaving enemy ports. Now the roles were reversed: the United States was a naval belligerent and Britain the foremost neutral. The Union took the traditional British position on the question of the blockade's effectiveness, while the Confederacy reiterated the traditional American position. Britain could have found grounds to declare the blockade illegal had it chosen to do so, for Confederate envoys presented long lists of ships that had run the blockade. But the British government had no desire to create a precedent that could boomerang against its navy in a future war. On February 15, 1862, Foreign Secretary Lord Russell pronounced the Union blockade legal so long as warships patrolled a port in strength "sufficient really to prevent access to it or create an evident danger of entering or leaving it." The Union blockade certainly met this criterion.[14]

In previous wars the British navy had developed the doctrine of "continuous voyage" to justify the seizure of cargoes on ships plying between neutral ports if there was reason to believe that these cargoes were destined ultimately for an enemy port. The United States had rejected this doctrine a half-century earlier, but now the Union navy carried it even further than Britain had done. War materiel destined for the Confederacy usually proceeded from a European port to another neutral port near the Southern coast. There it was transferred to blockade runners. Union warships began to seize British merchant ships before they reached Nassau, Havana, and other trans-shipment ports. In the *Springbok* case (1863), a New York prize court upheld the seizure of the British ship *Springbok,* bound for a neutral port, on the grounds that its cargo was destined ultimately for the Confederacy. Despite furious protests from merchants, the British government took no action except to record the precedent.

In 1863, the Union navy extended the continuous voyage principle to ground transportation. By that year one of the busiest neutral ports for Confederate goods was Matamoras, a Mexican city just across the mouth of the Rio Grande from Texas. In February 1863, the navy seized the British ship *Peterhoff* near St. Thomas in the Caribbean. Bound for Matamoras, the *Peterhoff* carried military supplies. A prize court upheld the seizure because of evidence that this materiel would have been trans-shipped by land across the border into the Confederacy. Once again the British press clamored for retaliation against the arrogant Yankees, but the government accepted the American doctrine of "continuous transportation" and stored up the precedent for future use. A half-century later, during the early years of World War I, this particular chicken came home to roost when Britain applied the doctrine of continuous transportation against American exports to neutral Holland of war goods destined ultimately for Germany.

---

[14]Ephraim D. Adams, *Great Britain and the American Civil War,* 2 vols. (New York, 1925), I, 263.

 The *Trent* Affair

One case of Union interference with a British ship did come close to causing an Anglo-American war. On November 8, 1861, the *U.S.S. San Jacinto* stopped the British mail packet *Trent,* bound from Havana to St. Thomas. On board the *Trent* were James Mason of Virginia and John Slidell of Louisiana, Confederate commissioners traveling to London and Paris. Captain Charles Wilkes of the *San Jacinto* sent a boarding party to apprehend Mason and Slidell, and then carried them away to a Union prison in Boston. This event caused celebration in the North and turned Wilkes into a hero. The House of Representatives voted him a special medal. But when the news reached England, press and public reacted with violent anger. Prime Minister Viscount Palmerston told a tense cabinet: "You may stand for this but damned if I will!"[15] The British navy dispatched reinforcements to its North American squadron. The army made ready to send an expeditionary force to Canada. War talk was common on both sides of the Atlantic.

But neither side could profit by such a war, and both soon realized it. "One war at a time," said Lincoln. The British government prepared a tough note (but not an ultimatum) demanding an apology and the release of Mason and Slidell. Prince Albert, almost on his deathbed, softened the note by adding a suggestion that perhaps Wilkes's action had been unauthorized. This provided the Union government a way to give in without losing face. Wilkes had in fact acted on his own. The legality of his action was clouded by the ambiguities of international law. The right of search and seizure of contraband on the high seas was well established. But whether diplomats were "contraband" was less clear. If Wilkes had put a prize crew on board the *Trent* and brought it before a prize court, the British would have had no case against the United States. Secretary of State Seward made use of this technicality to admit that Wilkes had acted wrongly. On December 26, Lincoln ordered the release of Mason and Slidell, and the British accepted this in lieu of an apology. The crisis was over. Mason and Slidell proceeded to London and Paris, where they spent a futile three years trying to win foreign recognition and intervention.

---

[15]Allan Nevins, *The War for the Union: The Improvised War, 1861–1862* (New York, 1959), p. 388.

Chapter Fourteen

The Spring-time of Northern Hope

Every blow tells fearfully against the rebellion. The rebels themselves are panic-stricken, or despondent. It now requires no very far reaching prophet to predict the end of this struggle.

—New York Tribune,
May 23, 1862

Although Union arms would soon win a string of stirring victories, January 1862 was a month of gloom in Washington. The release of Mason and Slidell in the aftermath of the *Trent* affair had produced a feeling of letdown. Northern banks and the U.S. Treasury had just suspended specie payments (see page 223). News of war contract scandals dominated front pages. The Army of the Potomac had done nothing significant for six months except to send four regiments to disaster at Ball's Bluff, and now General McClellan had fallen ill with typhoid fever. Even General George Thomas's victory at Logan's Cross-Roads near Mill Springs in Kentucky (see page 176) did little to brighten the gloom, for it produced no further advance. On the back of a letter from General Henry Halleck, commander of the Department of Missouri, explaining why Halleck's troops could not make a forward move along the Mississippi, Lincoln wrote: "It is exceedingly discouraging. As everywhere else, nothing can be done." The despondent President dropped into the office of Quartermaster General Montgomery Meigs one day and said: "General, what shall I do? The people are impatient; Chase has no money; . . . the General of the Army has typhoid fever. The bottom is out of the tub. What shall I do?"[1]

On January 27, Lincoln issued "General War Order No. 1" directing a forward movement of all armies on February 22 (Washington's birthday). A rather clumsy device which Lincoln hoped would assuage public impatience and prod McClellan, this

---

[1]Roy P. Basler (ed.), *The Collected Works of Abraham Lincoln,* 9 vols. (New Brunswick, N.J., 1953–1955), V, 95; T. Harry Williams, *Lincoln and His Generals* (New York, 1952), pp. 55–56.

order had no military effect. But it did force McClellan to tell Lincoln of his plan to transport the Army of the Potomac by water down the Chesapeake Bay to land them for a flank attack on the Confederate troops at Centreville and Fredericksburg. While Lincoln was mulling over this plan, dramatic news arrived from the West.

Forts Henry and Donelson

The Confederate government in 1861 had appointed Albert Sidney Johnston (not to be confused with Joseph E. Johnston in Virginia) commander of its Western Department. A native of Kentucky but an adoptive Texan, one of the highest-ranking officers in the old army, Johnston had been offered a top Union command but had chosen to go with the South. When Union troops under Don Carlos Buell and Ulysses S. Grant occupied northern Kentucky in the fall of 1861, Johnston established through the southern part of the state a defensive line anchored by concentrations of forces at Bowling Green and at Columbus, on the Mississippi River. Buell planned a spring campaign against Bowling Green, but while he planned, Grant acted.

The weakest links in Johnston's line were Forts Henry and Donelson, twelve miles apart on the Tennessee and Cumberland rivers just south of the Kentucky-Tennessee border. A Union fleet of three wooden and four iron-armored gunboats (with more under construction) gave the Yankees control of the rivers. Commanding this fleet was Flag Officer Andrew Foote, a tough, teetotaling Connecticut Yankee who saw eye to eye with Grant about the strategic importance of Forts Henry and Donelson. Halleck saw it too, and authorized Grant to attack Fort Henry. Accompanied by the fleet, Grant brought 15,000 men up the Tennessee River (southward), landed them four miles below the fort, and prepared to attack it in the rear while the fleet shelled it from the river. As it turned out, the gunboats did the job alone before the infantry arrived on the scene. Fort Henry was badly sited on low ground, threatened almost as much by the rising river as by the approaching Yankees. At 1 P.M. on February 6, Foote's gunboats opened a heavy bombardment; the fort replied valiantly and disabled one ironclad with a shot into the boiler. But the Rebels were outgunned. After most of the garrison had escaped by land to Fort Donelson, the Confederate commander surrendered in midafternoon.

The consequences of this brief action were momentous. The Union gunboats now ranged all the way up the Tennessee to Florence, Alabama. Grant organized his troops for the overland march against Donelson while the ironclads steamed back downriver and up the Cumberland for another joint effort with the army. Johnston faced a desperate dilemma. His defensive line was pierced; his rail link between Bowling Green and Memphis was cut by Federal control of the Tennessee River; the Confederate stronghold at Columbus on the Mississippi was flanked by Grant at Fort Henry. If Donelson also fell, Johnston's main force at Bowling Green would have Grant in its rear while facing Buell in front, and Nashville itself could not be held. If he put every available man into Fort Donelson, he risked losing them; if he retreated to a new defensive line in central Tennessee, Donelson's small garrison would fall like a ripe plum into Grant's lap. Johnston compromised by sending half of his troops from Bowling Green to Donelson, which brought the force there to 17,000 men, and

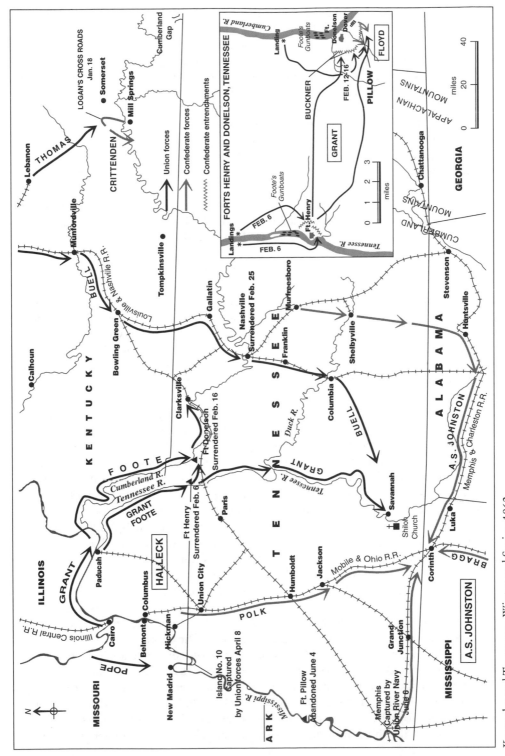

Kentucky and Tennessee, Winter and Spring 1862

retreating with the rest toward Nashville. The general who took command at Donelson was none other than John B. Floyd, the Virginia politician who had been sent to Kentucky after his failure in western Virginia.

Grant's confident forces converged on Donelson, where reinforcements increased his army to 27,000 men. Grant planned to have these troops surround the fort on the land side while Foote's flotilla pounded it into submission as it had done to Fort Henry. But Donelson proved a much tougher prospect. The fifteen-acre earthwork fort protected a dozen heavy guns sited on a bluff above the river. Outside the fort ran a circle of trenches along ridges overlooking steep wooded ravines. Good troops should have been able to hold these trenches against at least twice their number if the fearsome gunboats could be kept at bay. The battle began auspiciously for the Confederates. They repulsed a premature Federal infantry probe on February 13. Next day the armored gunboats moved up to the attack, but these monsters turned out not to be invincible after all. Well-aimed fire by the Rebel batteries damaged three of them after a fierce duel, and the wounded Foote called off the attack.

Although the Confederates had won the first round, Floyd and his subordinates still considered themselves to be in a bad fix. The Yankees had them besieged by land and water; surrender seemed only a matter of time. That night a council of Confederate officers decided to try a breakout attack on the morning of February 15 to enable the garrison to escape. As the Union soldiers on the right wing were getting ready for breakfast, 10,000 screaming Rebels suddenly burst from the woods with muskets blazing. After several hours of hard fighting, in which Colonel Nathan Bedford Forrest's battalion of dismounted cavalry particularly distinguished itself, the Southerners forced back the Union right and opened the road to Nashville.

What happened next has been the subject of controversy. Having opened the escape route, Confederate General Gideon J. Pillow ordered his men back to the trenches, and after some hesitation Floyd approved the order. Some historians consider this action inexplicable; others believe that the Rebel commanders, having succeeded in their plan, lost their nerve. The truth seems to be that the Confederate soldiers, exhausted and disorganized by their long fight in subfreezing weather, needed a pause to regroup and to fetch their equipment before marching away.

But this pause proved fatal. Grant had been absent during the fighting, conferring with Foote on his flagboat three miles downstream where the wind had blown the noise of battle away from him. Returning to find his right wing routed, he faced the crisis calmly. Reasoning that the Confederates must have weakened their own right to attack his, Grant ordered his left division to assault the trenches in their front. With a yell, Iowa and Indiana boys carried the first line of thinly held trenches while Grant on the right personally helped regroup the demoralized Illinois regiments for a counterattack that regained most of what they had lost in the morning.

During the night of February 15–16, Confederate officers once again held a council of war and decided, over Forrest's bitter objections, to surrender. Facing possible indictment for fraud and treason for actions he had committed as secretary of war under Buchanan, Floyd turned the command over to Pillow. Pillow, who as a politician was also apprehensive about falling into Federal hands, turned his command over to General Simon B. Buckner, who was not amused by these antics. While Floyd and Pillow escaped with 2,500 men in boats and Forrest led his 700 troopers out through a flooded road, Buckner prepared to surrender the remaining 13,000. Ironically, Buckner had once lent money to Grant when he was down and out in the old army. But when Buckner requested the terms of surrender, Grant replied: "No terms except an unconditional and immediate surrender can be accepted. I propose to move immediately upon your works."[2]

These words made Grant famous. But the consequences of his triumph at Donelson were more than personal. The fall of the fort lifted morale in the North and depressed it in the South. From London, Confederate envoy James Mason wrote that "the late reverses at Fort Henry and Fort Donelson have had an unfortunate effect on the minds of our friends here."[3] Worse was yet to come. With the Cumberland River now controlled by the Union navy, Nashville was no longer tenable, and the Confederates evacuated it on February 23. An important industrial and transport center, the city was also the first Confederate state capital to fall to the Yankees.

What was left of Albert Sidney Johnston's command retreated to the rail junction of Corinth in northern Mississippi. There they were joined by the garrison that had evacuated Columbus, Kentucky, and by reinforcements from the lower South. In March, Grant established his forward base at Pittsburg Landing on the Tennessee River only twenty miles from Corinth. He was reinforced by three new divisions, one of them commanded by William Tecumseh Sherman. Halleck was now in overall command of the Tennessee-Missouri theater. He ordered Buell's Army of the Ohio forward from Nashville to join Grant's Army of West Tennessee for a joint offensive of 75,000 Union troops against the 45,000 Confederates now concentrated at Corinth.

The Battle of Shiloh

But Johnston had no intention of waiting for Grant to attack him. Joined by General Beauregard, who had been sent west after quarreling with Jefferson Davis in Virginia, Johnston accepted Beauregard's plan to regain the initiative by a sudden strike at Grant's 40,000 men before they could be reinforced by Buell, who was delayed by flooded rivers and destroyed bridges. Johnston had one big advantage—no one on the Union side expected him to take the offensive. At Pittsburgh Landing the Yankee troops spent their time drilling instead of entrenching, for their commanders were so offensive minded that they took no defensive precautions.

Johnston planned to march his army from Corinth to a bivouac near Federal lines, from where he would launch a dawn attack on April 4. But from the outset things went wrong. Johnston learned what McDowell had learned at Bull Run nine months earlier—a large body of green troops could not move quickly from one place to another. The Confederates consumed three days in this march of eighteen miles. Certain that the advantage of surprise had been lost and that Buell had joined Grant by now, Beauregard wanted to call the whole thing off and return to Corinth. By all

---

[2]Ulysses S. Grant, *Personal Memoirs*, 2 vols. (New York, 1885–1886), I, 311.

[3]Ephraim D. Adams, *Great Britain and the American Civil War*, 2 vols. (New York, 1925), I, 272–273.

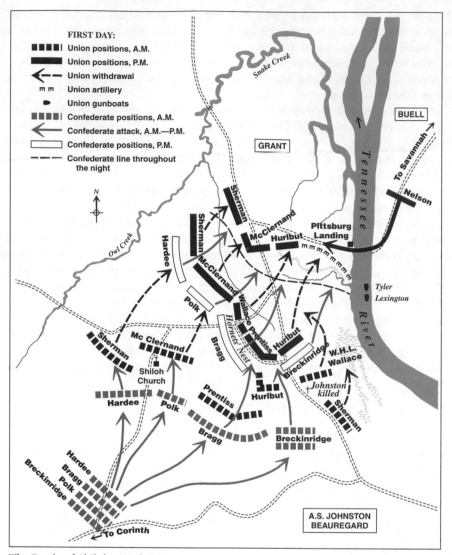

FIRST DAY:

Union positions, A.M.

Union positions, P.M.

Union withdrawal

m m Union artillery

Union gunboats

Confederate positions, A.M.

Confederate attack, A.M.—P.M.

Confederate positions, P.M.

Confederate line throughout the night

The Battle of Shiloh, April 6, 1862

odds he should have been right. The Confederates had made a great deal of noise getting into position. They had skirmished with cavalry pickets in front of Sherman's division. Grant knew the Rebels were up to something, perhaps an attack on his detached division five miles downriver at Crump's Landing, but he telegraphed Halleck that he had "scarcely the faintest idea of an attack (a general one) being made upon us." To a nervous colonel in his division who reported a Rebel buildup in the woods, Sherman said contemptuously: "Take your damned regiment back to Ohio. Beauregard is not such a fool as to leave his base of operations and attack us in ours. There is no enemy nearer than Corinth." But at that very moment, two miles away, Johnston was making his decision. Having finally got his army close to the enemy, he would not hear of retreat. "I would fight them if they were a million," Johnston told his corps commanders on the evening of April 5. "Gentlemen, we shall attack at daylight tomorrow."[4]

Next morning the first wave of the Rebel assault hit Sherman's camps near a small log church named Shiloh. The Yankees were not taken entirely by surprise, as some newspaper reports later stated. Union patrols had gone forward at first light, had encountered Confederate skirmishers, and had fallen back noisily toward their own lines, giving the two front divisions (those of Sherman and of Benjamin Prentiss, which were both composed of green troops) time to brace themselves for the gray wave coming toward them.

During that long day the 40,000 Confederates drove back the 33,000 Federals (Grant's detached division did not arrive on the field until dark) slowly but surely, with appalling losses on both sides. Brigades and regiments lost cohesion in the thick woods and small clearings, and the battle broke down into a series of vicious firefights. Breakfasting at his headquarters seven miles downriver, Grant heard the sound of the firing. He ordered the vanguard of Buell's arriving troops forward to the battlefield, commandeered a steamboat, and hastened to the front, where in cooperation with his division commanders, he labored to shore up faltering blue lines. By midafternoon a pattern had emerged. Both Union flanks had been bent backward, but Prentiss, with the remnants of his division and parts of others, held a line in the center along a sunken road that Confederates aptly named "the hornets' nest." While personally directing one of the attacks near this sector, Johnston was hit in the leg by a stray bullet. Almost before he realized he had been wounded, he bled to death from a severed artery—the highest-ranking general on either side killed in the war. Beauregard took command. Instead of containing and bypassing the hornets' nest, the Southerners brought up sixty-two guns and loosed an artillery barrage in an attempt to break the Yankee center. The relentless Rebels finally surrounded Prentiss, who surrendered his 2,200 survivors in late afternoon, having gained time for Grant to establish a strong defensive line along the ridge at Pittsburg Landing. Toward evening the first brigade of Buell's army crossed the river to join Grant; two gunboats and fifty guns on the ridge poured a heavy artillery fire into Confederate ranks; and Beauregard sensibly decided against sending his exhausted troops on one final twilight assault.

The Rebels had driven the bluecoats back more than two miles but had not achieved a breakthrough. Now the odds were with Grant. His missing division commanded by Lew Wallace finally arrived from downriver, while three of Buell's divisions crossed during the night. On the morrow Grant's strength would be augmented by 25,000 fresh troops, while the Confederates could expect no reinforcements. During the night, lightning flashed and rain fell on the 2,000 dead and 10,000 wounded lying on the battlefield. Few soldiers on either side could sleep. The gunboats lobbed eight-inch shells into the bivouacs of exhausted Confederates all night long. When sodden morning finally came, the determined Yankees counterattacked all along the line. Yard by yard they pushed the Rebels back over yesterday's battleground until

---

[4]Bruce Catton, *Grant Moves South* (Boston, 1960), p. 218; Shelby Foote, *The Civil War: A Narrative. Fort Sumter to Perryville* (New York, 1958), pp. 329, 331.

in midafternoon Beauregard broke off resistance and began a weary retreat through the mud to Corinth. The Federals seemed satisfied to regain their original camps and made only a feeble pursuit, which was checked by Forrest's cavalry.

Retreat and Pursuit after Battle

The Confederates were in a bad way on the retreat to Corinth. One corps commander, Braxton Bragg, wrote on the morning after the battle: "Our condition is horrible. Troops utterly disorganized and demoralized. Road almost impassable. No provisions and no forage."[5] But as after Bull Run, the victors were as disorganized and spent as the vanquished. Although some of Buell's troops were comparatively fresh, Grant himself could not give orders to them, and Buell lacked the killer instinct.

Pursuit of a beaten enemy after a major Civil War battle was never as easy as it might appear on paper. The soldiers were exhausted. Often they had marched many miles before fighting and had eaten and slept little for several days. So long as the action was at its height, adrenalin kept them going, but the slightest pause after hours of fighting produced an emotional letdown and an overpowering thirst that made the search for water a top priority. A Union soldier wrote home after Shiloh: "We chased them one-quarter mile, when we halted . . . and threw ourselves on the ground and rested. Oh, mother, how tired I was, now the excitement of the action was over. . . . The dead and wounded lay in piles. I gave water to some poor wounded men, and then sought food in an abandoned camp near us." After another battle one of the survivors said: "I never saw so many broken down and exhausted men in all my life. I was sick as a horse, and as wet with blood and sweat as I could be, and many of our men were vomiting with excessive fatigue. . . . Our tongues were parched and cracked for water, and our faces blackened with powder and smoke."[6]

A beaten army usually had an incentive to retreat quickly despite fatigue, but it was harder to motivate the victors to further exertion. After a few battles—notably Antietam and Gettysburg—the Union armies had fresh reserves of veteran troops who should have been used in vigorous pursuit. But most of the time, as at Shiloh, the men were too fought-out to do anything but rest and marvel upon their survival. And during or after many Civil War battles, as at Shiloh, rain churned the roads into mud, hindering pursuit.

Shiloh was the most ghastly bloodbath in the history of the Western Hemisphere thus far, though later Civil War battles would put it in seventh place in this respect. More than 1,700 men were killed and 8,000 wounded on *each* side. Of the 16,500 total wounded, over 2,000 more men would soon die. Shiloh was America's baptism in real war. "O it was too shocking too horrible," wrote one Confederate survivor. "God grant that I may never be the partaker in such scenes again. . . . When released from this I shall ever be an advocate of peace."[7]

---

[5]Catton, *Grant Moves South*, p. 247.

[6]Kenneth P. Williams, *Lincoln Finds a General: A Military Study of the Civil War*, 5 vols. (New York, 1949–1959), III, 389; Sam R. Watkins, *"Co. Aytch": A Confederate Soldier's Memoir* (reprint, New York, 1962), p. 160.

[7]Bruce Catton, *Terrible Swift Sword* (Garden City, N.Y., 1963), p. 236.

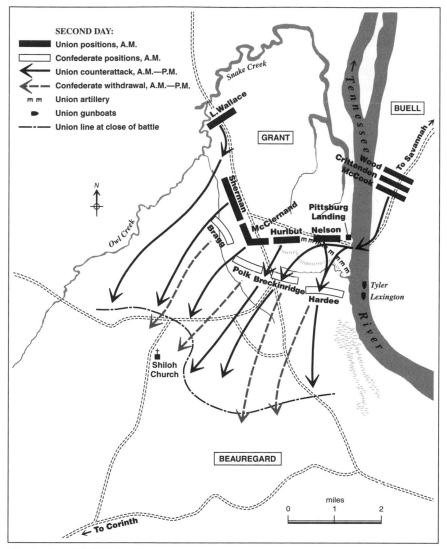

The Battle of Shiloh, April 7, 1862

Other Union Triumphs in the West

For a time in the spring of 1862, the Confederacy appeared to be finished. Four hundred miles west of Shiloh and one month earlier, Union victory in the battle of Pea Ridge had cleared the Rebels (except for guerrillas) out of Missouri and achieved Union control of northern Arkansas. After Frémont's departure from Missouri in November 1861 (see pages 170 to 172), General Samuel R. Curtis had taken field command of the main

Union army in the state. In a winter campaign, Curtis's 12,000 men maneuvered Sterling Price's 8,000 Confederate Missourians into Arkansas, where Price once again linked up with Ben McCulloch's small army. The combined Rebel force of 16,000 men (including two Cherokee and one Creek Indian regiments)[8] came under the overall command of the aggressive Earl Van Dorn. Curtis had deployed his bluecoats just south of Pea Ridge in northern Arkansas. Avoiding a frontal attack, Van Dorn executed an all-night flanking march around the north side of Pea Ridge and fell upon the Federal rear on the morning of March 7. Curtis's scouts had warned him of the Confederate maneuver, so he faced his army about to receive the attack. His artillery dispersed the Indian regiments, a sharpshooter killed General McCulloch, and the blue lines held against repeated infantry assaults by superior numbers. Next morning, correctly judging that Van Dorn was running short of ammunition, Curtis counterattacked and scattered the Rebels in several directions.

Meanwhile, the Confederacy had made its boldest bid to fulfill antebellum Southern ambitions to win the Southwest. A small army composed mostly of Texans pushed up the Rio Grande valley into New Mexico in 1861. The following February they launched a deeper strike to capture Santa Fe. With luck, they hoped to push even farther north and west to gain the mineral wealth of Colorado and California gold mines. A good many Southerners lived in these Western territories and in California.

At first, the Confederate drive up the Rio Grande went well. The Texans won a victory over Unionist New Mexico militia and a handful of regulars at the battle of Valverde, a hundred miles south of Albuquerque, on February 21, 1862. They continued up the valley, occupied Albuquerque and Santa Fe, and pushed on toward Fort Union near Santa Fe. But Colorado miners who had organized themselves into Union regiments and had carried out the greatest march of the war, over the rugged Rockies in winter, met the Texans in the battle of Glorieta Pass on March 26–28. The battle was a draw tactically, but a unit of Coloradans destroyed the Confederate wagon train, forcing the Southerners into a disastrous retreat to Texas. Of the 3,700 who had started out to win the West for the Confederacy, only 2,000 made it back. The Confederates had shot their bolt in this region; the far West and Southwest remained safe for the Union.

With the Confederates in retreat both east and west of the Mississippi, it was time to secure the great river itself. The Rebels had fortified Island No. 10 on the Mississippi (see map on page 245), where the river made a large **S** curve near the Kentucky-Tennessee border. So long as the Confederates held this island, no Yankee boats could go down the river. Halleck ordered General John Pope to organize 20,000 troops into an Army of the Mississippi to cooperate with the river navy in a campaign

---

[8]The Cherokees were the most prominent of the five "civilized tribes" (the others were the Chickasaws, Choctaws, Creeks, and Seminoles). Earlier in the century, whites in the Southeastern states had driven most of these Indians from their ancestral lands, and the government had resettled them in the Indian Territory (present-day Oklahoma). In 1861, the Confederacy negotiated treaties of alliance with certain chiefs of the five tribes, who sent delegates to the Confederate Congress and furnished troops to the Southern army. But nearly half of the Indians in the civilized tribes remained loyal to the Union. In general, the full-blooded Indians stayed with the Union and the "half-breeds" went with the Confederacy. Some of the latter owned Negro slaves. Most of the fighting of pro-Union against pro-Confederate Indians was confined to the Indian Territory; the battle of Pea Ridge was the main exception. The Cherokee leader Stand Watie rose to the rank of brigadier general in the Confederate army, and did not surrender his troops to the Union until a month after the last of the other Confederate armies had surrendered.

ADMIRAL DAVID G. FARRAGUT. Although a native of Tennessee, in 1861 he remained loyal to the American flag under which he had served for half a century. He told fellow Southerners who joined the Confederacy that "you fellows will catch the devil before you get through with this business." They would catch much of it from Farragut himself, who became the first full admiral in the history of the U.S. Navy.

LIBRARY OF CONGRESS

to take Island No. 10. Pope drove the Confederates away from the Missouri side of the river; his engineers cut a canal through the swamps so that transports could by-pass the island; two of the armored gunboats fought their way past the island batteries; then Pope used the gunboats and transports to ferry his men across the river below the island, where they seized the Tennessee bank. Trapped by Yankee troops and gunboats on all sides, the 4,500-man garrison surrendered itself and 109 heavy guns on April 8—the same day that beaten Confederates were stumbling through the mud from Shiloh to Corinth.

The Fall of New Orleans

As the North celebrated these victories in Tennessee, news came from the lower South of a stunning naval achievement—the capture of New Orleans. Believing the main Federal threat to the lower Mississippi would come from upriver, the Confederate high command had stripped the Gulf coast of troops (who fought at Shiloh) and had sent eight Rebel gunboats northward to confront the Union river fleet above Memphis. This left only 3,000 militia to defend New Orleans by land and two un-completed ironclads, a few armed steamboats, and two forts flanking the river seventy miles below the city to defend it against a thrust from the Gulf. It was the South's bad luck that this was the way the Federals came and that the expedition was led by the most remarkable naval commander of the war, David G. Farragut.

Tennessee-born and married to a Virginian, Farragut nevertheless remained loyal to the stars and stripes. Sixty years old at the outbreak of the Civil War, he had joined the navy as a midshipman at the age of nine and had fought in the War of 1812 and the Mexican War. A combative man, Farragut believed in carrying the war as far inland as water would float his ships. In 1862, his Gulf Expeditionary Force consisted of twenty-four wooden warships carrying 245 guns, nineteen mortar boats, and

15,000 soldiers under the command of Benjamin Butler. In mid-April, the fleet moved upriver to the forts below New Orleans. There the mortar boats under the command of Commodore David D. Porter commenced a week-long bombardment that fired 17,000 thirteen-inch shells without putting the forts out of action. Growing impatient with these spectacular but ineffective fireworks, Farragut decided to run his ships past the forts. At 2 A.M. on April 24, the fleet weighed anchor and moved single file up the channel. The forts opened fire with a hundred guns; the ships replied with their broadsides; the intrepid Confederate fleet tried to ram some of the Union ships and to push fire rafts against others (they almost set Farragut's flagship afire). One of the Union officers described the scene as resembling "all the earthquakes in the world and all the thunder and lightning storms together, in a space of two miles, all going off at once."[9] Despite the sound and the fury, Farragut got through with only one ship sunk and three disabled. He steamed to New Orleans, where the helpless militia fled from the fleet's guns without firing a shot. Yankee sailors and marines took possession of the city April 29. Downriver, the troops in the two Confederate forts mutinied and surrendered to Butler, who left a regiment to garrison them and brought the rest of his men up to occupy the South's largest city and principal port.

Farragut did not rest. He sent seven ships on up the river where Baton Rouge became the second state capital to fall, surrendering like New Orleans, with Union ships' guns trained on its streets. Natchez also surrendered without resistance, but Vicksburg—with its heavy guns sited on the bluff—refused to yield, and Farragut dropped back downriver. From New Orleans to Vicksburg, the Mississippi was a 400-mile Union highway by the end of May. Not to be outdone, the river fleet in the north fought its way down to Memphis, where on June 6 Federal ironclads and rams sank or captured seven of the eight boats in the Confederate river fleet while the unhappy citizens of Memphis watched from the bluffs. The city then surrendered.

The Pace of Union Triumphs Slows

While the U.S. navy was winning this series of dazzling victories, what were the western armies doing? After Shiloh the Confederates concentrated all available men at Corinth, bringing their total strength up to 70,000 men, of whom a quarter were on the sicklist. Halleck brought together more than 100,000 Federals on the old Shiloh battlefield, took personal command of them, and began to advance on Corinth, entrenching his troops at every stop and moving at a glacial pace. A textbook soldier, Halleck believed more in the eighteenth-century idea of capturing "strategic points" than in destroying the enemy's army. Thus, the vital rail junction at Corinth was his objective. If Beauregard would evacuate the place without a fight, Halleck would be happy. Beauregard did, slipping away at the end of May in what Halleck regarded as a Union triumph but Grant came to regret, for he believed that a determined effort might have destroyed part of the Confederate army.

At this time, however, Grant was under a cloud. He had never lost his reputation from the old army days as a heavy drinker, and after he had achieved prominence at Donelson, rumors of his drinking began to circulate again. After Shiloh, whispers

---

[9]Catton, *Swift Sword,* p. 261.

U.S.S. PENSACOLA.   A twenty-three-gun steam sloop, the *Pensacola* was a typical wooden ship of the saltwater Union navy. Using steam for speed and combat, she could switch to sails for long-distance cruising. Farragut preferred wooden ships to the new ironclads, contending that a shot could pass clean through a wooden ship and do less damage than when penetrating an ironclad. Whatever the merit of this argument, the *Pensacola* was the second ship in Farragut's line during the run past the forts below New Orleans. She took many direct hits but kept on going.

made the rounds that the Union army had been surprised there because its commander was drunk. Lincoln was not taken in by these unfounded reports.[10] To one visitor bearing such a tale, the President said: "I can't spare this man; he fights."[11]

But Halleck evidently thought he could spare him, for in the Corinth campaign he put Grant on the shelf by appointing him "deputy commander" and giving him

---

[10]The stories about Grant's drinking were an example of the way in which rumors about famous people, built on a tiny substratum of truth, are ballooned by newspapers and gossip into "fact." In 1854, Captain Grant, stationed at a California military outpost, apparently began drinking heavily in an attempt to overcome boredom and loneliness for his wife and children. He resigned from the army to avoid a court martial for neglect of duty, and tried a variety of occupations without notable success until he joined the army again as colonel of an Illinois volunteer regiment in 1861. In his rise to three-star rank by 1864, Grant inspired jealousy in the hearts of many other ambitious officers, who helped spread the stories of his drinking. Grant may indeed have been an alcoholic in the modern medical meaning of that term—a meaning nonexistent in his time, when excessive drinking or a weakness for alcohol was considered a moral weakness. In any case, with one possible exception, Grant did not get drunk during the war; there is no evidence that he had been drinking heavily before Shiloh or at any other time during active military operations. For a good discussion of this matter, see Lyle W. Dorsett, "The Problem of Grant's Drinking During the Civil War," *Hayes Historical Journal,* 4 (1983). See also Kevin Anderson, "Grant's Lifelong Struggle with Alcohol," *Columbiad,* 2 (Winter 1999), 16–26.

[11]Catton, *Grant Moves South,* p. 371.

nothing to do. Grant requested a transfer and even considered resigning from the army, but at Sherman's urging he stayed on. After Halleck went east in July, Grant took command of all Union forces in western Tennessee and northern Mississippi.

Before then, however, Halleck had divided his large army into several parts. Buell took 35,000 men to begin a frustrating (and in the end unsuccessful) campaign against Chattanooga. Other troops went to Arkansas to deal with new Confederate moves there. The rest dispersed to occupy cities and guard lines of communication in the 45,000 square miles of Confederate territory they had conquered in the past four months. Many historians have been critical of Halleck's policy of dispersal. They argue that if 50,000 men had been kept together after capturing Corinth, they could have marched southward to take Vicksburg, Jackson, even Mobile. The argument has some merit. But it slights the need to detach large numbers of troops to guard supply lines, to administer occupied cities, and to deal with all the problems of conquered territory. It also overlooks the problem of disease in a deep-South summer campaign.

The Confederates at Corinth had suffered fearfully from sickness in the spring of 1862. Several Union generals, including Halleck, Pope, and Sherman, fell ill (Sherman with malaria) after the Federals had occupied the city. Disease also plagued the initial Union campaign against Vicksburg. In June 1862, Farragut again brought his fleet and 3,200 army troops upriver with orders to take Vicksburg. The Union river fleet came down from Memphis to help. Defending Vicksburg were sixty heavy guns and 10,000 soldiers under Van Dorn. The navy's mortars and guns pounded the defenses day after day, with little effect. The army troops dug a canal across a neck of land formed by a hairpin bend in the river, in the hope that the current would widen it into a new channel to enable Northern shipping to bypass Vicksburg. But the river refused to cooperate. Shielded on three sides by the river and by impassable swamps, Vicksburg could be attacked by land only from the east, where it was protected by a high ridge. Not only would the number of troops needed for such an attack be large and the problem of supplying them formidable, but two-thirds of the Union soldiers and sailors already on hand were prostrated by malaria, dysentery, and typhoid. With hundreds of men dying of disease and the river level falling (endangering Farragut's deep-water ships), the Federals gave up the first Vicksburg campaign at the end of July. Farragut withdrew southward, the river fleet northward, and for the time being the Confederates owned the Mississippi for 200 miles between Vicksburg and Port Hudson, Louisiana, which they also fortified.

Despite the failure to capture Vicksburg in 1862, the four months from the fall of Fort Henry on February 6 to the fall of Memphis were a period of remarkable Union success in the West. "Every blow tells fearfully against the rebellion," exulted the *New York Tribune* on May 23, 1862. "The rebels themselves are panic-stricken, or despondent. It now requires no very far reaching prophet to predict the end of this struggle."

The Rebels were indeed despondent in May 1862. Not only had they been pushed back in the West, but in the East McClellan's 100,000-strong Army of the Potomac was within five miles of Richmond. Other Union forces in Virginia outnumbered the Confederates on every front and seemed poised for advances that would crush the rebellion before the Fourth of July. But by that date the brilliant generalship of Lee and Jackson had turned the tide in Virginia and ended Northern hopes for quick victory.

Jackson and Lee Strike Back

*His name might be Audacity. He will take
more chances, and take them quicker than
any other general in this country.*

—Confederate Colonel Joseph Ives, speaking of Robert
E. Lee,
June 1862

257

The Peninsula and Valley Campaigns in Virginia

With the approach of Virginia's spring in 1862, General McClellan planned an elaborate flanking maneuver with the Army of the Potomac against the Confederates at Centreville to avoid a costly frontal attack. Anticipating such a move, Confederate commander Joseph E. Johnston spoiled it in early March by retreating forty miles south to Culpeper. There, he was in a better position to protect Richmond against a threat from any direction. While McClellan pondered his next move, Northern journalists who visited the vacated Confederate lines discovered several logs painted black to resemble cannons plus other evidence that Johnston's position had not been so strong nor his army so large as McClellan had claimed. The "Quaker guns" caused McClellan much embarrassment and fed growing Republican suspicions that he really did not want to smash the Rebels. On March 11, Lincoln relieved McClellan as general in chief, on the ground that he could not exercise responsibility for all Union armies when he was about to take the field as head of a campaigning army. This was logical, but it also carried overtones of distrust for McClellan.

With the Confederates now ensconced behind the Rappahannock River, McClellan proposed to shift his own campaign farther south by transporting the Army of the Potomac down the Chesapeake Bay to Fortress Monroe at the tip of the peninsula formed by the York and James rivers. This had the advantage of placing the army's base near Richmond with only two rivers to cross before reaching the Confederate capital. But it made Richmond instead of the Southern army the primary objective, a reversal of what Lincoln thought the priorities should be. It also had the defect, in Lincoln's eyes, of leaving Washington unprotected against a Rebel attack from the west or south. McClellan promised to leave enough troops in the vicinity of Washington to protect the capital. He also assured Lincoln that his move to the Virginia peninsula would compel the Confederates to turn southeast, away from Washington, to meet the threat to Richmond. Lincoln reluctantly approved the plan.

In late March a fleet of more than 300 vessels began ferrying 70,000 soldiers plus horses, wagons, supplies, and 300 cannon from Alexandria to Fortress Monroe. General Irvin McDowell's strong corps of 35,000 men remained at Fredericksburg with orders to march southward later to cooperate with McClellan in a joint attack on Confederate defenses guarding the lower peninsula. In addition to the Army of the Potomac, two other Union armies were operating in the Virginia theater: 25,000 men in the Shenandoah Valley under Nathaniel Banks, and another 8,000 in West Virginia under John C. Frémont, whom Lincoln had appointed to this command in response to congressional pressures. McClellan counted some of these troops among those he had left behind to protect Washington. McClellan also left fewer regiments in the actual Washington defenses than he had promised to leave, and nearly all of them were new recruits. The President became concerned for the safety of the capital and annoyed with McClellan's apparent indifference to this concern.

Believing Banks had more than enough men in the valley to cope with Stonewall Jackson's small army there, Lincoln ordered one of Banks's divisions to Manassas, which was closer to Washington. But this reckoned without Jackson's extraordinary talents. Deeply religious, idiosyncratic, secretive, and unpredictable, Jackson proved to be one of the best generals of the Civil War. His orders were to prevent Banks from sending any part of his army from the valley to eastern Virginia. With only 4,200 men, Jackson on March 23 boldly attacked a division more than twice as large at Kernstown, a village just south of Winchester. He was repulsed with heavy losses, but this tactical defeat turned out to be a strategic victory with important consequences. Reasoning that Jackson must have more men than previously thought, Lincoln ordered all of Banks's army to remain in the valley and detached a division from McClellan to reinforce Frémont in West Virginia. To keep enough troops near Washington to protect the capital, Lincoln ordered McDowell's corps to remain near Fredericksburg instead of joining McClellan's forces as originally planned.

McClellan's Advance toward Richmond

The retention of McDowell's corps was the first of several actions that caused McClellan and his supporters to charge that the Republican administration did not want him, a Democratic general, to succeed. No evidence exists to support this charge. In any event, by the first week of April McClellan had 70,000 men (with 30,000 more soon to arrive) facing 17,000 Confederates entrenched across the lower peninsula near the old Revolutionary battlefield of Yorktown. Instead of attacking, McClellan settled down for a siege. He overestimated the number of enemy troops holding the Yorktown defenses. The Confederate commander, General John B. Magruder, did his best to encourage McClellan's illusions. A lover of amateur theatricals, Magruder staged a show for the Federals. He paraded his troops back and forth and shifted his artillery around to give the impression that he had more men than he did.

Lincoln was disappointed with McClellan's failure to smash through the Yorktown defenses before Johnston could shift the bulk of his army to the peninsula. On April 9, the President warned McClellan that a prolonged siege would only confirm suspicions of the general's unwillingness to fight. "It is indispensable to *you* that you strike a blow . . . . I have never written you, or spoken to you, in a greater kindness of feeling than now, nor with a fuller purpose to sustain you . . . . *But you must act.*" McClellan's only action was to inch forward with his siege while Johnston brought 40,000 more men to the peninsula. After looking at the Yorktown lines, Johnston commented that "no one but McClellan could have hesitated to attack."[1]

By the beginning of May, McClellan finally got his siege guns in position. But instead of waiting for them to pound his defenses to pieces, Johnston evacuated the trenches on the night of May 3 and pulled back toward Richmond. Several Union divisions pursued the retreating Rebels and attacked the rear guard at Williamsburg on May 5. After sharp fighting, the Confederates withdrew during the night, having delayed the pursuit long enough to protect the retreating supply wagons. Further Union pursuit bogged down in heavy rains that turned the roads into a morass. The rains persisted for nearly a month, during which there was much sickness, much corduroying (laying of planks or logs) of bottomless roads, much building of bridges over swollen creeks, and much cursing—but little fighting.

The Confederate retreat compelled the evacuation of Norfolk, which opened the James River to Union warships. Five gunboats including the *Monitor* steamed up the river on May 15 to attack the Confederate fort at Drewry's Bluff, seven miles below Richmond. The government prepared to evacuate the capital, but the Union navy took a beating at Drewry's Bluff. The *Monitor's* guns could not be elevated enough to hit the Confederate artillery on the bluff 100 feet above; the other gunboats suffered heavy damage from the Rebel guns and from sharpshooters along the banks who picked off Yankee sailors on the decks. If Richmond was to be taken, McClellan's army would have to take it.

By May 20, Johnston had established a defensive line five miles from the city, where 60,000 Confederates faced 100,000 Federals. Citing the reports of Allan Pinkerton's agents, McClellan estimated Johnston's army at 150,000 and demanded reinforcements before he would attack. Lincoln promised him McDowell's 40,000 men, who could now march down from Fredericksburg to link up with McClellan's right wing while still remaining between the Confederate army and Washington. But once again Stonewall Jackson's exploits in the Shenandoah Valley upset the Federal campaign against Richmond.

---

[1] Roy P. Basler (ed.), *The Collected Works of Abraham Lincoln,* 9 vols. (New Brunswick, N.J., 1953–1955), V, 184–185; Johnston to Robert E. Lee, April 22, 1862, *O.R.,* Ser. 1, Vol. 11, pt. 3, pp. 455–456.

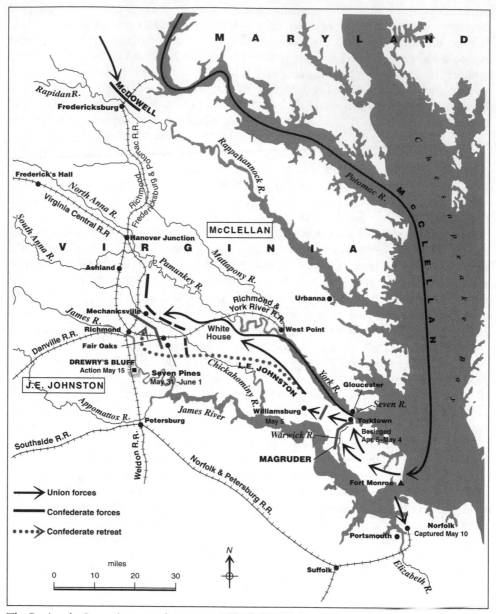

The Peninsula Campaign, March 17–June 1, 1862

Jackson in the Valley

After the battle of Kernstown in March, Jackson had withdrawn up the valley (southward) while Banks followed cautiously, harassed by Rebel guerrillas and cavalry raids. By late April, Jackson had recruited new troops and had been reinforced by a division under General Richard Ewell, bringing his total strength to 17,000 facing

AN IRONCLAD THAT
FAILED: THE *U.S.S. GALENA*.
Built at the same time as the
Monitor, the *U.S.S. Galena*
was a six-gun corvette plated
with three-inch iron armor.
During the attack on Drewry's
Bluff, a ten-inch shot broke
through her armor and
shattered her hull, while the
larger *Monitor* took similar
punishment without injury.
This settled the decision for
the future of ironclads in
favor of the more substantial
Monitor class of ships.

LIBRARY OF CONGRESS

Banks's 15,000 to the north (one of Banks's divisions had been recalled to reinforce
the campaign against Richmond) and Frémont's 15,000 scattered at several points to
the west. From Richmond, Robert E. Lee, now serving as Jefferson Davis's military adviser, suggested to Jackson another diversionary attack in the valley that would prevent further Union reinforcements being sent to the Richmond front. Jackson was just
the man to turn such a suggestion into action. Keeping his plans secret even from his
own officers to prevent leaks, he marched half his troops *eastward* across the Blue
Ridge, put them on trains near Charlottesville, and took them back west to Staunton,
an important supply base threatened by part of Frémont's army. Having mystified the
enemy by this zigzag movement, Jackson drove two of Frémont's brigades northward
after a sharp engagement in the mountains west of Staunton on May 8.

While guerrillas kept Frémont off balance, Jackson turned east again to discover
that still another of Banks's divisions had been ordered to join McDowell for the expected linkup with McClellan. Since this was just what Jackson wanted to prevent,
he moved quickly to attack Banks. Reduced to 8,000 men, Banks retreated down the
valley turnpike to Strasburg and sent one regiment to Front Royal to guard the head
of the Luray Valley. Jackson feinted as if to follow Banks to Strasburg, but suddenly
swerved east to cross Massanutten Mountain to Luray, where he picked up Ewell's
division and marched to Front Royal to overwhelm the Union garrison there on May
23. In all these movements, Jackson's cavalry under Turner Ashby screened the maneuvers (that is, prevented Union cavalry from getting close enough to find out what
Jackson was up to) with great success. The Rebel infantry marched so fast and far in
this campaign that they became known as "Jackson's foot cavalry."

Confused by the swiftness and secrecy of Jackson's movements, Banks was surprised by the Front Royal attack. The Confederates were now on his flank ten miles away with a force twice as large as his own. Jackson urged his troops forward to cut off Banks's retreat to his base at Winchester, but the weary foot cavalry, having marched seventy miles on bad roads in the preceding four days, moved slowly for once. Banks got most of his army into position at Winchester, but Jackson followed relentlessly with a night march and attacked at dawn May 25. After a brief resistance, the Federals broke. The remnants of Banks's force streamed northward toward the Potomac. Jackson hoped to pursue and annihilate the enemy, but his exhausted infantry could not move fast enough, and Ashby's ill-disciplined cavalry had dissolved as a fighting force after looting captured Yankee supplies. Although Banks got most of his men across the Potomac, Jackson's army had captured, wounded, or killed 3,000 Federals and had seized a bonanza of wagons, supplies, medicine, guns, and horses.

Exaggerated reports of Banks's rout caused panic in the North. Jackson was reported to be crossing the Potomac with 40,000 men to march on Washington. Lincoln did not believe this. His response was spurred not by a fear for the capital but by a desire to trap and destroy Jackson's force before it could withdraw up the valley. The President once again suspended McDowell's move toward Richmond and ordered him to send 20,000 men to Strasburg to get in Jackson's rear. He ordered Frémont to move with 15,000 men from the Alleghenies to the valley turnpike at Harrisonburg to block Jackson there if he got that far. He told Banks to reorganize and recross the Potomac to pursue Jackson from the north. If all went well on this military chessboard, Jackson's force would be trapped by 40,000 converging Federals.

Lincoln has been criticized for playing into Lee's and Jackson's hands, since the object of Jackson's valley campaign was to prevent McDowell from reinforcing McClellan. But Lincoln's decision to destroy Jackson first can be defended as a sound military plan. In the end it failed because his generals moved too slowly and did not coordinate their movements. Frémont approached Strasburg from the west instead of from the south as Lincoln had directed. On May 30, Frémont and General James Shields, commander of McDowell's lead division, were only twenty miles apart and converging with 25,000 men on Jackson's escape route through Strasburg. Both were closer to Strasburg than the Confederates were. But while the Union forces were slowed by muddy roads, by Confederate cavalry demonstrations, and by lack of aggressiveness, Jackson's army escaped by forced marches southward on the macadamized valley pike before the trap could be sprung.

Frémont and Shields chased Jackson southward by separate roads on either side of Massanutten Mountain. Confederate cavalry beat the Union horsemen to three key bridges in the Luray Valley, which they burned, delaying Shields' pursuit, while Jackson's rear guard burned a bridge on the valley pike to slow Frémont. The only remaining bridge where the two Union armies could link up was at Port Republic, a village sixty miles south of Strasburg. Jackson arrived there first and secured the bridge with his own division while leaving Ewell's 6,500 men to confront Frémont's 12,000 at Cross Keys, another village a few miles to the north. There Frémont attacked Ewell feebly on June 8, sending in only five of his twenty-four regiments before lapsing into an ineffective artillery bombardment. Next day Jackson brought half of Ewell's men to Port Republic to participate in an attack on two brigades of Shields'

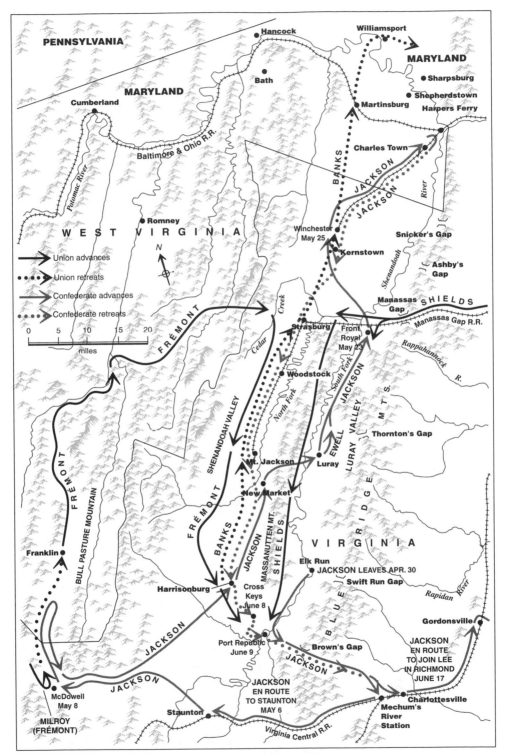

Jackson's Shenandoah Valley Campaign, May–June 1862

division. Outnumbering the Federals two to one, Jackson hoped to dispose of them quickly and then turn around for an attack on Frémont. It did not work out that way. Shields' men proved tougher than expected. Jackson drove them away only after hours of heavy fighting that left his army too bruised to go after Frémont. The Confederates withdrew to the Blue Ridge, burning the Port Republic bridge to delay any pursuit by Frémont.

Jackson's valley campaign is still studied in military schools as an example of how a small army utilizing geography and mobility can achieve numerical battlefield supremacy over larger but divided enemy forces. In a period of one month (May 8–June 9), Jackson's army of 17,000 men marched 350 miles, fought and won four battles against three separate armies whose combined numbers were twice their own, inflicted twice as many casualties as they suffered, captured large quantities of much-needed material, and immobilized nearly 60,000 Union troops. Three times Jackson caused Lincoln to suspend plans for McDowell's full corps to reinforce McClellan: in March after the battle of Kernstown, in May after the battle of Winchester, and again in June after Port Republic. Although one of McDowell's divisions finally did join McClellan, three others remained in or near the Shenandoah Valley to deal with whatever the fearsome Jackson decided to do next. McClellan later told the congressional Committee on the Conduct of the War that "had the command of General McDowell joined the Army of the Potomac in the month of May . . . we would have had Richmond within a week."[2] Though one may well doubt this in view of McClellan's reluctance to attack regardless of how many troops he had, it remains true that Jackson's valley campaign accomplished everything Lee and Davis had hoped it would. It also extended the streak of Confederate victories in Virginia that gave the Rebels a psychological edge over the enemy.

The Battle of Seven Pines and the Accession of Lee

While Jackson was escaping Lincoln's trap at Strasburg on May 31, the armies on the peninsula were fighting a major battle five miles from Richmond. The Chickahominy River flowed between Richmond and McClellan's supply base on the York River. To protect this base and to link his right wing with the expected advance of McDowell's corps from the north, McClellan had posted his troops in such a way that the two wings of his army were divided by the Chickahominy. Bordered by swampy ground in the best of times, the river had turned into a raging torrent from May's heavy rains. A tremendous storm on May 30 threatened to wipe out the four bridges that formed the only links between the two halves of the Union army. Taking advantage of this storm, Johnston on May 31 hurled two-thirds of his army against one of the two Union corps south of the river.

If well executed, this attack might have dealt McClellan a crippling blow. But verbal instead of written orders led to confusion on the Southern side. Johnston's battle plan required an advance of three divisions from three different directions. This proved too complicated for his inexperienced and undermanned staff to handle.

---

[2]Edward T. Downer, *Stonewall Jackson's Shenandoah Valley Campaign, 1862* (Charlottesville, 1959), p. 27.

General James Longstreet's division took a wrong road and became tangled with another Confederate division. The attack scheduled for dawn was not launched until afternoon. Several brigades never got into action, and others went in piecemeal. This gave Union generals time to bring up reinforcements. McClellan ordered General Edwin Sumner, a leather-lunged veteran of forty-two years in the pre-Civil War army, to bring his corps across the Chickahominy and shore up the Union flank. Despite water coursing knee-deep over the bridge, tough old "Bull" Sumner got his men and even his artillery across. His lead division counterattacked the Rebels and stopped their advance at nightfall. Next morning the Confederates renewed the assault with even less success than the previous day. By afternoon they had been driven back almost to their starting point along the road between Seven Pines and Fair Oaks (the battle is known by both names). It had been a confused, bloody conflict, fought in woods and swamps where coordination was impossible and where some wounded soldiers drowned as they sank into the sloughs. With about 42,000 men engaged on each side, the Rebels suffered 6,000 casualties and the Yankees 5,000.

The battle had no important strategic consequences, but it did have a profound impact on the top commanders of both sides. McClellan was unnerved by the sight of "mangled corpses" strewn over the battlefield. "Victory has no charms for me when purchased at such a cost," he wrote. McClellan's concern for his men was one cause of his popularity with them. But it also made him forget the hard fact that soldiers exist to fight and possibly to die.[3] It reinforced his preference for maneuver and siege rather than battle.

If Seven Pines accentuated the Union commander's caution, it had the opposite effect on Confederate leadership. General Johnston was wounded during the first day's fighting. His replacement was Robert E. Lee. Because Lee had not distinguished himself earlier in western Virginia (see page 175), his appointment evoked few cheers in the South. McClellan appraised his new opponent as "cautious & weak under grave responsibility . . . wanting in moral firmness when pressed by heavy responsibility . . . likely to be timed & irresolute in action." But a Southern officer who knew Lee well noted that despite his quiet demeanor and aristocratic bearing, he was a man of daring. "His name might be Audacity. He will take more chances, and take them quicker than any other general in this country."[4]

Lee named his command the Army of Northern Virginia. He began immediately to plan an offensive against McClellan's superior numbers. On June 12, he sent General J. E. B. Stuart on a cavalry reconnaissance to discover McClellan's exact position. A bold, dashing, romantic figure, the very image of a cavalier, Stuart was a superb cavalry leader. Not only did he get the information Lee wanted; he also rode completely around McClellan's army, a three-day adventure in which 1,200 men circled an enemy of 100,000, captured prisoners, destroyed Union supplies, outwitted pursuing enemy cavalry, and returned with the loss of only one man. Stuart told Lee that McClellan's right flank was "in the air" (unprotected by any natural barrier such as a river or mountain) and vulnerable to envelopment.

---

[3]George B. McClellan, *McClellan's Own Story* (New York, 1886), p. 398; T. Harry Williams, *Lincoln and His Generals* (New York, 1952), p. 106.

[4]McClellan to Lincoln, April 20, 1862, quoted in Stephen W. Sears (ed.), *The Civil War Papers of George B. McClellan* (New York, 1989), pp. 244–245; Douglas Southall Freeman, *R. E. Lee: A Biography*, 4 vols. (New York, 1934–1935), II, 92.

The Seven Days Battles

McClellan had moved most of his army south of the Chickahominy, leaving only Fitz-John Porter's reinforced corps of 30,000 on the north bank. Lee decided to launch an attack on this corps. To do so, he planned to bring Jackson's army from the valley to fall on Porter's flank with 18,000 men while 45,000 of the peninsula troops crossed the Chickahominy to assault his front. The risk in this was that while he reinforced his own left to assault McClellan's right, the 70,000 Federals south of the Chickahominy might smash through the remaining 25,000 Confederates in front of them. But knowing McClellan, Lee considered the risk worth taking. During the third week of June, Jackson moved his men with all possible secrecy by rail and road to a point just north of Richmond from which he could coordinate his attack with Lee's.

McClellan meanwhile had been promising Lincoln that he would begin an advance as soon as the weather improved and the "necessary preliminaries" had been completed, but, he asked, couldn't the government send him more men? His complaints about lack of support and reinforcements had little foundation. Though he never received McDowell's entire corps (see page 263), one of its larger divisions had reached him, and since April his original army had been reinforced by a total of 35,000 men. On June 20, he had nearly 100,000 combat troops. Even after Jackson arrived, the Confederates would have fewer than 90,000 soldiers, yet McClellan's wretched intelligence service inflated this to 200,000—which he cited as a reason for delay. Nevertheless, on June 25, McClellan made a reconnaissance in force—evidently the beginning of his long-promised offensive.

But the next day, Lee launched his attack across the Chickahominy. From then on the Rebels had the initiative. At first, though, little went right with their offensive—and surprisingly, the fault lay mainly with Jackson. Lee's plan had called for Jackson's three divisions to fall on Porter's right and rear, which would be a signal for the divisions from Lee's army to assault the Union front near the village of Mechanicsville. But Jackson's famed foot cavalry never got to the battlefield on June 26. Tired of waiting, the lead Confederate division in the center under A. P. Hill attacked in midafternoon, drove the Union pickets from Mechanicsville, but were then mowed down with heavy loss by bluecoats posted behind a boggy creek east of the village. Less than three miles away, Jackson heard the firing but did not come to Hill's aid. Jackson's strange behavior on this and subsequent days of what became known as the Seven Days battles has been explained in various ways. Union burning of bridges and felling of trees across the already bad roads are said to have slowed his march to Mechanicsville; Lee's orders are said to have been vague and Confederate staff work inadequate; Jackson's troops were weary from their valley campaign and the subsequent march to Richmond; Jackson himself was exhausted and lethargic after several near-sleepless nights. Whatever the reason, Jackson did not exhibit the same drive on the peninsula as he had in the valley.

During the night of June 26–27, Porter pulled his corps back to a strong line behind Boatswain's Swamp, just east of Gaines' Mill. Lee followed and launched an all-out assault with 57,000 men against Porter's reinforced 34,000 on the afternoon of

ROBERT E. LEE   THOMAS J. (STONEWALL) JACKSON

J. E. B. (JEB) STUART

THREE GENERALS WHO TURNED THE WAR AROUND IN 1862.
All of them Virginians, they forged the Army of Northern Virginia into a superb fighting force that carried out Lee's "offensive-defensive" strategy of defending Confederate territory by taking the offensive against the Army of the Potomac on four occasions during the year from Lee's accession to command in June 1862 until Jackson's death after Chancellorsville in May 1863.

June 27. Once again Jackson was slow getting into position on the Confederate left, and Lee's center divisions were repeatedly hurled back until a final attack all along the line at sundown pierced the blue defenses. Porter withdrew across the Chickahominy during the night.

What had the troops south of the river been doing while this fighting went on to the north? Once again John Magruder's theatrical talents were called into play. Lee told him to maneuver and demonstrate in such a way as to make McClellan think that he planned to attack. Magruder repeated his Yorktown performance. His artillery boomed out; his infantry marched and countermarched; officers stood in the woods within hearing of Union lines and shouted orders to imaginary regiments; some units made brief sallies against Yankee positions. The ruse worked. Indeed, McClellan telegraphed Washington that he had been "attacked by greatly superior numbers" on *both* sides of the Chickahominy—though in fact he had a numerical superiority of two and a half to one south of the river.[5]

McClellan decided to transfer his base across the peninsula to the more secure James River. He issued orders that night for the army to retreat southward to the James. He then sent a dispatch to Secretary of War Stanton which revealed that the events of the day had unhinged him:

I have lost this battle because my force was too small . . . . The government must not and cannot hold me responsible for the result . . . . I have seen too many dead and wounded comrades to feel otherwise than that this Government has not sustained this army . . . . If I save this army now, I tell you plainly that I owe no thanks to you or to any other persons in Washington. You have done your best to sacrifice this army.[6]

The man who wrote these words was a beaten general. No matter that he commanded an army superior in numbers and equipment to its enemy. Napoleon had said that in warfare it was not men who really counted, but *the man*—the commanding general. McClellan was proving it.

Lee intended to strike the Union army in the flank and rear during its withdrawal. His plans were excellent on paper but too complicated for his subordinates to execute. Twice they attacked portions of the retreating bluecoats—at Savage Station on June 29 and at Glendale on June 30. Each time the Confederates failed to coordinate their attacks; at Glendale they managed to get only two of eight divisions into action. Twice more Jackson tarried—once by spending all day building a bridge over the Chickahominy instead of fording it (the river had dropped); and once by allowing himself to be held by artillery and a broken bridge in the White Oak Swamp instead of throwing his divisions across the fords and onto the Union flank at Glendale.

On July 1, the Federals established a formidable line across Malvern Hill, a 150-foot high slope flanked by deep ravines and with a long, open field of fire in front. The blue artillery placed 100 guns across the front, with another 150 on the flanks and in reserve. This position looked too strong to attack, but Lee thought the litter of abandoned equipment left behind by the retreating Yankees indicated demoralization. One more push, he believed, might destroy them before they reached the James and the protection of their gunboats. Confederate batteries loosed an artillery

---

[5] *O.R.,* Ser. 1, Vol. 11, pt. 3, p. 266.

[6] *O.R.,* Ser. 1, Vol. 11, pt. 1, p. 61. An amazed colonel in the telegraph office deleted the last two sentences before sending the dispatch to Stanton.

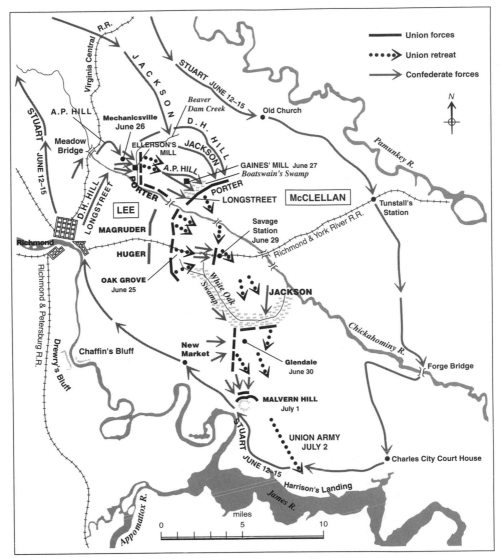

The Seven Days Battles, June 25–July 1, 1862

barrage to soften up the position, but the Union guns knocked them out with counter-battery fire of surgical efficiency. Lee decided to order an infantry assault anyway. What followed, in Confederate General Daniel H. Hill's words, "was not war—it was murder."[7] Attack after attack was cut to pieces by Union cannon firing shells and canister. Northern artillery superiority counted for more at Malvern Hill than in any other battle of the war. For probably the only time on either side in the

---

[7]Daniel H. Hill, "McClellan's Change of Base and Malvern Hill," in *Battles and Leaders of the Civil War,* 4 vols. (New York, 1887), II, 394.

war, half of the Confederate casualties were caused by artillery fire. Afterward, Hill declared that with Confederate infantry and Yankee artillery he could whip any army in the world.

Malvern Hill was the last battle of the Seven Days. The bluecoats retreated to rest and refit at Harrison's Landing, while the Rebels licked their wounds. Although Lee's achievement during his first month of command was extraordinary, he was disappointed that McClellan had gotten away without suffering greater damage. In an uncharacteristic burst of temper, Lee snapped at one of his generals that this had happened "because I cannot have my orders carried out."[8] Lee subsequently corrected the weaknesses in his staff and command structure by transferring several generals out of the Virginia theater and grouping the army's eight infantry divisions into two corps under Longstreet and Jackson.

Whatever defects existed in the Southern command were exceeded by McClellan's deficiencies as a fighting general. In all the Seven Days, the Union army actually lost only one battle—Gaines' Mill—and the Confederates suffered 20,000 casualties to the Federals' 16,500 (6,000 of the latter were missing, mostly captured; if killed and wounded only are counted, Southern losses were nearly 20,000 and Northern about 11,000). These casualty rates indicated Lee's much greater aggressiveness than McClellan's; indeed, for the war as a whole, the armies commanded by Lee suffered the highest proportion of killed and wounded for any Civil War general, while those commanded by McClellan experienced almost the lowest. After Malvern Hill the Confederates were hurting badly. Several Union generals, including even McClellan's protégé Fitz-John Porter, recommended a counterattack. When McClellan instead ordered a retreat to Harrison's Landing, hot-tempered division commander Philip Kearny was reported to have said: "We ought instead of retreating to follow up the enemy and take Richmond . . . . I say to you all, such an order can only be prompted by cowardice or treason."[9]

Among the Dead and the Living

Like Shiloh in the West, the Seven Days inaugurated war in earnest in the East. Gone forever was the light-hearted romanticism with which so many Yanks and Rebs had marched off to war. The colonel of a New York Zouave regiment (see page 181) wrote after returning from the fighting on the peninsula:

What a contrast between the departure and the return! We had started out in the spring gay, smart, well provided with everything. The drums beat, the bugles sounded, the flag with its folds of immaculate silk glistened in the sunshine. And we were returning before the autumn, sad, weary, covered with mud, with uniforms in rags . . . . Where were the red pantaloons? Where were the Zouave jackets? [Where were] those who had worn them? . . . Killed at Williamsburg, killed at Fair Oaks, killed at Glendale, killed at Malvern Hill; wounded or sick in the hospitals.[10]

Soldiers who served on burial details after battles sometimes wrote horribly eloquent descriptions of the experience: "The sights and smells that assailed us were simply indescribable—corpses swollen to twice their original size, some of them ac-

---

[8]Foote, *Fort Sumter to Perryville,* p. 509.
[9]Bruce Catton, *Mr. Lincoln's Army* (Garden City, N.Y., 1951), p. 149.
[10]Ibid., p. 166.

THE VETERANS OF '62:
CONFEDERATE AND UNION
SOLDIERS AT EASE.
At left: Confederate soldiers,
with a slave, in camp. *Below:*
Union infantrymen taking a
rest break. Compare these
photographs with those of
Georgia and Vermont recruits
(*pages 182 and 183*).

LIBRARY OF CONGRESS

LIBRARY OF CONGRESS

tually burst asunder with the pressure of foul gases and vapors. The odors were so nauseating . . . that in a short time we all sickened and were lying with our mouths close to the ground, most of us vomiting profusely." But many men became hardened to the sight of death. "We don't mind the sight of dead men no more than if they was dead Hogs," wrote one Yankee, while a reflective Rebel mused: "I cannot describe the change nor do I know when it took place, yet I know that there is a change for I look on the carcass of a man now with pretty much such feeling as I would were it a horse or hog."[11] The boys of '61 had become the veterans of '62.

---

[11]Bell I. Wiley, *The Life of Johnny Reb* (Indianapolis, 1943), pp. 35, 75; Bell I. Wiley, *The Life of Billy Yank* (Indianapolis, 1952), p. 79.

As the war became grimmer and more destructive, the attitudes of soldiers on both sides toward each other evolved into something of a paradox. On the one hand, the level of hatred escalated with the level of killing. After the Seven Days, a Virginia private wrote in his diary: "May God avenge us of our infernal enemies . . . . 'Forgive your enemies' is the Divine precept [but] how can one forgive such enemies as we are contending against? Despoiling us of our property, driving us from our homes & friends and slaying our best citizens on the field are hard crimes to forgive." A Georgia lieutenant wrote to his wife in the spring of 1862: "Teach my children to hate them with bitter hatred that will never permit them to meet under any circumstances without seeking to destroy each other." As the invaders rather than the invaded, Yankee soldiers less often expressed such naked hatred. But Billy Yank was capable of savage ferocity. During the peninsula campaign, many stories of Rebel atrocities against prisoners and wounded men circulated in Union camps. Believing such stories, a New York regiment swore that they would retaliate in kind. When a Confederate picket whose surrender they had demanded shot one of them, the enraged New Yorkers seized him and, as an observer reported, "put a rope around his neck and hoisted him on a tree, made a target of his suspended body, then cut him down, bayoneted him in a dozen places, then dragged him to the road where they watched till long trains of wagons made a jelly of his remains."[12]

On the other hand, the fraternization between Johnny Reb and Billy Yank has become legendary. Speaking the same language, sharing a common history and many aspects of a common culture, calling each other—in some cases literally—brother or cousin, Yanks and Rebs sometimes stacked muskets during quiet times and swapped tobacco (scarce in the North) for coffee (almost unobtainable in the South), played cards, and mutually cursed their officers or the politicians who had caused the war. A typical incident occurred on July 4 in a patch of blackberries between the picket lines near Malvern Hill. "Our boys and the Yanks made a bargain not to fire at each other," a Southern private wrote, "and went out in the field, leaving one man on each post with the arms, and gathered berries together and talked over the fight, traded tobacco and coffee and exchanged newspapers as peacefully and kindly as if they had not been engaged for the last seven days in butchering each other."[13] Such incidents—and there were many—symbolized the irony and tragedy of civil war.

The Union Army and "Hard War"

McClellan's failure in front of Richmond plunged Northern opinion from springtime euphoria to summertime despair. "The feeling of despondency here is very great," reported a prominent New Yorker in July. Democrats attacked Lincoln and Stanton for not sustaining McClellan; many Republicans denounced McClellan as a proslavery traitor and Lincoln as a dolt for keeping him in command. The President was

---

[12]Wiley, *Johnny Reb.,* p. 308; James M. McPherson, *For Cause and Comrades: Why Men Fought in the Civil War* (New York, 1997), p. 149; Wiley, *Billy Yank,* p. 348.

[13]Foote, *Fort Sumter to Perryville,* pp. 518–519.

downhearted, but he refused to panic. "I expect to maintain this contest until suc-cessful, or till I die, or am conquered, or my term expires, or Congress or my coun-try forsakes me," he declared.[14] Gone were the hopes for a peace of reconciliation. Neither side would compromise; neither side would back down; neither side would give up until forced to do so by utter, devastating defeat.

A year earlier, the Union defeat at Bull Run had shocked the North into a grim-mer, more determined commitment to victory. Thousands of new recruits had flocked to the colors, and the government had reorganized the command structure. In 1862, after the Seven Days, the pattern repeated itself, but this time the response of the Northern public was considerably less united and confident.

The first task was to recruit new levies to reinforce the armies for renewed of-fensives. Fearing that a call for recruits after the retreat in Virginia would be inter-preted as a sign of panic, Lincoln arranged for Northern governors to "request" the President to call upon the states for 300,000 new three-year volunteers so that "the recent successes of Federal arms may be followed up." Lincoln did so on July 2, as-signing each state a quota based on population.[15] Once again, would-be colonels and captains traveled through their counties and urged men to sign up to fight for God and country. The New York abolitionist James S. Gibbons, who, though a Quaker, possessed "a reasonable leaning toward wrath in cases of emergency," wrote a patriotic song to be sung at recruiting rallies: "We are Coming, Father Abra-ham, Three Hundred Thousand More."

But this time the 300,000 were slow to come forward. War weariness had replaced war enthusiasm. Several newspapers urged conscription. But so strong was the hos-tility to a draft that the government decided to exhaust every alternative first. Nev-ertheless, it became necessary to institute a quasi-draft in the fall of 1862. On August 4, Secretary of War Stanton issued a requisition on the states for 300,000 nine-month militiamen (this was in addition to the three-year volunteers called for a month ear-lier). Invoking a provision of the recently passed Militia Act (July 17), Stanton an-nounced that states failing to meet their quotas would be subject to a militia draft. Under the complicated regulations issued by the War Department, each three-year recruit above a state's volunteer quota was equal to four nine-month men against its militia quota. This provision was designed to put pressure on the states to stimulate volunteering in order to avoid a draft. For the most part it worked—but clumsily and with warnings of trouble ahead. Most states eventually met their quotas, though some had to resort to a state militia draft to do so. This produced antidraft violence in several areas, especially among Irish-Americans in the Pennsylvania coalfields and German-Americans in Wisconsin. Some states allowed drafted men to hire substi-tutes. Several states and localities paid bounties of $100 or more to three-year vol-unteers. They justified the bounties as a means to provide support for the families of men who left good jobs to join the army. But these payments introduced a merce-nary factor into volunteering that would become worse as time went on. The calls

[14]Samuel L. M. Barlow to Henry D. Bacon, July 15, 1862, S. L. M. Barlow Papers, Henry E. Huntington Library; Basler, *Works of Lincoln,* V, 292.

[15]Basler, *Works of Lincoln,* V, 296–297.

of July and August 1862 ultimately produced 421,000 three-year volunteers and 87,000 nine-month militiamen. This was accomplished without national conscription, but only because of the implied threat of conscription.

These measures raised fresh levies for the army. But what about new leaders to command them? In June, Lincoln had summoned John Pope from Mississippi to take command of the newly created Army of Virginia, formed from the separate armies of Frémont, Banks, and McDowell, which had made such a poor showing against Jackson in the Shenandoah Valley. Successful in the western theater, Pope had also won the support of radical Republicans with statements criticizing McClellan and opposing slavery. But Pope got off on the wrong foot with his new command. On July 14, he issued an address to the troops comparing the eastern armies unfavorably with those in the West, "where we have always seen the backs of our enemies." He wanted the Army of Virginia to discard such ideas as "taking strong positions and holding them" or securing "lines of retreat." He said, "Let us study the probable lines of retreat of our opponents, and leave our own to take care of themselves. Let us look before us and not behind. Success and glory are in the advance, disaster and shame lurk in the rear."[16] Whether or not Stanton wrote these words, as Pope later claimed, they were hardly the best way to win the loyalty of eastern soldiers.

Pope's next act also raised hackles. He announced that his army would confiscate Rebel property for its own use when necessary, would execute guerrillas and hold citizens responsible for aiding and abetting them, and would drive out of Union lines those citizens who refused allegiance to the United States and treat them as spies if they returned. These harsh orders made Pope a hated man in the Confederacy, where they were regarded as confirmation of Yankee inclinations toward pillage and murder. Robert E. Lee wrote that "this miscreant Pope" must be "suppressed." He could forgive one of his nephews for siding with the Union, said Lee, but he could never forgive him for joining Pope's staff.[17]

Although Pope's orders concerning guerrillas and civilians were not enforced, those concerning Rebel property were being carried out by this and other Union armies, with or without specific orders. Civilian property in the path of invading armies became a prime target of hard war. The campaigns in northern Virginia during the next several months left whole counties devastated. If a bridge was out, construction battalions did not hesitate to tear down the nearest house or barn to rebuild it. All the trees and fence rails for miles disappeared to feed soldiers' campfires. No farmer's livestock or corn crib was safe. Even in McClellan's command, soldiers pillaged some of the fine old plantation homes on the James River. Although Southern legend has magnified the wanton destruction committed by Yankee invaders, the reality was bad enough. Soldiers justified their behavior with the argument that it made no sense to fight a war against traitors while leaving their property untouched. This was unassailable logic. The same logic underlay a confiscation act passed by Congress on July 17, 1862 (see page 293). It also underlay the orders that went out from Washington to General Grant in August:

---

[16]*O.R.*, Ser. 1, Vol. 12, pt. 3, pp. 473–474.

[17]Douglas Southall Freeman, *R. E. Lee, a Biography,* 4 vols. (New York, 1934–1935), II, 264.

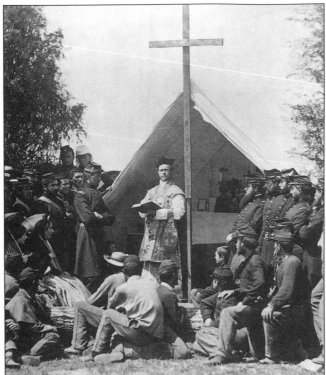

HOW FOLKS AT HOME
THOUGHT SOLDIERS
SPENT THEIR SPARE TIME
This photo portrays Sunday
morning mass in May 1861
for the 69th New York
Infantry, an Irish regiment.
The regiment was camped
near Washington, which
explains the presence of
women.

LIBRARY OF CONGRESS

It is very desirable that you should clear out West Tennessee and North Mississippi of all organized enemies. If necessary, take up all active sympathizers, and either hold them as prisoners or put them beyond our lines. Handle that class without gloves, and take their property
for public use. As soon as the corn gets fit for forage get all the supplies you can from the
rebels in Mississippi. It is time that they should begin to feel the presence of the war.[18]

One Union general who did not agree with this method of waging war was Mc-
Clellan. On July 8, Lincoln came to Harrison's Landing to see for himself the condition of the Army of the Potomac after the Seven Days. Following the consultations,
McClellan handed Lincoln a letter outlining his views on the proper conduct of the
war. "It should not be a war looking to the subjugation of the people of any State,"
he wrote. "Neither confiscation of property, political execution of persons, territorial
organization of States, or forcible abolition of slavery should be contemplated for a
moment . . . . A declaration of radical views, especially upon slavery, will rapidly disintegrate our present armies."[19]

Lincoln said nothing as he read this document. But it is not hard to infer what he
thought. McClellan's views were similar to Lincoln's own views—six months earlier.
But much had changed in those six months. The war had taken on a remorseless

---

[18]*O.R.*, Ser. 1, Vol. 17, pt. 2, p. 150.
[19]George B. McClellan, *McClellan's Own Story* (New York, 1886), pp. 487–489.

HOW SOLDIERS REALLY SPENT THEIR SPARE TIME.
These soldiers of the 56th Massachusetts Infantry are playing cards. Gambling was the most common pastime in the army. The rear areas of battlefields were littered with cards and dice thrown away by soldiers turned suddenly penitent in the face of battle and possible death.

MASSACHUSETTS COMMANDERY MILITARY ORDER OF THE LOYAL LEGION AND THE U.S. ARMY MILITARY HISTORY INSTITUTE

quality. No longer was it a limited war to suppress an insurrection and encourage Southern Unionists to return their states unchanged to the old Union. Instead, it was becoming a "hard war" to destroy the "slave power" that had led the old South into rebellion and to incorporate a new South into a transformed Union. Lincoln had already decided to draft an emancipation proclamation (see pages 294–295). McClellan's ideas on war aims were becoming anachronistic. Worse still, they seemed to be a bid for the Democratic presidential nomination two years hence. Prominent New York Democrats were already sounding out McClellan on this question. The general's expressed preference for a "soft" war underscored Republican suspicions that his heart was not in the cause. If Lincoln wanted an aggressive, hard-hitting general, one who believed that the war could be won only by grim, no-holds-barred fighting, it appeared that McClellan was not the man.[20]

The Second Battle of Bull Run

On July 11, Lincoln called Halleck from the west to become general in chief of all the armies. McClellan considered this a slap in the face, for he now would have to serve under a man "whom I know to be my inferior."[21] Lincoln hoped that "Old Brains" would coordinate the strategies of all Union armies and plan bold new offensives. But in this he was to be disappointed. Halleck turned out to be pedantic, fussy, and unimaginative. He soon settled into the routine of office work and seldom undertook the tasks of strategic planning and command for which Lincoln had brought him to Washington. The President later described Halleck as "little more . . . than a first-rate clerk." Yet Halleck's talents should not be dismissed too lightly. He

---

[20]The best study of the evolution of a "hard war" policy is Mark Grimsley, *The Hard Hand of War: Union Military Policy Toward Southern Civilians, 1861–1865* (Cambridge, 1995).

[21]McClellan to Samuel L. M. Barlow, July 23, 1862, Barlow Papers.

was an efficient administrator. He could translate the War Department's civilian directives into military language for the generals, and translate military reports into language that the government could understand. His orders and reports were clear and precise. These were important abilities in the mushrooming wartime military bureaucracy. A clerk Halleck may have been, but at least he was a first-rate clerk.[22]

The first problem facing Halleck was what to do with McClellan's army of 90,000 at Harrison's Landing. Give me 50,000 reinforcements, said McClellan, and I will take Richmond. Soon he upped the request to 100,000 and estimated that Lee had 200,000 men facing him. Sadly disillusioned, Lincoln told a cabinet member that if he gave McClellan 200,000 men, the general would suddenly discover that Lee had 400,000. Lincoln had hoped that a simultaneous advance on Richmond by McClellan's 90,000 from the east and Pope's 45,000 from the north would catch Lee's army in a giant pincers. But Pope and McClellan despised each other; McClellan showed few signs of advancing; and his army was being crippled by illness, with the worst part of the sickly season on the swampy peninsula still to come. Lincoln and Halleck finally decided to withdraw the Army of the Potomac from the peninsula and send it by water to reinforce Pope for an offensive from the north.

McClellan protested bitterly against this decision. His opposition to it and his contempt for the administration[23] did not augur well for the speed and efficiency with which he would carry out the task of reinforcing a general he disdained. And since many of his officers and men shared these opinions, it was a serious question how well they would fight under Pope when they reached him.

Even before McClellan received his orders to withdraw from the peninsula, Lee had sent Jackson with 24,000 men to counter Pope's southward thrust. Hoping to repeat his valley tactics, Jackson decided to pounce on two advanced Union divisions commanded by his old adversary Banks before the rest of the Union forces could concentrate. But this time Banks attacked first, at Cedar Mountain on August 9. In the early fighting, the outnumbered Yankees pushed the Rebels back and even routed the famous Stonewall Brigade, Jackson's original command. But Jackson brought up reinforcements and punished the bluecoats severely.

After this engagement, Lee gambled that McClellan was leaving the peninsula for good. He took another 30,000 troops north to engage Pope in a showdown battle before the Army of the Potomac could reinforce him. In ten days of maneuvering, Lee drove the Federals back across the Rappahannock but failed to create a favorable opportunity for attack. With the advance divisions of McClellan's army joining Pope, Lee decided on a typically bold but dangerous maneuver. He split his army in half and sent Jackson's corps on a wide flanking march around Pope's right to sever his supply line. In two days (August 25–26), Jackson's foot cavalry legged more than fifty miles to fall on the huge Union supply depot at Manassas. It was one of the war's great marches. Jackson was back in stride. His hungry and footsore soldiers seized all the Union supplies they could eat or carry away and burned the rest. (See map on page 280.)

---

[22]Stephen E. Ambrose, *Halleck: Lincoln's Chief of Staff* (Baton Rouge, 1962), *passim.*

[23]At this time McClellan was writing privately that Lincoln "was an old stick, and of pretty poor timber at that," Stanton was an "unmitigated scoundrel," and the administration as a whole was "a set of heartless villains . . . . I cannot express to you the infinite contempt I feel for these people." (McClellan to Mrs. McClellan, July 13, 17, 18, McClellan Papers, Library of Congress; McClellan to Samuel L. M. Barlow, July 15, S. L. M. Barlow Papers, Henry E. Huntington Library.)

LIBRARY OF CONGRESS

WRECKAGE LEFT BY JACKSON'S TROOPS AT THE UNION SUPPLY BASE, MANASSAS, VIRGINIA, 1862

Pope hoped to turn this disaster into an opportunity to smash Jackson before Lee with Longstreet's corps could join him. But first he had to find Jackson. The wily Stonewall moved his three divisions by separate routes from Manassas to a wooded ridge just west of the old Bull Run battlefield. As a succession of contradictory reports of the Rebels' whereabouts poured into Pope's headquarters on August 28, he issued confusing and contradictory orders in a vain attempt to run Jackson to earth. The seemingly pointless marching and countermarching caused officers and men, especially those in Fitz-John Porter's corps, to curse Pope as a blunderer. A Democrat like McClellan, Porter felt even more hostile than his chief toward Pope and the antislavery Republicans who backed him. Two weeks earlier Porter had written a Democratic editor that the administration had botched the Virginia campaign so badly that it deserved to fail. He concluded with a shocking statement: "Would that this army was in Washington to rid us of incumbents ruining our country."[24]

At sunset on August 28, one of Pope's divisions found Jackson. As this division marched unaware next to the Confederates hiding in the woods, Jackson could not resist the temptation to attack them. In a fierce, stand-up battle along the Warrenton

---

[24]Porter to Manton Marble, August 10, 1862, in T. Harry Williams, *Lincoln and His Generals* (New York, 1952), p. 148.

turnpike, the bluecoats stood off twice their numbers until dark. Once again a flurry of orders went out to Federal units, which at dawn on August 29 began to concentrate in front of Jackson. The Southerners had taken position along the cuts and fills of an unfinished railroad. As Pope's divisions arrived in Jackson's front during the day, the Union general hurled them piecemeal against the Rebel defenses. Porter's corps came up on the Union left in a position to move against Jackson's flank, but having no specific orders and misled by a dust cloud that Stuart's cavalry kicked up to convince him that a strong body of infantry was in his front, Porter did nothing. Although not there yet, infantry support was on its way to Jackson, for Pope had neglected to send a strong force to block Thoroughfare Gap, through which Longstreet's corps had forced its way the previous evening. At midday on August 29, Longstreet (accompanied by Lee) did arrive in front of Porter. Not realizing that these enemy troops had come up, Pope belatedly ordered Porter to attack Jackson's flank in late afternoon. Declining to obey because of Longstreet's presence, Porter stayed put. For this he was later court-martialed and cashiered from the service.[25]

By nightfall on August 29, the right half of the Union army had battered itself in six bloody assaults against Jackson's corps while the other halves of both armies had remained idle. That night the Confederates pulled back some units to strengthen their lines and to prepare for another flanking maneuver the next day. Still unaware that Longstreet's 30,000 men were on the field, Pope misinterpreted these moves as a preparation for a retreat. During the afternoon of August 30, he sent forward his own advance divisions to cut off the supposed retreat, but they quickly found Jackson in line and ready. Once again vicious fighting raged along the unfinished railroad. Some Confederate regiments ran short of ammunition and hurled rocks at the Yankees. The bluecoated attackers penetrated the Southern line at several points, forcing Jackson to call for help. At this moment Lee ordered Longstreet to counterattack with his entire corps against the Union left. With a mighty rebel yell, Longstreet's men swept forward against little opposition, for Pope had stripped the Federal left to reinforce the assault on Jackson. Longstreet's counterattack forced the whole Union line back more than a mile, where a desperate twilight stand on Henry House Hill finally halted the Confederates. During the night the dispirited, defeated Union troops retreated wearily to Centreville. Instead of following directly, Lee sent

---

[25]Until November, Porter remained in command of the Army of the Potomac's 5th Corps. The court-martial trial took place in December 1862 and January 1863. Pope accused Porter of deliberately disobeying the attack order. Porter contended that he could not obey the order because Confederate troops were in his front and connecting with Jackson's flank. This was in fact true, though the court-martial board did not know it at the time. Only with the capture of Confederate records and the testimony of Southern officers after the war did the truth become known. After a great deal of controversy, Porter finally won a reversal of the court-martial verdict in 1886. The controversy has continued for a century. To some degree, Porter was the victim of Republican hostility toward McClellanite officers. But Porter's own undisguised hostility toward Pope, toward Republicans, and toward emancipation, as well as his failure to do anything at all with his 11,000 men on August 29 while the battle raged nearby, left him open to the just suspicion that he did less than he might have done to cooperate with Pope. [Otto Eisenschiml, *The Celebrated Case of Fitz-John Porter* (Indianapolis, 1950); Kenneth P. Williams, *Lincoln Finds a General*, 5 vols. (New York, 1949–1959), I, 324–330, II, 785–789; Wallace J. Schutz and Walter N. Trennery, *Abandoned by Lincoln: A Military Biography of General John Pope* (Urbana, Ill., 1990), pp. 139–142, 199–213.]

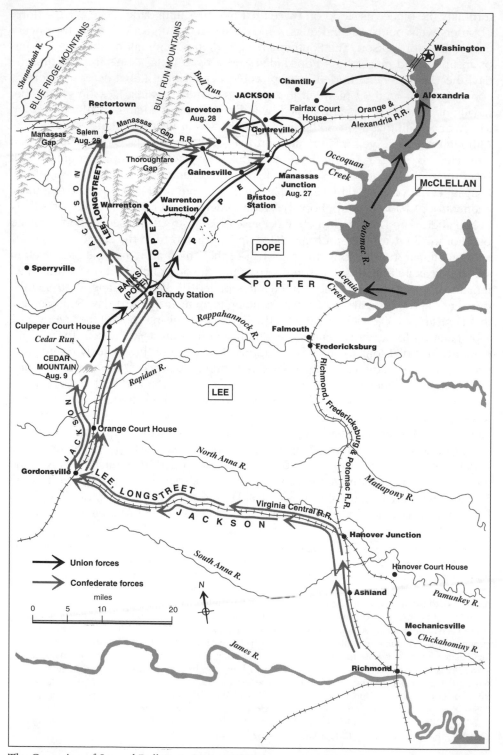

The Campaign of Second Bull Run, August 1862

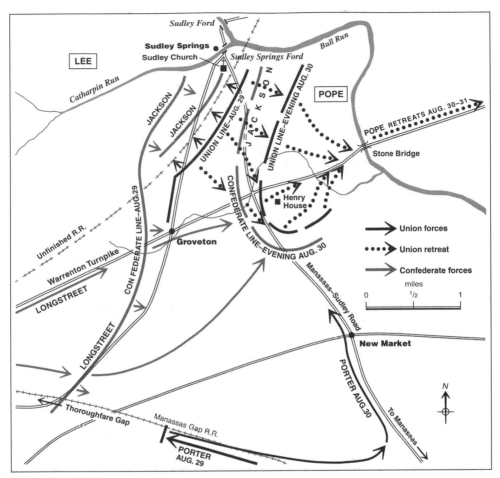

The Second Battle of Bull Run, August 29–30, 1862

Jackson's tired, hungry men on another wide flanking march around Pope's right through a drenching rainstorm. On September 1, these troops ran into two Union divisions, who stopped them at Chantilly in a sharp clash during a torrential downpour. Meanwhile, Pope pulled the rest of the army back to the Washington defenses.

Once again the Union army had suffered a humiliating defeat near Manassas. With just over 50,000 men Lee had inflicted 16,000 casualties on Pope's 60,000 at a cost of only 9,200 casualties to the Confederates. The defeat was all the more shocking to the North because it came on the heels of boastful dispatches from Pope that he was about to "bag" Jackson. Bitter recriminations followed the battle. Pope blamed McClellan and Porter for lack of cooperation. McClellan himself had been at Alexandria, where he had resisted Halleck's orders to send one of his corps to Pope as fast as possible. While the battle raged to the south on August 29, McClellan suggested to Lincoln that the best course might be to concentrate all available troops for the defense of Washington and "leave Pope to get out of his scrape" by himself. After the battle, Lincoln told his private secretary that McClellan's behavior had been "unpardonable." He "wanted Pope defeated." Four of the seven cabinet members signed a letter asking Lincoln to dismiss McClellan. Stanton thought McClellan ought to be court-martialed and Chase said he should be shot.[26]

But McClellan was neither shot nor fired. Lincoln retained him in command of the Army of the Potomac, which absorbed the Army of Virginia, while the luckless Pope was exiled to an unimportant command in the Midwest. Republicans found this a bitter pill to swallow. But in the circumstances Lincoln felt he had no choice. The army was demoralized and almost on the edge of mutiny against Pope, whom many soldiers considered responsible for their defeat. Although Lincoln had lost confidence in McClellan and had even tried to offer the top command to Ambrose E. Burnside (who declined), he knew that McClellan was the only man who could reorganize the army and restore its morale. Admitting that McClellan had "acted badly" in "breaking down Pope without regard to the consequences to the country," the President told confidants that "there is no remedy. McClellan has the army with him." No one else could "lick these troops of ours into shape half as well as he . . . . If he can't fight himself, he excels in making others ready to fight."[27] And this was all the more imperative, for Lee was taking his ragged, awesome butternut scarecrows across the Potomac to invade Maryland, in a campaign that was to have fateful consequences for the future of the country and of slavery.

---

[26]*McClellan's Own Story*, pp. 514–15; Michael Burlingame and John R. T. Ettlinger *Inside Lincoln's White House: The Complete Civil War Diary of John Hay* (Carbondale, Ill., 1997), pp. 37, 39; Gideon Welles, *The Diary of Gideon Welles*, ed. Howard K. Beale, 3 vols. (New York, 1960), I, 93–106.

[27]Burlingame and Ettlinger, *Inside Lincoln's White House*, p. 37; Welles, *Diary*, I, 113.

Chapter Sixteen

Slavery and the War: Northern Politics, 1861–1862

To fight against slaveholders, without fighting against slavery, is but a half-hearted business. . . . War for the destruction of liberty must be met with war for the destruction of slavery.

—Frederick Douglass,
1861

The military, diplomatic, and political maneuvers during the first two years of the war took place in the sometimes unacknowledged context of the slavery issue. Slavery was the fundamental cause of the sectional conflict that had led to war. The South had seceded to protect its peculiar institution from the perceived Republican threat to its future. Although a significant amount of internal disaffection existed in the Confederacy, the North suffered more disunity over war aims than the South. The South fought for independence. So long as the North fought simply for restoration of the Union, Northern unity was impressive. But the hard question of what kind of Union was to be restored soon divided the North. Was it to be a Union without slavery, as abolitionists and radical Republicans hoped? Or "the Union as it was, the Constitution as it is," as Democrats insisted? Was the South to be *restored* to the Union with its rights and power intact, or *reconstructed* in the image of the free-labor North? Disagreement about ends soon became disagreement about means as well. Was it to be an all-out war fought for absolute victory or a limited war looking toward an early peace conference to restore the Union through compromise?

War Aims and Politics in the North

Lincoln's Leadership

Northern unity in the spring and summer of 1861 had been fragile along several political fault lines. The Republican party was a coalition of men who a few years earlier had been Whigs, Democrats, Know-Nothings, Free Soilers, or abolitionists. Northern Democrats still bore the scars of battles between the Douglas and Buchanan wings of the party. In the loyal border states, several factions competed for leadership of the new "Unionist" parties. Lincoln's task was to mold these disparate elements into a government that could win the war at the same time that it defined what victory would mean. This proved to be a difficult task, almost an impossible one. Lincoln's greatness as a war leader resulted from his success in accomplishing this task.

When contemporaries asked Lincoln what his policy was on one issue or another, he sometimes replied: "My policy is to have no policy." To the exasperated questioner, this answer seemed flippant or evasive. Lincoln did not mean it that way. He did have a policy—to win the war and restore the Union. But since the questioners often represented sharply opposed viewpoints on how to do this, he knew that to answer their questions about specific issues prematurely might destroy the delicate balance of support for the war effort. Lincoln was a master of timing. He knew how to make a series of small decisions that laid the groundwork for a large decision. He knew how to wait for the right moment to announce major policies such as emancipation, in the meantime enduring the criticisms of those who denounced his weak leadership. To abolitionists he appeared to move too slowly; for conservatives he moved much too fast. But as the President himself once told a subordinate, if half the people think you have gone too far and the other half not far enough, you have probably done just about right.

Lincoln's relations with his cabinet provide a good example of his leadership. The cabinet represented every Republican viewpoint from border-state conservatism (Attorney General Edward Bates) to antislavery radicalism (Secretary of the Treasury Chase). It contained former Whigs (Seward, Bates, Secretary of the Interior Caleb Smith, and Lincoln himself), former Democrats (Secretary of the Navy Gideon Welles and Postmaster General Montgomery Blair), a Free Soiler (Chase), and Secretary of War Simon Cameron, a former Democrat who had occasionally collaborated with Whigs and Know-Nothings. Considered too radical on the slavery issue for the presidential nomination in 1860, Seward became one of the most conservative members of the cabinet during the war. Edwin M. Stanton, who replaced the inept Cameron in January 1862, was a former Buchanan Democrat who became, next to Chase, the most radical member of the cabinet. Four cabinet officers—Seward, Chase, Bates, and Cameron—had been Lincoln's rivals for the presidential nomination in 1860. Cutting across these currents of ideology and politics were long-standing personal rivalries between several pairs of individuals in the cabinet.

Such a cabinet promised discord rather than harmony. But with tact, patience, and a sense of humor, the President welded them into an effective team. On purely administrative matters, Lincoln allowed each secretary to run his own department. But on matters of policy, the President made the important decisions. He announced, rather than presented to the cabinet for debate, such important actions as the Emancipation Proclamation and the appointment or dismissal of army commanders. Chase complained that on vital war issues the cabinet as a whole was "so rarely consulted that they might as well not be consulted at all." Lincoln preferred to confer individually with cabinet members on such issues. He worked most closely with Stanton and Seward. The President's unique blend of firmness and deference, the iron fist of decision clothed in the velvet glove of humor and tact, enabled him to dominate his subordinates without the appearance of domination. "The relations between him and his Secretaries were perfectly cordial always and unaffected," recalled the assistant secretary of war, "without any appearance of his thinking himself the boss, but it was always his will, his order, that determined a decision."[1]

Lincoln's relations with Congress exhibited the same combination of deference and firmness. On matters of finance and domestic legislation unconnected with the war, he deferred to congressional leadership. In this respect he fitted the Whig tradition of a weak executive. But in all matters relating to the war and reconstruction, Lincoln exercised more power than perhaps any other president. His interpretation of the president's war powers was breathtakingly broad. "I conceive that I may in an emergency do things on military grounds which cannot be done constitutionally by Congress," he said.[2] Since his entire presidency was a time of emergency, he did many things that caused Democrats and even some Republicans to denounce his "tyranny" and "dictatorship."

Lincoln's actions during the first eight days of the war established the tone for his use of executive power. Instead of calling Congress into immediate session after the bombardment of Fort Sumter (as Jefferson Davis did), he called them to meet July 4. In the meantime Lincoln took a number of bold steps on his own authority. His proclamation of blockade on April 19 was in effect a declaration of war.[3] By executive order on May 3, he expanded the regular army and navy beyond the number authorized by law. He also issued a call for three-year volunteers, normally a congressional prerogative. In four proclamations from April to July, Lincoln suspended

---

[1] Allan Nevins, *The War for the Union: The Improvised War 1861–1862* (New York, 1959), pp. 204, 205.

[2] John G. Nicolay and John Hay, *Abraham Lincoln: A History*, 10 vols. (New York, 1890), IX, 119–120.

[3] The legality of this proclamation came before the Supreme Court in 1863 in the *Prize Cases* (67 U.S. 35). Plaintiffs argued that ships seized for violation of the blockade before July 13, 1861, when Congress declared the existence of a state of war, had been captured illegally. By a vote of 5 to 4, the Court upheld the President's action as legal under his emergency war powers. Three of the five justices in the majority were Lincoln appointees. Chief Justice Taney issued a dissent maintaining that the power to suppress insurrection was not the power to wage war. But the majority decided that from the moment Lincoln declared the blockade, the United States was at war.

the writ of habeas corpus in various parts of the country. He also turned over $2 million to a New York committee for "military measures necessary for the defence and support of the government" despite the Constitution's enjoinder that "no money shall be drawn from the Treasury, but in Consequence of Appropriations made by Law" (Article I, Section 7).[4]

The special session of Congress in the summer of 1861 retroactively approved Lincoln's executive actions to mobilize and increase the army "as if they had been done under the previous express authority" of Congress.[5] Two-thirds of the Democrats and border-state Unionists either abstained or voted with the Republican majority. Most Democrats also voted for measures to raise additional troops and to finance the war.[6] The opposition party had not yet divided into the factions later known as War Democrats and Peace Democrats. The germ of that division was present in the minds of Democrats who opposed or reluctantly supported some of the war measures. But thus far the spirit of bipartisanship prevailed.

The Meaning of Union

It prevailed because for most Northerners the concept of Union was endowed with such transcendent values as to amount almost to a religion. The rebellion "has outraged the Constitution, set at defiance all law, and trampled under foot that flag which has been the glorious and consecrated symbol of American Liberty," declared a Chicago newspaper. Four years later, in his second inaugural address, Lincoln summarized the meaning of the war with these words: "Both parties deprecated war; but one of them would *make* war rather than let the nation survive; and the other would *accept* war rather than let it perish. And the war came."[7]

Lincoln gave voice to the Northern conviction that secession challenged the whole basis of constitutional government by majority rule. Most republics through history had collapsed into tyranny or fragmented into quarreling fiefdoms. Would the United States follow that dismal pattern? "This is essentially a People's contest," said Lincoln in 1861.

On the side of the Union it is a struggle for maintaining in the world that form and substance of government whose leading object is to elevate the condition of men . . . to afford all an unfettered start, and a fair chance in the race of life. . . . The central idea pervading this struggle is the necessity . . . of proving that popular government is not an absurdity. We must settle this question now, whether in a free government the minority have the right to break up the government whenever they choose.[8]

---

[4]Roy P. Basler (ed.), *The Collected Works of Abraham Lincoln,* 9 vols. (New Brunswick, N.J., 1953–1955), IV, 347, 353–354, 364, 414, 419, V, 241–242.

[5]Edward McPherson (ed.), *The Political History of the United States During the Great Rebellion,* 2d ed. (Washington, D.C., 1865), p. 150.

[6]Because of the confused nature of party allegiances in the border states, the precise number of Republicans and Democrats in this Congress is hard to specify. In the House there were 106 Republicans, 42 Democrats, and 28 "Unionists," mostly from the border states. The Senate contained 31 Republicans, 10 Democrats, and 7 Unionists.

[7]*Chicago Daily Journal,* April 17, 1861, in Howard C. Perkins (ed.), *Northern Editorials on Secession,* 2 vols. (New York, 1942), II, 808–809; Basler, *Works of Lincoln,* VIII, 332.

[8]Basler, *Works of Lincoln* IV, 438; Tyler Dennett (ed.), *Lincoln and the Civil War in the Diaries and Letters of John Hay* (New York, 1939), p. 19.

The struggle is "not altogether for today," continued Lincoln; "it is for a vast future." It "embraces more than the fate of these United States. It presents to the whole family of man the question whether," as Lincoln expressed it in the Gettysburg Address two years later, a nation "conceived in Liberty, and dedicated to the proposition that all men are created equal . . . can long endure."[9] European liberals were fired by the same vision of the Union cause. The triumph of the Confederacy, wrote John Stuart Mill, "would be a victory of the powers of evil which would give courage to the enemies of progress and damp the spirits of its friends all over the civilized world. [The American war is] destined to be a turning point, for good or evil, of the course of human affairs."[10]

This vision helped to unite the North in 1861. It soon burst forth in song. The most popular song in the Union army was "John Brown's Body," set to the tune of a familiar camp-meeting hymn. First sung by a Massachusetts regiment in the spring of 1861, it spread through all Union armies by year's end. Its sprightly rhythm made it a perfect marching song. It was adaptable to any number of extemporized verses— profane or religious, ribald or sublime. The most popular version spoke of John Brown's body moldering in the grave, of his departure to become a soldier in the army of the Lord, and of hanging Jeff Davis on a sour apple tree. Whatever the verse, the chorus always ended with John Brown's soul marching on.

Julia Ward Howe, whose husband Samuel Gridley Howe had aided the real John Brown, enshrined this song in the national literature. After visiting an army camp near Washington in November 1861, she awoke in the middle of the night with a creative urge to write down the words of "The Battle Hymn of the Republic." Upon publication in the *Atlantic Monthly,* this exalted version of the John Brown song also became popular, though the idea of hanging Jeff Davis on a sour apple tree remained more fashionable in the army. The words of the "Battle Hymn," next to those of the Gettysburg Address, have come down through the years as the noblest expression of what the North was fighting for. Both somehow gave meaning to the power of God's terrible swift sword, which had struck down so many men who had given their last full measure of devotion that freedom might live.

The Slavery Issue

The problem with this lofty rhetoric of dying to make men free was that in 1861 the North was fighting for the restoration of a slaveholding Union. In his July 4 message to Congress, Lincoln reiterated the inaugural pledge that he had "no purpose, directly or indirectly, to interfere with slavery in the States where it exists." Three weeks later, Congress passed almost unanimously the Crittenden-Johnson resolution affirming that the war was being fought not for the purpose "of overthrowing or interfering with the rights or established institutions of those States," but only "to defend and

---

[9]Basler, *Works of Lincoln,* V, 53, VII, 23.

[10]Belle B. Sideman and Lillian Friedman (eds.), *Europe Looks at the Civil War* (New York, 1960), pp. 117–118.

maintain the supremacy of the Constitution and to preserve the Union."[11] Little wonder that, at this stage of war, European liberals began to ask: Since "the North does not proclaim abolition and never pretended to fight for anti-slavery," how "can we be fairly called upon to sympathize so warmly with the Federal cause?"[12]

Most of the congressional Republicans who voted for the Crittenden-Johnson resolution were of course antislavery men. Lincoln also had more than once branded slavery "an unqualified evil to the negro, the white man, and to the State. . . . The monstrous injustice of slavery . . . deprives our republican example of its just influence in the world—enables the enemies of free institutions, with plausibility, to taunt us as hypocrites."[13]

Precisely. So why did Lincoln not respond to this taunt by proclaiming the war to be fought for freedom as well as for union? Because as President of *all* the states, he still considered himself bound by the constitutional guarantee of slavery in the states. The Union government fought the war on the theory that, secession being illegal, the Confederate states were still legally in the Union although temporarily under control of insurrectionists. The need to retain the loyalty of the border slave states was another factor in Lincoln's and Congress's assurances on slavery. Beyond that was the desire for bipartisan support of the war. Nearly half of the voters in the free states had cast anti-Lincoln ballots in the 1861 election. The Northern Democrats were a proslavery party. Any sign of an antislavery war policy in 1861 might divide the North and alienate most Democrats.

The Antislavery Argument

Abolitionists and some Republicans disagreed with this analysis. Several prominent antislavery congressmen abstained or voted against the Crittenden-Johnson resolution. For many abolitionists, freedom for the slaves was a more important value than union. Now that the "convenant of death" had been broken by Southern secession, Garrisonian abolitionists supported the war for the Union because they believed that the "death grapple with the Southern slave oligarchy" must become a death grapple with slavery itself. As the black leader Frederick Douglass put it in May 1861: "The American people and the Government at Washington may refuse to recognize it for a time; but the 'inexorable logic of events' will force it upon them in the end; that the war now being waged in this land is a war for and against slavery."[14]

But since the North was fighting for a Constitution that protected slavery, emancipationists had to find extraconstitutional reasons for a blow against bondage—reasons compelling enough to overcome the inertia of indifference, conservatism, and racism that had for so long sustained Northern toleration of slavery. Abolitionists

---

[11]Basler, *Works of Lincoln*, IV, 263; *Congressional Globe*, 37th Cong., 1st sess. (1861), 222–223.

[12]*Saturday Review*, September 14, 1861, quoted in Ephraim D. Adams, *Great Britain and the American Civil War*, 2 vols. (New York, 1925), I, 181; *Economist* (London), September 1861, quoted in Karl Marx and Friedrich Engels, *The Civil War in the United States*, ed. Richard Enmale (New York, 1937), p. 12.

[13]Basler, *Works of Lincoln*, II, 255, III, 92.

[14]William Lloyd Garrison to Oliver Johnson, April 19, 1861, W. L. Garrison Papers, Boston Public Library; *Douglass' Monthly*, May 1861.

quickly hit upon the "military necessity" argument for emancipation. By insisting that slavery was crucial to the Southern war effort and its abolition necessary for Northern success, they hoped to put their cause on the broadest possible platform—a platform that could appeal to all Unionists whether Republican or Democrat, radical or conservative, egalitarian or racist. Although they themselves wanted emancipation for reasons of justice and morality, they avoided these themes in their early wartime rhetoric. "You will observe that I propose no crusade for abolition," wrote Charles Sumner in November 1861. Emancipation "is to be presented strictly as a measure of military necessity . . . rather than on grounds of philanthropy. . . . Abolition is not to be the object of the war, but simply one of its agencies."[15]

It was easy enough to prove slavery's military value to the Confederacy. The three and a half million slaves in the eleven Confederate states constituted nearly 40 percent of their population and a majority of their labor force. Southern newspapers boasted that slavery was "a tower of strength to the Confederacy" because it enabled the South "to place in the field a force so much larger in proportion to her white population than the North."[16] More than half the workers in Confederate iron, salt, and lead mines were slaves. By 1864, blacks constituted one-third of the labor force at the Tredegar Iron Works in Richmond and three-quarters at the naval works in Selma, two of the Confederacy's main ordnance plants. At least half the nurses in Confederate military hospitals were black. Slaves worked as cooks, servants, teamsters, construction laborers, and even musicians in the Confederate armies. So important were slaves in all these capacities that the military authorities impressed them into service from the beginning of the war, well before the Confederacy began drafting white men into the army. Well might Frederick Douglass exclaim that "the very stomach of this rebellion is the negro in the form of a slave. Arrest that hoe in the hands of the negro, and you smite the rebellion in the very seat of its life."[17]

Abolitionists maintained that emancipation could be accomplished under the "laws of war." With the proclamation of the blockade and the decision to treat Rebel captives as prisoners of war, the conflict had taken on the character of a war rather than a domestic insurrection. Slavery in the Confederate states, insisted abolitionists, no longer enjoyed constitutional protection but came instead under international law. Confiscation of enemy property was a belligerent right recognized by international law. Slaves were enemy property; some of this property was being used in direct aid of the rebellion and was therefore doubly liable to confiscation.

Slave property was unlike any other; it possessed a mind and a will. Many slaves saw the Civil War as a potential war for freedom as soon as the abolitionists did. And they were in a better position than most abolitionists to help make it so. By voting with their feet for freedom—by escaping from their masters to Union military camps in the South—they could force the issue of emancipation on the Lincoln administration. This the slaves did from the beginning of the war, first by twos and threes, eventually by hundreds as Union armies penetrated deeper into the Confederacy. By creating a situation in which Union officials would either have to return them to slavery

---

[15]Edward L. Pierce, *Memoir and Letters of Charles Sumner,* 4 vols. (Boston, 1877–1893), IV, 49.

[16]*Montgomery Advertiser,* November 6, 1861.

[17]*Douglass' Monthly,* July 1861.

or acknowledge their freedom, escaping slaves took the first step toward achieving freedom for themselves and making the conflict a war for freedom as well as for union. They turned the theory of confiscation into a reality.

The first move toward applying this theory came in May 1861 from an unlikely source: General Benjamin Butler, a former Breckinridge Democrat commanding Union troops at Fortress Monroe on the Virginia coast. A shrewd politician, Butler had felt the antislavery wind blowing from his home state of Massachusetts and was ready for the first step in his pilgrimage to the radical wing of the Republican party. When three slaves who had been working on Confederate fortifications escaped to Butler's lines on May 23, he refused to return them to their masters and labeled them "contraband of war." This phrase caught on, and for the rest of the war slaves who came within Union lines were known as contrabands. Word soon got around among slaves on the Virginia peninsula. By August, a thousand contrabands were in Butler's camps, and abolitionists were making plans to establish schools and send missionary teachers to them.

The belligerent right of confiscation was incorporated into a law signed by Lincoln on August 6, 1861, which authorized the seizure of all property, including slaves, used in military aid of the rebellion. This confiscation act applied to only a handful of slaves then within reach of Union forces, and it did not specifically emancipate them. But like Butler's contraband policy, it was the thin edge of the wedge of emancipation. It also marked a departure from the Crittenden-Johnson resolution passed only two weeks earlier. During those two weeks, the meaning of Union defeat at Bull Run had sunk in. The war was not going to be short and easy. The reassessment of war policies produced a harder attitude toward the rebellion. Most Republicans were now willing to consider at least limited steps against slavery as a means of victory if not yet as an end in itself. But Democrats were not. Congress passed the confiscation act by a party-line vote. It was the first real breach in the bipartisan war front.

As the conflict moved toward "hard war" in subsequent months, this breach became wider. The slavery issue dominated the 1861–1862 session of the Union Congress. When the Congress reassembled in December 1861, fifty-three House Republicans who had voted for the Crittenden-Johnson resolution in July changed their votes, and the House thereby refused to reaffirm the resolution. The question of what to do about slavery not only divided Republicans from Democrats but also served increasingly to define the differences among three factions in the Republican party: conservative, moderate, and radical.

Slavery and the Republican Party

All Republicans were in some sense antislavery. But differences of degree did exist. Conservatives hoped for the ultimate demise of bondage, but they were gradualists, believing in voluntary action by the states rather than in coercive federal action, and preferred to link emancipation with the colonization of freed slaves abroad. The radicals were deep-dyed antislavery advocates who wanted to abolish the institution immediately, through the war power of the national government. The moderates were a less easily defined group. They disliked slavery and hoped to see it abolished

NATIONAL ARCHIVES

ARRIVAL OF CONTRABANDS IN UNION LINES

sooner rather than later, but they feared the social consequences of precipitate action. Early in the war they were hard to distinguish from the conservatives, but the imperatives of hard war drove them ever closer to the radicals as the intensity of the conflict increased.

The foremost moderate was Lincoln himself, who said in his first annual message to Congress on December 3, 1861: "In considering the policy to be adopted for suppressing the insurrection, I have been anxious and careful that the inevitable conflict for this purpose shall not degenerate into a violent and remorseless revolutionary struggle."[18] The President's gradualist temperament and his pragmatic conviction that most Northerners, as well as the border-state Unionists, would not tolerate radical action against slavery had lain behind his modification of General Frémont's emancipation order in Missouri in September 1861 (see page 171). For the same reasons, Lincoln took another action in December that angered radicals. Without consulting the President, Secretary of War Cameron had included in his report to Congress a section endorsing the freeing and arming of slaves who came into Union lines. When Lincoln learned of this, he ordered the report recalled and the section deleted. Within weeks Cameron, like Frémont before him, was removed from his post. In both cases, lax administration and corruption in war contracts were the principal reasons for removal. But to radicals it appeared that vigorous antislavery men were being combed out of the government and the army while proslavery generals such as McClellan and Buell were riding high.

---

[18]Basler, *Works of Lincoln*, V, 48–49.

Unlike Lincoln, abolitionists and radical Republicans did believe in a "remorseless and revolutionary" war. An abolitionist editor wanted the Civil War to become "the glorious Second American Revolution" to complete the unfinished business of the first—"a National Abolition of Slavery."[19] In an editorial on January 24, 1862, that must have chilled the hearts of conservatives, the *New York Tribune* compared the crisis of the Union to the crisis of France during the Revolution of 1789. Beset by internal factions and threatened by counterrevolution within and foreign intervention without, the French Republic survived only by exporting the revolution to all Europe. "Like the French leaders of 1793," said the *Tribune*, "we must offer liberty and protection to the oppressed, and war to the oppressors." The most radical of the congressional Republicans, Thaddeus Stevens, was equally outspoken. "Free every slave—slay every traitor—burn every Rebel mansion, if these things be necessary to preserve this temple of freedom," said Stevens. We must "treat this [war] as a radical revolution, and remodel our institutions."[20]

Although the radicals never constituted a majority of Republicans, they were the most aggressive faction in the party. A vigorous, determined minority with a clear vision of what it wants and how to get it always has an advantage, especially in time of crisis. The radicals controlled key committee chairmanships in Congress. In the Senate, Charles Sumner and Henry Wilson of Massachusetts were chairmen respectively of the Committee on Foreign Affairs and the Committee on Military Affairs, John P. Hale of New Hampshire chaired the Naval Affairs Committee, Zachariah Chandler of Michigan headed the Committee on Commerce, and Benjamin Wade of Ohio served as chairman of both the Committee on Territories and the Joint Committee on the Conduct of the War. In the House, the radical Pennsylvanians Galusha Grow and Thaddeus Stevens held the two most important positions—Speaker and chairman of the Ways and Means Committee. Several moderate Republican senators who usually supported radical positions in 1862 also held important committee chairmanships, notably Lyman Trumbull of Illinois (Judiciary Committee) and William Pitt Fessenden of Maine (Finance Committee).

New England was the mother of congressional radicalism. Of the ten most prominent radicals in the House, five (including Stevens and Grow) had been born and raised in New England. In the Senate, eight of the twelve radicals and nine of the thirteen moderates, but only two of the seven conservative Republicans, were natives of New England. The influence of New England in the Senate was extraordinary. Senators from that region held eleven committee chairmanships, and men born in New England chaired five of the eleven remaining committees. Only one New England senator did not hold a committee chairmanship. New England had been the taproot of abolitionism and the cutting edge of modernization in the antebellum era; now the region also played a dominant role in forging the modernizing antislavery legislation of the Civil War.

---

[19] *Principia*, May 4, 1861.

[20] Margaret Shortreed, "The Anti-Slavery Radicals, 1840–1868," *Past and Present*, no. 16 (November 1959), 77.

Congress and Slavery

Congress could not have escaped the question of slavery in the 1861–1862 session even if it had wanted to. The Union navy's conquest of the South Carolina coastal islands had brought 10,000 contrabands within Union lines; hundreds of others were trickling in weekly wherever blueclad troops were encamped in slave territory; the Union advances in Tennessee and Louisiana brought in scores of thousands more. The legal status of these contrabands remained unclear, but some Northern commanders in Virginia and South Carolina were already treating them as free people. On the other hand, Union generals in the border states returned fugitives claimed by loyal masters, and General Halleck in Missouri issued an order excluding contrabands from his lines altogether. Without guidance from Washington, the contraband question in military zones was mired in confusion and contradiction.

Congressional Republicans attacked slavery on several fronts. By mid-January no less than seven different bills dealing with emancipation and confiscation of Rebel property had been reported out of committees. The first action was a new article of war enacted March 13; it prohibited army officers, under pain of court-martial, from returning fugitive slaves to their masters. Next on the agenda, April 16, came the abolition of slavery in the District of Columbia, with an average compensation to owners of $300 per slave. This was followed by legislation to create schools for black children in Washington and to permit blacks to testify in District of Columbia courts. In June, Congress prohibited slavery in all territories and ratified a new treaty with Britain for more effective suppression of the Atlantic slave trade.

Important as these acts were, they only nibbled at the edges of slavery. More far-reaching was a bill for the confiscation of Confederate-owned property. This was a hard-war measure based on the "laws of war" and the constitutional power of Congress to punish treason (Article III, Section 3). As finally enacted on July 17, this second confiscation act authorized the seizure of the property of persons in rebellion against the United States and specified that all of their slaves who came within Union lines "shall be deemed captives of war and shall be forever free."[21]

This measure went far beyond the first confiscation act of the previous August. It altered the character and purpose of the war. Yet in practical terms both its immediate and long-term effects were marginal. Confiscation and emancipation under the law would depend on legal proceedings to determine whether owners had been engaged in rebellion. And because Lincoln believed that the question of wartime emancipation must be handled by the president as commander-in-chief, he took little action under the second confiscation act as such. The emancipation provisions of the act were soon overshadowed by the President's own executive acts against slavery.

Lincoln and Slavery

For several months in the spring and summer of 1862, however, it appeared that Lincoln intended to do nothing against slavery. In May, General David Hunter, commander of Union forces occupying islands and enclaves along the south Atlantic

---

[21]McPherson, *Political History,* pp. 196–198.

coast, issued an order emancipating all slaves in the "Department of the South," theoretically including all of South Carolina, Georgia, and Florida. Lincoln revoked the order, stating that he reserved to himself the authority to make such a momentous decision. Abolitionists and radicals condemned the President. "Stumbling," "halting," "prevaricating," "irresolute," "weak," "besotted," were some of the adjectives they applied to Lincoln. "He has evidently not a drop of anti-slavery blood in his veins," wrote William Lloyd Garrison. "A curse on that [border-state] 'loyalty' which is retained only by allowing it to control the policy of the Administration!"[22]

Garrison was wrong. By the spring of 1862, Lincoln had become convinced that the war must end slavery. But he still wished to achieve emancipation gradually, with the least possible amount of revolutionary disruption. This helps to explain his proposal in 1862 for voluntary border-state emancipation. On March 6, the President sent a special message to Congress recommending the passage of a joint resolution offering financial aid to any state "which may adopt gradual abolishment of slavery." Congress passed the resolution, with Republicans unanimously in favor and Democrats 85 percent opposed. But border-state spokesmen complained of federal coercion, bickered about the amount of compensation and about Congress's constitutional right to appropriate funds for this purpose, and expressed fears of race war and economic ruin even if emancipation took place gradually over a thirty-year period as Lincoln had suggested. Disappointed, the President again appealed to the border states in May 1862. If they adopted his plan, said Lincoln, the changes produced by emancipation "would come gently as the dews of heaven, not rending or wrecking anything." But if they did nothing, the radicals would preempt the ground. "You cannot," admonished the President, "be blind to the signs of the times."[23]

But the border-state representatives remained blind to the signs, despite the increasing momentum of emancipation sentiment in the North. "The great phenomenon of the year," observed a conservative Boston newspaper in the summer of 1862, "is the great intensity which this [emancipation] resolution has acquired. A year ago men might have faltered at the thought of proceeding to this extremity in any event. The majority do not now seek it, but, we say advisedly, they are in great measure prepared for it." On July 12, Lincoln once more brought border-state representatives to the White House. This time his plea for cooperation was backed by a blunt warning: "The incidents of the war can not be avoided. If the war continue long . . . the institution in your states will be extinguished by mere friction and abrasion . . . and you will have nothing valuable in lieu of it." In revoking General Hunter's emancipation edict "I gave dissatisfaction, if not offense, to many whose support the country cannot afford to lose. And this is not the end of it. The pressure, in this direction is still upon me, and is increasing. By conceding what I ask, you can relieve me." Lincoln's plea again fell on deaf ears. By a vote of 20 to 9, the border-state representatives rejected his plan.[24]

---

[22] *Liberator,* December 6, 1861, July 25, 1862.

[23] Basler, *Works of Lincoln,* V, 222–223.

[24] *Boston Advertiser,* August 20, 1862; Basler, *Works of Lincoln,* V, 317–319; Allan Nevins, *The War for the Union: War Becomes Revolution* (New York, 1960), pp. 148–149.

That evening Lincoln made up his mind to issue an emancipation proclamation that he had begun drafting several days earlier, after McClellan had been driven back from Richmond in the Seven Days battles. The President had come to the conclusion stated a year earlier by Frederick Douglass that "to fight against slaveholders, without fighting against slavery, is but a half-hearted business, and paralyzes the hands engaged in it." On July 13, Lincoln privately told Seward and Welles of his decision. On July 22, he convened the cabinet to inform his ministers officially. Montgomery Blair, the Postmaster General, opposed the issuance of a proclamation, for he feared that it might throw the fall elections to the Democrats. All other cabinet members endorsed it with varying degrees of enthusiasm. But Seward pointed out that because of the "depression of the public mind, consequent upon our [military] reverses," the proclamation "may be viewed as the last measure of an exhausted Government, a cry for help." He suggested that Lincoln "postpone its issue until you can give it to the country supported by military success."[25]

Lincoln accepted Seward's shrewd advice. But the wait turned out to be two long, agonizing months during which Northern morale dropped to its lowest point thus far, public opinion became further polarized on the issue of slavery, and the army in Virginia suffered its second ignominious defeat at Bull Run.

The Copperheads

The war placed Northern Democrats in a difficult position. The party gradually divided into "war" and "peace" wings. The War Democrats generally supported whatever military measures seemed necessary to defeat the Confederacy. Some War Democrats became Republicans, and a few—such as General Benjamin Butler and Secretary of War Edwin M. Stanton—eventually moved all the way to the radical wing of the party. The Peace Democrats initially supported the preservation of the Union by military force. But as the conflict moved toward total war, they began to denounce the Republicans' determination to destroy and remake the South in the Northern free-labor mold. Opposition to Republican war policies sometimes became opposition to a continuation of the war itself. This was not necessarily a pro-Confederate position, despite Republican efforts to portray it as such. Peace Democrats urged restoration of the Union through negotiation and compromise, but at times the more hot-headed among them spoke or acted in such a way as to give substance to Republican charges of disloyalty. The relative strength of the two Democratic factions fluctuated with Northern fortunes in the war. On many vital issues, however, such as emancipation and military arrests, both factions united in opposition to the administration.

As Northern morale plummeted during the summer of 1862, the hopes of the Peace Democrats, or Copperheads, rose correspondingly. Like so many political labels, "Copperhead" was a term of reproach invented by opponents. In the fall of

---

[25]*Douglass' Monthly,* September 1861; Gideon Welles, *The Diary of Gideon Welles,* ed. Howard K. Beale, 3 vols. (New York, 1960), I, 70–71; Francis B. Carpenter, *Six Months at the White House with Abraham Lincoln* (New York, 1866), p. 22.

1861, some Republican newspapers in Ohio likened antiwar Democrats to the poisonous copperhead snake. The term soon caught on and was often applied indiscriminately to all Democrats; but it is used here interchangeably with Peace Democrats only. Although the Copperheads drew support from every socioeconomic group in the North, their greatest strength was concentrated among the Butternuts of the southern Midwest and the immigrant Catholics of the cities. Both of these groups disliked blacks, abolitionists, temperance reformers, New England Yankees, and the modernizing changes that were upsetting the traditional bases of their culture. As the war took on the dimensions of a Republican antislavery crusade, the Butternuts and ethnic Catholics became increasingly antiwar.

Economic issues continued during the war to exacerbate the anti-New England sentiments of the southern Midwest. The region's representatives in Congress voted solidly against the national bank acts, income tax and tariff legislation, and other wartime financial measures. They revived Jacksonian rhetoric to denounce "this monstrous Bank Bill" and "the money monopoly of New England." "The design is to destroy the fixed institutions of the States, and to build up a central moneyed despotism," said one Midwestern Democrat in 1863; another asked: "Shall we sink down as serfs to the heartless, speculative Yankee for all time to come—swindled by his tariffs, robbed by his taxes, skinned by his railroad monopolies?"[26]

Ethnocultural hostilities reinforced these anti-New England economic attitudes. It was the "Constitution-breaking, law-defying, negro-loving Pharaseeism of New England" that had driven the South to secession, said Congressman Samuel S. Cox of Ohio in 1863. The Yankee "tendency to make government a moral reform association . . . is the special curse of the nation at the present time." Much of the Roman Catholic press joined this attack on the "New England Negrophiles" and "canting Abolition Puritans [who] brought on this war."[27]

There was even talk in the southern Midwest of organizing the region into a "Northwest Confederacy" to make peace with the South and to reconstruct the old Union with New England left out. Although in hindsight such a project appears fantastic, it was seriously proposed during the war. "The erection of the States watered by the Mississippi and its tributaries into an independent Republic," said Cox, "is the talk of every other western man."[28] Confederate agents worked quietly to encourage antiwar sentiment in the Midwest. The Knights of the Golden Circle (the secret society formed in the 1850s to promote Southern expansion into the Caribbean) organized chapters in the Midwest to promote the Northwest Confederacy. Although Republicans exaggerated the extent of such activity in their attempt to stigmatize the Democrats as disloyal, the existence of the Knights of the Golden Circle and similar societies was not a myth.

---

[26]Frank L. Klement, "Economic Aspects of Middle Western Copperheadism,"*Historian,* 14 (Autumn 1951), 39–40; Wood Gray, *The Hidden Civil War: The Story of the Copperheads* (New York, 1964; first printed 1942), p. 125.

[27]Samuel S. Cox, "Puritanism in Politics," in Samuel S. Cox, *Eight Years in Congress* (New York, 1865), pp. 283, 290; Cuthbert E. Allen, "The Slavery Question in Catholic Newspapers, 1850–1865," U.S. Catholic Historical Society, *Historical Records and Studies,* 26 (1936), 145, 160.

[28]Cox, "Puritanism in Politics," p. 283.

The radical changes set into motion by Republican war policies threatened Copperhead values and traditions. This was why Peace Democrats adopted the slogan "The Constitution as it is and the Union as it was." Continuation of the war, they said, would produce "terrible social change and revolution." The "most radical, revolutionary, and disorganizing doctrines" were "brought into vogue by the war; doctrines which sweep away the whole fabric of our institutions." The foremost Copperhead was Congressman Clement L. Vallandigham of Ohio, descendant of a Virginia family and married to the daughter of a Maryland planter. Vallandigham knew what kind of Union he wanted restored. "It is the desire of my heart," he wrote, "to restore the Union, the Federal Union as it was forty years ago." But if this Republican war continued, he said in January 1863, "I see nothing before us but universal political and social revolution, anarchy and bloodshed, compared with which the Reign of Terror in France was a merciful visitation."[29]

Democrats and Emancipation

Opposition to emancipation became the chief rallying cry not only of Copperheads but of nearly all Democrats. "We mean that the United States . . . shall be the white man's home . . . and the nigger shall never be his equal," said a Democratic senator in a typical statement. A wealthy and powerful New York Democrat declared that "the verdict of impartial history will surely put Jeff Davis, bad as he is, far above the abolition herd who have brought this revolution upon us." And Archbishop John Hughes of New York announced that Catholics "are willing to fight to the death for the support of the constitution, the government, and the laws of the country. But if . . . they are to fight for the abolition of slavery, then, indeed, they will turn away in disgust from the discharge of what would otherwise be a patriotic duty."[30] Rarely in American history has an issue so sharply polarized political parties as emancipation polarized them in 1862. This can be demonstrated by an analysis of congressional votes on four antislavery measures in 1862: the article of war forbidding the return of fugitives, emancipation in the District of Columbia, prohibition of slavery in the territories, and the second confiscation act. Senate and House Republican votes on these bills were 99 percent aye, while Democratic votes were 96 percent nay. Given the persistence of anti-abolition and antiblack sentiments among the constituents of many Republican congressmen, this virtually unanimous support of emancipation measures testified to the power of ideology and the pressures of war to overcome "politics as usual." But it also promised trouble for Republicans at the polls in the fall of 1862, as Montgomery Blair had warned (see page 295).

Racial fears motivated the anti-abolition sentiments of many Northern whites. The Democratic press exploited these fears. It dwelt on the theme that emancipation would turn loose a flood of freed blacks into the North. "The hundreds of thousands,

[29]Joel H. Silbey, *A Respectable Minority: The Democratic Party in the Civil War Era, 1860–1868* (New York, 1977), p. 101; Frank L. Klement, *The Limits of Dissent: Clement L. Vallandigham and the Civil War* (Lexington, Ky., 1970), p. 79.

[30]*Congressional Globe*, 37th Cong., 2nd sess. (1862), 1923; Samuel L. M. Barlow to Henry D. Bacon, January 23, 1862, Barlow Papers, Henry E. Huntington Library; Benjamin J. Blied, *Catholics and the Civil War* (Milwaukee, 1945), pp. 44–45.

if not millions of slaves [the confiscation act] will emancipate will come North and West," proclaimed the *Cincinnati Enquirer,* "and will either be competitors with our white mechanics and laborers, degrading them by the competition, or they will have to be supported as paupers and criminals at the public expense." Other editors warned of the "two or three million semi-savages" who would come north to mix with "the sons and daughters" of white workingmen. A New York Democratic newspaper ran frequent stories and editorials under such headlines as "White Supremacy or Negro Amalgamation?" "Can Niggers Conquer Americans?" "Shall the Working Classes Be Equalized with Negroes?" A German-language newspaper in Milwaukee issued a call to action: "Workingmen! Be Careful! Organize yourselves against this element which threatens your impoverishment and annihilation."[31]

With such advice from their leaders, it was little wonder that in 1862 white laborers erupted into mob violence against blacks in a half-dozen cities across the North. Most of the rioters were Irish-Americans, who attacked black employees or strikebreakers in such occupations as stevedore and deckhand. The mobs sometimes surged into black neighborhoods and assaulted people on the streets and in their homes. In southern Illinois, Butternut farmers and farmhands attacked contrabands who had been brought in from Tennessee to help with the harvest.

Fears of emancipation were not confined to Butternuts and Irish. Republicans ruefully admitted that large parts of the North were infected with racism. "Our people hate the Negro with a perfect if not a supreme hatred," said Congressman George Julian of Indiana. Senator Lyman Trumbull of Illinois conceded that "there is a very great aversion in the West—I know it to be so in my State—against having free negroes come among us. Our people want nothing to do with the negro."[32] The same could be said of many soldiers who would be required to fight to free the slaves, if the Republican antislavery policy was to succeed.

✑ The Union Army and Emancipation

The racial sentiments of Northern soldiers reflected the society from which they came. Although some men had joined the army to fight against slavery, the overwhelming majority had enlisted to fight for flag and country, and many of them strongly resisted the idea that they should risk their lives to free the slaves. Typical of soldiers' attitudes in 1861–1862 was the private who wrote: "I came out to fight for the restoration of the Union and to keep slavery [from] going into the territories & not to free the niggers." Some Northern soldiers made no bones about their racism. "I think the best way to settle the question of what to do with the darkies," wrote a New Yorker in 1861, "would be to shoot them."[33]

---

[31]V. Jacque Voegeli, *Free but Not Equal: The Midwest and the Negro During the Civil War* (Chicago, 1967), p. 6; Forrest G. Wood, *Black Scare: The Racist Response to Emancipation and Reconstruction* (Berkeley, 1968), p. 35; Frank L. Klement, *The Copperheads in the Middle West* (Chicago, 1960), p. 14.

[32]Voegeli, *Free but Not Equal,* pp. 1, 18.

[33]Bell I. Wiley, *The Life of Billy Yank* (Indianapolis, 1952), pp. 42, 109.

As time went on, however, the demands of a war in which white Southerners were enemies and black Southerners were potential allies converted most Yankee soldiers to a belief in emancipation—if not as an act of justice, at least as a necessity of war. A Minnesota soldier wrote in March 1863:

I have never been in favor of the abolition of slavery until since this war has detirmend me in the conviction that it is a greater sin than our Government is able to stand—and now I go in for a war of emancipation. . . . I am satesfied that slavery is . . . an institution that belonged to the dark ages—and that it ill becomes a nation of our standing to perpetuate the barbarous practice. It is opposed to the Spirit of the age—and in my opinion this Rebelion is but the death strugle of the overgrown monster.[34]

Contrabands welcomed Yankee soldiers as liberators, gave them food, showed them where valuables were hidden at abandoned plantations, served as guides and scouts and spies for the invading forces. Slaves often sheltered escaped Union prisoners of war and helped them on their way back to Northern lines. This friendliness was bound to affect the attitudes of Northern soldiers, some of whom repaid it by teaching contrabands to read and write or by helping them in other ways. An antislavery company of Ohio soldiers took up a collection to send a promising contraband to Oberlin College. Other freed slaves received similar help to go north.

Most of the positive references to blacks in soldiers' letters date from the second half of the war, and the majority were written by men from New England and other antislavery areas of the upper North. Social class also made a difference in racial attitudes: officers and men with a fair amount of education were more likely to be antislavery than privates and men with less schooling. Among the latter, especially in the first two years of war, crude racism was the rule. These soldiers often treated with cruel callousness the slaves who naively welcomed them as liberators. A trooper stationed in South Carolina wrote in November 1861: "About 8–10 soldiers from the New York 47th Regiment chased some Negro women but they escaped, so they took a Negro girl about 7–9 years old, and raped her." A Connecticut soldier wrote from Virginia that some of his messmates had grabbed "two nigger wenches . . . turned them upon their heads, & put tobacco, chips, sticks, lighted cigars & sand into their behinds."[35] But about the same time a Massachusetts private wrote from Maryland that "the whole Reg[imen]t seem to have become completely abolitionized." And while the Emancipation Proclamation, when it finally came, sharply divided Northern soldiers for a time, many agreed with a private from upstate New York who exulted that "the contest is now between Slavery & freedom, & every honest man knows what he is fighting for."[36]

---

[34]Ibid., p. 44.

[35]Ibid., p. 114.

[36]James Glazier to parents, December 8, 1861, James Glazier Papers, Henry E. Huntington Library; Constant Hanks to his mother, April 20, 1863, Hanks Papers, Perkins Library, Duke University. For an analysis of the attitudes of Union soldiers toward emancipation, see James M. McPherson, *For Cause and Comrades: Why Men Fought in the Civil War* (New York, 1997), pp. 117–130.

Colonization of Freed Slaves

In sum, although the Yankee army eventually became an army of liberation, some of its members were at best reluctant liberators. An Illinois soldier who approved of emancipation nevertheless declared in October 1862 that "I am not in favor of freeing the negroes and leaving them to run free and mingle among us nether is Sutch the intention of Old Abe but we will Send them off and colonize them."[37] Such indeed was Lincoln's expressed intention at that time. The President invited five Washington black leaders to the White House on August 14, 1862, and urged them to consider the idea of emigration. Slavery was "the greatest wrong inflicted on any people," Lincoln told them. But even if the institution were abolished, racial differences and prejudices would remain. "Your race suffer very greatly, many of them, by living among us, while ours suffer by your presence." Black people had little chance for equality in the United States. More than that, "there is an unwillingness on the part of our people, harsh as it may be, for you free colored people to remain with us. . . . I do not mean to discuss this, but to propose it as a fact with which we have to deal. I cannot alter it if I would. . . . It is better for us both, therefore, to be separated." Lincoln implored his listeners to recruit several hundred fellow blacks for a pilot colonization project to demonstrate the feasibility of this "solution" of the race problem.[38]

Northern blacks and abolitionists predictably condemned the President's proposal. For thirty years they had been fighting colonization and they were not about to stop now, on the eve of victory for their cause. The wealthy Philadelphia black abolitionist Robert Purvis bluntly addressed Lincoln in print: "It is in vain you talk to me of 'two races' and their 'mutual antagonism.' In the matter of rights, there is but one race, and that is the *human race*. . . . Sir, this is our country as much as it is yours, and we will not leave it." Most radical Republicans expressed the same viewpoint, at least in private. Chase complained in his diary of the racism inherent in Lincoln's proposal. "How much better would be a manly protest against prejudice against color!—and a wise effort to give freemen homes in America."[39]

But this was still a minority opinion in the North. From Thomas Jefferson to Abraham Lincoln, America's foremost statesmen had come to a similar conclusion: emancipation could work only if the freed slaves were colonized abroad. Otherwise, the South would endure the horrors of race war and the freed people would either suffer extermination or degenerate into a vicious class of welfare clients. The actual prospect of emancipation in 1862 intensified these concerns. Abolitionists "may prattle as they wish about the end of slavery being the end of strife," warned a Boston conservative, but "the great difficulty will then but begin! The question is the profound and awful one of race."[40]

---

[37]Wiley, *The Life of Billy Yank*, p. 112.

[38]Basler, *Works of Lincoln*, V, 370–375.

[39]Purvis in *New York Tribune*, September 20, 1862; David Donald (ed.), *Inside Lincoln's Cabinet: The Civil War Diaries of Salmon P. Chase* (New York, 1954), p. 112.

[40]*Boston Post*, quoted in *Boston Commonwealth*, October 18, 1862.

Whatever its substantive merits, colonization was good politics. Having made up his mind to issue an emancipation proclamation, Lincoln thought it best to sugarcoat this strong pill with colonization. Even some radicals accepted this reasoning. "I believe practically [colonization] is a damn humbug," said one, "but it will take with the people."[41] Congress appropriated $600,000 in 1862 to finance the voluntary colonization of freed slaves. Radical Republicans initially opposed this, but half of them eventually changed their minds when it became clear that the appropriation was necessary to ensure passage of the confiscation act of 1862.

In the end, colonization did turn out to be a humbug. Lincoln managed to recruit 450 blacks for settlement on an island off the coast of Haiti. But the colony suffered from smallpox and from the malfeasance of the white promoter who had contracted with the government to manage the venture. The administration admitted its mistake in 1864 and sent a naval vessel to bring back the 368 survivors. By then the momentum of war had carried Northern opinion beyond the conservatism of 1862, and no more was heard of colonization. An abolitionist pronounced a fitting epitaph upon this sorry episode: "Thus does the boasted wisdom of 'Conservatism' turn out to be folly, while the 'fanaticism' of the 'crazy Radicals' is proved by experience to be the highest wisdom."[42]

Lincoln's Circumlocution on Emancipation, August–September 1862

A strategy of caution and indirection governed Lincoln's public statements during the ten weeks between his decision to issue an emancipation proclamation and the date he actually did so. During this interval of plunging Northern morale, radicals attacked Lincoln from the left for his retention of McClellan in command and his refusal to proclaim emancipation, while Democrats sniped at the President from the right and hoped for victory in the fall elections. Through it all Lincoln remained outwardly calm and noncommittal. He refused to disclose the emancipation proclamation prematurely, lest it drive conservatives and War Democrats into the arms of the Copperheads. At the same time, he threw out hints of what was coming, lest the radicals desert him completely. Never was Lincoln's sense of timing better demonstrated than in these difficult late summer days of 1862.

An example of Lincoln's strategy was his reply on August 22 to Horace Greeley's open letter in the *New York Tribune* entitled "The Prayer of Twenty Millions." Greeley complained that the "Union cause has suffered from a mistaken deference to Rebel Slavery." He implored Lincoln to turn the war into a crusade for freedom. In an unusual public response, the President carefully explained: "My paramount object in this struggle *is* to save the Union, and is *not* either to save or to destroy slavery. If I could save the Union without freeing *any* slave I would do it, and if I could save it by freeing *all* the slaves I would do it; and if I could save it by freeing some and leaving others alone,

---

[41]Voegeli, *Free but Not Equal,* p. 45.
[42]*National Anti-Slavery Standard,* March 19, 1864.

I would also do that." In closing, Lincoln stated that this represented his "view of *official* duty; and I intend no modification of my oft-expressed personal wish that all men everywhere could be free."[43] Here was something for both conservatives and radicals: an assertion that union, not emancipation, was the Northern war aim; but also a hint that emancipation might become necessary to save the Union.

Lincoln similarly balanced the pros and cons of emancipation in his September 13 reply to a group of Chicago clergymen who had borne to Washington a petition for freedom. The President agreed that "slavery is the root of the rebellion, or at least its *sine qua non*." He also agreed that "emancipation would help us in Europe, and convince them that we are incited by something more than ambition. . . . And then unquestionably it would weaken the rebels by drawing off their laborers, which is of great importance." On the other hand, with Confederate armies on the offensive and Union armies reeling, "what *good* would a proclamation of emancipation from me do? . . . I do not want to issue a document that the whole world will necessarily see must be inoperative, like the Pope's bull against the comet! Would *my* word free the slaves, when I cannot even enforce the Constitution in the rebel states?"[44]

Here again was something for both sides. Lincoln's statements could be read as indicating that he believed an emancipation edict useless. But with his actual proclamation tucked away in a desk drawer as he spoke, what the President really meant was that a proclamation would be useless until Union arms won a big victory. Then, perhaps, he could enforce emancipation *and* the Constitution in the South. For as Lincoln met with the Chicago delegation, his mind was preoccupied with the fateful military drama unfolding in Maryland.

---

[43]Basler, *Works of Lincoln,* V, 388–389.
[44]Ibid., V, 419–425.

Chapter Seventeen

The First Turning Point: Antietam and Emancipation

The character of the war has very much changed within the last year. There is now no possible hope of reconciliation with the rebels. . . . We must conquer the rebels or be conquered by them. . . . Every slave withdrawn from the enemy is the equivalent of a white man put hors de combat.

—Union General-in-Chief Henry W. Halleck,
March 31, 1863

 The Battle of Antietam

Under ordinary circumstances, Lee's victorious but exhausted army should have gone into camp for rest and refitting after Second Bull Run. Food was low, thousands of men were shoeless, and the Union forces in his front were nearly twice as large as his own. But Lee had beaten the odds before by taking great risks; he now proposed to take a greater one in a bold campaign to win Maryland for the Confederacy, earn diplomatic recognition from Britain and France, and perhaps even force the Union to sue for peace. An invasion of the North would also take the armies out of war-ravaged Virginia during the fall harvest and enable the hungry Rebel soldiers to live off the enemy's country for a time.

Screened by Stuart's cavalry, the Army of Northern Virginia on September 4, 1862, began splashing across the Potomac forty miles upriver from Washington. But already thousands of men were falling behind because they lacked shoes or because they were sick from eating green corn and green apples. Many others would drop out from exhaustion or bloody feet before the showdown battle. The Confederates concentrated at Frederick on September 7. Disappointingly few Marylanders flocked to the Rebel standard, for western Maryland was Unionist in sentiment. Lee hoped to move west of South Mountain (an extension of the Blue Ridge into Maryland) to open a supply line into the Shenandoah Valley. Before he could do so, however, he needed to eliminate the 10,000-man Union garrison at Harpers Ferry. On September 9, he ordered Jackson's corps and portions of Longstreet's to converge on Harpers Ferry and capture it. After accomplishing this, they were to rejoin the rest of the army for a planned move to cut the Pennsylvania Railroad at Harrisburg. Once again—for the third time in three campaigns—Lee divided his army, contrary to the maxims of military textbooks. It had worked before because Lee's appraisals of his opponent's defects had been accurate. Counting on McClellan's slowness, he expected to reunite the army before the Federals caught up with him.

Meanwhile, McClellan had whipped the Army of the Potomac back into shape and was moving northward with 80,000 men to locate the Rebels, whose numbers he estimated at 120,000 (two and a half times their actual strength). On September 13, McClellan had a stroke of luck such as few generals have ever had. In an abandoned Confederate encampment near Frederick, a Union corporal found a copy of Lee's orders wrapped around three cigars, lost by a careless Southern officer. The orders gave McClellan a picture of the whereabouts of Lee's army, divided into five parts: three separate columns converging on Harpers Ferry; two divisions at Hagerstown; and another division at Boonsboro, near Turner's Gap, where the National Road crossed South Mountain. Each of the five parts was at least eight or ten miles from any of the others; the two most widely separated parts were thirty miles from each other with the Potomac between them; McClellan with most of his army was only twelve miles from the nearest Confederate unit. As historian Bruce Catton has written, "no Civil War general was ever given so fair a chance to destroy the opposing army one piece at a time." McClellan was jubilant. To one of his generals, he said, "Here is a paper with which if I cannot whip 'Bobbie Lee,' I will be willing to go home."[1]

But instead of marching immediately to force the gaps through South Mountain and attack Lee's scattered divisions, McClellan moved with his usual caution and deliberation. After all, those wily Rebels still outnumbered him—in his mind. Eighteen hours passed before McClellan got his troops on the road. By the time two of his corps reached Turner's Gap and another arrived at Crampton's Gap five miles to the south, Lee had been warned and had rushed troops to defend the passes. Union General William B. Franklin's 6th Corps pushed through Crampton's Gap on the afternoon of September 14 and rolled southward toward Maryland Heights overlooking Harpers Ferry, but then stopped timidly when some of the Confederate

---

[1]Bruce Catton, *Terrible Swift Sword* (Garden City, N.Y., 1963), p. 449; Stephen W. Sears, *Landscape Turned Red: The Battle of Antietam* (New Haven, 1983), p. 115.

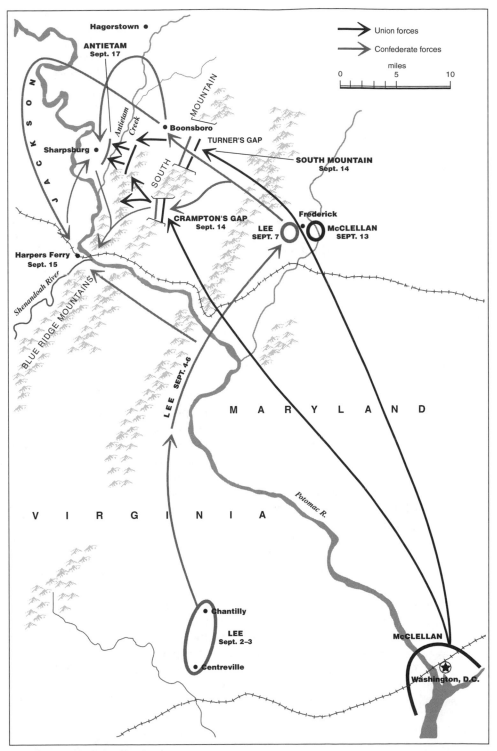

Lee's Invasion of Maryland, 1862

brigades besieging the Ferry turned to meet them. Meanwhile, after a fierce day-long battle at Turner's Gap, in which the outnumbered Confederate suffered 2,700 casualties to the Union's 1,800, Lee withdrew toward the village of Sharpsburg. His invasion plans were wrecked, but McClellan's slowness had given him an extra day to extricate his scattered army from destruction. Lee prepared orders for a retreat to Virginia. But when he learned that Jackson's troops had captured Harpers Ferry and its garrison on the morning of September 15, he changed his mind and ordered the army to concentrate and accept battle at Sharpsburg.

The ensuing battle of Antietam (or Sharpsburg, as the South called it) was a story of desperate defense by the Confederates and missed opportunities by the Federals. Lee's troops occupied the low ridge just east of the village running north and south four miles, with his left flank on the Potomac and his right on Antietam Creek. For some reason (perhaps because they lacked spades and axes), the Confederates did not entrench, a neglect that would be unthinkable a year later. Because of straggling and because of his losses at South Mountain, Lee had fewer than 40,000 men to face McClellan's 75,000. And on the afternoon of September 15, before Jackson could join him from Harpers Ferry, Lee had only 19,000 troops at Sharpsburg. But again McClellan moved cautiously, and the chance for an attack with overwhelming numbers on the 15th slipped away. Next morning Jackson's divisions started arriving from Harpers Ferry, but still the Federals did not attack, despite having more than 60,000 men on the ground to Lee's 30,000. The hours ticked away while McClellan matured plans for an attack on the morrow, by which time all of McClellan's troops and all but A. P. Hill's division of Lee's army (which had stayed at Harpers Ferry to supervise the surrender) would be in line.

The Union 1st and 12th corps under Joseph Hooker and Joseph Mansfield crossed the Antietam on the afternoon of September 16 and prepared to assault next day the Confederate left, held by Jackson. The 9th Corps under Burnside was to force its way across the creek on the Confederate right. The other three Union corps would be held in reserve to reinforce these attacks and to smash through the Confederate center when and if Lee weakened it to reinforce both wings.

It was a good battle plan. Hooker got it off to a good start with a furious attack at dawn in which he lived up to his sobriquet of Fighting Joe. His 12,000 men swept forward from a grove known ever after as the North Woods. Artillery and musketry blasted a forty-acre cornfield in which Confederate infantry were waiting. "In the time I am writing," Hooker later reported, "every stalk of corn in the northern and greater part of the field was cut as closely as with a knife, and the slain lay in rows precisely as they had stood in their ranks a few minutes before. It was never my fortune to witness a more bloody, dismal battlefield."[2] Many other participants who later wrote of this battle agreed that the fighting was the most intense of their experience. A half-savage "fighting madness" took possession of men and drove them to acts of courage or desperation beyond human ken. The blue brigades surged through the cornfield and up to the edge of the West Woods near a small whitewashed church of the pacifist Dunkard sect. There John B. Hood's gray division finally stopped the Federals and drove them back across the cornfield. Soon afterward, fresh Union troops from Mansfield's corps charged

---

[2]*O.R.*, Ser. 1, Vol. 19, p. 218.

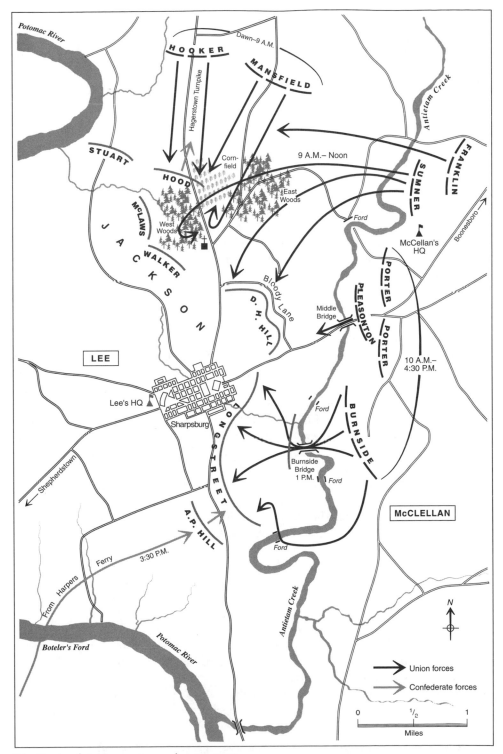

The Battle of Antietam, September 17, 1862

from the East Woods through the cornfield and pushed the broken Confederate lines into and through the West Woods. But once more the Union attack ran out of steam as men went down by the hundreds. Mansfield was killed and Hooker wounded, and most of their shattered divisions pulled back to reorganize after three hours of unmitigated hell. In midmorning Union General Edwin Sumner led his 2nd Corps forward against the West Woods. His lead division had penetrated the position deeply when suddenly two Confederate divisions appeared on its flank and poured a deadly fire into the Yankee brigades, cutting down 2,200 men in twenty minutes. Then a counterattack by Jackson across the cornfield was beaten back with staggering losses. The cornfield had become a no-man's land. It was so full of bodies that, in one soldier's recollection, a man could have walked through it without stepping on the ground.

Before noon the battle on the Confederate left was over. Each side had fought the other to exhaustion. Thirteen thousand men lay dead or wounded. The Union attacks had failed because they were delivered seriatim instead of simultaneously. The Confederates had had time to shift troops and to bring up reserves to meet the assaults. McClellan must bear part of the blame for this. His battle dispositions had prevented Mansfield from going in together with Hooker, while he personally had delayed Sumner's attack for more than an hour.

McClellan was also responsible for the failure to exploit a Union breakthrough in the center. Two divisions of Sumner's corps had veered left from the assault in the West Woods and had bumped into a Confederate line at a sunken farm road, known thereafter as Bloody Lane. There for three hours the Rebels had hung on desperately in their ready-made trench until a misunderstood order allowed two Union regiments to enfilade the road and drive out those defenders not already lying dead or wounded in its tracks. The Confederate center was wide open. "There was no body of Confederate infantry in this part of the field that could have resisted a serious advance," wrote a Southern general. "When Rodes' brigade left the sunken road," added one of Longstreet's artillery officers, "Lee's army was ruined, and the end of the Confederacy was in sight."[3] Franklin was on hand with 8,000 fresh troops of his 6th Corps to exploit the breakthrough. He begged McClellan to unleash him, but the commanding general, shaken by the morning's carnage and fearing a counterattack by an army that he still believed outnumbered him, refused with the words that "it would not be prudent to make the attack."[4] Somewhat later, another Union general urged McClellan to send one division of Franklin's corps and the two uncommitted divisions of Porter's 5th Corps through the weakened Confederate center, but again McClellan refused.

Meanwhile, what of Burnside on the Union left? Throughout the morning McClellan had repeatedly ordered him to push his strong 9th Corps across the Antietam and roll up the Confederate right. But this was easier said than done, for the one bridge over the creek in that sector was well covered by Confederate artillery and riflemen. Nevertheless, Burnside could have done better than he did. The Antietam at that season was fordable in several places, yet Burnside had focused his attention on the bridge. In the early afternoon, some of his brigades finally found fords; at about the same time, other troops forced a crossing over the bridge. But then Burnside delayed to deploy his divisions and did not begin to push forward against the weakened Confederate right

---

[3]Frederick Tilbert, *Antietam* (National Park Service, Washington, D.C., 1961), pp. 36, 39.
[4]*O.R.,* Ser. 1, Vol. 19, p. 377.

CONFEDERATE DEAD AS THEY FELL NEAR THE WEST WOODS IN THE BATTLE OF ANTIETAM.   These pictures reveal the horrors of war in a way that words cannot convey. These and many other photographs of the Antietam battlefield were taken, two days after the battle, by Alexander Gardner and James Gibson, who worked for the famous photographer Mathew Brady. A month later, the photographs went on exhibit at Brady's studio in New York City, where thousands of people viewed these scenes of carnage. This was the first time in American history that the public could vicariously witness the devastation and suffering of war.

until 3 P.M. For a time this blue advance swept all before it, reaching the outskirts of Sharpsburg itself, only half a mile from Lee's line of retreat to the Potomac fords. Again all seemed lost for the Confederates when suddenly, double-timing onto the field with a rebel yell, came A. P. Hill's division, which had marched seventeen miles in seven hours from Harpers Ferry. Some of Hill's veterans wore captured blue uniforms, which increased the surprise when they smashed the Federal flank and stopped the last Union advance of the day.

Night fell on a battlefield whose horrors defied description: 2,100 Yankees and nearly 2,000 Rebels were dead, and another 18,000 (split almost evenly between the two armies) were wounded, 2,500 of them mortally. It was the bloodiest single day of the war.[5] Whole units on both sides were virtually wiped out; regimental and even brigade losses of 50 percent were common. A British military observer who visited

---

[5]By way of comparison: on D-Day in World War II, American forces suffered 6,000 casualties— about one-fourth the number of casualties at Antietam. More Americans were killed or mortally wounded in combat in a single day at Antietam as in the War of 1812, the Mexican War, and the Spanish-American War *combined*.

LIBRARY OF CONGRESS

CONFEDERATE DEAD NEAR THE SHELL-MARKED DUNKARD CHURCH

LIBRARY OF CONGRESS

CONFEDERATE DEAD IN BLOODY LANE. In the *New York Times* of October 20, 1862, a reporter described the exhibit: "Mr. Brady has done something to bring home to us the terrible reality and earnestness of war. If he has not brought bodies and laid them in our door-yards and along streets, he has done something very like it. . . . [But] there is one side of the picture that the sun did not catch, one phase that has escaped photographic skill. It is the background of widows and orphans, torn from the bosom of their natural protectors by the red remorseless hand of Battle. . . . Homes have been made desolate, and the light of life in thousands of hearts has been quenched forever. All of this desolation imagination must paint—broken hearts cannot be photographed."

the battlefield ten days later wrote that "in about seven or eight acres of wood there is not a tree which is not full of bullets and bits of shell. It is impossible to understand how anyone could live in such a fire as there must have been here."[6]

What had been achieved by this valor and sacrifice? The battle was a tactical draw; but for the Confederates it was a strategic defeat. Lee had gone north with high hopes of ending the war at one stroke; his crippled army limped back to Virginia with these hopes shattered. Yet McClellan's failure was the greater. Several times he had had victory in his grasp only to lose it by faulty generalship and timidity. Never did more than 20,000 Federals go into action simultaneously. This allowed Lee to shift men from quiet to threatened sectors. Twenty thousand Union troops, more than a quarter of the army, were scarcely engaged at all. This makes a mockery of McClellan's statement in a letter to his wife: "The spectacle yesterday was the grandest I could conceive of—nothing could be more sublime. Those in whose judgment I rely tell that I fought the battle splendidly & that it was a masterpiece of art."[7]

The sun rose on September 18 to show the battered Confederates still in place. McClellan received 13,000 reinforcements during the morning. With the 20,000 previously uncommitted, this gave him more fresh men than Lee had left in his whole army. Yet McClellan did not renew the attack, and Lee escaped across the Potomac on the night of September 18. A feeble pursuit on September 20 was repulsed by the Rebel rear guard. Lee retreated unmolested to Winchester, while the Federals buried the dead and set up field hospitals for the wounded. Not for five weeks would the main body of the Army of the Potomac again cross into Virginia. Lincoln seized upon Antietam as the victory he had been waiting for to issue the Emancipation Proclamation (see page 316). But the President was sorely disappointed by this renewed demonstration of McClellan's failure to close in on the enemy for the kill. For the moment, however, Lincoln postponed major military decisions in the eastern theater because events in the West were reaching a crisis.

The Confederate Invasion of Kentucky

After Beauregard had evacuated Corinth, Mississippi, at the end of May, his standing with Jefferson Davis had fallen even lower. Davis replaced him as commander of the Confederate Army of Mississippi with Braxton Bragg, a stern disciplinarian who had previously led a corps in this army. In July Bragg divided his army into three parts. He left 16,000 men under Earl Van Dorn and another 16,000 under Sterling Price to defend Mississippi. The remaining 30,000 he took by a roundabout rail route to Chattanooga to help Edmund Kirby Smith's 18,000 Confederate troops defend east Tennessee against Buell's advancing Army of the Ohio. Bragg arrived in Chattanooga before Buell could get there, even though the Federals had only one-fourth as far to go and had started six weeks earlier.

---

[6]Jay Luvaas, *The Military Legacy of the Civil War: The European Inheritance* (Chicago, 1959), pp. 18–19.

[7]McClellan to Ellen Marcy McClellan, September 18, 1861, McClellan Papers, Library of Congress.

Buell's problems illustrated the difficulties of railroad logistics in enemy territory. Until this time, Union forces in the West had supplied themselves mainly by river. But a drought in the summer of 1862 made Buell dependent on the railroad, which he had to rebuild as he moved eastward through northern Alabama. Guerrilla raids reduced his normally slow movements to a snail's pace. A Democrat like McClellan, Buell believed in a "soft" war and was unwilling to deal harshly with guerrillas or to subsist his army off the countryside. As he approached Chattanooga in July, he opened a new rail supply line through Nashville to Louisville. But his troubles had just begun. Cavalry raids by Nathan Bedford Forrest and John Hunt Morgan repeatedly cut this railroad and stopped Buell's advance. The hapless Union cavalry could do little against the daredevil Rebel horsemen, who lived off the country and melted back into the population after a raid.

Meanwhile, when Bragg reached Chattanooga he turned to the offensive. Jefferson Davis ordered Bragg and Kirby Smith to draw Buell out of Tennessee by invading Kentucky. Confederate leaders believed Kentuckians to be eager for liberation from their Yankee oppressors. The invading armies took along 15,000 extra rifles to arm the men they expected to join them. At first things went well. The 10,000 troops with Kirby Smith bypassed the Union force holding Cumberland Gap and marched all the way to central Kentucky, where on August 30 they defeated and captured most of the Union garrison at Richmond (just south of Lexington). With 30,000 men Bragg struck northward from Chattanooga, moving quickly across Tennessee, and marched into Kentucky on a parallel route 100 miles to the west of Smith. Buell had to abandon his stalled campaign against Chattanooga and race northward to prevent the Rebels from capturing Louisville.

Despite their apparent success, the ragged, shoeless Confederates learned in Kentucky as in Maryland that it was one thing to invade Union territory but quite another to stay there. Confederate soldiers were outstanding at marching and fighting, but the South lacked the logistical capacity to convert a large-scale raid into a genuine invasion. And despite the Confederate flags and the smiles of pretty girls as Southern troops marched through their towns, Kentuckians proved no more ready than Marylanders to join up. Those 15,000 rifles stayed in their wagons. Kirby Smith did seize the state capital at Frankfort and prepared to inaugurate a Confederate governor. But this meant little so long as Buell's army remained in Kentucky and another 80,000 Northern recruits drilled in Louisville and Cincinnati. Unless these soldiers could somehow be eliminated, most residents of the Bluegrass State would think twice about declaring open allegiance to the Confederacy, no matter how strong their Southern sentiments might be.

By mid-September, Buell had received three divisions of reinforcements from Grant and now had an army of 50,000. Meanwhile, the Confederates captured another 4,000-man garrison at Munfordville, Kentucky. Criticism of Buell rose to a crescendo in the North. Whatever the underlying weaknesses of the Confederate invasion, it appeared to be a brilliant success. The Rebels had captured 8,000 Union soldiers, had drawn another 50,000 out of Tennessee, and were threatening Louisville and even Cincinnati. Buell seemed to have done nothing to stop them. Halleck warned a Western officer that unless Buell "does something very soon" he would be removed. "The Government seems determined to apply the guillotine to all unsuccessful generals," continued Halleck. "It seems rather hard to do this where the general is not at fault, but perhaps with us now, as in the French Revolution, some harsh measures are required."[8] At the end of September, Lincoln did try to replace Buell with George Thomas; but he suspended the order when Thomas protested that commanders should not be changed on the eve of battle.

The Battle of Perryville

Buell finally moved out to fight the Rebels. He sent two divisions on a feint toward Frankfort, which disrupted the inauguration of the Confederate governor and diverted Kirby Smith's troops and one division of Bragg's army from the main battle. The rest of Buell's army moved in three columns toward Perryville, where Bragg concentrated his remaining forces to meet them. The preliminaries of the ensuing battle were much influenced by the search for water, for the drought had dried up all but the larger streams. One Union corps detoured to find water; when advance units of another reached Perryville at dusk on October 7, they immediately attacked in a vain attempt to gain control of Doctor's Creek two miles west of town. A brigade in Philip Sheridan's division attacked again at dawn and carried not only the creek but the heights beyond. A small, bandy-legged man only thirty-one years old, Sheridan possessed an indomitable will and driving force. After he had seized the heights and held them against a counterattack, the rest of Buell's army filed into position on the left and right to form a line six miles long.

But then the initiative went over to the Confederates, who had only 16,000 men on the field, one-third as many as Buell. General Leonidas Polk, who in addition to commanding a corps in Bragg's army was an Episcopal bishop, launched an all-out attack on the Union left, leaving only two brigades of infantry and one of cavalry to demonstrate against the Union center and right. The Rebels rolled up the green troops on the Federal left, driving them back more than a mile and killing two generals before resistance stiffened. Sheridan meanwhile grasped the opportunity to counterattack against the weak Confederates in his front and sent them flying back two miles through the village of Perryville.

By nightfall, then, the troops on the northern half of the battlefield had swung counterclockwise in a huge quarter-circle. The right half of Buell's army had not fought at all. Through a freak of wind and atmospheric conditions known as acoustic shadow, they had heard nothing and did not even realize that a battle was going on a mile or two to their left. For the same reason, Buell himself remained unaware of the fighting until late afternoon. For those engaged (23,000 Federals, 15,000 Confederates), the casualties were heavy: 4,200 Yankees and 3,400 Rebels killed, wounded, or missing. Buell planned to attack with his whole army next morning, but Bragg slipped away during the night to join Kirby Smith's forces. Even united, however, the two Confederate armies were outnumbered. They were also short of supplies, and encumbered with many sick and wounded. In a despondent mood, Bragg decided to withdraw from Kentucky. Buell pursued timidly and failed to attack the retreating Confederates, despite good opportunities.

---

[8]*O.R.*, Ser. 1, Vol. 16, pt. 2, p. 421.

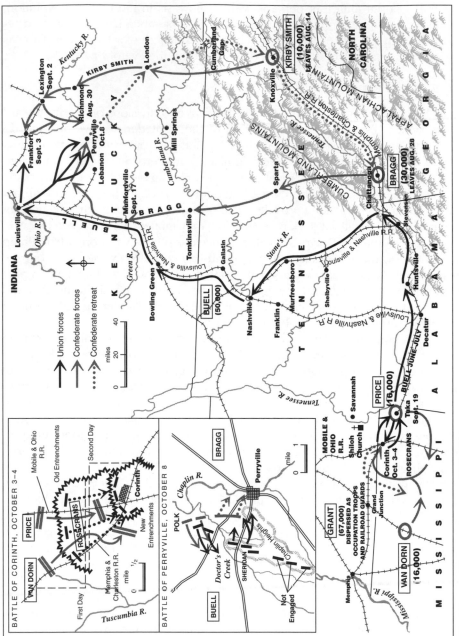

The Western Theater, Summer–Fall 1862

The Battles of Iuka and Corinth

One reason for Bragg's decision to withdraw was a series of actions 300 miles away, in northern Mississippi. The mission of Van Dorn's and Price's small Confederate armies there was to keep Grant from reinforcing Buell and, if possible, to strike northward themselves in coordination with Bragg's invasion. But Grant and Rosecrans[9] frustrated both objectives. Several thousand of the Union soldiers who fought at Perryville, including Sheridan, were among the reinforcements Grant had sent Buell. And in two battles—at Iuka and Corinth—Rosecrans blocked the plans of Price and Van Dorn to invade west Tennessee.

In mid-September, Price occupied Iuka in northeast Mississippi. Grant formed a plan to trap these 14,000 Confederates between two converging Union forces. Rosecrans with 9,000 men came up from the south, while 8,000 troops from the Army of the Mississippi under General Edward Ord approached along the railroad from the west. But the difficult procedure of bringing two separate forces together on the battlefield went awry, as it often did in those days before radio communication. Rosecrans came up late and was attacked by Price on September 19; but he held his own while an acoustic shadow kept Ord from hearing the sound of battle. That night Price, realizing he was in a trap, escaped by an unblocked road and moved to join Van Dorn forty miles to the west, while the Federals marched back to their base at Corinth.

On October 3, the combined armies of Van Dorn and Price launched a fierce attack against an equal number of bluecoats (22,000) under Rosecrans at Corinth. After driving the Yankees back two miles in their initial thrust, the Rebels halted for the night. When they renewed the attack next morning, stiffened Union resistance cut them to pieces. The Confederates retreated southward; Rosecrans's force was too crippled for effective pursuit, and a fresh brigade sent by Grant managed only to pick up a few hundred Rebel stragglers. In the two battles of Iuka and Corinth, Union casualties totaled 3,300, and the Confederates lost 5,700 men, a quarter of their force.

From September 17 to October 8, three attempted Confederate invasions of Union territory were turned back. It was the South's most ambitious bid for victory through coordinated military offensives. Lee would again invade the North in June 1863, but never again would all the principal Confederate armies march northward simultaneously. Although none of the three big battles—Antietam, Perryville, and Corinth—was an unequivocal Union victory, together they marked a turning point of crucial importance. They ended the chance for European recognition of the Confederacy, and they changed the character of the conflict from a war for union to a war for union and freedom.

---

[9]When General Pope was transferred to the eastern theater in June, Rosecrans came west to take command of the Army of the Mississippi.

SOME OF THE FIFTY-SIX CONFEDERATES KILLED IN A CHARGE ON A UNION BATTERY IN THE BATTLE OF CORINTH, OCTOBER 4, 1862

The Preliminary Emancipation Proclamation

Five days after the battle of Antietam, Lincoln called the cabinet together to announce his decision to issue the Emancipation Proclamation. For months, the President reminded his advisers, he had tried to persuade the border states to act against slavery. Now "we must make the forward movement" without them. "They [will] acquiesce, if not immediately, soon; for they must be satisfied that slavery [has] received its death-blow from slave-owners—it could not survive the rebellion." As for Northern Democrats, Lincoln no longer cared to conciliate them, for "their clubs would be used against us take what course we might."[10]

---

[10]Gideon Welles, *The Diary of Gideon Welles,* ed. Howard K. Beale, 3 vols. (New York, 1960), I, 142–145; John G. Nicolay and John Hay, *Abraham Lincoln: A History,* 10 vols. (New York, 1890), VI, 158–163.

The edict dated September 22, 1862, was actually a preliminary proclamation, for it declared that the slaves in states still in rebellion on January 1, 1863, "shall be then, thenceforward, and forever free." The proclamation justified emancipation solely on grounds of military necessity, endorsed voluntary colonization of freed slaves, and reiterated Lincoln's plea for gradual emancipation in the loyal slave states. This conservative approach was deliberate. Still uncertain of the country's response to such a revolutionary step, the President announced it in a manner designed to cushion the shock and make emancipation appear a necessary means of winning the war. Most radicals and abolitionists understood this. "A poor *document,* but a mighty *act*" was Massachusetts' radical Governor John Andrew's comment on the proclamation. A Garrisonian abolitionist conceded that from a purist's viewpoint the proclamation had a number of defects. But "I cannot stop to dwell on these. Joy, gratitude, thanksgiving, renewed hope and courage fill my soul."[11]

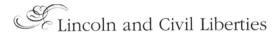 Lincoln and Civil Liberties

Two days after signing the Emancipation Proclamation, Lincoln issued a second edict; this one suspended the writ of habeas corpus and authorized military trials for "all Rebels and Insurgents, their aiders and abettors within the United States, and all persons discouraging volunteer enlistments, resisting militia drafts, or guilty of any disloyal practice."[12] Democrats denounced this action as the tyrannical twin of emancipation. The two proclamations provided the opposition with its main issues in 1862 congressional elections. Before turning to these elections, it is necessary to examine the question of civil liberties in the wartime North.

Although no consistent policy of newspaper censorship existed during the war, the government did use its military control of the telegraph after January 1862 to regulate reporters' dispatches. The Post Office occasionally excluded "treasonable" newspapers from the mails. Generals sometimes barred certain newspapers from their departments on the ground that they provided military information to the enemy. On several occasions the government shut down particular newspapers for limited lengths of time. Most of this suppression took place in occupied portions of slave states, though a few famous cases occurred in the North itself. Northern mobs destroyed the offices and presses of several Copperhead newspapers. At least two such mobs were led by Union soldiers, who were not punished for their acts.

During 1861, the State Department was responsible for enforcing internal security. Seward organized a secret service network of agents and informers whose zeal frequently exceeded their discretion. The government arrested hundreds of men in the border states and detained them without trial. In Maryland, federal troops imprisoned

<hr>

[11]Henry G. Pearson, *The Life of John A. Andrew,* 2 vols. (Boston, 1904), II, 51; Samuel May, Jr., to Richard Webb, September 23, 1862, Samuel May, Jr., Papers, Boston Public Library.

[12]Roy P. Basler (ed.), *The Collected Works of Abraham Lincoln,* 9 vols. (New Brunswick, N.J., 1953–1955), V, 436–437.

the mayor and police chief of Baltimore, several members of the legislature, and a state judge. The army also arrested and punished numerous spies, saboteurs, and guerrillas in the occupied portions of the South and border states.

By executive order in February 1862, Lincoln transferred responsibility for internal security to the War Department. Stanton reduced the number of arrests and established a commission to examine the cases of prisoners then being held. Most of them were released upon taking an oath of allegiance. Arrests almost ceased during the spring, when the North was confident of soon winning the war. But the reverses of summer, mushrooming Copperhead sentiment, and resistance to the militia draft in the fall of 1862 produced a new wave of military arrests. Lincoln's September 24 proclamation suspending habeas corpus was aimed mainly at this draft resistance.

Union authorities arrested at least 15,000 civilians during the war. Was this an excessive repression of civil liberties? Many contemporaries thought so. They did not question the arrest of enemy agents and saboteurs or the military trials of guerrillas and spies in active war zones. Some critics even sanctioned military arrest and trial of draft evaders and of persons encouraging desertion or draft resistance, although some of these activities occurred in Northern states where the civil courts were functioning. But they condemned the arbitrary arrest of editors, public officials, and other persons whose only crime was to write or speak against the administration's war policies or in favor of peace. Some of those arrested were victims of wild rumors of conspiracy that became an inevitable part of war psychology. Some were imprisoned for months without any charges having been brought against them. All this seems to confirm that the administration's record on civil liberties was a bad one.

Yet there was often a thin line between verbal antiwar activities and those that were obviously treasonable. Was an inflammatory speech urging recruits to refuse to fight in an "abolitionist war" an exercise of free speech, or was it aiding and abetting the enemy? Lincoln stated the question graphically: "Must I shoot a simple-minded soldier boy who deserts, while I must not touch a hair of a wily agitator who induces him to desert? . . . I think that in such a case, to silence the agitator, and save the boy, is not only constitutional, but, withal, a great mercy." The President insisted that in a time of grave emergency it was better to arrest too many than too few. "Under cover of 'Liberty of speech,' 'Liberty of the press' and 'Habeas Corpus,' " he wrote, the Rebels "hoped to keep on foot amongst us a most efficient corps of spies, informers, suppliers, and aiders and abettors of their cause." The civil courts were too slow to handle these cases in the emergency; and if released on writs of habeas corpus to await trial, these persons would continue their treasonable activities. The purpose of military arrests was preventive, not punitive. These were strong measures, Lincoln admitted, unconstitutional in times of peace but constitutional "in cases of rebellion or invasion." "I can no more be persuaded," wrote Lincoln in one of his homely but effective metaphors, "that the government can constitutionally take no strong measure in time of rebellion, because it can be shown that the same could not be lawfully taken in time of peace, than I can be persuaded that a particular drug is not good medicine for a sick man, because it can be shown to not be good food for a well one."[13]

---

[13]Ibid., VI, 263, 266–267.

One of the most thorough students of wartime civil liberties defends the Lincoln administration. Most prisoners, he found, were treated well during their confinement. Most were in prison "for good reason." Most were released after relatively short detentions unless convicted for actual crimes such as espionage or treason. When military commissions tried civilians, it was usually for a military crime committed in a war zone. (The notable exceptions of the Vallandigham and Milligan cases are discussed in Chapters 20 and 24.) The overwhelming majority of the 15,000 arrests occurred in the occupied South or in the border states that because of guerrilla activity and espionage were really part of the war zone. "Considering the imperative demands of the emergency, a fair amount of restraint was shown in the making of arrests. . . . The Government smarted under great abuse without passing an Espionage Act or a Sedition Law. Freedom of speech was preserved to the point of permitting the most disloyal utterances."[14] Although troops patrolled the polls in border states to exclude voters who had not taken an oath of allegiance, free elections took place throughout the war, administration candidates often suffered defeat, and for a time in 1864 it appeared that Lincoln himself would not be reelected. Compared with the draconian enforcement of espionage and sedition laws in World War I and the internment of Japanese-Americans during World War II, the infringement of civil liberties during the much greater internal crisis of 1861–1865 seems mild indeed. Be that as it may, Democrats capitalized on "arbitrary arrests" in the 1862 elections. Resentment of the militia draft also worked in their favor. But the most important single issue, judged by the volume of rhetoric, was the Emancipation Proclamation.

The Elections of 1862 in the North

Democrats called on voters to repudiate the Republicans before Lincoln could issue the final emancipation proclamation on January 1. In New York, where Democratic gubernatorial candidate Horatio Seymour hoped the election would catapult him into national prominence, party organs announced that "a vote for Seymour is a vote to protect our white laborers against the association and competition of Southern negroes." Midwestern Democratic orators proclaimed that "every white man in the North, who does not want to be swapped off for a free Nigger, should vote the Democratic ticket."[15]

Many observers regarded the outcome of the elections as a sharp rebuke of the Republicans and of emancipation. Democrats scored a net gain of thirty-two seats in the House. Nearly all of this gain came in the lower North—New York, New Jersey, Pennsylvania, Ohio, Indiana, and Illinois. The Democrats also won the governorships of New York and New Jersey, and gained control of the legislatures in New Jersey, Illinois, and Indiana. (Only the fortuitous circumstance that the gubernatorial

---

[14]James G. Randall, *Constitutional Problems Under Lincoln*, rev. ed. (Urbana, Ill., 1951), chaps. 6–8, 19–20; quotations from pp. 154, 155, 520. See also Mark E. Neely, Jr., *The Fate of Liberty: Abraham Lincoln and Civil Liberties* (New York, 1991).

[15]*New York World*, October 18, 1862; V. Jacque Voegeli, *Free but Not Equal: The Midwest and the Negro During the Civil War* (Chicago, 1967), p. 55.

and legislative elections in Pennsylvania and Ohio were held in odd years and that Republican governors had been elected to four-year terms in Illinois and Indiana in 1860 prevented these state governments from being controlled by Democrats after 1862.) Democrats were exuberant. Typical newspaper headlines proclaimed: "Abolition Slaughtered" and "No Emancipation." According to Ohio Congressman Samuel S. Cox, the election had brought forth a new commandment: "Thou shalt not degrade the white race by such intermixtures as emancipation would bring."[16]

Several historians have concurred in this interpretation of the 1862 elections. "The verdict of the polls," wrote one, "showed clearly that the people of the North were opposed to the Emancipation Proclamation, opposed to governmental encroachment on individual rights, and opposed to conscription."[17] But in fact the elections showed nothing of the kind. Democratic gains occurred in regions of the party's traditional strength. And the Republicans actually made a net *gain* of five seats in the Senate while suffering the *smallest* net loss of House seats by the majority party in an off-year election in twenty years. Republicans carried all of New England, the upper North, the two Pacific states, and the border states. To be sure, federal troops excluded secessionist sympathizers from the polls in the border states; but even without these states, the Republicans would have retained control of Congress and of all but two governorships and three state legislatures. If the election was in any sense a referendum on emancipation and on Lincoln's conduct of the war, a majority of Northern voters endorsed these policies.

When Congress convened in December 1862 for its lame-duck session, Republicans emphatically reaffirmed emancipation. First they rejected a Democratic-sponsored House resolution which declared that anyone in the government who proposed to wage war "for the overthrowing or interfering with the rights or established institutions of any of the States" was guilty of "a high crime against the Constitution." Then by a straight party vote, the House adopted a resolution endorsing the Emancipation Proclamation.[18] Finally Congress passed a bill to require emancipation as a condition of West Virginia statehood.[19]

Lincoln's message to Congress on December 1 recommended a constitutional amendment to provide for compensated, gradual (extending to 1900) emancipation in every state "wherein slavery now exists." This was not an alternative to an emancipation proclamation. Lincoln also said that no proceedings under the September 22 proclamation would be delayed by his proposal, and that all slaves freed "by the chances of war" would remain "forever free." The President made it clear that one way or another the war must accomplish a new birth of freedom.

Fellow citizens, *we* cannot escape history. . . . The fiery trial through which we pass, will light us down, in honor or dishonor, to the latest generation. . . . The dogmas of the quiet past, are

---

[16]Voegeli, *Free but Not Equal*, p. 64.

[17]William B. Hesseltine, *Lincoln and the War Governors* (New York, 1948), p. 265.

[18]*Congressional Globe*, 37th Cong., 3rd sess. (1862), 15, 92.

[19]The enabling act specified that all persons born after July 4, 1863, should be free; all others under the age of twenty-five would become free on their twenty-fifth birthday. West Virginia incorporated these provisions into its 1863 constitution. But the gradualist features were soon swept aside by the Thirteenth Amendment.

inadequate to the stormy present. . . . As our case is new, so we must think anew, and act anew. . . . In *giving* freedom to the *slave,* we *assure* freedom to the *free.* . . . We must disenthrall ourselves, and then we shall save our country.[20]

Lincoln privately reassured Republicans that he would not falter on emancipation. "The President is firm," Charles Sumner told Boston friends. "He says that he would not stop the Proclamation if he could, and he could not if he would."[21]

On January 1, Lincoln signed the document, proclaiming freedom to all slaves in the portions of Confederate states not then occupied by Union troops.[22] Southern leaders damned the proclamation as an infamous incitement to slave insurrection or as a hypocritical Yankee trick, which "emancipated" only those slaves beyond Northern reach and left the others in slavery. Democratic and conservative reaction in the North ran a similar gamut. A good many radicals were troubled by the exemption of border states and occupied areas of the Confederacy. They wriggled uncomfortably under the jibe of the London *Spectator* that the principle of the proclamation was "not that a human being cannot justly own another, but that he cannot own him unless he is loyal to the United States."[23]

But such criticism missed the point. The proclamation was a war measure directed against enemy resources. Under the laws of war, the President and army had the right to seize these resources; but they had no constitutional power over slaves not owned by the enemy. Already 100,000 or more contrabands within Union lines in Tennessee, Louisiana, Virginia, and elsewhere were free by the realities of war. West Virginia was committed to freedom. Strong emancipation parties were rising in Missouri, Maryland, and Tennessee that would soon disenthrall these states as well. The Emancipation Proclamation announced a new war aim. Thenceforth, the Union army became officially an army of liberation. The North was now fighting to create a new Union, not to restore the old one.

The Removal of McClellan and Buell from Command

In September 1862, some Republicans had been apprehensive about how the Union armies, especially the Army of the Potomac with its hierarchy of Democratic officers, would react to the Emancipation Proclamation. Although there was reason for worry, few soldiers actually threw down their arms or refused to fight for black freedom. Much

---

[20]Basler, *Works of Lincoln,* V, 537.

[21]Sumner to Samuel Gridley Howe, December 28, 1862, Sumner-Howe Correspondence, Houghton Library, Harvard University.

[22]The portions of the Confederacy exempted from the proclamation were several counties in Virginia, several parishes in Louisiana, and the entire state of Tennessee. Because these areas (with the exception of eastern Tennessee) were occupied by Union troops and governed by military or civil authorities appointed or sanctioned by the President, they were in effect part of the Union and therefore not subject to the Emancipation Proclamation, which as a war measure could apply only to enemy territory. Eastern Tennessee was exempted because Lincoln considered its white inhabitants loyal to the Union.

[23]*Spectator* (London), October 11, 1862.

muttering occurred in the ranks, to be sure. A private in the Army of the Potomac reported that his messmates were saying "they will not fight to put niggers on a par with white men, that they had been duped & that they only enlisted for the preservation of the Union & nothing else."[24]

More representative, however, was a lieutenant in the 2nd Minnesota who had once bitterly opposed emancipation but had changed his mind by February 1863. "Slavery and Aristocracy go hand in hand," he wrote to his fiancée, who did not agree with his new opinions. "An Aristocracy brought on this war—that Aristocracy must be broken up . . . it is rotten and corrupt. . . . We did not think so one year ago & you will think differently too a year hence." Early in 1863, General in Chief Halleck passed the word to Grant that "the character of the war has very much changed within the last year. There is now no possible hope of reconciliation with the rebels. . . . We must conquer the rebels or be conquered by them. . . . Every slave withdrawn from the enemy is the equivalent of a white man put *hors de combat*."[25]

But McClellan and some of his fellow officers in the Army of the Potomac reacted to the Emancipation Proclamation just as their Republican critics feared they would. McClellan privately condemned it for "inaugurating servile war." General Fitz-John Porter called it "the absurd proclamation of a political coward" and said that it was "resented in the army" by fighting men who were "tired of the war and wish to see it ended soon and honorably."[26] Some officers even urged McClellan to march the army on Washington to compel a reversal of the proclamation. A staff officer admitted having said that Lee's army had not been destroyed at Sharpsburg because "that is not the game; the object is that neither army shall get much advantage of the other; that both shall be kept in the field till they are exhausted, when we will make a compromise and save slavery." Lincoln cashiered the officer, and explained: "I thought his silly, treasonable expressions were 'staff talk' and I wished to make an example."[27] McClellan felt that this "staff talk" was becoming such a problem that he issued a special order on October 7 pointing out that it was the government's duty to make policy and the army's to execute it. At the same time, however, McClellan included in this order a none too subtle reference to the upcoming congressional elections: "the remedy for political errors, if they are committed, is to be found only in the action of the people at the polls."[28]

Although McClellan's Democratic politics obviously hurt him with the administration, it was his military shortcomings that finally brought his downfall. Believing that he had fought a "masterpiece" at Antietam, the general at first expected to have things his own way. Three days after the battle, he wrote to his wife: "I have insisted

---

[24]Augustus Auberne to Samuel L. M. Barlow, January 17, 1863, S. L. M. Barlow Papers, Henry E. Huntington Library.

[25]John Beatty to Laura Maxfield, Feb. 20, 1863, Beatty Papers, Minnesota Historical Society; *O.R.,* Ser. I, Vol. 24, pt. 3, p. 157.

[26]McClellan to William H. Aspinwall, September 26, 1862, in *Battles and Leaders of the Civil War,* Extra-Illustrated ed., Vol. VIII, Henry E. Huntington Library; Porter to Manton Marble, September 30, 1862, in Nevins, *War Becomes Revolution,* pp. 238–239.

[27]Basler, *Works of Lincoln,* V, 442–443, 508–509; Nicolay and Hay, *Abraham Lincoln,* VI, 186–188.

[28]*O.R.,* Ser. 1, Vol. 19, pt. 2, pp. 395–396.

LINCOLN WITH MCCLELLAN AND OFFICERS NEAR THE ANTIETAM BATTLEFIELD, OCTOBER 3, 1862

that Stanton shall be removed & that Halleck shall give way to me as Comdr. in Chief. . . . The only safety for the country & for me is to get rid of both of them."[29] Rarely had even McClellan been so blind to reality. The truth was that his failure to follow up Antietam vigorously was soon to end his military career. Telegram after telegram from Washington urged him to give the Rebels a knockout punch while they were still groggy. Back to Washington went as many telegrams full of reasons for delay: the enemy outnumbered him; he must drill the new recruits; and most amazing of all in view of the condition of Lee's army, he could not march until his men were provided with new clothing and shoes!

Lincoln visited the army October 1–4 and personally urged McClellan to get moving. After returning to Washington, the President had Halleck send an order to McClellan that any other general would have considered peremptory: "Cross the Potomac and give battle to the enemy. Your army must move now while the roads are good." Still McClellan did not move. On October 10–12, Stuart's cavalry once more made a circuit around the entire Union army. They raided Pennsylvania as far north as Chambersburg, evaded the Union horsemen sent after them, and

---

[29]McClellan to Ellen McClellan, September 20, 1862, McClellan Papers, Library of Congress.

brought away 1,200 horses and dozens of prisoners with the loss of only two troopers. When, several days later, McClellan explained that his advance must be further delayed until he could replace worn-out horses, Lincoln fired back a sarcastic telegram: "Will you pardon me for asking what the horses of your army have done since the battle of Antietam that fatigues anything?"[30]

McClellan's angry response to this goading was expressed in a letter to his wife: "The good of the country requires me to submit to all this from men whom I know to be greatly my inferior socially, intellectually, and morally! There never was a truer epithet applied to a certain individual than that of the 'Gorilla.' "[31] As McClellan was writing this letter, his army was finally beginning to move. But it took six days to cross the Potomac (which Lee's army had crossed in one night after Antietam), and another seven to move fifty miles south to the vicinity of Warrenton, Virginia. Lee divided his smaller force and placed Longstreet's corps between the enemy and Richmond, while Jackson stayed in the valley on McClellan's flank.

Once again the fast-marching Rebels had taken the initiative away from the ponderous Yankees. Lincoln's patience snapped. On November 7, he relieved McClellan from command of the Army of the Potomac and appointed a reluctant Burnside in his place. To his private secretary, Lincoln explained his decision: "I peremptorily ordered him to advance. . . . [He kept] delaying on little pretexts of wanting this and that. I began to fear he was playing false—that he did not want to hurt the enemy. I saw how he could intercept the enemy on the way to Richmond. I determined to make that the test. If he let them get away I would remove him. He did so & I relieved him."[32]

Another general who let the enemy get away was also relieved at the end of October. Like McClellan, Don Carlos Buell was a Democrat who made no secret of his opposition to emancipation. But unlike McClellan he was unpopular with his troops, who realized that they had not been used well in the Perryville campaign. When the exhausted and outnumbered Confederates retreated from Kentucky to Chattanooga, Lincoln urged Buell to go after them, smash them, and secure east Tennessee. But even though more than half of Buell's Army of the Ohio had not fought at Perryville, the general considered it necessary to refit and reorganize before he could renew the offensive. This sounded like McClellan. The exasperated President could not "understand why we cannot march as the enemy marches, live as he lives, and fight as he fights, unless we admit the inferiority of our troops and our generals."[33] Because Buell would not march and fight as Lincoln wished, the President replaced him with William S. Rosecrans. With this change of command, the name of the army was also changed to the Army of the Cumberland, about this time its Confederate opponents changed their name from the Army of Mississippi to the Army of Tennessee.

[30] *O.R.,* Ser. 1, Vol. 19, pt. 1, p. 72; Basler, *Works of Lincoln,* V, 474.

[31] McClellan to Ellen McClellan, undated, McClellan Papers.

[32] Tyler Dennett (ed.), *Lincoln and the Civil War in the Diaries and Letters of John Hay* (New York, 1939), pp. 218–219.

[33] *O.R.,* Ser. 1, Vol. 16, pt. 2, p. 627.

Europe and the War, 1862

The summer and fall of 1862 were punctuated by flurries of diplomatic activity whose rhythms were dictated by the changing military situation. Lee's victories in Virginia seemed to confirm European opinion that the Confederacy could never be conquered. When news of the Seven Days battles reached France, Napoleon III instructed his foreign secretary: "Demandez au government anglais s'il ne croit pas le moment venu de reconnaître le Sud." On July 18, the British Parliament debated a motion for recognition of the Confederacy. Although the motion was withdrawn as premature, the debate convinced Foreign Secretary Lord Russell that "the great majority are in favor of the South." Chancellor of the Exchequer William Gladstone wrote on July 26 that "it is indeed much to be desired that this bloody and purposeless conflict should cease." Gladstone later said in a speech at Newcastle that "Jefferson Davis and other leaders of the South have made an army; they are making, it appears, a navy; and they have made what is more than either, they have made a nation." Coming from such an influential source, this was taken as a signal that Britain was about to recognize the Confederacy. The American legation in London was plunged into gloom. "The current here [is] rising every hour and running harder against us than at any time since the Trent affair," wrote Henry Adams, son and secretary of Charles Francis Adams, the American minister to Britain.[34]

News of the second battle of Bull Run and of Lee's invasion of Maryland caused the Southern current to run even faster. Russell suggested to Prime Minister Palmerston a joint British and French offer of mediation. If the North refused, he wrote on September 17, "we ought ourselves to recognize the Southern States as an independent State." Palmerston was more cautious. He wanted to await the outcome of the battle then raging in Maryland. "If the Federals sustain a great Defeat [the North] may be brought to a more reasonable State of Mind [and] be at once ready for Mediation, and the Iron should be struck while it is hot. If, on the other hand, they should have the best of it, we may wait awhile and see what may follow."[35]

The results of the battle of Antietam reinforced Palmerston's caution. Although the idea of mediation remained alive for several more weeks, Palmerston now opposed immediate action. "The whole matter is full of difficulties," he wrote in October, "and can only be cleared up by some more decided events between the contending armies. . . . We must continue merely to be lookers-on till the war shall have taken a more decided turn."[36] When Napoleon III suggested at the end of October that France, Britain, and Russia jointly propose a six-month armistice and a suspension

---

[34]Shelby Foote, *The Civil War: A Narrative. Fort Sumter to Perryville* (New York, 1958), p. 523; D. P. Crook, *Diplomacy During the American Civil War* (New York, 1975), pp. 84, 92; Worthington C. Ford (ed.), *A Cycle of Adams Letters, 1861–1865,* 2 vols. (Boston, 1920), I, 166.

[35]Ephraim D. Adams, *Great Britain and the American Civil War,* 2 vols. (New York, 1925), II, 38, 41; Kinley J. Brauer, "British Mediation and the American Civil War: A Reconsideration," *Journal of Southern History,* 38 (February 1972), 57.

[36]Adams, *Great Britain and the Civil War,* II, 44.

of the blockade, pro-Union Russia refused. The British cabinet discussed a joint French-British overture in November; but only Gladstone and Russell favored it, and no action was taken.

As the meaning of Antietam and the Emancipation Proclamation sank in, it became clear that antislavery Britain could not recognize a proslavery Confederacy whose prospects for victory no longer appeared bright. A dramatic upsurge of pro-Northern opinion took place in Britain. On January 23, Henry Adams wrote from London to his brother in the Army of the Potomac: "The Emancipation Proclamation has done more for us here than all our former victories and all our diplomacy. It is creating an almost convulsive reaction in our favor. . . . We are much encouraged and in high spirits. If only you at home don't have disasters, we will give such a checkmate to the foreign hopes of the rebels as they have never yet had."[37]

But Union arms did suffer more disasters in the winter and spring of 1862–1863. Confederate hopes rose and Northern morale plummeted once again.

---

[37]Ford, *Cycle of Adams Letters*, I, 243.

The Winter of Northern Discontent

Exhaustion steals over the country. Confidence and hope are dying.

—Montgomery Meigs,
Union Quartermaster General, December 30, 1862

327

The Battle of Fredericksburg

In Virginia the newly appointed commander of the Army of the Potomac, Ambrose E. Burnside, seemed ready in November 1862 to apply Lincoln's formula for military success—fast marching and hard fighting. Instead of continuing south from Warrenton using the vulnerable Orange and Alexandria Railroad as his supply line, Burnside proposed to feint in that direction while he moved most of his army to Falmouth, across the Rappahannock from Fredericksburg. There he could be supplied by water and a short, secure rail line; from there he could cross the river to march directly on Richmond. Burnside moved rapidly; his leading corps covered the forty miles to Falmouth in two days, and the whole army was there by November 19. The swiftness of this maneuver surprised Lee, who for several days lost track of Burnside's whereabouts. The Yankees for once seemed to have stolen a march on the Rebels.

But when the Federals reached Falmouth, things began to go wrong. The pontoons Burnside had ordered for bridging the Rappannannock had unaccountably gone astray. (Pontoons were flat-bottomed boats anchored in a line to support a floating bridge across rivers too deep to ford.) The pontoons did not arrive until the end of November—the result of bungling by Halleck and several engineer officers— and this allowed Lee to concentrate his army on the heights behind Fredericksburg before the Federals could bridge the river. A Union reconnaissance in force fourteen miles downriver found the Confederates too strong for an unopposed crossing there, so Burnside went ahead with his plan to cross at Fredericksburg itself. Under cover of fog before dawn on December 11, the engineers began to place the pontoons. When the fog lifted, Rebel sharpshooters hiding in buildings along the bank began to pick them off. Union artillery shelled the town, but snipers still fired from the rubble. Finally, volunteers from three blue regiments crossed in boats for an assault that drove the sharpshooters away in street-by-street fighting. The bridges were completed, and next day the huge army crossed the river to deploy an attack as soon as the fog lifted on December 13.

Lee placed his 74,000 men along seven miles of hills west and south of the town. Swampy ground near the river on the left and steep, rough terrain in the center prevented Federal attacks at those points, so the main defenses were concentrated at Marye's Heights directly behind the town, held by Longstreet's corps, and at Prospect Hill, held by Jackson, three miles to the south. The 113,000 Union troops were organized in three "grand divisions" of two corps each. The left grand division under General William B. Franklin was to attack Jackson's position, the right grand division under Edwin V. Sumner was to assault Marye's Heights, and Hooker's center division was to function as a reserve to exploit breakthroughs.

The Federals first attacked Jackson's position. A blue division commanded by George Gordon Meade temporarily pierced the Rebel line before being driven back by a fierce counterattack. With proper support, Meade might have broken through the Confederate right; but Franklin never managed to get more than half of the 50,000 men under his command into action despite imperative orders from Burnside in midafternoon to renew the attack with his whole force.

Franklin's failure on the Union left spoiled any slim chance for a Northern victory that day, for the odds on the right were hopeless. Longstreet's riflemen were posted along a sunken road behind a stone wall at the base of Marye's Heights. Artillery on the heights commanded the half-mile stretch of open ground over which Union attackers had to advance. As one of Longstreet's officers put it: "A chicken could not live on that field when we open on it." The blueclad soldiers were no chickens. They launched seven courageous but futile assaults against Marye's Heights. "It can hardly be in human nature for men to show more valor, or generals to manifest less judgment," wrote a newspaper correspondent. A New York infantryman said that "we might as well have tried to take Hell."[1]

When the blessedly early December dark finally fell, the ground in front of the stone wall was covered for acres with dead and dying men. The Union army had suffered 12,600 casualties, the Confederates fewer than 5,000. And nothing had been achieved. While the wounded endured untold agonies during the freezing night, Burnside was beside himself with grief for his bleeding army and anger at Franklin's failure to exploit his opening on the Union left. Burnside's subordinates talked him out of the wild idea of personally leading a charge next day at the head of his old corps. After a truce to bury the dead, the Federals pulled back over the river on the night of December 15.

---

[1]James Longstreet, "The Battle of Fredericksburg," in *Battles and Leaders of the Civil War,* 4 vols. (New York, 1887), III, 79; Shelby Foote, *The Civil War: A Narrative. Fredericksburg to Meridian* (New York, 1963), p. 44; Allan Nevins, *The War for the Union: War Becomes Revolution* (New York, 1960), p. 348.

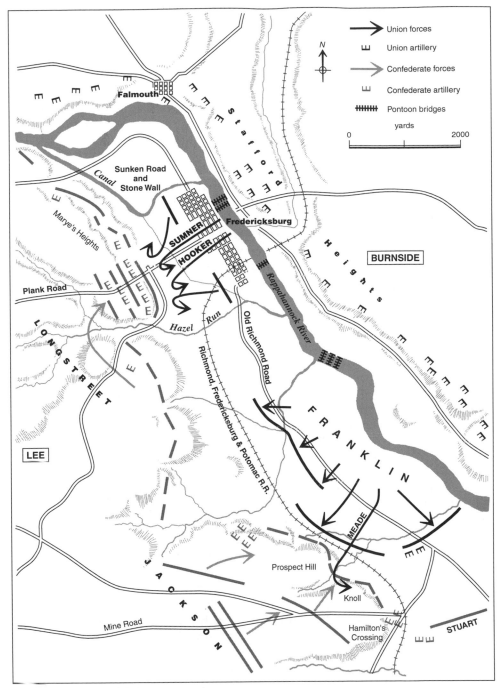

The Battle of Fredericksburg, December 13, 1862

A Crisis of Confidence in the North

While the South breathed a sigh of relief after Fredericksburg, Northern despair became acute. *Harper's Weekly* cried out that the people were filled with anguish. "They have borne, silently and grimly, imbecility, treachery, failure, privation, loss of friends and means, almost every suffering which can afflict a brave people. But they cannot be expected to suffer that such massacres as this at Fredericksburg shall be repeated." Quartermaster General Montgomery Meigs wrote that "exhaustion steals over the country. Confidence and hope are dying." When Lincoln learned of the outcome at Fredericksburg, he said to an associate: "If there is a worse place than Hell, I am in it."[2]

Lincoln's hell was made worse by a political crisis that Fredericksburg brought to a head. The military defeat was a catalyst for all the discontent and rumors festering in Washington. Republican dissatisfaction with the administration's conduct of affairs focused specifically on Secretary of State Seward. Distrusted by radicals since his role in compromise efforts during the secession winter of 1860–1861, Seward was believed to be the "evil genius" of the cabinet, the "unseen hand" whose conservative influence over Lincoln had undermined vigorous presidential leadership—especially on questions concerning slavery and the appointment of army commanders. In two long caucus meetings on December 16 and 17, every Republican senator but one voted to request a reorganization of the cabinet to secure "unity of purpose and action." This resolution was aimed at Seward. It was inspired by Secretary of the Treasury Chase, Seward's main rival in the cabinet and a close associate of radical senators whose power would be enhanced if the senatorial scheme succeeded.

This affair was the gravest challenge thus far to Lincoln's leadership. It also created a constitutional crisis of the first order. If Lincoln "caved in" to the senatorial demand, as he put it, he would lose control of his administration. The United States would move closer to a parliamentary form of government. When word of the senatorial caucus leaked out, new rumors swept Washington that the whole cabinet, perhaps even Lincoln himself, would resign. The President was "awfully shaken" by the crisis. Branding the charge of Seward's "malign influence" an "absurd lie," Lincoln unburdened himself to a friend. "What do these men want? . . . They wish to get rid of me, and I am sometimes half disposed to gratify them. . . . Since I heard last night of the proceedings of the caucus I have been more distressed than by any event of my life. . . . We are now on the brink of destruction. It appears to me the Almighty is against us, and I can hardly see a ray of hope."[3]

Lincoln had regained his composure by the time he met with a delegation of eight senators on December 19. Seward had already submitted his resignation in order to relieve the pressure, but Lincoln did not reveal this. He listened with little

---

[2] *Harper's Weekly*, December 27, 1862; Meigs to Burnside, December 30, 1862, in *O.R.*, Ser. 1, Vol. 21, p. 917; Lincoln quoted in William Henry Wadsworth to Samuel L. M. Barlow, December 16, 1862, Barlow Papers, Henry E. Huntington Library.

[3] Samuel Wilkeson to Sydney Howard Gay, December 19, 1862, Gay Papers, Columbia University Library; Orville Hickman Browning, *The Diary of Orville Hickman Browning*, eds. Theodore C. Pease and James G. Randall, 2 vols. (Springfield, Ill., 1927–1933), I, 600–601.

comment to the senators' speeches "attributing to Mr. Seward a lukewarmness in the conduct of the war, and seeming to consider him the real cause of our failures." Without committing himself, the President invited the delegation back the next day for further discussions. When they returned, Lincoln exhibited his political virtuosity in a bravura performance. The senators were surprised to find that the President had arranged to have the entire cabinet on hand except Seward. In a tactful but forceful speech, Lincoln said that whenever possible he consulted the cabinet about important decisions but that he alone made the decisions; that members of the cabinet sometimes disagreed but that all supported a policy when it had been decided upon; and that Seward was a valuable member of the administration. Then the President turned to the cabinet for confirmation. All eyes fastened on Chase, who was neatly put on the spot. Chase had told the senators that Seward was responsible for cabinet disharmony; if he now denied it he would lose face with them, but if he reaffirmed it he would lose the confidence of the President. Chase mumbled a brief endorsement of Lincoln's statement but tried to save face by expressing regret that major decisions were not more fully discussed by the cabinet. Deflated by the whole experience and disappointed with Chase, the senators knew that Lincoln had won.

Much embarrassed, Chase next day came to the White House to offer his resignation. "Let me have it," said the President eagerly. Chase reluctantly handed over his letter of resignation; Lincoln read it and said triumphantly: "This cuts the Gordian knot. I can dispose of this subject now without difficulty." The Republican senators could not have Seward's resignation without losing Chase as well. Lincoln used a characteristic metaphor to describe his triumph: "Now I can ride; I have a pumpkin in each end of my bag." The President refused both resignations; the cabinet remained unchanged; the crisis was over; the murky political atmosphere suddenly cleared. This was not the first confrontation between the President and congressional Republicans, nor was it the last. But on this occasion Lincoln proved himself master. And he did so without making any enemies. It was an instructive lesson in political skill.[4]

The War in the West: The Battle of Stones River

Military news from the West offered little encouragement to offset Northern gloom following Fredericksburg in the East. The Confederates had reorganized their western command structure after the failure of the Kentucky invasion in 1862. Joseph Johnston came to Chattanooga in November to take overall charge of the Western Department, giving the Confederacy unity of command in that theater. General John C. Pemberton went to Vicksburg as head of Confederate forces in Mississippi. Bragg remained in command of the Army of Tennessee, which concentrated at Murfreesboro thirty miles south of Nashville. West of the Mississippi, the Confederates had 25,000

---

[4]The best contemporary accounts of this affair are Gideon Welles, *The Diary of Gideon Welles,* ed. Howard K. Beale, 3 vols. (New York, 1960), I, 194–204, and Pease and Randall, *Diary of Browning,* I, 596–604. The best secondary accounts are Nevins, *War Becomes Revolution,* pp. 350–365; Phillip Shaw Paludan, *The Presidency of Abraham Lincoln* (Lawrence, Kansas, 1994), pp. 170–177; and David Herbert Donald, *Lincoln* (New York, 1995), pp. 398–406.

troops in Arkansas. One thin gleam of cheer to the Union cause occurred on December 7 at Prairie Grove in northwest Arkansas, where 10,000 of these Rebel troops attacked two Union divisions only to be surprised and driven off when another blue division suddenly materialized on the Confederate flank. The victory at Prairie Grove kept northern Arkansas under Union control, but the Confederates remained strong enough to prevent a thrust at Little Rock. The main Union efforts in the West were to be directed against Vicksburg and against Bragg's army in central Tennessee.

When Union General William S. Rosecrans took over the Army of the Cumberland on October 30, he knew that the administration expected him to drive the Rebels out of central Tennessee. After many delays caused by cavalry raids in their rear, Rosecrans's 42,000 troops marched from Nashville the day after Christmas to confront Bragg's 36,000-strong Army of Tennessee at Murfreesboro. They found the Confederates drawn up astride Stones River, a shallow stream a mile northwest of town. On the night of December 30, the two armies bivouacked only a few hundred yards apart. Their bands engaged in a musical battle in the still winter air, one side blaring out "Dixie" in challenge to the other's "Yankee Doodle," and so on. Finally, one band began to play "Home, Sweet Home." Others took it up until all the bands in both armies were playing and thousands of soldiers, Yankees and Rebels together, sang the familiar words. Perhaps some of them wondered at the tragic irony of a war in which they could sing together one night and butcher each other on the morrow.

For Bragg had no intention of retreating or even of remaining on the defensive. He concentrated most of his army on the left for a dawn attack against the Union right—with the intention of rolling it up, pinning the Federals against the river, and cutting them off from their supply line. The Confederates struck at dawn December 31, once again catching the Yankees at breakfast as they had at Donelson and Shiloh. Two blue divisions on the Union right crumpled under the onslaught. Gray cavalry got in the Union rear and caused havoc among supply and ammunition wagons. But Rosecrans rose to the challenge of disaster. He personally rode back and forth along the front lines, rallying troops; his chief of staff, riding beside him, was decapitated by a cannonball. Sheridan's division on the Union right center stood firm, giving Rosecrans time to form a new line in front of the Nashville Pike. There the Confederate attack stalled before noon.

The fighting had been among the hardest of the war. The roar of artillery and rifles was so loud that soldiers picked cotton from the stalks and stuffed it into their ears. On the Union left center, fragments of several brigades held a patch of woods along the railroad known as the Round Forest. This became the hinge of the reorganized Union line, and Bragg decided to launch an all-out attack to break it. To do the job, he brought across the river the large division commanded by John C. Breckinridge. This division hurled itself against the Round Forest during the afternoon but was repulsed time after time with heavy loss.

No bands played on the field that night; instead, this New Year's Eve was filled with the groans and cries of the wounded. Bragg wired Richmond that he had won a great victory, and indeed it appeared that he had. He also said that "the enemy is falling back," but the enemy was not. Some of Rosecrans's generals advised him to

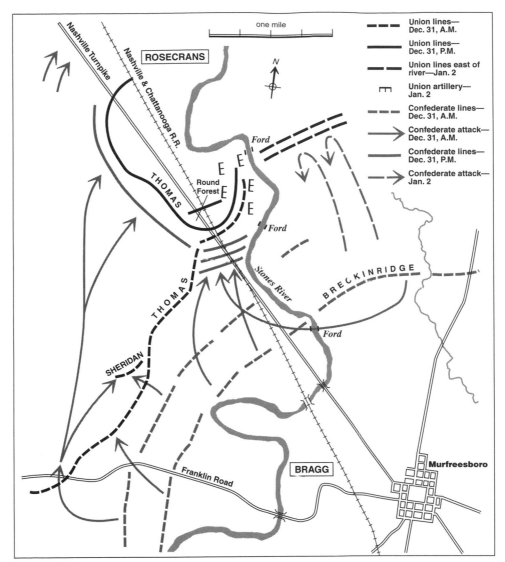

The Battle of Stones River, December 31–January 2, 1862–1863

retreat, but "Old Rosy" (as his troops called him) decided to hold on. There was little fighting next day, though both armies shifted a division to the east side of the river. When he discovered the Federals still in place on January 2, Bragg ordered (over the objections of his subordinates) an assault on the Union troops east of the river. Breckinridge's division drove the blue infantry off the hill, but the Union artillery—fifty-eight guns massed across the river—hit the Rebels in the flank at point-blank range and cut them to pieces.

Next day the torn armies held their positions, knowing that one side or the other would soon have to retreat. The combined casualty rate was the highest of the war: the Confederates had lost 33 percent of their men either killed, wounded, or missing; the Federals 31 percent. Bragg's generals had lost confidence in him; and Southern soldiers were suffering from a lack of supplies and from the incessant winter rains. The Union army, however, had received new supplies from Nashville and appeared ready to stay in position forever. So on the night of January 3–4, the Confederates began withdrawing to a new line behind the Duck River, thirty-five miles to the south. And there they went into winter quarters.

Thus did Rosecrans snatch victory from the jaws of defeat. Northern morale, depressed by the debacle at Fredericksburg, rose at the news from Stones River, despite the heavy casualties. Lincoln was profoundly grateful. "God bless you and all with you," he wired Rosecrans. "I can never forget, whilst I remember anything," the President later wrote the general, that "you gave us a hard victory which, had there been a defeat instead, the nation could scarcely have lived over."[5]

_Ce_ The War in the West: Vicksburg

Lincoln's gratitude for the outcome at Stones River was the greater because it came on the heels of bad news from Vicksburg. After the failure of Union naval forces to bombard that river fortress into submission during the summer of 1862, the Confederates had time to strengthen this "Gibraltar of the West" before the Yankees could organize another effort to capture it. As commander of the Union Department of the Tennessee, Grant in November 1862 launched an overland invasion through northern Mississippi to attack Vicksburg from the rear. In the meantime, Lincoln appointed Nathaniel P. Banks to succeed the controversial Benjamin Butler as commander of Union troops in Louisiana. Lincoln wanted Banks to lead an expedition up the Mississippi to attack Vicksburg from the south while other Union forces besieged it from the north. But the administrative problems of occupied Louisiana and the strong Confederate fort at Port Hudson prevented Banks from sending any force farther north than Baton Rouge. Without informing Grant, Lincoln also authorized another political general, John A. McClernand of Illinois, to command a downriver expedition from Memphis against Vicksburg. When Grant learned of this, he demanded clarification of his authority in the Mississippi theater. The government assured him that he had control of all 75,000 troops in his department, which included the territory between the Tennessee and Mississippi rivers as far south as Vicksburg. Distrusting McClernand, Grant sent Sherman to take charge of the troops assembling in Memphis for McClernand's expedition. When McClernand arrived at Memphis in late December, he discovered that instead of having his own army he was merely a corps commander under Grant and that Sherman had already taken his corps downriver for an attack on the Vicksburg defenses to be coordinated with Grant's overland invasion.

---

[5]Roy P. Basler (ed.), _The Collected Works of Abraham Lincoln,_ 9 vols. (New Brunswick, N.J., 1953–1955), VI, 39, 424.

McClernand was furious; but Lincoln sustained Grant's authority, and there was nothing McClernand could do about it. The West Pointer Grant had scored a victory over the politician McClernand.

Competition also existed between Confederate Generals Van Dorn and Forrest, but it took a different form. In mid-December, they led simultaneous cavalry raids against Grant's supply line. With 2,100 men Forrest eluded numerous Union patrols, killed, wounded, or captured more than 2,000 Federals, cut the railroad and telegraph for a stretch of sixty miles north of Jackson, Tennessee, captured 10,000 rifles and other equipment, and got away with the loss of only 500 men. Meanwhile, Van Dorn's 3,500 cavalry forced the surrender of the Union garrison at Holly Springs and destroyed Grant's supply depot at that place. Once again, small cavalry forces proved their ability to paralyze a large army dependent on a rail supply line deep in enemy territory. Grant was forced to call off his advance on Vicksburg and return to Tennessee.

Grant's change of plans endangered Sherman's part of the campaign, for his river-based attack was keyed to the expectation that the Confederates would weaken their Vicksburg defenses in meeting Grant's rear attack. Because Forrest had cut the telegraph, Sherman had no way of knowing that Grant had been stopped. The Rebels concentrated 14,000 troops on the Chickasaw Bluffs three miles north of Vicksburg. Sherman had to occupy these bluffs if he was to reach dry land for a move against Vicksburg itself. Although the Union attackers outnumbered the defenders by more than two to one, the Confederates were entrenched on high ground with ample artillery to cover the sandbars over which the Federal infantry must cross the swamp-bordered bayou. The Union assault on December 29 was hopeless from the start. Sherman's four divisions suffered nearly 1,800 casualties to the Confederates' 200. The Yankees withdrew to their marshy, disease-ridden camp twenty miles upriver from Vicksburg, while the Northern public learned that yet another December offensive had been snuffed out.

This was the situation when Rosecrans's ambiguous victory at Stones River temporarily lightened Lincoln's gloom. During the next four months (January–April 1863), there were no major battles on any front as the armies waited for spring to dry the roads. Grant spent this time trying fruitlessly to get his army on high ground east of the Mississippi for a campaign against Vicksburg. His greatest obstacle was topography. Vicksburg was built on a 200-foot bluff that gave its artillery command of the river and made the idea of frontal assault suicidal. West of the river a maze of bayous and swamps blocked military operations except at low water, and the winter of 1862–1863 was exceptionally wet. East of the river and extending in a 250-mile arc from Vicksburg to Memphis was a line of hills that enclosed the Delta, a strip of low-lying land averaging sixty miles in width. Today it is rich, well-drained farmland; but in 1863 much of it was a network of swamps, rivers, and junglelike forests. Only east and south of Vicksburg was there dry land suitable for military operations. Grant's problem was to get there with a large enough army—and its supplies—to defeat the enemy and reestablish contact with the Union fleet, which controlled the river north of Vicksburg.

On the map the simplest way to reach that dry land would appear to be an overland invasion from Tennessee, but Grant had already tried that without success. And to move back upriver to Memphis and start over again by land would look like a retreat. For better or worse, then, the campaign against Vicksburg would be based on the river. Grant came downriver in late January to take command personally of the troops encamped on the west bank just above Vicksburg because in his absence the distrusted McClernand was the ranking general.

A Winter of Failures

During the winter, Grant tried five different routes to get his army and supplies across the river. Three involved attempts to bypass the Vicksburg batteries in order to get gunboats, transports, and troops below the city for a secure crossing: (1) Sherman's corps renewed excavation of the canal started the previous summer, but they abandoned the effort in March when rising water flooded the area without cutting the hoped-for deepwater channel through the canal. (2) Other troops started a separate canal several miles to the north to link the river with a series of bayous that rejoined the Mississippi below Vicksburg, but the bayous proved too shallow for anything but the lightest transports. (3) Another corps began an ambitious project to open a 400-mile route from Lake Providence, far above Vicksburg, through a series of bayous and rivers all the way to the Red River far below. After expending enormous labor sawing off trees below the water, the army abandoned this route also (because it was suitable only for shallow-draft steamboats) in favor of two apparently more promising efforts to flank Vicksburg on the north by transporting troops through the endless waterways of the Delta.

The first of these, the Yazoo Pass expedition, blew up a levee opposite Helena, which enabled gunboats to enter a labyrinth of rivers tributary to the Yazoo. These treacherous waterways, where gunboats constantly ran aground and low-hanging branches banged against their smokestacks, caused the naval officer in charge to suffer a nervous breakdown. At a narrow part of the channel, where the gunboats could not maneuver, the Confederates concentrated heavy artillery and loosed a barrage that forced the Yankee fleet to turn back. Finally, there was the Steele's Bayou expedition, another attempt to get the navy through the interconnected waterways of the Delta. David Porter, now commander of the Mississippi River Squadron, took eleven gunboats on this venture through twisted channels scarcely wider than the boats themselves. As the strange flotilla penetrated deeper into the jungle, Rebel axemen felled trees across the river ahead of and behind the boats. For a time it appeared that they might trap and capture the whole fleet. But Sherman disembarked his infantry, drove the Confederates off, and the weary sailors maneuvered their tree-battered craft back to the Mississippi.

Success in the Spring

Despite these setbacks, Grant never lost confidence that he would take Vicksburg. No campaign better illustrated his coolness under pressure, his will to succeed, and his quiet ability to impart that will to subordinates. On the home front, though, a rising clamor of criticism branded Grant as a drunkard and a failure. Democrats made political capital of the alarming death rate from typhoid and dysentery among the Union troops floundering in the Mississippi and Yazoo swamps. Nervous Re-

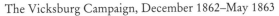

The Vicksburg Campaign, December 1862–May 1863

publicans implored Lincoln to get rid of Grant. "I think Grant has hardly a friend left, except myself," said the President. But "what I want . . . is generals who will fight battles and win victories. Grant has done this, and I propose to stand by him."[6] Lincoln's faith was not misplaced. By late March, Grant had matured a plan that had been forming in his mind for some time. Since the attempts to bypass Vicksburg had failed, he would have Porter run the gunboats and supply boats right past the batteries while the troops marched down the west bank to rendezvous with the fleet below Vicksburg. There the men would be ferried across for a campaign against the soft underbelly of Pemberton's defenses. It was a simple plan but a daring one.

Once the operation began, there was no turning back; once across the river, Grant would be cut off from his base until he could fight his way back to the Mississippi at or above Vicksburg.

Sherman and Porter opposed the plan, while Lincoln was skeptical. But like Lee, Grant was a great general because he was willing to take great risks. He sent two of his three corps southward on April 5. They made their arduous way through bottomless mud, towing makeshift rafts through the bayous, building bridges, corduroying roads, and cutting new roads as they went. On the moonless night of April 16–17, eleven of Porter's boats drifted quietly downriver toward Vicksburg. Suddenly the sky was lit by bonfires set along the banks by Rebel spotters. The heavy guns of Vicksburg opened on the fleet as the boats churned at full speed past the four-mile gauntlet of shot and shell. Every boat was hit; most were set afire; one sank. But the others got through with only thirteen men wounded. A few nights later, six transports towing twelve barges tried the same feat with less luck—six of the barges and one transport (containing medical supplies) went to the bottom, but all crewmen were rescued.

Grant now had most of his army south of Vicksburg with supplies to support it for a while. The troops were ferried across to the high ground at Bruinsburg, thirty-five miles south of Vicksburg. As he later recounted, Grant experienced

. . . a degree of relief scarcely ever equaled since. . . . I was now in the enemy's country, with a vast river and the stronghold of Vicksburg between me and my base of supplies. But I was on dry ground on the same side of the river with the enemy. All the campaigns, labors, hardships, and exposures, from the month of December previous to this time . . . were for the accomplishment of this one object.[7]

Grant's landing in Mississippi was unopposed because he had ordered two diversionary movements that deceived Pemberton into dispersing most of his troops elsewhere. On the day that Grant crossed the river with two of his corps, Sherman with the other feinted an attack north of Vicksburg in the vicinity of Chickasaw Bluffs. At the same time, Colonel Benjamin Grierson was leading one of the most spectacular cavalry raids of the war. A former music teacher from Illinois, Grierson had built a fine cavalry brigade which demonstrated that Union horsemen were finally coming up to the Confederate standard. Starting with 1,700 men, Grierson pounded down into Mississippi toward Pemberton's railroad supply line east of Jackson. Constantly driving off the Confederate cavalry sent after him, Grierson's troopers tore up fifty miles of railroad and lured a division of Confederate infantry into a futile effort to trap them. The Yankees finally reached Union lines at Baton Rouge sixteen days and six hundred miles from their starting point, having killed or wounded one hundred Rebels and captured five hundred at a cost of only twenty-four men.

It was an exploit worthy of Forrest or Stuart at their best. It also meant that when Grant's 23,000 men reached Port Gibson on May 1, there were only 8,000 Confederates to meet them. After the Federals had smashed through these defenders, Grant brought Sherman's corps downriver. He now had 44,000 men to oppose Pemberton's 32,000 plus a few thousand troops that Johnston was desperately trying to assemble

---

[6]Foote, *The Civil War . . . Fredericksburg to Meridian*, p. 217.

[7]Ulysses S. Grant, *Personal Memoirs*, 2 vols. (New York, 1885–1886), I, 480–481.

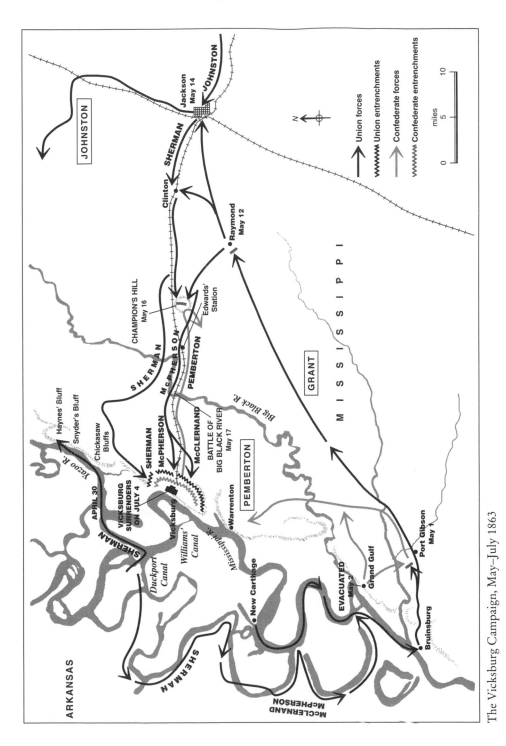

The Vicksburg Campaign, May–July 1863

in Jackson, the state capital. Grant ordered wagons and vehicles seized from nearby plantations to be filled with ammunition and other essential supplies, and told his troops to fill their haversacks with all the rations they could carry; then he cut loose from his river base and his telegraph communications with the North. His army would "live off the country" until it could fight its way back to Vicksburg.

For the next two weeks, Grant disappeared from sight, so far as anyone in the North could see. During that time his army marched 130 miles, fought and won four battles against separate enemy forces that, if combined, would have been nearly as large as Grant's own, and penned the Confederates up in the Vicksburg defenses. In the words of a British military historian, this campaign was "a brilliant vindication of the tactical maxim to hit hard, hit often, and keep on hitting."[8]

The Confederates were confused by the swiftness and unexpected direction of Grant's movements. Instead of marching directly against Vicksburg, he struck eastward toward Jackson. Grant's strategy was to seize the capital, defeat Johnston there, and having abolished this threat to his rear, to turn west and defeat the main Southern army near Vicksburg. In their attempts to counter these moves, the Confederates suffered from divided counsel. Johnston urged Pemberton to move out and join forces with him to attack Grant as far from Vicksburg as possible. But Pemberton had orders from Jefferson Davis to hold Vicksburg at all costs, so he refused to venture far from the river. A native of Pennsylvania who had chosen to side with his wife's Virginia compatriots, Pemberton was reluctant to provoke suspicions of his loyalty to the Confederacy by taking undue risks. On May 12, one Union corps cut up a small Confederate detachment at Raymond, just west of Jackson. On the 14th, two corps drove Johnston's scratch army out of Jackson. Sherman's corps remained to wreck the city's railroad and industrial facilities, while Grant turned westward with the rest of his army to strike Pemberton. That luckless general had been edging southward with the idea of cutting Grant's (nonexistent) supply line. On May 16, the two Union corps (29,000 men) ran into part of Pemberton's army (21,000) at Champion's Hill, about halfway between Jackson and Vicksburg.

The ensuing battle was the most decisive of the campaign. It could have been even more decisive but for McClernand's poor generalship. While General James B. McPherson's corps attacked vigorously on the Union right, McClernand was slow and hesitant on the left. Pemberton shifted troops to the points of heaviest fighting, where attacks and counterattacks surged back and forth. As Rebel regiments began falling back in disorder, Pemberton decided to withdraw. One of his divisions was cut off and was forced to escape to the southeast, away from Vicksburg. Not counting this division, Pemberton lost 3,851 men in the battle (to Grant's 2,441). But Grant thought he might have destroyed more of the Rebel force if McClernand had been more alert.

Next day the advancing Yankees came up against the Confederate rear guard at the Big Black River, ten miles east of Vicksburg. A headlong assault routed the unnerved defenders, most of whom retreated over the river, burning the bridge and leaving behind 1,700 men to be captured by the Federals. Ignoring yet another appeal from Johnston to march northward for a junction with his army, Pemberton withdrew to the

---

[8]Frederick E. Whitton, *The Decisive Battles of Modern Times* (London, 1923), p. 45.

Vicksburg defenses and called in scattered brigades that had been guarding the bluffs and river crossings nearby. Explaining his decision to defend Vicksburg, Pemberton wrote: "I still conceive it to be the most important point in the Confederacy."[9]

Grant's reinforced army of 45,000 surrounded Vicksburg on the land side, while Union gunboats cut it off from the river. Believing the Confederates demoralized by their defeats, Grant on May 19 ordered an assault against the Vicksburg trenches. But the Rebels had recovered their morale, and for the first time in the campaign they repulsed the bluecoats. This seemed to confirm the maxim that one soldier in trenches was the equal of at least three in the open. The Vicksburg trenches and fortifications were the strongest defensive works of the war. They were situated on a ridge fronted by deep gullies and protected by felled trees whose branches entangled enemy attackers.

Despite this, Grant decided to launch another assault on May 22, preceded by careful preparation and artillery bombardment. He wanted to avoid a siege during the sickly summer months. He also feared that a prolonged siege would enable Johnston to build up a strong army in his rear. At 10 A.M. on the 22nd, all three corps launched a simultaneous attack along a four-mile front. The attackers made temporary penetrations of the enemy works at several points but could not hold them against murderous Confederate volleys. In the two assaults of May 19 and 22, the Federals lost as many men (about 4,200) as in the previous three weeks of marching and fighting.

The repulse of these assaults compelled Grant to settle down to a siege. The dramatic May campaign of movement and battle was over. But even at its height, this campaign had attracted less public attention in both North and South than events in the Virginia theater.

Joe Hooker and the "Finest Army on the Planet"

Morale in the Army of the Potomac had dropped to rock bottom after the defeat at Fredericksburg. Four generals who wanted McClellan restored to command complained directly to Lincoln of Burnside's incompetence. One of the complainers was William B. Franklin, who as commander of the left wing had failed to exploit the only Union breakthrough in the battle. Several anti-McClellan officers also criticized Burnside, especially General Hooker, who indulged in loose talk to newspaper reporters about Burnside's bungling, the administration's stupidity, and the need for a "dictator" to run the country. Much of this feeling filtered into the ranks. A soldier from Maine wrote that "the great cause of liberty has been managed by Knaves and fools the whole show has been corruption, the result disaster, shame and disgrace." To make matters worse, Burnside was a poor administrator. With the resources of a rich country at his back and army warehouses bulging with supplies, troops in winter quarters at Falmouth suffered from poor food, poor medical care, slack discipline, and sickness—including even scurvy. Desertions increased in January 1863 to at least 200 a day. An officer described this winter of 1862–1863 as "the Valley Forge of the war."[10]

---

[9]*O.R.*, Ser. 1, Vol. 24, pt. 1, p. 273.

[10]Bell I. Wiley, *The Life of Billy Yank* (Indianapolis, 1952), p. 280; Alan T. Nolan, *The Iron Brigade: A Military History* (New York, 1961), p. 193.

LIBRARY OF CONGRESS

CO. C, 110TH PENNSYLVANIA INFANTRY, AFTER THE BATTLE OF FREDERICKSBURG. This regiment suffered heavy casualties; at the time this photograph was taken, the full complement of one hundred men in Co. C was down to about twenty-five. Note the weary slouch of the enlisted men in contrast to the ramrod-straight posture of the officer, who was probably an old-army man.

The final straw was an aborted campaign that became famous as the "Mud March." Determined to recoup his fortunes, Burnside ordered the army to move up the Rappahannock, cross the river, and flank the Confederates above Fredericksburg. The general's detractors opposed the plan. "Franklin has talked so much and so loudly to this effect," wrote one officer, "that he has completely demoralized his whole command and so rendered failure doubly sure. His conduct has been such that he surely deserves to be broken."[11] The movement began on dry roads amid unusually benign weather on January 20. But that night a heavy rain turned the roads into ooze and bogged down the whole army hub-deep in mud. Triple-teams of horses could not budge the artillery or the pontoon wagons. Rebel soldiers across the river watched this with glee and held up mocking signs with arrows pointing "This Way to Richmond."

After two days, Burnside gave it up and ordered the army back to camp. He then went to Washington and threatened to resign unless Lincoln approved the dismissal of troublemaking generals, beginning with Franklin and Hooker. Lincoln did trans-

---

[11]Charles S. Wainwright, *A Diary of Battle,* ed. Allan Nevins (New York, 1962), pp. 157–158.

fer Franklin and several other generals out of the Army of the Potomac. But recognizing that Burnside had lost the confidence of his men, the President also accepted Burnside's resignation and assigned Hooker to the command!

This action was less startling than it appeared. Although he had intrigued against Burnside, Hooker was popular with the troops and the public. Lincoln knew that he had a reputation as a drinker and a womanizer; but he also knew him as an aggressive, hard-driving general and hoped he could infuse this spirit into the army. With the appointment Lincoln also gave Hooker an admonitory letter: "I have heard, in such a way as to believe it, of your recently saying that both the Army and the Government needed a Dictator. Of course it was not *for* this, but in spite of it, that I have given you the command. Only those generals who gain successes, can set up dictators. What I now ask of you is military success, and I will risk the dictatorship."[12]

Hooker started well. He shook up the commissary and quartermaster services, upgraded the food, cleaned filthy camps, improved field hospitals, and cut the sick rate in half. He tightened discipline but at the same time granted furloughs liberally. He abolished the grand divisions, reinstituted the old corps, and increased unit pride by devising insignia badges for each corps. He increased the efficiency of the cavalry by reorganizing it into one corps instead of leaving it scattered by brigades or regiments throughout the army. Morale rose, desertions declined, and many absentees rejoined the colors after Lincoln on March 10 promised amnesty to deserters who returned. Within two months Hooker produced a remarkable transformation in the army's spirit. A soldier put it best: "Under Hooker, we began to *live*."[13]

Never modest, Hooker boasted that he had created "the finest army on the planet." The question was not whether he would take Richmond, he told the President, but when. He hoped that God Almighty would have mercy on the Rebels because Joe Hooker would have none. This gasconade disturbed Lincoln. It reminded him ominously of John Pope. A shrewd judge of character, the President feared that Hooker's boasting was a cloak to mask his insecurity. He remarked pointedly that "the hen is the wisest of all the animal creation because she never cackles until the egg is laid." Lincoln may have heard the old army story that Hooker was a superb poker player "until it came to the point where he should go a thousand better, and then he would flunk." When the President visited the army in April, his parting words to Hooker were: "In your next fight, put in all your men."[14]

The Battle of Chancellorsville

In none of the previous battles had the Army of the Potomac used its full strength. If Hooker had followed Lincoln's advice, he might have won a great victory with his army of 115,000, nearly twice the 60,000 Lee had with him along the Rappahannock

---

[12]Basler, *Works of Lincoln,* VI, 78–79.

[13]Bruce Catton, *Glory Road* (Garden City, N.Y., 1952), p. 161.

[14]Ibid., p. 157; Darius N. Couch, "The Chancellorsville Campaign," in *Battles and Leaders of the Civil War,* 4 vols. (New York, 1887), III, 155.

(Longstreet had taken two divisions for detached service south of the James River.) The Army of Northern Virginia had also gone through a hard winter. Men were on reduced rations, and horses were dying because all the forage in Virginia's fought-over countryside had been consumed. But the soldiers' morale remained high. They had constructed twenty-five miles of trenches along the river, which gave them confidence that they could hold off any number of Yankees.

Hooker had no intention of repeating Burnside's futile frontal assaults. He devised an excellent tactical plan and executed it well—up to a point. Leaving two-fifths of his infantry near Fredericksburg to feign another direct assault, he marched the rest far upriver where they swarmed across the fords, captured the surprised Confederate pickets, and moved eastward to close in on the Rebel rear. (Meanwhile Hooker had sent most of his rejuvenated cavalry on a deep raid to cut Lee's supply line. This turned out to be a mistake because the raid did little serious damage and left Hooker short of cavalry for reconnaissance in the coming battle.) On the evening of April 30, 40,000 bluecoats were still in Lee's front at Fredericksburg while 70,000 were only eight or ten miles from his rear in the vicinity of Chancellorsville, a crossroads hostelry in the Wilderness of Virginia, an area of thick second-growth forest and tangled underbrush with few clearings.

Hooker and his generals were jubilant. The 5th Corps commander George Gordon Meade declared: "Hurrah for old Joe! We're on Lee's flank and he doesn't know it."[15] This was not quite true; Lee knew where the Federals were, but he faced a dilemma in deciding what to do about it. His only apparent choices were to retreat toward Richmond, which would expose his army to attacks on both flanks, or to face the army about to meet the larger threat from Chancellorsville, which would expose him to a rear attack from the force at Fredericksburg.

Typically, Lee did neither. Once again he took a bold risk by dividing his army, leaving 10,000 men under Jubal Early to hold the Fredericksburg trenches and marching the rest toward Chancellorsville. The Federals there moved eastward two miles on May 1 to the open country beyond the Wilderness. But when they clashed with advance Confederate units, Hooker suddenly ordered his troops back to defensive positions near Chancellorsville. His corps commanders protested, for this meant surrendering the initiative to Lee. It also meant that the dense woods of the Wilderness would neutralize Union numerical and artillery supremacy. Many theories have been advanced to explain this strange decision by a general previously known as "Fighting Joe." The most likely explanation is that faced with the responsibility of commanding an entire army in a showdown battle, Hooker lost his nerve. The poker player who faltered when it was time to raise his opponent a thousand was not the man to raise a gambler like Lee when the stakes were much greater.

From the afternoon of May 1, Hooker was psychologically "a whipped man," as one of his generals later wrote. Once again Lee read his enemy's weakness like a book. Stuart's cavalry discovered that Hooker's right flank three miles west of Chancellorsville was "in the air." Although the Confederate army was already divided, Lee decided to divide it again. On May 2, he sent Jackson with 28,000 men

---

[15]Ernest B. Furgurson, *Chancellorsville 1863: The Souls of the Brave* (New York, 1992), p. 110.

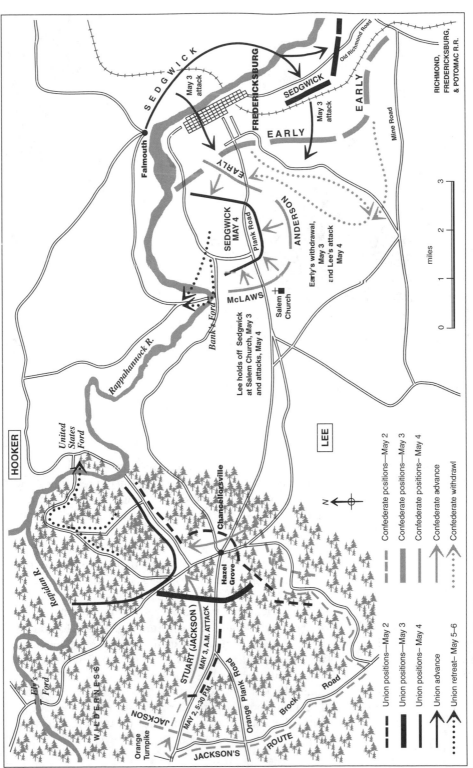

The Battle of Chancellorsville, May 2–6, 1863

LIBRARY OF CONGRESS

A PORTION OF THE CONFEDERATE LINE AT THE STONE WALL BELOW MARYE'S HEIGHTS AT FREDERICKSBURG, CARRIED BY UNION TROOPS ON MAY 3, 1863. The photographer took this picture only twenty minutes after the Yankee assault carried the trenches.

on a roundabout fourteen-mile march to attack the Union flank, while the remaining 18,000 Confederate military stood wary watch against three times their number. It was Lee's riskiest gamble yet, for if Hooker discovered it he could drive a wedge between these two parts of Lee's army before Jackson could get his troops deployed for an attack on Hooker's right.

Federal scouts detected Jackson's movements, and Hooker warned General Oliver O. Howard, commander of the 11th Corps holding the right flank, to strengthen his defenses. But instead of ordering an all-out assault on Jackson's marchers as they crossed his front, Hooker sent only two divisions on a reconnaissance in force. Reports from this reconnaissance that Jackson's troops were moving southward (see map) convinced Hooker that the Confederates were retreating! Both Hooker and Howard relaxed their vigilance, despite repeated warnings by Union pickets in Howard's corps that the Rebels were building up to something in the woods.

Many of the 12,000 men in the 11th Corps were playing cards or cooking supper at 5:30 when Jackson's screaming Rebels burst out of the woods and crumbled the Union flank like a dry leaf. The 11th Corps contained many German-American regiments. In the eyes of the rest of the army, they had a poor reputation, which this day's fighting did nothing to improve. Some of the regiments fought stubbornly after their initial surprise, but they never had a chance to regain formation. The Confederates pushed them back more than two miles before various blue brigades formed a solid line and brought the onslaught to a halt at dark. Eager to cut the Federals off from the river, Jackson rode ahead to reconnoiter for a night attack. As he was returning to his own lines, a jumpy Confederate company, thinking that Jackson's party were Union cavalry, loosed a volley that wounded the general. Early the next morning, his left arm was amputated; when Lee learned of this, he said: "He has lost his left arm; but I have lost my right arm."[16]

Despite the success of Jackson's attack, Hooker still had a good chance to defeat Lee the next day. The two parts of the Confederate army in the Wilderness were separated by the Union forces, which outnumbered them and held the high ground at Hazel Grove, one of the few clearings where artillery could operate effectively. Under the mistaken assumption that Hazel Grove was an exposed salient, Hooker committed his greatest blunder when he ordered it abandoned at dawn. The alert Stuart, temporarily commanding Jackson's corps, quickly moved fifty guns to the hill, from where they pounded the Union defenses while the Confederate infantry launched repeated assaults. The bluecoats gave ground grudgingly, inflicting heavy casualties.

Only half of Hooker's force was engaged, but forgetting Lincoln's advice to "put in all your men," the general refused to order two idle corps into action. During the fighting Hooker was stunned when a cannonball struck a column of the Chancellor House on which he was leaning. Although groggy, he would not turn the army over to the senior corps commander, who wanted to throw every Union division into the battle. Instead, Hooker ordered a fallback to a new position north of Chancellorsville.

Meanwhile in Fredericksburg, the 25,000 remaining bluecoats had finally carried the heights beyond the town. When Lee learned that this force was coming up on his rear, he once again divided his army at Chancellorsville, leaving Stuart with 25,000 men to contain the 75,000 Federals there while he marched with the rest to reinforce Early's 10,000. In sharp fighting halfway between Chancellorsville and Fredericksburg on May 3–4, the Confederates drove the outnumbered Unionists on this front across the river while Hooker remained idle with his large force only a few miles to the west. Lee then returned to confront Hooker, who gave up the battle and crossed to the north bank of the Rappahannock on May 6.

The defeat was a bitter, humiliating one for "the finest army on the planet." But it was primarily Hooker rather than the army who was defeated. Morale in the ranks did not suffer after this battle as after Fredericksburg, despite the 17,000 Union casualties (compared with 13,000 Confederate) in four days of fighting. Chancellorsville has been called "Lee's greatest masterpiece," but that was so mainly because Hooker's battlefield generalship was the worst of the war. And in the end the South may have lost more than it gained despite its great victory, for on May 10 Jackson died of pneumonia, which had set in after he was wounded.

---

[16]Douglas Southall Freeman, *Lee's Lieutenants*, 3 vols. (New York, 1942–1944), II, 669.

Lincoln received the news of Chancellorsville with an "ashen" face, according to a visitor. "My God! my God!" he exclaimed. "What will the country say!"[17] Coming on the heels of the other failures in this winter of despair (so far as the public knew, Grant was still bogged down in the bayous near Vicksburg), Chancellorsville might be a mortal blow to the Union cause. But instead, it turned out to be the darkness before the dawn. In the summer and fall of 1863, several crucial Union victories would turn the conflict in favor of the North.

---

[17]Noah Brooks, *Washington in Lincoln's Time* (New York, 1896), pp. 57–58.

Chapter Nineteen

The Second Turning Point: Gettysburg, Vicksburg, and Chattanooga

Yesterday we rode on the pinnacle of success—today absolute ruin seems to be our portion.

—Josiah Gorgas,
Confederate Ordnance Chief, July 28, 1863

349

The Gettysburg Campaign

Southern elation over the victory at Chancellorsville masked intensifying problems for the Confederacy. The blockade was tightening; inflation was worsening; Grant was closing in on Vicksburg; Banks was approaching Port Hudson; Rosecrans appeared ready to push Bragg out of central Tennessee; the Federals were preparing a combined army-navy operation against Charleston; and the Army of the Potomac remained poised on the north bank of the Rappahannock. On all fronts the South was hemmed in by superior numbers.

During May, the Confederate cabinet and leading generals held several conferences to hammer out a strategy for dealing with this situation. Longstreet proposed that he take two divisions west to reinforce Bragg for an offensive against Rosecrans. If successful, such an effort would not only liberate Tennessee but also force Grant to relax his grip on Vicksburg. But Lee opposed this plan. The railroads were too rickety to carry a large force to the West, he said; the coming summer would compel the unacclimated Northern troops at Vicksburg to retreat anyway; the most important theater was Virginia, where, instead of being weakened, the Army of Northern Virginia should be reinforced for another invasion of the North. This would relieve the threat to Richmond, enable the army to supply itself from the rich Pennsylvania countryside, reduce the pressure on Confederate armies in the West by forcing Union armies there to send reinforcements to the East, strengthen the Peace Democrats in the North by demonstrating the unbeatable power of the South, reopen the question of European recognition of the Confederacy, and perhaps accomplish the capture of Washington or other Northern cities. Lee's great prestige enabled him to carry his point. The government approved his plan for an invasion.

Lee has been criticized for his narrow preoccupation with the Virginia theater. A Virginian who had gone to war to defend his state, he lacked a large strategic vision encompassing the South as a whole. The Confederacy was losing the war in the West, even if it appeared to be winning in Virginia. Lee's belief that an invasion of Pennsylvania would force Grant and Rosecrans to weaken their grip in the West was wishful thinking. On the other hand, had it not been for Lee's extraordinary tactical victories in Virginia, the South might have lost the war earlier. And if the Confederates had won the ensuing battle of Gettysburg, nothing would ever have been heard of the defects in Lee's strategic vision.

The return of Longstreet's divisions to the army and reinforcements from elsewhere brought Lee's strength up to 75,000 men. Early in June they began to move. Trying to penetrate Stuart's cavalry screen to find out what the Rebels were up to, Union horsemen crossed the Rappahannock June 9 and precipitated the largest cavalry battle of the war, at Brandy Station near Culpeper. Although eventually driven back across the river, the Yankee troopers gave a good account of themselves. Richmond newspapers reproached Stuart and his "puffed up cavalry" for having been surprised at Brandy Station. This criticism rankled the South's *beau sabreur.* His eagerness to erase the stain by another dramatic ride was to have serious consequences for the forthcoming campaign.

But at first all went well. The advance Confederate units (Jackson's old corps, now commanded by Richard Ewell) captured or scattered Union garrisons at Winchester and elsewhere in the Shenandoah Valley, and crossed the Potomac in mid-June. The invaders intended to live off the land in Pennsylvania, as Grant's troops had done in Mississippi. Rebel foraging parties stripped the fertile Pennsylvania countryside of horses, livestock, and food. They cleaned out stores of shoes and clothing, paying or promising to pay with Confederate money. They levied tribute on merchants and banks in the towns—$28,000 from York, for example. Most ominously, Confederate scouting parties rounded up black people (including some born free in Pennsylvania) and sent them south, claiming that they were escaped slaves. A Chambersburg woman described the capture of several black women and children, who were "driven by just like we would drive cattle."[1]

The Army of the Potomac groped uncertainly toward the Rebels as they began moving north. Hooker suggested to Lincoln that he could cut in behind the Confederate force and capture Richmond. Lincoln vetoed this proposal and gave Hooker some sound strategic advice: "I think *Lee's army,* and not *Richmond,* is your true objective point."[2] Although Hooker moved quickly to keep his army between the Confederates and Washington, he began to complain that the Rebels outnumbered him, that the government was not supporting him, and that he could never win unless he had the administration's confidence. This sounded distressingly like McClellan. Lincoln began to suspect that Hooker was afraid to fight Lee again. The President had earlier considered removing Hooker from command; when the general submitted his resignation over a quarrel with Halleck about the Harpers Ferry garrison, Lincoln accepted it and on June 28 appointed a surprised George Gordon Meade to the command.

On the day Meade assumed command, two of Lee's three corps were at Chambersburg; part of Ewell's corps was at York and the rest near Harrisburg. Stuart's cavalry had taken off on a deep raid around the Union rear. Similar raids against McClellan had made Stuart famous, but this one would earn him only rebuke for depriving Lee of his "eyes" when he most needed them. Lee hoped to cross the Susquehanna and rip up the Pennsylvania Railroad between Harrisburg and Lancaster. But in Stuart's absence, he did not know where the Union army was. When a scout reported that it was across the Potomac and heading north, Lee hurriedly sent couriers to call in his scattered divisions. Lee intended to concentrate at Cashtown, a village eight miles west of Gettysburg. Meade had disposed his army to cover all the approaches to Washington and Baltimore. Neither had planned to fight at Gettysburg. But early on the morning of July 1, a Confederate infantry brigade on its way to seize a rumored cache of shoes in Gettysburg clashed with two Union cavalry brigades west of the town. The Northern cavalry commander, John Buford, had recognized the strategic importance of this town, where a dozen roads converged from every point on the compass. Buford dismounted his troopers to hold back the charging Rebels, while couriers on both sides pounded up the roads to summon reinforcements. Thus began the most crucial battle in American history.

---

[1]Edwin B. Coddington, *The Gettysburg Campaign: A Study in Command* (New York, 1968), pp. 153–179, esp. p. 161; James C. Mohr, *The Cormany Diaries: A Northern Family in the Civil War* (Pittsburgh, 1982), pp. 328–330.

[2]Lincoln to Hooker, June 10, 1863, in Roy P. Basler (ed.), *The Collected Works of Abraham Lincoln,* 9 vols. (New Brunswick, N.J., 1953–1955), VI, 257.

The Battle of Gettysburg

Since they were closer to Gettysburg, the Confederates were able to achieve a faster concentration. They got 25,000 men into action July 1 against the Union's 19,000. Through the long hours of that day, it was a story of outnumbered bluecoats desperately holding off repeated gray attacks before finally giving way. In midmorning the tough Union 1st Corps came up to relieve Buford's cavalry and stop the slashing Confederate attacks of A. P. Hill's corps west of the town. The commander of the 1st Corps, John F. Reynolds, was killed early in this action. During the early afternoon, the Union 11th Corps arrived and took up a position north of the town, where they met Ewell's troops coming down from the north. Outgunned along both flanks, the luckless Union "German Corps" (see page 346) was once again routed by Jackson's old corps, causing the Union position west of Gettysburg also to collapse after some of the war's hardest fighting. Northern troops retreated in disorder through the town to take up a position on Cemetery Hill. Ironically, a sign on the cemetery gate read: "All persons found using firearms in these grounds will be prosecuted with the utmost rigor of the law."

Lee arrived at Gettysburg in midafternoon. Still without Stuart and uncertain where the rest of the Union army was, he was reluctant to bring on a general engagement. But the success of his troops changed his mind. He gave Ewell discretionary orders to take Cemetery Hill "if practicable." When Jackson had commanded this corps, such an order would have produced an all-out assault. But Ewell hesitated. He knew that the Federals had dug in on the hill and placed a lot of artillery up there, and in the end he decided not to attack. As darkness fell, one of the many "ifs" of Gettysburg was already being debated: If Ewell had attacked Cemetery Hill on July 1, could he have taken it, and if he had, would the outcome of the battle and of the war have been the same?

During the night and next morning, most of the remaining troops in both armies reached the battlefield. The Federal position resembled a fishhook, with the barbed end curving from Culp's Hill to Cemetery Hill and the shank running southward along low-lying Cemetery Ridge to the eye at two other hills, Little Round Top and Round Top. With Culp's Hill and the Round Tops anchoring the flanks, and the convex shape of the line allowing reinforcements to be shifted rapidly from one point to another, the Union line was admirably suited to defense. The concave Confederate line was nearly twice as long, and communication from one part to another was difficult.

After studying the Union position on the morning of July 2, Longstreet concluded that it was too strong to be attacked. He urged Lee to make a flanking march to the south, where the Confederates could get between the Union army and Washington, pick a good defensive position of their own, and force Meade to attack them. But Lee's fighting blood was up. He believed his army invincible. Without adequate cavalry, a flanking movement such as Longstreet advocated would be dangerous. With limited supplies and a vulnerable line of communications, Lee thought that he had to fight or retreat. Therefore, he rejected Longstreet's advice and resolved to attack

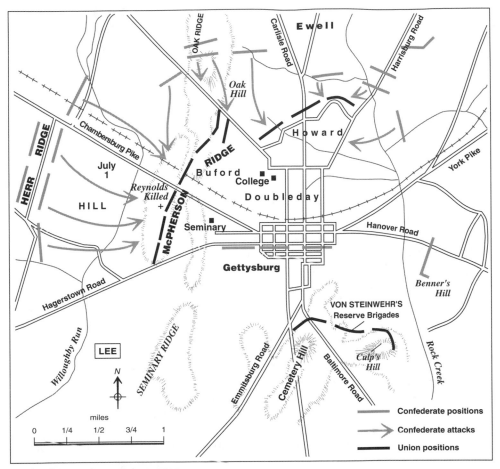

Battle of Gettysburg, July 1, 1863

the Union flanks. Ewell still thought the right flank too strong, so Lee ordered Longstreet to make the primary assault on the Union left while Ewell, at the sound of Longstreet's artillery, was to make a secondary attack on Cemetery and Culp's hills to prevent Meade from shifting reinforcements to his left.

Although Longstreet had disagreed with Lee's plan for attack, he carried it out as well as possible under the circumstances.[3] Because the most direct route to the attack point was under observation from a Union signal station, Longstreet's troops had to countermarch on a different route and did not attack until late afternoon. Commanding the Union 3rd Corps holding the Federal left was Daniel Sickles, an ex-Tammany politician who had achieved notoriety when he murdered his wife's

---

[3]For more than a century, controversy has persisted over Longstreet's role in the battle of Gettysburg. The Virginians who dominated the writing first of memoirs and then of histories of the Army of Northern Virginia seemed eager to blame Longstreet for loss of the battle—in part to exonerate Virginians who might otherwise be blamed, including Lee himself as well as Ewell and Stuart. They

(cont.)

lover. Contrary to orders, Sickles had advanced his corps from the low ground at the south end of Cemetery Ridge to higher ground along the Emmitsburg road, creating a salient in the Union line. Sickles's advance had left Little Round Top undefended. When Union General Gouverneur K. Warren discovered this, he realized that Confederate capture of the hill would allow Rebel artillery to enfilade the entire Union line. Warren quickly rushed two brigades of the 5th Corps to Little Round Top minutes ahead of the charging Confederates. Desperate fighting raged back and forth across the rocky slopes of the hill in which the 20th Maine, holding the left flank of the entire Army of the Potomac, particularly distinguished itself. The Yankees held on to Little Round Top, but Sickles's salient to the northwest was driven back in vicious fighting at places that became famous: the Peach Orchard; the Wheat Field; and Devil's Den, a maze of boulders across a boggy creek from Little Round Top. Confederate units attacked with great élan, but Union forces fought with fierce determination backed by timely command decisions in shifting reinforcements to threatened points. The main Federal line on Cemetery Ridge held firm. By dusk the exhausted Rebels on the right had given up the attack.

Over on the left, Ewell's guns had opened when Longstreet began his attack, but instead of sending his infantry against Culp's and Cemetery hills, Ewell engaged in a fruitless three-hour artillery duel with Union batteries. When his infantry finally went forward, two brigades penetrated the Union defenses on the east side of Cemetery Hill (held by the hapless 11th Corps) and another occupied some Union trenches on the southern slope of Culp's Hill that had been vacated earlier by troops sent to reinforce the Union left. But in Ewell's sector, a lack of coordination among the attacking brigades robbed the Confederates of any chance to exploit their breakthrough. The successful attacks had come at dusk, and they were unsupported; Union reinforcements drove the Rebels off Cemetery Hill and stopped them short of the summit of Culp's.

A. P. Hill's corps had been crippled the first day; Longstreet's (except George Pickett's division, which did not arrive until evening) was mangled the second day. Longstreet again pleaded with Lee to maneuver around the Federal left. But Lee would not hear of it. He knew that three Federal corps (1st, 3rd, and 11th) had been equally mauled in two days of fighting. In a rare failure of insight into the psychology of his opponents, Lee believed that Union morale had been sapped by these losses. He also thought that the attacks on the Union flanks had forced Meade to

---

[3]charged Longstreet with tardiness and reluctance in executing the attacks of both July 2 and 3, which they assumed would have succeeded if carried out with more speed and vigor. Most historians now disagree with this analysis, however, and are more likely to attribute Confederate defeat to Lee's overconfident aggressiveness in attacking strong positions, and to effective leadership and superb fighting by the Union army. For discussions of this controversy, see Glenn Tucker, *Lee and Longstreet at Gettysburg* (Indianapolis, 1968); Thomas L. Connelly, *The Marble Man: Robert E. Lee and His Image in American Society* (New York, 1977); William Garrett Piston, *Lee's Tarnished Lieutenant: James Longstreet and His Place in Southern History* (Athens, Ga., 1987); and several of the essays in Gary W. Gallagher (ed.) *The Second Day at Gettysburg* (Kent, Ohio, 1993), Gallagher (ed.), *The Third Day at Gettysburg & Beyond* (Chapel Hill, 1994), and Gabor S. Boritt (ed.), *The Gettysburg Nobody Knows* (New York, 1997). Michael Shaara's novel *The Killer Angels* (New York, 1974) provides a sympathetic account of Longstreet's actions and his state of mind at Gettysburg.

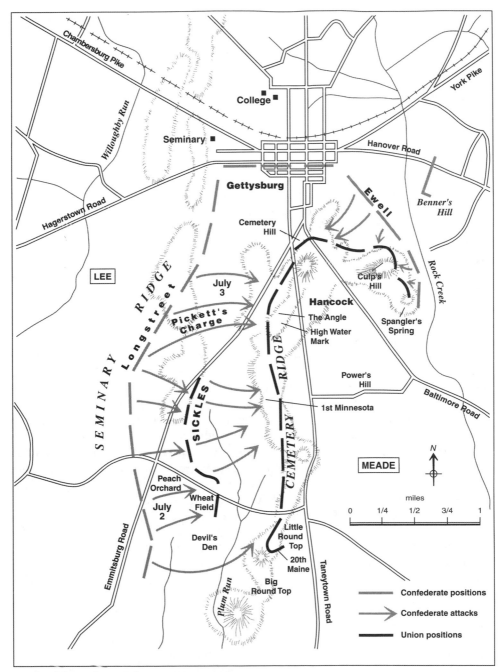

Battle of Gettysburg, July 2-3, 1863

weaken his center. Over Longstreet's objections Lee decided to mass three divisions, led by Pickett's fresh troops, for an assault on the Union center. It was a poor decision. Northern morale was high; Meade expected the attack on his center; and the point selected for attack was held by two divisions of Winfield Scott Hancock's 2nd Corps, some of the best troops in the Army of the Potomac.

Before Pickett's charge on the third day at Gettysburg, however, shooting broke out at dawn on Culp's Hill, where the Federals had attacked to regain their lost trenches. In six hours of hard fighting, they not only won the trenches but drove most of the Rebels off the hill altogether. An eerie silence fell upon the field at noon. Longstreet was massing 143 guns to soften up the Union center prior to the infantry assault. Stuart's cavalry, which had arrived only the night before, swung out to the east of the battlefield to come in behind the Union center when Pickett hit it in front. But Stuart's troopers never got closer than two and a half miles to the Union rear, for they were intercepted and defeated by Union cavalry in a three-hour clash distinguished by the headlong charges of a blue brigade commanded by twenty-three-year-old General George Armstrong Custer.

About one o'clock, two signal guns shattered the silence at Gettysburg. Suddenly, the air was filled with Confederate shells. Union batteries replied, and the heaviest artillery duel of the war ensued. At first, the Confederate shelling was accurate and damaging, but as the guns' recoils dug their trails into the ground the shots began to go high, falling in the rear of the Union infantry crouched behind a stone wall and breastworks. The smoke was so thick that Southern artillery observers could not tell the effect of their fire. After more than an hour, many Union batteries began to fall silent, in order to conserve ammunition for the expected Confederate assault and to deceive the Rebels into thinking that the blue artillery had been disabled.

The ruse worked. Confederate cannoneers believed their fire knocked out the Yankee batteries. Just before three o'clock, the Southern artillery ceased firing and the gray infantry stepped out. As 13,000 Rebels approached the Union lines in parade-ground order, the blue artillery belched forth, cutting great gaps in Confederate ranks. Then the Northern infantry fired volley after volley into the thinning Southern columns. A handful of Rebels charged over the stone wall but were immediately shot down or captured. Two of the three brigade commanders in Pickett's own division were killed and the third badly wounded. All thirteen of his colonels were killed or wounded. The casualties among officers in several other brigades were almost as high. Scarcely half of the attackers in the war's most famous charge returned to their own lines, where General Lee rode among them trying to console them with the words: "It's all my fault." "You must help me." "All good men must rally."

Aftermath of the Battle

Lee and Longstreet worked feverishly to patch up a defensive line to receive the expected Union counterattack. But no counterattack came. The wounded Hancock pleaded with Meade to go over to the offensive. But Meade, a careful, cautious man who had been in command only six days, three of them fighting for his army's life, was in no mood to take chances. He said later that he did not want to follow "the

LIBRARY OF CONGRESS

UNION AND CONFEDERATE DEAD AT GETTYSBURG. These photos were taken by Northern photographers Alexander Gardner and Timothy O'Sullivan on July 5, three days after the soldiers had been killed and just before burial crews began their grisly task of gathering and burying the bloated and mangled corpses. One picture shows Union soldiers killed in the assault of Longstreet's corps near the Wheat Field. The other focuses on a Rebel soldier blown apart by a shell in the same sector of the battlefield.

LIBRARY OF CONGRESS

bad example [Lee] had set me, in ruining himself attacking a strong position."[4] Late in the afternoon, some of Meade's 20,000 reserves did move forward from the area of Little Round Top, flushing out Longstreet's rear guard which was pulling back from its advanced positions of the previous day. But Meade ordered no general counterattack. He feared that his troops were too exhausted and disabled by casualties, and did not know yet how badly Lee's army was crippled or how short it had run of artillery ammunition. The Army of the Potomac suffered 23,049 casualties in the battle: 3,155 killed, 14,528 wounded (more than 2,000 of them mortally), and 5,365 missing. Confederate casualties were higher—at least 24,000, one-third of the 75,000 effectives in Lee's army on the eve of the battle.

Meade's caution did not end with the battle itself. After remaining in position during July 4, Lee's army began the sad retreat to Virginia in a rainstorm exactly one month after it had started north with such high hopes. From the outset Lincoln had viewed the Confederate invasion more as an opportunity than as a threat—an opportunity to cripple and perhaps to destroy the Rebel army far from its home base. At the President's urging, General-in-Chief Halleck sent repeated messages to Meade instructing him to "push forward, and fight Lee before he can cross the Potomac."[5] Union cavalry harassed Lee's retreat and destroyed his pontoon bridge over the Potomac. Since the river was too high from recent rains to be forded, Lee was in a tight spot. Straggling and desertions had reduced his army to 42,000 effectives, while reinforcements had brought Meade's strength back up to 85,000. Yet Meade, personally exhausted and in an ill temper from Halleck's prodding messages, followed Lee slowly and hesitated to attack the fortified lines that the Confederates had constructed at Williamsport while their engineers worked with desperate haste to build a new bridge. On the night of July 13–14, the Rebels escaped across the river over their new bridge and at a ford made possible by the falling river level.

When Lincoln learned of this, he was inconsolable. "On only one or two occasions have I ever seen the President so troubled, so dejected and discouraged," wrote Secretary of the Navy Gideon Welles. "We had them in our grasp," said Lincoln. "We had only to stretch forth our hands & they were ours. And nothing I could say or do could make the Army move."[6] When Halleck sent word to Meade of the President's dissatisfaction, the testy general offered his resignation. This was a serious matter, for despite his slowness Meade had won great public acclaim for Gettysburg. An administration that sacked a general after such a victory would look foolish, if not worse. Halleck reassured Meade of the government's confidence in him and refused to accept his resignation. Lincoln sat down to write Meade a letter to assuage the general's anger. But the President's own unhappiness caused the letter to come out differently than he intended, so he never sent it. "My dear general," he wrote after congratulating Meade on his victory. "I do not believe you appreciate the magnitude

---

[4] *O.R.,* Ser. 1, Vol. 27, pt. 3, p. 539.

[5] *O.R.,* Ser. 1, Vol. 27, pt. 1, p. 83.

[6] Gideon Welles, *The Diary of Gideon Welles,* ed. Howard K. Beale, 3 vols. (New York, 1960), I, 371; Michael Burlingame and John R.T. Ettlinger (eds.) *Inside Lincoln's White House: The Complete Civil War Diary of John Hay* (Carbondale, Ill., 1997), p. 62.

of the misfortune involved in Lee's escape. He was within your easy grasp, and to have closed upon him would, in connection with our other late successes, have ended the war. As it is, the war will be prolonged indefinitely."[7]

The "other late successes" to which Lincoln alluded were the capture of Vicksburg and Port Hudson, and Rosecrans's expulsion of Bragg from central Tennessee.

Union Victories in the West

The Fall of Vicksburg and Port Hudson

At Vicksburg the Union army had inexorably tightened its siege lines during the six weeks after the unsuccessful assault of May 22 (see page 340). Engineers tunneled under the Confederate line and exploded a mine on June 25, but the supporting attack failed to achieve a breakthrough. Another mine was readied for July 6, when Grant planned an all-out assault, but before then the Rebels had had enough. Reduced to quarter rations, subjected to artillery and mortar bombardment around the clock and sharpshooter fire during the day, the garrison was exhausted and near starvation. Civilians who had remained in Vicksburg lived in caves and shared the soldiers' meager diet, supplemented toward the end with mule meat and rats. Their only hope for salvation was Joseph Johnston, who had organized odds and ends of troops into an army of 30,000 men poised across the Big Black River twenty miles to the east. But Johnston lacked sufficient supplies, weapons, and transportation for these men, while Grant's lines had been reinforced to 70,000 tough, well-armed veterans. Johnston reported to Richmond on June 15: "I consider saving Vicksburg hopeless."[8]

So did many of the besieged Vicksburg soldiers, who on June 28 sent General Pemberton a petition that concluded: "If you can't feed us, you had better surrender."[9] On July 3, Pemberton came through the lines under a flag of truce to discuss surrender terms with Grant. Neither, of course, knew of the climactic events taking place at that moment far away in Pennsylvania. The Vicksburg garrison formally surrendered July 4. The 30,000 Confederate prisoners were paroled (that is, they pledged not to bear arms until exchanged), and many of them drifted away to their homes never to fight again.

Before dark on July 4, Sherman took 50,000 men to go after Johnston's hovering army. These Confederates retreated to Jackson, where Johnston hoped to induce Sherman to hurl his infantry against the strong entrenchments. But after some sharp skirmishing, Sherman began to surround the city in order to starve out the defenders, as at Vicksburg. This was just what Johnston feared, so on the night of July 16 he withdrew stealthily, abandoning central Mississippi to the Federals.

Nor was this the full extent of Confederate losses. Union General Banks had besieged Port Hudson on May 23 with 15,000 soldiers and several warships of Farragut's fleet. The trenches and the natural defenses of ravines, woods, and bayous surrounding Port

[7]Basler, *Works of Lincoln,* VI, 327–328.
[8]*O.R.,* Ser. 1, Vol. 24, pt. 1, p. 227.
[9]Allan Nevins, *The War for the Union: The Organized War 1863–64* (New York, 1971), p. 71.

LIBRARY OF CONGRESS

UNION TRENCHES AT VICKSBURG.   These dugouts and mortar shelters protected the soldiers of the 45th Illinois against artillery fire on the center of the Union line at Vicksburg. The house owned by local planter James Shirley miraculously survived the siege and still stands, in what is today the Vicksburg National Military Park.

Hudson rivaled those of Vicksburg. Banks tried two assaults, on May 27 and June 14, both of which were repulsed with Union casualties ten times greater than those of the defenders. After the second assault, Banks was content to starve out the garrison, which suffered even more from hunger than Vicksburg. One Confederate soldier wrote in his diary that the men had eaten "all the beef—all the mules—all the Dogs—and all the Rats."[10] The news of Vicksburg's surrender gave the Port Hudson commander no choice but to do likewise, on July 8. The Confederacy was cut in twain. The Mississippi River was now a Union highway. On July 16, a merchant steamboat tied up at the wharf in New Orleans, having traveled unmolested from St. Louis. Rebel snipers on the river-banks were still to be feared, but Lincoln was essentially correct when he announced that "the Father of Waters again goes unvexed to the sea."[11]

Grant's Vicksburg campaign is generally regarded as the most successful of the war. With casualties of fewer than 10,000, his army had killed or wounded 10,000 of the enemy and captured another 37,000 (30,000 at Vicksburg and 7,000 previously), including fifteen generals. They had also taken 172 cannon and 60,000 rifles. A distinguished British military historian has written that "we must go back to the cam-

---

[10]Bell I. Wiley, *The Life of Johnny Reb* (Indianapolis, 1943),p. 94.
[11]Basler, *Works of Lincoln,* VI, 409.

paigns of Napoleon to find equally brilliant results accomplished in the same space of time with such small loss." Lincoln was delighted with the outcome at Vicksburg, so different from the lost opportunity after Gettysburg. "Grant is my man," said the President, "and I am his the rest of the war."[12]

The losses at Gettysburg and Vicksburg shook the Confederacy to its foundations. "I see no prospect now of the South ever sustaining itself," wrote a Confederate private captured at Vicksburg. "We have lost the Mississippi and our nation is Divided and they is not a nuf left to fight for." A Rebel soldier who had fought at Gettysburg wrote afterward to his sister: "We got a bad whiping. . . . They are awhiping us . . . at every point. . . . I hope they would make peace so that we that is alive yet would get home agane." The loss of Vicksburg left Jefferson Davis "in the depths of gloom. . . . We are now in the darkest hour of our political existence." And Confederate Ordnance Chief Josiah Gorgas wrote in his diary on July 28, 1863:

Events have succeeded one another with disastrous rapidity. One brief month ago we were apparently at the point of success. Lee was in Pennsylvania threatening Harrisburgh, and even Philadelphia. Vicksburgh seemed to laugh all Grant's efforts to scorn. . . . Now the picture is just as sombre as it was bright then. . . . It seems incredible that human power could effect such a change in so brief a space. Yesterday we rode on the pinnacle of success—today absolute ruin seems to be our portion. The Confederacy totters to its destruction.[13]

The Confederates Retreat from Tennessee

Added to the Southern list of woes in July 1863 was the retreat of Bragg's army from central Tennessee. After the battle of Stones River at the end of 1862 (pages 331 to 333), the two bruised armies shadowboxed warily with each other south of Murfreesboro for nearly six months. Although Rosecrans's Army of the Cumberland had nearly twice as many infantry regiments as the Army of Tennessee, the Confederates were superior in cavalry. Nathan Bedford Forrest and Joseph Wheeler led several mounted raids against Rosecrans's communications, while John Hunt Morgan began a spectacular but relatively unproductive raid that carried him all the way into Indiana and Ohio before he and most of his men were finally captured. Guerrillas also played havoc with the Federals' supply lines. In retaliation, Rosecrans sent a mule-mounted raid (he was short of horses) deep into the Confederate rear to cut the railroad between Chattanooga and Atlanta, but Forrest caught up with the raiders in Alabama and captured them.

Washington put increasing pressure on Rosecrans to begin his campaign against Bragg. Just as Lincoln's patience was about to run out, Rosecrans finally got moving, on June 23. Once started, he maneuvered his 63,000 men with speed and skill despite rain that fell steadily for two weeks. The 45,000 Confederates held a strong defensive position behind four gaps in the Cumberland foothills. Feinting with his cavalry and one infantry corps toward the western gaps, Rosecrans sent three corps through and around the other gaps with such force and swiftness that the Confederates were knocked aside or flanked almost before they knew what had hit them.

---

[12] J. F. C. Fuller, *Grant and Lee* (London, 1933), p. 184; T. Harry Williams, *Lincoln and His Gener* (New York, 1952), p. 272.

[13] Bell I. Wiley, *The Road to Appomattox* (Memphis, 1956), pp. 64–65; Dunbar Rowland (ed.), *Jefferson Davis, Constitutionalist,* 10 vols. (Jackson, Miss., 1923), V, 548, 554; Frank Vandiver (ed.), *Civil War Diary of General Josiah Gorgas* (University, Ala., 1947), p. 55.

Forced back to Tullahoma, Bragg received another rude surprise when a blue brigade of mounted infantry armed with new seven-shot Spencer rifles got around to the Confederate rear and threatened their rail lifeline. Once again Bragg fell back, this time all the way to Chattanooga. In little more than a week's time and at a cost of only 560 casualties, Rosecrans had pushed the enemy almost into Georgia. Piqued by dispatches from Washington announcing the great victories at Gettysburg and Vicksburg, Rosecrans wired back that he hoped the War Department would not overlook his own achievement just "because it is not written in letters of blood."[14]

Chattanooga was a city of great strategic importance. Situated in a gap carved by the Tennessee River through the Cumberland Mountains, the city formed the junction of the Confederacy's two east-west railroads and the gateway both to east Tennessee and to the war industries of Georgia. Having already split the Confederacy in two with the capture of Vicksburg, Northern armies could split it in three by a penetration into Georgia via Chattanooga.

Lincoln prodded Rosecrans to attack the Confederates in Chattanooga quickly while they were off balance. But the stiff-backed general insisted that he could not advance until all the railroads and bridges were repaired and new supply bases fully stocked. Rosecrans also wanted his left flank protected by a simultaneous advance of another Union army from Kentucky to Knoxville. This was the newly formed Army of the Ohio, commanded by Ambrose E. Burnside, who had been sent to the west after removal from command of the Army of the Potomac. In mid-August, both Union armies began to advance. Burnside's 24,000 troops compelled the outnumbered Confederate defenders of Knoxville to surrender or retreat. Most of them joined Bragg's main army around Chattanooga. Burnside entered Knoxville September 3, finally achieving Lincoln's cherished goal of liberating east Tennessee.

Meanwhile, Rosecrans again demonstrated his ability to move a large army quickly and cleverly once he got started. Feinting with three brigades toward the crossings above Chattanooga, Rosecrans crossed most of his troops over the Tennessee River at several places below the city. Deceived by the feint and bewildered by "the popping out of the rats from so many holes," Bragg realized that his formidable defenses in Chattanooga had been flanked by the appearance of Union divisions south of the city.[15] As the Federals drove eastward across rugged mountain passes toward Bragg's lifeline, the Western and Atlantic Railroad, the Confederate general evacuated Chattanooga September 9.

The Battle of Chickamauga

For the second time in two months, Rosecrans had maneuvered Bragg out of a strategically important position. But now Bragg reached into his own bag of tricks. He sent "deserters" into Union lines with planted stories of Confederate demoralization and retreat. Rosecrans pressed forward eagerly to cut off this supposed retreat. He

---

[14] *O.R.,* Ser. 1, Vol. 23, pt. 2, p. 518.

[15] Daniel Harvey Hill, "Chickamauga—The Great Battle of the West," in *Battles and Leaders of the Civil War,* 4 vols. (New York, 1887), III, 644.

sent each of his three corps through separate mountain gaps twenty miles apart. But instead of retreating, Bragg was concentrating his army southeast of Chattanooga for strikes against the isolated Union fragments. He had already been reinforced by two divisions from Johnston in Mississippi. This brought Bragg's numbers almost to a par with Rosecrans's. And at an important conference in Richmond, Davis and Lee decided to send Longstreet with two more divisions to Bragg. The Confederate railroad administration mobilized its scanty resources to transport 12,000 men and all their equipment, artillery, and animals from Virginia to northern Georgia. Since the direct route through Knoxville was blocked by Burnside's troops, the Confederate reinforcements had to be sent 965 roundabout miles via Atlanta over broken-down lines of varying gauges. The process took ten days; fewer than two-thirds of the troops arrived in time for the battle, but they made a decisive difference.

Before Longstreet arrived, Bragg had three chances to trap fragments of Rosecrans's separated army, but each time his corps commanders found excuses for failing to obey attack orders. These abortive Confederate maneuvers alerted Rosecrans to his danger. He ordered a concentration of his own forces in the valley of Chickamauga Creek a dozen miles south of Chattanooga. As the first of Longstreet's regiments detrained on September 18, Confederate units forced their way across the Chickamauga in an attempt to turn the Union left and cut the Federals off from their base at Chattanooga. Next morning, a full battle erupted. The fighting was some of the most vicious but confused of the war. Much of the battlefield was covered with heavy woods and dense undergrowth. Visibility was limited; brigades and divisions fought in isolation from one another, with little apparent relationship to any overall plan. A Union general described Chickamauga as "a mad, irregular battle, very much resembling guerrilla warfare on a vast scale."[16]

Although neither side gained any advantage on September 19, several division-size Confederate attacks had forced the Federals to contract their lines. Most of the pressure had been on the Union left, commanded by General George H. Thomas. Thomas expected the Confederates to attack his corps again in the morning and persuaded Rosecrans to strengthen the left. Bragg did indeed intend to hit the Union left; but his attack on the morning of September 20 started sluggishly, and with the help of reinforcements Thomas stopped the repeated Confederate assaults with heavy loss to both sides.

Then a lucky break turned the battle in the Confederates' favor. A Union staff officer, failing to see a blue division in line amid the smoke and trees, reported a gap on the Federal right. Rosecrans ordered another division to close this supposed gap, thereby creating a true gap when the latter division pulled out of line to plug the nonexistent one. By coincidence, Longstreet just then launched an assault directly at the breach created by this false Union move. The yelling Rebels burst through the gap at noon, cutting off two blue divisions from the rest of the army, rolling up the right flank of the remainder, and threatening to come in on the rear of Thomas's forces while they were desperately engaged in their front. Rosecrans was caught in the rout of the Union right and fled with the broken divisions to Chattanooga. But Thomas kept his head and kept two-thirds of the army on the field. With the aid of

---

[16]Bruce Catton, *Never Call Retreat,* Pocket Books ed. (New York, 1967), p. 235.

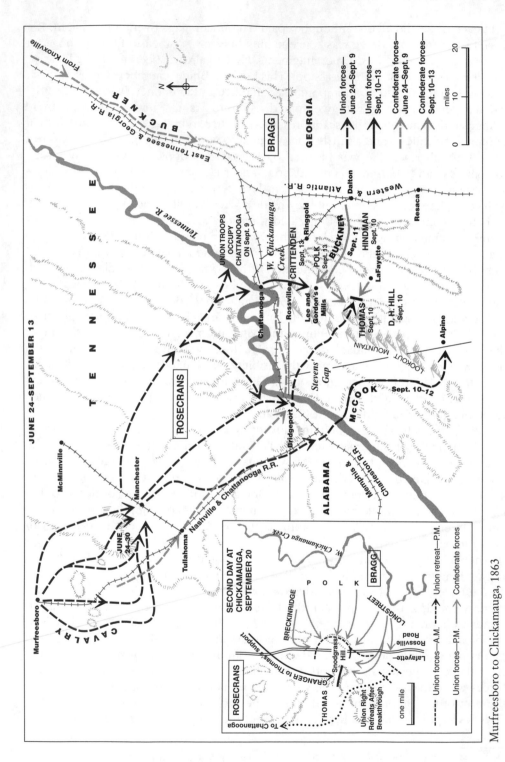

Murfreesboro to Chickamauga, 1863

two reserve brigades whose timely arrival staved off total disaster, he formed a new line on the Union right and repulsed several all-out Confederate attacks. That night the Federals withdrew toward Chattanooga. For his superb generalship, Thomas was thereafter known as "the Rock of Chickamauga."

Chickamauga was an important Confederate tactical victory. "We have met with a severe disaster," Rosecrans wired Washington. When the news reached Richmond, a government clerk wrote exultantly in his diary: "The effects of this great victory will be electrical. The whole South will be filled again with patriotic fervor, and in the North there will be a corresponding depression. . . . Surely the Government of the United States must now see the impossibility of subjugating the Southern people, spread over such a vast extent of territory."[17]

But the Southern triumph was purchased at the cost of 18,454 casualties, nearly 30 percent of the force engaged. Union casualties were nearly as great (16,170); but the North could replace its losses while the South could not. Chickamauga turned out to be the last significant offensive victory by any Confederate army. And it also proved to be a triumph without strategic consequences. Rosecrans still held Chattanooga, for Bragg had failed to follow up his victory.

Mutual recriminations racked the Confederate high command. All of Bragg's leading generals accused their commander of poor battlefield tactics because he had not exploited Longstreet's breakthrough and had not renewed the attack next day while the Federals were still disorganized. For his part the quarrelsome, fault-finding Bragg accused several subordinates of slowness or refusal to obey orders. He dismissed two corps commanders. The bickering grew so bad that Jefferson Davis made the long trip from Richmond to Bragg's headquarters to resolve the ugly dispute. The Confederate president handled the affair in the worst possible way. In Bragg's presence he asked each of the chief generals whether he thought the army needed a new leader. Each said yes, whereupon Davis decided to keep Bragg in command! Two of the South's premier generals, Johnston and Beauregard, were available for the post but Davis disliked both of them; he continued to hold a high opinion of Bragg, an opinion shared by few others.

The Battles for Chattanooga

Lincoln handled his command problems with more deftness after Chickamauga. The Confederates had bottled up Rosecrans in Chattanooga: Bragg's forces occupied Missionary Ridge east of the city and placed artillery on the brow of massive Lookout Mountain, which commanded all approaches from the south and west. The only supply line open to the Yankees was a circuitous road over mountains to the north, all but impassable in wet weather and vulnerable to Rebel cavalry in all weather. Nevertheless, the Union government decided to reinforce Rosecrans. The War Department ordered 17,000 troops under Sherman to move eastward from Mississippi and transferred 20,000 men of the Army of the Potomac 1,200 miles by rail from Virginia

---

[17] *O.R.*, Ser. 1, Vol. 30, pt. 1, p. 142; John B. Jones, *A Rebel War Clerk's Diary* (New York, 1935), II, 50.

to Chattanooga. Lincoln reactivated Joseph Hooker to command the two Army of the Potomac corps in their new theater of war. The transfer of these troops was the most impressive logistic achievement of the war. The North sent nearly twice as many men from Virginia to Tennessee over a greater distance in less time than the Confederates had done the previous month.

But there was no point putting these men into Chattanooga so long as the troops already there could not be supplied. The Army of the Cumberland was in danger of slow starvation. By mid-October, thousands of horses had died and the men were reduced to quarter rations. Rosecrans seemed paralyzed by his defeat at Chickamauga and unable to cope with the crisis. On October 17, Lincoln placed all of the Union military departments between the Appalachians and the Mississippi under the overall command of General Grant. Grant's first action was to replace Rosecrans with Thomas as commander of the Army of the Cumberland. His second was to go personally to Chattanooga. As one officer later wrote, when Grant arrived "we began to see things move. We felt that everything came from a plan."[18] Grant put in motion a previously designed operation to break the supply blockade. While one blue brigade drifted silently downriver on bridge pontoons to Brown's Ferry on the night of October 27, two other columns marched overland to attack Rebel outposts guarding approach roads to the ferry. At dawn the Federals struck, drove away the Confederates, repelled a counterattack, laid the bridge over the river, and thereby established a new supply route (dubbed "the Cracker Line" by hungry bluecoats) beyond the range of Confederate artillery on Lookout Mountain.

Having stationed insufficient force in Lookout Valley to prevent this coup, Bragg committed a bigger mistake on November 4 when, at President Davis's behest, he sent Longstreet with 15,000 men (followed later by 5,000 more) to drive Burnside out of Knoxville. Longstreet himself thought this a foolish move, for it reduced Bragg's strength to 45,000 at a time when the arrival of Hooker's troops boosted Federal strength to nearly 60,000. Longstreet also considered his force too small for the job assigned to it. And so it proved. The Confederate attack on the Knoxville defenses November 29 was repulsed with heavy Southern losses.

Back in Chattanooga the arrival of Sherman with another 17,000 men of the Army of the Tennessee on November 15 gave the Federals the initiative. For the first time in the war, parts of the Union's three main armies—the Cumberland, the Tennessee, and the Potomac—operated in concert, with Grant as commander of the combined forces. Bragg held a six-mile line on 400-foot high Missionary Ridge with trenches at the base and the top and an unfinished line of rifle-pits halfway up the steep slope. Three Confederate brigades held 1,100-foot high Lookout Mountain. All Civil War experience taught that a frontal assault against Missionary Ridge would be suicidal, so Grant's battle plan called for Sherman's four divisions of the Army of the Tennessee to make a flank attack against the north end of the ridge while Hooker with three divisions was to force his way over or around Lookout Mountain, cross the intervening valley to Missionary Ridge, and attack the Rebel left flank there. Thomas's Army of the Cumberland was assigned the secondary role of threatening the Confederate center to prevent reinforcements from being sent to either flank.

---

[18]Catton, *Never Call Retreat,* p. 247.

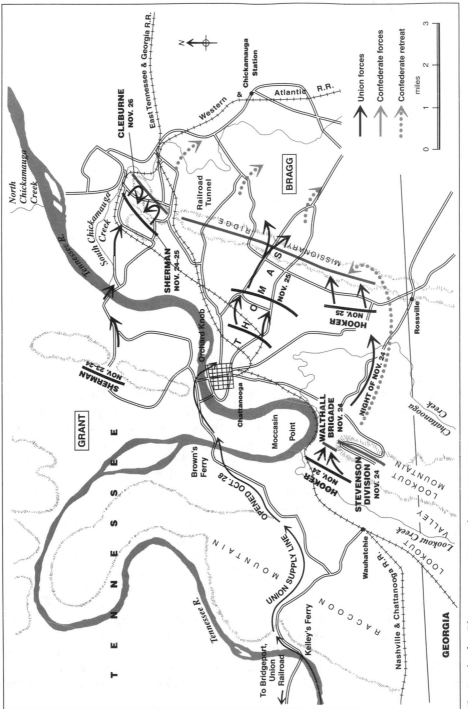

The Battles for Chattanooga, November 24–25, 1863

Eager to avenge their defeat at Chickamauga, Thomas's troops chafed under this passive role and burned to make Grant eat his words that "they could not be got out of their trenches to assume the offensive."[19]

Hooker's divisions carried out their initial assignment handsomely on November 24, driving the outnumbered Rebels off Lookout Mountain in a series of skirmishes obscured by a fog that caused the fighting there to be labeled "The Battle Above The Clouds." Next morning, the fog dissolved at sunrise to reveal the Stars and Stripes flying from the pinnacle of Lookout Mountain in full view of both armies. Meanwhile, Sherman's divisions had run into trouble. Having gained the crest of one hill at the north end of Missionary Ridge, they discovered that it was only a spur separated by a rock-strewn ravine from the main ridge defended by Patrick Cleburne's oversize division, the best unit in Bragg's army. Sherman's battle-hardened westerners assaulted this position without success on the morning of November 25. Grant sent reinforcements, but still Sherman got nowhere.

As Hooker finally approached the opposite end of Missionary Ridge after being delayed several hours by the destruction of the bridge over Chattanooga Creek, Grant ordered Thomas to make a diversionary attack against the first line of Rebel trenches at the base of Missionary Ridge. Led by two of the divisions that had been routed at Chickamauga, Thomas's boys moved out with spirit and took these lower trenches. Once there, however, they were exposed to fire from the Confederates in the second and third lines of trenches at the midpoint and top of the ridge. Some of the blue regiments began to move up the slope. Soon the whole line swept forward with exultant yells and cleared the second line of trenches. "Who ordered those men up the hill?" Grant asked angrily. No one had ordered it. The only orders were the impromptu commands of front-line officers after their men had already started. As Grant and Thomas watched in amazement from their command post a mile in the rear, the blue line swarmed all the way to the top of the ridge in an assault apparently more hopeless than Pickett's at Gettysburg.

But Bragg's engineer officers had made the mistake of locating the upper trenches on the topographical crest of the ridge rather than several yards lower on the "military crest," from which the line of fire would not have been blocked by intervening swells in the ground. The oncoming Yankees therefore found ravines and dips through which they could advance under cover until they got close enough to enfilade the Rebel defenses. Seized with panic, the Confederates broke and ran or surrendered, by thousands. The victorious Federals were "completely and frantically drunk with excitement," wrote an officer. They yelled "Chickamauga! Chickamauga!" in derisive triumph as they watched the graybacks rush "wildly down the hill and into the woods, tossing away knapsacks, muskets, and blankets as they ran."

Believing that "an army was never whipped as badly as Bragg's was," Grant hoped to organize a vigorous pursuit to finish off the Rebels. But Cleburne's division, which had not yielded an inch, conducted an effective rear-guard action that enabled Bragg to establish a strong defensive line near Dalton, Georgia, twenty-five miles to the south. After some skirmishing, both armies went into winter quarters as harsh weather came on.[20]

---

[19]Shelby Foote, *The Civil War: A Narrative. Fredericksburg to Meridian* (New York, 1963), p. 843.

[20]Quotations in these paragraphs are from ibid., p. 856, and Catton, *Never Call Retreat*, p. 253.

The storming of Missionary Ridge was one of the most remarkable feats of the war. As Grant said with a smile when someone mentioned that Bragg had believed the position impregnable: "Well, it *was* impregnable."[21] The Army of the Cumberland had fully redeemed Chickamauga. More than that, it completed the cycle of victories begun at Vicksburg and Gettysburg that disabled the Confederacy, though some of the war's bloodiest fighting still lay ahead. The loss of Chattanooga also sealed Bragg's fate. The general admitted privately to Davis that "the disaster admits of no palliation, and is justly disparaging to me as a commander. . . . I fear we both erred in the conclusion for me to retain command here after the clamor raised against me."[22] Davis reluctantly appointed Joseph Johnston to succeed Bragg as commander of the Army of Tennessee.

The victory at Chattanooga confirmed Grant as the Union's greatest general. From there he went on in March 1864 to become general-in-chief of all Union armies. The other three generals who with Grant became the architects of final Union victory—Sherman, Thomas, and Sheridan—also fought at Chattanooga. All four came out of the western theater; two of them, Grant and Sheridan, went east in 1864 to try their victory formula with the Army of the Potomac.

The War and Foreign Policy, 1863

In January 1863, Henry Adams had written from London that Confederate hopes of foreign recognition were dead unless Union arms suffered another disaster. Chancellorsville was such a disaster. Lee's subsequent invasion of Pennsylvania and Grant's initial failure to take Vicksburg revived the efforts for recognition. On June 22, Napoleon III discussed with pro-Confederate members of the British Parliament a movement for joint recognition of the South. Unfortunately for this movement, the man selected to present the motion in Parliament was John Roebuck, whom Henry Adams aptly described as "rather more than three-quarters mad." In a rambling speech on June 30, Roebuck indiscreetly revealed the details of his talk with Napoleon III. Parliament erupted in chauvinistic anger at the idea of following French leadership. Palmerston denied that the government had received any official communications from Paris on this matter (this was a bit of casuistry). Napoleon was chagrined by Roebuck's breach of confidence, and the whole affair ended in a fiasco that discredited Roebuck in particular and pro-Confederate partisans in general. Then came news of Gettysburg and of the fall of Vicksburg, which gave the coup de grace to Southern hopes in Britain. "It is now conceded at once that all idea of intervention is at an end," wrote Henry Adams on July 23. "The only remaining chance of collision is in the case of the ironclads. We are looking after them with considerable energy, and I think we shall settle them."[23]

---

[21]Foote, *Fredericksburg to Meridian,* p. 859.

[22]Ibid., p. 868.

[23]Worthington C. Ford (ed.), *A Cycle of Adams Letters, 1861–1865,* 2 vols. (Boston, 1920), II, 40, 60.

The Laird Rams

Adams's reference to ironclads concerned the "Laird rams," which provoked a near crisis in Anglo-American relations in 1863. The source of the trouble lay in Britain's equivocal interpretation of her own Neutrality Act of 1819, which forbade the "equipping, furnishing, fitting out, or arming" of warships to be used against any nation with which Britain was at peace. In June 1861, the Georgian James D. Bulloch had arrived in Liverpool with a mission to buy or build warships for the Confederacy. A tough, clever agent, Bulloch did a remarkable job with limited resources. He contracted for the construction of two powerful commerce raiders that eventually became the *Florida* and the *Alabama*. Between them these raiders sank or captured more than a hundred American merchant ships (see page 194). Bulloch's antagonist in Liverpool was U.S. Consul Thomas H. Dudley, who employed spies, informers, and double agents to amass evidence that these and other vessels were being built as Confederate warships in violation of British law. Bulloch countered with agents of his own who forged registry papers, fed Dudley's informers false information, and created such a fog of doubt that the true purpose of these ships could not be legally proved before they left England.

The British applied a narrow, technical interpretation of their neutrality law. So long as the ships were built but not "fitted out and armed" as warships in British territory, said Foreign Secretary Lord Russell, they did not violate the law. The *Florida* left Liverpool unarmed and was later converted to a commerce raider in the Bahamas (which itself *was* British territory). By July 1862, the evidence that "No. 290" would do the same was so strong that Russell ordered her seized. But while the order was being delayed by legal quibbles and bureaucratic negligence, Bulloch got wind of it from a double agent and sent the completed ship to sea on a "trial run" before the seizure order arrived. The ship never returned to port; she sailed to the Azores, where by prearrangement she was fitted out as a commerce destroyer and began her career as the *Alabama*.

Bulloch had also contracted with the Laird shipbuilding firm for the construction of two ironclad warships equipped with seven-foot underwater iron spikes attached to their prows. More powerful than anything afloat, these "Laird rams" were designed to destroy the wooden ships of the Union blockade fleet. Bulloch did everything possible to disguise their true purpose. But Dudley's spies piled up a mountain of evidence that they were being built for the Confederacy. All through the summer of 1863, American Minister Charles Francis Adams bombarded the Foreign Office with veiled threats of war if the rams were allowed to escape. Russell replied lamely that he could do nothing in the absence of airtight evidence. On September 5, Adams penned an angry note that concluded with the words: "It would be superfluous in me to point out to your Lordship that this is war."[24]

Next day, the British government detained the ships, and later it purchased them for the Royal Navy. When the diplomatic correspondence was published, Adams became something of a hero in the United States, for it appeared that his "this is war"

---

[24]Ephraim D. Adams, *Great Britain and the American Civil War*, 2 vols. (New York, 1925), II, 144.

note had forced John Bull to back down. In fact, the British government had decided to detain the rams two days before receiving Adams's note. But Adams did deserve much of the credit for the outcome. His firm protests during the preceding months, together with Seward's equally firm line with the British minister in Washington, kept unrelenting pressure on the British government. English merchants and naval officers, fearing the consequences in a future war if a neutral United States built destroyers for Britain's enemies, also brought pressure to bear on Her Majesty's government.

To the Confederacy, the seizure of the Laird rams came as a crowning blow in a year filled with foreign policy disappointments. All hope for British recognition and mediation had vanished. Now the opportunity to build warships in Britain seemed to be disappearing as well. In frustration, the Confederacy expelled British consuls (who were still officially accredited to the United States) from Southern cities and transferred Commissioner James Mason from London to Paris. This was the equivalent of breaking off diplomatic relations, but it hurt Britain not at all and did nothing for the Confederacy except perhaps to salve its injured dignity. From now on, Confederate diplomacy would be focused on France.

Intrigues in Mexico

Affairs in that quarter initially seemed promising. The French Emperor's sympathies were notoriously pro-Southern. Since 1862, Napoleon III had been involved in an imperial adventure in Mexico whose success would be imperiled by Union victory. Mexican political and financial instability in 1861 had provoked a joint military expedition by Britain, France, and Spain to collect debts owed by Mexico to foreign creditors. Britain and Spain withdrew their troops in 1862 after negotiating a settlement. But Napoleon III imposed impossible demands on the weak Mexican government and sent additional troops (35,000 by 1863), who seized Mexico City and overthrew the liberal leader Benito Juarez in June 1863.

Meanwhile, the Confederacy had concluded quasi-alliances with anti-Juarez chieftains in the northern provinces of Mexico, which profited from the contraband trade across the Texas border. By 1863, a key goal of Southern diplomacy was an agreement with France whereby the Confederacy would recognize a French-controlled regime in Mexico in return for French recognition of the Confederacy. When Napoleon III engineered the selection of Archduke Ferdinand Maximilian of Austria as emperor of Mexico, Confederate envoys approached Maximilian with proposals for an alliance. Although the Austrian was willing, his master Napoleon III did not really want to risk war with the United States. Secretary of State Seward skillfully steered American foreign policy between the two extremes of a surrender of the Monroe Doctrine or an open rupture with France. He warned Napoleon III politely but firmly that the United States would not tolerate foreign interference in Mexico, but at the same time he dropped vague hints that his country might recognize Maximilian if France continued to refuse recognition of the Confederacy.

This carrot-and-stick approach worked. Increasingly embroiled in European conflicts, Napoleon III gradually lost interest in Mexico. He held Confederate envoys at arm's length and clamped down on the construction of Southern warships in France.

The last serious Confederate bid for European recognition and support had failed. And after the collapse of the Confederacy in 1865, Napoleon III's Mexican adventure had a tragic denouement for the naive Maximilian. The United States sent 50,000 battle-hardened veterans to the Texas-Mexican border after Appomattox, while Seward put increasing pressure on France to pull her troops out of Mexico. When France did so in 1866, Maximilian's government fell and Maximilian himself was executed a year later by Juarez's partisans.

Chapter Twenty

War Issues and Politics in 1863

You say you will not fight to free negroes.
Some of them seem willing to fight for
you. . . . [When final victory is achieved]
there will be some black men who can
remember that, with silent tongue, and
clenched teeth, and steady eye, and well-
poised bayonet, they have helped mankind
on to this great consummation, while, I fear,
there will be some white ones, unable to
forget that, with malignant heart, and
deceitful speech, they have strove to hinder it.

—Abraham Lincoln,
August 26, 1863

Northern military victories in the second half of 1863 powerfully affected domestic politics in both the Union and the Confederacy. North of the Potomac, these victories reversed the erosion of home-front support for the war, erosion that had been accelerating during the first half of the year. Gettysburg in particular produced joyous celebration and renewed confidence in the North. "The results of this victory are priceless," wrote a New Yorker when he learned the outcome of the battle in Pennsylvania.

"Government is strengthened fourfold at home and abroad. . . . Copperheads are palsied and dumb for the moment at least."[1] But before Gettysburg, the Copperheads had grown in strength until they threatened social disruption, political realignment, and a faltering of the Northern war effort.

Vallandigham and the Copperhead Drive for Power

In the spring of 1863, Clement L. Vallandigham was campaigning for the Democratic gubernatorial nomination in Ohio. Looking for an issue to propel himself into martyrdom and the nomination, he found an unwitting ally in General Burnside, whose political judgment proved to be no wiser than his military judgment had been at Fredericksburg. After his removal from command of the Army of the Potomac, Burnside had been appointed head of the Department of the Ohio, with headquarters at Cincinnati.[2] There he found himself in the heart of Copperhead country during a period of rising antiwar sentiment. On April 19, he issued "General Order No. 38," which declared that "treason" in his department would no longer be tolerated.

In a speech on May 1, Vallandigham deliberately challenged this order by repeating all the themes he had been stating for months: the war was a wicked failure; the Emancipation Proclamation should be repudiated; conscription and the suspension of habeas corpus were unconstitutional; "King Lincoln" ought to be dethroned by the voters; and the North ought to stop fighting, declare an armistice, and invite the Confederates to a peace conference to restore the old Union, without New England if necessary. By Burnside's definition this was treason. At 2 A.M. on May 5, a company of soldiers broke into Vallandigham's home in Dayton and arrested him.

A review of political events in the North during the previous five months will provide background for an understanding of this action. Although historians disagree on the size of Vallandigham's following, it was large enough to constitute a threat to the Northern will to continue the war during this winter of discontent. Scores of Democratic politicians and editors were urging resistance to emancipation, the draft, even the war itself. A former governor of Illinois declared that "with the objectives announced in this [emancipation] proclamation as the avowed purpose of the war, the South cannot and ought not to be subdued." A Democratic editor in Iowa considered the Emancipation Proclamation cause for a counterrevolution in the North. If the people "possessed a tithe of the spirit which animated Rome when Cataline was expelled," he wrote, "they would hurl [Lincoln] into the Potomac [along with]

---

[1] Allan Nevins and Milton H. Thomas (eds.), *The Diary of George Templeton Strong, 1835–1875*, 4 vols. (New York, 1952), III, 330.

[2] Both the Union and Confederate armies established territorial organizations known as "departments." Each department was headed by a commanding general who was responsible for military operations and for army administrative duties within his territorial jurisdiction. The boundaries and names of some departments changed frequently—a source of great confusion to students of the war. The most active Union departments were those in the war zones and in the occupied portions of the Confederacy. But the Union border states and the Northern states themselves were also organized into military departments, where troops were responsible for repelling invasions, quelling internal uprisings, preventing espionage and sabotage, and enforcing conscription. In 1863, the Department of the Ohio comprised the states of Ohio, Illinois, Indiana, Michigan, and Kentucky east of the Tennessee River.

Cabinet, Congress, and all." Several Democratic county conventions in the Midwest resolved that "an experience of two years has taught us, that the Union can never be restored by force of arms," called for a "cessation of hostilities," and pledged defiantly that "we will not render support to the present Administration in carrying on its wicked abolition crusade against the South; . . . we will *resist* to the *death* all attempts to draft any of our citizens into the army." Nor were such sentiments confined to Midwestern Democrats. A large meeting of party faithful in New York resolved that "this war of the General Government against the South is illegal, being unconstitutional, and should not be sustained." And Horatio Seymour, a lukewarm War Democrat whose election as governor of New York had propelled him to national party leadership, said in his inaugural address that the "bloody, barbarous, revolutionary" emancipation policy would ruin the country.[3]

Talk is cheap, and much of this rhetoric was little more than loose talk. But such talk could be dangerous when it led to action, as it did in Illinois and Indiana. The 1862 elections in these states had produced Democratic legislatures that confronted Republican governors (elected in 1860) in a bitter showdown over war policy. The lower houses of both legislatures adopted resolutions calling for an armistice and a peace conference. The Illinois house even named commissioners to such a conference. The Indiana legislature contemptuously rejected Republican Governor Oliver P. Morton's annual message and voted instead to endorse the "exalted and patriotic sentiments" of New York's Governor Seymour. Democrats in both states introduced bills that could have resulted in the withdrawal of state troops from the war.

Governor Richard Yates of Illinois ended the threat in his state by invoking an obscure constitutional clause to adjourn the legislature. Indiana's Governor Morton could not do this, nor could he successfully veto any bills, for Indiana's constitution required only a simple majority to override a veto. But the same constitution specified that two-thirds of the legislature must be present to constitute a quorum. With Morton's connivance, Republicans absented themselves from the state senate to deny a quorum. For two years the iron-willed Morton ran the state without a legislature—and without any appropriations. He financed state operations with loans from banks and railroads, grants from Republican counties, and a subsidy of $250,000 from the War Department. This was an unconstitutional procedure, but these were revolutionary times. "If the Cause fails," Morton reminded Secretary of War Stanton, "you and I will be covered with prosecutions, imprisoned, driven from the country." "If the Cause fails," replied Stanton melodramatically, "I do not care to live."[4]

The Peace Democrats had an impact in Richmond as well as in Northern states. A Confederate War Department clerk reported in February 1863 that "several citizens from Illinois and Indiana" had arrived in the Southern capital:

. . . to consult our government on the best means of terminating the war; or, that failing to propose some mode of adjustment between the Northwestern States and the Confederacy,

---

[3]The former Illinois governor, the county Democratic conventions, and the New York meeting are quoted in Wood Gray, *The Hidden Civil War: The Story of the Copperheads* (New York, 1942), pp. 115, 123, 147; the Iowa editor is quoted in Frank L. Klement, *The Copperheads in the Middle West* (Chicago, 1960), p. 44; Seymour is quoted in Allan Nevins, *The War for the Union: War Becomes Revolution* (New York, 1960), p. 394.

[4]Albert G. Riddle, *Recollections of War Times* (New York, 1895), p. 321.

and new combination against the Yankee [i.e., New England] States and the Federal adminis-tration. . . . I have no doubt, if the war continues throughout the year, we shall have the spec-tacle of more Northern men fighting against the United States Government than slaves fight-ing against the South.[5]

Copperhead newspapers openly encouraged desertion from the army. Men who read these newspapers wrote such letters as the following to their sons in the army: "I am sorry you are engaged in this . . . unholy, unconstitutional, and hellish war . . . Come home, if you have to desert, you will be protected." Desertions were highest among troops from Copperhead areas. Declaring that they would "lie in the woods until moss grew on their backs rather than help free the slaves," all but thirty-five men of the 128th Illinois deserted early in 1863. When the 109th Illinois learned of the Emancipation Proclamation, half of its men deserted and the other half became so insubordinate that General Grant disbanded the regiment. Both regiments came from the Butternut counties of southern Illinois.[6]

To counter the Peace Democrats, Republicans and War Democrats organized Union Leagues and Loyal Leagues in Northern cities. These Leagues sponsored lec-tures, published pamphlets and editorials, and organized political rallies. The women's rights movement also threw itself into this effort. Elizabeth Cady Stanton and Susan B. Anthony formed the Women's Loyal National League in the spring of 1863 to harness the patriotic energies of Northern women. The WLNL circulated petitions endorsing the Emancipation Proclamation and calling for a constitutional amendment to end slavery everywhere. Although women could not vote, this petition campaign had a potent political impact, eventually obtaining nearly 400,000 signatures.

The first successes of the Union League movement occurred in the spring elec-tions of 1863,[7] especially in New Hampshire and Connecticut, where Democrats were making strong efforts to elect antiwar governors. These elections presented a crucial challenge to Republicans. If Peace Democrats could win in New England, they would certainly win elsewhere. Union leagues mobilized all their resources, the national government used its patronage to the utmost, and the War Department fur-loughed home soldiers to vote (experience had shown that front-line soldiers voted overwhelmingly Republican). Even with all this help, the Republicans won just 51.6 percent of the vote in Connecticut and 43.8 percent in New Hampshire. Only the presence of a third-party War Democratic candidate in the latter state denied the Peace Democrat a majority and threw the contest into the legislature, which elected the Republican candidate.

It was in this political atmosphere filled with rumors of conspiracies that Burnside arrested Vallandigham for speaking against the war. A military commission sentenced the Ohioan to imprisonment for the duration of the conflict. A federal judge refused to issue a writ to release Vallandigham to the custody of civil courts. Democrats—and even some Republicans—denounced these proceedings. The government's ac-

---

[5]John B. Jones, *A Rebel War Clerk's Diary,* 2 vols. (New York, 1895), I, 249, 253.

[6]Gray, *Hidden Civil War,* p. 133; Bruce Catton, *Glory Road* (Garden City, N.Y., 1952), p. 246.

[7]Unlike today, states then held state elections at various times of the year—some in the spring, some in August, September, or October, and several (as now) in November.

tion was "cowardly, brutal, infamous," said Governor Seymour of New York. "It is not merely a step toward revolution, it *is* revolution. . . . It establishes military despotism. . . . If it is upheld, our liberties are overthrown."[8]

Ohio Democrats unanimously nominated the martyred Vallandigham for governor. Although Lincoln was embarrassed by this affair, he refused to repudiate General Burnside or the military commission that had convicted Vallandigham. Instead, with a shrewd stroke, the President tarnished the Copperhead's martyrdom by commuting his sentence from imprisonment to banishment. Federal troops escorted Vallandigham under flag of truce to General Bragg's lines in Tennessee. Vallandigham escaped from the South on a blockade runner and went to Canada, from where he tried to direct his gubernatorial campaign in Ohio. His lawyers took the case to the Supreme Court, where they argued that the trial of a civilian by a military court outside the war zone was unconstitutional. But in February 1864 the Court refused to review the proceedings of the military commission, thereby in effect upholding Vallandigham's conviction.[9]

Black Men in Blue

The Vallandigham affair occurred amid a rising crescendo of Democratic Negrophobia. The administration's decision to recruit black regiments swelled the crescendo. "This is a government of white men, made by white men for white men, to be administered, protected, defended, and maintained by white men, " thundered a Democratic congressman in opposition to a black soldier bill in February 1863. Forty-three Democratic congressmen signed a round robin condemning the enlistment of black soldiers as part of a wicked Republican plot to establish "the equality of the black and white races."[10]

In a way they were right. One result of black soldiers fighting for the North was to advance the revolution of freedom a long step toward equality. This had been the purpose of Northern blacks and abolitionists who had urged the enlistment of black soldiers in the first place. As Frederick Douglass put it: "Once let the black man get upon his person the brass letters, U.S.; let him get an eagle on his button, and a musket on his shoulder and bullets in his pocket, and there is no power on earth which can deny that he has earned the right to citizenship."[11]

---

[8]William B. Hesseltine, *Lincoln and the War Governors* (New York, 1948), p. 331.

[9]In 1866, after the passions of war had partly cooled, the Supreme Court overturned a similar military conviction in 1864 of an Indiana Copperhead, Lambdin P. Milligan, on the grounds that when the civil courts are functioning, civilians must be tried therein even in wartime. This principle would have voided Vallandigham's conviction. But the effect of the Court's decision on Vallandigham was moot, since he had returned to Ohio in 1864 and had been allowed by the Lincoln administration to remain there undisturbed and even to participate actively in politics (see Chapter 24).

[10]*Congressional Globe,* 37th Cong., 3rd sess. (1863), Appendix, 93; Forrest G. Wood, *Black Scare: The Racist Response to Emancipation and Reconstruction* (Berkeley, 1968), p. 42.

[11]*Douglass' Monthly,* August 1863.

Although blacks had fought as soldiers in the Revolution and in the War of 1812, they were quickly disarmed afterward. A federal law of 1792 banned black men from the state militias, and no blacks had ever been allowed to enlist in the regular army. When antislavery generals in 1862 undertook to enroll black soldiers in Kansas and in occupied portions of Louisiana and South Carolina, the administration refused to sustain them. So long as the North was fighting only to restore the Union—the old Union—the Lincoln administration felt obliged to keep it "a white man's war."

Blacks in the Navy

The navy, however, had always had some black sailors. From the beginning of the war, the Union navy took whatever men it could get, including free blacks from Northern seaports and contraband slaves from the South. Most of these men served in menial capacities as firemen and stewards. But some performed combat duty. In May 1862, a South Carolina slave, Robert Smalls, achieved one of the best-publicized exploits of the war when he commandeered the Confederate vessel *Planter* in the Charleston Bay and ran it out to the Union blockading fleet. "Captain " Smalls served as a pilot in the Union navy for the rest of the war and went on to a prominent political career afterward. In all, nearly ten thousand black men served in the Union navy. They played a vital part in the war at sea.[12]

Recruitment of Black Soldiers

Black involvement in the navy encouraged Republicans who by 1862 wanted to enlist blacks to fight on land as well. What better way to employ able-bodied contrabands than to arm them to fight for the Union—and for their own freedom? This argument became even more compelling when the shortage of Northern white volunteers caused the government to order a militia draft in the summer of 1862. Two laws enacted on July 17, 1862, set the stage for the enlistment of black soldiers. One section of the confiscation act authorized the President to employ contrabands for the suppression of the rebellion "in such manner as he may judge best." And a section of the militia act authorized the enrollment of blacks for "any military or naval service for which they may be found competent."[13]

Neither of these laws required the President to enlist blacks as soldiers. For the time being, Lincoln chose to interpret the laws as granting him authority to enroll contrabands as laborers—which of course the army had been doing for more than a year. But Lincoln had probably made up his mind to arm blacks and was waiting for the right moment to announce it. On August 4, 1862, the President told a delegation from Indiana that "to arm the negroes would turn 50,000 bayonets from the loyal Border States against us that were for us." He said the same to a Chicago del-

---

[12]The number of black sailors was 9,596, as calculated by David L. Valuska, "The Negro in the Union Navy: 1861–1865," Ph.D. dissertation, Lehigh University, 1973.

[13]Edward McPherson, *The Political History of the United States During the Great Rebellion,* 2d ed. (Washington, D.C., 1865), pp. 197, 274.

egation six weeks later. But meanwhile, on August 25, Secretary of War Stanton had quietly authorized the Union commander on the South Carolina coastal islands to recruit 5,000 freedmen as soldiers.[14]

By early 1863, Lincoln had become an enthusiastic proponent of enlisting black soldiers. "The colored population is the great *available* and yet *unavailed of,* force for restoring the Union," the President told the military governor of Tennessee in March. "The bare sight of 50,000 armed and drilled black soldiers upon the banks of the Mississippi, would end the rebellion at once. And who doubts that we can present that sight, if we but take hold in earnest?"[15]

The administration proceeded to back these words with action. The War Department created the Bureau of Colored Troops to coordinate recruiting. In Louisiana, General Banks began to form a "Corps d'Afrique." A Northern abolitionist who had organized two black regiments for Massachusetts, George L. Stearns, took his recruiting service to Nashville to enroll black soldiers there. Generals in occupied Virginia and North Carolina formed black regiments. Most important of all, the government sent General Lorenzo Thomas to the Mississippi Valley to recruit freedmen as soldiers. A desk general with no prior field service, Thomas proved remarkably successful at his task. He combined administrative ability with the tact necessary to persuade hard-bitten, race-conscious Western soldiers to accept the new policy. By the end of the war, Thomas had raised 76,000 black troops, 41 percent of the total.

In the summer of 1863, an Illinois soldier in Grant's army wrote that "an honest confession is good for the soul. . . . A year ago last January I didn't like to hear anything of emancipation. Last fall accepted confiscation of Rebels' negroes quietly. In January took to emancipation readily, and now . . . am becoming so [color] blind that I can't see why they will not make soldiers. . . . I almost begin to think of applying for a position in a [black] regiment myself."[16] This man's "confession" hints at one of the conditions that made black regiments acceptable: all commissioned officers and some NCOs were to be white men. The chance for a commission helped convert many a white soldier to the policy of arming blacks—and also produced some racist officers who had little regard for the men they led.

The appointment of white officers could be justified at first on the ground that few blacks had any military experience. In regiments composed of former slaves, few of the soldiers were even literate. But black regiments recruited in the North also had white officers, even though some black soldiers in these regiments were potential officer material. And as time went on, the reluctance to promote capable black men from the ranks was clearly a result of race prejudice. Abolitionists and black leaders attacked this discriminatory policy, but they achieved limited success. In the 166 black regiments organized during the war, fewer than 100 black officers were commissioned (exclusive of surgeons and chaplains), none higher than captain.

---

[14]Roy P. Basler (ed.), *The Collected Works of Abraham Lincoln,* 9 vols. (New Brunswick, N.J., 1953–1955), V, 357, 423; *O.R.,* Ser. 1, Vol. 14, pp. 377–378.

[15]Basler, *Works of Lincoln,* VI, 149–150.

[16]Charles W. Wills to his sister, June 26, 1863, in Wills, *Army Life of an Illinois Soldier, Letters and Diary of the Late Charles Wills* (Washington, D.C., 1906), pp. 183–184.

Another discrimination that prevailed until 1864 was a difference in pay between black and white soldiers. Under the militia act of 1862 the pay of blacks was fixed at $10 monthly, while white privates received $13 plus a $3.50 clothing allowance. Abolitionists eloquently denounced this discrimination. Frederick Douglass obtained an interview with Lincoln on August 10, 1863, to protest inequalities in pay and status. As Douglass later remembered it, the President told him that:

. . . the employment of colored troops at all was a great gain to the colored people—that the measure could not have been successfully adopted at the beginning of the war, that the wisdom of making colored men soldiers was still doubted—that their enlistment was a serious offense to popular prejudice . . . that they were not to receive the same pay as white soldiers seemed a necessary concession to smooth the way to their employment at all as soldiers.[17]

Although partly remedied in 1864, the inequality of pay was only one of several signs that black regiments were considered second-class soldiers. Some regiments functioned initially as labor battalions to dig trenches, load and unload supplies, and perform heavy fatigue duty for white troops. Even when organized in combat units, black soldiers often carried inferior arms and equipment. Lincoln originally planned to use black troops to garrison forts, protect supply dumps and wagon trains, and perform rear-area duties, thereby releasing white regiments for front-line operations. Three considerations underlay this idea: (1) skepticism about whether blacks would make good combat soldiers; (2) a belief that freedmen were better acclimated to garrison duty in the deep South, where Northern soldiers suffered much sickness; and (3) rear-area duties would reduce the possibility of capture.

This last factor was a serious matter, for the Confederate government had threatened captured officers and men of black regiments with death or enslavement. In retaliation, Lincoln on July 30, 1863, issued an executive order stating that for every Union prisoner killed in violation of the laws of war, a Rebel captive would be similarly executed, and for every Union soldier enslaved, a Confederate prisoner would be placed at hard labor. This order had only part of the desired effect. The Confederacy did not execute captured officers of black regiments, and it generally treated captured blacks who had been free before the war as normal prisoners of war. But several instances occurred of the murder of black soldiers after their surrender in action, mostly notably at Fort Pillow, Tennessee, on April 12, 1864. A few captured freedmen were evidently executed, some were returned as slaves to their former masters, and some black captives were put to forced labor on Confederate fortifications. Because of the difficulty of obtaining accurate information on Southern treatment of black captives, the Lincoln administration did not implement eye-for-an-eye retaliation. The Confederates also refused to exchange black prisoners, thereby bringing to a halt the prisoner exchange program and contributing to the tragic overcrowding and high death rate of war prisoners in 1864 (for more on this, see Chapter 24).

The substitution of black for white troops in fatigue, labor, and garrison duty helped win over white soldiers to the arming of blacks. But it also placed a stigma of inferiority on black regiments. Even some abolitionists wondered whether slaves

---

[17]Frederick Douglass, *The Life and Times of Frederick Douglass* (Hartford, 1882), pp. 386–387.

BLACK SAILORS AND SOLDIERS.   The first photo (*top*) shows the racially mixed crew of the Union gunboat *Hunchback*, which operated along the coastal rivers in Virginia and North Carolina. The second photo (*bottom*) is of Co. E of the 4th U.S. Colored Troops.

BLACK SAILORS AND
SOLDIERS.
The third (*right*) shows two
black soldiers on picket
duty posing for the
photographer in a firing
position.

LIBRARY OF CONGRESS

who had been conditioned all their lives to fear and obey whites would stand in battle against those same whites. Loyal Northerners "have generally become willing that [blacks] should fight," said the *New York Tribune* on May 1, 1863, "but the great majority have no faith that they will really do so. Many hope they will prove cowards and sneaks—others greatly fear it." Colonels of black regiments pleaded with generals to send them into combat to give the men a chance to prove themselves.

Black Soldiers in Combat

Two actions involving black troops in the Vicksburg campaign converted many white skeptics. On May 27, two Louisiana black regiments participated in an assault on Port Hudson, the Confederate stronghold downriver from Vicksburg. Although the assault was repulsed with heavy Union casualties, the courageous fighting of the black soldiers opened many Northern eyes. One white officer wrote: "You have no idea how my prejudices with regard to Negro troops have been dispelled by the battle the other day." The *New York Times* commented that this battle "settles the question that the negro race can fight." Eleven days later, newly organized contraband regiments at Milliken's Bend on the Mississippi above Vicksburg helped beat off a Confederate attempt to smash through Union defenses west of the river. "The bravery of the blacks in the battle at Milliken's Bend completely revolutionized the sentiment of the army with regard to the employment of negro troops," wrote the assistant secretary of war, who was with Grant's army. "I heard prominent officers who formerly in private had sneered at the idea of the negroes fighting express themselves after that as heartily in favor of it."[18]

Although blacks fought in several major actions during the next two years, they continued to do more garrison and fatigue duty and less fighting than white troops. This was reflected in the casualty rates of the two groups. Nearly 6 percent of white Union troops were killed in action, compared with 1.7 percent for black soldiers. On the other hand, the rate of death from disease among black troops (18 percent) was almost twice as high as among Northern white soldiers. As garrison troops, many black regiments suffered from the high disease rates typical of soldiers confined to one place, where their water supply turned foul and they built up deadly accumulations of bacteria. Black regiments also received poorer medical care than whites. There were few black surgeons to draw upon (only eight were commissioned), and white doctors were not notably eager to volunteer for black units.

By October 1863, fifty-eight black regiments had been organized. Much of the initial Northern opposition to them had faded. Indeed, Union recruiters in the occupied South sometimes used press-gang techniques to round up unwilling or bewildered contrabands and draft them into the army. In the North, even Irish-Americans had come to see some advantages in black men stopping Rebel bullets that might otherwise come their way. This was the theme of a popular song by "Private Miles O'Reilly" (Irish-born journalist and army officer Charles G. Halpine) entitled "Sambo's Right to Be Kilt":

> Some tell us 'tis a burnin' shame
> To make the naygers fight;
> An' that the thrade of bein' kilt
> Belongs but to the white;
> But as for me, upon my soul!
> So liberal are we here,
> I'll let Sambo be murthered instead of myself
> On every day in the year.[19]

By 1864, the Democratic position on black soldiers had retreated to opposing equal pay, bounties, and status for them. The black man's only right, it seemed, was the right to be killed. At the prodding of abolitionists, congressional Republicans finally passed a bill in June 1864 to equalize the pay of white and black soldiers. But the opposition had forced some compromises in this legislation. To obtain conservative Republican support, congressional leaders had to accept a bill making equal pay retroactive only to January 1, 1864, except for blacks who had been free before the war; they would receive equal pay from the date of their enlistment. The legislation also failed to equalize federal bounties for soldiers who had been slaves. Other forms of discrimination also persisted to the war's end. Yet even with all of these injustices, the enrollment of 179,000 black soldiers and 10,000 black sailors

---

[18] *National Intelligencer,* August 24, 1863; *New York Times,* June 11, 1863; Charles A. Dana, *Recollections of the Civil War* (New York, 1898), p. 86.

[19] William Hanchett, *Irish: Charles G. Halpine in Civil War America* (Syracuse, 1970), p. 70.

was of crucial significance for the future. By fighting for the Union, black men would help to achieve freedom for their race. By helping the North win the war, they would also help win equal citizenship for blacks after the war.

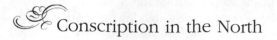Conscription in the North

By early 1863, it had become clear that the North, like the South a year earlier (pages 202 and 203), would be compelled to adopt conscription. The militia draft of the previous fall had been the handwriting on the wall. The enlistment terms of the nine-month men recruited then (ninety regiments) would expire in mid-1863. The same was true of forty regiments of two-year men who had enlisted in 1861. Although some of these men could be expected to reenlist, scarcely any new recruits were coming forward. Therefore the Enrollment Act of March 3, 1863, made every able-bodied male citizen (plus aliens who had filed for naturalization) aged twenty to forty-five eligible for the draft.

Although ostensibly a conscription law, the real purpose of the Enrollment Act was to stimulate volunteering. Under the presidential calls for men that preceded each Union draft (July 1863 and March, July, and December 1864), the War Department assigned each congressional district a quota based on a percentage of its eligible males minus the number of men who had already served in the army. But each district was given fifty days to fill this quota with volunteers. Drafting would be resorted to for only the number of men short of the quota. State and local officials used all the means at their command to secure sufficient volunteers to escape the stigma of conscription.

The principal means of stimulating volunteering were bounties. In time, this became one of the worst evils of the Union's recruiting system (largely avoided in the South because the Confederacy, lacking money, relied more on compulsion than inducement[20]). As the supply of recruits dwindled, competition for volunteers compelled districts to raise the bidding. Wealthy districts enticed men away from their home districts to enlist where they could get the most money. In October 1863, the federal government got into the act with a $300 bounty for three-year volunteers. By 1864, it was possible for recruits in some districts to parlay federal, state, and local bounties into a total payment of more than $1,000. Northern governments paid out more than half a billion dollars in bounties during the war. A large number of "bounty brokers" sprang up to obtain recruits (and to take a share of their bounties as a commission). The system also generated a class of "bounty jumpers," who enlisted in one district, collected their bounty, deserted, and repeated the process somewhere else. Some recruits got away with this several times; one claimed to have done it thirty-two times.

Equally notorious were the practices of substitution and commutation. The Union draft law, unlike its Confederate counterpart, contained no provision for occupational exemptions. Only those who were medically unfit or the sole support of wid-

---

[20]Several Southern states and counties offered small bounties, usually $50, to volunteers. The Confederate Congress authorized an additional $50 for three-year volunteers on December 11, 1861, and voted on February 17, 1864, to give every enlisted man a $100 bond.

ows, indigent parents, orphan siblings, or motherless children were exempt. But the Northern law did follow the initial Confederate example of allowing a drafted man to provide a substitute. To prevent the price of substitutes from rising to astronomical heights as it had in the South, the law permitted a drafted man the alternative of paying a $300 commutation fee, which exempted him from that particular draft but not from future drafts.

Although the idea of buying oneself out of the draft seems shocking today, in 1863 it was sanctioned by long precedent. Inevitably, however, fraud and accusations of injustice became associated with these practices. "Substitute brokers" grew rich by collecting a percentage of the substitute's hire price. Collusion between brokers and examining surgeons sent unfit recruits to the army. Veteran volunteers who were risking their lives resented a system that permitted others to buy their way out of the risk. These veterans often ostracized substitutes who joined their units. Officers reported mixed but mostly negative opinions of the soldierly qualities of substitutes, whose desertion rate appears to have been higher than average.

The privilege of hiring a substitute or paying a $300 commutation fee to escape the draft also provoked workingclass resentment. Since $300 represented more than half a year's wages for an unskilled workingman, the cry arose (as it had in the South a year earlier) that this practice made it a rich man's war and a poor man's fight. In response to growing protests, Congress in July 1864 abolished the commutation privilege except for conscientious objectors. As opponents of this move had predicted, the price of substitutes immediately soared, making it even harder for poor men to buy their way out of the draft. But this class discrimination was greater in appearance than in reality. As matters turned out, nearly as large a proportion of workingmen as of other classes avoided the draft. Several city councils appropriated funds to pay the exemption fee or to hire substitutes for men whose names were drawn. Political organizations like Tammany Hall did the same for their members. Employers established draft insurance funds to buy the exemption of employees if they were drafted. Some insurance companies even offered "draft insurance" whereby for a modest annual premium an individual could buy a policy that would pay his exemption fee or buy a substitute if his name was drawn. In this way, thousands of men escaped serving. In the poorest districts of New York City, for example, 98 percent of the men drafted paid commutation or hired substitutes.[21]

The Civil War draft has generally been accounted a costly, sordid failure. Only 46,000 men were drafted directly into the Union army, and another 118,000 furnished substitutes. Taken together, these 164,000 men along with several thousand from earlier militia drafts constituted barely 8 percent of the Union soldiers. Thus conscription does indeed appear to have been a failure. But when one recalls that the real purpose of the draft was to stimulate volunteering, a different picture emerges.

---

[21]The two fullest studies of the Union draft are Eugene C. Murdock, *One Million Men: The Civil War Draft in the North* (Madison, 1971), and James W. Geary, *We Need Men: The Union Draft in the Civil War* (DeKalb, Ill., 1991). See also Eugene C. Murdock, "Was It a 'Poor Man's Fight'?"; *Civil War History*, 10 (1964), 241–245; Peter Levine, "Draft Evasion in the North During the Civil War, 1863–1865," *Journal of American History*, 67 (1981), 816–834; and James W. Geary, "Civil War Conscription in the North: A Historiographical Review," *Civil War History*, 32 (1986) , 208–228.

Nearly a million men enlisted or reenlisted voluntarily during the two years that the draft was in effect. Thus despite its defects, the system did work. But it worked with such creaking inefficiency and apparent injustice that it became a model of how not to conduct a draft in future wars.

A Socioeconomic Profile of Civil War Soldiers

The notion that the Civil War was a rich man's war and a poor man's fight has been pervasive and persistent. How true is it? In addition to data on the draft cited above, statistics on the civilian occupations of Union and Confederate soldiers cast doubt on the notion. Table 20.1 compares the occupations of Union soldiers prior to their enlistment with the occupations of all males in the states from which the soldiers came.[22] At first glance the stereotype of a "poor man's fight" seems to be confirmed, for the white-collar and professional occupations appear to have been underrepresented in the army. But it should be remembered that most soldiers were young men (the median age was 23.5, and nearly two-fifths of the soldiers were 21 or younger at the time of enlistment), whereas the 1860 occupational profile represents men of *all* ages. Studies of occupational mobility in nineteenth-century America have shown that a substantial number of young men starting out as laborers or farm laborers moved into the white-collar or professional classes later in life. When this is taken into account, the Union army appears to have been quite representative of the Northern population. If anything, unskilled laborers were underrepresented—partly because of the underrepresentation of Irish-Americans, which is discussed below.

Occupational data on Confederate soldiers are scanty. The only scholar to study this subject has been Bell Wiley, who drew a sample of 9,057 men from the company rolls of regiments from seven states. The results are presented in Table 20.2. From this sample it appears that unskilled laborers were underrepresented in the Confederate army, while the white-collar and particularly the professional categories were, given the youth of soldiers, proportionally overrepresented.

Unless the farmers who enlisted in both armies were poorer than those who stayed home (which from other evidence seems unlikely, despite the notorious "20-Negro" draft exemption in the Confederacy), these occupational samples indicate that in neither North nor South was it especially a poor man's fight.

---

[22]The data for the 1860 occupations of males in the Union and Confederate states in Tables 20.1 and 20.2 were compiled from the occupational tables in the 1860 census. The samples of the previous occupations of Union soldiers are from (1) a U.S. Sanitary Commission survey of the occupations of 666,530 Union soldiers from all Union states except Maryland and Delaware; (2) Bell I. Wiley's sample of 13,392 white Union soldiers in 114 companies from all the free states plus Missouri. (California, Oregon, and the territories are not included in these data because they contributed a negligible number of soldiers to Civil War armies.) Both the Sanitary Commission and Wiley samples were drawn from company muster rolls. Both were generally representative of the proportion and distribution of soldiers from the various states. The Sanitary Commission data were reported in Benjamin A. Gould, *Investigations in Military and Anthropological Statistics of American Soldiers* (New York, 1869). I am grateful for the generosity of the late Professor Wiley in supplying me with copies of his research data on the occupations of Union soldiers as well as similar data on the occupations of Confederate soldiers, analyzed in Table 20.2.

Table 20.1   Previous Occupations of Samples of White Union Soldiers Compared with 1860 Occupations of All Males in Union States from Which The Soldiers Came

Occupational Categories	Union Soldiers (U.S. Sanitary Commission Sample)	Union Soldiers (Bell Wiley Sample)	All Males (From 1860 Census)
Farmers and farm laborers	47.5%	47.8%	42.9%
Skilled laborers	25.1	25.2	24.9
Unskilled laborers	15.9	15.1	16.7
White-collar and commercial	5.1	7.8	10.0
Professional	3.2	2.9	3.5
Miscellaneous and unknown	3.2	1.2	2.0

Table 20.2   Previous Occupations of Confederate Soldiers from Alabama, Arkansas, Georgia, Louisiana, Mississippi, North Carolina, Virginia Compared with 1860 Occupations of White Males in These States

Occupational Categories	Confederate Soldiers	White Males (From 1860 Census)
Planters, farmers, and farm laborers	61.5%	57.5%
Skilled laborers	14.1	15.7
Unskilled laborers	8.5	12.7
White-collar and commercial	7.0	8.3
Professional	5.2	5.0
Miscellaneous and unknown	3.7	0.8

Another long-lived Civil War myth is that the Yankees recruited an army of "foreigners" to do their fighting. "Yankees indeed!" said an indignant Southern woman to a New York officer in 1864. "Your whole army is made up of Irish, Dutch, and negroes." The *Richmond Examiner* declared that the Union army was composed mainly of "the riff-raff of Germany and Ireland." [23] But the facts are quite different. Of the 2,100,000 men in the Union army and navy, an estimated 500,000 (24 percent) were foreign-born and 190,000 (9 percent) were black. Not only did immigrants constitute a minority of the Northern soldiers but they were actually underrepresented in proportion to their share of the male population of military age. While 26 percent of the white soldiers in the Union army were foreign-born, 29 percent of the white males of military age residing in the Union states had been born abroad. One possible explanation for this underrepresentation of immigrants is that nondeclarant aliens were not subject to the draft, so immigrants who had not yet filed for citizenship were free from the compulsion of conscription. The data we have indicate that

---

[23]Southern woman and *Richmond Examiner* quoted in Ella Lonn, *Foreigners in the Union Army and Navy* (Baton Rouge, 1951), p. 576n.

two of the four principal ethnic groups among the foreign-born—the British and German Protestants—enlisted in proportion to their percentage of the male population, but that the Irish and German Catholics did not. The reason for this may have been the overwhelming commitment of Catholics to the Democratic party and their opposition to what became an increasingly Republican and antislavery war.[24]

Since 90 percent of the foreign-born lived in the states that remained in the Union, the number and proportion of immigrants were of course much greater in the Union army than in the Confederate army. But the widely held belief that "with very few exceptions" Confederate regiments were "composed exclusively of native-born Americans" is also a myth. The careful scholarship of Ella Lonn has yielded data indicating that 9 or 10 percent of the Confederate soldiers were foreign-born. Since only 7 1/2 percent of the white males of military age in the South were immigrants, this means that the foreign-born were proportionately overrepresented in the Southern armies in contrast to their underrepresentation in the Northern forces.[25] The reason for this is not clear. It may be related to the higher percentage of substitutes in the Confederate army, who were drawn partly from the immigrant aliens not subject to the draft, and partly to the South's failure to use black soldiers, whose enlistment in the Union army reduced the pressure on the foreign-born manpower pool.

Draft Resistance and Riots in the North

Although the poor and the foreign-born did not bear a disproportionate burden of the fighting, the appearance of class bias in the exemption and substitution provisions of conscription caused popular resentment. The Union draft became a catalyst for Democratic and ethnocultural opposition to the war. Democratic newspapers and politicians whipped up antidraft sentiment. The prospect of being drafted into a war to free the slaves was doubly infuriating to the Negrophobic Democratic constituency. Antidraft protests in some cites flared into violence. Armed bands in several Butternut districts of the Midwest attacked and murdered draft officials.

The twin sparks of antidraft and antiblack discontent set off a major explosion in New York City. Rioting began on July 13, 1863. Mobs of Irish workers roamed the streets, burned the draft office, sacked and burned the homes of prominent Republicans, and tried unsuccessfully to demolish the *New York Tribune* building. The mob's chief target was the black population. Chanting "kill the naygers," they lynched a dozen blacks and burned down the Colored Orphan Asylum. Because most of the militia had gone to Pennsylvania for the Gettysburg campaign, the city was especially vulnerable to the snowballing violence. On the fourth day of rioting,

---

[24]Data on the percentage of foreign-born soldiers in the Union army were derived from Gould, *Investigations in Military and Anthropological Statistics of American Soldiers,* pp. 15–29; Lonn, *Foreigners in the Union Army and Navy,* esp. pp. 581–582; and Wiley, *Billy Yank,* pp. 306–313. The proportion of foreign-born males of military age in the Union states has been calculated from the population tables of the 1860 and 1870 published census reports.

[25]Ella Lonn, *Foreigners in the Confederacy* (Chapel Hill, N.C., 1940), pp. 200–240, esp. pp. 200, 218–220.

the police and several regiments of soldiers that had been rushed to New York from Pennsylvania finally brought the city under control. The toll of the riot was staggering. Contemporary estimates of the number killed ranged up to 1,200, but recent research has scaled this down to about 120, most of them rioters killed by police and troops. It was the worst riot in American history. It vividly exposed the complex racial, ethnic, and class tensions that lay close to the surface of American society.

One result of the riot was a renewed surge of anti-Irish feeling among middle- and upper-class New Yorkers. This was part of a general wave of revulsion against Peace Democrats in the months after July 1863. Even non-Copperhead Democrats were caught in this backlash. Governor Seymour's reputation suffered most. Rushing to the city on the second day of violence, he had tried to calm the rioters with a speech in which he addressed them as "my friends." Republican newspapers never let him forget this slip. Indeed, many Northerners considered Seymour responsible for inspiring the riot with his speeches denouncing emancipation and conscription.

After the antidraft violence in New York and elsewhere died down, the draft went forward. Although Northern war weariness and defeatism would once again produce a rise in Copperhead prospects in the summer of 1864, never again would the Peace Democrats be as strong as they were in the spring of 1863. Even before the New York riots, antiwar sentiment had begun to decline in most parts of the North because of the Union successes at Gettysburg and Vicksburg. Northern attitudes toward emancipation and black people also turned a corner in a positive direction in July 1863, not least because of the contribution of black regiments to the Union cause.

Emancipation Confirmed

On July 18, two days after the New York drafts riots had subsided, two Union brigades assaulted a Confederate earthwork known as Fort Wagner, guarding the entrance to Charleston Bay. Part of an unsuccessful campaign to capture Charleston, the attack was beaten back with heavy loss. This was hardly unusual in Civil War battles. What made this attack unique, however, was that it was led by a black regiment, the 54th Massachusetts. The courageous fighting of the 54th and its long casualty list made the regiment famous. Coming only days after white rioters had marched through New York City attacking blacks, this example of black soldiers giving their lives for the Union could not have been more dramatic. Every Republican newspaper drew the obvious moral: black men who fought for the Union were more deserving of rights than white men who rioted against it. This battle "made Fort Wagner such a name to the colored race as Bunker Hill had been for ninety years to the white Yankees," observed the *New York Tribune*.[26]

Until July 1863, the proponents of emancipation and black soldiers had been on the defensive. Now they could go over to the offensive, just in time for the vital state elections to be held in the fall of 1863. Radical editors and orators spoke with a new

[26]James M. McPherson, *The Struggle for Equality: Abolitionists and the Negro in the Civil War and Reconstruction* (Princeton, 1964), p. 211.

boldness and pride. No longer was emancipation a political liability. No longer was it to be defended only as a military necessity. Republicans now championed it as a long-delayed revolution of justice and right. The theme of brave black soldiers and cowardly Copperhead traitors became a staple of Republican rhetoric. Lincoln set the tone on August 26 in a public letter that became an important document in the forthcoming political campaign. Addressing the foes of emancipation, he wrote:

You say you will not fight to free negroes. Some of them seem willing to fight for you. . . . Some of the commanders of our armies in the field who have given us our most important successes, believe the emancipation policy, and the use of colored troops, constitute the heaviest blow yet dealt to the rebellion.[27] . . . [When final victory is achieved] there will be some black men who can remember that, with silent tongue, and clenched teeth, and steady eye, and well-poised bayonet, they have helped mankind on to this great consummation; while, I fear, there will be some white ones, unable to forget that, with malignant heart, and deceitful speech, they have strove to hinder it.[28]

Although some Peace Democrats dimly perceived the changed current of Northern opinion, they still tried to swim in the same old direction. In the words of a Democratic newspaper headline, their platform for the 1863 fall elections was "No Abolitionism, No Emancipation, No Negro Equality." Campaign speakers rang all the changes on the "nigger-worshipping Republican party." Young girls at party rallies in Ohio carried banners bearing the slogan: "Father, save us from Negro Equality."[29]

The most important fall elections were those in Ohio and Pennsylvania. All eyes focused on Ohio, where the exiled Clement Vallandigham directed his campaign for governor from Windsor, Canada. The Democratic gubernatorial candidate in Pennsylvania was State Supreme Court Justice George W. Woodward, a Copperhead sympathizer. These elections, and less publicized contests elsewhere, became virtual referendums on Lincoln's war policies. The President was "nervous" about the outcome, according to Gideon Welles. "He told me that he had more anxiety in regard to the election results . . . than he had in 1860 when he was chosen."[30] His anxiety was soon dispelled. The elections proved to be a ringing endorsement of the administration. Republicans swept the board everywhere, especially in Ohio, where Vallandigham went down to a crushing defeat by more than 100,000 votes. The Republicans won three-fourths of the seats in the next Ohio legislature. Even in Horatio Seymour's New York, the Republicans carried nearly two-thirds of the legislative districts.

As in the spring elections, the soldier vote was important for Republicans. Several states had arranged for their soldiers to cast absentee ballots. In addition, the War Department had again furloughed home thousands of soldiers to states that did not

---

[27]This was a reference to a letter from Grant to Lincoln on August 23: "I have given the subject of arming the negro my hearty support. This, with the emancipation of the negro, is the heaviest blow yet given the Confederacy. . . . By arming the negro we have added a powerful ally. They will make good soldiers and taking from the enemy weakens him in the same proportion they strengthen us." (Lincoln Papers, Library of Congress.)

[28]Basler, *Works of Lincoln*, VI, 408–410.

[29]Frank L. Klement, *The Limits of Dissent: Clement L. Vallandigham and the Civil War* (Lexington, Ky., 1970), p. 245; V. Jacque Voegeli, *Free but Not Equal* (Chicago, 1967), p. 126.

[30]Gideon Welles, *The Diary of Gideon Welles*, ed. Howard K. Beale, 3 vols. (New York, 1960), I, 470.

permit absentee voting, especially Pennsylvania and New York. While this temporarily weakened the Army of the Potomac, the administration considered political victory well worth the military risk. The fighting men voted 92 percent for the Republican candidates (compared with 56 percent of the "home voters"). Ohio soldiers cast only 5 percent of their ballots for Vallandigham.[31] The soldier vote seemed to confirm the Republican thesis that patriotism equaled Republicanism.

The 1863 fall elections advanced the cause of emancipation. If the Emancipation Proclamation had been submitted to a referendum a year earlier, said an Illinois newspaper in December 1863, "there is little doubt that the voice of a majority would have been against it. And yet not a year has passed before it is approved by an overwhelming majority." Early in 1864, an upper-class New Yorker wrote that "the change of opinion on this slavery question since 1860 is a great historical fact. . . . Who could have predicted it? . . . God pardon our blindness of three years ago." In his annual message to Congress in December 1863, Lincoln admitted that the Emancipation Proclamation had been followed by "dark and doubtful days." But since the fall elections "the crisis which threatened to divide the friends of the Union is past."[32]

One sign of this change was the growing prestige of abolitionists. After crying in the wilderness for so many years, they suddenly found themselves prophets with honor. Contrasting the mobs that had attacked abolitionists in 1860 with the cheers that greeted them now, the *New York Tribune* observed: "It is not often that history presents such violent contrasts in such rapid succession." The veteran abolitionist Lewis Tappan reflected that "all true reformers have been ridiculed & despised in their own day. We are coming out of the slanderous valley sooner than most reformers have done, for we have lived to hear old opponents say, 'I was wrong.' "[33]

Perhaps the best comment on 1863 as the *annus mirabilis* was an entry in the diary of a Baltimore free black: "This year has brought about many changes that at the beginning were or would have been thought impossible. The close of the year finds me a soldier for the cause of my race. May God bless the cause, and enable me in the coming year to forward it on."[34]

Political Disaffection within the Confederacy

If the events of the latter half of 1863 boosted the cause of Union and emancipation in the North, they intensified the long-festering bitterness of political divisiveness in the South.

The Old South had been as proud of its political leadership as of its military prowess. The section that had produced Washington, Jefferson, Madison, Jackson, Calhoun, and Clay (born in Virginia) was confident that its statesmen as well as its soldiers would put the Yankees to shame. With such high expectations, the reality of mediocre political leadership came as a shock to many Southerners. The Confederate

---

[31]The voting percentages are calculated from data in *The Tribune Almanac for 1864*, pp. 55–69.

[32]Voegeli, *Free but Not Equal*, p. 131; Nevins and Thomas, *Diary of George Templeton Strong*, III, 408; Basler, *Works of Lincoln*, VII, 49–50.

[33]McPherson, *Struggle for Equality*, pp. 85, 132.

[34]The Diary of Christopher Fleetwood, Manuscripts Division, Library of Congress.

Congress made few positive contributions to the war effort. Much of its legislation was too little and too late. An outstanding example was the failure to pass a comprehensive tax measure until halfway through the war. Some important laws were repealed or amended so often that confusion reigned and enforcement became impossible. Congressmen expended much time and energy in grandiloquent or billingsgate oratory, procedural details, and personal quarrels. Both houses met often in secret session and published no record of their debates. This produced exaggerated and disquieting rumors of what went on. But Vice President Stephens said sarcastically that perhaps it was best Congress met in secret session "and so kept from the public some of the most disgraceful scenes ever enacted by a legislative body."[35]

Many of these "disgraceful scenes" resulted from the oversized Southern sense of honor and penchant for violence. Two of the Confederacy's most famous politicians, Benjamin Hill of Georgia and William L. Yancey of Alabama, became embroiled in a name-calling Senate debate one day in 1863 that ended with Hill throwing an ink bottle at Yancey, cutting open his cheek. Congressman Henry S. Foote of Tennessee had several fights with other congressmen in which he brandished a variety of weapons, including his fists, an umbrella, a bowie knife, and a revolver. In April 1863, the journal clerk of the House shot and killed the chief clerk in Richmond's capitol square. To make matters worse, the public drunkenness of several congressmen became a notorious feature of Richmond life. An influential South Carolinian wrote to Robert M. T. Hunter, president pro tem of the Senate, in 1863: "Pardon me, is the majority always drunk? The People are beginning to think so."[36] By 1863, the reputation of Congress had sunk to a low point from which it never recovered.

Having been schooled for decades in the tactics of obstruction when the South was part of the United States, Confederate politicians found it hard to shed old habits. After a visit to Richmond in 1863, an Alabamian concluded that "many men who were highly gifted in tearing down the old government are worth but little in building up a new one."[37] Then, too, the army rather than Congress attracted many of the Confederacy's ablest leaders. Several members of the Confederate constitutional convention and the provisional Congress went into the army in 1861. Less experienced men took their places. Fewer than one-third of the Confederate lawmakers had previously served in the U.S. Congress. By way of comparison, more than half the members of the wartime Union Congresses had served there before.

The Confederate cabinet also suffered from the greater attractiveness of military service. Two of Davis's initial choices for cabinet posts declined the appointments to accept a brigadier's commission instead. Two others resigned from the cabinet in 1861 to put on a uniform. Except for Judah P. Benjamin, who was successively attorney general, secretary of war, and secretary of state, the Confederate cabinet contained no men equal in ability and stature to Seward, Chase, Stanton, and Welles in Lincoln's cabinet. Critics of the Davis administration described the cabinet as a "farce" or a "ridiculous cipher." These descriptions were unjust. Nevertheless, the cabinet

---

[35]E. Merton Coulter, *The Confederate States of America 1861–1865* (Baton Rouge, 1950), p. 141.

[36]Clement Eaton, *A History of the Southern Confederacy,* Collier Books ed. (New York, 1961 [1954]), p. 63.

[37]Thomas B. Alexander and Richard E. Beringer, *The Anatomy of the Confederate Congress* (Nashville, 1972), p. 40.

was a relatively undistinguished body that, like Congress, contributed little toward solving the Confederacy's pressing problems. High turnover hindered administrative efficiency. Sixteen different men served in the six cabinet posts, compared with twelve men in the seven positions of the Union cabinet. The Confederacy had five secretaries of war and three secretaries of state, compared with the Union's two and one in these vital offices.

Criticism of Jefferson Davis

Southern criticisms of Congress and the cabinet were as nothing compared with the abuse heaped on Jefferson Davis. The president was a "false and hypocritical . . . wretch," wrote the powerful Robert Toombs. A prominent Mississippian considered Davis "a miserable, stupid, one-eyed, dyspeptic, arrogant tyrant."[38] Davis's most bitter enemies were Georgians, especially Vice President Alexander Stephens and his half brother Linton. "Mr. Davis is *mad,* infatuated, " wrote Linton Stephens. "He is a *little, conceited, hypocritical, snivelling, canting, malicious, ambitious, dogged* knave and fool." Although Alexander Stephens considered Davis "weak and vacillating, timid, petulant, peevish, obstinate," he claimed to have "no more feeling of resentment toward him" than toward "my poor old blind and deaf dog." Modern historians avoid such vitriolic criticisms. But some of them agree with David M. Potter, who wrote that Davis's leadership constituted "a record of personal failure significant enough to have had a bearing on the course of the war. . . . If the Union and Confederacy had exchanged presidents with one another, the Confederacy might have won its independence."[39]

But no single person can be made to bear such a load of blame for Confederate defeat. Many of the South's wartime problems were beyond the president's control. Nevertheless, it is true that Davis had important defects as a leader. Austere, humorless, wracked by pain from neuralgia and dyspepsia that grew worse as wartime pressures mounted, he often offended others with ill-tempered, biting remarks. He had a knack for making enemies. As an administrator, he wasted time and energy on minor details. He held long cabinet meetings that "from his uncontrollable tendency to digression," wrote Secretary of the Navy Mallory, "consumed four or five hours without determining anything; while the desk of every chief of a Department was covered with papers demanding his attention."[40] A West Point graduate whose first ambition had been to command the Confederate armies, Davis tried to run the War Department himself. Two of the five secretaries of war went to Davis "for instructions about every little matter";[41] another resigned after Davis reversed a decision about which the secretary had *not* consulted the president. Unlike Lincoln, Davis was more concerned with proving himself right than with getting results. He

---

[38]Coulter, *Confederate States,* pp. 375, 386.

[39]James Z. Rabun, "Alexander Stephens and Jefferson Davis," *American Historical Review,* 58 (1953), 307, 310; A. Stephens to Herschel V. Johnson, April 8, 1864, in *O.R.,* Ser. 4, Vol. 3, p. 280; David M. Potter, "Jefferson Davis and the Political Factors in Confederate Defeat," in David Donald (ed.), *Why the North Won the Civil War* (Baton Rouge, 1960), pp. 102, 112.

[40]Joseph T. Durkin, *Stephen R. Mallory: Confederate Navy Chief* (Chapel Hill, N.C., 1954), p. 176.

[41]Edward Younger (ed.), *Inside the Confederate Government: The Diary of Robert Garlick Hill Kean* (New York, 1957), p. 100.

JEFFERSON DAVIS. Austere, ascetic, humorless, utterly dedicated to the Confederate cause, Davis suffered from ill health that frequently prostrated him with sickness and sometimes caused him to lash out at his critics, who grew more numerous and vociferous as the war went badly for the Confederacy. The lines of pain and determination are etched in his face in this photograph.

LIBRARY OF CONGRESS

was unable to admit mistakes, and he lacked Lincoln's ability to work with critics and with those who disagreed about the best means toward a common end. Davis also lacked Lincoln's political acumen, his common touch, his talent for communicating with all classes of people, and his eloquence in defining the purpose and meaning of the war.

Significant opposition to Davis did not surface until the second year of the war. Basking in the aftermath of victory at Manassas, the administration enjoyed smooth sailing in the latter half of 1861. Organized political parties had disappeared during the secession crisis. With a common concern for unity against the Yankees, Southern Democrats and Whigs by mutual consent did not revive their party organizations. No candidates opposed Davis and Stephens in the November 1861 presidential election. Congressional candidates in this election ran without opposition in many districts. The campaign generated no issues, and voting was light. When Davis took the oath of office during a rainstorm on February 22, 1862 (until then he had been provisional president), the government still presented a facade of nonpartisan unity.

But that rainstorm would prove to be an ill omen. Military reverses and policy actions provoked the emergence of an anti-administration faction in the spring of 1862. Forts Henry and Donelson and Roanoke Island had fallen to blue armies just before Davis was inaugurated. On the day after the inauguration, Nashville surrendered to the Federals. New Orleans, Memphis, and most of Tennessee soon followed. Davis's own Mississippi plantation was taken over by the Yankees. Inflation was beginning to tighten its fatal grip on the Southern economy. Congress enacted the unpopular Conscription Act in April. Even more controversial was a law passed on February 27, 1862, that authorized the president to suspend the writ of habeas corpus.

Habeas Corpus and States' Rights in the Confederacy

In 1861, some Confederate military commanders, like their Union counterparts, arrested civilians for disloyal activities and refused to surrender them to the courts when presented with writs of habeas corpus. The Davis administration neither sanctioned nor disavowed these acts. Faced with Grant's invasion of Tennessee and McClellan's imminent invasion of Virginia in February 1862, the Confederate Congress empowered Davis to suspend the writ "in such cities, towns and military districts as shall, in his judgment, be in such danger of attack by the enemy as to require the declaration of martial law for their effective defence."[42] Davis thereupon proclaimed martial law in several parts of the Confederacy. Southern generals in some western districts did the same on their own authority. Davis rebuked them and revoked their actions, but in the crisis of invasion and battle in the West, orders of revocation from Richmond carried little weight. In August 1862, General Bragg even proclaimed martial law in Atlanta, far from the battlefront, because of its importance as a transport and supply center.

These actions aroused cries of protest from Southerners who feared that "military despotism" would undermine the constitutional liberties they were fighting for. "This is the worst that can befall us," wrote Vice President Stephens. "Far better that our country should be overrun by the enemy, our cities sacked and burned, and our land laid desolate, than that the people should thus suffer the citadel of their liberties to be entered and taken by professed friends." Governor Joseph Brown of Georgia denounced "the wicked act" suspending habeas corpus as "high-handed usurpation."[43]

Because of such protests, Congress allowed the law to expire in February 1863. During the next year, several state judges issued writs to release men charged with desertion, disloyalty, or draft evasion. This made it impossible for Confederate officials in some areas to enforce conscription. The situation became desperate following the defeats at Vicksburg, Gettysburg, and Chattanooga. Desertion increased, and secret Unionist societies became more bold in upcountry districts. In February 1864, Congress complied with Davis's pleas for a new act to suspend habeas corpus but specified that the law would expire on July 31.

Davis possessed the authority to suspend the writ of habeas corpus for a total period of only eighteen months. And he used the authority more sparingly than Lincoln, who unlike the Confederate president had exercised this power for nearly two

---

[42]James M. Mathews (ed.), *Public Laws of the Confederate States of America* (Richmond, 1862), p. 1.

[43]George C. Rable, *The Confederate Republic: A Revolution Against Politics* (Chapel Hill, 1994), p. 251; Joseph Brown to Alexander Stephens, February 20, 1864, in Ulrich B. Phillips (ed.), *The Correspondence of Robert Toombs, Alexander H. Stephens, and Howell Cobb* (Washington, D.C., 1913), p. 633; Allen D. Candler (ed.), *The Confederate Records of the State of Georgia*, 4 vols. (Atlanta, 1909–1911), II, 305.

years before obtaining congressional sanction for it in March 1863. Nevertheless, this issue stirred up at least as much anti-administration rancor in the Confederacy as in the Union. Along with conscription and the impressment of supplies, it fueled the emergence of opposition factions that hindered the government's effectiveness in the last half of the war.

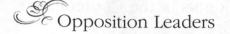 Opposition Leaders

Although every state contained anti-administration spokesmen, opposition centered in North Carolina and especially in Georgia. Governor Zebulon Vance of North Carolina was jealous of his state's prerogatives. He quarreled with the administration over everything—from the appointment of generals from North Carolina to the use of cargo space on state-owned blockade runners. At the same time, though, Vance was an energetic governor who did much to equip North Carolina soldiers fighting in Confederate armies and to provide assistance to their families at home. In Georgia a trio of powerful politicians—Toombs, Stephens, and Brown—evolved into the most outspoken anti-administration bloc. Disappointed at his failure to be elected president of the Confederacy, Toombs had tried the army without much success. He resigned his brigadier's commission in March 1863 and thereafter became a bitter critic of Davis. Vice President Stephens left Richmond in 1862 and rarely returned during the rest of the war, preferring to remain in Georgia and snipe at every measure that increased Jefferson Davis's "dictatorial power." Governor Brown was a political maverick whose growing dislike of "centralizing" war measures drove him to obstructive resistance.

Whatever their motives, opponents of Davis cloaked their opposition in the rhetorical garb of states' rights. "My position is the position of the old State Rights leaders from the days of 1798 to the present," wrote Brown in 1862. "I entered into this revolution to contribute my mite to sustain the rights of states and prevent the consolidation of the Government, and I am still a rebel till this object is accomplished, no matter who may be in power."[44] It should be noted, however, that Brown like Vance did a great deal to mobilize residents of his state for the war effort even as he quarreled with the Davis administration in Richmond. In particular, Brown provided food and salt to Georgia families that were suffering because of wartime shortages, inflation, and the absence of husbands or sons in the army. This kind of effort by state governors helped make it possible for Confederate armies to keep fighting and did something to offset the negative impact of states' rights opposition to conscription, martial law, and other centralizing measures. Recent scholarship has tended to minimize the importance of the states' rights problem that was emphasized so strongly by earlier historians.[45]

---

[44]Phillips (ed.), *Correspondence of Toombs, Stephens, and Cobb,* p. 598.

[45]For a sample of earlier scholarship, see Frank L. Owsley, *State Rights in the Confederacy* (Chicago, 1925), which maintained that on the tombstone of the Confederacy should be carved the epitaph: "Died of State Rights." For revisionist studies, see Paul D. Escott, *After Secession: Jefferson Davis and the Failure of Confederate Nationalism* (Baton Rouge, 1978), and Richard E. Beringer, Herman Hattaway, Archer Jones, and William N. Still, Jr., *Why the South Lost the Civil War* (Athens, Ga., 1986), chap. 10.

The Disadvantages of No-Party Politics

The Lincoln administration also confronted strong opposition, which grew more powerful during periods of military defeat. But a vital difference in the structure of Union and Confederate politics tempered Northern divisiveness: the North had political parties, the South did not. The absence of parties in the South paradoxically produced an opposition that became unmanageable precisely *because* it was nonpartisan. Without the institution of parties, the opposition became personal, factional, and sometimes irresponsible. Under the Confederate constitution, Davis was ineligible for reelection, so he had no motive to create a party organization. In the absence of a party with its ties of loyalty, patronage, and self-interest, Davis had no institutional means to rally support for his policies. In the North, by contrast, Lincoln was the leader of a vigorous, well-organized party. Moreover, the existence of an equally well-organized opposition served to unify the Republicans on crucial issues. While Lincoln faced criticism from radical Republicans, the momentum of the war pushed moderates toward the radical policies of emancipation and total war, uniting the party in elections and in important congressional votes. Nearly all the Northern state governors were Republicans, which created ties of loyalty and mutual interest between the states and the national government.

The Confederate congressional elections in November 1863 illustrated the problems of no-party politics. Unfortunately for the Davis administration, these elections occurred at a time of low morale and divisiveness in the South following the setbacks at Gettysburg and Vicksburg. The head of the War Department's administrative bureau in Richmond caught this mood in a diary entry in November: "The irretrievable bankruptcy of the national finances, the tenacity with which the President holds to men in whom the country has lost all confidence, the scarcity of means of support . . . are producing deep disgust."[46] The record of the Davis administration was the principal issue in the elections, but candidates announced for or against government policies on an individual, not a party basis. Instead of being channeled through an identifiable organization, the opposition came from every direction and was difficult to counter. Openly anti-administration candidates scored significant gains in the congressional elections, though they fell short of gaining control of the House by about fifteen seats and of the Senate by two seats. But while the Davis administration preserved a narrow majority in Congress, the lack of a party organization made it hard to mobilize that majority.[47]

---

[46]Edward Younger (ed.), *Inside the Confederate Government: The Diary of Robert Garlick Hill Kean* (New York, 1957), p. 119.

[47]This interpretation of the disadvantages of no-party politics and the benefits of the North's two-party system was suggested by Eric L. McKitrick, "Party Politics and the Union and Confederate War Efforts," in William Nisbet Chambers and Walter Dean Burnham, eds., *The American Party Systems: Stages of Political Development* (New York, 1967), pp. 117–151. For a different view, which challenges the notion that the bitter partisan wartime contests in some Northern states were healthy for the body politic, see Mark E. Neely, Jr., "The Civil War and the Two-Party System," in James M. McPherson, ed., *"We Cannot Escape History": Lincoln and the Last Best Hope of Earth* (Urbana, Ill., 1995), pp. 86–104.

An ominous feature emerged in these elections: the beginnings of a peace move-ment in parts of the South. It was particularly strong in North Carolina. The western part of that state, like east Tennessee, contained many Unionists; the state as a whole contained an even larger number of reluctant Confederates. Desertion from North Carolina regiments rose alarmingly after Gettysburg. A secret peace society, the Or-der of the Heroes of America, was founded in upcountry North Carolina. Armed clashes occurred between Confederate soldiers and bands of deserters-guerrillas. Eight of the ten congressmen elected from North Carolina opposed the Davis ad-ministration; at least five of them were "reported to be in favor of peace." What this meant was not clear: reunion with the North, or a peace concluded by an inde-pendent Confederacy with the United States, or a withdrawal of North Carolina from the Confederacy and a separate peace with the North?

The foremost peace advocate in the state, William W. Holden, insisted that an armistice and peace negotiations would lead to an independent Confederacy. In this respect, he was a Southern counterpart to Northern Copperheads. But like them, Holden lived in a fantasy world if he thought that peace overtures offered in the con-text of defeat and discouragement could lead to anything but surrender. Neverthe-less, Holden, editor of North Carolina's largest newspaper, the Raleigh *North Car-olina Standard,* gained a large following and decided to run for governor in 1864. In the end, Governor Vance trounced Holden and was triumphantly reelected on a platform declaring that the only way to achieve peace was to win the war. But the upswelling of peace sentiment in North Carolina and in upcountry districts of other states during the winter of 1863–1864 was a portent of trouble.

The alignment in the new Congress elected in 1863 was loosely pro- and anti-administration. One notable feature marked this alignment: the strongest support for the administration came from areas occupied by Union troops—Kentucky and Missouri (both of which had been admitted to full representation in the Confeder-ate Congress in 1861), Tennessee, and large portions of Louisiana, Arkansas, Mis-sissippi, and Virginia. Regular elections were impossible there, of course, so most incumbents were "reelected" by a handful of refugees and by soldiers from those districts. These congressmen had the strongest of motives for supporting the ad-ministration's war policies, for only through victory could they go home again. They provided the votes in Congress for higher taxes that would not be levied on their constituents and for tougher conscription laws that would take no men from their districts. The portions of the South still under Confederate control—where such measures would fall most heavily—elected a majority of anti-administration con-gressmen in 1863.

Politics and the military situation were not the only factors that affected these elec-tions. By 1863, the economic impact of the war had exacerbated Southern weak-nesses even as it augmented Northern strengths. The Confederacy seemed to be los-ing the war on the home front as well as on the battle front. The next chapter examines these developments.

Behind the Lines

Nothing that I had ever heard or read had given me the faintest idea of the horrors witnessed here.

—Kate Cumming,

nurse at the Confederate field hospital in Corinth, Mississippi, April 1862

The War's Economic Impact on the North

Union military and diplomatic successes in 1863 were matched by a booming economy. As the South grew weaker from invasion and destruction, the North grew stronger from the stimulus of war production and victory. "It was a favorite theory of the rebel leaders, at the beginning of the rebellion, that the withdrawal of Southern trade from the North would . . . 'make grass grow in the streets of New York,' "[1] commented the *New York Sun* toward the war's end. But the "vast increase of Northern and military trade" more than made up for the loss of Southern business. "There never was a time in the history of New York when business prosperity was more general . . . than within the last two or three years."[2]

Agriculture

The war record of Northern agriculture was especially impressive. American wheat production had increased 73 percent during the decade 1849–1859. Yet despite secession of the South and disruption in the loyal border states, the Union states grew

---

[1]This had indeed been a Southern theory. Several Southern newspapers in June 1861 reprinted an editorial from the *Louisville Courier* entitled "Grass in Their Streets." One person claimed to have seen grass actually growing in a busy New York street. Others described New York's "silent streets, the deserted hotels. . . . The glory of the once-proud metropolis is gone . . . for the trade of the South will never return. . . . Gotham must fall." (*Richmond Daily Examiner,* June 4, July 16, 1861, quoted in Rembert Patrick, *Jefferson Davis and His Cabinet* [Baton Rouge, 1944], pp. 17–19.)

[2]*New York Sun,* March 24, 1865.

more wheat in 1862 and again in 1863 than the entire country had grown in the previous record year of 1859. Corn production also increased in the Northern states to above prewar levels. Because of crop failures in western Europe from 1860 to 1862, American exports of wheat, corn, pork, and beef doubled during the war, even as the Union army consumed more food per man than any previous army in history.

The unique achievement of increasing exports during an internal war occurred while one-third of the farm labor force was absent in the army. The expanded use of machinery in Northern agriculture made this possible. The 1850s had been a decade of rapid mechanization in grain farming, and the production of reapers and mowers tripled during the war. The addition of a self-raking device to many reapers represented a further labor-saving advance. Reapers, mowers, and other implements enabled women and children to make up for the absence of their menfolk at the front. "Yesterday I saw the wife of one of our parishioners driving the team in a reaper; her husband is at Vicksburg," wrote an Illinois clergyman in 1863. Another observer wrote:

So perfect is machinery that men seem to be of less necessity. . . . We have seen, within the past few weeks, a stout matron whose sons are in the army, with her team cutting hay. . . . She cut seven acres with ease in a day, riding leisurely upon her cutter. This circumstance is indicative of the great revolution which machinery is making in production.[3]

"Revolution" was not quite the right word to describe farm mechanization. Rather it was a war-induced *acceleration* of prewar modernizing trends. The same things were happening in other aspects of food production and processing. Canned fruits and vegetables and condensed milk had made their first appearance before the war. But the needs of the Union armies gave these industries a crucial boost. The output of canned fruits and vegetables grew from five million to thirty million cans in the 1860s. Gail Borden had established his first condensed milk plant in 1859. Army contracts enabled him to expand production to 17,000 quarts per month by the summer of 1862. A year later, his plants were producing this much each day.[4]

Transportation

The transport sector of the economy performed almost as well as agriculture. All forms of internal water transport increased in volume, despite the closing of the Mississippi in the early part of the war. Heavy military traffic moved on the river networks above Vicksburg to support Union armies in the western theater. The east-west Great Lakes and canal traffic continued to grow, especially with the large grain shipments destined for armies in the eastern theater and for export. The Erie Canal carried 54 percent more tonnage annually during the war than in the 1850s. This growth of internal water commerce plus the demands of the Union navy caused a boom in shipbuilding, even though Confederate commerce raiders drove most of the

---

[3]Emerson D. Fite, *Social and Industrial Conditions in the North During the Civil War* (New York, 1910), p. 9; George Winston Smith and Charles Judah (eds.), *Life in the North During the Civil War* (Albuquerque, 1966), p. 167.

[4]Paul W. Gates, *Agriculture and the Civil War* (New York, 1965), pp. 141, 193; Joe B. Frantz, *Gail Borden: Dairyman to a Nation* (Norman, Okla., 1951), p. 255.

ROLLING STOCK OF THE U.S. MILITARY RAILROADS AT ALEXANDRIA, VIRGINIA

merchant marine off the high seas. The United States built almost twice as much merchant tonnage in the four war years as in the previous four years of peace. The 1864 total was not exceeded until 1908.[5]

Large as it was, the wartime expansion of water transport was outstripped by the railroads. The railroad construction boom of the 1850s had produced excess capacity, especially west of the Alleghenies; but the demands of war soon pushed the railroads to and beyond their capacity. Several Northern roads doubled their traffic volume between 1860 and 1865. Some also doubled their earnings. A few paid dividends for the first time. Of all major Northern railroads, only the Baltimore and Ohio was vulnerable to enemy destruction. But even the B&O benefited from increased wartime traffic.

Heavy war traffic compelled the double tracking of busy corridors, the building of new bridges across several rivers, the standardization of gauges or the adding of a third rail or extra car wheels so that freight could be shipped across lines of different gauges without transloading, and the construction of Union terminals to avoid delays in transferring freight or passengers across a city from one railroad to another. Much of the pressure for such improvements came from the government. In January 1862, Congress authorized the President to take control of any railroad "when in his judgment the public safety may require it." Although Lincoln rarely invoked this authority, its existence provided an incentive for railroads to give priority to military traffic. The government made heavy demands on the four different railroads in the

---

[5]These statistics and those in subsequent paragraphs are compiled from the relevant tables in *Historical Statistics of the United States* (Washington, D.C., 1975), and from Ralph Andreano (ed.), *The Economic Impact of the American Civil War* (Cambridge, Mass., 1962), Appendix.

corridor between Washington and New York. These companies double tracked much of their line and connected their tracks through Philadelphia in 1863. Nevertheless, the New York-Washington corridor remained something of a bottleneck throughout the war. Although several Northern officials talked of building a government-owned through line there, nothing came of the idea.

But in the occupied South, the War Department went into the railroad business in a big way. The United States Military Railroads, created in February 1862, began life with a few miles of line in northern Virginia. As invading Union armies lengthened their supply lines, the USMRR took over additional captured Southern railroads and built new ones. By war's end the USMRR was operating 2,105 miles of track with 419 engines and 6,330 cars, making it the largest railroad in the world at that time.

Industry

While the war stimulated the transport sector of the economy, its impact on Northern industry was uneven. The largest single industry, cotton textiles, suffered a 74 percent decline in output because of the war-created cotton famine. This was only partly offset by the woollen industry's doubling of production. The second largest consumer industry, shoe manufacturing, was hit hard by loss of its Southern market, though army contracts soon filled much of the gap. Loss of the Southern market also injured other industries in the first year or two of fighting, until war production brought a boom in 1863–1864. Iron production dropped by 14 percent in the first two years of war but by 1864 had reached a level for the Union states alone 29 percent higher than for the entire country in the previous record year of 1856. Coal production dropped in 1861 before rising to a new high in later years, so that the output of Northern coal mines alone was 21 percent greater during 1861–1865 than that of Northern and Southern mines combined during 1856–1860. Other war-related industries—firearms, gunpowder, leather (for harnesses), copper (for rifle percussion caps), wagon building, and others—grew rapidly from the beginning of the war. These industries helped the manufacturing index for the Union states alone to rise by 1864 to a level 13 percent higher than that for the country as a whole in 1860.

The war also accelerated the spread of mechanization and the factory system. As one of the first American industries to adopt the principle of machine-made interchangeable parts a half century earlier, firearms production was capable of rapid expansion during the war despite shortages of skilled workers. The experiences of two other Northern industries illustrate how the war quickened the trend toward mechanization. The invention of the sewing machine had established the ready-made clothing business by the 1850s. But the sudden wartime demand for army uniforms acted as a catalyst for further mechanization and standardization. The number of sewing machines doubled between 1860 and 1865. The War Department furnished clothing manufacturers with a series of graduated measurements for soldiers. This led to the concept of standard "sizes" for uniforms and, after the war, for civilian clothes. The war also accelerated the application of new technology to the production of shoes. A generation earlier, the making of shoes had begun to move from the small shop to the factory. The adaptation of the sewing machine to leather had accelerated this process in the 1850s, and in 1858 a Massachusetts inventor, Lyman Blake, had patented an improved machine to sew the uppers to soles. The war created a market for Blake's invention because the old method of hand sewing was too slow for filling army contracts, especially since many skilled shoemakers had joined the army. In 1862, the Massachusetts entrepreneur Gordon McKay purchased and improved Blake's patent and began selling the machines to shoe manufacturers. By the end of 1863, these machines had stitched two and a half million shoes.

The Civil War and Economic Growth

These and other war-fueled changes in the Northern economy prompted an earlier generation of historians to proclaim that the Civil War launched the industrial revolution in America. This was part of what Charles and Mary Beard meant when they labeled the Civil War "the Second American Revolution." But in recent decades, economic historians have attacked this thesis on two fronts. They have argued that (1) the basic innovations that produced economic modernization had taken place from the 1820s to the 1850s, and while the war may have accelerated some of these trends it produced no fundamental changes of direction; and (2) the decade of the 1860s witnessed an actual slowing of the rate of economic growth and therefore the war may have retarded rather than promoted industrialization.[6]

The first of these arguments is persuasive. The transportation revolution, the factory, the American system of mass production, and most of the technological innovations of nineteenth-century industrialization antedated the war. Clearly, then, the Civil War did not *begin* the modernization of the American economy. The war was a triumph for modernization, but not a cause of it.

The second argument also appears valid at first glance. By most statistical indexes, the rate of American economic growth was lower in the 1860s than in any other decade between 1840 and 1930. The commodity output of the American economy increased 51 percent in the 1840s, 62 percent in the 1850s, 62 percent in the 1870s, 63 percent in the 1880s, and 36 percent in the 1890s—but only 22 percent in the 1860s. Output per capita actually decreased by 3 percent in the 1860s, compared with an average decennial increase of 20 percent in the other five decades. Value added by manufacture increased only 25 percent during the 1860s, compared with a decennial average increase of 94 percent for the rest of the nineteenth century after 1839. Agricultural output grew 15 percent in the 1860s, compared with a 35 percent average growth for the other decades. Only 1,000 miles per year of new railroad were built during the war, compared with an annual average of 3,000 miles for the rest of the period from 1850 to 1873. Taken together, these statistics, according to a leading economic historian, "support a conclusion that the Civil War retarded American industrial growth."[7]

---

[6]See especially Thomas C. Cochran, "Did the Civil War Retard Industrialization?" *Mississippi Valley Historical Review*, 48 (September 1961), 197–210; David T. Gilchrist and W. David Lewis (eds.), *Economic Change in the Civil War Era* (Greenville, Del., 1965); Stanley L. Engerman, "The Economic Impact of the Civil War," *Explorations in Entrepreneurial History*, 2nd Ser., III (1966), 176–199; and Patrick O'Brien, *The Economic Effects of the American Civil War* (Highlands, N.J., 1988). For an excellent summary and evaluation of the literature on this question, consult Phillip Shaw Paludan, "What Did the Winners Win?" The Social and Economic History of the North during the Civil War," in James M. McPherson and William J. Cooper, Jr. (eds.), *Writing the Civil War: The Quest to Understand* (Columbia, S.C., 1998), pp. 174–188.

[7]Cochran, "Did the Civil War Retard Industrialization?" p. 205.

But the statistics in the foregoing paragraph include the South. Given the war's enormous destruction of resources, productive capacity, and consumer buying power in the South, it is hardly surprising that the 1860s were a decade of low growth for the country as a whole. While the Union states experienced a high growth rate during the war, economic dislocation in the Confederacy more than counterbalanced that growth. The accelerated growth rate after the war reflected in part the rebuilding of the shattered Southern economy and represented a catching-up process after the lag of the 1860s. Between 1840 and 1860, the per capita commodity output of the American economy had increased an average of 1.45 percent annually. After the slight decline of the 1860s, the per capita growth rate between 1870 and 1880 averaged 2.6 percent a year. After 1880, the rate dropped to under 2 percent again. Thus the per capita output of the American economy in 1880 stood at the same level as if the 1840–1860 rate had steadily continued and the Civil War had never occurred.[8]

In a statistical sense, then, the war neither accelerated nor retarded the long-term growth rate. But it did radically alter the sectional distribution of wealth and output. In 1860, the per capita wealth of white Southerners had been 95 percent higher than that of Northern whites; by 1870, Northern per capita wealth was 44 percent greater than that of Southern whites. In 1860, the per capita, commodity output (including agriculture) of North and South had been about equal; by 1870, the North's per capita output was 56 percent greater than the South's. In 1860, the South's share of national wealth had been 30 percent; by 1870, it was 12 percent.[9]

Nonmilitary Wartime Legislation

Sectional shifts in political power were equally dramatic. The war freed not only the slaves; it also freed modernizing Northern capitalism from the shadow of Southern ideology. The consequences of this liberation became evident as early as 1862. Wartime financial legislation created a uniform currency (the greenbacks and national banknotes) and a national banking structure. The absence of Southern Democrats from Congress also made possible the passage in 1862 of three important laws that reflected Whig-Republican modernizing purposes: the Homestead Act, the Land-grant College Act, and the Pacific Railroad Act.

The Homestead Act granted ownership of 160 acres of public land to a settler after five years of residence on his claim. A key plank in the 1860 Republican platform, "free land" had a long history as a cause frustrated by Southerners in Congress and by President Buchanan's veto in 1860. Freed of the Southern incubus, Republicans enacted the measure on May 20, 1862. Before the war's end, nearly 20,000 farmers had taken up three million acres under the law, which eventually accounted for the settlement and ownership of more than eighty million acres.

---

[8]Engerman, "The Economic Impact of the Civil War," p. 184.

[9]Lee Soltow, *Men and Wealth in the United States 1850–1870* (New Haven, Conn., 1975), p. 65; Stanley Engerman, "Some Economic Factors in Southern Backwardness in the Nineteenth Century," in John F. Kain and John R. Meyer (eds.), *Essays in Regional Economics* (Cambridge, Mass., 1971), pp. 291, 300. The complex and differential impacts of the war on the North and the South and on different sectors of the economy are summarized in Roger L. Ransom, *Conflict and Compromise: The Political Economy of Slavery, Emancipation, and the American Civil War* (Cambridge, 1989), pp. 255–284.

The Land-grant College Act (generally known as the Morrill Act after its sponsor, Congressman Justin Morrill of Vermont) laid the groundwork for several great universities. The Morrill Act, based on the principle of proportional representation, granted to a state 30,000 acres of public land for each congressman and senator. The proceeds from the sale of this land were to be used for the establishment in each state of at least one college for the teaching of "agricultural and mechanical arts." For a generation, educational reformers had urged such a measure to make higher education more relevant to the economic pursuits of most Americans, but Southerners and Democrats had previously blocked it. Buchanan had vetoed a land-grant bill in 1859. Lincoln signed the Morrill Act on July 2, 1862. In its impact on higher education, this was the most important instance of federal aid to education in American history.

The Pacific railroad bill had enjoyed bipartisan support in the 1850s but had bogged down in sectional disputes over whether the tracks should follow a southern or northern route. This question was settled by secession. The bill enacted on July 1, 1862, stipulated an eastern terminus at Omaha and a western terminus at San Francisco Bay. It provided a minimum grant of 6,400 acres of public land (later doubled) and $16,000 in federal loans for each mile of railroad built. From this act grew the Union Pacific and Central Pacific (later Southern Pacific) railroads, which joined their tracks at Promontory, Utah, in 1869. In 1864, Congress chartered the Northern Pacific Railroad (St. Paul to Seattle) and authorized even larger land grants. These and subsequent land grants to other railroads ultimately totaled 120 million acres.

In practice, these three laws sometimes conflicted with one another. The goal of free land for settlers was at times frustrated by grants to railroads or states, which held the land as collateral for bank loans or sold it to the highest bidder. But the Republicans who passed these laws intended them as complementary measures to advance the cause of free-soil modernizing capitalism: the Homestead Act offered farmers capital in the form of land; the Morrill Act was an investment in human capital that would help these farmers—and "mechanics"—become more prosperous and productive; and the land grants and loans to railroads injected large doses of social overhead capital into the economy.

The 37th Congress (1861–1863) enacted legislation that permanently altered the social and economic landscape. The Legal Tender Act, the National Bank Act, the Homestead Act, the Morrill Act, the Pacific Railroad Act, the Internal Revenue Act, and the Confiscation Act represented the triumph of modernizing capitalism. By confirming this triumph, Northern victory in the war produced an expansive optimism. "The truth is, the close of the war with our resources unimpaired," wrote Senator John Sherman to his brother in 1865, "gives an elevation, a scope to the ideas of leading capitalists, far higher than anything ever undertaken in this country before. They talk of millions as confidently as formerly of thousands."[10]

---

[10]Rachel Sherman Thorndike (ed.), *The Sherman Letters* (New York, 1894), p. 258. Three studies that chronicle and measure the modernizing impact of this legislation are Leonard P. Curry, *Blueprint for Modern America: Nonmilitary Legislation of the First Civil War Congress* (Nashville, 1968); Richard F. Bensel, *Yankee Leviathan: The Origins of Central State Authority in America, 1859–1879* (New York, 1990); and Heather Cox Richardson, *The Greatest Nation of the Earth: Republican Economic Policies during the Civil War* (Cambridge, Mass., 1997).

Labor and the War

One group in the North that viewed this wartime expansiveness with skepticism were blue-collar workers. More than one-third of them were foreign-born, primarily Irish, who lacked enthusiasm for Republican war aims and policies. A good many workers refused to join the middle-class applause for the triumph of modernizing capitalism, especially when they did not fully share in the wartime prosperity. Wage increases lagged 25 percent or more behind price increases until the final months of the war, when wages began to catch up.

One reason for this wage lag was a change in the composition of the labor force. More than half a million skilled and semiskilled workers enlisted in the Union army. To replace them, employers hired or promoted semiskilled and unskilled persons, including women and children. The number of women in the manufacturing labor force increased by 40 percent during the war, and the number of children sixteen and younger may have increased by almost as much. They remained concentrated in the industries that had traditionally employed them—textiles, garment making, and shoes. But some women worked in munitions plants and other previously all-male enterprises. The proportion of women in the manufacturing labor force increased from one-fourth in 1860 to one-third by 1865, though it fell back to the previous level after the war as men returned from the army. Women and other replacements for skilled male workers were paid less for the same work, and because they lacked experience in these jobs, their productivity was also lower—which helps to explain the 3 percent decline in per capita output as well as part of the decline in real wages.

In two other areas of employment, women made substantial gains during the war. This probably caused an increase of efficiency even as it lowered salaries in these occupations because women were paid less than men. The war accelerated the feminization of the teaching profession that had already begun in the Northeast and now spread rapidly to other parts of the country. It also brought women into the government civil service in a significant way. During the 1850s, a few women (including Clara Barton, who became a famous wartime nurse) had worked briefly as clerks in the U.S. Patent Office. The huge expansion of government bureaucracy after 1861 and the enlistment of many male clerks in the army created a demand that was filled by hundreds of women who in many cases did a better job than the men they replaced. When the bureaucracy shrank and men returned after 1865, some of these women clerks lost their positions. But their foothold in the civil service proved to be permanent. By 1875, the number of women in government jobs was double the wartime high. The example was not lost on the private sector, which began hiring women as clerks, bookkeepers, "typewriters" (a new invention of the 1870s), telephone operators (another new invention), and the like. The Civil War began the process which by the twentieth century had feminized clerical work.

During the war, workers occasionally went on strike for higher wages to keep up with the rising cost of living. Many of these strikes were successful, especially those conducted by skilled workers in 1863–1864. Thereafter, the wages of most skilled workers remained abreast of the cost of living. It was mainly the unskilled and the semiskilled, especially women, whose earnings fell further and further behind. Seamstresses (many of whom made uniforms for the army) experienced particularly egregious exploitation. Many of them labored seventy or more hours a week for a pittance of two to four dollars. "We are unable to sustain life for the prices offered by contractors, who fatten on their contracts by grinding immense profits out of the labor of their operatives," several seamstresses informed President Lincoln. In 1863, a group of New York seamstresses formed the Workingwomen's Protective Union. A delegation from the Philadelphia branch of this union held an unprecedented two-hour meeting with Lincoln in 1865. The President responded sympathetically, ordering an increase in their wages for war contracts, but by then the war was almost over. The union survived, though, and grew dramatically after the war.[11]

Successful wartime strikes produced a new feeling of unity and strength among skilled workers. Most strikes, and the unions that grew out of them, were spontaneous and local; but from these emerged a number of national unions, which became the basis for an upsurge of labor activism after the war. From a low point in the late 1850s, labor union membership rose sharply until the early 1870s, when a larger percentage of the industrial labor force belonged to unions than at any other time in the nineteenth century.

Most foreign-born workers were Democrats who shared the party's hostility to modernization and emancipation; while most native-born workers were Republicans who approved the free-labor ideology even to the extent of rejoicing in emancipation. Several labor leaders articulated the same views as radical Republicans concerning the need to destroy the oppressive premodern labor system of the South and to give all workers equal opportunity and equality under law. Massachusetts Senator Henry Wilson, who had been a shoemaker in his youth, boasted that by abolishing slavery, the Republican party had "made labor honorable . . . throughout the country and in so doing that grand work we have done more for labor . . . than was ever achieved by all the parties that arose in this country from the time the Pilgrims put their feet upon Plymouth Rock up to the year 1860.[12]

Several abolitionists and radical Republicans became active in postwar labor reform movements, most notably Wendell Phillips and Benjamin Butler. But the postwar era revealed a growing difference between Republicans and labor leaders in their understanding of the free-labor ideology. The workers moved beyond the Republican belief in equality of rights and opportunity. They began to demand, in the words of labor leader Ira Steward, an "equal *share* in the wealth their industry creates [italics added]."[13] By 1870, two-thirds of working Americans were wage earners rather than self-employed. To many of them, the free-labor ideology of competitive capitalism, individualism, social mobility, self-made men, and the harmony of classes seemed increasingly irrelevant to their dependent, wage-earning status. They were becoming conscious of labor as a special interest group, a separate class whose needs conflicted with the privileges of capital. The Civil War was both a climactic triumph of the free-labor ideology and the catalyst of a more class-conscious labor movement that eventually rejected this ideology as serving the interests of conservative capitalism.

---

[11]David Montgomery, *Beyond Equality: Labor and the Radical Republicans 1862–1872* (New York, 1967), p. 97; Mary Elizabeth Massey, *Bonnet Brigades* (New York, 1966), pp. 144–146, 345.

[12]Phillip Shaw Paludan, *"A People's Contest": The Union and the Civil War* (New York, 1988), p. 179.

[13]Montgomery, *Beyond Equality,* pp. 90–91.

Economic Discontent in the South

The effort to build an industrial economy geared for war on the base of an overwhelmingly agricultural society created great strains in the South. Nearly all of the able-bodied white manpower went into the army. Slaves and free blacks made up part of the deficit, especially in heavy industries like the Tredegar Iron Works in Richmond. But the Confederacy also had to call women into the labor force, a radical departure from Southern tradition which had placed white women on a pedestal. In reality, of course, many of these women had always worked as hard as men: yeoman farmers' wives, who managed household and livestock and worked in the fields at harvest; planters' wives, who ran a large domestic establishment and oversaw its slaves. But they had deferred to ultimate male control, and now the men were gone. Farm and plantation wives found themselves managing the whole enterprise. Only 10 percent of the workers in the South's tiny antebellum manufacturing sector had been women. During the war this proportion rose dramatically as white women went into textile mills and even armaments plants. Explosions in Confederate ordnance factories and arsenals killed at least one hundred women—who were as surely war casualties as men who died in battle. As in the North, many women also went to work for the first time in government offices. A small army of them in the Confederate Treasury spent their days signing the endless stream of notes that rolled off the printing presses to feed the spiraling inflation of the Southern economy.

Strains in Southern Agriculture

Ironically in this agricultural economy, the most serious shortages were salt to preserve meat, and food itself, despite the conversion of thousands of acres of cotton to food crops from 1862 on. The causes of these increasingly severe shortages were manifold. The antebellum South had imported most of its salt from the North or abroad, and efforts to develop domestic sources during the war never caught up with demand. Almost all of the South's railroad iron and locomotives had also come from the North or England; without a sufficient industrial base to develop replacement capacity, the Confederacy's railroads rapidly deteriorated even where they were not destroyed by the armies. With military shipments on the rails having priority, food for domestic consumption rotted in warehouses while women and children went hungry. Union conquest of food-producing areas of the Confederacy in 1862 was followed by a drought that summer which reduced harvests drastically. The steady leakage of slaves to Yankee lines and the restlessness of those who remained behind eroded the black agricultural labor force, while more than half a million white farmers, planters, planters' sons, and even overseers went into the Confederate army.

Farmers' wives had to do the work formerly done by their husbands as well as their own; planters' wives had to manage the field hands as well as the domestic servants. Many of them were overwhelmed by the prospect. "What is to become of the women and children if you call out *all* the men?" asked a Mississippi woman. "I feel it is more than I can bear, as I have been accustomed to trust to [my husband] entirely to manage and provide for the family having little or no knowledge of what ought to be done on the farm."[14] She soon learned what had to be done, and so did thousands of others like her. A Confederate officer from Georgia who owned a large plantation praised his wife's management. Despite this "new onus" with its "many trials and burdens . . . she assumes it bravely, and right ably and skillfully does she direct." But other women succumbed to panic and depression when they were left alone with no adult white male within miles. "I have no brother *no one* on whom I can call for aid," a young planter's wife wrote to the governor of Alabama in September 1862. "I am living *alone* now, with only my child a little girl of 2 years old. I am now surrounded on all sides by plantations of negroes—many of them have not a white [man] on them. I am now begging you will not you in kindness to a poor unprotected woman and child give me the power of having my overseer recalled."[15] It was appeals like this, plus the felt need to maintain slave discipline, that caused Congress in October 1862 to amend the conscription law to exempt one white man on every plantation with twenty or more slaves.

Enacted at a time when severe shortages and actual malnutrition began to pinch the families of yeoman farmers, however, this "20-Negro exemption" exacerbated class tensions in the Confederacy. "Never did a law meet with more universal odium," reported an alarmed Mississippian to Jefferson Davis in December 1862. "Its influence upon the poor is calamitous. . . . It has aroused a spirit of rebellion in some places." Another Mississippian reported that "the poorer classes of [soldiers'] families" were suffering "for want of *corn* and *salt*. . . . In the name of God, I ask is this to be tolerated? Is this war to be carried on and the Government upheld at the expense of the Starvation of the Women and children?"[16] State governments and many counties appropriated funds for the families of soldiers; at one time more than a third of the families in Alabama received public assistance. But these funds were pitifully small and got smaller as inflation ate away at them. And it was not only the poor who went hungry. A middle-class woman whose husband was in the army wrote an anguished entry in her diary: "Very miserable and wretched. Can get nothing to eat and no clothes for anybody. Can hear nothing from my husband." John Jones, a War Department official whose once-adequate salary had been eroded by inflation, wrote in his diary in March 1863 that "the shadow of the gaunt form of famine is upon us." Jones had lost twenty pounds; "my wife and children are emaciated." Even the rats in his kitchen were so hungry that they ate bread crumbs from his daughter's hand "as tame as kittens. Perhaps we shall have to eat them!"[17]

---

[14]George C. Rable, *Civil Wars: Women and the Crisis of Southern Nationalism* (Urbana, Ill., 1989), pp. 74, 78.

[15]John Rozier (ed.), *The Granite Farm Letters: The Civil War Correspondence of Edgeworth and Sallie Bird* (Athens, Ga., 1988), p. 184; James M. McPherson, *Battle Cry of Freedom: The Civil War Era* (New York, 1988), p. 611. For an analysis of the fears of white women left on plantations from which all white men had gone into the army, which quotes many such letters, see Drew Gilpin Faust, *Mothers of Invention: Women of the Slaveholding South in the American Civil War* (Chapel Hill, 1996), chap. 3.

[16]*O.R.*, Ser. 1, Vol. 17, pt. 2, p. 790; Charles W. Ramsdell, *Behind the Lines in the Southern Confederacy* (Baton Rouge, 1994), pp. 28–29.

[17]Rable, *Civil Wars*, p. 98; John B. Jones, *A Rebel War Clerk's Diary*, ed. Earl Schenck Miers (New York, 1958), pp. 170, 243, 164.

Bread Riots and Hyperinflation

The Confederacy's worst food crisis occurred in the spring of 1863, as the remnants of the drought-ravaged crops of the previous year ran out. Starving civilians knew—or suspected—that storekeepers and government warehouses still had food that they were holding for higher prices or for the army. In a dozen or more places that spring, starving women staged bread riots. Many of them were wives of soldiers; armed with knives or revolvers, they stalked into shops owned by men they denounced as "speculators" and asked the price of bacon or cornmeal. Upon hearing it, they denounced such "extortion" and took what they wanted. The most menacing riot occurred in Richmond itself on April 2, 1863. Several hundred women—many of them wives of workers at the Tredegar Iron Works—gathered in a church and proceeded to the governor's home to demand release of emergency stocks of food in government warehouses. The governor said he could not do anything for them, whereupon the crowd's mood grew ugly. Shouting "Bread or Blood!" and joined by boys and a few men, they began roaming the streets, smashing store windows and taking shoes, clothing, even jewelry as well as food. The mayor and governor appealed to them in vain to desist. A hastily assembled company of militia confronted them with loaded muskets. At this moment Jefferson Davis arrived on the scene, climbed onto a cart, threw his pocket change into the crowd to attract their attention, and made a speech appealing to Southern patriotism and asking them to disperse peacefully. The crowd responded with sullen silence except for a few jeers from the boys. Davis icily warned the mob to break up and go home or he would order the militia to fire. Whether he would really have done so—and whether the militia would have obeyed such an order—will never be known. Within the five-minute grace period Davis gave them, the crowd melted away into the streets and alleys of Richmond. Police arrested forty-four women and twenty-nine men as members or accessories of the mob; twelve women were convicted, and some of them may have served short jail sentences.[18]

Better weather and a more bountiful harvest in 1863 eased the Confederacy's food crisis, but only slightly. Malnutrition weakened thousands of Southerners, especially children and the elderly, who became prey to diseases that killed them during the war—casualties that must be added to the death toll in this deadliest of American wars. Hunger and exposure were especially severe among the 250,000 or more white refugees who uprooted themselves as Yankee invaders approached and fled to more secure areas, which were overwhelmed by the flood. And the twin disasters to Confederate arms at Vicksburg and Gettysburg accelerated the inflation that crushed so many Southern families. Prices rose 58 percent in the three months after Gettysburg. "A poor woman yesterday applied to a merchant in Carey Street to purchase a barrel of flour," wrote a Richmond diarist on October 22, 1863. "The price he demanded was $70. 'My God!' exclaimed she, 'how can I pay such prices? I have seven children; what shall I do?' 'I don't know, madam,' said he, coolly, 'unless you eat your children.'"[19]

---

[18]Good descriptions of the riot can be found in Emory M. Thomas, *The Confederate State of Richmond* (Austin, 1971), pp. 117–122; Emory M. Thomas, *The Confederate Nation: 1861–1865* (New York, 1979), pp. 201–206; and Rable, *Civil Wars*, pp. 108–110.

[19]Jones, *Rebel War Clerk's Diary*, p. 296.

Four months later, flour in Richmond cost $250 a barrel. Caught in a cruel dilemma whose causes they ill understood, many Southerners sought scapegoats for their misery. The most common targets were "speculators" and "extortioners," who were thought to have cornered supplies in order to profit from the consequent rise in prices. The press and pulpit rang with denunciations of these "contemptible wretches," who would "bottle the universal air and sell it at so much a bottle" if they could. Jefferson Davis spoke out against "the attempt of groveling speculators to forestall the market and make money out of the lifeblood of our defenders." As in the case of other people at other times, some Southerners focused their anger on Jewish merchants who had, in the words of Confederate congressmen, "swarmed here as the locusts of Egypt. They ate up the substance of the country, they exhausted its supplies, they monopolized its trade. . . . The end of the war [will] probably find nearly all the property of the Confederacy in the hands of Jewish Shylocks."[20]

There were "speculators" in the Confederacy, of course; but most merchants, whether Jew or Gentile, were trying to make an honest living in difficult times. They were more the victims than the cause of inflation. Though they may have sold goods at a 50 percent profit, they gained little if the general price level had increased 45 percent between the time they bought and sold the goods. Several Confederate states passed laws "to suppress monopolies," by which they meant wholesalers who allegedly profited from cornering the market in necessities. The Confederate tax law of April 1863 assessed a retroactive 10 percent levy on the profits of wholesalers. None of these laws was enforceable because proof of conspiracy and assessment of profit were virtually impossible amid the financial chaos of the Confederacy.

The Impressment Act of 1863 was also aimed in part at speculators. Because farmers and merchants often refused to sell food and supplies to the army at prices set by the government, commissary and quartermaster officers resorted to the impressment of supplies. This produced bitter outcries. To remedy abuses and regularize the process, Congress on March 26, 1863, passed "An Act to Regulate Impressments," which laid down guidelines for impressment officers and provided for arbitration whenever these officers could not agree with the seller on what constituted a fair price. Like so much Confederate financial legislation, however, this law failed to accomplish its purpose. With the spurt of inflation after Gettysburg and Vicksburg, the disparity between the impressment price and the market price widened to an unbridgeable gap. Indeed, farmers were becoming reluctant to accept Confederate money at any price. Army officers desperate for supplies seized what they wanted and offered the angry farmer an IOU receipt. At the end of the war, an estimated half billion dollars of these unpaid receipts were outstanding.

The impressment policy intensified rather than relieved shortages and inflation, because many farmers hid their crops and drove their livestock into the woods when impressment officers came near. Others refused to plant a crop at all. Impressment also turned many Southerners against the Confederacy. Farmers in a Louisiana district expressed a widely shared sentiment when they told a Confederate officer "that they would prefer seeing the Yankees to seeing our cavalry." Nearly every Southern governor denounced impressment. States' rights advocates, particularly Governor

---

[20]E. Merton Coulter, *The Confederate States of America 1861–1865* (Baton Rouge, 1950), pp. 225, 231–232, 227.

Joseph Brown of Georgia, did everything they could to harass impressment officers. Davis's political enemies used impressment as one of the main issues in their attacks on the administration. "It is far better for a free people to be vanquished in open combat with the invader," thundered William L. Yancey, than to "yield liberties and their constitutional safeguards to the stealthy progress of . . . military dictatorship."[21] But no matter how despicable, impressment was necessary in large parts of the South; without it the army would have been hard-pressed to obtain any supplies.

Trading with the Enemy

Another apparently necessary evil in the Confederacy was trade with the Yankees. Trading with the enemy is as old as war. Americans had proven themselves adept at it during the Revolution and in the War of 1812. They proved even more adept in the Civil War, which offered greater temptations and opportunities than most wars. The South had large quantities of a commodity much in demand—cotton—and a great need for shoes, salt, medicine, munitions, and other goods that had to be obtained mainly from the outside world. The North and South had been economically interdependent before the war, and all the regulations of governments and generals could not stop a commerce more profitable in war than it had ever been in peace. When cotton could be bought for 10 or 20 cents a pound in Memphis or New Orleans and sold for 80 cents in Boston or New York, and when salt could be obtained for $1.25 a sack in the North and sold for $60 in the Confederacy, enterprising men would find a way to trade cotton for salt. While the Confederacy embargoed cotton exports, Southerners sold cotton to Yankee or European speculators and Confederate officials looked the other way because the gold and greenbacks this brought in could buy guns and shoes. And while the Union government blockaded the South, it allowed— or at least did not suppress—a trade that partly undermined the blockade.

In 1861, both governments had officially prohibited trade with the enemy. But across a frontier a thousand miles long, much of it running through border states whose allegiance was divided, there was a great deal of smuggling through lonely woods and across unpatrolled rivers in the dark of night. Illicit trade was carried on by sea as well. New York merchants shipped war goods to Bermuda or Nassau, where they were trans-shipped to blockade runners for Wilmington or Charleston.

With the Union conquest of large areas of the South in 1862, opportunities for contraband trade vastly increased. Under the dictum that "commerce should follow the flag," the Treasury Department issued permits for legitimate trade in occupied territory. This liberal trade policy had two purposes: to restore normal commercial activity in conquered areas and to woo Southern citizens back into the Union—for in theory, only those who took an oath of allegiance could sell cotton or purchase goods from the North. In practice, the permit system never worked well. Hordes of unlicensed as well as licensed traders flocked into occupied areas with greenbacks,

---

[21]Stephen E. Ambrose, "Yeoman Discontent in the Confederacy," *Civil War History,* 8 (September 1962), 262; Frank L. Owsley, *State Rights in the Confederacy* (Chicago, 1925), p. 229.

gold, bacon, shoes, blankets—or even gunpowder—to exchange for cotton sold by planters or agents, some of whom had taken the oath of allegiance in good faith but many of whom had not. Through Memphis flowed a huge trade in contraband goods that made their way into Rebel lines and did much to sustain Confederate forces in Mississippi and Tennessee during 1862–1863.

Generals Grant and Sherman deplored this commerce. "We cannot carry on a war and trade with a people at the same time," wrote Sherman.[22] He issued a number of orders to limit or stop the trade; but some of them were overridden by Washington, and others proved impossible to enforce. Southern women were effective smugglers in this age of hoop skirts and multiple petticoats. One search of a Memphis woman whose crinolines looked suspicious revealed that tied to her girdle were twelve pairs of boots containing medicine, whiskey, and other items. On another occasion, an elaborate funeral procession in Memphis bore a coffin from the city that turned out to be full of medicine for General Van Dorn's Confederate army.

More serious was the participation of Northern soldiers in this trade. The lure of profits or bribes "has to an alarming extent corrupted and demoralized the army," lamented a War Department official sent to investigate affairs in Memphis. "Every colonel, captain, or quartermaster is in secret partnership with some operator in cotton; every soldier dreams of adding a bale of cotton to his monthly pay." In 1863, Grant wrote that this commerce "is weakening us of at least 33 percent of our force. . . . I will venture that no honest man has made money in West Tennessee in the last year, whilst many fortunes have been made there during that time."[23]

Some of the Northern merchants who flocked to Memphis were Jewish, which caused Grant to issue on December 17, 1862, one of the most ill-considered orders of his career: "The Jews, as a class violating every regulation of trade established by the Treasury Department and also [military] orders, are hereby expelled from the department within twenty-four hours from the receipt of this order." Grant's action roused something of a storm in the North. Within three weeks came word from Washington to revoke the order, which Grant promptly did. "The President has no objection to your expelling traitors and Jew peddlers" who traded with the enemy, Halleck informed Grant, but since the order "proscribed an entire religious class, some of whom are fighting in our ranks, the President deemed it necessary to revoke it."[24]

One top Union general who did nothing to discourage trade with the enemy—indeed, quite the contrary if his critics are to be believed—was Benjamin Butler, commander of the occupying forces in New Orleans from April to December 1862.

---

[22] *O.R.,* Ser. 1, Vol. 17, pt.:2, p. 141.

[23] Ibid., Vol. 52, pt. 1, p. 331, Vol. 24, pt. 3, p. 538.

[24] Ibid., Vol. 17, pt. 2, pp. 424, 530, 544, Vol. 24, pt. 1, p. 9. Several other Union commanders, including Sherman, also singled out Jewish traders for condemnation. Some Confederate officials did the same. These "Jew extortioners," wrote a War Department clerk in Richmond, "have injured our cause more than the armies of Lincoln." (John B. Jones, *A Rebel War Clerk's Diary at the Confederate States Capital,* 2 vols. [New York, 1935; first printed Philadelphia, 1866], I, 221.) These comments were as irrational as such attitudes usually are, for only a fraction of the traders and speculators were Jewish. Like all wars, the Civil War had its seamy as well as heroic side, its profiteers as well as patriots, but neither the former nor the latter belonged predominantly to any class or ethnic group.

Butler was one of the most ambiguous and controversial figures of the war. His rule in New Orleans earned him international notoriety and the undying hatred of Southerners. One of his first acts was to issue an order that any woman who continued to insult Union soldiers "shall be regarded and held liable to be treated as a woman of the town plying her avocation."[25] A few weeks later, Butler executed a civilian who had torn down the United States flag from a public building. As far away as London and Paris these actions increased foreign sympathy for the Confederacy. Closer to home, one of the mildest epithets that Southerners applied to Butler was "Beast." Jefferson Davis issued a proclamation branding him an outlaw and ordering that if captured he was "to be immediately executed by hanging."[26]

But Beast Butler gave New Orleans the most efficient and healthful administration it had ever known. He cleaned up the foul sewers, established new drainage systems and health regulations, and embarked on an ambitious public works program that provided jobs for the poor and the unemployed. Many of the funds for this program came from Butler's confiscation of public and private Confederate property, actions which earned him another nickname, "Spoons" Butler, because he and his officers allegedly stole Southerners' silver.

Butler also took steps to revive the city's economy from its blockade-induced depression. But much of the trade he promoted involved the exchange of cotton and sugar for such military items as salt, shoes, and provisions that found their way to the Confederate army. The unsavory atmosphere of corruption and profiteering that permeated New Orleans won Butler an unenviable reputation. Nothing illegal was ever proved against the general himself (a frustrated Treasury agent reported that Butler was "such a smart man, that it would, in any case, be difficult to discover what he wished to conceal"). But his brother Andrew, who had accompanied him to New Orleans as a colonel, reportedly made a fortune by means that would not bear examination.[27] Butler's replacement, General Nathaniel Banks, curbed the worst abuses, but he could never entirely stop the contraband trade. A foreign observer wrote that even "a Chinese wall from the Atlantic to the Pacific" could not stop the traffic when so much money was at stake.[28]

In March 1863, the Union Congress passed the Captured Property Act, which was intended to diminish private trading by making all Confederate-owned cotton subject to seizure by the government. In January 1864, the Treasury issued strict regulations to govern the purchase of non-Confederate cotton (that is, cotton owned by persons who had taken the oath of allegiance). In July 1864, Congress abolished the permit system by which civilians had carried on trade in occupied territory.

---

[25]Although perhaps ill-advised, this order was issued after considerable provocation. New Orleans women insulted Northern soldiers in every conceivable fashion. The last straw was when a lady in the French Quarter emptied the contents of a chamber pot on Admiral Farragut's head.

[26]Jessie A. Marshall (ed.), *Private and Official Correspondence of General Benjamin F. Butler During the Period of the Civil War,* 5 vols. (Norwood, Mass., 1971), I, 490; Frank Moore (ed.), *The Rebellion Record: A Diary of American Events, with Documents, Narratives, Illustrative Incidents, Poetry, Etc.,* 12 vols. (New York, 1862–1868), VI, 291–293.

[27]Gerald M. Capers, *Occupied City: New Orleans Under the Federals, 1862–1865* (Lexington, Ky., 1965), pp. 83–84.

[28]Coulter, *Confederate States,* p. 287.

BENJAMIN BUTLER.
One of the most complex
and ambiguous figures of
the Civil War, Butler was a
nimble-footed Democratic
politician from
Massachusetts who became
one of the most political of
Union generals and radical
of Republicans. At the 1860
Democratic convention, he
had supported Jefferson
Davis's nomination for
president of the United
States! Davis returned the
favor during the war by
branding Butler an "outlaw"
to be executed if captured
by Confederate forces.

LIBRARY OF CONGRESS

But these laws and regulations had little impact on the illicit trade. The administration enforced them in such a way as to allow the continued payment for cotton with cash, which then found its way into Confederate hands. Lincoln permitted this because he believed that cotton purchased by Northerners benefited the Union more and the Confederacy less than the same cotton exported through the blockade to Europe. The President explained his reasoning to one irate general who had tried to suppress the cotton trade in his department. Cotton prices had risen to more than six times their prewar level, noted Lincoln. "And yet the enemy gets through at least one sixth part as much in a given period, say a year, as if there were no blockade, and receives as much for it, as he would for a full crop in time of peace," enabling the South to earn foreign exchange for the purchase of arms and supplies. It was therefore "not merely a concession to private interest and pecuniary greed" to allow private traders to buy cotton, because every bale that went North was one less available for export. "Better give him *guns* for it than let him, as now, get both guns and ammunition for it."[29]

---

[29]Roy P. Basler (ed.), *The Collected Works of Abraham Lincoln* (New Brunswick, N.J., 1953–1955), VIII, 163–164.

Confederate generals were no more successful in stopping the trade than were their Union opposites. Southern civilians near Union lines were quick to take the oath of allegiance in order to sell cotton. And just as bribes tempted Northern soldiers to look the other way when contraband supplies went through the lines, "a pair of boots and a bottle of whiskey" accomplished the same purpose with Confederate pickets. Everyone involved was "corrupted and demoralized," complained a Confederate officer. "The fact is that cotton, instead of contributing to our strength, has been the greatest element of our weakness here. Yankee gold is fast accomplishing what Yankee arms could never achieve—the subjugation of [our] people." The Confederate government agreed—in theory. "All trade with the enemy is demoralizing and illegal, and should, of course, be discountenanced," wrote the Secretary of War in Richmond. "But at the same time . . . the Army cannot be subsisted without permitting trade to some extent." Jefferson Davis reluctantly sanctioned the commerce, but only if "the necessity should be absolute."[30]

For the South, the necessity was nearly always absolute. The contraband trade unquestionably helped the Confederacy more than the Union, Lincoln's arguments and the complaints of Confederate officers to the contrary notwithstanding. The judgment of historian James Ford Rhodes on the trade seems fair: "For the South it was a necessary evil; for the North it was an evil and not a necessary one."[31] It was also an evil that contributed to the climate of corruption and profiteering that marred the postwar decade.

Disease and Medical Care in Civil War Armies

Disease was the principal killer of Civil War soldiers. Two soldiers died of disease for every one killed in battle. And for every man who died of disease, scores of others were on the sick list at any given time. Sickness and physical disability were the main reasons why the initial 1,000-man enrollment in a regiment was often cut in half by the time the unit first went into battle.

Physical examinations of recruits were often cursory and sometimes nonexistent. In July 1862, an investigation of Union enlistment procedures concluded that "the careless and superficial medical inspection of recruits made at least 25 per cent of the volunteer army raised last year not only utterly useless, but a positive incumbrance."[32] Medical examinations thereafter became more rigorous. But even healthy recruits had a hard time staying healthy when they were exposed to the new disease environment created by the crowding together of thousands of men. In both armies, soldiers from rural areas proved to be more susceptible to disease than those from cities, who had already been exposed to many of the bacteria that struck down farm boys. Recruits from the Midwestern states in the Union army suffered a disease mortality rate 43 percent higher than those from the more urban states of the Northeast.

---

[30] *O.R.,* Ser. 4, Vol. 2, pp. 151, 173–175, 334–335, Vol. 3, pp. 646–648.

[31] James Ford Rhodes, *History of the United States from the Compromise of 1850,* 7 vols. (New York, 1892–1906), V, 420.

[32] *O.R.,* Ser. 3, Vol. 2, p. 236.

Disease hit Civil War armies in two waves. The first was an epidemic of childhood maladies—mainly measles and mumps—that many men encountered for the first time. Though rarely fatal, these illnesses could temporarily incapacitate large numbers of new troops. The second wave consisted of camp and campaign diseases caused by bad water, bad food, exposure, and mosquitoes. These included the principal killer diseases of the Civil War: dysentery and diarrhea, typhoid, and malaria. Primitive or careless sanitation in army camps often contaminated the water and left wastes exposed to flies and rodents. Even when medical officers ordered proper sanitary procedures, soldiers sometimes paid little attention. "Our poor sick, I know, suffer much," wrote Robert E. Lee in 1861, but "they bring it on themselves by not doing what they are told. They are worse than children, for the latter can be forced."[33]

Because the Civil War soldier was ten times more likely to die of disease and eight times more likely to die from a battlefield wound than the American soldier in World War I, numerous historians have concluded that "the medical services represent one of the Civil War's most dismal failures."[34] The war certainly had its share of incompetent or drunken surgeons, bureaucratic blundering in the army medical corps, officers careless of their men's health, and medical old-fogyism. But these represented only one side of the story. *By the standards of the time,* Civil War medical care and army health were unusually good. Although the ratio of disease to battle deaths was two to one, this compared favorably with ratios of seven to one in the Mexican War (1846–1848) and six to one in the Spanish-American War (1898). The ratio for the British army in the Crimean War (1854–1856) was nearly four to one; in the Napoleonic Wars it had been eight to one. The allied armies in the Crimea had a disease mortality of 25 percent in less than two years, compared with the Civil War armies' 13 percent in four years (10 percent for the Union army, 20 percent for the Confederates). The U.S. surgeon general was right when he wrote proudly that the Union army's mortality rate from disease and wounds was "lower than had been observed in the experience of any army since the world began."[35]

But by twentieth-century standards, the morbidity and mortality rates of Civil War armies are shocking. As the wartime surgeon general later explained with benefit of hindsight, "the Civil War was fought at the end of the medical Middle Ages."[36] Louis Pasteur, Joseph Lister, and other Europeans were just beginning the research in bacteriology that within a generation would revolutionize medical knowledge. Civil War doctors did not know what caused dysentery, or typhoid, or malaria. Ideas concerning the importance of sanitation or good water or balanced diet were in their infancy. Notions of sepsis and antisepsis hardly existed yet; few were aware of the need to sterilize surgical instruments to prevent infection; medicine could not conceive of antibiotics because biotics were scarcely known. The large caliber and low

---

[33]Robert E. Lee, Jr., *Recollections and Letters of General Robert E. Lee* (New York, 1904), p. 46.

[34]Peter J. Parish, *The American Civil War* (New York, 1975), p. 147.

[35]William Q. Maxwell, *Lincoln's Fifth Wheel: The Political History of the United States Sanitary Commission* (New York, 1956), p. 245. The comparative statistics in this paragraph are from ibid., p. 5; George W. Adams, *Doctors in Blue: The Medical History of the Union Army in the Civil War,* Collier Books ed. (New York, 1961), p. 169; and E. B. Long, *The Civil War Day by Day: An Almanac, 1861–1865* (Garden City, N.Y., 1971), p. 711.

[36]Allan Nevins, *The War for the Union: The Organized War, 1863–1864* (New York, 1971), p. 312.

muzzle velocity of Civil War rifles meant that the soft lead bullets often remained in an arm or leg wound instead of going through. The only way surgeons knew how to prevent gangrene or septicemia or pyemia or osteomyelitis—especially if a bone was shattered—was to amputate. A controversy raged among Civil War surgeons between "conservatives" who wanted to save as many limbs as possible, and "radicals" who believed that amputation saved more lives than it threatened. The radicals were probably right, given the medical knowledge and techniques of the time. Although many amputees died of shock or infection, their mortality rate was lower than in any previous war—in part because of the recent invention of chloroform and ether. Nevertheless, the field hospital with its piles of severed arms and legs after a major battle is one of the most graphic and grisly images of the Civil War. Even in quiet times, unwounded but sick soldiers tried to avoid army hospitals. This era constituted what historians have called "the heroic age" of medicine in which large doses of drugs containing mercury or opium were prescribed for almost any ill to which the body was prone. Soldiers who complained that "the Doctors kills more than they cours" were not far wrong.[37] Doctors knew no better because of the primitive state of their art. Their ignorance was not personal, but a fact of history.

Although the Civil War did not produce any striking advances in medical knowledge, it did generate important innovations in army medical care. Inadequate and amateurish in 1861, the medical services were greatly expanded and professionalized by 1863. When Fort Sumter fell, the surgeon general of the United States was an eighty-year-old veteran of the War of 1812. His successor, aged sixty-four, was equally complacent with the somnolent bureaucracy of the old army. But from the time of the appointment of thirty-three-year-old William A. Hammond as surgeon general in April 1862, the Union Army Medical Bureau was blessed with vigorous, progressive leadership. So was its Confederate counterpart, within the limits of its smaller resources. In April 1861, the U.S. army had only 113 surgeons, of whom 24 resigned to go with the South. By the war's end, more than 15,000 surgeons had served in the Union and Confederate forces. Before the war, the army had no general hospitals; in 1865, there were more than 350, many of them of the new "pavilion" type that became the standard military hospital for half a century because the hublike cluster of well-ventilated buildings housing forty to sixty patients each prevented an outbreak of infection in one building from spreading to the others.

During the first year or more of the war, procedures for battlefield treatment of the wounded were chaotic. Regimental musicians (many of them younger than eighteen), cooks, teamsters, and other noncombatants were detailed as stretcher-bearers; and civilians were frequently employed as ambulance drivers. More often than not these men and boys bolted in panic when the fighting became hot, leaving the wounded to lie untended for hours or days. Consequently, combat soldiers would often drop out of line to carry wounded friends to the rear, thus reducing the army's fighting strength. To remedy this situation, General McClellan in August 1862 authorized the creation of a trained ambulance corps for the Army of the Potomac. This worked so well that it was adopted by other Union armies and finally mandated by Congress in March 1864. Members of the ambulance corps moved over the battle-

---

[37]Bell Irvin Wiley, *The Life of Johnny Reb: The Common Soldier of the Confederacy* (Indianapolis, 1943), p. 267.

field during and after the fighting, administered first aid to wounded soldiers, carried them to brigade or division field hospitals in the rear, and drove the horse-drawn ambulances that evacuated the wounded from field to base hospitals. The Confederates developed a similar "infirmary corps." These units became models for most armies of the world down to World War I.

Much of the pressure for creation of the ambulance corps and for other reforms came from the United States Sanitary Commission. Organized early in the war, the Sanitary Commission sought government sanction as a civilian agency to help the Army Medical Bureau prevent the health problems that had decimated the British and French armies in the Crimea. After overcoming the army's hostility to "meddling" civilians, the Sanitary Commission received official War Department recognition in June 1861.

The Sanitary Commission became the principal agency through which Northern women aided the war effort. Although its national officers and most of its salaried agents were men, the volunteer workers who ran its 7,000 local auxiliaries, collected supplies, organized the great "Sanitary Fairs" to raise money, and worked as nurses were mostly women. The commission established depots for the distribution of clothing, food, and medicine to the army. It provided meals and lodging to convalescent and furloughed soldiers on their way to and from the front. It sent sanitary inspectors to regimental camps to instruct officers and men in such matters as latrines, drainage, water supply, and cooking. It supplied soldiers with vegetables, an item often lacking in the standard army ration. It gathered emergency stockpiles of medicines and bandages and rushed them to battlefield hospitals. It sent its own nurses and doctors to work in army hospitals. It chartered ships to evacuate wounded from Shiloh and from the Virginia peninsula in 1862, and provided ambulance service on the peninsula when the army's ambulances proved inadequate.

Sanitary Commission officials criticized the surgeon general and his staff in 1861 as "venerable do-nothings and senile obstructionists." The old-army establishment retaliated with angry cries against "sensation preachers, village doctors, and strong-minded women."[38] But so popular was the Sanitary Commission with the soldiers, so obvious its effectiveness, and so great its influence in Congress that it was able to push through a bill to reorganize the Medical Bureau and to secure Hammond's appointment as surgeon general in 1862. This inaugurated an era of partnership between the Medical Bureau and the commission productive of such reforms as the ambulance corps.[39]

Other voluntary associations supplemented the work of the Sanitary Commission. Several state societies provided services for soldiers and support for their families. The Western Sanitary Commission, a separate organization, carried on relief and medical work for Union troops in Missouri and Arkansas. The Roman Catholic Sisters of Charity supplied army hospitals with the best-trained nurses in the country. In November 1861, a group of Protestant ministers and YMCA officials organized the

---

[38]Adams, *Doctors in Blue,* p. 68.

[39]The commission and General Hammond ran afoul of Secretary of War Edwin M. Stanton in 1863 for reasons not entirely clear. Stanton sometimes obstructed the commission's activities. He disliked Hammond and forced his dismissal in 1864. By then, however, the reforms Hammond had instituted had become standard army procedure.

UNIVERSITY OF ROCHESTER MEDICAL CENTER

TREATMENT OF UNION WOUNDED.
Clockwise from top left: A photograph of a simulated amputation, taken at the Union army base, Fortress Monroe, Virginia, in 1861. The "patient's" face is blocked by the surgeon's assistant, who is holding the leg with a clamp while the surgeon pretends to saw it off. The spectators are soldiers in a Zouave regiment. The second and third photos show amputees and other wounded Union soldiers

LIBRARY OF CONGRESS

convalescing outside the base hospital at Fredericksburg. Notice the Sanitary Commission nurse sitting in the doorway. The fourth photo was taken at the Armory Square military hospital in Washington, an example of the pavilion-style hospitals built during the war. This clean, cheerful hospital ward shows Union medical care at its best.

LIBRARY OF CONGRESS

MASSACHUSETTS COMMANDERY MILITARY ORDER OF THE LOYAL LEGION AND THE U.S. ARMY MILITARY HISTORY INSTITUTE.

Christian Commission, which gave more than spiritual comfort to the troops. Christian Commission volunteers provided food and nursing care to wounded soldiers, supplied most of the books and pamphlets in hospital libraries, and distributed blankets, warm clothing, and even medicines to convalescent soldiers. Such activities sometimes brought them into rivalry with the Sanitary Commission, whose more secular leadership frowned on the evangelical enthusiasm of the Christian Commission.

The contribution of volunteer agencies to the Union army's health was significant. They also had a long-term impact on medical history. The Sanitary Commission evolved a philosophy of scientific inquiry, hard-headed efficiency, and disciplined humanitarianism that became a hallmark of postwar philanthropy. It provided the model for the American Public Health Association, founded in 1872 by men who had been active in the Sanitary Commission. The APHA played an important role in the subsequent modernization of American medicine and public health.

Organized relief and medical work in the South was less centralized than in the North. No counterpart of the Sanitary or Christian commissions existed in the Confederacy, though local soldiers' aid and hospital relief societies sprang up everywhere. These societies performed valuable services, but Confederate soldiers still fared less well in medical care than their Union counterparts. One of every six wounded Rebels died of his wounds, compared with one of seven Yankees. The percentage of Confederate soldiers who died of disease was twice that of Union soldiers (it should be noted that the percentage killed in action was also twice as large). This was less the fault of the Confederate medical corps than of the shortages, economic breakdowns, and destruction of resources that plagued all aspects of the Confederate war effort. Sick or wounded soldiers could not get enough food or the right kind of food. Although most accounts also mention shortages of medicines caused by the Union blockade, the fullest study of Confederate medical services maintains that domestic manufacture and illicit trade with the North largely remedied these shortages.[40] But the gradual collapse of Southern railroads caused deficiencies when and where medicines were most needed.

Women and Medical Care

In both North and South, women played a vital role in Civil War medicine. Not only did they do most of the hard work in civilian volunteer agencies, but many thousands also served as professional and volunteer nurses in army hospitals. One woman, Mary Walker, served as a surgeon in the Union army in 1864. She was captured in Georgia by the Confederates, who expressed amazement "at the sight of a *thing* that nothing but the debased and depraved Yankee nation could produce."[41]

The male hostility that Walker had to overcome before receiving her appointment was encountered on a smaller scale by women who volunteered as nurses. Nevertheless, the illustrious example of Florence Nightingale in the Crimean War had begun to dignify the profession of nursing, which previously had been stigmatized as a menial occupation. Women were assumed to possess finer and gentler natures than men and were therefore thought to make the best nurses. Yet a somewhat contradictory feeling also existed in 1861, especially in the South, that the rough, masculine, and embarrassingly physical atmosphere of a military hospital was no place for a respectable woman, particularly if she was young, pretty, and unmarried. The

---

[40]H. H. Cunningham, *Doctors in Gray: The Confederate Medical Service* (Baton Rouge, 1958).
[41]Mary Elizabeth Massey, *Bonnet Brigades* (New York, 1966), p. 62.

Union government in June 1861 appointed Dorothea Dix, the famous reformer of asylums for the insane, as superintendent of female nurses. Dix specified that all nursing applicants must be "plain in appearance" and at least thirty years old. "Dragon Dix . . . won't accept the services of any *pretty* nurses," complained one disappointed applicant. "Just think of putting such an old thing over everyone else. . . . Some fool man did it."[42] Women who managed to pass Dix's scrutiny had to contend with the prejudices of army surgeons such as the one who complained that every preacher in the North "would recommend the most troublesome old maid in his congregation as an experienced nurse." The surgeon said he had been plagued by several of these women, "each one with spectacles on her nose and an earnest gaze in her eyes, to see the man she was to take possession of." An increase in the death rate occurred at the hospital after they arrived, he added, "probably caused by the spectacles."[43]

Northern women slowly overcame such prejudices. They were aided by an order of Surgeon General Hammond in July 1862 that at least one-third of the nurses in army general hospitals must be women (most of the rest were detailed or convalescent soldiers). About 3,200 women served as army nurses in the North, one-quarter of the total number of nurses. The Confederate army was slower to use "respectable" white women as nurses, though many slave women served in army hospitals from the beginning. Nevertheless, in the South too the example of Florence Nightingale and the desire to play a part in the Confederate war effort caused many white women of "good families" to defy the opposition of fathers or brothers and become volunteer nurses. One of them was twenty-seven-year-old Kate Cumming of Mobile, who went to Corinth, Mississippi, after the bloodbath at Shiloh in April 1862. "As to the plea of its being no place for a refined lady," she wrote in her diary, "I wondered what Miss Nightingale and the hundreds of refined ladies of Great Britain who went to the Crimea, would say to that!" Her first encounter with a military hospital—a Corinth hotel with hundreds of wounded soldiers covering every square foot of space and an overpowering stench in the fetid air—almost caused her to turn around and go home. "Nothing that I had ever heard or read had given me the faintest idea of the horrors witnessed here," But she rolled up her sleeves and set to work "all night, bathing the men's wounds, and giving them water. . . . We have to walk, and when we give the men anything kneel, in blood and water; but we think nothing of it."[44]

The dedicated example of hundreds of Kate Cummings overcame the initial skepticism of Confederate army surgeons. One of them, in Danville, Virginia, expressed a strong preference for women nurses over the detailed soldiers who had been performing that duty, "rough country crackers" who did not "know castor oil from a gun rod nor laudanum from a hole in the ground."[45] In September 1862, the Confederate Congress officially authorized women nurses. Thereafter, the Southern army welcomed them, though white women constituted a smaller proportion of army nurses

---

[42]Ibid., p. 47.

[43]Bruce Catton, *Grant Moves South* (Boston, 1960), pp. 53–54.

[44]Richard B. Harwell (ed.), *Kate: The Journal of a Confederate Nurse* (Baton Rouge, 1959), pp. xii, 14, 15.

[45]Cunningham, *Doctors in Gray*, p. 72.

in the Confederacy than in the Union. But in both North and South, additional thousands of women worked as hospital volunteers or as employees of the Sanitary Commission, Christian Commission, and the like. Some of the volunteers were Lady Bountiful types and disliked by the soldiers, but most were dedicated, hard-working people who earned respect and praise from officers and men.

Women nurses worked mainly in general hospitals away from the fighting front. But some also shared the hardships and dangers of field hospitals. Clara Barton, later the founder of the American Red Cross, served in several Union battlefield hospitals. Several women labored at the base hospitals after Shiloh and during the fighting near Richmond in the summer of 1862. Many Northern women came to Gettysburg in 1863, where they helped care for thousands of Confederate as well as Union wounded. Mary Ann Bickerdyke was the best known of the front-line women nurses. A widow from Illinois known affectionately to soldiers as "Mother Bickerdyke," she made the health of enlisted men in the Army of the Tennessee her special concern. With the support of Generals Grant and Sherman, she overcame opposition from surgeons and high-ranking officers. She was one of the few civilians whom Sherman allowed with his army, and she won the lifelong respect of this crusty general.

The work of women as nurses in the Civil War advanced the professional status of nursing in the United States. In 1861, the Women's Central Relief Association set up a training program for nurses in New York City. Several other nursing schools were founded in Northern cities during or soon after the war. In this respect, also, the Civil War gave an important impulse to the modernization and professionalization of medicine.

Wartime Reconstruction and the Freedpeople

What McClellan was on the battle-field—
"Do as little hurt as possible!"—Lincoln is in
civil affairs—"Make as little change as
possible!"

—Wendell Phillips,
March 27, 1864

On December 8, 1863, Lincoln issued a "Proclamation of Amnesty and Reconstruction." Under his constitutional authority to grant pardons for offenses against the United States, he offered "full pardon" and restoration of property "except as to slaves" to those engaged in rebellion who would swear an oath of allegiance to the United States and to all laws and proclamations concerning slavery. (Civil and diplomatic officials of the Confederate government, high army and navy officers, and certain other prominent Confederates were exempted from this offer.) Whenever in any state the number of voters taking the oath reached 10 percent of the number who had voted in the 1860 election, this loyal nucleus could reestablish a state government to which Lincoln promised executive recognition. "Any provision which may be adopted by such State government in relation to the freed people of such State, which shall recognize and declare their permanent freedom, provide for their education, and which may yet be consistent, as a temporary arrangement, with their present condition as a laboring, landless, and homeless class, will not be objected to by the national Executive." To Congress, of course, belonged the right to determine whether the representatives and senators from such states would be seated.[1]

This document was the product of much thought. Addressing itself to the main social and political issues of the war, it laid down the following policies: (1) acceptance of emancipation accomplished thus far was to be a prerequisite of reconstruction; (2) for the time being, however, Southern states might enact contract labor laws or other measures to bring order out of the chaos caused by sudden emancipation; (3) political restoration of states to the Union was to be a relatively easy process that would impose no harsh punishments for treason, confiscate no property except slaves, and require no more than 10 percent of the voting population to begin the process.

Lincoln formulated these provisions in the context of Northern military success during the second half of 1863. Union troops now occupied nearly all of Tennessee and large parts of Louisiana, Arkansas, Mississippi, and Virginia. A policy for the restoration (or "reconstruction") of elected civil governments in these areas had become necessary. Lincoln's proclamation was designed to meet this necessity. In addition, the President hoped that his liberal promise of amnesty would cause many lukewarm Confederates to renew their allegiance to the Union and thereby further weaken the Confederacy. But these complex provisions divided the Republican party and produced a confrontation between President and Congress. To unravel the complexities requires an analysis of three separate but interrelated issues: emancipation, the status of the freedpeople, and political reconstruction.

Emancipation

Although all Republicans wanted to make emancipation a condition of reconstruction, many of them—including Lincoln—doubted whether wartime actions against slavery would remain legally in effect after the war was over. Based on the war power to seize enemy property, those actions might not have constitutional validity in peacetime. Republicans generally agreed that those slaves who had come within Union lines had been freed by the confiscation acts, by the Emancipation Proclamation, or by the military orders of Union commanders in the occupied South—such as those of General Nathaniel Banks, which abrogated the slave code of Louisiana's antebellum Constitution. Lincoln said repeatedly that so long as he was President no person who had been freed would be returned to slavery. But would the courts sustain this position after the war? What about the three million slaves in the Confederacy who had not come within Union lines, and the half million in the border states to whom these measures did not apply? And even if abolition became a condition of reconstruction, there was nothing in the Constitution to prevent a state from reestablishing slavery once it was back in the Union.

---

[1] Roy P. Basler (ed.), *The Collected Works of Abraham Lincoln* (New Brunswick, N.J., 1953–1955), VII, 53–56.

By the end of 1863, Republicans had concluded that the only safe course was a constitutional amendment to abolish slavery everywhere. "Such alone can meet and cover all cavils," said Lincoln.[2] In April 1864, the Senate passed the Thirteenth Amendment by a vote of 38 to 6, with two Democrats joining the Republican majority. But Democratic gains in the 1862 congressional elections enabled Northern Democrats and border-state conservatives to block passage in the House, where the 93-to-65 vote for the amendment (with only three Democrats voting aye) on June 15, 1864, fell thirteen votes short of the necessary two-thirds.[3]

Passage of the Thirteenth Amendment by the House would have to await the next session of Congress, after Republican victory in the presidential election of 1864 showed the direction of Northern opinion (see Chapter 25). Meanwhile, the initiative for further constitutional steps toward emancipation went over to the border states and to occupied portions of Confederate states. Two years earlier, the border states had turned down an offer of compensated, gradual emancipation. Now the issue was immediate, uncompensated abolition. As Lincoln had predicted in 1862, the "abrasion" of war had been grinding up the institution of slavery in these states until little but the legal shell was left.

In Maryland and Missouri, the absence of many proslavery men who were fighting in the Confederate armies and the disfranchisement of other Confederate sympathizers by their refusal to take a loyalty oath enabled antislavery Union men to gain political control of these states in 1864. Even so, the struggle for emancipation was close. On June 24, a Maryland constitutional convention adopted an amendment abolishing slavery. In the referendum on the new constitution, a majority of civilian ballots went against the abolition amendment, and only a vote of 2,633 to 263 in its favor by Maryland Union soldiers provided the razor-thin margin for ratification on October 13, 1864. In Missouri, a state constitutional convention passed an abolition amendment on January 11, 1865. Once again, the referendum on the new constitution (which contained several other controversial features, including wholesale disfranchisement of Rebel sympathizers) was characterized by an exceedingly close vote. Only a majority of the soldier votes in favor of the constitution overcame a slight majority of the civilian votes against it to produce a margin of 1,862 votes for ratification out of a total of 85,478 votes cast.

The closeness of these votes and the disfranchisement of many men who would otherwise have voted against the new constitutions meant that emancipation in Maryland and Missouri was scarcely the "voluntary" measure that Lincoln had initially hoped for. The same can be said of the other three states that abolished slavery before the end of the war: Louisiana, Arkansas, and Tennessee. In 1864, constitutional conventions with delegates from the occupied portions of Louisiana and Arkansas abolished slavery as part of their reorganization under Lincoln's "10 percent plan" of reconstruction, and the eligible voters dutifully ratified the new constitutions. A convention in Tennessee adopted an emancipation amendment on

---

[2]Ibid., p. 380.
[3]*Congressional Globe,* 38th Cong., 1st sess. (1864), 2995.

January 10, 1865, and Unionist Tennessee voters ratified it on February 22. Although a larger percentage of voters took part in this election than in Louisiana and Arkansas, the total still fell far short of a majority of all potential voters.

In most parts of these five states, the commercially oriented urban population and the prosperous nonslaveholding farmers generally supported the movements for emancipation. In Maryland, for example, the conflict over abolition took place between what an historian later described as "the static, agricultural, society of the tidewater counties" and "the growing commercial, industrial, and farm interests of the north and west." The narrow victory for emancipation, according to one of its proponents from Baltimore, pointed toward a "new alliance with Northern progress and prosperity."[4]

The strength of the tradition-oriented Democrats prevented the development of strong emancipation movements in Kentucky and Delaware, even though the latter was virtually a free state with fewer than 2,000 of its 22,000 black people in slavery. Formal emancipation did not occur in Kentucky and Delaware until the Thirteenth Amendment was ratified eight months after the end of the war.

The Status of the Freedpeople

No single generalization can encompass the variety of ways in which freedom came to the slaves. Many thousands became "contrabands" when their masters fled before invading Northern armies and the slaves stayed behind to welcome the Yankees as liberators. Other slaves, learning of the proximity of blueclad regiments, left the plantations and made their way to Union lines. Tens of thousands trailed Sherman's army as it sliced through Georgia and the Carolinas in 1864–1865 (see Chapter 25). Some slaves helped Northern soldiers loot the Big House; others helped the mistress bury the silver. Trusted house servants and drivers were often the first to desert the plantation for the Yankees; others remained faithful to master to the end. Many contrabands served as guides and scouts for Union commanders; others feigned ignorance or refused to give information to the invaders. Only one generalization is safe: most slaves welcomed freedom, no matter how ambiguous or disillusioning it proved to be. By the war's end, perhaps one and a half million of the three and a half million slaves in the Confederacy had been directly affected by Northern invasion, and more than half a million of these were within areas of firm Union control.

The Union government never developed a uniform, consistent, considered wartime policy for dealing with these half million contrabands. Authority was fragmented among the army, the Treasury Department (which controlled confiscated property), and various missionary and freedmen's societies organized in the North to bring relief and education to the freedpeople. The army officers in command of occupation forces held ultimate power. From their initial attempts to cope with the influx of contrabands, some semblance of a "policy" emerged. In its early stages, this policy was attended with much confusion, hardship, and injustice.

---

[4]Charles L. Wagandt, *The Mighty Revolution: Negro Emancipation in Maryland, 1862–1864* (Baltimore, 1964), p. 264.

The contrabands crowded into improvised camps, where disease took a fearful toll. Yankee soldiers sometimes "confiscated" the meager worldly goods the blacks had managed to bring with them. Sexual contacts between soldiers and black women caused the spread of venereal disease. To bring order out of chaos, to prevent demoralization of the troops and exploitation of the contrabands, Union commanders established separate freedpeople's villages, appointed army officers as superintendents of freedmen, detailed squads of soldiers to protect these villages against Yankee exploiters and Confederate guerrillas (this became a major function of black regiments), supplied rations, clothing, and medicine to the contrabands, called upon missionary and voluntary associations in the North for help, and moved as quickly as possible to mobilize able-bodied freedmen as laborers and eventually as soldiers.

In all of this, the army's first priority was military efficiency. Humanitarianism was distinctly secondary. The army did not conceive of itself as a reform society. Its chief purpose was to organize the contrabands in such a way as to minimize their interference with military operations and to maximize their labor for support of these operations. The army and navy used contrabands as teamsters, stevedores, pioneers (construction workers), hospital orderlies and nurses, cooks, laundresses, servants, woodchoppers to cut fuel, and so on.

The only difference between these jobs and the same kinds of work that slaves did for the Confederate army was that Union laborers were free and received wages. But sometimes this was a distinction with little difference. While Confederate officers impressed black laborers without their consent, Union officers often did the same. Contraband laborers for the Union theoretically received wages, but many of them seldom saw a dollar because their wages had been deducted for clothing, family support, rations, or medical care. And while Confederate officers or overseers may have been harsh taskmasters, some Yankee quartermasters and freedmen's superintendents matched them in this respect. Many contrabands could be excused for wondering what difference there was between their old status and the new one.

The same question could be asked by a good many freedpeople who worked on plantations seized by the Union invaders. Some lessees of these plantations were dollar-hungry Yankees; others were Southerners who had taken the oath of allegiance. In the lower Mississippi valley, a number of planters took the oath and continued to operate their plantations with former slaves, the only difference being the payment of wages. But the same things seemed to happen to these wages as to those of black army laborers. A Northern worker might have had trouble recognizing the system as free labor. Under regulations issued by General Banks for occupied Louisiana, and copied by army officers in the Mississippi valley north of Louisiana (two-thirds of the freedmen under organized union control lived in these two areas), labor was defined as " a public duty," idleness and vagrancy as "a crime." All able-bodied freedmen not otherwise employed were required to labor on the public works. A contraband could choose his employer; but once he signed a contract, he must remain with this employer for the full year of the contract. The regulations stipulated minimum wages plus rations and housing. But so many deductions were allowed for clothing, medical care, days lost because of illness, and the like, that in effect most plantation hands wound up working for room and board. Provost marshals were ordered to enforce the "continuous and faithful service, respectful deportment, correct discipline and perfect subordination" of the workers.[5] Abolitionists denounced these regulations as a parody of free labor. Their anger was intensified by revelations of the bad character of many white lessees and of collusion between them and some provost marshals, who functioned much as the old slave patrol had done.

But this was only one side of the story. Some army officers were men of compassion and concern for the freedpeople's welfare. This was especially true of Colonel John Eaton, an army chaplain appointed by Grant as head of freedmen's policy in the Mississippi valley, and of General Rufus Saxton, military governor of the South Carolina and Georgia offshore islands. Many of the freedmen in occupied territory, particularly those with skills, commanded good wages. The army intervened as often to protect workers from abuses by planters as to enforce planter discipline over workers. Not all plantation lessees were Simon Legrees. The very concept of written contracts and wages was itself new in the plantation South. It was a major step from a quasi-feudal toward a modern free-labor society.

Not all captured plantations were leased to private parties. Many remained under government control. Freedpeople on these plantations worked under the direction of superintendents sent by the Northern freedmen's aid societies. This was the common pattern on the South Carolina offshore islands and in occupied portions of Virginia and North Carolina. These superintendents, unlike lessees or owners, often had more interest in helping the contrabands make the transition to freedom than in making a profit on the crop. But the profit motive also existed. A major theme of the proslavery argument had been the necessity of slavery for the South's staple-crop economy. Northern antislavery people were eager to demonstrate the profitability of free black labor. Although the chaos and disruption of war reduced crop yields below antebellum standards, the war-inflated price of cotton assured profits to most growers—so antislavery people pronounced the free-labor experiment a success.

To be sure, the practice of organizing plantation workers under white supervision—whether that of benevolent "superintendents" or profit-maximizing lessees—was only another form of paternalism. But the officers and civilians who confronted the masses of uprooted, ragged, suffering contrabands believed that they faced a condition, not a theory. After the army had drained off most of the able-bodied adult male contrabands as laborers and soldiers, the freedmen's superintendents were left with women and children and the aged and infirm. Some degree of paternalism was inevitable in these circumstances. The alternative would have been neglect and an appalling death rate that would have been cause for greater condemnation than the charge of paternalism.

As it was, the mortality rate in contraband camps was perhaps as high as 25 percent during the war. Shocking as this may seem, it becomes less so when compared to the nearly 20 percent disease death rates of Confederate soldiers and black Union soldiers, who included no old people or children in their ranks. White refugees displaced by the war also suffered high mortality rates. The worst ravages of disease and death among contrabands occurred *before* the Union armies and philanthropic societies acted to organize, discipline, and succor these black refugees. One reason

---

[5]*O.R.,* Ser. 1, Vol. 15, pp. 666–667, Vol. 34, pt. 2, pp. 227–231, Ser. 3, Vol. 4, pp. 166–170.

for their determination to put all able-bodied contrabands to work was to disperse them away from the unhealthy camps, where congestion, dirt, and epidemics took a grim toll.

The Question of Land for Freedpeople

An obvious alternative to the paternalism of white superintendents or lessees was to lease or sell confiscated lands directly to the freedmen. This was urged by Northern radicals and increasingly practiced in the occupied South. By the last year of the war, nearly 20 percent of the agricultural land under Union control was being independently farmed by blacks. The outstanding example occurred on the plantations of Jefferson Davis and his brother Joseph at Davis Bend south of Vicksburg. In 1864 and 1865, black farmers, many of them former slaves of the Confederacy's president, leased several thousand acres at Davis Bend and raised successful cotton and food crops. They cleared a profit of $159,000 on the 1865 cotton crop. These freedmen formed a self-governing colony with black sheriffs and justices of the peace elected by themselves. Freedpeople in other parts of the South were able to buy land during the war.

Such opportunities gave black people a small start toward the status of independent farmers—a status that had become their chief aspiration. Most abolitionists and radical Republicans also envisioned a future South of landowning black farmers. But this vision encountered powerful obstacles. While the freedmen on the South Carolina islands bought 5,000 acres in 1863–1864, for example, Northern investors bought 20,000 acres (some of this land was later resold to blacks). Many of these Northern purchasers, like Northern lessees elsewhere, foreshadowed the postwar attitude of Southern planters in their preference for a landless black labor force rather than a small-holding black yeomanry.

The Constitution seemed to bar genuine land reform in the South. In July 1862, Lincoln had threatened to veto the second Confiscation Act because, in his view, its expropriation of real estate owned by Confederates violated the constitutional ban on bills of attainder that worked a forfeiture of property beyond the life of offenders.[6] At the President's insistence, Congress passed an explanatory resolution abrogating any intention to attaint the heirs of Confederates. This of course nullified the value of the Confiscation Act as an instrument of land redistribution. The Direct Tax Act of 1861, under which South Carolina island lands had been sold for nonpayment of taxes, offered another possibility for reallocating Southern land; but formidable legal and administrative problems loomed there as well.

---

[6]Article III, Section 3, of the Constitution states: "The Congress shall have Power to declare the Punishment of Treason, but no Attainder of Treason shall work Corruption of Blood, or Forfeiture except during the Life of the Person attainted." The second Confiscation Act had provided for the seizure of the property of Confederates as a punishment for their treason against the United States. But since this provision would have prevented the children of those so punished from inheriting this property ("corruption of blood"), Lincoln threatened to veto it unless Congress modified the act to prevent this. Since the English precedents on which this section of the Constitution was based applied only to real estate, Lincoln believed that property in slaves would be exempt from the ban on corruption of blood—in other words, slaves could be permanently confiscated, but land could not.

Radicals were impatient with what they regarded as constitutional quibbles. "By all the laws and usages of civilized nations," said one abolitionist, "rebels against a government forfeit their property." Without land the freedmen would be only half free. "To be safe, peaceable, and permanent," insisted radicals, reconstruction "must be primarily economical and industrial; it must commence by planting a loyal population in the South, not only as its cultivators but as its rightful and actual owners. . . . No such thing as a free, democratic society can exist in any country where all lands are owned by one class of men and cultivated by another."[7]

Lincoln's amnesty proclamation in December 1863 further undermined the chances of land reform by restoring property (except slaves) to Confederates who took the oath of allegiance. "If the President can restore to these traitors all their rights to the land," said one angry abolitionist, "the Confiscation Act is a farce, and the war will have been a gigantic failure."[8]

Early in 1864, radical Congressman George W. Julian introduced a bill to extend the Homestead Act of 1862 to confiscated lands in the South. Julian's bill would have granted forty or eighty acres to each head of a freed family, Southern Unionist, and Union army veteran. Although this proposal seemed to conflict with Lincoln's policy, Julian claimed to have secured the President's agreement to sign a repeal of the 1862 resolution limiting confiscation to the life of the offender. Whatever the truth of this claim, the House and Senate each passed in different forms a repeal of the 1862 resolution. But constitutional scruples and the conservatism of some Republicans, who hesitated to tamper with the property rights even of Rebels, prevented final passage of the repeal or of Julian's land redistribution bill. The closest Congress would come to such legislation was a provision in the law of March 3, 1865, creating a Freedmen's Bureau. This provision stipulated that forty acres of abandoned or confiscated land could be leased to each Southern freedman or Unionist with an option to buy after three years with "such title thereto as the United States can convey."[9]

A large land redistribution program was already under way when Congress passed this bill. Ironically, the man who initiated it—William Tecumseh Sherman—had little use for radicals or freedmen. When Sherman's army reached Savannah in December 1864 after its march through Georgia, thousands of ragged freedpeople were straggling in its wake (see Chapter 25). After a conference with twenty black leaders, who told him that "the way we can best take care of ourselves is to have land," Sherman issued a special order on January 16 designating the coastline and riverbanks thirty miles inland from Charleston to Jacksonville as an area for the resettlement of freedpeople on forty acres of land per family. They would receive "possessory titles" to this land until Congress "shall regulate the title." By the end of June 1865, the army had settled more than 40,000 freedpeople in this area. The future would determine whether Congress was capable of converting the "possessory titles" into true ownership.[10]

---

[7]_Liberator,_ February 5, 1864; _Boston Commonwealth,_ January 15, 1864; James McKaye, _The Mastership and Its Fruits: The Emancipated Slave Face to Face with His Old Master_ (New York, 1864), p. 37.

[8]_Boston Commonwealth,_ March 4, 1864.

[9]George W. Julian, _Political Recollections_ (Chicago, 1884), pp. 245–246; _U.S. Statutes at Large,_ XIII, 507–509.

[10]James M. McPherson, _The Struggle for Equality_ (Princeton, 1964), pp. 257–259.

Freedmen's Education

Land ownership was one prop of the radical vision of the future; another was education. In the end, the quest for education was more successful than the quest for land. The Northern crusade to plant schools in the South was one modernizing innovation that really took hold in the former Confederacy. A Northern missionary in occupied Louisiana wrote in 1863 that he was surrounded by:

. . . negroes in uniform, negroes in rags, negroes in frame houses, negroes living in tents, negroes living in rail pens covered with brush, and negroes under brush piles without any rails, negroes living on the bare ground with the sky for their covering; all hopeful . . . every one pleading to be taught, willing to do anything for learning. They are never out of our rooms, and their cry is for "Books! Books!" and "when will school begin?"[11]

Abolitionists took the lead in forming freedmen's aid societies all over the North. "The duty of abolitionists to their clients will not cease with the technical abolition of slavery," wrote one. Freedmen's education was the next stage of the movement. "Our duty is to *see the negro through*."[12] Aid societies sent at least a thousand teachers to the South during the war. They were the forerunners of 2,000 more who went in the early postwar years. "We have come to do anti-slavery work, and we think it noble work and mean to do it nobly," wrote one of the first Northern teachers to arrive at Beaufort, South Carolina, in 1862. A generation later, the black leader W. E. B. Du Bois wrote that these missionary teachers, three-quarters of them women, were unsung Civil War heroines and heroes who "fought the most wonderful peace-battle of the 19th century. . . . [They] came not to keep the Negroes in their places, but to raise them out of the defilement of the places where slavery had wallowed them. . . . This was the gift of New England to the freed Negro."[13]

Not all of the teachers were white. The first freedmen's school, established at Fortress Monroe, Virginia, in September 1861, was taught by a free black woman. During the 1860s, perhaps 20 percent of the 4,000 teachers in freedmen's schools were black. Southern blacks founded and supported many of these schools from their own resources.

As Du Bois implied, however, freedmen's education was predominantly a New England enterprise. Three-fifths of the white teachers were born in New England. The largest of the freedmen's societies was the American Missionary Association (Congregational), which received most of its support from New England. The strongest of the secular societies was the New England Freedmen's Aid Society. One teacher wrote that he thought of his mission as the founding in Alabama of "a real New England civilization." Another hoped that the Yankee schoolmarm's crusade would furnish enough teachers "to make a New England of the whole South."[14]

---

[11] *Liberator,* January 8, 1864.

[12] *National Anti-Slavery Standard,* January 7, 1865; *Friends' Review,* December 28, 1872.

[13] Rupert S. Holland (ed.), *Letters and Diary of Laura M. Towne* (Cambridge, Mass., 1912), p. 8; W. E. B. Du Bois, *The Souls of Black Folk* (New York, 1903), p. 100.

[14] James M. McPherson, *The Abolitionist Legacy: From Reconstruction to the NAACP* (Princeton, 1975), pp. 161–163.

LIBRARY OF CONGRESS

CONTRABAND LABORERS AND FREEDMEN'S TEACHERS.
The photograph above shows contraband laborers building a stockade in Union-occupied Alexandria, Virginia. Note that the blacks are doing the work while whites stand around and supervise. The right-hand photo shows the integrated teaching staff of a freedmen's school near Norfolk, Virginia.

MASSACHUSETTS COMMANDERY MILITARY ORDER OF THE LOYAL LEGION AND THE U.S. ARMY MILITARY HISTORY INSTITUTE

The Northern teachers conceived of education as being much broader than the three R's. They hoped to implant in the South the values of the Protestant ethic and the free-labor ideology. At the core of these values was the concept of the necessity and nobility of work. The best kind of discipline was *self*-discipline. The freedmen "need to be held to the Puritan doctrine of the dignity of labor," wrote one abolitionist missionary. Slavery had degraded the nobility of work by associating it with bondage. To help the freedpeople "unlearn the teachings of slavery," the schools drilled students in "lessons of industry, of domestic management and thrift"; they taught that "industry is commendable and indispensable to freedom, and indolence both wicked and degrading." Freed slaves, the missionaries believed, needed "the New England church and school to . . . beget order, sobriety, purity, and faith" and teach them to become "like Northerners, in industry, economy, and thrift."[15]

The freedmen's schools reached an estimated 200,000 blacks during the war. After Appomattox, the expanded freedmen's education program reached a much larger number. These schools began an assault on illiteracy that was later continued by the South's new public school system, built on the foundations of Northern missionary schools.

An important partner of the privately supported freedmen's societies was the Freedmen's Bureau, which spent a third of its budget from 1865 to 1870 on schools. Its full name was the Bureau of Refugees, Freedmen, and Abandoned Lands. First proposed in 1863, the Bureau's establishment was delayed until March 3, 1865, by disagreement between the House and Senate over whether it should be in the War or Treasury Department. Congress finally placed it in the War Department. The Bureau's operations were modeled on the army's wartime experience in the occupied South. It functioned as a relief agency for displaced refugees of both races; it drafted and enforced labor contracts between planters and freedmen; and it cooperated with voluntary associations in the operation of freedmen's schools.

The Government and the Freedpeople

The record of the Union government toward the freedmen was a mixture of success and failure, humanitarianism and exploitation, kindness and cruelty. The government's policy often seemed confused and shortsighted; but the government was faced with an unprecedented situation. There was no tradition of government responsibility for a huge refugee population, no bureaucracy to administer a large welfare and employment program. The Union army and government were groping in the dark. They created the precedents. No other society in history had liberated so many slaves in so short a time; no other army had ever carried through such a social revolution. No other country had established a Freedmen's Bureau to deal with the problems of emancipated slaves; no other society had poured so much effort and money into the education of ex-slaves. Small as these efforts may have been, they were revolutionary by the standards of their time.

Political Reconstruction

The fate of any freedmen's policy depended ultimately on the conditions of political reconstruction. Lincoln preferred a moderate approach to this question. The President was an old Whig of the Henry Clay school. He had enjoyed cordial relations with Southern Whigs in antebellum days. He knew that many of these men had been conditional Unionists in 1861. His 10 percent reconstruction plan was an appeal to these old Whigs and other Unionists to come forward and reassert their allegiance

---

[15]Ibid., pp. 212, 188.

to the Union. For Lincoln, the task of reconstruction was one of restoration rather than revolution. Not restoration of the Union "as it was," to be sure, for the new Union would not have slavery. But the President was willing to permit pardoned Southern leaders to "adopt some practical system" to cushion the shock of the "total revolution of labor" and thus enable blacks and whites to "gradually live themselves out of their old relation to each other."[16]

Abolitionists and radicals did not want to cushion the shock of revolution. "The whole social system of the Gulf States [must] be taken to pieces," said Wendell Phillips. "This is primarily a social revolution. . . . The war can only be ended by annihilating that Oligarchy which formed and rules the South and makes the war—by annihilating a state of society."[17] Next to Phillips, Congressman Thaddeus Stevens was the most outspoken advocate of reconstruction as revolution. Described by contemporary European observers as "the Robespierre, Danton, and Marat" of one of the "most radical revolutions known to history," Stevens declared that reconstruction must "revolutionize Southern institutions, habits, and manners. . . . The foundations of their institutions . . . must be broken up and relaid, or all our blood and treasure have been spent in vain."[18]

Such sentiments were shared by many radical officers and officials in the occupied South. Northern values and institutions must prevail after the war, wrote a Massachusetts colonel in South Carolina, and they could do this only by "changing, revolutionizing, absorbing the institutions, life, and manners of the conquered people." A Treasury agent in Louisiana said in 1864 that "there [can] be no middle ground in a revolution. It must work a radical change in society; such [has] been the history of every great revolution."[19] But moderates also cited history to support their *evolutionary* approach. "The history of the world," wrote General Banks (in charge of Lincoln's reconstruction program in Louisiana), "shows that revolutions which are not controlled and held within reasonable limits, produce counter-revolution."[20]

These contrasting viewpoints framed the struggle within the Republican party over the terms of reconstruction during the first half of 1864. The outcome was a stalemate, but the contest came close to splitting the party and threatening Lincoln's reelection.

Lincoln's policy was based on his theory of the indissoluble Union. Since the states could not legally secede, they were still in the Union. The task of reconstruction, therefore, was to establish a process whereby loyal citizens could regain control of their states. In a practical sense, however, the Confederate states were unquestionably *out* of the Union. Most congressional Republicans did not wish to allow Rebels to come back into the Union merely by taking a loyalty oath. Distrusting former Confederates, Republicans wished to entrust reconstruction only to undoubted

---

[16]Basler, *Works of Lincoln,* VI, 365, VII, 51.

[17]McPherson, *Struggle for Equality,* pp. 370, 249; *Liberator,* August 8, 1862.

[18]For a perceptive treatment of Stevens, see Hans L. Trefousse, *Thaddeus Stevens: Nineteenth-Century Egalitarian* (Chapel Hill, 1997).

[19]H. B. Sargent to John Andrew, January 14, 1862, Andrew Papers, Massachusetts Historical Society; John C. Collins quoted in Petyon McCrary, *Abraham Lincoln and Reconstruction: The Louisiana Experiment* (Princeton, 1978), p. 228.

[20]Banks to Lincoln, December 20, 1863, quoted in McCrary, *Lincoln and Reconstruction,* p. 224.

Unionists. They intended to impose conditions that would guarantee the freedom and civil rights of blacks. To justify such interference with the constitutional rights of states, they developed a variety of theories. Thaddeus Stevens declared that since the Southern states had indeed gone out of the Union they should be treated as "conquered provinces." This was too radical for most Republicans, who leaned toward Charles Sumner's argument that by seceding, Southern states had committed "state suicide." Having thus forfeited their rights under the Constitution, they had reverted to the status of territories that could be readmitted as states only when they met the conditions laid down by Congress. But this concept of territorialization was also too strong for some Republicans. More than one-fourth of the House Republicans joined with Democrats and border-state congressmen to defeat a territorialization reconstruction measure in 1862.

Meanwhile, Lincoln seized the initiative from Congress by appointing military governors for the occupied portions of four Confederate states in 1862. Although this was a pragmatic response to the need for an interim authority to administer occupied territory, Lincoln clearly intended it as a first step toward presidential reconstruction (that is, the shaping of reconstruction policy by executive decision rather than by congressional legislation). At the same time, moderate Republicans in Congress worked out an ingenious alternative to territorialization. Article IV, Section 4, of the Constitution specifies that "the United States shall guarantee to every State in this Union a Republican form of Government." The framers had intended "republican" to mean only nonmonarchical. But like other parts of the Constitution, this phrase was capable of new interpretations to fit new conditions. For Republicans in 1863, rebellion and slavery could be construed as denials of a republican form of government. This raised certain awkward questions. If slavery was unrepublican in Confederate states, what about loyal border states? Nevertheless, by 1863, a consensus had emerged among Republicans to base reconstruction on this clause of the Constitution. Neither the congressional idea of territorialization nor the presidential theory of indestructible states disappeared, but both were subsumed under the concept of a republican form of government, whose ambiguity could justify almost anything.

But the phrase "republican form of government" did not abolish the differences between Lincoln's approach and that of the radicals. The President's policy of pardoning Rebels and letting them take part in reconstruction, said Wendell Phillips, "leaves the large landed proprietors of the South still to domineer over its politics, and makes the negro's freedom a mere sham." Once these pardoned Confederates regained power, warned Phillips, "the Revolution may be easily checked with the aid of the Administration, which is willing that the negro should be free but seeks nothing else for him. . . . What McClellan was on the battle-field—'Do as little hurt as possible!'—Lincoln is in civil affairs—'Make as little change as possible!' "[21]

Not only did radicals want land reform in the South; many of them began to urge black suffrage as well. They did so on grounds of justice and expediency. For a generation, abolitionists had been trying to win equal voting rights for blacks in the North; they were now prepared to extend that struggle to the South. Unless enfranchised, they said, the freed slaves would never be able to protect themselves against

---

[21]Phillips to Benjamin Butler, December 13, 1863, Butler Papers, Library of Congress; Phillips to George W. Julian, March 27, 1864, Giddings-Julian Papers, Library of Congress; *Liberator,* May 20, 1864.

a counterrevolution by the old master class. Abolitionists also maintained that the freedmen constituted the only large bloc of unconditional Unionists in the lower South. Without their voting power, a reconstructed state would stand on a fragile foundation of loyalty. Was it justice or sound policy to deny the ballot to men who had worked and fought for the Union while giving this precious right to men who had fought against it? "The negro has earned land, education, rights," Phillips told packed lecture halls in early 1864. "Before we leave him, we ought to leave him on his own soil, in his own house, with the ballot and the school-house within reach. Unless we have done it, the North has let the cunning of politics filch the fruits of war."[22]

This doctrine was too advanced for most Republicans in 1864. The Northern electorate, only recently converted to emancipation as a war measure, was scarcely ready yet for political equality. But if at this time only the most radical spokesmen publicly favored black suffrage, the history of the war indicated that where the radicals led, a majority of Republicans would eventually follow. Salmon P. Chase wrote after private talks with several Republicans in late 1863: "I find that almost all who are willing to have the colored men fight are willing to have them vote."[23]

Louisiana

Events in Louisiana brought into sharp perspective the difference between Lincoln's approach toward reconstruction and that of the radicals. In New Orleans, a substantial portion of the middle class and the skilled artisan class, which included some of the 10,000 antebellum free Negroes, provided the nucleus for a genuinely radical reconstruction. Many of these people had opposed secession. They had little stake in slavery and less liking for it. In 1863, their political leaders formed the Free State General Committee and urged the calling of a convention to write a new state constitution. "It seems to me as though I was in a new world," wrote a Treasury agent working with the Free State Committee. "A large majority are as radical as we ever were. A colored delegation of intelligent free men were admitted, which was more than would have been done in Ohio."[24] General Banks, however, favored the moderate Unionist faction in Louisiana over the radical Free State Committee. Instead of calling a constitutional convention as the radicals wished, Banks set up an election of state officers and congressmen under the antebellum constitution, modified by a military order which abolished slavery. Eager to hasten the reconstruction process in Louisiana as a model for other states, Lincoln told Banks to go ahead.

Banks was in a position to influence the results of the election. The Union army controlled the voter registration process. Banks dispensed patronage to leaders of the moderate faction. Many voters would think twice before going against the wishes of the general in command of the occupation forces. Not surprisingly, the moderates easily won the election held on February 22, 1864. Banks's role in this outcome angered the radical Free State men and alienated powerful congressional Republicans. To repair some of the damage, Lincoln urged Banks to put pressure on the moder-

---

[22]*Liberator,* February 5, 1864.

[23]Hans L. Trefousse, *The Radical Republicans* (New York, 1969), p. 285.

[24]McCrary, *Lincoln and Reconstruction,* p. 199.

ates to frame a liberal state constitution at the convention now scheduled for April. Meanwhile, the Free State committee sent two leaders of the New Orleans black community to Washington bearing a petition for black suffrage. Impressed by the education and eloquence of these men, Lincoln wrote a letter to Michael Hahn, newly elected governor of occupied Louisiana. The constitutional convention would decide the qualifications for voters in the new era. "I barely suggest for your private consideration," wrote the President, "whether some of the colored people may not be let in—as, for instance, the very intelligent, and especially those who have fought gallantly in our ranks. They would probably help, in some trying time to come, to keep the jewel of liberty within the family of freedom."[25]

This letter demonstrated Lincoln's readiness to meet the radicals halfway. But he needed to do more than "barely suggest" black suffrage to get it adopted in Louisiana. Despite pressure from Banks, the convention gave the legislature only discretionary power to enfranchise blacks. The new constitution did prohibit slavery and create a public school system for both races. But this did not mollify radicals. The ratification vote on the constitution represented only 10 percent of the adult white males in the state. Congressional Republicans considered this too slender a basis for reconstruction, especially since none of the radicals—the most reliable Unionists—were part of Louisiana's new government. If this was the showcase of Lincoln's reconstruction policy, a growing number of congressional Republicans wanted no part of it.

The Wade-Davis Bill

But Congress had some recourse—it had the power to exclude representatives from Louisiana, and it did so. It also denied admission to congressmen elected under Lincoln's policy from occupied portions of Arkansas, and it refused to count the electoral votes from both of these states, as well as those from Tennessee, in the 1864 presidential election. Going beyond these negative actions, Congress tried to regain the initiative on reconstruction. "Everybody abounds in schemes for settling the troubles in the rebel states," wrote one jaded congressman, "and at least six plans a day are offered in the shape of a Bill."[26] After nearly five months of debate, the Republicans on July 2, 1864, passed a bill sponsored by Congressman Henry Winter Davis of Maryland and Senator Benjamin Wade of Ohio. The Wade-Davis measure differed from Lincoln's program in several important respects: instead of requiring only 10 percent of the voters to take an oath of allegiance to begin the process, it required 50 percent; instead of allowing this group to elect new state officers, it required the election, first, of delegates to a constitutional convention; instead of permitting all white men who took the oath of allegiance to vote in such an election, it enfranchised only those who could take an "iron-clad oath" swearing that they had never voluntarily supported the rebellion; and it enacted specific legal safeguards of the freedmen's liberty, which were to be enforced by federal courts.

---

[25]Basler, *Works of Lincoln*, VII, 243. For a discussion of Lincoln's policy toward Louisiana that sees him as working toward the same ends as the radical Republicans, see LaWanda Cox, *Lincoln and Black Freedom: A Study in Presidential Leadership* (Columbia, S.C., 1981), pp. 46–139.

[26]Herman Belz, *Reconstructing the Union: Theory and Policy During the Civil War* (Ithaca, 1969), p. 173.

Like Lincoln's program, however, the Wade-Davis bill confined the reconstruction process to white voters. At one point in its progress through the congressional labyrinth, the bill had enfranchised all "loyal" men; but in the last-minute rush to get it passed before adjournment, Wade consented to a white-only amendment to save the bill. Most radicals (the radicals constituted about one-third of the Republican congressmen and senators at this time) would probably have preferred to include black suffrage. But they went along with the deletion in order to have some program with which "to go before the country" in the forthcoming elections. They also expected the 50 percent requirement and the stringent restrictions on white voters to postpone reconstruction until the war was over, when the increasing radicalism of the North might sustain a black suffrage requirement.

Despite the nearly unanimous vote of congressional Republicans for the Wade-Davis bill, Lincoln exercised the little-used constitutional provision for a pocket veto, whereby the president can kill a bill passed at the end of a session merely by refusing to sign it. Lincoln issued a statement explaining his action: he was unwilling to approve a measure that would commit him to any single plan of restoration, especially since it would destroy the fragile governments of Louisiana and Arkansas that he was trying to nurse along. But Lincoln stated a willingness to enforce the Wade-Davis plan in any state "choosing to adopt it"—surely a remote possibility when the milder presidential plan was available as an alternative.[27]

Goaded to fury by Lincoln's cool defiance of Congress, Wade and Davis published a blistering manifesto on August 5. "Congress passed a bill; the President refused to approve it, and then by proclamation puts as much of it in force as he sees fit. . . . A more studied outrage on the legislative authority of the people has never been perpetrated." Throwing down the gauntlet in behalf of congressional Republicans, Wade and Davis warned Lincoln that "if he wishes our support, he must confine himself to his Executive duties—to obey and to execute, not to make the laws—to suppress by arms armed rebellion, and leave political reorganization to Congress."[28]

Reconstruction and Presidential Politics

Seldom has a president been so sharply attacked by leaders of his own party in the midst of a political campaign whose outcome might determine the nation's life. But this came as little surprise, for the reconstruction issue had long been embroiled in intraparty factionalism. In early 1864, Lincoln's renomination had been by no means assured. The prevailing tradition was a one-term presidency. No president had been elected to a second term since 1832, and no incumbent had been renominated by his party since 1840. Several Republicans believed themselves at least as well qualified as Lincoln for the office.

Foremost among these was Salmon P. Chase, whose ambition overwhelmed his judgment. Chase used Treasury patronage to build a political machine for his nomination in 1864. This effort won the support of radicals disenchanted with Lincoln's

---

[27]Basler, *Works of Lincoln*, VII, 433–434.
[28]*New York Tribune*, August 5, 1864.

reconstruction policy. But Chase's supporters played their hand so badly that once again, as in the cabinet crisis of December 1862 (see pages 329 and 330), the secretary was outsmarted and humiliated. In early February, a pro-Chase pamphlet entitled *The Next Presidential Election* circulated in the Midwest under the frank of prominent Republican congressmen. Several days later Chase's manager, Senator Samuel C. Pomeroy of Kansas, sent out a "strictly private" circular touting the secretary's presidential potential. The Pomeroy Circular was soon leaked to the press. The reaction to these documents turned the premature Chase boom into a boomerang. Lincoln proved to have greater support in the party than expected. While Chase had been creating a machine in the Treasury Department, the President had used the patronage of other departments to build a strong organization in nearly every Northern state. Republican legislatures or conventions in fourteen states—including Chase's home state of Ohio—passed resolutions endorsing Lincoln's renomination. The Republican National Committee did the same. The Chase movement collapsed.[29]

The hopes of some anti-Lincoln radicals next focused on General John C. Frémont. After resigning his Shenandoah Valley command in June 1862, Frémont had cooled his heels in New York, "awaiting orders." Ever since his abortive emancipation edict of 1861 in Missouri, he had been something of a hero to abolitionists and radical German-Americans. Representatives of these groups met on May 31 in Cleveland to nominate Frémont for president on a platform calling for a constitutional amendment to "secure all men absolute equality before the law" and to distribute confiscated Rebel land "among the soldiers and settlers."[30]

But this apparently radical platform was tainted by evidence that Democrats had infiltrated the movement. One plank of the platform condemned the administration's suppression of free speech and suspension of habeas corpus—which were Democratic issues. The convention named itself the "Radical Democratic party," which pretty well summed up this political marriage of strange bedfellows. Although some abolitionists followed Wendell Phillips in supporting Frémont's candidacy, most concurred with William Lloyd Garrison's observation that Frémont had become the catspaw of wily War Democrats hoping to divide and conquer the Republicans. No prominent Republican endorsed Frémont.

When the Republican national convention met in Baltimore on June 7, Lincoln's managers had matters well in hand. Only the radical Missouri delegation opposed the President's renomination. Calling itself the National Union party to broaden its appeal, the convention nominated the Tennessee War Democrat Andrew Johnson for vice president in an attempt to attract War Democrats and loyal Southerners to the party's banner. Avoiding the knotty problem of reconstruction, the platform endorsed Lincoln's war measures, rejected any peace terms except unconditional surrender of the Confederacy, and endorsed a constitutional amendment to abolish slavery.

---

[29]The embarrassed Chase offered to resign after the Pomeroy Circular became public, but Lincoln preferred to keep him in the cabinet, where he would be less of a threat to the President's renomination. Four months later, however, when Chase again offered his resignation over a patronage dispute, Lincoln—now safely renominated—accepted it.

[30]Ibid., June 1, 1864.

This demonstration of party harmony concealed persistent divisions caused by the reconstruction issue. At least one-third of the congressional Republicans were unhappy with Lincoln's nomination. Behind the scenes, several radicals continued to maneuver for some way to replace Lincoln with a more acceptable nominee. The President's pocket veto of the reconstruction bill had crystallized Republican discontent. The Wade-Davis Manifesto formed part of an ill-coordinated scheme for a new convention to nominate General Benjamin Butler for president. War Democrats were expected to rally behind this ticket, Frémont would withdraw his candidacy, and recognizing the inevitable, Lincoln himself would then step down.

In the murky political atmosphere of August 1864, a good many intelligent men actually believed that such a fantastic scheme could work. To understand why, we must turn to the story of the 1864 military campaigns. For in the final analysis, it was not the issue of reconstruction but the issues of war and peace on which the 1864 election turned. The high hopes for military victory with which the North had begun the year had turned to despair as Grant and Sherman appeared to be stymied before Richmond and Atlanta, after fighting a series of battles with staggering casualties. By August, war weariness and defeatism had settled over the Northern political landscape like a heavy fog in which people blindly groped their way.

Chapter Twenty-Three

Military Stalemate, 1864

Whatever happens, there will be no turning back.

—Ulysses S. Grant to Abraham Lincoln, *May 1864*

The apparent reversal of military fortunes in the summer of 1864 was all the more shocking to the North because the Confederacy's prospects had appeared so bleak at the beginning of the year. With fewer than half as many men under arms as the North, the South had no more reserves of manpower to draw on while the North could mobilize hundreds of thousands of new volunteers and draftees. Tennessee was occupied by Union troops, the Trans-Mississippi Department was cut off from the rest of the Confederacy, the railroad system of the South was in shambles, and supplies of all kinds were lacking. Southern leaders were quarreling with one another over responsibility for the defeats of 1863, and powerful Northern armies were poised for the kill. A Confederate War Department official wrote in his diary on November 6, 1863: "I have never actually despaired of the cause . . . [but now] steadfastness is yielding to a sense of hopelessness."[1]

But all was not so hopeless as it seemed. Morale among front-line Confederate troops remained high, aided by a wave of religious revivals in the winter camps. Southern soldiers were nearly all veterans, while the expiration of Northern three-year enlistments in 1864 foretold a decline in the fighting quality of blue regiments. True, many Confederate three-year enlistments also expired in 1864, but a recent amendment to the conscription law required all of these men to reenlist.

In contrast, Northern men whose enlistments expired were free to leave the army. If all of them did so, nearly half of the combat troops—the best half, veterans with three years' experience—would melt away. Instead of compelling these men to reenlist, the Union government relied on persuasion and inducement: an appeal to patriotism and unit pride, plus a thirty-day furlough and a $400 federal bounty (in addition to state and local bounties for many soldiers) to those who reenlisted. More

---

[1]Edward Younger (ed.), *Inside the Confederate Government: The Diary of Robert Garlick Hill Kean* (New York, 1975), p. 119.

than half of the three-year veterans reenlisted,[2] some with fanfare and parades, but most, perhaps, in the spirit expressed by two privates in a Massachusetts regiment that had fought in all the Army of the Potomac's major battles and suffered heavy losses. "They use a man here," said one, "just the same as they do a turkey at a shooting match, fire at it all day and if they don't kill it raffle it off in the evening; so with us, if they can't kill you in three years they want you for three more—but I will stay." And his messmate added: "If new men won't finish the job, old men must."[3]

Without these "veteran volunteers" (who wore a special chevron on their sleeves), the Union armies would have become hollow shells in 1864. This was all the more true because of the unpromising character of many new recruits. Bounty men, substitutes, and conscripts poured into the camps of veteran regiments to bring them up to strength. The boys of '61 were appalled by these "off-scourings of northern slums," these "dregs of every nation . . . branded felons . . . thieves, burglars and vagabonds." With some exaggeration, a New Hampshire veteran wrote that "such another depraved, vice-hardened and desperate set of human beings never before disgraced an army." Another old soldier remarked that "if those fellows are trusted on picket, the army will soon be in hell."[4] Many of the new soldiers deserted as soon as they got a chance. "The men we have been getting in this way nearly all desert," Grant informed the War Department in September 1864," and out of five reported North as having enlisted we don't get more than one effective soldier."[5] These factors reduced the North's numerical superiority much below appearances. Coupled with the South's advantages of fighting on the defensive, they went a long way toward evening the odds for Confederate survival.

Union Military Strategy in 1864

In 1864, the North developed a unified command system to coordinate strategy on all fronts. This had been Lincoln's purpose when he appointed Halleck general in chief in 1862, but Halleck had abdicated the responsibility. In March 1864, Grant came to Washington to assume Halleck's title.[6] But Grant had no intention of becoming a desk general. He thenceforth made his headquarters with the Army of the Potomac, becoming in effect its strategic field commander while Meade remained its titular and tactical commander. Halleck agreeably stepped down to become chief of staff. He stayed in Washington, where his office served as a communications and operations center for Grant's orders to the far-flung armies under his control.

---

[2] Approximately half of the three-year veterans in the Army of the Potomac reenlisted. The percentage of reenlistments in the western armies was higher.

[3] Bruce Catton, *A Stillness at Appomattox* (Garden City, N.Y., 1957), p. 36.

[4] Ibid., pp. 25–29; Bell I. Wiley, *The Life of Billy Yank* (New York, 1952), pp. 343–344.

[5] *O.R.,* Ser. 1, Vol. 42, pt. 2, p. 783.

[6] Congress had revived the rank of lieutenant-general, previously held only by George Washington (Winfield Scott had held this rank by brevet only). Lincoln promoted Grant to lieutenant-general and appointed him general in chief of all the armies.

LIEUTENANT-GENERAL ULYSSES S. GRANT AT HIS FIELD HEADQUARTERS NEAR COLD HARBOR, 1864. In his first command, as colonel of an Illinois regiment in 1861, Grant discovered that the enemy colonel "had been as much afraid of me as I had been of him. . . . The lesson was valuable." In 1864, he infused this lesson into the officer corps of the Army of the Potomac, who had previously been more afraid of Lee than they thought Lee was of them.

LIBRARY OF CONGRESS

Lincoln at last had a general in chief whose strategic ideas accorded with his own. He could trust Grant to act decisively without the constant prodding necessary with previous commanders in the Virginia theater. Grant believed that in the past the various Union armies had "acted independently and without concert, like a balky team, no two ever pulling together."[7] This had allowed the Confederates to shift troops from one point to another to meet the most pressing danger. For two years, Lincoln had been trying to get his armies to advance simultaneously on several fronts, and now Grant worked out such an overall plan. He issued orders to five Union armies stretched over a thousand miles of front to begin coordinated campaigns as early in the spring as possible.

The Army of the Potomac, with about 115,000 men, would attack the 64,000-strong Army of Northern Virginia. "Lee's Army will be your objective point," Grant told Meade. "Wherever Lee goes, there you will go also."[8] Two small armies in Virginia would operate on the perimeters of the main action: Benjamin Butler was to move from Fortress Monroe up the James River with 30,000 men to threaten Richmond from the south and prevent reinforcements from being sent to Lee. At the same time Franz Sigel, now in command of the scattered Union forces in West Virginia,

---

[7] *O.R.*, Ser. 1, Vol. 46, pt. 1, p. 11.

[8] Ibid., Vol. 33, pp. 827–828.

was to move up the Shenandoah Valley to prevent its resources and defenders from going to Lee's aid. As Lincoln aptly described the auxiliary role of Butler and Sigel: "Those not skinning can hold a leg."[9]

Next to Virginia, the most important theater would be Georgia, where Sherman's 100,000 faced Johnston's 50,000 (reinforced to 65,000 as the campaign began). Grant directed Sherman "to move against Johnston's army, to break it up and to get into the interior of the enemy's country as far as you can, inflicting all the damage you can against their war resources."[10] Banks was to move from New Orleans against Mobile, and after capturing that important port he was to strike northeast through Alabama into Georgia to cooperate with Sherman in a pincers movement that would crush all Confederate resistance in that area.

Failure of the Auxiliary Campaigns

Like most military plans, however, this one went awry, partly because the Confederate armies still had a great deal of defensive punch, but also because the Union's political generals—Banks, Butler, and Sigel—did not do their jobs. Indeed, Banks's Mobile campaign did not even get started, though this was not entirely his fault.

The Red River Campaign

Ever since the fall of Vicksburg, Grant and Banks had wanted to move against Mobile. But Lincoln had ordered Banks's Army of the Gulf to invade Texas instead. The President desired a Union military presence in Texas as a warning to France, which was in the process of setting up a puppet government in Mexico. Banks had been unable to do more than plant the flag in a few enclaves along the Texas Gulf coast in 1863. But in March 1864, he undertook an ambitious campaign up the Red River of Louisiana, with the intention of capturing Shreveport and using it as a jumping-off point for an expedition into Texas.

The Confederates had 30,000 combat troops scattered in various detachments around the Trans-Mississippi Department under the overall command of Edmund Kirby Smith. The main Rebel force in Louisiana was commanded by Richard Taylor, son of former President Zachary Taylor. Banks had an army of 27,000 men (10,000 of them borrowed from Sherman), supported by a powerful fleet of river ironclads under Admiral David Porter. Cooperating with Banks was a Union army of 15,000 moving south from Little Rock. From the outset, Grant had considered this campaign a wasteful diversion. He ordered Banks to get it over with quickly, garrison Shreveport, and return most of his troops to New Orleans to launch the campaign against Mobile. But Banks started late and conducted his campaign poorly. On April 8, Taylor's forces routed Banks's advance divisions at Sabine Crossroads, forty miles south of Shreveport. Next day, the Federals made a stand at Pleasant Hill and struck the pursuing Confederates a sharp blow.

---

[9]Michael Burlingame and John R. T. Ettlinger (eds.) *Inside Lincoln's White House: The Complete Civil War Diary of John Hay* (Carbondale, Ill., 1997), p. 194.

[10]*O.R.,* Ser. 1, Vol. 32, pt. 3, p. 246.

A vigorous general might have followed up this tactical victory with a fast march to Shreveport, but Banks decided instead to retreat. He had learned that the Union column from Arkansas could not link up with him because bad roads and Confederate cavalry had forced it back to Little Rock. Worse still, the abnormally low Red River was dropping fast and threatening to maroon Porter's entire fleet above the rapids at Alexandria. Calamity was averted by a Wisconsin colonel with a lumbering background, who supervised the construction of a series of ingenious dams that floated the fleet over the rapids. Banks's army returned downriver too late for a drive against Mobile, and the 10,000 troops borrowed from Sherman went to Mississippi to cope with Forrest instead of joining Sherman in Georgia. Lincoln's Texas campaign never made it to that state. The Confederates still controlled Texas, northern Louisiana, and southern Arkansas. And with French support, Maximilian had become emperor of Mexico (see page 371). Banks was relieved of field command, though he remained in charge of the military administration of southern Louisiana.

The James River and Shenandoah Valley Campaigns

While Banks was coming to grief in Louisiana, Butler and Sigel were failing to carry out their part of Grant's strategy in Virginia. Butler brought his 30,000 well-armed troops up the James River and landed fifteen miles south of Richmond on May 5. From there he might have cut the railroads linking Richmond to the South, occupied Petersburg, or even smashed his way into the capital itself against the scratch force of 5,000 troops and an equal number of government clerks serving as emergency militia. Any of these actions would have crippled Lee, who was then engaged in a desperate battle with Grant sixty miles to the north, for the railroad between Richmond and Petersburg was Lee's lifeline.

In the end, Butler failed to accomplish any of these objectives. Instead of attacking boldly, Butler's troops entrenched, tore up only a few miles of track, then advanced cautiously toward Richmond on May 12. General Beauregard, in charge of the capital's defenses, had by then assembled an army equal in size to Butler's mobile force (about 18,000 men). Beauregard launched a counterattack on May 16 near Drewry's Bluff, seven miles from Richmond. Although both sides suffered heavy casualties, the Federals were forced back to their trenches across the narrow neck of land between the James and Appomattox rivers just north of Petersburg. The Confederates then entrenched their own line across the neck. As Grant later put it, Butler's army was "as completely shut off from further operations directly against Richmond as if it had been in a bottle strongly corked."[11] Not only had Butler failed to strike a blow against Lee's rear; he could not even prevent Beauregard from sending nearly 7,000 reinforcements to the hard-pressed Army of Northern Virginia.

Despite this sorry performance, Butler's political influence was too great for Lincoln to remove him from command. But the hapless Franz Sigel did not escape this fate. Advancing up the Shenandoah Valley, Sigel was defeated at New Market on May 15 by a Confederate force of 5,000 in a battle remembered chiefly for a spirited charge by 247 teenage cadets from the Virginia Military Institute. Sigel had

---

[11] Ibid., Vol. 46, pt. 1, p. 20.

failed in his dual mission—to cut the railroad from the valley to Richmond and to prevent reinforcements being sent to Lee. On May 21, Lincoln relieved him of command.

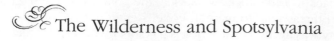 The Wilderness and Spotsylvania

Having planned that Butler and Sigel would each hold a Rebel leg while the Army of the Potomac did the skinning, Grant now realized that this army would have to do the job by itself. It would be no easy task, for in two weeks of fighting the Army of the Potomac had already suffered more casualties than in any comparable period of the war.

On May 4, the blue divisions began crossing the Rapidan for a campaign that the North expected would win the war within a month or two. Grant intended to move around Lee's right to force his army out of its trenches and into open battle. Lee accepted the challenge, but he planned to hit the Yankees in the flank before they emerged from the dense second-growth forest known as the Wilderness, where Federal numerical and artillery superiority would count for little. Lee had brought Joe Hooker to grief in the Wilderness exactly one year earlier in the battle of Chancellorsville. He hoped to repeat the performance with Grant.

The Battle of the Wilderness

On May 5, Lee's advance units came into contact with Grant's southward-marching men. The surprised Federals faced right and attacked, bringing on two days of vicious fighting in woods so thick that soldiers seldom saw their enemies but fired at the spot where the sound and smoke indicated they were. Whole brigades got lost in the forest; officers had little control over the confused movements of their men; muzzle flashes from thousands of rifles set the underbrush on fire; scores of wounded men burned to death. Most of the fighting surged back and forth near the intersections of the two main roads through the Wilderness. At the end of the first day, Union forces still held the vital intersections.

That night Grant ordered Winfield Scott Hancock, commander of the army's crack 2nd Corps, to throw everything he had into an assault on the Confederate right at dawn. The Union generals knew that Longstreet's corps had not come up in time for the first day's fighting. They hoped to roll up Lee's flank before Longstreet could arrive next morning. At first, Hancock's attack on May 6 went well. It drove the Rebels right back a mile to a clearing where Lee had his command post. On the verge of a smashing success, the blue brigades became disorganized by their advance through the tangled woods. At that moment, the leading units of Longstreet's fresh troops double-timed into the clearing from the opposite side. Agitated by his brush with disaster, Lee tried personally to lead these troops against the re-forming Yankee line. But the gray soldiers shouted "General Lee to the rear" and restrained him, while Longstreet directed a counterattack that rocked the Federals back on their heels.

Later in the morning, Longstreet sent part of his corps along the cut of an unfinished railroad, from which they launched a surprise assault on Hancock's exposed flank. Now it was the Confederates' turn to lose all cohesion as they drove the Yan-

A GRISLY OMEN.   These skeletons of Union soldiers killed at Chancellorsville in May 1863, their shallow graves uncovered by erosion or animals, greeted living Union soldiers exactly a year later, at the beginning of the Wilderness campaign. The Wilderness promised to turn many of them into skeletons as well.

kees back through the woods. Riding forward to reconnoiter, Longstreet was shot by his own men in the confusion of smoke and noise. (In a similar accident, Stonewall Jackson had been shot a year earlier less than four miles from the spot where Longstreet fell. Longstreet survived but was out of action for five months.) Thereafter most of the steam went out of the Confederate attack on this flank, as Hancock got his men behind breastworks protecting the road intersection. There they repulsed a final Rebel assault in late afternoon. Near twilight, a Confederate attack three miles to the north bent the other Union flank back at right angles and captured several hundred prisoners, including two generals.

It was a situation reminiscent of Chancellorsville, when a successful Rebel assault on the Union right near this same spot had been a prelude to defeat. But Grant was no Joe Hooker. When an overwrought officer rushed up and said, "General Grant, this is a crisis. . . . I know Lee's methods well by past experience; he will throw his whole army between us and the Rapidan, and cut us off completely from our communications," Grant replied with some asperity: "I am heartily tired of hearing about what Lee is going to do. Some of you always seem to think he is suddenly going to turn a double somersault, and land on our rear and on both flanks at the same time. Go back to your command, and try to think what we are going to do ourselves, instead of what Lee is going to do."[12]

Grant suited action to words. The Union right was stabilized, darkness fell, and next day—May 7—both armies lay exhausted behind their breastworks. In two days of fighting, the Federals had suffered more than 17,000 casualties, the Confederates at least 11,000—about 17 percent of each army. Once again Lee had won an apparent victory over superior numbers. In the past each time this had happened, the Army of the Potomac had retreated. Weary veterans were certain it would be the same this time. "Most of us," wrote one soldier, "thought it was another Chancellorsville, and that next day we should recross the river." During the day the movement of supply wagons and artillery toward the rear seemed to confirm this expectation. But when night fell and the men received orders to march *south,* the realization suddenly dawned that whether the Wilderness had been a victory or a defeat, this army was no longer going to retreat. Even though they had just been through hell and the move southward promised more hell, the smoke-grimed Yanks felt a sense of elation. "Our spirits rose," one of them later recalled. "We marched free. The men began to sing." Before the campaign began, Grant had promised Lincoln that "whatever happens, there will be no turning back." Now the eastern troops learned that this general from the west meant to infuse his own brand of aggressiveness into the Army of the Potomac. When Grant cantered unobtrusively along the road next to the 5th Corps on the night of May 7–8, the men recognized him and sent up a cheer—not the parade-ground cheer of McClellan's time, but the veteran's yell of hard-earned respect.[13]

The Battles of Spotsylvania

Grant's objective was the crossroads at Spotsylvania Courthouse a few miles southeast of the Wilderness. There his communications through Fredericksburg would be safe, and with the Union army poised between Lee and Richmond, the Rebels would be forced to fight in open territory on ground of Grant's choosing. But Lee foiled the move. He had ordered Longstreet's corps, now commanded by Richard Anderson, to make a forced march to Spotsylvania on the night of May 7–8. While Anderson marched swiftly, the leading Union divisions were delayed by Rebel cavalry and by their own cavalry blocking the road. On the morning of May 8, Anderson's men scrambled behind hastily improvised breastworks north of Spotsylvania just in time to turn back a Federal assault. As more troops on both sides filed into line, exhausted after their all-night march, Grant renewed the attack without avail. The bluecoats had lost the race for Spotsylvania.

---

[12]Horace Porter, *Campaigning with Grant* (New York, 1897), pp. 69–70. In his memoirs, written twenty years after the Civil War, Grant noted that many Northerners, including officers in the Army of the Potomac, attributed "almost superhuman abilities" to Lee. But "I had known him personally" when both were junior officers in the Mexican War, "and knew that he was mortal." *Personal Memoirs of U.S. Grant,* 2 vols. (New York, 1885–1886), I, 192.

[13]Catton, *Stillness at Appomattox,* p. 91; Shelby Foote, *The Civil War: A Narrative. Red River to Appomattox* (New York, 1974), pp. 189–191.

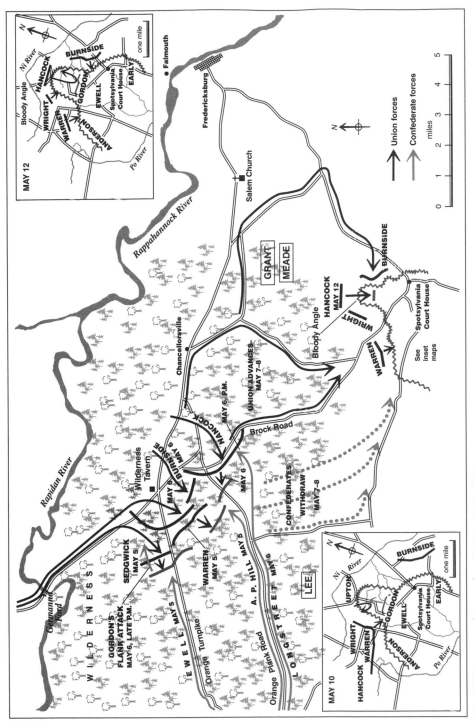

The Wilderness and Spotsylvania, May 5–12, 1864

The ragged men in gray, by now masters of entrenchment, threw up formidable breastworks along a five-mile line of trenches covering Spotsylvania in the shape of a huge inverted U. Grant tried to flank the west end of this line, but Lee shifted troops to meet this threat. Believing that the Confederate center was thereby weakened, Grant ordered two assaults on the afternoon of May 10. The first was repulsed, but the other, led by twenty-four-year-old Colonel Emory Upton, achieved a temporary breakthrough. Organizing his twelve specially picked regiments in four compact lines under cover of woods 200 yards from the Rebel trenches, Upton took them across no-man's land at a sprint. Yelling like maniacs, the Yankees overran the works before the Confederates could fire more than a couple of volleys. But the failure of a supporting division to exploit this opening enabled the Rebels to organize a counterattack that drove Upton back with heavy losses.

Upton's temporary success won him promotion to brigadier general and persuaded Grant to try the same tactics with a whole corps. Upton had hit the northwest face of a salient in the Confederate line dubbed the "mule shoe" because of its shape. Grant decided to launch a large-scale assault against the tip of the salient, considered the weakest point because its convexity caused the fire of defenders to diverge. At 4:30 A.M. on May 12, Hancock's 2nd Corps burst out of the rain and fog and overran the Confederate trenches with unexpected ease. The yelling bluecoats swept forward a half mile, capturing twenty guns and three thousand prisoners. But their very success disorganized the Federals into an exultant, yelling mob. Before their officers could reorganize them, a Confederate counterattack blunted the Union advance. Once more Lee tried to lead this counterattack personally, but with the sure knowledge that if he was killed or captured their cause was lost, the soldiers again shouted "General Lee to the rear" as they ran forward. Hancock's men were driven back to the trenches they had initially captured, which they held against repeated gray attacks.

While this was going on, the Union 6th Corps assaulted the Confederate trenches a few hundred yards down the west side of the salient. Here was the famous "Bloody Angle," where some of the most savage fighting of the war took place. Blue and gray slugged it out for endless hours in the rain. Fighting madness turned men into killing machines. Individual soldiers would leap up onto the parapets of the trenches and fire down into them as fast as comrades could pass loaded rifles up to them. When one was shot down, another would jump up to take his place. Killed and wounded men lay in the trenches three deep, where some of them were trampled entirely under the muck of mud and blood. The intensity of firing blasted trees and logs into splinters; minie balls cut down one oak nearly two feet thick. "I never expect to be fully believed when I tell what I saw of the horrors of Spotsylvania, " wrote an officer in the 6th Corps, "because I should be loath to believe it myself, were the case reversed."[14] All day and through half the night, the Confederates grimly held these trenches while Lee's engineers worked desperately to complete a new line a mile to the rear. When the fighting finally stopped after midnight and the Rebels abandoned the mule shoe, the Federals had suffered 7,000 casualties and the Confederates nearly as many, most of them along a quarter mile of trenches.

---

[14]Gordon C. Rhea, *The Battles for Spotsylvania Court House and the Road to Yellow Tavern, May 7–12, 1864* (Baton Rouge, 1997), p. 294.

GENERALS IN THE ARMY OF THE POTOMAC'S 2ND CORPS IN 1864. Seated is Winfield Scott Hancock, commander of the corps. Standing are the division commanders (*from left to right*): Francis C. Barlow, David B. Birney, and John Gibbon. All four men had been wounded the previous summer at Gettysburg, where they had played key roles in Union victory. They returned to uniform in time to play equally important roles in the Wilderness.

LIBRARY OF CONGRESS

Grant had dented but failed to break Lee's defenses. He now attempted to maneuver the Confederates out of these defenses, first by swinging half the army around the Rebel right and then countermarching for an attack on the left flank. Continual rain slowed these movements, while Lee was able to shift troops on his shorter interior lines to counter them. Although intermittent heavy fighting occurred during this week of maneuvering, which brought total Union and Confederate casualties at Spotsylvania to about 18,000 and 12,000, respectively, there were no more battles like those of May 10 and 12. During one of the lulls, a Union staff officer reflected on the fraternization between pickets of the two armies:

These men are incomprehensible—now standing from daylight to dark killing and wounding each other by thousands, and now making jokes and exchanging newspapers! . . . The great staples of conversation are the size and quality of rations, the marches they have made, and the regiments they have fought against. All sense of personal spite is sunk in the immensity of the contest.[15]

On May 11, Grant had sent a dispatch to Washington promising "to fight it out on this line if it takes all summer." Northern newspapers picked up this phrase and garnished it with exaggerated reports of Union success at Spotsylvania. These reports, said one veteran correspondent, produced "delirium" in the North; "everybody

---

[15]George R. Agassiz (ed.), *Meade's Headquarters, 1863–1865, Letters of Colonel Theodore Lyman* (Boston, 1922), p. 106.

seemed to think that the war was coming to an end right away."[16] Lincoln was distressed by such attitudes, for he feared that the end was still far off and that excessive optimism now might lead to a severe letdown later, especially when the casualty lists came in.

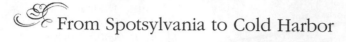

From Spotsylvania to Cold Harbor

Grant's determination to fight it out at Spotsylvania was based on the assumption that Butler and Sigel would so disrupt Lee's supply lines and threaten his rear that the Rebels would have to come out of their trenches to fight or retreat. On May 9, Grant had also sent the Union cavalry, 10,000 strong and now commanded by fiery Phil Sheridan, on a raid deep in Lee's rear. The blue troopers destroyed supply depots, tore up miles of track, bested the outnumbered Rebel horsemen in several engagements, killed Jeb Stuart and another Confederate general, and broke through the outer defenses of Richmond before being driven off. It was a spectacular raid, and if Butler and Sigel had not suffered their humiliating defeats at precisely this time, the Army of Northern Virginia might well have been cut off and forced out of its trenches. But the damage from Sheridan's raid was soon repaired (though the loss of Stuart was irreparable), and Lee's supply lines remained open.

Grant learned the bad news about Butler and Sigel at the same time that his tactical maneuvers of May 14–19 were failing to dislodge Lee. The Union commander therefore ordered another long flanking movement to place his army between Lee and Richmond. But once again Lee anticipated the move and marched his army twenty miles southward to entrench a strong line behind the North Anna River before the Federals got there. After probing the Confederate defenses, Grant decided not to risk an assault. Instead, he again moved to his left and crossed the Pamunkey River on May 28. Once more he found the Rebels already entrenched behind Totopotomoy Creek, less than ten miles northeast of Richmond. So yet again—for the fifth time in the campaign—Grant sidled to the left in an attempt to turn Lee's flank. Sheridan's cavalry seized a dusty, desolate crossroads known as Cold Harbor[17] and held it against Confederate infantry until their own infantry came up. Lee desperately shifted his line to the right; more Yankee foot soldiers arrived and drove back the Confederate line on the evening of June 1. Grant ordered an all-out attack at dawn next morning to smash through the Rebels before they could fully entrench. But half of the Union army was still on the road, trying to make forced night marches over poorly mapped terrain in stifling heat. One corps got lost and finally staggered into line long after dawn. Many of the men were too weary even to stay awake, much less to fight, so Grant had to postpone the attack for twenty-four hours. This gave the 59,000 gray soldiers all the time they needed to entrench a six-mile line with its flanks protected by the Totopotomoy and Chickahominy.

---

[16] *O.R.,* Ser. 1, Vol. 36, pt. 2, p. 627; Noah Brooks, *Washington in Lincoln's Time* (New York, 1895), p. 148.

[17] So named because the tavern there provided drinks and overnight accommodations but no hot meals.

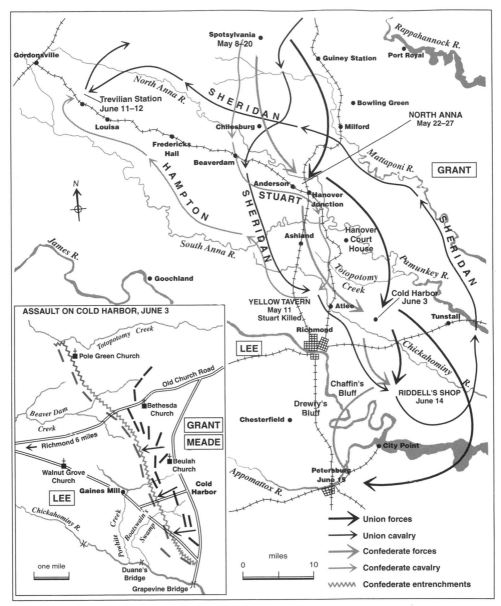

From Spotsylvania to Petersburg, May–June, 1864

Despite the strength of the Confederate defenses, Grant decided to go ahead with his attack. He had run out of room to maneuver, for another flanking move would only drive the Rebels into their even stronger Richmond fortifications. The blue veterans knew what to expect at dawn on June 3. The night before, many of them pinned slips of paper with name and address on their coats so their bodies could be identified after the battle. One soldier wrote in his diary: "June 3. Cold Harbor. I was

SHERIDAN AND HIS CAVALRY COMMANDERS. Wesley Merritt, Philip Sheridan, George Crook, James W. Forsyth, and George Armstrong Custer. By the summer of 1864, the cavalry corps of the Army of the Potomac, once its weakest arm, had become perhaps the finest fighting force of the war, playing a crucial role in Sheridan's victories in the Shenandoah Valley during the fall.

LIBRARY OF CONGRESS

killed." The diary was found on his body after the battle. The June 3 attack at Cold Harbor was one of the most costly failures of the war. "I regret this assault more than any one I have ever ordered," Grant said afterward.[18] Delivered by 50,000 Union troops against three miles of the Confederate line held by 30,000 defenders, the attack was decimated by massed frontal and enfilading fire from the dug-in Rebel infantry and artillery. Seven thousand Union soldiers were killed or wounded, most of them in the first few minutes; the Confederates lost only 1,500.

The Shenandoah Valley and Petersburg

Some historians have mistakenly described Grant's campaign against Lee as a war of attrition. Grant's hammering assaults, they argue, demonstrated that he was willing to accept heavy losses because he knew they could be replaced while Lee's could not. In the end it worked out that way, but not because Grant intended it. He had planned a war of maneuver and open battle. It was Lee who turned it into a war of attrition. Once the boldest and most offensive-minded of generals, Lee could no

---

[18]Porter, *Campaigning with Grant,* p. 179.

THE GRIM HARVEST OF WAR. This photograph was taken in April 1865 at the Cold Harbor battlefield, where a reburial detail exhumed the remains of Union soldiers killed the previous June for interment in a national cemetery at Cold Harbor. After the war, Congress legislated the establishment of national military cemeteries on or near Civil War battlefields, prisons, and army posts—for the reinterment of Union soldiers. The creation of the Gettysburg cemetery in 1863 and the establishment of cemeteries at Vicksburg, Chattanooga, and other sites occupied by Union forces during the war provided models for the postwar cemeteries, the largest of which became Arlington National Cemetery. American armed forces veterans since 1865 are also eligible for burial in these Civil War-created cemeteries.

longer risk his limited manpower in battle outside the trenches. The Confederates could no longer hope to "win" the war with the tactics or strategy of Chancellorsville or Gettysburg. By remaining on the defensive, however, they could hope to hang on long enough and to inflict losses enough on the Yankees to make *them* give up trying to win. This strategy was beginning to work in June 1864. In the North, many who had expressed extravagant hopes that Grant would win the war in a month now denounced him as a "butcher." The Copperheads came to life and began to declaim that the Republicans would persist in this insane war to liberate the slaves until every white man was killed—unless the voters elected a Peace Democrat as president in November.

For political as well as military reasons, therefore, Grant wanted to avoid a war of attrition and siege. Once again he planned a series of coordinated maneuvers to cut Lee's communications, flank him out of his trenches, and force him into the open for a showdown battle. But once more he was frustrated by the Confederates' quick response to his moves and by the poor performance of some of his own generals.

Out in the Shenandoah Valley, General David Hunter had replaced Sigel as commander of the Union forces. Although a West Point graduate and a professional soldier, Hunter was also a radical antislavery man who was appointed to this command in part to gratify radical Republicans. Grant ordered Hunter to advance up the valley, to cut its railroad links with Richmond, and to destroy the Confederate supply depot at Lynchburg. Meanwhile, Grant sent part of Sheridan's cavalry to tear up the railroad east of the valley. After accomplishing this, Sheridan was to join Hunter for a raid on the James River Canal and the railroads southwest of Richmond. At the same time, the Army of the Potomac would cross the James southeast of Richmond to cut Lee's rail links through Petersburg and to crush the Army of Northern Virginia when it fought to protect these lifelines, as it must.

Hunter started well. He routed a small Confederate force at Piedmont and moved toward Lynchburg. Exasperated by guerrilla attacks on their supplies, his ill-disciplined soldiers looted and burned as they went. They burned the Virginia Military Institute in Lexington on June 11, an action that infuriated Southerners everywhere. Alarmed by this threat to his rear, Lee dispatched more than 10,000 troops under Jubal Early to attack Hunter and sent most of his cavalry to intercept Sheridan. Now commanded by Wade Hampton of South Carolina, the Rebel cavalry clashed with the Yankee horsemen June 11–12 in a drawn battle near Trevilian Station. Learning that Hunter was ninety miles away from him behind the Blue Ridge Mountains, Sheridan abandoned the attempt to join him and returned eastward after doing only minor damage to the railroads. Meanwhile the Confederates under Early had moved faster than Hunter. They concentrated at Lynchburg a force as large as Hunter's and repelled weak Federal attacks there on June 18. Short of supplies and ammunition, with Confederate cavalry and guerrillas across his escape route to the north, Hunter retreated into West Virginia. Not only had he failed in the mission Grant had set for him; he had left the whole Shenandoah Valley open to Early's veterans.

Before Grant learned of Hunter's and Sheridan's rebuffs, his own maneuver against Petersburg had also miscarried. The operation started brilliantly. On the night of June 12–13, the Army of the Potomac silently pulled out of its trenches at Cold Harbor and moved southward. For three days, Lee remained uncertain about Grant's movements. Thinking that this was another short-range flanking maneuver, the Confederates entrenched a new line east of Richmond and skirmished with the Union cavalry screen while Yankee engineer troops built the longest pontoon bridge in history (2,200 feet) across the James River. By June 15, two blue corps were south of the river and the rest were on their way while Lee's entire army was still on the north side. General Beauregard held the formidable Petersburg defenses with only 2,500 troops against the oncoming 18th Corps, which outnumbered him by seven to one. If Petersburg fell, Richmond would have to be evacuated, Lee's army would be cut off—and perhaps the war would be over.

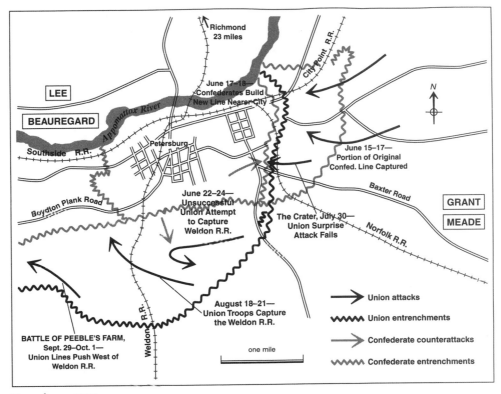

Petersburg, 1864

But with this opportunity in their hands, Union corps commanders fumbled. Coming up to the Petersburg defenses on the afternoon of June 15, General William F. Smith's 18th Corps carried part of the thinly defended line. One of the Union's few successes that day was the capture of two artillery batteries by a division of black soldiers. There was irony in this, for two years earlier Smith had been one of McClellan's protégés—a Democrat and an opponent of emancipation who had been transferred out of the Army of the Potomac in the reshuffle after Fredericksburg. Now back in Virginia with a chance to redeem himself by leading his white and black troops into Petersburg, he hesitated, overestimated Rebel strength, and then decided against making a night attack despite the bright moonlight.

More such failures occurred during the next three days. Although Beauregard received reinforcements from Lee's army, the bluecoats still outnumbered him by four or five to one on June 16. A Northern assault late that day carried part of the enemy line; but lack of coordination among the various Union corps enabled Beauregard to prevent a breakthrough. The story was the same next day, for though the Yankees captured more positions and it seemed to Beauregard that "the last hour of the Confederacy had arrived," poor staff work down the chain of command in the Union army produced delays and contradictory orders that paralyzed the advance. That night Beauregard pulled his line back another mile, almost to the outskirts of Petersburg, while Lee marched the rest of his lean veterans to these trenches as fast as they could go. Grant planned an assault for June 18, before all of them could arrive. As on previous days he left the tactical arrangements to Meade. This may have been a mistake, for once again the command system of the Army of the Potomac operated sluggishly. The short-tempered Meade finally sent bristling messages to his generals: "I find it useless to appoint an hour to effect cooperation. . . . What additional orders to attack you require I cannot imagine. . . . Finding it impossible to effect cooperation by appointing an hour for attack, I have sent an order to each corps commander to attack at all hazards and without reference to each other."[19]

Part of the problem was that officers and men alike were infected with what might be termed the "Cold Harbor syndrome"—a reluctance to make head-on assaults against trenches. "The men feel just at present a great horror and dread of attacking earthworks again," said one general; while another wrote that the soldiers had been "foolishly and wantonly sacrificed" in suicidal attacks against trenches. On the afternoon of June 18, a veteran unit refused to obey an order to charge a strongly held point in the Confederate line, and yelled to a regiment of new men preparing for the assault: "Lie down, you damn fools, you can't take them forts!" The rookies went in anyway, and lost 632 of their 850 men.[20]

Grant and Meade finally called off the attacks. The Federals had bungled their chance to take Petersburg before Confederate reinforcements made it impossible. The Yankees lost more than 11,000 men in four days of fighting, the Rebels fewer than half that many. The Army of the Potomac had been bled white in the fighting from the Wilderness to Petersburg, suffering about 64,000 casualties, which by grim coincidence equaled the number of combat troops in Lee's army at the beginning of the campaign. These losses, plus the expiration of service for another 18,000 men during the spring and summer, caused the Army of the Potomac to lose its fighting edge. Lee had also lost half of his original army; but the remainder, plus reinforcements and Beauregard's veterans, were protected by miles of elaborate trenches, redans, forts, and abatis. Grant reluctantly settled down for the siege he had hoped to avoid. The Union cavalry and infantry made periodic raids to cut Lee's rail and road communications south of Petersburg. Although these actions achieved only partial success, they did worsen Lee's already serious supply problems. Grant also extended his entrenched lines inexorably south and west, to force Lee to thin his defenses by stretching his own lines.

The Battle of the Crater

The most promising Federal bid to break these defenses—the famous battle of the Crater—ended in tragic fiasco, once again illustrating the bad luck and incompetent officers that plagued the Army of the Potomac. Holding a section of the Union line opposite a Confederate artillery redan was the 48th Pennsylvania, containing many coal miners from Schuylkill County. One day the regiment's colonel, Henry Pleas-

---

[19] *O.R.,* Ser. 1, Vol. 40, pt. 2, pp. 167, 179, 205.
[20] Catton, *Stillness at Appomattox,* pp. 168, 170, 198.

ants, overheard a soldier say that "we could blow that damned fort out of existence if we could run a mine shaft under it."[21] A civil engineer, Pleasants liked the idea and persuaded General Burnside (now a corps commander in the army that had once been his) to endorse it. Meade's engineers scoffed at the project as "claptrap and nonsense," for the shaft would have to run more than 500 feet to reach Confederate lines, requiring ventilation holes that the Rebels would be sure to see. But Pleasants devised an ingenious (and invisible) ventilation system, and his men drove the shaft under the enemy lines without any help from the army's engineer corps. They then filled it with four tons of gunpowder.

Initially skeptical, Grant grew hopeful that the mine would blow a hole in the Confederate trenches through which a heavy assault could roll up the lines right and left and drive straight into Petersburg itself. In Burnside's 9th Corps were three white divisions that had seen hard fighting since the Wilderness, and one black division that had seen no real combat at all. Despite the successful record of black troops on several fronts, including the June 15 attack on the outer defenses of Petersburg, most officers in the Army of the Potomac still doubted their fighting ability. But Burnside, a New Englander with antislavery sympathies, decided to give his black division special assault training to lead the attack. The soldiers reacted with enthusiasm to this assignment. "Both officers and men," wrote one of the brigade commanders, "were eager to show the white troops what the colored division could do."[22]

The explosion of the mine was scheduled for the predawn darkness of July 30. The black division was ready to lead off, but at the last minute Meade, with Grant's approval, ordered the white divisions to be sent in first. The generals evidently still distrusted the combat reliability of this division; moreover, they did not want to be accused of using black soldiers as cannon fodder. Testifying later before the Committee on the Conduct of the War, Grant said that if black troops had led the assault and the battle turned out badly, it would have been said "that we were shoving those people ahead to get killed because we did not care anything about them. But that could not be said if we put white troops in front."[23]

Deflated by Meade's order to change the attack formation, Burnside provided poor tactical leadership. The mine blew 300 Rebels high into the air and blasted a hole 170 feet long, 60 feet wide, and 30 feet deep. It was the most awesome spectacle of the war. For 200 yards on either side of the crater the stupefied Confederates abandoned their trenches and ran for the rear. But from then on everything went wrong for the Federals. Unprepared for its mission, the leading white division went forward in disorganized fashion while its commander stayed in the rear calming his nerves by swilling rum begged from the surgeon. The bluecoats came to the edge of the crater, gaped at the sight, and milled around in confusion. Many of them went *into* the crater instead of fanning out right and left and forming for a further advance. Generals in the rear sent up more troops; the crater became packed with disorganized men; the Confederates recovered from the shock, brought up artillery, and fired at Yankees in the crater as at fish in a barrel; the Southern infantry counterattacked

---

[21] Ibid., p. 220.

[22] Dudley T. Cornish, *The Sable Arm: Negro Troops in the Union Army* (New York, 1956), p. 273.

[23] Ibid., p. 274.

and pushed back the few Federal units that had moved out from the crater. By the time the black division went into action, the battle was lost. Soldiers had to push their way through panic-stricken white troops streaming to the rear. The blacks fought well under the circumstances and suffered more casualties than any other division, but they too were driven back in confusion. Many Rebel soldiers, enraged beyond reason that the Yankees had sent former slaves against them, bayoneted or shot black men who were trying to surrender.

Admitting failure, Grant finally called off the attack. "It was the saddest affair I have witnessed in the war," he wired Washington. "Such opportunity for carrying fortifications I have never seen and do not expect again to have." Confederate General William Mahone, who organized the counterattack, wrote that for an hour after the explosion "there was nothing to prevent the . . . cutting [of] the Confederate army in twain . . . opening wide the gates to the rear of the Confederate capital."[24] After the Crater, the siege of Petersburg went on about as before. A huge hole in the ground remains to this day as a monument to a lost opportunity.

Early's Raid on Washington

This fiasco did not exhaust the Union's bitter cup of defeat during July 1864. On the same day as the battle of the Crater (July 30), Confederate cavalry from the Shenandoah Valley rode into the town of Chambersburg, Pennsylvania, and burned much of it to the ground when its citizens refused to pay a tribute of $500,000. This was Jubal Early's parting shot in a raid that had carried his small army to the outskirts of Washington itself three weeks earlier. After Early had driven David Hunter's Union forces out of the valley in June, his 14,000 gray veterans, many of whom had fought in the valley under Jackson, marched north in an attempt to repeat Jackson's 1862 strategy of relieving the pressure on Richmond by threatening Washington. The Rebels crossed the Potomac July 5, scattered a scratch force of Federals at the Monocacy River east of Frederick on July 9, and came up to the fortifications northwest of Washington itself on July 11. The defenses were manned initially by a handful of troops, hastily mobilized government clerks, and raw militia, for Grant had combed out most of the garrison for front-line service in Virginia. In response to the government's call for help, Grant sent the 6th Corps from Petersburg. These tough veterans filed into the works on July 11. After studying the situation, Early decided that he had better retreat to Virginia before being crushed between these troops in his front and Hunter's force, finally on its way from West Virginia, in his rear.

To Lincoln's and Grant's disgust, Early got away safely after burning the house of Postmaster General Blair in Maryland and levying $220,000 on the cities of Hagerstown and Frederick in addition to burning Chambersburg. Union pursuit was hampered by conflicts of authority among generals commanding four separate departments. In early August, Grant cut through this red tape by abolishing these departments and sending Sheridan to the valley as overall commander of a newly created Department and Army of the Shenandoah, consisting of the 6th Corps and two cavalry divisions from the Army of the Potomac, Hunter's former

---

[24] *O.R.,* Ser. 1, Vol. 40, pt. 1, p. 17; William Mahone, "The Crater," in James H. Stine, *History of the Army of the Potomac* (Philadelphia, 1892), pp. 675–676.

Army of West Virginia, and two divisions transferred from the Louisiana theater. Grant ordered the hard-driving Sheridan to go after Early and "follow him to the death." Since the Shenandoah Valley was a source of food for Lee's army and a favorite stamping ground for guerrillas, Grant also told Sheridan to destroy the valley's crops so thoroughly that "crows flying over it for the balance of the season will have to carry their provender with them."[25]

The Atlanta Campaign, May–July 1864

Sheridan would do just that, but first he had to organize his new command. Far to the south, another general who would soon achieve fame as a destroyer of Confederate resources was also resting and reorganizing in preparation for a final move against Atlanta. In three months, Sherman's army had inflicted nearly 28,000 casualties on the Confederates while suffering only 25,000 themselves. In Virginia, by comparison, while the Confederates had lost about 36,000, they had exacted nearly twice that number in return.

Overview of the Campaign

This contrast in casualty ratios reflected the different tactics in the two theaters. Grant and Lee both favored attack and all-out battle as a means of destroying the enemy. Sherman and Johnston engaged in a war of maneuver. Rather than assault the Confederates' strong defensive positions, Sherman executed a series of flanking movements that forced Johnston repeatedly to fall back to protect his communications. Only once, at Kenesaw Mountain, did Sherman order a frontal assault, with no more success than Grant at Cold Harbor. Although Johnston retreated toward Atlanta as Lee did toward Richmond, such maneuvers in Virginia usually occurred *after* big battles; in Georgia they occurred *without* large-scale fighting. Johnston lost fewer men in the first month of his campaign than Lee did in two days at the Wilderness.

Nearly half of all Confederate casualties in the Atlanta campaign from May through July would occur in the last two weeks of July, after John B. Hood replaced Johnston as commander of the Army of Tennessee. Dissatisfied with Johnston's Fabian strategy, the Confederate government put Hood in his place with the expectation that this hard-fighting transfer from Lee's army would attack and smash the Yankees. Hood did attack, three times, but it was the Yankees who did the smashing. Hood's battered army returned to its trenches, while Sherman settled down for a siege of Atlanta.

The strategy of the Atlanta campaign was dictated by railroads and topography. Atlanta's importance as a rail junction (and manufacturing center) made it a Union objective that came to overshadow Sherman's primary goal of destroying the Confederate army. The mountainous ridges and steep valleys of northern Georgia formed defensive barriers far stronger than the rolling countryside and sluggish rivers of eastern Virginia. For their supplies, both armies in Georgia were tied to the same rickety single-track railroad running between Chattanooga and Atlanta. Neither army could operate for long out of reach of this railroad; both Sherman and Johnston had

---

[25]Bruce Catton, *Grant Takes Command* (Boston, 1969), pp. 343, 347.

to protect the tracks in their rear at all costs. As Johnston retreated, his supply line grew shorter and more secure while Sherman's grew longer and more vulnerable. But the Yankee repair crews became so proficient that they could rebuild bridges and re-lay rails almost as fast as the Rebels destroyed them.

Narrative of the Campaign

Sherman's combat forces of 100,000 men were grouped in three separate "armies": 61,000 in the Army of the Cumberland under George Thomas; 25,000 in what had once been Sherman's Army of the Tennessee, now commanded by James B. McPherson; and the small Army of the Ohio under John M. Schofield. Johnston's Army of Tennessee numbered 50,000 effectives (soon to be reinforced by 15,000 from Alabama). At the beginning of May, they were entrenched along a rugged, sheer-faced ridge straddling the railroad twenty-five miles south of Chattanooga. Sherman had no intention of assaulting this "terrible door of death." Instead, Thomas and Schofield feinted at the Confederate line while McPherson's fast-marching army swung wide to the right through a mountain gap south of Johnston's left flank to cut the railroad at Resaca. One of the most promising young generals in the army, who had won Grant's and Sherman's praise as a corps commander in the Vicksburg campaign, McPherson performed the first part of his assignment flawlessly. His troops burst through the thinly defended gap on May 9 with a chance to sever Johnston's lifeline and catch the Confederates in a pincers. "I've got Joe Johnston dead!" cried Sherman when he learned of this success.

But McPherson found the Resaca defenses held by the advance brigades of the Alabama reinforcements, whose numbers he overestimated. Instead of attacking, the Federals skirmished cautiously. Thus alerted to this danger on his flank, Johnston skillfully withdrew his whole army on the night of May 12–13 to a prepared defensive position covering Resaca. Although McPherson's caution was justified by his discretionary orders, Sherman was disappointed. "Well, Mac, you have missed the opportunity of a lifetime," Sherman told him. But despite his failure, McPherson remained Sherman's most trusted subordinate.[26]

For three days the two armies probed for an opening in each other's lines around Resaca. While this was going on, Sherman sent part of McPherson's army on another swing to the right. Johnston again fell back to protect his rear. The Confederates stopped briefly fifteen miles to the south, at Adairsville, and skirmished with the pursuing bluecoats before continuing ten miles farther to Cassville, where they turned to fight. Sherman's forces were now spread over a twenty-mile front. On May 19, Johnston planned to attack Schofield's isolated corps on the Union left. He ordered Hood's corps to roll up Schofield's flank while Leonidas Polk's corps held him in front. Hood had come to Georgia with Longstreet for the battle of Chickamauga the previous September and had remained there after Longstreet returned to Virginia. Hood's left arm was crippled from a Gettysburg wound, and his right leg had been amputated at Chickamauga. But these wounds did not abate his pugnacity. During the Atlanta campaign, he complained of Johnston's tendency to retreat without fighting. But given the chance on May 19 to fight, Hood muffed it. Alarmed by a false report of enemy infantry on his flank, he went on the defensive. Johnston's plan for a counterattack

---

[26]Albert Castel, *Decision in the West: The Atlanta Campaign of 1864* (Lawrence, Kans., 1992), p. 150.

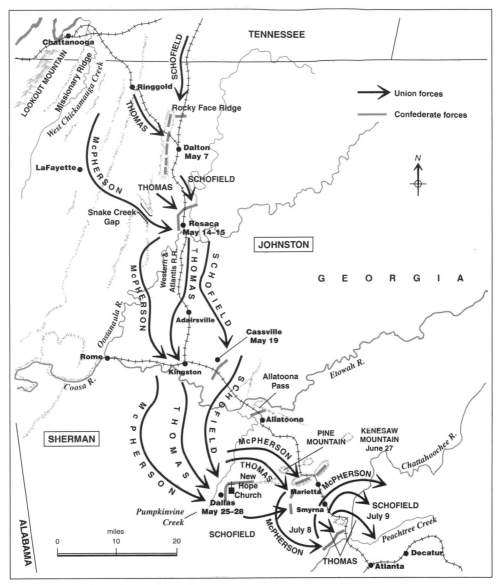

The Campaign for Atlanta, May–July 1864

had to be scrapped. Again the Confederates fell back, first to a line behind Cassville, then eight miles farther south to a strong position on a high ridge behind the Etowah River at Allatoona pass.

In two weeks of much marching and little fighting, the Atlanta campaign had begun to resemble the intricate steps of a minuet. The two armies faced each other; Sherman sidestepped gracefully to his right and forward, Johnston stepped back to conform, and after nodding to each other they repeated the process. Johnston stepped back each time to trenches previously dug by slaves. As the Yankees came up to each new position they constructed their own network of trenches and log breastworks. Sherman organized freed slaves into a "pioneer corps" to assist this work. Southern newspapers began to criticize Johnston for his constant retreats. His apparent unwillingness to fight distressed Jefferson Davis in the same way that McClellan's similar behavior had affected Lincoln two years earlier. But Johnston's defenders pointed out that he was trading space for time and luring Sherman deeper into hostile territory, where sooner or later the Yankees would dash themselves to pieces against the trenches.

Instead of obliging Johnston by attacking at Allatoona, Sherman filled his wagons with twenty days' rations, cut loose from the railroad, and sent his whole army around Johnston's left flank toward the road junction at Dallas, Georgia—fifteen miles in Johnston's rear and only thirty miles from Atlanta. Johnston's efficient cavalry detected the move, and once again the Confederates marched swiftly to entrench a new line near Dallas before the Federals got there. For several days at the end of May, the two armies fought and skirmished in this vicinity, especially around a Methodist meeting house called New Hope Church but renamed "Hell-Hole" by the Yankees. Thick pine woods made this area as difficult for offensive operations as the Wilderness in Virginia. Adding to Sherman's discomfiture were heavy rains, which began in late May and continued for a month, turning the red clay roads into bottomless mire and crippling the armies' mobility. Sherman sidestepped his lines a mile or two eastward each day. Johnston conformed to every move until by the second week of June both armies were again astride the railroad with the Confederate right anchored on Kenesaw Mountain just north of Marietta.

During these maneuvers the volatile Sherman grew edgy. Although the Confederates had retreated seventy miles, the wily Johnston had used the terrain skillfully to avoid the open, decisive battle that Sherman sought. Meanwhile, far away in Mississippi, Forrest's cavalry routed a force twice its size at Brice's Crossroads on June 10. Fearing that Forrest would now move into Tennessee to cut the railroad between Nashville and Chattanooga, Sherman ordered two infantry divisions plus cavalry to move out from Memphis "and follow Forrest to the death, if it cost 10,000 lives and breaks the Treasury. There never will be peace in Tennessee till Forrest is dead."[27] The Union troops drew Forrest into battle at Tupelo, Mississippi, and defeated him. Forrest was wounded during the fighting, but refused to conform to Sherman's wish and later returned to action.

The neutralization of Forrest temporarily relieved Sherman of concern about Tennessee. But Johnston was still entrenched along a seven-mile line in his front, blocking the way to Atlanta. Sherman decided to make a head-on assault. His reasons for doing so are not entirely clear. He was apparently worried that this campaign of maneuver and entrenchment was robbing his men of their fighting edge. "A fresh furrow in a plowed field will stop the whole column, and all begin to entrench," he complained. "We are on the offensive and . . .must assail and not defend."[28] Sherman reasoned that Johnston must have weakened his center to protect his flanks against

---

[27]*O.R.*, Ser. 1, Vol. 39, pt. 2, p. 121.
[28]Ibid., Vol. 38, pt. 4, p. 507.

another turning maneuver, so he ordered an attack on the Rebel center June 27. The main assaults were carried out by three divisions against two hills south of Kenesaw Mountain proper, while the rest of the army feinted against the mountain and the flanks. But Johnston was not caught napping. His troops repelled the blue attacks with a loss of only 600 men while inflicting five times that many casualties.

These losses were small compared with those in Virginia, but costly enough to cause Sherman to renew his flanking tactics. Once more he sent McPherson on a wide swing around the Confederate left. Once more Johnston fell back, this time to a position north of the Chattahoochee River only eight miles from Atlanta. Instead of attacking this line as Johnston hoped he would, Sherman sent cavalry to his right on a pretended search for a crossing in that direction and massed Schofield's army to force a crossing on the opposite flank. Schofield surprised the Rebel pickets and pushed his corps across a quickly built pontoon bridge before Johnston was aware of the danger. One corps of McPherson's mobile Midwesterners followed, proving that they could move to their left as well as to their right. With nearly a third of the Union army across the river on his flank, Johnston abandoned his line and withdrew behind Peachtree Creek on the night of July 9–10.

Removal of Johnston from Command

Southern criticism of Johnston rose to a crescendo. Hostility between Johnston and Jefferson Davis had been smoldering since 1861. As Davis saw it, in 1862 Johnston had retreated all the way up the Virginia peninsula to Richmond and might have lost the capital had not fortune put Robert E. Lee in his place. In 1863, Johnston had failed to come to the aid of Vicksburg's besieged defenders. Now he had been driven all the way back to Atlanta without a real battle. The Confederate cabinet unanimously recommended the general's removal from command. "Johnston is determined not to fight," said Secretary of State Judah Benjamin. "It is of no use to re-enforce him, he is not going to fight."[29]

Johnston later insisted that he had planned to attack the Federals as they crossed Peachtree Creek. But at the time he refused to commit himself to any specific course of action. In reply to a telegram from Davis on July 16, Johnston said that his plan must "depend upon that of the enemy. It is mainly to watch for an opportunity to fight for advantage. We are trying to put Atlanta in condition to be held . . . by the Georgia militia, that army movements may be freer and wider." To the administration, Johnston's last sentence implied an intention to abandon Atlanta, just as a year earlier he had ordered Pemberton to give up Vicksburg. The consequences of losing Atlanta would be enormous. In the eyes of both North and South, the city had become a symbol of Confederate resistance second only to Richmond. Johnston's apparent unwillingness to defend the city or to strike Sherman a blow sealed his fate. On July 17, the secretary of war informed him that "as you have failed to arrest the advance of the enemy to the vicinity of Atlanta, far in the interior of Georgia . . . you are hereby relieved of command." Hood took over the army.[30]

---

[29]William C. Davis, *Jefferson Davis: The Man and His Hour* (New York, 1991), p. 560.
[30]*O.R.,* Ser. 1, Vol. 38, pt. 5, pp. 882–883, 885.

This action was controversial then and remains so today. Johnston was popular with his troops, who appreciated the Fabian strategy that kept the army intact and minimized casualties. Many officers distrusted Hood's aggressiveness. Sherman later wrote that "the Confederate Government rendered us most valuable service" by removing Johnston. Hood's reputation as an offensive fighter, said Sherman, "was just what we wanted . . . to fight in open ground, on any thing like equal terms, instead of being forced to run up against prepared intrenchments."[31] Many historians have criticized Davis for removing Johnston. But their appraisals, like Sherman's, have benefited from hindsight. Political and military circumstances made it as difficult for Davis to retain Johnston in command in 1864 as it had been for Lincoln to keep McClellan in 1862.

The Battles for Atlanta

The conditions of Hood's appointment virtually compelled him to attack as soon as possible. After crossing the Chattahoochee, Sherman had sent McPherson on another flanking march to the east to get astride the railroad between Atlanta and the Carolinas, break it up, and prevent any possibility of Lee or Hood reinforcing each other by rail. While McPherson's boys were ripping up the tracks, Hood on July 20 launched an assault on the flank of Thomas's Army of the Cumberland, separated from the other two Union armies by a gap of two miles. Hood hoped to hit two of Thomas's corps while they were crossing Peachtree Creek, but his attack started late, the bluecoats were ready, and the Rebels dashed themselves to pieces against Yankee breastworks. During the night Hood withdrew two miles into the Atlanta fortifications. Sherman invested the city on the north and east. Hood discovered that McPherson's left flank east of the city was in the air, and on the night of July 21–22 he sent a corps on a long march to roll up that flank next morning. The Confederate attack gained some initial success, including the killing of McPherson, but by hard fighting the Army of the Tennessee restored its lines and drove the gray infantry back into the Atlanta defenses with heavy casualties.

Sherman named Oliver O. Howard to succeed McPherson and promptly ordered him to take the Army of the Tennessee on a long swing around the west side of Atlanta to strike toward the city's remaining rail links to the south. At the same time, Sherman sent his cavalry in three columns to tear up the same railroads farther south. Four divisions of Confederate infantry moved out to counter Howard's thrust. In a battle near Ezra Church on July 28, the Yankees for the third time in nine days punished the attackers fearfully. In these three battles Hood lost more than 13,000 men, compared with Union casualties of 6,000. Confederate morale declined and desertions increased. Less than three weeks after he had given Hood command of the army with tacit orders to attack, Jefferson Davis instructed the general not to risk any more assaults. But Hood's last attack at Ezra Church did halt Howard's envelopment

---

[31]William T. Sherman, "The Grand Strategy of the Last Year of the War," in *Battles and Leaders of the Civil War,* 4 vols. (New York, 1887), IV, 253; William T. Sherman, *Memoirs,* 2d ed. rev., 2 vols. (New York, 1886), II, 72.

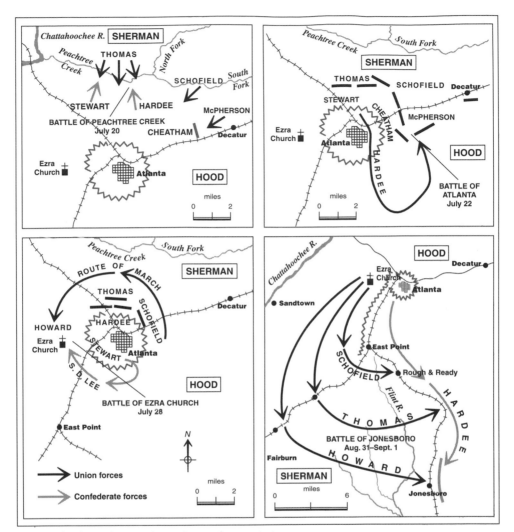

The Battles for Atlanta, July 20–September 1, 1864

short of the railroad. And Confederate cavalry commander Joseph Wheeler brilliantly countered the mounted Union thrusts (thereby confirming Sherman's low opinion of his own cavalry, which had been frequently outmaneuvered by Rebel horsemen during the campaign). Wheeler divided his mounted force into three columns, each of which headed off and defeated the blue troopers before they could do serious damage to the railroad.

Foiled in his attempts to cut Hood's lifeline and pry him out of Atlanta, Sherman settled down for an artillery bombardment of the city's defenses while he contemplated his next move. In three months he had driven the Confederates back ninety miles while inflicting more losses on the enemy than suffered by his own army. No other strategic offensive of the war except Grant's Vicksburg campaign accomplished so much at such relatively low cost. One of the foremost military theorists of the twentieth century, the British writer B. H. Liddell Hart, considered Sherman the greatest Civil War general because his employment of mobile tactics and the "indirect approach" in this campaign overcame the bloody stalemate of trench warfare in a fashion that could have been profitably studied by World War I generals.[32]

But in July 1864 little of this was evident to the Northern people, who saw only that Sherman was checked before Atlanta just as Grant was before Petersburg. The hopes of May for quick victory had been drowned in the sorrows of 100,000 Northern battle casualties. "Who shall revive the withered hopes that bloomed at the opening of Grant's campaign?" asked the *New York World*. "Patriotism is played out," declared another Democratic newspaper. "All are tired of this damnable tragedy. . . . Each hour is but sinking us deeper into bankruptcy and desolation."[33] Northern war weariness augured ill for the Republicans in the forthcoming presidential election, which was shaping up as a referendum on the war.

---

[32]Basil H. Liddell Hart, *Sherman: Soldier, Realist, American* (New York, 1929), esp. chaps. 16–18. In contrast Albert Castel, *Decision in the West,* is critical of Sherman for alleged missed opportunities that might have resulted in quicker and more complete success.

[33]*New York World,* July 12, 1864; Frank L. Klement, *The Copperheads in the Middle West* (Chicago, 1960), p. 233.

The Third Turning Point: The Election of 1864

This morning, as for some days past, it seems exceedingly probable that this Administration will not be re-elected. Then it will be my duty to cooperate with the President elect, as to save the Union between the election and the inauguration; as he will have secured his election on such ground that he cannot possibly save it afterwards.

—Abraham Lincoln,
August 23, 1864

471

Peace Feelers

Northern war weariness in the summer of 1864 revived the prospects of Peace Democrats. Clement Vallandigham boldly returned from his year-long exile in Canada. Not wanting to martyr him again, Lincoln allowed Vallandigham to stay and to speak out against the war. Democratic conventions in the Midwest adopted resolutions calling for an armistice and peace negotiations. Democratic congressmen introduced resolutions of similar purport. Although a coalition of Republicans and War Democrats voted down these resolutions, peace sentiment seemed to have gained so much momentum that Republicans despaired of the party's chances in the fall elections.

The most despairing was Horace Greeley, the eccentric but influential editor of the *New York Tribune*. A radical but also something of a pacifist, Greeley was notorious for his vagaries. He had oscillated between militancy and defeatism since 1860. In early 1864, he supported the Chase-for-President movement because Lincoln was not radical enough. But in midsummer he wrote to the President: "Our bleeding, bankrupt, almost dying country . . . longs for peace—shudders at the prospect of fresh conscriptions,[1] of further wholesale devastations, and of new rivers of human blood." If the administration did not do something to meet this longing, "we shall be beaten out of sight next November."[2]

Greeley's letter launched one of the most bizarre incidents of the war. Through an intermediary, the *Tribune* editor had learned that Confederate emissaries were in Niagara Falls, Canada, prepared to open peace negotiations. Confederate agents were indeed there, but they had no accreditation as peace negotiators. Rather, they were part of the Confederacy's secret service network sent to Canada to plot the escape of Southern prisoners from war prisons, to rig the gold market in New York, to establish contacts with Peace Democrats, and to do anything else they could to undermine the Union war effort. Greeley urged Lincoln to give these "negotiators" safe conduct to Washington. Lincoln had a pretty good idea of what the Rebel agents were up to, but he authorized Greeley to make contact with them and to bring to Washington "any person anywhere professing to have any proposition of Jefferson Davis in writing, for peace, embracing the restoration of the Union and abandonment of slavery."[3]

This put Greeley on the spot, for it made him responsible for verifying the credentials of the negotiators. The editor balked, but Lincoln sent his private secretary, John Hay, to New York to prod Greeley into action. Together Hay and Greeley went to Niagara Falls, where they held two interviews with the Confederate agents. These conversations succeeded only in revealing the Southerners' lack of credentials. Having obtained Lincoln's statement of peace terms, the agents leaked these terms and their own reply to the Associated Press. The Confederate reply was intended for propaganda purposes. Lincoln's terms, it charged, meant further death and destruction, for they precluded negotiations by prescribing conditions known to be unacceptable to the South.

Similar publicity surrounded a second peace mission that occurred simultaneously with the Greeley fiasco. In this case, two unaccredited Northern emissaries sought and obtained an interview with Jefferson Davis to discuss peace terms. The two were freelance journalist James R. Gilmore and Colonel James Jaquess of the 73rd Illinois Infantry. Jaquess was a Methodist clergyman with a good war record who yearned for an honorable way to stop Christians from slaughtering each other. Lincoln believed that he had nothing to lose and perhaps something to gain from this mission. He al-

---

[1] On July 18 Lincoln issued a call for 500,000 new volunteers, with deficiencies in district quotas to be filled by a draft in September. When one Copperhead editor read this call, he exulted: "Lincoln is deader than dead." [Frank L. Klement, *The Copperheads in the Middle West* (Chicago, 1960), p. 233.]

[2] Greeley to Lincoln, July 7, August 8, 1864, Lincoln Papers, Library of Congress.

[3] Roy P. Basler (ed.), *The Collected Works of Abraham Lincoln,* 9 vols. (New Brunswick, N.J., 1953–1955), VII, 435.

lowed Gilmore and Jaquess to pass through the lines to Richmond, where Davis and Secretary of State Judah Benjamin received them on July 17. In a candid interview, the two Northerners conveyed Lincoln's peace terms: Union, abolition, amnesty, and perhaps partial compensation to owners of emancipated slaves. Davis knew that Lincoln could not commit Congress on the last point. But it mattered little, for the Confederate president insisted on no peace terms short of Southern independence. "Amnesty, Sir, applies to criminals," Davis told the emissaries. "We have committed no crime. . . . Extermination [is] preferable to such dishonor. . . . We will [fight] on *unless you acknowledge our right to self-government.*"[4]

Gilmore's account of this meeting was published in a Boston newspaper on July 22—by coincidence the same day that the first detailed reports of the Greeley negotiations were published. In retrospect it became clear that each side in both of these affairs was more interested in scoring propaganda points than in opening serious negotiations. Each president knew that the other's terms were unacceptable. But neither could ignore the significant peace movements among his people. Several peace candidates had won seats in the 1863 Confederate congressional elections; antiwar and pro-Union sentiments in upcountry districts of North Carolina, Alabama, and elsewhere were stronger than ever; advocates of peace negotiations included the Confederate vice president himself. By publicizing the unofficial peace missions, each side hoped to show its own people that the enemy's conditions for negotiations would mean the loss of everything they were fighting for: in the case of the South, independence and slavery; in the case of the North, Union and emancipation.

The Confederacy won greater short-run benefits in this propaganda war. Because Lincoln's peace terms included both Union and emancipation, Northern Democrats were able to exploit a belief that the North could have peace if the government would drop its insistence on emancipation. "Tens of thousands of white men must yet bite the dust to allay the negro mania of the President," ran a typical Democratic editorial. During August this notion gained ground, as stalemate continued on the battlefronts and Northern morale plunged to rock bottom. "The people are wild for peace," wrote the shrewd New York politico Thurlow Weed. "Lincoln's re-election is an impossibility." Bleak reports from Republican state chairmen poured in to Henry J. Raymond, chairman of the Republican National Committee (and also editor of the *New York Times*). "I fear that the desire for peace," wrote Raymond, "aided by the impression that Mr. Lincoln . . . is fighting not for the Union but for the abolition of slavery, and by the draft, the tax, the lack of victories . . . will overbear [the administration] and give control of everything to the Opposition."[5]

On August 22, Raymond suggested to Lincoln a plan to counteract the false notion that "we *can* have peace with Union if we would." He urged the President to appoint a commission to offer the Confederates peace on the sole condition of Union, with "all remaining questions" (i.e., slavery and the terms of reconstruction) to be adjusted later. If Davis spurned this offer, as Raymond was sure he would, the

---

[4]Edward C. Kirkland, *The Peacemakers of 1864* (New York, 1927), pp. 85–96; Hudson Strode, *Jefferson Davis,* 3 vols. (New York, 1955–1964), III, 74–81.

[5]*Columbus Crisis,* August 3, 1864, quoted in V. Jacque Voegeli, *Free but Not Equal* (Chicago, 1967), p. 146; Francis Brown, *Raymond of the Times* (New York, 1951), pp. 259–260.

ABRAHAM LINCOLN IN 1864.
Lincoln considered himself the ugliest man he had ever known; few contradicted him. Yet the beard and the lines limned in his face by the pressures of his job gave his countenance a nobility familiar to the millions who have viewed the image of this much-portrayed president. Because of the time-shutter requirements of photography in the 1860s, none of the pictures of this man with a famous sense of humor shows him smiling.

LIBRARY OF CONGRESS

rejection would "dispel all the delusions about peace that prevail in the North, silence the clamors and damaging falsehoods of the opposition, [and] . . . reconcile public sentiment to the War, the draft, & the tax as inevitable necessities." Lincoln went so far as to incorporate Raymond's suggestions into a draft of instructions for a peace commission. He also drafted a letter to a Democratic editor that concluded with the words: "If Jefferson Davis . . . wishes to know what I would do if he were to offer peace and re-union, saying nothing about slavery, let him try me."[6]

But Lincoln did not send this letter. Nor did he appoint a peace commission as Raymond had urged. At a meeting on August 25, the President convinced the editor that such a course would be misconstrued in the North as a retreat from emancipation. This would be "worse than losing the Presidential contest—it would be ignominiously surrendering it in advance," for it would alienate antislavery Republicans by seeming to confirm their suspicions of Lincoln's softness on slavery. Beyond that, it would also appear to be a betrayal of the "solemn promise" of freedom embodied in the Emancipation Proclamation.[7]

---

[6]Basler, *Works of Lincoln,* VII, 517–518, 501.
[7]Ibid., pp. 518, 500, 507.

Lincoln knew about the flurry of meetings among Republican dissidents who hoped to replace him with a different candidate. By the last week of August, these dissidents had gone so far as to prepare a call for a new Republican national convention to nominate another candidate. This movement was motivated partly by radical hostility to Lincoln's reconstruction policy and partly by a despairing conviction that the President could not win reelection. Lincoln shared the latter conviction. On August 23, he wrote the following memorandum and asked his cabinet to endorse it, sight unseen: "This morning, as for some days past, it seems exceedingly probable that this Administration will not be re-elected. Then it will be my duty to cooperate with the President elect, as to save the Union between the election and the inauguration; as he will have secured his election on such ground that he cannot possibly save it afterwards."[8]

The Democrats Nominate McClellan

When he wrote these words, Lincoln expected the Democrats to nominate McClellan on a peace platform. After his removal from command of the Army of the Potomac in November 1862, McClellan had lived quietly in New Jersey and New York. Many of his friends had worked for his restoration to command, and failing in that had urged him to seek vindication through politics. In the fall of 1863, McClellan declared his open opposition to the administration by publicly endorsing the Democratic candidate for governor of Pennsylvania, and by the end of the year he had discreetly made known his availability for the presidency. McClellan's views on the war had not changed since 1862. He still opposed emancipation but favored restoration of the Union by military victory. This made him objectionable to the peace wing of the party, which favored an armistice followed by negotiations. Because of the intraparty conflict and the uncertainty of Union military prospects, the Democrats postponed their convention from July 4 to August 29—nearly three months after the Republican convention that had renominated Lincoln. When the Democrats finally met in Chicago, they "bridged the crack" between the party's two wings by nominating McClellan while allowing Peace Democrats to write the platform and name the vice-presidential candidate (George Pendleton of Ohio). The platform denounced "arbitrary military arrest," "suppression of freedom of speech and of the press," and "disregard of State rights"—a code phrase for slavery, which the Republicans proposed to abolish by a federal constitutional amendment that would override the "state rights" that protected the institution. The key plank declared that "after four years of failure to restore the Union by the experiment of war . . . [we] demand that immediate efforts be made for a cessation of hostilities, with a view to an ultimate convention of the states, or other peaceable means, to the end that, at the earliest practicable moment, peace may be restored on the basis of the Federal Union."[9]

---

[8]Ibid., p. 514.

[9]Edward McPherson, *The Political History of the United States During the Great Rebellion,* 2d ed. (Washington, D.C. , 1865), pp. 419–420.

This plank presented McClellan with a dilemma. Could he run on a platform that put peace first and Union second? Beset by pressures from both wings of the party, McClellan agonized over the wording of his letter of acceptance. The first two drafts endorsed the idea of an armistice, qualified by a proviso that fighting would be renewed if negotiations broke down. But the general's War Democratic friends convinced him that this would be seen as a capitulation to the Confederacy, for few intelligent men believed that if once stopped, the war could be started again. Thus the final version of McClellan's letter reversed the platform's priorities: Union first, then peace. When "our present adversaries are ready for peace, upon the basis of the Union," negotiations could begin in "a spirit of conciliation and compromise. . . . The Union is the one condition of peace—we ask no more."[10]

This letter satisfied most War Democrats and upset some Peace Democrats to the extent that they contemplated a bolt. But they had nowhere else to go, so most of them, including Vallandigham, remained in the fold. In their campaign speeches, the Peace Democrats emphasized the platform while the War Democrats stressed McClellan's letter. This schizophrenia gave Republicans a field day. "The truth is," said a Republican orator, "neither you nor I, nor the Democrats themselves can tell whether they have a peace platform or a war platform. . . . Upon the whole it is both peace and war, that is peace with the rebels but war against their own government."[11]

The Democratic convention helped end Republican divisions. Faced with a tangible threat from a party half opposed to the war and wholly opposed to emancipation, radicals suddenly realized that Lincoln was their only alternative to disaster. The President's insistence on abolition as a condition of peace now began to work in his favor among antislavery people. The plans for a new Republican convention perished. On September 22, Frémont withdrew his third-party candidacy. The next day, Lincoln requested and received the resignation of Postmaster General Montgomery Blair. The Blair family was identified with conservative Republican factions in Maryland and Missouri. Montgomery Blair had been quietly reestablishing old Democratic ties. Radicals suspected that the Blairs had gained a dangerous influence in the administration. Lincoln's request for Blair's resignation was the quid pro quo for Frémont's withdrawal. Republicans went into the campaign as a united party.

---

[10]Charles R. Wilson, "McClellan's Changing Views on the Peace Plank of 1864," *American Historical Review,* 38 (April 1933), 498–505. The three drafts of McClellan's letter showing the transition from peace to Union as the first priority are in the S. L. M. Barlow Papers, Henry E. Huntington Library. The denial by McClellan's most recent biographer that the general endorsed an armistice in his initial drafts, and subsequently changed the wording of his letter of acceptance, is not entirely convincing. See Stephen W. Sears, *George B. McClellan: The Young Napoleon* (New York, 1988), pp. 375–376, and Sears, "McClellan and the Peace Planks of 1864: A Reappraisal," *Civil War History,* 36 (1990), 57–64. Sears ignores or minimizes the meaning of such phrases in McClellan's first three drafts of the letter as his expression of "cordial concurrence" with the platform's call for a "cessation of hostilities," and his statement that "we have fought enough to satisfy the military honor of the two sections." These phrases were deleted in the final draft. See also David E. Long, *The Jewel of Liberty: Abraham Lincoln's Reelection and the End of Slavery* (Mechanicsburg, Pa., 1994), pp. 243–244.

[11]William F. Zornow, *Lincoln and the Party Divided* (Norman, Okla., 1954), p. 139.

Mobile Bay

On the very day that Lincoln had written his defeatist memorandum of August 23, the final act in a three-week drama at Mobile Bay closed this port to blockade runners. It also chalked up the first of a string of Union victories that would end the summer of Northern discontent and mock the Democrats' description of the war as a failure.

After Farragut's fleet had run the forts below New Orleans and captured that city in April 1862, the next obvious saltwater target was Mobile. But Farragut's warships were needed for operations on the Mississippi, and Grant's plans for a campaign against Mobile after the fall of Vicksburg were aborted by Banks's miscarried Red River expedition (see pages 446 and 447). Not until the summer of 1864 could troops and ships be spared for Mobile. The city lay at the head of a bay whose entrance thirty miles to the south was protected by three forts, a minefield, and four warships—including the huge ironclad *Tennessee*. Farragut assembled fourteen wooden ships and four ironclads to hammer the forts from the sea while 5,500 blue soldiers invested them by land. On the morning of August 5, the Union fleet engaged the forts in a spectacular duel of heavy guns. Suddenly, the leading Union ironclad blew up and sank, the victim of a mine. This brought the fleet to a halt under a punishing fire from the two largest forts. But Farragut took his wooden flagship *Hartford* to the head of the line, where he gave the order that immortalized him in the annals of the U.S. Navy: "Damn the torpedoes! Full speed ahead!"[12] The *Hartford* pushed through the minefield safely; the fleet followed; and after passing into Mobile Bay beyond range of the forts, the Union ships turned their attention to the plucky Confederate vessels and pounded them into submission. By 10 A.M., the Federals controlled the waters of Mobile Bay; during the next eighteen days, they forced the forts one after another to surrender. The city of Mobile itself remained in Southern hands, but isolated from the sea it was thereafter of little use to the Confederacy.

The Fall of Atlanta

Important as it was, the victory at Mobile Bay was eclipsed by the capture of Atlanta. After the battles of late July, both armies had sidestepped their trenches southwest from the city, Hood to protect his railroads, and Sherman in an attempt to get at them. In desperation Hood sent his cavalry to cut Sherman's rail communications, but Union crews repaired the damage. On August 25, Sherman launched his final stroke. Pivoting on its right wing, the blue army swung counterclockwise in another flanking move. Completely hoodwinked, Hood thought that his cavalry raid had forced the Federals to fall back. He telegraphed news of his great victory to Richmond, while special trains carried cheering Georgians into Atlanta for a celebration.

---

[12]Whether Farragut shouted these exact words is uncertain. But it is certain that he ordered the fleet through the minefield, with his flagship in the lead.

But even as the celebrants entered the city, the bluecoats reached the railroads twenty miles to the south and began making "Sherman neckties" of the rails—by heating them over bonfires of ties and wrapping them around trees. Finally alerted to his danger, Hood sent two corps to attack the Union troops at Jonesboro. But the Federals, although outnumbered, repulsed the Confederates on August 31. Next day, they counterattacked and drove the Rebels away (see map on page 469). In imminent peril of being surrounded, Hood evacuated the rest of his army and the Georgia militia from Atlanta on the night of September 1–2, after burning everything of military value in the city. The Federals marched into Atlanta the next day and Sherman telegraphed Washington: "Atlanta is ours, and fairly won."

This news electrified the North. "Glorious news this morning—*Atlanta taken at last!!!*" wrote a New Yorker on September 3. "It is (coming at this political crisis) the greatest event of the war." Newspapers praised Sherman as the greatest general since Napoleon. Lincoln, Grant, and Halleck sent effusive congratulations to the red-haired general, whose Atlanta campaign, the President predicted, would become "famous in the annals of war."[13] Overlooked in this chorus of praise was the escape of Hood's army. But the symbolic importance of Atlanta had become so great that the political consequences of its fall eclipsed all else. One Republican newspaper capsulized these consequences in its headline on the fall of Atlanta: "Old Abe's Reply to the Chicago Convention. Is the War a Failure?" The *Richmond Examiner* sadly made the same point from the Southern viewpoint. The "disaster at Atlanta," it lamented, came "in the very nick of time" to "save the party of Lincoln from irretrievable ruin. . . . It will obscure the prospect of peace, late so bright. It will also diffuse gloom over the South."[14] In this war of peoples as well as of armies, such a political achievement more than balanced the military survival of Hood's battered and depleted force.

🛸 Sheridan in the Valley

The next bad news for the South came from Shenandoah Valley. Jubal Early's summer campaign in that vale of Union defeats, climaxed by his march to the outskirts of Washington itself, was one reason why so many Northerners had considered the war a failure. After Grant had sent Sheridan in August to whip Early and lay waste the valley's resources, the two opposing armies in the valley had sparred and skirmished for a month. In contrapuntal harmony, the Army of the Potomac meanwhile attacked first the left of the Confederate lines before Richmond and then the right below Petersburg, forcing Lee to recall a division from the valley and giving Sheridan a two to one numerical advantage over Early. Informed of this by Rebecca Wright, a Quaker schoolteacher in Winchester and a Unionist, Sheridan decided to strike. On September 19, he attacked the Confederate defenses east and north of Winchester. A botched order that tangled one Union corps in its own wagon train

---

[13]Allan Nevins and Milton H. Thomas (eds.), *The Diary of George Templeton Strong,* 4 vols. (New York, 1952), III, 408–481; Basler, *Works of Lincoln,* VII, 533.

[14]Wood Gray, *The Hidden Civil War: The Story of the Copperheads* (New York, 1942), p. 189; Lloyd Lewis, *Sherman: Fighting Prophet* (New York, 1932), p. 409.

caused the fight to go badly for the Federals at first. But with superb battlefield leadership, Sheridan straightened out the mess and sent his cavalry in a picture-book charge against the Rebel flanks while the infantry assaulted the center. Early's left flank crumpled, while the stubborn defenders in the center fell back step by step through the town and then streamed southward through the night to organize a new defensive position along a ridge known as Fisher's Hill, two miles south of Strasburg.

Sheridan came after the Confederates without letup. On September 22, he sent one of his three infantry corps to work its way around the Confederate left at Fisher's Hill while the other two demonstrated in front. Near sunset the flanking corps emerged yelling from the woods to mow down the surprised Confederates on that end, while two miles away their blue comrades converted the demonstration into an attack that sent the whole Rebel line reeling in retreat. Casualties in these two battles were equal on each side—about 5,500—but this represented a loss of nearly one-third of Early's army. The broken Confederates retreated all the way to Brown's Gap eighty miles south of Winchester.

These victories further strengthened Lincoln's reelection bid. James A. Garfield, formerly a general and now a congressman from Ohio, wrote on September 23 that "Sheridan has made a speech in the Shenandoah Valley more powerful and valuable to the Union cause than all the stumpers in the Republic."[15]

Sheridan did not rest on his laurels. His 35,000 men moved up the valley like locusts, carrying out the second part of Grant's orders. On October 7, he reported: "I have destroyed over 2,000 barns filled with wheat, hay, and farming implements; over seventy mills filled with flour and wheat; have driven in front of the army over 4,000 head of stock, and have killed and issued to the troops not less than 3,000 sheep." This was just the beginning. By the time he was done, he said, "the Valley, from Winchester up to Staunton, ninety-two miles, will have little in it for man or beast."[16]

Here was hard war in earnest. Nor was the destruction all on one side. Rebel guerrillas swarmed in the rear of Sheridan's army burning wagon trains and shooting teamsters, couriers, and stragglers. The guerrillas forced Sheridan to detach a third of his front-line force and prevented him from carrying out Grant's original orders to move east across the Blue Ridge and come up on Lee's rear at Petersburg. The bushwhackers also provoked Federal troops into a scorched-earth retaliation that went far beyond Sheridan's initial orders to destroy only property of military value. Thousands of valley residents—Rebel, Unionist, and neutral alike—became penniless, ragged refugees.

Having destroyed the valley's resources, Sheridan withdrew northward in mid-October and prepared to return the 6th Corps to Grant. But the irrepressible Early refused to be counted out. He had been reinforced to three-fifths of the enemy's strength. While Sheridan was in Washington conferring on future plans for his army, Early planned to launch a surprise attack across the north fork of the Shenandoah River against the Union left behind Cedar Creek, near Middletown. Three divisions of gray infantry moved silently into position on the night of October 18–19 and overran

---

[15]Bruce Catton, *Never Call Retreat,* Pocket Books ed. (New York, 1967), p. 369.
[16]*O.R.,* Ser. 1, Vol. 43, pt. 1, pp. 30–31.

the tents of the 8th Corps at dawn. Seven thousand bluecoats fled to the rear in panic. It was the most effective surprise attack of the war. The Rebels kept going and drove the other two Union corps back four miles.

But then the attack ran out of steam. Believing that he had won a great victory, Early did little to stop his men from breaking ranks to plunder the Yankee camps. But half of the blue divisions had not been routed, and the rest were re-forming under the electrifying leadership of Sheridan. The Union commander had returned to Winchester the previous afternoon. When the sounds of battle twelve miles to the south reached him on the morning of October 19, he mounted his horse and galloped toward the battlefield in a ride soon to be celebrated in song and story. As he rode, Sheridan encountered stragglers streaming toward the rear, who stopped and cheered when they saw him. "God *damn* you, don't cheer me!" Sheridan yelled at them. "If you love your country, come up to the front! God *damn* you, don't cheer me! There's lots of fight in you men yet! Come up, God damn you! Come up!"[17]

They continued to cheer, but they also turned around and followed him. The effect of this man's presence on the beaten army was extraordinary. By midafternoon, Sheridan had gotten the stragglers into line and organized a counterattack against the disorganized Confederates. By nightfall, the blue tide had not only washed back over the four miles lost in the morning but had driven the enemy eight miles farther south. Early's army, thrice routed in a month, virtually ceased to exist as a fighting force. For all practical purposes the war in the valley was over except for Rebel guerrilla actions, which continued to tie down large Union detachments.

The Petersburg Front

Sherman and Sheridan had given the Confederacy a one-two punch; now Grant hoped to follow up with a knockout blow. At the end of September, the Army of the Potomac had struck both ends of Lee's lines simultaneously. North of the James the Federals captured Fort Harrison, part of the Richmond defenses, but had been unable to achieve a breakthrough either there or southwest of Petersburg. Again at the end of October, Grant unsuccessfully attacked both flanks. This time the hardest fighting occurred on the Petersburg front, where Union forces tried an end run around the Confederate trenches to strike the railroad entering Petersburg from the west. But Lee's ragged veterans foiled the move and drove the Federals back with heavy losses.

In most of these actions, the new troops in the Army of the Potomac—substitutes, draftees, and bounty men—performed poorly. Large numbers of them surrendered without putting up much of a fight. This was especially true in the once-proud 2nd Corps, which had suffered by far the greatest number of casualties in the bloodletting from the Wilderness to Petersburg. Not until the 6th Corps and Sheridan's cavalry could return from the valley would the Army of the Potomac be capable of real offensive action. Grant failed to strike his knockout blow; but he had forced Lee again to stretch his defensive lines, which now extended thirty-five miles—from the Williamsburg Road east of Richmond to Hatcher's Run southwest of Petersburg. Lee

---

[17]Quoted in Catton, *Never Call Retreat,* p. 374, from a letter of a Union army surgeon written on the day of the battle.

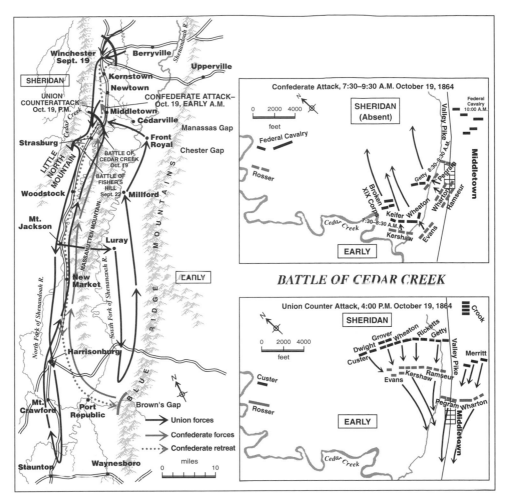

Sheridan's Shenandoah Valley Campaign, 1864

warned Davis that his lines were so thin that unless reinforced "I fear a great calamity will befall us."[18] But the onset of Virginia's coldest winter of the war curtailed operations and postponed the calamity until spring.

The Copperhead Issue in the 1864 Election

As military victories cleared away the political clouds, Republicans lost no opportunity to accuse their opponents of disloyalty. At its mildest, this tactic consisted of arguments that the Rebels desired McClellan's election. Republicans made much of Grant's dispatches from the Petersburg front. "The enemy are exceedingly anxious

---

[18]Clifford Dowdey (ed.), *The Wartime Papers of R. E. Lee* (Boston, 1961), p. 868.

to hold out until after the Presidential election," wrote Grant. "They hope for a counter revolution. . . . Deserters come into our lines daily who tell us that the men are nearly universally tired of the war, and that desertions would be much more frequent, but they believe peace will be negotiated after the fall elections."[19]

Grant and the Republicans may have been more right than they realized. Confederate leaders did indeed believe that McClellan's election would ensure the success of their cause. Vice President Stephens considered the Democratic platform "the first ray of light I have seen from the North since the war began." A Southern army surgeon assumed that if McClellan won, "the war is over. The thought is indescribable. May we not be disappointed." A Confederate secret service agent in Canada sent to Richmond a report on the Northern Democrats: "The platform means peace, unconditionally. . . . McClellan will be under the control of the true peace men. . . . At all events, he is committed by the platform to cease hostilities and to try negotiations. . . . An armistice will inevitably result in peace. The war cannot be renewed if once stopped, even for a short time."[20]

Republicans also did their best to identify Democrats with the antiwar secret societies in the North. The largest of these shadowy organizations had been the Knights of the Golden Circle, which faded away in 1863 when revelations of its ties with the Confederacy destroyed its usefulness. It was replaced by the Order of American Knights, whose membership was concentrated in the southern Midwest. Most members of this order seem in turn to have been absorbed by the Sons of Liberty, formed in February 1864 with none other than Clement Vallandigham as Supreme Grand Commander.

Federal agents infiltrated the Sons of Liberty and compiled a long list of charges against it, which were published in time for Republican use in the 1864 campaign. Among other things, the organization was said to have entered into a conspiracy with Confederate agents to capture a Union warship on Lake Erie, to liberate Southern prisoners of war at several Midwestern prison camps, to burn Northern cities, to stir up antidraft resistance, to foment an armed uprising to form a "Northwest Confederacy," and in general to raise so much hell that Yankee armies in the South would have to come home to deal with the civil war in their rear. Union detectives arrested numerous leaders of these alleged plots, especially in Indiana. Among those tried by a military commission in that state was one Lambdin P. Milligan, whose conviction was reversed two years later in a famous Supreme Court ruling that civilians could not be tried by military tribunals when the civil courts were open.

Republican orators, editors, and pamphleteers drew upon these exposés to link the Democratic party with treason. After all, was not Vallandigham the commander of the Sons of Liberty, and had he not written the Democratic platform? "REBELLION IN THE NORTH!! EXTRAORDINARY DISCLOSURE! Val's Plan to Overthrow the Government! Peace Party Plot!" ran a typical Republican headline. Pamphlets rolled off the presses with such titles as: *Copperhead Conspiracy in the North-West: An Exposé of the Treasonable Order of the Sons of Liberty*. So pervasive was this theme that the Republicans fixed the Copperhead label on the entire Democratic party, a stigma from which the party did not recover for a generation.

---

[19]Grant to Elihu Washburne, August 16, 1864, quoted in Bruce Catton, *Grant Takes Command* (Boston, 1969), p. 355; Grant to Stanton, September 13, 1864, in *O.R.*, Ser. 3, Vol. 4, p. 713.

[20]E. Merton Coulter, *The Confederate States of America* (Baton Rouge, 1950), p. 544; Clement C. Clay to Judah Benjamin, September 12, 1864, in *O.R.*, Ser. 4, Vol. 3, pp. 637–638.

Several historians have discounted the stories of Copperhead conspiracies as "a figment of Republican imagination . . . a political apparition." Without question the Republicans exaggerated or fabricated many of these conspiracies. On the other hand, evidence for some of them was a good deal more than mere "lies, conjecture and political malignancy," as one historian has termed it.[21] Perhaps the sworn testimony of Union detectives or of Copperheads who turned state's evidence should be taken with a grain of salt; but the official reports of Confederate agents cannot be disregarded. Several reports from agents in Canada turned up in captured Confederate archives after the war. These documents revealed that several hundred thousand dollars had been distributed to Midwestern Democrats, including candidates for state offices: the nominee for governor of Illinois had accepted $40,000 from a Canadian-based Confederate agent, and two large peace rallies in Illinois had been financed largely by Rebel gold. Detectives found caches of weapons paid for with Confederate secret service money in the homes of Copperheads. There were several plots to free Confederate prisoners, including one to stage an uprising in Chicago during the Democratic national convention to cover the liberation of war prisoners from nearby Camp Douglas.

Most of these fantastic plots, of course, never succeeded. This was owing to two factors: the loose security of the secret societies, which allowed federal agents to infiltrate them; and the inability of Northern conspirators to mobilize more than a handful of men when the time came for real action. Numerous Confederate agents showed up at the Chicago Democratic convention, but the expected legions of armed Copperheads never appeared. The disillusioned Southerners concluded that the Northern peace movement was all talk and no action. The only major operations that took place were those carried out by Confederate agents on their own: a raid across the border on October 19, 1864, that netted $200,000 from the banks of St. Albans, Vermont; and an attempt on November 25 to burn several New York hotels and other buildings, which fizzled out when the nineteen fires set by Southern agents were extinguished after damaging only a few buildings.[22]

Another invasion of Missouri by Sterling Price was also connected with efforts by Confederate agents to ignite uprisings in Union territory. Price had accepted the title of "military commander" of the Order of American Knights. With 12,000 soldiers he moved into Missouri from Arkansas in September 1864 hoping that the Knights would soften Union defenses by sabotage. As elsewhere, however, these civilian commandos accomplished little. But Confederate guerrilla bands did wreak havoc in the Union rear; on one occasion "Bloody Bill" Anderson's men took twenty-four unarmed

---

[21]Frank L. Klement, *The Copperheads in the Middle West* (Chicago, 1960), p. 205; Frank L. Klement, *The Limits of Dissent: Clement L. Vallandigham and the Civil War* (Lexington, Ky., 1970), p. 294. See also Richard O. Curry, "The Union as It Was: A Critique of Recent Interpretations of the Copperheads," *Civil War History,* 13 (March 1967), 25–39, and Frank L. Klement, *Dark Lanterns: Secret Political Societies, Conspiracies, and Treason Trials in the Civil War* (Baton Rouge, 1984).

[22]For a sober summary of the evidence about these activities, see Stephen Z. Starr, "Was There a Northwest Conspiracy?" *The Filson Club Historical Quarterly,* 38 (October 1964), 323–341. Two full-scale studies that tend to exaggerate the dimensions of treasonable Copperhead activities are Gray, *Hidden Civil War,* and George Fort Milton, *Abraham Lincoln and the Fifth Column* (New York, 1942). Of the two, Gray is the more reliable. The two most recent studies of the 1864 election, Long, *The Jewel of Liberty* and John C. Waugh, *Reelecting Lincoln: The Battle for the 1864 Presidency* (New York, 1997), take seriously the undercover activities of Copperheads and Confederate agents in the North.

Union soldiers off a train in Centralia and murdered them in cold blood. Anderson then joined Price's army as it headed up the Missouri River. Despite all this, the Confederate invasion came to grief. Union forces and Missouri militia hammered Price at Pilot Knob and in several small battles near Kansas City. Price retreated into Indian territory at the end of October after losing half his force. Bloody Bill Anderson was killed in one of these battles, and many of the guerrilla bands were broken up—though individuals like the James and Younger brothers survived to carry the guerrilla-outlaw tradition into postwar Missouri.

The fullest summary of activities by the Confederate secret service and their Northern allies during the 1864 political campaign was Jacob Thompson's report to the Confederate secretary of state on December 3, 1864. Thompson was a Mississippian who had been secretary of the interior under Buchanan. His prewar affiliations with Northern Democrats made him an ideal person to head the secret service in Canada. He established contacts with several Peace Democrats, including Vallandigham. "I was received among them with cordiality, and the greatest confidence [was] at once extended to me." Thompson detailed his distribution of $300,000 to purchase arms, hold meetings, and subsidize newspapers. "Money has been advanced to Mr. Churchill, of Cincinnati, to organize a corps for the purpose of incendiarism in that city," he wrote. Thompson had faith in arson as a weapon against the North: "A great amount of property has been burned" (this was an exaggeration), and "[we must continue] to burn whenever it is practicable, and thus make the men of property feel their insecurity and tire them out with the war." Indeed, Thompson was preparing to burn his own records, for "I have so many papers in my possession, which in the hands of the enemy would utterly ruin and destroy very many of the prominent men in the North."[23]

One can readily imagine what use Republicans would have made of this document had they possessed it in 1864. As it was, Democratic "treason" was their most effective issue. Democrats retaliated with charges of "tyranny"; but this and other standard party issues—inflation, debt, corruption, conscription, violation of civil liberties—failed to catch fire. So did personal attacks on Lincoln such as the following, which appeared in a New York Catholic weekly: "Abe Lincoln—passing the question as to his taint of Negro blood . . . is altogether an imbecile. . . . He is brutal in all his habits. . . . He is filthy. He is obscene. . . . He is an animal!"[24]

Even racism had lost much of its potency as a Democratic issue. This was not for lack of trying. Democratic newspapers published snide speculations on Lincoln's black ancestry. Campaign orators rang all the changes on "the negro-loving, negro-hugging worshippers of old Abe." A pair of reporters for the leading Democratic paper, the *New York World,* added a new twist when they wrote anonymously a pamphlet entitled *Miscegenation: The Theory of the Blending of the Races, Applied to the American White Man and Negro*. The pamphlet, purportedly written by an abolitionist, advocated miscegenation (a new word, coined by the real authors) as a solution of the race problem. It predicted that if Republicans won the election they would carry the war into its next stage, "a war looking, as its final fruit, to the blending of the white and the black." Democrats did all they could to exploit the miscegenation

---

[23] *O.R.,* Ser. 1, Vol. 43, pt. 2, pp. 930–936.
[24] *Freeman's Journal,* August 20, 1864.

issue with doggerel poetry, salacious political cartoons portraying black men kissing white women in the "millennium of abolitionism" after Lincoln's reelection, sensational stories of New England schoolmarms in the occupied South who had produced mulatto babies, and the like. But there is little evidence that all this won many new voters for the Democrats. On the contrary, it may have turned some intelligent voters away in disgust.[25]

The Prisoners of War Issue

One issue indirectly connected with race, which the Democrats exploited only slightly, was the matter of prisoner of war exchanges. The Democratic platform denounced the administration's "shameful disregard" of "our fellow-citizens who now are, and long have been, prisoners of war in a suffering condition."[26] The plight of war prisoners, especially in Georgia's notorious Andersonville prison, was one reason for Northern war weariness in the summer of 1864. Democrats attributed the breakdown in prisoner exchanges to Republican insistence on the equal treatment of black prisoners. But the Democrats did not make much of this issue, probably because they felt it might backfire. Most Northerners bitterly blamed the South for the suffering of Union prisoners. A party already regarded as pro-Southern was not likely to win many friends on this issue.

The emotional and often misunderstood question of war prisons and prisoner exchanges reached a crisis in 1864. The overcrowding and the appalling death rate at Andersonville became a scandal in both North and South. The stockade was built in early 1864 to accommodate 15,000 prisoners, but by August it was packed with nearly 33,000 men. Thirteen thousand prisoners died at Andersonville. The commandant of the prison, Henry Wirz, was later convicted of war crimes and hanged. Some historians consider Wirz's conviction a miscarriage of justice resulting from the North's need for a scapegoat. They maintain that Northern captives fared no worse on the average than Southern prisoners in Northern camps. Union prisoners received the same rations as Confederate soldiers; if these were meager by 1864, it was because the Yankees had destroyed so many of the South's resources. And so far as Andersonville was concerned, its horrors were the product of a breakdown in exchanges for which, according to this view, the North was responsible.

These are complex questions. It is true that Northern propaganda exaggerated the conditions in Southern prisons. Prisoner memoirs were one of the most sensationalized forms of Civil War literature. It is hard to separate fact from fiction in these memoirs, most of which were written by Northerners. Perhaps the greatest exaggerations concerned Libby Prison, a large warehouse in Richmond that housed as many as 1,300 Union officers. These captives had a roof over their heads, better food and medical care, and more privileges than the enlisted men imprisoned at Belle Isle, Andersonville, and other Confederate prisons where conditions were far worse than at Libby.

---

[25]For a summary of the race issue in the 1864 campaign, see Forrest G. Wood, *Black Scare: The Racist Response to Emancipation and Reconstruction* (Berkeley, 1968), pp. 53–79.

[26]McPherson, *Political History of the Rebellion*, p. 420.

But because the Libby prisoners were more highly educated and articulate, and because they included several colonels and even a general with important political or journalistic connections in the North, their stories during and after the war reached the public more prominently than those of enlisted men. These stories made things seem worse at Libby than, in context, they really were. The same is true of the Union prison for Confederate officers at Johnson's Island in Lake Erie near Sandusky, Ohio. The mortality of prisoners at Johnson's Island was 2 percent and at Libby not much greater—compared with 29 percent at Andersonville, and 24 percent for the Union prison at Elmira, New York. Libby also earned fame because of a spectacular escape attempt on February 9, 1864, when 109 officers crawled to freedom through a tunnel before they were discovered—and 48 of them recaptured. The commandant at Libby earned infamy in the North by placing 200 pounds of gunpowder under the floor and threatening to blow up the prison if its inmates tried another breakout.

The following is probably a fair generalization about prison conditions: with the exception of Andersonville, average conditions at Southern prisons were not much worse than those at Northern prisons. In truth, these conditions were usually bad. Prisoners on both sides suffered from poor sanitary facilities, bad water, disease, trigger-happy guards, boredom, and mental depression. Insufficient clothing and blankets caused cold-weather distress among unacclimated Confederate prisoners at Camp Douglas near Lake Michigan, on Johnson's Island in Lake Erie, and at Elmira, New York. On the other hand, with respect to food and shelter the Confederate prisoners in the North fared better than their Yankee counterparts in the South. While most Northern prison camps housed captured Rebels in barracks, several Confederate camps—including the two largest, Andersonville and Belle Isle (an island in the James River near Richmond)—provided no shelter, and prisoners suffered from exposure. Medical care for prisoners on both sides was probably no worse than for soldiers in general—which is to say that by modern standards it was poor. But shortages of medicine in the South (for which the Union blockade was partly responsible) affected Yankee prisoners as it did Southern soldiers and civilians.

These factors—poorer food, inadequate shelter, and shortages of medicine—help to explain why the death rate for Union captives in Southern prisons was at least 28 percent higher than for Confederate prisoners in the North.[27] Another way of analyzing the figures shows that Confederate prisoners were 29 percent less likely to die in Yankee prisons than to die of disease in their own army, while Union prisoners

---

[27]Like most Civil War statistics, data on prisoners are at best inexact; this is especially true for the South because so many Confederate records were destroyed or lost during the evacuation of Richmond in April 1865. The most reliable figures indicate that of the 194,743 Union soldiers imprisoned for various lengths of time, 30,218 (15.5 percent) died in prison, while of the 214,865 imprisoned Confederates 25,976 (12.1 percent) died in captivity. Thus the death rate for Union prisoners was 28 percent higher than for Confederates. [General F. C. Ainsworth, Chief of the U.S. Record and Pension Office, to James Ford Rhodes, June 29, 1903, in James Ford Rhodes, *History of the United States from the Compromise of 1850*, 7 vols. (New York, 1893–1906), V, 507–508.] Other, less reliable figures show a Union death rate of 17.8 percent, which would have been 48 percent higher than the Confederate rate cited in this same report. (*O.R.*, Ser. 2, Vol. 8, pp. 946–948.) For discussions of this question, see William B. Hesseltine, *Civil War Prisons: A Study in War Psychology* (Columbus, Ohio, 1930), pp. 254–256, and Lonnie R. Speer, *Portals to Hell: Military Prisons of the Civil War* (Mechanicsburg, Pa., 1997), xxiv, 341.

were 68 percent more likely to die in Southern prisons than in their own army. No evidence exists to support Northern charges of deliberate Confederate cruelty to prisoners—except for captured black soldiers, some of whom were shot and others reenslaved. The difference in death rates can be accounted for primarily by the collapse of the Southern economy in the war's last year, when the number of prisoners reached its maximum.

On the other hand, it is as hard for the modern historian as it was for Northerners in 1864 to understand why Union prisoners at Andersonville were not allowed to build huts out of wood from the abundant pine forests that surrounded the prison. This would have saved many lives. One Georgia woman was shocked by what she saw at Andersonville. "My heart aches for the poor wretches, Yankees though they are, and I am afraid that God will suffer some terrible retribution to fall upon us for letting such things happen. If the Yankees ever should come to South-West Georgia . . . and see the graves there, God have mercy on the land!"

"And yet, what can we do?" she continued. "The Yankees themselves are really more to blame than we, for they won't exchange these prisoners, and our poor, hard-pressed Confederacy has not the means to provide for them, when our own soldiers are starving in the field."[28] The breakdown in the prisoner exchange program was indeed the main reason for the overcrowding of prisons in 1864, but the responsibility for this breakdown was more complex than this Georgia woman implied.

During the war's first year, Lincoln had refused to negotiate an exchange cartel lest this be construed as official recognition of the Confederacy. But field commanders arranged many informal exchanges. The large number of prisoners captured by both sides in 1862 increased the pressure on the Union government to accept a cartel, which it finally did in July. By the terms of this agreement, each side exchanged its prisoners for an equal number held by the enemy, with the surplus on one side or the other to be released on parole until formally exchanged.

Under this cartel, the war prisons were almost emptied by the fall of 1862. But the agreement broke down in 1863. The initial cause of this breakdown was the Confederacy's response to the Emancipation Proclamation and to the Union army's enlistment of black soldiers. Condemning these actions as "the most execrable measure recorded in the history of guilty man," Jefferson Davis announced that henceforth the officers of black regiments plus all Union officers captured in states affected by the Emancipation Proclamation would be turned over to state governments to be executed as "criminals engaged in servile insurrection." Captured black soldiers were also to be turned over to "the respective States to which they belong to be dealt with according to the laws of said States." The Confederate Congress endorsed these policies, which were of course a violation of the cartel, to say nothing of their other qualities. To ensure that the Confederates did not carry out these policies, Union Secretary of War Stanton ordered all exchanges of Confederate officers stopped so that these captives could be held as hostages against the Confederate threat to execute Union prisoners.[29]

---

[28]Eliza Frances Andrews, *The War-Time Journal of a Georgia Girl, 1864–1865* (New York, 1908), pp. 78–79.
[29]*O.R.,* Ser. 2, Vol. 5, pp. 797, 808, 940–941, 128, 696.

LIBRARY OF CONGRESS

WAR PRISONERS AND PRISONS.   The first photo in this series (*above*) shows a group of captured Confederate cavalrymen in Virginia in 1864. Note the contrast between the uniforms of the Union guards and the nondescript clothing of many Rebels. The men in the second photograph (*page 489, top*) are Confederate war prisoners at Camp Douglas near Chicago. Note the heated barracks and the healthy appearance of the prisoners. Such photographs gave Northern viewers a somewhat rosy impression of good treatment of Southern prisoners, which they contrasted with the sufferings of Union prisoners at Andersonville, seen in the next two pictures. The third photograph (*page 489, center*) shows the flimsy shelters rigged up by prisoners at Andersonville from whatever materials they had at hand. The sluggish stream in the foreground served as both sewer and water supply for the prisoners, some of whom are staring at the camera in the fourth picture (*page 489, bottom*). These Andersonville photographs, taken by a Southern cameraman in August 1864 at the height of the stockade's prisoner population, were published in the North after the war and exacerbated public anger over the prisoner treatment issue, an issue that perpetuated sectional bitterness long after the war. The fifth photograph (*page 490*) added to this bitterness. This man was among several Union prisoners suffering from dysentery and other maladies at Belle Isle prison camp near Richmond, prisoners who were returned to Union lines under special exchange in 1864. Although hardly typical of Union prisoners, the condition of these prisoners—whose photographs were published in the North—reinforced Northern beliefs in the Confederacy's fiendish treatment of captured Yankees.

CHICAGO HISTORICAL SOCIETY

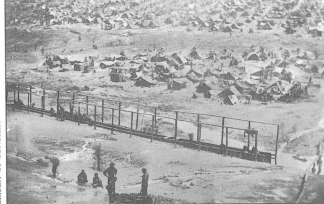

LIBRARY OF CONGRESS

MASSACHUSETTS COMMANDERY MILITARY ORDER OF THE LOYAL LEGION AND THE U.S. ARMY MILITARY HISTORY INSTITUTE

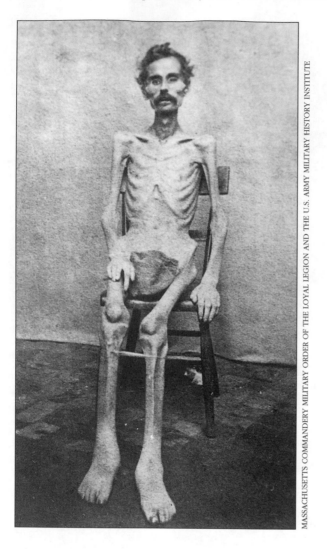

MASSACHUSETTS COMMANDERY MILITARY ORDER OF THE LOYAL LEGION AND THE U.S. ARMY MILITARY HISTORY INSTITUTE

Although official exchanges of officers largely came to an end by June 1863, some exchanges and paroling of enlisted men continued. Grant and Banks paroled the 36,000 men captured at Vicksburg and Port Hudson in July, but soon thereafter the Confederate War Department put thousands of these men back into the army (in time for some of them to fight in the battles at Chattanooga). The Union government regarded this as an outrageous violation of the cartel. Disputes about it brought all exchanges to a halt. By December 1863, 26,000 Confederate prisoners were being held in the North and 13,000 bluecoats in the South—numbers large enough to create pressure for a renewal of exchanges. But the Southern refusal to include captured black soldiers and their officers in any exchange proved a major obstacle. "The enlistment of our slaves is a barbarity," declaimed the head of the Confederate Bureau of War. "No people . . . could tolerate . . . the use of savages [against them]." The

Confederate exchange agent declared that the South would "die in the last ditch" before "giving up the right to send slaves back to slavery as property recaptured."[30] In reply, Stanton insisted that for the North to negotiate a Jim Crow cartel would be "a shameful dishonor. . . . When [the Rebels] agree to exchange all alike there will be no difficulty." When Grant became general in chief, he took the same position. "No distinction whatever will be made in the exchange between white and colored prisoners," he ordered on April 17, 1864. And there must be "released to us a sufficient number of officers and men as were captured and paroled at Vicksburg and Port Hudson. . . . Non-acquiescence by the Confederate authorities in both or either of these propositions will be regarded as a refusal on their part to agree to the further exchange of prisoners."[31]

There matters stood while the battles of May-July 1864 poured an unprecedented number of prisoners into overcrowded stockades. In August, the Confederates offered a man-for-man exchange but again refused to assure Union authorities that captured freedmen would be included.[32] By this time Grant had become convinced that any exchange would benefit the Confederacy more than the Union. "It is hard on our men held in Southern prisons not to exchange them," he wrote, "but it is humanity to those left in the ranks to fight our battles." Every exchanged Confederate "becomes an active soldier against us at once," whereas most of the released Yankees would go home or into the hospital because of expired enlistments or broken-down health. "We have got to fight until the military power of the South is exhausted, and if we release or exchange prisoners captured it simply becomes a war of extermination."[33]

These statements are often cited as proof that the Union insistence on equal treatment for black prisoners was merely a cover for the real reason it refused an exchange—to wear down the Confederacy by attrition. Thus, the argument goes, the North rather than the South was responsible for the horrors of Andersonville.

But the evidence does not sustain this thesis. When Lee on October 1 suggested a man-for-man exchange of prisoners recently captured in Virginia, Grant provisionally accepted a partial exchange but asked Lee for assurance that black soldiers would be included. When Lee replied that "negroes belonging to our citizens are not considered subjects of exchange and were not included in my proposition," Grant closed the affair with the statement that since the Union government was "bound to secure to all persons received into her armies the rights due to soldiers," Lee's refusal to grant blacks those rights "induces me to decline making the exchanges you ask."[34] When the two opposing secretaries of the navy worked out an arrangement in October 1864 for the exchange of captured sailors, the Lincoln administration insisted that black personnel be included—and they were. This was the first real break in the exchange impasse. During the winter of 1864-1865, the two sides exchanged thousands of sick and wounded prisoners without regard to color. In January 1865,

---

[30]Edward Younger (ed.), *Inside the Confederate Government: The Diary of Robert Garlick Hill Kean* (New York, 1957), pp. 92–93; *O.R.*, Ser. 2, Vol. 6, pp. 441–442, 647–649.

[31]*O.R.*, Ser. 2, Vol. 6, p. 226, Vol. 7, pp. 62–63.

[32]Ibid., Vol. 7, pp. 578–579, 606, 688, Vol. 8, p. 150; Benjamin F. Butler, *Autobiography* (Boston, 1892), p. 605.

[33]*O.R.*, Ser. 2, Vol. 7, pp. 607, 615.

[34]Ibid., pp. 906–907, 909, 914.

the Confederate exchange agent offered to exchange "all" prisoners, and this offer the Union government accepted.[35] The Confederacy was about to enroll slaves in its own armies (see pages 514 and 515), and since the continued refusal to exchange black prisoners would then have become absurd, it was quietly abandoned. During February and March 1865, the exchanges went forward at the rate of nearly a thousand men per day—until the end of the war liberated all remaining prisoners.

✑ The Reelection of Lincoln

The 1864 election was a referendum on the war and emancipation. No one could be entirely sure what the consequences of a Democratic victory would be: Confederate independence, restoration of the Union with slavery, or something else. But the consequences of a Republican victory were certain: the doom of slavery and the continuation of war until the South surrendered. Knowing this, voters went to the polls on November 8 and reelected Lincoln by a majority of 212 to 21 in the electoral college. McClellan carried only New Jersey, Kentucky, and Delaware. Lincoln's majority of 55 percent of the popular vote was a healthy increase from the 48 percent he had received in the same states four years earlier. Only one free state (New Jersey) elected a Democratic governor in 1864. Republicans won an extraordinary 145 of the 185 seats in the next House of Representatives (the Senate would have a 41-to-10 Republican majority). Seldom in American history has one party won such a lopsided victory in congressional elections. The Republican gains over 1860 came mainly from the soldier vote (discussed below) and from the border states, where troops excluded secessionist voters and may have intimidated some potential McClellan voters.

One remarkable fact about the 1864 election was that it took place at all. No other country before World War II held general elections in the midst of war. Britain twice in the twentieth century canceled elections because of wartime emergencies. The American experiment of holding an election during a *civil* war whose result would determine the nation's future is unique in history. Yet no one in 1864 proposed to postpone the election. As Lincoln himself explained: "We can not have free government without elections; and if the rebellion could force us to forego, or postpone a national election, it might fairly claim to have already conquered and ruined us." The outcome, said Lincoln after his reelection, proved that "a people's government can sustain a national election in the midst of a great civil war."[36]

Equally remarkable was the soldier vote in 1864. No other society had tried the experiment of letting its fighting men vote in an election that might decide whether they were to continue fighting. By 1864, nineteen states had made it possible for their troops to vote in the field. Seven of these provided that soldier votes should be deposited with other votes, leaving twelve states in which the army vote would be separately tabulated. The remaining Northern states—most notably Illinois and Indiana—made no provision for absentee voting by soldiers. Democrats in Illinois and Indiana had blocked such legislation, for with good reason they feared the soldier vote.

---

[35]Gideon Welles, *The Diary of Gideon Welles,* ed. Howard K. Beale, 3 vols. (New York, 1960), II, 168–172; *O.R.,* Ser. 2, Vol. 7, p. 1007, Vol. 8, pp. 98, 123, 504.

[36]Basler, *Works of Lincoln,* VIII, 101.

Although McClellan's name still evoked enthusiasm among many officers and men in the Army of the Potomac, few soldiers wished to vote for a party that declared the war a failure. A Democratic victory, wrote one veteran officer, would mean "inglorious peace and shame, the old truckling subserviency to Southern domination." Another soldier, a lifelong Democrat, said that "we all want peace, but none *any* but an *honorable* one. I had rather stay out here a lifetime (much as I dislike it) than consent to a division of our country."[37]

Republicans considered the soldier vote crucial in certain states. As commander in chief, Lincoln could do something about this. Military operations came to a halt in early November as thousands of soldiers from states without absentee balloting received furloughs to go home and vote. Democrats charged fraud in Indiana, where thousands of Republican votes were said to have been cast by out-of-state soldiers. On the other hand, Democratic commissioners from New York who went to the front to collect soldier votes were arrested and convicted (one of them having confessed) of stuffing ballot boxes with forged McClellan votes. There were other accusations of fraud and harassment, but on the whole the army vote was marred by no more irregularities than normal in nineteenth-century elections. Lincoln won an extraordinary 78 percent of the separately tabulated soldier vote (119,754 out of 154,045). The Republican majority was probably as large among soldiers who went home to vote or whose ballots were not separately counted. Even in the Army of the Potomac, only 29 percent of the men voted for McClellan.

The soldier vote provided the margin of victory in several congressional districts. It probably also provided Lincoln's margin in New York and Connecticut (and possibly in Indiana and Maryland). Although the President would have won without the army vote, the four-to-one Republican majority of soldier ballots was an impressive mandate for Lincoln's policy of war to victory. The men who would have to do the fighting had voted by a far larger margin than the folks at home to finish the job.[38]

The message of Lincoln's reelection was clear to everyone. "The overwhelming majority received by Mr. Lincoln and the quiet with which the election went off will prove a terrible damper to the Rebels," wrote Grant to a friend. "It will be worth more than a victory in the field both in its effect on the Rebels and in its influence abroad." Union soldiers in the trenches at Petersburg "cheered until they were hoarse" when they heard the news of Lincoln's victory. "At a point where the lines came within a few rods of each other," wrote a Yankee private, "our men heard a voice from behind the rebel breastworks. 'Say, Yank.' 'Hilloa, Johnny.' 'Don't fire, Yank.' 'All right, Johnny.' 'What are you'uns all cheering for?' 'Big victory on our side.' 'What is it, Yank?' came the eager response. 'Old Abe has cleaned all your fellers out up North.' 'You don't say so, Yank?' 'Fact; gobbled the whole concern; there is not peace men enough left in the whole North to make a corporal's guard.' "[39]

---

[37]Bruce Catton, *A Stillness at Appomattox* (Garden City, N.Y., 1957), p. 323; John Berry to Samuel L. M. Barlow, August 27, 1864, Barlow Papers.

[38]The best account of the soldier vote is Oscar O. Winther, "The Soldier Vote in the Election of 1864," *New York History*, 25 (1955), 440–458. Long, *Jewel of Liberty*, p. 285, and Waugh, *Reelecting Lincoln*, p. 354, have slightly different figures but similar percentages for the soldier vote.

[39]Catton, *Grant Takes Command*, p. 384; Paul M. Angle and Earl Schenck Miers (eds.), *Tragic Years, 1860–1865 (New York, 1960), p. 290.

McClellan and his friends were disappointed but accepted the outcome with resignation. One of the general's close friends expressed relief that the Democrats would not be saddled with the responsibility for ending the war. "We engaged in an *impossible* fight," he wrote of the election campaign. "We undertook to interrupt a revolution before the completion of its cycle, and we fortunately failed." To the perceptive correspondent of the London *Daily News,* the turn in the tide of Northern opinion since midsummer showed that the North was "silently, calmly, but desperately in earnest . . . in a way the like of which the world never saw before. . . . I am astonished the more I see and hear of the extent and depth of [this] determination . . . to fight to the last."[40]

Richmond also understood the message of Lincoln's reelection. But Jefferson Davis put on a brave official front and insisted that the Confederacy remained "as erect and defiant as ever. Nothing [has] changed in the purpose of its Government, in the indomitable valor of its troops, or in the unquenchable spirit of its people. . . . There is no military success of the enemy which can accomplish its destruction."[41] It was this last-ditch defiance that Sherman set out to break in his famous march from Atlanta to the sea.

---

[40]Samuel L. M. Barlow to Fitz-John Porter, November 17, 1864, Barlow Papers; Allan Nevins, *The War for the Union: The Organized War to Victory,* 1864–1865 (New York, 1971), p. 141.

[41]Dunbar Rowland (ed.), *Jefferson Davis, Constitutionalist,* 10 vols. (Jackson, Miss., 1923), VI, 386.

Chapter Twenty-Five

The End of the Confed- eracy

We are not only fighting hostile armies, but a hostile people. . . . We cannot change the hearts of those people of the South, but we can make war so terrible . . . [and] make them so sick of war that generations would pass away before they would again appeal to it.

—William Tecumseh Sherman,
1863, 1864

 From Atlanta to the Sea

Soon after occupying Atlanta in September, Sherman decided to evacuate most of its civilian population. He wanted to use the city as a military base without the burden of feeding and protecting civilians or of guarding against spies and guerrillas in their midst. "I had seen Memphis, Vicksburg, Natchez, and New Orleans," explained Sherman, "all captured from the enemy, and each at once was garrisoned by a full division of troops, if not more; so that success was actually crippling our armies in the field by detachments to guard and protect the interests of a hostile population."[1]

When Atlanta's mayor and General Hood protested Sherman's "cruelty," the Northern general seized the opportunity to lecture them on the wickedness of rebellion. "War is cruelty and you cannot refine it," Sherman told the mayor. The South had started the war and boasted of its ability to whip the Yankees. "Now that the war comes home to you, you feel very different. You deprecate its horrors, but did not feel them when you sent car-loads of soldiers and ammunition . . . to carry war into Kentucky and Tennessee." The only road to peace was relentless war until the Confederacy surrendered. The evacuation orders for Atlanta "were not designed to meet the humanities of the case, but to prepare for the future struggles in which millions of good people outside Atlanta have a deep interest. We must have peace, not only at Atlanta, but in all America." To Hood, who had denounced Sherman's action as "preeminent in the dark history of war" for "studied and ingenious cruelty," Sherman replied with angry words for "you who, in the midst of peace and prosperity, have plunged a nation into war . . . who dared and badgered us to battle, insulted our flag . . . turned loose your privateers to plunder unarmed ships; expelled Union families by the thousands [and] burned their houses. . . . Talk thus to the marines, but not to me, who have seen these things."[2]

Sherman had long pondered the nature and purpose of this war. He had concluded that "we are not only fighting hostile armies, but a hostile people." Defeat of Southern armies was not enough to win the war; the railroads, factories, and farms that supplied and fed them must be destroyed; the will of the civilian population that sustained the armies must be crushed. Sherman expressed more bluntly than anyone else the meaning of hard war. He was ahead of his time in his understanding of psychological warfare, and he was in a position to practice it. "We cannot change the hearts of those people of the South, but we can make war so terrible . . . [and] make them so sick of war that generations would pass away before they would again appeal to it." In Tennessee and Mississippi, Sherman's troops had burned and destroyed everything of military value—and much that was not—within their reach. Now Sherman proposed to do the same in Georgia. He urged Grant to let him cut loose from his base and march his army through the heart of Georgia, living off the land and destroying all the resources not consumed by the army. The psychological impact of such a campaign, said Sherman, would be greater even than its material impact. "If we can march a well-appointed army right through [Jefferson Davis's] territory, it is a demonstration to the world, foreign and domestic, that we have a power which Davis cannot resist. This may not be war, but rather statesmanship."[3]

Lincoln and Grant were reluctant to authorize such a risky move while Hood's army and Forrest's cavalry still roamed in Sherman's rear. With 40,000 men Hood was too weak to attack Sherman; but he was strong enough to move northward along

---

[1]William T. Sherman, *Memoirs*, 2d ed. rev., 2 vols. (New York, 1886), II, 111.

[2]Brooks D. Simpson and Jean V. Berlin (eds.) *Sherman's Civil War: Selected Correspondence of William T. Sherman, 1860–1865* (Chapel Hill, 1999), pp. 704–709.

[3]*O.R.*, Ser. 1, Vol. 39, pt. 3, p. 660; John Bennett Walters, "General William T. Sherman and Total War," *Journal of Southern History*, 14 (August 1948), 463, 470.

Sherman's communications, gobble up small garrisons, and destroy the railroad back to Chattanooga. In October this was precisely what he tried to do. Sherman followed, leaving one corps to garrison Atlanta. For two weeks the armies skirmished and maneuvered back through the same territory they had fought over from May to August. Forrest's and Wheeler's cavalry also caused havoc in Union-occupied territory from northeast Alabama to western Tennessee.

The Confederate strategy was to force Sherman to abandon Atlanta and disperse his army by chasing the marauding Rebels. But after driving Hood into northern Alabama, Sherman pleaded with Grant not to play the Southern game. "If I turn back now, the whole effect of my campaign will be lost," he said. "It will be a physical impossibility to protect the [rail] roads, now that Hood, Forrest, and Wheeler, and the whole batch of devils, are turned loose without home or habitation. By attempting to hold the roads, we will lose a thousand men monthly and will gain no result." Instead, Sherman proposed to send Thomas with two corps to Tennessee, where with reinforcements and new troops his total force of 60,000 would be more than a match for Hood. Meanwhile, Sherman with 62,000 men would "move through Georgia, smashing things to the sea. . . . Instead of being on the defensive, I would be on the offensive. . . . I can make the march, and make Georgia howl!"[4]

Sherman won his point. Grant accepted his trusted subordinate's judgment and approved the march; Thomas returned to Nashville to organize his conglomerate army; and Sherman readied his hard-bitten veterans for their march to make Georgia howl. To oppose them, the Confederacy could scrape together no more than a few thousand cavalry and the Georgia militia. Yet Sherman's proposed march of 285 miles to Savannah was one of the most dangerous and unorthodox of military undertakings. "To leave the enemy in his rear, to divide his army, to cut himself adrift from railroad and telegraph, from supplies and reinforcements, and launch not a mere raiding force of cavalry but a great army into a hostile country" was, in the words of a British military expert, "either one of the most brilliant or one of the most foolish things ever performed by a military leader"—depending on how it came out.[5]

The Yankees left Atlanta November 15 after burning everything of military value in the city. Inevitably, the flames spread, consuming much of the business district and leveling one-third of Atlanta. As Sherman stood on a hill overlooking the burning city and watched his men march by, a band struck up "John Brown's Body" and the soldiers began to sing. "Never before or since," wrote Sherman a decade later, "have I heard the chorus of 'Glory, glory, hallelujah!' done with more spirit, or in better harmony of time and place."[6] The army moved in four parallel columns of infantry with the cavalry weaving back and forth from one flank to the other. Most of what little fighting occurred was done by the cavalry, which skirmished with Confederate horsemen who tried futilely to obstruct the march. Only once (November 22) did a division

---

[4] *O.R.*, Ser. 1, Vol. 39, pt. 3, pp. 162, 202, 595.

[5] Lloyd Lewis, *Sherman: Fighting Prophet* (New York, 1932), p. 457; B. H. Liddell Hart, *Sherman* (New York, 1929), p. 330.

[6] Sherman, *Memoirs*, II, 179.

WILLIAM TECUMSEH
SHERMAN.
The grim determination of
this general who made
famous the phrase "war is
hell" confronts the viewer.
Sherman's philosophy and
practice of hard war
anticipated twentieth-
century conflicts which
involved the home front
and the civilian population
as a crucial part of warfare.
But while an advocate of
hard war, Sherman favored
a soft peace whose
generosity to defeated
Confederates would have
restored all their political
power.

LIBRARY OF CONGRESS

of the Georgia militia attack a Yankee infantry brigade, which repulsed it easily and was horrified to discover afterward that the 600 Georgians they had killed or wounded were mostly old men and boys.

The 62,000 bluecoats moved at a leisurely pace of ten miles a day, giving them plenty of time to cut a swath of destruction fifty miles wide through the heart of the Confederacy. The devastation wrought by Sherman's army has become legendary. The legend has much basis in fact. Although Sherman's orders empowered only of-ficial foraging parties to gather food and forbade the destruction of civilian property, these orders lost their authority as they filtered down through the ranks. The men were in a devil-may-care mood; they knew about Sherman's philosophy of hard war; and officers from the lowliest lieutenant up to Sherman himself were confessedly lax in enforcing discipline. One soldier wrote that "we had a gay old campaign. . . . De-stroyed all we could not eat, stole their niggers, burned their cotton & gins, spilled their sorghum, burned & twisted their R. Roads and raised Hell generally."[7]

---

[7]Bruce Catton, *Never Call Retreat,* Pocket Books ed. (New York, 1967), p. 395. An excellent study of the temperament and behavior of Sherman's army is Joseph T. Glatthaar, *The March to the Sea and Beyond: Sherman's Troops in the Savannah and Carolinas Campaigns* (New York, 1985). For other balanced accounts that include the perspective of the civilian population affected by the march, see Lee Kennett, *Marching Through Georgia: The Story of Soldiers and Civilians During Sherman's Campaign* (New York, 1995), Part III, and Mark Grimsley, *The Hard Hand of War: Union Military Policy Toward Southern Civilians, 1861–1865* (Cambridge, 1995), pp. 190–200.

Much of the unauthorized pillaging and burning of civilian property was carried out by "bummers"—foragers who were not under control of their officers, plus stragglers, deserters (Confederate as well as Union), and native freebooters in the guise of Georgia Unionists. And some of the scorching of Georgia's earth was done by the Rebel cavalry and by the Georgia militia, obeying orders from Richmond to remove all "negroes, horses, cattle and provisions from [the path] of Sherman's army, and burn what you cannot carry. . . . Obstruct and destroy all roads in Sherman's front, flank, and rear, and his army will soon starve in your midst."[8]

One group of Georgians who greeted the bluecoats not as avenging demons but as the army of the Lord were the blacks. Slaves were usually the first property liberated by the Yankee soldiers. Sherman tried to prevent all but able-bodied black males (whom he organized into labor battalions) from following the army, for he worried that thousands of black camp followers would reduce his mobility and consume supplies. But he had limited success. Thousands of freedpeople—old and young, male and female, sick and lame—fell in with the army. Officers and soldiers took black women into their units as cooks and concubines and hired black men as servants and porters. Three-generation families trailed the army in plantation wagons. Many tragedies accompanied this exodus. An Indiana officer wrote: "Babies tumbled from the backs of mules to which they had been told to cling, and were drowned in the swamps, while mothers stood by the roadside crying for their lost children."[9] Dozens of freedpeople drowned trying to cross a river after the army's rear guard had taken up the pontoon bridge. Of at least 25,000 blacks who joined the columns at one time or another, most fell out from weariness, hunger, or sickness. Fewer than 7,000 made it all the way to the coast.

Although myth has exaggerated the ruin that "Sherman's vandals" left in their wake, the sober truth was devastating enough. Sherman estimated the damage "at $100,000,000; at least $20,000,000 of which has inured to our advantage, and the remainder is simple waste and destruction." Georgia would thenceforth send few supplies to Confederate armies. An Alabama-born member of Sherman's staff who had initially deplored the destruction eventually came to share his chief's view of its psychological value in producing "among the *people of Georgia* a thorough conviction of the personal misery which attends war. . . . If that terror and grief and even want shall help to paralyze their husbands and fathers who are fighting us . . . it is mercy in the end."[10]

Sherman's march did indeed have this effect on Southern morale. A Georgia editor admitted that "a kind of gloom overshadows the face of many, their minds have lost buoyancy." And a Rebel soldier wrote: "i hev conkludud that the dam fulishness uv tryin to lick shurmin Had better be stoped. we hav bin gettin nuthin but hell & lots uv it ever sinse we saw the dam yankys & I am tirde uv it. . . . Thair thicker an lise on a hen and a dam site ornraier."[11]

---

[8]Sherman, *Memoirs*, II, 179.

[9]Lewis, *Sherman*, p. 440.

[10]*O.R.*, Ser. 1, vol. 44, p. 13; Mark A. DeWolfe Howe (ed.), *Marching with Sherman: Passages from the Letters and Campaign Diaries of Henry Hitchcock* (New Haven, 1927), pp. 125, 168.

[11]E. Merton Coulter, *The Confederate States of America* (Baton Rouge, 1950), pp. 549–550.

The bluecoats came up to Savannah December 10 and found its strong defenses held by 10,000 Confederates. Sherman sent one division to capture Fort McAllister on the Ogeechee River south of Savannah. This reopened the Union army's communications with the outside world, through the navy. Then Sherman closed in on Savannah itself. The Confederates evacuated the city December 21 before the Federals could surround and trap them. In a typically jaunty gesture, Sherman telegraphed Lincoln: "I beg to present you, as a Christmas gift, the city of Savannah, with 150 heavy guns and plenty of ammunition, and also about 25,000 bales of cotton."[12] Published in Northern newspapers on Christmas Eve, this telegram set off another wave of celebration all the more euphoric because it came on the heels of Union victories in Tennessee that had all but wrecked Hood's army.

The Battles of Franklin and Nashville

As Sherman moved out of Atlanta in November, Hood moved into Tennessee. His strategy was one of boldness born of desperation. He hoped to draw Sherman after him. Failing that, he intended to take his 39,000 men all the way through Tennessee and Kentucky to the Ohio River and then turn eastward to join Lee in Virginia. To achieve these goals, all he had to do was march 700 miles and defeat Thomas's 60,000 men in Tennessee, beginning with two veteran corps under John Schofield stationed near Pulaski.

Ill-equipped for a winter campaign (thousands of his men wore shoes so poor that they were marching barefoot within two weeks), Hood moved northward on November 19 with Forrest's cavalry leading the way. The Confederates flanked Schofield's smaller force (30,000 men) out of Pulaski. Schofield retreated to the Duck River at Columbia, only forty miles south of Nashville. Hood left two divisions to demonstrate against the Federals at Columbia and sent the cavalry and the rest of his infantry on a long swing around the Union left. Belatedly realizing the danger to his rear, Schofield quickly retreated northward toward Franklin on November 29.

Up to this time everything had gone well for Hood. Most of his army was in Schofield's rear where it could pounce on the retreating Federals. But then everything began to go wrong. A series of contradictory or poorly understood orders caused Hood's corps and division commanders to delay until too late an attack on a single blue division holding the main road at Spring Hill. That night Schofield's whole command escaped silently along this road to Franklin, where they entrenched a strong defensive position.

Frustrated and enraged, Hood blamed his subordinates for the lost opportunity at Spring Hill and foolishly ordered a frontal assault at Franklin on November 30. His corps commanders urged him instead to flank the position. But Hood's blood was up; he refused to listen, and almost as if to discipline the army, he ordered the attack to proceed even though two of his divisions were far in the rear and he would not have numerical superiority over the blue veterans waiting behind stout breastworks. The outcome was predictable. The Confederates attacked with reckless valor

---

[12] *O.R.,* Ser. 1, Vol. 44, p. 783.

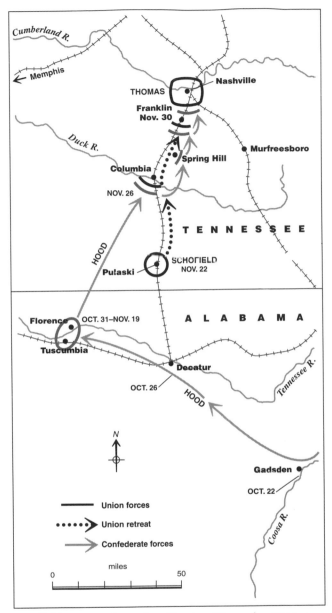

Hood's Tennessee Campaign, October–November 1864

but were cut to pieces. The total of 6,300 Southern casualties was nearly three times the Federal loss. The casualties among Confederate officers were appalling: twelve generals and fifty-four regimental commanders were killed, wounded, or captured.

His army crippled, Hood's only sensible course was to retreat. Instead, it was Schofield who retreated to join the rest of Thomas's army at Nashville. Hood followed and entrenched his troops on the hills south of the city, but he had run out of options.

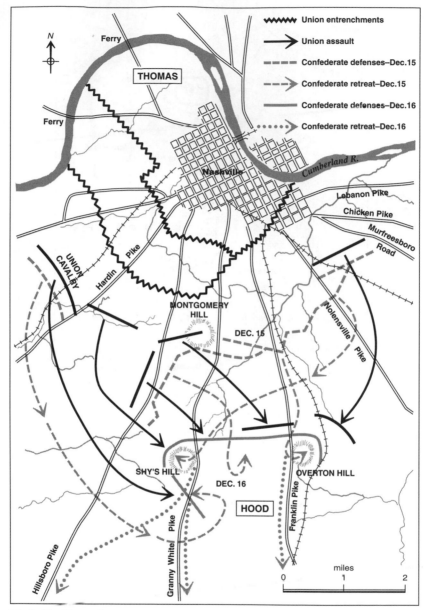

Nashville, December 15–16, 1864

His forces were too weak to attack the Nashville defenses; it was logistically impossi-ble for them to continue north, and Hood believed that a retreat would demoralize his army. In truth the army was already demoralized as it awaited the inevitable attack. Thomas took his time preparing for this attack—so much time that the impatient Grant was on the verge of removing him from command when, after a further delay caused by an ice storm, the Union troops finally moved out December 15.

A diversionary attack by a division containing two black brigades held most of one Confederate corps in position on the right, while Thomas launched 40,000 men in a bruising assault against the left. The Rebels hung on grimly through the short December day and withdrew two miles to a new position during the night. Next day the black troops again feinted against the right while the main attack rolled back the left. Dismounted Union cavalry carrying seven-shot Spencer carbines worked their way around to the Confederate rear, while a simultaneous infantry attack in front caused two of Hood's three corps to disintegrate. The Rebels streamed southward in the darkness and rain, which hindered Union pursuit. The battle of Nashville was one of the most crushing Union victories of the war. At the cost of only 3,000 casualties, the Federals had inflicted more than twice that many. The remnants of the shattered Southern army did not stop until they reached Tupelo, Mississippi, where the crestfallen Hood resigned in January. Of the 50,000 infantry he had inherited from Johnston in July, fewer than 15,000 were left. Dozens of these men deserted every day. For all practical purposes, the Army of Tennessee ceased to exist.

Adoption of the Thirteenth Amendment

The destruction of Hood's army coincided with the final step toward the constitutional destruction of slavery. Democratic opposition had defeated the Thirteenth Amendment in the House the previous June. In December, Lincoln urged Democrats to put aside partisanship and join the Republicans in passing the amendment. The next Congress would have a three-fourths Republican majority and would easily pass it. The President was prepared to call the new Congress into special session on March 4, 1865, for this purpose. But he preferred that such a historic achievement be accomplished as a bipartisan measure. When the amendment came before the House in January, the administration lobbied earnestly to persuade a dozen or more Democrats to change their previous negative votes.

Some Democrats responded favorably. A New York representative reminded his party that it had come to grief in the last election "because we [would] not venture to cut loose from the dead carcass of negro slavery."[13] But most Democrats seemed determined, like Jefferson Davis, to die in the last ditch in defense of the past. Right up to the time of the roll call on January 31, nobody could predict confidently which way it would go. As a few Democrats early in the alphabet voted aye, tense Republican faces began to relax into smiles. Sixteen of the eighty Democrats voted aye; eight others had absented themselves. The vote was 119 to 56—enough to pass the amendment with seven votes to spare. When the result was announced, the most tumultuous celebration in the history of Congress took place. Republican members jumped to their feet and cheered, clapped each other on the back, and shouted triumphant congratulations to their colleagues. In the galleries, black onlookers embraced each other and wept tears of joy. The House voted to take the rest of the day off "in honor of this immortal and sublime event."[14]

---

[13] *Congressional Globe*, 38th Cong., 2nd sess. (1865), 525–526.
[14] Ibid., p. 531.

Those black celebrants were symbols of the great changes wrought by the war; until 1864, black people had not been allowed in congressional galleries. Blacks were also invited to White House receptions in 1865 for the first time. Federal legislation in 1864–1865 prohibited the exclusion of witnesses from federal courts on grounds of race, forbade segregation on streetcars in the District of Columbia, and repealed an 1810 law that had barred blacks from carrying the mail. Several Northern states and cities outlawed segregation in public transportation during or soon after the war. Northern states with black laws—laws that denied blacks certain civil rights—repealed these discriminatory laws between 1863 and 1866. Several states where blacks could not vote scheduled referendums on constitutional amendments to enact black suffrage. Perhaps the most vivid symbol of these changes was an event that occurred February 1, 1865. On that day Chief Justice Salmon P. Chase admitted John Rock of Massachusetts as a practicing lawyer before the U.S. Supreme Court. The only unusual aspect of this proceeding was that Rock was black, a member of a race whom Chase's predecessor had eight years earlier declared ineligible for U.S. citizenship.

Within three months after congressional passage of the Thirteenth Amendment, every Northern state legislature in session but one had ratified it. They were joined by the legislatures of Maryland, Missouri, and West Virginia plus the provisional Unionist legislatures of Louisiana and Tennessee. Only New Jersey, Kentucky, and Delaware—the states carried by McClellan in 1864—refused to ratify the amendment. The rest of the former Confederate states ratified it in the fall of 1865 as a condition of restoration under Andrew Johnson's reconstruction policy. When the amendment became part of the Constitution in December 1865, the institution that had tormented and nearly destroyed the republic existed no more.

⚜ Desertion from the Confederate Armies

While these winds of racial change were blowing over the North in early 1865, the Confederacy was visibly collapsing. Army desertions rose to alarming proportions. At the end of 1864, more than half of the 400,000 soldiers on the Confederate rolls were absent from the army, many of them deserters. General Beauregard admitted that desertion had become an "epidemic." In one month during the winter, the Army of Northern Virginia lost nearly 8 percent of its combat strength by desertion.

The Civil War desertion rate was high in both armies. Accurate statistics are elusive because of incomplete records and the difficulty of distinguishing between genuine deserters and those who for a variety of reasons were temporarily absent—with or without leave. There appear to have been about 200,000 Union deserters, of whom 80,000 were caught and returned to the army and 147 were executed. At least 104,000 Confederates deserted; 21,000 of them were caught and returned. Deserters thus constituted approximately 9.6 percent of the Union forces and 12.2 percent of the Confederate forces.

Until the fall of 1864, the desertion rate had been about the same on both sides. It was the "epidemic" of Confederate desertions in the winter of 1864–1865 that lifted the Southern rate higher for the war as a whole. Hunger, cold, and misery at the front, and the desperate plight of soldiers' families back home caused many desertions. Thousands of Confederate soldiers went home in response to such letters from their wives as this one in December 1864: "We haven't got nothing in the house to eat but a little bit o meal. . . . Try to get off and come home and fix us all up some and then you can go back. . . . If you put off a-coming, 'twont be no use to come, for we'll all hands of us be out there in the garden in the grave yard with your ma and mine."[15]

The most important cause of Confederate desertions in the war's final months was the belief that "our cause was hopeless and that further sacrifices were hopeless." A soldier in Lee's army who had previously testified to high morale in the ranks wrote in January 1865 that "the successful and . . . unopposed march of Sherman through Georgia, and the complete defeat of Hood in Tennessee, have changed the whole aspect of affairs." Lee was convinced that such "discouraging sentiment" was the main cause of "this defection in troops who have acted so nobly and borne so much. . . . Unless it can be changed, [it] will bring us calamity. . . . Hundreds of men are deserting nightly. . . . I don't know what can be done to put a stop to it."[16]

The Fall of Fort Fisher and the Failure of Peace Negotiations

Worse was yet to come. Lee's threadbare army drew its meager supplies from the interior of the Carolinas, as yet untouched by invasion, and from Wilmington, North Carolina, the main port still open to blockade runners. Grant sent an expedition to close off Wilmington, and Sherman set out on his second march of destruction, this one through the Carolinas.

Wilmington was defended by a network of forts at the mouth of the Cape Fear River twenty miles below the city. The most important of these was Fort Fisher, a huge earthwork mounting seventy-five guns. The treacherous channels and the formidable defenses at the mouth of the Cape Fear made it impossible for Union ships to run past the forts as they had at New Orleans and Mobile. Thus Wilmington had remained the principal blockade-running port. In the fall of 1864, the Union command fitted out an army-navy expedition to capture Fort Fisher. Much to Grant's chagrin, Benjamin Butler took command by virtue of his seniority in the Department of North Carolina. Butler conceived the idea of filling an old ship with 215 tons of gunpowder and running it into the shallows to explode next to the fort. This project was a fiasco, for the explosion on the night of December 23 did no damage to the fort. The navy then bombarded Fisher with 640 tons of metal, and Butler landed some of his 6,500 troops. But he decided that the fort was too strong for an assault, and embarked them again.

For Grant this was the last straw. He had long been looking for an excuse to remove Butler from command. With the election over, the administration no longer needed to treat Butler with kid gloves, so on January 8 his checkered military career

---

[15]Bessie Martin, *Desertion of Alabama Troops from the Confederate Army* (New York, 1932), p. 148.

[16]Bell I. Wiley, *The Life of Johnny Reb* (Indianapolis, 1943), p. 134; Ella Lonn, *Desertion During the Civil War* (New York, 1928), p. 28.

LIBRARY OF CONGRESS

U.S. MARINES.   Marines such as these served on board Union naval ships and participated in such sea-launched attacks as the assault on Fort Fisher in January 1865.

came to an end. Grant promptly sent another expedition; this one consisted of 8,000 troops (including two black brigades) under General Alfred H. Terry, supported by the largest naval fleet of the war—fifty-eight ships mounting 627 guns. For two days this fleet blitzed Fort Fisher, disabling all but two of its guns. On January 15, 2,000 sailors and marines assaulted Fisher's seaward face while half of the 8,000 army troops attacked the land face and swarmed over the parapets. With the fall of Fisher the other forts were also evacuated, Yankee ships sailed into the Cape Fear, and the last major Confederate port was sealed off from the world.

Vice President Alexander Stephens considered the loss of Fort Fisher "one of the greatest disasters which had befallen our Cause from the beginning of the war."[17] The disaster brought to a head the growing peace sentiment in the Confederacy. Two weeks after the fall of Fort Fisher, Stephens participated in yet another futile effort to negotiate a peace. In response to unofficial Union overtures borne to Richmond by Francis P. Blair, Jefferson Davis appointed three commissioners headed by Stephens to meet Northern representatives "with a view to secure peace to the two

[17]Alexander Stephens, *A Constitutional View of the Late War Between the States,* 2 vols. (Philadelphia, 1868–1870), II, 619.

countries." Lincoln expressed his willingness to receive commissioners whom Davis "may informally send to me with the view of securing peace to the people of our common country."[18]

This crucial difference in wording should have warned the Confederates what to expect. At the nadir of Northern morale six months earlier, Lincoln had insisted on reunion and emancipation as conditions of peace; he was unlikely to recede from this position with Union arms now victorious everywhere. Yet at a meeting with Lincoln and Seward aboard the Union steamer *River Queen* at Hampton Roads, Virginia, on February 3, the Confederate commissioners professed surprise at Lincoln's refusal to consider even an armistice without prior Southern submission to these terms. On procedural issues—the method of Southern political restoration, the timing and implementation of emancipation, even the question of compensation to slaveholders—Lincoln was prepared to be flexible, even at the cost of opposition within his own party. On the question of emancipation, Lincoln insisted that there would be "no receding . . . on the Slavery question." Some historians have interpreted these words to mean that only those slaves who had been emancipated by coming into Union lines or by state constitutional amendments would remain legally freed, with the status of the others to be determined once peace was restored and the Emancipation Proclamation, as a war measure, ceased to apply. These historians have relied on Alexander Stephens's account of the meeting (written down several years later, it should be noted)—for no other detailed record of the meeting exists. Stephens maintained that Lincoln had urged him to go home to Georgia and persuade the legislature to take the state out of the war and to ratify the Thirteenth Amendment *prospectively,* to take effect in five years, thereby mitigating the evils of immediate emancipation. This statement by Stephens makes his whole account suspect, for Lincoln was too good a lawyer to suggest such an absurdity as "prospective" ratification of a constitutional amendment. The President had just played a leading role in getting Congress to pass the Thirteenth Amendment, and he was using his influence to get every Republican state legislature as well as those of Maryland, Missouri, and Tennessee to ratify it. At the Hampton Roads conference, he insisted on reunion and emancipation as nonnegotiable terms of peace. The Confederate commissioners therefore returned home having failed to gain any of their objectives. This was probably what Jefferson Davis had expected and wanted, for he lived in a fog of unreality where victory still seemed possible. Since the North refused "to permit us to have [peace] on any other basis than our unconditional submission to their rule," Davis told his Congress, war to the bitter end was the only honorable alternative.[19]

---

[18]Roy P. Basler (ed.), *The Collected Works of Abraham Lincoln,* 9 vols. (New Brunswick, N.J., 1953-1955), VIII, 275–276.

[19]Dunbar Rowland (ed.), *Jefferson Davis, Constitutionalist,* 10 vols. (Jackson, Miss., 1923), VI, 466. Stephens's account is in his *Constitutional View,* II, 599–624. For the treatments of this affair by the historians referred to, see Richard N. Current, *The Lincoln Nobody Knows* (New York, 1958), pp. 243–247, and Ludwell H. Johnson, "Lincoln's Solution to the Problem of Peace Terms, 1864–1865," *Journal of Southern History,* 34 (1968), 581–586. A succinct account of the Hampton Roads Conference can be found in William C. Harris, *With Charity for All: Lincoln and the Restoration of the Union* (Lexington, Ky., 1997), pp. 238–239.

Lincoln's second inaugural address, delivered a month later, demonstrated with Old Testament eloquence where he stood on slavery and the war. "American Slavery is one of those offences which, in the providence of God . . . He now wills to remove [through] this terrible war, as the woe due to those by whom the offence came," said the President as he began his second term. "Fondly do we hope—fervently do we pray—that this mighty scourge of war may speedily pass away. Yet if God wills that it continue, until all the wealth piled by the bondman's two hundred and fifty years of unrequited toil shall be sunk, and until every drop of blood drawn with the lash, shall be paid by another drawn with the sword, as was said three thousand years ago, so still it must be said 'the judgments of the Lord, are true and righteous altogether.' "[20]

Sherman's March through the Carolinas

In February, Sherman's 60,000 avengers brought the scourge of war to South Carolina in a campaign more devastating than their march from Atlanta to the sea. Sherman's intent was to smash his way through the Carolinas, destroying all war resources in his path and spreading demoralization among the populace as he moved up on Lee's rear to catch the Army of Northern Virginia in a vise between his army and Grant's.

The logistical accomplishments of this march were among the most stunning in the history of warfare. The earlier march through Georgia had taken place against token opposition in dry fall weather along lines parallel to the principal rivers. This one went half again as far and crossed many rain-swollen rivers and swamps in the middle of an unusually wet winter against increasing opposition, as the Rebels desperately scraped together an army in their futile attempt to block the blue bulldozer. Counting rest days and delays caused by skirmishes and fights, Sherman's forces averaged nearly ten miles a day for forty-five days. During twenty-eight of those days, rain fell.

The Confederates expected the weather and terrain to stop Sherman. Joseph Johnston believed that "it was absolutely impossible for an army to march across lower portions of the State in winter." But the Yankees did it. Pioneer battalions (100 white soldiers and 75 black freedmen) cut down whole forests to corduroy roads; entire brigades exchanged rifles for spades and axes to build bridges. At night the men—Sherman included—sometimes roosted in trees to escape the flooded ground. Yet in all this, only 2 percent of the army fell sick. When the Federals came to the Salkiehatchie River, Confederate General William J. Hardee assured his superiors: "The Salk is impassable." The bluecoats bridged it and got the army over without loss of a wagon or gun. "I wouldn't have believed it if I hadn't seen it," said Hardee ruefully. Johnston later wrote: "When I learned that Sherman's army was marching through the Salk swamps, making its own corduroy roads at the rate of a dozen miles a day and more, and bringing its artillery and wagons with it, I made up my mind that there had been no such army in existence since the days of Julius Caesar."[21]

---

[20]Basler, *Works of Lincoln,* VIII, 333.
[21]Lewis, *Sherman,* pp. 484, 490.

THE FRUITS OF WAR. The first two photographs (*left and below*) show the ruins of Charleston after a year of Union shelling and after Confederate troops had set fire to large parts of the city when they pulled out in February 1865. The photographer accompanying the Union occupation forces posed freed slave children in one picture and an aged freedman in the other to serve as symbols of the new South rising from the ashes of the old.

LIBRARY OF CONGRESS

U.S. ARMY FIELD ARTILLERY AND FORT SILL MUSEUM, FORT SILL, OKLAHOMA

The second two pictures (*right and below*) show the ruins of Richmond after the Confederates set the city afire while evacuating it in April 1865. The photographer posed Union soldiers in the rubble of the top picture for similar symbolic purposes.

LIBRARY OF CONGRESS

LIBRARY OF CONGRESS

Sherman feinted one wing of his army toward Charleston and the other toward Augusta. The Confederates sent reinforcements to both cities. But the Federals pushed straight northward, cutting the railroad between the two cities without going near either. With its communications to the interior cut off, Charleston surrendered on February 18 to the Union forces that had besieged it from the sea for nearly two years. The Union officer who formally received the surrender was the colonel of a black regiment. His men were the first to take possession of the proud city where some of them had been slaves. They marched in singing "John Brown's Body" while Charleston's black population cheered mightily. The first task of these occupying troops was to extinguish the fires that evacuating Confederates had set to destroy cotton, military supplies, warehouses, and shipping, but which had spread to other parts of the city.

Queen city of the South, the taproot of secession, Charleston's fall was the most dramatic sign of the Confederacy's collapse. For abolitionists, a visible symbol of the mighty revolution was the presence in Charleston of George Thompson Garrison, son of the *Liberator's* editor and a lieutenant in the 55th Massachusetts Colored Infantry. Two months later William Lloyd Garrison himself, along with many other abolitionists, arrived in the city to take part in a ceremonial raising of the Stars and Stripes over Fort Sumter four years to the day after the flag had been lowered in surrender.

Before Sherman began his march into South Carolina, Chief of Staff Halleck had wired him: "Should you capture Charleston, I hope that by some accident the place may be destroyed, and if a little salt should be sown upon its site it may prevent the growth of future crops of nullification and secession."[22] Charleston escaped this fate, but much else in South Carolina did not. In Northern eyes the state deserved special punishment for its fire-eating role in provoking the war. Many Southerners by 1865 shared this viewpoint. During Sherman's march through Georgia, civilians repeatedly said to the Yankees: "Why don't you go over to South Carolina and serve them this way? They started it." The bluecoats were willing. Sherman reported that "the whole army is burning with an insatiable desire to wreak vengeance upon South Carolina. I almost tremble at her fate, but feel that she deserves all that seems in store for her."[23] Sherman's orders in South Carolina were the same as in Georgia: seize or destroy all forage and property of military value, but leave civilian property alone. Bummers respected these orders even less than they had in Georgia, and Sherman did little to restrain them. A Union officer noted that "in Georgia few houses were burned; here few escaped." The soldiers made little distinction between civilian and military property. They "would sometimes stop to tell me that they were sorry for the women and children," wrote a woman whose house was plundered, "but South Carolina must be *destroyed*. South Carolina and her sins was the burden of their song." A pillaging private put it succinctly: "Here is where treason began, and, by God, here is where it shall end!"[24]

The greatest outrage charged against Sherman was the burning of Columbia, the capital of South Carolina. Union soldiers entered Columbia on February 17; by next morning half the city was in ashes. The controversy over responsibility for this act has not yet abated. Southern partisans maintained that the Yankees deliberately put Columbia to the torch. Sherman and his officers insisted that the flames spread from cotton set afire by Confederate cavalry as they evacuated the city. As usual, the truth appears to lie between these claims. Civil order had broken down in Columbia even before Sherman's troops arrived. Great quantities of liquor were stored in the city; Confederate cavalrymen, hoodlums, and slaves had broken into these supplies and were rampaging through the streets, looting and setting fire to cotton. Hundreds of Union soldiers got drunk on February 17; liberated convicts from the jail and escaped Union prisoners from a nearby prisoner-of-war camp joined the inebriated rampage. Sober Union soldiers helped to put out fires started by burning cotton, but when night fell on February 17

---

[22] *O.R.,* Ser. 1, Vol. 44, p. 741.

[23] Lewis, *Sherman,* p. 446; *O.R.,* Ser. 1, Vol. 44, p. 799.

[24] Lewis, *Sherman,* pp. 493, 489; James G. Randall and David Donald, *The Civil War and Reconstruction,* 2d ed. (Lexington, Mass., 1969), p. 432.

and the wind rose to a gale, the social and meteorological combustibility of the city exploded into flame at scores of places. Soldiers and officers, Sherman included, worked through the night to contain the fires, but only a wind shift at 4 A.M. prevented the entire city from being consumed. No single group—Confederate cavalry, drunken bluecoats, vengeful prisoners, slaves, or criminals—was solely responsible for the burning of Columbia, but neither could any of them be entirely absolved of blame. Columbia was yet another victim of a war that brought more tragedy and destruction to the United States than all its other wars combined.[25]

Sherman's wrecking crew moved on to North Carolina, where they encountered an old antagonist, Joseph E. Johnston. On February 6, Robert E. Lee had become general in chief of the Confederate armies. Although Lee's popularity in the South was so great that he could have assumed dictatorial powers had it been in his character to do so, the only power of his new office that he exercised was to restore Johnston to command. Johnston's task of stopping Sherman was a forlorn hope. By bringing together several scattered units, he could muster barely 22,000 men to oppose Sherman's 60,000, soon to be joined by 30,000 bluecoats moving inland from the North Carolina coast. Johnston's only hope was to strike part of Sherman's army while it was isolated from the rest. On March 19 at Bentonville (near Raleigh), Johnston thought he saw his opportunity. With about 17,000 infantry, he attacked an equal number of Federals on the left wing of Sherman's advance. The surprised Yankees dug in and held their ground. Next day, the rest of Sherman's divisions began to arrive, but before Sherman was ready to order a general assault, the Confederates retreated northward. The Federals went on to Goldsboro to rest and refit after their seven weeks of marching and fighting.

Destruction of Confederate Resources

Behind them Sherman's troops left 425 miles of desolation that would never again support a Rebel army. And even as these weary Union veterans trudged into Goldsboro, two Union armies 700 miles to the southwest launched simultaneous strikes that laid waste the only remaining undamaged part of the Confederacy east of the Mississippi. Forty thousand men moved in two columns from Mobile Bay and Pensacola against the city of Mobile. In a three weeks' campaign, they took Mobile and captured or scattered its 10,000 defenders. Meanwhile, the twenty-seven-year-old cavalry commander James H. Wilson led the largest, longest, and most destructive cavalry raid of the war from northwest Alabama to southern Georgia. Armed with Spencer seven-shot carbines, Wilson's 13,000 troopers had twice the firepower and three times the mobility of an infantry corps. Smashing their way through Alabama, the blue horsemen defeated Forrest's once-feared cavalry in six engagements, killed or wounded 1,000 Confederates and captured 6,000, and climaxed the 500-mile raid on May 10 by capturing the fleeing Jefferson Davis at Irwinsville, Georgia. Along the

---

[25]The fullest and fairest discussion of this event is Marion Brunson Lucas, *Sherman and the Burning of Columbia* (College Station, Tex., 1976).

way they tore up railroads, wrecked 600 locomotives and freight cars, demolished dozens of munitions factories and arsenals, seized or burned enormous quantities of cotton, and destroyed 300 pieces of artillery and 10,000 small arms.

In 1861, many foreign observers had considered the Confederacy unconquerable because its large area, poor roads, and rugged terrain would defeat an invader just as Russia's vast distances had defeated Napoleon in 1812. But contrary to predictions, the South was not only invaded and conquered, it was utterly destroyed. By 1865, the Union forces had penetrated an area almost as large as France, Spain, and Germany combined. These forces destroyed two-thirds of the assessed value of Southern wealth, two-fifths of the South's livestock, and one-quarter of her white men between the ages of twenty and forty. More than half the farm machinery was ruined, and the damage to railroads and industries was incalculable. While total Northern wealth increased by 50 percent from 1860 to 1870, Southern wealth decreased by 60 percent (or 30 percent if the slaves are not counted as wealth).[26] These figures provide eloquent testimony to the tragic irony of the South's counterrevolution of 1861 to preserve its way of life. They also testify to the capacity of a modernizing society to overcome the barriers of distance and terrain in history's first "modern" war.

The Reconstruction Issue in the Winter of 1864–1865

While the Confederacy disintegrated, the Northern Congress tried again to define the conditions of reconstruction. Under Lincoln's 10 percent plan (see pages 425 and 426), Unionist governments were functioning in occupied portions of Louisiana and Arkansas. A new government was forming in Tennessee. Despite the earlier clash between Lincoln and the radicals over reconstruction, the President now hoped that Congress would recognize these governments. The spirit of Republican harmony growing out of the 1864 election augured well for a compromise between President and Congress. Lincoln's appointment of Salmon P. Chase as chief justice in December was a gesture of goodwill toward the radicals. So also was a sentence in the President's annual message indicating a willingness to support "more rigorous measures than heretofore" toward the postwar South.[27]

The President and House Republican leaders worked out a compromise whereby Congress would recognize the Lincoln-nurtured governments of Louisiana and Arkansas in return for presidential approval of legislation for the rest of the Confederacy similar to the Wade-Davis bill vetoed the previous July. This compromise measure initially enacted black suffrage in the remaining Southern states, but moderates modified it to enfranchise only black army veterans and literate blacks. During January and February 1865, a bewildering series of committee and floor votes in the House defeated several versions of the bill. Radicals voted against measures that

---

[26]James L. Sellers, "The Economic Incidence of the Civil War in the South," *Mississippi Valley Historical Review,* 14 (1927), 179–191; Stanley Engerman, "Some Economic Factors in Southern Backwardness in the Nineteenth Century," in John F. Kain and John R. Meyer (eds.), *Essays in Regional Economics* (Cambridge, Mass., 1971), pp. 300–302; *U.S. Census,* 1870, Vol. III, pp. 8–11.

[27]Basler, *Works of Lincoln,* VIII, 152.

did not enfranchise blacks or that recognized the existing Louisiana government. Conservative Republicans opposed measures that required black suffrage. Democrats voted against all reconstruction bills. As a result, no bill could be passed. In the Senate, an incongruous alliance of Democrats and radicals blocked a proposal to recognize the reconstruction government of Louisiana.[28]

Moderates regretted the breakdown of compromise efforts. But radicals were just as happy to postpone the reconstruction question until the war was over. "In the meantime," wrote a radical congressman, "I hope the nation may be educated up to our demand for universal suffrage."[29] The next Congress, elected in the Republican sweep of 1864, was sure to be more radical. The President might also become more radical. From 1861 to 1865, Lincoln had moved steadily to the left: from limited war to hard war; from gradual, compensated emancipation to immediate, universal abolition; from opposition to the arming of blacks to enthusiastic support for it; from the idea of restoring the Union to the idea of reconstructing it; from the colonization of freed slaves to the enfranchisement of black soldiers and literate blacks. At the close of the war, Lincoln again appeared to be moving closer to the radical position. In a speech on April 11, he reasserted his flexible, pragmatic approach to reconstruction. The Louisiana precedent was not necessarily applicable to other states, said the President, and he was not unalterably committed to it even in Louisiana if this proved "adverse to the public interest." At the end of his speech, Lincoln promised "some new announcement" on reconstruction in the near future. But three days later, John Wilkes Booth robbed the nation of that announcement forever.[30]

The Confederate Decision to Arm Slaves

With most of its territory overrun, its armies melting away, and its economy ruined, the Confederacy in March 1865 was clearly doomed. Yet Davis and Lee still had two cards to play in a desperate bid to stave off the inevitable. The first was the enlistment of slaves in the Confederate army. The second was an effort to unite Lee's and Johnston's 70,000 ragged, half-starved troops to strike Sherman's 90,000 and Grant's 115,000 in succession. Both enterprises were born of fantasy out of despair, but Southern leaders expressed a determination to "die in the last ditch" before they succumbed.

In 1863, the North's enlistment of black soldiers had prompted a few iconoclasts in the South to wonder whether the Confederacy might also tap this reservoir of manpower. General Patrick Cleburne openly suggested the arming of slaves early in 1864, but Jefferson Davis squelched the proposal. It could not stay squelched. As the Confederate armies disintegrated during the winter of 1864–1865, the Southern press and politicians endlessly debated the idea of drafting slaves. By the end of 1864, Davis and his cabinet supported the idea. Two years earlier Davis had denounced the North's arming of contrabands as "the most execrable measure recorded in the

---

[28]These complex events are chronicled in Herman Belz, *Reconstructing the Union: Theory and Policy During the Civil War* (Ithaca, 1969), chap. 9 and in Harris, *With Charity for All*, pp. 229–238.

[29]*Boston Commonwealth*, March 4, 1865.

[30]Basler, *Works of Lincoln*, VIII, 399–405.

history of guilty man." But much had happened since then. As a Confederate diarist put it on Christmas Day, "when the question is between slavery and independence, slavery must go."[31]

But to Southerners for whom the purpose of the war was the defense of slavery, the idea of arming black men was an "inconsistent self-stultification." "What did we go to war for, if not to protect our property?" asked Robert M. T. Hunter of Virginia, president pro tem of the Confederate Senate. Howell Cobb, one of the South's most powerful political generals, insisted that "if slaves will make good soldiers our whole theory of slavery is wrong. . . . The day you make soldiers of them is the beginning of the end of the revolution." Cobb's fellow Georgian Robert Toombs thundered that "the worst calamity that could befall us would be to gain our independence by the valor of our slaves. . . . The day that the army of Virginia allows a negro regiment to enter their lines as soldiers they will be degraded, ruined, and disgraced."[32]

It was Robert E. Lee who finally overcame this opposition. Never a strong proponent of slavery, Lee believed that if emancipated, the slaves would fight for "their country" more readily than for the Yankees. "We must decide whether slavery shall be extinguished by our enemies and the slaves be used against us, or use them ourselves," wrote Lee. "I think we could at least do as well with them as the enemy, and he attaches great importance to their assistance." So great was Lee's prestige (the *Richmond Examiner* said that "the country will not deny to General Lee . . . *anything* he may ask for") that the Confederate Congress on March 13 narrowly passed a bill to enlist black soldiers.[33] Impending disaster converted the counterrevolution of 1861 to the revolution of 1865—but not quite. Despite Lee's recommendation that slave soldiers be freed, the bill did not require this. Whether the slaves would have fought for the South with or without a promise of freedom remained a moot question. Before any regiments could be organized, the war was over.

From Petersburg to Appomattox

It was over because the Army of the Potomac had finally brought the Army of Northern Virginia to bay. For almost four years, these armies had slaughtered each other across a narrow front of 200 miles while the principal Union armies in the West had marched victoriously through a thousand miles of Rebel territory. This gave rise to a cockiness among Western troops. Lean, hard men from the farms and the frontier, they expressed contempt for the "paper collar" Eastern soldiers. When Western and Eastern Union troops came together, they traded insults and sometimes blows. An Indiana private declared in 1863 that "the war would never end were it left to the

---

[31]Edward Younger (ed.), *Inside the Confederate Government: The Diary of Robert Garlick Hill Kean* (New York, 1957), p. 182.

[32]Robert F. Durden, *The Gray and the Black: The Confederate Debate on Emancipation* (Baton Rouge, 1972), p. 184; *O.R.,* Ser. 4, Vol. 3, 1010; Shelby Foote, *The Civil War: A Narrative from Meridian to Appomattox* (New York, 1974), pp. 766, 860.

[33]Durden, *The Gray and the Black,* pp. 199, 206, 208. See also Ervin L. Jordan, Jr., *Black Confederates and Afro-Yankees in Civil War Virginia* (Charlottesville, 1995), chap. 11.

fighting of the band box army in the east. . . . They have been in but one Confederate state while we have been through five." An Illinois soldier thought that "the Potomac Army is only good to draw greenbacks and occupy winter quarters." For their part, Eastern soldiers considered Western troops an "armed rabble" who owed their military success to the inferiority of the Western Confederate armies. "The Western rebels are nothing but an armed mob," wrote one Army of the Potomac veteran in 1864, "and not anything near so hard to whip as Lee's well disciplined soldiers."[34]

Most historians of the Union armies have accepted the Westerners' image of themselves. And it cannot be denied that from Donelson to Atlanta, the Western armies won most of their battles and conquered large chunks of territory while the Army of the Potomac could do no better than a stalemate in Virginia. But this was the result less of differences in the fighting qualities of Eastern and Western soldiers than of differences in the quality of generalship, both Union and Confederate. All four of the Union's best generals—Grant, Sherman, Sheridan, and Thomas—came out of the West. Of the South's most successful generals—Lee, Jackson, Longstreet, Stuart, and Forrest—only Forrest was a Westerner. When Longstreet took part of his corps to Georgia in 1863, he provided the leadership that exploited the breakthrough at Chickamauga, the only clear victory won by the Confederate Army of Tennessee. When the 11th and 12th Corps of the Army of the Potomac went from Virginia to Chattanooga a month later, these troops, considered the weakest units in the Eastern army, became good fighting men in a Western army. It was not the men who had changed but their leaders.

The Western armies did less hard fighting than the Army of the Potomac. Not all contemporaries recognized this. A Wisconsin private who marched with Sherman wrote that "the Potomac Army has no doubt done some hard fighting, but it has been on a different scale than ours, and the most of it was done in the newspapers."[35] He could not have been more wrong. Of the fourteen bloodiest battles of the war (those with combined Union and Confederate casualties of 17,000 or more), ten were fought between the Army of Northern Virginia and the Army of the Potomac. Of the fifty Southern regiments with the highest percentage of battle casualties, forty fought in the Eastern theater. Of the fifty highest-casualty Union regiments, forty-one were in the Eastern armies. Six of the seven Union army corps with the highest battle casualties fought in the Army of the Potomac. This army alone suffered more than half the battle deaths in the entire Union armed forces. The proportion of battle deaths among soldiers from New England and the Middle Atlantic states was 23 percent higher than among those from Western states.[36]

---

[34]Bell I. Wiley, *The Life of Billy Yank* (Indianapolis, 1952), pp. 321–323; Lewis, *Sherman,* p. 362. An historian of the principal Confederate armies agrees that Lee's army was superior in fighting power to western Confederate armies. [Richard M. McMurry, *Two Great Rebel Armies: An Essay in Confederate Military History* (Chapel Hill, 1989).]

[35]Wiley, *Billy Yank,* p. 322.

[36]These data were compiled from Thomas L. Livermore, *Numbers and Losses in the Civil War* (Boston, 1901), and William F. Fox, *Regimental Losses in the American Civil War* (Albany, 1889).

The Fall of Petersburg and Richmond

Although a Westerner, Grant was sensitive to the Army of the Potomac's pride and to its resentment of the Westerners' claims of superiority. Thus he was anxious to finish the war before Sherman's army came up on Lee's rear and took credit for the final victory. Grant's greatest worry now was that he would wake up one morning to find that Lee's army had slipped away during the night to join Johnston in North Carolina. This was precisely what Lee intended to do. Before pulling out of the trenches, however, he gambled on one last assault against Grant's position east of Petersburg to compel him to shorten his encircling lines by sending reinforcements from the left. In the predawn darkness of March 25, sham Confederate deserters who had been fraternizing with Union pickets suddenly seized the surprised Yankees and spearheaded an attack that captured Fort Stedman, an earthwork in the Union line. Rebel brigades poured through the gap and soon occupied nearly a mile of Union trenches. But they could not hold them in the face of enfilading artillery fire and an infantry counterattack. By midmorning the Confederates had been driven back with a loss of 4,800 men.

Grant now seized the initiative. He sent two infantry corps and 12,000 cavalry to flank the Confederate right, tear up the last open railroad into Petersburg, and block Lee's escape route to the southwest. At a road junction called Five Forks, Sheridan's cavalry and the 5th Corps on April 1 struck 10,000 Confederates in front and flank and routed them, inflicting more than 5,000 casualties at a cost of only 1,000 to themselves. When Grant learned of Sheridan's success, he ordered an assault all along the Petersburg lines at dawn the next day. The remaining Confederates put up a desperate struggle, falling back from one line of trenches to the next during a long and bloody day that cost the Federals 4,000 killed and wounded. Grant hoped to trap Lee's army in Petersburg, but during the night the Rebels escaped across the Appomattox River and retreated westward. Meanwhile, the Confederate government and all troops in the area evacuated Richmond after blowing up bridges, factories, and arsenals, and burning all tobacco and government property that could not be removed. By dawn on April 3, Richmond was a blazing inferno.

Among the first Union soldiers to take possession of the city were black troopers of the 5th Massachusetts Cavalry, commanded by Charles Francis Adams, Jr., eldest son of the minister to Britain and grandson of President John Quincy Adams. Once again, as at Charleston, the first task of the occupation troops was to put out the fires, which they had done by nightfall, but only after most of the business and industrial sections of Richmond were destroyed. Next day, President Lincoln visited the ruined city, escorted by a troop of black cavalry. Richmond blacks turned out by the thousands to cheer every step of their way. "I know I am free," shouted one, "for I have seen Father Abraham and felt him." A black correspondent of one of the leading Northern newspapers, T. Morris Chester of the *Philadelphia Press,* sat quietly in the Confederate Capitol, writing a dispatch describing the scene. For Richmond whites this was tangible evidence, if any more was needed, of the shattering revolution that had turned their world upside down.[37]

---

[37] *Philadelphia Press,* April 11, 12, 1865.

U.S. ARMY MILITARY HISTORY INSTITUTE

LIBRARY OF CONGRESS

VICTORS AND VANQUISHED. *Above:* Union soldiers resting in the trenches after fighting at Petersburg. *Left:* A fourteen-year-old Confederate soldier killed in the Petersburg trenches during the final Union assault on April 2, 1865. Nothing could testify more powerfully than these two pictures to the contrast in the strength and resources of the two sides at the war's end.

The Road to Appomattox

While these events took place in Richmond, Lee's army of 35,000 was trying to escape from 80,000 Federals in hot pursuit. Sheridan's cavalry and two infantry corps raced parallel to the fleeing Confederates on their left to prevent Lee from turning southward, while two other infantry corps stayed on their rear, picking up hundreds of exhausted Rebel stragglers. On April 6, at Sayler's Creek near Farmville, the Federals cut off and captured 7,000 Confederates after a battle in which the bluecoats lost only 1,200 men. "My God! Has the Army been dissolved?" agonized Lee as he watched the climax of this action. On April 8, Sheridan got in front of what was left of Lee's army and captured two trainloads of rations at Appomattox Station, 100 miles west of Petersburg. When a final Confederate attempt to break through the encircling ring on the morning of April 9 revealed two blue infantry corps in line behind the cavalry, Lee realized that the game was up. One of his artillery officers suggested that the army scatter to the woods and carry on the war as guerrillas. But Lee would have none of this. The guerrillas, he said, "would become mere bands of marauders, and the enemy's cavalry would pursue them and overrun many sections they may [otherwise] never have occasion to visit. We would bring on a state of affairs it would take the country years to recover from." No, said Lee, "there is nothing left for me to do but to go and see General Grant, and I would rather die a thousand deaths."[38]

Lee Surrenders

But go he did, to the house of Wilmer McLean in the village of Appomattox Courthouse. Ironically, McLean had owned a house near Manassas, Virginia, in 1861 that had been used as a Confederate headquarters in the first battle of Bull Run. He had moved to this remote corner of Virginia to escape the ravages of contending armies, only to witness the final act of the war in his living room. Lee arrived resplendent in full-dress uniform; Grant, whose headquarters wagon had not kept up in the mad dash to cut off the Confederates, came to this historic meeting in a faded campaign blouse and with trousers tucked into mud-spattered boots. The only general in American history to capture three separate armies (at Donelson, Vicksburg, and now Appomattox), Grant proposed generous terms that paroled Lee's whole army and allowed them to take their horses or mules home "to put in a crop." As the two generals shook hands, Grant felt "sad and depressed" at "the downfall of a foe who had fought so long and valiantly, and had suffered so much for a cause, though that cause was, I believe, one of the worst for which a people ever fought."[39]

Some Union officers were so awestruck by the news of Lee's surrender that they could hardly believe it. One colonel who had fought in Virginia for three years wrote two weeks after the capitulation at Appomattox: "None of us realize even yet that [Lee] has actually surrendered. I had a sort of impression that we should fight him all our lives." But as news of the surrender spread through Union camps on April 9,

---

[38]Douglas Southall Freeman, *R. E. Lee: A Biography,* 4 vols. (New York, 1934–1935), IV, 120–123.
[39]Ulysses S. Grant, *Personal Memoirs,* 2 vols. (New York, 1885), II, 489.

the soldiers began to celebrate. "The air is black with hats and boots, coats, knapsacks, shirts and cartridge boxes," wrote one veteran who tried to describe the scene. "They fall on each others' necks and laugh and cry by turns. Huge, lumbering, bearded men embrace and kiss like schoolgirls, then dance and sing and shout, stand on their heads and play leapfrog with each other." Every band in the army struck up, each trying to outdo the others in volume and spirit.[40] As the telegraph flashed the news of Lee's surrender through the North, which was just recovering from its celebration of the fall of Richmond, new and wilder jubilation broke out.

The Assassination of Lincoln and the End of the War

Suddenly, the rejoicing turned to grief as once more the telegraph clicked out momentous news—but this time news of terrible, grave import—the assassination of Lincoln. On April 14, the careworn fifty-six-year-old President had relaxed by attending a comedy at Ford's Theater. In the middle of the play, John Wilkes Booth gained entrance to Lincoln's box and shot him in the head. Jumping to the stage (where he broke his leg), Booth shouted "Sic semper tyrannis" and hobbled out a rear door, escaping on horseback before anyone in the theater could stop him.

An aspiring young actor overshadowed by the greater fame of his father and his older brother Edwin, John Wilkes Booth was a frustrated, unstable egotist who supported the Confederacy and hated Lincoln. He had plotted for months to kidnap Lincoln and hold him hostage for concessions to the Confederacy. To help in this mad scheme, he recruited several allies from Washington's underworld of drifters, Rebel spies, and Confederate deserters. The fall of Richmond and Lee's surrender ruined the kidnapping venture, so Booth decided instead to murder Lincoln, Vice President Johnson, and Secretary of State Seward. The accomplice assigned to assassinate Johnson lost his nerve; Seward suffered serious stabbing wounds but survived. On April 26, Union troops finally tracked down the Maryland-born Booth and shot him to death in a burning barn in Virginia. A military court convicted eight accomplices of collusion in the assassination. Four were hanged, and the rest were sentenced to life imprisonment. Some contemporaries and historians believed that in two of these cases a miscarriage of justice occurred: Mary Surratt, keeper of a boardinghouse where several of the conspirators lived and planned the kidnapping; and Dr. Samuel Mudd, who treated Booth's broken leg after the assassination but claimed that he did not recognize Booth or know what he had done. Recent research, however, has made it clear that Mrs. Surratt was part of the kidnapping plot and may have known about Booth's intention to kill Lincoln, while Dr. Mudd was closely associated with Booth and knew more about the kidnapping plot and the assassination than he admitted. Mrs. Surratt was hanged and Mudd was imprisoned but pardoned (along with the other imprisoned conspirators) in 1869.

Booth's death before he could stand trial spawned numerous conspiracy theories purporting to reveal the true story of the assassination. Many Northerners believed that Jefferson Davis and other Confederate officials had conspired with

---

[40] *War Diary and Letters of Stephen Minot Weld, 1861–1865* (Boston, 1979), p. 396; Bruce Catton, *Grant Takes Command* (Boston, 1969), p. 469.

Booth; others thought Andrew Johnson was somehow involved. One of the wilder theories is that Booth, a secret convert to Roman Catholicism, killed Lincoln at the order of the Jesuits. Most popular of the modern conspiracy theories has been the thesis that Secretary of War Stanton plotted the assassination in behalf of a clique of radical Republicans who wanted to get rid of Lincoln because of his "soft" reconstruction policy. Still other writers maintain that the man killed in Virginia was not Booth but someone else with his initials who looked like the actor. None of these theories is supported by any credible evidence. Booth and his accomplices appear to have acted on their own. But recent scholarship has established that the Confederate Secret Service was involved in the kidnapping plot, and that high Confederate officials including Secretary of State Judah Benjamin and perhaps Jefferson Davis were aware of this plot. Much of the evidence on this matter is circumstantial rather than solid, however, especially for Confederate involvement in Booth's decision to assassinate Lincoln.[41]

The Martyred President

On April 15, 1865, Andrew Johnson took the oath as President of a nation in shock and mourning. People wept in the streets for the martyred Lincoln. General Grant wept openly during the funeral services in the White House on April 19. Millions stood silently along the tracks as a nine-car train carried Lincoln's body the thousand miles from Washington back home to Springfield, Illinois. In a nation with an abiding religious heritage, the murder of the President on Good Friday seemed to be more than a coincidence. For black people, especially, Lincoln's death at the moment of victory over slavery made of him a Christ-like figure. The event clothed with new meaning the last verse of Julia Ward Howe's "Battle Hymn of the Republic": "As He died to make men holy, Let us die to make men free."

Anger as well as sorrow marked the Northern mood in the weeks after the assassination. There were bitter cries for vengeance against not only the assassination conspirators but against all Confederate leaders, who were considered to be ultimately responsible for the death not only of Lincoln but also of the 360,000 Union soldiers who had been killed in the war. But such cries were contrary to the teachings of the Christ to whom Lincoln was now being compared. They also seemed to be contrary to the moving peroration of Lincoln's second inaugural address: "With malice toward none; with charity for all; with firmness in the right, as God gives us to see the right, let us strive . . . to bind up the nation's wounds [and to achieve] a just, and lasting peace."[42]

---

[41]For a summary and analysis of various assassination theories, see William Hanchett, *The Lincoln Murder Conspiracies* (Urbana, Ill., 1983) and William G. Eidson, "Recent Scholarship on the Lincoln Assassination," *The Filson Club History Quarterly,* 62 (April 1988), 220–250. The case for Confederate involvement in at least the kidnapping plot, and for Mrs. Surratt's and Dr. Mudd's culpability, is made by William A. Tidwell, James O. Hall, and David Winfred Geddy, *Come Retribution: The Confederate Secret Service and the Assassination of Lincoln* (Jackson, Miss., 1988) and William A. Tidwell, *April '65: Confederate Covert Action in the American Civil War* (Kent, Ohio, 1995). Almost everything known about Booth is brought together in John Rhodehamel and Louise Taper (eds.) *"Right or Wrong, God Judge Me": The Writings of John Wilkes Booth* (Urbana, Ill., 1997).

[42]Basler, *Works of Lincoln,* VIII, 333.

The tension in this passage between "charity" and "firmness" would mark Northern attitudes toward the South for months after the assassination, just as it had marked Lincoln's wartime leadership. His greatness as president had lain in his ability to resolve these and other tensions in such a manner as to maintain the Northern will to fight through many moments of doubt, discouragement, and division.

Subject to moods of depression (which he called "the hypo"), Lincoln had learned to transcend despair in his personal life just as the Union under his leadership was able to transcend its national despair. The President told anecdotes not only as parables to illustrate points about larger issues but also to dissolve anxiety in laughter. Lincoln loved to frolic with his two youngest sons, eleven-year-old Willie and eight-year-old Tad. In February 1862, both fell ill, probably with typhoid fever. Tad recovered, but Willie did not; on February 20 he died. (In a sad parallel two years later, five-year-old Joseph Davis, son of the Confederate president, fell from a balcony of the executive mansion in Richmond and died of a skull fracture.) Abraham and Mary Lincoln were almost prostrated with grief at Willie's death. Abraham recovered to face the problems of emancipation, political opposition, and military defeats and to overcome them; Mary suffered a nervous breakdown and never fully regained her mental balance. The anguish in the White House was a microcosm of the ordeal experienced by the nation during Lincoln's four years and six weeks as president. No other president endured such personal affliction while in office; no other president faced such a national crisis. Lincoln's success in surmounting both is a measure of his humanity and his greatness.

The End of the War

During the weeks after Lincoln's death, while President Johnson was trying to get accustomed to his new office and several Confederate armies were still in the field, Secretary of War Stanton was the government's strong man. Brusque and excitable, Stanton feared that the assassination was part of a Rebel plot to overthrow the government. He ordered the arrest of many Confederate sympathizers; those implicated in the assassination were harshly treated and their legal rights all but ignored.

In the midst of these events came news of the surrender terms negotiated by Sherman and Johnston. These terms aroused in Stanton a different set of suspicions. An advocate of hard war, Sherman had always hoped for a soft peace once the Rebels were thoroughly whipped. He had opposed the arming of blacks; he had little faith in black equality; he opposed the radical program of reconstruction. In the spirit of what Sherman thought Lincoln's policy would have been, he went far beyond Grant's surrender terms for Lee's army and negotiated with Johnston what amounted to a peace treaty. It provided for the recognition of existing Southern state governments when their officials had taken the oath of allegiance; it allowed disbanded Confederate troops to deposit their arms in state arsenals; and it guaranteed to Southerners "their political rights and franchises, as well as their rights of person and property."

Normally astute and chary of political involvement, Sherman here committed a major blunder. Not only did he exceed his authority, but he also failed to see that this agreement could be interpreted as recognizing insurgent governments, guaranteeing property in slaves, and taking the question of reconstruction out of the hands of the President and Congress. Grant conveyed to Sherman the cabinet's unanimous disapproval of the terms, and Sherman unhesitatingly negotiated a new surrender agreement with Johnston on April 26 that duplicated the Grant-Lee terms. There the matter might have rested except that Stanton, distrustful of Sherman's motives (Democrats were beginning to sing his praises), released to the press a distorted version of the affair that put Sherman in a bad light. Stanton's fears were unfounded; his action, though sincere, was unjust, and Sherman never forgave the secretary of war.[43]

Everyone in Washington, Stanton most of all, was under great pressure during the weeks after the assassination. Although Lee had surrendered, Jefferson Davis and his cabinet remained at large, moving southward as fast as the dilapidated railroads could carry them. Davis exhorted his people to fight on, "operating in the interior," where the enemy's extended lines of communication would "render our triumph certain."[44] Even after Johnston surrendered, Davis spoke of moving the government to the trans-Mississippi states and carrying on the war. To the Union government it appeared that guerrilla warfare might go on for years. But most Southerners had had more than enough. Lee's example was stronger than Davis's rallying cries. In Alabama on May 4, General Richard Taylor surrendered the remaining Confederate forces east of the Mississippi. Union cavalry captured Jefferson Davis and his entourage in Georgia on May 10. On May 26, General Edmund Kirby Smith surrendered the trans-Mississippi army. These events of May brightened the skies in Washington. The problems of peace still lay ahead, but the war was definitely over.

Demobilization of the Union Armies

Two feared consequences of the war did not materialize. (1) There was no bloodbath of vengeance. No Confederates were tried for treason. Jefferson Davis was imprisoned without trial for two years but then released to live a quiet life and write his memoirs. This absence of reprisals was almost unique in the history of rebellions, especially those waged on the scale of this one. (2) The army did not become a power in American life. To be sure, every elected president until 1904 save one (Grover Cleveland) had fought in the Union army and owed his political success in part to his war record. But none of them, not even Grant, was a "military" president; all except Grant were civilians who had sprung to arms in the crisis of 1861 and returned to civilian life as quickly in 1865.

Before they went home, however, the Army of the Potomac and Sherman's army held a Grand Review in Washington on May 23–24. For two days, the armed might of the republic marched in a giant parade down Pennsylvania Avenue before thousands of cheering spectators. As Sherman's long-striding Westerners came swinging by on the second day, some people in the stands began to sing "John Brown's Body." The soldiers picked it up, and soon thousands of voices were thundering the great marching song of the Union armies in a city once trod by slaves. Nothing could have testified more eloquently to the revolution wrought by the war.

---

[43]Stanton's motives and personality have eluded the analytical efforts of many historians. Efficient, incorruptible, hardworking, and intensely dedicated to the Union, he was a superb secretary of war. At the same time, he was secretive, high-strung, brusque, sometimes devious in personal relationships, and often insensitive to the feelings of others.

[44]Rowland, *Jefferson Davis,* VI, 530.

LIBRARY OF CONGRESS

THE GRAND REVIEW.   Part of the Army of the Potomac marching down Pennsylvania Avenue in the victory parade of May 23, 1865.

After the Grand Review, the victorious veterans scattered quietly to their homes. The Union armies were demobilized with remarkable swiftness. Within two months 641,000 men had been mustered out. The navy shrank from 530 to 117 warships by the end of 1865. By November 1866, only 65,000 men remained in an army that eighteen months earlier had numbered more than a million. Although some veterans experienced psychological problems and others never fully recovered from wounds or the physical hardships of their service, most returning soldiers seemed to readjust readily to civilian life. "When I returned home I found that the farm work my father was then engaged in was cutting and shucking corn," wrote an Illinois veteran.

So, the morning after my arrival, September 29th, I doffed my uniform of first lieutenant, put on some of my father's old clothes, and proceeded to wage war on the standing corn. The feeling I had while engaged in this work was sort of queer. It almost seemed, sometimes, as if I had been away only a day or two, and had just taken up the farm work where I had left off.[45]

The Imprint of War

But in truth, nothing would ever be the same again for this Illinois veteran—or for anyone else in the country. The war left an indelible imprint on the nation's consciousness. A thrice-wounded infantry captain and future Supreme Court justice put it best: "The generation that carried on the war has been set apart by its experience," said Oliver Wendell Holmes in 1884. "Through our great good fortune, in our youth our hearts were touched with fire. It was given to us to learn at the outset that life is a profound and passionate thing."[46] The Civil War generated a greater outpouring of memoirs, regimental histories, popular literature, and scholarly studies than any other war in American history—perhaps more than all of them combined. Civil War roundtables multiply and flourish into the twenty-first century. The Civil War monuments on town squares in thousands of communities far outnumber the monuments to other notable events in the American past. For generations, Southerners dated their history by reference to "before the war" or "since the war"—and nobody had to ask which war they meant. In the 1960s, "The Battle Hymn of the Republic" became one of the inspirational songs of the civil rights movement, while the Confederate flag and "Dixie" served as symbols of Southern resistance to that movement. These symbols remain powerful in America today.

One reason for the Civil War's profound impact was its human cost. Approximately 620,000 soldiers lost their lives (360,000 Union and 260,000 Confederate), a toll that nearly equals the 680,000 American fighting men killed in all the other wars combined in which the United States has been involved. There was scarcely a family in North or South that did not mourn a relative or friend killed in the war. Veterans' organizations—the Grand Army of the Republic and the United Confederate Veterans—kept war memories alive and became potent political forces in their respective sections. In time, heroic myths and romance glazed over the war's grim realities. But these myths themselves, especially in the South, soon became an important reality—a lens through which people viewed their world, providing a perspective that governed their lives.

The Civil War marked a decisive turn in the nature of American nationality. Buried forever was the notion of the Union as a voluntary confederation of sovereign states. The word "Union" gradually gave way to "nation." The name "United States" became construed as a singular rather than plural noun. The war strengthened the national government at the expense of the states. Before 1861, only the post office among

---

[45]Leander Stillwell, *The Story of a Common Soldier, or Army Life in the Civil War* (Erie, Kansas, 1917), p. 154. For an important and thought-provoking study that identifies a higher percentage of psychiatric casualties and a higher incidence of post-traumatic stress disorder among Civil War veterans than previously recognized, see Eric T. Dean, Jr., *Shook Over Hell: Post-Traumatic Stress, Vietnam, and the Civil War* (Cambridge, Mass. 1997).

[46]Oliver Wendell Holmes, Jr., *Speeches* (Boston, 1913), p. 11.

federal agencies touched directly the lives of most Americans. Citizens paid their taxes to local or state governments and settled most of their disputes in state courts. For money, they used the notes of banks chartered by state legislatures. When war came in 1861, the President called first on the state militia. State governors took the lead in recruiting, equipping, and officering the volunteer regiments. But the centralizing pressures of war changed all this. By 1863, the War Department prescribed enlistment quotas for states and drafted men directly into the army if states failed to meet the quotas. The President declared martial law and stationed soldiers in every state, where their powers of detention superseded those of state courts. The United States government levied a host of direct taxes and created an internal revenue bureau to collect them. It printed paper money, established a national banking system, and taxed state banknotes out of existence. It confiscated the property and freed the slaves of Southern citizens, and it set up a social welfare agency—the Freedmen's Bureau—to override state law in the governance of the freedpeople. The first eleven amendments to the Constitution had limited the power of the federal government; the Thirteenth Amendment established a precedent by which the next six amendments restricted state powers or expanded those of the national government.

The war's impact fell most heavily on the South. Emancipation made the deepest dent of all in the social order. Seventy years later, aged ex-slaves interviewed by the Federal Writers Project recalled with vivid clarity the day they had learned of their freedom. For many, it was still the central event of their lives. So sweeping was this transformation that contemporaries described it in the language of revelation and revolution. North Carolina freedmen believed that "these are the times foretold by the Prophets, 'When a Nation shall be born in a day.' "[47] A Memphis newspaper marveled in 1865: "The events of the last five years have produced an entire revolution in the social system of the entire Southern country." The chaplain of a black regiment occupying Wilmington described the whites who stared at the soldiers as uncertain "whether they are actually in another world, or whether this one is turned wrong side out." One black soldier, recognizing his former master among a group of Confederate prisoners he was guarding, shouted a greeting: "Hello, massa; bottom rail on top dis time!"[48]

In 1865, the bottom rail did indeed appear to be on top. Whether it would stay there depended on the events of Reconstruction.

---

[47]Leon F. Litwack, *Been in the Storm So Long: The Aftermath of Slavery* (New York, 1979), p. 171; William McKee Evans, *Ballots and Fence Rails: Reconstruction on the Lower Cape Fear* (New York, 1967), p. 87.

[48]Eugene D. Genovese, *Roll, Jordan, Roll: The World the Slaves Made* (New York, 1974), p. 110; Litwack, *Been in the Storm So Long*, pp. 96, 102.

Part Two Timeline

1861:
- **April–June:** Virginia, Arkansas, North Carolina, and Tennessee secede and join Confederacy
- **April 19:** Mob attacks Massachusetts troops in Baltimore Lincoln declares blockade of Confederacy
- **May 10:** Union soldiers and Confederate mob clash in St. Louis
- **June 10:** "Battle" of Boonville, Missouri
- **July 11:** Battle of Rich Mountain (West Virginia)
- **July 13:** Battle of Carrick's Ford (West Virginia)
- **July 21:** First Battle of Bull Run (Manassas) (Virginia)
- **July 26:** McClellan takes command of Army of the Potomac
- **August 6:** Union Congress passes first Confiscation Act
- **August 10:** Battle of Wilson's Creek (Missouri)
- **August 29:** Union capture of Fort Hatteras, North Carolina
- **August 30:** Fremont declares martial law, frees slaves of Confederate supporters in Missouri
- **September 3:** Confederate forces enter Kentucky
- **September 6:** Union forces enter Kentucky
- **September 11:** Lincoln rescinds Fremont's emancipation edict
- **October 21:** Battle of Balls' Bluff (Virginia)
- **November 7:** Union capture of Port Royal (South Carolina)
- **November 8:** USS *San Jacinto* seizes Mason and Slidell from British ship *Trent*
- **November 26:** Convention in Wheeling forms new state of West Virginia
- **December 26:** Lincoln administration releases Mason and Slidell

1862:
- **January 19:** Battle of Logan's Cross Roads, Kentucky (Mill Springs)
- **February 6:** Capture of Fort Henry (Tennessee)
- **February 8:** Battle of Roanoke Island (North Carolina)
- **February 16:** Grant captures Fort Donelson (Tennessee)
- **February 21:** Battle of Valverde (New Mexico)
- **February 25:** Union Congress passes Legal Tender Act
- **March 7–8:** Battle of Pea Ridge (Arkansas)
- **March 8:** CSS *Virginia* (*Merrimack*) sinks USS *Cumberland* and USS *Congress*
- **March 9:** Fight between USS *Monitor* and CSS *Virginia* (*Merrimack*)
- **March 23:** Battle of Kernstown (Virginia)
- **March 26–28:** Battle of Glorieta Pass (New Mexico)
- **April 6–7:** Battle of Shiloh (Tennessee)
- **April 8:** Union capture of Island No. 10 (Tennessee)
- **April 16:** Confederate Congress enacts conscription
- **April 29:** Fall of New Orleans

May 9: General Hunter issues order freeing slaves in South Carolina, Georgia, and Florida

May 15: Union naval attack on Drewry's Bluff (Virginia) fails

May 19: Lincoln rescinds Hunter's emancipation order

May 20: Union Congress passes Homestead Act

May 25: Battle of Winchester (Virginia)

May 30: Confederates evacuate Corinth, Mississippi

May 31–June 1: Battle of Seven Pines; Lee takes command of Army of Northern Virginia

June 6: Capture of Memphis

June 8: Battle of Cross Keys (Virginia)

June 9: Battle of Port Republic (Virginia)

June 25–July 1: Seven Days Battles (Virginia)

June 26: Mechanicsville

June 27: Gaines' Mill

June 29: Savage Station

June 30: Glendale and White Oak Swamp

July 1: Malvern Hill

July 1: Union Congress passes Pacific Railroad Act

July 2: Union Congress passes Morrill Land-Grant College Act

July 17: Union Congress passes second Confiscation Act

August 9: Battle of Cedar Mountain (Virginia)

August 29–30: Second Battle of Bull Run (Manassas)

September 14: Battles of Turner's Gap and Crampton's Gap (South Mountain range, Maryland)

September 17: Battle of Antietam (Sharpsburg) (Maryland)

September 19: Battle of Iuka (Mississippi)

September 22: Lincoln issues preliminary Emancipation Proclamation

October 3–4: Battle of Corinth (Mississippi)

October 8: Battle of Perryville (Kentucky)

October–November: Democrats make gains in Union congressional elections

November 7: Burnside replaces McClellan as commander of Army of the Potomac

December 7: Battle of Prairie Grove (Arkansas)

December 13: Battle of Fredericksburg (Virginia)

December 29: Battle of Chickasaw Bluffs (Mississippi)

December 31, 1862–January 2, 1863: Battle of Stones River (Murfreesboro) (Tennessee)

1863: *January 1:* Lincoln issues Emancipation Proclamation

January 25: Hooker replaces Burnside as commander of Army of the Potomac

February 25: Union Congress passes National Bank Act

March 3: Union Congress enacts conscription

April 2: Bread riot in Richmond

April–July: Grant's Vicksburg campaign (Mississippi)

May 1: Battle of Port Gibson

May 12: Battle of Raymond

May 14: Capture of Jackson

May 16: Battle of Champion's Hill

May 17: Battle of Big Black River

May 19 and 22: Failed assaults on Vicksburg defenses

July 4: Surrender of Vicksburg

May 1–6: Battle of Chancellorsville (Virginia)

June 9: Battle of Brandy Station (Virginia)

June 20: West Virginia officially enters Union

June 28: Meade replaces Hooker as commander of Army of the Potomac

July 1–3: Battle of Gettysburg (Pennsylvania)

July 9: Surrender of Port Hudson

July 13–16: Draft riots in New York

September 9: Confederates evacuate Chattanooga (Tennessee)

September 19–20: Battle of Chickamauga (Georgia)

November: Confederate congressional elections strengthen anti-Davis faction

November 24: Battle of Lookout Mountain (Chattanooga)

November 25: Battle of Missionary Ridge (Chattanooga)

November 29: Battle of Knoxville (Tennessee)

December 8: Lincoln issues Proclamation of Amnesty and Reconstruction

December 16: Johnston replaces Bragg as commander of Army of Tennessee

1864:

April 8: Battle of Sabine Crossroads or Mansfield (Louisiana)

April 9: Battle of Pleasant Hill (Louisiana)

May 5–6: Battle of the Wilderness (Virginia)

May 11: Battle of Yellow Tavern; mortal wounding of Stuart (Virginia)

May 12–19: Battle of Spotsvylvania (Virginia)

May 14–15: Battle of Resaca (Georgia)

May 15: Battle of New Market (Virginia)

May 16: Battle of Drewry's Bluff (Virginia)

May 25–28: Battles near Dallas and New Hope Church (Georgia)

June 3: Failed assault at Cold Harbor (Virginia)

June 8: Lincoln renominated

June 10: Battle of Brice's Crossroads (Mississippi)

June 11–12: Battle of Trevilian Station (Virginia)

June 15–18: Failed assaults at Petersburg (Virginia)

June 27: Battle of Kenesaw Mountain (Georgia)

July 2: Union Congress passes Wade-Davis bill; Lincoln pocket-vetoes it

July 11: Jubal Early's forces reach outskirts of Washington

July 14: Battle of Tupelo (Mississippi)

July 17: Hood replaces Johnston as commander of Army of Tennessee

July 20: Battle of Peachtree Creek (Georgia)

July 22: Battle of Atlanta
Peace negotiations in Niagara Falls and Richmond publicized

July 28: Battle of Ezra Church (Georgia)

July 30: Battle of the Crater (Virginia)
Burning of Chambersburg (Pennsylvania)

August 5: Wade-Davis Manifesto
Battle of Mobile Bay (Alabama)

August 23: Lincoln writes memorandum predicting defeat in presidential election

August 31: Democrats nominate McClellan for president

August 31–September 1: Battle of Jonesboro (Georgia)

September 2: Fall of Atlanta

September 19: Battle of Winchester (Opequon Creek) (Virginia)

September 22: Battle of Fisher's Hill (Virginia)

October 19: Battle of Cedar Creek (Virginia)

November 8: Lincoln reelected

November 15–16: Sherman's army leaves Atlanta on March to the Sea

November 30: Battle of Franklin (Tennessee)

December 15–16: Battle of Nashville

December 22: Sherman occupies Savannah

1865: *January 15:* Capture of Fort Fisher (North Carolina)

January 31: House passes 13th Amendment

February 17–18: Burning of Columbia (South Carolina)

February 18: Fall of Charleston

March 3: Congress creates Freedmen's Bureau

March 13: Confederate Congress passes Negro soldier bill

March 19: Battle of Bentonville (North Carolina)

March 25: Battle of Fort Stedman (Virginia)

April 1: Battle of Five Forks (Virginia)

April 2: Petersburg and Richmond fall

April 6: Battle of Sayler's Creek (Virginia)

April 9: Lee surrenders to Grant at Appomattox

April 14: Booth assassinates Lincoln

April 26: Johnston surrenders to Sherman

May 10: Jefferson Davis captured

May 23–24: Grand Review of Union armies in Washington

May 26: Last substantial Confederate army surrenders

December 6: 13th Amendment ratified

Part Three Reconstruction

The Problems of Peace

We tell the white men of Mississippi that the men of the North will convert the State of Mississippi into a frog pond before they will allow such laws to disgrace one foot of the soil in which the bones of our soldiers sleep and over which the flag of freedom waves.

—Chicago Tribune,
December 1, 1865, on the Mississippi black code

The Aftermath of War

The South in 1865 presented a bleak landscape of destruction and desolation. Burned-out plantations, fields growing up in weeds, and railroads without tracks, bridges, or rolling stock marked the trail of the conquering Union armies. The collapse of Confederate authority left large areas without law and order. Roaming bands of guerrillas and deserters plundered defenseless homes. Hundreds of thousands of freedpeople and white refugees suffered from disease, exposure, and hunger. As just one example of the horrors left by the war, a pile of sixty-five horses and mules killed by Sherman's army lay unburied near Columbia, South Carolina, for six weeks because the troops had carried off all spades and other implements.

Having swept through the South as destroyers, Yankees remained there as restorers. Into the vacuum of devastation and chaos moved the occupation forces, the Freedmen's Bureau, and Northern relief agencies. The 200,000 occupation troops functioned as the main source of law and order. The army placed the ex-Confederate states under martial law. Military courts punished criminals, and Freedmen's Bureau courts regulated relations between former slaves and their former masters. Army hospitals treated thousands of Southern civilians, both black and white. During the summer of 1865, the Freedmen's Bureau issued 150,000 daily rations (one-third of them to white refugees), and the army fed at least as many more Southern civilians. The Freedmen's Bureau continued to provide food relief even after the postwar crisis eased; between 1865 and 1870, the Bureau issued nearly twenty-two million rations.

But not every agency of the government contributed to rehabilitation. The Treasury Department sent special agents into the South to seize whatever Confederate cotton had survived the war. However honest these agents may have been when they left Washington, several of them succumbed to temptation when they reached their destinations. At prices of $200 a bale or more, cotton still exercised its wartime power to corrupt. Some Treasury men and army officers seized privately owned cotton, stamped it "C.S.A.," and sold it on their own accounts or extorted bribes from the owners not to do so. In this way, sizable amounts of the South's only remaining form of liquid wealth were siphoned away. In 1865, Congress levied a tax of 2.5 cents a pound on cotton and in 1866 raised it to 3 cents. Although the purpose of this tax, like that of similar taxes on Northern products, was to help pay the cost of the war, the impost appeared vengeful to the South. It also retarded the region's economic recovery. Congress finally repealed the cotton tax in 1868.

The Attitudes of Southern Whites

Contradictory appraisals of the Southern mood were sent north by army officers, government officials, and the multitude of journalists who flocked southward after Appomattox. Stories of continued defiance toward Yankees and violence against freedmen mingled with reports of submission and docility.

Southern whites were a proud people who had staked all and lost all. Hatred of their conquerors was a natural repsonse. "Day by day and hour by hour does the deep seated enmity I have always had . . . for the accursed Yankee nation increase & burn higher," wrote a young planter late in the war. "They have slaughtered our kindred . . . destroyed our prosperity as a people & filled our whole land with sorrow. . . . I have vowed that if I should have children—the first ingredient of the first principle of their education shall be uncompromising hatred & contempt of the Yankee." An innkeeper in North Carolina told a Northern journalist in 1865 that the Yankees had killed his soldier sons, burned his house, and stolen his slaves. "They've left me one inestimable privilege—to hate 'em. I git up at half-past four in the morning, and sit up till twelve at night, to hate 'em."[1]

Observers agreed that such attitudes were less prevalent among Confederate soldiers than among noncombatants, especially women. The soldiers had had enough of defiance, at least for the time being.[2] The experience of fraternization across the lines with Billy Yank and the liberal surrender terms, which protected Confederate soldiers from punishment for treason, also worked for the reconciliation of veterans to defeat. But noncombatants had endured the suspense and agony of war with no outlet for their anger. Many had been forced to watch helplessly as the invaders destroyed their property. After the fighting ended, their pent-up bitterness exploded in expressions of hatred and often in violence. The freed slaves and Southern white Unionists sometimes became surrogate victims of attacks by frustrated Southerners

---

[1] James L. Roark, *Masters Without Slaves: Southern Planters in the Civil War and Reconstruction* (New York, 1977), p. 86; John T. Trowbridge, *A Picture of the Desolated States and the Work of Restoration, 1865–1868* (Hartford, 1868), p. 577.

[2] Two or three years later, however, Confederate veterans would play a dominant role in the Ku Klux Plan and similar organizations.

who did not dare to assault the real symbols of their humiliation, Yankee soldiers. For Southern white women, behavior such as the following incident in July 1865, described by a Northern reporter, provided an outlet for repressed rancor:

A day or two ago a Union officer, yielding to an impulse of politeness, handed a dish of pickles to a Southern lady at the dinner-table of a hotel in this city [Savannah]. A look of unspeakable scorn and indignation met him. "So you think," said the lady, "a Southern woman will take a dish of pickles from a hand that is dripping with the blood of her countrymen?"[3]

This woman's hostility sprang in part from awareness of the human disaster caused by the war. About one-third of the Confederate soldiers were married, so some 85,000 of the 260,000 Southern war dead left behind the same number of widows and perhaps 200,000 fatherless children. (The number of widows and fatherless children in the North was larger, but their percentage of the Northern population was much smaller.) Countless other young Southern white women would never marry or would marry late because so many potential husbands had been killed. A complex psychological mixture of grief, bitterness, and pride underlay the formation by Southern women of Confederate memorial associations, which sent commissioners to Civil War battlefields to disinter the remains of Southern soldiers who had been hastily buried, often in mass graves, and bring them home for reinterment with dignity in hundreds of Confederate cemeteries throughout the South. These solemn ceremonies assuaged grief and also formed the basis of the "Lost Cause" mentality that underlay Southern defiance of Reconstruction and the creation of a Southern mythology about the Old South, slavery, and the Civil War, a mythology that persisted for generations and still persists under the auspices of the United Daughters of the Confederacy and similar organizations.

During the early postwar months, however, many Southerners experienced successive waves of shock, despair, and apathy before feeling anger, which is a sign of reviving spirits. "*We* give up to the *Yankees!*" wrote a shocked woman when she learned of Lee's surrender. "How can it be? . . . Have we suffered all—have our brave men fought so desperately and died so nobly for this?" In June 1865, the daughter of a Georgia planter looked forward to nothing more than "a joyless future of probable ignominy, poverty, and want [with] God alone knowing where any of us will end a life robbed of every blessing and already becoming intolerable."[4] A South Carolina planter told a Northern journalist: "We are discouraged: we have nothing left to begin anew with. I never did a day's work in my life, and don't know how to begin." Many years later, an Alabama ex-slave recalled the return home of Confederate soldiers after the war: "I seen our 'Federates go off laughin' an' gay; full of life an' health. Dey was big an' strong, asingin' Dixie an' dey jus knowed dey was agoin' to win. I seen 'em come back skin an' bone, dere eyes all sad an' hollow, an' dere clothes all ragged. Dey was all lookin' sick. De sperrit dey lef' wid jus' been done whupped outten dem."[5]

---

[3]Eric L. McKitrick, *Andrew Johnson and Reconstruction* (Chicago, 1960), p. 40.

[4]James P. Shenton (ed.), *The Reconstruction: A Documentary History* (New York, 1963), p. 18; Robert M. Myers (ed.), *The Children of Pride: A True Story of Georgia and the Civil War* (New York, 1972), p. 1273.

[5]Trowbridge, *Picture of the Desolated States,* p. 291; Leon F. Litwack, *Been in the Storm So Long: The Aftermath of Slavery* (New York, 1979), p. 108.

PRESIDENT ANDREW JOHNSON.
The most self-consciously plebeian of American presidents, he found no room in his definition of the common people for nonwhites. Unlike Lincoln, Johnson demonstrated no capacity for growth and flexibility in his attitudes.

LIBRARY OF CONGRESS

While this mood of despondency lasted, Southern whites might have submitted to almost any terms of reconstruction the government imposed. "They expected nothing," wrote a Northern journalist; "were prepared for the worst; would have been thankful for anything. . . . They asked no terms, made no conditions. They were defeated and helpless—they submitted." In many cases this submissiveness barely concealed the underlying hatred. Nevertheless, even South Carolinians admitted that "the conqueror has the right to make the terms, and we must submit."[6]

The Attitudes of Northern Whites

But the conquerors could not agree on what terms to impose. Contradictory and shifting moods chased each other across the Northern landscape. In the immediate aftermath of Lincoln's assassination, a cry for the punishment of traitors rent the air. The new President seemed to endorse the demands for a draconian policy. "*Treason* is a crime; and *crime* must be punished," he said. "Traitors must be punished and impoverished. Their great plantations must be seized and divided into small farms, and sold to honest, industrious men."[7]

Johnson, like Lincoln, was a self-made man of humble background. The death of his father, a porter in North Carolina, left the family in poverty and made necessary young Andrew's apprenticeship to a tailor. The apprentice learned the trade, moved to the

---

[6]Whitelaw Reid, *After the War: A Tour of the Southern States 1865–1866* (Cincinnati, 1866), p. 296; Sidney Andrews, *The South Since the War* (Boston, 1866), p. 95.

[7]Hans L. Trefousse, *Andrew Johnson: A Biography* (New York, 1989), p. 197; Brooks D. Simpson, *The Reconstruction Presidents* (Lawrence, Kansas, 1998), p. 68.

mountain country of east Tennessee, married a shoemaker's daughter (who taught him to write), and scrambled up the ladder of success. Johnson acquired a farm and slaves. He served as state legislator, governor, congressman, senator, vice president, and finally, by an accident of history, as president of the United States. A Jacksonian Democrat and a self-proclaimed champion of the common people, Johnson never lost his fierce plebeian pride. "Some day I will show the stuck-up aristocrats who is running the country," he had vowed early in his Tennessee career. "A cheap purse-proud set they are, not half as good as the man who earns his bread by the sweat of his brow."[8]

As President, Johnson had his chance to show the Southern aristocrats—whom he blamed for secession—who was running things. He investigated the possibilities of indicting leading Confederates for treason and of confiscating their property under the 1862 Confiscation Act. Radical Republicans who had opposed Lincoln's reconstruction policy were gratified that Providence had "trained a Southern loyalist in the midst of traitors, a Southern democrat in the midst of aristocrats, to be lifted at last to the presidency of the United States, that he might be charged with the duty of dealing punishment to these self-same assassins of the Union."[9]

As the postassassination furor subsided, however, the mood toward traitors softened. Johnson gave no more speeches branding treason an odious crime. The joyous Northern celebrations of victory and the grim reports of Southern destitution purged vengeance from the hearts of many Yankees. A spirit of magnanimity toward a fallen foe began to manifest itself. "We want true union and concord in the quickest possible time," declared the influential *Springfield* (Mass.) *Republican* on June 10, 1865. "Are these ends to be gained by reproaches and invectives; by prolonging the spirit and the evils of the war after the war itself has terminated?"

But this sentiment coexisted uneasily with a conviction that the "fruits of victory" must not be sacrificed by premature leniency. Magnanimity must be tempered by justice. What were these fruits of victory? For most Republicans they included, at a minimum, absolute repudiation of secession, guarantees for the freedom and civil rights of emancipated slaves, security and political power for Southern Unionists, and at least temporary political disqualification of leading ex-Confederates.

Northern ideas on reconstruction ranged across a spectrum of alternatives. At one end was the Democratic alternative of self-reconstruction. Such a policy would have allowed the existing Southern state governments to proclaim their loyalty to the Union, to supervise the election of new congressmen and senators, and then to carry on as if the war had never occurred. Self-reconstruction would have met none of the minimum Republican conditions. It would have preserved ex-Confederates in power, shut out Unionists, jeopardized the rights of the freedmen, and perhaps imperiled their freedom itself—since the restored legislatures would have had the option of not ratifying, and therefore defeating, the Thirteenth Amendment.

At the opposite end of the spectrum was the radical vision of reconstruction as revolution. Radicals desired to overthrow the power of the Southern ruling class by disfranchisement and confiscation. They wanted to enfranchise the freedmen and grant them confiscated land. They wished to reshape the South in the Republican image of the free-labor North. Congressman George W. Julian of Indiana, one of the

---

[8]McKitrick, *Andrew Johnson and Reconstruction*, p. 87.
[9]Kenneth M. Stampp, *The Era of Reconstruction* (New York, 1965), pp. 52–53.

most radical of the Republicans, described his vision of the new South: in place of "large estates, widely scattered settlements, wasteful agriculture, popular ignorance, social degradation, the decline of manufactures, contempt for honest labor, and a pampered oligarchy," Republicans would plant "small farms, thrifty tillage, free schools, social independence, flourishing manufactures and the arts, respect for honest labor, and equality of political rights."[10]

Between these two extremes lay options ranging from partial to full enfranchisement of the freedmen, temporary to long-term disfranchisement of varying categories of ex-Confederates, and an assortment of proposals for economic assistance to freed slaves, including government loans to enable them to buy land. For two years after Appomattox, moderate Republicans struggled to forge a policy somewhere in the middle of this spectrum while President Johnson moved toward the Democratic position and broke with the party that had put him in office.[11]

 Presidential Reconstruction, 1865

Although Johnson initially seemed to agree with radicals on the need to punish Rebels, his fundamental convictions clashed with Republican ideology in two crucial respects. A Jacksonian Democrat to the core, Tennessean Andrew Johnson shared Tennessean Andrew Jackson's suspicion of banks, corporations, bondholders, and New England. He opposed the Whig/Republican policy of using government to promote economic development. His enemies list included both the plantation aristocracy and the "bloated, corrupt aristocracy" of the commercial-industrial economy emerging in the Northeast.

The President also proved to be hostile toward the Republican vision of the freedmen's place in society. Although in 1864 Johnson had told Tennessee blacks that he would be their "Moses" to lead them out of bondage, he never subscribed to the liberal tenets of antislavery ideology. He had owned slaves himself, and he was committed to white supremacy. When a Union army officer had commented during the war that the government was turning the conflict into a crusade to free the slaves, Johnson exclaimed: "Damn the negroes! I am fighting these traitorous aristocrats, their masters." In 1866, a delegation of blacks headed by Frederick Douglass visited the White House to urge the merits of black suffrage as a condition of reconstruction. The President parried their arguments and afterwards remarked to his secretary: "Those d——d sons of b——s thought they had me in a trap! I know that d——d Douglass; he's just like any nigger, and he would sooner cut a white man's throat than not." Johnson told a Democratic senator that "white men alone must manage the South."[12]

---

[10]Michael Les Benedict (ed.), *The Fruits of Victory: Alternatives in Restoring the Union, 1865–1877*, rev. ed. (Lanham, Md., 1986), pp. 97–98.

[11]The Republicans had nominated Johnson, a War Democrat from an occupied Confederate state, for vice president in 1864 in an attempt to broaden their appeal beyond the Republican electorate and to fit their new appellation as the "Union party." (See page 441.)

[12]Clifton Hall, *Andrew Johnson, Military Governor of Tennessee* (Princeton, 1916), p. 221; Hans L. Trefousse, *Andrew Johnson*, p. 242; Eric Foner, *Reconstruction: America's Unfinished Revolution 1863–1877* (New York, 1988), p. 180.

FREDERICK DOUGLASS. Born a slave, Douglass learned to read, acquired knowledge of a world beyond bondage, and escaped to freedom in 1838 at the age of twenty-one. He joined the abolitionist movement, became one of its leaders, and by 1850 was considered the foremost black spokesman for freedom and equal rights. During the war he recruited black soldiers for the Union army; two of his sons fought in the Massachusetts 54th Infantry.

LIBRARY OF CONGRESS

These differences between Johnson and the Republicans only gradually became clear to the latter. In the meantime, attention focused on the reconstruction process. The President decided not to call Congress into special session during the long interval between March and December 1865. Johnson, like Lincoln, conceived of reconstruction (which he preferred to call restoration) as primarily an executive function. He also believed in Lincoln's theory of indestructible states. The rebellion had been one of individuals, not states, said Johnson, and although the individuals might be punished, the states retained all their constitutional rights.

On May 29, 1865, the President issued two significant proclamations. The first offered amnesty and restitution of property, except slaves, to all who would take an oath of allegiance, with the exception of several categories. These categories included Confederate civil and diplomatic officials; army officers above the rank of colonel and naval officers above the rank of lieutenant; all who had resigned as congressmen, federal judges, or military officers to join the rebellion; state governors under the Confederacy; those who had mistreated prisoners of war or were under arrest for other military crimes; and all persons owning taxable property with an estimated value of more than $20,000. The last-named exemption, which had been absent from Lincoln's amnesty proclamation of December 8, 1863, was Johnson's way of humbling the purse-proud aristocrats. Johnson's proclamation offered those in the exempted categories the opportunity to apply for individual pardons.

Johnson's second proclamation named a provisional governor for North Carolina and directed him to call an election of delegates to frame a new state constitution. Only white men who had taken an oath of allegiance and had received amnesty could take part in this process. In subsequent weeks, Johnson issued similar proclamations for six other Southern states. He also recognized the Lincoln-sponsored governments of Louisiana, Arkansas, and Tennessee, and designated the wartime loyalist government that had administered the part of Virginia under Union military control as the official government of that state.

The provisional governors appointed by Johnson had opposed secession in 1861, though most of them had subsequently chosen to go with their states. The President hoped that these governors would build a new party in the South, a party composed of Unionists and lukewarm Confederates. Most of the delegates elected to the state constitutional conventions in 1865 had indeed been conditional or outright Unionists in 1861. Up to this point, Johnson's policy seemed to be working as intended. As the conventions met, the President made clear the minimum conditions they must fulfill (despite the inconsistency of such conditions with his theory of unimpaired state rights): the abolition of slavery, the nullification of secession, and the repudiation of all state debts incurred during the period of the Confederacy (on the grounds that, secession being illegal, all obligations incurred in its behalf were null and void).

Republican Responses to Presidential Reconstruction

Most Republicans initially supported Johnson's actions. But many abolitionists and radicals immediately criticized the President's policy. They feared that the restriction of suffrage to whites would open the door to oppression of the freedmen and restoration of the old power structure. Charles Sumner considered the President's proclamations to be "madness." "Nothing since Chancellorsville," he wrote privately, "has to my mind been so disastrous to the National Cause." Radicals noted that the abolition of slavery automatically gave the South a dozen more congressmen by nullifying the three-fifths compromise and counting the entire black population in the basis for representation. Thus Johnson's policy would reward rebellion by increasing the South's power in national politics—unless blacks were enfranchised to offset the Rebel vote. "Is there no way to arrest the insane course of the President?" lamented Thaddeus Stevens in June 1865.[13]

Most Republicans did not yet share Stevens's and Sumner's alarm. Although a majority of them probably believed that black men should participate to some degree in the reconstruction process, they were not yet ready to condemn the President's policy. They looked upon that policy as only a beginning—an "experiment" that could be expanded or modified to include black suffrage at a later stage. Just as Johnson was requiring Southern states to abolish slavery and to repudiate the Confeder-

---

[13]Howard K. Beale, *The Critical Year: A Study of Andrew Johnson and Reconstruction* (New York, 1930), pp. 63–64.

ate debt, so he would recognize the wisdom of requiring them to extend at least a limited franchise to blacks. "Loyal negroes must not be put down, while disloyal white men are put up," wrote a moderate Republican. "But I am quite willing to see what will come of Mr. Johnson's experiment." If Southern states did not voluntarily enfranchise freedmen, said another moderate, the President "will then be at liberty to pursue a sterner policy."[14]

In an attempt to arouse Northern opinion and to put pressure on Johnson, radicals organized a "Universal and Equal Suffrage Association" and launched a barrage of speeches, pamphlets, and editorials. Johnson did respond to the pressure, but not in a manner calculated to ease anxieties. On August 15, he telegraphed Provisional Governor William L. Sharkey of Mississippi, who presided over the first state convention to meet under Johnson's plan. The President suggested that if the new constitution were to enfranchise literate blacks and those who owned property worth $250, "you would completely disarm the adversary and set an example the other states would follow. This you can do with perfect safety, and . . . as a consequence, the radicals, who are wild upon negro franchise, will be completely foiled."[15]

This was a revealing telegram. It showed that Johnson already viewed the radicals as "adversaries" to be "foiled" by a token measure. Scarcely one in nine adult black males in the South could have qualified to vote under these criteria. Such a small number of black voters would pose no immediate threat to white supremacy. And Johnson was probably correct in his belief that their enfranchisement would satisfy moderate Republicans of the South's good intentions. It would also put the South on a higher plane than the North, where only six states allowed blacks to vote on any terms. Johnson's communication to Sharkey invites comparison with Lincoln's letter to the reconstruction governor of Louisiana a year earlier (see page 439). Both presidents tried the same tactic of noncompulsory persuasion; but Lincoln had made no reference to adversaries, and his suggested inclusion of black soldiers would have nearly doubled the potential black electorate. Johnson excluded soldiers because he knew that they were the most humiliating symbol of Southern defeat and the most provocative threat to white supremacy.

In any case, Southern whites paid no more attention to Johnson's suggestion than they had to Lincoln's. None of the conventions made any provision for black suffrage in their new constitutions. The provisional governor of South Carolina explained why: "This is a white man's government, and intended for white men only. . . . The Supreme Court of the United States has decided [in the Dred Scott case] that the negro is not an American citizen."[16] Johnson made no more gestures in the direction of black enfranchisement. He stated that voting qualifications were a state matter and that it was beyond his constitutional right to interfere. But his radical critics pointed out that under the Constitution the president had no right to appoint provisional governors either, or to require states to abolish slavery and repudiate debts. He had taken these extraconstitutional steps because the Constitution prescribed no

---

[14]McKitrick, *Andrew Johnson and Reconstruction,* p. 78 and n.

[15]Edward McPherson, *The Political History of the United States During the Period of Reconstruction* (Washington, D.C., 1875), p. 19.

[16]McKitrick, *Andrew Johnson and Reconstruction,* p. 167.

process for the unforeseen task of restoring states after a civil war. Thus, to require black suffrage as a condition of reconstruction would be no more unconstitutional than these other actions. But Johnson refused to budge, and Republicans grew discouraged about the prospects for success on the suffrage issue.

The Black Suffrage Issue in the North

Their discouragement was deepened by the outcome of three Northern state referendums in the fall of 1865. The legislatures of Connecticut, Wisconsin, and Minnesota placed on the ballot constitutional amendments to enfranchise the few black men in those states. Everyone recognized that, in some measure, the popular vote on these amendments would serve as a barometer of Northern opinion on black suffrage. Democrats mounted an antisuffrage campaign that exploited race prejudice in the usual manner. Republican leaders worked for passage of the amendments but fell short of success in all three states. The results were subject to conflicting interpretations. In each state a switch of about 5 percent of the votes would have reversed the outcome.[17] Most Republican voters had cast their ballots for the amendments. This could be interpreted as a Republican mandate for black suffrage. On the other hand, the defeat of the amendments could be seen as a mandate against black suffrage by a majority of Northern voters. This was how contemporaries interpreted it. Moderate Republican congressmen were therefore unwilling to force a showdown with the President on the issue. Even radicals conceded that the cause of black suffrage as a condition of reconstruction had suffered a setback. "We feel humiliated and ashamed" by the Connecticut vote, confessed one. "It jeopardizes—at least delays—the permanent settlement of the questions in dispute in the rebellious States."[18]

The Revival of Southern Defiance

At the same time, however, alarming signs in the South began to convince even moderate Republicans that Johnson's program was not working well. Reports filtered northward of a growing number of assaults on freedmen and Unionists. The old-time "secesh" manners of defiance and haughtiness seemed to have replaced the earlier docility of ex-Confederates. In September 1865, a leading Alabama politician scoffed at Republican insistence on guarantees of Southern loyalty and good behavior. "It is you, proud and exultant Radical, who should give the guarantees, guarantees that you will not again . . . deny to any portion of the people their rights." Two months later Wade Hampton, one of the antebellum South's richest planters and a Confed-

---

[17]The referendum votes on black suffrage were:

Conn. (Oct. 2, 1865)	Minn. (Nov. 7, 1865)	Wis. (Nov. 7, 1865)
For: 27,217 (45%)	For: 12,170 (45%)	For 46,588 (46%)
Against: 33,489 (55%)	Against: 14,840 (55%)	Against: 55,591 (54%)

Assuming that in each state virtually all the Democrats voted against black suffrage, the percentage of Republicans in each state who voted for it can be calculated, using the 1864 presidential election as a base to determine the proportion of each state's voters who were Republican. The Republicans voting for black suffrage amendments were, therefore, approximately as follows: Connecticut 85 percent, Minnesota 75 percent, and Wisconsin 80 percent.

[18]*Boston Commonwealth,* October 7, 1865.

erate war hero, said that "it is our duty to support the President of the United States *so long as he manifests a disposition to restore all our rights as a sovereign State"* (italics added).[19] This sounded like 1860 all over again. Little wonder that some Republicans began to question whether the South had learned anything from the war.

Political events in the South added to Republican concern. Ex-Confederates in Louisiana reorganized the Democratic party and wooed the governor (elected as lieutenant governor under Lincoln's policy in 1864) to their side. He began to replace Unionist officeholders with former Confederates. Louisiana Unionists, now allied with the Republican party, cried in alarm to Washington. "Hatred of the Government and to the Union men," reported one, "is now more intense than it was in 1860 & 1861, and were we without the Protection of the Federal troops in this State the union men would be persecuted and driven out of the country."[20]

Similar reports came from other Southern states in the fall of 1865. Johnson's own provisional governor of North Carolina wrote the President: "I regret to say that there is much of a rebellion feeling still in this state. In this respect I admit I have been deceived. In May and June last these rebellious spirits would not have dared to show their heads even for the office of constable; but leniency has emboldened them."[21] At the state constitutional conventions held during the fall, delegates spent a great deal of time quibbling over the details of Johnson's requirements. Several states repealed rather than repudiated their secession ordinances, thereby yielding no principle; Mississippi and South Carolina refused to repudiate their Confederate debt; Mississippi and Texas failed to ratify the Thirteenth Amendment; Georgia reserved the right to seek compensation for emancipated slaves.

These actions did not sit well with the North—or with Johnson. But the President seemed unable to do more than plead ineffectively with Southerners to be more circumspect. And worse was yet to come. In the first elections held under the new constitutions, the voters elected to the United States Congress no fewer than nine Confederate congressmen, seven Confederate state officials, four generals, four colonels, and Confederate Vice President Alexander Stephens. An even larger number of prominent ex-Rebels won election to state offices. To apprehensive and angry Republicans, it appeared that the Rebels, unable to capture Washington in war, were about to do so in peace.

Johnson and the South

Although these developments distressed Johnson, he bore much of the responsibility for them. In August, Provisional Governor Sharkey had taken steps to reorganize the Mississippi militia, using Confederate veterans as a nucleus. The professed reason for this action was to curb an outbreak of robberies and assaults. But the true reason seems to have been a desire to reassert states' rights and to bring pressure on the federal government to reduce the number of occupation troops, most of whom were black. The

---

[19]Michael Perman, *Reunion Without Compromise: The South and Reconstruction 1865–1868* (Cambridge, 1973), p. 82; Andrews, *The South Since the War,* p. 391.

[20]Michael Les Benedict, *A Compromise of Principle: Congressional Republicans and Reconstruction, 1863–1869* (New York, 1974), p. 120.

[21]McKitrick, *Andrew Johnson and Reconstruction,* p. 211.

commander of the occupation forces, General Henry W. Slocum, issued an order prohibiting the militia organization. Sharkey thereupon bombarded Washington with imperious telegrams insisting on the need for a state police force. The President, who had initially disapproved of Sharkey's action, meekly backed down. He endorsed the militia and sent a telegram reproving Slocum and General Carl Schurz, who was in Mississippi on an inspection tour and had supported Slocum. "The [Southern] people must be trusted with their Government," the President lectured the generals, "and if trusted my opinion is they will act in good faith and restore their former constitutional relations with . . . the Union." This spectacle of a president yielding to a provisional governor—and in the process humiliating two major generals who had fought gallantly at Gettysburg and elsewhere—delighted Southerners and outraged Republicans. A Southern friend told the President: "Your endorsement of [Sharkey's] militia call, electrified the whole South. From that day to this, I have met with no man who has not a kind word to say of President Johnson." But a Republican paper warned that "if rebels in Mississippi are to be thus armed, then also will they be in every state. . . . What can be hatched from such an egg but another rebellion?"[22]

Johnson's action in this affair was only one of several presidential signals that encouraged Democrats to think of him as one of their own. Southern Democrats who had once denounced the President as a renegade and demagogue now praised him fulsomely as the man "who had the courage to place himself as a breakwater between the Radicals of the North and the prostrate people of the bleeding South." Northern Democrats similarly flattered Johnson. Their only chance for political power lay in a revival of the antebellum alliance with Southern Democrats. Johnson's policy promised to facilitate such an alliance. Democratic newspapers began to hint that Johnson could receive the party's presidential nomination in 1868. Every Northern Democratic state convention that met in 1865 passed resolutions of "cordial and hearty approval" of the President's course. A veteran Jacksonian advised Johnson: "The Democracy of the North look to the South to reinstate them in power. If you so act, towards the South, as to command their confidence and support you will carry the Democratic party and unite the North West and South in your support."[23]

This was a heady prospect. Johnson was after all a Democrat, even though he had been elected to his office by Republicans. The President indeed hoped to construct a new political coalition, composed of Northern Democrats and conservative Republicans plus Southern Unionists. Excluded from this coalition would be radical Republicans on one extreme and "traitors" on the other. But something was going wrong with the Southern part of the plan. The purse-proud aristocrats and traitors had gotten into the coalition and were elbowing aside the genuine Unionists, with Johnson's apparent blessing. On September 11, 1865, a delegation from nine Southern states called on the President to express their "sincere respect" for his "desire and intention to sustain Southern rights in the Union." In his reply, Johnson waxed eloquent on his "love, respect, and confidence" toward the Southern people and his intent to be "forbearing and forgiving" toward their past sins.[24]

---

[22]Perman, *Reunion Without Compromise*, p. 100; *Boston Commonwealth*, September 30, 1865.

[23]Perman, *Reunion Without Compromise*, pp. 170–171; McKitrick, *Andrew Johnson and Reconstruction*, p. 73.

[24]McKitrick, *Andrew Johnson and Reconstruction*, pp. 173, 183.

What explains this transformation from the Johnson of April, who spoke menacingly about the crime of treason, to the Johnson of September, who spoke of forgiveness? For one thing, the President was a Southerner. He had no more liking for the radical Yankee ethos than most Southerners had. Moreover, his experiences during the summer and fall of 1865 convinced him that the Southern whites, including ex-Confederates, were his real friends. They praised his policy and flattered his ego, while radical Republicans criticized him openly and moderates exchanged worried words in private.

Of special significance was the matter of presidential pardons for those excluded from the amnesty proclamation. The White House was thronged day after day with supplicants for pardon or their tearful female relatives or "pardon brokers." The President felt a deep sense of gratification when members of the haughty Southern ruling class humbly confessed the error of their ways and promised to be good. To one group of Southerners, Johnson said that their expression of loyalty "excites in my mind feelings and emotions that language is totally inadequate to express." "I remember the taunts, the jeers, the scowls with which I was treated," the President continued. He was happy to "have lived to see the realization of my predictions and the fatal error of those whom I vainly essayed to save from the results" of secession.[25]

In this mood, Johnson bestowed pardons liberally—an average of a hundred a day in September 1865. Altogether he granted 13,500 special pardons out of about 15,000 applications. With pardons in their pockets, ex-Confederates seemingly faced no further obstacles to a bid for a return to power in their states. But this was too much for even conservative Republicans to swallow. Since the Republicans controlled Congress, they could exercise their right to exclude Southern representatives and senators, pending further consideration of the whole reconstruction question.[26] Their determination to do so was intensified by evidence of a Southern intention to restrict the freedpeople to a twilight zone of quasi-freedom.

Land and Labor in the Postwar South

The news of freedom came to slaves in many different ways. Because the Thirteenth Amendment was not finally ratified until December 1865, some uncertainty persisted until then about the precise legal status of slavery. But in the spring of 1865, Union army officers and Freedmen's Bureau agents had announced the abolition of slavery in the occupied South and warned that planters who thenceforth refused to pay

---

[25]Ibid., p. 173.

[26]Article I, Section 5, of the Constitution states that each house of Congress "shall be the Judge of the Elections, Returns, and Qualifications of its own Members." The Republican majority of Congress, therefore, could use this power to exclude Southerners until they met qualifications established by Congress. The words "readmission," "restoration," and "reconstruction" were used interchangeably by contemporaries to designate the process by which the former Confederate states would resume their place in the Union on an equal basis with other states. Once "restored," these states would be represented in Congress, would have their electoral votes counted in presidential elections, and would exercise the normal functions of state governments free of extraordinary intervention by the U.S. Army or by federal courts.

wages to their black workers would be subject to confiscation of property. Owners called their slaves together and announced, with varying degrees of civility or surliness, that they were free. Where owners failed to do so, Yankee officers or freedmen from a neighboring plantation brought the news. In one way or another, emancipation had penetrated to the most remote corners of the South by the fall of 1865.

Many freedmen stayed to work as wage earners on the same plantation where they had formerly worked as slaves. But for others, leaving the old place was an essential part of freedom. In slavery times, the only way to become free was to escape from the plantation, and the impulse persisted after the war. "You ain't, none o' you," a black preacher told his flock, "gwinter feel rale free till you shakes de dus' ob de Ole Plantashun offen yore feet an' goes ter a new place whey you kin live out o' sight o' de gret house." When a Northern missionary asked a freedwoman why she had left her cabin on a Georgia plantation for the uncertainties of postwar Atlanta, the woman responded: "To 'joy my freedom."[27]

Freedpeople also left the plantations to search for relatives separated from them in slavery, to accept offers of higher wages elsewhere, or to seek protection and rations at army posts or Freedmen's Bureau offices. The latter were usually located in cities and larger towns, and much of the black migration in the early postwar months was from country to city. Southern whites viewed this urban influx as a serious health, welfare, and crime problem. The movement away from plantations also created a labor shortage at a time when the South desperately needed to plant crops and repair war devastation. The occupation forces shared the concern of Southern whites for recovery and labor stability. The army urged and sometimes forced unemployed blacks to sign contracts for farm labor. Sensitive to charges in both the Northern and Southern press that the Freedmen's Bureau was fostering a welfare ethic among ex-slaves, some Bureau officers cut off rations to able-bodied blacks to compel them to work. City officials invoked vagrancy laws for the same purpose. By the fall of 1865, many footloose freedmen had returned to their old plantations or to others in the same county. But mobility remained a hallmark of freedom; when it came time to sign contracts for the new year, more than a few blacks left their old employers in search of better opportunities elsewhere.

The Issue of Land for the Landless

They would, of course, have preferred to work for themselves rather than for white folks. Many freedmen believed that only the ownership of land could make their freedom real. "What's de use of being free if you don't own land enough to be buried in?" asked one black man. "Might juss as well stay slave all yo' days." A black army veteran said: "Every colored man will be a slave, & feel himself a slave until he can raise him own *bale of cotton* & put him own mark upon it & say dis is mine!"[28] Freed slaves who had managed to save a little money tried to buy land in 1865. Demobi-

---

[27]Litwack, *Been in the Storm So Long*, p. 296; Tera W. Hunter, *To 'Joy My Freedom: Southern Black Women's Lives and Labors after the Civil War* (Cambridge, Mass., 1997), p. 2.

[28]Reid, *After the War*, p. 564; Thomas Wentworth Higginson, Journal, entry of November 21, 1863, Higginson Papers, Houghton Library, Harvard University.

lized black soldiers purchased land with their bounty money, sometimes pooling their resources to buy an entire plantation on which several black families settled. But for most ex-slaves the purchase of land was impossible. Few of them had money, and even if they had, whites often refused to sell or even to rent them land for fear of losing a source of cheap labor or of encouraging notions of independence.

If they could not buy land, many freedmen in 1865 expected the government to grant or lease them land. This hope—for "forty acres and a mule"—was no delusion. By June 1865, the Freedmen's Bureau had placed nearly ten thousand families on almost half a million acres of plantation lands abandoned by planters who had fled Union armies along the coastal rivers in Georgia and South Carolina. General William T. Sherman had assigned this land to the freedmen in his famous Order No. 15 (see page 432). Sherman also turned over horses and mules captured from the enemy. Elsewhere in the South, the Freedmen's Bureau controlled nearly a million acres of abandoned or confiscated land, part of which it leased to freed slaves. The Bureau also provided some freedmen with tools and draft animals, to be paid for with the proceeds from their crops.

If these actual examples of forty acres and a mule were not enough to encourage the freedmen's hopes, many Bureau agents and Union soldiers—especially black troops—circulated rumors that the government intended to give blacks their former masters' land. Reports came from the North of powerful Republicans who favored the confiscation and redistribution of plantations. In a speech at Lancaster, Pennsylvania, on September 6, Thaddeus Stevens urged the confiscation of land owned by wealthy ex-Confederates. Stevens proposed to allocate forty acres of this land to each adult freedman and to sell the remainder to finance war pensions and repay the war debt. "Strip a proud nobility of their bloated estates," said Stevens in a later congressional speech; "send them forth to labor, and teach their children to enter the workshops or handle the plow, and you will thus humble the proud traitors."[29]

The freedmen, therefore, seemed to have good reason to hope for government assistance in obtaining land. But President Johnson's amnesty proclamation and the failure of Congress to pass effective legislation dashed most of their hopes. Presidential amnesty and pardon included the restoration of property. By midsummer 1865, pardoned planters were returning home to claim estates held by the Freedmen's Bureau or under cultivation by freedmen. General Oliver O. Howard, commissioner of the Freedmen's Bureau, refused to honor the planters' claims without a direct order from the President to do so. Howard considered the amnesty proclamation inapplicable to abandoned or confiscated property "which by law has been set apart [for use] by refugees and freedmen."[30] Annoyed at this unauthorized interpretation of his policy, the President on August 16 ordered Howard to restore the property of all pardoned Confederates. But Howard and several of the Bureau's assistant commissioners continued to stall. They hoped to retain as much land as possible until Congress met in December, when new legislation might confirm the freedmen's possession of at least some of the land under Bureau control.

---

[29] *Congressional Globe,* 39th Cong., 1st sess. (1866), 1309.
[30] George R. Bentley, *A History of the Freedmen's Bureau* (Philadelphia, 1955), p. 93.

THADDEUS STEVENS. Sometimes known as "the Great Commoner," grim-visaged old Thad had fought for a public school system and black rights in Pennsylvania before the war. During Reconstruction, he was the strongest advocate of placing former slaves and their masters on an equal plane. When he died in 1868, he was buried in a black cemetery because the main cemetery in Lancaster, Pennsylvania, refused to accept blacks.

LIBRARY OF CONGRESS

Meanwhile, the pardoned owners of plantations affected by Sherman's Order No. 15 also clamored for restoration of their property. The Bureau's assistant commissioner for South Carolina was General Rufus Saxton, a native of Massachusetts and an abolitionist sympathizer. On the grounds that Sherman's order was "as binding as a statute," Saxton refused to give up plantations occupied by freedpeople. But Andrew Johnson rejected this argument and directed the return of the properties to their former owners. With the support of Howard and the tacit encouragement of Secretary of War Edwin M. Stanton, Saxton dragged his feet to give Congress time to confirm the freedmen's title to these plantations. Senator Charles Sumner introduced a bill for this purpose in December 1865, but it failed to get out of committee. In the meantime Johnson cracked down on the Bureau, removed Saxton from office, and forced the return of the land. Some freedmen refused to give up their farms until the army compelled them to do so at bayonet point. Blacks protested eloquently against this betrayal of a promise, but in the absence of legislation by Congress there was little they or the Bureau could do about it.

In February 1866, Congress did pass a bill that extended the life of the Freedmen's Bureau and included a provision confirming the freedmen's possession for three years of lands occupied under the Sherman order. But Johnson vetoed the bill and Congress failed to pass it over the veto. Republicans finally managed to enact a revised Freedmen's Bureau bill over the President's veto in July 1866, but this law did not include the section confirming the Sherman grants. Instead, it offered the freedmen who had been dispossessed of these properties the opportunity to buy government-held land (at a price below market value) on the South Carolina and Georgia offshore islands. In this way more than two thousand dispossessed freed families obtained title to land; but this achievement marked a sad denouement to the high hopes of 1865. By the end of 1866, nearly all the arable land once controlled by the Freedmen's Bureau had been returned to its ex-Confederate owners.

Congress made one other effort to place freedpeople on land of their own: the Southern Homestead Act of June 21, 1866. This law set aside forty-four million acres of public land in five Southern states (Alabama, Arkansas, Florida, Louisiana, and Mississippi) for individual grants of eighty acres to settlers who resided on and cultivated the land for five years. To give the freedmen and Unionist whites first chance at this land, the law stipulated that no one who had supported the Confederacy could file a claim before January 1, 1867. Generous in conception, the Southern Homestead Act was largely a failure in practice. Most of the remaining public land in these states was of poor quality. And few freedmen possessed the capital to settle on land distant from their homes, to purchase seed, tools, livestock, and building materials, and to support themselves while waiting for the first crop to mature. General Howard ordered Freedmen's Bureau agents to provide settlers with transportation to their claims, but many agents were indifferent or sluggish about complying. Fewer than seven thousand freedmen claimed homesteads, and only a thousand of these fulfilled the requirements for final ownership.

Land reform did not become a part of Reconstruction. Thaddeus Stevens's confiscation bill got nowhere in Congress. Despite the warnings of abolitionists that "to give [the slaves] only freedom, without the land, is to give them only the mockery of freedom which the English or the Irish peasant has," confiscation was too radical for most Republicans. The constitutional prohibition against bills of attainder that forfeited property beyond the lives of offenders was a major stumbling block (see pages 431 and 432). Moderates who wished to win the heartfelt loyalty of Southern whites to a restored Union could hardly expect to do so by taking away their land. Many Republicans expressed doubts about the ethics as well as the legality and expediency of confiscation. "People who want farms work for them," declared the *New York Tribune*. "The only class we know that takes other people's property because they want it is largely represented in Sing Sing."[31]

The free-labor ideology envisaged upward mobility through hard work, thrift, and the other Protestant ethic virtues. Many Northern proponents of this ideology believed the freedmen would gain more by working and sweating to buy land than by having the government grant them special favors. But radicals who wanted confiscation insisted that the freedmen had already "earned" the land by their lifetime of toil in slavery. Whatever the merits of this argument, it did not prevail. Most freedmen did not achieve the economic independence they had hoped for. Instead, they had to work for white landowners, who in many cases were their former masters.

---

[31]James M. McPherson, *The Struggle for Equality: Abolitionists and the Negro in the Civil War and Reconstruction* (Princeton, 1964), pp. 411–412.

The "Labor Question" and the Freedmen's Bureau

Some of these former masters still perceived their workers as slaves in all but name. "They esteem the Negro the property of the white man by natural right," wrote a Freedmen's Bureau agent in September 1865, "and however much they may confess that the President's Proclamation broke up the relation of the individual slaves to their owners, they still have the ingrained feeling that the black people at large belong to the whites at large." Slavery had been a form of compulsion, and "three fourths of the [white] people assume that the negro will not labor except on compulsion," wrote a Northern reporter. "The whites seem wholly unable to comprehend that freedom for the negro means the same thing as freedom for them."[32]

This should not have been surprising. Proslavery convictions held for a lifetime could hardly be overcome in a few months. In reorganizing their labor force, some planters tried to replicate slavery as closely as possible—even to the extent of hiring overseers, who punished recalcitrant workers with whippings. When freedmen refused to work under these conditions or walked away from the plantation to seek better terms elsewhere, planters complained of a labor shortage and said in an "I told you so" manner that such behavior proved blacks would work only under compulsion.

Into this uncertain situation stepped the Freedmen's Bureau. As Commissioner of the Bureau, General Oliver O. Howard had his headquarters in Washington. Army generals were assigned as assistant commissioners for each former slave state, with headquarters in the state's capital or in its largest city. Most of the Bureau's 550 local agents were junior army officers from middle-class Northern backgrounds. Some of them had taken a job with the Bureau because they were interested in the freedmen. Others were marking time until they could make plans for their civilian careers. Their racial attitudes ranged from radical to conservative, though most felt some degree of liberal sympathy for the freedpeople. The Bureau also appointed some civilian agents, including a few black men. Although there were too few agents to reach every corner of the South, these agents—backed by the army's occupation troops—nevertheless had considerable potential power to shape postwar Southern labor relations.

Once it became clear that no large-scale land redistribution would take place, the Bureau proceeded to patch together a new relationship between planters and the freedmen. Agents encouraged or required planters and laborers to sign written contracts that specified the amount and kind of work to be done, the wages to be paid, and other conditions of employment. Wages ranged from eight to fifteen dollars a month plus food, housing, and sometimes clothing and medical care. Payment took the form of cash or a share of the crop. Planters came to prefer the latter, both because money was scarce and because share wages, which could not be paid until after the harvest, gave laborers an interest in the crop and deterred them from breaking their contracts.

The Bureau tried to protect freedmen from exploitation. Its agents adjudicated thousands of disputes concerning the interpretation or violation of contracts, crimes by or against freedmen, and the like. After Southern states passed laws allowing blacks to

---

[32]Samuel Thomas to Oliver O. Howard, September 21, 1865, Freedmen's Bureau Records, National Archives, Record Group 105, Box 3, Vol. 1; Andrews, *The South Since the War,* p. 398.

testify in civil courts, the Bureau allowed these courts to handle such disputes—under the watchful eyes of agents. Some of the agents did not like what they saw. "The admission of Negro testimony will never secure the Freedmen justice before the courts of this state when that testimony is considered valueless by the judges and juries who hear it," wrote one agent. "It is of no consequence what the law may be, if the majority be not inclined to have it executed." None of the reconstruction governments in 1865–1866 allowed blacks to serve on juries. After two months of watching the Mississippi courts function, the assistant commissioner of the Bureau in the state reported that their rulings "with reference to the freedmen are a disgrace."[33]

On the strength of these and similar reports, General Howard urged Congress to create "Freedmen's United States Courts" to supersede the state courts. The revised Freedmen's Bureau bill, passed over Johnson's veto in July 1866, empowered the Bureau to establish special courts to function as military tribunals until Congress declared the rebellious states restored to the Union.[34] These "courts," which in most cases consisted only of a Bureau agent, remained in existence until 1868. But state courts continued to handle many cases concerning freedmen because some Bureau commissioners and military commanders, guided by Johnson's continuing hostility to the Bureau, were reluctant to override civil courts.

Not surprisingly, Southern whites denounced the Bureau as "a curse," a "ridiculous folly," a "vicious institution." Wade Hampton wrote in 1866: "The war which was so prolific of monstrosities, new theories of republican government, new versions of the Constitution . . . gave birth to nothing which equals in deformity and depravity this 'Monstrum horrendum informe ingens.' " Planters insisted that they could "make the nigger work" if the interfering agents would only leave them alone. "The Bureau doesn't seem to understand the possibility of a white man's being right in a contest or difference with a negro," complained one Southerner. Another added: "The fairest minded of all these [Bureau] officials seemed not to be able [to] comprehend the difference between the 'nigger' freedman and the white northern laborer."[35]

These complaints reflected a dislike of the Bureau more for what it symbolized—conquest and emancipation—than for what it did. In reality, the Bureau often functioned as an ally of planters by getting idle freedmen back to work and by enforcing contracts whose terms often favored employers. While publicly abusing the Bureau, a good many Southerners privately admitted that without it the postwar labor situation would have been even more chaotic. In late 1865, many freedmen refused to sign contracts for the next year because they expected soon to get their forty acres and a mule. This led to a short-lived but intense "Christmas insurrection" scare among whites. To the Freedmen's Bureau fell the unhappy task of disabusing the

---

[33]Samuel Thomas to Oliver O. Howard, September 21, 1865, loc. cit.

[34]The Supreme Court's decision in *ex parte Milligan* (April 1866) ruled that military courts could not try civilians in areas remote from a war theater. President Johnson believed that this decision rendered the Bureau courts invalid. But congressional Republicans insisted that the war was not over until Congress said so, and in the meantime the South was a war zone where military tribunals could dispense justice.

[35]Bentley, *History of the Freedmen's Bureau,* pp. 104, 159; Walter Lynwood Fleming (ed.), *Documentary History of Reconstruction,* 2 vols. (Cleveland, 1906), I, 368; Roark, *Masters Without Slaves,* p. 154.

freedmen about land redistribution and of compelling them to sign contracts. In 1867, a Bureau official summed up his experience with the contract system: "It has succeeded in making the Freedman work and in rendering labor secure & stable— but it has failed to secure to the Freedman his just dues or compensation."[36]

The Bureau's enforcement policies varied greatly according to the priorities and convictions of individual commissioners and agents. In 1865, the assistant commissioners in South Carolina, Louisiana, Mississippi, and Tennessee demonstrated more sympathy for the freedmen than did those in Alabama and Georgia. In 1866, President Johnson removed some of the most liberal commissioners and appointed conservatives in their places. Some Bureau agents mixed socially with local whites and soon adopted the latter's viewpoints. Despite all this, however, agents appear to have tilted toward the freedmen in most disputes that came before them. A historian who studied a sample of 286 cases handled by fifteen Bureau courts in eight states found that 194 (68 percent) of them were decided in favor of the freedmen.[37]

The Black Codes

The Bureau also overruled or suspended the more oppressive features of the "black codes" adopted by Southern states in 1865–1866. One of the first tasks facing legislatures elected under Johnson's reconstruction program was the passage of laws to regulate the new status of blacks. Much of this legislation was unexceptionable: it authorized freedmen to own property, make contracts, sue and plead in the courts, and contract legal marriages. Under pressure from the Johnson administration and the Freedmen's Bureau, Southern states also permitted black testimony in court cases where blacks were parties. But the codes excluded blacks from juries and prohibited racial intermarriage. Some of them required segregation in public facilities. Several also prescribed more severe punishment of blacks than whites for certain crimes. These provisions raised an outcry from abolitionists. But the North as a whole was in no position to condemn them, for numerous Northern states excluded blacks from juries, banned racial intermarriage, permitted discriminatory law enforcement, and allowed or required segregated schools; and several Northern states until recently had denied blacks the right to testify against whites.

The provisions of the black codes relating to vagrancy, apprenticeship, labor, and land, however, provoked Republican accusations of an intent to create a new slavery. The Mississippi and South Carolina codes, passed first, were the harshest in these respects. They defined vagrancy in such a broad fashion as to allow magistrates to arrest almost any black man whom they defined as unemployed, fine him for vagrancy, and hire him out to a planter to pay off the fine. Both states required blacks to obtain special licenses for any occupation other than agriculture. Mississippi prohibited freedmen from renting or leasing land outside cities. South Carolina

---

[36]Bentley, *History of the Freedmen's Bureau,* p. 151. For a critical but balanced appraisal of the Freedmen's Bureau and the contract system, see Foner, *Reconstruction,* pp. 164–169. The essays in Paul A. Cimbala and Randall Miller (eds.) *The Freedmen's Bureau and Reconstruction* (New York, 1999) provide a range of appraisals of Bureau activities in all of the Southern states.

[37]Bentley, *History of the Freedmen's Bureau,* p. 159.

defined white employers as "masters" and black employees as "servants." Several states stipulated that freedpeople under eighteen without adequate parental support (the courts to define "adequate") could be bound out as apprentices, with their former owner given preference as the master. Some states forbade employers to "entice" laborers away from their jobs by offering higher wages.

The army and the Freedmen's Bureau suspended the enforcement of those parts of the black codes that discriminated between the races. The most important impact of the codes, therefore, was not in their operation but rather in the impression they made on the North. Whatever the shortcomings of their own racial attitudes, many Northerners were incensed by the South's apparent attempt to overturn one of the main results of the war. "We tell the white men of Mississippi," thundered the *Chicago Tribune,* "that the men of the North will convert the State of Mississippi into a frog pond before they will allow such laws to disgrace one foot of the soil in which the bones of our soldiers sleep and over which the flag of freedom waves."[38] The black codes strengthened the resolve of Republican congressmen to keep the South on probation until they could work out means to protect the freedpeople and to guarantee the fruits of victory. In this mood, the members of the Thirty-ninth Congress gathered in Washington in December 1865.

---

[38] *Chicago Tribune,* December 1, 1865.

Chapter Twenty-Seven

The Origins of "Radical" Recon- struction

*They would not cooperate in rebuilding
what they destroyed, [so] we must remove
the rubbish and rebuild from the bottom.
Whether they are willing or not, we must
compel obedience to the Union, and
demand protection for its humblest citizen.*

—Congressman James A. Garfield,
February 8, 1867

The Schism between President and Congress

Although Republicans enjoyed a three-to-one majority in the Thirty-ninth Congress, the old divisions between radicals, moderates, and conservatives hindered unity on reconstruction. Conservatives were generally satisfied with Andrew Johnson's policy, though some of them wished to pass additional legislation to protect the freedmen from violence and discrimination. Moderates agreed with radicals that the President's policy did not go far enough to safeguard the fruits of Northern victory. But they believed that Northern voters would not support the radical policy of black suffrage. They also wanted to prevent a break with Johnson, for they feared that such a break could benefit only the Democrats.

All Republicans, however, were united in a determination not to admit Southern representatives to Congress in December 1865. By prearrangement, the clerk of the House omitted the names of Southern representatives from the roll at the opening session, and both houses immediately voted to create a joint committee of fifteen (nine representatives, six senators) to formulate a reconstruction policy. Republicans did not construe this action as a defiance of Johnson, for in his message to Congress the President, while asserting that the Southern states had fulfilled his requirements for restoration, conceded the right of Congress to judge the qualifications of its own members. Johnson also affirmed that "good faith requires the security of the freedmen in their liberty and their property, their right to labor, and their right to claim the just return of their labor."[1]

This seemed to provide a basis for accommodation between the President and the moderate majority of Republicans. The composition of the congressional joint committee reflected a desire for accommodation. Although Thaddeus Stevens was a member, moderates dominated the committee. Senator William Pitt Fessenden of Maine became chairman, to the chagrin of Charles Sumner, who had hoped to be chairman but was not even placed on the committee. The joint committee held extensive hearings, at which army officers, Freedmen's Bureau agents, Southern Unionists, and freedmen testified to a rising wave of neo-Confederate hostility and violence. This testimony convinced Republicans of the need for a new constitutional amendment plus additional legislation to guarantee loyalty and to protect blacks. Although Northern Democrats predicted that the President would oppose any such measures, Fessenden maintained cordial relations with Johnson and expressed confidence that the President would cooperate with Congress.

Meanwhile Lyman Trumbull of Illinois, chairman of the Senate Judiciary Committee and one of the most influential Republican moderates, drafted two bills to protect the freedpeople. The first extended the life of the Freedmen's Bureau, expanded its legal powers, and authorized it to build and support schools. Trumbull's second bill defined the freedmen's civil rights and gave federal courts appellate jurisdiction in cases concerning these rights. Trumbull conferred with Johnson several times about this legislation and believed that he had the President's approval. The Freedmen's Bureau bill sped through both houses with virtually unanimous Republican support.

But on February 19, 1866, Johnson dismayed his Republican supporters by vetoing the bill. His convictions of white supremacy and states' rights prevailed over any concern about harmony with the congressional majority. The Constitution, declared the veto message, never contemplated a "system for the support of indigent persons." The jurisdiction of military courts over civil matters in time of peace was unconstitutional. Finally, said Johnson in a passage that rang ominously in Republican ears, the bill defied the Constitution because at the time of its passage "there was no Senator or Representative in Congress from the eleven States which are to be mainly affected by its provisions." The authority of Congress to judge the qualifications of its members "cannot be construed as including the right to shut out, in time of peace, any State from the representation to which it is entitled by the Constitution."[2] If this interpretation stood up, *any* legislation passed by Congress in the absence of Southern representation would be unconstitutional.

Moderates found the veto a bitter pill to swallow. An unhappy Lyman Trumbull told the Senate: "I thought in advocating [the bill], that I was acting in harmony with the views of the President. I regret exceedingly the antagonism his message presents

---

[1] *Congressional Globe,* 39th Cong., 1st sess. (1865), Appendix, 2–3.

[2] Edward McPherson, *The Political History of the United States During the Period of Reconstruction* (Washington, D.C., 1875), pp. 68–72.

to the expressed views of Congress. . . . He believes that the freedman will be protected without it; I believe he will be tyrannized over, abused, and virtually reenslaved without some legislation by the nation for his protection."[3] Trumbull introduced a motion to pass the measure over the President's veto. But five conservative Republicans who had previously voted for the bill now voted against it, and the motion fell just short of the required two-thirds majority.

Johnson knew that his veto would move him toward an alliance with Democrats. The latter organized mass meetings to celebrate and endorse the veto. After one of these meetings in Washington on February 22, the celebrants trooped to the White House to serenade Johnson, who favored them with one of the most remarkable presidential speeches ever delivered. Acting as though he were back on the stump in Tennessee, Johnson denounced the radicals as traitors who did not want to restore the Union. Charging that they were plotting to assassinate him, the President compared the radicals to Judas and himself to Christ.

If my blood is to be shed because I vindicate the Union and the preservation of this government in its original purity and character, let it be shed; let an altar to the Union be erected, and then, if it is necessary, take me and lay me upon it, and the blood that now warms and animates my existence shall be poured out as a fit libation to the Union.[4]

Many Americans were mortified by the President's behavior. "Was he drunk?" they wondered. Radicals who had long since turned against Johnson said to their moderate colleagues, "I told you so!" Senator Fessenden conceded privately that "the President's recent exhibitions of folly and wickedness" had disillusioned him. "He has broken the faith, betrayed his trust, and must sink from detestation to contempt."[5]

Despite Johnson's virtual declaration of war against congressional Republicans, most moderates still wished to avoid an irrevocable break. Their hopes centered on a modified Freedmen's Bureau bill and on Trumbull's civil rights bill. Congress passed the latter with nearly unanimous Republican support March 13, 1866.[6] Designed to nullify the Dred Scott decision and the black codes, the bill defined blacks as U.S. citizens and guaranteed their rights to own or rent property, make and enforce contracts, and have access to the courts as parties and witnesses. In general, it affirmed the right of blacks to enjoy "full and equal benefit of all laws and proceedings for the security of person and property as is enjoyed by white citizens." Although the civil rights bill mandated the transfer of legal proceedings from state to federal courts if the former discriminated by race, it would not nullify the traditional federal system, said Trumbull, for it would "have no operation in any State where the laws are equal."[7] Nor would the bill enfranchise blacks, authorize them to sit on juries, or require desegregated schools and public accommodations. Republicans therefore expected Johnson to sign this moderate bill despite his states' rights convictions.

---

[3]Eric McKitrick, *Andrew Johnson and Reconstruction* (Chicago, 1960), p. 292.

[4]McPherson, *Political History,* pp. 58–63.

[5]McKitrick, *Andrew Johnson and Reconstruction,* p. 297n.

[6]The House passed the bill by a vote of 111 to 38; the Senate passed it by a vote of 33 to 12.

[7]Michael Les Benedict (ed.), *The Fruits of Victory: Alternatives in Restoring the Union, 1865–1877* (Lanham, Md., 1986), p. 24.

But on March 27, Johnson sent in a veto message that once again asserted the illegality of legislation passed in the absence of Southern congressmen. The bill was unconstitutional, said the President, because it invaded the exclusive jurisdiction of state courts. It discriminated against whites by "establish[ing] for the security of the colored race safeguards which go infinitely beyond any that the General Government has ever provided for the white race" and by granting newly freed slaves the privilege of citizenship while immigrants had to wait five years for this boon.[8]

Like the first veto, this one provoked Democratic elation and Republican gloom. A Democratic editor gave thanks that Johnson did not believe "in compounding our race with niggers, gipsies, and baboons." If Congress could declare blacks citizens, said another party newspaper, "how long will it be . . . before it will say the negro shall vote, sit in the jury box, and intermarry with your families? Such are the questions put by the President." For most Republicans, this veto was the last straw. Johnson had deprived "every friend he has of the least ground upon which to stand and defend him," said a moderate congressman.[9]

If Johnson's goal had been to isolate the radicals and to create a broad conservative/moderate coalition in support of his policy, he had badly miscalculated. "Instead of driving off from him a small minority of the Republican party, or even half of it," observed a leading moderate newspaper, he "drives off substantially the whole of it." A Philadelphia editor commented astutely: "The demand of the President is that the Republican party shall, to suit him, stultify itself and its whole past career and principles. By this simple process he has managed to make the term radical synonymous with the entire mass of the dominant party."[10]

The Fourteenth Amendment

Although Johnson had indeed driven moderates closer to the radical position, they were not yet prepared to go the whole way to reducing the Southern states to territories and enacting black suffrage therein. Instead, they concentrated on passing the civil rights bill and a revised Freedmen's Bureau bill over the President's vetoes—which they accomplished April 9 and July 16, 1866—and on drafting a constitutional amendment as the basis for readmission of the Southern senators and representatives to Congress. All through the winter and spring of 1866, the Joint Committee on Reconstruction labored to fashion an amendment acceptable to a broad spectrum of Northern opinion. Such an amendment must: (1) provide a constitutional (as opposed to merely legislative) guarantee of the rights and security of freedmen; (2) insure against a revival of neo-Confederate political power; and (3) enshrine in the Constitution the sanctity of the national debt and the repudiation of the Confederate debt. Radicals on the joint committee also pushed for an amendment to enfranchise

---

[8]McPherson, *Political History,* pp. 74–78.

[9]LaWanda Cox and John H. Cox, *Politics, Principle, and Prejudice: Dilemma of Reconstruction America* (New York, 1963), pp. 212, 202.

[10]Cox and Cox, *Politics, Principle, and Prejudice,* p. 206; Michael Les Benedict, *A Compromise of Principle: Congressional Republicans and Reconstruction* (New York, 1974), p. 165.

blacks or disfranchise ex-Confederates, or both; moderates, believing that these proposals went too far, softened them to temporary disfranchisement of Confederates
and an indirect inducement for the states themselves to enfranchise blacks.

On April 30, the joint committee finally submitted to Congress a five-part constitutional amendment. After lengthy debate, on June 13 the revised Fourteenth
Amendment emerged from both houses with the necessary two-thirds majority. Section 1 defined all native-born or naturalized persons, including blacks, as citizens
(thus nullifying the Dred Scott decision) and prohibited the states from abridging the
"privileges and immunities" of citizens, from depriving "any person of life, liberty, or
property" without due process of law, and from denying to any person "the equal
protection of the laws."[11] Section 2 provided for the proportional reduction of the
congressional representation of any state that withheld suffrage from a portion of its
adult male citizens. Section 3 disqualified from holding office any person who as a
member of the federal or state governments had taken an oath to support the Constitution and afterward had broken that oath by engaging in rebellion. Congress
could remove this disability by a two-thirds vote. (This section replaced a harsher
committee recommendation to disfranchise until 1870 all persons who had voluntarily participated in the rebellion.) Section 4 guaranteed the national debt and repudiated the Confederate debt; Section 5 gave Congress the power to enforce the
amendment by "appropriate legislation."

This complex amendment has been the basis of more litigation than any other
part of the Constitution. Nearly all of this litigation has concerned Section 1, and
much of it has been occasioned by the ambiguity of the phrases "privileges and immunities," "due process of law," and "equal protection of laws." This ambiguity was
intentional. Its purpose was to leave the greatest possible scope for a future broadening of the meaning of these phrases. One unintended consequence of this section was an interpretation of the clause prohibiting states from depriving persons
of property without due process as a limitation of the states' power to regulate corporations (legal "persons"). But since the 1930s, Section 1 has been used mainly to
protect and expand the civil rights of black citizens. Whether the "equal protection"
clause was meant to outlaw racial segregation in schools and public facilities has
been the subject of a prolific juridical literature. The framers probably did not so intend it, but in recent decades the courts have interpreted this clause to strike down
segregation.

---

[11]Although the Civil Rights Act of 1866 had defined blacks as citizens, the incorporation of this
provision into a constitutional amendment would insure against any future Dred Scott-type denial of their
citizenship. But the wording of the Fourteenth Amendment did leave a loophole. It states that all persons
born or naturalized in the United States are "citizens of the United States and of the State wherein they
reside. No State shall make or enforce any law which shall abridge the privileges or immunities of citizens
of the United States" (italics added). The failure to add "or of the State wherein they reside" to this last
sentence created an opening for the Supreme Court to distinguish between the rights of state and national
citizenship, which it did in the *Slaughterhouse* decision of 1873. Since the Court in this case defined the
rights of national citizenship narrowly, *Slaughterhouse* reduced the potential jurisdiction of the federal
government over state abridgments of the rights of *state* citizenship. In recent decades, however, the
courts have used the equal protection of the laws clause of the Fourteenth Amendment to broaden vastly
the powers of the federal government for enforcement of civil rights.

In 1866, Section 1 of the amendment was less controversial than Sections 2 and 3. Southerners and Democrats denounced Section 3 as a vindictive punishment of men who had already suffered enough for their sins. Radicals, on the other hand, believed that it did not go far enough to penalize traitors and to protect the country against their political resurgence. Abolitionists and radicals also denounced Section 2 as a cowardly evasion of Congress's duty to enfranchise the freedmen. This section was indeed an ingenious contrivance worthy of a better cause. By reducing Southern representation in the House and the electoral college in proportion to the unenfranchised black population, it protected the North against an increase of Southern white political power. It penalized Southern states for withholding suffrage from blacks but allowed Northern states to do so with impunity, since their black population was too small to make a difference in the basis of representation. Abolitionists considered Section 2 a "wanton betrayal of justice and humanity," a "fatal and total surrender." It "is only fitted to protect the North and the white race, while it leaves the Negro to his fate," declared the American Anti-Slavery Society. "It is the blighted harvest of the bloodiest sowing the fields of the world ever saw."[12]

Radicals nevertheless had to accept the Fourteenth Amendment as the best they could get and to hope that future events would move the country toward black suffrage. The amendment became the Republican platform for the 1866 congressional elections, which were shaping up as a Northern referendum on reconstruction. Implicit in the process by which Congress passed the amendment was a commitment to readmit Southern states when they ratified it, though the lawmakers did not make this commitment explicit. When Tennessee, controlled by ex-Whig enemies of Andrew Johnson, ratified the amendment in July 1866, Congress promptly admitted its senators and representatives despite radical lamentations that this action would establish a precedent for admission of other states without black suffrage.

 The Election of 1866

After Congress passed the Fourteenth Amendment, some moderates hoped that Andrew Johnson would recognize defeat, cease his opposition, and cooperate to make reconstruction work. But they reckoned without his stubbornness. The President's fighting blood was up. He issued a statement implying that the amendment was illegal because it had been passed by a Congress from which Southern states were absent. Johnson prepared to fight the 1866 congressional elections on this issue. By the logic of the two-party system, this would push him into the Democratic camp. But a few conservative Republicans, led by the old New York Whig leaders William H. Seward, Thurlow Weed, and Henry J. Raymond (editor of the *New York Times*), still remained with the President. They hoped to build a Johnson coalition of conservatives from both old parties into the nucleus of a new party.

---

[12]James M. McPherson, *The Struggle for Equality* (Princeton, 1964), pp. 352, 354; Kenneth M. Stampp, *The Era of Reconstruction* (New York, 1965), p. 142; Eric Foner, *Reconstruction: America's Unfinished Revolution* (New York, 1988), p. 255.

The first step in building this coalition had been the formation of the National Union Executive Committee in April 1866. Two months later, this committee issued a call for a National Union convention to meet at Philadelphia in August. Johnson played an active role in preparations for the convention. He expected it to mobilize a majority of Northerners in favor of his policy. The conservative Republican leaders of the movement tried to keep Democrats inconspicuous in the preconvention maneuvering, in order not to alienate Republicans who might be scared off by a copper tinge. But this proved to be difficult. Johnson's partisans had overestimated the potential Republican support for their movement. The President's actions had united nearly the whole of the party against him. Inevitably, therefore, most of the pro-Johnson congressional candidates in the North were Democrats. The Democratic tail soon began to wag the National Union dog. Hopes for a third force in American politics succumbed to the realities of the two-party system.

On August 14, delegates from both North and South met in the National Union convention at Philadelphia. The platform called for the immediate readmission of Southern states. To symbolize the theme of unity, delegates from Massachusetts and South Carolina marched into the hall in pairs, each delegate from one state locked arm in arm with a delegate from the other. When President Johnson learned of this dramatic gesture, he was overcome with emotion and pronounced the convention more important than any that had met since 1787.

In the end, however, the National Union movement failed. It suffered from three fatal weaknesses. The first, as noted, was its domination by Democrats. War memories were too fresh for most Northern voters to trust a party they still regarded as tainted by treason. Governor Oliver Morton of Indiana expressed this distrust in an 1866 speech that became a classic example of what was later known as "waving the bloody shirt." "Every unregenerate rebel," said Morton, "calls himself a Democrat."

Every bounty jumper, every deserter, every sneak who ran away from the draft calls himself a Democrat. . . . Every man who labored for the rebellion in the field, who murdered Union prisoners by cruelty and starvation, who conspired to bring about civil war in the loyal states . . . calls himself a Democrat. Every New York rioter in 1863 who burned up little children in colored asylums, who robbed, ravished and murdered indiscriminately . . . called himself a Democrat. In short, the Democratic party may be described as a common sewer and loathsome receptacle, into which is emptied every element of treason North and South, every element of inhumanity and barbarism which has dishonored the age.[13]

A second weakness of the National Union movement was the hyperbole of its platform declaration that "there is no section of the country where the Constitution and the laws of the United States find more prompt and entire obedience than in [the Southern] states." The rising tide of violence against freedmen and Unionists, said Republicans, disproved this. Although Republicans exaggerated and exploited Southern violence for partisan purposes, the large degree of truth in this propaganda made it effective. The worst clashes occurred at Memphis in May 1866 and at New Orleans two months later. The affray in Memphis began with a quarrel between local whites and demobilized black soldiers; by the time it was over, white

---

[13]McKitrick, *Andrew Johnson and Reconstruction,* pp. 318–319.

mobs—which included many policemen—had rampaged through the black sections of town and killed at least forty-six people. With Memphis as an example, commented the *New York Tribune* sarcastically, "who doubts that the Freedmen's Bureau ought to be abolished forthwith, and the blacks remitted to the paternal care of their old masters, who 'understand the nigger, you know, a great deal better than the Yankees can.' "[14]

On July 30 in New Orleans, a mob—again aided by police—assaulted the delegates to a black suffrage convention. This assemblage was a reconvened remnant of the 1864 Louisiana constitutional convention. The delegates had gathered to consider the enfranchisement of blacks as a counterweight to the control of the state government by ex-Confederates. The mayor of New Orleans, who had received a special pardon from Johnson in order to assume office, obtained the President's approval of an order to prevent the convention from assembling. But the commander of the occupation forces refused to sanction this suppression and sent troops to protect the delegates. The troops arrived late, however, and by the time they got there the mob had killed thirty-seven blacks and three of their white allies. Republicans pointed to this as yet another example of what could be expected from Johnson's policy. The President did not help his cause by a speech in St. Louis on September 8, a speech in which he blamed Republicans for provoking the mob and expressed no regret for the victims.

The third weakness of the National Union movement was Andrew Johnson himself. Back in Tennessee, Johnson had been an effective stump speaker. He believed that he could repeat his success on the national scene by taking the case for his policy directly to the people. Against the advice of friends, he broke precedent and went on the campaign trail in a "swing around the circle" from Washington to Chicago and St. Louis and back to Washington (August 28–September 15). For Johnson, this whistle-stop tour was a disaster. He allowed himself to be drawn into shouting contests with hecklers. He bandied insults with hostile crowds. The content of his speeches seldom varied: the South was loyal; the real traitors were radicals who refused to readmit Southern representatives; and he, Andrew Johnson, was willing to give his life if necessary for the salvation of the Union and the Constitution. "He who is opposed to the restoration of this Government and the reunion of the States is as great a traitor as Jeff Davis or Wendell Phillips," he shouted at Cleveland. "Why not hang Thad. Stevens and Wendell Phillips?" Just as he had done in Washington during the preceding winter, the President reminded those who condemned his generous pardoning policy that Jesus had come to earth to forgive men rather than to condemn them. "He died and shed His own blood that the world might live. . . . If more blood is needed, erect an altar, and upon it your humble speaker will pour out the last drop of his blood as a libation for his country's salvation."[15]

---

[14]*New York Tribune,* May 22, 1866.

[15]Edward McPherson, *Political History,* p. 135; McKitrick, *Andrew Johnson and Reconstruction,* p. 432. For an excellent analysis of the "Swing around the Circle," see Hans L. Trefousse, *Andrew Johnson: A Biography* (New York, 1989), pp. 262–266.

Johnson had lost control of himself. And the elections showed that he had also lost control of the country. Even the confident Republicans were astonished by the one-sided nature of their victory. The party retained its three-to-one majority in both houses of Congress and gained ascendancy in every Northern state as well as in West Virginia, Missouri, and Tennessee.

The Reconstruction Acts of 1867

If ever a party won a mandate, the Republicans did so in the congressional elections in the fall of 1866. But a mandate for what? Insofar as the elections had turned on a specific issue, that issue was the Fourteenth Amendment. Yet the adoption of the amendment required ratification by at least four of the unreconstructed states plus all the states the Republicans had carried. Some far-sighted Southerners read the Northern election returns correctly. They recognized that if the South did not "take the present terms, harder ones will be proposed." But most Southern whites refused to cooperate with their conquerors. Typical of their attitude was the reason offered by the governors of North and South Carolina for refusing to ratify the amendment: "If we are to be degraded we will retain some self-esteem by not making it self-abasement. . . . Worse terms may be imposed by Congress, but they will be *imposed* and not *voluntarily accepted*."[16]

Andrew Johnson also stood fast. Although "we are beaten for the present," explained one of the President's allies, "our cause will live. If all the states not represented refuse to ratify the amendment . . . the extreme Rads will go . . . for reorganizing the southern states on negro suffrage. . . . That will present the issue squarely . . . and on that we can beat them at the next Presidential election."[17] When the legislatures of Virginia and Alabama seemed willing to ratify the amendment, Johnson dissuaded them. All Southern legislatures rejected the Fourteenth Amendment, in many cases unanimously. Having spurned the easiest terms they could have hoped for, they sat back to watch Congress try to decide what to do next.

This Southern attitude exasperated moderate Republicans. "They would not cooperate in rebuilding what they destroyed," said one moderate, so "we must remove the rubbish and rebuild from the bottom. Whether they are willing or not, we must compel obedience to the Union, and demand protection for its humblest citizen."[18] Southern and presidential intransigence accomplished what the radicals alone could not have accomplished: the conversion of moderates to black suffrage as the cornerstone of reconstruction.

---

[16]McKitrick, *Andrew Johnson and Reconstruction*, p. 451n; Michael Perman, *Reunion Without Compromise: The South and Reconstruction 1865–1868* (Cambridge, 1973), pp. 238, 239.

[17]Cox and Cox, *Politics, Principle, and Prejudice*, p. 230.

[18]Benedict, *Fruits of Victory*, p. 33.

During the three-month session of Congress following the congressional elections of 1866,[19] Republicans debated and passed a Reconstruction Act whose final terms represented a compromise between moderates and radicals—a compromise hammered out in an exhausting sequence of committee wrangles, caucus decisions, floor debates, parliamentary maneuvers, all-night sessions, and frayed tempers. During this process, the Democrats tried to play the role of spoiler, voting first with the radicals on amendments to make the law stronger and then with the moderates to defeat the amended measures.

Three of the radicals' objectives went beyond what moderate Republicans were willing to accept: (1) long-term disfranchisement of ex-Confederates, to give blacks and Unionists a chance to put the new state governments on a solid footing before a counterrevolution of Southern Democrats could destroy them; (2) confiscation and redistribution of land, to give the freedmen an economic basis for their new political power; and (3) federally supported schools, to enable Southern blacks to acquire the literacy, skills, and self-confidence to protect their freedom and rights. Recognizing that they had no chance to achieve these aims in the final short session of this Congress, radicals supported a bill simply to nullify the existing Southern governments and to place the territorialized states under military rule—in the hope that the new Congress, elected in 1866 and somewhat more radical than its predecessor, would enact more thorough measures.

Radicals believed that reduction of ex-Confederate states to the status of territories would have positive benefits in and of itself. During territorial probation, they hoped, the Freedmen's Bureau, freedmen's aid societies, Northern soldiers, Northern settlers, and Northern capital could educate the freedpeople up to the level of their new responsibilities, protect them with military force, make Southern whites feel the heavy hand of national power until they gave up hope of defying it, and rebuild the South in the Northern self-image of "small farms, thrifty tillage, free schools, closely-associated communities, social independence, respect for honest labor, and equality of political rights."[20]

But this idealized vision of a free-labor South was not to be fulfilled, at least not by the legislation of the Thirty-ninth Congress. Although the House passed a bill for territorialization and military government, Senate moderates believed that Congress must enact a comprehensive law setting forth the conditions of restoration. Other-

---

[19]This was still the 39th Congress, elected in 1864. Under the Constitution as it then existed, Congress met on the first Monday in December of the year *after* it was elected. This meant that thirteen months elapsed between the election of most congressmen and the date of their first meeting, unless the president called them into special session or Congress itself provided by law for a different meeting date. The second regular session of any given Congress, meeting in December of the second year after its election, expired on the following March 4. This second session was therefore known as the "short" session, since it lasted only three months—from early December to March 4. The second session of the Congress elected in 1864, therefore, met in December 1866. This situation was changed by the Twentieth Amendment to the Constitution, adopted in 1933, which stipulated that a Congress would meet on January 3 of the year following the year of its election, and would not expire until January 3 two years later.

[20]David Donald, *The Politics of Reconstruction 1863–1867* (Baton Rouge, 1965), pp. 62–63.

wise, the divisive issue of reconstruction would drag on indefinitely and Northern voters might lose patience with the Republican failure to come up with a "policy." Therefore the Senate passed a measure that, like the House bill, divided the ten un-reconstructed states[21] into five military districts and declared the existing civil governments in these states to be provisional only, subject to the overriding authority of the occupation forces. But the Senate bill also provided that after any of the states had called a new constitutional convention elected by manhood suffrage, had adopted a new constitution that included black suffrage, and had ratified this constitution and the Fourteenth Amendment to the federal Constitution, the state's representatives would be readmitted to Congress. Those persons disqualified by the Fourteenth Amendment from holding office were barred from voting for convention delegates and from voting on the ratification of the new constitution. But the bill did not require the states to keep them disfranchised thereafter. The House concurred with the Senate bill, and after Johnson vetoed this Reconstruction Act on March 2, both houses passed it over his veto the same day.

Although the radicals accepted this measure as the best they could get for the time being, Indiana Congressman George W. Julian expressed their misgivings about it in a speech to the House. Southern states, he warned:

. . . are not ready for reconstruction as independent States. . . . If these districts were to-day admitted as States, with the precise political and social elements which we know to exist in them, even with their rebel population disfranchised and the ballot placed in the hands of radical Union men only, irrespective of color, the experiment would be ruinous. . . . The power of the great landed aristocracy in these regions, if unrestrained by power from without, would inevitably assert itself. . . . What these regions need, above all things, is not an easy and quick return to their forfeited rights in the Union, but *government,* the strong arm of power, out-stretched from the central authority here in Washington, making it safe for the freedmen . . . safe for northern capital and labor, northern energy and enterprise, and northern ideas. . . . To talk about suddenly building up independent States where the material for such structures is fatally wanting is nonsense. States must *grow,* and to that end their growth must be fostered and protected.[22]

Although future events would confirm Julian's forebodings, the Reconstruction Act seemed radical, even revolutionary, in 1867. That was how Johnson described it in his veto message. With their huge majority, Republicans no longer worried about the President's capacity to prevent the enactment of reconstruction laws. But as Commander in Chief of the army and as head of the branch of government charged with executing the laws, Johnson still possessed great power to frustrate the enforcement of legislation. And the President made clear his intention to use this power. Therefore, while it worked out the terms of the Reconstruction Act, Congress also passed a series of measures to limit the President's authority.

---

[21]Including all of the states that had seceded except Tennessee, which had been readmitted after ratifying the Fourteenth Amendment in 1866.

[22]Benedict, *Fruits of Victory,* pp. 115–116.

Limitations on Presidential Power

The first was a bill enacted on January 22, 1867, calling the Fortieth Congress into special session immediately after the expiration of the Thirty-ninth on March 4. This ensured that the legislators could maintain oversight of their reconstruction program during the interval before the first regularly scheduled session of the Fortieth Congress met in December. Second, Congress on March 2 passed, over Johnson's veto, the Tenure of Office Act, which required the continuance in office of any government official dismissed by the President until the Senate confirmed a new appointee. This was designed to stop Johnson's dismissal of Republican officeholders who supported the congressional reconstruction policy. In its final form, the Tenure of Office Act also required Senate consent for the dismissal of cabinet officers. This was intended to protect Secretary of War Stanton, who now supported the congressional policy and was in a crucial position to influence its enforcement. The third measure to curb Johnson's powers was a rider to an army appropriations bill (passed on March 2) providing that all presidential orders to the army must be issued through the general of the army (Grant), who could not be removed without the Senate's consent. Grant had earlier favored a mild reconstruction policy, but Southern violence toward freedmen and Unionists had convinced him of the need for a stronger policy. The appropriations rider was designed to prevent Johnson from nullifying the military enforcement of reconstruction by orders issued independently of Grant.

The Second Reconstruction Act

The Reconstruction Act of March 2 had spelled out the process by which Southerners could take the initiative to restore their states to congressional representation, but it had created no machinery to compel them to act. This soon proved to have been a mistake. Southern whites expressed a preference to remain in limbo under military rule, rather than to cooperate in the establishment of new constitutions with black suffrage. But most Republicans wanted to get on with the task of political reconstruction. On March 23, therefore, the special session of the new Congress passed a supplementary Reconstruction Act that required the generals in command of Southern military districts to register eligible voters and to set the machinery in motion for the election of delegates to constitutional conventions. With the passage of this act, black leaders and Unionist whites (soon to be called "scalawags") along with Northern settlers in the South (soon to be called "carpetbaggers") began in earnest to organize a Republican party in the Southern states. The army undertook the task of registering voters, including freed slaves. The nation had completed another stage in the revolution that had begun with emancipation—"the maddest, most infamous revolution in history," according to a hostile South Carolinian.[23]

---

[23]Stampp, *Era of Reconstruction*, p. 170.

Recon-struction and the Crisis of Impeach-ment

*He has thrown down the gauntlet to
Congress, and says to us as plainly as words
can speak it: "Try this issue now betwixt me
and you; either you go to the wall or I do."*

—Congressman Austin Blair,
*speaking of President Andrew Johnson, February 24,
1868*

567

Johnson's Continued Defiance of Congress

Andrew Johnson also considered reconstruction a mad, infamous revolution. The President retained considerable capacity to weaken the enforcement of reconstruction, despite Congress's efforts to tie his hands in this regard. He could appoint conservative generals to administer Southern military districts. He could interpret the Reconstruction Acts narrowly in order to give the existing civilian governments maximum control over the registration of voters and the election of convention delegates. He could use his executive powers in a dozen ways to obstruct or delay the Southern political revolution. For these reasons, a growing number of radicals concluded that reconstruction could never work so long as Johnson remained in office. They launched a drive to impeach the President and replace him with Benjamin Wade, who as president pro tem of the Senate was next in line for the presidency.

The First Impeachment Effort

Impeachment was an extreme step. The Constitution empowers the House to impeach by a simple majority and the Senate to convict by a two-thirds majority any official for "Treason, Bribery, or other high Crimes and Misdemeanors" (Article II, Section 4). The House had used this power only five times in the past, and the Senate had voted conviction only twice. Both cases concerned district judges. Never previously had Congress contemplated using the impeachment weapon against a president.

Moderate Republicans shrank from such a prospect. They maintained that an official could be impeached only for conduct that, if he were a private citizen, would be indictable as a crime. Much as they deplored Johnson's political perversity, they did not believe that he had committed any crimes. Radicals, however, contended that impeachment was not a criminal proceeding but rather a means of punishing a public official for "grave misuse of his powers, or any mischievous nonuse of them—for any conduct which harms the public or perils its welfare."[1] Johnson deserved such punishment, they insisted, for his wholesale pardons of ex-Rebels, his defiance of Congress, his intimation that Congress was an illegal body, his disgraceful public speeches, his complicity by inaction in the New Orleans massacre, and his general obstruction of the will of the Northern people.

On January 7, 1867, radicals managed to get the House to pass a resolution calling for an impeachment investigation. But the Judiciary Committee, designated to conduct the investigation, was dominated by moderates. Although the committee held extensive hearings, these only demonstrated that without further and greater provocation by Johnson, impeachment would come to nothing. Nevertheless, in February 1867 a moderate warned: "If [Johnson] fails to execute the laws, in their spirit as well as in their letter . . . if, holding the South in his hand, either by direct advice or personal example he shall encourage them to such resistance to progress as may tend to defeat the public will . . . the President may, after all, come to be regarded as an 'obstacle' which must be 'deposed.' "[2]

For a time Johnson seemed to heed such warnings. He let it be known that he intended to carry out the reconstruction laws. He appointed generals recommended by Stanton and Grant to command the five Southern military districts. These generals supported the congressional policy.

The Southern Response to the Reconstruction Acts

In the South, too, prominent ex-Confederates advised their people to accept the inevitable and to comply with the laws. By cooperating with the reconstruction process, some Southern whites hoped to influence it in a moderate direction. Members of the upper class, in their professed role as paternal protectors of the freedpeople, even hoped to control a substantial portion of the black vote. They organized interracial political meetings and barbecues at which they urged the freedmen to vote with their fellow Southerners rather than with alien Yankees. This was part of a persistent effort in postwar Southern politics, led mainly by former Whigs, to

---

[1] New York Tribune, October 27, 1866.

[2] Michael Les Benedict, The Impeachment and Trial of Andrew Johnson (New York, 1973), p. 25.

create a moderate third force independent of both Democrats and Republicans. Enfranchisement of the freedmen seemed to offer the proponents of this effort an opportunity they were quick to grasp.

But the imperatives of the two-party system doomed this endeavor, just as they had doomed the National Union movement in the North the previous year. Moreover, the Republicans soon demonstrated their ability to mobilize black voters *en masse* under their banner. The party of Lincoln and emancipation had an unbeatable advantage in this respect.

The nucleus of a Southern Republican party had existed for two years in the form of unconditional Unionists and postwar settlers from the North. So long as the franchise was limited to whites, however, this nucleus was a small minority of Southern voters except in a few staunchly Unionist areas such as east Tennessee. With passage of the Reconstruction Acts, the Republicans would become a potential majority party in at least half of the Southern states if they could win the allegiance of the freedmen. This they did easily. The principal agency for recruiting blacks into the Republican party was the Union League. Founded in the North during the war as an anti-Copperhead organization, the Union League moved into the South after Appomattox. During the spring of 1867, branches of the Union League mushroomed in the South to organize and instruct the freedmen in their new political duties.

In many districts the Freedmen's Bureau aided the League in this task. Indeed, some Bureau agents served simultaneously as Union League officials and, in their military capacity, as supervisors of voter registration under the Reconstruction Acts. These partisan activities gave white Southerners another reason to condemn the Bureau—not only did it intervene in their economic relations with black laborers, but now it was also helping to mobilize these laborers into an alien political party.

As Republican success in winning black voters became clear, many Southern whites who had initially urged cooperation with reconstruction changed their tune. They hoped that, somehow or other, President Johnson or the Northern Democrats could yet reverse the process and overthrow the radicals.

Their faith in Johnson was not entirely misplaced. Although the President had promised to carry out the Reconstruction Acts, he believed them unconstitutional and planned to weaken their impact by executive interpretation. An opportunity to do so arose from several actions by the army as it began to enforce the acts. The voter registration boards in many Southern districts construed the disfranchisement provisions broadly to apply to men who had held any office, down to cemetery sexton, before the war and had thereafter supported the rebellion. Some generals removed state and local officials from office for alleged obstruction and for other causes. Johnson rebuked General Philip Sheridan, commander of the Louisiana-Texas district, who had evicted several high officials. The President asked Attorney General Henry Stanbery to rule on the legality of Sheridan's action and on the disfranchisement criteria of the registration boards. Stanbery's opinion, issued in June 1867, interpreted the Reconstruction Acts in the narrowest possible fashion. He ruled that the army's supremacy over civil governments was confined to police duties; that commanders could not remove civilian officials; that only those antebellum officeholders who had taken an oath before the war to support the United States Constitution could be disfranchised for rebellion; and that registrars must accept without question a prospective voter's oath that he had not participated in rebellion.

Military commanders expressed dismay at this ruling, especially its final provision, which Sheridan described as opening "a broad macadamized road for perjury and fraud to travel on." If sustained, Stanbery's opinion would go a long way toward nullifying the intent of the Reconstruction Acts because former Confederates would dominate the voting for new constitutional conventions. Stanton and Grant protested against the opinion; Grant informed commanders that it did not have the force of an order and told them to continue enforcing their own construction of the law.

Congress reassembled in July to plug the loopholes opened by Stanbery's ruling. On July 19, the Republicans passed, over Johnson's veto, a third Reconstruction Act, which declared Southern provisional governments subordinate in all respects to military rule, confirmed the power of commanders to remove officials from office, authorized registration boards to reject a voter's oath if they believed it falsely sworn, and defined, more broadly than Stanbery had done, the categories of prewar officeholders who were liable to disfranchisement.

The Second Impeachment Effort

This accomplished, congressional radicals wanted to revive impeachment. The President, they asserted, had demonstrated that he had no intention of enforcing the law in good faith. But moderates still feared that impeachment might make a martyr of Johnson. They managed to head off the radical effort. Among themselves, however, they complained that "the President . . . *does* continue to do the most provoking things. If he isn't impeached it won't be his fault."[3]

As if to thumb his nose at the moderates who were trying to save him, Johnson again took the offensive as soon as Congress adjourned. Democrats had long been imploring him to dismiss Secretary of War Stanton, the only cabinet member who supported the congressional reconstruction program. But for reasons never made clear, the President had not previously done so, and the Tenure of Office Act now seemed to make it impossible for him to remove Stanton without Senate approval. By waiting until Congress adjourned, however, Johnson could suspend Stanton until the Senate reconvened several months later. This was what he did on August 12, 1867.

The President persuaded Grant to become interim secretary of war. This sent shock waves through the Republican party. Grant was the most popular man in the country. Despite his well-known aversion to politics, he seemed almost certain to be drafted as a presidential candidate in 1868. Did Grant's acceptance of office under Johnson mean that he agreed with the President's actions? Republicans soon breathed easier as it became clear that he did not. Grant had strongly urged Johnson not to suspend Stanton. He accepted the interim appointment only to serve as a buffer between the President and the army, in order to prevent Johnson from doing more mischief. When Johnson informed Grant on August 17 of his intention to replace Sheridan with a more conservative general as commander of the Louisiana-Texas district, Grant penned an earnest letter, which he leaked to the press, imploring him not to do so. Sheridan was a great general and a good administrator who had done as much as any man to overcome the Rebels in war and peace, said Grant. "His removal will only be regarded as an effort to defeat the laws of Congress. It will

---

[3]Ibid., p. 56.

be interpreted by the unreconstructed element in the South . . . as a triumph. It will embolden them to renewed opposition to the will of the loyal masses, believing that they have the Executive with them."[4]

Johnson disregarded this advice. He removed Sheridan, and for good measure, he also removed General Daniel Sickles, commander of the Carolinas district, who had offended Southern whites with his aggressive enforcement of the Reconstruction Acts. Grant did his best to cushion the impact of these changes by ordering the new commanders not to restore civilian officials deposed by their predecessors—which in Sheridan's district included the governors of both Louisiana and Texas.

But the President had once again demonstrated his ability to contravene the spirit of the reconstruction laws, and this gave the impeachment movement another shot in the arm. "What does Johnson mean to do?" worried a former attorney general. "Does he mean to have another rebellion on the question of Executive powers & duties?" The publisher of a moderate Republican newspaper asked a friend in Washington: "Is the President crazy, or only drunk? I am afraid his doings will make us all favor impeachment."[5] Several Republican editors who had opposed impeachment changed their minds and came out in its favor during the fall of 1867. One moderate Republican on the House Judiciary Committee switched his negative vote to affirmative, enabling the committee to recommend by a 5 to 4 vote the President's impeachment on general grounds of "usurpation of power." Before the House could vote on this resolution, however, the off-year state elections in the North produced Democratic gains that seemed to portend a conservative shift in public opinion.

Once again circumstances made state elections into a quasi-referendum on reconstruction and especially on black suffrage. Having enfranchised Southern blacks, Republicans felt compelled by reproaches of hypocrisy to try their best to enfranchise blacks in the Northern states that still denied them the ballot. Unless they did so, conceded one abolitionist, "our whole demeanor toward the southern states" would be "like that of the Pharisee toward the Publican."[6] All but two state Republican platforms in 1867 endorsed the principle of equal suffrage in Northern states. Republican legislatures in five states placed constitutional amendments for this purpose on the ballot, three of them to be voted on in 1867.

But voters in Ohio, Minnesota, and Kansas rejected black suffrage. At least 80 percent of the Republican voters in Ohio and Minnesota favored the proposal, but solid Democratic opposition caused it to lose narrowly in both states. The issue helped Democrats win control of the Ohio legislature. The party also made major gains in other Northern states, where black suffrage as well as impeachment and radical reconstruction in general were important issues. As usual, Democrats went all out to exploit racism in the campaign. "Any Democrat," observed a French newspaper correspondent, "who did not manage to hint in his speech that the negro is a degenerate gorilla, would be considered lacking in enthusiasm."[7]

---

[4]Edward McPherson, *The Political History of the United States During the Period of Reconstruction* (Washington, D.C., 1875), p. 307.

[5]Benedict, *Impeachment*, pp. 58–59.

[6]Parker Pillsbury to Gerrit Smith, November 27, 1867, Gerrit Smith Papers, Syracuse University Library.

[7]Georges Clemenceau, *American Reconstruction 1865–1870*, trans. Margaret MacVeagh (New York, 1928), p. 131. For an analysis of the 1867 elections, see Eric Foner, *Reconstruction: America's Unfinished Revolution, 1863–1877* (New York, 1988), pp. 313–316.

Democrats magnified their gains in the 1867 elections into a "Great Reaction" against Republicans, "*a revulsion of popular feeling in the North*. . . . Judging from the history of Counter Revolutions . . . the days of Radical domination are numbered." Andrew Johnson made a "victory speech" to a group of serenaders at the White House. One of the President's aides chortled: "I almost pity the Radicals. After giving ten states to the negroes, to keep the Democrats from getting them, they will have lost the rest. . . . Any party with an abolition head and a nigger tail will soon find itself with nothing left but the head and the tail."[8]

These predictions of Republican demise proved premature. But the elections did strengthen moderates in the party at the expense of radicals. Party leaders became chary of the suffrage issue in the North. In Horace Greeley's words, "the Negro question lies at the bottom of our reverses. . . . We have lost votes in the Free States by daring to be just to the Negro." The elections also blunted the impeachment drive. "We shall have burdens enough to carry in the next campaign," said Greeley, "without making Mr. Johnson a martyr and carrying him also." A Washington correspondent reported the impeachment movement "dead, unless the President, by fresh outrages, gives it a new impetus."[9] The House confirmed this observation on December 7 by voting down an impeachment resolution, 108 to 57.

The Impeachment and Acquittal of Johnson

But Johnson's subsequent actions once more raised the issue from the dead. General Winfield Scott Hancock, a Democrat and Johnson's choice to replace Sheridan as commander of the Louisiana-Texas district, reversed many of Sheridan's policies and thereby set back Republican efforts. Johnson publicly commended Hancock. Then on December 28, the President replaced two radical-leaning generals in the Georgia-Alabama-Florida district with conservatives who were expected to follow Hancock's example. These moves encouraged the growing Southern resistance to reconstruction. Having failed to elect a majority of delegates to any of the ten constitutional conventions that met during the winter of 1867–1868, Southern Democrats organized to defeat or delay ratification of the new constitutions long enough for the much-heralded Northern reaction to overturn reconstruction by a Democratic victory in the 1868 presidential election. "Will the white men of the North and the Great West fail to come to the rescue?" asked an Atlanta newspaper rhetorically. "We answer for them—THEY WILL NOT FAIL."[10]

Southern Republicans[11] expressed dismay at this newly demonstrated power of the President to strengthen their enemies. "Unfriendly military management has killed us," wrote Alabama Republican leaders. "The removal of Genls. Pope and

---

[8]Michael Perman, *Reunion Without Compromise: The South and Reconstruction 1865–1868* (Cambridge, 1973), pp. 320–321; C. Vann Woodward, "Seeds of Failure in Radical Race Policy," in Harold Hyman (ed.), *New Frontiers of the American Reconstruction* (Urbana, Ill., 1966), p. 137; Ira Brown, "Pennsylvania and the Rights of the Negro, 1865–1887," *Pennsylvania History,* 28 (January 1961), 51.

[9]*Independent,* November 14, 21, 1867; *New York Tribune,* December 9, 1867.

[10]Perman, *Reunion Without Compromise,* p. 317.

[11]For analyses of the Southern Republicans, see pages 578 and 597 to 603.

Swayne has taken from the work of Reconstruction two able and experienced leaders. . . . Their removal is followed by such an outburst of rebel hostility that . . . no man to-day can enter the canvass without taking his life in his hands. . . . The rebels have had all their own ways in many counties. . . . What next can we do?"[12]

While these events were taking place in the South, a singular drama was unfolding in Washington. General Grant was still serving as interim secretary of war while the Senate decided whether to concur in the President's suspension of Stanton. If the Senate refused to concur, Johnson hoped to challenge the constitutionality of the Tenure of Office Act in the courts. But to do this, he needed Grant's cooperation. Johnson thought he had obtained the general's promise not to turn the War Department back to Stanton if the Senate overruled the secretary's suspension. But when Grant learned on January 14 that the Senate had done so, he vacated the office and Stanton moved back in. Johnson charged Grant with bad faith. The astonished and angry general replied that, on the contrary, he had made clear his intention not to violate the Tenure of Office Act. A bitter exchange of letters between the two men made front-page copy. Johnson may have gotten the better of this verbal contest, but in making an enemy of Grant the President further eroded his own political support and boosted the general's prestige among Republicans.

Foiled in his attempt to use Grant to gain control of the War Department, Johnson decided to challenge Congress directly. He issued an order on February 21 removing Stanton and nominating Adjutant General Lorenzo Thomas as interim secretary of war. When this news reached Congress, uproar ensued. Republican senators urged Stanton to disobey the order. The dour war secretary barricaded himself in his office and refused to yield the keys when the hapless Thomas showed up the next morning with a hangover after a Washington's Birthday ball at which he had drunk too much in celebration of his new job.

The House Votes Impeachment

Johnson's apparent violation of the Tenure of Office Act changed the minds of many Republican moderates who had previously opposed impeachment. "He has thrown down the gauntlet," wrote one moderate, "and says to us as plainly as words can speak it: 'Try this issue now betwixt me and you; either you go to the wall or I do.' "[13] On February 24, 1868, the House impeached the President by a party-line vote of 126 to 47. Befitting the Republicans' angry mood, they took this action *before* drawing up the charges against Johnson. The House then created a committee of prosecutors whose members included some of the most radical men in Congress: Thaddeus Stevens, George Julian, Benjamin Butler, John Logan, and George Boutwell. In the manner of a grand jury indictment, the charges they drafted contained eleven counts framed in prolix legal language designed to cover every conceivable "high crime or misdemeanor" allegedly committed by the President. The first eight counts

---

[12]Hans L. Trefousse, *Impeachment of a President: Andrew Johnson, the Blacks, and Reconstruction* (Knoxville, 1975), p. 119; Eric McKitrick, *Andrew Johnson and Reconstruction* (Chicago, 1960), p. 500n.; Michael Les Benedict, *A Compromise of Principle: Congressional Republicans and Reconstruction, 1863–1869* (New York, 1974), p. 290.

[13]Benedict, *Compromise of Principle*, p. 299.

dealt with his attempt to remove Stanton and to appoint a successor without the Senate's consent. The ninth article charged Johnson with trying to persuade the army commander in the District of Columbia to violate the Command of the Army Act by accepting orders directly from the President. The tenth article, written by Butler, accused the President of trying to "excite the odium and resentment of all the good people of the United States against Congress and the laws by it duly and constitutionally enacted." The final "omnibus" article in effect drew together all the charges in the previous ten.

On Trial before the Senate

The Constitution empowers the Senate to try cases of impeachment, with the Chief Justice functioning as presiding judge when the President of the United States is the defendant. The trial began March 4 and continued, with interruptions, for eleven weeks. This protracted process worked in the President's favor by cooling the passions that had come to a climax with his attempted removal of Stanton.

Johnson's defense counsel included some of the leading lawyers in the country: Henry Stanbery, the attorney general; William M. Evarts, a future secretary of state; and Benjamin R. Curtis, a former justice of the Supreme Court who had written the principal dissenting opinion in the Dred Scott case. During the trial, these men demonstrated a good deal more legal acumen than did the House prosecutors (called "managers"). The case for the defense rested on three arguments: a government official can be impeached only for criminal offenses that would be indictable in ordinary courts; Johnson had committed no crime by seeking to test the constitutionality of the Tenure of Office Act; and in any case, because this law applied only to cabinet officers "during the term of the president by whom they may have been appointed," it did not apply to Stanton, who had been appointed by Lincoln.

To these arguments the impeachment managers replied: Johnson was serving out Lincoln's term and therefore the Tenure of Office Act did cover Stanton; to allow a president to disobey a law in order to test it in court would set a dangerous precedent; and regardless of whether Johnson was guilty of any crime, impeachment was a political rather than a criminal process. On this last point, Benjamin Butler maintained that an impeachable offense was "one in its nature or consequences subversive of some fundamental or essential principle of government, or highly prejudicial to the public interest, and this may consist of a violation of the Constitution, of law, of an official oath, or of duty . . . or, without violating a positive law, by the abuse of discretionary powers."[14]

Butler's statement got to the heart of the case for impeachment. Johnson was really on trial for two years of relentless opposition to the Republican reconstruction program. His crime, in the words of a congressman, was "the one great overshadowing purpose of reconstructing the rebel States in accordance with his own will, in the interests of the great criminals who carried them into the rebellion." Impeachment was also the culmination of a long power struggle between Congress and the executive, a struggle that went back to the Lincoln administration. "The great ques-

---

[14] *The Trial of Andrew Johnson . . . for High Crimes and Misdemeanors,* 3 vols. (Washington, D.C., 1868), I, 88.

tion to be decided," wrote one partisan of impeachment, was whether "the National Legislature [is] to be as omnipotent in American politics as the English is in English politics. . . . May we not anticipate a time when the President will no more think of vetoing a bill passed by Congress than the British crown thinks of doing?"[15]

But some moderates feared the creation of a precedent by which a two-thirds majority of Congress could remove any president who happened to disagree with them. This might destroy the constitutional balance of powers in the American political system. Despite their disgust with Johnson, these moderates did not want to cripple the Presidency. "Whether Andrew Johnson should be removed from office, justly or unjustly, [is] comparatively of little consequence," wrote a conservative senator, "but whether our government should be Mexicanized and an example set which would surely, in the end, utterly overthrow our institutions, [is] a matter of vast consequence."[16] Several moderates also distrusted the radical Benjamin Wade, who would become president if the Senate convicted Johnson.

These concerns enabled troubled Republican senators to seize upon the legal uncertainties of the case to justify their doubts about impeachment. Moderate senators who abhorred Johnson's reconstruction policies but wished to vote against impeachment sought through intermediaries to reach an understanding with the President. For the first time, Johnson responded to such overtures. He conducted himself with dignity and restraint during the trial. He gave no more speeches or interviews denouncing Congress. He promised to enforce the Reconstruction Acts, and he did so. After discreet negotiations with moderate senators, Johnson appointed as secretary of war General John M. Schofield, whose efficiency and impartiality as commander of the Virginia military district commended him to all factions.

These actions strengthened the President's prospects for acquittal. But intense pressure from Republican constituencies kept the issue in doubt until the end. Every Republican state convention endorsed conviction. Southern Republicans continued to predict Rebel resurgence if Johnson remained in office. Rumors of bribes and other sinister machinations floated through Washington. When the Senate on May 16 finally voted on the eleventh article of impeachment (the omnibus article), the roll call took on the dimensions of high drama. Not until West Virginia's Republican Senator Peter G. Van Winkle, near the end of the alphabet, voted nay did it become clear that Johnson was acquitted. The vote was 35 to 19; the nay votes of seven Republicans and twelve Democrats had caused the total for conviction to fall one vote short of the necessary two-thirds. Identical votes on articles 2 and 3 on May 26 came as an anticlimax. The impeachment managers conceded defeat. Although the seven "recusant" Republican senators endured recriminations for a time, the impeachment passions soon died down as the party closed ranks for the presidential election. Although Johnson continued to veto reconstruction bills, they were passed over his vetoes and the reconstruction process went forward without further presidential hindrance. A crisis that had shaken the constitutional system to its foundations ended without fundamentally altering the system.

---

[15] *House Reports,* No. 7, 40th Cong., 1st sess. (1867), 2; William R. Brock, *An American Crisis: Congress and Reconstruction 1865–1867* (London, 1963), p. 260.

[16] Benedict, *Impeachment,* p. 179.

✐ The Supreme Court and Reconstruction

During the impeachment controversy, Congress and the Supreme Court also engaged in a power struggle from which the Court backed away before a final showdown. The Court's ruling in the *Milligan* case (1866)—that military trials of civilians in nonwar zones were unconstitutional—seemed to invalidate martial law in the South.[17] Congressional Republicans denounced the *Milligan* decision as a "piece of judicial impertinence which we are not bound to respect."[18] They introduced a rash of bills and constitutional amendments to curb the Court's power by requiring at least a two-thirds majority of justices to declare an act of Congress unconstitutional, to restrict the Court's appellate jurisdiction, to enable a two-thirds majority of Congress to override a Court ruling, and even to abolish the Court. The House did pass a bill making a two-thirds Court majority necessary to declare legislation unconstitutional, but the Senate failed to act on the measure. With one exception, noted below, Congress failed to enact any proposals to curb the Court's power.

Republican attacks on the Court may have convinced some justices that discretion was the better part of valor. In 1867, the Court dismissed suits by state officials in Mississippi and Georgia seeking an injunction to prevent federal officials from enforcing the Reconstruction Acts. But early in 1868, the case of *ex parte McCardle* threatened a collision between Court and Congress. This case arose from the military arrest in November 1867 of a Mississippi editor named William McCardle for publishing inflammatory articles against reconstruction. After a federal circuit court had denied his petition for a writ of habeas corpus, McCardle appealed to the Supreme Court under the Habeas Corpus Act of 1867, which, ironically, Congress had passed to protect freedmen against imprisonment under state black codes. While McCardle's appeal was pending, Congress on March 27, 1868, repealed the statute on which it was based, thus depriving the Supreme Court of appellate jurisdiction. The Court acquiesced, despite the wish of conservative justices to accept the case on other grounds in order to rule on the constitutionality of the Reconstruction Acts.

This was not quite the craven surrender by the Court that some historians have said it was. Article III, Section 2, of the Constitution empowers Congress to regulate the Supreme Court's appellate jurisdiction. By refusing jurisdiction in this and in the earlier Mississippi and Georgia cases, the Court in effect declared that the reconstruction of ex-Confederate states was a political rather than a constitutional problem—a position explicitly affirmed in *Texas v. White* (1869), a decision concerning the illegality of secession. Because secession was impossible *de jure,* the restoration of states that had gone out of the Union *de facto* was an extraconstitutional and therefore essentially a political process legitimated by the constitutional duty of the national government to guarantee each state a republican form of government.

. [17]Justice David Davis, who wrote the *Milligan* decision, said in February 1867 that he did not mean it to apply to "insurrectionary" states, which could be regarded as still in a state of war until Congress declared otherwise. But Republicans feared that a majority of the Court might well declare the Reconstruction Acts unconstitutional if a case arising from military rule came before it. For an earlier reference to the Milligan case, see page 551n.

[18]Brock, *American Crisis,* p. 262.

Congressional reconstruction demonstrated the resilience of the Constitution. Despite the shock of secession and civil war, reconstruction proceeded in a fashion that left the country's basic institutions intact. The presidency survived the gravest threat it had ever experienced. Although the Supreme Court backed down from a potential confrontation with Congress in 1868, the Court retained its stature as a coordinate branch of government with sufficient power to strike down vital reconstruction legislation in the 1870s (see Chapter 32). For better or worse, Thaddeus Stevens's attempt to substitute revolutionary legitimacy for constitutional legitimacy failed. The crisis of war and reconstruction temporarily altered but did not destroy the balance of powers among the three branches of the federal government.

Readmission of Southern States

While great political and constitutional issues were being decided in Washington, the reconstruction of Southern states moved forward. When the registration of voters ended in September 1867, approximately 735,000 blacks and 635,000 whites were enrolled in the ten unreconstructed states. Blacks constituted a majority of voters in five states: South Carolina, Mississippi, Louisiana, Florida, and Alabama. An estimated 10 to 15 percent of the potential white electorate was disfranchised by the Reconstruction Acts; another 25 to 30 percent failed to register because of apathy or of opposition to the whole process.

Having failed to attract black voters, Democrats searched for other ways to control or defeat reconstruction. The presence of twenty thousand federal troops discouraged open violence. But some white landowners and employers used economic threats to keep their black employees home on election day. Some Democratic leaders urged their followers to abstain from voting in the hope that the ballots in favor of holding a constitutional convention would fall short of the required majority of registered voters. Even if this tactic failed, they said, a large white abstention would discredit the elections in the eyes of Northern moderates. "A change at the North is our only hope for civil liberty in this country," wrote a North Carolinian, "and I am quite willing the Radicals should make themselves blacker and blacker, until they become in the sight of all men—especially, all good men—*black and all black!*"[19]

Fewer than half of the registered white voters (compared with four-fifths of the blacks) voted in the elections for conventions, held during the fall of 1867, and only half of the voting whites cast ballots in favor of holding a convention. Nevertheless, in every state the proconvention vote exceeded the requisite majority of registered voters. About three-quarters of the delegates elected to these conventions were Republicans; most of the remainder called themselves Conservatives—out of deference to the former Whigs among them who could not yet accept the label Democrat. Of the Republican delegates, about 45 percent were Southern whites, 30 percent were blacks, and 25 percent were Northern men who had settled in the South since the war. Blacks were a majority of delegates in the South Carolina and Louisiana conventions; Northern whites were a majority in none.

---

[19]Perman, *Reunion Without Compromise,* p. 317.

Southern white Republican delegates were mostly wartime Unionists who represented upcountry districts; they were particularly numerous in the conventions of Virginia, North Carolina, Georgia, and Arkansas. Most of the Northern-born delegates were former Union army officers or Freedmen's Bureau agents who had decided to make their future in the new South. They had, on the average, more education than the other classes of delegates and more wealth than the other classes of Republican delegates. They exercised leadership in the conventions out of proportion to their numbers, serving as presidents of four of the conventions and as chairmen of nearly half of the committees. The black delegates were the elite of their race. At least half of them had been free before the war, and most of those who had been slaves belonged to the upper strata of slave society. About four-fifths of the black delegates were literate. Their predominant occupations were clergyman, teacher, artisan, and landowning farmer; very few were field hands or unskilled laborers.

The Constitutional Conventions

Hostile Southern whites ridiculed the "Bones and Banjoes Conventions" that met during the winter of 1867–1868. They described the delegates as "ragamuffins and jailbirds . . . baboons, monkeys, mules." In typical phrases, Louisiana conservatives branded the new constitution as a "base conspiracy against human nature . . . the work of ignorant Negroes co-operating with a gang of white adventurers."[20]

Such caricatures long dominated the historical image of these conventions. The reality, however, was quite different. The delegates generally conducted themselves with order and decorum. Although a certain amount of wrangling took place among different factions of the Republican majority, this was normal in American politics. But the momentous character of these conventions was far from normal. For the first time, blacks and whites were working and voting together to write the fundamental law of their states.

The constitutions they produced were among the most progressive in the nation. Many of their provisions were modeled on the most advanced features of Northern state constitutions. In their enactment of universal manhood suffrage, they were ahead of most Northern states. All of the new constitutions mandated statewide systems of public schools for both races. Most of the constitutions increased the state's responsibility for social welfare beyond anything previously known in the South. Some constitutions established state boards of public charities. Several of them enacted prison reforms and reduced the number of capital crimes. These new public services made necessary a large increase in the property tax. But most states provided homestead exemptions that aided the small landowner by exempting real and personal property up to $2,000 or $3,000 from attachment for debts. This feature was popular with Southern white delegates representing constituents whose small holdings were threatened by the shaky postwar Southern economy. The increased taxes on real property were popular with black delegates and some Northerners, who hoped they might force the sale of excess land at a price affordable to black farmers. Although some radical delegates urged the

---

[20]Foner, *Reconstruction,* p. 317; Kenneth M. Stampp, *The Era of Reconstruction 1867–1877* (New York, 1965), p. 170; Joe Gray Taylor, *Louisiana Reconstructed, 1863–1877* (Baton Rouge, 1974), p. 148; John Hope Franklin, *Reconstruction: After the Civil War* (Chicago, 1961), p. 105.

confiscation of land, no convention took such action. The only gesture in this direction was the authorization by the South Carolina convention of a state land commission to buy property at market value and resell it in small tracts on liberal terms.

These measures won more or less solid support from the majority Republican coalition. Other issues, however, divided this coalition, with most Northern whites and the black delegates on one side and many Southern white Republicans joining their Conservative colleagues on the other. One such issue was public school segregation. Heated debates on this question occurred in nearly every convention. Most conventions resolved it by tabling motions either to mandate segregated schools or to prohibit them. No state constitution required the schools to be segregated, and only two—those of South Carolina and Louisiana—forbade racial segregation in public schools. In practice, however, desegregation prevailed only at the University of South Carolina and in several Louisiana elementary schools, mostly in New Orleans.

Another divisive issue was disfranchisement of ex-Confederates. North and South Carolina, Georgia, Florida, and Texas finally adopted constitutions that disfranchised no one for participation in the rebellion. Arkansas, Alabama, Louisiana, Virginia, and Mississippi disfranchised certain categories of ex-Confederate leaders.[21] The unpopularity of these disfranchisement provisions with white voters and even with some black voters helped bring about the initial defeat of the Virginia and Mississippi constitutions, which did not go into effect until the disfranchisement clauses were removed. Alabama and Louisiana repealed disfranchisement soon after returning to full statehood. Arkansas, which disfranchised a larger class of former Rebels than any other ex-Confederate state, did not remove these disabilities until 1872—the last Southern state to do so.

Readmission to Congressional Representation

Once the constitutions were written, the next step was to submit them to the voters. Still hoping to thwart reconstruction by delaying it beyond the 1868 election, Conservatives mounted a well-organized effort to defeat ratification. Most Southern whites could not believe that a majority of Northern voters would sustain the "infamous" Republican attempt to impose "Negro rule" on the South. If ratification of the new Southern state constitutions could be defeated, the hoped-for Democratic victory in the presidential election would reverse the process of reconstruction and restore Southern states to self-government without black suffrage. To defeat ratification, many Southern whites resorted to violence to intimidate or eliminate black voters. A secret organization of night-riding terrorists with the ominous name of Ku Klux Klan made its first serious forays in these elections.

But the main Conservative tactic was to boycott the polls. If enough whites could be persuaded or coerced to stay home, the vote in favor of the constitution might fall short of a majority of registered voters. This tactic worked in the first state to hold its ratification election, Alabama, on February 4, 1868. Although the vote in favor of the constitution was 70,812 to 1,005, this was only 43 percent of the 168,813 registered voters. Perplexed and angry congressional Republicans passed on March 11 a fourth Reconstruction Act that required for ratification of a constitution only a majority of

---

[21] At this time (1868) ex-Confederates were still disfranchised in Missouri, Tennessee, and West Virginia.

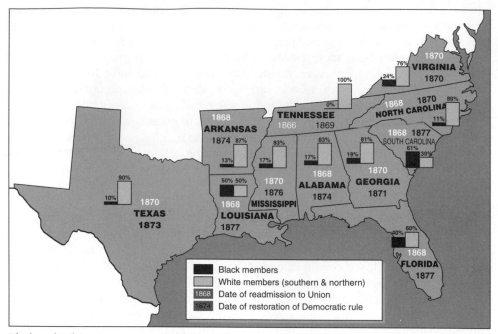

Black and White Participation in Constitutional Conventions, 1867–1868; dates of readmission to Union and Restoration of Democratic Rule

those actually voting. During the next two months, six states ratified their constitutions by voting majorities ranging from 51 percent (Arkansas) to 72 percent (South Carolina).[22] Republicans won control of the state offices and legislatures at the same elections. The legislatures promptly assembled and ratified the Fourteenth Amendment, thus completing the requirements for readmission.

Despite the apparent success of reconstruction, many congressional Republicans felt reluctant to take the final step of readmission. Once these states were restored to self-government, the presence of federal troops would have to be reduced. The Conservative/Democratic party had already demonstrated its potential for winning power in several states, especially after disfranchised whites regained the ballot. The Republican coalition had demonstrated its fragility and the vulnerability of its black constituency to intimidation. What was to prevent Southern Democrats from dismantling a new constitution, black suffrage and all, if they recovered control of a state? Beware of "hastening back States where rebelism is pervading them from end to end," warned a radical Senator. "There are not ten men . . . who believe it is a safe thing to do at this time," said another.[23]

---

[22]In Arkansas and Georgia, the proratification total was only 36 percent and 46 percent, respectively, of those states' registered voters.

[23]Benedict, *Compromise of Principle,* p. 317.

But political necessities dictated readmission. Northern voters would rap Republican knuckles in the 1868 election if uncertainty and "bayonet rule" still prevailed in the South. "Things cannot drift along in this way forever," declared a House Republican leader. "Those States must be admitted some time. There must be an end of the confusion, the anarchy now prevailing. We must have civil law and civil order. We cannot always control those States by the bayonet."[24] Swallowing their doubts, Republicans in June 1868 readmitted seven states (including Alabama) to representation in Congress. The enabling acts included a "fundamental condition" that the constitutions of these states must never be amended to deprive blacks of the right to vote. Such a condition was of dubious constitutionality and enforceability (the Constitution granted Congress no power to impose or enforce such conditions), but it may have assuaged the qualms of some congressmen.

The restoration of Texas, Virginia, and Mississippi was delayed until 1869. The vast expanse of Texas and the disarray of the Republican party there slowed the completion of the state's constitution. In Virginia, Republican factionalism and the unpopularity of stringent disfranchisement provisions in the new constitution prevented the scheduling of a ratification election. And in Mississippi, a disfranchisement clause provoked Conservatives to organize an aggressive campaign that defeated ratification on June 22, 1868, by a majority of 7,600 votes. Violence and intimidation had kept an estimated 20,000 Republican voters from the Mississippi polls despite the presence of 2,000 soldiers in the state.

In 1869, Texas finally completed its constitution and was readmitted the next year. The disfranchisement clauses in Virginia and Mississippi were voted on separately and defeated, and these states were then admitted with their purged and ratified constitutions. "Reconstruction" appeared to be completed. But events were soon to demonstrate that it had barely begun.

---

[24]Ibid., p. 319.

The First Grant Administration

I have no powder to burn killing negroes. I intend to kill radicals. . . . There is not a radical leader in this town [Memphis] but is a marked man, and if trouble should break out, none of them would be left alive.

—Nathan Bedford Forrest,
Grand Wizard of the Ku Klux Klan, 1868

The Election of 1868

Just as the 1864 presidential election had been a referendum on Republican war policies, so the 1868 contest shaped up as yet another plebiscite on reconstruction. In 1864, the Democrats had run against Lincoln's policy of prosecuting the war relentlessly until the Confederacy and slavery both ceased to exist. In 1868, they ran on a platform that pledged to turn back the clock on reconstruction. Like the Bourbon monarchy in France a half-century earlier, the Democrats seemed to have learned nothing and forgotten nothing from the experiences that had almost revolutionized them out of existence. The outcome in 1868 proved them to be as far out of step with the Northern electorate as they had been during the war.

The Republican Convention

For almost a year before the Republican convention met in May 1868, Ulysses S. Grant seemed sure to become the party's nominee. Grant's only serious rival was Salmon P. Chase, a perennial candidate whose ambitions were not satisfied by the chief justiceship of the Supreme Court. Most radicals favored Chase in 1867 and distrusted Grant because of the general's antebellum Democratic leanings and his early postwar identification with Johnson's reconstruction policy. But several developments muted these reservations about Grant: his endorsement of the congressional program in 1867; the Democratic gains in the off-year 1867 elections, which convinced many radicals that they needed to nominate a war hero rather than one of their own in 1868; and Grant's bitter break with Johnson in January 1868. Moreover,

Chase's conduct of the impeachment trial, in which he had made clear his sympathy for the President's acquittal, caused the chief justice virtually to be read out of the Republican party. The Republican convention unanimously nominated Grant on a platform that pointed with pride to "the assured success of the reconstruction policy of Congress."

One nagging problem marred the self-congratulatory mood of the convention—the problem of black suffrage in Northern states. Radicals insisted that the party must come out unequivocally for equal suffrage everywhere: "To dodge the issue, or to cover it out of sight under some meaningless generality, would be moral depravity and political folly."[1] But moderates believed that equivocation was political wisdom, not folly. Republican campaigns for Northern suffrage had hurt the party in the 1867 elections. In April 1868, Michigan voters defeated a new constitution that included black suffrage by a margin of 61 to 39 percent—which meant that at least 20 percent of the Republicans had voted against it. "Discreditable as the fact may be, it is pretty evident that the enfranchisement of the colored race in the Northern States will have to wait," declared a moderate newspaper. "The more immediate interests of reconstruction might be jeopardized by forcing the issue at this juncture."[2]

The platform committee at the national convention was the scene of a sharp struggle on this issue between radicals and moderates. Victory finally went to the moderates. The convention adopted the committee's plank, which stated that while black suffrage in ex-Confederate states "was demanded by every consideration of public safety, of gratitude, and of justice," the "question of suffrage in all the loyal States properly belongs to the people of those States." Abolitionists and radicals denounced this "mean-spirited . . . foolish and contemptible" plank. Charles Sumner predicted accurately that "the Democrats will have a great opportunity in exposing its Janus-faced character."[3]

The Democratic Convention

In contrast to the Republicans, Democrats had a plethora of candidates for the presidential nomination. Four leaders emerged from the pack by the eve of the party's July convention: Congressman George Pendleton of Ohio (the vice-presidential candidate in 1864); Senator Thomas Hendricks of Indiana; General Winfield Scott Hancock, whose outstanding war record might neutralize part of Grant's advantage in that respect; and Andrew Johnson. Although the President evoked sympathy in the party for his battles against the radicals, he carried too many liabilities; he dropped out of contention by the third ballot. Pendleton, Hancock, and Hendricks each in turn came close to winning a majority on the eighth, eighteenth, and twenty-second ballots, respectively, but each fell far short of the necessary two-thirds. At the end of the twenty-second ballot, a few states changed their votes to Horatio Seymour. The effect on the exhausted convention was electric. State after state jumped on the bandwagon. Seymour had repeatedly refused to be a candidate, and now his friends

---

[1]*Independent,* May 4, 1868.

[2]*Springfield Republican,* quoted in *The Revolution,* April 23, 1868.

[3]Charles Sumner to Frank Bird, May 28, 1868, Bird Papers, Houghton Library, Harvard University; *Independent,* May 28, 1868.

had to hustle him out of the hall to prevent him from declining the nomination on the spot. In the end the suave, frail ex-governor of New York bowed to necessity and accepted the dubious honor of running against Grant.

The Democratic platform branded the Reconstruction Acts "a flagrant usurpation of power . . . unconstitutional, revolutionary, and void," and demanded "the abolition of the Freedmen's Bureau, and all political instrumentalities designed to secure negro supremacy." This became the party's battle cry. Vice-presidential candidate Frank Blair of Missouri set the tone for the campaign with a public letter that became famous as the Brodhead letter. "There is but one way to restore the Government and the Constitution, and that is for the President-elect to declare these acts null and void, compel the army to undo its usurpations at the South, disperse the carpet-bag State Governments, [and] allow the white people to reorganize their own governments."[4]

The Race Issue and the Ku Klux Klan

Unabashed by Republican outcries against such statements, Blair repeated them throughout the campaign. The Republican state governments in the South were "bastard and spurious" governments, he said. "The white race is the only race in the world that has shown itself capable of maintaining free institutions of a free government," but Southern white men were being "trodden under foot by an inferior and barbarous race." The Democrats would restore to Southern whites their "birthright." In this effort "we shall have the sympathy of every man who is worthy to belong to the white race." Other Democrats, especially in the Midwest and South, took their cue from Blair. If the Democrats won a majority of white voters in November, said a Wisconsin editor, they should "march to Washington . . . and take their seats, and reinaugurate the white man's government."[5]

Republicans replied in kind. They waved the bloody shirt (a campaign technique of associating Democrats with the Southern violence that had left many a Unionist with blood on his shirt). They contrasted the final sentence of Grant's letter accepting the nomination—"Let us have peace"—with Blair's call for a counterrevolution. In an electorate weary from four years of war and three years of political warfare over reconstruction, Grant's statement struck a responsive chord. Republicans made the most of it. Grant in the White House would bring a surcease of conflict; a Democratic victory would inaugurate "government by assassination and violence, instead of government by law."[6]

Some Southern Democrats seemed determined to prove the Republicans right. In several states, the Ku Klux Klan and similar organizations launched a reign of terror. Efforts by federal troops to prevent this violence were hindered by their inability to impose martial law now that the states were "reconstructed." The hastily organized state militias could do no better.

---

[4]John Hope Franklin, "Election of 1868," in Arthur M. Schlesinger, Jr. (ed.), *History of American Presidential Elections*, 4 vols. (New York, 1971), II, 1269; *Independent,* July 16, 1868.
[5]Edward McPherson, *The Political History of the United States During the Period of Reconstruction* (Washington, D.C., 1875), pp. 381, 382; Charles H. Coleman, *The Election of 1868* (New York, 1933), p. 155; Franklin, "The Election of 1868," p. 1259; *La Crosse Democrat,* quoted in *National Anti-Slavery Standard,* March 7, 1868.
[6]Franklin, "The Election of 1868," p. 1262.

The Klan had been founded two years earlier in Pulaski, Tennessee. Like the Confederate army, in whose ranks many Klansmen had served, this secret order recruited members from all classes of Southern white society. Among its leaders were two dozen or more Confederate generals and colonels headed by Nathan Bedford Forrest, the Klan's "Grand Wizard." By 1868, the Klan had evolved from a harmless fraternal order into a hooded terrorist organization dedicated to the preservation of white supremacy. It punished freedmen who left their employers or complained of low wages or acted in an "insolent" manner toward whites. It whipped teachers of freedmen's schools and burned down their schoolhouses. But above all, Klansmen terrorized and murdered Republican leaders and voters. The Klan and similar groups, such as the Knights of the White Camelia, became in effect "the military arm of the Democratic party."[7]

The Klan professed to act in the name of law and order. "It is, indeed, unfortunate that [our people] should be compelled to have recourse to measures of violence and blood to do away with lawless tyrants and wrong-doers," declared a Louisiana newspaper. "But who is to blame? . . . Assuredly not we people of the South, who have suffered wrongs beyond endurance. Radicalism and negroism . . . are alone to blame. . . . These northern emissaries of advanced political ideas, and of progressive social reforms . . . have met the fate they deserved." In August 1868, General Forrest publicly warned Republican leaders that they would suffer dire consequences if they dared to use the militia against the Klan: "I have no powder to burn killing negroes. I intend to kill radicals. . . . There is not a radical leader in this town [Memphis] but is a marked man, and if trouble should break out, none of them would be left alive."[8]

During the 1868 campaign, the Klan and similar organizations were most active in Louisiana, Georgia, Arkansas, and Tennessee. Although Republicans managed to carry the last two states, they did so at a great cost. More than two hundred political murders were reported in Arkansas, including the ambush killing of a Republican congressman on October 22. The death toll in Georgia was lower, but the incidence of threats and beatings higher. These tactics kept thousands of Republicans from the polls. In twenty-two Georgia counties with a total registration of more than 9,300 black voters, Grant tallied only 87 votes. The Republicans received no votes at all in eleven Georgia counties. In this manner, a Republican majority of 7,000 in the April state election became a Democratic majority of 45,000 in the presidential election.

Even worse was Louisiana, where according to the subsequent report of a congressional committee, more than a thousand persons, mostly blacks, were killed between April and November 1868. Two riots near Shreveport left more than one hundred dead, and a major outbreak at Opelousas, in St. Landry Parish, produced an estimated death toll of two hundred. A Democratic leader in St. Landry believed that this affair had taught blacks a "wholesome lesson." He was evidently right, for on election day not a single Republican voted in the parish. Indeed, seven parishes that had cast a total of 4,707 Republican ballots in April recorded none in November.

---

[7] George C. Rable, *But There Was No Peace: The Role of Violence in the Politics of Reconstruction* (Athens, Ga., 1984), p. 95.

[8] Allen W. Trelease, *White Terror: The Ku Klux Klan Conspiracy and Southern Reconstruction* (New York, 1971), pp. xiv, 46.

RUTHERFORD B. HAYES PRESIDENTIAL CENTER

LIBRARY OF CONGRESS

TWO KLANSMEN AND GENERAL NATHAN BEDFORD FORREST.   As a secret terrorist organization, the Ku Klux Klan was not eager for publicity that would reveal the identities of its members. The disguises were intended to protect their anonymity as well as to frighten black and Republican victims. Though General Forrest never admitted it, he was the Klan's "Grand Wizard." Many former Confederate soldiers belonged to the Klan, giving it the character of a military guerrilla force.

Twenty-one parishes with a previous Republican vote of 26,814 reported only 501 ballots for Grant. In the state as a whole, a Republican majority of 58 percent in April was transformed into a Democratic majority of 71 percent in November.

Although by these means the Democrats managed to carry Louisiana and Georgia and to cut down the Republican majority elsewhere in the South, this probably hurt the party in the North more than it helped in the South. It lent substance to Republican charges that Rebels and Copperheads were trying to achieve by terrorism what they had failed to achieve by war. The similarity of Northern voting patterns in 1868 to those of 1864 was remarkable. Grant received virtually the same proportion of the Northern vote (55 percent) as Lincoln had received in 1864. In scarcely any state did the vote change by more than one or two percentage points. Only 7 percent of the counties in the North switched from Democratic to Republican or vice versa. Seymour carried only three Northern states: Oregon, New Jersey, and New York, the last by one percentage point—as a result, probably, of Tammany frauds in New York City. Seymour won three of the five border states (Delaware, Maryland, and Kentucky) and two of the eight reconstructed Confederate states, giving him 80 electoral votes to Grant's 214. The Democrats made a slight net gain of congressional seats, but the Republicans retained majorities of two-thirds in the House and four-fifths in the Senate.

The Fifteenth Amendment

During the year after Grant's election, Congress was preoccupied with the unfinished tasks of reconstruction. The most important was a constitutional amendment to enfranchise black men in every state. Without such an amendment, the future of black suffrage might be doubtful in Southern states where Democrats managed to regain control. Moreover, the inequity of requiring black suffrage in the South (by the Reconstruction Acts) but not in the North bothered many Republicans. "We have no moral right to impose an obligation on one part of the land which the rest will not accept," wrote a radical. "We can have no peace until this right is made national."[9]

Although Iowa and Minnesota finally adopted black suffrage by referendums in 1868, black men still could not vote in eleven of the twenty-one Northern states or in any of the five border states. One-sixth of the country's black people lived in these states. Most of them would vote Republican if enfranchised. Therefore, as a Republican congressman pointed out, "party expediency and exact justice coincide for once."[10] Since Republicans controlled twenty-five of the thirty-three state legislatures (not including the unreconstructed states of Texas, Mississippi, Virginia, and Georgia[11]), they could ratify a constitutional amendment without having to face the obstacle of referendums, which had so often defeated state suffrage amendments.

The drafting of the Fifteenth Amendment consumed the short session of Congress that met between Grant's election and his inauguration on March 4, 1869. Three versions of the amendment emerged from a variety of proposals: the first version would forbid states to deny citizens the right to vote on grounds of race, color, or previous condition of servitude; the second would in addition forbid states to impose literacy, property, or nativity qualifications for suffrage; the third would affirm simply that all male citizens aged twenty-one years or older had the right to vote. Whereas the first two versions would merely impose restrictions on state power, the third envisaged a radical enlargement of national power.

---

[9]*Zion's Herald,* December 10, 1868.

[10]*National Anti-Slavery Standard,* November 14, 1868. But justice and expediency did not coincide to make possible the enfranchisement of women at this time. Although the women's rights movement pushed for the inclusion of a clause in the Fifteenth Amendment giving women the right to vote, and some radical Republicans sympathized with this effort, there was not a sizable constituency among male voters to overcome powerful conservative prejudices against the idea of women voting. Consequently, the National Woman Suffrage Association, founded in 1869 by Elizabeth Cady Stanton and Susan B. Anthony, opposed the Fifteenth Amendment.

[11]For the special case of Georgia, see page 589.

After much tugging and hauling, Congress passed the first and most conservative version of the amendment. Many radicals feared that this version would not prevent Southern states from disfranchising most blacks by means of literacy or property qualifications. "Let it remain possible," warned one congressman, "to still disfranchise the body of the colored race in the late rebel States and I tell you it will be done."[12] But moderates believed that anything stronger than a limited prohibition of discrimination on grounds of race might defeat ratification in the necessary three-fourths of the states: legislatures might balk at giving up most of their control over voting regulations; a good many Northerners as well as Southerners doubted the wisdom of a perpetual guarantee of the right to vote to illiterate men; and a ban on nativity restrictions might prevent ratification by the three far-west states, where anti-Chinese sentiment was rising. Thus the final form of the Fifteenth Amendment, which forbade states to deny the right to vote only on grounds of race, color, or previous condition, left loopholes that enabled Southern states a generation later to disfranchise most black voters. They accomplished this by subterfuges that were clearly contrary to the purpose of the Fifteenth Amendment, however, and could not have done so if the will to enforce the amendment that existed in 1869 had still existed in 1899.

Congress passed the Fifteenth Amendment on February 26, 1869. Within four months, the seventeen Republican legislatures then in session had ratified it and the four Democratic legislatures in session had rejected it. Whether the necessary ratification by eleven more states could be obtained when the rest of the legislatures met in the fall was uncertain. But the delay of reconstruction in Virginia, Mississippi, and Texas gave Congress an opportunity to strengthen the chances of ratification. The lawmakers required these three states to ratify the Fifteenth as well as the Fourteenth Amendment as a prerequisite for readmission. They did so, and all three states were restored in early 1870.

This left only Georgia in the limbo of nonstatehood. That state's congressmen had initially resumed their places in June 1868, but an egregious violation by white Georgians of the spirit of reconstruction had caused Congress to remand the state to military rule. The Georgia legislature in 1868 was evenly divided between Republicans and Conservatives. Some of the Southern white Republicans, however, soon defected to the Conservatives. These new allies expelled twenty-eight black legislators on the grounds that the state constitution did not specifically declare blacks eligible for office. Twenty-four of the legislators who voted for expulsion were later proved to be ineligible for office themselves under the disqualifying clause of the Fourteenth Amendment! Outraged congressional Republicans rescinded Georgia's readmission. The black members returned to the legislature, the ineligible whites departed, the legislature ratified the Fifteenth Amendment, and Georgia's representatives returned to Congress in 1870.

With Georgia's ratification, the Fifteenth Amendment became part of the Constitution on March 30, 1870. Many Republicans shared the conviction that this achievement was "the last great point that remained to be settled of the issues of the war." Now it was time to turn to other problems long neglected because of preoccupation

---

[12]Michael Les Benedict, *A Compromise of Principle: Congressional Republicans and Reconstruction, 1863–1869* (New York, 1974), p. 332.

with sectional strife. Ever since the annexation of Texas a quarter-century earlier, the nation had known scarcely a moment's respite from this strife. "Let us have done with Reconstruction," pleaded the *New York Tribune* in April 1870. "The country is tired and sick of it. . . . LET US HAVE PEACE."[13]

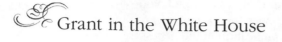

Grant in the White House

Few presidents have carried more prestige and goodwill into the office than Ulysses S. Grant. His supporters were eager to address the problems of currency and finance, civil service reform, foreign policy, and other "new issues" demanding attention now that reconstruction was "settled." But Grant's own inexperience and errors of judgment, the venality of some of his associates, and above all the persistent and apparently insolvable problems of reconstruction dashed the hopes with which many Americans had viewed his inauguration.

Several of the new President's appointments to government positions gave rise to complaints about nepotism and cronyism. Grant named some of his wife's numerous relatives to office. Other posts, including several places on the White House staff, went to former army colleagues. Two of the latter—General Orville Babcock, Grant's private secretary, and General William Belknap, who became secretary of war—were later charged with accepting bribes and left the government in disgrace. The President gave the impression of a lack of discernment in his choice of associates. But Grant was the victim more of circumstances than of his own shortcomings. Honest himself, he sometimes remained too supportive of dishonest subordinates who betrayed his confidence. Grant also became the victim of a "bad press" by reform-minded journalists whose sometimes unjust criticisms were taken at face value by generations of historians who have labeled Grant one of the worst of American presidents. This undeserved ranking underestimates the intractable problems faced by the country during Grant's tenure and overlooks the positive achievements of his administration.[14]

The *Alabama* Claims

In foreign policy, the Grant administration achieved one great success and one failure. The success was the settlement of damage claims against Britain for the wartime destruction caused by the *Alabama* and other British-built Confederate cruisers. The United States accused Britain of negligence and violation of neutral obligations in allowing these ships to be built. Damage claims by American owners of destroyed

---

[13] *Northwestern Christian Advocate*, February 9, 1870; *New York Tribune*, April 18, 1870.

[14] The historiographical pendulum is beginning to swing in Grant's favor, however. More positive evaluations of his presidency can be found in Geoffrey Perret, *Ulysses S. Grant: Soldier & President* (New York, 1997), and especially in Frank J. Scaturro, *President Grant Reconsidered* (Lanham, Md., 1998), which includes a critical review of earlier Grant scholarship. A biography of Grant scheduled for publication in 2000, by Jean Smith, contains a balanced appraisal of Grant's presidency. See also the chapter on Grant in Brooks D. Simpson, *The Reconstruction Presidents* (Lawrence, Kansas, 1998), pp. 133–196.

ships and cargoes amounted to more than $15 million. But the British government refused to admit responsibility. For several years, strained relations existed between the two countries. Newspapers on both sides of the Atlantic traded bellicose threats.

During the final months of Andrew Johnson's administration, the United States and Britain negotiated a treaty for adjudication of these *Alabama* claims." But the terms of the treaty leaned toward the British interpretation, so the U.S. Senate rejected it in April 1869 by a vote of 54 to 1. Charles Sumner, chairman of the Senate Foreign Relations Committee, delivered a belligerent speech in which he demanded reparation not only for direct damages but also for "indirect damages," including prolongation of the war by British actions and by Southern expectations of British intervention. Sumner hinted that the cession of Canada would be a fair indemnity for these damages. Although no precedent for indirect damages existed in international law, Sumner's extreme demands evoked a sympathetic response from many Americans who still resented Britain's role in the Civil War.

Sumner's speech raised the ante to a point that appeared to doom hopes for a negotiation of the *Alabama* claims. For more than a year, no apparent progress took place on this matter. But behind the scenes, Secretary of State Hamilton Fish, scion of a prominent New York family—and Grant's best cabinet appointee—worked quietly to reopen negotiations. The outbreak of the Franco-Prussian War in July 1870 forced the precedent-conscious British to think about the consequences for their merchant marine if Britain should be drawn into a war and a neutral United States should build commerce raiders for an enemy power. Meanwhile, Sumner had broken with the administration over the annexation of Santo Domingo (discussed later). To punish the senator for this and to neutralize his power to block a compromise on the *Alabama* claims, Republican senators who supported the administration deposed Sumner from his chairmanship of the Foreign Relations Committee in March 1871. Fish worked out the creation of a Joint High Commission to negotiate terms for settlement of the *Alabama* claims and of other differences between the two countries. In May 1871, the commission completed the Treaty of Washington, which established an international tribunal to arbitrate American claims. The British made several concessions in this treaty, including an expression of regret for the depredations of the *Alabama* and other ships built in Britain.

The U.S. Senate promptly ratified the Treaty of Washington. The tribunal that met at Geneva in December 1871 consisted of arbitrators from the United States (Charles Francis Adams), Britain, Switzerland, Italy, and Brazil. The Americans pressed extravagant claims before this body. They maintained that indirect damages should include the entire cost of the war after July 4, 1863, on the grounds that only British support enabled the South to go on fighting after Gettysburg and Vicksburg. The outraged British threatened to withdraw from arbitration if the Americans persisted with this "preposterous" argument. Fish and Adams quietly let it be known that the United States would not insist on indirect damages. With American acquiescence, the neutral members of the tribunal ruled out indirect claims. By a 4-to-1 vote (Britain dissenting), the arbitrators in September 1872 finally declared that the British government had failed to exercise "due diligence" to prevent the building and arming of the *Alabama, Florida,* and *Shenandoah,* and awarded the United States $15.5 million for the damage done by these ships. It was a victory for American diplomacy, for the peaceful settlement of international disputes, and for better Anglo-American relations.

The Santo Domingo Affair

Grant's foreign policy failure was the attempt to annex Santo Domingo (today the Dominican Republic). This project grew out of a revival of Manifest Destiny following the triumph of American nationalism in the Civil War. Many Republicans now shared what had once been primarily a Democratic sentiment. Secretary of State Seward's purchase of Alaska from Russia in 1867 set a precedent for the acquisition of noncontiguous territory. The Civil War had demonstrated the need for an American naval base in the Caribbean, so Seward also negotiated a treaty with Denmark for the purchase of the Virgin Islands. The Senate killed this treaty, but the idea of expansion into the Caribbean did not die.

Land speculators, commercial developers, promoters of fabulous gold and silver mines, and naval officers who wanted a Caribbean base and dreamed of an Isthmian canal formed a Dominican lobby in Washington. The wily Dominican dictator Bonaventura Baez favored American annexation to bolster his power against revolutionary elements. Less self-interested supporters of annexation in the United States, including Grant, believed that American ownership would bring peace and stability to a country of chronic revolutions, develop its rich resources, open the gateway for the extension of beneficent American influence throughout the Caribbean, and get the canal project started.

The more Grant thought about it, the more desirable annexation became. He hoped to make it the showpiece foreign policy achievement of his administration. But his lack of political experience betrayed him. He acted as if he were still a general who needed only to give orders, instead of a president who must line up political support. Without consulting congressional leaders or the cabinet, Grant in July 1869 sent his private secretary, Orville Babcock, to Santo Domingo to investigate the possibilities. The enthusiastic Babcock exceeded his instructions and brought back a treaty of annexation. Ignoring the irregularities of this procedure, Grant presented the treaty to his astonished cabinet. Secretary of State Fish, who was cool to the whole idea, said nothing. Other members of the cabinet did the same. Finally, Secretary of the Interior Jacob Cox broke the embarrassed silence. "But, Mr. President, has it been settled, then, that we *want* to annex Santo Domingo?"[15]

It was settled in Grant's mind. He sent Babcock back to Santo Domingo with State Department authorization to renegotiate the treaty in a proper fashion. Babcock did so, returning a second time with a treaty that made Santo Domingo a U.S. territory and declared its 120,000 people to be American citizens, all at a bargain price of $1.5 million. A plebiscite of Santo Domingans approved annexation. In January 1870, Grant proudly submitted the treaty to the Senate—where the trouble began.

Charles Sumner's Foreign Relations Committee reported the treaty adversely. Sumner and Carl Schurz, now a senator from Missouri, led the anti-annexation forces. They castigated the corrupt promoters who had bought up land in the expectation of windfall profits from annexation. They invoked the traditional Whig/Republican hostility to expansion. Schurz questioned the wisdom of incorporating a new mixed-blood Catholic population into a polity that already had more than enough trouble

---

[15]Allan Nevins, *Hamilton Fish: The Inner History of the Grant Administration* (New York, 1936), p. 271.

with racial problems. Sumner feared that the acquisition of Santo Domingo would threaten the independence of neighboring Haiti, which except for Liberia was the only self-governing black republic in the world. "These islands by climate, occupation, and destiny . . . belong to the colored people," said Sumner. "We should not take them away. No greed of land should prevail against the rights of this race."[16]

Angered by this opposition, Grant lobbied personally with senators in behalf of the treaty. He insisted that annexation would benefit the poverty-stricken black people of both Santo Domingo and Haiti by bringing American capital, enterprise, and political institutions to the island. Grant privately denounced Sumner in harsh terms. This unhappy breach between President and senator was exacerbated by a heavy-handed administration effort to obtain protreaty votes from Southern Republican senators, who might otherwise have been inclined to follow Sumner's lead. Attorney General E. Rockwood Hoar, a Massachusetts friend and ally of Sumner, had offended Southern Republicans with some of his appointments of federal attorneys and marshals. Hoar was also at odds with Benjamin Butler, an administration ally and emerging factional leader in the Massachusetts Republican party. To gratify Butler and secure Southern votes for the treaty, Grant dismissed Hoar on June 15, 1870, and replaced him with an obscure Georgian, Amos Akerman. The President also obliged Senator Roscoe Conkling, a treaty supporter, by appointing one of Conkling's political lieutenants to the patronage-rich collectorship of the New York port—an appointment that later bore rotten fruit in a corruption scandal. These maneuvers availed little except to alienate a growing number of Republicans from the administration. On June 30, 1870, the Senate defeated the treaty by a tie vote of 28–28, with nineteen Republicans joining the nine Democrats in opposition.

A bitter President took revenge on Sumner by dismissing the senator's protégé John Lothrop Motley from his post as minister to Britain. The administration justified this action on the grounds that Motley, like Sumner, was hindering a settlement of the *Alabama* claims by his extreme position. But Sumner's friends interpreted it as an attempt to punish the senator. The open warfare between Grant and Sumner became more savage during the winter of 1870–1871. Grant reopened the question of annexing Santo Domingo, even though his Senate supporters conceded that the project was dead. Seizing the opportunity, Sumner excoriated the President in a Senate speech that accused Grant of following in the footsteps of Franklin Pierce, James Buchanan, and Andrew Johnson. This was too much. Soon after Sumner's speech, pro-administration senators deposed him as chairman of the Foreign Relations Committee.

These events divided the Republican party. Both sides in the squabble over Santo Domingo had demonstrated traits of petty vindictiveness. Sumner's vain ego and righteous moralism seemed to grow more excessive with age. But to many of the senator's friends among the old Free Soilers and Conscience Whigs, Grant's vendetta seemed to be an attack on the idealism that had made the Republican party great. They feared that the party was falling into the hands of spoilsmen and opportunists such as Conkling and Butler who had no roots in the antislavery movement and no

---

[16]Edward L. Pierce, *Memoir and Letters of Charles Sumner,* 4 vols. (Boston, 1877–1879), IV, 448.

commitment to moral ideals. This breach between "old" and "new" Republicans (to oversimplify a complex reality) was widened by the movement for civil service reform that gained momentum during Grant's first administration.

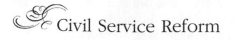 Civil Service Reform

The "spoils system"—by which the victors in an election rewarded party workers with appointments to public office—was one of the most venerable institutions in American politics. The hope of office was the glue that kept the party faithful together when the party was out of power. An assessment of 2 or 3 percent on government salaries kept party coffers filled when in power. But in the 1860s, a growing number of reformers attacked this system as wasteful and corrupt. They urged that government officials be appointed on the basis of merit rather than party fidelity. Representative Thomas Jenckes of Rhode Island introduced at every session of Congress from 1865 to 1871 a bill to create a civil service commission to administer competitive examinations for appointment to office. Although Jenckes's bill never got out of committee, support for some kind of action continued to grow until civil service reform became one of the most powerful reform movements of the 1870s.

Its proponents were mainly well-educated professional men who resided in the Northeast. Most were Republicans, identified with the old Conscience Whig element of the party. They admired the incorruptible efficiency of the British civil service and wanted to emulate it. Professional politicians looked askance at such notions. To them, patronage was the lifeblood of democracy. They accused the reformers of elitism and ridiculed them as dilettantes trying to play at the serious business of politics.

At the beginning of Grant's administration, reformers had high hopes for this nonpolitical President. Grant seemed to share their reform sentiments. Like all new occupants of the White House, he suffered the unwanted entreaties of swarms of office seekers. "Patronage is the bane of the Presidential office," Grant told a friend. "There is no man in the country so anxious for civil service reform as the President. . . . He is necessarily a civil service reformer because he wants peace of mind."[17]

But Grant's record on this issue was mixed. On the positive side, Secretary of the Treasury Boutwell, Secretary of the Interior Cox, and Attorney General Hoar instituted impartial examinations for certain kinds of promotions and appointments in their departments. Grant's annual message to Congress in December 1870 urged reform legislation. Although the lawmakers balked at this, they did pass a joint resolution authorizing the President to appoint a commission to prescribe new rules for civil service appointments. To head the commission, Grant named George William Curtis, editor of *Harper's Weekly* and a leading reformer. The commission recommended competitive examinations for various grades of civil service positions. It also urged the abolition of party assessments on salaries. Grant promulgated the regulations by executive order to go into effect on January 1, 1872. But Congress refused to appropriate suffi-

---

[17]Howard N. Meyer, *Let Us Have Peace: The Story of Ulysses S. Grant* (New York, 1966), p. 202.

cient funds to enable the Civil Service Commission to enforce the new rules effectively. Although some government departments implemented part of the regulations, a thoroughgoing reform of the spoils system was not achieved in the 1870s.

Those Republicans in Congress who had been most closely identified with Grant in the Santo Domingo affair also played a prominent role in crippling the Civil Service Commission. This raised doubts among reformers about the President's sincerity on the issue. Several of Grant's appointments to the customs service and to the internal revenue service disappointed reformers. The use of patronage and the sacrifice of Attorney General Hoar in the Santo Domingo treaty fight appalled them. In October 1870 came another shock: the conscientious Secretary of the Interior Jacob Cox resigned after a bitter fight with spoilsmen who were trying to subvert his appointments policy. Congressman James Garfield said of this development: "It is a clear case of surrender on the part of the President to the political vermin which infest the government and keep it in a state of perpetual lousiness."[18]

The Roots of Liberal Republicanism

Cox, Hoar, Sumner, Motley—to reformers it looked as if the President was sacrificing the best elements of the party to its worst elements. By 1871, a new noun, "Grantism," had entered the language. It stood for all the things that reformers thought were wrong with postwar America: spoilsmanship and corruption in government; crude taste and anti-intellectualism in culture; dishonesty in business; and a boundless materialism, a get-rich-quick acquisitiveness of the sort satirized by Mark Twain and Charles Dudley Warner in their 1873 novel, whose title—*The Gilded Age*—gave a name to the era.

It was, of course, unfair to saddle Grant with responsibility for these things. He genuinely desired reform, and his administration deserved credit for several important achievements. Moreover, the corruption in the federal government paled in comparison with knavery elsewhere. The pilfering in the New York customs house was not in the same league with the massive depredations of the Tweed Ring in the same city. The New York legislature was a notorious marketplace for buying and selling politicians. It was said of the Pennsylvania legislature that the Standard Oil Company could do anything with it except to refine it. The postwar relaxation of tensions and the explosive economic growth after the 1867 recession heightened speculative fever and loosened standards in the whole society. The wartime expansion of the government bureaucracy and of government contracts had opened new vistas for the unscrupulous. At the same time, the emergence of a strong postwar reform movement focused a harsh light on dark corners of corruption hitherto unillumined because of preoccupation with the sectional problem. During the Grant administration, many government agencies actually made progress toward eliminating abuses that had flourished in the Johnson and even in the Lincoln administrations.

Whether unfair or not, however, Grant became the scapegoat for many of the perceived ills of the country. His association with some of the unsavory promoters of Santo Domingo's annexation, his vendetta against Sumner, and the apparently

---

[18]William B. Hesseltine, *Ulysses S. Grant, Politician* (New York, 1935), p. 218.

growing influence of such men as Conkling and Butler in his administration sparked a revolt by reform Republicans. They hoped at first to win control of the party, purge the spoilsmen, and replace Grant with a reform nominee for president in 1872. But this proved impossible, so the reformers bolted the party and organized their own "Liberal Republican" party. Their goal, as Carl Schurz phrased it in his keynote address to the Liberal Republican convention in 1872, was to create a government "which the best people of this country will be proud of."[19] (For more on the Liberal Republicans, see pages 610ff.)

When Liberals looked to the South, they discovered that some of the "best people" there were former Confederates, many of them disqualified from holding office or otherwise denied power by Republican regimes. From the Liberal viewpoint, Grantism in the South was as bad as Grantism in Washington. "Carpetbag-Negro government" and "bayonet rule" became the foremost issues in the 1872 election.

---

[19] *Speeches, Correspondence, and Political Papers of Carl Schurz,* 6 vols. (New York, 1913), II, 359.

The Southern Question, 1869–1872

We are not prepared for this suffrage. But we can learn. Give a man tools and let him commence to use them, and in time he will learn a trade. So it is with voting. We may not understand it at the start, but in time we shall learn to do our duty.

—William Beverly Nash,
ex-slave delegate to the South Carolina constitutional convention, 1868

597

Southern Republicans: Blacks, Carpetbaggers, and Scalawags

The Southern Republican party during Reconstruction was unique in the history of American politics. The party had no indigenous roots in the region. Most whites perceived it as an alien instrument of hateful change. In the North the Republican party represented the most prosperous, educated, and influential elements of the population; in the South most of its adherents were poor, illiterate, powerless—and black. The wonder is not that the Southern Republicans were ousted from power after only a few years, but that they ever held power at all.

About 80 percent of the Southern Republican voters were black men. Although most of them were landless ex-slaves, their leaders came primarily from the elite strata of the black community. Of the black men elected to state or federal office, at least four-fifths were literate and about one-third had been free before the war. Several had been born and educated in the North. About two-fifths practiced professional occupations, with clergymen forming the largest single category; nearly a third were farmers, most of them owning the land they farmed; more than a quarter were artisans or small businessmen (carpenters, blacksmiths, etc.). Although less is known about the blacks who held local office, the proportion of professionals and antebellum free men appears to have been lower and the proportion of farmers, artisans, and illiterate men higher than among those who filled state and federal positions.

Of the fourteen black congressmen and two black senators elected in the South from 1868 through 1876, all but three had obtained some secondary school education. Four had attended college. Several black state officeholders had also enjoyed exceptional educational opportunities. Jonathan Gibbs, secretary of state in Florida from 1868 to 1872 and state superintendent of education from 1872 to 1874, was a prewar graduate of Dartmouth College and of Princeton Theological Seminary. Francis L. Cardozo, who served as South Carolina's secretary of state for four years and as state treasurer for another four, had attended the University of Glasgow and theological schools in Edinburgh and London.

Neither the black leaders nor their constituents were so ignorant or incompetent as the traditional image of Reconstruction has portrayed them. It is true that four-fifths of the black voters and perhaps one-quarter of the black officeholders could not read and write. The fault for this, however, lay not with Reconstruction but with the old regime that had denied them education. Although contemporary accounts cited examples of black men who went to the polls with a basket to carry home the promised "vote," and of county treasurers who could neither read nor count, such stories provide a distorted picture of reality. The abilities of most black officials equaled the responsibilities of their offices. And most black voters understood what they were doing. Illiteracy did not preclude such an understanding for blacks, any more than it did for Irish immigrants in the North. Participation in Union League meetings and the experience of voting were themselves a form of education. "We are not prepared for this suffrage," conceded William Beverly Nash, an untutored ex-slave delegate to the South Carolina constitutional convention in 1868. "But we can learn. Give a man tools and let him commence to use them, and in time he will learn a trade. So it is with voting. We may not understand it at the start, but in time we shall learn to do our duty."[1] Black churches and fraternal organizations grew rapidly in numbers and organizational strength during the Reconstruction. Along with the Union League, they provided a forum that educated the freedmen in their rights and responsibilities as citizens and voters.

Linked to the myth of black incompetence was the legend of the "Africanization" of Southern governments during Reconstruction. A Northern journalist, James Shepherd Pike, presented a classic indictment of "Negro rule" in his 1873 book about South Carolina entitled *The Prostrate State*. Describing the state house of representatives, Pike wrote:

The Speaker is black, the Clerk is black, the door-keepers are black, the little pages are black, the chairman of the Ways and Means is black, and the chaplain is coal-black. At some of the

---

[1] John Hope Franklin, *Reconstruction: After the Civil War* (Chicago, 1961), p. 87. For a good discussion of black officeholders and their backgrounds, see Eric Foner, *Reconstruction: America's Unfinished Revolution 1863–1877* (New York, 1988), pp. 350–362. Biographical information and statistical tables on 1,510 black officeholders during Reconstruction can be found in Eric Foner, *Freedom's Lawmakers: A Directory of Black Officeholders during Reconstruction* (rev. ed., Baton Rouge, 1996).

desks sit colored men whose types it would be hard to find outside of Congo. . . . It is the dregs of the population habilitated in the robes of their intelligent predecessors, and asserting over them the rule of ignorance and corruption. . . . It is barbarism overwhelming civilization by . . . the rude form of the most ignorant democracy the world ever saw.[2]

This theme of "Negro supremacy," by which the "barbarous African" exercised "uncontrolled power" in ten Southern states, was a staple of Democratic propaganda. It became enshrined in many textbooks and in the popular memory of Reconstruction.

In sober truth, however, blacks held no more than 15 or 20 percent of the offices even at the height of Reconstruction in the early 1870s. Only 6 percent of the Southern congressmen from 1868 to 1877 were black. Although several black men served as lieutenant governors, secretaries of state, and state treasurers, none was ever nominated or elected governor.[3] Only one black man, Jonathan J. Wright of South Carolina, became a justice of a state supreme court. And only in South Carolina did blacks hold office in numbers approaching their proportion of the population. In the state legislature, 61 percent of the representatives and 42 percent of the senators from 1868 through 1876 were black. Blacks held 52 percent of all state and federal elective offices in South Carolina during those years. In no other state legislature did blacks ever have a majority in either house. Such was the reality of "Negro rule."

Although whites cast only about 20 percent of the Southern Republican votes, they dominated the party's leadership. Settlers from the North provided about 30 percent of the Republican officeholders while contributing at most 2 or 3 percent of the Republican votes. These carpetbaggers did even better in the higher offices: more than half the Republican governors and nearly half the Republican congressmen and U.S. senators were migrants from the North.

"Carpetbagger" and "scalawag" are among the most pejorative words in the American political lexicon. This book will use these terms, without their negative connotations, because they have become part of the language of history. The term "scalawag" supposedly came from Scalloway, a tiny Scottish island noted for its scrubby cattle and horses. To Southern Democrats, "scalawag" seemed an eminently suitable word to describe Southern whites who joined the Republicans, for such men were "vile, blatant, vindictive, unprincipled . . . the mean, lousy and filthy kind that are not fit for butchers or dogs." Democrats professed to prefer "the blackest man that can be found to the vilest renegades of the South . . . those who have dishonored the dignity of the white blood, and are traitors alike to principle and race." Carpetbaggers acquired their cognomen from the carpetbags containing their worldly goods that they allegedly carried southward on their way to plunder a helpless people. "Gangs of itinerant adventurers, vagrant interlopers," as Southerners described them, they were "too depraved, dissolute, dishonest and degraded to get the lowest of places in the states they had just left."[4]

---

[2]James S. Pike, *The Prostrate State: South Carolina Under Negro Government* (New York, 1874), pp. 15, 12.

[3]The black lieutenant governor of Louisiana, P. B. S. Pinchback, served as governor from December 9, 1872, until January 13, 1873, while the governor was suspended during impeachment proceedings.

[4]Franklin, *Reconstruction,* pp. 93, 98, 101; E. Merton Coulter, *The South During Reconstruction* (Baton Rouge, 1947), pp. 124–126.

Although some scalawags and carpetbaggers fit these stereotypes, most did not. On the average, Southern Republican leaders were neither more nor less honest and able than their counterparts in the other party or in other regions. If anything, they possessed more courage and—particularly in the case of the carpetbaggers—more idealism than the average politician, for they served in the front lines of progressive and unpopular change.

Most of the carpetbaggers were Union army officers who had stayed on in the South after the war. Some served as Freedmen's Bureau agents; some were teachers or superintendents of freedmen's schools; others liked the climate or the economic opportunities in the new frontier of the postwar South and decided to settle there. Nearly two-thirds of the carpetbag congressmen and senators practiced a profession—law, medicine, engineering, or teaching. Half of the senators were college graduates. Indeed, the carpetbaggers may have been the best-educated group of Americans in politics, North or South. Many of them brought not skimpy carpetbags but rather considerable capital, which they invested in the South. They also invested human capital—themselves—in a drive to modernize the region's social structure, revive its crippled economy, and democratize its politics. If this crusade provoked Southern hostility, carpetbaggers knew that as members of an invading army they had not been exactly welcomed to the region in the first place.[5]

Many scalawags shared the carpetbaggers' vision of a new South. The Republicans, said a North Carolina scalawag, were the "party of progress, of education, of development. . . . Yankees and Yankee notions are just what we want in this country. We want their capital to build factories and work shops, and railroads. . . . We want their energy and enterprise to operate these factories, and to teach us how to do it." An Arkansas scalawag asked voters: "Do you want good roads throughout your state? Do you want free bridges? Do you want free schools and the advantages of education for your children?" If you do, he concluded, vote Republican.[6]

Scalawags evolved mainly from the Unionists of 1860–1861. Most of them lived in the upland counties of eastern Tennessee, western North Carolina and Virginia, and northern Georgia, Alabama, and Arkansas. They had never liked the plantation regime and were as likely to have fought against the Confederacy as for it. They became Republicans because the party promised to overthrow the power of the planter class. A Republican handbill of 1868 addressed to the "Poor White Men of Georgia" expressed this sentiment: "Let the slave-holding aristocracy no longer rule you. Vote for a constitution which educates your children free of charge; relieves the poor debtor from his rich creditor; allows a liberal homestead for your families; and more than all, places you on a level with those who used to boast that for every slave they were entitled to three fifths of a vote in congressional representation."[7]

---

[5]For the best analyses of the carpetbaggers, see Richard N. Current, "Carpetbaggers Reconsidered," in David Pinkney and Theodore Ropp (eds.), *A Festschrift for Frederick B. Artz* (Durham, N.C., 1964), pp. 139–157, and Richard N. Current, *Those Terrible Carpetbaggers: A Reinterpretation* (New York, 1988).

[6]Carl N. Degler, *The Other South: Southern Dissenters in the Nineteenth Century* (New York, 1974), pp. 218, 226.

[7]Ibid., pp. 217–218.

Republicans also drew some support from former Whigs in the black belt and in the cities. Reluctant secessionists in 1861, many of these men were loath to join the Democrats after the war. Heirs of the futile antebellum attempts to foster Southern commercial and industrial development, these erstwhile Whigs turned to the Republicans as the party of modernization. Eight of the ten white Republican counties in Mississippi adjoined two new railroad lines built to open up a lumbering industry. Whiggish scalawag leaders in Alabama expected Republicans to promote "the revival of industry and prosperity" by mobilizing private and public capital. "Unite north and south Alabama by railroads," wrote a scalawag editor, "and do it by state aid, as a great State necessity."[8]

Thus the Southern Republican party in 1870 was a fragile coalition of blacks and whites, natives of the South and the North, hill-country yeomen and low-country entrepreneurs, illiterates and college graduates. The party was weakest along the seams where these disparate elements joined. Scalawags were particularly prone to defection because of their vulnerability to the charge of racial treason. For a Southern white man to defy the mores of his society required courage and conviction. An old friend of one scalawag refused to speak to him because "any white man who will go around with nigger clubs is too low to speak to a gentleman." A Mississippi Republican wrote sadly in 1872: "Even my own kinspeople have turned the cold shoulder to me because I hold office under a Republican administration."[9]

Democrats did their best to rip the Republicans apart along the racial seam. "THE GREAT and paramount issue is: SHALL NEGROES or WHITE MEN RULE NORTH CAROLINA?" proclaimed the state's leading Conservative newspaper. "All other issues are . . . subordinate and should be kept so." Such tactics whittled away scalawag strength. "It is hard . . . to carry the eternal nigger," confessed one white Republican. Black candidates for office hurt the Republicans' chances with white voters. "Should the negroes insist on having a negro on the ticket," said a North Carolina scalawag in 1868, "it will kill it dead."[10]

Sensitive to this problem, many black leaders initially maintained a low profile. But as time passed, they began to insist on a role more commensurate with their voting strength. "Are not in all States, and in all parties, the classes who have the largest majorities first considered?" asked a black South Carolinian in 1870. "No people have become a great people who had not their own leaders."[11]

This drive for black power produced an increasing number of black officeholders for a few years after 1870. But it also eroded white Republican strength, especially in states and counties with black majorities, where scalawags soon began to defect to the Conservatives.[12] The whites who tended to stay with the Republican party the longest were those in the upland regions where there were fewer blacks,

---

[8]Ibid., pp. 208–209.

[9]Ibid., p. 254.

[10]Otto H. Olsen, "Reconsidering the Scalawags," *Civil War History,* 12 (December 1966), 314; Degler, *Other South,* p. 233.

[11]Thomas Holt, *Black Over White: Negro Political Leadership in South Carolina During Reconstruction* (Urbana, Ill., 1977), pp. 106–107.

[12]Most Democratic organizations in the South continued for several years to call themselves "Conservatives" or "Democratic and Conservative" to ease the transition for erstwhile Whigs.

and the carpetbaggers. As outsiders, carpetbaggers were less susceptible to local pressures; with antebellum roots in the Republican party, they would not easily turn their coats. Since many of them had worked for black education and equal rights, they were not likely to be shocked by the sight of black men in office. "The radicals of northern birth," noted a Tennessee Republican, "having naturally more antislavery feeling . . . [than] native Tennessee loyalists are more ready to sustain new rights or claim privileges for the blacks than the other section of the radical party and as a result . . . have a larger share of the confidence of the colored population."[13]

This did not mean that harmony and sweetness prevailed between carpetbaggers and blacks. On the contrary, tensions among them often erupted into verbal conflict. Black leaders accused carpetbaggers of paternalism for wishing to limit blacks to minor offices. For their part, some carpetbaggers predicted disaster if black Republicans tried to break away from white tutelage too soon. "There is not," wrote a South Carolina carpetbagger in 1871, "enough virtue and intelligence among the Blacks to conduct the government in such a way as will promote peace and prosperity."[14]

But the frictions between carpetbaggers and blacks paled in comparison with those between carpetbaggers and scalawags. More radical than native white Republicans on racial issues, the Northerners sometimes voted with blacks on such sensitive matters as the desegregation of public accommodations and schools. Other, less ideological, frictions grew out of internal party battles for power and patronage. A white Republican in Alabama lamented: "What can a native Union man do, expect, or calculate on in the future? The Carpetbaggers have already landed everything that is Republican in Hell. . . . The political offices, University, Schools, all carpetbagged!"[15]

Another weak seam in the Republican fabric joined the predominantly mulatto antebellum free Negroes and the largely black ex-slaves. In Louisiana and South Carolina, the early monopolization of black leadership by the mulatto class aroused the color and class tensions never far from the surface in the black community. Mulatto-black frictions sometimes became more serious than black-white divisions in the party. A mulatto candidate for the 1868 constitutional convention in South Carolina reportedly said: "If ever there is a nigger government—an unmixed nigger government—established in South Carolina, I shall move." On the other side, a black leader said of the mulattoes: "To what race do they belong? . . . I know that my ancestors trod the burning sands of Africa, but why should men in whose veins run a great preponderance of white blood seek to specially ally themselves with the black man, prate of 'our race,' when they are simply mongrels."[16]

In contrast with these Republican divisions, Southern Democrats became increasingly united during the early 1870s. As "outs" pursuing the single goal of expelling the hated black/carpetbag governments, they achieved a concord that eluded

---

[13]Degler, *Other South,* p. 258.
[14]Holt, *Black Over White,* p. 104.
[15]Degler, *Other South,* p. 256.
[16]Holt, *Black Over White,* pp. 59–60.

the unstable Republican coalition. A study of the relative cohesion[17] of each party in the South Carolina legislature found that from 1868 to 1876, the Democrats maintained an average score of 75 percent compared with the Republicans' 45 percent.[18]

In nearly every state, a significant number of Republicans went over to the Democrats/Conservatives in at least one important election. This paved the way for the "redemption" (a Democratic term) of one state after another by conservative coalitions. The redemption process began with Virginia in 1869; Tennessee followed later in the same year, North Carolina and Alabama in 1870 (though Republicans regained control of the latter in 1872, only to lose it again in 1874), Georgia in 1871, Texas in 1873, and Arkansas in 1874. Although the Republicans' national victory in the 1872 election temporarily interrupted this process, the party's strength in the South ebbed from the outset of radical Reconstruction.

◯ᖗ Southern Republicans in Power

During their brief terms in office, however, Southern Republicans did score some modernizing advances. They established statewide public school systems for both races and provided state aid to railroad construction.[19] They continued the work of rebuilding levees, bridges, roads, public buildings, and other facilities destroyed by the war. They created industrial commissions to attract investment in Southern enterprises. They reorganized and modernized the judicial system. In some states they passed civil rights and antidiscrimination laws that, though seldom enforced, nevertheless evinced at least a theoretical commitment to racial equality.

Many of these achievements cost money—more money than Southern states had ever spent in peacetime. Emancipation nearly doubled the number of citizens requiring state services. A public school system had to be built almost from scratch, and though the Freedmen's Bureau and Northern freedmen's aid societies provided financial help in the initial stages, the schools still absorbed large amounts of state funds. The rehabilitation of war-ravaged properties and loans to railroads soaked up much more. As a consequence, state and county expenditures, taxes, and debts mushroomed during the early years of Republican rule. Tax rates in 1870 were three or four times as high as in 1860. Although Southern taxes in the 1870s were no higher on the average than those in rural Midwestern states, the war had destroyed wealth and slashed property values and thereby reduced the Southern tax base. Emancipation had further reduced it, for a significant source of revenue under the old regime had been a tax on slaves. Thus the small white landowner paid a larger share of a larger taxation than he had done under slavery. This alone soured many whites on the Republicans. Property owners formed taxpayers associations in nearly every

---

[17]A political science concept that measures the degree to which members of the same party vote alike on legislative roll calls.

[18]Holt, *Black Over White,* p. 123.

[19]These two activities are discussed in the next chapter.

Southern state to demand retrenchment. Their inability or refusal to pay taxes crippled schools and social services, and the ensuing fiscal chaos discredited Republican state governments in the eyes of many Northerners as well as Southerners.

The Corruption Issue

The much-advertised corruption of Reconstruction regimes also discredited the Republicans. "Such a Saturnalia of robbery and jobbery has seldom been seen in any civilized country," wrote a contemporary observer soon after the end of Reconstruction. "As voting power lay with those who were wholly unfit for citizenship, and had no interest, as taxpayers, in good government . . . greed was unchecked and roguery unabashed." This interpretation became engraved as historical truth. "Saddled with an irresponsible officialdom," wrote one scholar in a passage typical of most historical analyses until the 1950s, "the South was now plunged into debauchery, corruption, and private plundering unbelievable—suggesting that government had been transformed into an engine of destruction."[20]

Seldom has the truth been so distorted. To be sure, many of the Reconstruction governments were scarcely models of efficiency or honesty. Railroad promoters bribed legislators and governors for favored treatment. Officials awarded inflated contracts to friends and accepted kickbacks as their reward. Some of the funds for schools and public services stuck to the fingers of administrators. The state lottery in Louisiana seemed to corrupt everyone it touched. State printing contracts became a lucrative business. In South Carolina the printing costs for the eight-year period 1868–1876 exceeded total printing expenditures for the preceding eighty years. The South Carolina legislature voted a bonus of $1,000 to the Speaker of the House after he had reportedly lost that amount at a horse race. South Carolina's governors Robert Scott (1868–1872) and Franklin Moses (1872–1874) probably deserved much of the calumny heaped on their heads.

But Louisiana's carpetbag governor Henry Clay Warmoth (1868–1872), perhaps the most calumniated of all, may have been more sinned against than sinning. Corruption certainly flourished in Louisiana during his administration. But so had it flourished earlier, and so would it continue to flourish long afterward. Warmoth probably did as much or more to stem corruption as to participate in it. In 1870, he told a delegation from New Orleans that had petitioned for good government:

You charge the Legislature with passing, corruptly, many bills looking to the personal aggrandizement of individuals and corporations. Let me suggest to you that these individuals and corporations are your very best people. For instance, this bank bill that is being lobbied through the Legislature now by the hardest kind of work. We have been able to defeat this bill twice in the House, and now it is up again. Who are doing it? Your bank presidents . . . whispering bribes into these men's ears to pass this measure. How are we to defend the State against the interposition of these people who are potent in their influence?

---

[20]For perceptive commentaries on traditional scholarship about the corruption issue, see Kenneth M. Stampp, *The Era of Reconstruction 1865–1877* (New York, 1965), chap. 1, and Mark W. Summers, *The Era of Good Stealings* (New York, 1993), chap. 11. Quotations from James Bryce, *The American Commonwealth,* 3d ed., 2 vols. (New York, 1895), II, 476–477; Coulter, *South During Reconstruction,* p. 148.

On another occasion, Warmoth told a congressional committee: "These much-abused members of the Louisiana legislature are at all events as good as the people they represent. Why, damn it, everybody is demoralizing down here. Corruption is the fashion."[21]

As Warmoth suggested, Republican corruption must be put in perspective. For one thing, many Democrats participated in and profited from it. A Louisiana Democrat confessed that not "all the evils . . . result from the carpetbaggers and negroes—the democrats are leagued with them when anything is proposed which promises to pay."[22] For another, much that was accounted corruption could better be described as the inefficiency of inexperienced governments trying to deal with unprecedented problems amid the chaos of the postwar South. Moreover, some of the "extravagance" of Reconstruction governments was a fiction. The state debts provide an illustration. Contemporary writers and historians alike have wrung their hands in despair at the apparently huge increases in these debts. In 1867, at the beginning of Republican Reconstruction, the total indebtedness of the eleven Southern states was about $175 million. During the next four years, it rose to $305 million. But when this increase of $130 million is analyzed, nearly $100 million turns out to have consisted of state endorsements of railroad bonds. For the states, these were contingent debts secured by liens on railroad property. If the railroads defaulted, as some did, their assets became the property of the state to be applied against the indebtedness. State endorsement of railroad bonds had long been a common practice in both North and South. During Reconstruction the Southern states experienced little real increase in their indebtedness from these ventures, while they ultimately benefited from the railroad expansion that resulted.

Finally, the graft that took place in the South must be set in a national context. All the Southern governments combined probably stole less from the taxpayers than did the Tweed Ring in New York. The South Carolina and Louisiana legislatures were more exotic but perhaps no more corrupt than those of New York and Pennsylvania. Southern railroad "rings" could not hold a candle to the buccaneer Wall Street operators Jim Fisk and Jay Gould. The postwar era of relaxed standards and entrepreneurial aggressiveness affected the South as it affected the rest of the country.

The Amnesty Question

In truth, Southern Democrats abhorred *corrupt* government less than *Republican* government. An honest Republican regime was in some respects more alarming than a dishonest one, for it belied their accusations of black incompetence and carpetbag roguery. The charges of corruption were part of a Democratic campaign to discredit Southern Republicans. The campaign succeeded because a good many Northerners were prepared to believe black people incapable of responsible participation in government. Some Yankees also began to feel a sense of guilt for the sufferings of white Southerners. As the decade of the 1870s began, a movement in behalf of forgiveness and reconciliation gathered momentum in the North.

---

[21]Richard N. Current, *Three Carpetbag Governors* (Baton Rouge, 1967), p. 60; Roger W. Shugg, *Origins of Class Struggle in Louisiana* (Baton Rouge, 1939), p. 227.

[22]Foner, *Reconstruction,* p. 387.

Carl Schurz and Horace Greeley emerged as the most prominent leaders of this movement. Schurz headed a drive to end the disfranchisement of former Confederates in Missouri. This issue split the state's Republican party, which had controlled Missouri since the war. In 1870, the "Liberal" Republicans bolted the party and, with Democratic support, carried the state. Meanwhile, Horace Greeley's *New York Tribune* orchestrated a campaign for reconciliation with the South and total amnesty for ex-Rebels. Greeley insisted that Reconstruction could never work without the cooperation of the "better class" of Southern whites. To continue a policy of force and proscription, he warned, would only drive all whites into the Democratic party and intensify Ku Klux terrorism. But restraint and amnesty would encourage the growth of a moderate Southern Republican party dominated by the region's "natural leaders," especially those who like Greeley had once been Whigs. In the spring of 1871, Greeley carried this message to the South in a well-publicized lecture tour. Some Republicans who had grown disillusioned with Grant began to mention Greeley as a possible presidential candidate in 1872.

But most Republicans denounced Greeley's suggestions as a formula for disaster. Many of them no longer opposed amnesty in the narrow sense of removing the remaining political disqualifications of ex-Confederates. But in the lexicon of the Liberal movement, amnesty meant more than that. It connoted total forgiveness of Rebels and a willingness to entrust to their stewardship the results of Northern victory. The time for this had not yet come, according to *Harper's Weekly,* because the majority of Southern whites still consisted of those "who hate the government, who hold to paramount allegiance to the State, who hunt and harass the colored race, who compose the Ku-Klux."[23]

The Klan Issue

Terrorism persisted in many parts of the South after the 1868 elections. The Klan's excesses reputedly caused Grand Wizard Forrest to disband the order in 1869. But Forrest's ability to enforce any such directive was limited. The Klan had never been centrally controlled. Local bands, whether they called themselves Ku Klux Klans or something else, had operated on their own before 1869 and continued to do so after that date. Legend has it that the Klan now became dominated by irresponsible lower-class elements and that the South's Democratic leaders turned against it. The most scholarly history of the order, however, finds little evidence for this. Various kinds of information on Klan members—arrests by state militia or federal troops, grand jury indictments, convictions, and confessions—indicate that while in some areas poor whites did predominate, Klansmen came from all social classes and the leaders were often prominent men or the sons of prominent men.[24] Most

---

[23] *Harper's Weekly,* November 11, 1871.

[24] Allen W. Trelease, *White Terror: The Ku Klux Klan Conspiracy and Southern Reconstruction* (New York, 1971), pp. 296, 354, and passim. See also George C. Rable, *But There Was No Peace: The Role of Violence in the Politics of Reconstruction* (Athens, Ga., 1984), esp. chap. 6.

Klansmen were in their twenties and early thirties, and most were probably Confederate veterans. Their hit-and-run guerrilla tactics made them, in effect, a paramilitary arm of the Southern Democratic party's effort to overthrow Republican rule in the South.

One purpose of Klan violence was the social and economic control of the black population. Black schools, perceived as a threat to white supremacy, received special attention. Scores of black schoolhouses went up in flames. Democratic newspapers sometimes made fun of such occurrences. In 1869, an Alabama newspaper facetiously reported the appearance of a comet whose tail had dropped to the ground and burned several schools. "The antics of the tail of this wonderful comet have completely demoralized free-nigger education in these counties; for negroes are so superstitious that they believe it to be a warning for them to stick, hereafter to 'de shovel and de hoe,' and let their dirty-backed primers go."[25]

But the Klan's principal purpose remained political. The level of violence rose during the months before an election. Alleged Republican misrule served as the main justification for Klan activities. As the *Yorkville* (S.C.) *Enquirer* phrased it in 1871: "The intelligent, honest white people (the tax-payers) of this county shall rule it! We can no longer put up with negro rule, black bayonets [i.e., Negro militia], and a miserably degraded and thievish set of lawmakers. . . . We are pledged to stop it; we are determined to end it, even if we are 'forced, by force, to use force.' " Once this force had overthrown Republican rule, Democratic leaders counseled peace and order. In February 1871, editor Henry W. Grady of the *Rome* (Ga.) *Commercial,* who may have been a Klan member himself, advised all members of "secret organizations" to "*remain perfectly quiet and orderly, for the present. . . .* The exciting elections have all passed; the good cause has triumphed; the enemies of Georgia are beat to the dust. . . . Let the harsh asperities that were necessary during the 'reign of terror' pass away like a dream."[26]

Northern leaders wondered aloud why Southern Republicans could not defend themselves and maintain order. It was not for lack of trying. Republican sheriffs formed posses to go after the Klan. Governors organized militia companies and sent them to trouble spots. But the sheriff of Fayette County, Alabama, explained why such efforts often failed:

When I gather my posse . . . I could depend on them; but as soon as I get home, I meet my wife crying, saying that they have been there shooting into the house. When we scatter to our houses, we do not know at what time we are to be shot down; and living with our lives in our hands in this way, we have become disheartened, and do not know what to do.[27]

The militia accomplished little more. If the troops were whites, their commander might doubt their reliability because the Klan was known to have infiltrated some militia companies. Several governors, particularly in South Carolina, organized black militia units. But the occasional use of these troops inflamed white fury to a fever pitch and tended to exacerbate rather than to subdue violence. Governors became

---

[25]Trelease, *White Terror,* p. 259.
[26]Ibid., pp. 369, 327.
[27]Ibid., pp. 268–269.

reluctant to employ black militia for fear of starting an all-out race war. Even federal troops seemed ineffective against the Klan before 1871. For one thing, few cavalry units were stationed in the South (except on the Texas frontier), and infantry could not cope with the hit-and-run tactics of the mounted Klan. For another, the army in Southern states operated under the constraints of civil law.

If law enforcement officers did manage to apprehend Klansmen, what then? Even in Republican counties it proved difficult to empanel a jury that would convict, no matter what the evidence. Although federal troops might be able to protect witnesses and jurors during a trial, they could not prevent retaliation on a dark night months later. And sometimes the intimidation occurred during the trial itself. To cite one example, the district attorney in northern Mississippi saw a case fall apart when five key witnesses were murdered. The example was not lost on witnesses elsewhere.

Martial law and the large-scale use of troops seemed to be the only answer to Klan violence. But state legislatures were reluctant to give their governors authority for these actions. Only in Arkansas and Tennessee did state forces carry out successful campaigns against the Klan. In 1868–1869, Arkansas's governor, Powell Clayton, a tough Union army veteran with anti-guerrilla experience in Missouri, organized reliable white and black militia companies, put them under the command of former Union officers, and sent undercover agents to infiltrate the Klan. He proclaimed martial law in ten counties, attacked and scattered the Klan, arrested and tried Klansmen in military courts, and executed several of them by firing squad. This broke the back of the Klan in Arkansas. Governor William G. Brownlow of Tennessee mobilized a similar militia effort in 1869. The legislature gave him authority to declare martial law, which he did in nine counties. All of these counties were in middle and western Tennessee, while the militia came from solidly Republican eastern Tennessee. Little fighting occurred, for the Klan leaders decided to disband their forces before the militia arrived. Few arrests and no convictions took place. Although this campaign appeared to have achieved success, other forms of intimidation persisted, and the Republicans lost control of Tennessee in the fall of 1869.

North Carolina's Governor William W. Holden came to grief because of his attempt to stamp out the Klan. County sheriffs and civil courts proved helpless to contain a rising wave of terror that swept over the state in early 1870. The legislature authorized Holden to proclaim a state of insurrection but refused him the power to declare martial law or to suspend the writ of habeas corpus. Knowing that nothing short of these actions would do the job, Holden in effect declared martial law by executive order. The militia arrested scores of Klansmen, while dozens of others turned state's evidence in hope of a light sentence. In response to mounting pressures, Holden dropped his plan to try the offenders in military courts. As usual, none of those arrested could be convicted in civil courts. After the Democrats won control of the legislature in 1870, they impeached and convicted Holden in March 1871 for having illegally declared martial law. He was the first governor in American history to be removed from office by impeachment.

Congressional Legislation against the Klan

In several states, the Klan and Klan-like organizations grew bolder during 1870. The death toll mounted into the hundreds. Southern Republicans desperately petitioned the national government for help. Tough legislation to enforce the Fourteenth and Fifteenth Amendments became major items of congressional business. A stumbling block to such legislation was the federal system, under which the states had jurisdiction over the crimes of murder, assault, arson, and the like. In the view of many moderate Republicans, the prosecution of such crimes by federal officials would stretch the Constitution to the breaking point. Nevertheless, the clauses of the Fourteenth and Fifteenth Amendments giving Congress the power to enforce their provisions by appropriate legislation seemed to provide constitutional sanction for a departure from tradition. On May 31, 1870, Congress passed an enforcement act that made interference with voting rights a federal offense punishable in federal courts. The key section of this law defined as a felony any attempt by one or more persons to deprive another person of his civil or political rights.

This section became the basis for subsequent prosecutions and convictions of Klansmen. But during the first year of the law's existence, President Grant and Attorney General Hoar did little to enforce it. Their Southern policy relied more on the velvet glove than on the iron fist. By 1871, however, it was clear that the government's soft tactics were failing; Klan violence was on the rise. Grant and his new attorney general, Amos Akerman, readied the iron fist. On February 28, 1871, Congress passed a second enforcement act, which established machinery for the federal supervision of registration and voting. But the most important law was the enforcement act passed by a special session on April 20, 1871, popularly known as the Ku Klux Act. This law strengthened the felony and conspiracy provisions of the 1870 law, authorized the president to use the army to enforce it, and empowered him to suspend the writ of habeas corpus in areas that he declared to be in a state of insurrection. Although this last provision fell short of true martial law (indicted persons would still be tried in civil courts), it was a significant step in that direction. The Ku Klux Act also gave the courts power to purge suspected Klansmen from juries by an oath backed with stiff penalties for perjury.

Under these laws, the Grant administration cracked down on the Klan. Government detectives infiltrated the order and gathered evidence of its activities. In 1871, a congressional committee also conducted an investigation of the Klan that produced twelve volumes of testimony documenting its outrages. The President sent several companies of cavalry south to cope with the fast-riding Klansmen. Because Grant was sensitive to Democratic charges of "military despotism," however, he used his powers sparingly. He suspended the writ of habeas corpus in only nine counties of South Carolina. There and elsewhere, especially in North Carolina and Mississippi, federal marshals aided by soldiers arrested thousands of Klansmen. Hundreds of others fled their homes to escape arrest. Federal grand juries handed down more than three thousand indictments. Several hundred defendants pleaded guilty in return for suspended sentences. The Justice Department dropped charges against nearly two thousand others in order to clear clogged court dockets for trials of major offenders. About 600 of the latter were convicted and 250 acquitted. Of those convicted, most received fines or light jail sentences, but 65 were imprisoned for sentences up to five years in the federal penitentiary at Albany, New York.

Most arrests of Klansmen took place in 1871–1872, though their trials dragged on until 1875.[28] The government's main purpose was to destroy the Klan and to restore law and order in the South, rather than to secure mass convictions. Thus the courts granted clemency to many convicted defendants, and Grant used his pardoning powers liberally. By 1875, all the imprisoned men had served out their sentences or received pardons. The government's vigorous action in 1871–1872 did bring at least temporary peace and order to large parts of the former Confederacy. As a consequence, the 1872 election was the fairest and most democratic presidential election in the South until 1968.

# The Election of 1872

Despite Grant's restraint in enforcing the Ku Klux Act, bayonet rule became a central issue in the 1872 election. In the end, however, the administration's Southern policy proved to be more of a political asset than a liability.

As the probability of Grant's renomination was becoming a near certainty by early 1872, Republicans disaffected from his administration decided to form a third party. This movement began in Missouri, where Liberal Republicans with Democratic support had recently wrested control of the state from the regular Republicans. On January 24, 1872, the Missouri Liberals issued a call for a national convention to meet at Cincinnati in May. Pursuant to this call, Republican dissidents in every state had organized themselves around the Liberal banner and elected convention delegates.

The Liberal Republican Convention

The men who gathered at Cincinnati represented a broad range of viewpoints. Some shared the laissez-faire ideals of nineteenth-century British liberalism: individual liberty, limited government, and free trade. They opposed the protective tariffs favored by most Republicans; they supported civil service reform and expressed disillusionment with Grant's failures in this area; and they urged amnesty and an end to bayonet rule in the South. Having changed parties at least once before in their careers—from Whig or Democrat to Republican, with perhaps the Free Soil party as an intermediate step—many of them did not regard the Republican party as a permanent institution. The party had won the war, preserved the Union, abolished slavery, and reconstructed the South. These were glorious achievements. But Liberals believed that unprincipled spoilsmen and politicos had captured the party. Therefore, the time had come again, as in 1848 and 1854, to form a new party to apply the old ideals to the new issues of the 1870s.

---

[28]Arrests and trials under the legislation of 1870 and 1871 continued for two decades after 1875, but at a much diminished rate. Supreme Court decisions in 1876 (see page 637) struck down significant portions of the enforcement acts, and a Democratic Congress repealed most of this legislation in 1894.

The idealistic Liberals rubbed elbows at Cincinnati with political brokers who cared little for any of these issues. From both the North and the South arrived delegates who had lost factional or patronage battles within the party and who saw the Liberal movement as a means to recoup their political fortunes. This would make them unlikely proponents of civil service reform. To complicate the picture further, every shade of tariff opinion found expression at the convention. Therefore the tariff plank of the platform emerged as a meaningless compromise. (In the meantime, Congress in 1872 lowered tariff rates by an average of 10 percent and removed the duties on coffee and tea altogether, thereby robbing the issue of some of the potential it might have had.) The platform did take a firm stand on civil service reform. Under Grant, it declared, the bureaucracy had "become a mere instrument of partisan tyranny and personal ambition . . . a scandal and reproach upon free institutions . . . dangerous to the perpetuity of republican government." Reform of these abuses, impossible under the "tyrannical" Grant administration, was "one of the most pressing necessities of the hour."[29]

Despite this emphasis on civil service reform, the Southern question became the main issue of the Liberal Republican movement. This happened primarily for two reasons: the party's need for a coalition with Democrats and the personality of the presidential nominee, Horace Greeley. In 1871, a number of dissident Republicans had begun to urge the Democratic party to repudiate its racist past and to accept the legitimacy of Reconstruction. This would pave the way for a coalition between the "better class of Democrats" and the anti-Grant Republicans. Many Northern Democrats were ready to bury the "dead issues" of the past and to undertake such a "New Departure" toward future success. When the arch-Copperhead himself, Clement Vallandigham, proposed resolutions to a county Democratic convention in May 1871 accepting the Fourteenth and Fifteenth Amendments as "the natural and legitimate results of war," the New Departure became a reality. A dozen state Democratic conventions adopted the resolutions in 1871. As a consequence, said the party's national chairman, "the game of charging us with disloyalty and Copperheadism is played out."[30]

This prediction turned out to be premature. Moreover, the Democratic endorsement of Reconstruction contained some small print. The party continued to adhere to its states' rights principles. Congressional Democrats voted against the enforcement acts of 1870–1871 and denounced the arrests of Klansmen as "tyranny" and "despotism." This created a problem for Liberal Republicans, many of whom had initially supported these laws. They tried to resolve the problem by endorsing the purpose of the laws but criticizing the use of "bayonets" to carry them out. This ambivalence found its way into the Liberal Republican platform. Two planks pledged fidelity to "the equality of all men before the law . . . equal and exact justice to all of whatever nativity, race, color, or persuasion." But two other planks demanded amnesty for all former Confederates, advocated "the supremacy of the civil over the military authority," called for "local self-government" (already a code phrase for

[29]William Gillette, "Election of 1872," in Arthur M. Schlesinger, Jr. (ed.), *History of American Presidential Elections,* 4 vols. (New York, 1971), II, 1335–1336.

[30]Lawrence Grossman, *The Democratic Party and the Negro: Northern and National Politics, 1868–1892* (Urbana, Ill., 1976), p. 26.

HORACE GREELEY. Despite his benign expression in this photograph, Greeley had a contentious career as editor of the *New York Tribune,* which he built into the leading Whig and then Republican newspaper. His vigorous stands on different sides of several issues over the years made him vulnerable to ridicule as a presidential candidate in 1872.

LIBRARY OF CONGRESS

white rule in the South), and condemned Grant's use of "arbitrary measures."[31] Since "bayonets" and "arbitrary measures" had proven to be the only way to protect equal rights in the South, these platform phrases were widely recognized as a bid for an alliance with the Democrats.

As for Greeley, his name was almost a household word. But some of the reasons for his fame worked against him as a candidate. During his nearly forty years as a journalist, he had lent his support to a wide range of unpopular, contradictory, or just plain quackish positions. His quixotic personality and cherubic appearance made him a cartoonist's delight. His temporary acquiescence in peaceful secession in 1861, his subsequent oscillation between advocacy of total war and negotiated peace, and his postwar support of a tough reconstruction policy combined with the forgiveness of Rebels had created an image of a muddling, confused mind. Greeley's long record of partisan attacks on Democrats made him an unlikely prospect to head a coalition with that party.

Despite all this, Greeley was the most influential newspaperman in the country. By 1871, he had also made himself the leading spokesman for amnesty, reconciliation, and self-government in the South. Even so, Greeley did not figure as a probable nominee in the preconvention maneuvering. The two leading candidates were diplomat Charles Francis Adams and Supreme Court Justice David Davis. Austere and impeccably correct, Adams received the support of New Englanders and principled reformers. The professional politicians leaned toward Davis. In effect, the two men

---

[31]Gillette, "Election of 1872," p. 1336.

neutralized each other, paving the way for Greeley to pick up Davis delegates and to emerge as the victor amid pandemonium on the sixth ballot. Adams's supporters, including Carl Schurz and most other founders of the Liberal movement, were stunned by Greeley's nomination. Some of them defected from the party and either endorsed Grant or sat out the campaign. But most of them swallowed their disappointment and prepared to do their best to elect Greeley.

The Campaign

In the spirit of the slogan "Anything to beat Grant," the Democratic national convention overlooked the enmities and barbs of four decades and endorsed Greeley's nomination. Liberals and Democrats set up fusion tickets at the state level. Early in the campaign, the Greeley candidacy seemed to develop a strong momentum.

But of the three issues that had initially impelled the Liberal movement—civil service reform, tariff reduction, and sectional reconciliation—Greeley was indifferent toward the first and hostile toward the second. This left amnesty and self-government as the "great watchwords" of the Liberal Republican party. In his acceptance letter, Greeley announced an intention to make Grant's "Federal subversion of the internal polity" of Southern states the main campaign issue "in the confident trust that the masses of our countrymen . . . are eager to clasp hands across the bloody chasm which has too long divided them."[32]

The Republican Congress acted to defuse the potential appeal of the Liberals' amnesty plank by removing the officeholding disqualification from all but a handful of ex-Confederates in May 1872. Apart from this, however, Greeley's stand on Southern questions turned out to be politically counterproductive. Most Northern voters did not yet trust the white South or the Democrats. *Harper's Weekly* cartoonist Thomas Nast, famous for the biting cartoons that had helped overthrow the Tweed Ring, did a similar job on Greeley. One cartoon showed the editor shaking hands "across the bloody chasm" with a Rebel who had just shot a Union soldier. Others pictured Greeley shaking hands across Andersonville prison and across a Ku-Kluxed black man. One that really hit below the belt showed the editor stretching a hand across Lincoln's grave to the ghost of John Wilkes Booth. Nast's most famous campaign cartoon portrayed Greeley as a pirate captain bringing his craft alongside the ship of state while Confederate leaders, armed to the teeth, hid below waiting to board and destroy it.

Although several former Free Soilers became Liberal Republicans, the mainstream of antislavery and abolitionist sentiment remained with the Republicans. So did nearly all black voters. Frederick Douglass spoke for the latter when he branded the Liberal movement "mischievous and dangerous." "Whatsoever may be the faults of the Republican party," said Douglass, "it has within it the only element of friendship for the colored man's rights." The Democratic endorsement of Greeley confirmed William Lloyd Garrison's belief that the Liberal movement was "simply a stool pigeon for the Democracy to capture the Presidency." And Lydia Maria Child, who though she could not vote was one of the most astute political observers among the abolitionists, wrote that while the Liberal and Democratic platforms professed to affirm equality before the law:

---

[32]Ibid., pp. 1358–1359.

IT IS ONLY A TRUCE TO REGAIN POWER ("PLAYING POSSUM").
H. G. "Clasp hands over the bloody chasm."
C. S. "Freely accept the hand that is offered, and reach forth thine own in friendly grasp."

ONE OF THOMAS NAST'S ANTI-GREELEY CARTOONS. This cartoon appeared in *Harper's Weekly,* August 24, 1872. Typical of Nast's complicated but powerful drawings, it shows Greeley about to "clasp hands across the bloody chasm" with a member of the Ku Klux Klan whose hand is dripping with the blood of a black woman he has murdered, as her husband is about to share the same fate. On the Klansman's left stands a Nast caricature of an Irishman, while in the background are scenes from the New York draft riot in 1863, when Irish-Americans lynched blacks. On the far right is Charles Sumner, whose bitterness toward Grant caused him to support Greeley in 1872. Nast depicts this unholy alliance as the essence of the Liberal Republican/Democratic coalition in 1872.

. . . the Rebels and Democrats have taken care to put in some loopholes through which they can creep out of all they have promised. They claim "self-government for the States," which means the "State Sovereignty" for which the Rebels fought. . . . They demand that "the nation should return to methods of peace, and the supremacy of civil over military authority," which means that when the Ku Klux Klan renew their plans to exterminate Republicans, white and black, they shall be dealt with by Southern civil authorities—that is, by judges and jurors who are themselves members of the Ku Klux associations.[33]

---

[33]James M. McPherson, "Grant or Greeley? The Abolitionist Dilemma in the Election of 1872," *American Historical Review,* 71 (October 1965), 49, 51.

As the campaign proceeded, the Greeley candidacy began to wilt. The makeshift Liberal organization proved to be no match for the well-financed Republican machine. Many Democrats who could not bring themselves to vote for Greeley decided to stay home on election day. Grant's apparent success in quashing the Klan helped him more than the corruption issue hurt him. On November 5, the President scored a solid victory over his challenger. Grant won 56 percent of the popular vote, the highest proportion for any candidate between 1828 and 1904. He carried every Northern state and ten of the sixteen Southern and border states. The Republicans regained a two-thirds majority in the House and preserved a similar majority in the Senate. Worn out from the campaign, despondent at its outcome, and grieving over the recent death of his wife, Greeley died three weeks after the election.

The Liberal Republican party also died. But the issues of reform and reconciliation remained alive, despite the apparent electoral mandate for a tough Southern policy. When the nation's booming prosperity collapsed into depression after the Panic of 1873, the Republicans became vulnerable to the kind of attacks on their record that had failed in 1872.

Chapter Thirty-One

Social and Economic Reconstruction

It took America three-quarters of a century of agitation and four years of war to learn the meaning of the word "Liberty." God grant to teach us by easier lessons the meaning of the words "equal rights."

—American Freedmen's Union Commission, *1866*

617

Education in the South

One of Reconstruction's proudest achievements was the planting in the South of a public school system for both races. It was a tender plant, buffeted by the storms of violence, corruption, taxpayer revolts, and Democratic counterrevolution. But it survived and grew to maturity, bringing literacy to the freedpeople and some semblance of a modern educational system to the South.

The work of freedmen's education societies expanded rapidly after the war. The former slaves remained eager for schooling. Next to ownership of land, blacks looked upon education as their best hope for advancement. "My Lord, ma'am, what a great thing larning is!" said a South Carolina freedman to a Northern teacher. "White folks can do what they likes, for they know so much more'na we." A black Mississippian vowed in 1869: "If I nebber does do nothing more while I live, I shall give my children a chance to go to school, for I considers education the next best ting to liberty."[1]

Many Southern whites disliked the idea of educating blacks because they feared that such education might threaten white supremacy. Other Southerners, more farseeing, recognized that education of the freedpeople was necessary to prepare

---

[1]Leon F. Litwack, *Been in the Storm So Long: The Aftermath of Slavery* (New York, 1979), pp. 472–473.

them for the responsibilities of freedom. But they feared that Yankee teachers would instill "false notions of equality" in black minds. Much of the violence against freedmen's schools took the form of attacks on Northern teachers. Southern moderates who sympathized with the idea of black education urged fellow whites to support black schools in order to forestall Yankee domination of the enterprise.

But such appeals availed little. Southern whites did next to nothing for black education in the early postwar years. By default, Northern missionaries, the federal government, and freedmen created a network of black schools from the elementary to college level. Protestant denominations, especially Congregationalists through the American Missionary Association, took the lead in these efforts. Many nonsectarian freedmen's aid societies also sprang up in the North. Most of these merged in 1866 to form the American Freedmen's Union Commission. Black denominations, especially the African Methodist Episcopal Church, also founded schools. In 1866, the Freedmen's Bureau became involved in education on a large scale.

This was a unique experiment in joint private and public support of education. The Freedmen's Bureau owned many of the school buildings, paid transportation for teachers from the North, and maintained a general oversight of affairs. The freedmen's aid societies and mission associations recruited and paid the teachers and determined the curriculum and content of the schooling. The initial preponderance of Northern teachers fell to less than half by 1870. In that year about half of the teachers were blacks and a handful were Southern whites. From 1865 to 1870, the expenditures for freedmen's education totaled approximately $9 million, of which the Freedmen's Bureau contributed $5 million, the Northern societies more than $3 million, and the freedmen the remainder. In 1870, there were 4,000 freedmen's schools with 9,000 teachers and more than 200,000 pupils. Despite these impressive statistics, only 12 percent of the 1,700,000 black children of school age (six to seventeen years old) were enrolled in 1870. The proportion of Southern white children attending some kind of school, however, was not much higher.

The establishment of public schools by the reconstructed state governments gave promise of an enlarged and permanent educational system. But the promise was not entirely fulfilled. The insecure tenure of these governments, the difficulty of collecting taxes, the waste and corruption in the disbursement of some school funds, the added expense of maintaining a dual school system for the two races, the shortage of qualified teachers and administrators especially for black schools, the persistent white hostility to black education, and the low population density of rural areas slowed the development of a public school system. Most of the good schools were located in the cities and larger towns, while schools in the countryside rarely functioned for more than three months a year if they functioned at all. Nevertheless, there was some progress. By 1876, more than half of the white children and nearly two-fifths of the black children of school age in the former slave states were enrolled in school. This represented a threefold increase in only six years. Though still a tender plant, the public school system had definitely taken root in the South.

With the establishment of public schools, the nonsectarian Northern freedmen's societies turned their properties over to the states and went out of existence. The denominational societies also deeded most of their elementary schools to the states, but they continued to operate academies and "colleges," the latter at first function-

LIBRARY OF CONGRESS

FREEDPEOPLE'S SCHOOLHOUSE.   The planting of schools for freed slaves and the creation of a public education system in the South was the proudest achievement of Reconstruction. At first, most of the teachers were Northern white women, but as time went on the schools themselves produced the next generation of black teachers.

ing mainly as secondary schools. The main purpose of these institutions was to train black teachers, clergymen, and other professional leaders—the group that the black leader W. E. B. Du Bois later called "the talented tenth." The American Missionary Association continued to lead the way in this endeavor. From the schools founded and sustained by this and other Northern Protestant societies evolved most of the leading black colleges: Fisk, Atlanta, and Dillard Universities; Talladega, Tougaloo, Morehouse, and Spelman Colleges; and many others. The efforts of these institutions and of the public schools slowly reduced the black illiteracy rate from more than 80 percent in 1870 to 45 percent by 1900.

The Segregation Issue

A school integration debate generated much heat but little light in the 1870s. Freedmen's aid societies confronted this question in their schools as early as 1865. Consistent with their abolitionist heritage, they welcomed both races to their schools. The American Freedmen's Union Commission declared in 1866 that although integration would "produce difficulties in the South," the policy was "inherently right" and the commission would never "shut out a child from our schools because of his color. . . . It took America three-quarters of a century of agitation and four years of war to learn the meaning of the word 'Liberty.' God grant to teach us by easier lessons the meaning of the words 'equal rights.' "[2]

---

[2] *American Freedman*, I (April 1866), 2–6.

In practice, however, few Southern whites chose to attend these schools. From 1867 to 1870, whites made up only 1 percent of the students enrolled in schools supervised by the Freedmen's Bureau. With the exception of one school, the few white students in the mission societies' secondary schools and colleges were mainly the children of Northern instructors who taught in these institutions. The exception was Berea College. Founded by the American Missionary Association in eastern Kentucky, Berea enrolled whites as well as blacks from 1866 on. For nearly forty years, until the Kentucky legislature banned integration in 1904, Berea's student population averaged about half black and half white, making it the most thoroughly integrated school in the United States.

Several Northern states moved toward the desegregation of public schools during Reconstruction. In 1866 and 1867, the legislatures of Rhode Island and Connecticut followed Massachusetts's earlier example and prohibited public school segregation. During the next decade Michigan, Minnesota, Iowa, and Kansas took similar action by legislative act or court decision. Although enforcement of these laws was spotty, most of the few black children in the upper North attended nonsegregated schools.

The South was another matter. White spokesmen, including scalawags, repeatedly warned that compulsory integration would destroy the fledgling public schools by driving all whites away. Only Louisiana and South Carolina mandated nonsegregated schools in their constitutions. Florida did so by statute in 1873. But implementation was nonexistent there and in most parts of Louisiana and South Carolina as well. In a few Louisiana parishes, white and black children apparently attended the same schools for a time. For several years in the 1870s, about one-third of the New Orleans public schools were mixed. Carpetbagger administrators compelled the admission of black students to the University of South Carolina in 1873. But this policy achieved dubious success. Nearly all of the whites withdrew from the university. By 1875, nine-tenths of the students were black, and the few remaining whites were mostly the sons of carpetbaggers or Northern missionaries. The achievement of integration in New Orleans resulted in part from the cosmopolitan ethnic heritage of the city, whose population contained a spectrum of colors that made it difficult to tell where "black" left off and "white" began. Even so, integration in New Orleans produced tension and violence. Several thousand white children transferred to private schools or dropped out of school altogether. The restoration of Democratic control in Louisiana and South Carolina in 1877 ended the South's first experiments in desegregated public education.

The Civil Rights Act of 1875

The federal government also got into the act of trying to legislate desegregation. In 1870, Senator Charles Sumner introduced a bill to prohibit racial discrimination in schools, juries, and all forms of transportation and public accommodations anywhere in the United States. Backed by an abolitionist campaign to mobilize public support for this effort to "remove the last lingering taint of slavery," Sumner reintroduced his bill at each subsequent session of Congress until his death in 1874. But many lawyers doubted the bill's constitutionality, for the Fourteenth Amendment seemed to ban only racial discrimination imposed by states and not that practiced by individuals or corporations. Although public schools clearly fell within the category of state agencies, doubt existed whether the equal protection clause of the amendment prohibited separate schools. The same Congress that passed the Fourteenth Amendment had also established a segregated public school system in the District of Columbia. Moreover, many radicals who sympathized with Sumner's purpose in theory expressed concern that the law might destroy Southern schools in practice. Even though segregated schools were based on an "unreasonable prejudice," wrote a radical editor, "we have lived long enough to know that this prejudice, so far as it exists, is not to be corrected by the legislative coercion of a civil rights bill. It is far better to have both [races] educated, even in 'separate' schools, than not to have them educated at all."[3]

Despite these doubts, the Senate passed Sumner's bill in May 1874—several senators probably voting aye only as a memorial gesture to Sumner, who had died two months earlier. But the House cut the school provision from the bill before passing it in February 1875. Even without the school clause, this law turned out to be far ahead of its time. Many congressmen who voted for it did not believe it would survive legal challenges or that it could be enforced if it did. The Justice Department made little effort to enforce the law. Although some railroads, streetcar lines, and even restaurants and theaters in the South as well as the North served blacks on a nonsegregated basis after passage of the law, most did not. Several discrimination cases made their way on appeal through the lower courts to the United States Supreme Court. In 1883, the Court ruled the 1875 law unconstitutional (except the provision relating to juries) on the grounds that the Fourteenth Amendment gave Congress no power to legislate against discrimination by individuals, only against discrimination by states.

The New Order in Southern Agriculture

Just as black education took a great leap forward during Reconstruction and then settled into a pattern of separate and unequal,[4] so the economic status of the freedmen at first improved dramatically but then settled into a pattern of exploitation and poverty. The problem of defining new labor relationships between former slaves and former masters lay at the core of Reconstruction. The United States was unique among societies that experienced the wrenching transition from a slave-labor to a free-labor economy because it granted freed slaves equal political rights. This revolutionary act had important consequences for social and economic relations in the new order. It "profoundly if temporarily affected the relationship of the state to the economic order," writes historian Eric Foner. "The freedmen won, in the vote, a form of leverage their counterparts in other societies did not possess. . . . Radical Reconstruction stands as a unique moment when . . . political authority actually sought to advance the interests of the black laborer." Republican state legislatures in the South

---

[3]*Independent,* June 4, 1874.

[4]The expenditures per student for white schools seem to have been 30 to 40 percent greater than those for black schools during the 1870s. This disparity persisted during subsequent decades, and it widened during the early twentieth century.

enacted certain taxes, lien laws to protect workers' wages and sharecroppers' rights to their fair share of the proceeds from sale of the crop, measures concerning credit, and other laws to defend the interests of the freedpeople. As a South Carolina planter complained in 1872, "under the laws of most of the Southern States ample protection is afforded to tenants and very little to landlords."[5] When Democrats regained control of one Southern state after another during the 1870s, one of their top priorities was to repeal these laws and replace them with a new version of the black codes that favored employers and landlords.

Economic studies of emancipation have revealed an apparently large rise in the freed slaves' standard of living during the early postwar years. Political power and friendly legislation played some part in this; but the main reason was economic. High cotton prices continued for several years after Appomattox. At the same time, chaotic postwar conditions and the wartime loss of lives created a labor shortage. In these circumstances, the freedmen possessed bargaining power to bid up the price of their labor. If a planter did not offer satisfactory wages, his workers could go elsewhere. This mobility of labor was the chief economic benefit of emancipation. The efforts of Southern whites to neutralize it by anti-enticement laws, vagrancy laws, violence, and other means could not fully overcome economic realities. In 1865, planters offered freed workers provisions and housing plus money wages of only $5 or $6 per month or share wages of one-tenth of the crop. By 1867, the freedmen had pushed this up to an average of $10 per month for a full hand (an adult male) or as much as one-third of the crop. From Texas came a typical report: "The old-line planters, who only a few weeks before had driven off their negroes, endeavored to secure their services by offering greater inducements. They offered part of the crop—first, one-fourth, then one-third, and now one-half—rather than let their plantations remain idle."[6]

Several economic historians have attempted to calculate the income gains of blacks during the first decade of freedom. The most painstaking of these analyses[7] is based on estimates of the shares of return going to each of the three inputs in cotton growing: capital (land, seed, implements, etc.), labor, and management. Under slavery, the slaves received only 22 percent of the return—in the form of food, clothing, and shelter. With freedom, labor's share jumped to 56 percent. For two reasons, however, not all of this increase represented a clear gain in black income. First, the South suffered a general decline in per capita output from prewar levels. Blacks got a bigger slice of the pie, but it was a smaller pie. Second, one of the benefits of freedom was no longer having "to work like slaves." Although many freedwomen, especially in towns and cities, had to labor as domestic servants in white households to help support their families, some chose to stay home and nurture their own children rather than work in the fields as they had done in slavery. Some freed children

---

[5]Eric Foner, *Nothing but Freedom: Emancipation and Its Legacy* (Baton Rouge, 1983), pp. 46, 52, 53.

[6]Robert Higgs, *Competition and Coercion: Blacks in the American Economy 1865–1914* (Cambridge, 1977), p. 49.

[7]Roger L. Ransom and Richard Sutch, *One Kind of Freedom: The Economic Consequences of Emancipation* (Cambridge, 1977); Roger L. Ransom and Richard Sutch, "Growth and Welfare in the American South of the Nineteenth Century," *Explorations in Economic History,* 16 (1979), 207–236.

Table 31.1   Per Capita Agricultural Income in Seven Cotton States

	1857	1879
Black	$ 28.95	$42.22
White	124.79	80.57
Average	74.28	60.13

went to school instead of the fields; their fathers could refuse to work "from dawn to dusk." The options of parenting, education, and leisure defined the meaning of freedom. They also helped to produce the labor shortage that bid up the price of labor but at the same time reduced the potential income of individual families by reducing the overall product of their labor.

After factoring all these variables into their calculations, economists Roger Ransom and Richard Sutch estimate that black per capita agricultural income in the cotton states increased by 46 percent between 1857 and 1879, with most of this increase coming in the first years of freedom. At the same time, the per capita agricultural income of whites declined by 35 percent. Put another way, black per capita income rose from a relative level of only 23 percent of white income under slavery to 52 percent of white income by the 1870s. While the freedmen enjoyed a standard of living only half as high as that of Southern whites, their *relative* gains since slavery represented the greatest proportionate redistribution of income in American history. Table 31.1 illustrates the changes in per capita income.[8]

Most of this income redistribution occurred at the expense of former slaveholders, who could no longer expropriate so large a share of their laborers' output. Postwar planters complained bitterly about their straitened circumstances. "The Negro laziness, and the fall in the price of cotton made me come out a loser, that is, in debt, after surrendering everything I made," wrote a Georgia planter in January 1868. "I worked harder than any negro I employed and made less, because they got their food and clothes for their families and I got nothing." Later in the year, the same planter professed to have "nothing to say that is not gloomy and discouraging. . . . We are more despondent, more degraded, more prostrate, and poorer today than we have ever been, and with negro legislatures, juries, and executive officers, we must sink into a deeper abyss. . . . If I could sell my land or raise enough money to pay my railroad fare, I would not stay here a week."[9]

The Evolution of Tenantry

The freedmen's bargaining power plus other economic factors also forced a reorganization of the methods of plantation labor. Slaves had generally worked in gangs under the supervision of an owner, overseer, or driver. Planters tried to reimpose this

---

[8]Table adapted from data in Roger L. Ransom and Richard Sutch, "Growth and Welfare in the American South of the Nineteenth Century," *Explorations in Economic History,* 16 (1979), 225.

[9]Samuel M. Browne to Samuel L. M. Barlow, January 26, April 9, 1868, S. L. M. Barlow Papers, Henry E. Huntington Library.

system after the war, with the payments of wages as the only new feature. But the effort soon broke down. The chronic shortage of cash in the postwar South made the payment of money wages difficult or impossible for many planters. Thus the practice arose of offering a share of the crop as payment. For planters this had the advantage of giving workers a stake in successful operations. To the freedmen it provided a sense of proprietorship. They began to demand that instead of working in gangs with payment of wages in shares or money, they be allowed to work a plot of land independently and pay a share of the crop as rent. Under this plan, the freedmen became, in effect, farm operators rather than farm laborers. They enjoyed at least partial independence from the day-to-day supervision of white men.

Share tenantry did not become universal. In fact, a bewildering variety of land and labor systems had come into existence by the 1870s and persisted for the next half-century or more. In 1880, one-quarter of the blacks employed in Southern agriculture (along with some whites) worked for wages. Of the remainder, which the census defined as "farm operators," two-thirds of the whites and one-fifth of the blacks owned part or all of the land they farmed. One-tenth of the whites and one-quarter of the black operators paid a fixed rent; one-quarter of the whites and slightly more than half of the blacks rented their land for a share of the crop. Fixed rent took one of two forms: payment in cash or payment in a specified number of pounds or bushels of the crop (standing rent). Share tenantry also took one of two forms, which outside observers sometimes failed to distinguish: share renting and share cropping. In the former, the landowner provided land and housing only; the renter provided livestock, seed, and implements as well as his labor, and paid one-fourth of the crop in rent. In share *cropping,* the cropper provided only his labor and received the proceeds from half the crop as his payment. Share cropping became more common than share renting, for most tenants lacked the capital to provide their own work animals, seed, and machinery.

The Ownership of Land

The various forms of land tenure ranked themselves in an ascending order of status, from sharecropping at the bottom to ownership at the top. Reconstruction brought a shift in relative percentages of white and black farm owners. On the eve of the Civil War, more than four-fifths of the white farmers and planters had owned their land. By 1880, three principal causes had reduced this proportion to two-thirds in the cotton South. The first was the movement of white upcountry farmers from marginal land to rich lowland soils in response to the demand for labor. In the process they exchanged the ownership of poor land for the promise of higher income as renters or croppers. The second reason some white owners lost their land was lack of capital, which forced them into debts that many could ultimately pay only by yielding their land to creditors. The third reason was increased taxation during Reconstruction, which forced some white farmers into tenantry. While this was happening, many freedmen who had emerged from slavery with almost nothing managed by hard work, thrift, and luck to buy land. By 1880, about one-fifth of the black farm operators owned land. The average number of acres they owned was less than half the average owned by whites, and black-owned land was worth less per acre than white-owned land. Nevertheless for a people who had owned nothing in 1865 to have done this well by 1880 was a significant achievement, all the more remarkable because it occurred while many white farmers were losing their land. These black gains and white losses help to explain some of the white violence against blacks during Reconstruction.

Despite the promises of 1865, the national government did little to help the freedmen obtain land (see pages 546 to 549). Three agencies that did offer assistance deserve mention, however: the freedmen's aid societies, the Freedman's Bank, and the South Carolina Land Commission.

Several of the freedmen's aid societies bought land in the South and resold it in small lots to freedmen, or they served as agents for Northern philanthropists doing the same. The most ambitious effort to encourage capital accumulation among blacks was the Freedman's Savings and Trust Company, founded in 1865 by anti-slavery whites and commonly called the Freedman's Bank. The bank established branches in the South that solicited deposits from freed slaves. During the nine years of the bank's life, more than 100,000 depositors maintained accounts totaling $57 million. Thousands of freedmen used these savings to buy homes, farms, and businesses. But the story of the Freedman's Bank had an unhappy ending. Petty embezzlements from branch offices, speculative investments in Washington real estate, and high-risk loans to insiders diminished the bank's reserves. The Panic of 1873 finished what these actions had begun. The bank failed in 1874. The 61,000 remaining depositors lost an average of $20 each.

The South Carolina Land Commission also had a mixed record of achievement adulterated by fraud. Created by the legislature in 1869, the commission was capitalized at $500,000 with power to buy land and resell it at cost with liberal credit terms in plots ranging from twenty-five to one hundred acres. Although corrupt administrators siphoned off some of its funds, the commission did manage to sell land to about 14,000 buyers, most of them black. When Democrats regained control of South Carolina in 1877, they preserved the Land Commission but changed its purpose. The Republican practice of lax foreclosure on defaulted mortgages came to an end, and the state thus recovered much of the black-owned land and resold it in large blocks to whites. When the commission closed its books in 1890, it had conveyed 68,000 acres to white purchasers and 44,000 to blacks.

The Crop Lien System

Whether they acquired land of their own or remained renters or croppers, black as well as white farmers found themselves squeezed by an exploitative credit system that impoverished many of them and retarded the growth of Southern agriculture.

After the war, planters and factors tried to rebuild the antebellum marketing structure, whereby factors purchased supplies, arranged credit, and marketed the crop through mercantile firms in the South's cities. But as the development of sharecropping and tenantry multiplied the number of farm operators, the factors found it impossible to serve the hundreds of thousands of new smallholders and tenants. Nor could small-town banks provide farmers with credit as they did in the Midwest. The war wiped out the South's banks, which had been none too plentiful in the first place. Even if bank loans had been available, few Southern farmers owned sufficient property for collateral. Yet they desperately needed credit to purchase seed, fertilizer, and supplies to sustain themselves until they could harvest and sell the crop. Into this credit vacuum stepped the rural crossroads merchant, whose store advanced supplies to the farmer on credit secured by a lien on his crop.

A complex relationship developed among landowners, country merchants, and tenants. In the old plantation areas, the landowners sometimes established their own stores. Successful merchants often became landowners themselves, either through purchase or by attachment of property for debt. Thus a black tenant could experience a double indebtedness to the same person, who might be his former master: he owed part of the crop in payment for rent, and part or all of the remainder in payment for food and supplies sold on credit. If a tenant made a good crop and got a good price for it, he might come out with a profit after paying his store bill. But if cotton prices dropped, or if drought or floods or army worms or any of a dozen other potential disasters reduced his crop, he was likely to find himself more deeply in debt at the year's end than at the beginning. Even farmers who owned their land suffered this spiral of indebtedness, which gripped the South ever more tightly as time went on.

The merchant received his goods on credit from an urban wholesaler who in turn was probably financed by a Northern bank or mercantile firm. Each middleman in this chain extracted profit and interest charges. The country merchant charged a premium of 50 to 60 percent above the cash price for goods sold on credit. In effect, this credit markup became the interest rate for his loan. Some merchants succumbed to the temptation to cheat debtors by doctoring their accounts. Most black sharecroppers were illiterate and powerless to resist such exploitation. Nor could they easily shop around for better prices, since the number of country stores averaged only one to every seventy square miles. The forces of law and order lined up on the side of planters and merchants after the overthrow of Reconstruction removed Republicans from power. Black farmers became increasingly the victims of racial and economic exploitation, which by 1880 had slammed the door to further upward mobility.

In another way also, the crop lien system imposed a vicious cycle on Southern agriculture. To repay their loans, many farmers had to plant their land up to the doorsills with the most marketable cash crop—cotton. This drove cotton prices down, intensified the South's one-crop economy, and exhausted the soil. The lower the price of cotton, the more a farmer must plant in order to meet his debts. This only drove the price down further. It also reduced the amount of land devoted to food crops. Farmers who might otherwise have produced their own cornmeal and bacon became even more dependent on merchants for these supplies. Before the war, the cotton states had been almost self-sufficient in food. In the postwar decades, however, they had to import nearly half their food at a price 50 percent higher than it would have cost Southern farmers to grow their own.

Everyone, from the university agronomist down to the lowliest sharecropper, understood that only diversification could break this cruel cycle. But the crop lien system locked Southern farmers into it. "We ought to plant less [cotton and tobacco] and more of grain and grasses," said a North Carolina farmer in 1887, "but how are we to do it; the man who furnishes us rations at 50 percent interest won't let us; he wants money crop planted. . . . It is cotton! cotton! cotton! Buy everything and make cotton pay for it."[10] As a result, the output of cotton more than doubled between 1869 and 1889; but the price of cotton dropped by half, while the cost of supplies to farmers decreased by only one-fifth.

The Poverty of Southern Agriculture

The drop in the price of cotton was one reason for the general postwar decline of Southern income. A second reason was emancipation, which reduced by one-third the hours worked by the black labor force. A third reason was the destruction of Southern wealth by the war. And a fourth was the reluctance of outside capital after 1870 to invest in Southern agriculture when more attractive opportunities beckoned elsewhere. Southern agriculture remained the most labor-intensive, capital-starved, and retarded sector of the American economy. Its per capita output did not reach the prewar level for more than a half-century after Appomattox. Southern per capita income, which had been two-thirds of the Northern average in 1860, declined to only two-fifths by 1880 and remained at that level for the rest of the century. The average income of blacks, which had jumped from one-quarter to one-half of the Southern white average between 1857 and 1879, leveled off at that point and did not begin again to increase relative to white income until the mid-twentieth century. The economic promise of emancipation, like the political promise of reconstruction, remained only half-fulfilled during the generation that experienced these events.

Postwar Commercial and Industrial Developments

Because the South remained primarily agricultural, retardation in that sector slowed development of the rest of the region's economy. While the per capita production of Northern agriculture and manufacturing increased by 30 and 45 percent respectively between 1860 and 1880, Southern per capita production declined by 19 and 2 percent. Whereas in 1860 the eleven Confederate states had possessed 10 percent of the country's manufacturing capital and 30 percent of its railroad mileage, these states in 1880 possessed only 5 percent of the manufacturing capital and 17 percent of the railroad mileage.

Postwar Railroad Development

The experience of railroad construction illustrated Southern handicaps. Democrats and Republicans alike recognized the crucial role of improved transportation for regional economic growth. Both parties advocated state aid to railroad construction. Reconstruction governments granted state lands to railroads and lent them a specified amount per mile of construction or backed railroad bonds with state credit. Local governments bought railroad stock. Antebellum state and local governments had done

---

[10]Ransom and Sutch, *One Kind of Freedom,* p. 161.

the same. Yet Republican-sponsored state aid to railroads during Reconstruction became controversial because the corruption that accompanied it provided Democrats with a potent political issue. Republicans were vulnerable not only because of corruption but also because they seemed to accomplish so little. From 1865 through 1879, only 7,000 miles of new track were laid down in the South compared with 45,000 miles in the North. The main reason for this was neither corruption nor inefficiency, however, but rather the destruction of Southern railroads by the war. Most investment and construction during the early postwar years went into rebuilding. Not until 1870 were Southern railroads restored to their prewar condition. Only then could new construction go forward with vigor, but the depression following the Panic of 1873 slowed the pace.

In the North, railroad construction and operations formed the leading edge of economic development for two decades after the war. Railroads were the nation's largest nonagricultural employers. Forward and backward linkages generated new industries and technologies. During these years the iron horse switched from wood to coal as a fuel, which helped to triple coal production between 1865 and 1880.[11] Railroads also replaced iron with steel rails during the postwar decades. The mass production of steel by the new Bessemer process thereupon zoomed from an insignificant 19,000 tons in 1867 to 1,247,000 tons in 1880. The development of a refrigerated railroad car in the 1870s made possible the long-distance transportation of processed meat. This in turn gave rise to a meat-packing industry centered in Chicago and spawned the classic cattle kingdom in Texas and the plains states. As the steel rails crisscrossed these states in the 1870s and 1880s, they helped to transform this kingdom from open-range grazing and the long cattle drive to tamer and more scientific methods of livestock agriculture.

Railroading also generated important technological innovations to improve the comfort, efficiency, and safety of its own operations: George Pullman developed the sleeping car in the 1860s; George Westinghouse invented the air brake in the 1870s; several men contributed to the development of the knuckle coupler to replace the dangerous link and pin method. In 1883, the railroad industry, weary of the scheduling havoc caused by a multitude of different local times, divided the country into four time zones and created the concept of standard time that exists today.

Anti-railroad Sentiment

While railroads contributed in crucial ways to economic growth, they gave rise to problems and criticism as well. Railroad construction proceeded at a frenetic pace from 1866 to 1873. During those years, as many miles of new rail (35,000) were laid down as in all the years from 1830 through 1865. The building of the first transcontinental line across 1,800 miles of sparsely settled plains and rugged mountains excited awe and admiration. The much-photographed driving of the golden spike that linked the Union Pacific and Central Pacific at Promontory Point, Utah, on May 10,

---

[11]Coal-generated steam also replaced wood and water as the principal source of industrial power after the war.

1869, became a symbol of the age. But the construction of these and other western lines also illustrated some of the problems associated with postwar railroads. The huge amount of risk capital necessary to build tracks across forbidding terrain in advance of settlement could be provided only by the government, in the form of land grants and loans. In a race to lay down as much trackage as possible to increase its subsidy, the Union Pacific built poorly and soon had to rebuild parts of the line. The financing of Union Pacific construction also produced one of the Gilded Age's foremost scandals—the Crédit Mobilier.

This exotic-sounding corporation was formed by the Union Pacific stockholders as a construction company to build the railroad. In their capacity as directors of one company—the Union Pacific—they awarded contracts to another company—the Crédit Mobilier—of which they were themselves also directors. Not uncommon in that age, this practice reduced the financial risk in railroad construction. But in this case the government was assuming much of the risk. And some of the Union Pacific-Crédit Mobilier directors could not resist the temptation to enrich themselves by padding construction contracts.

To make sure Congress did not inquire too closely into these affairs, a Massachusetts congressman named Oakes Ames—who happened to be head of a company that sold construction equipment to the Crédit Mobilier, as well as a director of the latter and a director of the Union Pacific—sold Crédit Mobilier shares at token prices to several influential congressmen in 1867 and 1868. Writing privately that "there is no difficulty in inducing men to look after their own property," Ames placed these shares "where they will do the most good to us."[12] In 1872, a New York newspaper exposed these transactions. Public outrage compelled a congressional investigation, which produced a censure of Ames and cast shadows across the careers of several other Republican politicians. The notion of conflict of interest, previously almost nonexistent, came into its own with the publicity surrounding this affair.

By this time, 1873, railroads were under fire from several directions. The building of a second transcontinental line, the Northern Pacific, precipitated a financial panic that burst the bubble of postwar prosperity. The economy plunged into a depression from which it did not begin to recover until 1878. The hero of Union Civil War finance, Jay Cooke, became the goat of the Panic of 1873. Cooke's Philadelphia banking firm had taken over financial management of the Northern Pacific in 1869. Despite a huge land grant and loans authorized by Congress, the company had not yet laid a mile of track. Under Cooke's management, the Northern Pacific began in 1870 to build westward from Duluth. Cooke pyramided every conceivable kind of equity and loan financing to keep the funds flowing to construction crews. Other banks, railroads, and industries were doing the same in a feverish cycle of expansion and speculation. In September 1873, the pyramid of paper collapsed. Badly overextended, Cooke's firm was the first to close its doors. Like dominoes, hundreds of other banks and firms succumbed to the panic. Of the country's 364 railroads, 89 went into bankruptcy. Eighteen thousand businesses failed in two years. Unemployment mounted to 14 percent by 1876, and "hard times" settled on the country like a pall.

---

[12]Allan Nevins, *The Emergence of Modern America, 1865–1878* (New York, 1927), p. 189.

Even before the panic, railroads in the Midwest had provoked hostility from their customers. Having initially welcomed the iron horse as a transportation link to distant markets, many farmers came to curse it for its monopoly grip on the transport lifeline. A decline in war-inflated crop prices exacerbated the situation. The price of wheat dropped by half between 1867 and 1870, and corn prices dropped by half between 1869 and 1872. Freight rates, though declining, did not go down by anything like this much. Farmers blamed the railroads for their distress. The railroads lent credence to this theory by keeping rates higher in areas of no competition (most farmers lived in districts served by only one line) than in areas with competing transport. Railroad companies also owned many of the grain elevators that came under attack for cheating farmers by classifying grain below its actual quality.

Farmers organized cooperative marketing and purchasing associations to bypass middlemen in selling crops and buying supplies. The umbrella organization for many of these cooperatives was the Patrons of Husbandry, or Grange, founded in 1867. But farmers could not build their own railroads. So they did the next best thing: they went into politics, organized "anti-monopoly" parties, and elected state legislators who worked with representatives of other shipping interests to enact "Granger laws" in a half-dozen states. These laws established state railroad commissions and fixed maximum freight rates and warehouse charges. Railroads challenged the laws in court. Eight of these "Granger cases" made their way to the U.S. Supreme Court, which handed down its decision in 1877 in *Munn v. Illinois*. The Court held that states could use their police powers to regulate businesses clothed with a "public interest"—common carriers, millers, innkeepers, and so on. Although sanctioned by the highest court, some of the Granger laws nevertheless proved hard to enforce. The campaign for effective railroad regulation remained very much alive.

Labor Strife

Railroads also became the focal point of labor unrest and violence. The railroad strikes of 1877 climaxed a decade of labor ferment and four years of depression.

The real wages of workers advanced by an average of 25 percent from 1865 to 1873—that is, actual wages rose slightly while the general price index declined 20 percent from its inflationary wartime level. Most of these gains accrued to skilled workers, while the unskilled, especially women and children, continued to labor long hours for marginal pay. And although skilled workers experienced improved living standards, the continuing mechanization of many trades eroded old craft skills and provoked anxieties about a loss of independence when craftsmen who had once controlled their own trades were forced to become employees of manufacturers who owned the new machines.

These crosscurrents of prosperity and unease produced a wave of unionization. Twenty-two new national trade unions came into existence alongside the ten that had been organized before and during the war. Many of these unions joined together to form the National Labor Union in 1866. The NLU's principal goal was to cut the average ten- or eleven-hour day to eight hours—with no reduction of wages. Unions tried to achieve this goal not only by collective bargaining and strikes but also by legislation. Several labor reform parties sprang up in the more industrialized states, particularly Massachusetts, where the party's gubernatorial candidate won 13 percent of the vote in 1870. Labor's political weight secured the passage of eight-hour laws in six states. But the laws proved to be full of loopholes and lacking in enforcement machinery. In 1872, politically oriented labor spokesmen formed the National Labor Reform party. These political activities caused tensions among union leaders, many of whom feared a diversion of energies from the more practical matter of collective bargaining for better wages and working conditions. The National Labor Reform party's presidential candidate in 1872 garnered only 0.5 percent of the popular votes. In the wake of this debacle, both the Labor Reform party and the NLU collapsed.

Industrial violence discredited unions in the eyes of many middle-class Americans. In 1875, headlines featured spectacular revelations about the "Molly Maguires" in the anthracite coalfields of eastern Pennsylvania. This area constituted a microcosm of ethnic and class tensions in American society. Most of the mine owners were Scots-Irish Presbyterians; many foremen and skilled miners were Welsh and English Protestants; and most of the unskilled workers were Irish Catholics. This was a volatile mixture. The skilled miners formed the Workingmen's Benevolent Association, which had won modest gains for its members by 1873. Many Irish belonged to the Ancient Order of Hibernians, whose alleged inner circle—the Molly Maguires[13]—planned and carried out a series of assassinations and other vendettas against owners, foremen, and workers. The trials and convictions of Molly Maguires (twenty were hanged for murder) in 1875–1877 not only discredited the order but also gave mine owners the opportunity to cripple the Workingmen's Benevolent Association by invoking a repressive campaign for law and order against all labor organizations.

The violent railroad strikes of 1877 aroused even greater fears and hatreds. During the previous three years several eastern railroads, citing declining revenues, had instituted wage cuts of as much as 35 percent (during the same period retail prices declined about 8 percent). Workers organized and tried without success to resist these cuts. But when the Baltimore and Ohio on July 16, 1877, announced its third 10 percent cut, workers at two points on the line spontaneously struck and prevented trains from moving. The strike spread to other eastern lines almost as fast as the telegraph could carry the news. Workers tied up rail traffic as far west as Chicago and St. Louis. Ten states called out the militia, which in some cases fired on the strikers but in other cases fraternized with them. In response to urgent requests from state governors, President Rutherford B. Hayes sent federal troops to more than a half-dozen cities. Troops, militia, and police finally brought the situation under control by the first week of August. At least a hundred strikers, troops, and innocent bystanders lost their lives, and hundreds more were injured. In the aftermath of the strikes, some railroads partially rescinded their wage cuts. But states and cities also strengthened their riot-control forces. The specter of class conflict that appeared during these strikes frightened many Americans with its desperate vision of the future.

---

[13]Named after an anti-landlord organization in Ireland that resisted the eviction of tenants.

These developments undercut Republican Reconstruction policy in the South. Labor strife, preoccupation with economic issues, and above all the depression from 1873 to 1878 distracted public attention from concern with the plight of blacks. Northern Republicans received most of their political support from entrepreneurial interests and the middle class, who were frightened by labor militancy and violence. Many of these Republicans grew increasingly sympathetic toward Southern whites who seemed to face similar threats of social disorder from lower-class blacks. Racial and class identity between Northern and Southern middle-class whites began to drive a wedge into the political coalition of Northern white and Southern black Republicans. The economic depression plus revelations of new scandals in the Grant administration further weakened the Republican party and helped pave the way for a retreat from Reconstruction.

The Retreat from Recon-struction

People are becoming tired of . . . abstract questions, in which the overwhelming majority of them have no direct interest. The negro question, with all its complications, and the reconstruction of the Southern States, with all its interminable embroilments, have lost much of the power they once wielded.

—Washington National Republican,
January 24, 1874

Reconstruction Unravels, 1873–1876

President Grant's landslide reelection in 1872 had seemed to confirm the nation's commitment to reconstruction. A majority of voters rejected the Liberal Republican appeal for "home rule" by the South's "best people." Republicans regained their two-thirds majority in Congress and retained control of seven of the eleven ex-Confederate states. The Ku Klux prosecutions proceeded apace.

But events during Grant's second term exposed the foundation of sand upon which these successes rested. A growing Northern disenchantment with Southern Republicans was the first sign of trouble. Although the Liberal and Democratic cry against bayonet rule and carpetbag corruption had left most Republican voters unmoved in 1872, the cry grew louder in subsequent years. Most of the controversy in 1873–1874 centered on Louisiana.

The Louisiana Imbroglio

A schism among Louisiana Republicans had produced two party tickets in 1872, one of them endorsed by the Democrats. The confused outcome of the election caused bitter wrangling over who had won. Each faction created its own "returning board" to canvass the returns and throw out fraudulent votes. The regular Republicans and the Liberal Republican/Democratic coalition each convened their own legislature and inaugurated their own governor. Congress refused to count Louisiana's electoral votes for either presidential candidate. Grant spoke for most Americans when he commented that "the muddle down there is almost beyond my fathoming."[1] A federal district judge finally declared the regular Republicans to be the legitimate government. Grant ordered federal troops to enforce the ruling.

The moral force of this action was tarnished by the unsavory reputation of the regulars. Grant himself privately conceded that the carpetbag governor, William P. Kellogg, was a "first-class cuss."[2] Some staunch Republican congressmen branded the Kellogg administration a "bogus government" kept in power only by federal bayonets. Louisiana whites refused to accept its legitimacy and, in effect, formed a shadow government supported by armed paramilitary units known as White Leagues. Controlling much of the countryside, White Leaguers launched attacks on Republicans and blacks wherever the opportunity presented itself. Sheriff's posses and the state's largely black militia did little to stop such attacks, and federal troops were too few to extend their power much beyond New Orleans. The worst violence occurred at Colfax in upstate Louisiana, where on April 13, 1873, a clash between black militia and armed whites left three white men and a hundred black men dead, half of the latter killed in cold blood after they had surrendered. Although the federal government indicted seventy-two whites for their part in the Colfax massacre, only nine of these came to trial and three were convicted. The U.S. Supreme Court eventually freed them in a ruling that declared unconstitutional those portions of the 1870 enforcement act under which they had been indicted.

Tension and violence escalated during the months preceding the 1874 elections. The worst of many rural incidents occurred at Coushatta, near Shreveport, where in late August the White League murdered six Republican officeholders. Two weeks later, on September 14, New Orleans became the scene of a battle between the police and the state militia on one side and the White League on the other. Although the casualties of thirty killed and one hundred wounded were about evenly divided, the White Leaguers defeated their opponents. Commander of the state forces was none other than former Confederate General James Longstreet, who had become a Republican after the war and adjutant general of the Louisiana black militia. His forces killed twenty-one White Leaguers and wounded nineteen, but suffered eleven killed and sixty wounded (including Longstreet) in the process of being routed by the White Leaguers. After this affray Grant sent in more federal troops. They put an end to large-scale violence and ensured a peaceful election, but they could do little to prevent intimidation and economic pressure against black voters on plantations and farms.

The election of state legislators in 1874 produced a new round of disputed results and military intervention. The Democrats appeared to have won a majority in the lower house. But the Republican returning board threw out the results of several parishes on grounds of intimidation. The board certified the election of fifty-three Republicans and fifty-three Democrats, with five cases undecided and referred to the lower house itself. When this body convened on January 4, 1875, the Democrats car-

---

[1]William Gillette, *Retreat from Reconstruction 1869–1879* (Baton Rouge, 1979), p. 107.
[2]William B. Hesseltine, *Ulysses S. Grant: Politician* (New York, 1935), p. 348.

ried out a well-planned maneuver to name a speaker, swear him in, and pass a motion to seat the five Democratic claimants before the befuddled Republicans could organize to prevent it. In response, Governor Kellogg asked federal troops to eject the five Democrats who had no election certificates. Labeling the White Leaguers "banditti" who should be tried by military courts, General Philip Sheridan upheld the conduct of his field commander, who had marched into the capitol and expelled the five Democrats.

This affair provoked an uproar in Congress and in the country. Most radicals endorsed the army's action. The White Leagues deserved no quarter, said one. "Crush them, utterly, remorselessly. . . . Better military rule for forty years than the South given over to lawlessness and blood for a day." But Democrats and a good many Republicans condemned this unprecedented military invasion of a legislature. "This is the darkest day for the future of the Republican party I have ever seen," wrote Congressman James Garfield. "The Louisiana question now appears to be the mill stone that threatens to sink our party out of sight."[3] "If this can be done in Louisiana," said Senator Carl Schurz, "how long will it be before it can be done in Massachusetts and in Ohio? . . . How long before a soldier may stalk into the national House of Representatives, and, pointing to the Speaker's mace, say, 'Take away that bauble!' "[4]

The Wavering Commitment of Northern Republicans

Congress finally imposed a compromise on Louisiana by which the Democrats gained control of the lower house in return for a promise not to disturb the remaining two years of Kellogg's term as governor. This compromise brought an uneasy peace to Louisiana. But other Southern states experienced growing disruption in 1874–1875: the Brooks-Baxter "war" between rival Republican factions in Arkansas; squabbling and schisms among Republicans in South Carolina and Florida; the formation of Democratic "rifle clubs," which attacked Republicans in Mississippi. Texas came under Democratic control in 1873, Arkansas and Alabama in 1874. A growing number of Northern Republicans were willing to concede these losses without a fight. A party leader in Maine admitted that voters were "tired and sick of carpet-bag governments." Grant's postmaster general lamented that the ranks of carpetbaggers contained "not one really first class man. . . . We have got a hard lot from the South, and the people will not submit to it any longer, nor do I blame them."[5]

The Republican commitment to black rights had never been very deep. Only the party's radical wing had supported racial equality with genuine conviction, and by 1874 the convictions of some had been shaken. The revolutionary achievements of the war and reconstruction—emancipation, civil equality, Negro suffrage, black participation in Southern governments—owed more to anti-Southern than to pro-black motivation. They sprang primarily from the military exigencies of war and the political exigencies of peace rather than from a considered social purpose. With the emergence

---

[3]James M. McPherson, *The Abolitionist Legacy: From Reconstruction to the NAACP* (Princeton, 1975), pp. 46, 40–41; Brooks D. Simpson, *The Reconstruction Presidents* (Lawrence, Kansas, 1998), p. 176.

[4]*Congressional Record*, 43rd Cong., 2nd sess. (1875), 367.

[5]Vincent P. De Santis, *Republicans Face the Southern Question: The New Departure Years, 1877–1897* (Baltimore, 1959), pp. 39–40.

of new issues of vital concern to Northern voters—depression, declining farm prices, wage cuts, unemployment, monetary uncertainty—these voters lost interest in the plight of faraway blacks for whom they had never felt much sympathy in the first place. The leading Republican newspaper in Washington observed in January 1874: "People are becoming tired of . . . abstract questions, in which the overwhelming majority of them have no direct interest. The negro question, with all its complications, and the reconstruction of the Southern States, with all its interminable embroilments, have lost much of the power they once wielded." A Republican politician said the same thing more bluntly a year later: "The truth is our people are tired out with this worn out cry of 'Southern outrages'!!! Hard times & heavy taxes make them wish the 'nigger,' 'everlasting nigger,' were in ———— or Africa."[6]

Republican setbacks in the 1874 elections intensified the party's disillusionment with reconstruction. Democrats won control of the next House of Representatives for the first time in eighteen years. They scored an astonishing net gain of seventy-seven seats in the House and ten in the Senate. And these gains occurred in every region of the country. Even Massachusetts elected a Democratic governor for the first time in a generation. An important cause of this Democratic "tidal wave" was the depression. As always, voters punished the party in power during hard times. But Republican analysts attributed their losses also to voter disgust with the party's Southern policy. They began to speak of "unloading" the dead weight of carpetbag-black governments before 1876 to avoid going down to defeat in the presidential election.

The unloading policy bore its first fruit in the Mississippi state election of 1875. Democrats in the state evolved the "Mississippi Plan" for this campaign. The plan's first step was to herd all whites into the Democratic party. Democrats used social and economic pressures, ostracism, and threats to compel the 10 or 15 percent of the state's whites who still called themselves Republicans to change sides. A white Republican who succumbed to these pressures explained that the Democrats made it "too damned hot for [us] to stay out. . . . No white man can live in the South in the future and act with any other than the Democratic party unless he is willing and prepared to live a life of social isolation and remain in political oblivion."[7]

A second step in the Mississippi Plan was a relentless intimidation of black voters. Democratic newspapers adopted the slogan: "Carry the election peacefully if we can, forcibly if we must." Economic coercion proved quite effective among black laborers and sharecroppers, who were informed that if they voted Republican they could expect no further work. But this alone was not enough. Democrats organized rifle clubs and turned party headquarters into arsenals. They discovered that their best political tactic was the "riot." When Republicans gathered together—for a Fourth of July picnic, a political rally, or whatever—armed whites would provoke an incident and then open fire. One of the earliest and deadliest such affairs was the Vicksburg riot prior to a county election in December 1874, in which at least thirty-five blacks and two whites were killed. Three months later the Vicksburg Democratic newspaper declared: "*The same tactics that saved Vicksburg will surely save the State,*

---

[6] *Washington National Republican,* January 24, 1874; Hesseltine, *Grant,* p. 358.
[7] Vernon Lane Wharton, *The Negro in Mississippi, 1865–1890* (Chapel Hill, N.C., 1947), p. 183.

and no other will."[8] Democrats in other parts of the state took the advice. Several riots erupted, smaller in scale than Vicksburg's but with about the same ratio of black-to-white casualties.

In September 1875, Governor Adelbert Ames—a native of Maine, a Medal of Honor winner in the war, and one of the ablest carpetbag governors—appealed to Washington for troops to control the violence. Grant intended to comply, but his attorney general and a delegation of Ohio Republicans dissuaded him. The Mississippi Republicans would lose the election even if troops were sent, they said, and the bayonet rule issue would tip the narrow balance in the forthcoming Ohio elections to the Democrats. In a letter informing Ames of the rejection of his request for troops, the attorney general lectured the governor: "The whole public are tired out with these annual autumnal outbreaks in the South, and the great majority are now ready to condemn any interference on the part of the government. . . . Preserve the peace by the forces in your own state, and let the country see that the citizens of Mississippi, who are . . . largely Republican, have the courage to *fight* for their rights."[9]

Ames did try to organize a loyal state militia. But he had difficulty doing so, and in any case he was reluctant to use his black troops for fear of provoking an even greater bloodbath, in which blacks would be the main victims. Instead, he negotiated an agreement with Democratic leaders whereby the latter promised peace in return for a disbandment of the militia. "No matter if they are going to carry the State," said Ames wearily, "let them carry it, and let us be at peace and have no more killing."[10]

Violence nevertheless continued, though an unusual quiet prevailed on election day itself. Republicans were conspicuous by their absence from the polls in several counties. In five of the state's counties with heavy black majorities, the Republicans polled twelve, seven, four, two, and zero votes, respectively. The Mississippi Plan converted a Republican majority of 30,000 at the previous election into a Democratic majority of 30,000 at this one.

The Supreme Court and Reconstruction

As the presidential election of 1876 approached, Republican governments had been "unloaded" in every Southern state except South Carolina, Louisiana, and Florida. Events in Washington meanwhile crippled the government's ability to protect Southern Republicans even if the will to do so had still existed. The Democratic House cut the Justice Department's appropriation in order to compel a reduction of its enforcement apparatus in the South. Even more damaging were two rulings by the U.S. Supreme Court in the spring of 1876. The two cases, *U.S. v. Reese* and *U.S. v. Cruikshank,* had started their ways through lower courts in 1873 and 1874, respectively. *Reese* concerned an attempt by whites in Kentucky to prevent blacks from voting; *Cruikshank* grew out of the indictment of whites involved in Louisiana's Colfax massacre. Circuit court rulings in both cases called into question the constitutionality of the 1870 enforcement act on which the indictments were based. While the cases

---

[8]Ibid., pp. 187, 190.

[9]Richard N. Current, *Three Carpetbag Governors* (Baton Rouge, 1967), p. 88.

[10]Wharton, *Negro in Mississippi,* p. 195.

were pending before the Supreme Court, the Justice Department suspended further prosecutions under the enforcement acts. "I do not believe that any convictions can be obtained under existing circumstances," wrote the attorney general in 1875. "Criminal prosecution under these acts ought to be suspended until it is known whether the Supreme Court will hold them constitutional or otherwise."[11]

The Court's rulings, when they finally came in 1876, were less than clear-cut. The indictments in both cases were dismissed, but mainly on grounds of technical defects in certain sections of the 1870 law. Nevertheless, the thrust of Chief Justice Morrison Waite's opinions in both cases narrowed the scope of the Fourteenth and Fifteenth Amendments. These amendments, according to the Court, empowered Congress to legislate only against discrimination by states. "The power of Congress . . . to legislate for the enforcement of such a guarantee, does not extend to the passage of laws for the suppression of ordinary crime within the States. . . . That duty was originally assumed by the States; and it still remains there."[12] The effect of the *Reese* and *Cruikshank* decisions, combined with the Northern loss of will to carry out reconstruction, was to inhibit further enforcement efforts.

Government Scandals

New scandals that came to light in 1875 and 1876 also demoralized Republicans. Although these scandals did not concern the South, their spillover effect discredited Grantism everywhere and further undermined the party's willingness to uphold carpetbag government. Suspicions of malfeasance pervaded nearly every level of the federal bureaucracy. The attorney general's wife and the secretary of the interior's son were accused of accepting bribes in return for influencing the policies of these departments. Both cabinet officials resigned in 1875. In March 1876, the House impeached Secretary of War William W. Belknap for accepting bribes (transmitted through his wife) in return for appointments to army post exchanges in Western territories. President Grant, unaware of the implications of his action, accepted Belknap's resignation before his trial by the Senate, thereby allowing him to escape conviction.

The most spectacular scandal of the decade was the "Whiskey Ring." This was an intricate network of collusion among distillers and government revenue agents, centered in St. Louis, whereby the government was cheated of millions of tax dollars annually. The man chiefly responsible for exposing the ring was Secretary of the Treasury Benjamin Bristow, appointed to the office in 1874 after his predecessor had resigned under suspicion of wrongdoing. Bristow assembled a team of incorruptible agents. On May 10, 1875, Bristow's men seized distilleries and internal revenue offices in three Midwestern cities. What they found revealed a deep vein of corruption, which may have reached into the White House itself. Grant's private secretary Orville Babcock—who had negotiated the ill-fated annexation treaty with Santo Domingo in 1870—was accused of participation in the ring. Shocked, Grant instructed Bristow to "let no guilty man escape." Federal grand juries brought indictments against more than 350 distillers and government officials. Bristow himself managed the cases against 176 men and obtained convictions of 100.

---

[11]Everette Swinney, "Enforcing the Fifteenth Amendment," *Journal of Southern History,* 27 (1962), 208.
[12]25 *Fed. Cas.* 707, p. 210; 92 *U.S. Reports,* 542.

But Babcock was not among those convicted. As the prosecutions went forward, Bristow became the hero of reform Republicans—including many who had denounced Grant and opposed his reelection in 1872. The President grew convinced that Bristow's actions, and especially the approving chorus from reformers, were really an indictment of his administration. He also came to believe that Bristow's zeal was motivated by a desire for the Republican presidential nomination. His stubborn anger aroused, Grant in February 1876 made a deposition in favor of Babcock's good character for use in his secretary's trial. The jury acquitted Babcock on grounds of insufficient evidence—and perhaps also because of Grant's deposition, which the reform press condemned. Grant's last year in office began inauspiciously.

That centennial year, 1876, witnessed one of the most tense presidential elections in American history—exceeded only by the election of 1860. The multiplying revelations of corruption in high places ensured that reform would emerge as one of the campaign's main issues. And disillusionment with Grantism in the South as well as in Washington ensured that no matter who won the election, the remaining carpet-bag governments were likely to be reformed out of existence.

The Election of 1876

Democrats gave notice of their intent to capitalize on the reform issue by nominating Samuel J. Tilden of New York for president. As chairman of the state Democratic party, Tilden had earned a reform reputation for his role in overthrowing the Tweed Ring. In 1874, he won the governorship and proceeded to expose the machinations of a "Canal Ring" that had defrauded the state with padded repair contracts on the Erie Canal. Tilden ran for president in 1876 on a platform that contained the word "reform" twelve times. Only a Democratic victory, declared the platform, could save the country "from a corrupt centralism which, after inflicting upon ten States the rapacities of carpet-bag tyrannies, has honeycombed the offices of the Federal Government itself with incapacity, waste, and fraud."[13]

The Republicans did not lack for reform candidates. Chief among them was Benjamin Bristow, fresh from his triumphs over the Whiskey Ring. But the preconvention favorite was James G. Blaine of Maine, a congressman since 1862 and Speaker of the House from 1869 to 1875. Possessing a magnetic personality and political talents of a high order, Blaine nevertheless fell victim to the reform wave. While Speaker of the House, he had purchased securities of the Little Rock and Fort Smith Railroad. When these securities declined in value, Blaine sold some of them to the Union Pacific for a price well above their market value. Both railroads had received land grants from the government and therefore had a keen interest in maintaining friendly relations with a man of Blaine's influence. Blaine's enemies discovered and publicized his railroad transactions. The congressman protested innocence of impropriety, but the damage was done. The prospect of running a tainted candidate in a campaign where reform would be a prime issue caused many Republicans to

---

[13]Arthur M. Schlesinger, Jr. (ed.), *History of American Presidential Elections 1789–1968,* 4 vols. (New York, 1971), II, 1437–1440.

blanch. Although the Maine congressman held his lead through six ballots at the Republican national convention, a coalition of Bristow supporters and anti-Blaine radicals joined together on the seventh to nominate Rutherford B. Hayes.

A Civil War general and three times governor of Ohio, Hayes was a good compromise candidate. His reform credentials were strong, and he was a moderate on Southern policy.[14] The Republican platform pledged both "permanent pacification" of the South and enforcement of "exact equality in the exercise of all civil, political, and public rights."[15] Since most white Americans had become convinced by 1876 that these two goals were contradictory, the party's future Southern policy remained a puzzle. Hayes received conflicting advice on how he should treat the Southern question in his acceptance letter, which would stand as a more important statement than the platform. Carl Schurz wanted Hayes to declare that "the Constitutional rights of local self-government must be respected." But the nominee objected to this phrasing. It seemed "to smack of the bowie knife and the revolver. 'Local self-government' has nullified the Fifteenth Amendment in several States, and is in a fair way to nullify the Fourteenth and Thirteenth." Hayes's letter contained something for everybody. To those disillusioned with carpetbag rule, it promised support for "honest and capable local government" in the South. On the other hand, it affirmed that "there can be no enduring peace if the constitutional rights of any portion of the people are permanently disregarded."[16]

This did little to clarify future Republican policy. And Hayes refused to say anything more for public consumption during the campaign. Despite his statement to Schurz, however, Hayes had for several years considered "bayonet rule" a failure. A former Whig himself, he hoped that the substitution of conciliation for coercion could win erstwhile Southern Whigs over to a Republican party purged of corrupt carpetbaggers. He believed that the goodwill and influence of Southern moderates would provide better protection for black rights than federal troops could provide.

But events in the South plus the Republicans' need for a campaign issue soon caused the party to take a hard line. In Hamburg, South Carolina, a minor Fourth of July incident between a company of black militia and two white men escalated four days later into a pitched battle between the militia and 200 whites. Afterward, five captured black men were shot and killed "while attempting to escape." This affair revived some of the old Republican militancy in the North and united South Carolina's whites behind a determined effort to elect a Democratic state ticket. Armed "Red Shirt" units mobilized to "bulldoze" Republican voters in South Carolina. Governor Daniel H. Chamberlain, a Massachusetts native and an alumnus of Yale College and Harvard Law School, called on the federal government for more troops. This time the Grant administration responded positively. The President personally branded the Hamburg massacre "cruel, blood-thirsty, wanton, unprovoked . . . a repetition of the course that has been pursued in other Southern States," whereby several of those states were governed "by officials chosen through fraud and violence such as would scarcely be ac-

---

[14]The nature of "moderation" on this issue will become clear in the following pages.

[15]Schlesinger, *American Presidential Elections,* p. 1441.

[16]De Santis, *Republicans Face the Southern Question,* p. 54; Schlesinger, *American Presidential Elections,* II, 1449–1450.

credited to savages."[17] The government not only sent additional troops to trouble spots, especially in South Carolina, but also placed several thousand deputy marshals and election supervisors on duty in the South. This show of force reduced violence at the polls. But it could do little to stop the threats and assaults that took place far away from the polls. Such tactics reduced the potential Republican tally in ex-Confederate states by an estimated 250,000 votes in 1876.

Southern outrages and the alleged danger of Rebels returning to power became staples of Republican campaign oratory. Even Hayes encouraged these bloody shirt tactics. "Our strong ground is the dread of a solid South, rebel rule, etc. etc.," he wrote to a fellow Republican. "I hope you will make these topics prominent in your speeches. It leads people away from 'hard times,' which is our deadliest foe." One of the most successful practitioners of this advice was Colonel Robert Ingersoll, the famous agnostic, whose speech to a GAR[18] convention in Indianapolis in September became a classic of the bloody shirt genre:

Every state that seceded from the United States was a Democratic State. . . . Every man that tried to destroy this nation was a Democrat. Every man that loved slavery better than liberty was a Democrat. The man that assassinated Abraham Lincoln was a Democrat. . . . Every man that raised blood-hounds to pursue human beings was a Democrat. . . . Soldiers, every scar you have got on your heroic bodies was given to you by a Democrat.[19]

But many Northern voters remained more concerned with hard times than with "the everlasting Negro question." On election eve, most Republican leaders privately expressed pessimism. If the Democrats could carry every former slave state (which they were confident of doing), they would need only 47 electoral votes from the North to win the 185 necessary for victory. New York and Indiana, or New York, New Jersey, and Connecticut, would do the trick. As it happened, Tilden won all four of these states. But on the day after the election, great uncertainty prevailed about whether he had carried all the Southern states.

The Disputed Returns

From South Carolina, Louisiana, and Florida came conflicting reports of the results. On the face of the returns from Louisiana and Florida, Tilden had carried both states and the Democrats had elected the governors and a majority of both legislatures. Although South Carolina reported a narrow victory for Hayes, the Democratic gubernatorial candidate Wade Hampton had apparently won his election and carried a Democratic majority into control of the next legislature. But accusations of force and fraud raised questions about these results. In all three states, the existing Republican administrations controlled the returning boards responsible for canvassing the accuracy and fairness of the returns. Louisiana Republicans had earlier shown what such boards could do by way of turning apparent Democratic majorities into Republican

---

[17]Hesseltine, *Grant,* p. 409.

[18]Grand Army of the Republic, the organization of Union army veterans, which became an influential political pressure group.

[19]Keith I. Polakoff, *The Politics of Inertia: The Election of 1876 and the End of Reconstruction* (Baton Rouge, 1973), pp. 115, 145–146.

victories. They prepared to do so again in 1876. Such a purpose was not necessarily a subversion of justice, as Democrats charged. On the contrary, it was the Democratic subversion of justice by force and intimidation that made the returning boards necessary. To cite just one example of what confronted the Louisiana board: a parish that in 1874 had recorded 1,688 Republican votes reported only one in 1876.

Several dozen "visiting statesmen"—national leaders of both parties—descended on the three states to oversee the canvasses by their returning boards. This process took place in the glare of national publicity amid rising tensions. The stakes were no less than the presidency itself. Even without these three states, Tilden had 184 electoral votes. Hayes needed all nineteen of their electors to win; Tilden needed only one. Well-founded rumors of bribery and perjury flew about. The Louisiana returning board converted an apparent Tilden majority of 7,500 into a Hayes majority of 4,500 and certified the election of a Republican governor and legislature by throwing out or modifying the returns from several bulldozed parishes. The South Carolina board ratified the victory of the Hayes electors and also invalidated enough Democratic votes to certify Governor Chamberlain's reelection with a Republican legislative majority. In Florida, the returning board changed an apparent Tilden victory into a Hayes victory but failed to overturn the Democratic capture of the governorship and legislature.

The official returns from these states, therefore, raised Hayes's electoral vote to the 185 necessary to elect him.[20] Democrats cried fraud and challenged the results. In South Carolina and Florida, they obtained court orders to certify the transmission to the electoral college of returns showing a Tilden victory. In Louisiana, the Democratic shadow governor whom the party claimed to have elected in 1872 signed the certificate transmitting alternate returns to Washington. Democrats and Republicans in Louisiana and South Carolina each inaugurated their own governors and legislatures. Only the presence of federal troops in these states maintained the facade of Republican governments, whose real authority scarcely extended beyond the capitol buildings. From December 1876 to April 1877, whites in Louisiana and South Carolina paid taxes to the Democratic governments. While the legal controversy remained unsettled, the Democrats maintained *de facto* control of both states.

The Compromise of 1877

This unprecedented situation presented Congress with a grave dilemma. A genuinely free and fair election would probably have produced Republican victories in South Carolina and Louisiana—and for that matter in Mississippi and North Carolina as well. Tilden's national plurality of 252,000 popular votes would have been neutralized by the estimated 250,000 Southern Republicans who had failed to vote because they were afraid to do so. On the other hand, Republican frauds may have canceled Democratic intimidation in Florida, thereby robbing Tilden of a legitimate majority in that state.

---

[20]One electoral vote from Oregon was contested on a technicality that made a Republican elector ineligible. But no one doubted that Hayes had carried Oregon. The Democratic challenge there was a diversionary tactic.

The Constitution offered no clear guidance in this crisis. The Twelfth Amendment states only that the electoral college shall transmit its votes to "the President of the Senate" (normally the vice president of the United States) "who shall, in the presence of the Senate and the House of Representatives, open all certificates and the votes shall then be counted." This was of little help. *Who* should count them? Since 1864, Congress had operated under the twenty-second joint rule, which required the concurrent vote of both houses to count the electoral votes of a state. But this rule had expired in 1875, and Congress—divided between a Republican Senate and a Democratic House—had failed to agree on its renewal. The constitutional provision requiring the House to choose a president (and the Senate a vice president) if no candidate had a majority of electoral votes was not applicable, for it could be invoked only after the votes had been counted. In 1876, the issue was how to count them.

While Congress grappled with this problem, passions in the country rose toward the danger level. Rumors circulated among Republicans of neo-Copperhead rifle clubs in both North and South that were reported to be preparing to inaugurate Tilden by force if necessary. Democrats held mass meetings and made angry speeches. Editor Henry Watterson of the *Louisville Courier-Journal* called for 100,000 Democrats to march on Washington for a demonstration. Talk of a new civil war abounded. President Grant quietly strengthened the army garrison in Washington.

But little substance underlay all the rumors and rhetoric. Few Southerners had any taste for another civil conflict. Congressman James Garfield reported to Hayes that "the leading southern Democrats in Congress, especially those who were old Whigs, are saying that they have seen war enough, and don't care to follow the lead of their northern associates who . . . were 'invincible in peace and invisible in war.' " Tilden himself discouraged Democratic militancy. "It will not do to fight," he told hotheaded partisans. "We have just emerged from one civil war, and it will not do to engage in another civil war; it would end in the destruction of free government."[21]

The Electoral Commission

Many interest groups pressed Congress for a compromise solution. Business spokesmen in particular pointed out that a prolonged crisis would only plunge the economy into a deeper depression. Congress created a joint committee to work on the problem. After sifting through dozens of proposals, the committee recommended the creation of an electoral commission to arbitrate the disputed returns. The commission's decisions would be final unless overruled by both houses of Congress. The commission was to contain fifteen members: five senators (three Republicans and two Democrats); five representatives (three Democrats and two Republicans); and five Supreme Court justices. In theory the latter would be impartial; but in fact two would be Democrats, two Republicans, and the fifth was expected to be David Davis of Illinois, a one-time Lincoln associate who had become a Liberal Republican in 1872 and was now an independent. Because Democrats expected Davis to side with them, they supported the idea of a commission with greater enthusiasm than did the

---

[21]C. Vann Woodward, *Reunion and Reaction: The Compromise of 1877 and the End of Reconstruction*, rev. ed. (New York, 1956), p. 23; Harry Barnard, *Rutherford B. Hayes and His America* (Indianapolis, 1954), p. 343.

Republicans. Democratic congressmen and senators voted 150 to 18 in favor of a commission, while Republicans opposed it by 84 to 57. President Grant signed the bill creating the commission on January 29, 1877.

Suddenly, however, news from Illinois sent a bolt of dismay through the Democratic camp. A coalition of Democrats and Greenbackers in the legislature elected Davis to the U.S. Senate. This action seems to have resulted from a miscalculation by certain Democratic leaders, including Tilden's nephew. They believed that such a gesture would cement Davis to the party and ensure his vote on the electoral commission. Instead, Davis accepted the senatorship (which he saw as a steppingstone to the presidency) and declined appointment to the commission. Since the Supreme Court contained no additional Democrats, the fifth Court appointee became the independent-leaning Justice Joseph Bradley.

The first case to come before the commission was Florida's. Democrats maintained that the state returning board had illegally reversed the outcome of the election there. Republicans replied that the certificate of election signed by the governor was the only valid one, and that the commission could not go behind these official returns unless it also went behind the local returns to investigate every aspect of the balloting. This could hardly be done before March 4, when the next president must be sworn in. The commission divided 7 to 7 according to party affiliation, with Justice Bradley yet to be heard from. An immense responsibility rested on his shoulders. On February 9, Bradley cast the deciding vote—to accept the official Florida returns.

Although Democrats cried foul and hinted darkly that Bradley had been bribed (no evidence supports this suspicion), the die was cast. If the commission would not go behind the returns from Florida, it would not do so for Louisiana or South Carolina. Tilden privately gave up and began to plan a European trip. On February 16, the commission endorsed the Hayes electoral votes from Louisiana, and on February 28 it did the same with respect to South Carolina. According to the legislation that established the commission, both houses of Congress would have to reject its rulings to overturn them. The Senate promptly approved them. But some House Democrats were not yet ready to give up. They conceived the idea of a filibuster to delay the formal completion of the count beyond March 4. Since neither candidate would then have a majority, the House could invoke its constitutional power to elect a president, and choose Tilden.

Negotiations behind the Scenes

While these ominous proceedings went forward in public, informal negotiations of various sorts occurred behind the scenes. The most important of these took place between Republican associates of Hayes and some of the more moderate Southern Democrats. The latter had a weak hand, but they played it with the unblinking bluff of an expert gambler. In any real showdown, the Democrats could scarcely hope to prevail. Republicans controlled the Senate, the Supreme Court, the presidency, and the army. Equally important, they still controlled the North's reservoir of patriotism. Once the electoral commission had made its decisions, Republicans could brand any resistance as insurrection. Northern Democrats, who had barely begun to shed their wartime Copperhead image, could scarcely afford to come out on the wrong side again in a national crisis. This helps to explain the refusal of Tilden and most other

Eastern Democrats to approve any scheme to resist Hayes's inauguration. Deserted by Northern allies, many Southern Democrats began to think about making the best possible bargain with the Republicans. Southerners who had once been Whigs were especially inclined toward this course. They cautiously established contacts with Hayes Republicans.

The latter were open to such contacts. Hayes had pretty much committed himself to the reform wing of the party. He intended to carry out civil service reform with vigor. He also hoped to rebuild the Southern Republican party on the foundations of Whiggery—as Lincoln had hoped to do a dozen years earlier. The interests of Northern Whiggish Republicans and Southern Whiggish Democrats intersected at several points. The latter wanted federal land grants and loans for the Texas and Pacific Railroad. They wanted federal subsidies to help rebuild the Mississippi River levees and to carry out other internal improvements. Most Northern Democrats opposed such subsidies, but the Republicans might support them in return for Southern acquiescence in Hayes's inauguration.

Southern Democrats who talked with Hayes's lieutenants also raised the possibility of a cabinet appointment and of federal patronage for themselves. Above all, they wanted to know what Hayes would do about Louisiana and South Carolina. Would he use the army to uphold the carpetbag regimes, or would he withdraw the troops and allow the Democrats who already governed these states in fact to do so in law as well? Hayes let it be known that he sympathized with all of these Southern aspirations—indeed, they coincided with his own views. In return, he asked only for promises of fair treatment of the freedmen and respect for their rights. The informal conversations also raised the possibility that enough Southern Democrats might vote with the Republicans to enable the latter to control the next House of Representatives (in which the Democrats would have a nominal majority of only ten or twelve).

Nothing as formal as a "deal" was concluded in any of these matters. But on both sides a series of unwritten "understandings" had emerged by late February. The threat of a filibuster to delay the electoral count enabled Southerners to nail down some of these understandings a little more firmly than they might otherwise have been able to do. With more than half of the Northern as well as Southern Democrats now refusing to support a prolonged filibuster, the delaying tactics collapsed, the count was completed, and Hayes was peacefully inaugurated.

So far as it was in his power to do so, Hayes carried out his part of the understandings. His cabinet choices foreshadowed the administration's new policy of reform and conciliation. They included Secretary of State William M. Evarts, one of Andrew Johnson's defense attorneys in the impeachment trial; Secretary of the Interior Carl Schurz, the leading Liberal Republican in 1872; and Postmaster General David M. Key, an ex-Confederate Tennessee Democrat, who promptly began to dispense some of the rich patronage of his office to Southern moderates. The administration lent its support to numerous internal improvements appropriations for the South. The section received more federal money in 1878 than ever before. Although the Hayes administration in the end did not sanction federal aid for construction of the Texas and Pacific Railroad, it did encourage the building, without subsidies, of the Southern Pacific, which finally linked the old South to the new Southwest in 1881. Most important, in return for pledges from the Democratic gubernatorial claimants in South Carolina and Louisiana to uphold black rights, in April 1877 Hayes ordered the federal troops withdrawn from the capitals. The Republican governments in those states immediately collapsed. Along with the other nine ex-Confederate states, South Carolina and Louisiana were now "redeemed."

Old-guard radicals, Blaine Republicans, and most abolitionists denounced Hayes's withdrawal of the troops as a betrayal of the freedmen. Benjamin Wade declared: "To have emancipated those people and then to leave them unprotected would be a crime as infamous as to have reduced them to slavery when they were free." With his old-time vehemence, William Lloyd Garrison excoriated Hayes's "policy of compromise, of credulity, of weakness, of subserviency, of surrender," a policy that sustained "might against right . . . the rich and powerful against the poor and unprotected." As for Southern promises to respect black rights, said Wendell Phillips, "the whole soil of the South is hidden by successive layers of broken promises. To trust a Southern promise would be fair evidence of insanity."[22]

But these voices could scarcely be heard above the national sigh of relief that the electoral crisis was over. Most Americans wanted no more reconstruction if it meant military intervention in state affairs. "I have no sort of faith in a local government which can only be propped up by foreign bayonets," wrote the editor of the *New York Tribune* in April 1877. "If negro suffrage means that as a permanency then negro suffrage is a failure."[23] In truth, Hayes had little choice but to remove the troops. Such action had been foreshadowed by Grant's refusal to intervene in the Mississippi election of 1875 and by the Supreme Court's rulings in the *Reese* and *Cruikshank* cases in 1876. The House of Representatives had already cut Justice Department appropriations and now threatened to withhold War Department appropriations if the army was again used in the South—at a time when Indian troubles on the frontier following Custer's disaster at Little Big Horn in 1876 and railroad strikes in the North in 1877 were making urgent demands on the army. Even prominent black leaders, most notably Frederick Douglass, endorsed Hayes's course. "What [is] called the President's policy," said Douglass in May 1877, "might rather be considered the President's necessity. . . . Statesmen often [are] compelled to act upon facts as they are, and not as they would like to have them."[24]

Although no Southern Democrats deserted their party to help the Republicans organize the House, the rest of the Compromise of 1877 seemed to be working out. Quiet fell on the region below the Potomac for the first time in a generation. In September 1877, Hayes proudly stated: "There has been no other six months since the war when there have been so few outrages committed upon the colored people." A year later, Hayes's principal political adviser still insisted that "it is only a question of time when there will arise a really Republican party in the South numbering in its ranks the intelligence, the culture, the wealth, the Protestantism of the Southern white people, who will give protection and support to the colored people."[25]

---

[22]Hans L. Trefousse, *The Radical Republicans: Lincoln's Vanguard for Racial Justice* (New York, 1969), p. 469; McPherson, *Abolitionist Legacy,* pp. 89–90.

[23]De Santis, *Republicans Face the Southern Question,* p. 113.

[24]McPherson, *Abolitionist Legacy,* p. 93.

[25]Ibid., p. 95; Michael Les Benedict, *The Fruits of Victory: Alternatives in Restoring the Union, 1865–1877* (Latham, Md., 1986), p. 78.

The New South

We have sown towns and cities in the place
of theories, and put business above politics.
We have challenged your spinners in
Massachusetts and your ironmakers in
Pennsylvania. . . . We have established
thrift in city and country. We have fallen in
love with work.

—Henry Grady,
editor of the Atlanta Constitution, 1886

The Persistence of the Southern Question

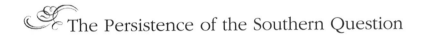

The 1878 congressional elections produced consternation among many supporters of Hayes's conciliatory Southern policy—including the President himself. Violence and intimidation characterized the campaigns in South Carolina and Louisiana despite their governors' pledges of fair dealing. Throughout the lower South, the Republican share of the vote in 1878 dropped sharply from the previous election. Only 62 of 294 counties with black majorities went Republican, compared with 125 two years earlier. Several black counties recorded not a single Republican ballot. Hayes's attempts to attract ex-Whig Southern Democrats into the Republican party produced no discernible results. The President expressed his disappointment in a newspaper interview. He had launched a new Southern policy, said Hayes, "with an earnest desire to conciliate the Southern leaders . . . and to soften the asperities of political strife." But now, he continued, *"I am reluctantly forced to admit that the experiment was a failure.* The first election of importance held since it was attempted has proved that fair elections with free suffrage . . . in the South are an impossibility."[1]

What could be done about this? Hayes promised "the most determined and vigorous action."[2] Federal marshals arrested twenty-two South Carolina whites for violations of federal election laws. Republicans called for new legislation to enforce the

---

[1]Stanley P. Hirshson, *Farewell to the Bloody Shirt: Northern Republicans and the Southern Negro, 1877–93* (Bloomington, Ind., 1962), p. 49.

[2]Ibid.

Fifteenth Amendment. They urged Congress to refuse to seat Southern representatives elected by violence and fraud. But all of this was futile. No Southern jury would convict whites indicted for electoral crimes. The Democrats already controlled the House, and after the 1878 elections they led the next Senate as well. No new enforcement legislation could be passed, and Democrats made clear their intent to block any presidential initiative under the existing laws. Five times in 1879 they attached riders to vital appropriations bills repealing what was left of the 1870–1871 enforcement acts. Five times Hayes vetoed these bills, even though some governmental operations ground to a halt as funds ran out. The Democratic congressional majority finally backed down. But the enforcement acts nevertheless remained a dead letter.

By 1879, even Republican radicals had come to recognize the futility of government action in the South under existing circumstances. Their only hope was to regain control of Congress. A solid North must outvote the solid South. How would this help Southern blacks? Northern solidarity, said a Republican newspaper, would teach Southern whites that they could not control the government by "intimidation, bulldozing [and] ballot-box stuffing. . . . We are not going to let any party rule this country that will not deal justly by the political rights of the Negro."[3]

During the 1879–1880 session of Congress, Republicans unfurled the bloody shirt in preparation for the 1880 presidential election. They made much of the "Rebel Brigadiers" who now ruled Congress. Southerners once again constituted a majority of Democratic congressmen. More than 90 percent of the Southern congressmen had served in the Confederate armed forces or government. Eighteen Confederate generals sat in Congress, a Confederate editor was secretary of the Senate, and the commander of a Confederate prisoner of war camp where, as one Republican editor put it, "many a poor boy met an inglorious death of starvation and disease," was chairman of the Senate Pensions Committee. It was enough to alarm any Union veteran who thought he had fought on the winning side. The Republican party, with the help of the Grand Army of the Republic, prepared to capitalize on this alarm in the 1880 election.

The Presidential Election of 1880

After remaining deadlocked through thirty-five ballots, the Republican national convention nominated the Ohio dark horse James Garfield for president on the thirty-sixth. A self-made man (like Lincoln, he was born in a log cabin), Garfield had risen to the rank of major general during the war and was elected in 1863 to Congress, where he had served until nominated for president in 1880. In an attempt to break the Republican monopoly on the patriotism issue, the Democrats—for the first and only time—also nominated a Union general, Winfield Scott Hancock, hero of Gettysburg.

Republicans portrayed Hancock as a figurehead candidate, a captive of the Southern Democrats with whom he had sympathized since the war. A GAR circular insisted that "a thousand Union Generals . . . could not palliate . . . the terrors and the torture, the bloodshed and massacre, with which the Democratic party has prepared, and again sets in the field, a Solid South against the Soldiers and Sailors of the pa-

---

[3]*Independent,* December 12, 1878.

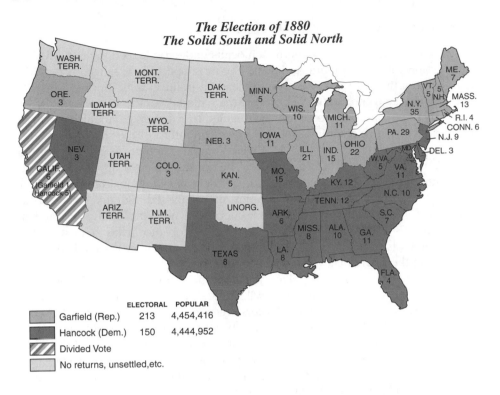

The Election of 1880
The Solid South and Solid North

	ELECTORAL	POPULAR
Garfield (Rep.)	213	4,454,416
Hancock (Dem.)	150	4,444,952
Divided Vote		
No returns, unsettled, etc.		

triotic North." Republicans did not hesitate to hit below the belt; a cartoon by Thomas Nast showed Hancock contemplating the graves of Confederate soldiers killed at Gettysburg, with the caption: "The 'Silent (Democratic) Majority.' General Hancock will miss them on Election Day."[4]

The Republican "solid North" strategy paid off. While Hancock carried every former slave state, Garfield carried all but three Northern states—all small ones—and thereby won a comfortable majority of electoral votes despite his razor-thin plurality of only ten thousand popular votes out of more than nine million cast. The Republicans won about 41 percent of the popular vote in the South, the same as in 1876.

But the Southern states with the largest percentages of black voters recorded sharp declines in their Republican totals. The Republican platform had pledged to protect all voters against "terrorism, violence or fraud." Such pledges were easier made than fulfilled. Although the party regained control of the House by a narrow margin, the balance of power in the Senate was held by a single independent elected from Virginia, William Mahone. This suggested a new Republican Southern strategy. President Hayes's effort to win former Whigs into the Republican party having failed, President-elect Garfield toyed with the idea of promoting coalitions between Republicans and the emerging independent parties in several Southern states. After Garfield's assassination in midsummer 1881, his successor, Chester Arthur, did his best to carry out such a coalition policy.

---

[4]Mary R. Dearing, *Veterans in Politics: The Story of the G. A. R.* (Baton Rouge, 1952), pp. 257–258, 262–263.

The Readjuster Movement in Virginia

After redeeming their states, Southern Democrats had experienced internal divisions over economic and other nonracial issues. The most spectacular schism occurred in Virginia, where the state debt became the leading political issue during the 1870s. Saddled with a large antebellum debt (twice the national per capita average in 1870) contracted at high interest rates, Virginia struggled to maintain payments despite the wartime destruction of resources and the loss of one-third of the state's white population resulting from the detachment of West Virginia. Attempts to get West Virginia to assume a share of the debt broke down. The conservative "Bourbons" who ruled Virginia during the 1870s insisted that the entire debt must be repaid in order to preserve the state's honor and credit. To do this, they imposed high taxes and slashed public services, especially schools. "Free schools are not a necessity," insisted the governor in 1878. "Our fathers did not need free schools to make them what they were. . . . [Schools] are a luxury . . . to be paid for, like any other luxury, by the people who wish their benefits."[5]

Such sentiments sparked a rebellion that split the Democrats into "Funders" and "Readjusters." Under the leadership of William Mahone, a railroad promoter and a former Confederate general, the Readjusters organized a separate party in 1879. Following the example of several other states, the Readjusters proposed to reduce the interest rate on Virginia's debt[6] and to repudiate that portion of it which should fairly have been borne by West Virginia. This would not only reduce ruinous taxes, said Readjusters, but would liberate the state's resources and energy for productive enterprises. It would increase the state's human capital—both black and white—by restoring the public schools. With support from black as well as white voters, the Readjusters in 1879 won control of the Virginia legislature. In 1881, they elected the governor and sent Mahone to the U.S. Senate.

The Readjusters fulfilled their promises. They scaled down the debt by one-third and reduced the interest rate from 6 to 3 percent. And they tripled the number of schools, teachers, and pupils. Black Virginians were prominent participants and beneficiaries in these actions. Readjuster/Republican coalitions elected several blacks to the legislature. One-third of the delegates to the 1881 Readjuster convention were blacks. The Readjuster government abolished the whipping post as a punishment for crime (a legacy of slavery), enrolled blacks as jurors, and repealed the poll tax, which had kept many poor men of both races from voting. Mahone also moved to consummate a formal merger with Virginia's Republican party.

This development projected Virginia's politics onto the national scene. Although some Northern Republicans expressed concern about the fiscal ethics of debt readjustment, most welcomed an alliance with a movement that shared progressive Republican values and promised to break the solid South. The debt question, said a Massachusetts radical, "has assumed in this movement a position of secondary im-

---

[5]Carl N. Degler, *The Other South: Southern Dissenters in the Nineteenth Century* (New York, 1974), p. 271.

[6]The deflationary trend added one or two percentage points per year to nominal interest rates in the 1870s and 1880s. The cumulative impact of deflation could therefore add 15 or 20 percent to the nominal interest rate after ten years. This burden produced widespread movements, especially during the 1873–1878 depression, to renegotiate interest rates downward on state debts.

portance; the real principles on which the party plumes itself are equal rights, a fair ballot, an honest count, and a thorough system of public education." Republicans liked the sound of Readjuster assertions that Virginia must abandon the "dead customs and effete traditions" of the old South and align itself with the "great and growing States of the North" to develop the industrial and human resources of the new South. An Indiana Republican praised Mahone as "the one *statesman*" the South had produced since the war. "He seems to have grasped the great fact that the South, with her great natural wealth, can be and ought to be made as rich, as powerful, and as prosperous as the most favored part of the country."[7] Senator Mahone voted with the Republicans to enable them to organize the Senate in 1881. In return, President Arthur gave Mahone control of the federal patronage in Virginia and sanctioned the creation of a Republican/Readjuster coalition there.

Readjuster success in Virginia inspired a proliferation of independent movements in other Southern states. Arthur used patronage to encourage these movements also. But none of them matched the Readjuster achievements. Moreover, while these movements paid lip service to black political rights, their voting constituencies consisted mainly of poor white farmers, who were not noted for sympathy with blacks. Even in Virginia, the race issue brought down the Republican/Readjuster coalition in 1883. Appealing to the traditions of white supremacy and white unity, Democrats denounced Readjusters as latter-day scalawags and exploited an election-eve race riot in Danville to sweep the legislative elections on the color-line issue. Mahone thereafter became leader of the Virginia Republican party, which came close to carrying the state in 1888. But independent parties elsewhere died out, and the South remained solid for the Democrats.

꧁ Ideology and Reality in the New South

With recovery from the depression after 1878, the American economy leaped forward. Steel production quadrupled during the 1880s. Railroad construction crews laid down 75,000 miles of new track during the decade, nearly doubling the 86,000 miles in existence at its beginning. Rapid industrial growth called forth a similar growth in the membership of labor unions. The Knights of Labor enrolled an estimated 700,000 members in 1886. The American Federation of Labor was founded the same year. Several major strikes and the Haymarket Square bombing in Chicago produced in 1886 the highest level of labor violence since the railroad strikes of 1877. Despite this, the economic mood of the 1880s remained optimistic.

The Ideology of the "New South"

The South shared this expansive mood. According to legend, the Democratic loss of the 1880 presidential election convinced forward-looking Southerners that they could not achieve salvation through politics. So they rolled up their sleeves and went to work to build a "New South" of commerce, cotton mills, and foundries. Like all legends, this

---

[7] *Boston Commonwealth*, June 11, 1881; James Tice Moore, *Two Paths to the New South: The Virginia Debt Controversy, 1870–1883* (Lexington, Ky., 1974), pp. 85–86; Degler, *Other South*, p. 287.

one embodied some truth. A new spirit of enterprise quickened Southern life in the 1880s. Prominent journalists and industrial promoters emerged as spokesmen for an ideology of economic modernization modeled on the Yankee example.

The New South creed was not entirely new in the 1880s. Several antebellum Southerners had futilely urged economic diversification and industrialization. After the war, many of the South's leading thinkers attributed the Confederacy's defeat to its lack of a modernized economy. Having lost the war, the South must imitate the victors. *"We have got to go to manufacturing to save ourselves,"* declared *DeBow's Review* in 1867.[8] Economic depression and a preoccupation with reconstruction politics delayed the emergence of a full-blown Southern ideology of modernization. But in the 1880s, that ideology came into its own.

Henry Grady, editor of the *Atlanta Constitution,* became the foremost proponent of the New South ideology. What the region needed, said Grady in 1880, was "fewer stump-speakers and more stump-pullers. . . . The defeat of Hancock will be a blessing in disguise if it only tends to turn our people from politics to work." This emphasis on the "gospel of work as the South's great need" became the litany of New South prophets. By 1886, Grady could say, in a speech to Northern businessmen which achieved instant fame, that the New South creed had already paid off: "We have sown towns and cities in the place of theories, and put business above politics. We have challenged your spinners in Massachusetts and your ironmakers in Pennsylvania. . . . We have established thrift in city and country. We have fallen in love with work."[9]

The Industries of the New South

Some real achievements lay behind Grady's rhetoric. Under the slogan "Bring the Cotton Mills to the Cotton," the Southern textile industry expanded rapidly during the 1880s. Along the piedmont from Virginia to Alabama, new cotton mills and company towns to house their workers sprang up. The labor force—40 percent women, 25 percent children, and almost entirely white—worked for wages about half as high as those in New England. The number of Southern cotton spindles increased ninefold between 1880 and 1900. In 1880, the South possessed only 5 percent of the country's textile-producing capacity; in 1900, the section possessed 23 percent, and it was well on the way to surpassing New England by 1930. Most of the initial capital for the Southern textile industry came from the South itself. But after 1893 an increasing amount came from the North, as New England mill owners began to see the advantages of relocating in the low-wage, nonunion Southern climate.

Another Southern industry developed from a regional agricultural crop—tobacco. Southerners provided most of the capital for this industry also. The reigning genius was James B. Duke of Durham, North Carolina. Duke's entrepreneurial talents and tactics rivaled those of John D. Rockefeller. In 1890, Duke incorporated the American Tobacco Company, which for a time achieved a virtual monopoly of tobacco manufacturing until broken up by Supreme Court decree in 1911. Unlike textile mills, tobacco factories employed substantial numbers of blacks.

---

[8]Paul M. Gaston, *The New South Creed: A Study in Southern Mythmaking* (New York, 1970), p. 25.

[9]Ibid., pp. 42, 108; Joel Chandler Harris (ed.), *Life of Henry W. Grady, Including His Writings and Speeches* (New York, 1890), p. 88.

Two New South industries dependent on Northern capital were railroads and iron. During the 1880s, the pace of railroad construction in the South exceeded the national average. In 1886, Southern railroads shifted from their traditional 5-foot gauge to the national standard of 4 feet 8 1/2 inches. This change integrated the Southern lines into the national network. It also served as a symbol of increasing Northern domination of Southern railroads. By 1890, Yankees constituted a majority of directors in companies that controlled two-thirds of Southern mileage. Northern control increased still more when the depression of 1893–1897 compelled the reorganization and consolidation of many Southern lines by Northern banking firms.

The Southern iron industry experienced spectacular growth in the 1880s. Most of the expansion was concentrated in northern Alabama, where the proximity of coal, limestone, and ore made the new city of Birmingham "the Pittsburgh of the South." In 1880, the former slave states had produced only 9 percent of the nation's pig iron; by 1890, that proportion had more than doubled. Northern capital figured prominently in this growth: during the 1880s, according to one observer, "the Federal brigadier was almost as prominent in the iron world of the South as the Confederate brigadier was in the political world at Washington."[10] Northern domination of the industry intensified in 1907, when U.S. Steel gained control of Tennessee Iron and Coal, the South's largest company.

Northern Perceptions of the New South

Southern proponents of industrialization welcomed this invasion of Yankee dollars. The South was still too poor to generate sufficient capital itself for heavy industry. The industrial "expositions" held in various Southern cities during the 1880s were designed primarily to attract the favorable attention of Northern and European investors. The rhetoric of some Yankee prophets of a New South outdid even that of their Southern counterparts. Edward Atkinson of Massachusetts, a textile manufacturer and antebellum Free Soiler, said in 1881 that the new Southern spirit of "vigor and energy" was "creating new conditions" of prosperity and racial comity that would soon excise the "cancer of slavery" and guide the New South "in the direction of peace, order, stability, and prosperity." In 1886, William D. Kelley of Pennsylvania, a former radical Republican congressman, published a book entitled *The Old South and the New* that pulled out all the stops. "Wealth and honor are in the pathway of the New South," wrote Kelley. "Her impulses are those which are impelling the advance of civilization. . . . She is the coming El Dorado of American adventure."[11]

Atkinson and Kelley represented a significant slice of Republican opinion in the 1880s. Both had been active in the antislavery movement. Both had supported a radical reconstruction policy. Political reconstruction having fallen short of unqualified success, however, they now placed their hopes in economic reconstruction. As they saw it, the modernization of the North had raised the standard of living for all classes and had promoted a progressive ethos; they hoped that Southern modernization would improve material conditions for both races, soften racial asperities, and give blacks leverage for upward mobility. The South might even become like New England, said a Boston radical. "With railroads and telegraphs traversing its domain

---

[10]C. Vann Woodward, *Origins of the New South, 1877–1913* (Baton Rouge, 1951), p. 128.

[11]James M. McPherson, *The Abolitionist Legacy: From Reconstruction to the NAACP* (Princeton, 1975), pp. 108–109.

should go schools, factories, shops, a better family and community feeling." In 1885, a Massachusetts Republican concluded that "work and money have brought into vogue new ideals, new tests and new ambitions in Southern society. Capital is, after all, the greatest agent of civilization . . . and the two races will move kindly together when wealth is more evenly divided between them."[12]

Education in the New South

The South experienced significant educational as well as economic growth in the 1880s. Although black higher education was still supported mainly by Northern missionary societies, several Southern states established their own black colleges or industrial institutes during the decade. Virginia provided some state aid to Hampton Institute, while Alabama appropriated a modest sum to help Booker T. Washington found Tuskegee Institute. The number of black students enrolled in secondary schools and colleges doubled during the 1880s, while enrollments in black elementary schools grew faster than the population.

But in many respects the Southern educational landscape remained bleak. In 1880, 20 percent of the whites and more than 70 percent of the blacks were still illiterate. Fewer than three-fifths of the white children and two-fifths of the black children of school age attended school. The South spent less than one-third as much per pupil as the North. In the rural South, the average school term was three months or less. "The typical Southern free school," wrote a sympathetic Northern observer in 1888, "is kept in a log house, with dirt or puncheon floor, without desks or blackboards." Millions of children were growing up without adequate schooling. "It is desperately important that those children should be educated. The North is rich and can educate its children. The South is poor and cannot."[13]

From this concern arose a movement for federal aid to education, with the funds to be apportioned among the states on the basis of illiteracy. This would channel three-quarters of the funds to the South. The idea of federal support for Southern schools had persisted since 1867, when Senator Charles Sumner had introduced legislation for this purpose. In 1872, the House had passed a bill to appropriate the proceeds from public land sales for public schools. But the Senate had failed to act, and the economic depression discouraged further efforts during the 1870s. The revelation by the 1880 census that more than six million Americans aged ten or older could not read and write revived the movement. The 1880 Republican platform pledged the party to work for federal aid. Surviving abolitionists urged generous appropriations for Southern education. "The North," said an antislavery veteran, "shared the responsibility for the sin of slavery, is responsible for emancipation and enfranchisement, and is therefore under a triple obligation to share the duty and the burden of equipping the emancipated Negro race for the duties of citizenship."[14]

In 1884, the Senate passed a bill introduced by Henry W. Blair of New Hampshire to grant the states $77 million (about $1.6 billion at 2000 prices) over seven years for public schools. The money would be apportioned on the illiteracy ratio, and each

---

[12]Ibid.

[13]Ibid., p. 130.

[14]*Independent*, June 11, 1891.

state would be required to match it with additional appropriations to its own school funds. Lower-South Democrats—whose states would benefit most—as well as Republicans voted for this bill. But the House, controlled by the Democrats from 1883 to 1889, refused to pass it. The Democratic opposition sprang from the party's commitment to states' rights, from fears that the bill would insert an opening wedge for the revival of Reconstruction, and from the suspicions of low-tariff Democrats that the measure was a protectionist trick to maintain high duties.[15] Although the Republican Senate passed the Blair bill a second time in 1886 and a third in 1888, the margin of passage was reduced in 1888, and the House as usual refused to consider it. When Blair brought his bill before the Senate a fourth time in 1890, three Republicans and four Southern Democrats switched their previous affirmative votes to negative, thereby killing the measure for good. Thus ended one of the more promising efforts to improve Southern schools.

Politics in the New South

Nevertheless, the mood of New South prophets both above and below the Potomac remained upbeat. Editor George William Curtis of *Harper's Weekly* in 1886 expressed the widely shared conviction that "political differences and the friction of races are yielding to the beneficent touch of healthy industrial enterprise."[16] Although more than a little wishful thinking underlay this belief, some evidence existed to support it. Racial violence had declined since the heyday of the Klan and the White League. The conservative white supremacists who ruled the South during the 1880s were hardly enlightened by modern standards, but their racism was less virulent than that of the next generation of Southern politicians. Although never allowed to exercise as much power as during Reconstruction, blacks continued to vote and to hold office in considerable numbers during the 1880s and into the 1890s. The Republican share of the two-party vote in the former slave states remained at about 40 percent in the presidential elections of 1884 and 1888. Republican strength in the upper South was impressive: besides the successful coalition with Readjusters in Virginia, the party won the Tennessee governorship when the Democrats split on the state debt issue in 1880, and it came within a whisker of winning the North Carolina governorship in 1884. At least one Southern black man served in every Congress from 1881 to 1901. Hundreds of blacks were elected to state legislatures during these years, and thousands to local offices. The complete suppression of black political participation came around 1900, not when federal troops ceased to enforce reconstruction in 1877.

But this point must not be overstated. Wherever black Republican majorities had the potential to exercise real power that might affect state politics, the Democrats took steps to negate that power. In the lower South, the suppression of Republican votes by intimidation and chicanery prevailed from the 1870s on. In a fair vote, at least South Carolina, Mississippi, and Louisiana would probably have gone Republican. But

---

[15] During most of the 1880s, the federal budget ran a surplus. Most Democrats wished to lower the tariff (a major form of taxation then) in order to bring the government's receipts down to the level of its expenditures. Most Republicans opposed tariff reduction. Democrats suspected that one reason for Republican support for federal aid to education was to eliminate the budget surplus and thereby to blunt the movement for lower tariffs.

[16] *Harper's Weekly*, December 25, 1886.

these were precisely the states that recorded the smallest Republican totals after 1876. Because the threat to white supremacy was greatest there, whites took the strongest steps to eliminate the threat. South Carolina passed an "eight box law" in 1882, which required voters to deposit votes for various offices in separate ballot boxes. This was in effect a literacy test that disfranchised many black voters. Georgia required payment of a poll tax. Several states passed complicated registration laws that discouraged blacks from voting. Ballot-box stuffing became a fine art. Democrats in South Carolina loaded the boxes with thin "tissue ballots." When counters discovered that the number of ballots exceeded the number of legal voters, they withdrew and discarded the larger, heavier ballots—all Republican.[17] Similar techniques prevailed elsewhere. White landowners deposited votes on behalf of their black sharecroppers. This helps to explain the large Democratic vote in the black districts of some states. As an Alabamian explained: "Any time it was necessary the black belt could put in ten, fifteen, twenty or thirty thousand Negro votes."[18]

Other Realities in the New South

Other blemishes also marred the New South's image of racial comity. The worst was the convict leasing system. Ironically, this form of neoslavery was a consequence of emancipation. Under the old regime, most slave crimes were punished on the plantation. The Southern prison system was therefore inadequate to accommodate the increase in convicted criminals after the war. Most states began leasing convicts to private contractors—coal-mining firms, railroad construction companies, planters, and so on. This practice proved so successful that the post-Reconstruction regimes expanded it. The state not only saved the cost of housing and feeding the prisoners but also received an income for leasing them; the lessees obtained cheap labor whom they could work like slaves. Indeed, the system seemed good for everybody—except the convicts. The cruelty and exploitation they suffered soon made convict leasing a national scandal. Ninety percent of the convicts were black, the result in part of discriminatory law enforcement practices. The convicts were ill fed, ill clothed, victimized by sadistic guards, and worked almost to death. The annual death rate among Mississippi convicts in the 1880s was about 11 percent; in Arkansas it was 25 percent. A group of convict laborers building a railroad in South Carolina suffered a death rate of 50 percent in 1878 and 1879. A grand jury investigation of a convict hospital in Mississippi in 1887 reported that most patients had "their backs cut in great wales, scars, and blisters, some with the skin peeling off in pieces as the result of severe beatings. . . . They were lying there dying, some of them on bare boards, so poor and emaciated that their bones almost came through their skin."[19]

Northerners who were otherwise friendly to the New South condemned "this newest and most revolting form of slavery" as "a state of things hardly credible in a civilized community." Thoughtful Southerners agreed; an official investigation in

---

[17]Ballots were then printed by the parties, not by the state. One of the reforms associated with the introduction of the Australian secret ballot system after 1888 was the printing of uniform ballots by the state governments.

[18]J. Morgan Kousser, *The Shaping of Southern Politics: Suffrage Restriction and the Establishment of the One-Party South, 1880–1910* (New Haven, Conn., 1974), p. 47.

[19]Woodward, *Origins of the New South*, p. 214.

Georgia pronounced convict leasing "barbaric," "worse than slavery," "a disgrace to civilized people."[20] Reform groups, many of them led by women, sprang up in the South to work for the abolition of convict leasing. But the practice proved difficult to reform. Too many powerful people profited from it. Part of the New South's industrial progress was based on it. Only in the first two decades of the twentieth century did Southern reformers gradually manage to overturn the system.

In other respects also, the glitter of the New South turned out to be more gilt than gold. While certain industries grew impressively, the Southern economy remained in colonial dependence on the North. Southern textile mills produced the coarser grades of yarn and cloth, often sending them to New England mills for higher-grade finishing. Northern ownership of Southern steel mills and railroads sometimes brought pricing and rate structures that discriminated against the South. Although the ex-Confederate states doubled their share of the national manufacturing capacity from 5 percent in 1880 to 10 percent in 1900, the latter figure was virtually the same as it had been in 1860. New South industrial progress had done no more than restore the region's antebellum standing relative to the North. In per capita income, the New South did not even do this well. Although Southern per capita income grew by 21 percent between 1880 and 1900, this barely kept pace with Northern growth and left the Southern average only two-fifths of the Northern—the same proportion it had been in 1880 and well below the two-thirds of 1860.

One reason for this failure to gain on the North was the low wages that prevailed in Southern industry. Another reason was the persistent anemia of Southern agriculture. The vicious cycle of debt and overproduction continued to drive down the price of cotton and to impoverish its growers. Except for occasional lip service to the virtues of crop diversification, most New South prophets said little and did less about agriculture. Nearly all new investment went into the nonagricultural sector. While manufacturing capital per capita increased by 300 percent in the ex-Confederate states between 1880 and 1900, the amount per capita invested in agriculture increased by only 29 percent.

The destitution of Southern agriculture led to explosive political consequences after 1890. The Populist movement and other "redneck revolts" overthrew several conservative regimes and permanently altered the Southern political landscape. Meanwhile an attempt to revive federal enforcement of voting rights fell just short of success. With its failure, the last lingering legacy of Reconstruction faded away.

Farewell to the Bloody Shirt

After the collapse of the Readjusters and of other independent movements in 1883, Northern Republicans pursued various and sometimes contradictory courses toward the South. In 1884, presidential nominee James G. Blaine at first hoped to win votes in the industrializing portions of the region on the tariff issue. When this hope proved illusory, Blaine unfurled the bloody shirt and charged that the suppression of Southern Republican votes had cost him the election, which he lost narrowly to Democrat

---

[20]McPherson, *Abolitionist Legacy*, p. 115; Woodward, *Origins of the New South*, p. 424.

Grover Cleveland. But a good many Republicans had become tired of the bloody shirt, especially since the party seemed to be able to do little to protect black voters even when it held national power. In 1888, still hoping that the presumed legions of old Southern Whigs could be won over on economic issues, the Republican National Committee concentrated almost exclusively on the tariff. Whatever the potency of this issue, the party's presidential nominee Benjamin Harrison won the presidency by carrying 233 of 248 Northern electoral votes, and even came close to cracking the solid South: a switch of less than one-half of 1 percent of the popular votes in Virginia and West Virginia would have put these states in the Republican column.

But in Mississippi, Louisiana, and South Carolina, the Republicans won respectively only 27, 26, and 17 percent of the vote. Such outrageous results constituted "an open attack on the Constitution," declared a Republican newspaper. "We dare not ignore the challenge."[21] Having won control of both houses of Congress as well as the presidency in 1888, some Republicans wished to respond to the challenge with new enforcement legislation. When Congress met in December 1889, seventeen contested Southern election cases confronted the lawmakers. The House decided eleven of them in favor of the Republican claimants. The testimony in these cases convinced many congressmen of the need for a new federal elections law based on the constitutional right of Congress to regulate the time, place, and manner of electing its members (Article I, Section 4).

Congressman Henry Cabot Lodge of Massachusetts took charge of the numerous bills introduced in the House and fashioned them into a single comprehensive measure. The Lodge bill authorized federal district judges to appoint election supervisors in any congressional district upon petition by 100 voters. The supervisors would have the power to inspect registration books, observe the voting, and advise voters of election procedures. Federal circuit courts were to appoint canvassing boards to certify the results of an election (the board's decision was to be final even if it conflicted with results reported by state boards) and to initiate proceedings against anyone charged with intimidation or fraud. Although this was a strong bill, it applied only to congressional elections and would do nothing to protect black voters in state and local contests, where matters vital to their interests were decided—schools, labor legislation, criminal punishments, and so on. Nevertheless, Democrats mounted a hysterical campaign against this "Force Bill," which, they said, would bring back the darkest days of "Black Reconstruction." Despite the furor, the House passed Lodge's bill by a straight party vote on July 2, 1890.

In the Senate, however, other legislation crowded the Lodge bill aside. Congress had already enacted a new pensions act, an anti-trust law, and an expanded silver coinage act. Still on the Senate docket was the McKinley tariff—the most comprehensive upward revision of import duties since the war. For many Republicans this complicated measure took precedence over an elections law. The Senate Republican caucus decided to postpone the latter until the next session in order to complete work on the tariff. This loss of momentum proved fatal to the Lodge bill. At the next

---

[21]McPherson, *Abolitionist Legacy,* p. 134.

session, a group of Western Republican senators, desiring still more generous silver coinage legislation, agreed to abandon the elections bill in return for Southern support of their silver bill. Unable to impose cloture to stop a Democratic filibuster, the Republican managers of the elections bill were compelled to give it up.

The death of the Lodge bill marked the end of the era. The abandonment of legislation on the "Southern question" in favor of bills dealing with tariffs, trusts, and silver signified the transformation of American concerns. The sectional and racial issues that had dominated every presidential election for the past half-century faded into insignificance for the next half-century. The generation that had fought the Civil War was passing away; a new generation with few memories of the war and little interest in its issues was emerging to leadership. The Lodge bill was the last black rights measure to come so close to passage until the Civil Rights Act of 1957. In 1894, the Democratic Congress repealed much of the 1870–1871 enforcement legislation. The era of Reconstruction died an unmourned death.

Epilogue

Southern Democrats correctly interpreted the failure of the Lodge elections bill as a signal of final Northern surrender. Before they could act on this signal, however, the emergence of Populism created a new crisis. The People's party, or Populists, grew out of the agricultural depression and rural unrest in Southern and Western states. When cotton prices plummeted nearly 50 percent in four years, to an all-time low of 4.5 cents a pound in 1894, farmers became desperate. The Southern Farmers' Alliance mobilized hundreds of thousands of farmers into a powerful political force. In several states—South Carolina, Tennessee, Florida, and Arkansas—the farmers' movement gained power within the Democratic party and did not form an independent party. But in other states, the farmers bolted the Democrats and in 1892 joined with rebellious Westerners to form the People's party—the largest third party since the Civil War.

In 1896, the national Democratic party absorbed the Populists and nominated William Jennings Bryan for president on a platform advocating the unlimited coinage of silver as a means to reverse declining farm prices and to end the depression that had begun with the Panic of 1893. Although Bryan carried every ex-Confederate state and most trans-Mississippi states, Republican William McKinley swept the North and also won Maryland, Kentucky, West Virginia, and Delaware. The Populist party was dead, while the Democratic party outside the South would appear moribund throughout the next fifteen years.

During its short life, however, Populism caused turmoil in the politics of a half-dozen Southern states. Republican/Populist coalitions won control of North Carolina for four years and fell short of success in a couple of other states only because of wholesale Democratic frauds. Democrats once again pulled out all the stops on the themes of "Negro domination" and "revival of Black Reconstruction" to discredit the Populist/Republican alliance. The viciousness of racist propaganda reached a new low, and violence rose almost to Reconstruction levels. When the dust settled after 1896, the Democrats had regained firm control of Southern politics and had crushed what turned out to be the last serious challenge to one-party rule in the South for the next sixty years.

As part of this process, Southern states disfranchised black voters. Democrats professed several motives for this action: it would purify Southern politics from chaos and corruption; it would eliminate illiterate and unqualified voters; it would make "normal" politics possible once more without the destructive specter of black rule. But the underlying purpose was a Democratic determination to consolidate one-party rule by disfranchising the opposition. Between 1889 and 1902, every ex-Confederate state followed Georgia's example and imposed a poll tax as a prerequisite for voting. In 1890, Mississippi established a literacy qualification, and other states followed suit:

South Carolina in 1895, Louisiana in 1898, North Carolina in 1900, Alabama in 1901, Virginia in 1902, and Georgia in 1908. The last five of these states allowed illiterates to vote if they owned property assessed at $300 or more. Since a good many white men could meet neither the literacy nor property qualifications, four states (Mississippi, South Carolina, Virginia, and Georgia) adopted "understanding" clauses, which allowed a registrar to enroll illiterate, propertyless men if they could demonstrate an understanding of a section of the state constitution when read to them. In effect, this gave registrars carte blanche to grant the ballot to whites and deny it to blacks—which is precisely what they did. Four states—Louisiana, North Carolina, Alabama, and Georgia—also enacted "grandfather" clauses, allowing men to vote if they could prove that they or their ancestors had voted before 1867—the year blacks were enfranchised. This barefaced violation of the federal Constitution was nullified by the Supreme Court—but not until 1915. The Supreme Court upheld the other suffrage provisions of Southern constitutions, for the Fifteenth Amendment forbade denial of the franchise only on grounds of race or color—not literacy, property, or tax paying. In *Williams v. Mississippi* (1898), the Court approved the Mississippi franchise restrictions and the understanding clause because they did not "on their face discriminate between the races."[1]

Two years earlier, in *Plessy v. Ferguson,* the Supreme Court had also sanctioned another dimension of the second-class citizenship fastened on blacks during this period—Jim Crowism. *Plessy* concerned a Louisiana statute requiring separate racial accommodations on railroad passenger cars. Before 1890, segregation in public accommodations was widespread but not universal in the South. Some railroads made blacks ride in "second-class" cars (usually the smoking car) even if they paid full fare. Challenges to this policy came before the newly created Interstate Commerce Commission, which ruled in 1889 that railroads must provide equal accommodations for both races. The ruling, however, did not require the *same* accommodations. This opened the floodgates for Jim Crow legislation. By 1891, seven states had passed laws mandating "separate but equal" railroad coaches. Although such accommodations were rarely equal in fact, the Supreme Court's ruling in *Plessy* legitimated the separate but equal doctrine and thereby put the stamp of approval on Jim Crow. Segregation by law soon prevailed in almost every aspect of Southern public life—streetcars, water fountains, restaurants, recreational facilities, and so on.

While Jim Crow laws formally placed blacks in a separate caste, disfranchisement virtually eliminated black voters as a factor in Southern politics for half a century. Poor white voters also got caught in the disfranchisement net. The poll tax and other restrictive measures reduced the white electorate by a quarter, and the absence of a two-party system lowered voter turnouts still more. Not until the last third of the twentieth century did a two-party system reemerge in the South. And not until the civil rights movement of the 1950s and 1960s produced a second Reconstruction did Southern blacks again achieve the rights and power they had possessed during the first.

---

[1]For good measure, after virtually eliminating black voters the Democrats established the "white primary," restricting the franchise to whites in primary elections to nominate party candidates. Since disfranchisement had all but destroyed the Republican party, the primary became the only meaningful election in the South.

Part Three Timeline

1865: Summer–Fall: Ex-Confederate states reorganize under Andrew Johnson's policy, enact black codes

December: Congress refuses to admit Southern representatives and senators under Johnson's plan

1866: Congress passes Freedmen's Bureau and Civil Rights bills over Johnson's veto

Congress passes Southern Homestead Act

Congress passes 14th Amendment

Race riots in Memphis and New Orleans

Republicans win three-fourths majority in congressional elections

1867: Congress passes Reconstruction Acts enfranchising freedmen

Efforts to impeach Johnson fail

1868: Most Southern states readmitted under congressional plan of Reconstruction

Johnson impeached but not convicted

14th Amendment ratified

Grant elected president

1869: Congress passes 15th Amendment

1870: Remaining Southern states readmitted under congressional plan

Annexation of Santo Domingo defeated in Senate

Congress passes legislation to enforce Reconstruction

15th Amendment ratified

1871: Treaty of Washington to arbitrate *Alabama* claims ratified

Congress passes "Ku Klux" Act; government begins to arrest and try Klansmen

1872: Liberal Republicans and Democrats nominate Greeley for president

Grant reelected

1873: Financial panic brings on economic depression

Colfax massacre in Louisiana

1874: Congressional elections give Democrats a majority in House

Street battles in New Orleans

1875: Army intervenes in Louisiana legislature

Congress passes Civil Rights Act

"Whiskey Ring" scandal

"Mississippi Plan" gives Democrats control of state

1876: Supreme Court eviscerates Reconstruction enforcement laws in *Cruikshank* and *Reese* decisions

Disputed presidential election between Hayes and Tilden

1877: Compromise of 1877 gives Hayes the presidency

Hayes withdraws federal troops from South Carolina and Louisiana; last Southern Republican governments collapse

Federal troops intervene in railroad strikes

1880: Garfield elected president

1881: Garfield assassinated; Chester Arthur becomes president

Readjuster movement in Virginia

1890: Lodge bill defeated in Senate

Mississippi constitution disfranchises most black voters; other Southern states follow Mississippi's example in subsequent years

1894: Democratic Congress repeals most Reconstruction enforcement legislation

1896: Supreme Court upholds "separate but equal" public facilities in *Plessy v. Ferguson*

1898: Supreme Court upholds Mississippi constitution of 1890 in *Williams v. Mississippi*

Glossary

Abatis. A network of felled trees in front of an entrenched position, with branches interlaced and facing the enemy's position to form an obstacle to attacking troops.

Blockade. A cordon of patrolling warships attempting to prevent vessels from entering or leaving enemy ports.

Bounty. A payment by the federal, state, or local government to induce men to enlist in the army.

Breastworks. A barricade of logs, fence-rails, stones, sandbags, or other material to protect troops fighting on the defensive. When erected in front of trenches, breastworks are covered with the dirt excavated from the trenches.

Breechloader. A rifle that is loaded at the breech, i.e., the rear of the barrel near the trigger.

Brevet rank. An honorary appointment of an army or navy officer to a rank above his regular rank, given as a reward for meritorious service but carrying no increase in authority.

Bushwhacker. Opprobious slang term for an irregular guerrilla soldier who fights from ambush or in hit-and-run attacks.

Caisson. A four-wheeled horse-drawn vehicle with a large box to carry artillery ammunition.

Cashier. To cashier an officer is to dismiss him from the service for disciplinary reasons.

Chattel slavery. A chattel is an article of personal, movable property. Slaves in the United States were chattels and could be bought or sold or moved from place to place, unlike serfs in Europe who were attached to the land.

Commissary Bureau. The administrative department of the army responsible for supplying food to the soldiers.

Contraband. Technically, contraband is enemy property or goods subject to seizure by a belligerent power in war. During the Civil War, "contrabands" became the popular name for freed slaves.

Corduroy (a road). To lay logs crosswise on a road to enable vehicles to avoid bogging down in mud.

Countermarch. To reverse the direction of marching troops and return to or near the starting point.

Court martial. A court of army or navy officers to try persons for offenses under martial (or military) law.

Demonstrate, demonstration. In military operations, a demonstration is a show of force on a given front without an actual attack, intended to distract enemy attention from the actual point of attack. Similar to a *feint*.

Earthworks. Military fortifications constructed of earth and logs.

Enfilade. To bring an enemy position under fire from the side or end instead of directly or obliquely from the front. The advantage of enfilading fire is twofold: shots that miss the initial target may hit men further down the line; the enemy has difficulty returning the fire effectively without risk of hitting their own men.

Envelop. To undertake an attack on one or both flanks or the rear of an enemy position; to encircle or surround.

Exchange cartel. An official agreement between governments at war with each other for the exchange of prisoners of war.

Feint.   A limited attack or movement of troops against one objective to mislead the enemy and cause him to weaken his defenses at the intended point of real attack. Similar to but more aggressive than a *demonstration*.

Fiat money.   Paper money declared legal currency by government decree (fiat) and not backed by, or necessarily converted into, gold or silver.

Field trenches.   Trenches constructed by an army fighting or maneuvering in an active campaign, as opposed to fortifications and trenches protecting a fixed strategic point such as a city.

Fire-eaters.   The popular term for aggressive spokesmen on behalf of Southern rights who denounced the North and advocated extreme measures to protect slavery, including secession.

Flank.   The side or end of a moving or stationary column or line of troops."To flank" an enemy position is to get around to its side or rear in order to *enfilade* the position. A "flanking march" is the movement of troops to get on the enemy's flank or rear.

Flotilla.   A group of warships and transports acting in concert with one another for a specific purpose. A flotilla generally contains a smaller number of ships than a fleet.

Forage.   As a noun, forage is grass, hay, or grain for horses and mules. Forage was as necessary for a Civil War army as petroleum is for a modern army. The verb "to forage" meant to seek food for humans as well as for animals.

Forced march.   A long march of troops at a fast pace made necessary by an impending battle or other emergency.

Guerrilla warfare.   Guerrillas are members of small armed bands that operate independently of the organized armed forces—often behind enemy lines, where they attack small detachments of enemy troops or destroy supply and transportation facilities. Guerrillas are sometimes civilians who take up arms temporarily and then return to their homes until called upon for another raid.

Lien.   A legal claim on the property of a debtor as security for payment of the debt.

Martial law.   Temporary government of a civilian population by military authorities, accompanied by the suspension or partial suspension of civil liberties and civil courts.

Mortar boat.   A specially constructed warship carrying a large mortar. A mortar is a short, large-caliber cannon designed to fire shells at a high angle so that they fall behind defensive fortifications too strong to be breached by direct artillery bombardment.

Muzzleloader.   A firearm loaded at the muzzle (end) of the barrel.

Ordnance Bureau.   The administrative department of the army responsible for supplying arms and ammunition (ordnance).

Parole.   An oath by a captured soldier, given in return for release from captivity, not to bear arms against the captors until formally exchanged for one of the captor's soldiers. To parole a captured soldier is to exact such an oath as a condition of his release.

Picket.   A soldier assigned to the perimeter of an army encampment or position to give warning of enemy movements.

Pincers movement.   A military operation by two or more cooperating forces to converge on and attack a single enemy from different directions, thereby catching the enemy in a "pincers."

Prize crew.   Crew put on board a captured enemy ship or a neutral ship carrying contraband to bring the captured ship into one of the captor's ports.

Quartermaster.   An officer responsible for supplying army units with uniforms, shoes, equipment (exclusive of ordnance), transportation, and forage. The Quartermaster Bureau or Quartermaster Corps is the army administrative department in charge of this function.

Ranger.   A soldier engaged in special service detached from organized army units, often operating behind enemy lines to gather information or to destroy facilities. "Ranger" and "guerrilla" were often used interchangeably during the Civil War.

Reconnaissance in force. A tentative or probing attack or other maneuver by a sizable number of troops, usually a brigade or larger, to gain information about the location, size, and movements of enemy forces.

Redan. Earthworks or breastworks thrown up in front of a cannon in the form of an inverted V to protect the gun and its crew from enemy fire.

Regular. An officer or soldier in the peacetime army, or "regular army," as distinguished from a "volunteer" in the "volunteer army" who enlisted for the specific purpose of fighting in the Civil War.

Repeating firearm. A gun that can be fired two or more times before reloading.

Repudiate (a debt). To cancel or refuse to pay a debt.

Returning board. A commission established to determine the validity of votes ("returns") cast in an election.

Salient. A portion of a defensive line or trench that juts out toward the enemy.

Screen (cavalry). A patrol of the front and flanks of an army to prevent enemy cavalry or scouts from getting close enough to the main army for observation.

Shotted guns. Cannons loaded with live ammunition.

Solid shot. Round cannonballs that do not explode.

Specie. Coined money, especially gold and silver. Specie payments are payments in coin, or the redemption of paper money on demand with coin equivalent. To suspend specie payments is to refuse to redeem paper money in coin.

Spike (a gun). To drive in and clinch a spike or nail in the vent (airhole where the powder is ignited) of a muzzleloading cannon in order to prevent the cannon being fired without major repairs.

Transport. An unarmed ship carrying troops or supplies.

Trooper. A cavalryman.

Volley. The simultaneous firing of their guns by an entire unit of soldiers.

Works. A general term to describe defensive military fortifications of all kinds.

Appendix

United States and Confederate States Constitutions

In most respects, the Confederate Constitution was a verbatim copy of the U. S. Constitution. The Confederates did make some important and revealing modifications, however, which are indicated below in italics.

U.S. Constitution

PREAMBLE

We, the people of the United States, in order to form a more perfect Union, establish justice, insure domestic tranquility, *provide for the common defence, promote the general welfare,* and secure the blessings of liberty to ourselves and our posterity, do ordain and establish this Constitution.

ART. I, SEC. 6, PAR. 2

. . . no person holding any office under the United States, shall be a member of either House during his continuance in office.

Confederate States Constitution

PREAMBLE

We, the people of the Confederate States, *each State acting in its sovereign and independent character,* in order to form a *permanent government,* establish justice, insure domestic tranquility, and secure the blessings of liberty to ourselves and our posterity—*invoking the favor and guidance of Almighty God*—do ordain and establish this Constitution.

ART. I, SEC. 6, PAR. 2

. . . no person holding any office under the Confederate States shall be a member of either House during his continuance in office. *But Congress may, by law, grant to the principal officer in each of the Executive Departments a seat upon the floor of either House, with the privilege of discussing any measure appertaining to his department.*

U.S. Constitution

ART. I, SEC. 7, PAR. 2

[The President may veto any bill passed by Congress, and his veto shall stand unless the bill is repassed by a two-thirds majority of each House.]

ART. I, SEC. 8, PAR. 1

The Congress shall have power to lay and collect taxes, duties, imposts and excises.

ART. I, SEC. 8, PAR. 3

[Congress shall have power] to regulate commerce with foreign nations, and among the several states, and with the Indian tribes.

No counterpart in the U.S. Constitution

Confederate States Constitution

ART. I, SEC. 7, PAR. 2

[Same provision regarding the veto, plus the following:] *The President may approve any appropriation and disapprove any other appropriation in the same bill. In such case he shall, in signing the bill, designate the appropriations disapproved; and shall return a copy of such appropriations, with his objections, to the House in which the bill shall have originated; and the same proceedings shall then be had as in case of other bills disapproved by the President.*

ART. I, SEC. 8, PAR. 1

The Congress shall have power to lay and collect taxes, duties, imposts, and excises . . . *but no bounties shall be granted from the treasury; nor shall any duties or taxes on importations from foreign nations be laid to promote or foster any branch of industry.*

ART. I, SEC. 8, PAR. 3

[Congress shall have power] to regulate commerce with foreign nations, and among the several States, and with the Indian tribes; *but neither this nor any other clause contained in the Constitution shall be construed to delegate the power to Congress to appropriate money for any internal improvement intended to facilitate commerce.*

ART. I, SEC. 9, PAR. 9

Congress shall appropriate no money from the treasury except by a vote of two-thirds of both Houses, taken by yeas and nays, unless it be asked and estimated for by some one of the heads of the departments, and submitted to Congress by the President.

ART. II, SEC. 1, PAR. 1

The executive power shall be vested in a President of the United States of America. He shall hold his office during the term of four years, and, together with the Vice President, chosen for the same term.

ART. II, SEC. 1, PAR. 1

The executive power shall be vested in a President of the Confederate States of America. *He and the Vice President shall hold their offices for the term of six years; but the President shall not be reeligible.*

U.S. Constitution

Confederate States Constitution

ART. IV, SEC. 2, PAR. 1

The citizens of each State shall be entitled to all privileges and immunities of citizens in the several States.

ART. IV, SEC. 2, PAR. 1

The citizens of each State shall be entitled to all the privileges and immunities of citizens of the several States, *and shall have the right of transit and sojourn in any State of this Confederacy, with their slaves and other property.*

No counterpart in the U.S. Constitution.

ART. IV, SEC. 3, PAR. 3

The Confederate States may acquire new territory; and Congress shall have power to legislate and provide governments for the inhabitants of all territory. . . . In all such territory, the institution of negro slavery, as it now exists in the Confederate States, shall be recognized and protected by Congress and by the territorial government; and the inhabitants of the several Confederate States and Territories shall have the right to take to such territory any slaves lawfully held by them.

Jefferson Davis's Inaugural Address

Montgomery, Alabama, February 18, 1861

Gentlemen of the Congress of the Confederate States of America, Friends, and Fellow-Citizens:

Called to the difficult and responsible station of Chief Executive of the Provisional Government which you have instituted, I approach the discharge of the duties assigned me with an humble distrust of my abilities, but with a sustaining confidence in the wisdom of those who are to guide and aid me in the administration of public affairs, and an abiding faith in the virtue and patriotism of the people. Looking forward to the speedy establishment of a permanent government to take the place of this, and which by its greater moral and physical power will be better able to combat with the many difficulties which arise from the conflicting interests of separate nations, I enter upon the duties of the office to which I have been chosen, with the hope that the beginning of our career as a confederacy may not be obstructed by hostile opposition to our enjoyment of the separate existence and independence which we have asserted, and which, with the blessing of Providence, we intend to maintain.

Our present condition, achieved in a manner unprecedented in the history of nations, illustrates the American idea that governments rest upon the consent of the governed, and that it is the right of the people to alter and abolish governments whenever they become destructive to the ends for which they were established. The declared compact of the Union from which we have withdrawn was to establish justice, ensure domestic tranquillity, provide for the common defence, promote the general welfare, and secure the blessings of liberty to ourselves and our posterity; and when in the judgment of the sovereign States now composing this confederacy, it has been perverted from the purposes for which it was ordained, and ceased to answer the ends for which it was established, a peaceful appeal to the ballot-box declared that, so far as they were concerned, the government created by that compact should cease to exist. In this they merely asserted the right which the Declaration of Independence of 1776 defined to be inalienable. Of the time and occasion of its exercise they as sovereigns were the final judges, each for itself. The impartial enlightened verdict of mankind will vindicate the rectitude of our conduct; and He who knows the hearts of men will judge the sincerity with which we labored to preserve the government of our fathers in its spirit.

The right solemnly proclaimed at the birth of the States, and which has been affirmed and reaffirmed in the bills of rights of the States subsequently admitted into the Union of 1789, undeniably recognizes in the people the power to resume the authority delegated for the purposes of government. Thus the sovereign States here represented, proceeded to form this confederacy; and it is by the abuse of language that their act has been denominated revolution. They formed a new alliance, but within each State its government has remained. The rights of person and property have not been disturbed. The agent through whom they communicated with foreign nations is changed, but this does not necessarily interrupt their international relations. Sustained by the consciousness that the transition from the former Union to the present confederacy has not proceeded from a disregard on our part of our just obligations or any failure to perform every constitutional duty, moved by no interest or passion to invade the rights of others, anxious to cultivate peace and commerce with all nations, if we may not hope to avoid war, we may at least expect that posterity will acquit us of having needlessly engaged in it. Doubly justified by the absence of wrong on our part, and by wanton aggression on the part of others, there can be no cause to doubt the courage and patriotism of the people of the Confederate States will be found equal to any measures of defence which soon their security may require.

An agricultural people, whose chief interest is the export of a commodity required in every manufacturing country, our true policy is peace, and the freest trade which our necessities will permit. It is alike our interest and that of all those to whom we would sell and from whom we would buy, that there should be the fewest practicable restrictions upon the interchange of commodities. There can be but little rivalry between ours and any manufacturing or navigating community, such as the northeastern States of the American Union. It must follow, therefore, that mutual interest would invite good will and kind offices. If, however, passion or lust of dominion should cloud the judgment or inflame the ambition of those States, we must prepare to meet the emergency and maintain by the final arbitrament of the sword the position which we have assumed among the nations of the earth.

We have entered upon a career of independence, and it must be inflexibly pursued through many years of controversy with our late associates of the Northern States. We have vainly endeavored to secure tranquillity and obtain respect for the rights to which we were entitled. As a necessity, not a choice, we have resorted to the remedy of separation, and henceforth our energies must be directed to the conduct of our own affairs, and the perpetuity of the confederacy which we have formed. If a just perception of mutual interest shall permit us peaceably to pursue our separate political career, my most earnest desire will have been fulfilled. But if this be denied us, and the integrity of our territory and jurisdiction be assailed, it will but remain for us with firm resolve to appeal to arms and invoke the blessing of Providence on a just cause.

As a consequence of our new condition, and with a view to meet anticipated wants, it will be necessary to provide a speedy and efficient organization of the branches of the Executive department having special charge of foreign intercourse, finance, military affairs, and postal service. For purposes of defence the Confederate States may, under ordinary circumstances, rely mainly upon their militia; but it is deemed advisable in the present condition of affairs, that there should be a well instructed, disciplined army, more numerous than would usually be required on a peace establishment. I also suggest that, for the protection of our harbors and commerce on the high seas, a navy adapted to those objects will be required. These necessities have, doubtless, engaged the attention of Congress.

With a Constitution differing only from that of our fathers in so far as it is explanatory of their well known intent, freed from sectional conflicts, which have interfered with the pursuit of the general welfare, it is not unreasonable to expect that the States from which we have recently parted may seek to unite their fortunes to ours, under the government which we have instituted. For this your Constitution makes adequate provision, but beyond this, if I mistake not, the judgment and will of the people are, that union with the States from which they have separated is neither practicable nor desirable. To increase the power, develop the resources, and promote the happiness of the Confederacy, it is requisite there should be so much homogeneity that the welfare of every portion would be the aim of the whole. Where this does not exist antagonisms are engendered which must and should result in separation.

Actuated solely by a desire to preserve our own rights, and to promote our own welfare, the separation of the Confederate States has been marked by no aggression upon others, and followed by no domestic convulsion. Our industrial pursuits have received no check, the cultivation of our fields progresses as heretofore, and even should we be involved in war there would be no considerable diminution in the production of the staples which have constituted our exports, in which the commercial world has an interest scarcely less than our own. This common interest of producer and consumer can only be intercepted by an exterior force which should obstruct its transmission to foreign markets, a course of conduct which would be detrimental to manufacturing and commercial interests abroad.

Should reason guide the action of the government from which we have separated, a policy so detrimental to the civilized world, the Northern States included, could not be dictated by even a stronger desire to inflict injury upon us; but if it be otherwise, a terrible responsibility will rest upon it, and the suffering of millions will bear testimony to the folly and wickedness of our aggressors. In the meantime there will remain to us, besides the ordinary remedies before suggested, the well known resources for retaliation upon the commerce of an enemy.

Experience in public stations of a subordinate grade to this which your kindness has conferred, has taught me that care and toil and disappointments are the price of official elevation. You will see many errors to forgive, many deficiencies to tolerate; but you shall not find in me either want of zeal or fidelity to the cause that is to me the highest in hope and of most enduring affection. Your generosity has bestowed upon me an undeserved distinction, one which I neither sought nor desired. Upon the continuance of that sentiment, and upon your wisdom and patriotism, I rely to direct and support me in the performance of the duties required at my hands.

We have changed the constituent parts but not the system of our government. The Constitution formed by our fathers is that of these Confederate States. In their exposition of it, and in the judicial construction it has received, we have a light which reveals its true meaning. Thus instructed as to the just interpretation of that instrument, and ever remembering that all offices are but trusts held for the people, and that delegated powers are to be strictly construed, I will hope by due diligence in the performance of my duties, though I may disappoint your expectation, yet to retain, when retiring, something of the good will and confidence which will welcome my entrance into office.

It is joyous in the midst of perilous times to look around upon a people united in heart, when one purpose of high resolve animates and actuates the whole, where the sacrifices to be made are not weighed in the balance, against honor, right, liberty, and equality. Obstacles may retard, but they cannot long prevent the progress of a movement sanctioned by its justice and sustained by a virtuous people. Reverently let us invoke the God of our fathers to guide and protect us in our efforts to perpetuate the principles which by his blessing they were able to vindicate, establish, and transmit to their posterity; and with a continuance of His favor ever gratefully acknowledged, we may hopefully look forward to success, to peace, to prosperity.

Abraham Lincoln's Inaugural Address

March 4, 1861

Fellow-Citizens of the United States:

In compliance with a custom as old as the Government itself, I appear before you to address you briefly, and to take, in your presence, the oath prescribed by the Constitution of the United States to be taken by the President, before he enters on the execution of his office.

I do not consider it necessary, at present, for me to discuss those matters of administration about which there is no special anxiety or excitement. Apprehension seems to exist among the people of the southern States, that, by the accession of a Republican Administration, their property and their peace and personal security are to be endangered. There has never been any reasonable cause for such apprehension. Indeed, the most ample evidence to the contrary has all the while existed, and been open to their inspection. It is found in nearly all the published speeches of him who now addresses you. I do but quote from one of those speeches, when I declare that "I have no purpose, directly or indirectly, to interfere with the institution of slavery in the States where it exists." I believe I have no lawful right to do so; and I have no inclination to do so. Those who nominated and elected me, did so with the full knowledge that I had made this, and made many similar declarations, and had never recanted them. And, more than this, they placed in the platform, for my acceptance, and as a law to themselves and to me, the clear and emphatic resolution which I now read:

"*Resolved,* that the maintenance inviolate of the rights of the States, and especially the right of each State to order and control its own domestic institutions according to its own judgment exclusively, is essential to that balance of power on which the perfection and endurance of our political fabric depend; and we denounce the lawless invasion by armed force of the soil of any State or Territory, no matter under what pretext, as among the gravest of crimes."

I now reiterate these sentiments; and in doing so I only press upon the public attention the most conclusive evidence of which the case is susceptible, that the property, peace, and security of no section are to be in anywise endangered by the now incoming Administration.

I add, too, that all the protection which, consistently with the constitution and the laws, can be given will be cheerfully given to all the States when lawfully demanded, for whatever cause, as cheerfully to one section as to another.

There is much controversy about the delivering up of fugitives from service or labor. The clause I now read is as plainly written in the constitution as any other of its provisions:

"No person held to service or labor in one State under the laws thereof, escaping into another, shall, in consequence of any law or regulation therein, be discharged from such service or labor, but shall be delivered up on claim of the party to whom such service or labor may be due."

It is scarcely questioned that this provision was intended by those who made it for the reclaiming of what we call fugitive slaves; and the intention of the lawgiver is the law.

All members of Congress swear their support to the whole Constitution—to this provision as well as any other. To the proposition, then, that slaves whose cases come within the terms of this clause "shall be delivered up," their oaths are unanimous. Now, if they would make the effort in good temper, could they not, with nearly equal unanimity, frame and pass a law by means of which to keep good that unanimous oath?

There is some difference of opinion whether this clause should be enforced by national or by state authority; but surely that difference is not a very material one. If the slave is to be surrendered, it can be of but little consequence to him or to others by which authority it is done; and should any one, in any case, be content that this oath shall go unkept on a merely unsubstantial controversy as to how it shall be kept?

Again, in any law upon this subject, ought not all the safeguards of liberty known in the civilized and humane jurisprudence to be introduced, so that a free man be not, in any case, surrendered as a slave? And might it not be well at the same time to provide by law for the enforcement of that clause in the Constitution which guaranties that "the citizens of each State shall be entitled to all the privileges and immunities of citizens in the several States?"

I take the official oath to-day with no mental reservations, and with no purpose to construe the Constitution or laws by any hypercritical rules; and while I do not choose now to specify particular acts of Congress as proper to be enforced, I do suggest that it will be much safer for all, both in official and private stations, to conform to and abide by all those acts which stand unrepealed, than to violate any of them, trusting to find impunity in having them held to be unconstitutional.

It is seventy-two years since the first inauguration of a President under our national Constitution. During that period fifteen different and very distinguished citizens have in succession administered the executive branch of the government. They have conducted it through many perils, and generally with great success. Yet, with all this scope for precedent, I now enter upon the same task, for the brief constitutional term of four years, under great and peculiar difficulties.

A disruption of the Federal Union, heretofore only menaced, is now formidably attempted. I hold that in the contemplation of universal law and of the Constitution, the Union of these States is perpetual. Perpetuity is implied, if not expressed, in the fundamental law of all national governments. It is safe to assert that no government proper ever had a provision in its organic law for its own termination. Continue to execute all the express provisions of our national Constitution, and the Union will endure forever, it being impossible to destroy it except by some action not provided for in the instrument itself.

Again, if the United States be not a government proper, but an association of States in the nature of a contract merely, can it, as a contract, be peaceably unmade by less than all the parties who made it? One party to a contract may violate it—break it, so to speak; but does it not require all to lawfully rescind it? Descending from these general principles we find the proposition that in legal contemplation the Union is perpetual, confirmed by the history of the Union itself.

The Union is much older than the Constitution. It was formed, in fact, by the Articles of Association in 1774. It was matured and continued in the Declaration of Independence in 1776. It was further matured, and the faith of all the then thirteen States expressly plighted and engaged that it should be perpetual, by the Articles of Confederation, in 1778; and, finally, in 1787, one of the declared objects for ordaining and establishing the Constitution was to form a more perfect Union. But if the destruction of the Union by one or by a part only of the States be lawfully possible, the Union is less than before, the Constitution having lost the vital element of perpetuity.

It follows from these views that no State, upon its own mere motion, can lawfully get out of the Union; that resolves and ordinances to that effect, are legally void; and that acts of violence within any State or States against the authority of the United States, are insurrectionary or revolutionary, according to circumstances.

I therefore consider that, in view of the Constitution and the laws, the Union is unbroken, and, to the extent of my ability, I shall take care, as the Constitution itself expressly enjoins upon me, that the laws of the Union shall be faithfully executed in all the States. Doing this, which I deem to be only a simple duty on my part, I shall perfectly perform it, so far as is practicable, unless my rightful masters, the American people, shall withhold the requisition, or in some authoritative manner direct the contrary.

I trust this will not be regarded as a menace, but only as the declared purpose of the Union that it will constitutionally defend and maintain itself.

In doing this there need be no bloodshed or violence, and there shall be none unless it is forced upon the national authority.

The power confided to me *will be used to hold, occupy, and possess the property and places belonging to the Government,* and collect the duties and imposts; but beyond what may be necessary for these objects there will be no invasion, no using of force against or among the people anywhere.

Where hostility to the United States shall be so great and so universal as to prevent competent resident citizens from holding the Federal offices, there will be no attempt to force obnoxious strangers among the people that object. While the strict legal right may exist of the Government to enforce the exercise of these offices, the attempt to do so would be so irritating, and so nearly impracticable withal, that I deem it better to forego for the time the uses of such offices.

The mails, unless repelled, will continue to be furnished in all parts of the Union.

So far as possible, the people everywhere shall have that sense of perfect security which is most favorable to calm thought and reflection.

The course here indicated will be followed, unless current events and experience shall show a modification or change to be proper; and in every case and exigency my best discretion will be exercised according to the circumstances actually existing, and with a view and hope of a peaceful solution of the national troubles, and the restoration of fraternal sympathies and affections.

That there are persons, in one section or another, who seek to destroy the Union at all events, and are glad of any pretext to do it, I will neither affirm nor deny. But if there be such, I need address no word to them.

To those, however, who really love the Union, may I not speak, before entering upon so grave a matter as the destruction of our national fabric, with all its benefits, its memories, and its hopes? Would it not be well to ascertain why we do it? Will you hazard so desperate a step, while any portion of the ills you fly from, have no real existence? Will you, while the certain ills you fly to, are greater than all the real ones you fly from? Will you risk the commission of so fearful a mistake? All profess to be content in the Union if all constitutional rights can be maintained. Is it true, then, that any right, plainly written in the Constitution has been denied? I think not. Happily the human mind is so constituted, that no party can reach to the audacity of doing this.

Think, if you can, of a single instance in which a plainly-written provision of the Constitution has ever been denied. If, by the mere force of numbers, a majority should deprive a minority of any clearly-written constitutional right, it might, in a moral point of view, justify revolution; it certainly would, if such right were a vital one. But such is not our case.

All the vital rights of minorities and of individuals are so plainly assured to them by affirmations and negations, guaranties and prohibitions in the Constitution, that controversies never arise concerning them. But no organic law can ever be framed with a provision specifically applicable to every question which may occur in practical administration. No foresight can anticipate, nor any document of reasonable length contain, express provisions for all possible questions. Shall fugitives from labor be surrendered by national or by state authorities? The Constitution does not expressly say. Must Congress protect slavery in the Territories? The Constitution does not expressly say. From questions in this class, spring all our constitutional controversies, and we divide upon them into majorities and minorities.

If the minority will not acquiesce, the majority must, or the government must cease. There is no alternative for continuing the government but acquiescence on the one side or the other. If a minority in such a case, will secede rather than acquiesce, they make a precedent which in turn will ruin and divide them, for a minority of their own will secede from them whenever a majority refuses to be controlled by such a minority. For instance, why not any portion of a new confederacy, a year or two hence, arbitrarily secede again, precisely as portions of the present Union now claim to secede from it? All who cherish disunion sentiments are now being educated to the exact temper of doing this. Is there such perfect identity of interests among the States to compose a new Union as to produce harmony only, and prevent renewed secession? Plainly, the central idea of secession is the essence of anarchy.

A majority held in restraint by constitutional check and limitation, and always changing easily with deliberate changes of popular opinions and sentiments, is the only true sovereign of a free people. Whoever rejects it, does, of necessity, fly to anarchy or to despotism. Unanimity is impossible; the rule of a majority, as a permanent arrangement, is wholly inadmissible. So that, rejecting the majority principle, anarchy or despotism in some form is all that is left.

I do not forget the position assumed by some that constitutional questions are to be decided by the Supreme Court, nor do I deny that such decisions must be binding in any case upon the parties to a suit, as to the object of that suit, while they are also entitled to very high respect and consideration in all parallel cases by all other departments of the government; and while it is obviously possible that such decision may be erroneous in any given case, still the evil effect following it, being limited to that particular case, with the chance that it may be overruled and never become a precedent for other cases, can better be borne than could the evils of a different practice.

At the same time the candid citizen must confess that if the policy of the government upon the vital questions affecting the whole people is to be irrevocably fixed by the decisions of the Supreme Court, the instant they are made, as in ordinary litigation between parties in personal actions, the people will have ceased to be their own masters, unless having to that extent practically resigned their government into the hands of that eminent tribunal.

Nor is there in this view any assault upon the court or the judges. It is a duty from which they may not shrink, to decide cases properly brought before them; and it is no fault of theirs if others seek to turn their decisions to political purposes. One section of our country believes slavery is right and ought to be extended, while the other believes it is wrong and ought not to be extended; and this is the only substantial dispute; and the fugitive slave clause of the constitution, and the law for the suppression of the foreign slave trade, are each as well enforced, perhaps, as any law can ever be in a community where the moral sense of the people imperfectly supports the law itself. The great body of the people abide by the dry legal obligation in both cases, and a few break over in each. This, I think, cannot be perfectly cured, and it would be worse in both cases after the separation of the sections than before. The foreign slave trade, now imperfectly suppressed, would be ultimately revived, without restriction, in one section; while fugitive slaves, now only partially surrendered, would not be surrendered at all by the other.

Physically speaking we cannot separate—we cannot remove our respective sections from each other, nor build an impassable wall between them. A husband and wife may be divorced, and go out of the presence and beyond the reach of each other, but the different parts of our country cannot do this. They cannot but remain face to face; and intercourse, either amicable or hostile, must continue between them. Is it possible, then, to make that intercourse more advantageous or more satisfactory after separation than before? Can aliens make treaties easier than friends can make laws? Can treaties be more faithfully enforced between aliens than laws can among friends? Suppose you go to war, you cannot fight always; and when, after much loss on both sides and no gain on either, you cease fighting, the identical questions as to terms of intercourse are again upon you.

This country, with its institutions, belongs to the people who inhabit it. Whenever they shall grow weary of the existing government, they can exercise their constitutional right of amending, or their revolutionary right to dismember or overthrow it. I cannot be ignorant of the fact that many worthy and patriotic citizens are desirous of having the national Constitution amended. While I make no recommendation of amendment, I fully recognize the full authority of the people over the whole subject, to be exercised in either of the modes prescribed in the instrument itself, and I should, under existing circumstances, favor, rather than oppose, a fair opportunity being afforded the people to act upon it.

I will venture to add, that to me the convention mode seems preferable, in that it allows amendments to originate with the people themselves, instead of only permitting them to take or reject propositions originated by others not especially chosen for the purpose, and which might not be precisely such as they would wish either to accept or refuse. I understand that a proposed amendment to the Constitution (which amendment, however, I have not seen) has passed Congress, to the effect that the Federal Government shall never interfere with the domestic institutions of States, including that of persons held to service. To avoid misconstruction of what I have said, I depart from my purpose not to speak of particular amendments, so far as to say that, holding such a provision to now be implied constitutional law, I have no objection to its being made express and irrevocable.

The chief magistrate derives all his authority from the people, and they have conferred none upon him to fix the terms for the separation of the States. The people themselves, also, can do this if they choose, but the Executive, as such, has nothing to do with it. His duty is to administer the present government as it came to his hands, and to transmit it unimpaired by him to his successor. Why should there not be a patient confidence in the ultimate justice of the people? Is there any better or equal hope in the world? In our present differences is either party without faith of being in the right? If the Almighty Ruler of nations, with his eternal truth and justice, be on your side of the North, or on yours of the South, that truth and that justice will surely prevail by the judgment of this great tribunal, the American people. By the frame of the Government under which we live, this same people have wisely given their public servants but little power for mischief, and have with equal wisdom provided for the return of that little to their own hands at very short intervals. While the people retain their virtue and vigilance, no administration, by any extreme wickedness or folly, can very seriously injure the Government in the short space of four years.

My countrymen, one and all, think calmly and well upon this whole subject. Nothing valuable can be lost by taking time.

If there be an object to hurry any of you, in hot haste, to a step which you would never take deliberately, that object will be frustrated by taking time; but no good object can be frustrated by it.

Such of you as are now dissatisfied still have the old Constitution unimpaired, and on the sensitive point, the laws of your own framing under it; while the new administration will have no immediate power, if it would to change either.

If it were admitted that you who are dissatisfied hold the right side in the dispute, there is still no single reason for precipitate action. Intelligence, patriotism, Christianity, and a firm reliance on Him who has never yet forsaken this favored land, are still competent to adjust, in the best way, all our present difficulties.

In your hands, my dissatisfied fellow-countrymen, and not in mine, is the momentous issue of civil war. The government will not assail you.

You can have no conflict without being yourselves the aggressors. You have no oath registered in Heaven to destroy the government; while I shall have the most solemn one to "preserve, protect, and defend" it.

I am loath to close. We are not enemies, but friends. We must not be enemies. Though passion may have strained it, it must not break our bonds of affection.

The mystic cords of memory, stretching from every battle-field and patriot grave to every living heart and hearthstone all over this broad land, will yet swell the chorus of the Union, when again touched, as surely they will be, by the better angels of our nature.

Speech by Confederate Vice President Alexander H. Stephens in Savannah

March 21, 1861

Mr. Mayor and Gentlemen of the Committee, and Fellow-Citizens

For this reception you will please accept my most profound and sincere thanks. The compliment is doubtless intended as much, or more, perhaps, in honor of the occasion, and my public position in connection with the great events now crowding upon us, than to me personally and individually. It is, however, none the less appreciated by me on that account. We are in the midst of one of the greatest epochs in our history. The last ninety days will mark one of the most memorable eras in the history of modern civilization . . . one of the greatest revolutions in the annals of the world—seven States have, within the last three months, thrown off an old Government and formed a new. This revolution has been signally marked, up to this time, by the fact of its having been accomplished without the loss of a single drop of blood. [Applause.] This new Constitution or form of government, constitutes the subject to which your attention will be partly invited. . . .

But not to be tedious in enumerating the numerous changes for the better, allow me to allude to one other—though last, not least: the new Constitution has put at rest *forever* all the agitating questions relating to our peculiar institutions—African slavery as it exists among us—the proper *status of* the negro in our form of civilization. *This was the immediate cause of the late rupture and present revolution.* JEFFERSON, in his forecast, has anticipated this, as the "rock upon which the old Union would split." He was right. What was conjecture with him, is now a realized fact. But whether he fully comprehended the great truth upon which that rock *stood and stands,* may be doubted. *The prevailing ideas entertained by him and most of the leading statesmen at the time of the formation of the old Constitution were, that the enslavement of the African was in violation of the laws of nature; that it was wrong in principle, socially, morally and politically.* It was an evil they knew not well how to deal with; but the general opinion of the men of that day was, that, somehow or other, in the order of Providence, the institution would be evanescent and pass away. This idea, though not incorporated in the Constitution, was the prevailing idea at the time. The Constitution, it is true, secured every essential guarantee to the institution while it should last, and hence no argument can be justly used against the constitutional guarantees thus secured, because of the common sentiment of the day. *Those ideas, however, were fundamentally wrong. They rested upon the assumption of the equality of races. This was an error.* It was a sandy foundation, and the idea of a Government built upon it—when the "storm came and the wind blew, it *fell.*"

Our new Government is founded upon exactly the opposite ideas; its foundations are laid, its cornerstone rests, upon the great truth that the negro is not equal to the white man; that slavery, subordination to the superior race, is his natural and moral condition. [Applause.] *This, our new Government, is the first, in the history of the world, based upon this great physical, philosophical, and moral truth.* This truth has been slow in the process of its development, like all other truths in the various departments of science. It is so even amongst us. Many who hear me, perhaps, can recollect well that this truth was not generally admitted, even within their day. The errors of the past generation still clung to many as late as twenty years ago. Those at the North who still cling to these errors with a zeal above knowledge, we justly denominate fanatics. All fanaticism springs from an aberration of the mind; from a defeat in reasoning. It is a species of insanity. One of the most striking characteristics of insanity, in many instances, is, forming correct conclusions from fancied or erroneous premises; so with the *anti-slavery* fanatics: their conclusions are right if their premises are. They assume that the negro is equal, and hence conclude that he is entitled to equal privileges and rights, with the white man. If their premises were correct, their conclusions would be logical and just; but their premises being wrong, their whole argument fails. I recollect once of having heard a gentleman from one of the Northern States, of great power and ability, announce in the House of Representatives, with imposing effect, that we of the South would be compelled, ultimately, to yield upon this subject of slavery; that it was as impossible to war successfully against a principle in politics, as it was in physics or mechanics. That the principle would ultimately prevail. That we, in maintaining slavery as it exists with us, were warring against a principle—a principle founded in nature, the principle of the equality of man. The reply I made to him was, that upon his own grounds we should succeed, and that he and his associates in their crusade against our institutions would ultimately fail. The truth announced, that it was as impossible to war successfully against a principle in politics as well as in physics and mechanics, I admitted, but told him it was he and those acting with him who were warring against a principle. They were attempting to make things equal which the Creator had made unequal.

✑ Proclamation Calling Militia and Convening Congress

April 15, 1861

By the President of the United States:
A Proclamation.

Whereas the laws of the United States have been for some time past, and now are opposed, and the execution thereof obstructed, in the States of South Carolina, Georgia, Alabama, Florida, Mississippi, Louisiana and Texas, by combinations too powerful to be suppressed by the ordinary course of judicial proceedings, or by the powers vested in the Marshals by law,

Now therefore, I, Abraham Lincoln, President of the United States, in virtue of the power in me vested by the Constitution, and the laws, have thought fit to call forth, and hereby do call forth, the militia of the several States of the Union, to the aggregate number of seventy-five thousand, in order to suppress said combinations, and to cause the laws to be duly executed. The details, for this object, will be immediately communicated to the State authorities through the War Department.

I appeal to all loyal citizens to favor, facilitate and aid this effort to maintain the honor, the integrity, and the existence of our National Union, and the perpetuity of popular government; and to redress wrongs already long enough endured.

I deem it proper to say that the first service assigned to the forces hereby called forth will probably be to re-possess the forts, places, and property which have been seized from the Union; and in every event, the utmost care will be observed, consistently with the objects aforesaid, to avoid any devastation, any destruction of, or interference with, property, or any disturbance of peaceful citizens in any part of the country.

And I hereby command the persons composing the combinations aforesaid to disperse, and retire peaceably to their respective abodes within twenty days from this date.

Deeming that the present condition of public affairs presents an extraordinary occasion, I do hereby, in virtue of the power in me vested by the Constitution, convene both Houses of Congress. Senators and Representatives are therefore summoned to assemble at their respective chambers, at 12 o'clock, noon, on Thursday, the fourth day of July, next, then and there to consider and determine, such measures, as, in their wisdom, the public safety, and interest may seem to demand.

In Witness Whereof I have hereunto set my hand, and caused the Seal of the United States to be affixed.

Done at the city of Washington this fifteenth day of April in the year of our Lord

[L.S.]   One thousand, Eight hundred and Sixty-one, and of the Independence of the

United States the Eighty-fifth.

By the President: ABRAHAM LINCOLN

WILLIAM H. SEWARD, Secretary of State.

The Emancipation Proclamation

By the President of the United States of America:
A Proclamation.

Whereas on the 22d day of September, A.D. 1862, a proclamation was issued by the President of the United States, containing, among other things, the following, to wit:

> That on the 1st day of January, A.D. 1863, all persons held as slaves within any State or designated part of a State the people whereof shall then be in rebellion against the United States shall be then, thenceforward, and forever free; and the executive government of the United States, including the military and naval authority thereof, will recognize and maintain the freedom of such persons and will do no act or acts to repress such persons, or any of them, in any efforts they may make for their actual freedom.
>
> That the Executive will on the 1st day of January aforesaid, by proclamation, designate the States and parts of States, if any, in which the people thereof, respectively, shall then be in rebellion against the United States; and the fact that any State or the people thereof shall on that day in good faith represented in the Congress of the United States by members chosen thereto at elections wherein a majority of the qualified voters of such States shall have participated shall, in the absence of strong countervailing testimony, be deemed conclusive evidence that such State and the people thereof are not then in rebellion against the United States.

Now, therefore, I, Abraham Lincoln, President of the United States, by virtue of the power in me vested as Commander in Chief of the Army and Navy of the United States in time of actual armed rebellion against the authority and Government of the United States, and as a fit and necessary war measure for suppressing said rebellion, do, on this 1st day of January A.D. 1863, and in accordance with my purpose so to do, publicly proclaimed for the full period of one hundred days from the day first above mentioned, order and designate as the States and parts of States wherein the people thereof, respectively, are this day in rebellion against the United States the following, to wit:

Arkansas, Texas, Louisiana (except the parishes of St. Bernard, Plaquemines, Jefferson, St. John, St. Charles, St. James, Ascension, Assumption, Terrebonne, Lafourche, St. Mary, St. Martin, and Orleans, including the city of New Orleans), Mississippi, Alabama, Florida, Georgia, South Carolina, North Carolina, and Virginia (except the forty-eight counties designated as West Virginia, and also the counties of Berkeley, Accomac, Northampton, Elizabeth City, York, Princess Anne, and Norfolk, including the cities of Norfolk and Portsmouth), and which excepted parts are for the present left precisely as if this proclamation were not issued.

And by virtue of the power and for the purpose aforesaid, I do order and declare that all persons held as slaves within said designated States and parts of States are and henceforward shall be free, and that the executive government of the United States, including the military and naval authorities thereof, will recognize and maintain the freedom of said persons.

And I hereby enjoin upon the people so declared to be free to abstain from all violence, unless in necessary self-defense; and I recommend to them that in all cases when allowed they labor faithfully for reasonable wages.

And I further declare and make known that such persons of suitable condition will be received into the armed service of the United States to garrison forts, positions, stations, and other places and to man vessels of all sorts in said service.

And upon this act, sincerely believed to be an act of justice, warranted by the Constitution upon military necessity, I invoke the considerate judgment and mankind and the gracious favor of Almighty God.

In witness whereof I have hereunto set my hand and caused the seal of the United States to be affixed.

> Done at the city of Washington, this 1st day of January A.D. 1863, and of the Independence of the United States of America the eighty-seventh.

By the President: ABRAHAM LINCOLN
WILLIAM H. SEWARD, Secretary of State.

✍ The Gettysburg Address

Lincoln's Speech at the Dedication of the National Military Cemetery on the Gettysburg Battlefield, November 19, 1863

Fourscore and seven years ago our fathers brought forth on this continent a new nation, conceived in liberty, and dedicated to the proposition that all men are created equal.

Now we are engaged in a great civil war, testing whether that nation, or any nation so conceived and so dedicated, can long endure. We are met on a great battlefield of that war. We have come to dedicate a portion of that field as a final resting place for those who here gave their lives that the nation might live. It is altogether fitting and proper that we should do this.

But, in a larger sense, we can not dedicate—we can not consecrate—we can not hallow—this ground. The brave men, living and dead, who struggled here, have consecrated it, far above our poor power to add or detract. The world will little note, nor long remember, what we say here, but it can never forget what they did here. It is for us the living, rather, to be dedicated here to the unfinished work which they who fought here have thus far so nobly advanced. It is rather for us to be here dedicated to the great task remaining before us—that from these honored dead we take increased devotion to that cause for which they gave the last full measure of devotion—that we here highly resolve that these dead shall not have died in vain—that this nation, under God, shall have a new birth of freedom—and that government of the people, by the people, for the people, shall not perish from the earth.

Proclamation of Amnesty and Reconstruction

By the President of the United States of America: A Proclamation.

Whereas, in and by the Constitution of the United States, it is provided that the President "shall have power to grant reprieves and pardons for offences against the United States, except in cases of impeachment;" and

Whereas a rebellion now exists whereby the loyal State governments of several States have for a long time been subverted, and many persons have committed and are now guilty of treason against the United States; and

Whereas, with reference to said rebellion and treason, laws have been enacted by Congress declaring forfeitures and confiscation of property and liberation of slaves, all upon terms and conditions therein stated, and also declaring that the President was thereby authorized at any time thereafter, by proclamation, to extend to persons who may have participated in the existing rebellion, in any State or part thereof, pardon and amnesty, with such exceptions and at such times and on such conditions as he may deem expedient for the public welfare; and

Whereas the congressional declaration for limited and conditional pardon accords with well-established judicial exposition of the pardoning power; and

Whereas, with reference to said rebellion, the President of the United States has issued several proclamations, with provisions in regard to the liberation of slaves; and

Whereas it is now desired by some persons heretofore engaged in said rebellion to resume their allegiance to the United States, and to reinaugurate loyal State governments within and for their respective States; therefore,

I, Abraham Lincoln, President of the United States, do proclaim, declare, and make known to all persons who have, directly or by implication, participated in the existing rebellion, except as hereinafter excepted, that a full pardon is hereby granted to them and each of them, with restoration of all rights of property, except as to slaves, and in property cases where rights of third parties shall have intervened, and upon the condition that every such person shall take and subscribe an oath, and thenceforward keep and maintain said oath inviolate; and which oath shall be registered for permanent preservation, and shall be of the tenor and effect following, to wit:

"I, —— ——, do solemnly swear, in presence of Almighty God, that I will henceforth faithfully support, protect and defend the Constitution of the United States, and the union of the States thereunder; and that I will, in like manner, abide by and faithfully support all acts of Congress passed during the existing rebellion with reference to slaves, so long and so far as not repealed, modified or held void by Congress, or by decision of the Supreme Court; and that I will, in like manner, abide by and faithfully support all proclamations of the President made during the existing rebellion having reference to slaves, so long and so far as not modified or declared void by decision of the Supreme Court. So help me God."

The persons excepted from the benefits of the foregoing provisions are all who are, or shall have been, civil or diplomatic officers or agents of the so-called confederate government; all who have left judicial stations under the United States to aid the rebellion; all who are, or shall have been, military or naval officers of said so-called confederate government above the rank of colonel in the army, or of lieutenant in the navy; all who left seats in the United States Congress to aid the rebellion; all who resigned commissions in the army or navy of the United States, and afterwards aided the rebellion; and all who have engaged in any way in treating colored persons or white persons, in charge of such, otherwise than lawfully as prisoners of war, and which persons may have been found in the United States service, as soldiers, seamen, or in any other capacity.

And I do further proclaim, declare, and make known, that whenever, in any of the States of Arkansas, Texas, Louisiana, Mississippi, Tennessee, Alabama, Georgia, Florida, South Carolina, and North Carolina, a number of persons, not less than one-tenth in number of the votes cast in such State at the Presidential election of the year of our Lord one thousand eight hundred and sixty, each having taken the oath aforesaid and not having since violated it, and being a qualified voter by the election law of the State existing immediately before the so-called act of secession, and excluding all others, shall re-establish a State government which shall be republican, and in no wise contravening said oath, such shall be recognized as the true government of the State, and the State shall receive thereunder the benefits of the constitutional provision which declares that "The United States shall guaranty to every State in this union a republican form of government, and shall protect each of them against invasion; and, on application of the legislature, or the executive, (when the legislature cannot be convened,) against domestic violence."

Any I do further proclaim, declare, and make known that any provision which may be adopted by such State government in relation to the freed people of such State, which shall recognize and declare their permanent freedom, provide for their education, and which may yet be consistent, as a temporary arrangement, with their present condition as a laboring, landless, and homeless class, will not be objected to by the national Executive. And it is suggested as not improper, that, in constructing a loyal State government in any State, the name of the State, the boundary, the subdivisions, the constitution, and the general code of laws, as before the rebellion, be maintained, subject only to the modifications made necessary by the conditions hereinbefore stated, and such others, if any, not contravening said conditions, and which may be deemed expedient by those framing the new State government.

To avoid misunderstanding, it may be proper to say that this proclamation, so far as it relates to State governments, has no reference to States wherein loyal State governments have all the while been maintained. And for the same reason, it may be proper to further say that whether members sent to Congress from any State shall be admitted to seats, constitutionally rests exclusively with the respective Houses, and not to any extent with the Executive. And still further, that this proclamation is intended to present the people of the States wherein the national authority has been suspended, and loyal State governments have been subverted, a mode in and by which the national authority and loyal State governments may be re-established within said States, or in any of them; and, while the mode presented is the best the Executive can suggest, with his present impressions, it must not be understood that no other possible mode would be acceptable.

Given under my hand at the city, of Washington, the 8th day of December, A.D. one thousand eight hundred and sixty-three, and of the independence of the United States of America the eighty-eighth.

By the President: ABRAHAM LINCOLN
WILLIAM H. SEWARD, Secretary of State.

Lincoln's Second Inaugural Address

March 4, 1865

Fellow Countrymen:

At this second appearing to take the oath of the presidential office, there is less occasion for an extended address than there was at the first. Then a statement, somewhat in detail, of a course to be pursued, seemed fitting and proper. Now, at the expiration of four years, during which public declarations have been constantly called forth on every point and phase of the great contest which still absorbs the attention, and engrosses the energies of the nation, little that is new could be presented. The progress of our arms, upon which all else chiefly depends, is as well known to the public as to myself; and it is, I trust, reasonably satisfactory and encouraging to all. With high hope for the future, no prediction in regard to it is ventured.

On the occasion corresponding to this four years ago, all thoughts were anxiously directed to an impending civil-war. All dreaded it—all sought to avert it. While the inaugeral [*sic*] address was being delivered from this place, devoted altogether to *saving* the Union without war, insurgent agents were in the city seeking to *destroy* it without war—seeking to dissolve the Union, and divide effects, by negotiation. Both parties deprecated war; but one of them would *make* war rather than let the nation survive; and the other would *accept* war rather than let it perish. And the war came.

One eighth of the whole population were colored slaves, not distributed generally over the Union, but localized in the Southern part of it. These slaves constituted a peculiar and powerful interest. All knew that this interest was, somehow, the cause of the war. To strengthen, perpetuate, and extend this interest was the object for which the insurgents would rend the Union, even by war; while the government claimed no right to do more than to restrict the territorial enlargement of it. Neither party expected for the war, the magnitude, or the duration, which it has already attained. Neither anticipated that the *cause* of the conflict might cease with, or even before, the conflict itself should cease. Each looked for an easier triumph, and a result less fundamental and astounding. Both read the same Bible, and pray to the same God; and each invokes His aid against the other. It may seem strange that any men should dare to ask a just God's assistance in wringing their bread from the sweat of other men's faces; but let us judge not that we be not judged. The prayers of both could not be answered; that of neither has been answered fully. The Almighty has His own purposes. "Woe unto the world because of offences! for it must needs be that offences come; but woe to that man by whom the offence cometh!" If we shall suppose that American Slavery is one of those offences which, in the providence of God, must needs come, but which, having continued through His appointed time, He now wills to remove, and that He gives to both North and South, this terrible war, as the woe due to those by whom the offence came, shall we discern therein any departure from those divine attributes which the believers in a Living God always ascribe to Him? Fondly do we hope—fervently do we pray—that this mighty scourge of war may speedily pass away. Yet, if God wills that it continue, until all the wealth piled by the bond-man's two hundred and fifty years of unrequited toil shall be sunk, and until every drop of blood drawn with the lash, shall be paid by another drawn with the sword, as was said three thousand years ago, so still it must be said "the judgments of the Lord, are true and righteous altogether."

With malice toward none; with charity for all; with firmness in the right, as God gives us to see the right, let us strive on to finish the work we are in; to bind up the nation's wounds; to care for him who shall have borne the battle, and for his widow, and his orphan—to do all which may achieve and cherish a just, and a lasting peace, among ourselves, and with all nations.

The Thirteenth, Fourteenth, and Fifteenth Amendments to the Constitution

ARTICLE XIII   [proposed 1 Feb. 1865; declared ratified 18 Dec. 1865]

Section 1. Neither slavery nor involuntary servitude, except as a punishment for crime whereof the party shall have been duly convicted, shall exist within the United States, or any place subject to their jurisdiction.

Section 2. Congress shall have power to enforce this article by appropriate legislation.

ARTICLE XIV   [proposed 16 June 1866; declared ratified 28 July 1868]

Section 1. All persons born or naturalized in the United States, and subject to the jurisdiction thereof, are citizens of the United States and of the State wherein they reside. No State shall make or enforce any law which shall abridge the privileges or immunities of citizens of the United States; nor shall any State deprive any person of life, liberty, or property, without due process of law; nor deny to any person within its jurisdiction the equal protection of the laws.

Section 2. Representatives shall be apportioned among the several States according to their respective numbers, counting the whole number of persons in each State, excluding Indians not taxed. But when the right to vote at any election for the choice of electors for President and Vice President of the United States, Representatives in Congress, the Executive and Judicial officers of a State, or the members of the Legislature thereof, is denied to any of the male inhabitants of such State, being twenty-one years of age, and citizens of the United States, or in any way abridged, except for participation in rebellion, or other crime, the basis of representation therein shall be reduced in the proportion which the number of such male citizens shall bear to the whole number of male citizens twenty-one years of age in such State.

Section 3. No person shall be a Senator or Representative in Congress, or elector of President and Vice President, or hold any office, civil or military, under the United States, or under any State, who, having previously taken an oath, as a member of Congress, or as an officer of the United States, or as a member of any State legislature, or as an executive or judicial officer of any State, to support the Constitution of the United States, shall have engaged in insurrection or rebellion against the same, or given aid and comfort to the enemies thereof. But Congress may by a vote of two-thirds of each House, remove such disability.

Section 4. The validity of the public debt of the United States, authorized by law, including debts incurred for payment of pensions and bounties for services in suppressing insurrection or rebellion, shall not be questioned. But neither the United States nor any state shall assume or pay any debt or obligation incurred in aid of insurrection or rebellion against the United States, or any claim for the loss or emancipation of any slave; but all such debts, obligations, and claims shall be held illegal and void.

Section 5. The Congress shall have power to enforce, by appropriate legislation, the provisions of this article.

ARTICLE XV [proposed 27 Feb. 1869; declared ratified 30 Mar. 1870]

Section 1. The right of citizens of the United States to vote shall not be denied or abridged by the United States or by any State on account of race, color, or previous condition of servitude.

Section 2. The Congress shall have power to enforce this article by appropriate legislation.

Bibliography

TABLE OF CONTENTS

ABBREVIATIONS

AH   *Agricultural History*

AHR   *American Historical Review*

CWH	Civil War History
JAH	Journal of American History
JEH	Journal of Economic History
JNH	Journal of Negro History
JSH	Journal of Southern History
MVHR	Mississippi Valley Historical Review
SAQ	South Atlantic Quarterly

Bibliographies on the Civil War—Reconstruction Era

The number of books and articles on the era of the Civil War and Reconstruction is so enormous that the following essay can provide only a selective listing of the most important of them. Students desiring more detailed bibliographies should consult the following guides, which are comprehensive to the dates of their publication: Don E. Fehrenbacher (ed.), *Manifest Destiny and the Coming of the Civil War* (1970); David Donald (ed.), *The Nation in Crisis, 1861–1877* (1969); and the relevant portions of Frank Freidel (ed.), *Harvard Guide to American History,* rev. ed. (1974). The essays by Charles Dew, Joe Gray Taylor, LaWanda Cox, and Harold Woodman in John B. Boles and Evelyn Thomas Nolen (eds.), *Interpreting Southern History* (1987), contain excellent reviews of scholarship on slavery, secession, the war, emancipation, Reconstruction, and the New South. For substantial bibliographies on slavery, consult John D. Smith, *Black Slavery in the Americas: An Interdisciplinary Bibliography,* 2 vols. (1983), and Joseph C. Miller (ed.), *Slavery and Slaving in World History,* 2 vols. (1998). The historiographical essays in James M. McPherson and William J. Cooper, Jr. (eds.), *Writing the Civil War: The Quest to Understand* (1998) focus mainly on the war years but contain references also to literature on the origins and consequences of the war. The same is true of the bibliographical essays in Steven E. Woodworth (ed.), *The American Civil War: A Handbook of Literature and Research* (1996). The December issue each year through 1977 of the quarterly journal *Civil War History* (1954–) classifies articles dealing with the Civil War era published in other journals during the previous year. Each issue of the *Journal of American History* and the May issue each year of the *Journal of Southern History* list articles published in other journals, including many articles on the Civil War era. The ongoing volumes of *Writings in American History* and *America: History and Life* contain classified listings of books and articles on all aspects of American history. A useful index of articles in a half-dozen popular magazines of Civil War history is Lee M. Meredith (ed.), *Guide to Civil War Periodicals,* 2 vols. (1991–98). For guides to the holdings of the U.S. Archives on the Civil War era, see Kenneth W. Munden and Henry Putney Beers, *The Union: A Guide to the Federal Archives Relating to the Civil War* (1986), and Henry Putney Beers, *The Confederacy: A Guide to the Archives of the Confederate States of America* (1986).

Biographical and Related Works

Biographies of important persons provide a great deal of information of value. The following is an alphabetical listing (by subject) of biographies of many of the principal figures of the Civil War and Reconstruction eras who receive prominent mention in this text. In some cases more than one biography is cited, and where relevant, diaries, collected letters, and other writings of individuals are also cited. In this section and throughout the bibliography, the date of publication in parentheses is for the original publication; many of the books have been reprinted in hardcover and/or paperback at later dates.

ADAMS, CHARLES FRANCIS
Duberman, Martin, *Charles Francis Adams* (1961).

Ford, Worthington C. (ed.), *A Cycle of Adams Letters, 1861–1865,* 2 vols. (1920). Wartime letters from Charles Francis Adams and his two sons Charles, Jr., and Henry.

ADAMS, HENRY
Adams, Henry, *The Education of Henry Adams* (1918).

Samuels, Ernest, *Henry Adams* (1989).

ANDREW, JOHN A.
Pearson, Henry G., *The Life of John A. Andrew, Governor of Massachusetts, 1861–1865,* 2 vols. (1904).

ATCHISON, DAVID
Parrish, William E., *David Rice Atchison of Missouri: Border Politician* (1961).

BANKS, NATHANIEL P.
Hollandsworth, James G., *Pretense of Glory: The Life of General Nathanial P. Banks* (1999).

BARTON, CLARA
Pryor, Elizabeth B., *Clara Barton: Professional Angel* (1987).

Oates, Stephen V., *Woman of Valor: Clara Barton and the Civil War* (1994).

BATES, EDWARD
Cain, Marvin R., *Lincoln's Attorney General: Edward Bates of Missouri* (1965).

Beale, Howard K. (ed.), *The Diary of Edward Bates, 1859–1866* (1933).

BEAUREGARD, PIERRE G. T.
Williams, T. Harry, *P. G. T. Beauregard: Napoleon in Gray* (1955).

BELL, JOHN
Parks, Joseph H., *John Bell of Tennessee* (1950).

BENJAMIN, JUDAH P.
Evans, Eli N., *Judah P. Benjamin: The Jewish Confederate* (1988).

BICKERDYKE, MARY ANN
Baker, Nina Brown, *Cyclone in Calico: The Story of Mary Ann Bickerdyke* (1952).

BIRNEY, JAMES G.
Fladeland, Betty, *James Gillespie Birney: Slaveholder to Abolitionist* (1955).

BLAIR, FRANCIS P., AND HIS SONS FRANCIS JR. (FRANK) AND MONTGOMERY
Smith, Elbert B., *Francis Preston Blair* (1980).

Smith, William E., *The Francis Preston Blair Family in Politics,* 2 vols. (1933).

Parrish, William E., *Frank Blair: Lincoln's Conservative* (1998).

BOOTH, JOHN WILKES
Bauer, Charles L., *So I Killed Lincoln: John Wilkes Booth* (1976).

Rhodehamel, John and Louise Taper (eds.), *"Right or Wrong, God Judge Me": The Writings of John Wilkes Booth* (1997).

BRADY, MATHEW
Meredith, Roy, *Mr. Lincoln's Camera Man: Mathew B. Brady*, 2d ed. rev. (1974).

BRAGG, BRAXTON
McWhiney, Grady, *Braxton Bragg and Confederate Defeat* (1969).

BRECKINRIDGE, JOHN C.
Davis, William C., *Breckinridge: Statesman, Soldier, Symbol* (1974).

BRISTOW, BENJAMIN
Webb, Ross Allan, *Benjamin Helm Bristow, Border State Politician* (1969).

BROWN, ALBERT GALLATIN
Ranck, James B., *Albert Gallatin Brown: Radical Southern Nationalist* (1937).

BROWN, JOHN
Boyer, Richard O., *The Legend of John Brown: A Biography and a History* (1973).

Oates, Stephen B., *To Purge This Land with Blood: A Biography of John Brown* (1970).

Villard, Oswald Garrison, *John Brown, 1800–1859: A Biography* (1910).

BROWN, JOSEPH E.
Parks, Joseph Howard, *Joseph E. Brown of Georgia* (1977).

BROWNLOW, WILLIAM G.
Coulter, E. Merton, *William G. Brownlow: Fighting Parson of the Southern Highlands* (1937).

BUCHANAN, JAMES
Klein, Philip S., *President James Buchanan* (1962).

Binder, Frederick M., *James Buchanan and the American Empire* (1994).

BUCKNER, SIMON B.
Stickles, Arndt M., *Simon Bolivar Buckner: Borderland Knight* (1940).

BUELL, DON CARLOS
Engle, Stephen D., *Don Carlos Buell: Most Promising of All* (2000).

BUFORD, JOHN
Longacre, Edward G., *General John Buford: A Military Biography* (1995).

BURNSIDE, AMBROSE E.
Marvel, William, *Burnside* (1991).

BUTLER, BENJAMIN
Trefousse, Hans, *Ben Butler: The South Called Him Beast* (1957).

West, Richard S., Jr., *Lincoln's Scapegoat General: A Life of Benjamin F. Butler* (1965).

CALHOUN, JOHN C.
Coit, Margaret, *John C. Calhoun, American Portrait* (1950).

Niven, John, *John C. Calhoun and the Price of Union* (1988).

Wiltse, Charles M., *John C. Calhoun*, 3 vols. (1944–1951).

CAMERON, SIMON
Bradley, Erwin S., *Simon Cameron, Lincoln's Secretary of War: A Political Biography* (1966).

CASS, LEWIS
Klunder, Willard C., *Lewis Cass and the Politics of Moderation* (1996).

CHASE, SALMON P.
Blue, Frederick, *Salmon P. Chase: A Life in Politics* (1987).

Niven, John, *Salmon P. Chase: A Biography* (1995).

Niven, John (ed.), *The Salmon P. Chase Papers,* 5 vols. (1993–1998).

CHESNUT, MARY BOYKIN
Muhlenfeld, Elizabeth, *Mary Boykin Chesnut: A Biography* (1981).

Woodward, C. Vann (ed.), *Mary Chesnut's Civil War* (1981).

CHESTER, T. MORRIS
Blacket, R. M. J. (ed.), *T. Morris Chester, Black Civil War Correspondent: His Dispatches from the Virginia Front* (1989).

CLAY, HENRY
Remini, Robert, *Henry Clay: Statesman for the Union* (1991).

Van Deusen, Glyndon G., *The Life of Henry Clay* (1937).

CLEBURNE, PATRICK
Symonds, Craig, *Stonewall of the West: Patrick Cleburne and the Civil War* (1997).

COBB, HOWELL
Simpson, John Eddings, *Howell Cobb: The Politics of Ambition* (1973).

COLT, SAMUEL
Rohan, Jack, *Yankee Arms Maker: The Story of Sam Colt and His Six-Shot Peacemaker* (1948).

COOKE, JAY
Larson, Henrietta Melia, *Jay Cooke, Private Banker* (1936).

COX, JACOB
Cox, Jacob D., *Military Reminiscences of the Civil War,* 2 vols. (1900).

COX, SAMUEL S.
Lindsey, David, *"Sunset" Cox, Irrepressible Democrat* (1959).

CRITTENDEN, JOHN J.
Kirwan, Albert D., *John J. Crittenden: The Struggle for the Union* (1962).

CUMMING, KATE
Harwell, Richard B. (ed.), *Kate: The Journal of a Confederate Nurse* (1960).

CURTIS, GEORGE WILLIAM
Milne, Gordon, *George William Curtis and the Genteel Tradition* (1956).

CUSTER, GEORGE A.
Monaghan, Jay, *Custer* (1959).

Weit, Jeffry D., *Custer* (1996).

DAVIS, DAVID
King, Willard L., *Lincoln's Manager: David Davis* (1960).

DAVIS, HENRY WINTER
Henig, Gerald S., *Henry Winter Davis: Antebellum and Civil War Congressman from Maryland* (1973).

DAVIS, JEFFERSON
Davis, William C., *Jefferson Davis: The Man and His Hour* (1991).

Allen, Felicity, *Jefferson Davis, Unconquerable Heart* (1999).

Monroe, Haskell M., Jr., Linda Lassell Crist, and others (eds.), *The Papers of Jefferson Davis,* 10 vols. so far (to 1864) (1971–).

Rowland, Dunbar (ed.), *Jefferson Davis, Constitutionalist: His Letters, Papers and Speeches,* 10 vols. (1923).

DE BOW, JAMES B. D.
Skipper, Otis Clark, *J. B. D. De Bow, Magazinist of the Old South* (1958).

DIX, DOROTHEA
Brown, Thomas J., *Dorothea Dix: New England Reformer* (1998).

DOUGLAS, STEPHEN A.
Johannsen, Robert W., *Stephen A. Douglas* (1973).

Milton, George F., *The Eve of Conflict: Stephen A. Douglas and the Needless War* (1934).

DOUGLASS, FREDERICK
Blight, David W., *Frederick Douglass' Civil War: Keeping Faith in Jubilee* (1989).

Foner, Philip S., *The Life and Writings of Frederick Douglass,* 4 vols. (1950–1955).

McFeely, William S., *Frederick Douglass* (1991).

Quarles, Benjamin, *Frederick Douglass* (1948).

EARLY, JUBAL
Osborne, Charles C., *Jubal: The Life and Times of General Jubal A. Early* (1992).

ERICSSON, JOHN
White, Ruth, *Yankee from Sweden: The Dream and the Reality in the Days of John Ericsson* (1960).

EVARTS, WILLIAM M.
Barrows, Chester L., *William M. Evarts: Lawyer, Diplomat, Statesman* (1941).

EVERETT, EDWARD
Reid, Ronald F., *Edward Everett: Unionist Orator* (1990).

EWELL, RICHARD S.
Pfanz, Donald C., *Richard S. Ewell: A Soldier's Life* (1998).

FARRAGUT, DAVID G.
Duffy, James P., *Lincoln's Admiral: The Civil War Campaigns of David Farragut* (1997).

Hearn, Chester G., *Admiral David Glasgow Farragut: The Civil War Years* (1997).

FESSENDEN, WILLIAM P.
Jellison, Charles A., *Fessenden of Maine: Civil War Senator* (1962).

FILLMORE, MILLARD
Rayback, Robert J., *Millard Fillmore: Biography of a President* (1959).

FINNEY, CHARLES GRANDISON
Hambrick-Stowe, Charles E., *Charles G. Finney and the Spirit of American Evangelicalism* (1997).

FISH, HAMILTON
Nevins, Allan, *Hamilton Fish: The Inner History of the Grant Administration* (1936).

FITZHUGH, GEORGE
Genovese, Eugene D., *The World the Slaveholders Made* (1969).

Wish, Harvey, *George Fitzhugh: Propagandist of the Old South* (1943).

FORREST, NATHAN BEDFORD
Hurst, Jack, *Nathan Bedford Forrest: A Biography* (1993).

Wills, Brian Steel, *A Battle From the Start: The Life of Nathan Bedford Forrest* (1992).

FOX, GUSTAVUS V.
Thompson, Robert M., and Richard Wainwright (eds.), *Confidential Correspondence of Gustavus Vasa Fox, Assistant Secretary of the Navy, 1861–1865,* 2 vols. (1918–1919).

FRÉMONT, JOHN C.
Rolle, Andrew, *John Charles Frémont: Character as Destiny* (1991).

GARFIELD, JAMES A.
Peskin, Allan, *Garfield: A Biography* (1978).

Williams, Frederick D. (ed.), *The Wild Life of the Army: Civil War Letters of James A. Garfield* (1964).

GARRISON, WILLIAM LLOYD
Mayer, Henry, *All on Fire: William Lloyd Garrison and the Abolition of Slavery* (1998).

Thomas, John L., *The Liberator: William Lloyd Garrison* (1963).

Merrill, Walter M., and Louis Ruchames (eds.), *The Letters of William Lloyd Garrison,* 6 vols. (1971–1981).

GEARY, JOHN W.
Tinkcom, Harry M., *John White Geary: Soldier-Statesman, 1819–1873* (1940).

GIDDINGS, JOSHUA
Stewart, James B., *Joshua Giddings and the Tactics of Radical Politics* (1970).

GORGAS, JOSIAH
Vandiver, Frank E., *Ploughshares into Swords: Josiah Gorgas and Confederate Ordnance* (1952).

Wiggins, Sarah Woolfolk (ed.), *The Journals of Josiah Gorgas, 1857–1878* (1995).

GRADY, HENRY
Nixon, Raymond B., *Henry W. Grady: Spokesman of the New South* (1943).

GRANT, ULYSSES S.
Lewis, Lloyd, *Captain Sam Grant* (1950).

Catton, Bruce, *Grant Moves South* (1960).

Catton, Bruce, *Grant Takes Command* (1969).

McFeely, William S., *Grant: A Biography* (1981).

Perret, Geoffrey, *Ulysses S. Grant: Soldier & President* (1997).

Grant, Ulysses S., *Personal Memoirs of U.S. Grant,* 2 vols. (1885).

John Y. Simon (ed.), *The Papers of Ulysses S. Grant,* 24 vols. so far (to 1873) (1967–   ).

GREELEY, HORACE
Hale, William H., *Horace Greeley: Voice of the People* (1950).

Van Deusen, Glyndon G., *Horace Greeley: Nineteenth-Century Crusader* (1953).

GREENHOW, ROSE O'NEAL
Ross, Ishbel, *Rebel Rose: Life of Rose O'Neal Greenhow, Confederate Spy* (1954).

GREGG, WILLIAM
Mitchell, Broadus, *William Gregg: Factory Master of the Old South* (1928).

GRIERSON, BENJAMIN
Leckie, William H., and Shirley A. Leckie, *Unlikely Warriors: General Benjamin H. Grierson and His Family* (1984).

GRIMKÉ, ANGELINA AND SARAH
Birney, Catherine H., *The Grimké Sisters: Sarah and Angelina Grimké* (1977).

Lerner, Gerda, *The Grimké Sisters from South Carolina: Rebels Against Slavery* (1967).

Lumkin, Katherine Du Pre, *The Emancipation of Angelina Grimké* (1974).

GROW, GALUSHA
Ilisevich, Robert D., *Galusha A. Grow: The People's Candidate* (1989).

HALE, JOHN P.
Sewell, Richard H., *John P. Hale and the Politics of Abolition* (1965).

HALLECK, HENRY W.
Ambrose, Steven E., *Halleck: Lincoln's Chief of Staff* (1962).

HAMLIN, HANNIBAL
Scroggs, Mark, *Hannibal: The Life of Lincoln's First Vice President* (1993).

HAMMOND, JAMES H.
Faust, Drew Gilpin, *James Henry Hammond and the Old South* (1982).

Bleser, Carol (ed.), *Secret and Sacred: The Diaries of James Henry Hammond, a Southern Slaveholder* (1988).

HAMPTON, WADE
Wellman, Manly Wade, *Giant in Gray: A Biography of Wade Hampton of South Carolina* (1949).

HANCOCK, WINFIELD SCOTT
Jordan, David M., *Winfield Scott Hancock: A Soldier's Life* (1988).

HARDEE, WILLIAM J.
Hughes, Nathaniel C., Jr., *General William J. Hardee: Old Reliable* (1965).

HAY, JOHN
Clymer, Kenton J., *John Hay: The Gentleman as Diplomat* (1975).

Dennett, Tyler, *John Hay: From Poetry to Politics* (1933).

HAYES, RUTHERFORD B.
Hoogenboom, Ari, *Rutherford B. Hayes: Warrior and President* (1995).

Williams, C. R. (ed.), *Diary and Letters of Rutherford Birchard Hayes,* 5 vols. (1922–1926).

HELPER, HINTON ROWAN
Bailey, Hugh C., *Hinton Rowan Helper: Abolitionist-Racist* (1965).

HIGGINSON, THOMAS WENTWORTH
Edelstein, Tilden G., *Strange Enthusiasm, A Life of Thomas Wentworth Higginson* (1968).

HILL, AMBROSE POWELL
Robertson, James I., Jr., *General A. P. Hill: The Story of a Confederate Warrior* (1987).

HILL, DANIEL HARVEY
Bridges, Hal, *Lee's Maverick General: Daniel Harvey Hill* (1961).

HOLDEN, WILLIAM W.
Harris, William C., *William Woods Holden: Firebrand of North Carolina Politics* (1987).

HOLMES, OLIVER WENDELL, JR.
Howe, Mark De Wolf, *Justice Oliver Wendell Holmes: The Shaping Years, 1841–1870* (1957).

Novick, Sheldon M., *Honorable Justice: The Life of Oliver Wendell Holmes* (1989).

HOOD, JOHN B.
McMurry, Richard M., *John Bell Hood and the War for Southern Independence* (1982).

HOOKER, JOSEPH
Hebert, Walter H., *Fighting Joe Hooker* (1944).

HOWARD, OLIVER O.
Carpenter, John A., *Sword and Olive Branch: Oliver Otis Howard* (1964).

HOWE, JULIA WARD
Clifford, Deborah Pickman, *Mine Eyes Have Seen the Glory: A Biography of Julia Ward Howe* (1979).

HUNTER, DAVID
Miller, Edward A., Jr., *Lincoln's Abolitionist General: The Biography of David Hunter* (1997).

HUNTER, ROBERT M. T.
Simms, Henry H., *Life of Robert M. T. Hunter: A Study in Sectionalism and Secession* (1935).

JACKSON, ANDREW
Remini, Robert, *The Life of Andrew Jackson* (1988).

JACKSON, THOMAS J.
Chambers, Lenoir, *Stonewall Jackson,* 2 vols. (1959).

Henderson, G. F. R., *Stonewall Jackson and the American Civil War,* 2 vols. (1919).

Robertson, James I., Jr., *Stonewall Jackson: The Man, the Soldier, the Legend* (1997).

Vandiver, Frank E., *Mighty Stonewall* (1957).

JOHNSON, ANDREW

Trefousse, Hans L., *Andrew Johnson: A Biography* (1989).

Graf, Le Roy P., Ralph W. Haskins, and Paul Bergeron (eds.). *The Papers of Andrew Johnson*, 15 vols. so far (to 1869) (1967–   ).

JOHNSTON, ALBERT SIDNEY

Roland, Charles P., *Albert Sidney Johnston: Soldier of Three Republics* (1964).

JOHNSTON, JOSEPH E.

Symonds, Craig L., *Joseph E. Johnston: A Civil War Biography* (1992).

JULIAN, GEORGE W.

Riddleberger, Patrick W., *George Washington Julian, Radical Republican* (1966).

LEE, ROBERT E.

Connelly, Thomas L., *The Marble Man: Robert E. Lee and His Image in American Society* (1977).

Freeman, Douglas Southall, *R. E. Lee: A Biography*, 4 vols. (1934–1935).

Nolan, Alan T., *Lee Considered: General Robert E. Lee and Civil War History* (1991).

Thomas, Emory M., *Robert E. Lee: A Biography* (1995).

Roland, Charles P., *Reflections on Lee: A Historian's Assessment* (1995).

Dowdey, Clifford (ed.), *The Wartime Papers of R. E. Lee* (1961).

Gallagher, Gary (ed.), *Lee the Soldier* (1996).

LINCOLN, ABRAHAM

Boritt, Gabor S. (ed.), *The Historian's Lincoln* (1988).

Current, Richard N., *The Lincoln Nobody Knows* (1958).

Donald, David Herbert, *Lincoln* (1995).

Donald, David, *Lincoln Reconsidered*, 2d ed. (1961).

Fehrenbacher, Don E., *Lincoln in Text and Context: Collected Essays* (1987).

Luthin, Reinhard, *The Real Abraham Lincoln* (1960).

Neely, Mark E., Jr., *The Abraham Lincoln Encyclopedia* (1982).

Neely, Mark E., Jr., *The Last Best Hope of Earth: Abraham Lincoln and the Promise of America* (1993).

Thomas, Benjamin P., *Abraham Lincoln* (1952).

Basler, Roy P., et al. (eds.), *The Collected Works of Abraham Lincoln,* 9 vols. (1953–1955); *The Collected Works of Abraham Lincoln—Supplement, 1832–1865* (1974); and *Second Supplement, 1848–1865* (1990).

Cuomo, Mario, and Harold Holzer (eds.), *Lincoln on Democracy* (1990).

LINCOLN, MARY TODD

Baker, Jean, *Mary Todd Lincoln: A Biography* (1987).

LONGSTREET, JAMES

Piston, William Garrett, *Lee's Tarnished Lieutenant: James Longstreet and His Place in Southern History* (1987).

Wert, Jeffry D., *General James Longstreet* (1993).

LYON, NATHANIEL
Phillips, Christopher, *Damned Yankee: The Life of Nathaniel Lyon* (1990).

MAHONE, WILLIAM
Blake, Nelson M., *William Mahone of Virginia: Soldier and Political Insurgent* (1935).

MALLORY, STEPHEN R.
Durkin, Joseph T., *Stephen R. Mallory: Confederate Navy Chief* (1954).

MANN, HORACE
Messerli, Jonathan, *Horace Mann: A Biography* (1972).

MASON, JAMES M.
Young, Robert W., *Senator James Murray Mason: Defender of the Old South* (1998).

MCCLELLAN, GEORGE B.
Sears, Stephen W., *George B. McClellan: The Young Napoleon* (1988).

Sears, Stephen W. (ed.), *The Civil War Papers of George B. McClellan* (1989).

MCLEAN, JOHN
Weisenburger, Francis P., *The Life of John McLean: A Politician on the United States Supreme Court* (1937).

MCPHERSON, JAMES B.
Whaley, Elizabeth J., *Forgotten Hero: General James B. McPherson* (1955).

MEADE, GEORGE GORDON
Cleaves, Freeman, *Meade of Gettysburg* (1960).

MEIGS, MONTGOMERY
Weigley, Russell F., *Quartermaster General of the Union Army: A Biography of M. C. Meigs* (1959).

MORGAN, JOHN HUNT
Ramage, James A., *Rebel Raider: The Life of General John Hunt Morgan* (1986).

MORTON, OLIVER P.
Foulke, William D., *Life of Oliver P. Morton,* 2 vols. (1899).

MOSBY, JOHN SINGLETON
Jones, Virgil C., *Ranger Mosby* (1944).

Siepel, Kevin H., *Rebel: The Life and Times of John Singleton Mosby* (1983).

NAST, THOMAS
Keller, Morton, *The Art and Politics of Thomas Nast* (1968).

OLMSTED, FREDERICK LAW
Roper, Laura, *FLO: A Biography of Frederick Law Olmsted* (1973).

PARKER, THEODORE
Commager, Henry Steele, *Theodore Parker* (1936).

PEMBERTON, JOHN C.
Ballard, Michael B., *Pemberton: A Biography* (1991).

PHILLIPS, WENDELL
Stewart, James Brewer, *Wendell Phillips: Liberty's Hero* (1986).

PICKETT, GEORGE E.
Gordon, Lesley J., *General George E. Pickett in Life & Legend* (1998).

Longacre, Edward G., *Leader of the Charge: A Biography of General George E. Pickett* (1995).

PIERCE, FRANKLIN
Nichols, Roy F., *Franklin Pierce: Young Hickory of the Granite Hills* (1958).

PIKE, JAMES SHEPHERD
Durden, Robert F., *James Shepherd Pike: Republicanism and the American Negro, 1850–1882* (1957).

PINKERTON, ALLAN
Mackay, James A., *Allan Pinkerton: The Eye Who Never Slept* (1996).

POLK, JAMES K.
Haynes, Samuel W., *James K. Polk and the Expansionist Impulse* (1997).

Quaife, Milo M. (ed.), *The Diary of James K. Polk During His Presidency*, 4 vols. (1910).

Weaver, Herbert, et al. (eds.), *The Correspondence of James K. Polk*, 7 vols. so far (1969–).

POLK, LEONIDAS
Parks, Joseph H., *General Leonidas Polk, C.S.A.: The Fighting Bishop* (1962).

POPE, JOHN
Cozzens, Peter, *General John Pope: A Life for the Nation* (1999).

PORTER, DAVID D.
West, Richard S., Jr., *The Second Admiral: A Life of David Dixon Porter* (1937).

PORTER, FITZ JOHN
Eisenschiml, Otto, *The Celebrated Case of Fitz John Porter* (1950).

PRICE, STERLING
Castel, Albert, *General Sterling Price and the Civil War in the West* (1968).

Shalhope, Robert E., *Sterling Price: Portrait of a Southerner* (1971).

QUANTRILL, WILLIAM C.
Castel, Albert, *William Clarke Quantrill: His Life and Times* (1962).

QUITMAN, JOHN A.
May, Robert, *John A. Quitman: Old South Crusader* (1985).

RAYMOND, HENRY J.
Brown, Francis, *Raymond of the Times* (1951).

REYNOLDS, JOHN F.
Nichols, Edward J., *Toward Gettysburg: A Biography of General John F. Reynolds* (1958).

RHETT, ROBERT BARNWELL
White, Laura A., *Robert Barnwell Rhett, Father of Secession* (1931).

ROSECRANS, WILLIAM S.
Lamers, William M., *The Edge of Glory: A Biography of General S. Rosecrans* (1961).

RUFFIN, EDMUND
Mathew, William M., *Edmund Ruffin and the Crisis of Slavery in the Old South* (1988).

Mitchell, Betty L., *Edmund Ruffin: A Biography* (1981).

Scarborough, William S. (ed.), *The Diary of Edmund Ruffin,* 3 vols. (1972–1989).

SCHOFIELD, JOHN M.
McDonough, James L., *Schofield: Union General in the Civil War* (1972).

SCHURZ, CARL
Trefousse, Hans, *Carl Schurz: A Biography* (1982).

SCOTT, WINFIELD
Eisenhower, John S. D., *Agent of Destiny: The Life and Times of General Winfield Scott* (1997).

Johnson, Timothy D., *Winfield Scott: The Quest for Military Glory* (1999).

SEWARD, WILLIAM H.
Van Deusen, Glyndon G., *William Henry Seward* (1967).

Taylor, John M., *William Henry Seward* (1991).

SEYMOUR, HORATIO
Mitchell, Stewart, *Horatio Seymour of New York* (1938).

SHERIDAN, PHILIP H.
Morris, Roy, Jr., *Sheridan: The Life and Wars of General Phil Sheridan* (1992).

Sheridan, Philip H., *Personal Memoirs,* 2 vols. (1888).

SHERMAN, JOHN
Burton, Theodore E., *John Sherman* (1906).

SHERMAN, WILLIAM TECUMSEH
Fellman, Michael, *Citizen Sherman* (1995).

Liddell Hart, Basil H., *Sherman: Soldier, Realist, American* (1929).

Marszalek, John F., *Sherman: A Soldier's Passion for Order* (1993).

Vetter, Charles E., *Sherman: Merchant of Terror, Advocate of Peace* (1992).

Sherman, William T., *Memoirs of General W. T. Sherman,* 2 vols., 2d ed. rev. (1886).

Simpson, Brooks D., and Jean V. Berlin (eds.), *Selected Correspondence of William T. Sherman, 1860–1865* (1999).

SICKLES, DANIEL
Swanberg, W. A., *Sickles the Incredible* (1956).

Knoop, Jeanne W., *"I Follow the Course, Come What May": Major General Daniel E. Sickles, USA* (1999).

SIGEL, FRANZ
Engle, Stephen D., *Yankee Dutchman: The Life of Franz Sigel* (1993).

SLIDELL, JOHN
Sears, Louis M., *John Slidell* (1925).

SMALLS, ROBERT
Miller, Edward A., Jr., *Gullah Statesman: Robert Smalls from Slavery to Congress, 1839–1915* (1995).

SMITH, EDMUND KIRBY
Parks, Joseph H., *General Edmund Kirby Smith* (1954).

SMITH, GERRIT
Harlow, Ralph V., *Gerrit Smith: Philanthropist and Reformer* (1939).

STANTON, EDWIN M.
Thomas, Benjamin P., and Harold M. Hyman, *Stanton: The Life and Times of Lincoln's Secretary of War* (1962).

STANTON, ELIZABETH CADY
Griffith, Elisabeth, *In Her Own Right: The Life of Elizabeth Cady Stanton* (1984).

STEPHENS, ALEXANDER H.
Schott, Thomas E., *Alexander H. Stephens of Georgia: A Biography* (1988).

Von Abele, Rudolph, *Alexander H. Stephens: A Biography* (1946).

STEVENS, THADDEUS
Trefousse, Hans L., *Thaddeus Stevens: Nineteenth-Century Crusader* (1997).

Palmer, Beverly Wilson, and Holly Byers Ochoa (eds.), *The Selected Papers of Thaddeus Stevens,* 2 vols. (1997).

STOWE, HARRIET BEECHER
Foster, Charles H., *The Rungless Ladder: Harriet Beecher Stowe and New England Puritanism* (1954).

Hedrick, Joan D., *Harriet Beecher Stowe: A Life* (1994).

STUART, JAMES E. B.
Davis, Burke, *Jeb Stuart, the Last Cavalier* (1957).

Thomas, Emory, *Bold Dragoon: The Life of J. E. B. Stuart* (1986).

SUMNER, CHARLES
Donald, David, *Charles Sumner and the Coming of the Civil War* (1960).

Donald, David, *Charles Sumner and the Rights of Man* (1970).

Palmer, Beverly Wilson (ed.), *The Selected Letters of Charles Sumner,* 2 vols. (1990).

SUMNER, EDWIN V.
Crocchiola, Stanley F. L., *E. V. Sumner, Major-General United States Army, 1797–1863* (1969).

TANEY, ROGER B.
Lewis, Walker, *Without Fear or Favor: A Biography of Chief Justice Roger Brooke Taney* (1965).

Swisher, Carl B., *Roger B. Taney* (1935).

TAPPAN, LEWIS
Wyatt-Brown, Bertram, *Lewis Tappan and the Evangelical War Against Slavery* (1969).

TAYLOR, ZACHARY
Bauer, K. Jack, *Zachary Taylor: Soldier, Planter, Statesman of the Old Southwest* (1985).

Hamilton, Holman, *Zachary Taylor,* 2 vols. (1941–1951).

THOMAS, GEORGE H.
Cleaves, Freeman, *Rock of Chickamauga: The Life of General George H. Thomas* (1948).

McKinney, Francis F., *Education in Violence: The Life of George H. Thomas and the History of the Army of the Cumberland* (1961).

TILDEN, SAMUEL J.
Flick, Alexander C., *Samuel Jones Tilden: A Study in Political Sagacity* (1939).

TOOMBS, ROBERT
Thompson, William Y., *Robert Toombs of Georgia* (1966).

TRUMBULL, LYMAN
Roske, Ralph J., *His Own Counsel: The Life and Times of Lyman Trumbull* (1979).

TYLER, JOHN
Chidsey, Donald B., *And Tyler Too* (1978).

VALLANDIGHAM, CLEMENT L.
Klement, Frank L., *The Limits of Dissent: Clement L. Vallandigham and the Civil War* (1970).

VAN BUREN, MARTIN
Cole, Donald B., *Martin Van Buren and the American Political System* (1984).

Niven, John, *Martin Van Buren: The Romantic Age of American Politics* (1983).

VAN DORN, EARL
Carter, Arthur B., *The Tarnished Cavalier: Major General Earl Van Dorn, C.S.A.* (1999).

VANCE, ZEBULON
Tucker, Glenn, *Zeb Vance: Champion of Personal Freedom* (1966).

WADE, BENJAMIN
Trefousse, Hans L., *Benjamin Franklin Wade: Radical Republican from Ohio* (1963).

WALKER, ROBERT J.
Shenton, James P., *Robert John Walker: A Politician from Jackson to Lincoln* (1961).

WALKER, WILLIAM
Carr, Albert H., *The World and William Walker* (1963).

WEBSTER, DANIEL
Remini, Robert, *Daniel Webster: The Man and His Time* (1997).

WELD, THEODORE
Abzug, Robert H., *Passionate Liberator: Theodore Dwight Weld and the Dilemma of Reform* (1980).

WELLES, GIDEON
Niven, John, *Gideon Welles: Lincoln's Secretary of the Navy* (1973).

Beale, Howard K., and Alan W. Brownsward (eds.), *The Diary of Gideon Welles* (1960).

WHEELER, JOSEPH
Dyer, John P., *"Fightin' Joe" Wheeler* (1941).

WIGFALL, LOUIS T.
King, Alvy L., *Louis T. Wigfall, Southern Fire-eater* (1970).

WILKES, CHARLES
Henderson, Daniel, *The Hidden Coasts: A Biography of Admiral Charles Wilkes* (1953).

WILMOT, DAVID
Going, Charles B., *David Wilmot, Free-Soiler* (1924).

WILSON, HENRY
Abbott, Richard H., *Cobbler in Congress: The Life of Henry Wilson* (1972).

WISE, HENRY A.
Simpson, Craig M., *A Good Southerner: The Life of Henry A. Wise of Virginia* (1985).

YANCEY, WILLIAM LOWNDES
DuBose, John Witherspoon, *The Life and Times of William Lowndes Yancey* (1892).

General Works on the Civil War—Reconstruction Era

Two eminent historians writing a half-century apart have produced magisterial multivolume narratives of America's sectional trauma: James Ford Rhodes, *History of the United States from the Compromise of 1850 to the McKinley-Bryan Campaign of 1896,* 8 vols. (1892–1919); and Allan Nevins, *Ordeal of the Union,* covering the years 1847–1857, 2 vols. (1947), *The Emergence of Lincoln,* covering 1857–1861, 2 vols. (1950), and *The War for the Union,* 4 vols. (1959–1971). Other important one-volume studies covering all or part of this period include Peter J. Parish, *The American Civil War* (1975), and William R. Brock, *Conflict and Transformation: The United States 1844–1877* (1973), both by British historians who offer valuable perspectives on the American experience; David Herbert Donald, *Liberty and Union* (1978); Arthur C. Cole, *The Irrepressible Conflict 1850–1865* (1934); James M. McPherson, *Battle Cry of Freedom: The Civil War Era* (1988); Joel Silbey, *The American Political Nation, 1838–1893* (1991); Richard H. Sewell, *A House Divided: Sectionalism and Civil War, 1848–1865* (1988); Roger L. Ransom, *Conflict and Compromise: The Political Economy of Slavery, Emancipation, and the American Civil War* (1989); Charles P. Roland, *An American Iliad: The Story of the Civil War* (1991); William L. Barney, *Battleground for the Union: The Era of the Civil War and Reconstruction* (1990); Richard Franklin Bensel, *Yankee Leviathan: The Origins of Central State Authority in America, 1859–1877* (1990); and Allen C. Guelzo, *The Crisis of the American Republic; A History of the Civil War and Reconstruction Era* (1995).

Charles A. Beard and Mary A. Beard's sweeping survey of American history, *The Rise of American Civilization,* 2 vols. (1927), interprets the Civil War as a "Second American Revolution," by which an industrializing North destroyed the agrarian civilization of the Old South. Refinements and modifications of this interpretation can be found in Barrington Moore, *Social Origins of Dictatorship and Democracy* (1966), chap. 3: "The American Civil War: The Last Capitalist Revolution"; Margaret Shortreed, "The Anti-Slavery Radicals, 1840–1868," *Past and Present,* no. 16 (1959), 65–87; and Raimondo Luraghi, *The Rise and Fall of the Plantation South* (1978). Carl N. Degler, "The Two Cultures and the Civil War," in Stanley Coben and Lorman Ratner (eds.), *The Development of an American Culture* (1970), pp. 92–119, emphasizes cultural differences between North and South.

Wilbur J. Cash, *The Mind of the South* (1941), evokes the impact of the sectional conflict on the South; while Robert Penn Warren, *The Legacy of the Civil War* (1964), a book published during the centennial commemoration of the conflict, critically appraises the war's meaning. Several essays in Arthur S. Link and Rembert W. Patrick (eds.), *Writing Southern History: Essays in Historiography in Honor of Fletcher M. Green* (1965), evaluate historical writing about the South during the middle decades of the nineteenth century. Carl N. Degler, *The Other*

South: Southern Dissenters in the Nineteenth Century (1974), offers a fresh and enlightening account of Southern whites who resisted the dominant institutions and developments in their region. Roger W. Shugg, *Origins of Class Struggle in Louisiana 1840–1875* (1939), focuses on non-elite whites in one state during the era. Superb insights into the mentality of the South's planter elite can be found in the massive collection of letters from the Jones family of Georgia, Robert M. Myers (ed.), *The Children of Pride* (1972).

Hans L. Trefousse, *The Radical Republicans: Lincoln's Vanguard for Racial Justice* (1969), analyzes the group in the North most committed to an overthrow of the Old South's institutions; while George M. Fredrickson, *The Black Image in the White Mind: The Debate Over Afro-American Character and Destiny, 1817–1914* (1972), traces the evolution of racial ideologies during the era.

Several individual historians have published collections of important and stimulating essays on the Civil War and related themes: C. Vann Woodward, *The Burden of Southern History,* 3d ed. (1993) and *American Counterpoint: Slavery and Racism in the North-South Dialogue* (1971); David M. Potter, *The South and the Sectional Conflict* (1968); Stephen B. Oates, *Our Fiery Trial: Abraham Lincoln, John Brown, and the Civil War Era* (1979); Eric Foner, *Politics and Ideology in the Age of the Civil War* (1980); James M. McPherson, *Drawn With the Sword: Reflections on the American Civil War* (1996); and Edmund Wilson, *Patriotic Gore: Studies in the Literature of the American Civil War* (1962).

Anthologies of essays and articles by various historians include: Charles Crowe (ed.), *The Age of Civil War and Reconstruction, 1830–1900,* rev. ed. (1975); Michael Perman (ed.), *Major Problems in the Civil War and Reconstruction* (1991); George M. Fredrickson (ed.), *A Nation Divided: Problems and Issues of the Civil War and Reconstruction* (1975); Robert P. Swierenga, (ed.), *Beyond the Civil War Synthesis: Political Essays on the Civil War Era* (1975); Irwin Unger (ed.), *Essays on the Civil War and Reconstruction* (1970); Harold D. Woodman (ed.), *The Legacy of the American Civil War* (1973); Walter J. Fraser, Jr., and Winifred B. Moore, Jr., *From the Old South to the New: Essays on the Transitional South* (1981); J. Morgan Kousser and James M. McPherson (eds.), *Region, Race and Reconstruction* (1982); Robert H. Abzug and Stephen E. Maizlish (eds.), *Race and Slavery in America* (1986); and Lloyd E. Ambrosius (ed.), *A Crisis of Republicanism: American Politics during the Civil War Era* (1990); David W. Blight and Brooks D. Simpson (eds.), *Union & Emancipation: Essays on Politics and Race in the Civil War Era* (1997); and Robert H. Abzug and Stephen E. Maizlish (eds.), *New Perspectives on Race and Slavery in America* (1986).

The history of political parties and presidential elections during the era is ably covered by several historians in Winifred E. A. Bernhard (ed.), *Political Parties in American History* (1973); Arthur M. Schlesinger, Jr. (ed.), *History of U.S. Political Parties,* 4 vols. (1973), vols. I and II; and Arthur M. Schlesinger, Jr. (ed.), *History of American Presidential Elections,* 4 vols. (1971), vol. II. The maps in Charles O. Paullin, *Atlas of the Historical Geography of the United States* (1932), provide a wealth of important data on the social, economic, and political history of this period. *Historical Statistics of the United States* (1975) and Donald B. Dodd and Wynette S. Dodd (eds.), *Historical Statistics of the South* (1973), are indispensable.

The Antebellum Years and the Coming of the Civil War

General Works

A brief introduction to the period is provided by John Niven, *The Coming of the Civil War* (1990). The fullest and most enlightening chronicle of the antebellum decade is David M. Potter, *The Impending Crisis 1848–1861* (1976). Avery Craven, *The Coming of the Civil War* (1942), blames extremists in both sections, particularly in the North, for whipping up popular passions that led to conflict. This "revisionist" interpretation can also be found in Avery Craven, *The Growth of Southern Nationalism 1848–1861* (1953). A less partisan history of the South, during an earlier period, is Charles S. Sydnor, *The Development of Southern Sectionalism, 1819–1848* (1948). Ulrich B. Phillips, *The Course of the South to Secession* (1939), sympathetically traces the emergence of a self-conscious Southern nationalism. William L. Barney, *The Road to Secession: A New Perspective on the Old South* (1972), is more critical of the South, while William W. Freehling, *The Road to Disunion: Secessionists at Bay 1776–1854* (1990), provides a hard-edged analysis of evolving Southern sectionalism. Don E. Fehrenbacher, *The South and Three Sectional Crises* (1980), analyzes the Missouri Compromise, the Compromise of 1850, and the Kansas-Nebraska controversy. A fuller study of these and other compromises is Peter B. Knupfer, *The Union as It Is: Constitutional Unionism and Sectional Compromise, 1787–1861* (1991). Two useful though difficult studies of the antebellum mentality are Paul C. Nagel, *One Nation Indivisible: The Union in American Thought, 1776–1861* (1964); and Major Wilson, *Space, Time, and Freedom: The Quest for Nationality and the Irrepressible Conflict, 1815–1861* (1974). George B. Forgie, *Patricide in the House Divided: A Psychological Interpretation of Lincoln and His Age* (1979), offers a fascinating and provocative view of the sectional conflict. A superb collection of primary sources on the social and cultural landscape of the pre-Civil War years can be found in David Brion Davis (ed.), *Antebellum American Culture* (1979).

The "causes" of the Civil War have been set forth in a voluminous and at times contentious literature. For an interesting analysis of this literature, begin with Thomas J. Pressly, *Americans Interpret Their Civil War,* 2d ed. (1962). Three fine anthologies of interpretive writings, reflecting all the major viewpoints, are Michael Perman (ed.), *The Coming of the American Civil War,* 3d ed. (1993); Hans L. Trefousse (ed.), *The Causes of the Civil War* (1971); and Kenneth M. Stampp (ed.), *The Causes of the Civil War,* 2d ed. (1974). For a brief, insightful view by an Australian scholar, see Alan A. Conway, *The Causes of the American Civil War: An Historical Perspective* (1961). Two British historians have offered varied insights: Bruce Collins, *The Origins of America's Civil War* (1981), and Brian Holden Reid, *The Origins of the American Civil War* (1996). Other useful essays that have appeared during the past forty years include David Donald, "American Historians and the Causes of the Civil War," *SAQ,* 59 (1960), 251–255; Lee Benson and Cushing Strout, "Causation and the American Civil War: Two Appraisals," *History and Theory,* 1 (1961), 163–185; William Dray, "Some Causal Accounts of the American Civil War," *Daedalus,* 91 (1962), 578–592, with comment by Newton Garner, 592–598; Eric Foner, "The Causes of the American Civil War: Recent Interpretations and New Directions," *CWH,* 20 (1974), 197–214; and Gabor S. Boritt (ed.), *Why the Civil War Came* (1996). A unique approach can be found in Stephen B. Oates, *The Approaching Fury: Voices of the Storm, 1820–1861* (1997). Bruce Levine, *Half Slave and Half Free: The Roots of the Civil War* (1992), skillfully blends social, economic, cultural, and political history.

The essays by Joel H. Silbey, *The Partisan Imperative: The Dynamics of American Politics Before the Civil War* (1985), offer the viewpoint of the "new" political history, while Don E. Fehrenbacher, "The New Political History and the Coming of the Civil War," *Pacific Historical Review,* 54 (1985), 117–142, provides a critique of this approach.

For the intellectual odyssey of a prominent Southern historian from a revisionist viewpoint that portrayed the conflict as needless and "repressible" toward a view that North-South differences were so fundamental as to make conflict perhaps "irrepressible" after all, see the following three books by Avery Craven: *The Repressible Conflict* (1939), *The Civil War in the Making, 1815–1860* (1959), and *An Historian and the Civil War* (1964). For the mature reflections of a Northern historian, see Kenneth M. Stampp, *The Imperilled Union: Essays on the Background of the Civil War* (1980).

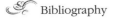

American Modernization, 1800–1860

For a stimulating though perhaps overstated exposition of the modernization thesis as applied to the antebellum United States, see Richard D. Brown, *Modernization: The Transformation of American Life 1600–1865* (1976). Daniel Boorstin, *The Americans: The National Experience* (1965), offers fascinating insights and details about the changes experienced by Americans during the first half of the nineteenth century. Charles Sellers, *The Market Revolution: Jacksonian America, 1815–1846* (1991), provides a critical perspective on this process.

Three readable and informative studies of economic developments during this period are Stuart Bruchey, *The Roots of American Economic Growth 1607–1861* (1965); Douglass C. North, *The Economic Growth of the United States 1790–1860* (1961); and Thomas C. Cochran, *Frontiers of Change: Early Industrialism in America* (1981). The relevant portions of Lance E. Davis et al., *American Economic Growth: An Economist's History of the United States,* 4th ed. (1972), and Lance E. Davis and Douglass C. North, *Institutional Change and American Economic Growth* (1971), are valuable. Peter Temin, *Causal Factors in American Economic Growth in the Nineteenth Century* (1975), provides a trenchant summary of the historiography of this subject, while Stanley L. Engerman and Robert F. Gallman, "U.S. Economic Growth, 1783–1860," *Research in Economic History,* 8 (1983), provide a succinct synthesis of the latest data and interpretations. Two valuable anthologies publish many relevant articles: Douglass C. North and Robert P. Thomas (eds.), *Growth of the American Economy to 1860* (1968); and Robert W. Fogel and Stanley L. Engerman, (eds.), *The Reinterpretation of American Economic History* (1971). Stanley Lebergott, "Labor Force and Employment, 1800–1861," in National Bureau of Economic Research, *Output, Employment, and Productivity in the United States after 1800* (1966), pp. 117–210, provides important data.

The "transportation revolution" and its impact on the American economy are best described in George Rogers Taylor, *The Transportation Revolution 1815–1860* (1951). For the role of steamboats, see Louis C. Hunter, *Steamboats on the Western Waters: An Economic and Technological History* (1949); and Eric F. Haites, James Mak, and Gary M. Walton, *Western River Transportation: The Era of Early Internal Development 1810–1860* (1975). Canals and railroads are treated in Carter Goodrich, *Government Promotion of American Canals and Railroads 1800–1860* (1960); Ronald E. Shaw, *Canals for a Nation: The Canal Era in the United States, 1790–1860* (1990); Ronald E. Shaw, *Erie Water West: A History of the Erie Canal* (1966); Carol Sheriff, *The Artificial River: The Erie Canal and the Paradox of Progress, 1817–1862* (1996); Albert Fishlow, *American Railroads and the Transformation of the Ante-Bellum Economy* (1965); and John R. Stover, *Iron Road to the West: American Railroads in the 1850's* (1979).

The best general treatment of agriculture during this period is Paul W. Gates, *The Farmers' Age: Agriculture 1815–1860* (1962). For the free states, see Jeremy Atack and Fred Bateman, *To Their Own Soil: Agriculture in the Antebellum North* (1987). Specialized studies of value include Leo Rogin, *The Introduction of Farm Machinery . . . During the Nineteenth Century* (1931); Clarence H. Danhof, *Change in Agriculture: The Northern United States 1820–1870* (1969); and a collection of shorter pieces, Thomas C. Cochran and Thomas B. Brewer (eds.), *Views of American Economic Growth: The Agricultural Era* (1966).

For the development of industry during the antebellum decades, Victor S. Clark, *History of Manufactures in the United States,* 3 vols. (1929), vol. I, is still indispensable. Thomas C. Cochran, *Frontiers of Change: Early Industrialism in America* (1981), is a readable brief interpretation. For the American system of manufactures, see Nathan Rosenberg (ed.), *The American System of Manufactures* (1969); John E. Sawyer, "The Social Basis of the American System of Manufacturing," *JEH,* 14 (1954), 361–379; Otto Mayr and Robert C. Post (eds.), *Yankee Enterprise: The Rise of the American System of Manufactures* (1982); Merrit Roe Smith,

Harper's Ferry Armory and the New Technology (1977); David A. Hounshell, *From the American System to Mass Production, 1800–1932* (1983); and Donald R. Hoke, *Ingenious Yankees: The Rise of the American System of Manufactures in the Private Sector* (1990). One important industry is analyzed in Peter Temin, *Iron and Steel in Nineteenth Century America: An Economic Inquiry* (1964). For the New England textile industry, see Caroline F. Ware, *The Early New England Cotton Manufacture* (1931); and Robert F. Dalzell, Jr., "The Rise of the Waltham-Lowell System and Some Thought on the Political Economy of Modernization in Ante-Bellum Massachusetts," *Perspectives in American History,* 9 (1975), 229–270. The impact of industrial change on the traditional economic order of farmers and craftsmen is analyzed in Thomas Dublin, *Women at Work: The Transformation of Work and Community in Lowell, Massachusetts, 1826–1860* (1979); Alan Dawley, *Class and Community: The Industrial Revolution in Lynn* (1976); Sean Wilentz, *Chants Democratic: New York City and the Rise of the American Working Class, 1788–1850* (1984); Steven J. Ross, *Workers on the Edge: Work, Leisure, and Politics in Industrializing Cincinnati, 1788–1890* (1985); Jonathan Prude, *The Coming of Industrial Order: Town and Factory Life in Rural Massachusetts 1810–1860* (1983); Christopher Clark, *The Roots of Rural Capitalism: Western Massachusetts, 1780–1860* (1990); Steven Hahn and Jonathan Prude (eds.), *The Countryside in the Age of Capitalist Transformation* (1985); Bruce Laurie, *Artisans into Workers: Labor in Nineteenth-Century America* (1989); and Winifred Barr Rothernberg, *From Marketplaces to Market Economy: The Transformation of Rural Massachusetts, 1750–1850* (1992).

Roger Burlingame, *March of the Iron Men: A Social History of Union Through Invention* (1938), is a sprightly history of technological innovation. More analytical is Brook Hindle, *Technology in Early America* (1966) while a good illustrated history is Brook Hindle and Steven Lubar, *Engines of Change: The American Industrial Revolution, 1790–1860* (1987). A stimulating attempt to explain the reasons for the openness of the United States to technological change can be found in H. J. Habakkuk, *American and British Technology in the Nineteenth Century* (1962). For qualifications of the Habakkuk thesis, see Carville Earle and Ronald Hoffman, "The Foundation of Modern Economy: Agriculture and the Costs of Labor in the United States and England, 1800–1860," *AHR,* 85 (1980), 1055–1094; Peter Temin, "Labor Scarcity and the Problem of American Industrial Efficiency in the 1850's," *JEH,* 26 (1966), 277–298; and Paul Uselding and Bruce Juba, "Biased Technical Progress in American Manufacturing, 1839–99," *Explorations in Economic History,* 11 (1973–74), 55–72. Also valuable are Nathan Rosenberg, *Technology and American Economic Growth* (1972); Siegfried Giedion, *Mechanization Takes Command* (1948); Irwin Feller, "Inventive Activity in Agriculture, 1837–1890," *JEH,* 22 (1962), 560–577; and Edwin T. Layton (ed.), *Technology and Change in America* (1973).

The identification of progress with technological change is traced in Arthur A. Ekirch, *The Idea of Progress in America 1815–1860* (1944); and Hugo A. Meier, "Technology and Democracy, 1800–1860," *MVHR,* 43 (1957), 618–640. For the distaste of some Americans for modernization, industry, and technology, see Leo Marx, *The Machine in the Garden: Technology and the Pastoral Idea in America* (1964); and John F. Kasson, *Civilizing the Machine: Technology and Republican Values in America* (1976). Carl Siracusa, *A Mechanical People: Perceptions of the Industrial Order in Massachusetts 1815–1880* (1979), analyzes the interaction of ideology and technology in one state. See also David A. Zonderman, *Aspirations and Anxiety: New England Workers and the Mechanized Factory System* (1992). For the spreading of Yankee culture and influence through the northern tier of the Middle West, see Lois K. Mathews, *The Expansion of New England 1620–1865* (1909). The clash of Yankee and Southern migrants in the Midwest is traced in Richard L. Power, *Planting Corn Belt Culture: The Impress of the Upland Southerner and Yankee in the Old Northwest* (1953). Stimulating insights on antebellum values can be found in Daniel T. Rodgers, *The Work Ethic in Industrial America*

1850–1920 (1978). Lee Soltow, *Men and Wealth in the United States 1850–1870* (1975), documents the distribution of wealth among people of various regional and ethnic groups.

Ronald G. Walters, *American Reformers 1815–1860* (1978), and Steven Mintz, *Moralists and Modernizers: America's Pre-Civil War Reformers* (1995), are stimulating interpretations of the connections between modernization and reform. A fascinating case study is provided by Paul E. Johnson, *A Shopkeeper's Millennium: Society and Revivals in Rochester, New York, 1815–1857* (1978). One of the principal reform movements associated with modernization is analyzed in the following books: Norman A. Clark, *Deliver Us from Evil: An Interpretation of American Prohibition* (1976); William J. Rorabough, *The Alcoholic Republic: America 1790–1840* (1979); Ian R. Tyrrell, *Sobering Up: From Temperance to Prohibition in Antebellum America 1800–1860* (1979); Robert L. Hampel, *Temperance and Prohibition in Massachusetts, 1813–1852* (1982); and Jed Dannenbaum, *Drink and Disorder: Temperance Reform in Cincinnati from the Washingtonian Revival to the WCTU* (1984).

The expansion and improvement of public education during the antebellum period is discussed in Lawrence A. Cremin, *American Education: The National Experience, 1783–1876* (1980); Frederick M. Binder, *The Age of the Common School 1830–1865* (1974); Albert Fishlow, "The Common School Revival: Fact or Fancy?" in Henry Rosovsky (ed.), *Industrialization in Two Systems* (1966), pp. 40–67; Lee Soltow and Edward Stevens, *The Rise of Literacy and the Common School in the United States: A Socioeconomic Analysis* (1981); and Carl F. Kaestle, *Pillars of the Republic: Common Schooling and American Society, 1780–1860* (1983). The relationship between education and modernizing capitalism is explored from different angles in the following works: Michael Katz, *The Irony of Early School Reform: Educational Innovation in Mid-Nineteenth Century Massachusetts* (1969); Michael B. Katz, "The Origins of Public Education: A Reassessment," *History of Education Quarterly,* 16 (1976), 381–407; Stanley K. Schultz, *The Culture Factory: Boston Public Schools 1789–1860* (1973); Carl F. Kaestle, *The Evolution of an Urban School System 1750–1850* (1973); and Carl F. Kaestle and Maris A. Vinovskis, *Education and Social Change in Nineteenth-Century Massachusetts* (1980).

For changes in the status of women and the rise of a women's rights movement, see Nancy F. Cott, *The Bonds of Womanhood: "Woman's Sphere" in New England, 1780–1835* (1977); Carl N. Degler, *At Odds: Women and the Family in America from the Revolution to the Present* (New York, 1980); Mary P. Ryan, *Cradle of the Middle Class: The Family in Oneida County, New York, 1790–1865* (1981); Catherine Clinton, *The Other Civil War: American Women in the Nineteenth Century* (rev. ed., 1999); Ellen Carol DuBois, *Feminism and Suffrage: The Emergence of an Independent Women's Movement in America 1848–1869* (1978); and Sylvia D. Hoffer, *When Hens Crow: The Women's Rights Movement in Antebellum America* (1995).

A great deal of important information on the attitudes of Democrats and Whigs toward issues related to modernization can be found in Herbert Ershkowitz and William G. Shade, "Consensus or Conflict? Political Behavior in the State Legislatures During the Jacksonian Era," *JAH,* 58 (1971), 591–621; Harry L. Watson, *Liberty and Power: The Politics of Jacksonian America* (1990); John Ashworth: *"Agrarians" and "Aristocrats": Party Political Ideology in the United States, 1837–1846* (1983); Lawrence F. Kohl, *The Politics of Individualism: Parties and the American Character in the Jacksonian Era* (1989); Ronald P. Formisano, *The Transformation of Political Culture: Massachusetts Parties, 1790's–1840's* (1982); William G. Shade, *Democratizing the Old Dominion: Virginia and the Second Party System, 1824–1861;* and Michael F. Holt, *Political Parties and American Political Development from the Age of Jackson to the Age of Lincoln* (1992). For the ideology of Democrats, see Bruce Collins, "The Ideology of the Ante-Bellum Northern Democrats," *Journal of American Studies,* 11 (1977), 103–121; Jean E. Friedman, *The Revolt of the Conservative Democrats: An Essay on American Political Culture and Political Development 1837–1844* (1979); and Jean Baker, *Affairs of Party: The Political Culture of Northern Democrats in the Mid-Nineteenth Century* (1983). Robert L. Kelley, *The*

Transatlantic Persuasion: The Liberal-Democratic Mind in the Age of Gladstone (1969), and Rush Welter, *The Mind of America, 1820–1860* (1975), also contain suggestive insights into the Democratic world view. Robert L. Kelley, *The Cultural Pattern in American Politics: The First Century* (1979), offers a sometimes oversimplified synthesis of the social and ideological matrix of politics. The "Butternuts" are analyzed in Nicole Ettleson, *The Emerging Midwest: Upland Southerners and the Political Culture of the Old Northwest, 1787–1861* (1996). Whig attitudes are sensitively analyzed in Daniel Walker Howe, *The Political Culture of American Whigs* (1979); and Thomas Brown, *Politics and Statesmanship: Essays on the American Whig Party* (1985); while G. S. Boritt, *Lincoln and the Economics of the American Dream* (1977), explores Lincoln's Whig economic philosophy. Michael F. Holt, *The Rise and Fall of the American Whig Party* (1999), is an exhaustive treatment of its subject.

For the efforts of state and federal governments to provide social overhead capital and in other ways to foster economic development, consult Carter Goodrich (ed.), *The Government and the Economy 1783–1861* (1967); Oscar Handlin and Mary Handlin, *Commonwealth: A Study of the Role of the Government in the American Economy: Massachusetts 1774–1861* (1947); Louis Hartz, *Economic Policy and Democratic Thought: Pennsylvania 1776–1861* (1948); Harry Scheiber, *The Ohio Canal Era: A Case Study of Government and the Economy* (1969); Milton S. Heath, *Constructive Liberalism: The Role of the State in Economic Development of Georgia to 1860* (1954); and Peter Wallenstein, *From Slave South to New South: Public Policy in Nineteenth Century Georgia* (1987). The growing friendliness of the courts toward entrepreneurial innovation is brilliantly explored in Morton J. Horwitz, *The Transformation of American Law 1780–1861* (1977). For analyses of the major economic issue dividing Whigs and Democrats, the following works are important: Bray Hammond, *Banks and Politics in America from the Revolution to the Civil War* (1957); William G. Shade, *Banks or No Banks: The Money Issue in Western Politics 1832–1865* (1972); Roger James Sharp, *The Jacksonians Versus the Banks: Politics in the States After the Panic of 1837* (1970); and Larry Schweikart, *Banking in the American South: From the Age of Jackson to Reconstruction* (1987).

The Antebellum South and Slavery

An old but still useful survey of the antebellum South is William E. Dodd, *The Cotton Kingdom* (1919). The most up-to-date textbook is William J. Cooper, Jr., and Thomas E. Terrill, *The American South: A History* (1990), chaps. 1–14. Two collections of essays by the leading Southern scholar of a previous generation contain much of value: Ulrich B. Phillips, *Life and Labor in the Old South* (1929) and *The Slave Economy of the Old South: Selected Essays*, ed. Eugene Genovese (1968). For an attempt to separate the myth from the reality of the Southern plantation society, see Francis Pendleton Gaines, *The Southern Plantation: A Study in the Development and Accuracy of a Tradition* (1925). Lewis C. Gray, *History of Agriculture in the Southern United States to 1860,* 2 vols. (1933), still stands as the most exhaustive treatment of its subject, though many of the studies of the Southern economy cited below have modified or amplified its findings. Good microstudies of specific localities can be found in Elinor Miller and Eugene D. Genovese (eds.), *Plantation, Town, and County: Essays on the Local History of American Slave Society* (1974), and O. Vernon Burton and Robert C. McGrath (eds.), *Class, Conflict, and Consensus: Antebellum Southern Community Studies* (1982). A fine study of an important state is John Hebron Moore, *The Emergence of the Cotton Kingdom in the Old Southwest: Mississippi, 1770–1860* (1988). Religion was a powerful force in the South's cultural life; for a sensitive interpretation, consult Donald G. Mathews, *Religion in the Old South* (1977). The essays in John B. Boles (ed.), *Masters & Slaves in the House of the Lord: Race and Religion in the American South, 1740–1870* (1988), offer rich fare. Much of our perception of what life was like in the antebellum South comes from travelers' accounts; an excellent bibliography of these is Thomas D. Clark (ed.), *Travels in the Old South: A Bibliography,* 3 vols. (1956–1959), especially vol. III: *The Ante-Bellum South.* The best-known and most influential traveler was Frederick Law Olmsted. For a modern abridgment of his three books on the South, read Arthur Schlesinger (ed.), *The Cotton Kingdom* (1953). Olmsted's observations and preconceptions are analyzed by several of the essays in Dana F. White and Victor A. Kramer (eds.), *Olmsted South: Old South Critic/New South Planner* (1979).

The economics of slavery and its relationship to Southern development—or lack thereof— have been the subject of a large scholarly literature, much of it anthologized in Harold D. Woodman (ed.), *Slavery and the Southern Economy* (1966); and Hugh G. J. Aitken (ed.), *Did Slavery Pay?* (1971). Gavin Wright, *The Political Economy of the Cotton South* (1978), contains important insights. For additional essays and primary sources on this issue, see William N. Parker (ed.), *The Structure of the Cotton Economy of the Antebellum South* (1970); and Stuart Bruchey (ed.), *Cotton and the Growth of the American Economy 1790–1860* (1967). Eugene D. Genovese, *The Political Economy of Slavery* (1965), argues vigorously that slavery inhibited Southern economic development. Robert W. Fogel and Stanley L. Engerman, *Time on the Cross: The Economics of American Negro Slavery* (1974), argue the opposite case even more vigorously, but parts of their argument have suffered withering attacks from all directions: see especially Kenneth M. Stampp et al., *Reckoning with Slavery* (1976), and Herbert G. Gutman, *Slavery and the Numbers Game* (1975). Two important contributions to the debate are Fred Bateman and Thomas Weiss, *A Deplorable Scarcity: The Failure of Industrialization in the Slave Economy* (1981), and Mark M. Smith, *Debating Slavery: Economy and Society in the Antebellum American South* (1999). See also Laurence Shore, *Southern Capitalists: The Ideological Leadership of an Elite, 1832–1885* (1986). Harold D. Woodman, *King Cotton and His Retainers: Financing and Marketing the Cotton Crop of the South* (1968), is an excellent study of the factoring system. For an account of the self-sufficiency of most parts of the South in food, see Sam B. Hilliard, *Hog Meat and Hoe Cake: Food Supply in the Old South 1840–1860* (1972). Three studies emphasize that despite the South's low rate of urbanization, the region did have important cities: Leonard P. Curry "Urbanization and Urbanism in the Old South: A Comparative View," *JSH,* 40 (1974), 43–60; Blaine A. Brownell and David R. Goldfield (eds.), *The City in Southern History* (1977); and David R. Goldfield, *Urban Growth in the Age of Sectionalism: Virginia, 1847–1861* (1977).

The institution of slavery has generated more historical writing than any other aspect of Southern history, unless it be the Confederacy itself. For surveys of slavery scholarship, consult David Brion Davis, "Slavery and the Post-World War II Historians," *Daedalus,* 103 (1974), 1–16; Michael Craton (ed.), *Slave Studies: Directions in Current Scholarship,* 6 (Summer 1979); Peter J. Parish, *Slavery: History and Historians* (1989); and Peter Kolchin, "American Historians and Antebellum Southern Slavery, 1959–1984," in William J. Cooper, Jr., et al. (eds.), *A Master's Due: Essays in Honor of David Herbert Donald* (1985), pp. 87–111. John B. Boles, *Black Southerners, 1619–1869* (1983), and Peter Kolchin, *American Slavery 1619–1877* (1993), provide good introductions to the subject, while C. Duncan Rice, *The Rise and Fall of Black Slavery* (1975), places slavery in the United States in a world context. Robert William Fogel, *Without Consent or Contract: The Rise and Fall of American Slavery* (1989), refines and revises the themes of *Time on the Cross* fifteen years later, places slavery in a world context, and contains new insights on the antislavery movements in Britain and the United States. A fine reference work is Randall M. Miller and John D. Smith (eds.), *Dictionary of Afro-American Slavery* (1988).

The two classic and sharply opposed studies of slavery in the United States are Ulrich B. Phillips, *American Negro Slavery* (1918), which portrays the institution as nonrepressive and beneficial to blacks; and Kenneth M. Stampp, *The Peculiar Institution* (1956), which portrays it as repressive and harmful to blacks. Two state studies that reflect the Phillips viewpoint are

Charles S. Sydnor, *Slavery in Mississippi* (1933); and James B. Sellers, *Slavery in Alabama* (1950); while state studies that tend to follow Stampp are Joe Gray Taylor, *Negro Slavery in Louisiana* (1963), and Randolph B. Campbell, *An Empire for Slavery: The Peculiar Institution in Texas* (1989). For the past three decades, nearly all studies of slavery have been influenced in one way or another by Stanley Elkins, *Slavery: A Problem in American Institutional and Intellectual Life*, 3d ed. (1976), which argues that slavery in the United States was more psychologically corrosive than in other slave societies and that this "closed" system reduced slaves to fawning, dependent, childlike "Samboes," a personality syndrome that black Americans have struggled for more than a century to overcome. The Elkins interpretation has provoked many challenges, most of which maintain that blacks underwent a wide variety of experiences and possessed a wide variety of personality types, by no means all of them dependent or Sambo-like. See especially Ann J. Lane (ed.), *The Debate Over Slavery: Stanley Elkins and His Critics* (1971); and many of the essays in such anthologies as Richard G. Brown and Stephen G. Rabe (eds.), *Slavery in American Society*, 2d ed. (1976), and Allen Weinstein, Frank Otto Gatell, and David Sarasohn (eds.), *American Negro Slavery: A Modern Reader*, 3d ed. (1979).

The principal book-length challenge to Elkins is John W. Blassingame, *The Slave Community: Plantation Life in the Antebellum South*, 2d ed. rev. (1979). Another account that stresses the slaves' ability to maintain a vital culture of their own despite the contrary pressures of slavery is George Rawick, *From Sundown to Sunup: The Making of the Black Community* (1972). The 1970s and 1980s produced a cornucopia of studies of black culture in slavery, most of which emphasize especially the creative role of religion and the strength of family and kinship networks as instruments of survival in a hostile world: Eugene D. Genovese, *Roll, Jordan, Roll: The World the Slaves Made* (1974); Herbert G. Gutman, *The Black Family in Slavery and Freedom 1750–1925* (1976); Nathan Huggins, *Black Odyssey: The Afro-American Ordeal in Slavery* (1977); Albert J. Raboteau, *Slave Religion: The "Invisible Institution" in the Antebellum South* (1978); Leslie H. Owens, *This Species of Property: Slave Life and Culture in the Old South* (1976); Charles Joyner, *Down by the Riverside: A South Carolina Slave Community* (1984); and Charles Joyner, *Remember Me: Slave Life in Coastal Georgia* (1989). William Dusinberre, *Them Dark Days: Slavery in the American Rice Swamps* (1996), investigates slave life and culture outside the cotton belt. The vital function of song and folklore is explored by Lawrence W. Levine, *Black Culture and Black Consciousness* (1977).

The experiences of those slaves who lived and worked in urban or industrial settings is traced in Richard C. Wade, *Slavery in the Cities* (1964); Robert S. Starobin, *Industrial Slavery in the Old South* (1970); Ronald L. Lewis, *Coal, Iron, and Slaves: Industrial Slavery in Maryland and Virginia 1715–1865* (1979); Charles B. Dew, *Bond of Iron: Master and Slave at Buffalo Forge* (1994); and Midori Takagi, *"Rearing Wolves to Our Own Destruction": Slavery in Richmond, Virginia, 1782–1865* (1999).

The complicated relationship of women, both black and white, to the institution of slavery is analyzed in Deborah Gray White, *Ar'n't I a Woman? Female Slaves in the Plantation South* (1985); Brenda Stevenson, *Life in Black and White: Family and Community in the Slave South* (1996); Larry E. Hudson, Jr., *To Have and to Hold: Slave Work and Family Life in Antebellum South Carolina* (1997); Jennifer Fleischner, *Mastering Slavery: Memory, Family, and Identity in Women's Slave Narratives* (1996); Catherine Clinton, *The Plantation Mistress: Woman's World in the Old South* (1982); Elizabeth Fox-Genovese, *Within the Plantation Household: Black and White Women of the Old South* (1988); and Marli F. Weiner, *Mistresses and Slaves: Plantation Women in South Carolina* (1998). Otto H. Olsen, "Historians and the Extent of Slave Ownership in the Southern United States," *CWH*, 18 (1972), 101–116, documents the relatively widespread ownership of this expensive property; while William K. Scarborough, *The Overseer: Plantation Management in the Old South* (1966), analyzes a group of whites who did not own slaves but were involved in their management. William L. Van Deburg, *The Slave*

Drivers: Black Agricultural Labor Supervisors in the Antebellum South (1979), portrays the role of the black slave foremen. One of the most tragic dimensions of slavery is treated in Frederic Bancroft, *Slave Trading in the Old South* (1931); and Michael Tadman, *Speculators and Slaves: Masters, Traders, and Slaves in the Old South* (1989). Two books by James Oakes analyze the relationships among masters, slaves, Southern culture, and regional and national political economy: *The Ruling Race: A History of American Slaveholders* (1982); and *Slavery and Freedom: An Interpretation of the Old South* (1990). The essays in Willie Lee Rose, *Slavery and Freedom* (1982), contain many incisive insights.

Although large-scale revolts were relatively infrequent in the United States, those that did occur, as well as plans and rumors of others, are narrated in Herbert Aptheker, *American Negro Slave Revolts* (1943); Joseph C. Carroll, *Slave Insurrections in the United States 1800–1865* (1938); and Stephen B. Oates, *The Fires of Jubilee: Nat Turner's Fierce Rebellion* (1975). Eugene D. Genovese, *From Rebellion to Revolution: Afro-American Slave Revolts in the Making of the Modern World* (1979), places the United States experience in hemispheric context. Merton L. Dillon, *Slavery Attacked: Southern Slaves and Their Allies* (1990), chronicles opposition and resistance to slavery by both blacks and whites in the South. The most common form of resistance was running away; the best study of this matter is John Hope Franklin and Loren Schweninger, *Runaway Slaves: Rebels on the Plantation* (1999).

Much of the evidence on which an understanding of slavery can be based has been published. See especially Willie Lee Rose (ed.), *A Documentary History of Slavery in North America* (1976). An exhaustive digest of legal cases can be found in Helen T. Catterall (ed.), *Judicial Cases Concerning American Slavery and the Negro*, 5 vols. (1926–1937). For a briefer selection, see Paul Finkelman (ed.), *Slavery and the Law* (1998), and for a detailed analysis based on laws and cases, see Thomas T. Morris, *Southern Slavery and the Law, 1619–1860* (1996). Some of the most important evidence concerning the institution are the words of slaves themselves. For a large sample of these, consult John W. Blassingame (ed.), *Slave Testimony: Two Centuries of Letters, Speeches, Interviews, and Autobiographies* (1977). Many escaped or freed slaves wrote autobiographies or narratives about their experiences; twenty of them are reprinted in Yuval Taylor (ed.), *I Was Born a Slave: An Anthology of Classic Slave Narratives* (1999). For an analysis of the narratives, see Charles H. Nichols, *Many Thousand Gone: The Ex-Slaves' Account of Their Bondage and Freedom* (1963). In the 1920s and 1930s, Fisk University and the WPA undertook to interview as many surviving ex-slaves as possible about their experiences in bondage. The transcripts of these interviews have been published in George P. Rawick (ed.), *The American Slave: A Composite Autobiography*, 41 vols. (1972–1979). Paul Escott, *Slavery Remembered: A Record of Twentieth Century Slave Narratives* (1979), is a quantitative analysis of these interviews; while Norman R. Yetman (ed.), *Life Under the "Peculiar Institution": Selections from the Slave Narrative Collection* (1970), publishes a sample of one hundred of them.

Some of the most fruitful insights concerning North American slavery are contained in studies comparing it to the institution in other New World societies. Frank Tannenbaum, *Slave and Citizen: The Negro in the Americas* (1947), and Herbert S. Klein, *Slavery in the Americas: A Comparative Study of Cuba and Virginia* (1967), maintain that slavery in North America was more repressive than in Latin America. Most of the other scholarship on the subject, however, has either modified or rejected important aspects of this interpretation. For anthologies of various writings on the subject, see Laura Foner and Eugene D. Genovese (eds.), *Slavery in the New World* (1969); Stanley L. Engerman and Eugene D. Genovese (eds.), *Race and Slavery in the Western Hemisphere: Quantitative Studies* (1975); and Vera Rubin and Arthur Tuden (eds.), *Comparative Perspectives on Slavery in New World Plantation Societies* (1977). The startlingly higher rate of slave survival and reproduction in the United States than elsewhere is documented in Philip D. Curtin, *The Atlantic Slave Trade: A Census* (1969). Two of the most challenging books in the field of comparative slavery are Carl N. Degler, *Neither Black Nor White: Slavery and Race Relations in Brazil and the United States* (1971); and Eugene D. Genovese, *The World the Slaveholders Made: Two Essays in Interpretation* (1969). An important study that compares slavery and race relations in the United States and South Africa is George M. Fredrickson, *White Supremacy: A Comparative Study in American and South African History* (1981), while Peter Kolchin, *Unfree Labor: American Slavery and Russian Serfdom* (1987), compares and contrasts these two institutions.

Although most writings about the slave South focus on the slaveowners and their slaves, two-thirds or more of the whites had no connection with slaveholding. The classic account of these people, which portrays them as a crucial element in the South's social and political structure, is Frank L. Owsley, *Plain Folk of the Old South* (1949). For a damaging critique of Owsley's interpretation, consult Fabian Linden, "Economic Democracy in the Slave South: An Appraisal of Some Recent Views," *JNH,* 31 (1946), 140–189. Another study emphasizing the inequality of wealth and economic power is Gavin Wright, " 'Economic Democracy' and the Concentration of Wealth in the Cotton South," *AH,* 44 (1970), 62–99. For other analyses of the image and reality of nonslaveholding whites, see Paul H. Buck, "The Poor Whites of the Ante-Bellum South," *AHR,* 31 (1925), 41–54; Shields McIlwaine, *The Southern Poor White* (1939); Forest McDonald and Grady McWhiney, "The Antebellum Southern Herdsman: A Reinterpretation," *JSH,* 41 (1975), 147–166, and "The South from Self-Sufficiency to Peonage: An interpretation," *AHR,* 85 (1980), 1095–1118; Eugene D. Genovese, "Yeoman Farmers in a Slaveholder's Democracy," *AH,* 49 (1975), 331–342; Bill Cecil-Fronsman, *Common Whites: Class and Culture in Antebellum North Carolina* (1992); J. Wayne Flynt, *Dixie's Forgotten People: The South's Poor Whites* (1979); Bruce Collins, *White Society in the Antebellum South* (1985); Steven Hahn, *The Roots of Southern Populism: Yeoman Farmers and the Transformation of the Georgia Upcountry, 1850–1890;* Paul D. Escott, *Many Excellent People: Power and Privilege in North Carolina, 1850–1900* (1985); and Stephanie McCurry, *Masters of Small Worlds: Yeoman Households, Gender Relations, and the Political Culture of the Antebellum South Carolina Low Country* (1995). Ralph W. Wooster, *The People in Power: Courthouse and Statehouse in the Lower South* (1969) and *Politicians, Planters, and Plain Folk: Courthouse and Statehouse in the Upper South 1850–1860* (1975), maintains that while nonslaveholders exercised a considerable degree of political power and held many offices, their percentage of officeholding decreased during the 1850s. Other studies that trace the relationship between yeoman and planters include J. William Harris, *Plain Folk and Gentry in a Slave Society: White Liberty and Black Slavery in Augusta's Hinterlands* (1985), and Harry L. Watson, "Conflict and Collaboration: Yeomen, Slaveholders, and Politics in the Antebellum South," *Social History,* 10 (1985), 273–298. An intriguing study which argues for the Celtic roots of Southern culture, especially the yeomen farmers, is Grady McWhiney, *Cracker Culture: Celtic Ways in the Old South* (1988).

The anomalous and difficult position of free blacks in a slave society is sensitively explored in Ira Berlin, *Slaves Without Masters: The Free Negro in the Antebellum South* (1974), and Michael P. Johnson and James L. Roark, *Black Masters: A Free Family of Color in the Old South* (1984).

The Ideological Conflict over Slavery

For the international context and pre-nineteenth-century background of slavery and the antislavery movement, three books are superb: David Brion Davis, *The Problem of Slavery in Western Culture* (1966) and *The Problem of Slavery in the Age of Revolution 1770–1823* (1975); and Edmund S. Morgan, *American Slavery, American Freedom: The Ordeal of Colonial Virginia* (1975). Two books that put the evolution of antislavery in the context of economic transformations are John Ashworth, *Slavery, Capitalism, and Politics in the Antebellum Republic,* Vol. I: *Commerce and Compromise, 1820–1850* (1995); and Thomas Bender (ed.), *The Antislav-*

ery Debate: Capitalism and Abolitionism as a Problem in Historical Interpretation (1992). Two books on the reform milieu of abolitionism are Alice Felt Tyler, *Freedom's Ferment* (1944); and Ronald G. Walters, *American Reformers 1815–1860* (1978). The evangelical impulse underlying and infusing reform movements is analyzed in Timothy L. Smith, *Revivalism and Social Reform in Mid-Nineteenth Century America* (1957) and Whitney R. Cross, *The Burned-Over District* (1950). For a conservative movement against slavery, see P. J. Staudenraus, *The African Colonization Movement 1816–1865* (1961).

A good introduction to scholarship on the abolitionists is Merton L. Dillon, "The Abolitionists: A Decade of Historiography," *JSH*, 35 (1969), 500–522. Two more decades of historiography are summarized in James L. Huston, "The Experiential Basis of the Northern Antislavery Impulse," *JSH*, 55 (1990), 609–640, which also provides its own interpretation of the movement. Two collections of essays that depict the state of abolitionist historiography at the times of their publication are Martin Duberman (ed.), *The Antislavery Vanguard* (1965); and Lewis Perry and Michael Fellman (eds.), *Antislavery Reconsidered: New Perspectives on the Abolitionists* (1979). The best brief narratives of the antislavery movement are James B. Stewart, *Holy Warriors: The Abolitionists and American Slavery* (rev. ed. 1996), and Paul Goodman, *Of One Blood: Abolitionism and the Origins of Racial Equality* (1998). Two older studies also deal with the movement as a whole: Louis Filler, *The Crusade Against Slavery* (1960); and Dwight L. Dumond, *Antislavery: The Crusade for Freedom in America* (1961). More specialized studies that have done much to shape our understanding of the abolitionists include Gilbert Hobbs Barnes, *The Antislavery Impulse 1830–1844* (1933); Aileen S. Kraditor, *Means and Ends in American Abolitionism* (1969); Carleton Mabee, *Black Freedom: The Nonviolent Abolitionists from 1830 Through the Civil War* (1970); Ronald G. Walters, *The Antislavery Appeal: Abolitionism After 1830* (1976); Russel B. Nye, *Fettered Freedom: Civil Liberties and the Slavery Controversy 1830–1860* (1949); Lawrence J. Friedman, *Gregarious Saints: Self and Community in American Abolitionism, 1830–1870* (1982); Louis Gerteis, *Morality and Utility in American Antislavery Reform* (1987); Edward Magdol, *The Antislavery Rank and File: A Social Profile of the Abolitionists' Constituency* (1986); and Herbert Aptheker, *Abolitionism: A Revolutionary Movement* (1989). Two studies of blacks in the antislavery movement are Benjamin Quarles, *Black Abolitionists* (1969); and James H. Pease and William H. Pease, *They Who Would Be Free: Blacks' Search for Freedom 1830–1861* (1974). Two important books on blacks in the North include material on abolitionism: Leon F. Litwack, *North of Slavery: The Negro in the Free States 1790–1860* (1961), and James Oliver Horton and Louise Horton, *In Hope of Liberty: Culture, Community, and Protest Among Northern Free Blacks, 1700–1860* (1997). Two anthologies offer samples of the abolitionists' own writings: John L. Thomas (ed.), *Slavery Attacked: The Abolitionist Crusade* (1965), and William H. Pease and Jane H. Pease (eds.), *The Antislavery Argument* (1965), while C. Peter Ripley, Roy E. Finkenbine, Michael F. Hembree, and Donald Yacovone (eds.), *Witness for Freedom: African American Voices on Race, Slavery, and Emancipation* (1993), contain the writings of many black abolitionists. For the activism of women in the movement, see Alma Lutz, *Crusade for Freedom: Women in the Antislavery Movement* (1968); Shirley Yee, *Black Women Abolitionists: A Study in Activism, 1828–1860* (1992); Julie Roy Jeffrey, *The Great Silent Army of Abolitionism: Women in the Antislavery Movement* (1998); and Jean Yellin and John Van Horne (eds.), *The Abolitionist Sisterhood: Women's Political Culture in Antebellum America* (1994). For antislavery political parties, consult Theodore Clarke Smith, *The Liberty and Free Soil Parties in the Northwest* (1897); Vernon L. Volpe, *Forlorn Hope of Freedom: The Liberty Party in the Old Northwest* (1990); Richard H. Sewell, *Ballots for Freedom: Antislavery Politics in the United States, 1837–1860* (1976); Frederick J. Blue, *The Free Soilers: Third Party Politics, 1848–1854* (1973); John H. Hammond, *The Politics of Benevolence: Revival Religion and American Voting Behavior* (1979); and Gerald Sorin, *The New York Abolitionists: A Case Study of Political Radicalism* (1971). Also valuable are the essays in Alan M. Kraut (ed.), *Crusaders and Compromisers: Essays on the Relationship of the Antislavery Struggle to the Antebellum Party System* (1983). For the divisive impact of the slavery controversy on Protestant denominations, refer to C. C. Goen, *Broken Churches, Broken Nation: Denominational Schisms and the Coming of the American Civil War* (1985); John R. McKivigan, *The War against Proslavery Religion: Abolitionism and the Northern Churches, 1830–1865* (1984); Richard Carwardine, *Evangelicals and Politics in Antebellum America* (1993); and Douglas M. Strong, *Perfectionist Politics: Abolitionism and the Religious Tensions of American Democracy* (1999). John R. McKivagan and Mitchell Snay (eds.), *Religion and the Antebellum Debate over Slavery* (1998), contains articles on both the antislavery and proslavery sides of the issue. William Lee Miller, *Arguing About Slavery: The Great Battle in the United States Congress* (1996), is an exhaustive study of the gag rule controversy.

The most lucid account of the free-labor ideology, which also contains a fine analysis of the Republican party in the 1850s, is Eric Foner, *Free Soil, Free Labor, Free Men: The Ideology of the Republican Party Before the Civil War* (new ed. 1995). Howard Floan, *The South in the Northern Eyes 1831–1861* (1953), and Stanley Harrold, *The Abolitionists and the South, 1831–1861* (1995), summarize various Northern images of the South. David Brion Davis, *The Slave Power Conspiracy and the Paranoid Style* (1969), analyzes the symbolic power of these images. Three Northern groups that were generally hostile to the antislavery movement are discussed in Philip S. Foner, *Business and Slavery: The New York Merchants and the Irrepressible Conflict* (1941); Bernard Mandel, *Labor, Free and Slave: Workingmen and the Anti-Slavery Movement in the United States* (1955); David R. Roediger, *The Wages of Whiteness: Race and the Making of the Working Class* (1991); and Madeline H. Rice, *American Catholic Opinion in the Slavery Controversy* (1943).

Antebellum Southern culture, values, and attitudes are analyzed in the following books, which disagree with each other on some points: David Bertelson, *The Lazy South* (1967); three books by Clement Eaton: *The Growth of Southern Civilization 1790–1861* (1961), *The Freedom of Thought Struggle in the Old South*, rev. ed. (1964), and *The Mind of the Old South*, rev. ed. (1967); and Rollin Osterweis, *Romanticism and Nationalism in the Old South* (1949). For a skillful weaving together of Northern and Southern perceptions of Southern reality, see William R. Taylor, *Cavalier and Yankee: The Old South and American National Character* (1961). Bertram Wyatt-Brown, *Southern Honor: Ethics and Behavior in the Old South* (1982) and the same author's *Yankee Saints and Southern Sinners* (1985) trace the sensitivity of Southern white men to criticism and aspersions on their honor, especially by Yankees. Also important on these themes are Kenneth S. Greenberg, *Masters and Statesmen: The Political Culture of American Slavery* (1985) and Kenneth S. Greenberg, *Honor and Slavery* (1996). The classic account of the proslavery ideology is William S. Jenkins, *Pro-Slavery Thought in the Old South* (1935). It should be supplemented with Mitchell Snay, *Gospel of Disunion: Religion and Separatism in the Antebellum South* (1993) and Eugene D. Genovese, *The Slaveholders' Dilemma: Freedom and Progress in Southern Conservative Thought, 1820–1860* (1993). A good selection of proslavery writings can be found in Eric L. McKitrick (ed.), *Slavery Defended: The Views of the Old South* (1963) and Drew Gilpin Faust (ed.), *The Ideology of Slavery: Proslavery Thought in the Antebellum South* (1981).

For the evolution of sectionalism in Southern thought and politics, see, in addition to the books cited in the first paragraph under "General Works" for the antebellum years, Jesse T. Carpenter, *The South as a Conscious Minority 1789–1861* (1930); Robert R. Russel, *Economic Aspects of Southern Sectionalism 1840–1861* (1924); Weymouth T. Jordan, *Rebels in the Making: Planters' Conventions and Southern Propaganda* (1958); Vicki Vaughan Johnson, *The Men and the Vision of the Southern Commercial Conventions, 1845–1871* (1992); Eric H. Walther, *The Fire-Eaters* (1992); Davis S. Heidler, *Pulling the Temple Down: The Fire-Eaters and the Destruction of the Union* (1994); Donald L. Robinson, *Slavery and the Structure of*

American Politics 1765–1820 (1971); Glover Moore, *The Missouri Controversy 1819–1821* (1966); Richard H. Brown, "The Missouri Crisis, Slavery, and the Politics of Jacksonianism," *SAQ,* 65 (1966); William W. Freehling, *Prelude to Civil War: The Nullification Crisis in South Carolina 1816–1836* (1966); and Lacy K. Ford, Jr., *Origins of Southern Radicalism: The South Carolina Up-country, 1800–1860* (1988). For the Southern propensity toward violence and martial values, see John Hope Franklin, *The Militant South 1800–1861* (1956), and Dickson D. Bruce, *Violence and Culture in the Antebellum South* (1979). Marcus Cunliffe, *Soldiers and Civilians: The Martial Spirit in America 1775–1865* (1968), argues with limited success that the extent of Southern militarism has been exaggerated. An important article that argues—also with limited success—that the similarities between the North and the South were more important than the differences is Edward Pessen, "How Different from Each Other Were the Antebellum North and South?" *AHR,* 85 (1980), 1119–1149; for a challenge to this argument, see James M. McPherson, "Antebellum Southern Exceptionalism: A New Look at an Old Question," *CWH,* 29 (1983), 230–244.

Texas, Mexico, and the Compromise of 1850

For the general context of politics within which sectionalism heated up during the 1840s, see Frederick Jackson Turner, *The United States 1830–1850* (1935); and William R. Brock, *Parties and Political Conscience: American Dilemmas 1840–1850* (1979). The westering impulse that propelled Americans to and across the Mississippi during this period, undergirding the ideology of Manifest Destiny, is chronicled in Malcolm J. Rohrbough, *The Trans-Appalachian Frontier . . . 1775–1850* (1978), and Ray Allen Billington, *The Far Western Frontier 1830–1860* (1956). The racial philosophies and economic interests that rationalized expansion are analyzed by Thomas R. Hietala, *Manifest Design: Anxious Aggrandizement in Late Jacksonian America* (1985) and Reginald Horsman, *Race and Manifest Destiny* (1981). Frederick Merk, *Manifest Destiny and Mission in American History* (1963) and *The Monroe Doctrine and American Expansion 1843–1849* (1967), explore the expansionism of the 1840s; while in *Slavery and the Annexation of Texas* (1972), Merk narrows the focus to Texas specifically. Three studies analyze the relationship between American expansionism and the coming of the war with Mexico: David Pletcher, *The Diplomacy of Annexation: Texas, Oregon, and the Mexican War* (1973); Norman E. Tutorow, *Texas Annexation and the Mexican War: A Political Study of the Old Northwest* (1978); and Dean B. Mahin, *Sword and Olive Branch: The United States and Mexico, 1845–1848* (1997).

Mexican viewpoints are described in Gene M. Brack, *Mexico Views Manifest Destiny: An Essay on the Origins of the Mexican War* (1975). Glen W. Price, *Origins of the War with Mexico: The Polk-Stockton Intrigue* (1967), charges Polk with deliberately provoking Mexico to war; while Charles G. Sellers, *James K. Polk, Continentalist 1843–1846* (1966) and Paul H. Bergeron, *The Presidency of James K. Polk* (1987), are more sympathetic to the American President. The most detailed study of the Mexican War is still Justin H. Smith, *The War with Mexico,* 2 vols. (1919). Modern studies include Otis A. Singletary, *The Mexican War* (1960); John Edward Weems, *To Conquer a Peace: The War Between the United States and Mexico* (1974); K. Jack Bauer, *The Mexican War* (1974); and John S. D. Eisenhower, *So Far from God: The U.S. War with Mexico 1846–1848* (1989). John H. Schroeder, *Mr. Polk's War: American Opposition and Dissent 1846–1848* (1973), documents antislavery and Whig opposition; while Ernest M. Lander, *Reluctant Imperialists: Calhoun, the South Carolinians, and the Mexican War* (1980), highlights the ambivalence of some Southerners toward the war. Robert W. Johannsen, *To the Halls of the Montezumas: The Mexican War in the American Imagination* (1985), focuses on the popularity of the war among Democrats and expansionists, while John D. P. Fuller focuses on the most extreme proponents of Manifest Destiny in *The Movement for the Acquisition of*

All Mexico (1936). The nature and experiences of the American army in Mexico are chronicled in James M. McCaffrey, *Army of Manifest Destiny: The American Soldier in the Mexican War, 1846–1848* (1992), and Richard Bruce Winders, *Mr. Polk's Army: The American Military Experience in the Mexican War* (1997).

For Northern Democrats and the Wilmot Proviso, see Chaplain Morrison, *Democratic Politics and Sectionalism: The Wilmot Proviso Controversy* (1967); and Eric Foner, "The Wilmot Proviso Revisited," *JAH,* 56 (1969), 262–279. The divisive impact of the slavery issue on Massachusetts Whigs is treated in Thomas H. O'Connor, *Lords of the Loom: The Cotton Whigs and the Coming of the Civil War* (1967); and Kinley J. Brauer, *Cotton Versus Conscience: Massachusetts Whig Politics and Southwestern Expansion 1843–1848* (1967). For evidence of how party rather than sectional divisions persisted until 1850 on issues unrelated to slavery, see Thomas B. Alexander, *Sectional Stress and Party Stress: A Study of Roll-Call Voting Patterns in the United States House of Representatives 1836–1860* (1967); and Joel H. Silbey, *The Shrine of Party: Congressional Voting Behavior 1841–1852* (1967). Michael A. Morrison, *Slavery and the American West: The Eclipse of Manifest Destiny and the Coming of the Civil War* (1997), shows how the slavery-expansion issue emerged as the dominant one in American politics. The Free Soil party and the 1848 presidential election are treated in Joseph Rayback, *Free Soil: The Election of 1848* (1970); Frederick J. Blue, *The Free Soilers: Third Party Politics 1848–1854* (1973); and John Mayfield, *Rehearsal for Republicanism: Free Soil and the Politics of Antislavery* (1980).

Robert R. Russel, "What Was the Compromise of 1850?" *JSH,* 22 (1956), 292–309, undertakes to clear away myths and errors but in the process creates some new ones of his own. The fullest study of the compromise is Holman Hamilton, *Prologue to Conflict: The Crisis and Compromise of 1850* (1964). The importance of the Texas-New Mexico boundary dispute is emphasized in Mark J. Stegmaier, *Texas, Mexico, and the Compromise of 1850* (1996). For the role of Daniel Webster, see Robert F. Dalzell, *Daniel Webster and the Trial of American Nationalism 1843–1852* (1972). The careers of the three great senators who played such an important part in the Compromise debate are portrayed in Merrill Peterson, *The Great Triumvirate: Webster, Clay, and Calhoun* (1987). The efforts of fire-eaters to capitalize on resentment of the events that led up to the compromise are treated in Thelma Jennings, *The Nashville Convention: Southern Movement for Unity 1848–1850* (1980); while the destructive impact of these events on the Southern Whigs is narrated in Arthur C. Cole, *The Whig Party in the South* (1913).

Filibusterers, Fugitives, and Nativists

The best accounts of Southern expansionism and filibustering in the 1850s are Robert E. May, *The Southern Dream of a Caribbean Empire 1854–1861* (1973); and Charles H. Brown, *Agents of Manifest Destiny: The Lives and Times of the Filibusterers* (1979). For attempts to obtain Cuba, consult Basil Rauch, *American Interest in Cuba 1848–1855* (1948); and Tom Chaffin, *Fatal Glory: Narciso Lopez and the First Clandestine U.S. War against Cuba* (1996). C. Stanley Urban has written several articles on this question; see especially "The Ideology of Southern Imperialism," *Louisiana Historical Quarterly,* 39 (1956), 48–73; "New Orleans and the Cuban Question During the Lopez Expeditions of 1849–1851: A Local Study in Manifest Destiny," *Louisiana Historical Quarterly,* 22 (1939), 1095–1167; and "The Abortive Quitman Filibustering Expedition, 1853–1855," *Journal of Mississippi History,* 18 (1956), 175–196.

The basic study of the passage and enforcement of the Fugitive Slave Law is Stanley W. Campbell, *The Slave Catchers* (1970). Other treatments of legal aspects of the Fugitive Slave Law and related matters include Paul Finkelman, *An Imperfect Union: Slavery, Federalism, and Comity* (1980); Robert M. Cover, *Justice Accused: Antislavery and the Judicial Process* (1975); and William M. Wiecek, "Slavery and Abolition Before the United States Supreme Court, 1820–1860," *JAH,* 65 (1978), 34–59. For Northern personal liberty laws, see Thomas D.

Morris, *Free Men All: The Personal Liberty Laws of the North 1780–1861* (1974). A scholarly study of the underground railroad is Larry Gara, *Liberty Line: The Legend of the Underground Railroad* (1961). For interesting insights, see also Larry Gara, "The Fugitive Slave Law: A Double Paradox," *CWH,* 10 (1964), 229–240. For the hostility of many Northern states toward blacks—fugitive or otherwise—see Eugene Berwanger, *The Frontier Against Slavery: Western Anti-Negro Prejudice and the Slavery Extension Controversy* (1971). The Shadrach rescue and the Christiana riot are vividly described in Gary Collison, *Shadrach Minkins: From Fugitive Slave to Citizen* (1997), and Thomas P. Slaughter, *Bloody Dawn: The Christiana Riot and Racial Violence in the Antebellum North* (1991), while the tragedy of Margaret Garner is chronicled in Steven Weisenburger, *Modern Medea: A Family Story of Slavery and Child-Murder in the Old South* (1998). Reaction in Boston to the Anthony Burns affair is analyzed in Albert J. Von Frank, *The Trials of Anthony Burns: Freedom and Slavery in Emerson's Boston* (1998).

For the impact of immigration on the ethnic and regional distribution of the American population, see William I. Greenwald, "The Ante-Bellum Population, 1830–1861," *Mid-America,* 36 (1954), 176–189. Among the numerous studies of immigrant life and culture, the following are especially useful: Oscar Handlin, *Boston's Immigrants* (1941); Robert Ernst, *Immigrant Life in New York City 1825–1863* (1949); Jay P. Dolan, *The Immigrant Church: New York's Irish and German Catholics 1815–1865* (1975); and Joseph P. Ferrie, *Yankeys Now: Immigrants in the Antebellum U.S., 1840–1860* (1998). Still the basic narrative of nativism is Ray Allen Billington, *The Protestant Crusade 1800–1861* (1938). See also William G. Bean, "Puritan Versus Celt, 1850–1860," *New England Quarterly,* 7 (1934), 70–89; Ira M. Leonard and Robert D. Parmet, *American Nativism, 1830–1860* (1971); and Dale T. Knobel, *Paddy and the Republic: Ethnicity and Nationality in Antebellum America* (1985). The response of Catholics to nativism is explored in Robert F. Hueston, *The Catholic Press and Nativism 1840–1860* (1976); and Vincent P. Lannie, "Alienation in America: The Immigrant Catholic and Public Education in Pre-Civil War America," *Review of Politics,* 32 (1970), 503–521. For the anti-Catholic sentiments of British Protestant immigrants, consult Charlotte Erickson, *Invisible Immigrants: The Adaptation of English and Scottish Immigrants in Nineteenth Century America* (1972). Case studies of one series of ethnic conflicts are provided by David Montgomery, "The Shuttle and the Cross: Weavers and Artisans in the Kensington Riots of 1844," *Journal of Social History,* 5 (1972), 411–456; and Michael Feldberg, *The Philadelphia Riots of 1844: A Study of Ethnic Conflict* (1975).

Joel Silbey, "The Civil War Synthesis in American Political History," *CWH,* 10 (1964), 130–40; and Joel Silbey (ed.), *The Transformation of American Politics 1840–1860* (1967), argue for the primacy of nonsectional issues during much of the antebellum period. Michael Holt, "The Politics of Impatience: The Origins of Know-Nothingism," *JAH,* 60 (1973), 309–331, maintains that nativism was the most powerful political impulse in the first half of the 1850s and that it was principally responsible for breaking up the Whig party. For three books that advance a similar thesis and maintain in addition that after the demise of the Know-Nothings nativist sentiment found its way into the Republican party, see Mark L. Berger, *The Revolution in the New York Party Systems 1840–1860* (1973); Ronald P. Formisano, *The Birth of Mass Political Parties: Michigan 1827–1861* (1971); and Michael F. Holt, *Forging a Majority: The Formation of the Republican Party in Pittsburgh* (1969). Holt modifies this position and offers important new insights on politics during the 1850s in *The Political Crisis of the 1850s* (1978). Two other books that set the ethnocultural dimension of American politics in a wider context are Paul Kleppner, *The Third Electoral System 1853–1892* (1979); and Robert Kelley, *The Cultural Pattern in American Politics: The First Century* (1979). The fullest account of the matrix of nativism, ideology, and politics that gave birth to the Republican party is William E. Gienapp, *The Origins of the Republican Party, 1852–1856* (1987). Gienapp sides with those who see nativism as an important driving force in this process: see also his "Nativism and the Creation of a Republican Majority in the North before the Civil War," *JAH,* 72 (1985), 529–559. But the best study of the ideology of the Republican party sees antislavery sentiment as uppermost: Eric Foner, *Free Soil, Free Labor, Free Men: The Ideology of the Republican Party before the Civil War* (1970). An important state study takes a similar position: Stephen E. Maizlish, *The Triumph of Sectionalism: The Transformation of Ohio Politics, 1844–1856* (1983). Several of the essays in Stephen E. Maizlish and John J. Kushma (eds.), *Essays on American Antebellum Politics, 1840–1860* (1982), debate this theme. Dale Baum, "The Political Realignment of the 1850's: Know Nothingism and the Republican Majority in Massachusetts," *JAH,* 64 (1978), 959–986, raises important questions about some aspects of the ethnocultural interpretation, and his *The Civil War Party System: The Case of Massachusetts, 1848–1876* (1984), maintains the primacy of the slavery issue in the origin of the Republican party. John R. Mulkern, *The Know-Nothing Party in Massachusetts: The Rise and Fall of a People's Party* (1990), documents the complex roots of this phenomenon, while Tyler G. Anbinder, *Nativism and Politics: The Know Nothing Party in the Northern United States* (1992), argues persuasively that antislavery sentiments were important in both the birth and demise of the Know-Nothings. Gilbert Osofsky, "Abolitionists, Irish Immigrants, and the Dilemmas of Romantic Nationalism," *AHR,* 80 (1975), 889–912, demonstrates the ambivalence of abolitionists toward nativism; while Thomas J. Curran, "Seward and the Know Nothings," *New York Historical Society Quarterly,* 51 (1967), 141–159, highlights the antinativism of the foremost Republican leader. The complex interplay between German immigrants, nativism, and antislavery is analyzed in Bruce Levine, *The Spirit of 1848: German Immigrants, Labor Conflict, and the Coming of the Civil War* (1992).

By 1856, the principal locale of the Know-Nothing political strength as a separate party had shifted to the South. For the movement there, see W. Darrell Overdyke, *The Know-Nothing Party in the South* (1950); James H. Broussard, "Some Determinants of Know-Nothing Electoral Strength in the South," *Louisiana History,* 7 (1966), 5–20; and Jean Baker, *Ambivalent Americans: The Know-Nothing Party in Maryland* (1977).

Politics and the Deepening Crisis, 1854–1860

Roy F. Nichols, "The Kansas-Nebraska Act: A Century of Historiography," *MVHR,* 43 (1956), 187–212, is a good introduction to the issues and the historiography of the vexed question of the Kansas-Nebraska Act. For the politics of the act, consult Roy F. Nichols, *The Democratic Machine 1850–1854* (1923); Larry Gara, *The Presidency of Franklin Pierce* (1991); Robert R. Russel, "The Issues in the Congressional Struggle Over the Kansas-Nebraska Bill, 1854," *JSH,* 29 (1963), 187–210; and Gerald W. Wolff, *The Kansas-Nebraska Bill: Party, Section, and the Coming of the Civil War* (1977). Frank H. Hodder, "The Railroad Background of the Kansas-Nebraska Act," *MVHR,* 12 (1925), 3–22, contains valuable material. Events in "Bleeding Kansas" are treated in James A. Rawley, *Race and Politics: "Bleeding Kansas" and the Coming of the Civil War* (1969); Thomas Goodrich, *War to the Knife: Bleeding Kansas, 1854–1861* (1999); and Gunja SenGupta, *For God and Mammon: Evangelicals and Entrepreneurs, Masters and Slaves in Territorial Kansas, 1854–1860* (1996). Two books by James C. Malin view the motives and actions of all parties, especially Northerners, with a jaundiced eye: *The Nebraska Question 1852–1854* (1953) and *John Brown and the Legend of Fifty-Six* (1942). A detailed study of John Brown that culminates with his arrival in Kansas is Richard O. Boyer, *The Legend of John Brown* (1973). Samuel A. Johnson, *The Battle Cry of Freedom: The New England Emigrant Aid Company in the Kansas Crusade* (1954), is an informative study of the New England efforts to colonize Kansas. For the twin impacts of "bleeding Sumner" and "bleeding Kansas," see William E. Gienapp, "The Crime Against Sumner: The Caning of Charles Sumner and the Rise of the Republican Party," *CWH,* 25 (1979), 218–245.

The troubled and divisive presidency of James Buchanan is chronicled in Elbert B. Smith, *The Presidency of James Buchanan* (1975). The crucial year 1857 is dissected skillfully by Kenneth M. Stampp, *America in 1857: A Nation on the Brink* (1990). The Panic of 1857 and its political consequences are analyzed in James L. Huston, *The Panic of 1857 and the Coming of the Civil War* (1987). Charges of corruption bedeviled the Buchanan administration: this issue is exhaustively investigated by Mark W. Summers, *The Plundering Generation: Corruption and the Crisis of the Union, 1849–1861* (1987).

The Dred Scott case has received a great deal of attention. Among the more noteworthy studies are Vincent C. Hopkins, *Dred Scott's Case* (1967); Walter Ehrlich, *They Have No Rights: Dred Scott's Struggle for Freedom* (1979); and Stanley I. Kutler (ed.), *The Dred Scott Decision: Law or Politics?* (1967). All other studies, however, have been largely superseded by Don E. Fehrenbacher's exhaustive and magisterial study, *The Dred Scott Case: Its Significance in American Law and Politics* (1978), which was published in an abridged version with the title *Slavery, Law, and Politics: The Dred Scott Case in Historical Perspective* (1981). For Taney's partisan and sectional motives in this case, see also Don E. Fehrenbacher, "Roger B. Taney and the Sectional Crisis," *JSH,* 43 (1977).

The most detailed studies of the Lincoln-Douglas debates are Harry V. Jaffa, *Crisis of the House Divided* (1959), and David Zarefsky, *Lincoln, Douglas and Slavery in the Crucible of Public Debate* (1990). The full text of the debates can be found in Paul M. Angle (ed.), *Created Equal? The Complete Lincoln-Douglas Debates of 1858* (1958). For the divisive impact of the debates and of Douglas's earlier stance in the Lecompton debate on the Democratic party, consult Roy F. Nichols, *The Disruption of American Democracy* (1948). Don E. Fehrenbacher, *Prelude to Greatness: Lincoln in the 1850s* (1962), assesses Lincoln's strategy in the debates. Damon Wells, *Stephen Douglas: The Last Years, 1857–1861* (1971), and William E. Baringer, *Lincoln's Rise to Power* (1937), are also valuable for the crucial years of the late 1850s. Robert W. Johannsen, *Lincoln, the South, and Slavery: The Political Dimension* (1991), argues that Lincoln's antislavery position was motivated in considerable part by political ambition.

Ronald T. Takaki, *A Pro-Slavery Crusade: The Agitation to Reopen the African Slave Trade* (1971), argues for the importance of the slave trade issue in the sectional confrontation of the late 1850s. See also Barton J. Bernstein, "Southern Politics and Attempts to Reopen the African Slave Trade," *JNH,* 51 (1966), 16–35; and James P. Hendrix, "The Efforts to Reopen the African Slave Trade in Louisiana," *Louisiana History,* 10 (1960), 97–123. The question of reopening the trade, and the increase of the illegal trade in the 1850s, are placed in long-term context in the following books: Peter Duigan and Clarence Clendenen, *The United States and the African Slave Trade, 1619–1862* (1963); W. E. B. Du Bois, *The Suppression of the African Slave Trade to the United States 1638–1870* (1896); Warren S. Howard, *American Slavers and the Federal Law 1837–1862* (1963); and Tom Henderson Wells, *The Slave Ship* Wanderer (1967).

A good introduction to the literature on John Brown and the trauma of Harpers Ferry is Stephen B. Oates, "John Brown and His Judges: A Critique of the Historical Literature," *CWH,* 17 (1971), 5–24. Jeffrey S. Rossback, *Ambivalent Conspirators: John Brown, the Secret Six, and a Theory of Slave Violence* (1982), offers important insights on the Harpers Ferry raid. See also Edward J. Renehan, Jr., *The Secret Six: The True Tale of the Men Who Conspired with John Brown* (1997). Paul Finkelman (ed.), *His Soul Goes Marching On: Responses to John Brown and the Harpers Ferry Raid* (1994), contains several important essays. For the relationship of black leaders with Brown, see Benjamin Quarles, *Allies for Freedom: Blacks and John Brown* (1974).

For the background of the Southern Democratic insistence on a slave code for the territories, which split the Democratic party in 1860, see Arthur Bestor, "State Sovereignty and Slavery: A Reinterpretation of Proslavery Doctrine, 1846–1860," *Journal of the Illinois State Historical Society,* 54 (1961), 117–180. A revisionist interpretation of the Southern Constitutional Unionists in 1860 finds them more of a Southern rights than a Union party: John V. Mering, "The Slave-State Constitutional Unionists and the Politics of Consensus," *JSH,* 43 (1977), 395–410. A useful narrative of the 1860 election in the South is Ollinger Crenshaw, *The Slave*

States in the Election of 1860 (1945). A fascinating eyewitness account of the four presidential nominating conventions can be found in William B. Hesseltine (ed.), *Three Against Lincoln: Murat Halstead Reports the Caucuses of 1860* (1960). For several brief essays on the 1860 election, see Norman A. Graebner (ed.), *Politics and the Crisis of 1860* (1961). The two basic studies of the election are Emerson D. Fite, *The Presidential Campaign of 1860* (1911); and Reinhard D. Luthin, *The First Lincoln Campaign* (1944). The question of the foreign-born vote, especially that of the Germans, is discussed by several historians in Frederick D. Luebke (ed.), *Ethnic Voters and the Election of Lincoln* (1971). Despite its title, Thomas B. Alexander's "The Civil War as Institutional Fulfillment," *JSH,* 47 (1981), 3–31, is really an intriguing study of several aspects of the election of 1860.

Secession and the Coming of War

Three essays that provide a good introduction to the historiography of secession are Ralph A. Wooster, "Secession of the Lower South: Changing Interpretations," *CWH,* 7 (1961), 117–127; William J. Donnelly, "Conspiracy or Popular Movement: The Historiography of Southern Support for Secession," *North Carolina Historical Review,* 42 (1965), 70–84; and James Tice Moore, "Secession and the States: A Review Essay," *Virginia Magazine of History and Biography,* 94 (Jan. 1986), 60–76. Statistical analyses of the elections of delegates to secession conventions and of votes in those conventions are provided by Peyton McCrary, Clark Miller, and Dale Baum, "Class and Party in the Secession Crisis: Voting Behavior in the Deep South," *Journal of Interdisciplinary History,* 8 (1978), 429–457; and Ralph Wooster, The *Secession Conventions of the South* (1962). An older but still valuable study of Southern secession is Dwight L. Dumond, *The Secession Movement 1860–1861* (1931). Studies of secession in individual states include: Harold Schultz, *Nationalism and Sectionalism in South Carolina 1852–1860* (1950); Steven A. Channing, *Crisis of Fear: Secession in South Carolina* (1970); Percy Lee Rainwater, *Mississippi: Storm Center of Secession 1856–1861* (1938); William L. Barney, *The Secessionist Impulse: Alabama and Mississippi in 1860* (1974); J. Mills Thornton, *Politics and Power in a Slave Society: Alabama 1800–1861* (1978); Michael P. Johnson, *Toward a Patriarchal Republic: The Secession of Georgia* (1977); Anthony G. P. Carey, *Parties, Slavery, and the Union in Antebellum Georgia* (1997); Elizabeth R. Varon, *We Mean to be Counted: White Women and Politics in Antebellum Virginia* (1998); Henry T. Shanks, *The Secession Movement in Virginia 1847–1861* (1934); Joseph Carlyle Sitterson, *The Secession Movement in North Carolina* (1939); Mary E. R. Campbell, *The Attitude of Tennesseans Toward the Union 1847–1861* (1961); Walter L. Buenger, *Secession and Union in Texas* (1984); and James M. Woods, *Rebellion and Realignment: Arkansas's Road to Secession* (1987). A superb study of the dilemma of Unionists in the upper South is Daniel W. Crofts, *Reluctant Confederates: Upper South Unionists in the Secession Crisis* (1989). For a state that did not secede, see William J. Evitts, *A Matter of Allegiances: Maryland from 1850 to 1861* (1974). The role of Southern newspapers is analyzed in Donald E. Reynolds, *Editors Make War: Southern Newspapers in the Secession Crisis* (1970); while good samples of editorials are reprinted in Dwight L. Dumond (ed.), *Southern Editorials on Secession* (1931). Another set of primary sources is Jon L. Wakelyn (ed.), *Southern Pamphlets on Secession* (1996). The formation of the Confederate government and Constitution is chronicled in William C. Davis, *"A Government of Our Own": The Making of the Confederacy* (1994).

Northern newspaper opinion is copiously presented in Howard C. Perkins (ed.), *Northern Editorials on Secession,* 2 vols. (1942). An old but still useful account of the Buchanan administration's handling of the crisis is Philip G. Auchampaugh, *James Buchanan and His Cabinet on the Eve of Secession* (1926). Robert C. Gunderson, *Old Gentleman's Convention* (1961); Jesse L. Keene, *The Peace Convention of 1861* (1961); and Mary Scrugham, *The Peaceable Americans of 1860–1861: A Study in Public Opinion* (1921), chronicle the futile efforts to find

a compromise formula. Kenneth M. Stampp, *And the War Came: The North and the Secession Crisis 1860–61* (1950), is the best overall study of its subject; while David M. Potter, *Lincoln and His Party in the Secession Crisis,* 2d ed., with new preface (1962), is still the best study of Republican policies. See also William E. Barringer, *A House Dividing: Lincoln as President Elect* (1945). Stampp, Potter, and other historians debate the secession question in George H. Knoles (ed.), *The Crisis of the Union 1860–1861* (1965).

John S. Tilley, *Lincoln Takes Command* (1941), and Charles W. Ramsdell, "Lincoln and Fort Sumter," *JSH,* 3 (1937), 259–288, offer pro-Southern interpretations that fasten upon Lincoln the responsibility for provoking the war. Also sympathetic to the Confederate position is Ludwell H. Johnson, "Fort Sumter and Confederate Diplomacy," *JSH,* 26 (1961), 441–466. More balanced are Richard N. Current, *Lincoln and the First Shot* (1963) and "The Confederates and the First Shot," *CWH,* 7 (1961), 357–369, and Grady McWhiney, "The Confederacy's First Shot," *CWH,* 14 (1968), 5–14. See also the Stampp and Potter studies cited in the preceding paragraph, for judicious interpretations of the Sumter crisis. The fullest narrative, with judicious interpretations, of the background and climax of the firing on Fort Sumter is Maury Klein, *Days of Defiance: Sumter, Secession, and the Coming of the Civil War* (1997).

The Civil War

General Works

Several bibliographical guides will introduce the student to the rich and massive literature on the war: Allan Nevins, Bell I. Wiley, and James I. Robertson (eds.), *Civil War Books: A Critical Bibliography,* 2 vols. (1967–1969); Ralph G. Newman and E. B. Long, *A Basic Civil War Library* (1964); David J. Eicher (ed.), *The Civil War in Books: An Analytical Bibliography* (1997); James I. Robertson (ed.), *Southern Historical Society Papers, Index-Guide* (1980); E. Merton Coulter, *Travels in the Confederate States: A Bibliography* (1968); Eugene C. Murdock, *The Civil War in the North: A Selective Annotated Bibliography* (1987); John H. Wright, *Compendium of the Confederacy: An Annotated Bibliography,* 2 vols. (1989); Dallas Irvine, *Military Operations of the Civil War: A Guide-Index to the Official Records of the Union and Confederate Armies, 1861–1865* (1980); and Gerald L. Cole, *Civil War Eyewitnesses: An Annotated Bibliography of Books and Articles, 1955–1986* (1988). Joseph T. Glatthaar, "The 'New' Civil War History: An Overview," *Pennsylvania Magazine of History and Biography,* 115 (July 1991), 339–369, is a useful survey. See also the comprehensive reference works and bibliographies listed on p. B–2.

Two multivolume studies by gifted writers who emphasize military aspects of the war will give the interested reader endless hours of pleasure: Bruce Catton, *The Centennial History of the Civil War,* 3 vols. (1961–1965), vol. I: *The Coming Fury,* vol. II: *Terrible Swift Sword,* vol. III: *Never Call Retreat;* and Shelby Foote, *The Civil War: A Narrative,* 3 vols. (1958–1974), vol. I: *Fort Sumter to Perryville,* vol. II: *Fredericksburg to Meridian,* vol. III: *Red River to Appomattox.* Bruce Catton has also written a good one-volume history of the war, *This Hallowed Ground* (1956), which treats mainly military events, as do Herman Hattaway, *Shades of Blue and Gray: An Introductory Military History of the Civil War* (1998), and James L. Stokesbury, *A Short History of the Civil War* (1995).

Two one-volume histories that concentrate on social history are William L. Barney, *Flawed Victory: A New Perspective on the Civil War* (1975), and Robert Cruden, *The War That Never Ended* (1973). A collection of essays edited by Randall M. Miller, Harry S. Stout, and Charles Reagan Wilson, *Religion and the American Civil War* (1998), provides rich fare.

Several studies focus mainly or entirely on the North during the war: Philip S. Paludan, *"A People's Contest": The Union and Civil War 1861–1865* (1988), which blends political, social, and economic history; Randall C. Jimerson, *The Private Civil War: Popular Thought During the Sectional Conflict* (1988); Earl J. Hess, *Liberty, Virtue, and Progress: Northerners and Their War for the Union* (rev. ed. 1998); and Maris Vinovskis (ed.), *Toward A Social History of the Civil War: Exploratory Essays* (1990). Three books that focus more on the social and cultural homefront in the North than on the actual war are Daniel Sutherland, *The Expansion of Everyday Life, 1860–1876* (1989); Kathleen Diffley, *Where My Heart Is Turning Ever: Civil War Stories and Constitutional Reform, 1861–1876* (1992); and Anne C. Rose, *Victorian America and the Civil War* (1992).

The two fullest narrative histories of the Confederacy are E. Merton Coulter, *The Confederate States of America 1861–1865* (1950), and Emory M. Thomas, *The Confederate Nation 1861–1865* (1979). Richard N. Current (ed.), *Encyclopedia of the Confederacy,* 4 vols. (1993) is a superb reference work. See also Jon L. Wakelyn, *Biographical Dictionary of the Confederacy* (1977), and Ezra J. Warner and W. Buck Yearns, *Biographical Register of the Confederate Congress* (1975).

For their wealth of factual data, with entries arranged in alphabetical or chronological order, the following reference works are valuable: Mark M. Boatner, *The Civil War Dictionary* (rev. ed., 1988); Patricia L. Faust (ed.), *Historical Times Illustrated Encyclopedia of the Civil War* (1986); Stewart Sifakis, *Who Was Who in the Civil War* (1988); James M. McPherson (ed.), *Biographical Encyclopedia of the Civil War,* 3 vols. (1999); Jay Robert Nash (ed.), *Encyclopedia of the Civil War,* 6 vols. (2000); E. B. Long, *The Civil War Day by Day: An Almanac* (1971); John S. Bowman, *The Civil War Almanac* (1982); and Chris Bishop, Ian Drury, and Tony Gibbons, *1400 Days: The Civil War Day by Day* (1990). Contemporary documents, newspaper articles, speeches, military reports, poetry, and other kinds of items dealing with the war were collected and published by Frank Moore (ed.), *Rebellion Record,* 12 vols. (1861–1868) and have been reprinted in a modern edition (1977). Another valuable reference work is Jon Ropert (ed.) *American Civil War: Literary Sources and Documents,* 3 vols. (1999).

Many stimulating books, essays, and collections of essays offer interpretations of the meaning of the war or of specific aspects of it: Herbert Aptheker, *The American Civil War* (1961); James A. Rawley, *Turning Points of the Civil War* (1966); Emory M. Thomas, *The Confederacy as a Revolutionary Experience* (1971); Bell I. Wiley, *The Road to Appomattox* (1956); Grady McWhiney (ed.), *Grant, Lee, Lincoln, and the Radicals: Essays on Civil War Leadership* (1964); James I. Robertson (ed.), *Rank and File: Civil War Essays in Honor of Bell Irvin Wiley* (1976); William R. Brock (ed.), *The Civil War* (1969); Frank E. Vandiver et al., *Essays on the American Civil War* (1968); Henry Steele Commager (ed.), *The Defeat of the Confederacy* (1964); and a fascinating volume of essays focusing on the American Civil War and the Franco-Prussian War in a comparative context, Stig Förster and Jörg Nagler (eds.), *On the Road to Total War: The American Civil War and the German Wars of Unification, 1861–1871* (1997). Many of these volumes address, at least implicitly, the question of why the North won the war; the following books address that question explicitly, offering a wide range of answers: David Donald (ed.), *Why the North Won the Civil War* (1960); Herman Hattaway and Archer Jones, *How the North Won: A Military History of the Civil War* (1982); Richard E. Beringer, Herman Hattaway, Archer Jones, and William N. Still, Jr., *Why the South Lost the Civil War* (1986), and an abridged version of this book which appeared in 1988 with the title *The Elements of Confederate Defeat: Nationalism, War Aims, and Religion;* Gabor S. Boritt (ed.), *Why the Confederacy Lost* (1992); and Gary W. Gallagher, *The Confederate War* (1997).

The science of photography and the enterprise of photographers and artists made the Civil War the most lavishly illustrated war in history before the twentieth century. A good introduction to the subject is W. Fletcher Thompson, Jr., *The Image of War: The Pictorial Reporting of the American Civil War* (1960). The most ambitious effort to collect and publish the best of the tens of thousands of war photographs is Francis T. Miller (ed.), *The Photographic History of the Civil War,* 10 vols. (1911; reprinted 1957). A more selective collection, with a higher quality reproduction of the original photographs made possible by modern technology, is Hirst D. Milhollen and Milton Kaplan (eds.), *Divided We Fought: A Pictorial History of the War 1861–1865,* with narrative by David Donald (1952). A modern enterprise augmented the Miller volumes with many previously unpublished photographs and a better reproduction of all photographs: William C. Davis (ed.), *The Image of War, 1861–1865,* 6 vols. (1981–1984). For excellent selections of the work of one of the war's best photographers, consult Alexander Gardner, *Gardner's Photographic Sketch Book of the Civil War* (1959). D. Mark Katz, *Witness to an Era: The Life and Photographs of Alexander Gardner* (1999) includes some two hundred of Gardner's Civil War photographs. Four other fine photographic histories are Bell Irvin Wiley and Hirst D. Milhollen, *They Who Fought Here* (1959); Bell Irvin Wiley and Hirst D. Milhollen, *Embattled Confederates: An Illustrated History of Southerners at War* (1964); Geoffrey Ward with Rich Burns and Ken Burns, *The Civil War: An Illustrated History* (1990); and Carl Moneyhon, *Portraits of Conflict: A Photographic History of Louisiana in the Civil War* (1990). A lavish volume that reproduces photographs as well as drawings and paintings, some in full color, is James M. McPherson (ed.), *The American Heritage New History of the Civil War,* with narrative by Bruce Catton (1996). Another volume of a similar genre is *Brother Against Brother: Time-Life Books History of the Civil War* (1990). The work of wartime artists and illustrators is reproduced in Stephen W. Sears (ed.), *The American Heritage Century Collection of Civil War Art* (1974), while Harold Holzer and Mark E. Neely, Jr., *Mine Eyes Have Seen the Glory: The Civil War in Art* (1993), contains full-color reproductions of contemporary and later artists' illustrations of the Civil War. Holzer and Neely, along with Gabor S. Boritt, have put together 140 Confederate engravings and prints, with a text explaining their provenance and impact, in *The Confederate Image: Prints of the Lost Cause* (1987). Neely and Holzer have edited a similar volume for the North, *The Union Image: Popular Prints of the Civil War North* (1999). The illustrations and text from the Union's two leading illustrated weeklies have been reprinted in modern editions: *Harper's Pictorial History of the Civil War* (1975) and *Frank Leslie's Illustrated History of the Civil War* (1977). Edwin Forbes was one of the most prolific contemporary illustrators of the War, for Leslie's; a generation later he put together many of his illustrations in a volume that has been reprinted in a modern edition: *Thirty Years After: An Artist's Memoir of the Civil War* (1993). Another classic illustrated history of the war, which was first published in the 1870s, has also been reprinted in a modern edition: Benson J. Lossing, *Pictorial Field Book of the Civil War,* 3 vols. (1997). One of America's best artists got his start as a wartime illustrator for *Harper's Weekly;* for a collection of his war drawings and paintings, see Julian Grossman, *Echo of a Distant Drum: Winslow Homer and the Civil War* (1974). William A. Frassanito has movingly re-created the battles of Antietam and Gettysburg through the use of contemporary and modern photographs in two rich volumes: *Antietam: The Photographic Legacy of America's Bloodiest Day* (1978) and *Gettysburg: A Journey in Time* (1975). Frassanito has also put together a fine photographic history of the epic Virginia military campaigns from the Wilderness to Appomattox in *Grant and Lee: The Virginia Campaigns, 1864–1865* (1983). A modern artist who has done many Civil War paintings is Mort Künstler; for a book of his paintings accompanied by a text written by James M. McPherson, see *Images of the Civil War* (1992).

Strategies, Commanders, Armies, and Soldiers

Civil War historiography is rich in studies of strategy, command, and tactics. Some of the best include the following: Archer Jones, *Civil War Command and Strategy: The Process of Victory and Defeat* (1992); Joseph G. Glatthaar, *Partners in Command: The Relationships Between Leaders in the Civil War* (1994); Thomas B. Buell, *The Warrior Generals: Combat Leadership in the Civil War* (1997); Albert Castel, *Winning and Losing the Civil War* (1996); John T.

Hubbell (ed.), *Battles Lost and Won: Essays from Civil War History* (1975); Steven E. Woodworth (ed.), *The Art of Command in the Civil War* (1999); and the Civil War chapters in Russell Weigley, *The American Way of War* (1973). H. B. C. Rogers, *The Confederates and Federals at War* (1973) offers a British perspective, while another British analyst, Paddy Griffith, *Battle Tactics of the Civil War* (1989), argues with mixed success that technology had not changed the tactical situation much since the Napoleonic era. Steven E. Woodworth (ed.), *Civil War Generals in Defeat* (1999) contains several provocative essays. Edward Hagerman, *The American Civil War and the Origins of Modern Warfare* (1988) analyzes the relationship between logistics and strategy. Several important articles are reprinted in *Military Analysis of the Civil War: An Anthology by the Editors of Military Affairs* (1977). For a provocative study that blends cultural and strategic analysis, see Charles Royster, *The Destructive War: William Tecumseh Sherman, Stonewall Jackson, and the Americans* (1991). Jay Luvaas, *The Military Legacy of the Civil War: The European Inheritance* (1959), analyzes the influence (and lack thereof) of the lessons of the American Civil War on European strategists and commanders.

Ezra J. Warner, *Generals in Gray: Lives of the Confederate Commanders* (1959), and Bruce S. Allardice, *More Generals in Gray* (1995), contain brief biographies of Confederate generals. Additional material on West Point graduates who went with the South can be found in Eliot Ellsworth, *West Point in the Confederacy* (1941). Frank E. Vandiver, *Rebel Brass: The Confederate Command System* (1956), disentangles a complicated story. A good introduction to the historiographical themes and disputes concerning Confederate strategy and leadership is Douglas Southall Freeman, *The South to Posterity: An Introduction to the Writing of Confederate History* (1939). In addition to his four-volume biography of Lee (cited in the biography section), Freeman has written the classic *Lee's Lieutenants: A Study in Command,* 3 vols. (1942–1944). Four detailed studies of Confederate strategy are Thomas L. Connelly and Archer Jones, *The Politics of Command: Factions and Ideas in Confederate Strategy* (1973); Archer Jones, *Confederate Strategy from Shiloh to Vicksburg* (1961); Joseph L. Harsh, *Confederate Tide Rising: Robert E. Lee and the Making of Southern Strategy, 1861–1862* (1998); and Joseph L. Harsh, *Taken at the Flood: Robert E. Lee and Confederate Strategy in the Maryland Campaign of 1862* (1999). The essays in Gabor S. Boritt (ed.), *Jefferson Davis's Generals* (1999), offer critical appraisals, while three books by Steven E. Woodworth set forth incisive and provocative interpretations: *Jefferson Davis and His Generals: The Failure of Confederate Command in the West* (1990); *Davis and Lee at War* (1995); and *No Band of Brothers: Problems of the Rebel High Command* (1999). Gary W. Gallagher, *Lee and His Generals in War and Memory* (1998), contains trenchant essays on Confederate leadership, strategy, and tactics as well as Southern mythology. Richard M. McMurry, *Two Great Rebel Armies: An Essay in Confederate Military History* (1989), found superior leadership to be the principal reason for the greater success of the Army of Northern Virginia than the Army of Tennessee. But critical and negative appraisals of Lee's strategy and tactics became something of a cottage industry in the 1990s; for a summary of and commentary on this scholarship, see Alan T. Nolan, "Historians' Perspectives on Lee," *Columbiad,* 2 (Winter 1999), 27–45. Grady McWhiney and Perry Jamieson, *Attack and Die: The Failure of Confederate Military Tactics* (1982), maintain that the Confederacy bled itself to death by offensive tactics and strategy, while Jack Welsh, *The Medical Histories of Confederate Generals* (1995), points out that the top Confederate commanders averaged twelve years older than their Union adversaries and that this made a significant difference in their vitality and judgment as the war went on. Confederate guerrilla operations are assessed in Albert Castel, *The Guerrilla War* (1974); Virgil Carrington Jones, *Gray Ghosts and Rebel Raiders* (1956); Jeffrey Wert, *Mosby's Rangers* (1990); Richard S. Brownlee, *Gray Ghosts of the Confederacy: Guerrilla Warfare in the West 1861–1865* (1958); and Thomas Goodrich, *Black Flag: Guerrilla Warfare on the Western Border, 1861–1865* (1995). William Clarke Quantrill was the most notorious Confederate raider; for his story, see Edward E. Leslie, *The Devil Knows How to Ride: The True Story of William Clarke Quantrill and his Confederate Raiders* (1996). Don

Bowen, "Guerrilla Warfare in Western Missouri, 1862–1865: Historical Extensions of the Relative Deprivation Hypothesis," *Comparative Studies in Society and History* (1977), 30–51, is an important article on the social background of Missouri guerrillas. The war in the Indian Territory was characterized mainly by guerrilla operations on both sides; see Steve Cottrell, *Civil War in the Indian Territory* (1995), and Laurence M. Hauptman, *Between Two Fires: American Indians in the Civil War* (1995). For a useful anthology of essays by historians, see Daniel E. Sutherland (ed.) *Guerrillas, Unionists, and Violence on the Confederate Home Front* (1999).

Ezra J. Warner, *Generals in Blue: Lives of the Union Commanders* (1964), provides brief biographies of all Union generals. For perceptive essays, see Gabor S. Boritt (ed.), *Lincoln's Generals* (1994). T. Harry Williams, *Lincoln and His Generals* (1952), and Kenneth P. Williams, *Lincoln Finds a General: A Military Study of the Civil War*, 5 vols. (1949–1959), are highly critical of McClellan and find much to praise in Grant and Sherman, a position argued explicitly by T. Harry Williams in his *McClellan, Sherman, and Grant* (1962). For more sympathetic appraisals of McClellan, consult Warren W. Hassler, *Commanders of the Army of the Potomac* (1962), and Thomas Rowland, *George B. McClellan and Civil War History* (1999). In a provocative and thought-stimulating study, Michael C. C. Adams attributes what he sees as a defensive and defeatist psychology in the Army of the Potomac in part to McClellan: see Adams, *Our Masters the Rebels: A Speculation on Union Military Failure in the East 1861–1865* (1978), reprinted in 1992 as *Fighting for Defeat*. Most of the essays in James M. McPherson, *Abraham Lincoln and the Second American Revolution* (1991), focus on the relationship between Lincoln's dual roles as political leader and commander in chief. Two other evaluations of Union military leadership that give Lincoln high marks as a strategist and emphasize his cordial relationship with Grant are Maurice Frederick, *Statesmen and Soldiers of the Civil War: A Study of the Conduct of War* (1926), and Colin R. Ballard, *The Military Genius of Abraham Lincoln* (1926). The British Military historian J. F. C. Fuller rates Grant as the best general in the Civil War in two books: *The Generalship of Ulysses S. Grant* (1929) and *Grant and Lee: A Study in Personality and Generalship* (1933). Northern military strategy impacted Union policies in portions of the Confederacy conquered and occupied by Union forces; for studies of this impact, see Mark Grimsley, *The Hard Hand of War: Union Military Policy toward Southern Civilians, 1861–1865* (1995); Stephen V. Ash, *When the Yankees Came: Conflict and Chaos in the Occupied South, 1861–1865* (1995); and Chester Hearn, *When the Devil Came Down to Dixie: Ben Butler in New Orleans* (1997).

The fullest bibliography of regimental histories and individual accounts of army life and service appears under two different titles and slightly different formats in Charles E. Dornbusch, *Regimental Publications and Personal Narratives of the Civil War*, 3 vols. (1961–1972) and *Military Bibliography of the Civil War*, 3 vols. (1961–1972) and a fourth volume (1987) compiled with the help of Robert K. Krick. Frederick H. Dyer, *A Compendium of the War of the Rebellion*, 3 vols. (1908; new ed. in 2 vols., 1961) contains a great deal of information about Union military units from battalion to army. Its counterpart for the Confederate army, in even greater detail, is Stewart Sifakis, *Compendium of the Confederate Armies*, 10 vols. (1992–1995). Another valuable aid to the student of the war's military events is William F. Amann, *Personnel of the Civil War*, 2 vols. (1961). A massive statistical profile of soldiers in the Union army can be found in Benjamin A. Gould, *Investigations in the Military and Anthropological Statistics of American Soldiers* (1869). Unit casualties in the Union armies, along with a great deal of other information, are provided in William Freeman Fox, *Regimental Losses in the American Civil War 1861–1865* (1889). The most judicious treatment of the sometimes confusing and controversial question of battle casualties is contained in Thomas L. Livermore, *Numbers and Losses in the Civil War* (1901).

The hard luck but eventually triumphant story of the Army of the Potomac is brilliantly brought to life by Bruce Catton in three volumes: *Mr. Lincoln's Army* (1951), *Glory Road* (1952), and *A Stillness at Appomattox* (1953). Thomas L. Connelly has written a history of the

Confederacy's principal western army that is as thorough if less readable: *Army of the Heart-land: The Army of Tennessee 1861–1862* (1967) and *Autumn of Glory: The Army of Tennessee 1862–1865* (1971). Other fine studies of Civil War armies during all or parts of their histories, focusing mainly on the rank and file, are Larry Daniel, *Soldiering in the Army of Tennessee* (1991); Joseph T. Glatthaar, *The March to the Sea and Beyond: Sherman's Troops in the Savannah and Carolinas Campaigns* (1985); J. Tracy Power, *Lee's Miserables: Life in the Army of Northern Virginia from the Wilderness to Appomattox* (1998); and Edward G. Longacre, *Army of Amateurs: Benjamin F. Butler and the Army of the James, 1863–1865* (1997).

Several histories of individual brigades are superb: Alan T. Nolan, *The Iron Brigade* (1961); James I. Robertson, Jr., *The Stonewall Brigade* (1963); Jeffry Wert's comparative history of these two celebrated brigades, *A Brotherhood of Valor: The Common Soldiers of the Stonewall Brigade, C.S.A., and the Iron Brigade, U.S.A.* (1999); Terry L. Jones, *Lee's Tigers: The Louisiana Infantry in the Army of Northern Virginia* (1987); and William C. Davis, *The Orphan Brigade: The Kentucky Regiments Who Couldn't Go Home* (1980). Of many fine regimental histories, there is space here to mention only four: John J. Pullen, *The Twentieth Maine: A Volunteer Regiment in the Civil War* (1957); Warren Wilkinson, *Mother, May You Never See the Sights I Have Seen* (57th Massachusetts) (1990); Lance J. Herdegen and William J. K. Beaudot, *In the Bloody Railroad Cut at Gettysburg* (1990), which, despite its title, is a history of the 6th Wisconsin; and Richard Moe, *The Last Full Measure: The Life and Death of the First Minnesota Volunteers* (1993).

Two of the genuine classics of Civil War literature are Bell I. Wiley's books on the experiences of common soldiers: *The Life of Johnny Reb* (1943) and *The Life of Billy Yank* (1952). Beginning with Gerald F. Linderman, *Embattled Courage: The Experience of Combat in the American Civil War* (1987), the following decade brought forth many studies of the combat motives and experiences of Civil War soldiers, based mainly (like Wiley's books, and unlike Linderman's) on the letters and diaries written during their service by soldiers in the most literate armies in history to that time: Reid Mitchell, *Civil War Soldiers: Their Expectations and Their Experiences* (1988); James I. Robertson, Jr., *Soldiers Blue and Gray* (1988); Joseph A. Frank and George A. Reaves, *"Seeing the Elephant": Raw Recruits at the Battle of Shiloh* (1989); Reid Mitchell, *The Vacant Chair: The Northern Soldier Leaves Home* (1993); two books by James M. McPherson, *What They Fought For, 1861–1865* (1994) and *For Cause and Comrades: Why Men Fought in the Civil War* (1997); Joseph Allan Frank, *With Ballot and Bayonet: The Political Socialization of American Civil War Soldiers* (1998); and William C. Davis, *Lincoln's Men: How President Lincoln Became Father to an Army and a Nation* (1999). Eric T. Dean, Jr., *Shook Over Hell: Post-Traumatic Stress, Vietnam, and the Civil War* (1997), compares the experiences of Civil War soldiers and American soldiers in Vietnam, and finds that the former had it much harder. One thing that enabled Civil War soldiers to endure their hardships and danger was religious faith; as products of the Second Great Awakening, Civil War armies were arguably the most religious in all of American military history. For a good discussion of this matter, see Gardiner Shattuck, *A Shield and Hiding Place: The Religious Life of the Civil War Armies* (1987). But like all soldiers, many of those in the Civil War also sought pleasure and solace with the opposite sex: see Thomas P. Lowry, *The Story the Soldiers Wouldn't Tell: Sex in the Civil War* (1994). Some members of what Victorians called the "fair sex" actually disguised themselves as men and enlisted as soldiers, or tried to: see Elizabeth D. Leonard, *All the Daring of the Soldier: Women of the Civil War Armies* (1999), and Lauren Cook Burgess (ed.), *An Uncommon Soldier: The Civil War Letters of Sarah Rosetta Wakeman, alias Pvt. Lyons Wakeman* (1994).

Richard Nelson Current, *Lincoln's Loyalists: Union Soldiers from the Confederacy* (1992), tells the story of men from Confederate states (mainly Tennessee) and West Virginia who fought for the Union. Two studies that detail the role of immigrants in the armies are Ella Lonn, *Foreigners in the Union Army and Navy* (1951), and William L. Burton, *Melting Pot Soldiers:*

The Union's Ethnic Regiments (1988). Ella Lonn, *Desertion During the Civil War* (1928); Bessie Martin, *Desertion of Alabama Troops from the Confederate Army* (1932); Richard Bardolph, "Inconsistent Rebels: Desertion of North Carolina Troops in the Civil War," *North Carolina Historical Review,* 41 (1964), 163–189; and Richard Reid, "A Test Case of the 'Crying Evil': Desertion Among North Carolina Troops During the Civil War," ibid., 58 (1981), 234–262 are detailed studies of this unhappy subject. Thomas P. Lowry, *"Don't Shoot that Boy!" Abraham Lincoln and Military Justice* (1999), treats the relationship between the notoriously soft-hearted President and the military justice system in the Union army.

Military Campaigns and Battles

The basic building blocks for the campaigns and battles of the war are the 128 volumes published by the U.S. government beginning a generation after war: *War of the Rebellion: A Compilation of the Official Records of the Union and Confederate Armies* (1880–1901). Two indispensable finding aids and indexes for these records are Alan Aimone and Barbara Aimone, *A User's Guide to the Official Records of the American Civil War* (1993) and *Military Operations of the Civil War: A Guide-Index to the Official Records of the Union and Confederate Armies, 1861–1865,* 5 vols. (1966–1980). The maps accompanying these official records, by contemporary cartographers, are valuable: George B. Davis et al., *The Official Military Atlas of the Civil War* (1895, reprinted 1978). But any of several modern Civil War atlases are easier to follow: Vincent J. Esposito (ed.), *The West Point Atlas of American Wars,* vol. I 1959); Craig L. Symonds, *A Battlefield Atlas of the Civil War* (1973); Richard O'Shea, *American Heritage Battle Maps of the Civil War* (1992); James M. McPherson (ed.) *The Atlas of the Civil War* (1994); and, by the editors of Time-Life Books, *Echoes of Glory: Illustrated Atlas of the Civil War* (1998). Participants in the war analyzed the major campaigns and battles in *The Annals of the Civil War* (1878) and *Battles and Leaders of the Civil War,* 4 vols., ed. by Robert U. Johnson and Clarence C. Buel (1887–1888). Both series have been reprinted in modern editions. For articles on individual battles reprinted from the magazine *Civil War Times Illustrated,* see James M. McPherson (ed.), *Battle Chronicles of the Civil War,* 6 vols. (1989). For narratives of the cavalry's role and development, three books are worthwhile: Samuel Carter, *The Last Cavaliers: Confederate and Union Cavalry in the Civil War* (1980); Edward C. Longacre, *Mounted Raids of the Civil War* (1975); and Stephen G. Starr, *The Union Cavalry in the Civil War,* 3 vols. (1979–1985).

The number of books about individual battles and campaigns is so huge that only a small sample of those about the most important battles can be listed here, in chronological order: William C. Davis, *Battle at Bull Run: A History of the First Major Campaign of the Civil War* (1977); William Garrett Piston and Richard W. Hatcher, *Wilson's Creek: The Second Battle of the Civil War and the Men Who Fought It* (2000); Byron Farwell, *Ball's Bluff: A Small Battle and Its Long Shadow* (1990); Nathaniel C. Hughes, Jr., *The Battle of Belmont: Grant Strikes South* (1991); Benjamin F. Cooling, *Forts Henry and Donelson: The Key to the Confederate Heartland* (1987); William L. Shea and Earl J. Hess, *Pea Ridge: Civil War Campaign in the West* (1992); Wiley Sword, *Shiloh: Bloody April* (1974); James Lee McDonough, *Shiloh: In Hell Before Night* (1978); Larry J. Daniel, *Shiloh: The Battle That Changed the Civil War* (1997); Larry J. Daniel and Lynn N. Bock, *Island No. 10* (1996); Chester G. Hearn, *The Capture of New Orleans,* 1862 (1995); Robert G. Tanner, *Stonewall in the Valley* (1976); Clifford Dowdey, *The Seven Days* (1974); Stephen W. Sears, *To the Gates of Richmond: The Peninsula Campaign* (1992); Robert K. Krick, *Stonewall Jackson at Cedar Mountain* (1990); John J. Hennessy, *Return to Bull Run: The Campaign and Battle of Second Manassas* (1993); Stephen W. Sears, *Landscape Turned Red: The Battle of Antietam* (1983); Gary W. Gallagher (ed.), *Antietam: Essays on the 1862 Maryland Campaign* (1989) and *The Antietam Campaign* (1999); Peter

Cozzens, *The Darkest Days of the War: The Battles of Iuka and Corinth* (1996); Benjamin F. Cooling, *Fort Donelson's Legacy: War and Society in Kentucky and Tennessee, 1862–1863* (1997); James Lee McDonough, *War in Kentucky: From Shiloh to Perryville* (1994); Vorin E. Whan, Jr., *Fiasco at Fredericksburg* (1961); Gary W. Gallagher (ed.), *The Fredericksburg Campaign* (1995); Daniel E. Sutherland, *Fredericksburg and Chancellorsville* (1998); Peter Cozzens, *No Better Place to Die: The Battle of Stones River* (1990); Ernest B. Furgurson, *Chancellorsville 1863* (1992); Stephen W. Sears, *Chancellorsville* (1996); Gary W. Gallagher (ed.), *Chancellorsville: The Battle and Its Aftermath* (1996); Stephen R. Wise, *Gate of Hell: Campaign for Charleston Harbor, 1863* (1994); Edwin B. Coddington, *The Gettysburg Campaign* (1968); Harry W. Pfanz, *Gettysburg: The Second Day* (1987); Harry W. Pfanz, *Gettysburg: Culp's Hill and Cemetery Hill* (1993); George R. Stewart, *Pickett's Charge* (1959); Carol Reardon, *Pickett's Charge in History and Memory* (1997); Gabor S. Boritt (ed.), *The Gettysburg Nobody Knows* (1997); and three books edited by Gary W. Gallagher, *The First Day at Gettysburg* (1992), *The Second Day at Gettysburg* (1993), and *The Third Day at Gettysburg & Beyond* (1994); Samuel Carter, *The Final Fortress: The Campaign for Vicksburg* (1980); Peter F. Walker, *Vicksburg: A People at War* (1960); Terrence J. Winschel, *Triumph & Defeat: The Vicksburg Campaign* (1999); Lawrence L. Hewitt, *Port Hudson: Confederate Bastion on the Mississippi* (1987); Steven E. Woodworth, *Six Armies in Tennessee: The Chickamauga and Chattanooga Campaigns* (1999); Peter Cozzens, *This Terrible Sound: The Battle of Chickamauga* (1992); James L. McDonough, *Chattanooga—A Death Grip on the Confederacy* (1984); Peter Cozzens, *The Shipwreck of Their Hopes: The Battle of Chattanooga* (1994); Wiley Sword, *Mountains Touched with Fire: Chattanooga Besieged, 1863* (1995); Ludwell H. Johnson, *Red River Campaign: Politics and Cotton in the Civil War* (1958); Noah Andre Trudeau, *Bloody Roads South: The Wilderness to Cold Harbor, May–June, 1864* (1989); Gordon C. Rhea, *The Battle of the Wilderness, May 5–6, 1864* (1994); Gary W. Gallagher (ed.), *The Wilderness Campaign* (1997); Gordon C. Rhea, *The Battles for Spotsylvania Court House and the Road to Yellow Tavern* (1997); Gary W. Gallagher (ed.), *The Spotsylvania Campaign* (1998); William Glenn Robertson, *Back Door to Richmond: The Bermuda Hundred Campaign, April–June 1864* (1987); Noah Andre Trudeau, *The Last Citadel: Petersburg, Virginia, June 1864–April 1865* (1991); James L. McDonough and James Pickett Jones, *War So Terrible: Sherman and Atlanta* (1987); Albert Castel, *Decision in the West: The Atlanta Campaign of 1864* (1992); Benjamin F. Cooling, *Jubal Early's Raid on Washington, 1864* (1989); Jeffry D. Wert, *From Winchester to Cedar Creek: The Shenandoah Campaign of 1864* (1987); Thomas A. Lewis, *The Guns of Cedar Creek* (1988); Gary W. Gallagher (ed.), *Struggle for the Shenandoah: Essays on the 1864 Valley Campaign* (1991); James L. McDonough and Thomas L. Connelly, *Five Tragic Hours: The Battle of Franklin* (1983); Wiley Sword, *Embrace an Angry Wind: The South's Last Stand at Franklin and Nashville* (1991); Winston Groom, *Shrouds of Glory: From Atlanta to Nashville: The Last Great Campaign of the Civil War* (1995); Burke Davis, *Sherman's March* (1980); Lee Kennett, *Marching Through Georgia* (1995); John B. Barrett, *Sherman's March Through the Carolinas* (1956); Marion Brunson Lucas, *Sherman and the Burning of Columbia* (1976); Rod Gragg, *Confederate Goliath: The Battle of Fort Fisher* (1991); Chris E. Fonvielle, Jr., *The Wilmington Campaign* (1997); James P. Jones, *Yankee Blitzkrieg: Wilson's Raid Through Alabama and Georgia* (1976); Burke Davis, *To Appomattox: Nine April Days, 1865* (1959); Noah Andre Trudea, *Out of the Storm: The End of the Civil War, April–June 1865* (1994).

The war in the trans-Mississippi and especially in the far West has been relatively neglected, but for good accounts of campaigns and battles in these theaters, see Robert L. Kerby, *Kirby Smith's Confederacy: The Trans-Mississippi South, 1863–1865* (1972); Ray C. Colton, *The Civil War in the Western Territories* (1959); Alvin M. Josephy, Jr., *The Civil War in the American West* (1991); Donald S. Frazier, *Blood & Treasure: Confederate Empire in the Southwest* (1995); and Thomas S. Edrington and John Taylor, *The Battle of Glorieta Pass, March 26–28, 1862* (1998).

The Armies: Organization, Logistics, Intelligence, Medical Care, Prisons

Three studies provide comprehensive coverage of the organization and supply of the Union army: Fred A. Shannon, *The Organization and Administration of the Union Armies 1861–1865,* 2 vols. (1928); Frank J. Welcher, *The Union Army, 1861–1865: Organization and Operations,* vol. I: *The Eastern Theater* (1989); vol. 2: *The Western Theater* (1993); and A. H. Meneely, *The War Department, 1861* (1928). There are few comparable studies for the Confederacy, but see Richard D. Goff, *Confederate Supply* (1969); Samuel B. Thompson, *Confederate Purchasing Operations Abroad* (1935); and Kenneth Radley, *Rebel Watchdog: The Confederate States Army Provost Guard* (1989). Jerrold Northrop Moore, *Confederate Commissary General: Lucius Bellinger Northrop and the Subsistence Bureau of the Southern Army* (1996), is a valiant effort to improve Northrop's image. Recruitment and conscription in the Confederacy and Union are treated in Albert B. Moore, *Conscription and Conflict in the Confederacy* (1924); Eugene C. Murdock, *Patriotism Limited: The Civil War Draft and the Bounty System* (1967) and Murdock, *One Million Men: The Civil War Draft in the North* (1971); and James W. Geary, *We Need Men: The Union Draft in the Civil War* (1991). See also Peter Levine, "Draft Evasion in the North during the Civil War, 1863–1865," *JAH,* 67 (1981), 816–834; and James W. Geary, "Civil War Conscription in the North: A Historiographical Review, *CWH* (1986), 208–228.

The later chapters of Paul A. C. Koistenen, *The Political Economy of American Warfare, 1606–1865* (1996), deal with economic mobilization and logistics during the Civil War. Benjamin W. Bacon, *Sinews of War: How Technology, Industry, and Transportation Won the Civil War* (1997), is disappointing. Robert V. Bruce, *Lincoln and the Tools of War* (1956), is a fascinating account of the President's role in ordnance innovation. Other valuable volumes dealing with arms and ammunition include Carl L. Davis, *Arming the Union: Small Arms in the Civil War* (1973), and William A. Albaugh and Edward N. Simmons, *Confederate Arms* (1957). The use of balloons for military reconnaissance is treated in F. Stansbury Haydon, *Aeronautics in the Union and Confederate Armies* (1941). Three volumes provide detailed coverage of the crucial role of railroads in military movements and supply: George E. Turner, *Victory Rode the Rails* (1953); Thomas Weber, *The Northern Railroads in the Civil War* (1952); and Robert C. Black, *The Railroads of the Confederacy* (1952). Two studies of railroad logistics argue, in different ways, that the Union made better use of its (admittedly superior) rail network than the Confederacy: Jeffrey N. Lash, *Destroyer of the Iron Horse: Joseph E. Johnston and Confederate Rail Transport, 1861–1865* (1991), and Roger Pickenpaugh, *Rescue by Rail: Troop Transfer and the Civil War in the West, 1863* (1999).

Intelligence operations during the Civil War have more often been romanticized than analyzed. Some of the more well-researched and sober studies are: James D. Horan and Howard Swiggett, *The Pinkerton Story* (1951); Oscar A. Kinchen, *Women Who Spied for the Blue and the Gray* (1972); Oscar A. Kinchen, *Confederate Operations in Canada and the North* (1970); James D. Horan, *Confederate Agent* (1954); Edwin C. Fishel, *The Secret War for the Union: The Untold Story of Military Intelligence in the Civil War* (1996); Donald E. Markle, *Spies and Spymasters of the Civil War* (1994); and two books by William A. Tidwell (the first with co-authors James O. Hall and David W. Gaddy), *Come Retribution: The Confederate Secret Service and the Assassination of Lincoln* (1988) and *April '65: Confederate Covert Action in the American Civil War* (1995), which present much circumstantial evidence linking Confederate intelligence with John Wilkes Booth.

Frank R. Freemon, *Microbes and Minie Balls: An Annotated Bibliography of Civil War Medicine* (1993), is a good introduction to the subject, along with the same author's *Gangrene and Glory: Medical Care During the Civil War* (1999). The basic medical records of the Union side were compiled by the U.S. War Department, Office of the Surgeon General, *The Medical and Surgical History of the War of the Rebellion,* 6 vols. (1875–1888). Stewart Brooks, *Civil*

War Medicine (1966), is a useful brief study. Valuable data and insights are contained in Paul E. Steiner, *Disease in the Civil War* (1968), and in Horace H. Cunningham, *Field Medical Services at the Battles of Manassas* (1968). Two monographs on Union medicine are excellent: George W. Adams, *Doctors in Blue: The Medical History of the Union Army* (1952); and George W. Smith, *Medicines for the Union Army: The United States Army Laboratories During the Civil War* (1962). The role of the Sanitary Commission is analyzed in William Q. Maxwell, *Lincoln's Fifth Wheel: The Political History of the United States Sanitary Commission* (1956). One prominent Northern woman active in the Sanitary Commission described her work in Mary Livermore, *My Story of the War: A Woman's Narrative of Four Years' Personal Experience as Nurse in the Union Army* (1888). A significant collection that delineates the role of women nurses for the Union is John R. Brumgardt (ed.), *Civil War Nurse: The Diary and Letters of Hannah Ropes* (1980). Louisa May Alcott's letters describing her experiences as a nurse in a Union hospital were published in 1863 as *Hospital Sketches* (reprinted 1960). Sister Mary Denis Maher, *To Bind Up the Wounds: Catholic Sister Nurses in the Civil War* (1989), tells the story of an important group. See also Ann Douglas Wood, "The War Within a War: Women Nurses in the Union Army," *CWH,* 18 (1972), 197–212. The work of two Southern women—Kate Cumming and Phoebe Yates Pember—as nurses for the Confederate forces is described in Richard B. Harwell (ed.), *Kate: The Journal of a Confederate Nurse* (1959), and Bell I. Wiley (ed.), *A Southern Woman's Story: Life in Confederate Richmond* (1959). The best study of Confederate medicine is Horace H. Cunningham, *Doctors in Gray* (1959); see also Glenna R. Schroeder-Lein, *Confederate Hospitals on the Move: Samuel H. Stout and the Army of Tennessee* (1994).

Given that one in seven Civil War soldiers spent some time in a prisoner-of-war camp, the relative neglect of this aspect of the Civil War is surprising. For a long time the only general study was William B. Hesseltine, *Civil War Prisons* (1930); it has been partly superseded by Lonnie R. Speer, *Portals to Hell: Military Prisons of the Civil War* (1997). The entire June 1962 issue (vol. 8) of *Civil War History* was devoted to articles on prisons; this issue was subsequently reprinted as a separate book edited by William B. Hesseltine, with the title *Civil War Prisons* (1962). Two good modern studies of Andersonville are Ovid L. Futch, *History of Andersonville Prison* (1968), and William Marvel, *Andersonville: The Last Depot* (1994). Other Confederate prisons are treated in Frank L. Byrne, "Libby Prison: A Study in Emotions," *JSH,* 24 (1958), 430–444; James I. Robertson, Jr., "Houses of Horror: Danville's Civil War Prisons," *Virginia Magazine of Biography and History,* 69 (1961), 329–345; Louis Brown, *The Salisbury Prison: A Case Study of Confederate Military Prisons* (1980); and William O. Bryant, *Cahaba Prison and the Sultana Disaster* (1990). Robert E. Denney charts an oft-romanticized aspect of the prison experience in *Civil War Prisons and Escapes: A Day-by-Day Chronicle* (1993). A fine study of one of the largest Union prisons is Dale Fetzer, Jr., and Bruce E. Mowday, *Unlikely Allies: Fort Delaware's Prison Community in the Civil War* (1999).

The Naval War

Myron J. Smith, *American Civil War Navies: A Bibliography* (1972), provides a list of sources. Also useful is U.S. Department of the Navy, Naval History Division, *Civil War Naval Chronology 1861–1865* (1971). The basic sources for a naval history of the war are the *Official Records of the Union and Confederate Navies in the War of the Rebellion,* 30 vols. (1892–1922). See also William N. Still, Jr. (ed.), *The Confederate Navy: Ships, Men, and Organization* (1997) and Don L. Canney, *Lincoln's Navy: The Ships, Men, and Organization* (1998). Four readable one-volume narratives are Bern Anderson, *By Sea and by River: The Naval History of the Civil War* (1962); Howard P. Nash, *A Naval History of the Civil War* (1972); William M. Fowler, Jr., *Under Two Flags: The American Navy in the Civil War* (1990); and Ivan Musicant, *Divided Waters: The Naval History of the Civil War* (1995). The essays in William

N. Still, Jr., John M. Taylor, and Norman C. Delaney, *Raiders and Blockaders: The Civil War Afloat* (1998), cover various themes. The fullest account is Virgil C. Jones, *The Civil War at Sea,* 3 vols. (1960–1962). For the war's most famous naval battle, consult William C. Davis, *Duel Between the First Ironclads* (1975). Additional references can be found in David R. Smith, *The Monitor and the Merrimac: A Bibliography* (1968). For the river war, five books are valuable: H. Allen Gosnell, *Guns on the Western Waters: The Story of River Gunboats in the Civil War* (1949); John D. Milligan, *Gunboats Down the Mississippi* (1965); James M. Merrill, *Battle Flags South: The Story of the Civil War Navies on Western Waters* (1970); Jack D. Coombe, *Thunder Along the Mississippi: The River Battles that Split the Confederacy* (1996); and Jay Slagle, *Ironclad Captain: Seth Ledyard Phelps and the U.S. Navy 1841–1864* (1996).

Union naval strategy and leadership are treated in Richard S. West, *Mr. Lincoln's Navy* (1957); James M. Merrill, *The Rebel Shore: The Story of Union Sea Power in the Civil War* (1957); and Richard West, *Gideon Welles: Lincoln's Navy Department* (1943). Rowena Reed, *Combined Operations in the Civil War* (1978), argues that the Union did not exploit its full potential for combined army-navy operations. Robert M. Browning, Jr., *From Cape Charles to Cape Fear: The North Atlantic Blockading Squadron in the Civil War* (1993), is an excellent study of this crucial blockading region. For vivid first-hand descriptions of naval operations and battles along the Atlantic coast by a Union officer who always seemed to be where the action was, see James M. McPherson and Patricia R. McPherson (eds.), *Lamson of the Gettysburg: The Civil War Letters of Lieutenant Roswell H. Lamson, U.S. Navy* (1997). The exploits of another derring-do naval officer are chronicled in Ralph J. Roske and Charles Van Doren, *Lincoln's Commando: The Biography of Commander W. B. Cushing, U.S.N.* (1957). Dennis J. Ringle, *Life in Mr. Lincoln's Navy* (1998), focuses on the common sailor's experiences.

For the Confederate navy, see Tom H. Wells, The *Confederate Navy: A Study in Organization* (1971); Raimondo Luraghi, *A History of the Confederate Navy* (1996); William N. Still, Jr., *Confederate Shipbuilding* (1969) and *Iron Afloat: The Story of the Confederate Armorclads* (1971); Milton F. Perry, *Infernal Machines: The Story of Confederate Submarine and Mine Warfare* (1965); and Mark K. Ragan, *Union and Confederate Submarine Warfare in the Civil War* (1999), which covers Union as well as Confederate experiments with submarines. For the blockade, blockade running, and the question of the blockade's effectiveness, see Robert Carse, *Blockade: The Civil War at Sea* (1958); Hamilton Cochran, *Blockade Runners of the Confederacy* (1958); Frank E. Vandiver (ed.), *Confederate Blockade Running Through Bermuda 1861–1865* (1947); Francis B. C. Bradlee, *Blockade Running during the Civil War* (1925); Stephen R. Wise, *Lifeline of the Confederacy: Blockade Running during the Civil War* (1988); and William M. Still, "A Naval Sieve: The Union Blockade in the Civil War," *Naval War College Review,* 36 (1983), 38–45. Confederate attempts to buy and build warships in Europe are chronicled in Frank J. Merli, *Great Britain and the Confederate Navy* (1970), and Warren F. Spencer, *The Confederate Navy in Europe* (1983). For Confederate cruiser warfare against Northern merchant ships, see George W. Dalzell, *The Flight from the Flag* (1943); Chester G. Hearn, *Gray Raiders of the Sea* (1992); and Edward C. Boykin, *Ghost Ship of the Confederacy: The Story of the* Alabama *and Her Captain* (1957). For the converging careers of the *Alabama* and *Kearsage* down to their date with destiny off Cherbourg, see William Marvel, *The* Alabama *and the* Kearsarge: *The Sailor's Civil War* (1996).

Foreign Relations

The most complete treatment of this complex subject is by an Australian historian: David P. Crook, *The North, The South, and the Powers 1861–1865* (1974). An abridged version of this book is titled *Diplomacy During the Civil War* (1975). Essays on the policies of various countries toward the American war can be found in Harold M. Hyman (ed.), *Heard Round the*

World: The Impact Abroad of the Civil War (1969). An old but still useful survey of European public opinion is Donaldson Jordan and Edwin J. Pratt, *Europe and the American Civil War* (1931). A good anthology of European opinion is Belle B. Sideman and Lillian Friedman (eds.), *Europe Looks at the Civil War* (1960). For the writings of two subsequently famous Europeans who were intensely interested in the Civil War, see Karl Marx and Friedrich Engels, *The Civil War in the United States,* ed. Richard Enmale (1937); and Saul K. Padover (ed.), *Karl Marx on America and the Civil War* (1972). Robert E. May (ed.), *The Union, the Confederacy, and the Atlantic Rim* (1995), focuses on the international dimensions of the Civil War.

Frank L. Owsley, *King Cotton, Diplomacy: Foreign Relations of the Confederate States of America* (1931; rev. ed. 1959), is exhaustive but partisan. It should be supplemented by Henry Blumenthal, "Confederate Diplomacy: Popular Notions and International Realities," *JSH,* 32 (1966), 151–171, and by Samuel B. Thompson, *Confederate Purchasing Operations Abroad* (1935). Charles M. Hubbard, *The Burden of Confederate Diplomacy* (1998) argues that the failures of Confederate diplomacy were a major factor in losing the war. For a fresh perspective on the Union secretary of state, see Norman Ferris, *Desperate Diplomacy: William H. Seward's Foreign Policy, 1861* (1976). A valuable study of an important subject is Stuart L. Bernath, *Squall Across the Atlantic: American Civil War Prize Cases and Diplomacy* (1970). James W. Daddysman, *The Matamoras Trade* (1984), discusses Confederate imports via Mexico and their foreign-policy consequences.

There is a large literature on the crucial question of Anglo-American relations during the war. The best starting point is Ephraim D. Adams's magisterial but dated *Great Britain and the American Civil War,* 2 vols. (1925). For more recent studies, see Brian Jenkins, *Britain and the War for the Union,* 2 vols. (1974–1980), and Howard Jones, *Union in Peril: The Crisis over British Intervention in the Civil War* (1992). Robin Winks, *Canada and the United States: The Civil War Years* (1960), deals with a subject that was never absent from the calculations of both Britain and the United States. For full treatments of a major Anglo-American crisis, consult Norman B. Ferris, *The Trent Affair* (1977), and Gordon H. Warren, *Fountain of Discontent: The Trent Affair and the Freedom of the Seas* (1981). Mary Ellison, *Support for Secession: Lancashire and the American Civil War* (1972), revises previous notions about the Union sympathies of British textile workers, but Philip S. Foner, *British Labor and the American Civil War* (1981), challenges many of her conclusions. A number of important articles offer revealing insights on British attitudes and policy: Eli Ginzberg, "The Economics of British Neutrality During the American Civil War," *AH,* 10 (1936), 147–156; Max Beloff, "Great Britain and the American Civil War," *History,* 37 (1952), 40–48; Wilbur D. Jones, "The British Conservatives and the American Civil War," *AHR,* 58 (1953), 527–543; Sheldon Vanauken, *The Glittering Illusion: English Sympathy for the Southern Confederacy* (1988); Joseph M. Hernon, "British Sympathies in the American Civil War: A Reconsideration," *JSH,* 33 (1967), 356–367; Kinley J. Brauer, "British Mediation and the American Civil War: A Reconsideration," *JSH,* 38 (1972), 49–64; and Donald Bellows, "A Study of British Conservative Reaction to the American Civil War," *JSH,* 51 (1985), 505–506. A useful collection of editorials and other material from the powerful *Times* of London is Hugh Brogan (ed.), *The* Times *Reports the American Civil War* (1975). For relations with France, see Lynn M. Case and Warren F. Spencer, *The United States and France: Civil War Diplomacy* (1970); and Alfred J. Hanna and Kathryn A. Hanna, *Napoleon III and Mexico: American Triumph Over Monarchy* (1971). The relationship of slavery and diplomacy is most fully treated in Howard Jones, *Abraham Lincoln and a New Birth of Freedom: The Union and Slavery in the Diplomacy of the Civil War* (1999).

The Border States

A still useful study of the border states, which also pays some attention to the southern portions of Midwestern Union states, is Edward C. Smith, *The Borderland in the Civil War* (1927). For Maryland, the best study is Jean H. Baker, *The Politics of Continuity: Maryland Political Parties*

from 1858 to 1870 (1973). See also Charles B. Clark, "Suppression and Control of Maryland 1861–1865," *Maryland Historical Magazine,* 54 (1959), 241–271. An older, pro-Confederate study of Kentucky is E. Merton Coulter, *The Civil War and Readjustment in Kentucky* (1926). It should be supplemented by William H. Townsend, *Lincoln and the Bluegrass: Slavery and Civil War in Kentucky* (1955); and Lowell Harrison, *The Civil War and Kentucky* (1975). Missouri is well covered in William E. Parrish, *Turbulent Partnership: Missouri and the Union 1861–1865* (1963), while the vicious, destructive impact of guerrilla warfare on the civilian population is treated by Michael Fellman, *Inside War: The Guerrilla Conflict in Missouri during the American Civil War* (1989). See also the works on guerrilla warfare cited p. B–38 and B–39; Hans C. Adamson, *Rebellion in Missouri: 1861* (1961); and Arthur R. Kirkpatrick, "Missouri's Secessionist Government, 1861–1865," *Missouri Historical Review,* 45 (1951), 124–137. The military conflict in the Missouri-Arkansas-Kansas theater is the subject of Jay Monaghan's sprightly *Civil War on the Western Border 1854–1865* (1955). Albert Castel, *A Frontier State at War* (1958), deals primarily with Kansas but covers also the vicious fighting along the Missouri-Kansas border. For West Virginia, the best single study is Richard O. Curry, *A House Divided: A Study of Statehood Politics and the Copperhead Movement in West Virginia* (1964). Noel C. Fisher, *War at Every Door: Partisan Politics and Guerrilla Violence in East Tennessee, 1860–1896* (1997), is an excellent study of that troubled region. See also W. Todd Groce, *Mountain Rebels: East Tennessee Confederates and the Civil War, 1860–1870* (1999). For several essays on the bitter conflict in the Appalachian South, see Kenneth W. Noe and Shannon H. Wilson (eds.), *The Civil War in Appalachia: Collected Essays* (1997). A border region study that extends back before the war and carries the story beyond it is Richard Lowe, *Republicans and Reconstruction in Virginia, 1856–1870* (1991).

Government and Politics in the North

Eric L. McKitrick, "Party Politics and the Union and Confederate War Efforts," in William Nisbet Chambers and Walter Dean Burnham (eds.), *The American Party Systems* (1967), pp. 117–151, is a brilliant comparison of the Union and Confederate political systems. A political scientist analyzes the impact of war-spawned centralized governments in both Union and Confederacy in Richard Franklin Bensel, *Yankee Leviathan: The Origins of Central State Authority in America, 1859–1877* (1990). For other perspectives on Northern politics and the Lincoln administration, see James M. McPherson (ed.), *"We Cannot Escape History": Lincoln and the Last Best Hope of Earth* (1995), and Gabor S. Boritt (ed.), *Lincoln the War President* (1992). The fullest study of the Lincoln administration is Phillip Shaw Paludan, *The Presidency of Abraham Lincoln* (1994). A good brief narrative of Northern wartime politics is James E. Rawley, *The Politics of Union* (1974). Allan Nevins, *The Statesmanship of the Civil War* (1953), contains several thoughtful essays; while James A. Rawley (ed.), *Lincoln and Civil War Politics* (1969), is a useful anthology reflecting various viewpoints. An invaluable collection of laws, congressional votes, and other official government documents is Edward McPherson (ed.), *The Political History of the United States During the Great Rebellion,* 2d ed. (1865). Two books by Allan G. Bogue analyze the Union Congress: *The Earnest Men: Republicans of the Civil War Senate* (1981) and *The Congressman's Civil War* (1989). Burton J. Hendrick, *Lincoln's War Cabinet* (1946), is readable and informative. A great deal of useful information as well as provocative interpretations can be found in William B. Hesseltine, *Lincoln and the War Governors* (1948). Lincoln's skillful use of political patronage is analyzed in Harry J. Carman and Reinhard H. Luthin, *Lincoln and the Patronage* (1943). T. Harry Williams, *Lincoln and the Radicals* (1941), posits a sharp conflict between the President and Republican radicals; while Hans Trefousse, *The Radical Republicans* (1969), emphasizes their cooperation. Christopher Dell, *Lincoln and the War Democrats* (1975), chronicles that uneasy relationship. David M. Silver, *Lincoln's Supreme Court* (1999), describes the institution that Lincoln made over with his opportunity to appoint five new justices. See also Herman Belz, *Abraham Lincoln, Constitutionalism, and Equal Rights in the Civil War Era* (1998). Bruce

Tap, *Over Lincoln's Shoulder: The Committee on the Conduct of the War* (1998), shows how closely policy and war-making were connected in this war of peoples.

In addition to the diaries of prominent figures listed in the biography section, two other diaries focus on Union politics: Michael Burlingame and John R. Turner-Ettlinger (eds.), *Inside Lincoln's White House: The Complete Civil War Diary of John Hay* (1997); and Theodore D. Pease and James G. Randall (eds.), *The Diary of Orville Hickman Browning*, 2 vols. (1927–1933).

Several studies of Northern states and localities contain important insights and information: John Niven, *Connecticut for the Union* (1965); Eugene H. Roseboom, *The Civil War Era 1850–1873* (1944), on Ohio; Kenneth M. Stampp, *Indiana Politics During the Civil War* (1949); Emma Lou Thornbrough, *Indiana in the Civil War Era, 1850–1880* (1965); Arthur C. Cole, *The Era of the Civil War 1848–1870* (1919), on Illinois; Richard N. Current, *The History of Wisconsin: The Civil War Era 1848–1873* (1976); William Gillette, *Jersey Blue: Civil War Politics in New Jersey 1854–1865* (1995); William J. Jackson, *New Jerseyans in the Civil War* (2000); and William Disinberre, *Civil War Issues in Philadelphia 1856–1865* (1965). Margaret Leech, *Reveille in Washington* (1941), chronicles life and politics in the capital during the war. Frank Freidel (ed.), *Union Pamphlets of the Civil War,* 2 vols. (1967), is an invaluable collection of Northern writings. J. Matthew Gallman, *The North Fights the Civil War: The Home Front* (1994), is a general survey of Northern society and the economy as well as politics. Several of the works cited in the section on "Economy and Society in the Wartime North" also contain material on politics.

Northern Democrats, especially the Copperheads, have received a great deal of attention. For a general survey, see Joel Silbey, *A Respectable Minority: The Democratic Party in the Civil War Era* (1977). Two useful articles are Leonard P. Curry, "Congressional Democrats, 1861–1863," *CWH,* 12 (1966), 213–229; and Jean H. Baker, "A Loyal Opposition: Northern Democrats in the Thirty-seventh Congress," *CWH,* 25 (1979), 139–155. The classic study of the Peace Democrats, which emphasizes their disloyalty to the Union war effort, is Wood Gray, *The Hidden Civil War: The Story of the Copperheads* (1942). See also George Fort Milton, *Abraham Lincoln and the Fifth Column* (1942). Frank L. Klement offers a much more sympathetic treatment, which stresses the anti-industrialist economic ideology of the Peace Democrats, in the following books and articles: *The Copperheads in the Middle West* (1960); *Dark Lanterns: Secret Political Societies, Conspiracies, and Treason Trials in the Civil War* (1984); "Economic Aspects of Middle Western Copperheadism," *Historian,* 14 (1951), 27–44; and "Middle Western Copperheadism and the Genesis of the Granger Movement," *MVHR,* 38 (1952), 679–694. For other studies that provide insights on the Democrats, consult Henry C. Hubbart, *The Older Middle West 1840–1880* (1936); Eugene Roseboom, "Southern Ohio and the Union, 1863," *MVHR,* 39 (1952), 29–44; G. R. Tredway, *Democratic Opposition to the Lincoln Administration in Indiana* (1973); and Hubert H. Wubben, *Civil War Iowa and the Copperhead Movement* (1980). Richard O. Curry, "The Union as It Was: A Critique of Recent Interpretations of the 'Copperheads,' " *CWH,* 13 (1967), 25–39, deemphasizes the dimension of disloyalty. But William G. Carleton, "Civil War Dissidence in the North: The Perspective of a Century," *SAQ,* 65 (1966), 390–402, and Stephen Z. Starr, "Was There a Northwest Conspiracy?" *Filson Club Historical Quarterly,* 38 (1964), 323–339, find considerable evidence to buttress the older view of Copperhead antiwar intrigues. For the antiblack sentiments of Democratic and Catholic newspapers, see Ray H. Abrams, "Copperhead Newspapers and the Negro," *JNH,* 20 (1935), 131–152; Joseph George, " 'A Catholic Family Newspaper' Views the Lincoln Administration: John Mullaly's Copperhead Weekly," *CWH,* 24 (June 1978), 112–132; and Cuthbert E. Allen, "The Slavery Question in Catholic Newspapers, 1850–1865," U.S. Catholic Historical Society, *Historical Records and Studies,* 26 (1936), 99–169.

The interrelationships between the peace movement of 1864, the presidential election, and the issues of emancipation and reconstruction are analyzed in Edward C. Kirkland, *The Peace-*

makers of 1864 (1927); William F. Zornow, *Lincoln and the Party Divided* (1954); David E. Long, *The Jewel of Liberty: Abraham Lincoln's Re-Election and the End of Slavery* (1994); and John C. Waugh, *Reelecting Lincoln: The Battle for the 1864 Presidency* (1997). Confederate hopes and expectations regarding the Union presidential election are documented in Larry E. Nelson, *Bullets, Ballots, and Rhetoric: Confederate Policy for the United States Presidential Contest of 1864* (1980). For the soldier vote, see Josiah H. Benton, *Voting in the Field* (1915); and Oscar O. Winther, "The Soldier Vote in the Election of 1864," *New York History,* 25 (1944), 440–458. The postelection Hampton Roads peace conference is discussed by Howard C. Westwood, "Lincoln and the Hampton Roads Peace Conference," *Lincoln Herald,* 81 (1979), 243–256.

Dean Sprague, *Freedom Under Lincoln* (1965), is a critical analysis of the Lincoln administration's curtailment of civil liberties. More approving of the administration is James G. Randall, *Constitutional Problems Under Lincoln,* rev. ed. (1951), which also treats many other legal and constitutional aspects of Union war policy. The fullest and richest study of the civil liberties question is Mark E. Neely, Jr., *The Fate of Liberty: Abraham Lincoln and Civil Liberties* (1990). On constitutional matters, see also Harold M. Hyman, *A More Perfect Union: The Impact of the Civil War and Reconstruction on the Constitution* (1973); and Phillip S. Paludan, *A Covenant with Death: The Constitution, Law, and Equality in the Civil War Era* (1975).

The portrayal of Lincoln and his administration's policies by the press is presented in Robert S. Harper, *Lincoln and the Press* (1951), and Herbert Mitgang (ed.), *Abraham Lincoln, a Press Report: His Life and Times from the Original Newspaper Documents* (1971). Charles M. Segal (ed.), *Conversations with Lincoln* (1961), conveniently brings together many reports of interviews and conversations with the President. The best summary and analysis of the many writings about the assassination is William Hanchett, *The Lincoln Murder Conspiracies* (1983).

Government and Politics in the Confederacy

A good introduction to the political history of the Confederacy is George C. Rable, *The Confederate Republic: A Revolution Against Politics* (1994). Three books that analyze the constitutional framework of the Confederate polity are Marshal L. De Rosa, *The Confederate Constitution of 1861: An Inquiry into American Constitutionalism* (1991); Charles R. Lee, *The Confederate Constitutions* (1963); and Curtis A. Amlund, *Federalism in the Southern Confederacy* (1966). Mark E. Neely, Jr., *Southern Rights: Political Prisoners and the Myth of Confederate Constitutionalism* (1999) treats the issue of civil liberties. On the Confederate Congress, Wilfred B. Yearns, *The Confederate Congress* (1960), is a valuable narrative, and Thomas B. Alexander and Richard E. Beringer, *The Anatomy of the Confederate Congress* (1972), is a quantitative analysis. Two books cover the cabinet and administrative departments of the Richmond government: Rembert Patrick, *Jefferson Davis and His Cabinet* (1944), and Burton J. Hendrick, *Statesmen of the Lost Cause* (1939). Bell I. Wiley, *The Road to Appomattox* (1956), is critical of Confederate political leadership, and Paul D. Escott, *After Secession: Jefferson Davis and the Failure of Confederate Nationalism* (1978), focuses the criticism specifically on Davis; while Frank E. Vandiver, *Jefferson Davis and the Confederate States* (1964), is a more favorable treatment of the Confederate president. Drew Gilpin Faust, *The Creation of Confederate Nationalism: Ideology and Identity in the Civil War South* (1988), traces efforts to mobilize and define nationalist sentiment. Two diaries yield important insights into the operations of the Richmond government: *John B. Jones, A Rebel War Clerk's Diary* (1866; reprinted 1935); and Edward Younger (ed.), *Inside the Confederate Government: The Diary of Robert Garlick Hill Kean* (1957).

For the classic statement that states' rights undermined the Confederacy, read Frank L. Owsley, *State Rights in the Confederacy* (1925). But May S. Ringold, *The Role of State Legislatures in the Confederacy* (1966), argues that most legislatures contributed constructively to the war effort. Several of the essays in W. Buck Yearns (ed.), *The Confederate Governors* (1984), make a similar point about the governors. For an analysis of one particularly divisive issue, see John B. Robbins, "The Confederacy and the Writ of *Habeas Corpus,*" *Georgia Historical Quarterly,* 55 (1971), 83–101. The following books deal with the two most recalcitrant Confederate states and their leaders: T. Conn Bryan, *Confederate Georgia* (1953); Louise B. Hill, *Joseph E. Brown and the Confederacy* (1939); Marc W. Kruman, *Parties and Politics in North Carolina, 1836–1865* (1983); John G. Barrett, *The Civil War in North Carolina* (1963); W. Buck Yearns and John G. Barrett (eds.), *North Carolina Civil War Documentary* (1980); and Richard E. Yates, *The Confederacy and Zeb Vance* (1958). Other states and regions are covered in Charles E. Cauthen, *South Carolina Goes to War 1861–1865* (1950); John K. Bettersworth, *Confederate Mississippi* (1943); Malcolm C. McMillan, *The Disintegration of a Confederate State: Three Governors and Alabama's Homefront, 1861–1865* (1986); James Marten, *Texas Divided: Loyalty and Dissent in the Lone Star State, 1856–1874* (1990); Dale Baum, *The Shattering of Texas Unionism: Politics in the Lone Star State During the Civil War Era* (1998); William H. Nulty, *Confederate Florida* (1990); Jefferson Davis Bragg, *Louisiana in the Confederacy* (1941); and William Blair, *Virginia's Private War: Feeding Body and Soul in the Confederacy, 1861–1865* (1998). See also the citations in the section on "Economy and Society in the Confederacy."

For disloyalty and Unionism in the South, consult Georgia Lee Tatum, *Disloyalty in the Confederacy* (1934); and Frank W. Klingberg, *The Southern Claims Commission* (1955). Disloyalty and Unionism have been most intensively studied in North Carolina; in addition to the books on that state cited above, see Marc W. Kruman, "Dissent in the Confederacy: The North Carolina Experience," *CWH,* 28 (1981), 193–313; Horace W. Raper, "William W. Holden and the Peace Movement in North Carolina," *North Carolina Historical Review,* 31 (1954), 493–516; William T. Auman and David D. Scarboro, "The Heroes of America in Civil War North Carolina," ibid., 58 (1981), 327–363; and William T. Auman, "Neighbor against Neighbor: The Inner Civil War in the Randolph County Area of Confederate North Carolina," ibid., 61 (1984), 59–92. For a community of Union sympathizers in Atlanta, see Thomas G. Dyer, *Secret Yankees: The Union Circle in Confederate Atlanta* (1999). Also important are Richard Nelson Current, *Lincoln's Loyalists: Union Soldiers from the Confederacy* (1992), and John L. Wakelyn (ed.), *Southern Unionist Pamphlets in the Civil War* (1999).

Economy and Society in the Wartime North

The basic study of the Northern home front, still valuable for insights as well as facts, is Emerson D. Fite, *Social and Economic Conditions in the North During the Civil War* (1910). For a good collection of primary sources, consult George W. Smith and Charles Judah (eds.), *Life in the North During the Civil War* (1966). For a review and analysis of the debate over the impact of the war on Northern economic growth, see Harry N. Scheiber, "Economic Change in the Civil War Era: An Analysis of Recent Studies," *CWH,* 11 (1965), 396–411, which is supplemented and updated by Patrick O'Brien, *The Economic Effects of the American Civil War* (1988). The most important writings on this question, along with some of the statistics for understanding it, are published in David Gilchrist and W. David Lewis (eds.), *Economic Change in the Civil War Era* (1965); and Ralph Andreano (ed.), *The Economic Impact of the American Civil War,* 2d ed. (1967). See also Stanley L. Engerman, "The Economic Impact of the Civil War," *Explorations in Entrepreneurial History,* 2nd Ser., 3 (1966), 176–199; Saul Engelbourg, "The Impact of the Civil War on Manufacturing Enterprise, *Business History,* 21 (1979), 148–162; and Stephen J. DeCanio and Joel Mokyr, "Inflation and the Wage Lag During the American Civil War," *Explorations in Economic History,* 14 (1977), 311–336. For agriculture, the basic works are Paul W. Gates, *Agriculture and the Civil War* (1965), which deals also with the South; and Wayne D. Rasmussen, "The Civil War: A Catalyst of Agricultural Revolution," *AH,* 39 (October 1965), 187–196. On war finance, the fullest study is Bray Hammond, *Sovereignty and an Empty Purse: Banks and Pol-*

itics in the Civil War (1970). Leonard P. Curry, *Blueprint for Modern America: Non-Military Legislation of the First Civil War Congress* (1968), analyzes the processes by which financial, banking, homestead, and railroad legislation was passed, while Heather Cox Richardson, *The Greatest Nation of the Earth: Republican Economic Policies during the Civil War* (1997), analyzes Republican ideology and policy formation.

For a newspaper-reading people, reports from the battle front were vital in shaping homefront morale. There are a number of good studies of Civil War journalism: J. Cutler Andrews, *The North Reports the Civil War* (1955); Louis M. Starr, *Bohemian Brigade: Civil War Newsmen in Action* (1954); and Bernard A. Weisberger, *Reporters for the Union* (1953). Of several books on Northern churches and the war, perhaps the most challenging is James H. Moorhead, *American Apocalypse: Yankee Protestants and the Civil War 1860–1869* (1978). See also Benjamin J. Blied, *Catholics and the Civil War* (1945), and Bertram Korn, *American Jewry and the Civil War* (1951). For Union army chaplains, see Warren B. Armstrong, *For Courageous Fighting and Dying: Union Chaplains in the Civil War* (1998). Two stimulating studies of the war's impact on leading Northern writers and thinkers are George M. Fredrickson, *The Inner Civil War: Northern Intellectuals and the Crisis of the Union* (1965); and Daniel Aaron, *The Unwritten War: American Writers and the Civil War* (1973). One of the best of all Civil War diaries is Allan Nevins and Milton Halsey (eds.), *The Diary of George Templeton Strong,* vol. 3 (1952). On the role of women in several crucial aspects of the war effort, see Agatha Young, *Women and the Crisis: Women of the North in the Civil War* (1959); Elizabeth D. Leonard, *Yankee Women: Gender Battles in the Civil War* (1994); and Jeanie Attie, *Patriotic Toil: Northern Women and the American Civil War* (1998). Mary Elizabeth Massey, *Bonnet Brigades* (1966), and Marilyn M. Culpepper, *Trials and Triumphs: The Women of the American Civil War* (1991), treat Southern as well as Northern women.

The social tinder that flamed into the New York draft riots of 1863 is analyzed in Basil L. Lee, *Discontent in New York City 1861–1865* (1943); Adrian Cook, *The Armies of the Streets: The New York City Draft Riots of 1863* (1974); and Iver Bernstein, *The New York City Draft Riots: Their Significance for American Society and Politics in the Age of the Civil War* (1990). A more general study of the impact of the war on New York City is Ernest A. McKay, *The Civil War and New York City* (1990). For Philadelphia, see J. Matthew Gallman, *Mastering Wartime: A Social History of Philadelphia during the Civil War* (1990); for Chicago, Theodore J. Karamanski, *Rally 'Round the Flag: Chicago and the Civil War* (1993); for Boston, Thomas H. O'Connor, *Civil War Boston* (1997). A fine study of social and economic tensions in the coal country is Grace Palladino, *Another Civil War: Labor, Capital, and the State in the Anthracite Regions of Pennsylvania* (1990).

Finally, several articles by Ludwell H. Johnson describe the sometimes tawdry but always profitable business of trading with the enemy: "The Butler Expedition of 1861–1862: The Profitable Side of War," *CWH,* 11 (1965), 229–236; "Northern Profit and Profiteers: The Cotton Rings of 1864–1865," *CWH,* 12 (1966), 101–115; "Trading with the Union: The Evolution of Confederate Policy," *Virginia Magazine of History and Biography,* 78 (1970), 308–325; and "Contraband Trade During the Last Year of the Civil War," *MVHR,* 49 (1963), 635–653. See also Joseph H. Parks, "A Confederate Trade Center Under Federal Occupation: Memphis, 1862 to 1865," *JSH,* 7 (1941), 289–314.

Economy and Society in the Confederacy

For a comprehensive overview of this subject, the best study is Charles W. Ramsdell, *Behind the Lines in the Southern Confederacy* (1944). Two collections of documents on the Confederate home front are Albert D. Kirwan (ed.), *The Confederacy* (1959); and W. Buck Yearns and John G. Barrett (eds.), *North Carolina Civil War Documentary* (1980). An anthology of useful articles by historians is Harry P. Owens and James J. Cooke (eds.), *The Old South in the Crucible of War* (1983).

For the tangled question of Confederate financial and monetary policy, consult the following: John C. Schwab, *The Confederate States of America 1861–1865: A Financial and Industrial History* (1901); Richard C. Todd, *Confederate Finance* (1954); Douglas B. Ball, *Financial Failure and Confederate Defeat* (1991); Eugene M. Lerner, "The Monetary and Fiscal Problems of the Confederate Government," *Journal of Political Economy,* 62 (1954), 506–522, and 63 (1955), 20–40; and Eugene M. Lerner, "Inflation in the Confederacy, 1861–1865," in Milton Friedman (ed.), *Studies in the Quantity Theory of Money* (1956), pp. 163–178. Two studies that argue perhaps too vigorously that the Civil War produced a forced modernization and industrialization of the Southern economy are Raimondo Luraghi, "The Civil War and the Modernization of American Society: Social Structure and Industrial Revolution in the Old South Before and During the War," *CWH,* 18 (1972), 230–250; and Emory M. Thomas, *The Confederacy as a Revolutionary Experience* (1971). For other studies of Confederate economic mobilization, see: Lester J. Cappon, "Government and Private Industry in the Southern Confederacy," in *Humanistic Studies in Honor of John Calvin Metcalf* (1941), pp. 151–189; Louise B. Hill, *State Socialism in the Confederate States of America* (1936); Charles B. Dew, *Ironmaker to the Confederacy: Joseph R. Anderson and the Tredegar Iron Works* (rev. ed. 1999); Mary A. De Credico, *Patriotism for Profit: Georgia's Urban Entrepreneurs and the Confederate War Effort* (1990); Mary Elizabeth Massey, *Ersatz in the Confederacy* (1952); and Ella Lonn, *Salt as a Factor in the Confederacy* (1933). For a sector of the Confederate economy that performed poorly, see John Solomon Otto, *Southern Agriculture during the Civil War* (1994). Some idea of the war's devastating economic impact on the South can be gleaned from James L. Sellers, "The Economic Incidence of the Civil War in the South," *MVHR,* 14 (1927), 179–191; Stanley L. Engerman, "Some Economic Factors in Southern Backwardness in the Nineteenth Century," in John F. Kain and John R. Meyer (eds.), *Essays in Regional Economics* (1971), pp. 279–306; and Claudia G. Goldin and Frank K. Lewis, "The Economic Cost of the American Civil War: Estimates and Implications," *JEH,* 35 (1975), 299–326.

Social historians of the home front in the Confederacy have made clear the suffering of people, both black and white, from shortages of everything, but have sometimes exaggerated the degree of class conflict and alienation of yeoman whites from the Confederacy. See Bell I. Wiley, *The Plain People of the Confederacy* (1943); Fred Arthur Bailey, *Class and Tennessee's Confederate Generation* (1987); Wayne K. Durrill, *War of Another Kind: A Southern Community in the Great Rebellion* (1990); David Williams, *Rich Man's War: Class, Caste, and Confederate Defeat in the Lower Chattahoochee Valley* (1998); and David Williams, *Plain Folk in a Rich Man's War: Class and Dissent in Confederate Georgia* (2000). For whites uprooted by the war, see Mary Elizabeth Massey, *Refugee Life in the Confederacy* (1964). Phillip Shaw Paludan, *Victims: A True Story of the Civil War* (1981), demonstrates the class conflicts underlying tensions between Unionists and Confederates in western North Carolina. There is a substantial literature on Richmond during the war: see especially Emory M. Thomas, *The Confederate State of Richmond: A Biography of the Capital* (1971); William J. Kimball, *Starve or Fall: Richmond and Its People 1861–1865* (1976); and Ernest B. Furgurson, *Ashes of Glory: Richmond at War* (1996). The experiences of people in three other Southern communities are chronicled in Daniel E. Sutherland, *Seasons of War: The Ordeal of a Confederate Community, 1861–1865* (1995), about Culpeper County; Steven Elliot Tripp, *Yankee Town, Southern City: Race and Class Relations in Civil War Lynchburg* (1997); and William W. Rogers, Jr., *Confederate Home Front: Montgomery during the Civil War* (1999).

For Southern white women and gender issues in the Confederacy, see George C. Rable, *Civil Wars: Women and the Crisis of Southern Nationalism* (1989); Drew Gilpin Faust, *Mothers of Invention: Women of the Slaveholding South in the American Civil War* (1996); and Edward D. C. Campbell and Kym S. Rice (eds.), *A Woman's War: Southern Women, Civil War, and the Confederate Legacy* (1997), Victoria E. Bynum, *Unruly Women: The Politics of Social*

and Sexual Control in the Old South (1992), covers the war years as well as the antebellum period. Catherine Clinton and Nina Silber (eds.), *Divided Houses: Gender and the Civil War* (1992), has essays on the North as well as the South. The same dual coverage is true of the first study of the war's impact on children, James Marten, *The Children's Civil War* (1998). Catherine Clinton, *Civil War Stories* (1998), also focuses on the impact of the war on women and children.

Immigrants were a small percentage of the Southern population, but they have received a full study in Ella Lonn, *Foreigners in the Confederacy* (1940). On the Southern press the best book is J. Cutler Andrews, *The South Reports the Civil War* (1970). Several of the books cited in the section on "Government and Politics in the Confederacy" also include material on the economy and society.

Slaves, Freedmen, and Wartime Reconstruction

For an introduction to this subject, read Clarence L. Mohr, "Southern Blacks in the Civil War: A Century of Historiography," *JHN,* 69 (1974), 177–195. A succinct Marxian interpretation can be found in Herbert Aptheker, *The Negro in the Civil War* (1938). Two readable narratives by Benjamin Quarles are *The Negro in the Civil War* (1953) and *Lincoln and the Negro* (1962). William Gladstone, *Men of Color* (1993), includes more than two hundred photographs as well as a narrative of the role of blacks in the war. Two books by James M. McPherson analyze the part taken by abolitionists and blacks in the efforts for emancipation and equal rights during the war: *The Struggle for Equality: Abolitionists and the Negro in the Civil War and Reconstruction* (1964); and *The Negro's Civil War,* 3d ed. (1991). See also Wendy Hammand Venet, *Neither Ballots Nor Bullets: Women Abolitionists and the Civil War* (1991). For the role of antislavery elements in the black as well as white churches, see Victor B. Howard, *Religion and the Radical Republican Movement, 1860–1870* (1990), and Clarence E. Walker, *A Rock in a Weary Land: A History of the African Methodist Episcopal Church During the Civil War and Reconstruction* (1981).

For the role of blacks in the Confederate as well as the Union war effort, the best introduction is Bell I. Wiley, *Southern Negroes 1861–1865* (1938). See also Ervin L. Jordan, Jr., *Black Confederates and Afro-Yankees in Civil War Virginia* (1995); James H. Brewer, *The Confederate Negro: Virginia's Craftsmen and Military Laborers 1861–1865* (1969); Clarence L. Mohr, *On the Threshold of Freedom: Masters and Slaves in Civil War Georgia* (1986); and David C. Rankin, "The Impact of the Civil War on the Free Colored Community of New Orleans," *Perspectives in American History,* 11 (1977–1978), 379–418. The desperate last-minute move in the Confederacy to emancipate and arm the slaves is chronicled and set in context by Robert F. Durden, *The Gray and the Black: The Confederate Debate on Emancipation* (1972).

John Hope Franklin, *The Emancipation Proclamation* (1963), tells the story of how this momentous decision came about. For Lincoln's ideas and actions on the race question, see also Benjamin Quarles, *Lincoln and the Negro* (1962); Hans L. Trefousse (ed.), *Lincoln's Decision for Emancipation* (1975); Don E. Fehrenbacher, "Only His Stepchildren: Lincoln and the Negro," *CWH,* 20 (1974), 293–310; and George M. Fredrickson, "A Man but Not a Brother: Abraham Lincoln and Racial Equality," *JSH,* 41 (1975), 39–58. The best single study of Lincoln's thinking and policies is LaWanda Cox, *Lincoln and Black Freedom: A Study in Presidential Leadership* (1981). The process of emancipation in border states is exhaustively studied in Charles L. Wagandt, *The Mighty Revolution: Negro Emancipation in Maryland 1862–1864* (1964); Barbara Jeane Fields, *Slavery and Freedom on the Middle Ground: Maryland during the Nineteenth Century* (1985); and Victor B. Howard, *Black Liberation in Kentucky: Emancipation and Freedom, 1862–1884* (1983). For the hopes and realities of freedom as experienced by the freedmen, Leon F. Litwack, *Been in the Storm So Long: The Aftermath of Slavery* (1979), is rich in information and insight. A wealth of primary documents accompanied by superb essays can be found in Ira Berlin et al. (eds.), *Freedom: A Documentary History of Emancipation* (5 vols. to date, 1982–   ), an abridged version of which was published in one volume as *Free at Last: A Documentary History of Slavery, Freedom, and the Civil War* (1992). The interpretive essays written as introductions were also published separately in 1992, as *Slaves No More: Three Essays on Emancipation and the Civil War*. Hostile Northern reactions to emancipation are treated in V. Jacque Voegeli, *Free but Not Equal: The Midwest and the Negro during the Civil War* (1967); Forrest G. Wood, *Black Scare: The Racist Response to Emancipation and Reconstruction* (1968); and James M. McPherson (ed.), *Anti-Negro Riots in the North, 1863* (1969). The impact of loss of mastery on slaveholders is sensitively studied in James L. Roark, *Masters Without Slaves: Southern Planters in the Civil War and Reconstruction* (1977).

For black soldiers in the Union army, the best studies are Dudley T. Cornish, *The Sable Arm: Negro Troops in the Union Army* (1956); Ira Berlin et al. (eds.), *The Black Military Experience,* Series II of *Freedom: A Documentary History of Emancipation* (1982); Joseph T. Glatthaar, *Forged in Battle: The Civil War Alliance of Black Soldiers and White Officers* (1990); Howard C. Westwood, *Black Troops, White Commanders, and Freedmen during the Civil War* (1992); and Noah Andre Trudeau, *Like Men of War: Black Troops in the Civil War 1862–1865* (1998). See also James G. Hollandsworth, Jr., *The Louisiana Native Guards: The Black Military Experience During the Civil War* (1995). The abolitionist commander of one of the first black regiments raised in the South, the 1st South Carolina (later the 33rd U.S. Colored Troops), wrote up his diary entries into a book first published in 1869 and reprinted many times since, Thomas Wentworth Higginson, *Army Life in a Black Regiment*. The wartime letters of the man who became the first commander of the most famous black regiment, Robert Gould Shaw of the 54th Massachusetts, have been published in Russell Duncan (ed.), *Blue-Eyed Child of Fortune: The Civil War Letters of Colonel Robert Gould Shaw* (1992). The letters of Corporal James Henry Gooding of the 54th have also been published in Virginia M. Adams (ed.), *On the Altar of Freedom: A Black Soldier's Civil War Letters from the Front* (1991). Another excellent anthology of black soldiers' letters is Noah Andre Trudeau (ed.), *Voices from the 55th: Letters from the 55th Massachusetts Volunteers, 1861–1865* (1996), while letters (mostly written for publication at the time in newspapers) from numerous black soldiers are published in Edwin S. Redkey (ed.), *A Grand Army of Black Men: Letters from African-American Soldiers in the Union Army* (1992).

The fullest study of wartime reconstruction efforts is Herman Belz, *Reconstructing the Union: Theory and Policy During the Civil War* (1969). Belz has also written two perceptive books that focus specifically on Republican policies toward the freedmen: *A New Birth of Freedom: The Republican Party and Freedmen's Rights* (1976); and *Emancipation and Equal Rights: Politics and Constitutionalism in the Civil War Era* (1978). A book that emphasizes, not always convincingly, Lincoln's conservatism is William Harris, *With Charity for All: Lincoln and the Restoration of the Union* (1997).

The complex and important question of federal policy toward freedmen and their former masters in the occupied South has been the subject of several excellent studies, which sometimes disagree concerning the motives and results of Northern policy: Louis S. Gerteis, *From Contraband to Freedman: Federal Policy Toward Southern Blacks, 1861–1865* (1973); Willie Lee Rose, *Rehearsal for Reconstruction: The Port Royal Experiment* (1964); John Eaton, *Grant, Lincoln and the Freedmen* (1907); Steven Joseph Ross, "Freed Soil, Freed Labor, Freed Men: John Eaton and the Davis Bend Experiment," *JSH,* 44 (1978), 213–232; John W. Blassingame, "The Union Army as an Educational Institution for Negroes, 1862–1865," *Journal of Negro Education,* 34 (1965); Peyton McCrary, *Abraham Lincoln and Reconstruction: The Louisiana Experiment* (1978); C. Peter Ripley, *Slaves and Freedmen in Civil War Louisiana* (1976); William F. Messner, *Freedmen and the Ideology of Free Labor Louisiana 1862–1865* (1978); Ted Tunnell *Crucible of Reconstruction: War, Radicalism, and Race in Louisiana, 1862–1877* (1984);

Joseph G. Dawson, *Army Generals and Reconstruction: Louisiana, 1862–1877* (1982); James T. Currie, *Enclave: Vicksburg and Her Plantations 1863–1870* (1979); Michael Wayne, *The Reshaping of Plantation Society: The Natchez District, 1860–1880* (1983); Ronald L. F. Davis, *Good and Faithful Labor: From Slavery to Sharecropping in the Natchez District 1860–1890* (1982); Janet Sharp Hermann, *The Pursuit of a Dream* (1981), a study of the Davis Bend experiment; Noralee Frankel, *Freedom's Women: Black Women and Families in Civil War Era Mississippi* (1999); Peter Maslowski, *Treason Must Be Made Odious: Military Occupation and Wartime Reconstruction in Nashville, Tennessee 1862–1865* (1978); John Cimprich, *Slavery's End in Tennessee, 1861–1865* (1985); and Steven V. Ash, *Middle Tennessee Society Transformed, 1860–1870: War and Peace in the Upper South* (1989). For two fascinating collections of letters from Northern whites who went to the South Carolina sea islands during the war to teach the freedmen, read Rupert S. Holland (ed.), *The Letters and Diary of Laura M. Towne* (1912; reprinted 1970); and Elizabeth Ware Pearson (ed.), *Letters from Port Royal 1862–1868* (1906; reprinted 1969).

Reconstruction

General Works

For good introductions to the issues and the historiography of Reconstruction, read Eric McKitrick, "Reconstruction: Ultraconservative Revolution," in C. Vann Woodward (ed.), *The Comparative Approach to American History* (1968), pp. 146–159; and Bernard A. Weisberger, "The Dark and Bloody Ground of Reconstruction Historiography," *JSH,* 25 (1959); 427–447. Also useful are Larry G. Kincaid, "Victims of Circumstance: An Interpretation of Changing Attitudes Toward Republican Policy Makers and Reconstruction," *JAH,* 57 (1970), 48–66; Gerald Grob, "Reconstruction: An American Morality Play," in George A. Billias and Gerald N. Grob (eds.), *American History: Retrospect and Prospect* (1971); Herman Belz, "The New Orthodoxy in Reconstruction Historiography," *Reviews in American History,* 1 (1973), 106–113; Michael Les Benedict, "Equality and Expediency in the Reconstruction Era: A Review Essay," *CWH,* 23 (1977), 322–335; Eric Foner, "Reconstruction Revisited," *Reviews in American History,* 10 (1982), 82–100; and Michael Les Benedict, "The Politics of Reconstruction," in John F. Marszalek and Wilson D. Miscamble (eds.), *American Political History: Essays on the State of the Discipline* (1997), pp. 54–107.

For the "Dunning" school of Reconstruction historiography, which sympathized with Southern whites and viewed the Republicans as vengeful or partisan oppressors, the best examples are William A. Dunning, *Reconstruction: Political and Economic* (1970); and Walter L. Fleming, *The Sequel of Appomattox* (1919). Even more extreme in its pro-Southern interpretation is Claude G. Bowers, *The Tragic Era* (1929).

For articles representative of the more pro-Republican "revisionist" interpretation, which emerged to maturity in the 1960s, see Kenneth M. Stampp and Leon F. Litwack (eds.), *Reconstruction: An Anthology of Revisionist Writings* (1969); and Edwin C. Rozwenc (ed.), *Reconstruction in the South,* 2d ed. (1972). Still the best single book representing the revisionist viewpoint is Kenneth M. Stampp, *The Era of Reconstruction* (1965). Also valuable are John Hope Franklin, *Reconstruction: After the Civil War* (1961); Harold M. Hyman (ed.), *New Frontiers of the American Reconstruction* (1966); Brooks D. Simpson, *The Reconstruction Presidents* (1998); and Michael Perman, *Emancipation and Reconstruction, 1862–1879* (1987). One of the earliest revisionists was the black scholar William E. B. Du Bois; see his "Reconstruction and Its Benefits," *AHR,* 15 (1910), 781–799. For a more radical, detailed, and Marxist interpretation by Du Bois, read his *Black Reconstruction . . . in America 1860–1880* (1935). A concise Marxist study is James S. Allen, *Reconstruction: The Battle for Democracy*

1865–1876 (1937); and a more recent account from a black power perspective is Lerone Bennett, *Black Power U.S.A.: The Human Side of Reconstruction* (1967). For the role of the press, see Mark Summers, *The Press Gang: Newspapers and Politics, 1865–1878* (1994).

The standard of Reconstruction scholarship for the 1990s was set by Eric Foner, especially in his major work, *Reconstruction: America's Unfinished Revolution, 1863–1877* (1988), which is notable particularly for its focus on the agency of the freedpeople in the process, and in an abridged version of this work entitled *A Short History of Reconstruction* (1990). See also Eric Foner and Olivia Mahoney, *America's Reconstruction: People and Politics after the Civil War* (1995). For additional incisive insights on the social and economic dimensions of Reconstruction, see Foner's *Nothing but Freedom: Emancipation and Its Legacy* (1983).

The basic laws and other major government documents concerning Reconstruction are published in Edward McPherson (ed.), *The Political History of the United States During the Period of Reconstruction* (1875). The constitutional developments of this period, set in the context of the antebellum and war years, are analyzed by Harold M. Hyman and William M. Wiecek, *Equal Justice Under Law: Constitutional Development, 1835–1875* (1982). Fascinating insights by a young French newspaper correspondent who later became famous as France's premier during World War I are contained in the articles published together as Georges Clemenceau, *American Reconstruction 1865–1870,* trans. Margaret MacVeagh (1928). Other collections of contemporary documents and primary sources include Walter L. Fleming (ed.), *A Documentary History of Reconstruction,* 2 vols. (1906; reprinted 1966); James P. Shenton (ed.), *The Reconstruction: A Documentary History* (1963); Richard N. Current (ed.), *Reconstruction* (1965); Staughton Lynd (ed.), *Reconstruction* (1967); Harold M. Hyman (ed.), *The Radical Republicans and Reconstruction 1861–1870* (1967); Robert W. Johanssen (ed.), *Reconstruction: 1865–1877* (1970); Michael Les Benedict (ed.), *The Fruits of Victory: Alternatives in Restoring the Union* (1986), which contains an excellent introduction; and Hans L. Trefousse and Louis L. Synder (eds.), *Reconstruction: America's First Effort at Racial Democracy* (rev. ed. 1999), which also includes a fine introduction.

Presidential Reconstruction and the Congressional Challenge, 1865–1868

For many years Howard K. Beale, *The Critical Year: A Study of Andrew Johnson and Reconstruction* (1930), which sympathizes with Johnson and attributes self-serving economic motives to congressional Republicans, stood as the accepted interpretation of presidential Reconstruction. But since 1960 this viewpoint has been severely and successfully challenged by an outpouring of books and articles that, while they do not uncritically champion the sincerity and wisdom of the Republicans, are invariably and sometimes strongly critical of Johnson: Eric L. McKitrick, *Andrew Johnson and Reconstruction* (1960); LaWanda Cox and John H. Cox, *Politics, Principle, and Prejudice 1865–1866* (1963); William R. Brock, *An American Crisis: Congress and Reconstruction 1865–1867* (1963); David Donald, *The Politics of Reconstruction 1863–1867* (1965); LaWanda Cox and John H. Cox, "Negro Suffrage and Republican Politics: The Problem of Motivation in Reconstruction Historiography," *JSH,* 33 (1967), 303–330; Glen M. Linden, *Politics of Principle: Congressional Voting on the Civil War Amendments and Pro-Negro Measures* (1976); Michael Les Benedict, "Preserving the Constitution: The Conservative Basis of Radical Reconstruction," *JAH,* 61 (1974), 65–90; Michael Les Benedict, *A Compromise of Principle: Congressional Republicans and Reconstruction* (1974); Patrick W. Riddleberger, *1866: The Critical Year Revisited* (1979); and Earl M. Maltz, *Civil Rights, the Constitution, and Congress, 1863–1869* (1990). David W. Bowen, *Andrew Johnson and the Negro* (1988), sees the President as motivated mainly by racism. J. Michael Quill, *Prelude to the Radicals: The North and Reconstruction in 1865* (1980), surveys Northern public opinion, while Edward L. Gambill, *Conservative Ordeal: Northern Democrats and Reconstruction, 1865–1869* (1981), dissects the tactics of this party. For a provocative interpretation of the South's manipulation of Andrew Johnson and the political system to soften Reconstruction and lay the basis for the revival of Democratic power, read Michael Perman, *Reunion Without Compromise: The South and Reconstruction 1865–1868* (1975). Dan T. Carter, *When the War Was Over: The Failure of Self-Reconstruction in the South, 1865–1867* (1985), finds Southern leaders to have been shortsighted during the period of presidential Reconstruction. Most of Andrew Johnson's early biographers were sympathetic. For a sampling of their writings, plus some of the subsequent critical interpretations, consult Eric L. McKitrick (ed.), *Andrew Johnson: A Profile* (1960). Two studies blend critical insights with an appreciation of Johnson's virtues and accomplishments: Albert Castel, *The Presidency of Andrew Johnson* (1979); and James Sefton, *Andrew Johnson and the Uses of Constitutional Power* (1979).

A number of specialized monographs have enlarged our understanding of the presidential Reconstruction years. Harold Hyman, *The Era of the Oath* (1954), and Jonathan Dorris, *Pardon and Amnesty Under Lincoln and Johnson* (1953), unravel the complexities of loyalty oaths and presidential pardons. Giles Vandal, *The New Orleans Riot of 1866: Anatomy of a Tragedy* (1983), analyzes that crucial event and its consequences. For the context of Northern politics in which congressional Republicans acted, see James C. Mohr (ed.), *Radical Republicans in the North* (1976), and James C. Mohr, *The Radical Republicans and Reform in New York During Reconstruction* (1973). The details of Southern black codes that provoked Northern anger are set forth in Theodore B. Wilson, *The Black Codes of the South* (1965). Mary Frances Berry, *Military Necessity and Civil Rights Policy: Black Citizenship and the Constitution 1861–1868* (1977), maintains that the government's need for black troops was an important factor in Republican policy after as well as during the war. The complex origins, ratification, meaning, and interpretations of the Fourteenth Amendment are dissected in the following six studies: Jacobus ten Broek, *The Antislavery Origins of the Fourteenth Amendment* (1951); Joseph B. James, *The Framing of the Fourteenth Amendment* (1956), and *The Ratification of the Fourteenth Amendment* (1984); Michael Kent Curtis, *No State Shall Abridge: The Fourteenth Amendment and the Bill of Rights* (1986); William E. Nelson, *The Fourteenth Amendment: From Political Principle to Judicial Doctrine* (1988); and James E. Bond, *No Easy Walk to Freedom: Reconstruction and the Ratification of the Fourteenth Amendment* (1997). For the Fifteenth Amendment, see William Gillette, *The Right to Vote: Politics and Passage of the Fifteenth Amendment* (1965). The question of white disfranchisement under the Reconstruction Acts is considered in William A. Russ, "Registration and Disfranchisement Under Radical Reconstruction," *MVHR*, 21 (1934), 163–180; and the role of the Supreme Court in the early years of Reconstruction is analyzed in Stanley I. Kutler, *Judicial Power and Reconstruction Politics* (1968).

For the sensitive and crucial role of the army and of General Grant in Reconstruction, three books are important: James Sefton, *The United States Army and Reconstruction* (1967); Martin E. Mantell, *Johnson, Grant, and the Politics of Reconstruction* (1973); and Brooks D. Simpson, *Let Us Have Peace: Ulysses S. Grant and the Politics of War and Reconstruction, 1861–1868* (1991). An old study of Andrew Johnson's impeachment, still valuable for the detail it provides, is David M. De Witt, *Impeachment and Trial of Andrew Johnson* (1903). Two modern studies whose sympathies lean toward the impeachers are Michael Les Benedict, *The Impeachment and Trial of Andrew Johnson* (1973); and Hans L. Trefousse, *Impeachment of a President: Andrew Johnson, the Blacks, and Reconstruction* (1975). Charles H. Coleman, *The Election of 1868* (1933), is still the fullest study of the subject.

The South during Reconstruction

After the war, as before, the South attracted many visitors who described the conditions of life and politics for readers back home. For an annotated bibliography of such writings, see Thomas D. Clark (ed.), *Travels in the New South,* 2 vols. (1962). Four books made up of collected articles by Northern journalists who toured the postwar South did much to shape Northern attitudes and policy: Sidney Andrews, *The South Since the War* (1866; reprinted 1970, with introduction by David Donald); John Richard Dennett, *The South as It Is 1865–1866* (1866; reprinted 1965, with introduction by Henry M. Christman); Whitelaw Reid, *After the War: A Tour of the Southern States 1865–1866* (1866; reprinted 1965, with introduction by C. Vann Woodward); and John T. Trowbridge, *A Picture of the Desolated States and the Work of Restoration 1865–1868* (1868). These writers generally presented a critical view of the racial attitudes of Southern whites; by the 1870s, however, the most widely read of the Northern journalists who visited the South sympathized with the plight of white Southerners, and their articles, also collected into books, did much to influence the Northern retreat from Reconstruction. Especially important in this respect were Edward King, *The Great South* (1875; reprinted 1969, with introduction by James M. McPherson); Charles Nordhoff, *The Cotton States in the Spring and Summer of 1875* (1875); and James Shepherd Pike, *The Prostrate State: South Carolina Under Negro Government* (1874; reprinted 1968, with introduction by Robert F. Durden). For an analysis of this last book and of its author, see Robert F. Durden, *James Shepherd Pike: Republicanism and the American Negro 1850–1882* (1957).

There is a large scholarly literature on the South and on individual Southern states during Reconstruction. Books and articles published before 1960 generally reflect the conservative Dunning viewpoint sympathetic to Southern whites and critical of Republicans, while those published since 1960 are usually "revisionist" of this viewpoint: E. Merton Coulter, *The South During Reconstruction* (1947); Jack B. Scroggs, "Carpetbagger Constitutional Reform in the South Atlantic States, 1867–1868," *JSH*, 27 (1961), 475–493; Otto H. Olsen (ed.), *Reconstruction and Redemption in the South: An Assessment* (1980); Walter L. Fleming, *Civil War and Reconstruction in Alabama* (1905); George H. Thompson, *Arkansas and Reconstruction* (1976); Jerrell Shofner, *Nor Is It Over Yet: Florida and the Era of Reconstruction* (1974); Alan Conway, *The Reconstruction of Georgia* (1966); Joe Gray Taylor, *Louisiana Reconstruction 1863–1877* (1974); James W. Garner, *Reconstruction in Mississippi* (1901); William C. Harris, *Presidential Reconstruction in Mississippi* (1967); William C. Harris, *The Day of the Carpetbagger: Republican Reconstruction in Mississippi* (1979); William McKee Evans, *Ballots and Fence Rails: Reconstruction on the Lower Cape Fear* (1966); Francis B. Simkins and Robert H. Woody, *South Carolina During Reconstruction* (1932); Thomas B. Alexander, *Political Reconstruction in Tennessee* (1950), which despite its early date, reflects much of the revisionist viewpoint; Jack P. Maddex, *The Virginia Conservatives 1867–1879* (1970); Carl H. Moneyhon, *The Impact of the Civil War and Reconstruction on Arkansas, 1850–1874* (1994); Richard Zuczeck, *State of Rebellion: Reconstruction in South Carolina* (1996); and Randolph B. Campbell, *Grass-Roots Reconstruction in Texas, 1865–1880* (1997). For modern studies of the border states, see especially Richard O. Curry (ed.), *Radicalism, Racism, and Party Realignment: The Border States During Reconstruction* (1969); and William E. Parrish, *Missouri Under Radical Rule* (1965). In addition, several of the books cited in the section above on "Slaves, Freedmen, and Wartime Reconstruction" cover the postwar Reconstruction years as well.

Most of the monographs on blacks and Republicans during Reconstruction express one variety or another of revisionism, whatever their date of publication: Robert Cruden, *The Negro in Reconstruction* (1969); Otis Singletary, *Negro Militia and Reconstruction* (1957); Horace Mann Bond, *Negro Education in Alabama: A Study in Cotton and Steel* (1939); Peter Kolchin, *First Freedom: The Responses of Alabama's Blacks to Emancipation and Reconstruction* (1972); Loren Schweninger, *James T. Rapier and Reconstruction* (1978), about an Alabama black leader; Joe M. Richardson, *The Negro in the Reconstruction of Florida 1865–1877* (1965); Elizabeth Studley Nathans, *Losing the Peace: Georgia Republicans and Reconstruction* (1964); John W. Blassingame, *Black New Orleans 1860–1880* (1973); Charles Vincent, *Black Legislators in Louisiana During Reconstruction* (1976); Vernon Lane Wharton, *The Negro in Mississippi 1865–1890* (1947); Alrutheus A. Taylor, *The Negro in South Carolina During the Recon-*

struction (1924); Joel Williamson, *After Slavery: The Negro in South Carolina During Reconstruction 1861–1877* (1965); Thomas Holt, *Black Over White: Negro Political Leadership in South Carolina During Reconstruction* (1977); Julie Saville, *The Work of Reconstruction: From Slave to Wage Laborer in South Carolina, 1860–1870* (1994); Alrutheus A. Taylor, *The Negro in Tennessee 1865–1880* (1941); Carl Moneyhon, *Republicanism in Reconstruction Texas* (1979); Alrutheus A. Taylor, *The Negro in the Reconstruction of Virginia* (1926); Robert F. Engs, *Freedom's First Generation: Black Hampton, Virginia, 1869–1902* (1980); Edmund L. Drago, *Black Politicians and Reconstruction in Georgia: A Splendid Failure* (1982); Michael W. Fitzgerald, *The Union League Movement in the Deep South: Politics and Agricultural Change during Reconstruction* (1989); James Smallwood, *Time of Hope, Time of Despair: Black Texans during Reconstruction* (1981); and Howard Rabinowitz (ed.), *Southern Black Leaders of the Reconstruction Era* (1982). For the shifting and uneasy relationship between the national Republican party and the South, see Richard H. Abbott, *The Republican Party and the South, 1855–1877* (1986); and Terry L. Seip, *The South Returns to Congress: Men, Economic Measures, and Intersectional Relationships, 1868–1879* (1983). Eric Foner, *Freedom's Lawmakers: A Directory of Black Officers during Reconstruction* (rev. ed., 1993), provides biographical information on 1,510 black officeholders.

For excellent revisionist writings on the carpetbaggers, see Richard N. Current, "Carpetbaggers Reconsidered," in David Pinkney and Theodore Ropp (eds.), *A Festschrift for Frederick B. Artz* (1964), pp. 139–157, *Three Carpetbag Governors* (1967), and *Those Terrible Carpetbaggers: A Reinterpretation* (1988); Sarah Van Woolfolk, "Carpetbaggers in Alabama: Tradition Versus Truth," *Alabama Review,* 15 (1962), 133–144; and Otto H. Olsen, *Carpetbagger's Crusade: The Life of Albion W. Tourgee* (1965). Albert Morgan, *Yazoo* (1884), is a fascinating autobiography by a Mississippi carpetbagger. See also Ted Tunnell (ed.), *Carpetbagger from Vermont: The Autobiography of Marshall Harvey Twitchell* (1989); and Ruth Currie-McDaniel, *Carpetbagger of Conscience: A Biography of John Emory Bryant* (1987).

Two articles debate the role of former Southern Whigs, some of whom became Republicans, in the postwar era: Thomas B. Alexander, "Persistent Whiggery in the Confederate South, 1860–1877," *JSH,* 27 (1961), 305–329; and John V. Mering, "Persistent Whiggery in the Confederate South: A Reconsideration," *SAQ,* 69 (1970), 124–143. For the question of the social origins and previous political affiliations of scalawags, see the following five articles: David Donald, "The Scalawag in Mississippi Reconstruction," *JSH,* 10 (1944), 447–460; Allen W. Trelease, "Who Were the Scalawags?" *JSH,* 29 (1963), 445–468; Otto H. Olsen, "Reconsidering the Scalawags," *CWH,* 12 (1966), 304–320; Warren A. Ellem, "Who Were the Mississippi Scalawags?" *JSH,* 38 (1972), 217–240; and James A. Baggett, "Origins of Upper South Scalawag Leadership," *CWH,* 29 (1983), 53–73. Sarah Woolfolk Wiggins, *The Scalawag in Alabama Politics 1865–1881* (1977), is a fine monograph on a state with significant scalawag strength; while Gordon B. McKinney, *Southern Mountain Republicans 1865–1900: Politics and the Appalachian Community* (1978), analyzes the single most persistent group of Southern white Republicans. For the violent counterrevolution of Southern Democrats against Republicans and Reconstruction, see Allen W. Trelease's exhaustive *White Terror: The Ku Klux Klan Conspiracy and Southern Reconstruction* (1972) and George C. Rable, *But There Was No Peace: The Role of Violence in the Politics of Reconstruction* (1984).

Social and Economic Reconstruction

Daniel Stowell, *Rebuilding Zion: The Religious Reconstruction of the South, 1863–1877* (1998), deals with both black and white churches. See also Reginald F. Hildebrand, *The Times Were Strange and Stirring: Methodist Preachers and the Crisis of Emancipation* (1995). For comparisons of the United States with other post-slave societies, see the essays in Frank McGlynn and Seymour Drescher (eds.), *The Meaning of Freedom: Economics, Politics, and Culture After Slavery* (1992). The experiences of women and families in the first decades of black freedom have recently attracted scholarly attention; see especially Tera W. Hunter, *To 'Joy My Freedom: Southern Black Women's Lives and Labors after the Civil War* (1997); Laura F. Edwards, *Gendered Strife and Confusion: The Political Culture of Reconstruction* (1997); Leslie A. Schwalm, *A Hard Fight for We: Women's Transition from Slavery to Freedom in South Carolina* (1997); and Peggy Cooper Davis, *Neglected Stories: The Constitution and Family Values* (1997), a study of the freedpeople's struggle for family rights in the postwar South.

Somewhat outdated but still valuable is George R. Bentley, *A History of the Freedmen's Bureau* (1955). William McFeely, *Yankee Stepfather: General O. O. Howard and the Freedmen* (1968), is overly critical of Howard and the Bureau for failures beyond their control. More fair-minded is Donald G. Nieman, *To Set the Law in Motion: The Freedmen's Bureau and the Legal Rights of Blacks, 1865–1868* (1979), which presents an incisive analysis of the Bureau's mixed record in protecting freedpeople's legal rights. Four good state studies of the Bureau are Martin Abbott, *The Freedmen's Bureau in South Carolina* (1967); Howard Ashley White, *The Freedmen's Bureau in Louisiana* (1970); Barry A. Crouch, *The Freedmen's Bureau and Black Texans* (1992); and Paul A. Cimbala, *Under the Guardianship of the Nation: The Freedmen's Bureau and the Reconstruction of Georgia* (1997). A stimulating collection of essays is Paul A. Cimbala and Randall Miller (eds.), *The Freedmen's Bureau and Reconstruction* (1999).

Henry Lee Swint, *The Northern Teacher in the South 1862–1870* (1941), is a relatively fair-minded study that nevertheless portrays the Yankee teachers as disruptive and naive egalitarians who needlessly alienated Southern whites. On the other hand Donald Spivey, *Schooling for the New Slavery: Black Industrial Education 1868–1915* (1978), and to a lesser extent, Ronald E. Butchart, *Northern Schools, Southern Blacks, and Reconstruction: Freedmen's Education 1862–1875* (1980); Robert C. Morris, *Reading, 'Riting,' and Reconstruction: Freedmen's Education in the South, 1865–1870* (1981); and James Anderson, *The Education of Blacks in the South, 1860–1935* (1988) are critical of Northern educators for almost the opposite reason—their alleged paternalism and attitudes of racial superiority toward blacks. James M. McPherson, *The Abolitionist Legacy: From Reconstruction to the NAACP* (1975); Jacqueline Jones, *Soldiers of Light and Love: Northern Teachers and Georgia Blacks 1865–1873* (1980); Joe M. Richardson, *Christian Reconstruction, The American Missionary Association and Southern Blacks, 1861–1890* (1986); and Robert Francis Engs, *Educating the Disfranchised and Disinherited: Samuel Chapman Armstrong and Hampton Institute, 1839–1893* (1999), explore much more sympathetically but not uncritically the contribution of Northern whites to freedmen's education. William Preston Vaughan, *Schools for All: The Blacks & Public Education in the South 1865–1877* (1974), focuses primarily on the question of segregation and desegregation in education. Roger A. Fischer, *The Segregation Struggle in Louisiana 1862–1877* (1974), deals with this issue in all aspects of public life including education. Of several articles on the Civil Rights Act of 1875, perhaps the most comprehensive is Alfred H. Kelly, "The Congressional Controversy Over School Segregation, 1867–1875," *AHR*, 54 (1959), 537–563. The most influential study of the segregation question in the Reconstruction and post-Reconstruction South is C. Vann Woodward, *The Strange Career of Jim Crow*, 3d rev. ed. (1974). For a fresh perspective on this issue, see Howard N. Rabinowitz, *Race Relations in the Urban South 1865–1890* (1977).

Since the 1970s many books have been published on the economic consequences of emancipation and the evolution of a new agricultural labor system to succeed slavery. Valuable summaries and critiques of this literature can be found in Harold D. Woodman, "Sequel to Slavery: The New History Views the Postbellum South," *JSH*, 43 (1977), 523–554; and Jonathan Wiener, Robert Higgs, and Harold Woodman, "Class Structure and Economic Development in the American South, 1865–1955," *AHR*, 84 (1979), 970–1006. The fullest and most persuasive analysis of the postwar Southern economy and the freedmen's place in it is Roger L. Ransom and Richard Sutch, *One Kind of Freedom: The Economic Consequences of Emancipation*

(1977). See also Roger L. Ransom and Richard Sutch, "Growth and Welfare in the American South of the Nineteenth Century," *Explorations in Entrepreneurial History,* 16 (1979), 207–235; and Edward Royce, *The Origins of Southern Sharecropping* (1993). Two studies that present an even more optimistic picture of Southern agriculture and the freedmen's economic gains are Stephen J. DeCanio, *Agriculture in the Postbellum South* (1974); and Robert Higgs, *Competition and Coercion: Blacks in the American Economy 1865–1914* (1977). See also Gerald D. Jaynes, *Branches without Roots: Genesis of the Black Working Class in the American South 1862–1882* (1988). Two Marxian-oriented studies that portray a persistence of planter domination and of quasi-slavery for blacks are Jonathan M. Wiener, *Social Origins of the New South: Alabama 1860–1885* (1978); and Jay Mandle, *The Roots of Black Poverty: The Southern Plantation Economy After the Civil War* (1978). A number of state and community studies appeared during the 1980s that expand and deepen our understanding of race, class, and the economy in the postwar South: Charles L. Flynn, Jr., *White Land, Black Labor: Caste and Class in Late Nineteenth-Century Georgia* (1983); Lewis N. Wynne, *The Continuity of Cotton: Planter Politics in Georgia, 1865–1892* (1985); Crandall A. Shifflet, *Patronage and Poverty in the Tobacco South: Louisia County, Virginia, 1860–1900* (1983); Orville Vernon Burton, *In My Father's House Are Many Mansions: Family and Community in Edgefield, South Carolina* (1985); O. Vernon Burton and Robert McMath (eds.), *Toward a New South: Studies in Post-Civil War Southern Communities* (1982); Thavolia Glymph and John J. Kushma (eds.), *Essays on the Postbellum Southern Economy* (1985); Joseph P. Reidy, *From Slavery to Agrarian Capitalism in the Slave Plantation South* (1992), a study of central Georgia; and Lynda J. Morgan, *Emancipation in Virginia's Tobacco Belt, 1850–1870* (1993).

On the face of it, much of the legislation passed in the post-Reconstruction South supports the quasi-slavery thesis, though questions remain concerning the degree of enforcement of these laws: see Harold D. Woodman, "Post-Civil War Southern Agriculture and the Law," *AH,* 53 (1979), 319–337; William Cohen, "Negro Involuntary Servitude in the South, 1865–1940: A Preliminary Analysis," *JSH,* 42 (1976), 31–60; and Daniel A. Novak, *The Wheel of Servitude: Black Forced Labor After Slavery* (1978). But see William Cohen, *At Freedom's Edge: Black Mobility and the Southern White Quest for Racial Control, 1861–1915* (1991), which revises his earlier position on the effectiveness of restrictive laws. An important perspective and a great deal of information are presented concisely in Gavin Wright, *Old South, New South: Revolutions in the Southern Economy Since the Civil War* (1986). A study that analyzes the experiences of Northerners who tried their hands at cotton planting after the war is Lawrence N. Powell, *New Masters: Northern Planters During the Civil War and Reconstruction* (1980).

LaWanda Cox, "The Promise of Land for the Freedmen," *MVHR,* 45 (1958), 413–440, discusses the various congressional and executive acts that first opened and then closed the door to significant land reform in the South. Eric Foner, "Thaddeus Stevens, Confiscation, and Reconstruction," in Stanley Elkins and Eric McKitrick (eds.), *The Hofstadter Aegis: A Memorial* (1974), pp. 154–183, describes Stevens's proposals for land reform. One effort to provide land to freedpeople is analyzed in Michael L. Lanza, *Agrarianism and Reconstruction Politics: The Southern Homestead Act* (1990). For the mixed record of the Freedmen's Bureau in helping blacks achieve land ownership, see Claude F. Oubre, *Forty Acres and a Mule: The Freedmen's Bureau and Black Land Ownership* (1978). Edward Magdol, *A Right to the Land: Essays on the Freedmen's Community* (1977), is a series of uneven but interesting essays on the experiences of the first generation of freedmen. Two institutions that began their work with great hopes but ended with disappointments are treated in Carol Rothrock Bleser, *The Promised Land: The History of the South Carolina Land Commission 1869–1890* (1969); and Carl R. Osthaus, *Freedmen, Philanthropy, and Fraud: A History of the Freedmen's Savings Bank* (1976).

The large hopes but limited achievements of railroad expansion in the postwar South are treated in Mark W. Summers, *Railroads, Reconstruction, and the Gospel of Prosperity: Aid under the Radical Republicans, 1865–1877* (1984); John F. Stover, *The Railroads of the South,*

1865–1900: A Study of Finance and Control (1955); and Carter Goodrich, "Public Aid to Railroads in the Reconstruction South," *Political Science Quarterly,* 71 (1956), 407–442. Scott Reynolds Nelson, *Iron Confederacies: Southern Railways, Klan Violence, and Reconstruction* (1999), examines the relationships among these developments.

National Politics and the Retreat from Reconstruction in the 1870s

For a broad survey of changes in Northern opinion about the "Southern Question," read Paul H. Buck, *The Road to Reunion 1865–1900* (1937). A more comprehensive and up-to-date study of the Reconstruction years themselves is William Gillette, *Retreat from Reconstruction: A Political History 1867–1878* (1979). Michael Perman, *The Road to Redemption: Southern Politics, 1869–1879* (1984), presents a challenging thesis about the process of redemption. While William B. Hesseltine's study of the Grant presidency, *Ulyssess S. Grant, Politician* (1935), contains material of value, it has been superseded in many respects by Frank J. Scaturro, *President Grant Reconsidered* (1998). Domestic as well as foreign affairs during the Grant administration are also treated in Allan Nevins, *Hamilton Fish: The Inner History of the Grant Administration* (1936). An exhaustive treatment of the most important foreign policy issue is Adrian Cook, *The Alabama Claims* (1975). For a detailed analysis of state and national politics during the postwar generation, see Morton Keller, *Affairs of State: Public Life in Late Nineteenth Century America* (1977). The important role of veterans' organizations in both Northern and Southern politics is described in Mary R. Dearing, *Veterans in Politics: The Story of the G.A.R.* (1952); Stuart McConnell, *Glorious Contentment: The Grand Army of the Republic, 1865–1900* (1992); and Gaines M. Foster, *Ghosts of the Confederacy: Defeat, the Lost Cause, and the Emergence of the New South* (1987). Nina Silber, *The Romance of Reunion: Northerners and the South, 1865–1900* (1993), examines the cultural processes of reconciliation.

The civil service reformers and Liberal Republicans are treated in Ari A. Hoogenboom, *Outlawing the Spoils: A History of the Civil Service Reform Movement* (1961); John G. Sproat, *"The Best Men": Liberal Reformers in the Gilded Age* (1968); and David M. Tucker, *Mugwumps: Public Moralists of the Gilded Age* (1998). Mark Wahlgren Summers, *The Era of Good Stealings* (1993), examines both the image and reality of corruption. For the Liberals and the 1872 election, see Earle Dudley Ross, *The Liberal Republican Movement* (1919); Matthew T. Downey, "Horace Greeley and the Politicians: The Liberal Republican Convention of 1872," *JAH,* 53 (1967), 727–750; Richard A. Gerber, "The Liberal Republicans of 1872 in Historiographical Perspective," *JAH,* 62 (1975), 40–73; and Wilbert H. Ahern, "Laissez Faire vs. Equal Rights: Liberal Republicans and Limits to Reconstruction," *Phylon,* 40 (1979), 520–565. An older study of the 1876 presidential election and its aftermath, still serviceable for its factual detail, is Paul L. Haworth, *The Hayes-Tilden Disputed Presidential Election of 1876* (1906). For a provocative interpretation of the negotiations by which the electoral dispute was settled, read C. Vann Woodward, *Reunion and Reaction,* rev. ed. (1956). But consult also Allan Peskin, "Was There a Compromise of 1877?" *JAH,* 60 (1973), 63–73; and C. Vann Woodward, "Yes, There Was a Compromise of 1877," *JAH,* 60 (1973), 215–223. Challenges to Woodward's interpretation can also be found in Keith I. Polakoff, *The Politics of Inertia: The Election of 1876 and the End of Reconstruction* (1973); and Michael Les Benedict, "Southern Democrats in the Crisis of 1876–1877: A Reconsideration of *Reunion and Reaction,*" *JSH,* 46 (1980), 489–524. Additional light on the question is shed by George C. Rable, "Southern Interests and the Election of 1876: A Reappraisal," *CWH,* 26 (Dec. 1980), 347–361. Ari Hoogenboom, *The Presidency of Rutherford B. Hayes* (1988), includes a perceptive treatment of the 1877 Compromise.

The changing attitudes of various groups in the North toward the role of government in protecting the equal rights of blacks are chronicled in Rayford W. Logan, *The Betrayal of the Negro: From Rutherford B. Hayes to Woodrow Wilson* (1965); James M. McPherson, *The Abolitionist Legacy: From Reconstruction to the NAACP* (1975); and Lawrence Grossman, *The Democratic*

Party and the Negro: Northern and National Politics, 1868–1892 (1976). The decline in federal efforts to enforce black voting rights is discussed in Everette Swinney, "Enforcing the Fifteenth Amendment," *JSH,* 27 (1962), 202–218. The role of the courts in enforcing and then retreating from enforcement of federal Reconstruction laws is brilliantly treated by Robert J. Kaczorowski, *The Politics of Judicial Interpretation: The Federal Courts, Department of Justice and Civil Rights 1866–1876* (1985). Xi Wang, *The Trial of Democracy: Black Suffrage and Northern Republicans, 1860–1910* (1997), shows the difficulty of enforcing the 15th Amendment in the South.

The New South

The New South ideology of industrial progress and modernization on the Yankee model is dissected in Paul M. Gaston, *The New South Creed* (1970). Gaston expands upon the influential thesis set forth by C. Vann Woodward, *Origins of the New South 1877–1913* (1951), that the economic and political leaders of the New South came from the rising middle class, which had little connection with the antebellum planter regime and its ideology. For a sympathetic evaluation of this thesis, see Sheldon Hackney, *"Origins of the New South* in Retrospect," *JSH,* 38 (1972), 191–216. For a critical evaluation, see James Tice Moore, "Redeemers Reconsidered: Change and Continuity in the Democratic South, 1870–1900," *JSH,* 44 (1978), 357–378. A summary and reflection on this question can be found in George B. Tindall, *The Persistent Tradition in New South Politics* (1975). Edward L. Ayers, *The Promise of the New South: Life after Reconstruction* (1992), and Howard N. Rabinowitz, *The First New South, 1865–1920* (1991), focus on social and cultural as well as political and economic history. Ted Ownby, *Subduing Satan: Religion, Recreation, and Manhood in the Rural South, 1865–1920* (1990), treats an important dimension of cultural history.

For the rise of the textile industry, see Patrick J. Hearden, *Independence and Empire: The New South's Cotton Mill Campaign, 1865–1901* (1982), and David L. Carlton, *Mill and Town in South Carolina, 1880–1920* (1982). Monographs containing additional information on economic and political developments in the post-Reconstruction South include Theodore Saloutos, *Farmer Movements in the South 1865–1933* (1960); Robert C. McMath, *Populist Vanguard: A History of the Southern Farmers' Alliance* (1975); Michael Schwartz, *Radical Protest and Social Structure: The Southern Farmers' Alliance and Cotton Tenancy* (1977); and Melton A. McLaurin, *The Knights of Labor in the South* (1978).

Numerous studies of individual Southern states address implicitly if not explicitly the Woodward thesis concerning the discontinuity of Southern leadership and ideology. In addition to Jonathan Wiener's *Social Origins of the New South,* cited in the section on Social and Economic Reconstruction, consult the following: William Warren Rogers, *The One-Gallused Rebellion: Agrarianism in Alabama 1865–1896* (1970); Sheldon Hackney, *Populism to Progressivism in Alabama* (1969); William Ivy Hair, *Bourbonism and Agrarian Protest: Louisiana Politics 1877–1900* (1969); Albert D. Kirwan, *Revolt of the Rednecks: Mississippi Politics 1877–1925* (1951); Dwight D. Billings, *Planters and the Making of a "New South": Class, Politics, and Development in North Carolina 1865–1900* (1979); William Cooper, *The Conservative Regime: South Carolina 1877–1890* (1968); Francis B. Simkins, *Pitchfork Ben Tillman: South Carolinian* (1944); Roger L. Hart, *Redeemers, Bourbons, and Populists: Tennessee 1870–1896* (1975); and Alwyn Barr, *Reconstruction to Reform: Texas Politics 1876–1906* (1971).

James Tice Moore, *Two Paths to the New South: The Virginia Debt Controversy 1870–1883* (1974), analyzes the Mahone movement in Virginia, which seemed to offer Northern Republicans the best opportunity during the 1880s to crack the solid South in alliance with Southern independent political movements. For independent movements in other states, see Michael R. Hyman, *The Anti-Redeemers: Hill-Country Political Dissenters in the Lower South from Redemption to Populism* (1990). Vincent P. DeSantis, *Republicans Face the Southern Question: The New Departure Years 1877–1897* (1959), and Stanley P. Hirshson, *Farewell to the Bloody Shirt: Northern Republicans and the Southern Negro 1877–1893* (1962), trace the continuing efforts of national Republican leaders to nurture a viable Republican party in the South. For an analysis of the last congressional effort before the 1950s to pass a voting rights bill, see Richard E. Welch, "The Federal Elections Bill of 1890: Postscripts and Prelude," *JAH*, 52 (1965), 511–526. The persistence of Southern Republicanism and the ultimately successful Democratic counterattack by means of disfranchisement are trenchantly recounted in J. Morgan Kousser, *The Shaping of Southern Politics: Suffrage Restriction and the Establishment of the One-Party South 1880–1910* (1974). For black politics during this period, see Bess Beatty, *A Revolution Gone Backward: The Black Response to National Politics, 1876–1896* (1987). Claude H. Nolen, *The Negro's Image in the South: The Anatomy of White Supremacy* (1967), narrates the evolution of a post-emancipation ideology of white supremacy; while C. Vann Woodward, *The Strange Career of Jim Crow*, 3d rev. ed. (1974), discusses the hardening code of segregation in the South after 1890. An important study that focuses mainly on the New South period is Joel Williamson, *The Crucible of Race: Black-White Relations in the American South Since Emancipation* (1984), which was also published in an abridged edition with the title *A Rage for Order: Black-White Relations in the American South Since Emancipation* (1986). Leon F. Litwack, *Trouble in Mind: Black Southerners in the Age of Jim Crow* (1998), chronicles black responses to their deteriorating status. The worst aspects of New-South race relations are studied in Fitzhugh Brundage, *Lynching in the New South* (1993); Matthew J. Mancini, *One Dies, Get Another: Convict Leasing in the American South, 1866–1928* (1996); and Alex Lichtenstein, *Twice the Work of Free Labor: The Political Economy of Convict Labor in the New South* (1996).

The politics and ideology of race and racism are also treated in the following state studies: William W. Rogers and Robert D. Ward, *August Reckoning: Jack Turner and Racism in Post-Civil War Alabama* (1973); Margaret Law Callcott, *The Negro in Maryland Politics 1870–1912* (1969); Frenise Logan, *The Negro in North Carolina 1876–1894* (1964); George B. Tindall, *South Carolina Negroes 1877–1900* (1952); Joseph H. Cartwright, *The Triumph of Jim Crow: Tennessee Race Relations in the 1880's* (1976); Lawrence D. Rice, *The Negro in Texas 1874–1900* (1971); Charles E. Wynes, *Race Relations in Virginia 1870–1902* (1961); and William Ivy Hair, *Carnival of Fury: Robert Charles and the New Orleans Race Riot of 1900* (1976). Robert C. Kenzer, *Enterprising Southerners: Black Economic Success in North Carolina, 1865–1915* (1997), is the best study of black entrepreneurs in the New South. Numerous articles and books address the complex question of the Southern Populists and the race issue. Three of the most important are C. Vann Woodward, *Tom Watson, Agrarian Rebel* (1938); Helen C. Edmonds, *The Negro and Fusion Politics in North Carolina 1894–1901* (1951); and Lawrence C. Goodwin, "Populist Dreams and Negro Rights: East Texas as a Case Study," *AHR*, 76 (1971), 1435–1456. The most comprehensive analysis of this question is Gerald H. Gaither, *Blacks and the Populist Revolt: Ballots and Bigotry in the "New South"* (1977).

Index

THE UNITED STATES AND CONFEDERATE STATES, 1861